W9-BRC-077

Here are your

1992 Year Book Cross-Reference Tabs

For insertion in your WORLD BOOK set

Put these Tabs in the appropriate volumes of your **World Book Encyclopedia** now. Then, when you later look up some topic in **World Book** and find a Tab near the article, you will know that one of your **Year Books** has newer or more detailed information about that topic.

How to use these Tabs

First, remove this page from THE YEAR BOOK.

Begin with the first Tab, **ARCHAEOLOGY**. Take the A volume of your **World Book** set and find the **Archaeology** article in it. Moisten the **ARCHAEOLOGY** Tab and affix it to that page.

Go on to the other Tabs. Your set may not have articles on some of the topics—**GENETIC ENGINEERING**, for example. In that case, put the Tab in the correct volume and on the page where it would go if there *were* an article. The **GENETIC ENGINEERING** Tab should go in the G volume on the same page as the **Genetics** article.

Special Report
ARCHAEOLOGY
1992 Year Book, p. 54

Special Report
CANADA
1992 Year Book, p. 113

Special Report
CENSUS
1992 Year Book, p. 127

Special Report
COMMUNISM
1992 Year Book, p. 441

Special Report
DANCING
1992 Year Book, p. 169

New World Book Article
ESTONIA
1992 Year Book, p. 483

Special Report
EUROPE
1992 Year Book, p. 208

Special Report
GENETIC ENGINEERING
1992 Year Book, p. 298

New World Book Article
IRAQ
1992 Year Book, p. 486

New World Book Article
LATVIA
1992 Year Book, p. 500

Special Report
LITERATURE FOR CHILDREN
1992 Year Book, p. 177

New World Book Article
LITHUANIA
1992 Year Book, p. 503

Special Report
MARSHALL, THURGOOD
1992 Year Book, p. 409

Special Report
MIDDLE EAST
1992 Year Book, p. 342

Special Report
MUSIC
1992 Year Book, p. 367

New World Book Article
RACES, HUMAN
1992 Year Book, p. 506

Special Report
SPAIN
1992 Year Book, p. 397

Special Report
TUNNEL
1992 Year Book, p. 425

Special Report
WATER
1992 Year Book, p. 456

Special Report
YUGOSLAVIA
1992 Year Book, p. 472

A Review of the Events of 1991

The 1992 World Book Year Book

The Annual Supplement to The World Book Encyclopedia

World Book, Inc.
a Scott Fetzer company

Chicago London Sydney Toronto

World Book, Inc.
525 West Monroe
Chicago, IL 60661

ISBN 0-7166-0492-2
ISSN 0084-1439
Library of Congress Catalog Card Number: 62-4818

Staff

Editorial Director
A. Richard Harmet

Editorial
Managing Editor
Darlene R. Stille

Associate Editor
Rod Such

Senior Editors
Douglas Clayton
David L. Dreier
Mark Dunbar
Lori Fagan
Carol L. Hanson
Barbara A. Mayes
Karin C. Rosenberg

Contributing Editors
Jinger Hoop
Joan Stephenson

Editorial Assistant
Ethel Matthews

Cartographic Services
H. George Stoll, Head
Wayne K. Pichler

Head, Index Services
Beatrice Bertucci

Senior Indexer
David Pofelski

Staff Indexer
Dennis P. Phillips

Art
Art Director
Alfred de Simone

Assistant Art Director
Richard Zinn

Senior Artist, Year Book
Lisa Buckley

Senior Artists
Cari L. Biamonte
Melanie J. Lawson

Photography Director
John S. Marshall

Senior Photographs Editor
Sandra M. Dyrlund

Photographs Editor
Julie Laffin

Production
Procurement
Daniel N. Bach

Manufacturing
Sandra Van den Broucke, Director
Carma Fazio

Pre-Press Services
Jerry Stack, Director
Barbara Podczerwinski
Madelyn Underwood

Proofreaders
Anne Dillon
Marguerite Hoye
Daniel Marotta

Research Services
Director
Mary Norton

Researchers
Karen McCormack
Kristina Vaicikonis

Library Services
Mary Ann Urbashich, Head

Publisher
William H. Nault

President, World Book Publishing
Daniel C. Wasp

Preface

During 1992, *The World Book Encyclopedia* celebrates its 75th anniversary. First published in 1917 in 8 volumes, *World Book* has grown to its present 22 volumes as new information and new features have been added to better serve its readers in homes, schools, and libraries. In the process, *World Book* has become the world's largest-selling encyclopedia, touching the lives of millions of users.

By the early 1920's, the editors recognized the need for a "supplement" to help owners of *World Book* keep their set up to date. At first, this "annual supplement" consisted of about 100 pages in loose-leaf form, punched to fit into a special binder that resembled the owner's set. By 1931, the "Annual" had a paperback cover. Then, in 1962, the content was expanded, new features added, and the annual supplement took on a new title and a new look: *The World Book Year Book,* bound in hardcover to match the *World Book.*

This 1992 edition provides dramatic testimony to the important updating role of *The Year Book.* Think about the many important events of 1991: the Persian Gulf War; final 1990 U.S. census results; and the upheaval in the Soviet Union. All this and much more is included in *The 1992 Year Book.*

The Year Book has been specially designed to update your *World Book* and provide a record of the year. The "World Book Year Book Update" section, arranged alphabetically like *World Book,* summarizes major events of the year in nearly 300 articles—from Advertising to Zoos. In most cases, the article titles are the same as those of the articles in *The World Book Encyclopedia* that they update.

World Book Year Book Update

We have made a major change in this section this year, based on research with *Year Book* owners. They suggested that the book would be easier to use if we placed the Special Reports—in-depth articles on topics of current interest—in the A to Z "Year Book Update" section. So you will find the Special Reports—some 15 of them—spread throughout this section. For example, a Special Report analyzing the reasons behind the collapse of Soviet Communism is found within the year's summary of events in the "Union of Soviet Socialist Republics" article.

The "World Book Supplement" section reprints new and significantly revised articles from the latest edition of *World Book.* In this 1992 edition, six articles are reprinted, including timely articles on the newly independent Baltic republics—Estonia, Latvia, and Lithuania.

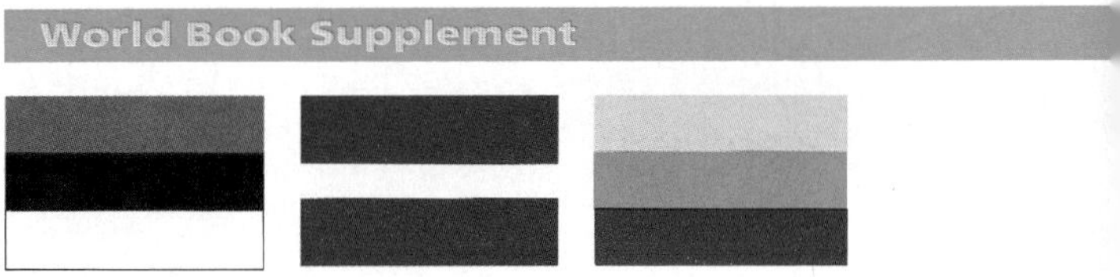

World Book Supplement

Estonia Latvia Lithuania

The other sections of the book each provide a special updating role. The "Year in Brief" provides a pictorial review of the top news stories of the year followed by a month-by-month chronology of the year's major events. The "Dictionary Supplement" lists words added to the latest edition of *The World Book Dictionary,* words that have become a permanent part of our ever-changing language.

The "Census Update" section is a special feature of *The 1992 Year Book.* In it, we provide final 1990 census figures for all 50 states—their cities and towns, metropolitan areas, and counties. Thus this Census section gives you a convenient source of the latest official figures for the many U.S. population figures in your *World Book.*

Two final features help direct you to the wealth of information contained in your *Year Book.* The "Cross-Reference Tabs," found in the front of the book, list key articles in *The 1992 Year Book.* Placed in the appropriate volumes of your *World Book,* they will direct you to more recent or more detailed information in *The Year Book.* "The Index," found at the back of this volume, covers the content of the current and two previous editions of *The Year Book.* Use this index when you are curious about a topic or event and want to find where it is covered in your *Year Books.*

We hope you will take a few minutes to become familiar with the organization and contents of *The 1992 Year Book.* Whether you are researching a topic for a school paper, looking up a particular event, or simply browsing through the dramatic events of the year, you will find it an invaluable addition to your World Book library.

The Editors

Page 25

Contents

The Year in Brief 10 to 37

A pictorial review of the top stories in the news and where to find information about them in this edition of ***The Year Book*** is followed by a month-by-month listing of some of 1991's major happenings.

World Book Year Book Update 38 to 478

The major world events of 1991 are reported in nearly 300 alphabetically arranged articles—from "Advertising" and "Europe" to "Persian Gulf" and "Zoos." Included are 15 Special Reports that provide an in-depth focus on especially noteworthy developments.

ARCHAEOLOGY: The Ancient Treasures of Iraq
by Elizabeth C. Stone 54-59
Ancient archaeological treasures were affected by the gulf war.

CANADA: Canada and Quebec at a Crossroads
by Kenneth McRoberts 113-124
French-speaking Quebec is thinking seriously about secession.

CENSUS: The 1990 Census: An American Self-Portrait
by Karin C. Rosenberg 127-136
The census tells Americans who they are and how they live.

DANCING: Two Legends of Dance
by Nancy Goldner 169-170
Profiles of Dame Margot Fonteyn and Martha Graham.

DEATHS: Dr. Seuss: Oh, the Places He Took Us!
by Ruth K. MacDonald 177-178
The famous author has a lasting place in children's literature.

EUROPE: The Rocky Road to European Unity
by Philip Revzin....208-215
Europe may have a single market by 1993 if all goes as planned.

MEDICINE: Genetic Medicine: Promise and Perils
by Jerry E. Bishop....298-309
Gene therapy is revolutionizing the field of medicine.

PERSIAN GULF: War in the Persian Gulf
by William R. Cormier 342-355
How an international coalition drove Iraq from oil-rich Kuwait.

POPULAR MUSIC: The Flap over Rap
by Alan Light....367-370
Rap music may be controversial, but it's a commercial success.

SPAIN: Spain Takes Center Stage in 1992
by Anne Spiselman 397-399
Spain will host the Olympics and a world's fair in 1992.

SUPREME COURT: A Champion of Civil Rights Retires
by Geoffrey A. Campbell and Linda P. Campbell 409-410
Retired Justice Thurgood Marshall leaves a legacy of dissent.

Page 177

Page 342

Page 42

TRANSIT: Light at the End of the Chunnel
by Laura van Dam 425-429
An underground tunnel will link England and France in 1993.

U.S.S.R.: Why Communism Failed in the U.S.S.R.
by Robert V. Daniels 441-446
The Soviet Communist Party proved to be unreformable.

WATER: Our Precious Ground Water
by Stanley N. Davis 456-467
Natural underground reservoirs are threatened by pollution.

YUGOSLAVIA: A Troubled Past Clouds Yugoslavia's Future
by David Lawday...472-475
Long-standing ethnic conflicts are tearing Yugoslavia apart.

Dictionary Supplement 479 to 481

A listing of new words added to the 1992 edition of ***The World Book Dictionary*** because they have become a part of our language.

World Book Supplement 482 to 513

Six new or revised articles are reprinted from the 1992 edition of ***The World Book Encyclopedia.***

483 Estonia

486 Iraq

493 Jazz

500 Latvia

503 Lithuania

506 Races, Human

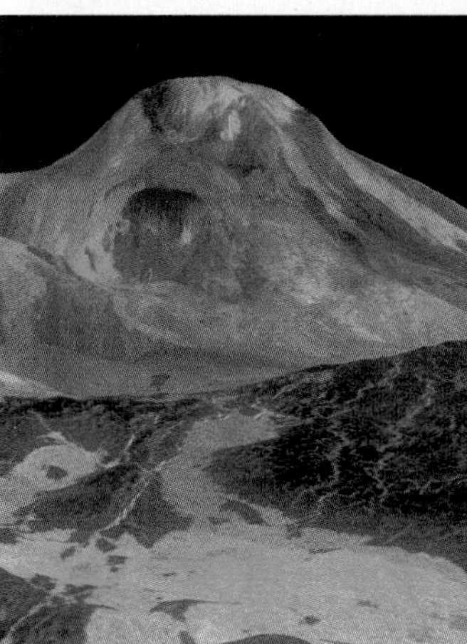

Page 74

Page 441

Census Supplement 514 to 552

A state-by-state listing, arranged alphabetically, of the population of almost every city in the United States, based on the 1990 census.

Index 553 to 572

A 20-page cumulative index covers the contents of the 1990, 1991, and 1992 editions of ***The Year Book.***

Cross-Reference Tabs

A tear-out page of Cross-Reference Tabs for insertion in ***The World Book Encyclopedia*** appears before page 1.

Contributors

Contributors not listed on these pages are members of ***The World Book Year Book*** editorial staff.

Alexiou, Arthur G., B.S.E.E., M.S.E.E.; Assistant Secretary, Committee on Climatic Changes and Ocean. **[Ocean]**

Andrews, Peter J., B.A., M.S.; free-lance writer; biochemist. **[Chemistry]**

Apseloff, Marilyn Fain, B.A., M.A.; Associate Professor of English, Kent State University. **[Literature for children]**

Arndt, Randolph C., Media Relations Director, National League of Cities. **[City]**

Barber, Peggy, B.A., M.L.S.; Associate Executive Director for Communications, American Library Association. **[Library]**

Berman, Howard A., B.A., B.H.L., M.A.H.L.; Rabbi, Chicago Sinai Congregation. **[Judaism]**

Bessman, Jim, contributor, *Billboard* magazine; Senior Editor, *Spin* magazine. **[Popular music]**

Bishop, Jerry E., B.S.J.; Deputy News Editor, *The Wall Street Journal.* **[Medicine,** Special Report: **Genetic Medicine: Promise and Perils]**

Blackadar, Alfred K., A.B., Ph.D.; Professor Emeritus, The Pennsylvania State University. **[Weather]**

Bourne, Eric, columnist, foreign affairs, *The Christian Science Monitor.* **[Eastern European country articles]**

Bower, Bruce, M.A.; Behavioral Sciences Editor, *Science News* magazine. **[Psychology]**

Bradsher, Henry S., A.B., B.J.; foreign affairs analyst. **[Asia and Asian country articles]**

Brett, Carlton E., B.A., M.S., Ph.D.; Professor of Geological Sciences, University of Rochester. **[Paleontology]**

Brock, Frances D., B.A., M.S.J.; free-lance writer. **[Advertising]**

Campbell, Geoffrey A., B.J.; Staff Reporter, *The Bond Buyer.* **[Supreme Court of the United States,** Special Report: **A Champion of Civil Rights Retires; Civil rights; Supreme Court of the United States]**

Campbell, Linda P., B.A., M.S.L.; National Legal Affairs Correspondent, *Chicago Tribune.* **[Supreme Court of the United States,** Special Report: **A Champion of Civil Rights Retires; Civil rights; Supreme Court of the United States]**

Campion, Owen F., A.B.; Associate Publisher. *Our Sunday Visitor* magazine. **[Religion; Roman Catholic Church]**

Cardinale, Diane P., B.A.; Assistant Communications Director, Toy Manufacturers of America. **[Toys and games]**

Carmody, Deirdre, B.A.; Media Reporter, *The New York Times* **[Magazine]**

Cormier, Frank, B.S.J., M.S.J.; former White House Correspondent, Associated Press. **[U.S. government articles]**

Cormier, Margot, B.A., M.S.J.; free-lance writer. **[U.S. government articles]**

Cormier, William R., M.S.J.; Newsman, International Desk, Associated Press. **[Persian Gulf,** Special Report: **War in the Persian Gulf]**

Cromie, William J., B.S., M.S.; science writer, Harvard University. **[Space exploration]**

Daniels, Robert V., A.B., M.A., Ph.D.; Professor Emeritus of History, University of Vermont. **[Union of Soviet Socialist Republics,** Special Report: **Why Communism Failed in the U.S.S.R.]**

Davis, Stanley N., B.S., M.S., Ph.D.; Professor Emeritus of Hydrology, University of Arizona at Tucson. **[Water,** Special Report: **Our Precious Ground Water]**

DeFrank, Thomas M., B.A., M.A.; White House Correspondent, *Newsweek* magazine. **[Armed forces]**

Dent, Thomas H., B.S.; Executive Director, The Cat Fanciers' Association. **[Cat]**

Dillon, David, B.A., M.A., Ph.D.; Architect Critic, *Dallas Morning News.* **[Architecture]**

Dirda, Michael, B.A., M.A., Ph.D.; writer and editor, *The Washington Post Book World.* **[Poetry]**

Ellis, Gavin, Assistant Editor, *New Zealand Herald.* **[New Zealand]**

Esposito, John L., B.A., M.A., Ph.D.; Loyola Professor of Middle East Studies, College of the Holy Cross. **[Islam]**

Evans, Sandra, B.S.J.; Staff Writer, *The Washington Post.* **[Washington, D.C.]**

Farr, David M. L., M.A., D.Phil.; Professor Emeritus, Carleton University, Ottawa. **[Canada; Canadian provinces articles; Mulroney, Brian]**

Fisher, Robert W., B.A., M.A.; Senior Economist/Editor, U.S. Bureau of Labor Statistics. **[Labor]**

Fitzgerald, Mark, B.A.; Midwest Editor, *Editor & Publisher* magazine. **[Newspaper]**

Friedman, Emily, B.A.; Contributing Editor, *Hospitals* magazine. **[Hospital]**

Garvie, Maureen, B.A., B.Ed., M.A.; Books Editor, *The* (Kingston, Ont.) *Whig-Standard.* **[Canadian literature]**

Gatty, Bob, Editor, Periodicals News Service. **[Food]**

Gillenwater, Sharon K., B.A.; Assistant Editor, *San Diego Magazine.* **[San Diego]**

Goldner, Nancy, B.A.; Dance Critic, *The Philadelphia Inquirer.* **[Dancing,** Special Report: **Two Legends of Dance; Dancing]**

Graham, Timothy J., City Editor, *The Houston Post.* **[Houston]**

Harakas, Stanley Samuel, B.A., B.D., Th.D.; Archbishop Iakovos Professor of Orthodox Theology, Hellenic College, Holy Cross Greek Orthodox School of Theology. **[Eastern Orthodox Churches]**

Haverstock, Nathan A., A.B.; Affiliate Scholar, Oberlin College. **[Latin America and Latin-American country articles]**

Heartney, Eleanor, B.A., M.A.; free-lance art critic. **[Art]**

Helms, Christine, B.A., Ph.D.; free-lance writer; consultant. **[Middle East and Middle Eastern country articles; North Africa country articles]**

Higgins, James V., B.A.; Auto Industry Reporter, *The Detroit News.* **[Automobile]**

Hill, Michael, B.A.; Television Critic, *Baltimore Evening Sun.* **[Television]**

Hillgren, Sonja, B.J., M.A.; Washington Editor, *Farm Journal.* **[Farm and farming]**

Inder, Stuart, former Editor and Publisher, *Pacific Islands Year Book.* **[Pacific Islands]**

Jacobi, Peter P., B.S.J., M.S.J.; Professor of Journalism, Indiana University. **[Classical music]**

Johanson, Donald C., B.S., M.A., Ph.D.; President, Institute of Human Origins. **[Anthropology]**

Keeney, Kathy, B.A.; Editor, *Modern Railroads* magazine. **[Railroad]**

King, Elliot W., M.S., M.A.; Editor, *Optical and Magnetic Report* magazine. **[Computer]**

Kisor, Henry, B.A., M.S.J.; Book Editor, *Chicago Sun-Times.* **[Literature]**

Knapp, Elaine S., B.A.; Editor, Council of State Governments. [**State government**]

Kolgraf, Ronald, B.A., M.A.; Publisher, *Adweek* magazine. [**Manufacturing**]

Lawday, David, M.A.; Europe Correspondent, *U.S. News & World Report.* [**Yugoslavia,** Special Report: **A Troubled Past Clouds Yugoslavia's Future**]

Lawrence, Al, B.A., M.A., M.Ed.; Executive Director, United States Chess Federation. [**Chess**]

Lawrence, Richard, B.E.E.; International Economics Correspondent, *The Journal of Commerce.* [**Economics; International trade**]

LeGall, Michel, Ph.D.; Associate Professor of Middle Eastern History, St. Olaf College. [**World Book Supplement: Iraq**]

Lewis, David C., M.D.; Professor of Medicine and Community Health, Brown University. [**Drug abuse**]

Liebenow, Beverly B., B.A.; author and free-lance writer. [**Africa and African country articles**]

Liebenow, J. Gus, B.A., M.A., Ph.D.; James J. Rudy Professor of Political Science and African Studies, Indiana University. [**Africa and African country articles**]

Light, Alan, B.A.; Associate Editor, *Rolling Stone* magazine. [**Popular music,** Special Report: **The Flap Over Rap**]

Litsky, Frank, B.S.; sportswriter, *The New York Times.* [**Sports articles**]

MacDonald, Ruth K., Ph.D.; Professor of English, Purdue University Calumet. [**Deaths,** Special Report: **Dr. Seuss: Oh, the Places He Took Us!**]

March, Robert H., A.B., S.M., Ph.D.; Professor of Physics, University of Wisconsin-Madison. [**Physics**]

Marschall, Laurence A., Ph.D; Professor of Physics, Gettysburg College. [**Astronomy**]

Marty, Martin E., Ph.D.; Fairfax M. Cone Distinguished Service Professor, University of Chicago. [**Protestantism**]

Mather, Ian J., B.A., M.A.; Diplomatic Editor, *The European,* London. [**Great Britain; Ireland; Northern Ireland**]

Maugh, Thomas H., II, Ph.D.; Science Writer, *Los Angeles Times.* [**Biology**]

McCarron, John F., B.S.J., M.S.J.; Financial Editor, *Chicago Tribune.* [**Chicago**]

McGinley, Laurie, B.S.J.; Reporter, *The Wall Street Journal.* [**Aviation**]

McRoberts, Kenneth, B.A., M.A., Ph.D.; Professor of Political Science, York University. [**Canada,** Special Report: **Canada and Quebec at a Crossroads**]

Merina, Victor, A.A., B.A., M.S.; Staff Writer, *Los Angeles Times.* [**Los Angeles**]

Merline, John W., B.A.; Correspondent, *Investor's Business Daily.* [**Consumerism**]

Moores, Eldridge M., B.S., Ph.D.; Professor of Geology, University of California at Davis. [**Geology**]

Moritz, Owen, B.A.; Urban Affairs Editor, New York *Daily News.* [**New York City**]

Morris, Bernadine, B.A., M.A.; Chief Fashion Writer, *The New York Times.* [**Fashion**]

Nguyen, J. Tuyet, B.A.; United Nations Correspondent, United Press International. [**United Nations**]

Nichols, Jennifer A., B.A.; Executive Editorial Assistant, American Correctional Association. [**Prison**]

Parming, Tonu, B.A., Ph.D.; Professor of Estonian Studies, University of Toronto. [**World Book Supplement; Estonia**]

Pennisi, Elizabeth, B.S., M.S.; Chemistry/Materials Science Editor, *Science News* magazine. [**Zoology**]

Prater, Constance C., B.S.J.; City-County Bureau Chief, *Detroit Free Press.* [**Detroit**]

Priestaf, Iris, B.A., M.A., Ph.D.; Geographer and Vice President, David Keith Todd Consulting Engineers, Inc. [**Water**]

Raloff, Janet, B.S.J., M.S.J.; Policy/Technology Editor, *Science News* magazine. [**Environmental pollution**]

Revzin, Philip, B.A., M.A.; Editor, *The Wall Street Journal Europe.* [**Europe,** Special Report: **The Rocky Road to European Unity; Europe and western European country articles**]

Rose, Mark J., M.A.; Managing Editor, *Archaeology* magazine. [**Archaeology**]

Shapiro, Howard S., B.S.; Cultural Arts Editor, *The Philadelphia Inquirer.* [**Philadelphia**]

Shewey, Don, B.F.A.; Contributing Writer, *Village Voice* and *American Theatre.* [**Theater**]

Smerk, George, B.S., M.B.A., D.B.A.; Professor of Transportation, School of Business, Indiana University. [**Transit**]

Spiselman, Anne, M.A., A.B.D.; free-lance writer. [**Spain,** Special Report: **Spain Takes Center Stage in 1992**]

Stein, David Lewis, B.A., M.S.; author; journalist, *The Toronto Star.* [**Toronto**]

Stone, Elizabeth C., B.A., M.A., Ph.D.; Associate Professor, State University of New York at Stony Brook. [**Archaeology,** Special Report: **The Ancient Treasures of Iraq**]

Swedlund, Alan, M.A,. Ph.D.; Professor of Anthropology, University of Massachusetts-Amherst. [**World Book Supplement: Races, Human**]

Tanner, James C., B.S.J.; Senior Energy Correspondent, *The Wall Street Journal.* [**Petroleum and gas**]

Thomas, Paulette, B.A.; Staff Writer, *The Wall Street Journal.* [**Bank**]

Tirro, Frank, B.M.E., M.M., Ph.D.; Professor of Music, Yale University. [**World Book Supplement: Jazz**]

Toch, Thomas W., B.A., M.A.; Associate Editor, *U.S. News & World Report.* [**Education**]

Tuchman, Janice Lyn, B.S., M.S.J.; Executive Editor, *Engineering News-Record.* [**Building and construction**]

van Dam, Laura, B.S., M.S.; Senior Editor, *Technology Review.* [**Transit,** Special Report: **Light at the End of the Chunnel**]

Vardys, V. Stanley, B.A., M.A., Ph.D.; Professor of Political Science, University of Oklahoma. [**World Book Supplement: Latvia; Lithuania**]

Vesley, Roberta, A.B., M.S.L.; former Library Director, American Kennel Club. [**Dog**]

Vizard, Frank, B.A.; Electronics Editor, *Popular Mechanics.* [**Electronics**]

Walter, Eugene, J., Jr., free-lance writer. [**Conservation; Zoos**]

Widder, Pat, B.A.; New York Financial Correspondent, *Chicago Tribune.* [**Stocks and bonds**]

Williams, Susan, B.A.; journalist, Sydney, Australia. [**Australia**]

Windeyer, Kendal; President, Windeyer Associates, Montreal, Canada. [**Montreal**]

Woods, Michael, B.S.; Science Editor, *The* (Toledo, Ohio) *Blade.* [**Industry articles and health articles**]

Wuntch, Philip, B.A., Film Critic, *Dallas Morning News.* [**Motion pictures**]

Year in Brief

January ■ February ■ March ■ April ■ May ■ June
July ■ August ■ September ■ October ■ November ■ December

A pictorial review of the top news stories of 1991 is followed by a month-by-month listing of highlights of some of the year's most significant events.

See pages 16 and 17 ▶

مدين
ity
ميناء عبدالله
Mina Abdulla

The Year's Major News Stories

From the war in the Persian Gulf to the breakup of the Soviet Union, 1991 was a year filled with momentous events. On these two pages are the stories that *Year Book* editors picked as the most memorable, the most exciting, or the most important of the year, along with details about where to find information about them in *The World Book Year Book*. *The Editors*

The end of the Soviet Union

The tricolored Russian flag, flying between the spires of St. Basil's Cathedral, replaced the Soviet hammer and sickle atop the Kremlin in Moscow on Dec. 25, 1991, when the Soviet Union dissolved. In the World Book Year Book Update section, see **Union of Soviet Socialist Republics,** pages 432 to 446. ▶

▲

The Persian Gulf War

With burning oil wells blackening the horizon behind them, American soldiers race across the desert during the ground attack in February that drove Iraqi troops from Kuwait. See **Armed forces,** page 63; **Persian Gulf,** Special Report, page 342.

▲

The Thomas hearings

Supreme Court nominee Clarence Thomas in October defended himself before a Senate committee and a national television audience against sexual harassment charges. See **Supreme Court,** page 407; **Thomas, Clarence,** page 420.

■ **Yugoslavia's civil war**

As Communism collapsed, there arose in the republics that make up Yugoslavia a long-repressed and complex mix of ethnic and nationalistic passions, which erupted into fierce fighting, mainly between the Croatian republic and the Serb-dominated federal army. See **Yugoslavia,** page 471.

◀ **Middle East peace conference**

Leaders of Israel and Arab nations gathered on October 30 in Madrid for the first round of peace talks. These were the first direct negotiations ever between Israel and its four Arab neighbors: Egypt, Jordan, Syria, and Lebanon. See **Middle East,** page 312.

◀ **Hostages freed**

All American and British hostages, including church envoy Terry Waite, after years of being held captive by radical groups in Lebanon were released between August and December. See **Lebanon,** page 277; **Middle East,** page 312.

◀ **Volcanic eruptions**

Eruptions in Japan and in the Philippines killed hundreds of people in 1991. The June eruption of Mt. Pinatubo in the Philippines buried towns under tons of ash and forced the closing of a U.S. air base. See **Geology,** page 226; **Philippines,** page 360.

■ **Independence for the Baltic states**

Estonia, Latvia, and Lithuania, long under Soviet domination, won freedom after a failed coup in the Soviet Union in August. See in the Year Book Update and the World Book Supplement sections, **Estonia,** pages 200 and 483; **Latvia,** pages 276 and 500; **Lithuania,** pages 288 and 503.

January 1991

S	M	T	W	TH	F	S
		1	2	3	4	5
6	7	8	9	10	11	12
13	14	15	16	17	18	19
20	21	22	23	24	25	26
27	28	29	30	31		

2 Salvadoran rebels shoot down a United States Army helicopter in eastern El Salvador and execute the two surviving members of its three-man crew.
6 Jorge Serrano Elías wins a runoff presidential election in Guatemala and takes office on January 14.
7 Secretary of Defense Richard B. Cheney cancels the $57-billion order for the A-12 attack plane, the biggest U.S. weapons program ever terminated.
An attempted coup by an associate of former dictator Jean-Claude Duvalier is thwarted by Loyalist troops in Haiti.
8 Pan Am Corporation files for bankruptcy protection, becoming the third major U.S. airline to do so, after Eastern and Continental.
9 Secretary of State James A. Baker III meets with Iraqi Foreign Minister Tariq Aziz, but the talks fail to produce a plan for Iraq's withdrawal from Kuwait.
11-13 Soviet troops and tanks storm the Lithuanian capital of Vilnius, seizing police and communications facilities and leaving as many as 13 people dead.
12 Congress authorizes President George Bush to use force to drive Iraq from Kuwait.
Gunmen fire on mourners at a funeral vigil for an African National Congress (ANC) leader in Sebokeng, South Africa, killing at least 35 people.
15 Iraq ignores the United Nations deadline for withdrawal from Kuwait.
Cape Verde's Prime Minister Pedro Pires resigns after his party loses, on January 13, the first multiparty election in that African nation.
17 The Persian Gulf War begins as the United States and its allies launch an air strike against Iraq and Iraqi-held Kuwait with 1,000 sorties in 14 hours.
18 Eastern Airlines ceases operations after flying for two years under bankruptcy protection.
21 King Harald V formally takes the throne of Norway, succeeding his father, King Olav V.
24 The Papua New Guinea government and leaders from Bougainville island sign a peace agreement expected to end fighting that began in 1988.
25 President Bush names Representative Edward R. Madigan (R., Ill.) as secretary of agriculture, replacing Clayton K. Yeutter, who was elected chairman of the Republican National Committee.
26 Somali rebels take control of Somalia's capital, Mogadishu. President Mohamed Siad Barre flees.
Tens of thousands of people in Washington, D.C., rally against the Persian Gulf War.
27 The New York Giants win football's Super Bowl XXV, defeating the Buffalo Bills 20-19, the narrowest margin of victory in any Super Bowl.
29 Nelson Mandela of the ANC and Chief Mangosuthu Gatsha Buthelezi of the Inkatha Freedom Party—the leaders of South Africa's two largest black groups—agree to end violence that has plagued relations between their organizations.
The first attempt to cure cancer by gene therapy begins at the National Cancer Institute in Bethesda, Md., when researchers inject genetically altered white-blood cells into two patients with melanoma.

▲ Running back Ottis Anderson carries the ball in the New York Giants' 20-19 victory over the Buffalo Bills in Super Bowl XXV on January 27.

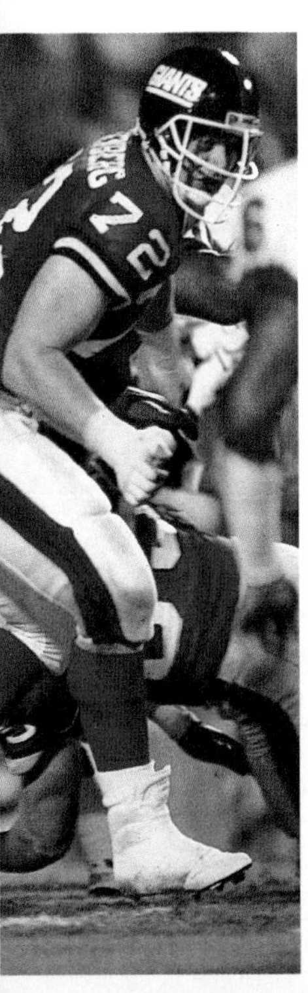

◀ Lithuanians erect barriers in Vilnius, the capital, to halt Soviet troops and tanks that stormed police and communications facilities from January 11 to 13.

Antiaircraft fire lights up the sky over Baghdad as the United States and its allies begin the air war against Iraq on January 17.
▼

February 1991

S	M	T	W	TH	F	S
					1	2
3	4	5	6	7	8	9
10	11	12	13	14	15	16
17	18	19	20	21	22	23
24	25	26	27	28		

1 A USAir jetliner collides with a commuter plane on a runway at Los Angeles International Airport, killing 34 people.
A deadly earthquake kills more than 1,200 people in Afghanistan and Pakistan.
3 A postage increase raises the cost of a first-class U.S. stamp from 25 to 29 cents.
7 A mortar shell explodes outside the London residence of Great Britain's prime minister. The Irish Republican Army (IRA) claims responsibility.
Jean-Bertrand Aristide, a Roman Catholic priest, becomes Haiti's first democratically elected president.
9 Citizens of Lithuania vote 9 to 1 in favor of independence from the Soviet Union.
Donald Cameron is elected premier of the Canadian province of Nova Scotia.
Criminal Type, a 5-year-old thoroughbred, wins Horse of the Year honors.
11 A federal grand jury indicts Detroit police chief William L. Hart on charges of embezzlement and income tax evasion. Hart denies the charges.
11, 18 Sudafed cold capsules poisoned with cyanide kill two people in Washington state.
12 An appeals court overturns television evangelist Jim Bakker's 45-year prison sentence, but the court upholds his 1989 conviction on 24 counts of fraud and conspiracy.
13 Allied bombs hit a building in Baghdad, Iraq, that the United States claims is a military command post but Iraq says is a civilian bomb shelter. At least 300 men, women, and children are killed.
17 The African nation of Cape Verde holds its first multicandidate presidential election since gaining independence in 1975. Opposition candidate Antonio Mascarenhas Monteiro wins by a landslide.
18 IRA bombings at two London train stations leave 1 person dead and more than 40 others wounded.
20 Albanian President Ramiz Alia dismisses the government of Premier Adil Çarçani in an attempt to end prodemocracy protests. On February 22, Alia appoints a new government, which is headed by Premier Fatos Nano.
23 A military coup topples the civilian government of Thailand's Prime Minister Chatchai Chunhawan.
24 The allied ground war begins against Iraq and Iraqi troops in Kuwait. In an elaborate deception, some troops begin a frontal assault along the border between Kuwait and Saudi Arabia, while other forces, undetected by the Iraqis, who lack satellites and reconnaissance aircraft, sweep into southern Iraq.
27 President Bush declares victory over Iraq in the Persian Gulf War and orders a cease-fire.
Bangladesh elects a new Parliament in which 139 of 300 seats go to the centrist Bangladesh Nationalist Party. Party leader Khaleda Zia becomes Bangladesh's first woman president on March 19.
28 Iraq agrees to end hostilities.
Voters in the Estonian and Latvian republics of the Soviet Union vote more than 3 to 1 in favor of independence in referendums.

American and Saudi Arabian troops victoriously enter the city of Kuwait on February 26, only two days after beginning the ground war against Iraq.

INTG. 91

March 1991

S	M	T	W	TH	F	S
					1	2
3	4	5	6	7	8	9
10	11	12	13	14	15	16
17	18	19	20	21	22	23
24	25	26	27	28	29	30
31						

3 A United Airlines jetliner crashes on approach to Colorado Springs Municipal Airport, killing all 25 people aboard.

Miguel Trovoada wins the first contested presidential election ever held in the African nation of São Tomé and Principé.

6 India's Prime Minister Chandra Shekhar resigns because of a dispute with former Prime Minister Rajiv Gandhi, whose support kept him in power.

10 El Salvador's ruling rightist party, the National Republican Alliance, wins 39 of 84 seats in voting for the National Assembly, enough to retain control with the support of its parliamentary allies.

14 Kuwait's ruler, Amir Jabir al-Ahmad al-Jabir al-Sabah, returns to his country after seven months in exile during Iraq's occupation.

15 The United States and Albania resume diplomatic relations for the first time since 1939.

Four Los Angeles police officers are indicted on felony charges in connection with the videotaped beating of an unarmed black motorist during a traffic stop on March 3. The officers plead innocent.

Canada's housing minister, Alan Redway, resigns after he was detained by police for joking that an acquaintance had a gun while passing through security at Ottawa International Airport. The acquaintance did not have a gun.

17 In the first national referendum ever held, the Soviet people vote in favor of keeping the 15 Soviet republics together. Although 77 per cent of the voters approved of unity, the margin is considered smaller than expected.

Finland's main opposition party, the Center Party, wins 55 of 200 seats in parliamentary elections and ends 25 years of dominance by the Social Democrats.

19 The Knight Commission on Intercollegiate Athletics, a panel of leading college educators, calls for sweeping reforms in college sports.

19-26 Lech Walesa makes the first-ever visit by a Polish president to the United States, stopping in Washington, D.C., Los Angeles, and Chicago.

20 British publisher Robert Maxwell assumes ownership of the New York *Daily News* after reaching labor agreements with striking newspaper unions.

The Supreme Court of the United States rules that employers cannot bar women from hazardous jobs because of a risk to unborn children.

24 Nicephore Soglo, prime minister of the African nation of Benin, wins election to the presidency in Benin's first presidential election since 1970.

25 The Western film *Dances with Wolves* wins seven Academy Awards, including best picture.

26 A military coup overthrows Mali's President Moussa Traoré.

Midway Airlines files for bankruptcy protection.

31 Albania's Communist party wins about two-thirds of the 250 seats in the legislature in Albania's first multiparty elections since 1944.

Kevin Costner stars in *Dances with Wolves,* which he also directed, and which won seven Academy Awards, including best picture, at the Oscar ceremonies on March 25.

▼

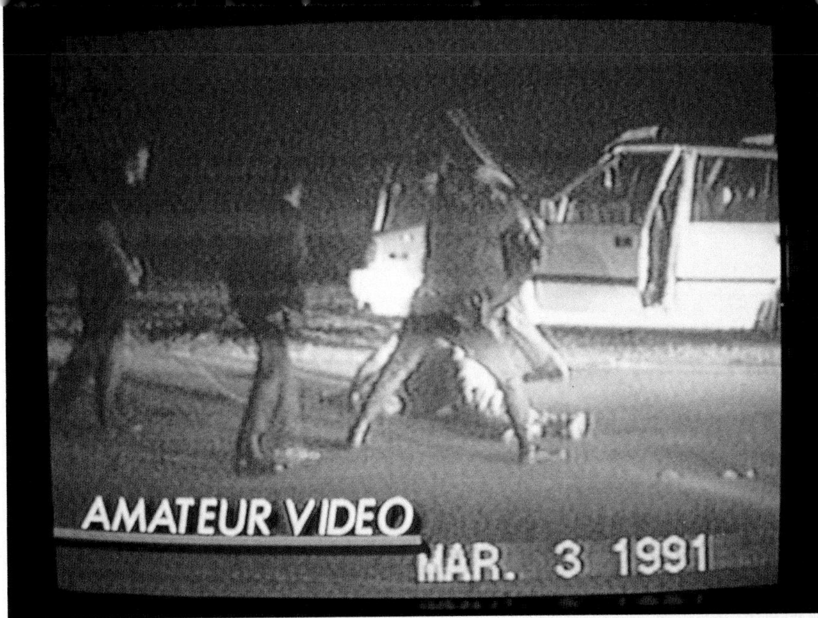

◀ A videotape made by an amateur captures the Los Angeles police beating black motorist Rodney King on March 3. Four policemen were charged in the incident on March 15.

April 1991

S	M	T	W	TH	F	S
	1	2	3	4	5	6
7	8	9	10	11	12	13
14	15	16	17	18	19	20
21	22	23	24	25	26	27
28	29	30				

1 Duke University wins the National Collegiate Athletic Association (NCAA) basketball championship, beating the University of Kansas 72-65.

2 Rita Johnston becomes the premier of British Columbia, Canada's first female premier, succeeding William N. Vander Zalm, who resigns after a government report found a conflict of interest in his 1990 sale of a theme park to a Japanese billionaire.

Government-imposed price increases double or triple the cost of many Soviet consumer items.

3 United States prosecutors drop tax-evasion and embezzlement charges against Representative Floyd H. Flake (D., N.Y.) and his wife, Elaine.

5 The space shuttle *Atlantis* lifts off from Cape Canaveral, Fla. The shuttle puts into orbit on April 7 an observatory to study gamma rays and returns to Earth on April 11.

11 A series of explosions damages the oil tanker *Haven* off Italy, and the tanker sinks on April 14 with most of its 41 million gallons (155 million liters) of crude oil aboard.

15 The 12-nation European Community lifts economic sanctions against South Africa in response to that nation's progress in dismantling apartheid.

16-18 Soviet President Mikhail Gorbachev makes the first-ever visit to Japan by the leader of the U.S.S.R. but fails to resolve a dispute over the Kuril Islands, four islands the Soviets wrested from Japan in 1945 at the end of World War II.

17 The Dow Jones Industrial Average (the Dow) closes above 3,000 for the first time in history, ending the day at 3,004.46.

18 Rail unions obey a back-to-work order under the Taft-Hartley Act, ending a one-day nationwide strike that suspended freight operations and also shut down some passenger lines.

19 Bishop George L. Carey of Bath and Wells is enthroned as archbishop of Canterbury, the spiritual head of the Church of England, succeeding Robert A. K. Runcie, who retired.

21 Canada's Prime Minister Brian Mulroney makes sweeping cabinet changes in an effort to deal more effectively with a threat of secession by Quebec.

23 Iceland's Prime Minister Steingrimur Hermannsson resigns after an inconclusive parliamentary election on April 20. Esko Aho succeeds him on April 26—at age 36, Iceland's youngest leader ever.

26 Tornadoes destroy hundreds of homes in the Midwestern United States and kill 25 people, including 20 in Kansas.

28 The space shuttle *Discovery* lifts off from Cape Canaveral on the first nonsecret military mission, testing instruments for the "Star Wars" missile defense system. The mission ends on May 6.

29 A powerful earthquake jolts the Soviet republic of Georgia, killing at least 360 people.

29-30 A killer typhoon hammers the coast of Bangladesh, causing at least 139,000 deaths.

A bloodless coup in the African nation of Lesotho deposes military ruler Justin M. Lekhanya.

Survivors of a typhoon that hit the coast of Bangladesh on April 29 survey the damage left behind by a storm that claimed at least 139,000 lives.

◀ A power slam gives the upper hand to Duke University in its 72-65 victory over the University of Kansas in the NCAA final on April 1.

May 1991

S	M	T	W	TH	F	S
			1	2	3	4
5	6	7	8	9	10	11
12	13	14	15	16	17	18
19	20	21	22	23	24	25
26	27	28	29	30	31	

1 Angola's leftist government and rebels backed by the United States agree to end a civil war that began in 1975. The peace pact is formally signed on May 31.
Oakland's Rickey Henderson steals the 939th base of his career, a new major league record.
3 Television's "Dallas" airs its last episode after 14 seasons, the second-longest series after "Gunsmoke," which ran for 20 years.
4-5 President Bush is hospitalized after experiencing an irregular heartbeat while jogging. His doctors later say the abnormal beat was due to an overactive thyroid gland.
5 The shooting of a Hispanic man by a black police officer during an arrest sparks rioting in the Mount Pleasant neighborhood of Washington, D.C.
9 Palm Beach, Fla., authorities charge William Kennedy Smith, nephew of Senator Edward M. Kennedy (D., Mass.), with sexual battery. Smith denies any wrongdoing.
12 Voters in Nepal go to the polls in that Asian nation's first multiparty election since 1959.
13 Winnie Mandela, wife of ANC leader Nelson Mandela, is found guilty of kidnapping in the 1988 abduction and beating of four youths. She is sentenced on May 14 to six years in prison, pending appeals.
14 Great Britain's Queen Elizabeth II arrives in Washington, D.C., for a 13-day royal visit.
Bush nominates Robert M. Gates, former deputy director of the Central Intelligence Agency, to succeed William H. Webster as the agency's director.
15 Edith Cresson becomes France's first woman prime minister, replacing Michel Rocard, who resigned to campaign for the presidency.
19 Voters in the Yugoslav province of Croatia vote overwhelmingly to secede from Yugoslavia.
21 Rajiv Gandhi is assassinated by a bomb during a campaign visit near Madras, India.
Ethiopia's President Mengistu Haile-Mariam resigns and flees into exile as rebels advance.
22 South Korea's Prime Minister Ro Jai Bong steps down after weeks of protests sparked by the fatal beating of a student by the police on April 26. Chung Won Shik succeeds Ro on May 24.
23 The Supreme Court of the United States rules that the government may prohibit federally funded family planning clinics from providing information about abortion.
24-25 A massive airlift evacuates more than 14,000 Ethiopian Jews, nearly the entire Jewish population of Ethiopia, to Israel.
25 The Pittsburgh Penguins win hockey's Stanley Cup, defeating the Minnesota North Stars four games to two.
Suriname's military-backed New Democratic Party captures a majority of seats in the National Assembly in elections.
26 An Austrian jetliner explodes shortly after taking off from Bangkok, Thailand, killing all 223 people aboard.
28 Ethiopian rebels seize the capital, Addis Ababa.

◀ Mourners accompany the funeral procession for Rajiv Gandhi, former prime minister of India, who was assassinated on May 21 during an election campaign stop near Madras.

Rebels seize the Ethiopian capital of Addis Ababa on May 28, after forcing President Mengistu Haile-Mariam to flee into exile.

▼

June 1991

S	M	T	W	TH	F	S
						1
2	3	4	5	6	7	8
9	10	11	12	13	14	15
16	17	18	19	20	21	22
23	24	25	26	27	28	29
30						

▲
Michael Jordan goes up and over Earvin (Magic) Johnson as the Chicago Bulls defeated the Los Angeles Lakers in the NBA championship, four games to one, on June 12.

4 **Albania's Council of Ministers Chairman** (Premier) Nano resigns after a nationwide strike. President Ramiz Alia appoints Ylli Bufi to replace Nano as caretaker prime minister.
5 **Algeria's President Chadli Bendjedid dismisses** Prime Minister Mouloud Hamrouche after 11 days of antigovernment demonstrations, replacing him with Sid Ahmed Ghozali.
The space shuttle *Columbia* lifts off from Cape Canaveral on a mission devoted to scientific and medical research.
5, 17 **South Africa repeals** the last legal foundations of apartheid (racial segregation), overturning the laws that segregated places of residence and employment. On June 17, the law that classified all South Africans by race is also repealed.
7 **About 200,000 people in Washington, D.C.,** cheer 8,800 returning Persian Gulf War veterans in a victory parade.
9 **Mount Pinatubo, a long-dormant volcano** in the Philippines, begins to erupt, killing 296 people, most of them on June 15 and 16.
12 **The Chicago Bulls win** the National Basketball Association championship, defeating the Los Angeles Lakers four games to one.
The Soviet republic of Russia holds the first direct presidential election in its history. Boris N. Yeltsin, a political and economic reformer, wins, defeating the candidate of the Soviet Communist party.
12, 15 **Indian voters return to the polls** for parliamentary elections that were interrupted by the May 21 slaying of Congress Party leader Rajiv Gandhi. The Congress Party wins the most seats but falls short of a majority. Congress leader P. V. Narasimha Rao becomes prime minister on June 21.
17 **Northern Ireland's four main political parties** begin talks on restoring self-government there.
Turkey's president Turgut Özal appoints Mesut Yilmaz as prime minister, succeeding Yildirim Akbulut, who resigned.
18 **The Louisiana legislature passes a bill** that prohibits virtually all abortions in the state, overriding a veto by Governor Charles E. (Buddy) Roemer III. In August, a federal district court judge rules the new law unconstitutional.
Wellington Webb is elected mayor of Denver, the first black to hold the office.
20 **House Majority Whip William H. (Bill) Gray III** resigns to become president of the United Negro College Fund.
The lower house of Germany's parliament votes to move the government from Bonn back to Berlin.
25 **The parliaments of the republics of Croatia and Slovenia** declare independence from Yugoslavia.
27 **Associate Justice Thurgood Marshall,** a noted champion of individual and civil rights, announces his resignation from the Supreme Court of the United States.

◀ Justice Thurgood Marshall at a press conference on June 28 cites age and health as his reasons for resigning from the U.S. Supreme Court.

A cloud of ash and deadly gas rises from Mount Pinatubo, a long-dormant volcano in the Philippines that erupted in June, killing 296 people.
▼

July 1991

S	M	T	W	TH	F	S
	1	2	3	4	5	6
7	8	9	10	11	12	13
14	15	16	17	18	19	20
21	22	23	24	25	26	27
28	29	30	31			

1 President Bush nominates Clarence Thomas, a conservative black judge, to replace Thurgood Marshall on the Supreme Court of the United States.
2 Fighting breaks out in Yugoslavia as the federal army attacks secessionists in Slovenia.
4 Colombia's President César Gaviria lifts a seven-year-long state of siege.
6-7 Tennis players Steffi Graf and Michael Stich, both of Germany, win the Wimbledon singles titles.
9 The International Olympic Committee readmits South Africa to the Olympics in response to the repeal of laws supporting apartheid.
Prosecutors in the Iran-contra investigation achieve a breakthrough with the guilty plea of former Central Intelligence Agency official Alan D. Fiers, Jr.
10 Russian President Boris Yeltsin takes office as Russia's first popularly elected leader.
President Bush lifts U.S. economic sanctions imposed on South Africa in 1986.
11 The shadow of the new moon falls upon Earth, producing the last total eclipse of the sun in North America in this century.
15 Chemical Bank and Manufacturers Hanover announce plans to merge in what would be the largest bank merger in U.S. history.
16 Soviet President Mikhail Gorbachev arrives in London to plead for Western aid at the economic summit of the Group of Seven industrial nations.
17 President Bush and Soviet President Gorbachev reach an agreement for a Strategic Arms Reduction Treaty (START), the first accord on long-range nuclear weapons in nearly 10 years. The two men formally sign the treaty on July 31.
18 An Israeli judge investigating a 1990 incident outside a mosque in Jerusalem, in which at least 17 Palestinians were shot and killed, rules that police provoked the incident.
21 Golfer Ian Baker-Finch of Australia wins the 120th British Open at Royal Birkdale in England.
22 Los Angeles police chief Daryl F. Gates, under fire for reports of brutality by officers under his command, announces his plans to retire in April 1992.
25 British astronomers report finding a planetlike object orbiting a distant star.
27 An oil spill begins fouling ocean beaches in Olympic National Park in Washington.
28 Montreal Expo Dennis Martinez pitches a perfect game against the Los Angeles Dodgers, only the 15th perfect game in major league history.
29 A New York grand jury indicts the Bank of Credit and Commerce International for the "largest bank fraud in world financial history," accusing the bank of defrauding depositors of $5 billion.
30 A jury in Haiti convicts the former leader of the Tontons Macoutes, the secret police under the Duvalier dictatorship, of attempting to overthrow Haiti's first democratically elected government.
31 The NAACP and the AFL-CIO announce their opposition to Clarence Thomas' appointment to the Supreme Court.

◀ The sun's corona encircles the moon during a total solar eclipse on July 11, the last total eclipse over North America in this century.

A Yugoslavian tank driver dashes for safety as a barricade burns during a battle on July 2 between the federal army and militia forces from the breakaway republic of Slovenia. ▼

◀ Reformer Boris Yeltsin takes office on July 10 as the first popularly elected president of the Russian republic.

August 1991

S	M	T	W	TH	F	S
				1	2	3
4	5	6	7	8	9	10
11	12	13	14	15	16	17
18	19	20	21	22	23	24
25	26	27	28	29	30	31

1 Israel agrees to participate in a Middle East peace conference, provided certain conditions are met on the makeup of the Palestinian delegation.
4 Ships and helicopters help rescue all 571 passengers and crew members from a sinking cruise ship off the coast of South Africa.
5 Soviet pole vaulter Sergei Bubka breaks the 20-foot (6.1-meter) mark in the outdoor pole vault.
7 The United Nations Security Council agrees to allow Iraq a one-time sale of oil but otherwise maintains economic sanctions against Iraq.
8 Lebanese kidnappers free hostage John McCarthy, a British journalist who was held captive for more than five years.
10 Police in Wichita, Kans., arrest 76 antiabortion demonstrators who tried to block access to a clinic where abortions are performed, bringing to 2,000 the number of arrests to date.
China agrees "in principle" to sign the Treaty on the Non-Proliferation of Nuclear Weapons, becoming the last major nuclear power to agree to its terms.
11 American Edward Austin Tracy is freed after being held hostage for five years in Lebanon. Terrorists also release Jérôme Leyraud of France.
Rookie golfer John Daly wins the PGA championship.
12 A general strike shuts down the capital of Madagascar after troops killed at least 51 people during antigovernment demonstrations.
15 Physicists report that they have created the tiniest electrical switch, consisting of a single atom—a discovery that may revolutionize the computer industry.
18 The Pan American Games end in Havana, Cuba, with the United States winning 352 total medals, including 130 gold medals. Cuba was second with 265 total medals, though it won more gold medals with 140. Canada was third with 127 medals.
19 Soviet hard-liners place President Mikhail Gorbachev under house arrest and impose a state of emergency in an attempted coup. The coup fails on August 21, its leaders are arrested, and Gorbachev returns to power on August 22.
Hurricane Bob sweeps along the East Coast from North Carolina to Maine, causing 16 deaths and knocking out electrical power for about 700,000 homes.
22 Cuban prisoners facing deportation seize 10 hostages at a federal prison in Talladega, Ala. Federal agents rescued the hostages on August 30.
24 Communist rule in the Soviet Union ends as President Gorbachev resigns as general secretary of the Communist Party and orders party units in the government disbanded.
25 Carl Lewis, at the age of 30, sets a world record in the 100-meter dash with a time of 9.86 seconds at the world championships in Tokyo. Five days later, Mike Powell of Alta Loma, Calif., broke the oldest record in track and field in the long jump.
28 A New York City subway train derails, killing 5 passengers and injuring more than 200. On September 3, the motorman was indicted on murder charges.

Soviet tanks assemble in Moscow following a coup attempt that began on August 19. But due to popular resistance led by Russian President Boris N. Yeltsin and the indecisiveness of the coup leaders, the coup crumbles on August 21, and its leaders are arrested.

September 1991

S	M	T	W	TH	F	S
1	2	3	4	5	6	7
8	9	10	11	12	13	14
15	16	17	18	19	20	21
22	23	24	25	26	27	28
29	30					

2 **President George Bush formally recognizes** the independence of Estonia, Latvia, and Lithuania. The Soviet Union extends its formal recognition on September 6, ending 51 years of occupation.
6 **Iran-contra prosecutors** obtain a grand-jury indictment of Clair E. George, formerly the third-highest- ranking officer in the Central Intelligence Agency, on 10 felony charges of perjury, false statements, and obstruction.
9 **Voters in Macedonia** overhelmingly approve a referendum on the republic's independence from Yugoslavia.
Canadian public employees, members of the Public Service Alliance of Canada, begin their first-ever general strike. The workers return to their jobs on September 18 as negotiations with the Treasury Board resume.
11 **Israel releases** 51 Arab prisoners and the bodies of 9 guerrillas, raising hopes for the release of the last remaining Western hostages in Lebanon.
Cuba reacts angrily to Soviet President Mikhail Gorbachev's announced plans to withdraw Soviet military personnel from Cuba and end economic aid.
15 **Sweden's Social Democrats** suffer their worst election defeat in more than 60 years, leading to the resignation of Prime Minister Ingvar Carlsson.
16 **Oliver L. North** is cleared of all charges brought against him in the Iran-contra affair. The ruling was made by U.S. District Court Judge Gerhard A. Gesell.
17 **The United Nations** (UN) admits seven new members—Estonia, Latvia, Lithuania, Marshall Islands, Micronesia, North Korea, and South Korea.
22 **The Dead Sea Scrolls,** the oldest known manuscripts of any books of the Bible, are made available without restrictions to researchers, officials of the Huntington Library in San Marino, Calif., announce.
23 **UN inspectors discover secret Iraqi** documents in a building in Baghdad detailing plans to make nuclear weapons, but Iraqi guards forcibly remove the inspectors and take the documents from them.
24 **Lebanese kidnappers release** Jack Mann, a 77-year-old British citizen, after more than two years of captivity.
25 **Rebels in El Salvador** reach an agreement with President Alfredo Cristiani for their reintegration into Salvadoran society, setting the stage for an end to 11 years of civil war.
27 **President Bush** announces unilateral reductions in short-range nuclear weapons and calls off 24-hour alerts for long-range bombers. On October 5, Soviet President Gorbachev responds to Bush's announcement with similar unilateral reductions.
29 **An Army colonel in El Salvador** is found guilty of murder and terrorism for ordering the deaths of six Jesuit priests who were killed in 1989, along with their housekeeper and the housekeeper's daughter.
30 **Haiti's first democratically elected** president, Jean-Bertrand Aristide, is arrested and sent into exile in a military coup that claimed at least 26 lives.

▲
Israeli soldiers release the body of an Arab guerrilla on September 11 as part of an agreement that raised hopes for the release of Western hostages.

Former White House aide Oliver L. North poses with his family after being cleared of all charges on September 16 in the Iran-contra affair. ▶

October 1991

S	M	T	W	TH	F	S
		1	2	3	4	5
6	7	8	9	10	11	12
13	14	15	16	17	18	19
20	21	22	23	24	25	26
27	28	29	30	31		

3 South African writer Nadine Gordimer, whose work was once suppressed because of its revelations about apartheid (racial separation), wins the Nobel Prize for literature.
Governor Bill Clinton of Arkansas throws his hat in the Democratic presidential race.
6 Soviet President Mikhail S. Gorbachev condemns anti-Semitism in the Soviet Union in a statement read on the 50th anniversary of the Nazi massacre of about 35,000 Jews at Babi Yar in the Ukraine.
7 Yugoslav air force jets bomb the office of Croatian President Franjo Tudjman, who narrowly escapes with his life, along with the president and prime minister of Yugoslavia, who are also Croatians.
13 The last Communist government in eastern Europe falls to the Union of Democratic Forces in parliamentary elections in Bulgaria.
15 The U.S. Senate confirms Clarence Thomas as associate justice of the Supreme Court by a narrow 52-48 margin, after three days of televised hearings on sexual harassment charges by a former colleague, Anita Hill.
16 A restaurant in Killeen, Tex., becomes the scene of the worst mass shooting in U.S. history when a gunman opens fire on patrons and employees, killing 23 people and then himself.
17 The U.S. House of Representatives rejects a ban on the sale and ownership of semiautomatic weapons by a vote of 247 to 177.
18 The Soviet Union restores diplomatic relations with Israel, having severed ties following the 1967 Six-Day War.
20 Twenty-five people are killed in a huge brush fire that swept through residential areas of Oakland, Calif., and destroyed more than 2,700 dwellings.
Former Ku Klux Klan leader David Duke wins a spot in a runoff election for Louisiana governor.
21 American hostage Jesse Turner is released by Lebanese kidnappers. Turner, a mathematics professor, had been held for more than 4 years.
23 Warring factions in Cambodia's 13-year-old civil war sign a peace treaty in Paris that guarantees a governmental role for the Khmer Rouge, the Communist group responsible for hundreds of thousands of deaths between 1975 and 1979 when it ruled the country.
27 The Minnesota Twins win baseball's World Series with a 1-0 victory over the Atlanta Braves in the 10th inning of the seventh game.
29 Trade sanctions against Haiti are expanded by the Administration of U.S. President George Bush to include all goods except basic food shipments and essential medicines in an effort to force coup leaders to restore democracy.
30 The Middle East peace conference—the first direct negotiations between Israel and nearly all its Arab adversaries—opens in Madrid, Spain.
31 Jury selection begins in a West Palm Beach, Fla., courtroom in the rape trial of William K. Smith, nephew of Senator Edward M. Kennedy.

▲ Minnesota Twins players surround pitcher Jack Morris, voted Most Valuable Player in the World Series, which the Twins won on October 27.

Fires sweep through an exclusive residential neighborhood in the hills overlooking Oakland, Calif., on October 20, killing 25 people. ▶

◀ The Senate Judiciary Committee hears testimony from Supreme Court nominee Clarence Thomas, prior to his confirmation on October 15.

November 1991

S	M	T	W	TH	F	S
					1	2
3	4	5	6	7	8	9
10	11	12	13	14	15	16
17	18	19	20	21	22	23
24	25	26	27	28	29	30

1 A disgruntled graduate student at the University of Iowa in Iowa City kills himself and five others after being passed over for an academic award.

4, 5 A two-day general strike, described as the most massive in the history of South Africa, paralyzes major cities as the African National Congress and its trade union affiliate demand a role in governing and an end to a value-added tax.

5 Pennsylvania voters elect Democrat Harris L. Wofford to the U.S. Senate, upsetting former U.S. Attorney General Richard L. Thornburgh, who led Wofford in an August public opinion poll by 44 points.

The U.S. Senate confirms Robert M. Gates as director of the Central Intelligence Agency by a vote of 64-31.

China and Vietnam restore normal relations after a 13-year rift as the leaders of the two countries meet in Beijing, China's capital.

The body of Robert Maxwell, billionaire owner of an international media empire, is found floating in the Atlantic Ocean off the Canary Islands after the crew of his yacht found him missing.

7 Earvin (Magic) Johnson, Jr., star basketball player for the Los Angeles Lakers, announces that he is infected with the virus that causes AIDS and is retiring from the National Basketball Association (NBA).

8 Hong Kong begins the forcible repatriation of Vietnamese boat people, starting with a group of 59 who were flown to Hanoi.

9 Tens of thousands of protesters in more than 100 German cities mark the anniversary of a Nazi attack on Jews by demonstrating against attacks on immigrant workers.

12 June Rowlands is elected the first woman mayor of Toronto.

14 The U.S. government indicts two Libyan intelligence agents in connection with the 1988 bombing of a Pan American World Airways jumbo jet over Lockerbie, Scotland, that killed 270 people.

Prince Norodom Sihanouk is cheered by tens of thousands of people in Phnom Penh as the former ruler returns to Cambodia under the terms of a peace settlement. On November 20, Sihanouk was declared president of the Supreme National Council.

15 President George Bush signs a compromise bill guaranteeing additional aid for some long-term jobless workers.

16 In a closely watched gubernatorial race, Democrat Edwin W. Edwards of Louisiana wins by a landslide in a runoff election over David Duke, a former Ku Klux Klan leader.

18 Hostages Terry Waite of the Church of England and American Thomas Sutherland are released by their Shiite Muslim captors in Lebanon.

20 The U.S. Senate confirms William P. Barr as the country's 77th attorney general.

21 President Bush signs into law the 1991 Civil Rights Act.

The United Nations (UN) Security Council recommends Boutros Ghali, Egypt's deputy prime minister, for the post of UN secretary-general.

▲ British hostage Terry Waite, left, and American hostage Thomas Sutherland, right, rejoice at their release on November 18.

Earvin (Magic) Johnson, Jr., ▶ announces on November 7 that he is infected with the virus that causes AIDS and is retiring from the NBA.

◀ Prince Norodom Sihanouk, former ruler of Cambodia, returns to Phnom Penh, the capital, on November 14 to take up residence after nearly 13 years of exile.

December 1991

S	M	T	W	TH	F	S
1	2	3	4	5	6	7
8	9	10	11	12	13	14
15	16	17	18	19	20	21
22	23	24	25	26	27	28
29	30	31				

1 Ukrainians vote by an overwhelming 9 to 1 margin in favor of independence from the Soviet Union. **France wins tennis' Davis Cup** for the first time since 1932.
2 American Joseph J. Cicippio of Norristown, Pa., arrives in Germany after being released by Shiite Muslim kidnappers in Lebanon who held him hostage for more than five years.
3 John Sununu, President Bush's chief of staff, resigns his position amid reports that he had become a political liability for the President.
3, 4 America's hostage ordeal comes to an end with the release on December 3 of Alann Steen and on December 4 of Terry A. Anderson, chief Middle East correspondent for The Associated Press and the longest-held hostage, a captive for nearly 7 years.
4 Pan American World Airways goes out of business, leaving about 9,000 people unemployed.
7 On the 50th anniversary of the bombing of Pearl Harbor, President Bush tells 2,000 survivors of the attack that it is time for reconciliation with Japan, and Japan's Prime Minister Kiichi Miyazawa expresses "deep remorse" for the "unbearable attack."
10 Leaders of the European Community agree on a treaty at a meeting in Maastricht, the Netherlands, that will bring their 12-nation common market to closer political and economic unity, including the establishment of a single currency by the end of the 1990's.
11 A jury in West Palm Beach. Fla., acquits William K. Smith, nephew of Senator Edward M. Kennedy (D., Mass.), of charges of rape and battery after deliberating for 77 minutes.
12 Reform Teamster Ronald Carey is elected president of the 1.6-million-member union and says, "It's goodbye to the Mafia."
13 North and South Korean leaders sign a treaty of reconciliation and nonaggression that they say is a first step toward reunification.
16 The Canadian government announces that the eastern reaches of the Northwest Territories, an area equal to about a fifth of Canada's land mass, will become the political domain of the 17,500 Eskimos who live there.
18 The General Motors Corporation announces a major restructuring that it says will result in the closing of 21 assembly plants and the loss of 70,000 jobs.
19 Australia's Prime Minister Robert Hawke is ousted by his former treasurer, Paul Keating, who pledges to help lift the economy out of recession.
21 Eleven former Soviet republics—all but Georgia—formally agree to join a Commonwealth of Independent States and declare that the Soviet Union has ceased to exist.
23 Germany recognizes the former Yugoslav republics of Croatia and Slovenia as independent states.
25 Soviet President Mikhail S. Gorbachev resigns his position as the eighth and last leader of the world's first Communist state. Most Western nations recognize the republic of Russia, headed by Boris N. Yeltsin, as the successor state to the Soviet Union.

William Kennedy Smith hugs his mother, Jean, after being found not guilty of rape and battery on December 11. His trial in West Palm Beach, Fla., was covered live on national television.
▼

▲ The tricolor flag of the Russian republic flies over the Kremlin on December 25, moments after the flag of the Soviet Union was lowered and that once-monolithic empire ceased to exist.

◀ President George Bush visits Pearl Harbor on December 7, the 50th anniversary of the Japanese attack that led to the U.S. entry into World War II.

World Book Year Book Update

...Persian Gulf War ■ Dr. Seuss ■ Genetic Medicine...

The major events of 1991 are summarized in nearly 300 alphabetically arranged articles—from "Advertising" to "Zoos." In most cases, the article titles are the same as those of the articles in **The World Book Encyclopedia** that they update. Included are 15 Special Reports that offer in-depth looks at particular subjects, ranging from the Persian Gulf War to the failure of Communism in the Soviet Union. The Special Reports can be found on the following pages under their respective Update article titles.

Archaeology 54
Canada..........................113
Census 125
Dance............................167
Deaths 175
Europe 206
Medicine........................296
Persian Gulf..................340
Popular music...............365
Spain.............................397
Supreme Court.............405
Transit...........................425
Union of Soviet Socialist Republics 441
Water............................456
Yugoslavia....................472

See pages 432 and 433 ▶

Advertising. Many advertisers in the United States altered their advertising plans for the first half of 1991 after war broke out in the Persian Gulf in January. Some of the changes came about because of policy decisions by the television networks.

Wartime ad losses. During the first days of the Gulf war, the National Broadcasting Company (NBC), CBS Inc., and Cable News Network (CNN) decided to cover the war without commercial interruptions. The American Broadcasting Companies (ABC) continued to run commercials, but some advertisers asked that their commercials not appear during the war coverage.

By the end of the first week of the war, all the networks had resumed televising commercials; still, many advertisers stayed off the air. The four networks later estimated that they had lost between $1 million and $3 million each in advertising revenues every day during the first two weeks of the war.

Because of the Gulf war, PepsiCo Incorporated and the Coca-Cola Company both scaled back advertising scheduled for broadcast on January 27 during the football Super Bowl, a major showcase for new advertising campaigns. Pepsi canceled a phone-in sweepstakes promotion, because it was concerned that too many calls might cripple the U.S. telephone system. The cola company instead ran ads that featured pianist and singer Ray Charles performing Pepsi's new slogan, "You've got the right one, baby. Uh-huh." Coca-Cola replaced its "Crack the Code" promotion—which involved viewers in a decoding game—with a simple all-print ad that paid tribute to the fighting forces in the Persian Gulf.

Advertising budgets continued to shrink in 1991 because of a nationwide recession. Advertisers shifted advertising dollars from such traditional media as television and magazines to direct mail and in-store promotions. By midyear, ad spending on the networks had dropped to $4.8 billion, down 7.1 per cent compared with the same six-month period in 1990, according to the Television Bureau of Advertising. Advertising revenues at the 170 magazines tracked by the Publishers Information Bureau, which monitors ad spending in print media, fell in the first eight months of 1991 to $3.9 billion, down 4.8 per cent over the same January through August period of 1990.

Misleading claims. Along with economic pressures came pressure from federal and state government agencies that were concerned about unfounded or misleading health and environmental claims made in advertising and on product labels. A leading watchdog over advertising claims was David A. Kessler, who became commissioner of the United States Food and Drug Administration (FDA) in February 1991.

Kessler made headlines on April 24, when his office seized 2,400 cases of Citrus Hill Fresh Choice orange juice from a Minneapolis, Minn., supermarket. He said that the term "fresh" in the brand's name was misleading because the juice was made by mixing water with a frozen concentrate. The manufacturer, the Procter & Gamble Company, changed the brand's name to Citrus Hill orange juice soon afterward.

Other companies also renamed products following FDA warnings. Chesebrough-Ponds Incorporated changed Ragu Fresh Italian brand pasta sauce to Ragu Fino Italian in May. In July, Kellogg Company's Heartwise cereal became Fiberwise cereal. The FDA proposed regulations for labeling on food packaging in November. The regulations define and limit the use of such claims as *cholesterol-free*, *low-fat*, and *lean*.

The Federal Trade Commission and a task force of state attorneys general sought to reduce public confusion about advertisers' environmental claims. The task force reviewed guidelines that would establish standards for advertisers to follow in using such terms as *biodegradable* and *recyclable*. Its *Green Report II*, published in May, proposed uniform definitions for environmental terms.

Banning tobacco ads. Laws governing tobacco advertising were reviewed in 1991 in Canada and the 12-nation European Community (EC or Common Market). On July 30, Canada's two-year-old ban on tobacco advertising was ruled unconstitutional by a superior court judge in Quebec. The judge ruled that the law violated free-speech guarantees. The EC was considering a proposal to ban all tobacco advertising, including sponsorships of cultural and sporting events by tobacco companies and in-store promotions of tobacco products. A final vote was expected in 1992. Meanwhile, a ban on all television advertising of tobacco took effect in EC nations on Oct. 1, 1991.

Bunny suit. A lawsuit that received much publicity in the United States was filed by the Eveready Battery Company against the Coors Brewing Company in April. Eveready sought to prevent Coors from airing a commercial that featured actor Leslie Nielsen mimicking the Energizer bunny, a battery-operated pink rabbit used in advertising Eveready batteries.

In May, U.S. District Court Judge Charles R. Norgle in Chicago ruled against Eveready and let the Coors ad run. The judge said that consumers would not confuse Nielsen with the bunny. In his ruling, Norgle wrote, "Although Mr. Nielsen dons rabbit ears, tail and feet, he by no means copies the majority of the Energizer bunny's 'look.'"

Awards. In June, the 31-year old Clio Awards went out of business. The Clio Awards were the advertising industry's equivalent of the Academy Awards for motion pictures. The privately funded annual awards ceremony was abruptly canceled because of financial difficulties and internal dissension.

A politician from Minnesota won the Grand Effie Award given by the New York chapter of the American Marketing Association for advertising that effectively sells a product. Senator Paul Wellstone (D., Minn.) became the first politician to win the award, which traditionally has gone to an advertiser of a consumer product. Frances D. Brock

In ***World Book,*** see **Advertising.**

Afghan rebels inspect the town of Khowst in eastern Afghanistan, captured from government forces on March 31 after years of fighting.

Afghanistan. International efforts to find a political solution to Afghanistan's civil war accelerated in 1991 as the collapsing Soviet Union reduced the military and economic support that had sustained the Afghan regime. Because it had been dependent on the Soviet Union for food and fuel, the Afghan government faced bleak prospects.

The United States and the Soviet Union agreed on September 13 to halt by Jan. 1, 1992, Soviet military aid to the Afghan regime and U.S. arms to its guerrilla opponents. The United States and the Soviet Union also agreed to try to recall major weapons that they had provided in the past and to urge other countries to stop sending weapons to Afghanistan. The agreement was intended to reduce the fighting that had continued since the Soviet Army left Afghanistan in 1989 and to open the way for a political settlement.

Afghan guerrillas captured the town of Khowst, 20 miles (32 kilometers) from the Pakistani border, on March 31, 1991, after years of fighting. The Afghan government charged that Pakistan's military forces had armed and directed the guerrilla campaign.

Negotiations. Efforts to arrange a peace settlement to the civil war focused on a plan proposed on May 21 by United Nations (UN) Secretary-General Javier Pérez de Cuéllar. Under the proposal, Afghanistan's current regime would be replaced by a transitional government that would hold elections. In September, Afghan Prime Minister Fazil Haq Khaliqyar indicated that President Najibullah (he uses only one name) would stand aside for a transitional regime that included other officials of the current government. A group of Afghan resistance leaders and Soviet officials meeting in Moscow agreed on November 15 to the UN proposal. But several other guerrilla groups rejected any arrangement under which members of the current Afghan regime would have a role in a new government.

Cooperation. During 1991, the governments of Pakistan and Iran, the rebels' chief backers, worked to encourage unity among rival guerrilla groups. At meetings held in Iran in autumn, most Afghan resistance groups agreed to work together. Despite some increased cooperation, however, conflict between rebel groups in Pakistan, including political assassinations, continued.

Karmal returns. Afghanistan's ruling circle was also torn by conflict. In June, a number of former Afghan leaders returned to Afghanistan from exile in Moscow, apparently with Soviet consent. Among them was former President Babrak Karmal, whom the Soviets had replaced with Najibullah in 1986.

Famine. A combination of spring floods, plant diseases, and early winter snow reduced wheat crops in central Afghanistan. As famine spread in late 1991, refugees fled the region. Henry S. Bradsher

See also **Asia** (Facts in brief table). In ***World Book,*** see **Afghanistan.**

Africa

Developments in Africa in 1991 demonstrated that African nations are attempting to solve many of the political and economic problems that have been holding the continent back. Several of Africa's long-standing civil wars ended or were winding down during the year, and prodemocracy movements gained momentum in a majority of African countries. Some nations also took steps to strengthen their economies. In South Africa, the dismantling of *apartheid* (racial separation) continued, and the two black groups that had been battling each other agreed to stop fighting and join in negotiating with the white government.

Foreign relations. African countries were more self-reliant than ever in 1991, but they also found themselves more influenced by nations elsewhere in the world than at any time since the colonial era. Growing ties between France, Portugal, and Great Britain and their former African colonies played an important part in the continent's economic development, peace negotiations, and cultural exchanges.

At the same time, Africa found itself receiving less attention from foreign governments that had been dependable patrons. The disintegrating Soviet Union and the nations of eastern Europe drastically curtailed their aid to Africa in 1991 and concentrated on meeting their own domestic needs. Likewise, the United States and the countries of western Europe targeted much of their aid and investment for eastern Europe. In addition, a great deal of Western money was spent on the 1991 Persian Gulf War.

The quest for peace. Although Africa on the whole was more peaceful in 1991 than it had been for years, fighting was still common on the continent. Most of Africa's 1991 conflicts, as they always have, involved large regions. A few, on the other hand, were localized affairs that went all but unnoticed by the rest of the world. Such was a rebellion of Tuareg and Arab minorities in northern Mali that was resolved in 1991. On March 7, with Algeria serving as mediator, the Mali government agreed to the rebels' demands for greater autonomy.

More typical was Africa's longest-running conflict, the civil war in Ethiopia. That war, which began in 1962 with a secessionist movement in the region of Eritrea against Emperor Haile Selassie, ended in 1991 with a victory by Eritrean rebels and their allies over a military government that succeeded Haile Selassie. The turning point came in 1990 when the Soviet Union cut off military aid to Ethiopia's President Mengistu Haile-Mariam. With that pillar of support gone, the Mengistu regime was weakened, and in

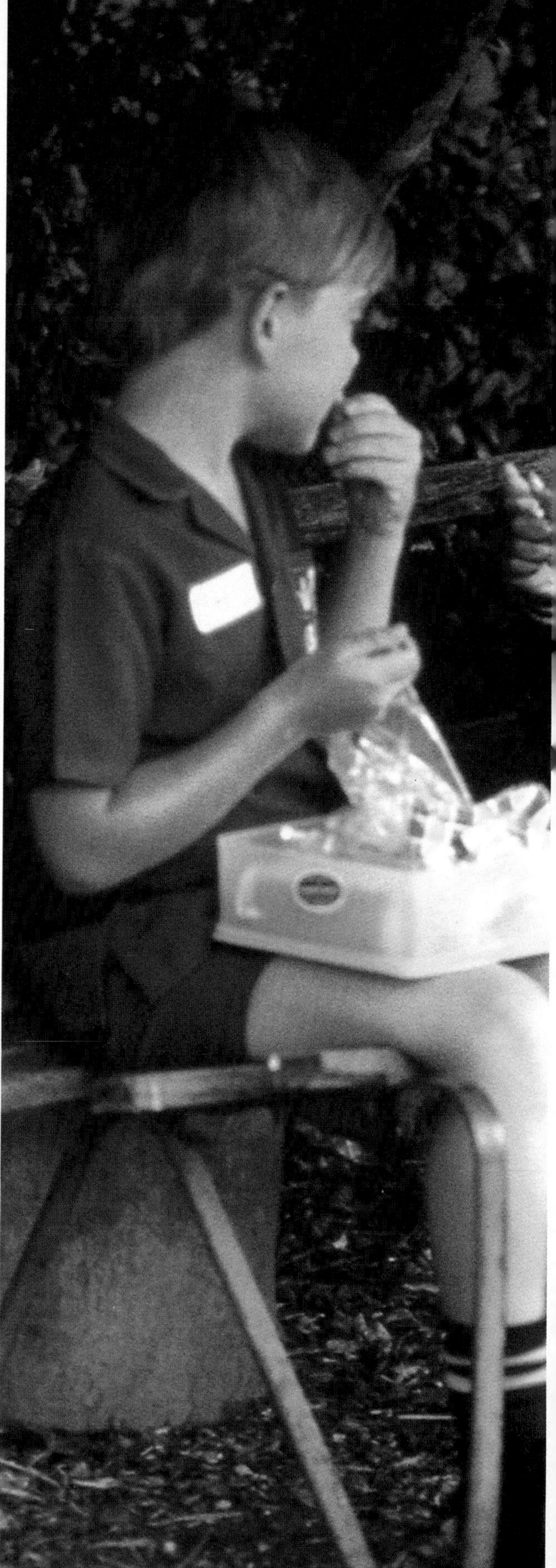

Boys at a newly integrated school in Johannesburg eat lunch together in January as South Africa moves to dismantle its system of racial segregation.

1991 the various rebel groups that had been opposing the government for years coordinated their efforts. In May, Mengistu fled into exile. Although that seemed to conclude the war, the question of secession for Eritrea and other issues were still unresolved.

The Ethiopian war has been rivaled in length by several other conflicts, such as the 16-year-old Angolan civil war, which also ended in May 1991. It, too, was a regional war, involving South Africa, Namibia, and Zaire. The United States and the Soviet Union had supported different sides in the struggle, but it was their cooperation that brought the two warring factions together in Portugal in 1990 to discuss peace. A cease-fire signed in May 1991 laid out a program for multiparty elections in 1992.

One conflict that seemed to be ending in 1990 but continued in 1991 was the civil war in Mozambique, being waged by the Mozambique National Resistance (Renamo). There have been many cease-fires in the war, including one agreed to in late 1990, but they were all later broken by Renamo. With no end to the war in sight as 1991 drew to a close, Malawi, Tanzania, and Zimbabwe continued to maintain troops in Mozambique to protect vital rail links.

That sort of regional cooperation aimed at ending, or at least limiting, hostilities in neighboring countries also helped bring stability to Liberia, which was torn apart by a civil war that began in late 1989. A five-nation peacekeeping force from the Economic Community of West African States, sent to Liberia in August 1990, arranged a cease-fire among the warring factions in 1991 and was preparing the country for elections in 1992.

Unresolved conflicts. Offsetting the 1991 success stories in the search for peace were several still-unresolved conflicts as well as some major failures. Fighting in Western Sahara between the rebel Polisario Front, which seeks independence for the area, and the Moroccan government, which administers it, ended with a September cease-fire. A vote on independence was set for January 1992. But Morocco was reportedly attempting to limit the registration of voters, so renewed hostilities in 1992 were a distinct possibility.

Signals were similarly mixed in Sudan, where Christians in the south have been waging war against the Muslim-Arab government of the north since 1983. In July 1991, it appeared that government victories and the promise of a federal constitution that would limit the imposition of Islamic law were bringing the rebels to the negotiating table. In November, however, fighting erupted again.

In Uganda, army troops reportedly committed atrocities in February and May 1991 against several ethnic minority groups in the north that had taken up arms against the government. That rebellion seemed likely to continue in 1992.

Other unresolved conflicts in 1991 included a civil war in Somalia. Although the three-year-old civil war seemed to end in January with the overthrow of President Mohamed Siad Barre, fighting between rival rebel groups broke out in November. Moreover, the issue of independence for the northern region of Somalia left the nation divided.

The quest for democracy. Although military coups have become much less common in Africa, they were far from dead in 1991 as a way of bringing about a change of government. During the year, rebel officers overthrew unpopular military regimes in Mali and Lesotho. But the coup leaders, unlike most of those in the past, moved quickly to prepare their countries for a return to civilian rule. In several other nations, military rulers continued to move toward a restoration of civilian government. Notable among them were Nigeria and Ghana, where regimes that had been in power for years were in the final stages of defining political parties and planning national elections in preparation for democratic rule in 1992.

In some cases, such as in Ethiopia and Angola, the possibility of returning to civilian government was a welcome consequence of ending years of civil war. In Liberia as well, preparations in 1991 for multiparty elections the following year were the result of the military overthrow in 1990 of President Samuel K. Doe.

In the general move toward democracy in Africa, the most dramatic changes in government in 1991 were brought about by private citizens. These "civilian coups" were termed Africa's "second wave of independence" by some observers, who compared them to the uprisings in the 1950's and 1960's that led to the end of colonial rule. Spurred on by prodemocracy developments in the former Soviet Union and eastern Europe, citizens in a majority of African nations in 1991 participated in mass demonstrations to protest one-party rule, human-rights violations, government corruption, inflation, and economic mismanagement.

The victories they won did not come easily. For example, Kenya's President Daniel T. arap Moi ignored public protests against his oppressive regime and refused until December to even discuss the possibility of multiparty elections. He had reportedly persisted in gross violations of human rights during the year, and only economic pressure from the United States and other donor nations compelled him to reform.

Other dictators were also forced in 1991 to accept multiparty elections. In several cases, however, the regime tried to thwart opposition parties with military force or by tampering with the electoral process. Such was the case in Ivory Coast, where early in the year President Félix Houphouët-Boigny faced riots and calls for his resignation. He had conceded to demands for a multiparty system in 1990, but in the October 1990 election he claimed to have received 80 per cent of the vote, an outcome that his opponents denounced as fraudulent.

In Madagascar, President Didier Ratsiraka in 1991 faced the most serious threat to his rule since seizing power in 1975. Beginning in June 1991, prodemocracy forces staged mass demonstrations demanding his res-

French troops, flown to Zaire to protect Westerners and restore order after Zairian soldiers went on a rampage, stand guard in Kinshasa in September.

ignation and a national conference to draft a new constitution. Ratsiraka seemed to be making concessions, but when 400,000 protesters gathered outside the presidential palace on August 10, he ordered his elite guard to fire on them. More than 50 people were killed and 300 wounded. At year-end, Ratsiraka appeared to be firmly in control.

In some African countries, including the Central African Republic and Gabon, dictators tried to defer or control political reform by merely appointing a new prime minister who would be more acceptable to the opposition. But some of these stalling efforts were ineffective. In Zaire, for instance, President Mobutu Sese Seko proposed one person after another for prime minister, only to have them rejected by the political opposition. When finally his fifth candidate was accepted in late September, it was Mobutu who was dissatisfied. He dismissed the man within weeks of appointing him.

Conferences lay democratic groundwork. The key instrument for political reform in 1991 was a series of national conferences convened to redraw the basic structures of a government and prepare for multiparty elections. One of the first such conferences had been held in Benin in 1990, and it led to an election in March 1991 that ended the 19-year rule of President Mathieu Kérékou. The opposition candidate, Nicephore Soglo, won 67 per cent of the vote and was installed as president on April 4. Elections also led to new governments in Cape Verde in February and São Tomé and Príncipe in March.

One of the most dramatic election results in 1991 was the defeat in March of one of Africa's "founding fathers"—President Kenneth Kaunda of Zambia. He had led his country to independence in 1964 and had been Zambia's only president. But his leadership had become increasingly ineffective and oppressive. As a result of a new constitution imposed on him in 1990, Kaunda had to stand for office. On Oct. 31, 1991, Kaunda was defeated by Frederick Chiluba, a labor union leader, who received 80 per cent of the vote. Chiluba was inaugurated on November 2.

Participants at the 1991 conferences drafted new multiparty constitutions providing guarantees for human rights and a schedule for elections. Most of the new constitutions rejected Marxism. Marxist principles had long held sway in many African nations, but they have become discredited across most of the continent in the 1990's, just as in eastern Europe.

South Africa underwent great change in 1991 as the government of State President Frederik Willem de Klerk took a number of significant steps to dismantle apartheid. In addition, a national convention was held for two days in December to lay the groundwork for a new constitution that would for the first time give the nation's black majority full democratic rights. But the country still experienced a great deal of strife during the year. Whites opposed to apartheid tried to thwart

Facts in brief on African political units

Country	Population	Government	Monetary unit*	Foreign trade (million U.S.$) Exports†	Imports†
Algeria	26,851,000	President Chadli Bendjedid; Prime Minister Sid Ahmed Ghozali	dinar (21.70 = $1)	8,164	7,396
Angola	10,591,000	President José Eduardo dos Santos	kwanza (89.75 = $1)	2,190	451
Benin	5,052,000	President Nicephore Soglo	CFA franc (278.81 = $1)	226	413
Botswana	1,375,000	President Quett K. J. Masire	pula (2.12 = $1)	1,300	1,100
Burkina Faso	9,526,000	Popular Front President, Head of State, & Head of Government Blaise Compaoré	CFA franc (278.81 = $1)	142	489
Burundi	5,771,000	President Pierre Buyoya	franc (199.19 = $1)	75	236
Cameroon	11,863,000	President Paul Biya	CFA franc (278.81 = $1)	924	1,271
Cape Verde	403,000	President Antonio Monteiro Mascarenhas; Prime Minister Carlos Alberto Wahnonde Carvalho Veiga	escudo (72.3 = $1)	7	112
Central African Republic	3,063,000	President André-Dieudonne Kolingba	CFA franc (278.81 = $1)	134	150
Chad	5,970,000	President Idriss Deby	CFA franc (278.81 = $1)	141	419
Comoros	552,000	President Said Mohamed Djohar	CFA franc (278.81 = $1)	12	52
Congo	2,106,000	President Denis Sassou-Nguesso; Prime Minister Andre Milougo	CFA franc (278.81 = $1)	751	544
Djibouti	431,000	President Hassan Gouled Aptidon; Prime Minister Barkat Gourad Hamadou	franc (177.72 = $1)	20	188
Egypt	56,506,000	President Hosni Mubarak; Prime Minister Atef Sedky	pound (3.33 = $1)	2,582	9,202
Equatorial Guinea	462,000	President Teodor Obiang Nguema Mbasogo; Prime Minister Cristino Seriche Bioko Malabo	CFA franc (278.81 = $1)	30	50
Ethiopia	49,263,000	Acting President Meles Zenawi	birr (2.07 = $1)	446	1,075
Gabon	1,249,000	President Omar Bongo; Prime Minister Casimir Oye-Mba	CFA franc (278.81 = $1)	1,288	732
Gambia	905,000	President Sir Dawda Kairaba Jawara	dalasi (9.06 = $1)	40	127
Ghana	15,966,000	Provisional National Defense Council Chairman Jerry John Rawlings	cedi (384 = $1)	1,014	907
Guinea	7,230,000	President Lansana Conté	franc (812.29 = $1)	553	509
Guinea-Bissau	1,032,000	President João Bernardo Vieira	peso (5,000 = $1)	15	49
Ivory Coast	13,600,000	President Félix Houphouët-Boigny	CFA franc (278.81 = $1)	2,792	2,100
Kenya	27,233,000	President Daniel T. arap Moi	shilling (28.60 = $1)	1,054	2,227
Lesotho	1,876,000	King Letsie III; Military Council Chairman Elias Phisoana Ramaema	loti (2.80 = $1)	55	526
Liberia	2,723,000	Interim President Amos Sawyer‡	dollar (1 = $1)	382	308
Libya	4,879,000	Leader of the Revolution Muammar Muhammad al-Qadhafi; General People's Committee Secretary (Prime Minister) Abu Said Omar Bourda	dinar (0.28 = $1)	6,683	5,879

*Exchange rates as of Nov. 29, 1991, or latest available data. †Latest available data.
‡Two rival rebel leaders, Charles Taylor and Prince Yormie Johnson, continued to press claims for the presidency.

Country	Population	Government	Monetary unit*	Foreign trade (million U.S.$) Exports†	Imports†
Madagascar	12,764,000	President Didier Ratsiraka; Prime Minister Victor Ramahatra	franc (1,912.87 = $1)	312	340
Malawi	9,399,000	President H. Kamuzu Banda	kwacha (2.77 = $1)	418	573
Mali	8,818,000	Acting President Amadou Toure; Prime Minister Soumana Sacko	CFA franc (278.81 = $1)	271	500
Mauritania	2,139,000	President Maaouya Ould Sid Ahmed Taya	ouguiya (83.23 = $1)	437	222
Mauritius	1,130,000	Governor General Sir Veerasamy Ringadoo; Prime Minister Sir Aneerood Jugnauth	rupee (15.54 = $1)	987	1,326
Morocco	26,334,000	King Hassan II; Prime Minister Azzedine Laraki	dirham (8.61 = $1)	3,308	5,492
Mozambique	16,517,000	President Joaquím Alberto Chissano; Prime Minister Mário da Graça Machungo	metical (1,766.81 = $1)	103	715
Namibia	1,994,000	President Sam Nujoma; Prime Minister Hage Geingob	rand (2.80 = $1)	935	856
Niger	8,180,000	Supreme Military Council President Ali Saibou; Prime Minister Aliou Mahamidou	CFA franc (278.81 = $1)	209	345
Nigeria	120,972,000	President Ibrahim Babangida	naira (9.80 = $1)	8,138	3,419
Rwanda	7,735,000	President Juvénal Habyarimana	franc (124.87 = $1)	101	369
São Tomé and Príncipe	132,000	President Miguel Trouoada	dobra (240 = $1)	9	17
Senegal	7,661,000	President Abdou Diouf; Prime Minister Habib Thiam	CFA franc (278.81 = $1)	606	1,023
Seychelles	70,000	President France Albert René	rupee (5.28 = $1)	31	164
Sierra Leone	4,370,000	President Joseph Momoh	leone (410 = $1)	138	189
Somalia	7,917,000	Interim President Ali Mahdi Mohamed	shilling (2,620 = $1)	104	132
South Africa	41,600,00	State President Frederik Willem de Klerk	rand (3.06 = $1)	18,969	17,075
Sudan	26,672,000	Prime Minister Umar Hasan Ahmad al-Bashir	pound (15 = $1)	509	1,060
Swaziland	844,000	King Mswati III; Prime Minister Obed Mfanyana Dlamini	lilangeni (2.80 = $1)	394	386
Tanzania	29,393,000	President Ali Hassan Mwinyi; Prime Minister John Malecela	shilling (234.55 = $1)	337	1,495
Togo	3,674,000	President Gnassingbé Eyadéma	CFA franc (278.81 = $1)	242	487
Tunisia	8,496,000	President Zine El-Abidine Ben Ali; Prime Minister Hamed Karoui	dinar (0.91 = $1)	3,595	5,550
Uganda	19,771,000	President Yoweri Museveni; Prime Minister George Cosmas Adyebo	shilling (917.58 = $1)	274	544
Zaire	38,338,000	President Mobutu Sese Seko	zaire (58,481.79 = $1)	1,108	771
Zambia	9,093,000	President Frederick Chiluba; Prime Minister Malimba Masheke	kwacha (84.62 = $1)	899	1,243
Zimbabwe	10,333,000	President Robert Mugabe	dollar (5.05 = $1)	1,420	1,043

de Klerk's effort, with the most extreme members of the opposition instigating acts of violence. Rival black groups also continued to battle one another, though an end to such violence seemed possible in September when the two largest black antiapartheid organizations signed an agreement.

Economic treaty. In June, the Organization of African Unity, an association of 50 African nations, produced a major treaty for the economic unification of the continent. The pact, which must be approved by two-thirds of the member nations, called for the creation of an African Economic Community modeled upon the European Community.

Health, conservation. African nations showed more concern for the health of their citizens in 1991, with many of them funding research and education programs on cholera, river blindness, and other widespread diseases. Some nations also began to face up to the problem of AIDS, which has hit Africa harder than any other continent.

A belated campaign to save the continent's endangered forests took hold in 1991. Most African nations were engaged in reforestation programs and were interested in the protection of endangered animal species, such as the elephant and the black rhinoceros.

J. Gus Liebenow and Beverly B. Liebenow

See also the various African country articles. In ***World Book,*** see **Africa.**

Agriculture. See **Farm and farming.**

AIDS. The fact that AIDS can strike anyone was dramatically emphasized when Los Angeles Lakers basketball star Earvin (Magic) Johnson, Jr., announced on Nov. 7, 1991, that he was infected with the human immunodeficiency virus (HIV), the virus that causes AIDS. Johnson retired from basketball to direct his energies in the cause of AIDS education. United States President George Bush then appointed him to serve on the National Commission on AIDS.

Health-care concerns. Concern that HIV-infected doctors and dentists might transmit the virus to their patients began to grow after the United States Centers for Disease Control (CDC) in Atlanta, Ga., verified in January that a Florida dentist had infected three patients. The CDC said it was the first instance in which a health-care worker had infected patients. Subsequently, two more of the dentist's patients were confirmed as having HIV infections. The first of these patients, Kimberly Bergalis, testified before a congressional panel on September 26 in favor of testing health-care workers for the AIDS virus. Bergalis died at her home in Fort Pierce, Fla., on December 8.

New guidelines for physicians, dentists, and other health-care workers infected with the AIDS virus were issued by the CDC in July. The guidelines advise that health-care workers who perform invasive procedures should voluntarily have tests for infection from both HIV and hepatitis B, a viral disease also spread by contact with infected blood.

AIDS definition. In August, the CDC revised its definition of AIDS. Effective in January 1992, the revised definition allows a diagnosis of AIDS when the number of *helper T cells* (a type of immune system cell) which HIV attacks, falls to 200 per cubic millimeter of blood or less. The normal level is about 1,000 per cubic millimeter of blood. Previously, doctors diagnosed AIDS when a person developed certain infections or forms of cancer. But these illnesses did not include those seen in HIV-infected intravenous drug abusers and women, groups with rising AIDS rates.

Drugs and tests. On Oct. 9, 1991, the U.S. Food and Drug Administration (FDA) approved dideoxyinosine (DDI) to treat AIDS patients who failed to respond to AZT (zidovudine). AZT is the only other drug approved to treat AIDS.

The FDA on September 26 approved the first one-step blood test for detecting infection with both HIV-1 and HIV-2. On September 30, an FDA advisory panel recommended that blood banks begin testing their blood supplies for both viruses by June 1992.

U.S. AIDS statistics. The CDC as of Nov. 30, 1991, reported 202,843 cases of AIDS and 130,687 deaths caused by AIDS since June 1981, when the disorder was first recognized. Michael Woods

In ***World Book,*** see **AIDS.**

Air pollution. See **Environmental pollution.**

Alabama. See **State government.**

Alaska. See **State government.**

Albania. A deteriorating economy plagued Albania's progress toward democracy in 1991. But in major steps toward restoring long-denied rights, the government lifted bans on religious worship and property ownership and granted Albanians the right to travel.

Albanian exodus. In March and September, thousands of Albanians fled their impoverished homeland, crossing the Adriatic Sea to Italy. As the exodus swelled, the Italian government sent many Albanians back. To halt the flow of hungry Albanians, Italy pledged food aid to Europe's poorest nation in June, followed by a loan for modernizing basic industries and financing exports. In September, Italy sent troops to Albania to ensure the rapid distribution of emergency food and medicine. The 12-nation European Community (EC or Common Market) also offered aid.

Political upheaval. On March 31, Albania held its first multiparty elections since 1923. In the elections, Albania's ruling Communist Party of Labor was almost eliminated as a political force in the towns and cities, but a big rural vote enabled the party to retain power and form a government.

A nationwide general strike in May and early June 1991 brought the economy to a standstill and forced the Communists to share power with the opposition. On June 5, Ylli Bufi, an economist and a Communist, was named prime minister in a broad-based coalition that was to remain in power until national elections, scheduled to take place in mid-1992.

Albanians seeking refuge from shortages of food and other goods in their impoverished homeland jump onto shore in Brindisi, Italy, in March.

A new cabinet was formed, consisting of Communists and non-Communists. Cabinet ministers agreed to give up their political party affiliations in an effort to achieve national unity and economic stabilization. An economist and a leader of the Democratic Party of Albania, Gramoz Pashko, became deputy prime minister in charge of economic reform.

In June, Albania's Communists held a party congress. They renamed themselves Socialists, expelled hard-liners, and installed a liberal economist, Fatos Nano, as party chairman.

Bufi's coalition faced an uphill task. By mid-1991, Albania's industrial output was down 50 per cent over the same period in 1990, exports met only one-fifth of the planned amount, and the foreign debt had quadrupled. Both inflation and unemployment continued to mount. A drought and the collapse of the state-run agricultural sector worsened the food shortage.

Bufi was forced to resign on December 4, after the largest non-Communist group, the Democratic Party, withdrew from the coalition formed in June. An interim government, headed by former Minister of Industry Vilson Ahmeti, was approved on December 15.

Diplomatic relations between Albania and the United States were renewed in March 1991, after a break of 52 years. The resumption of relations with Great Britain in May completed Albanian ties with the European countries. Eric Bourne

See also **Europe** (Facts in brief table). In ***World Book,*** see **Albania.**

Alberta. Alberta's efforts to diversify its economy in 1991 were set back by the failure of several government-backed enterprises. In April, a magnesium smelter in High River was closed. Alberta's government had supported the project with $103 million ($91 million U.S.) in loan guarantees. The smelter was supposed to turn magnesite ore into a metal stronger and lighter than aluminum. But the plant could not operate profitably because of low magnesium prices. The government also had to withdraw research support for a private supercomputer manufacturing business.

Critics of the provincial government's investments claimed that the Alberta Heritage Savings Trust Fund, set up by the province in 1976 with money from oil royalties, had fulfilled only one of its aims. It had improved the quality of life for Albertans through capital grants to parks and health care facilities. But it had not succeeded in moving the province's economy away from its dependence on the nonrenewable resources of oil and gas.

Balanced budget. Alberta's Progressive Conservative administration on April 4, 1991, introduced its first balanced budget in seven years. Higher taxes on tobacco and gasoline, combined with higher medicare premiums, were imposed. The government also initiated charges for some medical services, such as over-the-counter prescription drugs. David M. L. Farr

See **Canada,** Special Report: **Canada and Quebec at a Crossroads.** In *World Book,* see **Alberta.**

Islamic fundamentalists march in Algiers in February to protest government economic policies and to support Iraq during the Persian Gulf War.

Alexander, Lamar (1940-), a former Tennessee governor and university president, was sworn in as United States secretary of education on March 22, 1991. Long a proponent of improving U.S. schools, the new secretary was expected to help Bush make good on his pledge to be the "education President."

Andrew Lamar Alexander was born on July 3, 1940, in Knoxville, Tenn., and grew up in nearby Maryville. He attended Vanderbilt University in Nashville, Tenn., graduating with honors in 1962. In 1965, he earned a law degree at the New York University Law School.

From 1967 to 1970, after practicing law briefly in Knoxville, Alexander served in Washington, D.C., as an assistant to then Senator Howard Baker (R., Tenn.) and as a White House aide. He then returned to Tennessee to join a Nashville law firm.

Alexander, a Republican, was elected governor of Tennessee in 1979 and served until 1987. While serving as governor, he pushed for improvements in the state's public schools. In 1988, he was named president of the University of Tennessee system.

Alexander is an advocate of "Choice," a proposal that is a keystone of Bush's education policy. Under Choice, the federal government would provide tuition grants to states. Parents could use the grants to send their children to the schools of their choosing, including private or parochial schools. See **Education.**

Alexander is married to the former Leslee (Honey) Buhler. They have four children. David L. Dreier

Algeria. Algeria's experiment in democracy floundered in June 1991, only one year after the country held its first multiparty elections since 1962. Violent clashes between Islamic fundamentalists and police in Algiers, the capital, led President Chadli Bendjedid to declare a state of emergency and suspend all political activity on June 5, 1991. Elections finally took place on December 26, with the fundamentalist Islamic Salvation Front (FIS) winning 188 of 430 parliamentary seats. In contrast, the ruling National Liberation Front (FLN) captured only 15 seats. Runoff elections, which were expected to determine control of parliament, were scheduled for Jan. 16, 1992.

The unrest began in late May when Abassi Madani, leader of the FIS, called a general strike. The FIS had swept provincial and municipal elections in 1990. Madani charged that the government had changed election laws to give the ruling National Liberation Front an edge in parliamentary elections scheduled for June 27, 1991. He also demanded that the government hold a presidential election before the scheduled date in 1993. For 12 days, thousands of Madani's supporters clashed sporadically with authorities. An estimated 50 people died.

In response, Bendjedid postponed the parliamentary elections and gave Algeria's military forces broad powers to quell unrest. He also appointed Sid Ahmed Ghozali, a former foreign minister, as prime minister. Ghozali eased the crisis by announcing that parliamentary elections might be held by the end of 1991.

On June 28, however, after the army removed Islamic slogans from municipal buildings in Algiers, Madani threatened to call for a "holy war" if the government did not lift the state of emergency. On June 29, Ayatollah Ali Hoseini Khamenei, Iran's supreme spiritual leader, called on Algerians to stage an Islamic revolution, such as occurred in Iran in 1979. On June 30, 1991, the government arrested Madani and his deputy, and during July arrested about 5,000 FIS members, then lifted the state of emergency. Some analysts suggested that Madani's strategy of confrontation was intended to boost public support for the FIS.

Economic crisis. Earnings from oil and gas, which make up more than 97 per cent of the country's foreign revenues, totaled $13 billion in 1991. However, the government was forced to pay $8 billion in principal and interest on its $26-billion foreign debt. The Algerian government was also expected to spend approximately $10 billion to import raw materials, spare parts, food, and medicine. The inflation rate rose to an estimated 30 per cent, while unemployment remained at about 25 per cent. Christine Helms

See also **Persian Gulf,** Special Report: **War in the Persian Gulf; Africa** (Facts in brief table). In ***World Book,*** see **Algeria.**

Angola. See **Africa.**

Animal. See **Cat; Conservation; Dog; Zoology; Zoos.**

Anthropology. The discovery of prehuman fossilized bones believed to be from 3 million to 3.5 million years old was reported in March 1991. The bones, found at Hadar in Ethiopia, have expanded scientists' knowledge of the earliest known *hominid* species. (Hominids are human beings and their closest human and prehuman ancestors.) The fossils were found by a team of United States and Ethiopian scientists led by paleoanthropologists Donald C. Johanson, William H. Kimbel, and Robert C. Walter of the Institute of Human Origins in Berkeley, Calif.

The 18 fragmentary fossils consist of teeth, jaws, and a limb bone from 15 individuals that belonged to a species of delicately built apelike creatures called *Australopithecus afarensis.* The fossils are roughly the same age as other *A. afarensis* fossils found at the same site in the mid-1970's. The most complete skeleton found there was named "Lucy."

Analysis of the fossils has revealed new information about the physical characteristics of *A. afarensis.* One of the fossils, for example, is an upper jawbone that is larger than normal for the species. Johanson and his team suggest that the jawbone, which they believe is from a male, is evidence for the theory that *A. afarensis* males were considerably larger than the females of the species. A partial lower jaw contains a number of primitive physical traits similar to those found in the jaws of ancient apes dating to between 8 million and 12 million years ago. According to the sci-

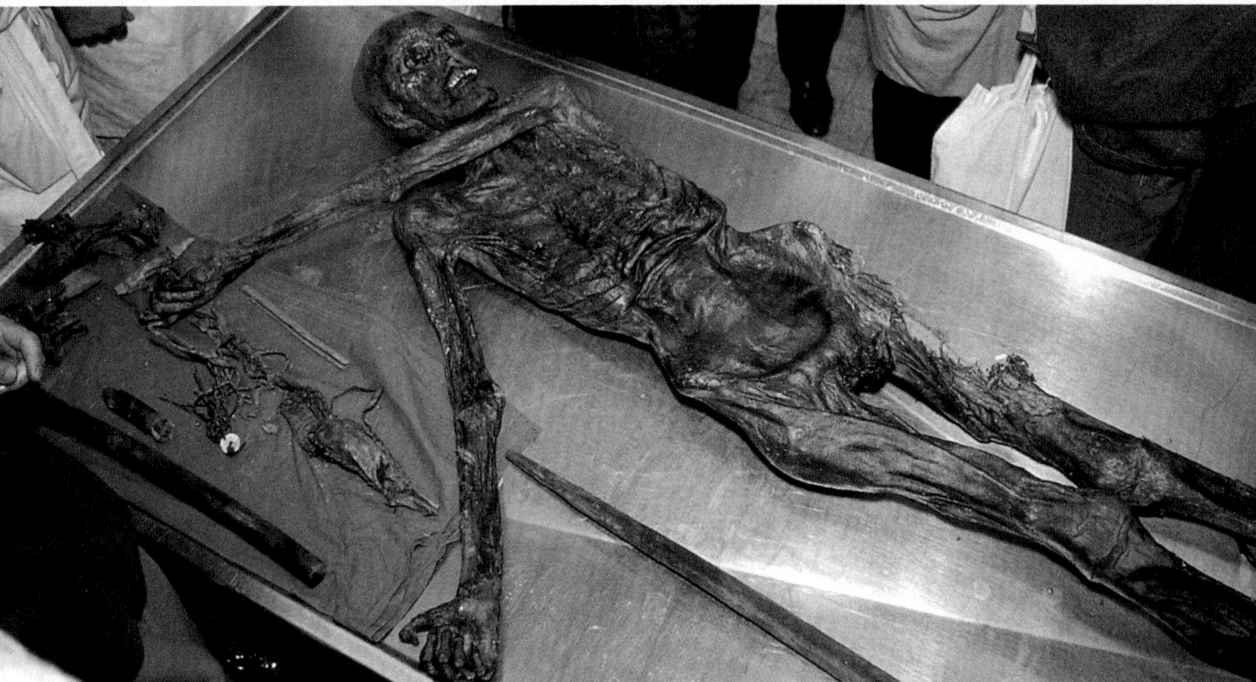

The preserved corpse of a man who died at least 4,600 years ago, perhaps in a snowstorm, was found on a glacier in Italy in September.

entists, this bolsters the view that hominids and present-day African apes shared a common ancestor.

The scientists found only one limb fossil, a powerfully built upper arm bone that had been damaged by chewing, probably by a hyena. Near the top end of the fossil were two large grooves where muscles had once been attached to the bone. The size of the grooves indicated that the muscles had been extremely powerful.

The manner in which *A. afarensis* used these powerful arm muscles is unclear. The muscles could have been used to hoist the body up by the arms. Most scientists believe that *A. afarensis* walked on two feet on the ground. The discovery of the arm bone, however, may fuel the debate about whether *A. afarensis* also spent part of its time in the trees.

Last common ancestor? The discovery of a fossil from a creature that may have been one of the last common ancestors of African apes and human beings was reported in June 1991. The fossil, which is about 10 million years old, was found in Namibia in southern Africa by a team of French and American scientists led by physical anthropologist Glenn C. Conroy of Washington University in St. Louis, Mo.

A preliminary analysis of the fossil, which consists of a partial lower right jaw with several teeth, suggests that it belongs to a previously unknown genus and species. The creature represented by the fossil was much smaller than an adult human being and may have weighed only 30 to 40 pounds (14 to 18 kilograms).

An African beginning. Additional support for the theory that modern human beings evolved from a small population of human ancestors living in Africa some 200,000 years ago was reported in September by a team of scientists from several U.S. universities. The study represented the most extensive research into human evolution done to date using mitochondrial deoxyribonucleic acid (mtDNA), a type of DNA found outside the nucleus of cells. DNA carries instructions for an organism's structure and life processes and is inherited from both parents. MtDNA, however, is inherited only from mothers. For this reason, researchers have theorized that any *mutations* (changes) found in mtDNA reflect random genetic changes that have occurred regularly over time. They also have theorized that the greater the number of mutations in the mtDNA from a population, the older that population is.

For their study, the scientists studied mtDNA from 121 native Africans, 15 Europeans, 20 Papua New Guineans, a native Australian, 24 Asians, and 8 black Americans. They reported that the mtDNA of the native Africans had the largest number of mutations. This suggests that the earliest modern human beings were African. The scientists also estimated that the ancestral Africans lived between 166,000 and 249,000 years ago. Donald C. Johanson

In *World Book,* see **Anthropology; Prehistoric people.**

Archaeology. A 40-year monopoly on access to the Dead Sea Scrolls, one of the greatest archaeological discoveries of the 1900's, was broken in 1991 by the actions of two scholars and of the Huntington Library in San Marino, Calif. The Dead Sea Scrolls are a collection of 2,000 complete and fragmentary manuscripts that were found in caves along the shore of the Dead Sea in the late 1940's and early 1950's. They contain a variety of religious texts, including all the books of the Old Testament except Esther.

In the early 1950's, the translation of the scrolls and the publication of that information was entrusted to a small group of scholars. Over the years, however, other scholars grew increasingly impatient with what they alleged was the slow pace of the publications team and with restrictions on access to the unpublished texts. The publications team, however, argued that limiting access was necessary to ensure the quality of the translations.

On Sept. 4, 1991, two scholars at Hebrew Union College in Cincinnati, Ohio, re-created the text of one of the unpublished scrolls using a computer and a previously published *concordance* of the text. (A concordance is a list of major words in a work with references to the passages in which they occur.)

Then on September 22, the Huntington Library announced that it would make its set of master photographic negatives of the scrolls available to all scholars. The negatives had been stored at the Huntington Library because of the risk of damage to the original scrolls, which are housed at the Rockefeller Museum in Jerusalem. Although the Israeli Antiquities Authority, which oversees the work on the scrolls, initially criticized the Huntington's decision, it reversed its policy in October and agreed to allow scholars access to the complete collection of photographs of the scrolls at the Rockefeller Museum.

Dating the scrolls. Results of the first use of a sophisticated form of a dating technique called radiocarbon dating on 14 of the Dead Sea Scrolls was reported in July. The tests confirmed that the scrolls date from the mid-100's B.C. to the late first century A.D. Scholars had previously suggested these dates for the scrolls based on analyses of the writing styles used in them.

Lost shepherd? The preserved body of a man who died at least 4,600 years ago was discovered on a glacier in northeastern Italy in September 1991. The body and the objects found with it represent the most complete archaeological find from the late Neolithic Period (New Stone Age) in Europe. This period, during which people were herding and farming, occurred in Europe from about 5,000 to 4,500 years ago.

Although nearly all the man's clothing had disintegrated, scientists found some scraps of fur and leather on the body. Parts of one boot, which was lined with straw, also survived.

The man, who may have been about 20 years old at the time of his death, was about 5 feet (1.5 meters)

Terra-cotta heads, possibly from an imperial tomb, are among thousands of figurines found near Xi'an, China, in 1990 and described in 1991.

tall and had tattoos on the inside of his knees and on his back. Artifacts found with the body included a copper ax, a bow, 14 arrows tipped with bone, a flint knife, and a flint and tinder—used for making fire—in a leather pouch.

Scientists established an age for the ancient corpse by obtaining radiocarbon dates for pieces of grass taken from a woven mat found with the body. Preliminary study of the body itself failed to reveal the cause of the man's death. Because the corpse was found in a ditch, scientists speculated that the man, who may have been a shepherd, had died while seeking shelter during a snowstorm. Other studies were planned to determine the cause of death and the state of the man's health before he died. Scientists also hoped to recover some of the man's *deoxyribonucleic acid* (DNA), the substance of which genes are made. The DNA analysis may reveal new information about the genetic relationships of late Neolithic Age people to modern Europeans.

Cave art discovery. The discovery of a cave decorated with prehistoric paintings and engravings was announced in October 1991 by French officials. The entrance to the cave, which lies beneath the surface of the Mediterranean Sea, was discovered by a scuba diver near Cassis, France, about 8 miles (13 kilometers) southeast of Marseille. The decorated chamber itself lies above sea level. French archaeologists reported that the art in the newly discovered cave may be as spectacular as the paintings at France's Lascaux Cave, which has some of the most beautiful examples of prehistoric cave art.

Depicted on the walls of the newly discovered cave are horses, ibex, red deer, bison, and other animals that lived in this part of Europe at the end of the Paleolithic Period (Old Stone Age). French scientists theorized that the paintings probably date from 10,000 to 20,000 B.C., just before the end of the last Ice Age. At that time, water from melting glaciers raised the level of the Mediterranean Sea above the cave's entrance. As a result, the decorated chamber has been closed off since that time.

Maya artifact ban. The United States on April 15 imposed an emergency ban on the import of all Maya artifacts from the Petén region of Guatemala. The United States acted at the request of Guatemala in an attempt to stop the growing U.S. sales of archaeological artifacts looted from the Petén. The Petén, a lowland area of tropical rain forests, was home to the Maya for more than 1,000 years, beginning about 900 B.C. More than 2,200 Maya sites exist in the region. As the international demand for pre-Columbian artifacts has grown, looting has become more widespread. Archaeologists believe 85 per cent of sites in the Petén have been plundered. Mark Rose

See also **Archaeology,** Special Report: **The Ancient Treasures of Iraq.** In ***World Book,*** see **Archaeology; Dead Sea Scrolls; Maya.**

The Ancient Treasures of Iraq

By Elizabeth C. Stone

Some of Iraq's ancient archaeological sites and treasures were among the victims of the Persian Gulf War and the civil uprisings that followed.

Exquisitely crafted gold objects are part of a spectacular treasure trove unearthed in three 2,400-year-old tombs at the ancient Assyrian city of Nimrud in the late 1980's. The treasure, the finest known examples of Assyrian artistry, includes, *clockwise from above,* a crown or belt, a fluted vase, a cuff, a pendant, and an anklet.

Glossary

Akkad: Northern half of Babylonia, where most early Mesopotamian cities arose.

Assyria: Area north of modern Baghdad, Iraq, that was an independent nation from about 1800 B.C. to 612 B.C.

Babylonia: Area south of Baghdad, made up of Sumer and Akkad, that was independent from about 3500 B.C. to the 500's B.C.

Cuneiform: First system of writing, based on wedge-shaped characters, that was developed about 3500 B.C. and used in Mesopotamia until the last centuries B.C.

Mesopotamia: Geographic and cultural area located between the Tigris and Euphrates rivers in what are now Iraq and northeastern Syria.

Sumer: Southern half of Babylonia that comprised the heartland of Mesopotamia.

The author:

Elizabeth C. Stone is an associate professor in the anthropology department at the State University of New York at Stony Brook.

Armies have clashed on the plains of Iraq, the birthplace of the world's first civilization, for at least 6,000 years. In 1991, war and civil conflict in Iraq once again took their toll of human life, property, and some of Iraq's—and the world's—most ancient and priceless treasures. See **Persian Gulf,** Special Report: **War in the Persian Gulf.**

By late 1991, Iraqi and foreign archaeologists were still unable to make a complete assessment of the damage caused by the Persian Gulf War and subsequent civil uprisings. Apparently, no ancient monuments or archaeological sites were destroyed by bombs dropped by the United States-led military force. However, a number of ancient structures and statues were cracked by shock waves generated by the blasts. Reports from areas outside Baghdad, Iraq's capital, were significantly bleaker. In the two civil uprisings that followed the war, many regional museums and the archaeological treasures they held suffered irreparable damage.

The heart of modern Iraq—the fertile plain between the Tigris and Euphrates rivers—was once the heartland of ancient Mesopotamia. The people who settled this featureless plain beginning 6,000 years ago were the first to develop cities, government, laws, and written records. The abundance and far-ranging content of those written records are the main reasons studying the origin and history of Mesopotamian civilization has been relatively easy for scholars—at least compared with investigations of early civilizations elsewhere. The writing system invented by the Mesopotamians about 3500 B.C. was based on tiny wedge-shaped characters. At first, scribes used these *cuneiform* symbols to tally and track the Mesopotamians' great agricultural wealth. Within 500 years, however, scribes were also recording myths, medical texts, business contracts, government edicts, and personal letters on cuneiform tablets.

The use of clay tablets to record this information is the single most important reason why so many cuneiform writings have survived. Unlike paper, papyrus, parchment, wood, or cloth, clay does not rot. As a result, cuneiform tablets thousands of years old are as legible to modern scholars as they were to the scribes who created them.

In no other early civilization was writing employed so widely or for such practical purposes. In most ancient societies, writing served the needs of political or religious rulers. The 3 million cuneiform tablets unearthed so far from the sites of ancient Mesopotamian libraries, schools, administrative centers, and even private homes have provided an incredibly intimate look at daily life in Mesopotamia.

Ancient Mesopotamia comprised a number of ethnic groups, languages, and political systems. Most scholars credit the Sumerians, who arrived in the region about 3500 B.C., with building the first cities and developing the first system of writing. By 2300 B.C., however, the inhabitants of Sumer included so many people who spoke Akkadian, a Semitic language closely related to modern Arabic and Hebrew, that this language replaced Sumerian. These Akkadian speakers—among them the Assyrians and Babylonians—dominated Mesopotamia until 539 B.C., when it was conquered by the Persians, ancestors of modern Iranians and Afghans.

Although the ancient Mesopotamians were successful farmers, their societies were mainly urban. Their cities, which had from 10,000 to 40,000

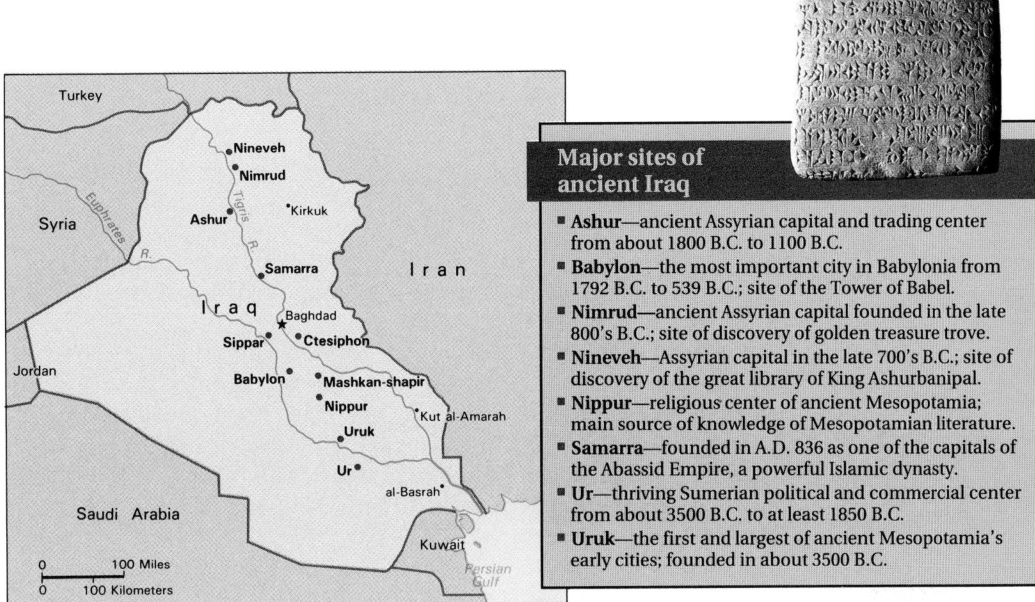

Major sites of ancient Iraq

- **Ashur**—ancient Assyrian capital and trading center from about 1800 B.C. to 1100 B.C.
- **Babylon**—the most important city in Babylonia from 1792 B.C. to 539 B.C.; site of the Tower of Babel.
- **Nimrud**—ancient Assyrian capital founded in the late 800's B.C.; site of discovery of golden treasure trove.
- **Nineveh**—Assyrian capital in the late 700's B.C.; site of discovery of the great library of King Ashurbanipal.
- **Nippur**—religious center of ancient Mesopotamia; main source of knowledge of Mesopotamian literature.
- **Samarra**—founded in A.D. 836 as one of the capitals of the Abassid Empire, a powerful Islamic dynasty.
- **Ur**—thriving Sumerian political and commercial center from about 3500 B.C. to at least 1850 B.C.
- **Uruk**—the first and largest of ancient Mesopotamia's early cities; founded in about 3500 B.C.

inhabitants, were linked to one another and to the region's rich farmlands by a network of rivers and canals. Two great institutions—the temple and the palace—dominated each city. The temple, built on a raised platform up to 50 feet (15 meters) high, was the city's visual focal point. The palace, usually an enormous structure, served as the seat of power for such kings as Sargon of Akkad and Hammurabi and Nebuchadnezzar II of Babylon.

At times, one great ruler or group dominated all of ancient Mesopotamia. At other times, smaller political units such as city-states or tribal groups competed for power. But at all times, the culture of Mesopotamia dominated the ancient Near East. The Akkadian language and cuneiform writing were used in diplomacy throughout the region.

After the followers of Islam conquered much of Mesopotamia in the A.D. 640's, the region continued to play an important role in Middle Eastern affairs. Baghdad and nearby Samarra were founded as capitals for the Abassid Caliphate, one of the most powerful of the early Islamic dynasties. At the height of its power in the 700's, this dynasty ruled an area stretching from modern Pakistan to modern Tunisia. By 800, Baghdad had more than 1 million inhabitants and was a world center of learning.

Archaeologists have been exploring Iraq's rich heritage since the mid-1800's. In the 1980's, they made a number of exciting discoveries. In northern Iraq, Iraqi and foreign archaeologists had devoted special efforts to the exploration of dozens of *salvage sites*—sites likely to be damaged or destroyed by development projects. Their findings there have provided important new insights into Mesopotamian civilization, especially regarding the developments that preceded the rise of the first cities.

Excavations at Samarra by British archaeologists, begun in the mid-1980's, revealed important new information about the layout of that former capital. In 1986, Iraqi archaeologists working at Sippar, near Baghdad, found a library with about 2,000 cuneiform tablets. In 1989, I led a

Civilization's cradle

Modern Iraq was once the heartland of ancient Mesopotamia, the birthplace of the world's first civilization at least 6,000 years ago. Archaeologists have learned about the ancient Mesopotamians by excavating the ruins of their cities, *above left,* and by reading the tablets, *top,* and other records these ancient people left behind. The Mesopotamians' writing system, the first ever developed, used wedge-shaped characters called *cuneiform* symbols.

team that identified the site of Mashkan-shapir, a 4,000-year-old trading center in southern Iraq.

The most important recent discoveries, however, have been at Nimrud (also called Kalhu), an ancient capital of the Assyrian Empire. There, Iraqi archaeologists in 1987, 1988, and 1989 uncovered three tombs containing the remains of Assyrian queens and the finest examples of Assyrian artistry ever found. The tombs were filled with approximately 1,000 exquisitely crafted gold vessels and pieces of jewelry, including crowns, bracelets, necklaces, and earrings.

Iraq's invasion of Kuwait in August 1990 had little immediate effect on archaeological projects in Iraq because, as usual, work had been suspended for the hot summer season. As of December 1991, archaeologists had yet to return to their digs. The injury to Mesopotamian archaeology was much greater than the interruption of excavations, however. The war and civil uprisings damaged some of Iraq's most important ancient sites and monuments.

At Samarra, the shock waves from allied bomb blasts cracked several Islamic monuments, causing significant damage. Bomb blasts also weakened the great arch at Ctesiphon, a vault nearly 90 feet (27 meters) tall and 150 feet (46 meters) deep, which is in grave danger of collapse after standing for 1,500 years. Apparently, the Iraq Museum in Baghdad suffered only minor damage, though some of its large stone sculptures that could not be moved to bomb shelters were cracked by bomb blasts. Most of the Islamic monuments in Baghdad—including the Abassid Palace, located next to the Department of Defense—were largely untouched.

The aftermath of the war may have exacted the greatest toll on Iraq's archaeological treasures. During the 1970's and 1980's, Iraq's Department of Antiquities had greatly expanded the number of regional museums in order to give Iraqis—and foreign visitors—a clearer sense of the richness of the country's Mesopotamian heritage. Although Iraq has many archae-

Ancient battle site

The skeletons of people killed during the fall of Assyrian Nineveh in 612 B.C., *bottom right*, were unearthed in 1989 by archaeologists from the University of California at Berkeley. The people died during a fight for the Halzi Gate, *bottom*, in an attack by Medes and Babylonians. Buried at one corner of the gate was a blue-painted figurine, *below*, which the Assyrians thought possessed protective powers.

Overturned and smashed display cabinets at the archaeological museum in Kirkuk stand empty in the aftermath of an uprising by Kurds in the northeastern part of Iraq in March and April 1991. In addition to stealing many of the objects on display at the museum, looters destroyed ancient statues and ground cuneiform tablets to dust.

ological sites, it has few standing ruins. What were once palaces, temples, and houses are now only great mounds of earth that yield their secrets through painstaking excavations. In the regional museums, visitors could see examples of jewelry, statues, and other objects found at these sites.

Unfortunately, all the regional museums in the Kurdish areas of northern Iraq were looted during the uprising there. Many of the museums in southern Iraq were also badly damaged in the rebellion by Shiite Muslims. The losses in the north are particularly keen because the museums there housed most of the artifacts found at the salvage sites. Because archaeologists had not yet thoroughly studied these objects and published their results, this material may be lost forever. The greatest damage reportedly occurred at the museum at Kirkuk in northeastern Iraq. There, looters smashed statues, ground cuneiform tablets to dust, and stole artifacts. The unpublished contents of cuneiform tablets found at Nippur and looted from the museum at Kut al-Amarah in southeastern Iraq may never be known. Some of the tablets may also have been destroyed by a blast, possibly caused by an allied bomb, that damaged the roof of the museum.

Archaeologists will not be able to make a full assessment of the damage until internal and international tensions have eased and they are able to conduct site-by-site evaluations. Although the human cost of the war overshadowed all other considerations, the damage to Iraq's ancient heritage will be an enduring scar on human history.

For further reading:

Oates, Joan. *Babylon.* Thames Hudson, 1986.

Roaf, Michael, and Postgate, Nicholas. *The Cultural Atlas of Mesopotamia and the Near East.* Facts on File, 1990.

Architecture. Architecture in the United States was affected by the economy and environmental concerns more than by any other issues in 1991. As overbuilding and the worsening savings and loan crisis slowed construction throughout the country, the number of new architectural projects shrank dramatically. The boom towns of a few years ago—New York, London, Washington, D.C., and Dallas—fell eerily quiet. Many architecture firms merged or folded, and even some of the giants, such as Skidmore, Owings, and Merrill of Chicago, had to reorganize to survive.

EuroDisneyland, the new international theme park near Paris, and the 1992 World Exposition in Seville, Spain, remained principal sources of architectural commissions for U.S. and foreign designers (see **Spain,** Special Report: **Spain Takes Center Stage in 1992**). The reunification of Germany in 1991 also served to foster a building boom in eastern Europe.

Completions. The Sainsbury Wing of the National Gallery in London opened in July 1991 to enthusiastic reviews. Some critics voiced surprise that the museum addition, which was designed by architect Robert Venturi, was influenced more by classical Greek and Roman architecture than by pop culture. Japanese architect Arata Isozaki completed a bold headquarters building at Walt Disney World in Orlando, Fla. It was the first of several projects Isozaki will design for the entertainment giant. Acclaimed Spanish architect Ricardo Bofill completed his first U.S. project, the Shepherd School of Music at Rice University in Houston.

E. Fay Jones's Thorncrown Chapel, set near Eureka Springs, Ark., was chosen by architects in 1991 as the best U.S. building constructed since 1980.

Awards. The year's top architectural awards went to designers who have been synonymous with the Post-Modern movement, which began in the 1960's and incorporated historic styles. Charles W. Moore in February 1991 received the gold medal for lifetime achievement from the American Institute of Architects for his colorful and whimsical buildings, which include the Piazza d'Italia in New Orleans and the Beverly Hills Civic Center in California. Venturi—who along with Moore championed the return of history, humor, and color to contemporary architecture—in April won the Pritzker Architecture Prize for lifetime achievement.

Modernism gains ground. The year's awards for Post-Modern designs notwithstanding, there was a new surge of interest during the year in Modern architecture. In addition to his building for Disney, Isozaki completed a new sports stadium in Barcelona, Spain, and was the subject of a major retrospective at the Los Angeles Museum of Contemporary Art, which he had designed in 1986. The exhibit demonstrated that Isozaki is one of the most inventive modern architects, capable of reviving tired ideas with bold forms and surprising uses of materials.

Isozaki also collaborated on the year's most important architectural exhibition: "Louis I. Kahn: In the Realm of Architecture," which opened at the Philadelphia Museum of Art in October 1991. Such buildings as the Kimbell Art Museum in Fort Worth, Tex., and the Salk Institute in La Jolla, Calif., display Kahn's austere sculptural forms and his poetic use of natural light. Kahn's designs have had a profound effect on contemporary architects, including Isozaki and his younger Japanese contemporary Tadao Ando. Ando's work, which combines reverence for nature with a love of such stark modern materials as concrete and steel, was featured in a provocative exhibition at the Museum of Modern Art in New York City.

The architectural event of the year occurred in October 1991 when the final design for the $360-million Getty Center in Los Angeles was unveiled. Architect Richard Meier, famous for his pristine white residences and museums, was chosen to create the art center. His model design consisted of a complex of six low buildings that includes a museum, library, computerized research center, and auditorium. While recognizably a Meier creation, the design is looser and more animated than his previous works and far more attuned to its surroundings. Construction on the Getty Center, which is being financed by the J. Paul Getty Trust, was scheduled to begin in the spring of 1992. Planners expected the complex to open in 1996.

Ecological concerns. In 1991, concern about environmental problems rekindled the search for ecologically sensitive structures, and architects focused on designs incorporating energy conservation and nontoxic building materials. The most visible effort on this new front was the completion of Biosphere II. Designed by Sarbid Architects, the 3-acre (1.2-hectare) sealed model of Earth's environment was constructed 30 miles (48 kilometers) north of Tucson, Ariz., and admitted its first residents in September. See **Newsmakers.**

Landmark decisions. In March, the Supreme Court of the United States let stand a lower court decision denying St. Bartholomew's Church, an Episcopal church in New York City, the right to demolish its parish house to allow for the building of a 47-story office tower. Church officials had challenged the city's landmark ordinance by claiming that the ordinance interfered with the church's mission to serve the poor and homeless. In rejecting that claim, the court reaffirmed both the legality of the city's landmark designation and the social and cultural importance of preserving great buildings.

In July, however, the Pennsylvania Supreme Court struck down Philadelphia's historic preservation law. The court ruled that when the city declared in 1987—without the owner's consent—that the Boyd Theater was a landmark, this represented an unlawful "taking" of private property. The ruling was without precedent in preservation law, and it raised fears that a flurry of similar challenges to municipal preservation ordinances might be forthcoming.

New baseball parks. America's favorite pastime began to revert to its traditional roots in 1991 with the rebirth of the old-fashioned baseball park. After two decades of domed stadiums, baseball fans once again demanded natural grass, blue skies, and intimacy with the action. The owners responded.

Chicago's new Comiskey Park, designed by HOK Sports Facilities Group for the White Sox, opened in April to mixed architectural reviews but widespread appreciation for its efforts to rekindle memories of older ball parks. In Baltimore, workers during 1991 were putting the finishing touches on the Orioles' new Oriole Park at Camden Yards, which also was designed by HOK and is located in downtown Baltimore. During the summer, the Texas Rangers, Cleveland Indians, and Detroit Tigers all announced plans to build traditional ball parks. David Dillon

In ***World Book,*** see **Architecture.**

Argentina. During the second half of 1991, there were several signs that the Argentine economy, long mired in recession, was at last on the road to recovery. The economic turnaround came suddenly in August, when inflation was held to 1.3 per cent, its lowest level in 25 years.

Buoyed by the good news, the average daily trading volume on the Buenos Aires Stock Exchange soared in August from $5 million to $115 million, evidence of a renewal of confidence in Argentina's financial fortunes under democratic rule. About half of the new investment in the financial market came from foreign investors in Japan, Europe, and the United States.

On August 26, the First Boston Corporation announced plans to underwrite a $60-million investment company that will target Argentina and be listed on the New York Stock Exchange. Following suit, the J. P. Morgan banking company announced plans to underwrite the first international Argentine debt issue in more than 12 years.

Much credit for the improved economic climate was assigned to Domingo Felipe Cavallo, who became Argentina's fourth economy minister in less than two years on January 29. Shortly after taking office, Cavallo introduced an orthodox stabilization program that took effect on April 1 and inspired a sustained surge of international confidence. Under the program, the government was required to maintain a fiscal surplus, the Central Bank was prohibited from printing money not backed by gold or foreign currency reserves, and a lower limit was placed on the value of the Argentine currency, which has fluctuated wildly in value in recent years.

Impressed by the program, the International Monetary Fund, an agency of the United Nations, pledged to provide Argentina with a $1-billion loan in July. In August, the World Bank announced it would lend Argentina nearly $500 million.

The optimism stirred by the economy helped blunt the impact of much-publicized scandals involving several of President Carlos Saul Menem's in-laws. His incumbent Peronist Party scored impressive results at midterm elections on September 8.

Yomagate. All during 1991, Argentines closely followed fresh revelations in a scandal involving members of the family of President Menem's estranged wife, who filed for a divorce on March 27. On July 19, her sister, Amira Yoma, the president's former appointments secretary, was indicted for complicity in a drug money-laundering scheme involving her ex-husband, a former Syrian army colonel, and her brother, a former deputy foreign minister. The Argentine press began calling the scandal Yomagate in reference to the Watergate political scandal that occurred in the United States in the 1970's.

President Menem initially defended his in-laws, but as more information became known, he sought to distance himself from the controversy. President Menem had troubles of his own as a result of his friendship with Ghaith Pharaon, the Argentine branch manager of the scandal-ridden Bank of Credit and Commerce International. See **Bank.**

Courting the United States. Reversing the traditional anti-American attitude associated with his Peronist Party, President Menem sought favor from the United States in 1991. Argentine Defense Minister Antonio Ermán González announced on May 29 that Argentina would cancel a secret ballistic missile program that the United States had opposed. González also announced cutbacks of 20,000 civilian and military personnel and the closing of unnecessary Argentine military bases.

Ecological disaster. On August 12, the Hudson volcano erupted on the Chilean side of the Andes Mountains just across the border from Argentina. Winds blew clouds of ash over about 25,000 square miles (65,000 square kilometers) of the sparsely inhabited Argentine province of Santa Cruz, an area with a delicate ecosystem. Some ecologists feared that the fallout would convert the area into a permanent desert. Scientists estimated that as many as a million sheep might perish from the catastrophe, as well as animals belonging to such endangered species as the *lesser rhea* (an ostrichlike bird) and the *guanaco* (a camellike animal). Nathan A. Haverstock

See also **Latin America** (Facts in brief table). In ***World Book,*** see **Argentina.**

Aristide, Jean-Bertrand (1953-   ), was sworn in as Haiti's first democratically elected president on Feb. 7, 1991. He was elected on Dec. 16, 1990, and replaced interim President Ertha Pascal-Trouillot.

On Sept. 30, 1991, the Haitian military overthrew Aristide. The Organization of American States organized a diplomatic effort to return Aristide to power. On November 22, Aristide and members of the Haitian National Assembly began talks in Colombia aimed at restoring him to the presidency. See **Haiti.**

Aristide was born in Port-Salut on Haiti's southern coast. He entered the Roman Catholic priesthood and rose to prominence in the early and mid-1980's as an opponent of the Duvalier family dictatorship that ruled Haiti from 1957 to 1986. The church expelled Aristide from the priesthood in December 1988 for teachings that it said advocated violence.

On Sept. 11, 1988, attackers burned Aristide's church, killing 13 worshipers and wounding 70 others. Many observers suspected the attackers were government secret police—the Tontons Macoutes—and in retaliation a group of army officers overthrew the government of Lieutenant General Henri Namphy.

Many Haitians respect Aristide as a visionary leader. Some critics charge that his radical politics discriminate against the middle and upper classes, however.

Mark Dunbar

Arizona. See **State government.**

Arkansas. See **State government.**

Armed forces. President George Bush announced a sweeping reduction of United States nuclear forces on Sept. 27, 1991. Bush said the proposed reductions were designed to take advantage of the collapse of the Soviet empire and the rise of democracy there and in eastern Europe. The initiatives represented the most dramatic attempt to stem the arms race in the history of the nuclear age and had profound implications for U.S. defense policy.

In a nationally televised address, Bush said he had ordered the worldwide withdrawal and destruction of all U.S. ground-launched, *tactical* (short-range) nuclear weapons, as well as all tactical nuclear weapons on U.S. submarines and warships. He also canceled the alert status of B-1 and B-52 *strategic* (long-range) bombers and ordered their nuclear weapons removed and placed in storage.

Bush removed 450 Minuteman II intercontinental ballistic missiles (ICBM's) from alert status and planned to accelerate the destruction of these weapons once the U.S. Senate ratified the recently negotiated Strategic Arms Reduction Treaty (START), signed by President Bush and Soviet President Mikhail S. Gorbachev in July. The ICBM modernization program was sharply curtailed, and Bush eliminated a program to build a replacement for the short-range nuclear attack missile carried by U.S. strategic bombers.

Bush challenged the Soviet Union to match his weapons cuts. He proposed accelerated negotiations

Commander of allied forces General H. Norman Schwarzkopf, Jr., points out battle plans on a map in February during the Persian Gulf War.

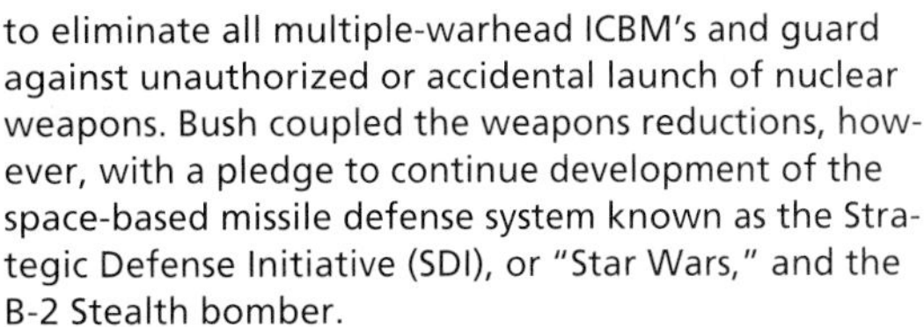

to eliminate all multiple-warhead ICBM's and guard against unauthorized or accidental launch of nuclear weapons. Bush coupled the weapons reductions, however, with a pledge to continue development of the space-based missile defense system known as the Strategic Defense Initiative (SDI), or "Star Wars," and the B-2 Stealth bomber.

On October 5, Soviet President Gorbachev announced that the Soviet Union would essentially match the U.S. nuclear weapons cutbacks. Gorbachev also ordered a one-year Soviet ban on nuclear testing and said that he would reduce the Soviet armed forces by 700,000 troops.

Strategic developments. On July 31, the United States and the Soviet Union signed the START treaty in Moscow. The treaty requires about a 30 per cent reduction in nuclear inventories. If ratified and if honored by the Commonwealth of Independent States, which replaced the Soviet Union in late December, the START accord would reduce U.S. nuclear weapons from 12,000 to 9,000, and what had been Soviet weapons from 11,000 to 7,000. The accord limited both sides to 6,000 nuclear warheads on 1,600 delivery vehicles. Ballistic missile warheads were limited to 4,900, with a limit of 1,100 warheads for land-based mobile missile systems. The START treaty, intended to be in effect until the year 2006, does not, however, cover the SDI program.

In an effort to simplify control of U.S. nuclear forces, President Bush announced on Sept. 27, 1991, that the Department of Defense would create a new Strategic Command (Stratcom) to begin operations on June 1, 1992. The command would merge control of the nuclear bombers and missiles of the Strategic Air Command (SAC) with that of the Navy's Trident ballistic missile submarines. Offutt Air Force Base in Omaha, Nebr., current headquarters of SAC, would be the Stratcom headquarters. Stratcom command would rotate between the Air Force and the Navy.

Persian Gulf War. The six-week war in the Persian Gulf, from Jan. 17 to Feb. 28, 1991, provided a dramatic backdrop for the U.S. military's increasingly sophisticated weaponry, most of which had never been tested in combat. For the most part, these weapons performed well. Advanced computer technology and a long-range cannon enabled the Army's M1A1 Abrams main battle tank to destroy enemy armor without being detected. The Department of Defense released videotapes of laser-guided "smart bombs" being delivered with pinpoint precision through enemy hangar doors and ventilator shafts. The Navy's Tomahawk cruise missile also proved its worth, destroying scores of targets such as command bunkers with great accuracy. The Army's Hellfire missile and the Air Force's F-117A Stealth fighter plane were also

The United States warship U.S.S. *Wisconsin* in January launches a Tomahawk cruise missile toward Iraqi positions during the Persian Gulf War.

Chairman of the U.S. Joint Chiefs of Staff, General Colin L. Powell, waves during a parade for U.S. Persian Gulf War troops in New York City in June.

praised for their effectiveness, though some Congressional and scientific critics later said that the plane, designed to elude detection by enemy radar, had been tracked by friendly radar on several occasions.

The performance of the Army's Patriot air-defense missile system was controversial. After Iraqi Scud missiles attacked Israeli population centers early in the war, the U.S. military rushed several Patriot batteries to Israel. The Patriots reportedly destroyed many of the Scud missiles subsequently launched against Israel. But a Patriot failure resulted in the war's worst single loss of allied life on February 25, when 28 U.S. soldiers were killed by a Scud missile that struck an Army barracks in Dhahran, Saudi Arabia. See **Persian Gulf,** Special Report: **War in the Persian Gulf.**

Conventional weapons. Development proceeded on a variety of new U.S. conventional weapons in 1991, including an experimental jet fighter, the SSN-21 Seawolf-class attack submarine, and a new family of armored vehicles. In June, the Department of Defense disclosed new details of a $15-billion radar-evading cruise missile that can be launched from the ground or air.

The Air Force awarded a contract for the F-22 Advanced Tactical Fighter to a team headed by the Lockheed Corporation in April. The new jet would replace the F-15 Eagle as the primary jet fighter in the mid-1990's. The total production contract was expected to reach $95 billion.

Technical problems continued to dog the B-1B bomber, the only major U.S. weapons system that did not participate in the Persian Gulf War. A government investigator told Congress in March that it might require $1 billion and 10 years of repairs and redesign to correct the plane's defects, which included engine flaws, a lack of electronic countermeasures to jam enemy radar, and an inability to fly safely in icy weather. In August, the Air Force confirmed that 13 of the planes had been grounded after cracks were discovered in the fuselage of 37 B-1B's.

The future of the B-2 Stealth bomber was also in doubt due to skyrocketing costs, technical difficulties, and the decline of the Soviet strategic nuclear threat. The Pentagon said in September that the $865-million plane had failed a test of its radar-evading capabilities. Cracks were also discovered in the fuselage that the Air Force said would cost $200 million to repair. On October 31, congressional opponents of the B-2 blocked any further purchase of the planes beyond the initial order of 15. The Defense Department had originally sought 132 planes.

In June, the United States and the Soviet Union resolved remaining differences over the Conventional Forces in Europe (CFE) treaty. The agreement cleared the way to implement the treaty, which 22 nations signed in November 1990. The CFE treaty would set limits on nonnuclear weapons in Europe.

***Iowa* apology.** The U.S. Navy formally apologized on Oct. 17, 1991, to the family of a sailor once accused of causing the 1989 explosion that killed him along with 46 others on the battleship U.S.S. *Iowa*. Admiral Frank B. Kelso, chief of naval operations, said that a two-year investigation had not established "clear and convincing proof" that Gunner's Mate Clayton Hartwig had deliberately set off the explosion in a gun turret. An independent investigation by the General Accounting Office, the investigative arm of Congress, released in August 1991 had cast doubt on the sabotage theory. A $2.35-billion lawsuit was filed against the Navy in April on behalf of the dead sailors. Families of the victims alleged that the tragedy was an accident caused by the Navy's failure to maintain equipment and by inadequate crew training. The *Iowa* had been decommissioned and retired from active service in October 1990.

Base closings. Budget realities and the diminishing threat from the Soviet Union prompted a new round of U.S. base closings. In July 1991, Congress approved the recommendation of an independent presidential commission to shut down 34 bases and reduce operations at 48 others. Major bases scheduled to close before the end of 1996 include Carswell Air Force Base, Texas; Fort Ord, Calif.; the Philadelphia Naval Shipyard; and the Long Beach, Calif., naval station. The Defense Department also planned to reduce overseas bases, particularly in Germany.

Defense budget. The Defense Department's budget request for the 1992 fiscal year, which began on

Oct. 1, 1991, was for $278.3 billion in spending authority, a decrease of $5.3 billion from the previous year and a 12 per cent decrease over two years after adjusting for inflation. The total request for defense, including the defense activities of the Department of Energy and other government agencies, was $290.8-billion. The budget request did not include the expenses of Operation Desert Storm. The largest budget items were a $4.8-billion request for four B-2 bombers and $4.6 billion for the SDI.

Personnel. United States military troop strength was 1,974,606 on October 31, a decrease of 71,752 from the previous year. A residual force of about 33,000 remained in the Persian Gulf region, most of them in Saudi Arabia and aboard naval ships in the Persian Gulf.

The controversy over whether women should serve in combat intensified in 1991 as a result of the deployment of more than 35,000 women soldiers to the Persian Gulf during Operation Desert Storm. All were banned from combat, but 5 of the 11 women who died during the war were listed as killed in action. Two women were captured as prisoners of war, and many served in combat support units in Iraq and Kuwait during the fighting. On August 2, the Senate authorized the Defense Department to permit women pilots to fly combat missions in future conflicts.

Philippine bases. The 100-year-old U.S. military presence in the Philippines appeared doomed in September when the Philippine Senate rejected a treaty that would have allowed the United States to operate its naval base at Subic Bay for 10 more years in return for $2.2 billion. A compromise announced by the Philippine government in October would allow American naval forces to withdraw from the Philippines over a three-year period.

The U.S. Defense Department had previously announced that it would abandon its huge Clark Air Base in the Philippines as a result of millions of dollars of damage from the volcanic eruption of nearby Mount Pinatubo in June. Naval forces withdrawn from Subic Bay would be relocated in Singapore, Guam, Japan, and Hawaii. See **Philippines.**

Command changes. President Bush reappointed Army General Colin L. Powell to a second two-year term as chairman of the Joint Chiefs of Staff in May. General Carl E. Vuono retired as U.S. Army chief of staff and was succeeded by General Gordon R. Sullivan in April. In July, General Carl E. Mundy, Jr., succeeded General Alfred M. Gray, Jr., as commandant of the Marine Corps. General Joseph P. Hoar of the Marine Corps replaced General H. Norman Schwarzkopf, Jr., as commander in chief of the Central Command in August. Naval first classman Juliane Gallina was appointed the first female commander of the brigade of midshipmen at the U.S. Naval Academy in Annapolis, Md., in April. Thomas M. DeFrank

In ***World Book,*** see the articles on the branches of the armed forces.

Art. A woman viewing an exhibit by the artist Christo was killed on Oct. 27, 1991, when a huge umbrella that was part of the exhibit blew away from its anchor, struck her, and hurled her against a rock. The exhibit, which was composed of 1,760 yellow umbrellas erected in California, and 1,340 blue umbrellas set up in Japan, had opened on October 9. It was to have stayed up for three weeks, but Christo ordered it shut down after the accident.

A worker in Japan who was dismantling the exhibit was also killed when his crane hit a high-tension wire, and he was electrocuted. Christo, who was born in Bulgaria but lives in New York City and does not use his last name, Javacheff, had worked on the umbrella project for seven years.

Money woes replaced obscenity and censorship as main concerns of the art world during 1991. Recessions, economic uncertainties produced by the Persian Gulf War, and a scandal involving Japanese art buyers cooled the art market just when funding agencies were encountering major budget cuts.

Because the United States Congress did not authorize any increase in the 1991 budget for the National Endowment for the Arts (NEA), the agency had to tighten its federal grants to artists. The federal government also ordered the agency to take $11.9 million from some of its existing programs and give it to state arts councils. This requirement imposed cuts in many grant categories and outright elimination of others.

Local funding cuts. The redistribution of NEA funds to states only partially compensated for budget cuts that some local arts councils also sustained. The New Jersey State Council on the Arts suffered the most, with a 40 per cent cut in its budget, which dropped from $19.7 million in 1990 to $11.7 million for 1991. New York State was also hit hard with a budget reduction of $4.3 million. Massachusetts lost $4.1 million, which will stall the construction of MASS MoCa, a $75-million contemporary-art museum proposed for rural North Adams, Mass. New York City's arts community felt the ax when Mayor David N. Dinkins slashed the arts budget by $24 million, a 28 per cent reduction from last year's funding.

Private foundations tried to pick up some of the slack in financial support. In January, the Lila Wallace-Reader's Digest Arts Stabilization Initiative announced an $8-million program to assist minority institutions. Art Matters, a New York foundation, launched a fund-raising effort to establish an independent grant of $10 million.

Art for sale. The market for art remained sluggish. In the spring, jitters over the Persian Gulf War and the continuing recession contributed to a decline in overall prices, which were 30 to 40 per cent lower than last year's bids.

For the seasonal spring auctions, New York City's main auction houses, Sotheby's and Christie's, persuaded sellers to accept more conservative presale estimates than had been the practice in recent years.

Sotheby's top price in 1991 was for Henri Matisse's *La Robe Persane* (1940), which sold for $4.5 million, half a million short of the expected minimum of $5 million.

Sotheby's contemporary art produced more sales vitality. Robert Rauschenberg's *Rebus* (1955), which sold for $6.3 million in 1988, fetched $7.3 million in April 1991. At Christie's London house, Edgar Degas's *Racehorses* (1875) sold in June for $9.7 million. The top bid at Christie's New York auction on May 1 was for Roy Lichtenstein's *Razzmatazz* (1968).

Christie's, in January, auctioned paintings owned by Imelda Marcos, the wife of former Philippine President Ferdinand Marcos. Christie's expected the paintings to sell for about $10 million, but they netted $15.4 million. Top prices went for an El Greco sketch for *The Coronation of the Virgin* (circa 1605), which sold for $2.3 million, and Raphael's *Saint Catherine of Alexandria* (1503), which sold for $1.6 million.

The fall auctions demonstrated that the overall art market remained weak. Total sales for Christie's and Sotheby's were expected to reach $250 million. But actual combined sales totaled only $130 million and were almost evenly split between the two houses.

American Indian masks purchased at Sotheby's in May were returned to the Hopi and Navajo tribes by buyer Elizabeth Sackler. Spurred by Native American protests and a 1990 law regarding the sale and exhibition of Indian ritual objects, the National Museum of the American Indian in Washington, D.C., also vowed to return Indian artifacts to tribes requesting them.

Financial scandals rocked the Japanese art market in 1991 when large Japanese corporations used purchases of impressionist and modern paintings to illegally transfer money and to evade taxes and financing regulations. Some executives were fined or sentenced to jail terms, and the scandals cooled Japanese participation in the auction market.

In the United States, an 18-month investigation of New York auction houses prompted the state Assembly to introduce legislation banning certain controversial practices. These included *chandelier bidding,* in which the auctioneer announces fictitious bids to drive up a selling price; the abolition of loans from auction houses to help buyers purchase artwork; and a statewide extension of New York City regulations that require auction houses to disclose their reserves and guarantees on individual lots.

Museum news. Museum acquisitions got a boost in 1991 when the U.S. Congress allowed a one-time revocation (for the 1991 tax year) of the 1986 Tax Reform Act. The act required art donators to claim as a tax deduction only the original price rather than the current market value of a donated work. Museum curators had claimed the act produced a 47 per cent decline in museum gifts nationwide.

New York City's Whitney Museum of American Art appointed David Ross as its director. Ross had been director of the Institute of Contemporary Art in Boston.

The Solomon R. Guggenheim Museum in New York City announced in April plans to open a satellite facility in the city's SoHo district. The museum plans to use a renovated downtown building for a large exhibition area, a library, and offices. The project was scheduled for completion by autumn 1993 and will be designed by Japanese architect Arata Isozaki.

The Metropolitan Museum of Art in 1991 became the beneficiary of a coveted collection of impressionist and postimpressionist works owned by publishing magnate Walter Annenberg. The former ambassador to Great Britain announced in March that his will bequeaths his $1-billion collection to the Met. The collection includes works by such renowned artists as Paul Cézanne, Claude Monet, Vincent van Gogh, Paul Gauguin, Pierre Auguste Renoir, Georges Seurat, Henri de Toulouse-Lautrec, Degas, Matisse, and Pablo Picasso.

In Paris, the Jeu de Paume reopened its doors in June and welcomed visitors to view its $10-million renovation and new collection of contemporary art. The museum had been empty since its holdings of impressionist art were moved to the Orsay Museum in 1986. The new space will exhibit art of the last three decades from both new and established artists.

Legal matters. The U.S. Congress in May enacted The Visual Artist's Rights Act, the most significant legislation affecting the art world in 1991. The new legislation protects artists by prohibiting art owners from mutilating or destroying the original artist's work, and it allows an artist to disclaim works altered in ways that harm his or her honor or reputation.

Several lawsuits during 1991 spotlighted obscenity and censorship issues, which have preoccupied the art community in recent years. In March, in San Francisco, a federal court ordered the Federal Bureau of Investigation (FBI) to return property confiscated in April 1990 from photographer Jock Sturges. Alleging that his photographs of nude children were pornographic, the FBI had seized negatives, prints, equipment, and diaries from the artist. Artists and civil libertarians hailed the court's decision as a victory for First Amendment rights.

In January 1991, Congress retracted an obscenity ban it had imposed in 1990 in favor of a gentler instruction to the NEA to consider "general standards of decency" when reviewing grant applications from artists. In September 1991, the Senate tried to resurrect curbs on "objectionable" art by passing legislation ordering the NEA not to grant money for "patently offensive" works. But the House rejected the measure in October.

Exhibitions. One of the most discussed shows of the year was "The West as America, Reinterpreting Images of the Frontier, 1820-1920," held at the Smithsonian Institution's National Museum of American Art. The exhibition of paintings, sculptures, graphics, and photographs of frontier life riled some art critics, politicians, and editorialists. They decried the museum's interpretations of the art as "preachy," "simplistic," and "having a political agenda." One museum label

An exhibit of umbrellas in California, above, and Japan by the artist Christo was closed in October after a windblown umbrella killed a woman.

for a painting depicting soldiers closing a fortress gate against Indians stated that the picture symbolized whites "closing the door on eastern Europeans and Asian immigrants" in the early 1900's.

"Degenerate Art: The Fate of the Avant-Garde in Nazi Germany" offered a partial reconstruction of the 1937 *"Entartete Kunst"* (degenerate art) exhibition of modernist works that had been confiscated by the Nazis from state museums. The exhibition opened at the Los Angeles County Museum of Art in February and moved to the Art Institute of Chicago in June. It was designed by architect Frank Gehry and included 150 works by German expressionists, Bauhaus abstract painters, and Jewish artists, as well as documentary material that explained the original show.

Several memorable retrospectives appeared in 1991. The Museum of Modern Art in New York City and the Los Angeles Museum of Contemporary Art jointly organized a retrospective of more than 100 works by abstract expressionist Ad Reinhardt. The show assembled Reinhardt's series of "black" paintings, which had not been shown together in the United States since the 1970's.

The Grand Palais museum in Paris premiered its first major retrospective of the work of Seurat, the neoimpressionist who painted with dots of unmixed color. The collection was also shown at the Metropolitan Museum of Art. Eleanor Heartney

In *World Book,* see **Art and the arts; Painting; Sculpture.**

Asia

Asia suffered from natural disasters in 1991 while groping toward peaceful resolutions to its largest wars. All Asian nations felt the effects of upheavals in the Communist world.

Natural disasters. Floods ravaged central and eastern China's Yangtze River Basin, the lower Mekong River in Cambodia and Vietnam, and central Afghanistan. Severe storms hit Japan, the Philippines, and Bangladesh. Damage was particularly severe in Bangladesh, where a cyclone pushed a wall of water over low-lying islands and the coastline on April 29, killing 139,000 people.

There were major earthquakes in Afghanistan, Pakistan, and India. The one in the Indian Himalaya on October 20 killed more than 360 persons. Volcanoes erupted in Japan and the Philippines. The eruption of Mount Pinatubo in the Philippines caused more than 700 deaths.

Peace efforts made progress in Cambodia and Afghanistan, two Asian countries that had suffered civil wars. But in the Philippines, Communist insurgents were still active, and ethnic and religious minorities fought for separate states in Bangladesh, Burma, India, Indonesia, and Sri Lanka.

The four factions fighting in Cambodia—the Communist regime installed in power by the Vietnamese in 1979 and the Communist Khmer Rouge whom they

Survivors of the cyclone that hit Bangladesh in April wait for food to be distributed by relief workers. About 139,000 people died in the storm.

ousted, plus two smaller non-Communist groups—signed a peace agreement in Paris on October 23. It provided for the four to run the country jointly under active supervision by the United Nations (UN), which would try to organize free elections by early 1993.

On May 21, the UN proposed a transitional coalition of factions in Afghanistan as a step toward free elections. But Islamic guerrillas continued their fight to oust the ruling regime, which had initially been Communist and later insisted that it had become nationalistic. The United States and the Soviet Union agreed on September 13 to quit arming the two sides.

Territorial disputes. In September, then Soviet President Mikhail S. Gorbachev and Russian President Boris Yeltsin signaled readiness to acknowledge Japan's claim to islands in the Kuril Island chain that had been seized by the Soviet Union at the end of World War II (1939-1945). Although some progress had been made toward settlement of the border dispute between China and the Soviet Union, that problem became more difficult as the individual republics of the former Soviet Union asserted more control over their borders. Japan, China, and Taiwan quarreled over the Senkaku Islands northeast of Taiwan. Countries around the South China Sea disputed ownership of the tiny—and possibly oil-rich—Spratly Islands.

The collapse of Communism in the old Soviet bloc affected much of Asia. Four countries that had depended upon Soviet economic assistance—North Korea, Vietnam, Afghanistan, and Mongolia—lost most of their aid. North Korea turned for help to China, which was unable to offer much due to its own economic problems. Vietnam's rice crop declined largely because it no longer received Soviet fertilizer.

Mongolia, which in 1990 replaced decades of Communist dictatorship with a shaky democracy, found more sympathy among non-Communist aid donors. As its former Soviet bloc patrons slashed trade and aid, Mongolia planned to move by 1993 from central economic planning to a market economy. The United States in 1991 sent Mongolia 25 Peace Corps volunteers to teach English and other skills.

India, which had adopted some aspects of Soviet economic planning and had developed extensive trade with the Soviets, also suffered from the turmoil in the Soviet economy. In 1991, India—a country that owed money to international agencies—found itself lending money to the Soviets to keep its exports flowing to the Soviet Union. It also found that spare parts for Soviet-made products became hard to obtain.

New economic bloc. The members of the Association of Southeast Asian Nations announced on October 8 the establishment of a free trade area. The members—Brunei, Indonesia, Malaysia, the Philippines, Singapore, and Thailand—agreed that the regional political group would create a single market for its 320 million people within 15 years.

Regional cooperation in South Asia, however, was set back by the postponement of the sixth annual summit conference of the region's seven leaders, who finally met in Colombo, Sri Lanka, on December 21. The six-week postponement occurred after King Jigme Singye Wangchuk of Bhutan said he could not attend for domestic reasons.

Bhutan's only newspaper reported that the king was being challenged by members of the National Assembly. They feared that the ethnic Bhutanese majority, which is Buddhist, was losing power to the ethnic Nepali minority, which is Hindu. In 1991, Nepali guerrillas were responsible for some violence in south Bhutan. Assembly members urged the king to crack

Hong Kong police carry a Vietnamese refugee aboard a plane bound for Hanoi. The forced return of boat people to Vietnam began on November 9.

down on the insurgents, but he sought to avoid actions that might lead to civil war.

Political developments. A number of Asian countries changed governments in 1991. Nepal had its first free elections in 32 years. The Nepali Congress Party that had won in 1959 won again, taking 110 out of 205 seats in parliament. Girija Prasad Koirala, a younger brother of the 1959 party leader whom the king had jailed in 1960, became prime minister. He faced difficult problems, including the deforestation of eroding mountainsides and dependence on declining foreign aid.

Singapore also held a free election, but opponents of the governing People's Action Party (PAP) ran for only 40 of the 81 parliamentary seats. Opposition parties ended up capturing only 4 of those seats. However, in the constituencies that were contested, the PAP's overall support dropped from 63 per cent in the 1988 elections to 61 per cent in 1991. This was seen as a setback for Prime Minister Goh Chok Tong.

On Sept. 8, 1991, Burma's military rulers formally annulled the result of a 1990 election in which they had been overwhelmingly rejected. The leader of the party that won the election, Aung San Suu Kyi, was held under house arrest. In October, Suu Kyi won the 1991 Nobel Peace Prize "for her nonviolent struggle for democracy and human rights."

In the Communist states of Vietnam and Laos, there were changes in party leadership. In Vietnam, Do Muoi moved up from prime minister to become the head of the party on June 27, and Vo Van Kiet replaced him as prime minister. In Laos, party leader Kaysone Phomvihan took over the presidency on August 15, and Khamtai Siphandon succeeded him as prime minister.

In Japan, leaders of the ruling Liberal-Democratic Party dumped popular Prime Minister Toshiki Kaifu and replaced him with Kiichi Miyazawa in November. In February, military leaders in Thailand deposed the civilian government of Chatchai Chunhawan. Under the banner of a National Peacekeeping Council, they named Anan Panyarachun as interim prime minister and promised elections in 1992.

Hong Kong held the first direct legislative elections in the British colony's history on Sept. 15, 1991. Only 39.2 per cent of the voters turned out to choose 18 members of the Legislative Council, which serves as a sounding board rather than as a decision-making body. The other 42 council members were appointed by Hong Kong's governor, Sir David Wilson, or chosen by the special-interest groups that dominate the prosperous British dependency that will become part of the People's Republic of China on July 1, 1997. The United Democrats of Hong Kong and their allies, who campaigned for more democracy, won 16 seats, while China-backed parties did poorly. However, Wilson did not name any United Democrats to his policy advisory group, the executive council.

Hong Kong newspapers interpreted the election results as a middle-class reaction against China's wish to control Hong Kong even before the British relinquish power in 1997. They also saw the results as a sign of fear of dictatorial rule once the Chinese take over. There was also widespread criticism of an agreement between Britain and China on an airport to be built in Hong Kong. The agreement granted China a large voice in the colony's affairs before 1997.

Refugee problems continued in 1991 in several parts of Asia. Few of the approximately 3 million Afghan refugees in Pakistan or some 2.5 million other Afghans in Iran started home. Neither did many of the more than 300,000 Cambodian refugees in Thailand. Hundreds of thousands of land mines in Afghanistan and Cambodia hampered efforts to return to normal life in the countryside. Large areas of once productive farmland in both nations were covered with land mines. Some had already exploded and crippled many people. Money and expertise for the dangerous job of removing the mines were scarce.

Boat people. One of the most politically sensitive refugee problems during 1991 involved people who had fled Vietnam by boat and tried to enter other countries. Malaysia decided on August 14 to close a camp through which 260,000 boat people had already passed, and it rejected further landings.

An international conference in 1979 had agreed that boat people would be temporarily received in Southeast Asian countries and then resettled in West-

Facts in brief on Asian countries

Country	Population	Government	Monetary unit*	Foreign trade (million U.S.$) Exports†	Imports†
Afghanistan	18,850,000	President and People's Democratic Party General Secretary Najibullah; Prime Minister Fazil Haq Khaliqyar	afghani (1,162.50 = $1)	238	798
Australia	17,116,000	Governor General Bill Hayden; Prime Minister Paul Keating	dollar (1.27 = $1)	39,628	38,880
Bangladesh	121,896,000	President Abdur Rahman Biswas; Prime Minister Khaleda Ziaur Rahman	taka (38.65 = $1)	1,305	3,524
Bhutan	1,586,000	King Jigme Singye Wangchuk	Indian rupee (25.82) = $1) & ngultrum (25.82 = $1)	71	138
Brunei	279,000	Sultan Sir Hassanal Bolkiah	dollar (1.67 = $1)	1,797	656
Burma (Myanmar)	43,435,000	State Law and Order Restoration Council Chairman Saw Maung	kyat (6.21 = $1)	325	261
Cambodia (Kampuchea)	7,302,000	Supreme National Council President Norodom Sihanouk; Cambodia People's Party Vice Chairman and Prime Minister Hun Sen	riel (1,000 = $1)	32	147
China	1,143,729,000	Communist Party General Secretary Jiang Zemin; Premier Li Peng; President Yang Shangkun	yuan (5.40 = $1)	62,089	53,369
India	889,417,000	President Ramaswamy Iyer Venkataraman; Prime Minister P. V. Narasimha Rao	rupee (25.82 = $1)	17,787	23,396
Indonesia	186,043,000	President Suharto; Vice President Sudharmono	rupiah (1,982 = $1)	25,675	21,837
Iran	59,601,000	Leader of the Islamic Revolution Ali Hoseini Khamenei; President Ali Akbar Hashemi Rafsanjani	rial (1,400 = $1)	12,300	12,000
Japan	124,595,000	Emperor Akihito; Prime Minister Kiichi Miyazawa	yen (130.15 = $1)	286,949	234,800
Korea, North	23,939,000	President Kim Il-sŏng; Premier Yon Hyong-muk	won (0.97 = $1)	2,400	3,100
Korea, South	44,458,000	President Roh Tae Woo; Prime Minister Chung Won Shik	won (754.50 = $1)	65,016	69,844
Laos	4,266,000	President Kaysone Phomvihan; Prime Minister Khamtai Siphandon	kip (705 = $1)	81	162
Malaysia	18,047,000	Paramount Ruler Azlan Muhibbuddin Shah ibni Sultan Yusof Izzudin; Prime Minister Mahathir bin Mohamad	ringgit (2.75 = $1)	29,418	29,261
Maldives	234,000	President Maumoon Abdul Gayoom	rufiyaa (10.80 = $1)	40	106
Mongolia	2,229,000	President Punsalmaagiyn Ochirbat; Prime Minister Dashiyn Byambasuren	tughrik (42.00 = $1)	388	1,000
Nepal	20,049,000	King Birendra Bir Bikram Shah Dev; Prime Minister Girija Prasad Koirala	rupee (42.70 = $1)	156	580
New Zealand	3,430,000	Governor General Dame Catherine Tizard; Prime Minister James B. Bolger	dollar (1.78 = $1)	9,435	9,489
Pakistan	129,808,000	President Ghulam Ishaq Khan; Prime Minister Nawaz Sharif	rupee (24.55 = $1)	5,522	7,356
Papua New Guinea	4,217,000	Governor General Sir Wiwa Korowi; Prime Minister Rabbie Namaliu	kina (0.95 = $1)	1,281	1,335
Philippines	65,275,000	President Corazon C. Aquino	peso (26.29 = $1)	8,186	12,206
Singapore	2,755,000	President Wee Kim Wee; Prime Minister Goh Chok Tong	dollar (1.67 = $1)	52,729	60,787
Sri Lanka	17,642,000	President Ranasinghe Premadasa; Prime Minister D. B. Wijetunge	rupee (42.57 = $1)	1,912	2,634
Taiwan	21,001,000	President Li Teng-hui; Premier Hao Po-ts'un	dollar (25.76 = $1)	66,200	52,200
Thailand	57,216,000	King Bhumibol Adulyadej; Interim Prime Minister Anan Panyarachun	baht (25.47 = $1)	22,972	32,829
Union of Soviet Socialist Republics	284,900,000	President Mikhail S. Gorbachev‡	ruble (0.57 = $1)	104,177	120,651
Vietnam	68,777,000	Communist Party General Secretary Do Muoi; Council of State Chairman Vo Chi Cong; Council of Ministers Chairman Vo Van Kiet	dong (12,880 = $1)	1,100	2,500

*Exchange rates as of Nov. 29, 1991, or latest available data. †Latest available data.
‡Gorbachev resigned on December 25, and the Soviet Union dissolved.

ern countries. But as large numbers continued to leave Vietnam, another conference in 1989 promised resettlement only to those who had escaped political persecution. Those who fled Vietnam to seek better economic conditions would be sent back.

Despite warnings that they would be turned away, thousands of boat people continued to sail to Hong Kong. Many Vietnamese who were considered economic, not political, refugees had been imprisoned in camps in Hong Kong for years because no Western country would resettle them.

Vietnam refused for years to take back boat people who did not want to go home. But on Oct. 29, 1991, the Vietnamese government signed an agreement with Britain for the return to Vietnam over the next three years of some 50,000 boat people in Hong Kong camps whom Britain did not consider political refugees. The agreement was made despite demonstrations in the camps against forced repatriation and threats of violence and suicide. On November 9, Hong Kong authorities began sending boat people back to Vietnam. The United States opposed forced repatriation but did not offer to resettle the refugees.

At the same time, some 100,000 persons joining relatives abroad or leaving after political imprisonment were flown out of Vietnam in 1991 under a UN "orderly departure program." Henry S. Bradsher

See also the articles on the individual Asian nations. In ***World Book,*** see **Asia.**

Astronomy. For astronomers who observe the universe by using instruments aboard spacecraft, 1991 was a year of frustration, as two spacecraft experienced malfunctions, but it was also a year of great success. One recently launched satellite operated flawlessly, opening up a new window on the universe at very short wavelengths. A radar survey of the planet Venus revealed remarkable new surface features. On Earth, millions of people saw a major eclipse of the sun. There were reports of a new planet discovered beyond the solar system, and several astronomers announced results that suggested the universe is much younger than previously thought.

Troubles for two spacecraft. The *Hubble Space Telescope,* still producing blurry images as a result of its improperly shaped mirror, developed several new problems in 1991. Two of the telescope's six gyroscopes failed, and a third showed signs of trouble. The gyroscopes are devices that enable the telescope to steady itself as it points at stars and are essential to its successful operation. Further trouble with the gyroscopes could cause *Hubble* to shut down.

The power supply on one of the *Hubble*'s six scientific instruments, the high-resolution spectrograph, also failed. This device was to be used for a detailed analysis of ultraviolet and visible light radiation from objects such as stars and galaxies. Despite these difficulties, the images produced by *Hubble,* when processed by complex computer programs, were clearer than any pictures of the planet produced by Earth-bound telescopes.

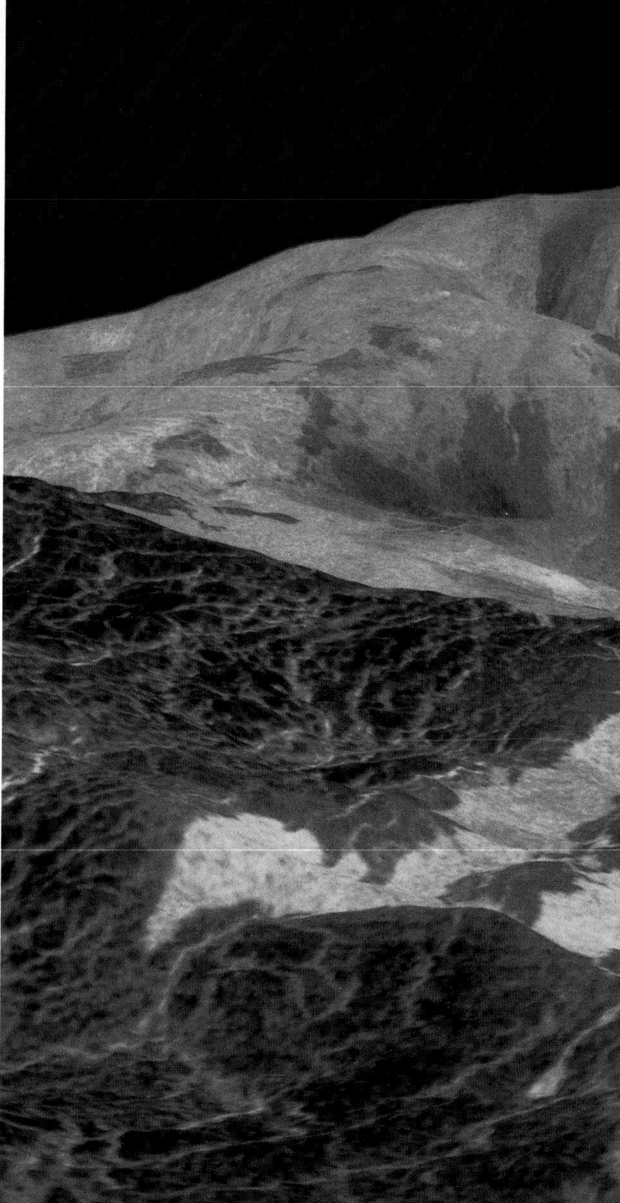

An image from the *Magellan* spacecraft, released in October, shows fresh lava flows around Maat Mons, indicating that Venus is volcanically active.

Galileo, a spacecraft on a long mission to orbit the planet Jupiter and probe its atmosphere, had difficulties in 1991 that may be more severe than those of the space telescope. *Galileo's* high-gain antenna, which permits it to send pictures back to Earth, would not open. If it cannot be opened before the spacecraft reaches Jupiter in 1995, the mission will be severely crippled.

Solar eclipse. On July 11, 1991, the shadow of the moon passed over Earth from the Pacific Ocean to

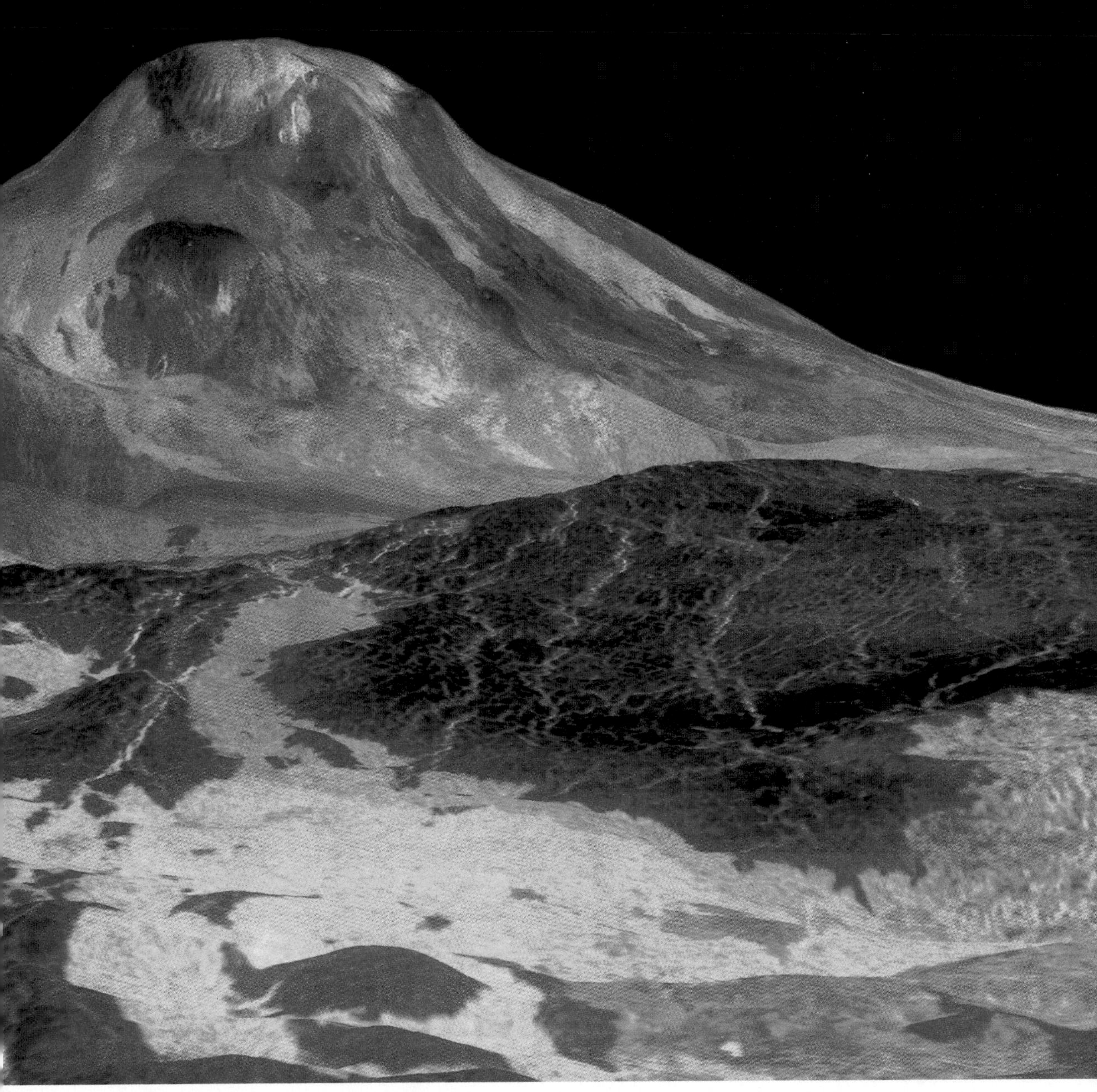

central Brazil, producing a total solar eclipse that was viewed by millions of people along its path. For observers in Baja California and mainland Mexico, it was one of the longest eclipses of the 1900's. With the sun totally blocked for almost seven minutes, several giant red flames called *prominences* extended from the edges of the sun and could have been easily visible to the naked eye—but looking directly at the sun during an eclipse can cause serious eye damage. Long streams of light from the corona, the outermost atmosphere of the sun, surrounded the sun like a pearly halo.

Astronomers in Paris used the eclipse to study motions of gas in the corona. Several other groups of astronomers, using cameras that recorded *infrared* (heat) radiation, took pictures of the eclipsed sun to search for a possible ring of small particles around the sun, such as the rings that circle the outer planets in the solar system. Astronomers found no such ring.

New views of Venus. The planet Venus is Earth's nearest neighbor in the solar system, but it is covered with thick clouds that have, until recently, hidden its surface from view. The *Magellan* satellite, which arrived at Venus in August 1990, is equipped with a radar device that bounces radio signals off the planet and produces strikingly detailed pictures of its surface, even through thick clouds. On May 15, 1991, *Magellan* completed its mission of mapping the entire planet and began to take second and third pictures of certain regions. *Magellan's* survey revealed a combination of features not found on any other planet.

Astronomy

Magellan found that Venus has craters similar to those formed on the moon when *meteoroids*—rocks that range in size from bits of dust to boulders—hit its surface. But the craters on Venus are fewer than those on the moon. Astronomers think this may be because most of the craters on Venus that formed more than a billion years ago have been covered by flows of lava that blanket more than 80 per cent of the planet.

Some of the craters on Venus are surrounded by flows of lava that appear to resemble flowers. Astronomers do not believe that these craters were formed by the impact of meteoroids. They seem to be volcanic in origin, according to astronomers. Unlike volcanoes on Earth, Venus' volcanoes cannot erupt into the thick atmosphere. Instead, lava swells upward from the crater and down its side, leaving the flowery patterns as it cools and solidifies.

On its way to Jupiter, the *Galileo* spacecraft passed Venus in February 1991. Astronomer David Gurnett of the University of Iowa in Iowa City announced in September that during the Venus fly-by, his plasma wave instrument aboard *Galileo* had detected radio signals from Venus that unmistakably resembled the static from lightning discharges. Lightning has been detected now in the atmospheres of Jupiter, Saturn, Uranus, and Neptune, but astronomers are puzzled about how lightning is generated in Venus' atmosphere, where the temperature is 1290° F. (700° C)—far too hot for the rain and clouds that are usually associated with lightning.

Gamma ray observatory. On April 27, 1991, the *Arthur Holly Compton Gamma Ray Observatory* (*GRO*) was successfully launched from Cape Canaveral, Fla. It carried four instruments designed to detect *gamma rays,* the most energetic form of electromagnetic radiation. Gamma rays have wavelengths even shorter than X rays and ultraviolet radiation. Earth's atmosphere blocks gamma rays, and the orbiting observatory was the first instrument able to survey the entire sky and look for gamma ray sources. The *GRO* has been particularly successful in detecting *gamma ray bursters,* strange objects that emit intense gamma radiation for short periods of time, from a thousandth of a second up to a few seconds.

New planet. On July 25, 1991, astronomer Andrew G. Lyne and his colleagues at the University of Manchester in England announced the discovery beyond the solar system of an object that may be a planet. The astronomers found the object while analyzing radio signals from a *pulsar,* PSR 1829-10, a dense spinning neutron star that emits regular pulses of radio waves. Five years of observations of the pulsar revealed regular delays in the arrivals of the pulses. Scientists thought that the tug of a small planet orbiting the neutron star may cause the delays. Some astronomers had difficulty accepting these results, however, because neutron stars supposedly form in *supernova outbursts,* huge explosions that should not leave any intact planets behind.

A younger universe? Several astronomers announced results in 1991 that suggest that our universe is younger than previously thought. Astronomers have long known that the galaxies, huge assemblages of stars, are all moving away from our own local group of galaxies. Most astronomers attribute this to the *big bang,* an explosion they believe started the expansion of the universe. By dividing the distances of galaxies by their speeds, astronomers are able to estimate how long the expansion has been occurring. In the past, many measurements suggested that the universe is between 15 billion and 20 billion years old. But new measurements from Earth, which is in the Virgo cluster of galaxies, to other galaxies in the cluster suggest that the expansion began about 10 billion years ago.

In June 1991, astronomer Robert McClure from the Dominion Astrophysical Observatory in British Columbia, Canada, and his colleagues announced that certain stars in the Virgo cluster appear brighter than previously supposed, indicating that they are closer to Earth than astronomers previously thought. The researchers used a telescope in Hawaii equipped with a special camera designed to remove the blurring effects of Earth's atmosphere. Research teams using different methods reported similar distances. Shorter distances may imply a younger age for the universe.

Laurence A. Marschall

See also **Space exploration.** In ***World Book,*** see **Astronomy.**

Australia. On Dec. 19, 1991, Australian Prime Minister Robert Hawke was toppled in a leadership challenge by parliamentary members of his party, the Australian Labor Party. In a 56 to 51 vote, the party elected former treasurer Paul Keating as its head. The leader of the governing party in Australia automatically becomes prime minister.

Keating had been treasurer since 1983, when Hawke and the Labor Party took office. In June 1991, Keating resigned from his dual offices of treasurer and deputy prime minister after failing in his first leadership challenge to Hawke. His second challenge succeeded, analysts said, because the Labor Party was concerned about its reelection chances as Australia's economy faltered and unemployment grew. At age 47, Keating was the youngest man to become Australia's prime minister. Keating promised to fight unemployment and focus on economic growth.

The conservative opposition coalition, led by John Hewson of the Liberal Party of Australia, had unveiled a comprehensive economic and tax package on November 21. The package included a consumption tax (called a goods and services tax). The package was to be the cornerstone in Hewson's bid to win the 1993 elections.

Agricultural woes. The east part of Australia was afflicted by severe drought, which contributed to Australia's lack of success in the struggle to trade its way out of a recession in 1991. The nation saw its traditional meat and wheat markets taken over by the United States, which was able to sell these products for a lower price because of subsidies paid to U.S. farmers. Australia has complained for several years that the United States "dumps" wheat on international markets, such as the Middle East, which usually buys 40 per cent of the Australian wheat crop. Dumping is the practice of exporting goods for less than they cost in the producing country, and this depresses world prices. On August 14, the Australian Senate passed a resolution asking the United States to minimize damage to countries such as Australia that do not subsidize wheat. Agricultural concerns were on the list of topics discussed when U.S. President George Bush visited Australia late in December.

A decrease in world demand for sugar contributed to a 24 per cent drop in net farm income in 1991. Up to 10 per cent of Australia's 5,700 sugar cane growers could lose their farms as a result of reduced demand for sugar. Australian wool producers also feared bankruptcy in 1991. In February, the Australian Wool Corporation (AWC), a government-backed organization that markets all Australian wool and buys unsold supplies, abandoned its minimum price in order to curtail wool production. Wool producers condemned the government's policy change, which forced them to slaughter 14 million sheep. In 1991, the number of sheep fell to 166 million and was forecast to drop to 130 million by 1995.

Economy. The government had some success in lowering interest rates and inflation in 1991. In early November, the federal reserve bank lowered the official interest rate 1.5 per cent to 9 per cent. The cut reflected a drop in inflation to 3.3 per cent at the end of October, the lowest level in 20 years.

The federal budget had a $1.9-billion surplus by July, far below the expected $8.11 billion. On August 20, Treasurer John Kerin issued his budget report for the 1991-1992 fiscal year, forecasting a budget deficit of $4.9 billion—the first deficit in four years. Kerin projected a slight rise in unemployment, to about 11 per cent of the work force, a drop to 3 per cent in inflation, and a 5 per cent rise in exports.

The Australian dollar slipped back to its 1990 value of 77 U.S. cents by the end of 1991, after climbing to 79 U.S. cents by September. (Monetary amounts in this article are in Australian dollars.)

State news. In May 1991 elections in New South Wales, the richest and most populous state, the Liberal-National coalition government was narrowly reelected but lost its majority representation. The coalition was forced to bargain with four independent members of the state parliament in order to govern. Reasons cited for the coalition's poor showing at the polls included a weak economy.

Banks. South Australia experienced financial scandal in 1991 similar to the 1990 scandals in Victoria and Western Australia involving the governments and failed merchant banks. Labor Premier John Bannon announced in March that the State Bank of South Australia lost $1 billion. Reportedly, the bankers had entertained lavishly to persuade customers to take loans, which remained unpaid.

Following the widespread collapse of corporations in 1990, due largely to their inability to repay enormous bank loans, banks in 1991 found themselves owning hotels, television networks, and media. Westpac Banking Corporation, Australia's largest bank, took possession of television network channel 7 and assumed financial control of the nation's oldest newspaper publisher, the John Fairfax Group. The family-owned Fairfax company was bankrupted late in 1990 when Warwick Fairfax attempted to buy out other family members. After a great deal of controversy, the banks accepted on Dec. 16, 1991, the $1.5-billion bid of the Tourang consortium. The consortium was led by Canadian Conrad Black, who is publisher of the *London Daily Telegraph* newspaper.

Aborigines. In May 1991, a royal commission released its final report concerning the deaths over a nine-year period of 99 Aborigines in police custody and jail. The commission, which had investigated for three years at a cost of more than $30 million, found that none of the prisoners had been murdered. Aborigines, Australia's indigenous people, die in prison at the same rate as non-Aborigines, the report concluded, but they are 29 times more likely than whites to be in prison. Aborigines are frequently jailed for drunkenness and other minor offenses. The report recommended that Aborigines should be imprisoned only as a last resort. Special alcohol clinics should be set up as an alternative to prisons, the report stated.

The commission recommended sweeping changes in police force operations, including eliminating violent treatment and abuse of Aborigines. It also urged governments to involve them in deciding, and delivering, appropriate management of their communities.

In June, in an unrelated development concerning Aborigines, the federal government decided against mining gold, platinum, and palladium at Coronation Hill on Aboriginal land in the Northern Territory because it is a sacred site of the Aborigines. In August, the government also decided against mining uranium at this same site.

Immigration. In August, a new study claimed that immigration adversely affects the national economy in both the short and long terms. Immigration has been a major issue in formulating Australia's foreign policy since the huge immigrant influx of the 1950's. The study showed that almost all immigrants reside in cities, where they encounter difficulty in finding work. Immigrants arriving in the last two years had an unemployment rate of 33 per cent, and most of them received unemployment and other welfare benefits. Australia's current annual level of immigration is about 110,000 people. Susan Williams

See also **Asia** (Facts in brief table). In ***World Book,*** see **Australia.**

Austria

Austria in 1991 continued to adapt to the increasing economic integration of western Europe into the 12-nation European Community (EC or Common Market) and to the collapse of Communist governments in eastern Europe and the Soviet Union. The civil war in neighboring Yugoslavia also concerned the Austrian government.

European relations. Although Austria was not yet an EC member, the government took a number of actions to help Austria compete more effectively within the EC's tariff-free economy, scheduled to go into effect by the end of 1992. These actions included speeding up a program to privatize state-owned companies and struggling to cut a high budget deficit. Austria had applied for EC membership in 1989, and even though the EC did not plan to admit new members before 1993, it was expected to give Austria's application first consideration.

The collapse of Communism in eastern Europe in 1990 and the breakup of Yugoslavia and the Soviet Union during 1991 brought Austria more worry than relief. Large numbers of eastern European immigrants used Austria as a bridge to enter western Europe, despite government efforts to stem the flow with immigration restrictions. The Austrian government worked alongside the EC to mediate the conflict between the breakaway Yugoslavian republics of Croatia and Slovenia and Yugoslavia's central government. Large Austrian companies and banks continued to invest in eastern Europe in 1991, particularly in neighboring Hungary, even though Austrian banks suffered losses on loans to Poland and some other eastern European countries.

In domestic affairs, the year's most important event was the June announcement by Austrian President Kurt Waldheim that he would not seek a second term in elections to be held in 1992. The former secretary-general of the United Nations was elected president in 1986 despite controversy over his alleged involvement in Nazi war crimes during World War II (1939-1945). Waldheim denied the allegations. In July, Austrian Chancellor Franz Vranitzky apologized publicly, on behalf of the Austrian people, for the country's role in the Holocaust against the Jews.

A coalition government of the Socialist Party and the conservative People's Party had taken office in December 1990. The coalition, headed by Socialist Party leader Vranitzky, began its term plagued by internal squabbling but during 1991 managed to reach consensus on such issues as future EC membership.

The Austrian economy, helped by a strong German demand for Austrian goods, continued to grow at an annual rate of about 3 per cent in 1991, slightly below the 1990 rate, but faster than most other nations in western Europe. Analysts expected investment in new factories and service companies, as well as demand for Austrian products, to stay strong. Philip Revzin

See also **Europe** (Facts in brief table). In ***World Book***, see **Austria.**

Automobile. Few years have been as rich in freshly designed cars and trucks or as poor in sales as 1991. Although there were dozens of attractive new models, sales of new cars and trucks in the United States fell to an estimated 12.5 million, down 11.3 per cent from the 14.15 million vehicles sold in 1990, and off 23.3 per cent from the previous sales peak of 16.32 million vehicles in 1986. Demand for new vehicles fell in every major market in the world except Germany. But even there, a car sales boom touched off by the 1990 reunification of East and West Germany slowed by the end of 1991. DRI Europe, a London-based economic forecasting house, estimated that worldwide car sales fell 2.9 per cent in 1991, dropping from 35.46 million in 1990 to 34.44 million in 1991.

With the U.S. economy in a recession and unemployment growing in 1991, it was clear that many consumers were too uncertain about their personal financial condition to invest in a new car. According to the Motor Vehicle Manufacturers Association, the U.S. auto industry's trade association, the average price paid for a new car in 1991 was $16,416.

New models. Despite consumer wariness, many new models were introduced in 1991. General Motors Corporation (GM) introduced two totally revamped car lines—a full-sized line represented by the Pontiac Bonneville, Oldsmobile 88, and Buick LeSabre; and a compact line consisting of the Buick Skylark, Oldsmobile Achieva, and Pontiac Grand Am. GM also introduced the restyled Cadillac Seville and Eldorado, Chevrolet and GMC Suburban trucks, and the Chevrolet Blazer and GMC Yukon sport-utility trucks.

Other notable restyled models included the Ford Taurus sedan; the F150 Flareside pickup truck; the Ford Crown Victoria and the Mercury Grand Marquis full-sized family cars; the Toyota Camry sedan and Paseo coupe; the Lexus SC400 and SC300 sport-luxury coupes; the Nissan NX 2000 coupe; a new line of Mercedes S-class sedans; the Audi 100 performance sedan; the Honda Civic and Prelude; the Subaru SVX sports car; the Acura Vigor luxury sedan; the luxury Mazda 929; and the Jaguar XJS sports coupe.

Chrysler redesigned its basic V-8 and V-6 engines in 1991. It also looked forward to the introduction of three important models in 1992—the Viper V-10 sports car; the Grand Cherokee sport-utility truck; and a new line of Dodge, Chrysler, and Eagle midsized cars code-named LH.

Hard times. Some names were missing from the long list of manufacturers offering cars or trucks for sale in the United States in 1991. Poor business conditions forced French automaker Peugeot and Britain's Sterling to withdraw from the U.S. market. There was speculation whether several other struggling firms, including Japan-based Suzuki Motor Company and Daihatsu, would be able to survive the slump.

American companies also scaled down their operations in response to diminishing sales. In the most dramatic announcement of the year, GM said on Decem-

The Zag, a concept car designed by Ford Motor Company's Ghia Studio in Turin, Italy, is a model for compactness and fuel efficiency in future cars.

ber 18 that in the next four years it would close 21 plants and lay off about 74,000 workers.

Slow sales in the United States and abroad, price discounts averaging more than $1,000 per vehicle, and heavy investments in future automotive products resulted in an especially difficult year for the three Detroit-based firms: GM, Ford Motor Company, and Chrysler Corporation. GM alone lost $2.21 billion in the first nine months of 1991. Its global sales revenue fell 6.7 per cent to $78.73 billion between January and September, compared with $84.4 billion in the same period in 1990.

Ford reported a nine-month loss of $1.78 billion, with sales in that period slumping 12.4 per cent to $54.15 billion from $61.8 billion in the same period in 1990. Chrysler in the first nine months of 1991 lost $892 million on sales of $21.1 billion, down 8.2 per cent from sales of $22.97 billion during the first nine months of 1990. It was the worst financial year in history for Detroit automakers.

Promising outlook. Most economists predicted that the car market would stage a weak recovery in 1992, climbing to around 13.5 million vehicle sales. Ford Treasurer David N. McCammon said he expected a new North American sales record would be achieved sometime in the mid-1990's, with rich rewards for companies that invest in new products while striving for greater efficiency in design, manufacturing, and marketing.

Chrysler declared that it would be one of the survivors of the 1991 slump. It opened a new $1.1-billion technical center near Detroit, intended both to keep the company on the leading edge of technological development and to reduce the amount of time it takes to bring new products to market. Ford invested in new plants, equipment, and production tooling at record levels in 1991, while GM planned capital spending in the neighborhood of $7 billion per year during the 1990's.

Many private investors agreed that better times were ahead for the Detroit firms. The three companies sold more than $4 billion worth of stock to the public in 1991 and placed those funds in the bank to help provide for future product spending. Ford offered the first public issue of preferred stock in its 88-year history.

Japanese competition. It also seemed likely by the end of 1991 that Detroit firms would be able to compete more effectively in the future with their Japanese rivals. Previous recessions had not hurt Japanese automakers in the United States. In 1991, however, they suffered along with GM, Ford, and Chrysler. Sales of Japanese cars and trucks—those that were imported, and those built in the United States—fell nearly 5 per cent during the year.

Japanese firms were beginning to rely more heavily in 1991 on their North American factories to support sales in the United States. Sales of cars and trucks imported from Japan fell 13 per cent in 1991, while output from Japanese-owned assembly plants in the United States continued to rise. In August, Toyota Motor Company began building pickup trucks at assembly plants in Fremont, Calif., and in Georgetown, Ky. Japanese automakers planned on being able to build 2.2 million vehicles in North America by 1995.

Nevertheless, trade conflicts between the United States and Japan intensified in 1991. Even though they were steadily beefing up their U.S. operations, Japanese automakers still relied on their home operations for cars, trucks, and the parts used in their American assembly plants. Analysts estimated that Japan's sales of automotive goods in the United States exceeded purchases of automotive goods from U.S. companies by $41 billion in 1991.

Japan's massive trade surplus in the automobile industry brought numerous complaints from U.S. automakers, trade unions, and the federal government. Faced with the possibility that their sales here would be restricted unless they did more to help the U.S. economy, Japanese firms announced that purchases of American-made parts for their assembly plants in the United States would more than double by 1995 to some $15 billion per year. And Toyota, Nissan Motor Company, and Honda Motor Company dropped restrictions that prevented Japanese dealers from selling Chevrolets, Dodges, and Fords. James V. Higgins

In *World Book,* see **Automobile.**

Automobile racing. In the United States, Rick Mears won the Indianapolis 500, the world's richest race, and Michael Andretti won the series for Indy-type cars. Internationally, Ayrton Senna of Brazil won the World Drivers Championship for the second year. United States and international officials considered using the same engines for both series to stimulate international competition and create a worldwide series on oval tracks for Indy-type cars.

Indianapolis 500. On May 26, on the 187th lap of the 200-lap race, Andretti, from Nazareth, Pa., passed Mears and took the lead. One lap later, Mears daringly roared by Andretti on the outside and went on to win by 3.1 seconds. The 39-year-old Mears, from Bakersfield, Calif., drove a car with a Penske chassis and a Chevrolet-Ilmor engine. He averaged 176.460 miles (283.994 kilometers) per hour. Mears joined A. J. Foyt and Al Unser, Sr., as the only four-time winners of this race. He and Roger Penske, his team owner, shared $1,219,704 from the purse of $7,009,150. The 56-year-old Foyt lasted only 25 laps before he ran over debris from an accident and broke his suspension. Willy T. Ribbs, the first black driver in the history of the race, lasted only six laps before his engine misfired.

The Indianapolis 500 was the showcase of the Championship Auto Racing Teams (CART) series of 17 races. Andretti clinched the series title on October 20, when he won the last race at Monterey, Calif. He led the series in earnings with $2.4 million.

Rick Mears enters the victory lane after winning the Indianapolis 500 in May for the fourth time, tying the record for Indy 500 wins.

Andretti's brother, Jeff, was named Rookie of the Year. John Andretti, Michael and Jeff's cousin, won on March 17 in Surfers Paradise, Australia, in the first CART race outside North America.

International drivers. The major international series consisted of 16 Grand Prix races, mostly in Europe, from March to November for Formula One open-wheeled cars. The 31-year-old Senna drove a McLaren with a new Honda V-12 engine.

In capturing his third world championship, Senna won seven races, compared with six in 1990. Nigel Mansell of England won five races in a Williams-Renault whose semiautomatic transmission made gear changes faster. Senna won the United States Grand Prix on March 10 in Phoenix. Nelson Piquet of Brazil captured the Canadian Grand Prix on June 2 in Montreal, Canada.

Senna seemed about to leave McLaren to join the Williams team for 1991 until he returned to McLaren for a salary of $12 million. He then signed with McLaren for 1992 for $17 million after Williams had offered a reported $23 million.

The Formula One cars were similar to the Indy-type cars, but lighter and with less-powerful engines. United States officials talked of adopting the Formula One 3.5-liter engines for Indy-type cars to attract manufacturers such as Ferrari, Renault, Mercedes, and Porsche to Indy-type racing.

NASCAR. The National Association for Stock Car Racing (NASCAR) staged the Winston Cup series for late-model sedans. The 29 races carried $21 million in prize money. Dale Earnhardt of Doolie, N.C., won his fifth series title and his second straight and led in earnings with $2.4 million. Davey Allison of Hueytown, Ala., in a Ford, and Harry Gant of Taylorsville, N.C., in an Oldsmobile, won five races each. Earnhardt won four. Ernie Irvan of Rockwell, N.C., in a Chevrolet, won the richest NASCAR race, the $2,181,370 Daytona 500 on February 17 in Daytona Beach, Fla.

Other races. For the first time, a Japanese car, a rotary-powered Mazda, won the premier endurance race, the 24 Hours of Le Mans, held from June 22 to 23 in France. Jaguar won the world title. In November, the endurance series was discontinued because of declining interest from manufacturers, but in December it was reinstated.

Geoff Brabham of Australia, in a Nissan, won a record fourth consecutive title in the International Motor Sports Association's series for prototype sports cars. Davy Jones won five of the 14 races in a Jaguar.

The National Hot Rod Association conducted 18 races from February to November over quarter-mile straightaways. Joe Amato of Old Forge, Pa., won a record fourth season title for top-fuel cars, the fastest group. Kenny Bernstein won six top-fuel races, and Amato won four. For the second consecutive year, John Force won the title in funny cars, and Darrell Alderman won in pro stock. Frank Litsky

In *World Book*, see **Automobile racing.**

Aviation. The economic recession in the United States and a sharp drop in air travel because of concerns about possible terrorist activities in connection with the Persian Gulf War pummeled the airline industry in 1991. Analysts predicted that the nation's airlines would lose at least $1.3 billion for the year, making it the second worst in airline history. The worst year was 1990, when increased fuel prices drove losses to $3.9 billion.

Airport security in the United States reached unprecedented levels in early 1991 during the Persian Gulf War. Curbside check-in of luggage was banned, and people who accompanied travelers were barred from going to the gate with passengers. These restrictions were lifted in May.

The Federal Aviation Administration (FAA) continued to improve airport security in general during 1991. The FAA required more intensive training of airport security personnel than in the past and assigned new federal security managers to major U.S. airports. These efforts were in response to an official British report released on March 22 regarding the 1988 terrorist bombing of Pan American World Airways Flight 103 over Lockerbie, Scotland, in which 259 people on board and 11 people on the ground were killed. The report found fault with Pan Am's baggage screening procedures that did not detect the bomb concealed in a radio-cassette player planted in a suitcase. On November 14, the U.S. Department of Justice indicted

Danger at the airport

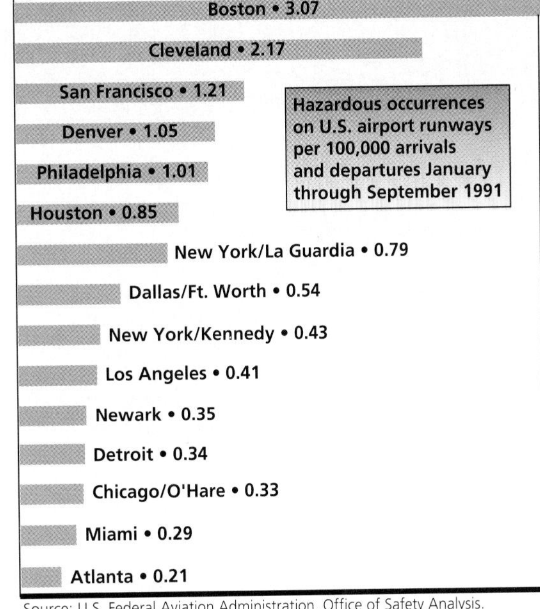

Source: U.S. Federal Aviation Administration, Office of Safety Analysis.

Boston's airport had the highest rate of hazardous occurrences on runways during 1991, and Atlanta's airport had the lowest rate.

A fire crew views the wreck of a USAir 737 jet that hit a SkyWest commuter plane awaiting take-off at Los Angeles International Airport on February 1.

two Libyan intelligence officials on charges that they were responsible for the Lockerbie bombing.

Failed airlines. Eastern Airlines, which had been struggling to emerge from bankruptcy for two years, failed to overcome financial problems. The 62-year-old carrier closed operations on January 18 and was liquidated. Eastern had employed 18,000 people.

Also in January, Pan Am Corporation, which operated Pan American World Airways, filed for protection from its creditors under federal bankruptcy laws. Pan Am was founded in 1927 and had been a leader in international aviation. During 1991, Pan Am sold some prime assets to Delta Air Lines, and Delta spent $115-million to offset Pan Am's losses. But finally, on December 3, Delta told a bankruptcy court that it would not provide any more money. The next day, December 4, Pan Am shut down operations, putting about 9,000 employees out of work.

Midway Airlines filed for bankruptcy protection on March 26. It was the first airline formed after the federal government deregulated the industry in 1978. On Nov. 13, 1991, Northwest Airlines withdrew from a tentative agreement to buy Midway assets, and Midway stopped flying the same day. About 4,300 employees lost their jobs as a result.

Other financial affairs. America West Airlines filed for bankruptcy protection in June, and Trans World Airlines (TWA) said in July that it planned to file for bankruptcy protection as early as January 1992. Northwest Airlines considered merging with

Continental Airlines, which had operated under bankruptcy-law protection since December 1990.

The parent companies of the nation's three largest airlines—American, Delta, and United—snapped up routes owned by ailing carriers. American agreed in May to buy three TWA routes from U.S. cities to London for $445 million. Delta bought Pan Am's shuttle service on the East Coast and other assets under a July agreement. United purchased Pan Am's London routes for more than $1 billion in cash and assumed liabilities, which was approved by the U.S. Department of Transportation in February.

Consumer groups and some members of the U.S. Congress feared that consolidation would limit competition and cause air fares to rise. But legislation designed to increase competition did not pass.

Airline investment. On January 23, Department of Transportation Secretary Samuel K. Skinner called for a further relaxation of a law that limits foreign investment in U.S. airlines as a way to attract funds to the ailing industry. Under the new policy, a foreign investor could hold as much as 49 per cent of a domestic airline's equity.

In September, American Airlines announced plans to cut $500 million from its ground-equipment purchases in 1992. American also said it would delay or not use options to buy $3.6 billion in airplanes.

Reducing aircraft noise. Under new FAA regulations issued on February 24, airlines must phase out the use of most of their older, noisier planes, called Stage 2 aircraft, by the year 2000 and replace them with newer, quieter planes, called Stage 3 aircraft. In cases of financial hardship, the airlines could be permitted to fly the noisier planes until the end of 2003. The rule also made it difficult for airports to impose their own, tougher noise restrictions on airlines.

Fatal crashes. There were a number of aircraft disasters during the year. A USAir 737 jet landing at Los Angeles International Airport hit a SkyWest commuter plane that was awaiting take-off on Feb. 1, 1991. An air traffic controller had cleared both planes to use the same runway. The accident killed 34 people. Several of those killed on the USAir plane died from toxic smoke and fumes given off by burning cabin materials rather than from the impact of the crash.

The National Transportation Safety Board (NTSB), which investigates accidents, blamed the crash on lax FAA management at the airport and faulty air traffic control procedures, which "created an environment" that allowed the controller to make a mistake. Consumer groups said there should be stricter standards for materials used in airplane cabins to cut down on toxic fumes during a fire.

On March 3, a United Airlines 737-200 jet crashed while approaching Colorado Springs Airport in Colorado, killing all 25 people aboard. In August, the NTSB, citing maintenance records indicating that the plane had experienced rudder-control "anomalies" twice before, urged the FAA to require the Boeing Company, the plane's manufacturer, to inspect the rudders of 727 and 737 aircraft. But the board said it did not know at that time whether a rudder problem caused the accident.

A Boeing 767 jet belonging to Lauda-Air, an Austrian charter air service, crashed in a jungle shortly after take-off from Bangkok, Thailand, on May 26, killing all 223 people aboard. In a preliminary report, investigators said that the thrust reverser on the left engine turned on accidentally in flight, making the plane uncontrollable. A thrust reverser helps slow a plane once it lands. On August 25, the FAA ordered the deactivation of thrust reversers on all planes with the same engine model as the Lauda-Air plane.

Small craft fatalities. On April 4, Senator John Heinz (R., Pa.) and six other people were killed when the private plane Heinz was aboard collided with a helicopter over a Philadelphia suburb (see **Philadelphia**). The next day, April 5, former Senator John Tower (R., Tex.) and 22 others were killed in the crash of an Atlantic Southeast Airlines commuter plane near Brunswick, Ga. By mid-October 1991, 67 people had been killed in accidents involving commuter aircraft. It was the worst year ever for commuter aircraft accidents in the United States. Laurie McGinley

In ***World Book,*** see **Aviation.**

Bahamas. See **Latin America.**

Bahrain. See **Middle East.**

Ballet. See **Dancing.**

Bangladesh. Khaleda Ziaur Rahman (known as Khaleda Zia), the 46-year-old widow of a Bangladeshi president who was assassinated in 1981, became prime minister on March 20, 1991. Her Bangladesh Nationalist Party (BNP) won 139 of 300 parliamentary seats in elections held on February 27. The Awami League, the other main party, led by Hasina Wazed, daughter of Bangladesh's independence leader, won only 88 seats. See **Ziaur Rahman, Khaleda.**

The elections came after a campaign by the BNP and the Awami League forced President Hussain Mohammad Ershad to resign on Dec. 6, 1990. Once Zia became prime minister, Acting President Shahabuddin Ahmed granted her most of the powers that the Constitution gave to the president.

Former President Ershad was elected to five different Parliament seats, even though he was under detention on corruption charges. His Jatiya Dal (National Party) won 35 seats in the election. On June 12, Ershad was convicted of illegal possession of firearms and sentenced to 10 years in jail.

Parliamentary system. Following the elections, the BNP and the Awami League agreed to end 16 years of autocratic presidential rule. On Aug. 6, 1991, the Parliament unanimously passed legislation for a return to a parliamentary form of government. In a referendum on September 15, more than 84 per cent of the voters supported the new legislation.

Zia's party won five additional parliamentary seats

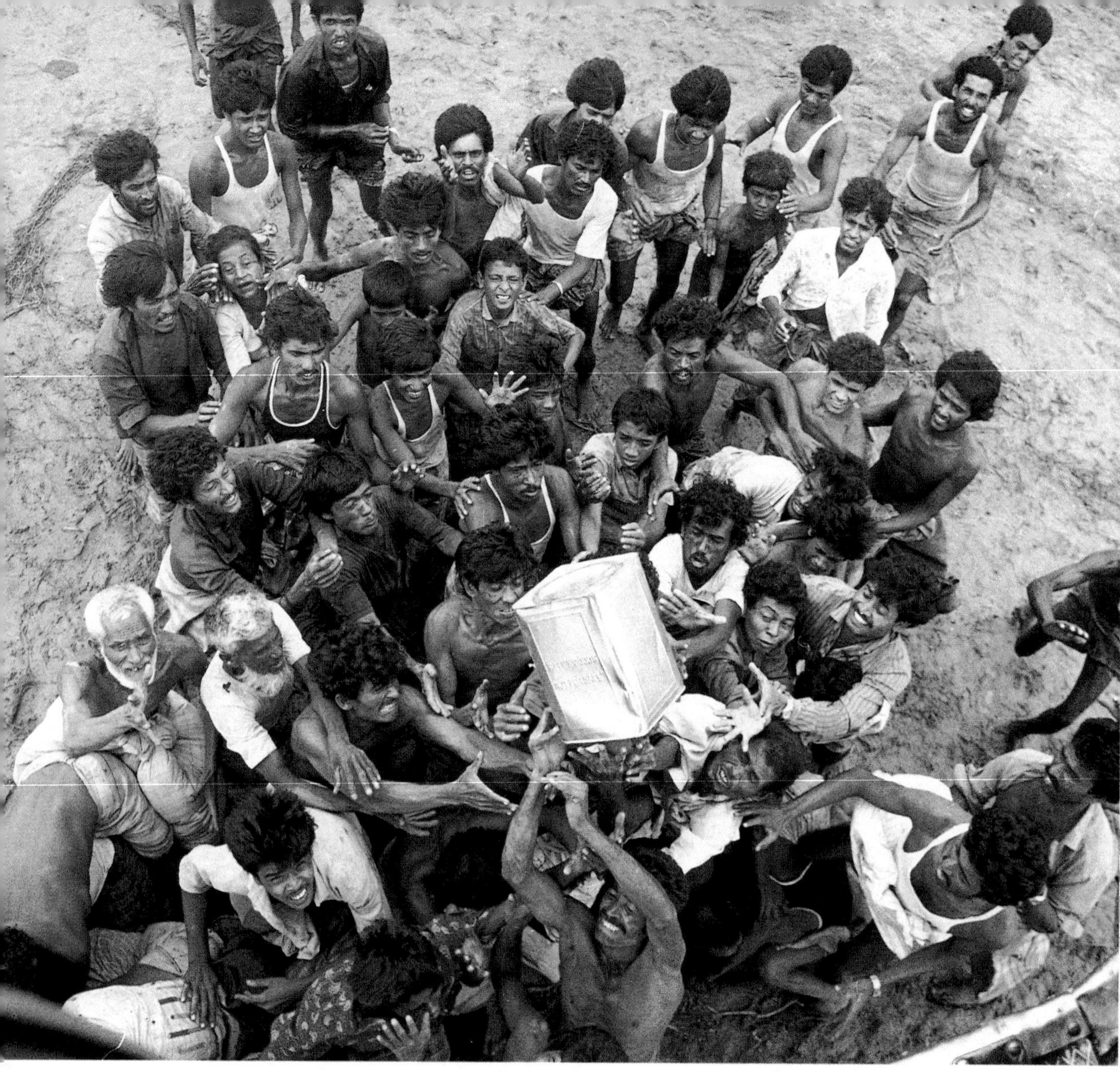

Bangladeshis scramble for packages of food and health supplies following the catastrophic cyclone that ravaged Bangladesh in April.

in elections held on September 11. These seats and others gained when independent members of Parliament joined the BNP, gave the party an absolute parliamentary majority for the first time. A new Cabinet headed by Zia was sworn in on September 19.

Ahmed then resigned as acting president and returned to his previous job as chief justice. On October 9, Parliament elected Abdur Rahman Biswas to be Bangladesh's figurehead president.

Deadly hurricane. A cyclone struck the southeastern coast of Bangladesh on April 29. This was Bangladesh's worst cyclone since 1970, when one killed about 266,000 people. Winds of 145 miles (233 kilometers) per hour drove waves 20 feet (6.1 meters) high over offshore islands and the low coastline.

Officials estimated that 139,000 persons were killed. A storm warning system enabled some people to take refuge in concrete shelters built after the destructive cyclone of 1970. But many people ignored warnings or had no place to hide on isolated islands as the storm swept away their simple huts.

Foreign aid helped bring food and water to people in devastated areas. About 8,000 American sailors returning home from the Persian Gulf War were diverted to help with relief and rebuilding efforts. A United Nations team estimated that rehabilitation and reconstruction would cost $1.78 billion—money the impoverished country did not have. Henry S. Bradsher

See also **Asia** (Facts in brief table). In ***World Book,*** see **Bangladesh.**

Bank. For the 12,500 banks in the United States, 1991 was a messy, difficult year. Bankers suffered a recession, a dwindling insurance fund for depositors, a wave of big mergers, scandals, and the biggest attempt by Congress to rewrite complex banking laws since the 1930's.

Bankers also took much of the blame from President George Bush for the weak economy. He said that bankers were causing a "credit crunch," by lending too little to allow businesses to expand.

FDIC woes. The biggest problem for bankers in 1991 was their shrinking bank industry insurance fund, part of the Federal Deposit Insurance Corporation (FDIC). Banks pay a small percentage of their deposits to the FDIC. If a bank fails, the FDIC dips into the fund and returns the depositors' money, up to $100,000 for each account.

But in recent years, a huge number of bank failures overwhelmed the fund. In the first week of 1991, there was every sign that the failures would continue. One of the biggest banks in the recession-torn Northeast—the Bank of New England Corporation—ran out of money. Bailing out the bank, with $20 billion in assets, would cost the FDIC fund about $3 billion.

For the FDIC, 1991 seemed frighteningly similar to the previous four years. From 1986 to 1990, about 800 banks with $140 billion in assets failed, bleeding the FDIC insurance fund of $23 billion. At the beginning of 1991, the FDIC had $8.5 billion in its coffers. At the end of the year, after roughly 160 more bank failures, it was all but broke. In late October 1991, federal regulators projected that the FDIC would be $9.6 billion short of money needed to insure failed banks in 1992.

In order to replenish the FDIC, federal banking regulators decided that the FDIC needed a $70-billion loan from taxpayers. Regulators feared that raising the money through higher insurance premiums to banks would simply break more banks. Instead, federal regulators decided, the banks would borrow the sum from the U.S. Treasury and pay it back over 15 years with future premiums.

In the final minutes of the U.S. congressional session that ended in November, banks got their $70-billion loan. In return, however, they were to increase their capital holdings, which act as a cushion against losses. That means lower bank profits but more protection for taxpayers.

Congress showed its nervousness about the industry in other ways. The Senate Banking Committee in November rejected President Bush's reappointment of Robert Clarke to his second term as comptroller of the currency, whose office regulates 3,900 national banks. The committee's Democratic majority blamed Clarke for not catching bank insolvencies soon enough and letting bad lending problems grow.

BCCI scandal. Fraud caused other losses. The Bank of Credit and Commerce International (BCCI), a worldwide banking company with offices in 69 countries,

Clark M. Clifford announces his resignation in August as chairman of First American Bankshares, a firm controlled by the scandal-ridden BCCI.

engaged in what some banking experts believe was the largest financial fraud in history. BCCI was founded by Agha Hasan Abedi, a Pakistani banker. His complex financial network served major corporations as well as drug dealers and terrorists. Although few U.S. depositors lost money, BCCI bilked thousands of depositors overseas and made large loans to insiders resulting in losses of more than $15 billion.

On July 5, banking regulators in seven countries closed offices of BCCI, alleging that the bank had engaged in fraud. Other investigations revealed that the bank had been involved in money laundering, drug trafficking, and secret weapons sales and that it used gangsterlike enforcement teams to collect loans. On December 19, BCCI pleaded guilty to U.S. fraud and racketeering charges and agreed to forfeit $550 million—all of its U.S. holdings—to the federal government, including the illegally purchased First American Bankshares Incorporated. Half of the $550 million was put aside to reimburse the bank's depositors.

Profits fall. In the April to June quarter, the profits of U.S. commercial banks slipped 12 per cent to $4.6 billion, compared with the same 1990 quarter. Regulators expected overall profits for 1991 to range from $15 billion to $16 billion, about the same lackluster profit as seen from 1988 to 1990.

Lower interest rates. In 1991, the Federal Reserve Board lowered its interest rate to 3.5 per cent. When business is sluggish, the Federal Reserve Board, which controls the U.S. supply of money, often lowers the interest rate it charges banks. Banks can then lower the interest rates they charge and encourage borrowing. Because many businesses and consumers had piled up record debt in the 1980's, lending scarcely increased, and the economy continued to crawl.

Bank mergers. The year also saw a wave of big bank mergers. Bank controllers believed that their operating costs would be lower if they merged with other banks and trimmed some staff from the combined companies. Some of the oldest and largest banks in the nation linked up. In August, the BankAmerica Corporation acquired its California rival, the Security Pacific Corporation, in a $4-billion transaction that created the nation's second largest bank next to New York City's Citicorp. The Chemical Banking Corporation announced in July that it would acquire its New York City rival, Manufacturers Hanover, making the new bank the third largest in the nation.

Resolution Trust Corporation. In the first two years of its bailout of failed savings and loans (S&L's), begun in 1989, the Resolution Trust Corporation took control of 563 S&L's and sold more than half of their assets. But the effort cost about $220 billion—three times more than the Bush Administration said it would in 1989. In March, Congress provided the RTC with $78 billion, but by the end of 1991, the RTC was out of money and Congress had to give it an additional $25 billion. Paulette Thomas

In ***World Book,*** see **Bank**.

Barr, William P. (1950-), was nominated by President George Bush on Oct. 16, 1991, to become the new United States attorney general. Barr, the deputy attorney general, had been serving as acting attorney general since the resignation in mid-August of Richard L. Thornburgh from the top Department of Justice post. The nomination was quickly approved by the Senate, and Barr was sworn into office on November 26.

Barr was born on May 23, 1950, in New York City. He attended Columbia University in New York, earning a bachelor's degree in 1971 and a master's degree two years later, both in Chinese studies.

From 1973 to 1977, Barr worked as a staff officer with the Central Intelligence Agency in Washington, D.C., meanwhile studying law at night at George Washington University. After receiving his degree in 1977, he joined a law firm in Washington.

In 1982, Barr accepted a position as deputy assistant director with the Domestic Policy Council in the Administration of President Ronald Reagan. He returned to private practice the following year but maintained the close contacts he had made in the White House. In 1989, after Bush's election to the presidency, Barr joined the Justice Department as an assistant attorney general. He was named deputy attorney general in July 1990.

Barr is married to the former Christine Moynihan. They have three children. David L. Dreier

Baseball. In 1991, for the first time in the 1900's, a major league team rose from last place to first in one year and played in the World Series. Two teams achieved that feat—the Minnesota Twins in the American League and the Atlanta Braves in the National League. In a dramatic series, the Twins prevailed.

The major leagues set unofficial attendance records of 56,888,512 for the season and a 27,403 average per game. *The New York Times* reported that opening-day salaries averaged $890,884, the highest ever, with 223 players earning $1 million or more and 32 players earning $3 million or more. In December, the New York Mets signed Bobby Bonilla, a free-agent outfielder, for $29 million over five years, making him the highest-paid player in professional team sports. And Nolan Ryan of the Texas Rangers, at age 44, continued to make pitching history.

American League. Minnesota won 15 consecutive games early in the season and finished 8 games ahead of the Chicago White Sox in the Western Division. In the Eastern Division, the Toronto Blue Jays finished 7 games ahead of the Boston Red Sox and the Detroit Tigers. For the first time, the pennant play-offs were played entirely in domed stadiums. Minnesota won the first game, lost the second, then won three consecutive games at Toronto and won the series, 4 games to 1. Jack Morris of Minnesota gained two pitching victories, and outfielder Kirby Puckett of Minnesota, with a .429 batting average, two home runs,

Final standings in major league baseball

American League

Eastern Division	W.	L.	Pct.	G.B.
Toronto Blue Jays	91	71	.562	
Boston Red Sox	84	78	.519	7
Detroit Tigers	84	78	.519	7
Milwaukee Brewers	83	79	.512	8
New York Yankees	71	91	.438	20
Baltimore Orioles	67	95	.414	24
Cleveland Indians	57	105	.352	34
Western Division				
Minnesota Twins	95	67	.586	
Chicago White Sox	87	75	.537	8
Texas Rangers	85	77	.525	10
Oakland Athletics	84	78	.519	11
Seattle Mariners	83	79	.512	12
Kansas City Royals	82	80	.506	13
California Angels	81	81	.500	14

American League champions—Minnesota Twins (defeated the Blue Jays, 4 games to 1)

World Series champions—Minnesota Twins (4 games to 3)

Offensive leaders

Batting average—Julio Franco, Texas	.341
Runs scored—Paul Molitor, Milwaukee	133
Home runs—José Canseco, Oakland; Cecil Fielder, Detroit (tie)	44
Runs batted in—Cecil Fielder, Detroit	133
Hits—Paul Molitor, Milwaukee	216
Stolen bases—Rickey Henderson, Oakland	58
Slugging percentage—Danny Tartabull, Kansas City	.593

Leading pitchers

Games won—Scott Erickson, Minnesota; Bill Gullickson, Detroit (tie)	20
Win average (15 decisions or more)—Scott Erickson, Minnesota (20-8)	.714
Earned run average (162 or more innings)—Roger Clemens, Boston	2.62
Strikeouts—Roger Clemens, Boston	241
Saves—Bryan Harvey, California	46
Shut-outs—Roger Clemens, Boston	4

Awards*

Most Valuable Player—Cal Ripken, Jr., Baltimore
Cy Young—Roger Clemens, Boston
Rookie of the Year—Chuck Knoblauch, Minnesota
Manager of the Year—Tom Kelly, Minnesota

National League

Eastern Division	W.	L.	Pct.	G.B.
Pittsburgh Pirates	98	64	.605	
St. Louis Cardinals	84	78	.519	14
Philadelphia Phillies	78	84	.481	20
Chicago Cubs	77	83	.481	20
New York Mets	77	84	.478	20½
Montreal Expos	71	90	.441	26½
Western Division				
Atlanta Braves	94	68	.580	
Los Angeles Dodgers	93	69	.574	1
San Diego Padres	84	78	.519	10
San Francisco Giants	75	87	.463	19
Cincinnati Reds	74	88	.457	20
Houston Astros	65	97	.401	29

National League champions—Atlanta Braves (defeated the Pirates, 4 games to 3)

Offensive leaders

Batting average—Terry Pendleton, Atlanta	.319
Runs scored—Brett Butler, Los Angeles	112
Home runs—Howard Johnson, New York	38
Runs batted in—Howard Johnson, New York	117
Hits—Terry Pendleton, Atlanta	187
Stolen bases—Marquis Grissom, Montreal	76
Slugging percentage—Will Clark, San Francisco	.536

Leading pitchers

Games won—Tom Glavine, Atlanta; John Smiley, Pittsburgh (tie)	20
Win average (15 decisions or more)—John Smiley, Pittsburgh (20-8)	.714
Earned run average (162 or more innings)—Dennis Martínez, Montreal	2.39
Strikeouts—David Cone, New York	241
Saves—Lee Smith, St. Louis	47
Shut-outs—Dennis Martínez, Montreal	5

Awards*

Most Valuable Player—Terry Pendleton, Atlanta
Cy Young—Tom Glavine, Atlanta
Rookie of the Year—Jeff Bagwell, Houston
Manager of the Year—Bobby Cox, Atlanta

*Selected by the Baseball Writers Association of America.

and six runs batted in, was voted the play-offs' Most Valuable Player.

National League. Atlanta won the division championship by one game over the Los Angeles Dodgers in the West. The Pittsburgh Pirates won by 14 games over the St. Louis Cardinals in the East. Pittsburgh's 98-64 record led the major leagues. Atlanta, in last place the three previous seasons, trailed the Dodgers by 9½ games at the all-star break on July 7. Atlanta rallied and clinched the division title on the next-to-last day of the season.

Play-offs. In the pennant play-offs, Pittsburgh won the fourth and fifth games in Atlanta and led, 3 games to 2. Then, in Pittsburgh, Atlanta won the sixth game, 1-0, behind the pitching of Steve Avery, and the seventh and decisive game on October 17, 4-0, behind the pitching of John Smoltz. Pittsburgh scored only 12 runs in seven games. Avery pitched 16⅓ shutout innings in two games and was voted the Most Valuable Player for the play-offs.

World Series. During the World Series, played between October 19 and 27, Minnesota won the first two games, 5-2 and 3-2. Atlanta won the next three, 5-4 in 12 innings, 3-2, and 14-5. Minnesota, trailing by 3 games to 2, won the sixth game, 4-3, on Puckett's leadoff home run in the 11th inning. Then Minnesota won the decisive seventh game, 1-0, on Gene Larkin's 10th-inning and bases-loaded fly-ball single over a drawn-in outfield. This exciting series was the first to have five games decided in a team's last at bat and

Oakland Athletics outfielder Rickey Henderson dives into third base on May 1, 1991, for his 939th career stolen base, breaking Lou Brock's record.

the first to have four games decided on the last pitch.

Morris held Atlanta to five hits in 7 innings in the first game, six hits in 6 innings in the fourth, and seven hits in a 10-inning shutout in the final game. The 36-year-old pitcher finished with a 2-0 record, an earned-run average of 1.17, and the Most Valuable Player trophy. Then he became a free agent and signed with Toronto for $10.85 million over two years.

Awards. Shortstop Cal Ripken, Jr., of the Baltimore Orioles, with a .323 batting average, 34 home runs, and 114 runs batted in, was voted the American League's Most Valuable Player. The National League honor went to third baseman Terry Pendleton of Atlanta, who led the league in hits (187) and total bases (303). The Cy Young Awards for pitchers went to Roger Clemens of Boston (18-10, 2.62 earned-run average, and 241 strikeouts) in the American League and Tom Glavine of Atlanta (20-11 and 2.55 earned-run average) in the National League.

The Associated Press all-star team comprised Cecil Fielder of Detroit at first base; Julio Franco of Texas at second; Pendleton of Atlanta at third; Ripken of Baltimore at shortstop; Barry Bonds of Pittsburgh, Ken Griffey, Jr., of the Seattle Mariners, and José Canseco of Oakland in the outfield; Mickey Tettleton of Detroit as catcher; Frank Thomas of the White Sox as the designated hitter; Clemens of Boston as the right-handed pitcher; Glavine of Atlanta as the left-handed pitcher; and Lee Smith of St. Louis as the relief pitcher.

Personalities. The year produced seven no-hit, no-run, games, including the seventh of Ryan's career and a perfect game by Dennis Martinez of the Montreal Expos. After the season, Texas exercised its option on Ryan, the all-time strikeout leader, to pitch in 1992 for $3.9 million. On the season's last day, David Cone of the Mets struck out 19 Philadelphia Phillies, equaling the National League one-game record.

In the American League, Fielder of Detroit was first in runs batted in (133) and tied for first in home runs (44), and first baseman Paul Molitor of the Milwaukee Brewers led in hits (216) and runs (133). Outfielder Howard Johnson of the Mets led the National League in home runs (38) and runs batted in (117).

On May 1, outfielder Rickey Henderson of Oakland broke Lou Brock's record of 938 stolen bases. In June, outfielder Otis Nixon of Atlanta stole six bases in one game, a National League modern record, but in September he was suspended for 60 days by Fay Vincent, the baseball commissioner, for having failed a drug test for the second time in two months. Vincent placed outfielder Lenny Dykstra of Philadelphia on one-year probation for involvement in high-stakes poker games, then Dykstra crashed his car while intoxicated and missed 65 games. The Kansas City Royals in March released outfielder Bo Jackson because of a hip injury. Jackson signed with the White Sox, recovered from the injury, and played in September.

Eight major league managers were fired during the season and five after the season. Former players without previous major league managing experience were named by five teams to manage—Butch Hobson by Boston, Buck Showalter by the New York Yankees, Bill Plummer by Seattle, Phil Garner by Milwaukee, and Gene Lamont by the White Sox.

Expansion. In June, the National League awarded franchises to Miami and Denver, starting in the 1993 season, for $95 million each. The unsuccessful bidders were Buffalo, N.Y.; Washington, D.C.; Tampa, Fla.; and Orlando, Fla. In all previous expansions, the teams in the expanding league split the franchise fees. This time, the American League demanded a share. When the leagues disagreed, Vincent awarded the American League 22 per cent of the $190 million, or $3 million per team. He also directed the American League teams to make an equal number of players available for the expansion draft to stock the new teams.

Hall of Fame. On January 8, the baseball writers elected to baseball's Hall of Fame infielder Rod Carew, a seven-time American League batting champion; pitcher Gaylord Perry, who won 314 games in 22 years; and pitcher Ferguson Jenkins, a 20-game winner in six successive seasons. In February, the Veterans' Committee chose second baseman Tony Lazzeri, who played on six Yankee championship teams in the 1920's, and Bill Veeck, a team owner between 1946 and 1980. Frank Litsky

See also **Henderson, Rickey.** In ***World Book,*** see **Baseball.**

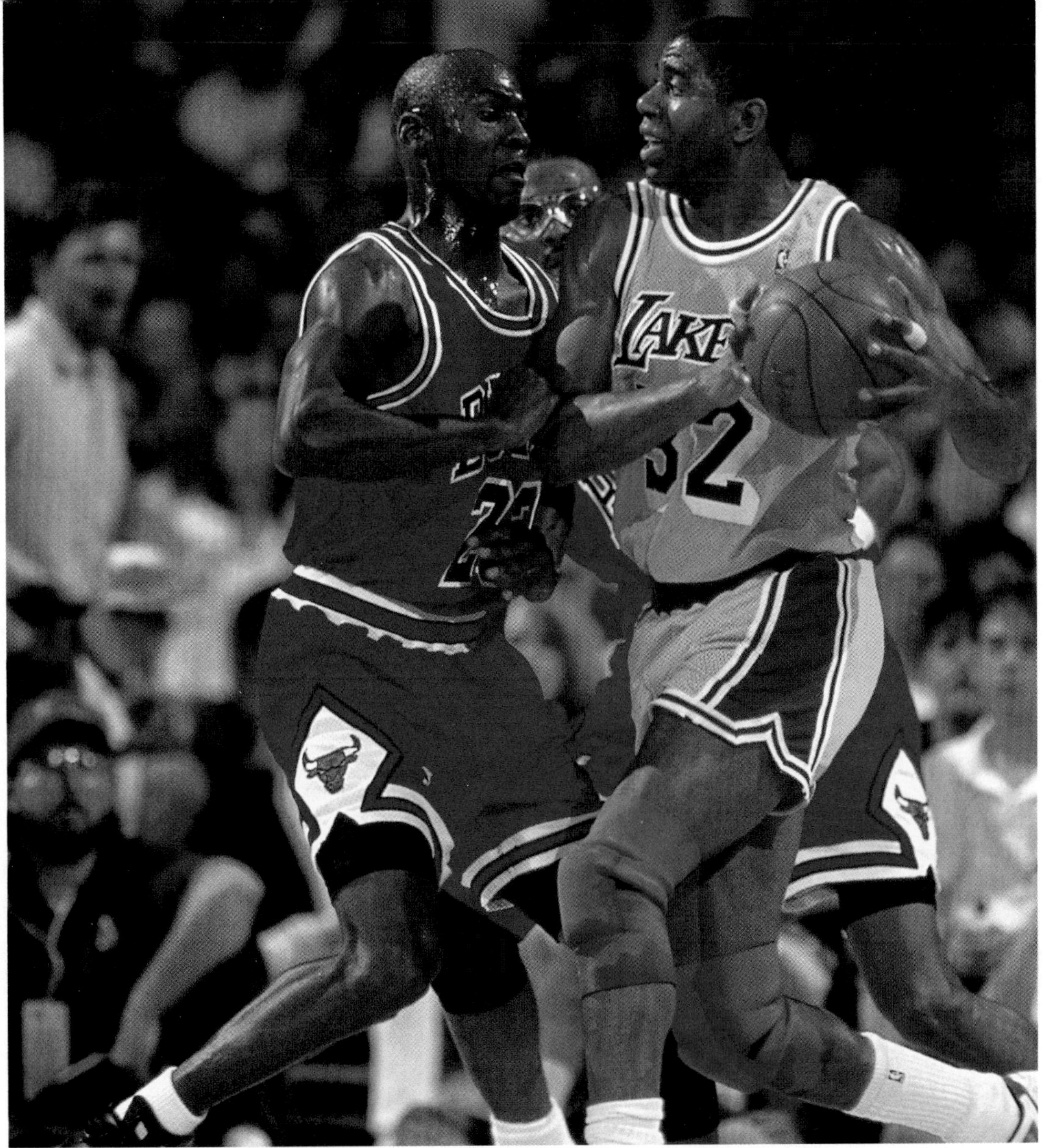

Michael Jordan of the Chicago Bulls guards Earvin (Magic) Johnson, Jr., of the Los Angeles Lakers in the final game of the NBA play-offs in June.

Basketball. The Duke University men, the University of Tennessee women, and the Chicago Bulls won major basketball championships during 1991. In international basketball competition, the usually dominant United States did poorly. The University of Nevada, Las Vegas (UNLV), men's team continued to attract wide attention with its adventures both on and off the court.

College. UNLV won the 1990 National Collegiate Athletic Association's (NCAA) postseason championship tournament and began the 1990-1991 season as the preseason favorite. But the team, the Runnin' Rebels, played under a cloud because the NCAA posed numerous questions about the integrity of UNLV's basketball program.

The NCAA continued its 14-year fight to impose sanctions on Jerry Tarkanian, UNLV's highly successful coach, for recruiting violations. Until 1990, federal courts barred UNLV from suspending Tarkanian, as the NCAA had directed. When that restriction was lifted, the NCAA barred UNLV from the 1991 postseason tournament.

UNLV appealed, saying it wanted to defend its championship. UNLV proposed that it be eligible for the 1991 tournament but be barred the following season from the tournament and television appearances. The NCAA agreed.

After that agreement, UNLV began a seemingly perfect season. It finished the regular season with a 30-0 record, the only major team without a defeat. In

The 1990-1991 college basketball season

College tournament champions

NCAA (Men) Division I: Duke
Division II: North Alabama
Division III: Wisconsin-Platteville

NCAA (Women) Division I: Tennessee
Division II: North Dakota State
Division III: St. Thomas (Minn.)

NAIA (Men): Oklahoma City
(Women): Fort Hays State (Kan.)

NIT (Men): Stanford
(Women): St. Mary's (Calif.)

Junior College (Men) Division I: Aquinas (Tenn.)
Division II: Danville Area (Ill.)
Division III: Herkimer County CC (N.Y.)
(Women): Odessa (Tex.)

Men's college champions

Conference	School
American South	New Orleans—Arkansas State (tie; reg. season) Louisiana Tech (tournament)
Atlantic Coast	Duke (reg. season) North Carolina (tournament)
Atlantic Ten	Rutgers (reg. season) Penn State (tournament)
Big East	Syracuse (reg. season) Seton Hall (tournament)
Big Eight	Kansas—Oklahoma State (tie; reg. season) Missouri (tournament)
Big Sky	Montana*
Big South	Coastal Carolina*
Big Ten	Ohio State—Indiana (tie; reg. season)
Big West	Nevada-Las Vegas (UNLV)*
Colonial A.A.	James Madison (reg. season) Richmond (tournament)
East Coast	Towson State*
Ivy League	Princeton
Metro Athletic	Southern Mississippi (reg. season) Florida State (tournament)
Metro Atlantic	Siena—La Salle (tie; reg. season) St. Peter's (tournament)
Mid-American	Eastern Michigan*
Mid-Continent	Northern Illinois (reg. season) Wisconsin-Green Bay (tournament)
Mid-Eastern	Coppin State (reg. season) Florida A&M (tournament)
Midwestern	Xavier (Ohio)*
Missouri Valley	Creighton*
North Atlantic	Northeastern*
Northeast	St. Francis (Pa.)—Fairleigh Dickinson-Teaneck (tie; reg. season) St. Francis (Pa.) (tournament)
Ohio Valley	Murray State*
Pacific Ten	Arizona
Patriot League	Fordham*
Southeastern	Kentucky (reg. season) Alabama (tournament)
Southern	Furman—East Tennessee State—Tennessee-Chattanooga (tie; reg. season) East Tennessee State (tournament)
Southland	Northeast Louisiana*
Southwest	Arkansas*
Southwestern	Jackson State*
Sun Belt	South Alabama*
Trans America	Texas-San Antonio (reg. season) Georgia State (tournament)
West Coast	Pepperdine*
Western	Utah (reg. season) Brigham Young (tournament)

*Regular season and conference tournament champions.

the wire-service polls, the Runnin' Rebels ranked first in the nation every week.

NCAA tournament. Of the 64 teams in the NCAA men's tournament, the four regional top seeds were UNLV (30-0), North Carolina (25-5), Arkansas (31-3), and Ohio State (25-3). UNLV and North Carolina won regional championships, along with Kansas and, for the fourth consecutive year, Duke.

Duke ended UNLV's season on March 30 in the national semifinals in Indianapolis. UNLV led by five points with little more than two minutes remaining, but Duke rallied to win, 79-77. Duke's win ended UNLV's 45-game winning streak and avenged a humiliating 103-73 loss to UNLV in the 1990 NCAA tournament championship game.

In the other semifinal game, Kansas upset North Carolina, 79-73. In the championship game on April 1 in Indianapolis, Duke defeated Kansas, 72-65. It was Duke's first championship.

On June 7, Tarkanian announced he would retire after the 1991-1992 season. His 23-year record at NCAA Division I colleges was 599-120, the best winning percentage in the history of major college basketball coaching.

The stars. Larry Johnson, UNLV's senior power forward, and Shaquille O'Neal, Louisiana State's sophomore center, won polls as Player of the Year. The Charlotte Hornets made Johnson the first choice in the National Basketball Association (NBA) draft. The Associated Press All-America team comprised Johnson and his teammate Stacey Augmon at forward; O'Neal at center; and Billy Owens of Syracuse and Kenny Anderson of Georgia Tech at guard.

The 1,316 four-year colleges that played men's basketball attracted 33,961,875 spectators, a record for the fourth consecutive year. The 1,199 colleges that played women's basketball drew 4,011,257 spectators, a record for the 10th consecutive year.

Women's collegiate. The best regular-season records among college teams were achieved by Penn State (29-1), Western Kentucky (28-2), Virginia (27-2), Purdue (26-2), and Arkansas (27-3). Virginia was the preseason favorite, and in the NCAA's 48-team postseason tournament, the regional top seeds were Virginia, Tennessee, Georgia, and Penn State. James Madison upset Penn State, 73-71, the first time in the tournament's 10-year history that the nation's top-ranked team had lost in its first tournament game.

In the national semifinals on March 29 in New Orleans, Tennessee defeated Stanford, 68-60, and Virginia defeated Connecticut, 61-55. On March 31, in the championship game, Tennessee beat Virginia, 70-67. Dawn Staley of Virginia was voted the Player of the Year.

Professional. In the NBA's 1990-1991 regular season, each of the 27 teams played 82 games. The Portland Trail Blazers won their first 11 games, and later in the season the Los Angeles Lakers won 16 straight games.

The division winners were Portland (63-19), Chicago (61-21), the Boston Celtics (56-26), and the San Antonio Spurs (55-27). The Lakers (58-24), with the third-best record in the league, still finished five games behind Portland in their division. Sixteen teams qualified for the play-offs.

In the play-offs, the Bulls breezed by the New York Knicks (3 games to 0), the Philadelphia 76ers (4-1), and the aging Detroit Pistons (4-0). Detroit had won the league championship the two previous years. The Lakers eliminated the Houston Rockets (3-0), the Golden State Warriors (4-1), and the Trail Blazers (4-2).

Play-off finals. The Bulls and their star guard, Michael Jordan, reached the championship round for the first time. After the Lakers won the first game of the four-of-seven-game finals, Jordan and guard-forward Scottie Pippen of the Bulls blanketed Earvin (Magic) Johnson, Jr., the Lakers' celebrated playmaker. The Lakers were further hurt by poor shooting and forward James Worthy's sprained left ankle.

The Bulls, coached by Phil Jackson, won the next four games, concluding with a 108-101 victory on June 12 in Inglewood, Calif., that clinched the NBA championship. The Bulls finished the play-offs with a 15-2 record.

Jordan was voted the regular season's Most Valuable Player (Johnson was second) and won the award again in the play-offs. In the play-off finals, Jordan averaged 31.2 points, 11.4 assists, and 6.6 rebounds per game. During the regular season, Jordan averaged 31.5 points per game and won his fifth consecutive NBA scoring title. Johnson became the NBA's all-time assists leader, breaking Oscar Robertson's previous record of 9,887.

The NBA's all-star team consisted of Jordan and Johnson at guard, David Robinson of San Antonio at center, and Karl Malone of the Utah Jazz and Charles Barkley of Philadelphia at forward. Jordan and Robinson were also voted to the all-defensive team.

Magic retires. Johnson shocked the world on November 7 when he said that he was retiring from basketball because he had contracted the HIV virus, which causes AIDS. In his 12 years in the NBA, Johnson was voted the league's Most Valuable Player three times (1987, 1989, 1990) and led the Lakers to the play-off finals nine times, winning five championships. Johnson said he would campaign for AIDS education and awareness. See **AIDS**.

International. Starting in 1982, the United States women's team had won 42 consecutive games in major international basketball competition. The United States men's team, however, its talent drained by the NBA, entered the Pan American Games, held from August 2 to 18 in Havana, Cuba, having lost its five previous major international tournaments.

United States teams had traditionally won Pan American gold medals, but this time neither team won the gold. Brazil beat the U.S. women and won the gold medal, while the men lost to Puerto Rico.

National Basketball Association standings

Eastern Conference

Atlantic Division	W.	L.	Pct.	G.B.
Boston Celtics*	56	26	.683	
Philadelphia 76ers*	44	38	.537	12
New York Knicks*	39	43	.476	17
Washington Bullets	30	52	.366	26
New Jersey Nets	26	56	.317	30
Miami Heat	24	58	.293	32
Central Division				
Chicago Bulls*	61	21	.744	
Detroit Pistons*	50	32	.610	11
Milwaukee Bucks*	48	34	.585	13
Atlanta Hawks*	43	39	.524	18
Indiana Pacers*	41	41	.500	20
Cleveland Cavaliers	33	49	.402	28
Charlotte Hornets	26	56	.317	35

Western Conference

Midwest Division	W.	L.	Pct.	G.B.
San Antonio Spurs*	55	27	.671	
Utah Jazz*	54	28	.659	1
Houston Rockets*	52	30	.634	3
Orlando Magic	31	51	.378	24
Minnesota Timberwolves	29	53	.354	26
Dallas Mavericks	28	54	.341	27
Denver Nuggets	20	62	.244	35
Pacific Division				
Portland Trail Blazers*	63	19	.768	
Los Angeles Lakers*	58	24	.707	5
Phoenix Suns*	55	27	.671	8
Golden State Warriors*	44	38	.537	19
Seattle SuperSonics*	41	41	.500	22
Los Angeles Clippers	31	51	.378	32
Sacramento Kings	25	57	.305	38

*Made play-off.

NBA Champions— Chicago Bulls (defeated Los Angeles Lakers, 4 games to 1)

Individual leaders

Scoring	G.	F.G.	F.T.	Pts.	Avg.
Michael Jordan, Chicago	82	990	571	2,580	31.5
Karl Malone, Utah	82	847	684	2,382	29.0
Bernard King, Washington	64	713	383	1,817	28.4
Charles Barkley, Philadelphia	67	665	475	1,849	27.6
Patrick Ewing, New York	81	845	464	2,154	26.6
Michael Adams, Denver	66	560	465	1,752	26.5
Dominique Wilkins, Atlanta	81	770	476	2,101	25.9
Chris Mullin, Golden State	82	777	513	2,107	25.7

Rebounding	G.	Tot.	Avg.
David Robinson, San Antonio	82	1,063	13.0
Dennis Rodman, Detroit	82	1,026	12.5
Charles Oakley, New York	76	920	12.1
Karl Malone, Utah	82	967	11.8

Both U.S. teams finished with bronze medals.

The United States expected the fortunes of its men's team to rise in the 1992 Olympics, when NBA professionals will be eligible for the first time. USA Basketball, the United States governing body for the sport, chose 10 NBA players for its 12-man squad.

The 10 were Jordan, Johnson, Pippen, and John Stockton of Utah at guard; Robinson and Patrick Ewing of New York at center; and Malone, Barkley, Chris Mullin of Golden State, and Larry Bird of the Boston Celtics at forward. Johnson's participation was questionable due to his illness, however. Remaining spots on the team were to be filled by collegiate players.

Frank Litsky

In ***World Book,*** see **Basketball.**

Bates, Kathy (1948-), won the Academy of Motion Picture Arts and Sciences Award for best actress on March 25, 1991. Bates, who is known for her portrayals of depressed or weird characters, was honored for her performance as a psychotic fan who imprisons an author in *Misery* (1990).

Kathleen Bates was born in Memphis, Tenn., on June 28, 1948. After graduating from Southern Methodist University in Dallas, where she studied theater, she moved to New York City. She made her first appearance off-Broadway in 1976 in *Vanities*. In the late 1970's, she joined the Actors Theatre of Louisville in Kentucky, where she played a starring role in the 1979 premiere of *Crimes of the Heart*.

Bates made her Broadway debut in 1980 in *Goodbye Fidel*. Her portrayal of a suicidal woman in the 1983 premiere of *'night, Mother* earned her an Antoinette Perry (Tony) nomination and an Outer Critics Award for best actress. In 1987, she won a Village Voice Off-Broadway (Obie) Award for her performance as a lonely waitress in *Frankie and Johnny in the Clair de Lune*. In addition, Bates appeared in the 1982 stage and film versions of *Come Back to the 5 & Dime, Jimmy Dean, Jimmy Dean*.

Bates, who made her motion picture debut in 1971 in *Taking Off*, moved to Los Angeles in 1985 to concentrate on film acting. Her film credits include *Arthur 2 on the Rocks* (1988), *Dick Tracy* (1990), and *Men Don't Leave* (1990). Barbara A. Mayes

Belgium in 1991 continued to play a central role in the political and economic integration of the 12-nation European Community (EC or Common Market). At the same time, the nation struggled with internal divisions between Dutch-speaking Flemings in Flanders and French-speaking Walloons in Wallonia.

Regional powers. The coalition government of Prime Minister Wilfried Martens faced parliamentary elections on Nov. 24, 1991. Right wing and environmental parties gained seats, while the governing coalition of Christian Democrats and Socialists lost them. By year's end, a new government had not yet been formed. Meanwhile, Martens headed a caretaker government.

The elections turned on Belgium's sluggish economy and on a controversial government plan to give more power to Belgium's three economic regions: Wallonia; Flanders; and Brussels, the nation's capital. Martens, a Fleming and a Christian Democrat, supported giving each region control over education. In addition, he proposed that each region have its own representatives in Belgium's foreign embassies and that the upper house of Belgium's Parliament become a body that represents the interests of specific regions rather than the policies of different political parties.

Much of the pressure to transfer political and economic power from the central government to the regions came from Flanders, Belgium's richest region. Some Flemings even favored complete separation from the rest of the country. French-speaking Walloons, on the other hand, were less eager for separation, because they feared that poorer, less industrialized Wallonia would fall further behind Flanders.

EC role. Martens in 1991 took himself out of the race to succeed Jacques Delors of France as president of the European Commission, the EC's executive branch, at the end of 1992. Brussels currently serves as the headquarters of the European Commission and the Council of Ministers, the legislative branch of the EC. The city hoped to cement its role as EC "capital" by becoming the permanent home of the European Parliament, the advisory branch of the EC, which currently meets in Strasbourg, France. The French government lobbied hard during 1991 to keep at least some of the Parliament's activities in Strasbourg. Martens felt he could better influence the future location of EC institutions if he remained Belgian prime minister.

Racial violence. Mounting tensions between native Belgians and growing numbers of immigrants, primarily from North Africa, led to rioting in Brussels in May. Clashes between police and rioters damaged shops and houses. The immigrants said they faced discrimination in jobs and housing and wanted to be better integrated into Belgian society. Philip Revzin

See also **Europe** (Facts in brief table). In ***World Book***, see **Belgium**.
Belize. See **Latin America**.
Benin. See **Africa**.

Bevilacqua, Anthony J. Cardinal (1923-), on June 28, 1991, was elevated to cardinal of the Roman Catholic Church by Pope John Paul II in Rome. The pope had appointed Bevilacqua bishop of Pittsburgh, Pa., on Oct. 7, 1983, and archbishop of Philadelphia on Dec. 8, 1987.

Bevilacqua was born on June 17, 1923, in New York City. He was ordained a priest on June 11, 1949, also in New York City, after completing his studies at the Seminary of the Immaculate Conception in Huntington, N.Y.

In 1956, Bevilacqua received a Doctor of Canon Law *summa cum laude* (with highest praise) from the Gregorian University in Rome, and in 1975, he received a Doctor of Laws in civil law from St. John's University in New York City. He has been admitted to the bars of several federal courts, including the Supreme Court of the United States in 1989.

From 1971 to 1983, Bevilacqua was director of the Catholic Migration and Refugee Office for the diocese of Brooklyn, a borough of New York City. From 1976 to 1980, he also taught immigration law at St. John's University. In 1982, Pope John Paul II appointed him to the Pontifical Council for the Pastoral Care of Migrants and Itinerant People.

Bevilacqua was appointed in November 1990 to serve on several committees of the National Conference of Catholic Bishops. Carol L. Hanson

Bhutan. See **Asia**.

Biology. Geneticists continued to make new discoveries in 1991. In July, researchers at Johns Hopkins University in Baltimore; Shriners Hospital for Crippled Children in Portland, Ore.; and the Mt. Sinai School of Medicine in New York City independently reported the discovery of the gene that causes *Marfan's syndrome*. The disorder, which affects 1 in 10,000 people worldwide with varying degrees of severity, is caused by defects in a protein in connective tissue. Characteristics of Marfan's include weakened arteries; a tall, lanky appearance; and enlarged hands and feet.

In May, a team headed by researchers at Emory University School of Medicine in Atlanta, Ga., reported the discovery of the gene that causes *fragile X syndrome*, the most common form of inherited mental retardation. The gene—the first that researchers have linked directly to intelligence—affects an estimated 1 in every 1,250 males and 1 in every 2,000 females. Its effects range from mild learning disabilities to severe retardation. French and Australian scientists in December announced the development of a test that can be used for prenatal diagnosis of the disorder—an accomplishment made possible by the gene's discovery.

Also in May, a multinational team headed by researchers at Northwestern University Medical School in Chicago reported finding the approximate location of the gene that causes *amyotrophic lateral sclerosis* (ALS), also known as Lou Gehrig's disease, for the famous baseball player who died of the illness in 1941. The discovery, scientists said, marks the first major advance toward determining the cause of ALS since it was first diagnosed more than 100 years ago. ALS, which some experts say may affect about 5,000 Americans every year, results in degeneration of the brain and spinal cord cells that control muscle function, leading to progressive muscle wasting and death.

Sexual orientation. A tiny portion of the human brain believed to help regulate sexual activity is smaller on average in homosexual men than in heterosexual men, a researcher at the Salk Institute for Biological Studies in La Jolla, Calif., reported in August 1991. The discovery, which follows similar results obtained in laboratory animals, provides the first specific evidence that biological factors may play a role in homosexuality in human beings.

The study found that a segment of the brain called the *interstitial nuclei of the anterior hypothalamus* (INAH 3) is about the same size in homosexual men as in heterosexual women. This finding, some experts speculate, suggests that the segment may influence sexual orientation in both sexes, though researchers have not yet studied the brains of homosexual women. Some scientists theorize that an individual's exposure to hormones in the womb may help determine the size of their INAH 3.

Bacteria and stomach cancer. Researchers at Stanford University in Stanford, Calif., in May reported finding the first strong evidence that a bacterium may play a role in the development of stomach cancer. Although a small number of cancers have been shown to be caused by viruses or by carcinogenic chemicals produced by molds and fungi, none had previously been linked to a bacterium. Most cancers are thought to be due to radiation or chemicals in the environment and to inherited susceptibility.

The researchers found that virtually all their patients with the most common type of stomach cancer were infected with an unusual bacterium called *Helicobacter pylori* (formerly called *Campylobacter pylori*). The bacterium was first discovered in 1982 by Australian scientists and has since been associated with gastritis—an inflammation of the stomach lining—and ulcers. As many as 30 per cent of the U.S. population is infected with the bacterium and, in some areas of the world, such as Colombia, the infection rate approaches 100 per cent. Researchers do not yet know how the bacterium is transmitted, why it apparently causes ulcers, or why it is linked to cancer only in some people.

Alzheimer's disease. Researchers had several major achievements in 1991 in the struggle to understand the cause of Alzheimer's disease, a degenerative brain disorder that affects as many as 4 million Americans. Its symptoms include memory loss, disorientation, and depression, and it eventually leads to death. The most notable biological sign of Alzheimer's is the presence of plaques (deposits) containing a protein called beta-amyloid in the regions of the brain that control memory and learning. In December, researchers from Mount Sinai Medical Center in New York City, the National Institute on Aging in Baltimore, and Yamanouchi Pharmaceutical Company of Tokyo announced they had produced genetically altered mice that develop such plaques. Experts predict that such an animal model will help scientists study the disease and test treatments.

Two other new studies suggest that the plaques are the disease's cause, rather than by-products of the disease process. In April, researchers at the City of Hope Medical Center in Duarte, Calif., reported that injecting beta-amyloid into the brains of mice caused the animals to forget tasks they had just learned. The study was the first demonstration that the protein could affect learning and memory.

In August, researchers at Harvard Medical School, Children's Hospital, and Massachusetts General Hospital, all in Boston, and the University of Alaska in Anchorage reported that injecting beta-amyloid into the brains of live rats caused the death of cells near the injection site. Scientists had previously demonstrated that beta-amyloid can kill brain cells grown in the laboratory, but had not done so in live animals. The researchers also discovered that injections of another human protein, substance P, helped prevent such cell death. Thomas H. Maugh II

See also **Medicine**, Special Report: **Genetic Medicine: Promise and Perils.** In ***World Book,*** see **Biology; Genetics.**

USA-II
DIET

Boating. The 1991 economic recession that gripped the United States and other nations hurt yachtsmen preparing for the 1992 America's Cup races off San Diego. Both U.S. syndicates contending for the defender's role had difficulty finding sponsors, and one of those syndicates lacked the money to build more than one boat.

Of the potential challengers, Great Britain dropped out, and Sweden and Slovenia-Croatia were having financial problems. The other challenging nations were New Zealand, Australia, Italy, France, Spain, Russia, and Japan. The challengers were scheduled to hold trials from January to April 1992 off San Diego.

At the same time, the two American syndicates were scheduled to meet in separate races. Then one defending and one challenging yacht would meet in May 1991 in a four-of-seven-race series.

New boat. Starting in 1958, the America's Cup races had been sailed in relatively slow 65-foot (20-meter) sloops. The yachts for the 1992 races came from the new International America's Cup Class. These were 75-foot (23-meter) carbon-fiber boats with 110-foot (34-meter) masts. They were faster, longer, lighter, and more powerful than the older yachts. They were also more expensive, costing $3 million rather than $500,000. The new boats met in their first world championship held from May 4 to 11, 1991, off San Diego. Italy defeated New Zealand in the final. Italy planned to have five boats in the America's Cup trials, and New Zealand planned to have four boats.

Among the American competitors were Bill Koch, a wealthy businessman from Palm Beach, Fla., and Dennis Conner, a skipper from San Diego who has won the America's Cup three times. Of the American boats, neither of Koch's two entries reached the semifinals. Conner's boat did, but he withdrew it because he didn't have enough sails to replace the ones that strong winds had ripped. He also feared that the heavy seas would damage his boat.

Other races. The BOC Challenge, a 27,000-mile (43,500-kilometer) single-handed race around the world, started on Sept. 13, 1990, off Newport, R.I., and ended there on April 23, 1991. Christophe Auguin, a 31-year-old Frenchman, won in the 60-foot (18-meter) *Groupe Sceta.* The Offshore Professional Tour conducted eight powerboat races from April to November 1991. Eike Batista, a 34-year-old Brazilian, won the series in the *Spirit of the Amazon*, a 50-foot (15-meter) superboat powered by four 1,100-horsepower turbocharged engines. Frank Litsky

In ***World Book,*** see **Boating; Sailing.**

Bolivia. See **Latin America.**

Books. See **Canadian literature; Literature; Literature for children.**

Botswana. See **Africa.**

Three-time America's Cup winner Dennis Conner sails *Stars & Stripes* in May off San Diego in preparation for the 1992 America's Cup.

Bowling. Despite a six-month suspension for losing his temper too often, 29-year-old Pete Weber became the star of the Professional Bowlers Association's (PBA) 1991 tour. The PBA tour included 34 bowling tournaments, which were held at various locations from January to December.

By April, Weber had won three times. One of his victories came on March 2 in Randallstown, Md., when Del Ballard, Jr., of Richardson, Tex., needing seven pins on his final ball to win, rolled the ball into the gutter. Weber won the United States Open in Indianapolis on April 13 by winning four straight matches. After the Tournament of Champions in April, with two appeals having been turned down, Weber began serving his six-month suspension. The suspension had been levied against Weber by Joe Antenora, the PBA commissioner.

In October, after 20 years as the PBA's chief executive officer, Antenora announced that he would retire at the end of the year. Michael J. Conner was named to succeed Antenora.

David Ozio of Vidor, Tex., won the $250,000 Firestone Tournament of Champions on April 27 in Fairlawn, Ohio. He won four tournaments during the year. Ballard won four, Weber won three, and John Mazza of Mount Clemens, Mich., won three. Ozio was the leading money-winner with $225,485.

Mike Miller of Albuquerque, N. Mex., who had never won on the tour, captured the PBA national championship on March 30 in Toledo, Ohio. In a roll-off, Doug Kent of Canandaigua, N.Y., won the American Bowling Congress Masters tournament on May 4, also in Toledo. On October 13, Walter Ray Williams, Jr., of Stockton, Calif., won the Japan Cup, only a few months after he had won the world horseshoe pitching championship.

Seniors. The seniors tour, expanding each year, totaled 11 tournaments from March to October. John Handegard of Las Vegas, Nev., who also competed on the PBA's regular tour, won three senior tournaments and led in earnings with $52,220. Gene Stus of Allen Park, Mich., won two titles, including the PBA senior championship on August 24 in Battle Creek, Mich., and had the highest average pinfall (221.48).

Earl Anthony of Cornelius, Ore., the sport's first $1-million earner, retired at age 53 after he finished second on June 20 at a tournament in Flint, Mich. He left with a flourish, rolling games of 258, 250, 268, and 236 before losing in the title game.

Women. The Ladies Pro Bowlers Tour (LPBT) held 22 tournaments from February to November. Nikki Gianulias of Vallejo, Calif., won four tournaments. Leanne Barrette of Oklahoma City, Okla., won three tournaments in 1991 and led in earnings with $87,617. Anne Marie Duggan of La Habra, Calif., won the $100,000 U. S. Open on May 30 in Fountain Valley, Calif., by beating Barrette, 196-185, in the final.

Frank Litsky

In ***World Book,*** see **Bowling.**

Boxing. Mike Tyson, who lost the world heavyweight championship in 1990, experienced difficulties outside the ring in 1991. He was indicted on September 9 in Indianapolis on charges of rape, and his November title bout against the current champion, Evander Holyfield, was called off, ostensibly because Tyson had suffered a rib injury.

In 1990, an unprepared Tyson had lost the title to James (Buster) Douglas, and Douglas later lost the title to Holyfield. Douglas faded from the picture, but the 25-year-old Tyson, from Catskill, N.Y., tried to fight his way back. On March 18, 1991, Tyson was taking a beating from Donovan (Razor) Ruddock of Canada in Las Vegas, Nev., until Tyson won on a controversial seventh-round technical knockout. Tyson also won a rematch with Ruddock on June 28 in Las Vegas.

Holyfield defends title. The unbeaten 28-year-old Holyfield, from Atlanta, Ga., defended his title on April 19 in Atlantic City, N.J., against George Foreman, a 42-year-old, 257-pound (117-kilogram) former champion who had spent four years on a comeback. Although Foreman put up a strong fight and was never knocked down, Holyfield won a clear-cut decision.

Just when a Holyfield-Foreman rematch had apparently been made, Holyfield signed instead to defend against Tyson on November 8 in Las Vegas. The fight was never held. First, Tyson was indicted on charges of raping an 18-year-old contestant in the Miss Black America pageant. He pleaded not guilty, and trial was set for January 1992. Then, three weeks before the fight, Tyson withdrew, saying he had injured his rib-cage in training. He wanted the fight postponed until January 1992, but Holyfield refused to risk fighting outdoors in Las Vegas in potentially cold weather.

Instead, Holyfield signed to defend on Nov. 23, 1991, in Atlanta against lightly regarded Francesco Damiani of Italy. When Damiani withdrew a week before the fight, citing an injured ankle, Bert Cooper, an obscure American boxer, replaced him. Cooper proved to be a tough opponent. He punished Holyfield against the ropes in what was ruled a third-round knockdown, but the champion recovered to win with a seventh-round technical knockout.

Other boxers. Holyfield and lightweight Pernell Whitaker were the only world champions universally recognized in 1991 by the World Boxing Council (WBC), the World Boxing Association (WBA), and the International Boxing Federation (IBF). Thomas Hearns of Detroit won his sixth world championship in five weight classes by outpointing the favored Virgil Hill on June 3 in Las Vegas for Hill's WBA light-heavyweight title. Hearns's old rival, Sugar Ray Leonard, took a beating from Terry Norris on February 9 in New York in a fight for Norris' WBC super-welterweight title. Leonard then retired again at age 34.

Frank Litsky

In ***World Book,*** see **Boxing; Foreman, George; Tyson, Mike.**

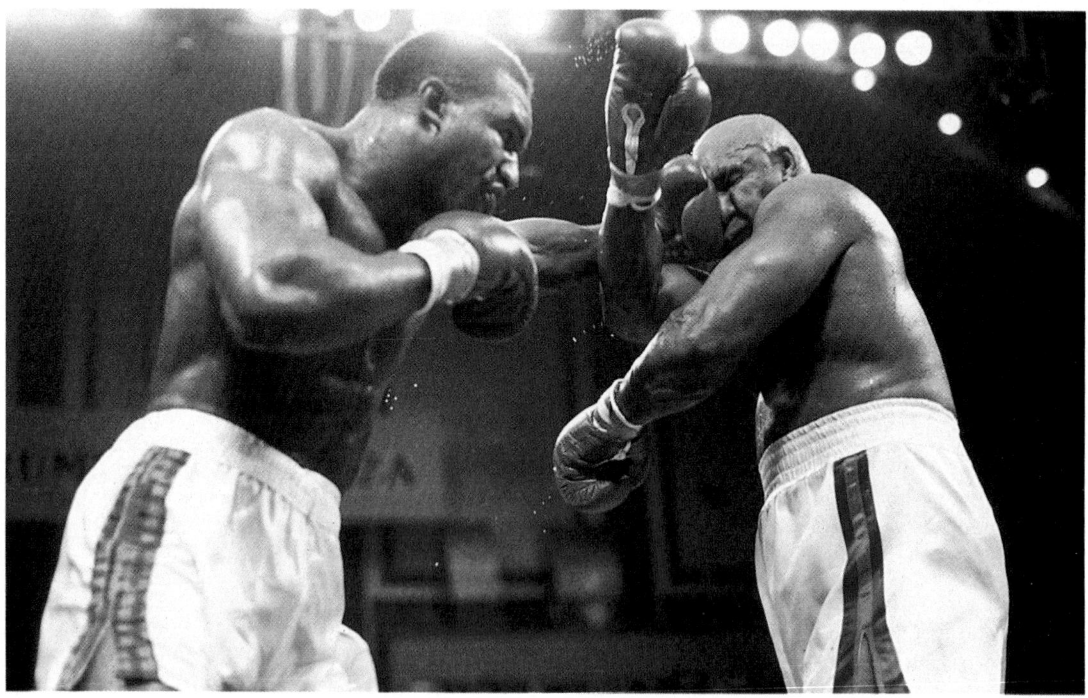

Heavyweight champion Evander Holyfield, left, lands a punch against George Foreman during their title fight on April 19. Holyfield won.

World champion boxers

World Boxing Association

Division	Champion	Country	Date won
Heavyweight	Evander Holyfield	U.S.A.	1990
Junior heavyweight	Robert Daniels	U.S.A.	1989
	Bobby Czyz	U.S.A.	March '91
Light heavyweight	Virgil Hill	U.S.A.	1987
	Thomas Hearns	U.S.A.	June '91
Super middleweight	Christophe Tiozzo	France	1990
	Victor Cordoba	Panama	April '91
Middleweight	Mike McCallum	Jamaica	1989
	vacant		
Junior middleweight	Julian Jackson	U.S. Virgin Islands	1987
	Gilbert Dele	France	March '91
	Vinny Pazienza	U.S.A.	Oct. '91
Welterweight	Aaron Davis	U.S.A.	1990
	Meldrick Taylor	U.S.A.	Jan. '91
Junior welterweight	Loreto Garza	U.S.A.	1990
	Edwin Rosario	Puerto Rico	June '91
Lightweight	Pernell Whitaker	U.S.A.	1989
Junior lightweight	Brian Mitchell	South Africa	1986
	Joey Gamache	U.S.A.	June '91
	Genaro Hernandez	U.S.A.	Nov.'91
Featherweight	Antonio Esparragoza	Venezuela	1987
	Yong-kyun Park	South Korea	April '91
Junior featherweight	Luis Mendoza	Colombia	1990
	Raul Perez	Mexico	Oct. '91
Bantamweight	Luisito Espinosa	Philippines	1989
	Israel Contreras	Venezuela	Oct. '91
Junior bantamweight	Khaosai Galaxy	Thailand	1984
	vacant		Dec. '91
Flyweight	Yukito Tamakuma	Japan	1990
	Elvis Alvarez	Colombia	March '91
	Yong-kang Kim	South Korea	June '91
Junior flyweight	Myung-woo Yuh	South Korea	1985
Minimumweight	Bong-jun Kim	South Korea	1989
	Hi-yong Choi	South Korea	Feb. '91

World Boxing Council

Division	Champion	Country	Date won
Heavyweight	Evander Holyfield	U.S.A.	1990
Cruiserweight	Massimiliano Duran	Italy	1990
	Anaclet Wamba	Congo	July '91
Light heavyweight	Dennis Andries	Great Britain	1990
	Jeff Harding	Australia	Sept. '91
Super middleweight	Mauro Galvano	Italy	1990
Middleweight	Julian Jackson	U.S. Virgin Islands	1990
Super welterweight	Terry Norris	U.S.A.	1990
Welterweight	Maurice Blocker	U.S.A.	1990
	Simon Brown	U.S.A.	March '91
	James McGirt	U.S.A.	Nov. '91
Super lightweight	Julio César Chávez	Mexico	1989
Lightweight	Pernell Whitaker	U.S.A.	1989
Super featherweight	Azumah Nelson	Ghana	1988
Featherweight	Marcos Villasana	Mexico	1990
	Paul Hodkinson	Great Britain	Nov. '91
Super bantamweight	Pedro Decima	Argentina	1990
	Kiyoshi Hatanaka	Japan	Feb. '91
	Daniel Zaragoza	Mexico	June '91
Bantamweight	Raul Perez	Mexico	1988
	Greg Richardson	U.S.A.	March '91
	Joichiro Tatsuyoshi	Japan	Sept. '91
Super flyweight	Sung-kil Moon	South Korea	1990
Flyweight	Sot Chitalada	Thailand	1989
	Muangshai Kittikasem	Thailand	Feb. '91
Light flyweight	Rolando Pascua	Philippines	1990
	Melchor Cob Castro	Mexico	April '91
	Humberto Gonzalez	Mexico	June '91
Strawweight	Ricardo Lopez	Mexico	1990

Brazil. When the unorthodox shock program she had put into place in 1990 failed to revitalize Brazil's economy, 37-year-old Zelia Cardoso de Mello, the nation's first female economy minister, resigned on May 8, 1991. Brazilian President Fernando Collor de Mello replaced her with Marcilio Marques Moreira, 59, Brazil's ambassador to the United States.

The cabinet shift helped smooth the way for the Brazilian president's visit from June 17 to 20 to the United States. Many U.S. government officials saw Cardoso de Mello's economic policies as too radical. On June 18, President Collor de Mello and President George Bush agreed to "close the chapter on past trade disputes and past debt problems." These included protectionist trade measures adopted by both nations and Brazil's ongoing dispute with the International Monetary Fund, an agency of the United Nations (UN), over ways to restore Brazil's credit rating.

Constitutional amendment. To curb spending and raise revenue, Brazil's new economy minister announced a proposal on August 22 to amend the 1988 Brazilian Constitution. Moreira called for an end to government employees' right to a job for life and to the monopoly enjoyed by Brazil's state-run telephone company. He also appealed for broad new powers to curb tax evasion and an end to the constitutional provision that the federal government must spend at least 18 per cent of its revenues on education.

Few political analysts saw much chance for the proposed amendment to win passage in the Brazilian Congress, however. Passage would require a three-fifths majority of both houses of the Brazilian Congress, where President Collor de Mello's party controls only 3 per cent of the votes.

To add to the president's woes, violent demonstrations broke out in September and October outside the Rio de Janeiro Stock Exchange over the Brazilian government's plan to sell the state-run Usiminas steel company to private investors. The Brazilian government had announced plans to raise $18 billion by selling at least 27 state-run companies.

Rain forest protection. To improve upon Brazil's image abroad and to respond to increased domestic environmental concerns, Collor de Mello on June 25 unveiled an ambitious new program to help protect the Amazon rain forest. The program would abolish tax subsidies that have encouraged companies to cut down areas of rain forest for farming or ranching. Responding to criticism from some U.S. senators when he visited the United States in June, Collor de Mello fired the head of Brazil's Indian protection agency for failing to make headway on a constitutionally mandated survey designed to protect 237 areas identified as Indian homelands.

In another policy shift, the Brazilian president announced that Brazil would entertain proposals for "nature for debt swaps." Such swaps allow groups interested in protecting the environment to help pay off Brazil's foreign debt at a reduced rate in exchange for a pledge by the Brazilian government to set aside protected land in the rain forest.

Development in the Amazon Basin. There were both positive and negative reports in 1991 about Amazon Basin development. Studies indicated the failure of a development program begun in the early 1980's in the state of Rondônia that was financed by the World Bank, a UN agency. Under the program, new roads were built to encourage settlement in the area. More than 100,000 families from overcrowded areas of the nation were provided free land. Development severely disrupted the state's indigenous Indian population, which fell from 35,000 in 1965 to about 6,000 in 1991. The new settlers also found that they were unable to raise enough corn and rice to feed their families because of the poor quality of the soil.

By contrast, investments in the neighboring state of Mato Grosso fueled an agricultural revolution that has tripled soybean and wheat production. The agricultural success helped Cuiabá, the capital city of Mato Grosso, grow from about 50,000 people in 1961 to more than 500,000 people in 1991. To help contine that progress, Olacyr de Moraes, one of the world's largest soybean producers, planned to build a $2.5-billion rail line linking Cuiabá with the port of Santos.

Nathan A. Haverstock

See also **Latin America** (Facts in brief table). In ***World Book,*** see **Brazil.**

Rita Johnston became Canada's first woman premier in April but relinquished the post after her party lost in British Columbia's October election.

British Columbia. A political dynasty ended in 1991 when the Social Credit Party, in office for 36 of the last 39 years, was ousted in a provincial election. The party sank amidst scandal and resignations. Thirteen Cabinet ministers had resigned due to allegations of improper conduct, and Premier William Vander Zalm was compelled to step down from office on April 2 after conflict-of-interest charges were leveled against him.

The provincial legislature chose Rita Johnston, a minister and deputy premier under Vander Zalm, to succeed him. Johnston became the first woman premier in Canadian history. But her tenure and the Social Credit control of the legislature ended on October 17 with a general election. Johnston lost her position, and the party lost all but seven legislative seats.

The New Democratic Party (NDP), advocating a mixture of public and private enterprise in the economy, swept to power by winning 51 seats in an expanded 75-seat legislature. Michael Harcourt, the party's leader since 1987, was a moderate and a consensus-builder. He espoused progressive views on social policy but was conservative in fiscal matters. The Liberal Party, shut out of British Columbia politics since the late 1970's, won 17 seats to become the NDP's official opposition. David M. L. Farr

See **Canada,** Special Report: **Canada and Quebec at a Crossroads.** See also **Johnston, Rita.** In ***World Book,*** see **British Columbia.**

Brown, Edmund Gerald, Jr. (1938-), declared his intention to seek the 1992 Democratic nomination for the presidency on Oct. 21, 1991. This was Brown's third campaign for the Democratic nomination, following unsuccessful bids in 1976 and 1980.

Brown has frequently presented himself as a political outsider. In campaign speeches during 1991, he claimed to represent nationwide disenchantment with recent Democratic and Republican politicians. He deplored political corruption and the necessity of raising huge sums of money in order to run for political office. Today's politicians, Brown insisted, are more concerned with being reelected than with solving national problems. He announced that contributions to his own campaign would be limited to $100 per donor.

Brown was born April 7, 1938. His father, Edmund G. (Pat) Brown, was governor of California from 1959 to 1967. Brown received his B.A. from the University of California at Berkeley in 1961 and a law degree from Yale University in New Haven, Conn., in 1964. In 1970, he was elected California's secretary of state, and he became governor of California in 1974. Brown was reelected governor in 1978, then ran for the U.S. Senate in 1982 but was defeated. From 1983 to 1989, he pursued private practice as a lawyer and traveled throughout the world. Between 1989 and 1991, he was chairman of the California Democratic Party.

Brown has never married. Douglas Clayton

Brunei. See **Asia.**

Buchanan, Patrick J. (1938-), announced his candidacy for the Republican presidential nomination on Dec. 12, 1991, bringing a conservative challenge to the renomination of President George Bush.

Buchanan has held no elective office. He has held White House staff positions but is known mainly as a conservative journalist. He entered the race calling himself a "nationalist" who believes in the "old republic" and traditional "Judeo-Christian values."

Patrick Joseph Buchanan was born on Nov. 12, 1938, in Washington, D.C. He received an undergraduate degree in English from Georgetown University in Washington, D.C., and a master's degree in journalism in 1962 from Columbia University in New York City. From 1962 to 1966, he worked for the St. Louis (Mo.) *Globe-Democrat* as an editorial writer and assistant editorial editor.

From 1969 to 1973, Buchanan served as a special assistant and consultant to former President Richard M. Nixon. He also worked as the White House director of communications under former President Ronald Reagan from 1985 to 1987. Buchanan has had a syndicated newspaper column with major newspaper companies for about 15 years. He also has been a co-host, moderator, and panelist on several television talk shows with political themes, including "The McLaughlin Group."

Buchanan has written three books on conservatism. He is married and has no children. Lori Fagan

Building and construction. Gripped by a continuing recession, the United States construction industry experienced a brief burst of optimism in February 1991. At that time, it appeared that the reconstruction of Kuwait, devastated by its invasion and occupation by Iraqi forces, could generate as much as $100-billion in construction work. The U.S. Army Corps of Engineers, the U.S. Department of Commerce, and other agencies were flooded with telephone calls from thousands of jobseekers at all levels of the building industry, from top construction managers to design firms to craftworkers.

Rebuilding Kuwait. This optimism was short-lived, however. By mid-March, it became clear that the damage toll had been overstated. Firms working for the Corps of Engineers, under a $1.2-billion contract with the Kuwaiti government, by then had moved into the country to restore emergency services. They found that the Kuwaiti oil fields were on fire, power transmission lines were down, and highways were battered. Most buildings, however, suffered more from vandalism than from structural damage. In July, U.S. government officials estimated that the five-year reconstruction of Kuwait would cost closer to $15 billion than $100 billion.

That estimate included restarting Kuwait's crippled power plants; restoring the ability of the Al Zour desalination plant to supply fresh water; and repairing and refurbishing damaged public buildings, including the headquarters of most government ministries. The burning oil fields affected all activities. Contractors issued surgical masks to protect work crews from the smoke. The smoke also hampered vision, making the repair of power lines difficult.

Gloomy U.S. outlook. The vast majority of jobseekers in the United States faced a gloomy outlook for work. At the end of August, awards for new building contracts had fallen 13 per cent over the same January-through-August period in 1990, according to economists at McGraw-Hill Incorporated, a leading source of construction industry data.

Of the $96 billion in new contracts awarded during the first eight months of 1991, $33.6 billion went for heavy construction, such as dams, waterways, sewerage, and highways. This amount fell 6 per cent below the amount awarded during the same eight-month period in 1990. Another $55.5 billion went to nonresidential construction in 1991, down 11 per cent from 1990. Multiunit housing, which includes hotels and motels as well as apartment buildings, dropped 39 per cent during the first eight months of 1991 as compared with the same eight-month period in 1990. Only $8.9 billion in new contracts was awarded.

The few bright spots were overwhelmed by poor showings in other categories. For example, contracts for new school buildings rose 10 per cent over the first eight months of 1990, but contracts for commercial buildings dropped 28 per cent.

Economists saw a ray of hope when new building contract awards averaged 2 per cent higher in the second quarter of 1991 than in the first quarter. This slight gain followed six consecutive quarters of decline. Economists also hoped that a modest upturn in housing starts at midyear—to a seasonally adjusted annual rate of 869,000 units—would jump-start the economy, as had happened in previous recessions. But by August, the number of new building permits had fallen almost 5 per cent from June, signaling fewer starts for the rest of the year.

Some experts blamed the persistence of the U.S. recession on a crisis in the banking industry. The banks showed reluctance to lend money, fearing that because of the recession the loans might not be repaid.

The recession pulled down demand in some areas to such low levels that suppliers of construction products and services were forced to lower prices. In April, a number of state and local officials in charge of public works reported rushing ahead with construction projects to take full advantage of the fiercely competitive environment. The Department of Transportation in Washington state reported that construction estimates bid for new projects fell below its own estimates by as much as 17 per cent.

Expo '92. Building activity reached fever pitch in Seville, Spain, in 1991, as teams from 110 countries raced to complete buildings and other structures for Expo '92 by the December 1991 deadline. Spain's world's fair, which runs from April to October 1992, commemorates the 500th anniversary of Christopher Columbus' voyage to the New World, which started from Spain. At the peak of construction activity in the summer of 1991, some 8,000 workers and 300 cranes worked on the exposition site on the island of La Cartuja, across from the main part of Seville.

Even though most of the pavilions will be dismantled after the six-month fair, they had to meet the same safety rules and structural criteria as buildings designed to last 50 years. Among the most dramatic buildings is the Pavilion of the Future, extending 920 feet (280 meters). The structure combines a curving steel roof, which rises like a wave from the ground, with a facade featuring pink granite arches.

Expo planners have made use of one unusual technique to cool visitors during Spain's blistering summer heat. The Avenue of Europe will have 12 fabric funnels, each rising 100 feet (30 meters). Spiral tubes inside the funnels will circulate water. As the water evaporates at the top of the funnels, it cools the air, which will then cool visitors below.

The most memorable structures of the exposition could well be two of the new bridges built to carry Expo visitors to La Cartuja. The Barqueta Bridge uses a single arch from which suspended cables hold a 551-foot (168-meter) roadway. The Alamillo Bridge is supported by a single tall tower made of concrete and steel that leans backward at an angle of 58 degrees to the ground. By leaning backward, the tower counters the pull of the cables extending from it. The cables suspend the roadway. See **Spain,** Special Report: **Spain Takes Center Stage in 1992.**

Linking Denmark. Danes worked to join by road and rail the island of Sjælland, where the Danish capital of Copenhagen is situated, with the peninsula of Jutland, which extends northward from the European continent. The $3-billion project, called the Great Belt, includes undersea tunnels and dramatic bridges, one of them suspended over a record 5,328-foot (1,624-meter) span. During April and early May, all four tunnel boring machines encountered mechanical problems after driving just 2,600 feet (790 meters) of their projected 10-mile (16-kilometer) distance. On top of earlier holdups, the stoppages could delay the completion of the project by well over a year, from mid-1993 to late 1994.

Chunnel progress. Work on the 31-mile (50-kilometer) English Channel Tunnel, known as the Chunnel, reached milestones in May and June 1991 when French and English crews digging two passages for trains met. The tunnel will connect Folkestone, England, with Calais, France, upon its completion in 1993. The Chunnel runs underseas for 23.5 miles (37.8 kilometers), making it the longest underwater tunnel in the world. Janice Lyn Tuchman

See also **Transit,** Special Report: **Light at the End of the Chunnel.** In ***World Book,*** see **Building construction.**

A single arch supports the Barqueta Bridge, which links the main part of Seville, Spain, with the nearby island of La Cartuja, site of Expo '92.

Bulgaria. In elections held Oct. 13, 1991, the Bulgarian Socialist (formerly Communist) Party lost its parliamentary majority to the opposition Union of Democratic Forces (UDF). But the Socialists drew many more votes than expected, denying the UDF a hoped-for majority with which to form a new government. In a large turnout, the UDF captured about 35 per cent of the vote to the Socialists' 33 per cent, giving the UDF 110 seats and the Socialists 106 seats in the new 240-member parliament.

Uncertainty ahead. The ethnic Turkish party, Movement for Rights and Freedom (MRF), won 24 seats and emerged as a potentially decisive force in the parliamentary stalemate. But UDF leader Filip Dimitrov, nominated by Bulgaria's President Zhelyu Zhelev to serve as prime minister, formed a minority government made up only of UDF members.

During the 1980's, ethnic tensions had mounted when Bulgaria's then-ruling Communist Party forced the country's ethnic Turks to adopt Slavic names and harshly discouraged them from practicing their religion, Islam. More than 300,000 ethnic Turks had fled to Turkey. Many of them returned after Communist hard-liners were overthrown in 1989. But a constitution passed by the Socialist-UDF coalition in July 1991 still failed to recognize Turks as a legal and distinct minority with full cultural and religious rights.

The new government started out with the unwritten support of the MRF members of parliament, and it promised to introduce legislation permitting extracurricular Turkish language classes in schools. But at best, Bulgaria appeared to face another period of uncertain government, with the Socialists forming a disruptive opposition and with demands escalating for new elections in early 1992.

Economic stagnation. Bulgaria took significant steps toward restructuring its economy in 1991. In February, parliament adopted the first legislation to privatize agriculture. The law would restore state-owned farmland to families who had formerly owned it or permit the sale of land to new owners. Another law eased the way for foreign investment and created favorable credit conditions for small businesses.

Overall, however, the economic stagnation of 1990 continued in 1991, with industrial output dropping 22.6 per cent in the first half of the year. There was no indication of an upturn in the second half. A serious decline in agricultural productivity resulted in chronic food shortages. Bulgaria also experienced trade losses as a result of the 1991 collapse of Comecon, the former East bloc trade alliance. Until 1991, Bulgaria had channeled 80 per cent of its foreign trade through Comecon. By midyear, unemployment rose to more than 200,000 people, and the government had to introduce new measures to protect the unemployed.

Eric Bourne

See also **Europe** (Facts in brief table). In ***World Book,*** see **Bulgaria.**

Burkina Faso. See **Africa.**

Burma. Aung San Suu Kyi, the leader of the opposition movement to the ruling military junta in Burma (also called Myanmar), was awarded the Nobel Peace Prize on Oct. 14, 1991. The junta, called the State Law and Order Restoration Council (SLORC), denounced the award as interference in its internal affairs. It refused to let Suu Kyi, who has been under house arrest since July 1989, receive official notification of the prize. University students demonstrated against the junta on December 10, when Suu Kyi's son accepted the Nobel Prize on her behalf in Norway. The junta then closed all universities. See **Nobel Prizes.**

Elections annulled. Junta member Lieutenant General Aung Ye Kyaw announced on September 8 that 1990 election results had been officially annulled. In the elections, Suu Kyi's party, the National League of Democracy (NLD), had won 82 per cent of the popular vote. The SLORC, however, refused to hand over power. In 1991, a majority of the NLD's election victors were in prison, hiding, or exile. Several were reported to have died in prison. Some NLD members formed a "parallel government" that camped along the border with Thailand.

Foreign diplomats reported that the junta had fired or disciplined some 15,000 civil servants in an effort to avoid any challenge to military rule. The junta reacted angrily to foreign criticisms of its human rights record, which the United Nations (UN) Human Rights Commission condemned in a report made public in February. The UN commission reported "serious and persistent allegations of torture and mistreatment" of prisoners.

Foreign support. Many nations ostracized Burma, but Southeast Asian countries refused to join international condemnation. Logging companies with ties to the army of neighboring Thailand saved Burma from bankruptcy by making deals to log Burma's forests on the Thai border. The Thai army also reportedly participated in military actions taken by the SLORC in 1991 to suppress insurgent guerrilla factions among the Karen, Mon, and Kachin ethnic minorities along the border with Thailand.

Burma used its logging income to order more than $1 billion worth of weapons, mostly from China. Meanwhile, the civilian economy was broke. Burma had been a wealthy nation before the army seized power in 1962. But in 1991, it ranked as one of the world's poorest. Speeches by government officials attacked free trade for profit, thus discouraging the foreign investment that the regime claimed to welcome.

Border refugees. The army forced thousands of Burmese Muslims living near the border with Bangladesh to cross over into Bangladesh. Burma's predominantly Buddhist army justified this action by calling the Muslims illegal immigrants. Henry S. Bradsher

See also **Asia** (Facts in brief table). In ***World Book,*** see **Burma.**

Burundi. See **Africa.**

Bus. See **Transit.**

As his wife, Barbara, looks on, President Bush in August talks by phone with Soviet President Mikhail S. Gorbachev after a failed coup in the Soviet Union.

Bush, George Herbert Walker (1924-   ), 41st President of the United States, concentrated more on foreign affairs than domestic issues in 1991—but at his political peril. Near year's end, Bush showed increasing concern about the nation's slumping economy and its potential impact on his campaign for reelection in 1992. He postponed until December a trip to Australia and the Far East after Democrats claimed that he was neglecting domestic problems. He recast the purpose of the trip as a mission to gain economic advantage and new jobs for Americans.

War with Iraq. As 1991 began, Bush was determined to force Iraq to evacuate Kuwait, which it had invaded in August 1990. With the support of United Nations (UN) resolutions, approved in late 1990, ordering Iraq to leave Kuwait, Bush left little doubt that he was ready to order military action if necessary.

The war began on January 17, when hundreds of warplanes struck targets in Iraq and its capital, Baghdad, and in Kuwait. On February 27, Bush proclaimed a cease-fire as the war ended in an Iraqi rout. The stunning allied victory boosted Bush's popularity to around 90 per cent in some national polls. Because most Democrats in Congress had voted against a "use of force" authorization on the eve of the fighting, there was talk among Republicans of Bush's winning reelection in 1992 almost by default.

But the postwar period produced new Mideast problems—Iraqi President Saddam Hussein, still in power, crushed revolts by Shiite Muslims in southern

Iraq and by Kurds in the north. Hussein's crackdown on the Kurds sent about 1.5 million refugees fleeing into Turkey and Iran, creating yet another problem for U.S. foreign policy. After much hesitancy, Bush in April sent U.S. troops into northern Iraq briefly to offer protection to Kurds returning to their homes. By late November, with the U.S. economy sagging, Bush's popularity had plummeted to 51 per cent.

Mideast peace conference. Capitalizing on the heightened prestige that the United States had garnered from the war, Bush sent his secretary of state, James A. Baker III, on eight negotiating trips to the troubled Mideast in search of a broad peace. The result was the start of formal peace talks in Madrid, Spain, on October 30, with Bush and Mikhail S. Gorbachev, then president of the Soviet Union, presiding. The meeting brought together Israel, Syria, Lebanon, Jordan, Egypt, and Palestinian representatives.

American-Israeli relations were strained as the result of actions taken during the year by Bush and members of his Administration. In pressuring Israel to attend the Madrid peace conference, Baker on May 22 termed the building of Israeli settlements in occupied Palestinian territory the biggest roadblock he faced in promoting peace. And in September, Bush insisted that action on a U.S. guarantee of $10 billion in loans to Israel be delayed until 1992.

Reducing the nuclear threat. Bush visited the Soviet Union from July 30 to August 1, and on July 31 in Moscow he and Gorbachev signed a Strategic Arms Reduction Treaty. Just weeks later, the abrupt collapse of the Communist Party in the Soviet Union inspired Bush to make a sweeping unilateral move to curb nuclear arms. On September 27, he ordered that all U.S. ground-based tactical nuclear weapons around the world be placed in storage and that nuclear-tipped cruise missiles be removed from U.S. ships and submarines. The President also took the U.S. Air Force's bomber fleet off constant alert and commanded that their nuclear weapons be placed in storage.

One of Bush's key motives in taking these actions was concern over what might happen with the many nuclear weapons in the disintegrating Soviet Union. By taking U.S. forces off alert and stowing nuclear missiles away, he hoped to spur Soviet officials into taking similar steps. On October 5, Gorbachev responded with a promise to destroy or store all Soviet short-range nuclear weapons based on land or sea. Gorbachev said he would go beyond the treaty that he and Bush signed on July 31 and cut an additional 1,000 strategic weapons.

Anticipating Soviet events. During his summer trip to the Soviet Union, Bush met privately with Boris Yeltsin, president of the Russian republic. He also traveled to Kiev, capital of Ukraine, which on August 24 declared its independence from the Soviet Union. Bush initially tried to discourage the breakup of the Soviet Union, but he soon came to recognize that the union's demise was inevitable.

To deal directly with rapid changes in the Soviet Union, Bush in June had nominated lawyer Robert S. Strauss, a pillar of the Democratic Party establishment, as ambassador to Moscow. Strauss received Senate confirmation on July 16 and went to Moscow in August. On August 29, Bush told a news conference that changes in the Soviet Union might present "an opportunity for a vastly restructured national security posture" and, perhaps, reduced defense spending.

At an economic summit meeting in London from July 15 to 17, 1991, Bush and other leaders of the major industrialized countries discussed the question of what might be done to help the Soviet Union. At a session with Gorbachev on July 17, they agreed to extend technical aid rather than financial assistance to the Soviets.

On September 2, after a brief delay requested by Gorbachev, Bush announced U.S. recognition of the breakaway Baltic states of Lithuania, Latvia, and Estonia as independent nations. On December 24, Bush announced U.S. recognition of the Russian republic as the successor state to the Soviet Union. The next day Gorbachev resigned, and the Commonwealth of Independent States, comprising 11 former Soviet republics, was established.

The ailing U.S. economy. Bush had hoped the U.S. economy would shake itself free of recession without help from the federal government. By late 1991, however, the economic news was nothing but bad. Taking note of growing public anger and pessimism, Bush on October 4 acknowledged that "all is not well" with the economy. He also began conferring with his Cabinet on what might be done about the situation. In November, Bush signed legislation extending unemployment benefits for jobless Americans, but at year-end he had yet to offer any comprehensive plan for stimulating the sluggish economy.

On December 30, Bush embarked on the trip to Australia and the Far East, a journey that was originally planned for November. The President intended to spend Jan. 7 to 10, 1992, in Japan, where he hoped to talk government officials into making Japanese markets more accessible to American products.

Sununu resigns. On April 21, 1991, *The Washington Post* reported that over a two-year period, Bush's chief of staff, John H. Sununu, had flown military jets on more than 60 trips, many described as personal or political in nature. Bush said he retained "full confidence" in Sununu, but he ordered White House travel policies tightened. Then Sununu took a government limousine to New York on personal business, forcing the President to place even stiffer curbs on staff travel. Some Administration officials also complained that Sununu was arrogant and difficult to deal with, and there was a growing feeling in the White House that the chief of staff had become a political liability.

On December 3, Sununu resigned. Two days later, Bush named Secretary of Transportation Samuel K. Skinner as his new chief of staff.

Bush strolls with former Presidents Reagan, Carter, Ford, and Nixon—the first gathering of the five—at the Reagan Library dedication in November.

Health matters. Bush had a medical checkup on March 27 and was found to be in excellent health. But on May 4, the 66-year-old President suffered an irregular heartbeat while jogging at the presidential retreat at Camp David, Md. He was taken by helicopter to the Naval Medical Center in Bethesda, Md. Bush was out of the hospital in two days but experienced recurrences of heart irregularity. On May 9, his doctors announced that the problem was being caused by Graves' disease, the same thyroid condition that had afflicted his wife, Barbara, since 1989. After the President was treated for that ailment, his heartbeat returned to normal.

Barbara Bush broke a bone in her left leg on January 13, when she crashed into a tree while riding a saucer sled down an icy slope at Camp David. She recovered with no complications.

Presidential library. Bush, who calls Texas his adopted home state, announced on May 3 that his presidential library would be built at Texas A&M University in College Station.

Income tax. The White House announced on April 15 that the Bushes paid $99,241 in federal income taxes on a 1990 adjusted gross income of $452,732.

Frank Cormier and Margot Cormier

See also **Congress of the United States; United States, Government of the.** In ***World Book,*** see **Bush, George Herbert Walker.**

Business. See **Bank; Economics; Manufacturing.**

Cabinet, U.S. On Dec. 3, 1991, John H. Sununu, chief of staff to President George Bush, resigned. The former governor of New Hampshire had drawn criticism for taking personal trips aboard United States government airplanes and had been blamed for contributing to Bush's declining domestic popularity in the autumn of 1991. See **Sununu, John H.**

Bush picked Samuel K. Skinner to replace Sununu. Skinner was transportation secretary before becoming chief of staff on December 16.

On Feb. 22, 1991, Lynn M. Martin was sworn in as secretary of labor. Martin succeeded Elizabeth H. Dole, who resigned in 1990 to head the American Red Cross. Like Skinner, Martin is from Illinois. She served 10 years in the U.S. House of Representatives before becoming labor secretary. In 1990, she ran unsuccessfully for a U.S. Senate seat. See **Martin, Lynn M.**

On Nov. 26, 1991, William P. Barr was sworn in as the new attorney general. He replaced Richard L. Thornburgh, who had resigned to run unsuccessfully for a U.S. Senate seat from Pennsylvania. (See **Barr, William P.**) On Dec. 26, 1991, Bush said he would nominate Barbara Franklin to be the new secretary of commerce. Franklin would replace Robert A. Mosbacher, who was slated to take over Bush's reelection campaign in January 1992. Mark Dunbar

In ***World Book,*** see **Cabinet.**

California. See **Los Angeles; San Diego; State government.**

Cambodia. Four warring factions in Cambodia (formerly Kampuchea) signed a peace treaty in Paris on Oct. 23, 1991. The treaty called for the United Nations (UN) to administer a transitional government, leading to elections by early 1993.

The agreement came after lengthy negotiations between Cambodia's Communist government, which was established by Vietnam in 1979, and the three guerrilla forces fighting it. One of the three factions, the Khmer Rouge, was also Communist. The brutal Khmer Rouge defeated an American-backed government in 1975, took control of the country, and was blamed for causing hundreds of thousands of deaths before being ousted by Vietnamese forces. One of the two non-Communist groups was headed by Prince Norodom Sihanouk, a former ruler of Cambodia, and the other was led by former Prime Minister Son Sann.

Peace plan. In addition to the rival Cambodian factions, the principal participants in the negotiations were Vietnam and the five permanent members of the UN Security Council—Great Britain, China, France, the Soviet Union, and the United States. The Council members had agreed in January 1990 to a peace plan, which led to the creation in September 1990 of a Supreme National Council (SNC) of representatives from the four rival factions. All four factions agreed to begin a cease-fire on May 1, 1991. A small UN observer team arrived on May 11 and found that fighting had dropped sharply but had not ended entirely.

Negotiations. The SNC was made up of six representatives from the three guerrilla groups and six representatives of the Communist regime. Sihanouk headed the delegation from the guerrilla groups. In meetings held in Pattaya, Thailand, from June 24 to 26, the SNC agreed to an unlimited cease-fire and a halt of foreign military supplies. Meeting again in Pattaya from August 26 to 29, the SNC agreed to a 70 per cent reduction of all Cambodian military forces and UN supervision of the remaining troops.

At the August meeting, the SNC called for "a liberal democratic and multiparty" political system for Cambodia. This led to the Paris meeting on October 23 at which SNC members signed the peace accord. The treaty gave the UN the job of monitoring the cease-fire, disarming the four groups, and organizing free elections.

Bitter memories. The accord said that the UN High Commissioner for Refugees would arrange the voluntary return home of 340,000 Cambodian refugees living across the border in Thailand. However, the Khmer Rouge, which had virtually imprisoned some of the refugees in border camps, planned to force refugees to relocate in areas where it would be able to control their votes in the scheduled elections. This revived bitter memories of the Khmer Rouge atrocities that occurred between 1975 and 1979.

Resentments against the Khmer Rouge erupted on Nov. 27, 1991, when a mob in Phnom Penh, the capital, attacked Khieu Samphan, the chief Khmer Rouge leader in the SNC. After a riot lasting four hours, Cambodian security forces finally rescued Khieu Samphan, who was bleeding profusely from a head wound. He immediately left Cambodia for Thailand. Fearing the likelihood of further attacks on Khmer Rouge leaders, the SNC held its next meeting in Thailand. On December 30, after a delay caused by rioting in Phnom Penh to protest government corruption, Khieu Samphan returned to the capital for the first SNC meeting there.

Communist Party compromise. The Communist regime held its party congress on October 17 and 18. At the congress, the party formally dropped its claim to single-party rule, insisting that it wanted "a democratic and free political system, a multiparty system." Heng Samrin was removed from his position as party chairman and placed in a ceremonial role. Chea Sim, who was known as a Communist Party hard-liner, became chairman, and the more liberal Hun Sen became party vice chairman.

In an apparent effort to counter the power of the Khmer Rouge, Hun Sen announced at the congress that the Communist Party would support Sihanouk as national president. On November 14, Sihanouk resumed living in Cambodia after living in exile since 1979. On Nov. 20, 1991, Hun Sen said he recognized Sihanouk as the "legitimate head of state."

Henry S. Bradsher

See also **Asia** (Facts in brief table); **Vietnam.** In ***World Book,*** see **Cambodia.**

Cameron, Donald (1946-), became the 21st premier of Canada's province of Nova Scotia on Feb. 26, 1991. The province's governing Tories elected Cameron by a narrow margin to replace the interim premier, Roger Bacon. As leader of the Progressive Conservative Party, Cameron forged his campaign from a platform that promised a smaller cabinet, a balanced budget, and the end of patronage.

Born in Egerton, Pictou County, N.S., on May 20, 1946, Cameron is the son of Helen and William Cameron. He earned a bachelor of science degree from McGill University in Montreal, Que., in 1968 and worked on the family's dairy farm for several years.

Cameron was first elected to Nova Scotia's legislature in 1974. He was elected again in 1978, 1981, 1984, and 1988. He held the position of minister of fisheries from 1978 to 1980 and was appointed minister of recreation from 1978 to 1979. He is a friend of Canada's Prime Minister Brian Mulroney. Cameron chaired the Nova Scotia legislature's 1987 hearings on the free-trade agreement between Canada and the United States. In 1988, he served as minister of industry, trade, and technology. Cameron has also been responsible for overseeing the Nova Scotia Research Foundation Corporation Act and the Advisory Council on Applied Science and Technology.

Cameron is married to the former Rosemary Simpson. They have three children. Lori Fagan

Cameroon. See **Africa.**

PUBLIC SERVICE ALLIANCE
PUBLIC SERVICE ALLIANCE
FAIT LA FORCE
PUBLIC SERVICE ALLIANCE
PUBLIC SERVICE ALLIANCE
IS
PUBLIC SERVI
ALLIANCE
ON STRIK
EN GREVE
ALLIANCE

Canada

Public discussion in Canada in 1991 centered on proposed changes to the Constitution and on whether Quebec would secede from the nation. Discussion of these topics became heated in 1991 partly because the Meech Lake Accord had not been approved by all 10 provinces in 1990. The accord was initiated by Prime Minister Brian Mulroney and his Progressive Conservative (PC) government and would have transferred several federal powers to the provinces and provided certain measures to preserve Quebec's "distinct society."

Because the accord failed, many Quebecers in 1991 supported independence for their province. Quebec Premier Robert Bourassa adopted a firm stance on what Quebec required from future constitutional negotiations. In June, Quebec passed a bill calling for a vote on independence to be held by October 1992.

Facing pressure from this deadline, the federal government in 1991 hammered out new constitutional proposals. In September, it presented them to the public, and a new round of public discussions began.

Public opinion. Early in the year, the federal government sounded out Canadians' opinions on the future of their country. A 12-member commission, the Citizens' Forum on Canada's Future, reported on June 27 that Canadians outside Quebec professed a stronger attachment to Canada than to their individual provinces. Loyalty to Canada was conditional in Quebec, however, where French is the official language and the culture is primarily influenced by its French history. More than three-fourths of Quebecers surveyed said that for Quebec to remain a part of the federation, English-speaking Canada had to recognize the province's special status. This conflicted with the equally strong view held elsewhere in Canada that equality among provinces is a basic principle of the federal union.

The commission found that the use of French and English as official languages in Canada was a major irritant outside Quebec and little appreciated inside Quebec. It recommended that the dual-language policy be reviewed. The commission also discovered many Canadians felt angry at their political leaders, partly due to the closed-door negotiations that had produced the Meech Lake Accord.

Constitutional proposals. A committee composed of 18 members of Mulroney's Cabinet spent most of the summer of 1991 working on a set of 28 constitutional proposals. The proposals were presented in September and were intended as a starting point for national-unity hearings to be held across Canada. A committee composed of members of the

Striking federal employees in Ottawa, Ont., in September 1991 demonstrate their displeasure with government policies affecting their jobs.

Senate and the House of Commons was to tour the country with the proposals and report their findings to Parliament by the end of February 1992. The parliamentary committee would then modify the proposals for presentation to Parliament and to the provinces.

The new proposals differed from the Meech Lake Accord in that they addressed desires for constitutional changes arising from all parts of Canada, rather than from Quebec alone. The reforms called for increased powers for the provinces and new authority for the federal government to manage the national economy.

Unlike the Meech Lake Accord, the new constitutional changes would not require unanimous approval from the provinces. Instead, the Mulroney government decided to revert to the Constitution's original amending formula, which requires approval by at least seven provinces containing at least 50 per cent of Canada's population. The constitutional revisions that were set before the Canadian people in 1991 targeted three main areas for change: the basic rights of Canada's peoples, a reformed Senate with more balanced provincial representation, and a cooperative economic union among the provinces.

The "Canada clause." Acting on suggestions frequently made during the debate on the Meech Lake Accord, the new proposals incorporated a "Canada clause," which defined the core values held by all Canadians. These included such principles as equal opportunity without regard to sex, race, color, religion, or disability; preservation of the environment; and Canada's respect for linguistic minorities.

The Canada clause also recognized Quebec's special responsibility "to preserve and promote its distinct society." The 1982 Charter of Rights and Freedoms, which has been part of the Constitution, was to be interpreted in such a way as to recognize Quebec as a "distinct society." For the first time, the meaning of this concept was spelled out as Quebec's language, culture, and civil law.

The proposals also addressed concerns of Canada's native peoples and called for aboriginal groups to be included in deliberations on the Constitution. It also guaranteed them a right to self-government within 10 years, the details of which would be worked out with federal and provincial governments. In addition, it suggested that native peoples be given special representation in a reformed Senate.

Reformed Senate. Responding to demands from Western provinces, the proposals contained a plan for an elected Senate with more equitable representation from the provinces. At present, the 104-member Senate, appointed by the prime minister, has more representatives from Ontario, Quebec, and the Maritime Provinces—the original members of the federation—than from the other provinces. For example, Quebec, with 6.5 million people, has 24 senators, while British Columbia, with about 3 million people, is allowed only 6 senators.

To make the Senate more responsive to the regions, the new revisions proposed that senators be elected by the provincial populations. It handed the parliamentary committee the sticky question of how many senators would be allowed for each province. The Western provinces had demanded an equal number for each province, but analysts believed the government was unlikely to adopt this recommendation. The plan also upheld the tradition that the prime minister and the Cabinet are responsible to the elected House of Commons.

The revisions placed limitations on the powers of a reformed Senate but retained the need for Senate consent for the passage of legislation. However, the proposals said the Senate would have no part in bills

Canada, provinces, and territories population estimates

	1991
Alberta	2,521,500
British Columbia	3,213,200
Manitoba	1,096,200
New Brunswick	726,800
Newfoundland	574,200
Northwest Territories	54,600
Nova Scotia	899,600
Ontario	9,906,400
Prince Edward Island	130,300
Quebec	6,845,000
Saskatchewan	996,800
Yukon Territory	26,900
Canada	**26,991,500**

City and metropolitan populations

	Metropolitan area 1991 estimate	City 1986 census*
Toronto, Ont.	3,812,100	612,289
Montreal, Que.	3,114,900	1,015,420
Vancouver, B.C.	1,587,500	431,147
Ottawa-Hull	891,000	
Ottawa, Ont.		300,763
Hull, Ont.		58,722
Edmonton, Alta.	842,100	573,982
Calgary, Alta.	742,900	636,104
Winnipeg, Man.	653,600	594,551
Quebec, Que.	630,200	164,580
Hamilton, Ont.	603,100	306,728
London, Ont.	376,900	269,140
St. Catharines-Niagara	364,400	
St. Catharines, Ont.		123,455
Niagara Falls, Ont.		72,107
Kitchener, Ont.	351,900	150,604
Halifax, N.S.	316,600	113,577
Victoria, B.C.	286,000	66,303
Windsor, Ont.	262,800	193,111
Oshawa, Ont.	250,200	123,651
Saskatoon, Sask.	205,000	177,641
Regina, Sask.	190,700	175,064
St. John's, Nfld.	164,800	96,216
Chicoutimi-Jonquière	159,100	
Chicoutimi, Que.		61,083
Jonquière, Que.		58,467
Sudbury, Ont.	150,600	88,717
Sherbrooke, Ont.	134,800	74,438
Trois-Rivières, Que.	131,800	50,122
Saint John, N.B.	124,600	76,381
Thunder Bay, Ont.	124,600	112,272

*Latest available data at time of publication.
Source: Statistics Canada.

Frank Iacobucci, right, is sworn in on Jan. 25, 1991, to serve as the first Italian-Canadian justice of the Supreme Court of Canada.

involving raising and spending money. Furthermore, the Senate would be given only a six-month suspensive veto on matters of national importance, such as international relations and military defense. The proposals also suggested that the Senate be given new authority to ratify senior appointments to federal institutions, such as the Bank of Canada and national regulatory agencies. Appointments to the Supreme Court would continue to be made by the federal government but would come from lists drawn up by the provinces.

Economic revisions. The constitutional proposals outlined plans for a stronger economic union. They included expanding the Constitution's "common market clause" to lift barriers to the free flow of "persons, goods, services, and capital" among the provinces.

The federal government would assume power to make laws for "the efficient functioning of the economic union" subject to the consent of seven provinces with at least 50 per cent of the population. A new body, the Council of the Federation, composed of federal, provincial, and territorial representatives, would endorse or revoke new economic legislation from the federal government. The council would also oversee new federal/provincial shared-cost programs, such as health and education.

The economic proposals called for the nation's central bank, the Bank of Canada, to be given a strong mandate to control inflation. To this end, the bank would work more closely with the provinces.

Federal spending in Canada

Estimated budget for fiscal 1991-1992*

Ministry (includes the department and all agencies for which a minister reports to Parliament):	Millions of dollars†
Agriculture	1,912
Atlantic Canada Opportunities Agency	358
Communications	
Canadian Broadcasting Corporation	1,034
Canadian Film Development Corporation	146
Other	812
Consumer and corporate affairs	203
Employment and immigration	2,155
Energy, mines, and resources	
Atomic Energy of Canada Limited	176
Other	927
Environment	1,019
External affairs	3,785
Finance	51,976
Fisheries and oceans	761
Forestry	147
Governor general	11
Indian affairs and northern development	3,833
Industry, science, and technology	
Canada Post Corporation	115
Other	2,675
Justice	653
Labour	253
National defence	12,850
National health and welfare	34,956
National revenue	2,175
Parliament	291
Privy Council	152
Public works	
Canada Mortgage and Housing Corporation	2,042
Other	1,503
Secretary of state	3,154
Solicitor general	
Royal Canadian Mounted Police	1,230
Other	1,234
Supply and services	359
Transport	3,054
Treasury Board	1,271
Veterans affairs	1,892
Western economic diversification	292
Total	**139,406**

* April 1, 1991, to March 31, 1992.
† Canadian dollars; $1= U.S. 87 cents as of Dec. 17, 1991.

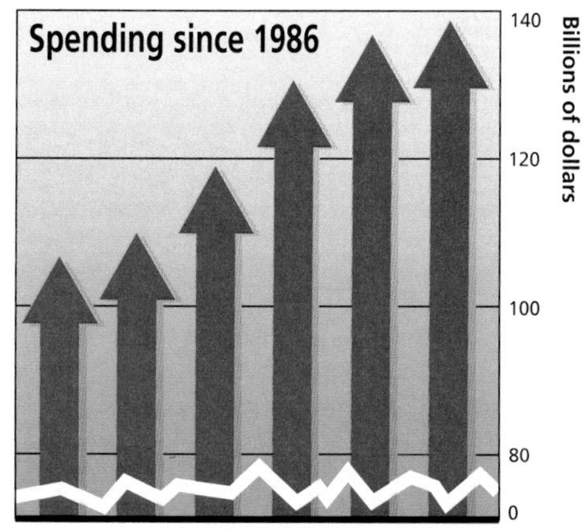

Source: Treasury Board of Canada.

The revisions would also transfer from the federal government to the provinces exclusive jurisdiction over job training, mining, forestry, tourism, recreation, housing, and municipal affairs. Provincial authority in the areas of culture and immigration would be expanded.

Mixed reaction. Initially, Canadians received the proposals with a hopeful but wary eye. The reforms appeared to be more acceptable to the populace than was the Meech Lake Accord. As time went on, however, the national-unity hearings became mired in political infighting. By October, polls showed that Canadians were rebuffing the proposals, and tensions between English-speaking Canada and Quebec were growing once again. At the end of November, the government announced an economic aid package for Quebec, and some parliamentary representatives responded angrily to what they considered to be preferential treatment for Quebec.

Quebecers were cool to the proposed constitutional reforms. They were especially concerned that the suggestions for an economic union might undermine Quebec's financial autonomy. Quebec's leaders also were uncertain that the narrowly defined "distinct society" clause would give Quebec the protection they believed it needed.

The reaction of native leaders was not positive, either. The Indian leadership refused to accept the suggested 10-year deadline in defining aboriginal self-government. The Assembly of First Nations, Canada's largest native organization, threatened to boycott the constitutional discussions but decided in November to participate.

By year-end, the federal government was scrambling to promote more successful dialogue. Federal officials proposed replacing the national-unity hearings with meetings with provincial prime ministers that would focus on specific constitutional issues. But Quebec refused to consider such an arrangement, and in November, Quebec's government said the 28 constitutional proposals were "unacceptable" as written. As the country studied the Mulroney government's proposals, it was apparent that many hard questions would have to be answered before a consensus on constitutional changes could be reached.

Cabinet changes. Mulroney on April 21, 1991, changed the positions of 23 members of his 39-member Cabinet. He created a new position, minister for constitutional affairs, and appointed Charles Joseph Clark to it. Clark was the secretary of state for external affairs and had been ousted by Mulroney as leader of the Progressive Conservatives in 1983. Michael H. Wilson, who had been minister of finance since the administration took office in 1984, was made minister for industry, science, technology, and international trade. Donald F. Mazankowski, the deputy prime minister, was appointed finance minister. Barbara J. McDougall, minister of employment and immigration, became the new secretary of state for external affairs.

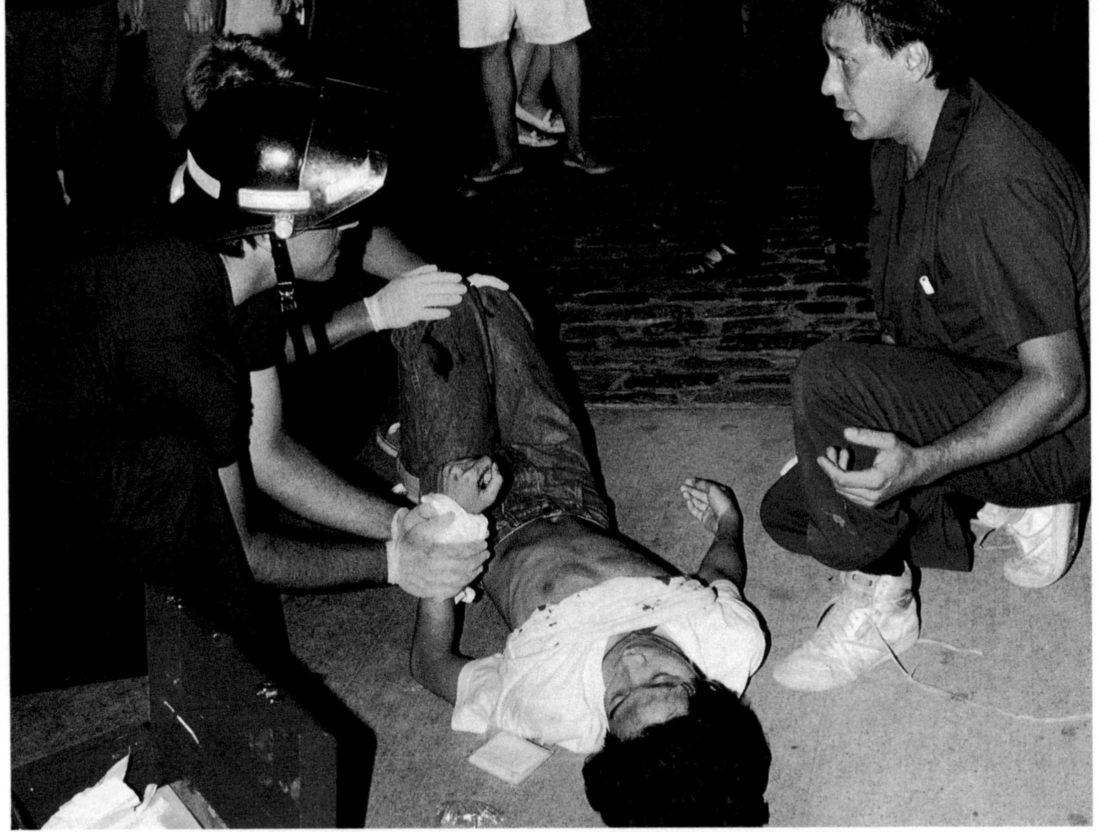

A Toronto youth falls victim to a rising tide of violence that police said originated with Asian gangs in many Canadian cities in 1991.

Mulroney and the PC's received record low ratings in an August 1991 Gallup poll. But the party operated from a comfortable majority in Parliament. Within the 295-seat House of Commons, the PC's held 159 seats. The Liberal Party had 81; the New Democratic Party had 44; the Bloc Québécois had 9; and the Reform Party had 1. In addition, 1 seat was held by an independent Conservative.

The economy began to pull out of the 1990 recession in April 1991. The recovery was helped by declining interest rates. In early December, the major private banks cut their prime lending rate to 8 per cent, the lowest level since 1968. Consumer spending in new housing increased, and exports of grain, lumber, and automobiles showed improvement. On June 30, the gross domestic product stood at $684 billion ($605 U.S.). The Canadian dollar hit a 13-year high on October 29, when it closed at 89.04 cents (U.S.).

Inflation, as measured by the Consumer Price Index, rose early in the year because of the introduction of the goods and services tax (GST) but settled back to 4.2 per cent in November. Yet unemployment remained disturbingly high. In August, unemployment reached 10.6 per cent of the population, the highest rate since 1985. By November 1991, it had fallen only slightly to 10.3 per cent.

Foreign trade faltered as the year went on. In September, statistics showed that for the first time since 1976, Canada imported more than it exported.

Budget. Minister of Finance Michael Wilson delivered his seventh budget on Feb. 26, 1991, and called for no major tax increases. However, premiums for unemployment insurance, paid by employees and employers, escalated 24 per cent. Total federal spending was expected to increase by 5.1 per cent to $159 billion ($140 billion U.S.) for the 1991-1992 fiscal year. Much of the increase would go to higher unemployment costs, wheat farmers, and expenditures arising from the Persian Gulf War.

Earnings from the GST, which were expected to total about $16 billion ($14 billion U.S.) for 1991-1992, were targeted to reducing the current national deficit of $30.5 billion ($27 billion U.S.). The government decided that for the next three years, transfer payments to the provinces for health care services and postsecondary education would be frozen at 1990 levels. The budget also limited increases in government spending to 3 per cent annually over the next five years.

Indian affairs were quiet in 1991 compared with the armed confrontations that occurred the previous year. The Assembly of First Nations, representing Canada's 500,000 status Indians (those living on reservations and governed by the Indian Act) elected Ovide Mercredi, 45, a Cree lawyer from Manitoba, as its national chief in June 1991. A believer in nonviolent methods of civil disobedience, Mercredi vowed to end the history of exclusion and rejection that he claimed marked Canada's treatment of native peoples. Mer-

The Ministry of Canada*

Brian Mulroney—prime minister
Charles Joseph Clark—president of the Queen's Privy Council; minister responsible for constitutional affairs
John Carnell Crosbie—minister of fisheries and oceans; minister for the Atlantic Canada Opportunities Agency
Donald Frank Mazankowski—deputy prime minister; minister of finance
Elmer MacIntosh MacKay—minister of public works
Arthur Jacob Epp—minister of energy, mines, and resources
Robert R. de Cotret—secretary of state of Canada
Henry Perrin Beatty—minister of communications
Michael Holcombe Wilson—minister of industry, science, and technology; minister for international trade
Harvie Andre—minister of state; leader of the government in the House of Commons
Otto John Jelinek—minister of national revenue
Thomas Edward Siddon—minister of Indian affairs and Northern development
Charles James Mayer—minister of state (grains and oilseeds); minister of Western economic diversification
William Hunter McKnight—minister of agriculture
Benoît Bouchard—minister of national health and welfare
Marcel Masse—minister of national defence
Barbara Jean McDougall—secretary of state for external affairs
Gerald Stairs Merrithew—minister of veterans affairs
Monique Vézina—minister of state (employment and immigration); minister of state (seniors)
Frank Oberle—minister of forestry
Lowell Murray—leader of the government in the Senate
Paul Wyatt Dick—minister of supply and services
Pierre H. Cadieux—minister of state (fitness and amateur sport); minister of state (youth); deputy leader of the government in the House of Commons
Jean J. Charest—minister of the environment
Thomas Hockin—minister of state (small businesses and tourism)
Monique Landry—minister for external relations; minister of state (Indian affairs and Northern development)
Bernard Valcourt—minister of employment and immigration
Gerry Weiner—minister of multiculturalism and citizenship
Douglas Grinslade Lewis—solicitor general of Canada
Pierre Blais—minister of state (agriculture); minister of consumer and corporate affairs
John Horton McDermid—minister of state (finance and privatization
Shirley Martin—minister of state (transport)
Mary Collins—associate minister of national defence; minister responsible for the status of women
William Charles Winegard—minister for science
Kim Campbell—minister of justice and attorney general of Canada
Jean Corbeil—minister of transport
Gilles Loiselle—minister of state (finance); president of the Treasury Board
Marcel Danis—minister of labour
Pauline Browes—minister of state (environment)
*As of Dec. 31, 1991.

Premiers of Canadian Provinces

Province	Premier
Alberta	Donald R. Getty
British Columbia	Michael Harcourt
Manitoba	Gary A. Filmon
New Brunswick	Frank J. McKenna
Newfoundland	Clyde K. Wells
Nova Scotia	Donald Cameron
Ontario	Robert K. Rae
Prince Edward Island	Joseph A. Ghiz
Quebec	Robert Bourassa
Saskatchewan	Roy Romanow

Government leaders of territories

Northwest Territories	Denis Paterson
Yukon Territory	Tony Penikett

credi's predecessor, Georges Erasmus, was named cochairman of a royal commission to inquire into the state of affairs among aboriginals. A seven-member commission was formed to address questions concerning native self-government, the legal status of Indian treaties, social problems of native communities, and economic development.

In a treaty set forth in December, Canada agreed to give Indians exclusive ownership to part of the Northwest Territories. The treaty marked the first change in Canada's borders since 1949.

Persian Gulf War. In January 1991, Canada supported the United Nations (UN) military action against Iraq. In all, 4,000 Canadian military personnel served in the gulf theater between August 1990 and April 1991. Three Canadian ships patrolled the Persian Gulf to help enforce the UN trade embargo, while CF-18 jet fighters undertook 2,700 sorties to protect naval vessels and escort United States bombing missions. Canadian aircraft also carried out air-to-ground attacks on Iraqi positions.

Trade. Canada decided in February to be a full participant in the free-trade negotiations between the United States and Mexico. Canadian representatives took their place at the bargaining table in June, intent on safeguarding the gains made through the 1989 trade agreement with the United States. Canada's trade with Mexico has been small, representing less than 1 per cent of the nation's total trade.

Environment. Meeting in Ottawa, Ont., on March 13, 1991, Mulroney and U.S. President George Bush signed an agreement to reduce the emissions that cause acid rain. The pact calls for Canada and the United States to cut back emissions of sulfur dioxide and other pollutants that contribute to acid rain. The United States promised to decrease its emissions by about 50 per cent of 1980 levels by the year 2000. Canada will cut its 1980 output in half by 1994.

Acid rain is rain that carries a high concentration of sulfuric and nitric acids, which can harm plants and fish. Environmental experts say that acid rain has damaged Canadian forests, harmed more than 150,000 lakes, and deadened 15,000 more lakes. Lakes and forests in the United States also have been hurt by acid rain. Canada had sought a treaty since 1979 to control this problem.

Military forces cut. The federal government on Sept. 17, 1991, announced plans for major reductions in Canada's military forces. Defense Minister Marcel Masse said that by 1995 Canada would close its two bases in Germany, bring home three squadrons of jet fighters in Europe, and reduce its troops in Europe from 6,600 to 1,100. The measures were part of an overall plan to reduce Canadian forces from 84,000 to 76,000 by 1994. David M. L. Farr

See also the Canadian provinces articles; **Cameron, Donald; Canadian literature; Iacobucci, Frank; Johnston, Rita; Montreal;** and **Toronto.** In ***World Book,*** see **Canada.**

Canada and Quebec at a Crossroads

By Kenneth McRoberts

Long-standing cultural and political tensions between the English-speaking majority of Canada and French-speaking Quebec have led this province to the brink of secession from Canada.

At various points in the 124 years since its creation, Canada has faced crises stemming from conflict between its English-speaking majority and its French-speaking minority, located primarily in the province of Quebec. By all appearances, Canada in 1991 was plunged into its worst crisis yet. In fact, the secession of Quebec from Canada had become a distinct possibility.

Quebec's legislature in 1990 passed a law calling for a popular referendum by October 1992 to determine whether Quebec should become a sovereign nation. Under sovereignty, the Quebec government would have the sole right to pass laws and collect taxes in Quebec. In all likelihood, the referendum on sovereignty for Quebec will be held only if the Canadian federal government and the other provincial governments cannot agree on a new constitutional arrangement that accommodates Quebec's demands for expanded powers and recognition of Quebec as a "distinct society." And it is possible, though far from certain, that such a referendum might pass.

Clearly, Canada and Quebec have reached a crossroads. To understand how Canada has come to such a critical stage, we first need to explore why Quebec's people have such a strong sense of distinctness.

Quebec's distinct identity

The most obvious basis for Quebec's sense of distinctness is language. About 25 per cent of the total Canadian population speaks mainly French. Of these, 89 per cent live in Quebec, where French-speaking people constitute an overwhelming majority. In Quebec, French is not simply a secondary language used at home and among family. For most Quebecers, it is the language in which they are educated, in which they work, and in which they watch television or read newspapers. In short, it is the language in which they live their lives. In fact, more than 70 per cent of the French-speaking people in Quebec cannot converse in English.

In addition, many of Quebec's institutions are distinct from those elsewhere in Canada. For example, Quebecers have a unique system of credit unions, their civil laws are based on the French Civil Code, and they have an independent labor union movement.

The Quebecers' strong sense of identity also is rooted in religion. In the past, Quebec's French-speaking people were closely linked with Roman Catholicism while the English-speaking people were identified with Protestantism. Although today's Quebecers are little inclined to define themselves in terms of the Roman Catholic Church, the long history of religious differences has left its mark.

Another major factor promoting a sense of distinctness is the fact that most French-speaking people of Quebec can trace their ancestry to the colony of New France, founded in 1608. Both the French and the English began exploring Canada in the 1500's, and both groups laid claim to land in Canada. But France established the first permanent settlement in Canada, which it called New France, and ruled the colony for about 150 years.

During this time, about 10,000 immigrants came to the colony, mainly from France, and by 1760, the colony's population was about 70,000. New France developed institutions that clearly distinguished it from the neighboring British colonies. French colonial authority was divided among the military governor, the *intendant* (the administrative head), and the Catholic bishop. The colony's legal system, called the Civil Code, was based upon French law. But the French-speaking colonists also developed a clear sense of difference from their mother country, referring to themselves as *Canadiens* or *habitants.*

The author:
Kenneth McRoberts is professor of political science at York University in Toronto, Canada, and author of the book *Quebec: Social Change and Political Crisis.*

The British conquest

French control over the colony came to an end after British troops captured Quebec City in 1759 and Montreal in 1760. In 1763, France signed the Treaty of Paris, giving most of its Canadian territory to Great Britain.

Where Quebec stands in Canada

Geographical Size: Ranks first among Canada's 10 provinces.

Population: Ranks second, with 25.5 per cent of Canada's 27 million people. Of Quebec's 6.5 million people, 5.4 million are French speaking.

Income: Holds 23.2 per cent of the nation's disposable income.

Labor: Employs 24.3 per cent of Canada's workers. Unemployment in Quebec as of mid-1990 was 2 per cent higher than the national average.

Manufacturing: Supplies about 23 per cent of Canada's products.

Natural resources: Ranks first in the production of hydropower, asbestos, and maple syrup.

Source: Statistics Canada; *The World Book Encyclopedia.*

The British renamed the colony Quebec and replaced French laws with British laws. Relatively few immigrants from France came to Quebec once French rule had ended.

From the British conquest onward, the French-speaking colonists were periodically confronted with threats to their cultural distinctiveness. Their struggles to stave off these threats, and their success in doing so, served to sharpen their sense of being a distinct nationality.

Initially, scholars maintain, British colonial authorities planned to eliminate totally Quebec's cultural heritage. Through an influx of British immigrants, the French-speaking people were to be assimilated. Under the Royal Proclamation of 1763, the Catholic Church was to lose all legal status. Furthermore, the colony had mainly traded with France, but now Great Britain replaced France as the focus of trade, and control over Quebec's economy swiftly passed to English-speakers. As a result, Quebec's French Canadians became increasingly dependent upon subsistence farming.

By the 1770's, it became apparent to British colonial officials that assimilation could not be readily achieved. English settlers were not migrating to Quebec in sufficient numbers. In fact, the royal proclamation was never fully enacted. Moreover, the unrest that would lead to the American Revolution was growing in the British colonies

The glory of Notre Dame Parish Church in Montreal symbolizes the central role of Roman Catholicism in the cultural heritage of French-speaking Quebecers.

A street in Quebec City displays signs written in French, the language most Quebecers speak almost exclusively. Quebec in 1977 banned the use of any language other than French on outdoor signs.

to the south. Therefore, British officials tried to solidify the allegiance of French Canadians by passing the Quebec Act of 1774.

This act restored the Catholic Church's rights and reestablished the Civil Code. It recognized the cultural distinctiveness of the French Canadians but in a way that reinforced the more conservative forces within that society. For example, the British authorities denied demands by the British inhabitants for a representative assembly. Some scholars say this was done out of deference to the Catholic Church, which at that time feared democratic institutions. At the same time, control of the colony's economy remained clearly in the hands of English-speaking merchants.

When a colonial assembly was finally created in 1791 through the Constitution Act, it was soon dominated by the French-English conflict. A new class of French-Canadian professionals—lawyers, doctors, and notaries—was able to use the assembly to pursue the economic interests of their constituents, who were mainly subsistence farmers, and to oppose the interests of the now significant British merchant class. At the same time, this new French-speaking leadership developed the idea that the people of Quebec constituted a distinct nation. Out of this conflict arose the Rebellions of 1837 by the French Canadians who sought to secure autonomy for the colony.

The Rebellions failed, and British colonial authorities returned to the old ideal of assimilation. In 1840, Quebec was united with Upper Canada (now Ontario) to form a new colony, the United Canadas, in which the French-speaking people would be a minority. Once again, the assimilationist project failed. Within the United Canadas' legislature, French-speaking leaders succeeded in securing recognition of their language and an informal veto over projects that affected their constituents.

In 1867, Britain passed the British North America Act, which created the Dominion of Canada, a federation of provinces that were once British colonies. Largely due to the insistence of French-Canadian leaders, the government structure divided authority between a federal government and the provincial governments. French Canadians, knowing they would be the minority within the federal government, intended to rely on Quebec's provincial government to protect their interests. They insisted that provincial governments be given exclusive jurisdiction over matters such as education and civil law—areas in which Quebec's cultural traditions were at stake. Economic matters were placed under federal jurisdiction.

Soon, though, English-speaking and French-speaking Canadians were divided again over various political questions. Usually, the federal government's position reflected the views of the English-speaking majority.

Relations between British and French Canadians seriously deteriorated in 1885 when the government hung Louis Riel, the leader of a *métis* (people of mixed white and Indian ancestry) rebellion and a hero in the eyes of French Canadians. Tension escalated further during World War I (1914-1918) and World War II (1939-1945), when the federal government imposed conscription on all Canadians for overseas military service. The French Canadians by this time had no allegiance to France. They felt that France had abandoned them to the British, and they also resented having to fight in what they regarded as the defense of Britain.

Serious as these conflicts may have been, they did not directly place in question Quebec's continued participation in the Canadian federation. In part, this was because French-Canadian leadership was dominated by conservatives who viewed Quebec as a traditional rural society that must rely upon the Catholic Church rather than the government to administer to its needs. During the first half of the 1900's, French-Canadian politi-

Quebec's history of tension

1534 Jacques Cartier sailed into the Gulf of St. Lawrence and claimed for France the region now known as Quebec.

1608 Samuel de Champlain (left, center) founded Quebec City.

cians, such as Maurice Duplessis, who governed Quebec from 1936 to 1939 and from 1944 to 1959, proclaimed themselves strong French-Canadian nationalists but did not call for constitutional changes to advance Quebec's interests.

Meanwhile, Quebec was undergoing important social and economic changes. By 1931, the majority of Quebec's French-speaking people were living in urban rather than rural areas, and a large proportion of them were working in industries that were, for the most part, controlled by the English-speaking Canadians. At the same time, there emerged a new class of French-speaking intellectuals who challenged both the position of the Catholic Church within French-Canadian society and the dominance of English speakers over the Quebec economy. They called for vigorous intervention by the Quebec state to address both matters.

Quebec's political power expands

In 1960, voters brought the Liberal Party and Jean Lesage to power. Unlike the Duplessis administration, the Lesage government intervened significantly in Quebec's society and economy. During the next six years, a period known as the *Quiet Revolution,* Quebec's government assumed functions held by the Catholic Church, such as the administration of schools, hospitals, and social services. In addition, it created state enterprises, such as government-owned public utilities, to carve out a new position for French Canadians in the economy of Quebec. Hence, French-Canadi-

1759 In the Battle of Quebec, British troops, transported by ship, captured the city.

1763 The Treaty of Paris gave Great Britain control of Quebec.

1774 Britain signed the Quebec Act, expanding Quebec's borders and recognizing French-Canadian rights.

1837 A French-Canadian revolt against the colonial government was swiftly crushed.

1885 French Canadians were outraged when federal authorities hung Louis Riel, the admired leader of a rebellion in what is now Saskatchewan Province.

an nationalism became defined as an explicitly Quebec nationalism.

A campaign grew for radical revisions in Canada's constitution that would give Quebec powers held by the federal government. These included the ability to deal directly with foreign governments; to set policies regarding immigration and communications; and to control all aspects of education, cultural activities, social security and pension programs, as well as the location and development of industry. Quebec also wanted decreased federal taxes so it could raise provincial taxes without overburdening its citizens.

In 1968, supporters of Quebec sovereignty formed a new political party called the Parti Québécois, led by René Lévesque. At the same time, members of the revolutionary group, the Front de Libération du Québec (FLQ), engaged in terrorist bombings and robberies in pursuit of the separatist cause. In 1970, the FLQ kidnapped two officials—James R. Cross, the British trade commissioner in Montreal, and Quebec Labor Minister Pierre Laporte—and ultimately killed Laporte.

Prime Minister Pierre Elliott Trudeau, a French Canadian who opposed independence for Quebec, led an effort to make the federal government bilingual through the Official Languages Act of 1969. He also wanted to strengthen the position of French minorities outside Quebec. The federal officials hoped that such changes would encourage French Quebecers to see all of Canada as their country.

In 1976, Quebec voters elected members of the Parti Québécois to 71 of the province's 110 legislative seats, and Lévesque became premier. After four years in power, the government held a referendum to secure a mandate for negotiating *sovereignty-association,* an arrangement that would make Quebec independent but allow it to maintain economic ties—such as free trade and, perhaps, a common currency—with Canada. But only 40 per cent of the voters gave their approval.

In 1980, the Trudeau government then initiated a new round of constitutional discussions intended to replace the British North America Act as the basic governing document of Canada. Nine of the 10 provinces agreed to constitutional changes, which became known as the Constitution Act of 1982, but Lévesque refused to sign the document, claiming that it did not meet Quebec's needs. Nevertheless, Quebec is bound by the Constitution Act.

1899 Resentment flared among Quebec's French Canadians when Canadian troops were sent to help Britain fight the Boer War in South Africa.

1917 When Quebecers objected to a military draft for overseas service during World War I, English Canadians accused them of being disloyal.

1944 Quebecers opposed a Canadian draft to fight overseas in World War II and elected the Union Nationale Party to promote French-Canadian rights and reduce federal "interference" in Quebec.

1960 The Liberal Party came to power in Quebec and took over some federal programs. Throughout the decade, Quebec separatist extremists staged demonstrations and bombings.

In 1985, the Liberal Party came to power in Quebec and Robert Bourassa, head of the party, became premier. He had previously served as premier between 1970 and 1976. In 1987, Bourassa and Prime Minister Brian Mulroney worked with the other provincial leaders to create a new package of constitutional revisions, popularly known as the Meech Lake Accord. Bourassa suggested that the Constitution formally recognize Quebec as a distinct society and that it grant all the provinces additional powers in four specific areas: nominating federal supreme court justices; screening immigration applicants; securing federal funding without participating in national shared-cost social programs; and the ability to veto some proposed constitutional amendments. These were all incorporated into the Meech Lake Accord, along with the right of the provinces to nominate members of the Senate. The accord received formal approval of all 10 provincial premiers and the Canadian prime minister.

To go into effect, the accord had to be ratified within three years. During this time, opposition to the proposed changes began to take hold throughout the country. English-speaking Canadians worried that the changes would weaken the federal government and that Quebec might gain too much power. In the end, two provinces—Manitoba and Newfoundland—failed to approve the accord by the June 1990 deadline and this plunged Canada into its present crisis.

After the failure of the Meech Lake Accord, several special commissions prepared reports on what each side wanted. The first, called "A Quebec Free to Choose," or the Allaire report, came from the Quebec Liberal Party. It called for a radical transfer of federal powers to Quebec. It

1968 Nationalists formed the Parti Québécois, led by René Lévesque, center.

1969 Canada made both English and French its official languages, but in 1974, Quebec declared that French is the official language of that province.

1970 Revolutionaries of the separatist group Front de Libération du Québec kidnapped a British trade commissioner and kidnapped and killed Quebec's labor minister. Canadian troops were sent to Quebec to safeguard officials and quell any public uprising.

also sought the abolition of the Canadian Senate and the termination of appeals from the Quebec courts to the Canadian supreme court.

A report from members of Quebec's legislature also demanded vastly expanded powers. It called for a popular vote on Quebec sovereignty to be held by October 1992—a recommendation the legislature adopted.

The federal government established the Citizens' Forum on Canada's Future to consult with a broad cross section of the populace. This commission reported that English-speaking Canadians were deeply committed to reform of federal institutions but opposed to any special arrangements for Quebec.

Constitutional change or a separate nation?

These conflicting interests have presented Canada with the enormous challenge of devising a constitutional package that English-speaking Canadians, all provincial governments, and French-speaking Quebecers will accept. Basically, there are two ways to resolve the present crisis: a revision of the Canadian federal system or sovereignty for Quebec. Each has its advantages and disadvantages that must be weighed and assessed.

The central issue in revising the Canadian federal system to meet Quebec's demands for additional powers is whether these same powers should be granted to all provincial governments. Broad decentralization of the federal government could transfer to all the provinces control of such areas as cultural policy, job training, regional economic development, energy and the environment, health care, social service programs, and unemployment insurance.

People in favor of across-the-board decentralization contend that the smaller provincial governments can identify and respond to public needs more efficiently. Those opposed to such sweeping changes believe that the increased power of provincial governments would lower the quality of services, such as health and social programs, which have largely been provided with federal funds. Poorer provinces want to see revenue transfers from wealthier provinces continued.

Concerns about decentralization might seem to warrant the granting

1982 Canada's Constitution was revised, but without the consent of the Quebec government.

1987 Canadian Prime Minister Brian Mulroney drafted a constitutional amendment, known as the Meech Lake Accord, intended to recognize Quebec as a "distinct society" and to reform relations between the provinces and the federal government. Ratification deadline was June 1990.

1990 The provinces of Manitoba and Newfoundland failed to ratify the Meech Lake Accord, and a new wave of separatist sentiment surged through Quebec.

1991 Quebec's premier, Robert Bourassa, announced that Quebec will vote by October 1992 on seceding from the nation unless Canada revises the federal Constitution to suit Quebec.

Items made in Quebec comprise about 23 per cent of Canada's domestically manufactured products. Quebec's leading manufactured goods are:

- Foods (dairy products, baked goods, meat packing, candy, canned fruits and vegetables, and livestock feed).
- Paper products.
- Primary metals (aluminum and steel).
- Transportation equipment.
- Chemicals.
- Electrical equipment.
- Metal products.
- Clothing.
- Wood.
- Printed materials.

Source: *1992 Canada Year Book.*

The manufacture of paper products is one of Quebec's leading industries, and one which contributes significantly to the Canadian economy.

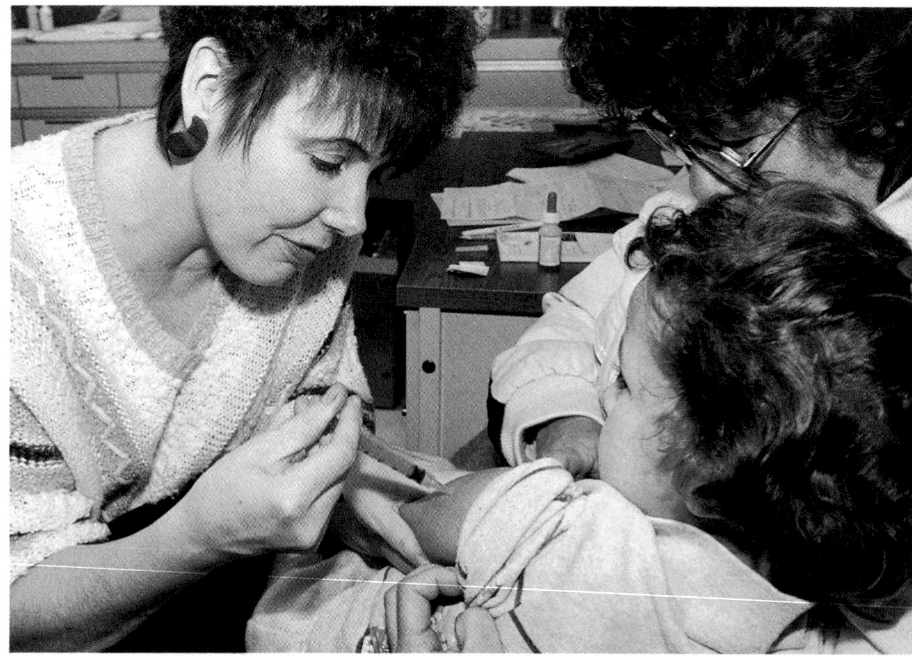

Those opposed to sovereignty point out that the Canadian government would no longer finance such programs as health care. Supporters of sovereignty claim that Quebec's increased tax revenues could cover such programs. Health care is one of several federally financed services Quebec would lose if it were to secede.

Independence poses pros and cons for Quebec

Pros

- International recognition of Quebec's nationhood.
- Liberty to govern itself without federal interference.
- Ability to control all the taxes raised in Quebec
- Elimination of federal/provincial duplication of services.
- Ability to establish direct foreign relations and to control immigration policies.
- Right to be solely responsible for Quebec's economy.
- Liberty to preserve the French language and culture.

Cons

- Loss of money spent by the federal government in Quebec; this loss might be greater than the money saved by not paying taxes to the federal government.
- Possible economic decline, especially during the transition period.
- Risk of losing the right to free trade with other Canadian provinces and with the United States.
- Possible loss of territory to the federal government and to native peoples.
- Loss of identification with a large nation that is influential in world affairs.
- Potential emigration of English-speaking Quebecers from the province.
- Need for Quebec to finance its portion of Canada's $400-billion ($354-billion U.S.) national debt.

of additional powers to Quebec alone. In effect, Quebec would assume functions which, in the rest of Canada, would continue to be fulfilled by the federal government. There are clear precedents for such an arrangement. For instance, In 1964 the Quebec government refused to participate in a new federal pension plan. As a result, Quebec has a pension plan administered by the provincial government while the rest of Canada is covered by a plan largely administered by the federal government.

Nonetheless, there are problems with this type of "asymmetrical federalism." There is particular concern over whether Quebec members of Parliament would vote on federal legislation that does not apply to Quebec. More fundamentally, English-speaking Canadians have become increasingly wedded to the principle of equality among the provinces. Any power or prerogative granted to one province, they argue, must be granted to all provinces.

Although there are profound problems confronting any plan to revise the federal system, a host of other problems surround the alternative of Quebec sovereignty. Clearly, sovereignty would be costly for Quebec. For instance, at the present time, Quebec is a net beneficiary of federal spending. The federal government is transferring more money to Quebec than it raises through taxes from Quebec. If Quebec were separate from Canada, these funds would disappear. Quebec separatists, however, point out that there have been times in the past when this situation was reversed. Moreover, they argue, with decision-making centered in one Quebec government, funds would be allocated more efficiently. In addition, wasteful duplication of programs by two levels of government would be eliminated.

Even more difficult to assess is the potential impact of sovereignty upon Quebec's economy. Its shipments of goods and services to Ontario have been considerably more important for Quebec's economy than exports to Quebec are for Ontario's economy. To minimize trade cutbacks, Quebec separatists have proposed establishing a customs union that would allow free movement of goods among the provinces. But some provinces claim they would not be interested in such an arrangement.

Quebec nationalists counter that a sovereign Quebec could rely upon its steadily growing trade with the United States, which is now covered by a free-trade agreement between Canada and the United States. But a sovereign Quebec would have to negotiate a new free-trade agreement with the United States, and some analysts claim that the new bargaining might leave Quebec with less favorable terms than it received under the U.S.-Canada Free Trade Agreement of 1989.

Most difficult of all to predict is how investors would react if Quebec became a separate nation. Economic experts say that in the short term some investors would curtail or postpone investment in the province and, perhaps, in all of Canada. With time, investor hesitation should ease and even disappear, and Quebec's economy might become stronger than it is now. Then Quebec's new, dynamic French-speaking business class would be better aided by a sovereign Quebec government. But it is impossible to predict with any accuracy how long the transition period might last.

The setting up of a new Quebec state would also call for negotiations with respect to Quebec's boundaries, and such negotiations could be extremely difficult. Some English-speaking minorities claim that the areas they occupy should remain in Canada. Native peoples have laid claim to lands in the northern part of the province, where Quebec operates hydropower projects that supply the province with 95 per cent of its electricity. Vast forests there supply Quebec's leading industry, paper and pulp manufacturing. Cree leaders warned in August 1991 that the Cree would seize half of Quebec's territory if the province seceded. Conceivably, the federal government might deny Quebec territory ceded to it after confederation. In each case, however, it is not clear that English-Canadian public opinion would support military intervention to impose these border changes if Quebec should declare itself a separate nation.

The next few years are bound to be fateful for Quebec and for Canada. While most Canadians want Quebec to remain a part of the nation, fundamental differences in the objectives of French-speaking and English-speaking Canadians have brought Canada to a crossroads. Although many questions about the nation's direction remain unanswered, one thing is for certain. If Quebec chooses to go its own way, Canada will be forever changed.

For further reading:

Fournier, Pierre. *A Meech Lake Post-Mortem: Is Quebec Sovereignty Inevitable?* McGill-Queen's University Press, 1991.

McRoberts, Kenneth. *Quebec: Social Change and Political Crisis.* McClelland & Stewart, 1988.

Resnick, Philip. *Toward a Canada-Quebec Union.* McGill-Queen's University Press, 1991.

Canadian literature. The Canadian recession took a toll on Canada's publishing industry in 1991 as book sales plummeted. Publisher Lester & Orpen Dennys closed its doors, as did Summerhill, Western Producer Prairie Books, and Hurtig Publishers.

Novels. Among the leading novels was *Murther and Walking Spirits* by Robertson Davies. A catchy combination of history, fictionalized autobiography, and technical virtuosity, it featured a just-murdered narrator.

A first novel by Rohinton Mistry, *Such a Long Journey,* about life in 1970's Bombay, won a nomination in Britain for the prestigious Booker Prize. Another powerful first novel, *News from a Foreign Country Came,* by poet and anthologist Alberto Manguel, used a sensuous prose style in a plot about a hidden Nazi past.

Katherine Govier's ambitious *Hearts of Flame* depicted the lives of a 1960's rock group descending into the world of the homeless in the 1990's. In *Evening Snow Will Bring Such Peace,* the second volume of the New Brunswick trilogy that began with *Nights Below Station Street,* David Adams Richards told the story of the beleaguered Basterache family. The somewhat melodramatic plot of Tom Marshall's *Changelings* explored the theme of multiple personalities caused by childhood sexual abuse. Michael Ignatieff's finely crafted historical fiction *Asya* followed his Russian heroine through the turbulent 1900's.

Short stories. The usual large number of short story collections was published in 1991. *Wilderness Tips* by Margaret Atwood was predictably hailed as a biting commentary on late 20th-century life. *Isobars* by novelist Janette Turner Hospital experimented with elliptical and dreamlike tales moving between Canada, Australia, and the United States. The stories in *Something Happened Here,* a typically accomplished book by Norman Levine, examined the haunting effect of the dead on the living. *The Divine Ryans* by Wayne Johnston was a funny and eloquent collection of tales about a Catholic boyhood in Newfoundland. M. T. Kelly's *Breath Dances Between Them* dealt with urban relationships in Toronto.

British Columbian Don Dickinson received attention for *Blue Husbands,* about a man who meets a talking crab. Douglas Glover's *A Guide to Animal Behavior* pushed at the traditional bounds of fiction with strange, often bizarre landscapes. And Terry Griggs's *Quickening* displayed fresh stylistic verve and humor.

From Ink Lake was a new anthology of Canadian stories written since 1930. Edited by Michael Ondaatje, the book undertook to represent "the geographical, emotional, and literary range of the country from fable to chronicle to intimate moment."

Poetry. Patrick Lane explored the relationship of father and son in *Mortal Remains.* Judith Fitzgerald's 12th book, *Rapturous Chronicles,* used fragmented imagery and language to document the progress of the century. And *Keep that Candle Burning Bright and Other Poems* collected the last works of the late Bronwen Wallace.

Biography and memoirs. One of the year's most talked about books was John Sawatsky's *Mulroney: The Politics of Ambition,* an exhaustively researched, unflattering biography of Canada's prime minister. *By Heart: Elizabeth Smart, A Life,* by poet, critic, and anthologist Rosemary Sullivan, was a sympathetic biography of the eccentric author of the feminist classic *By Grand Central Station I Sat Down and Wept.*

In *Zero Hour,* poet Kristjana Gunnars told the story of her father's death from a brain tumor. Lorne MacDonald's *Poor Polidori* illuminated a figure on the fringes of the famous circle of 19th-century romantic poets. In *Citizens Irving,* John DeMont took a critical look at one of the leading families in New Brunswick business. *The Danger Tree* by David MacFarlane re-created the history of the Goodyears of Newfoundland, the author's colorful relatives.

Politics. Canada's national-unity crisis also precipitated a deluge of titles on the future of Canada, many of them reflecting urgent concerns about the possible breakup of the nation. A flurry of books surfaced regarding the free-trade agreement between Canada and the United States.

Maude Barlow published two selections: *Parcel of Rogues: How Free Trade Is Failing Canada,* and (with co-author Bruce Campbell) *Take Back the Nation.* In *The Quick and the Dead,* journalist Linda McQuaig scrutinized globalization, free trade, the deficit, and the future of Canada's social programs. *Deconfederation*, by David Bercuson and Barry Cooper, speculated on various types of relations into which Canada and Quebec might enter. *The Unmaking of Canada* by Robert Chodis, Rae Murphy, and Eric Hamovitch and *The Betrayal of Canada* by Mel Hurtig, looked at Canada's relations with the United States.

Social issues. Several important books dealt with women's issues, and even more literature concerned native peoples. The lifelong activist Doris Anderson summed up the progress made by women in 12 Western countries in *The Unfinished Revolution.* In *Rock-A-Bye Baby,* the profile of a doomed young woman who committed suicide in prison, journalists Anne Kershaw and Mary Lasovich focused on how the federal prison system has failed women.

Native writers and native subjects were increasingly prominent in such works as *Occupied Canada* by Robert Hunter and Robert Calihoo; *The Last Stand of the Lubicon Cree* by John Goddard; and *Oka: People of the Pines* by Geoffrey York and Lorreen Pindera. Perhaps the most significant was Thomas Berger's *A Long and Terrible Season,* which assessed centuries of abuse of the original inhabitants of the Americas.

The right of Indians to exclusively publish the stories of their experience continued to be debated in 1991. Books by native people included Beth Brant's *Food & Spirits* and Lee Maracle's *Sojourner's Truth,* stories about being an Indian, a female, and a writer.

History. *Merchant Princes,* the third volume in Peter C. Newman's history of the Hudson Bay Company, ended the social historian's popular series. The many books on war included the late Dan Dancocks' *The D-Day Dodgers* about the Canadian war campaign in Italy between 1943 and 1945.

Awards. The 1990 Governor General's Literary Awards for books in English went to Nino Ricci for *Lives of the Saints* (fiction), Margaret Avison for *No Time* (poetry), Ann-Marie MacDonald for *Goodnight Desdemona (Good Morning Juliet)* (drama), Stephen Clarkson and Christina McCall for *Trudeau and Our Times* (nonfiction), Michael Bedard for *Redwork* (children's literature), and Jane Brierley for *Yellow-Wolf and Other Tales of the Saint Lawrence* (translation)—the English version of *Divers* by Philippe-Joseph Aubert de Gaspe.

The awards for French-language books went to Gerald Tougas for *La Mauvais Foi* (fiction), Jean-Paul Daoust for *Les Cendres bleues* (poetry), Jovette Marchessault for *Le Voyage magnifique d'Emily Carr* (drama), Jean-Francois Lisee for *Dans l'oeil de l'aigle* (nonfiction), Christiane Duchesne for *La Vraie Histoire du chien de Clara Vic* (children's literature), and Charlotte and Robert Melancon for *Le Second Rouleau* (translation), the French version of A. M. Klein's *The Second Scroll.* Maureen Garvie

In ***World Book,*** see **Canadian literature.**

Cape Verde. See **Africa.**

Cat. Ownership of cats in the United States climbed to record numbers in 1991. Statistics developed by MRCA Information Services indicate that the number of pet cats reached about 67 million, up from last year's estimate of 63 million. MRCA also estimates that 34 per cent of U.S. households have a cat, and the average number of cats per household is 2.1.

Because of an increasing number of stray animals, legislators across the country considered ways to avoid pet overpopulation problems. Mandatory spaying and neutering were suggested options.

The number of pedigreed cats registered in 1991 was about equal to 1990 registrations, according to the Cat Fanciers' Association, Incorporated, which registered close to 85,000 purebreds. Persian cats were still the most popular breed.

In 1991, the title of National Best Cat was awarded to Grand Champion Jovan The Legend, a brown tabby exotic shorthair male, bred and owned by Cheryl and Bob Lorditch of Cleona, Pa. The National Best Kitten Award went to Grand Champion Toshika's Secret Desire, a copper-eyed white Persian male, bred and owned by Penny and Gary Nordman of Elkhart, Ind. A blue-cream Persian spay, Grand Champion and Grand Premier Mystichill Mighty High achieved the award of Best Alter. Mighty High was bred by Diane Silverman of Tamarac, Fla., and is owned by Mark Hannon and John Watkins of Alexandria, Va. Thomas H. Dent

In ***World Book,*** see **Cat.**

Census. Controversy swirled in 1991 around the accuracy of the 1990 Census of Population conducted by the United States Bureau of the Census. In April 1991, a Census Bureau survey of 165,000 households estimated that the 1990 census had missed 4 million to 6 million people.

To adjust or not. According to the Census Bureau, blacks and Hispanics are undercounted in higher proportions than the population as a whole, because the bureau has a harder time locating them. Thus, undercounting affects cities with large minority populations that receive state and federal funds based on the census. New York City and several other large cities joined a suit to force the government to correct undercounts. Under the settlement of the suit, the government had to decide by July 1991 whether to adjust the figures according to the post-census survey.

On July 15, Robert A. Mosbacher, then secretary of the Department of Commerce—which includes the Census Bureau—announced that 1990 census figures would not be statistically adjusted to compensate for the estimated undercount. Mosbacher said there was insufficient evidence showing that the adjustments would improve the count's accuracy for most localities. His decision affected the redistribution of seats in the U.S. House of Representatives and state legislatures. The adjustment would have raised New York City's count, for example, by 230,000 people. California and other Western states would also have gained.

In the courts. New York City, Los Angeles, and a number of other cities filed suit to have the adjusted figures officially adopted, but no decision had been reached by the end of 1991. In a separate lawsuit, a federal judge in August ordered the Census Bureau to turn the adjusted figures over to California for use in redrawing its legislative districts. But the Supreme Court of the United States overturned the order in a 6-to-3 ruling in September.

In November, a House of Representatives subcommittee subpoenaed the adjusted figures so that states could use them in legislative redistricting. Congressional Democrats argued that Mosbacher's refusal to adjust was politically motivated because the inner cities, which vote largely Democratic, would have gained legislative seats, while heavily Republican suburbs would have lost. Commerce Department officials argued that the adjusted figures were seriously flawed.

On the move. Nearly 1 in 2 Americans moved from one home to another in the period from 1985 to 1989, according to figures released by the Census Bureau in December 1991. But mobility was expected to slow in the future, in part because of a recession and in part because people in their 20's and 30's—the most mobile generation—now make up a smaller percentage of the U.S. population. Karin C. Rosenberg

See also **City; Population.** In ***World Book,*** see **Census; Population.**

Central African Republic. See **Africa.**

Chad. See **Africa.**

The 1990 Census: An American Self-Portrait

By Karin C. Rosenberg

The latest figures from the United States Bureau of the Census reveal a changing picture of who Americans are and where and how they live.

Every 10 years since 1790, the United States has taken an inventory of its inhabitants known as the Census of Population. The official reason for taking a census is to determine the number of seats each state will fill in the U.S. House of Representatives. But the census serves many other purposes as well. One of its most important functions is to provide a picture of who Americans are and where and how they live. Over the past 200 years, census statistics have measured America's growth and reflected shifts in its living patterns.

For example, census data have charted America's shift from an overwhelmingly rural society to one that is predominantly urban. In 1790, only 1 American in 20 lived in an urban area, defined by the U.S. Bureau of the Census as a town or city of 2,500 or more people. Not until the 1920 census did urban residents overtake rural residents. By 1990, urban residents outnumbered rural residents 3 to 1.

The United States reached another milestone in 1990: For the first time, more than half the U.S. population lived in large metropolitan areas of more than a million people. During the 1980's, these metropolitan areas experienced steady growth on their fringes. As in the past, urban sprawl advanced as people moved to more and more distant suburbs to find affordable housing. At the same time, small towns were disappearing. Nearly three-quarters of U.S. towns with fewer than 2,500 inhabitants lost population during the 1980's, more than in any previous decade.

Another trend the 1990 census spotted was the growth of the suburban city: Of the 29 cities that surpassed the 100,000 population mark for the first time, 22 were suburbs of larger cities. These so-called satellite cities offered jobs as well as shopping and cultural activities. It has become increasingly common for people to both live and work in the suburbs.

Population growth, according to *demographers* (people who study population trends), usually indicates that an area is economically healthy. People tend to stay in or move to areas where jobs are available. And companies that hire new employees generally tend to be profitable.

Since the 1950 census, the Northeastern and Midwestern sections of the United States have grown far more slowly than have the Southern and Western regions. Industrial cities in the North have been hit especially hard, as the heavy industries on which they long depended have become less important to the U.S. economy. At the same time, the South and West have grown phenomenally, picking up nearly 90 per cent of America's population gain in the 1980's.

More than half the U.S. population growth from 1980 to 1990 occurred in just three states—California, Florida, and Texas. By 1990, 1 in 8 Americans lived in California, the nation's most populous state, and California's 29.8 million people surpassed Canada's entire population of 26.3 million. These population shifts foretell a dramatic swing in economic and political power from the Frostbelt to the Sunbelt.

Other shifts recorded by the 1990 census also point toward future social and political directions. For example, America is becoming more ethnically and racially diverse as its minorities increase faster than the population as a whole. By 1990, 1 in 4 Americans considered themselves nonwhite or Hispanic, according to census forms. In 1980, only 1 in 5 did.

This increased diversity also reflects how Americans see themselves. In 1990, the census recorded a big jump in the Native American population, which now numbers 1.8 million, three times its size in 1960. Experts theorize that many people who hid their Indian ancestry in the past now claim it proudly. Questions about Hispanic ancestry first appeared on the 1980 census in response to requests by Hispanic leaders. Hispanics, who make up 9 per cent of the U.S. population, are not considered a separate racial group, however. They may belong to white, black, or Indian racial groups.

A group to watch is the enormous generation born from 1946 through 1964, during the so-called baby boom. Baby boomers make up nearly a third of the nation's people and exert a powerful influence on American society. When they were young, during the 1960's and 1970's, they gave America the youth culture, the antiwar movement, and the phrase "Never trust anyone over 30." Baby boomers by 1990 had begun to enter middle age, and the nation has become preoccupied with health and fitness.

But the fastest-growing generation during the 1980's was age 65 and older. By 1990, a record number of Americans—12.5 per cent of the population—were retirement age. Demographers expect growth of this group to slow in the 1990's, however, when people born during the Great Depression of the 1930's begin to turn 65. Birth rates plunged during the depression as people's expectations for the future fell.

Getting the numbers

In March 1990, the Bureau of the Census mailed out nearly 90 million census forms to addresses across America. Much effort had gone into compiling the address lists, largely through purchases from firms that specialize in drawing up mailing lists. Census takers and postal workers dropped off census forms at millions of additional households, mainly those in rural areas without street addresses. In all, more than 100 million homes across American received 1990 census forms.

The Census Bureau prints two kinds of questionnaires. About 5 out of 6 households receive a short form with 14 questions. Half the questions ask about the age, sex, ancestry, marital status, and relationship of the household's residents. The other half relate to housing conditions, such as the number of rooms in a dwelling and whether the dwelling is owned or rented. Only 1 household in 6 receives a long form that asks 19 additional questions; for example, what kind of work the residents do; how they commute to work; and what, if any, disabilities they have.

The forms were due back on April 1. Processing began immediately, with clerical workers and computers checking forms for completeness. Census takers made follow-up telephone calls to obtain any missing information, such as children's ages. They also phoned or visited those who failed to return census forms. Neighbors were sometimes interviewed to obtain information on absent residents. Finally, local governments had an opportunity to review counts and to identify discrepancies between census lists and local records.

To achieve as accurate a count as possible, in 1990 the Census Bureau made its first effort ever to include Americans who have no homes. On the night of March 20, 1990, census takers in cities across the nation counted people spending the night in shelters for the homeless or sleeping in doorways, parks, abandoned buildings, and other such places. Census officials emphasized that the homeless count of 229,000 was far from inclusive, though it marked a start in the difficult task of locating the nation's homeless.

Once the census forms were completed, cameras photographed them on microfilm, and optical scanning devices transferred the information on the film to a computer tape. Computers then tabulated the information. The Census Bureau began releasing complete counts as they became available. But all the information from the long forms was not due out before late 1993.

Changes in smaller groups also emerge from census data. In 1790, U.S. families had an average of nearly six members. An average U.S. household in 1990, with 2.63 people, was less than half that size. Moreover, today's households are far less likely than ever before to consist of a married couple and their children. Before 1990, this traditional family group had always outnumbered other types of households in the United States. But the 1990 census found that married couples who lived without children—either because they had none or because their children were grown—formed the nation's most common household unit.

As households have shrunk in size, their number has proliferated. Divorce has created additional, smaller households, as has the tendency of young people to live alone and marry late. All these new households have required new housing, which for some years fueled the construction industry and real estate market.

The census breaks down population information by age, sex, and language, among other factors. Such information helps urban planners determine where to locate new schools, roads, hospitals, housing, and other facilities. Knowing how many Spanish-speaking preschoolers live in a particular school district, for example, could help school boards set hiring policies for teachers and decide where new elementary schools are needed. Similarly, a jump in a community's elderly population may indicate a need for more hospitals and public transportation. Some small towns seek to offset population losses by recruiting residents from America's many retirees, offering them a crime-free, low-cost place to live.

Businesses use census data to identify markets for their products or services. Many businesses would like to cash in on the enormous baby-boom market now approaching middle age. Opticians can expect to profit as baby boomers require reading glasses. Publishers may target this generation with more magazines that offer information on health and fitness or advice on investments. Other businesses have looked at the nation's expanding ethnic diversity to find new markets. For example, large cosmetics firms that previously targeted only whites have announced plans to bring out new lines aimed at blacks and Hispanics.

The most important uses of the census, however, go beyond spotting trends. Population figures determine how much federal funding the states and cities receive for such crucial budget items as education, public transportation, housing, and poverty programs. Poor Americans—those who depend most heavily on government-funded programs—abound in large U.S. cities. Yet the urban poor are also the people most likely to go uncounted by the census. Because undercounting can mean cuts in government funding, census results matter greatly to cities and states.

In 1790—three years after its Constitution was written—the United States became the first country to establish a complete, periodic census. Once America had introduced representative government, that government needed to know whom it represented. For 200 years, the census has provided a self-portrait of America and a foundation for government by the people.

Americans on the move

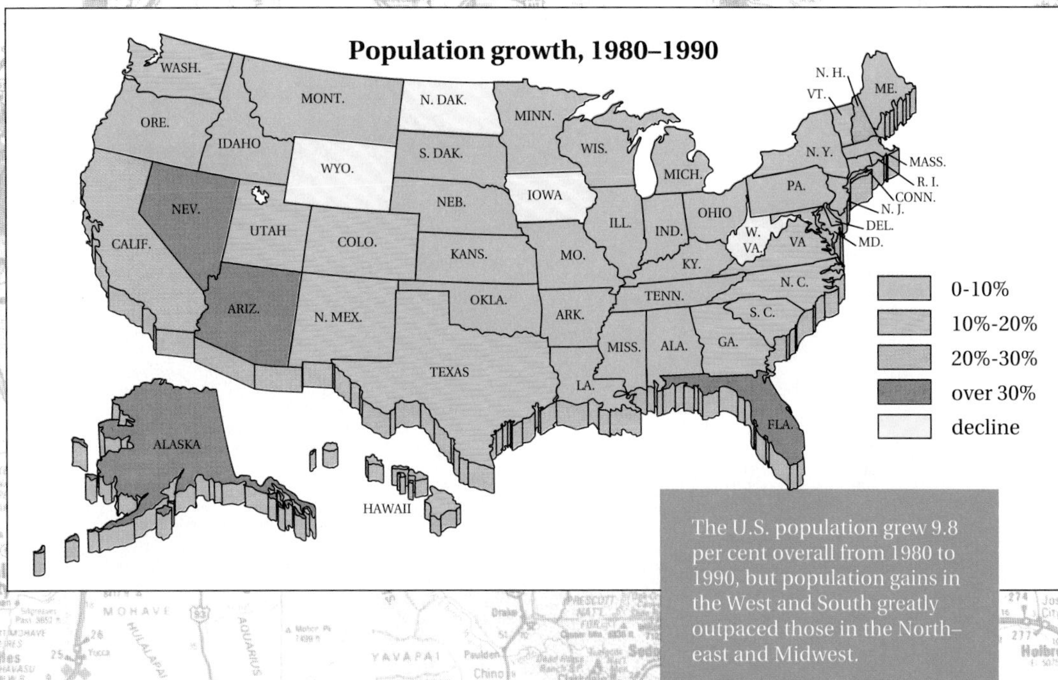

The U.S. population grew 9.8 per cent overall from 1980 to 1990, but population gains in the West and South greatly outpaced those in the Northeast and Midwest.

Biggest gainers and losers among major cities

As Americans trekked West and South during the 1980's, Sunbelt cities swelled and some large industrial cities, especially in the East and Midwest, shrank in population.

Gainers		Losers	
Orlando, Fla.	+53.3%	Pittsburgh, Pa	-7.4%
Phoenix	+40.6%	Buffalo, N.Y.	-4.3%
Sacramento, Calif	+34.7%	Cleveland	-2.6%
San Diego	+34.2%	Detroit	-1.8%
Dallas-Fort Worth	+32.6%	New Orleans	-1.4%
Atlanta, Ga.	+32.5%		

Biggest gainers and losers among the states

Nevada tallied the largest percentage gain of any state during the 1980's. With its small population, however, Nevada needed only 400,000 more people to register its dramatic 50 per cent spurt. The states that lost population depend heavily on farming or mining, two economic activities that suffered during the 1980's.

Gainers		Losers	
Nevada	+50.4%	West Virginia	-8.0%
Alaska	+37.4%	Iowa	-4.7%
Arizona	+34.9%	Wyoming	-3.7%
Florida	+32.8%	North Dakota	-2.1%
California	+25.8%		
New Hampshire	+20.5%		

The new American mix

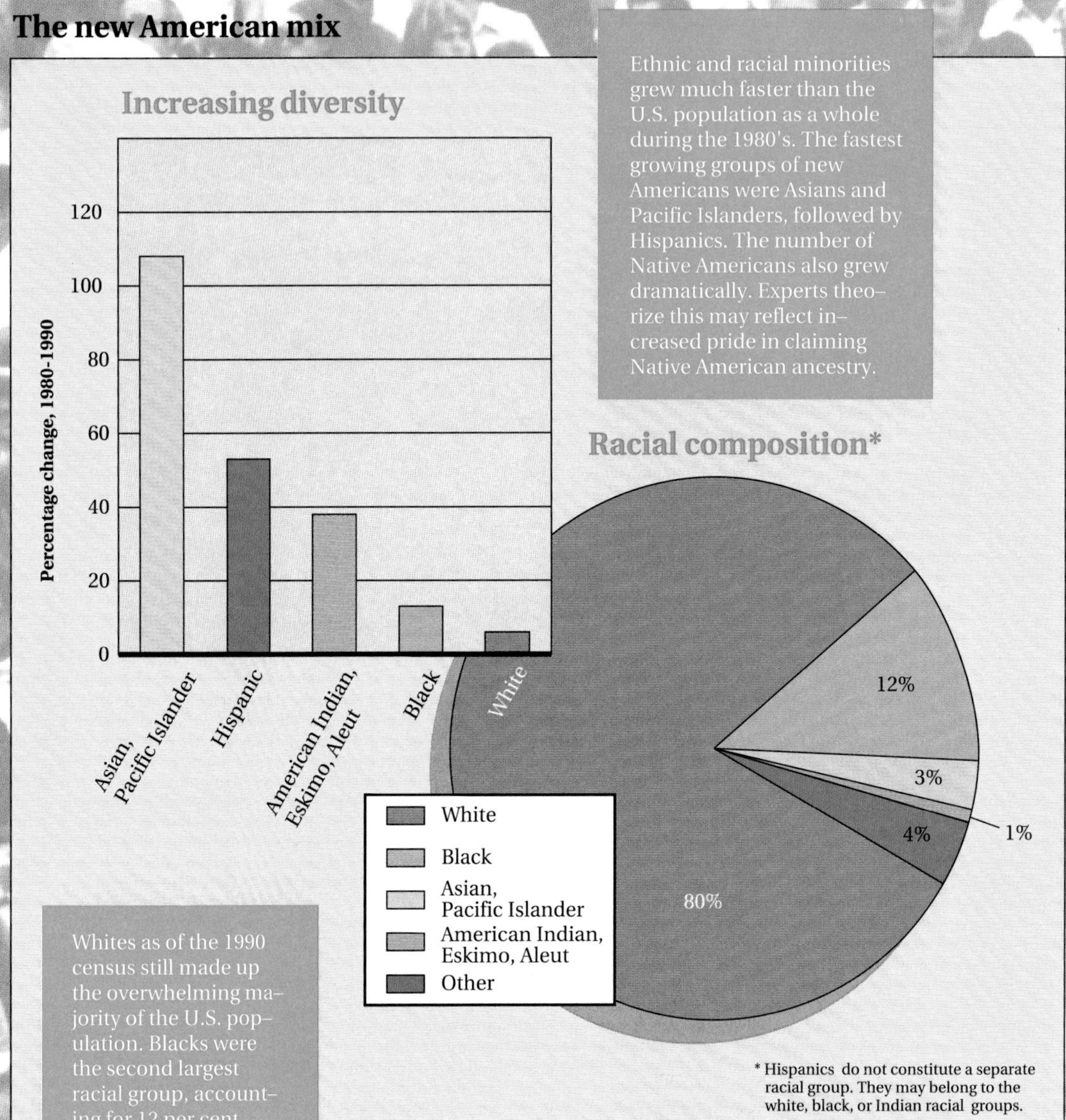

Ethnic and racial minorities grew much faster than the U.S. population as a whole during the 1980's. The fastest growing groups of new Americans were Asians and Pacific Islanders, followed by Hispanics. The number of Native Americans also grew dramatically. Experts theorize this may reflect increased pride in claiming Native American ancestry.

Whites as of the 1990 census still made up the overwhelming majority of the U.S. population. Blacks were the second largest racial group, accounting for 12 per cent.

* Hispanics do not constitute a separate racial group. They may belong to the white, black, or Indian racial groups.

Who is coming to America

Until the mid–1950's, America's immigrants arrived primarily from Europe. By 1990, at least 4 out of 5 U.S. immigrants came from non–European countries. Nearly 1 in 4 Americans claimed some African, Asian, Hispanic, or American Indian ancestry in 1990, up from 1 in 5 in 1980.

Fast–growing ethnic groups

Vietnamese	+135%
Asian Indians	+126%
Chinese	+104%
Filipinos	+ 82%
Mexicans	+ 54%
Puerto Ricans	+ 35%

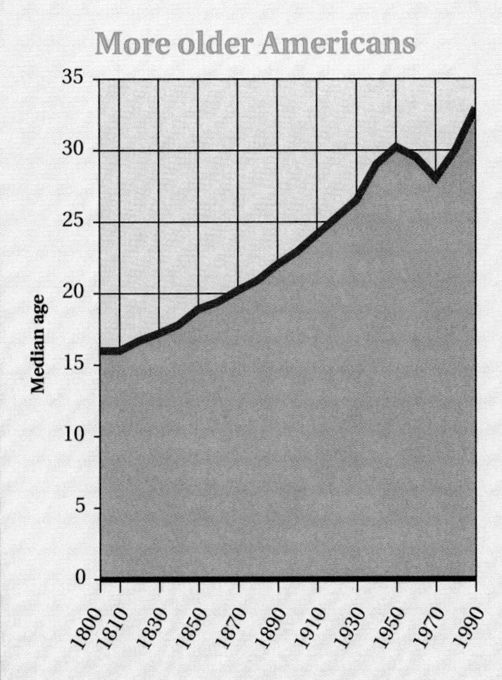

The median age in the United States was 32.9 in 1990, which meant that half the population was older than that and half was younger. In 1800, when the U.S. census first asked people's age, the median age was 16. The median age has risen partly because people live longer and partly because families have fewer children to add to the very young population of the United States.

The baby boom generation (born between 1946 and 1964), makes up nearly a third of the U.S. population. In the 1960's, this group, under age 25, was responsible for the "youth culture." But by 1990, the "boomers" were 26 to 44 years old and headed toward middle age.

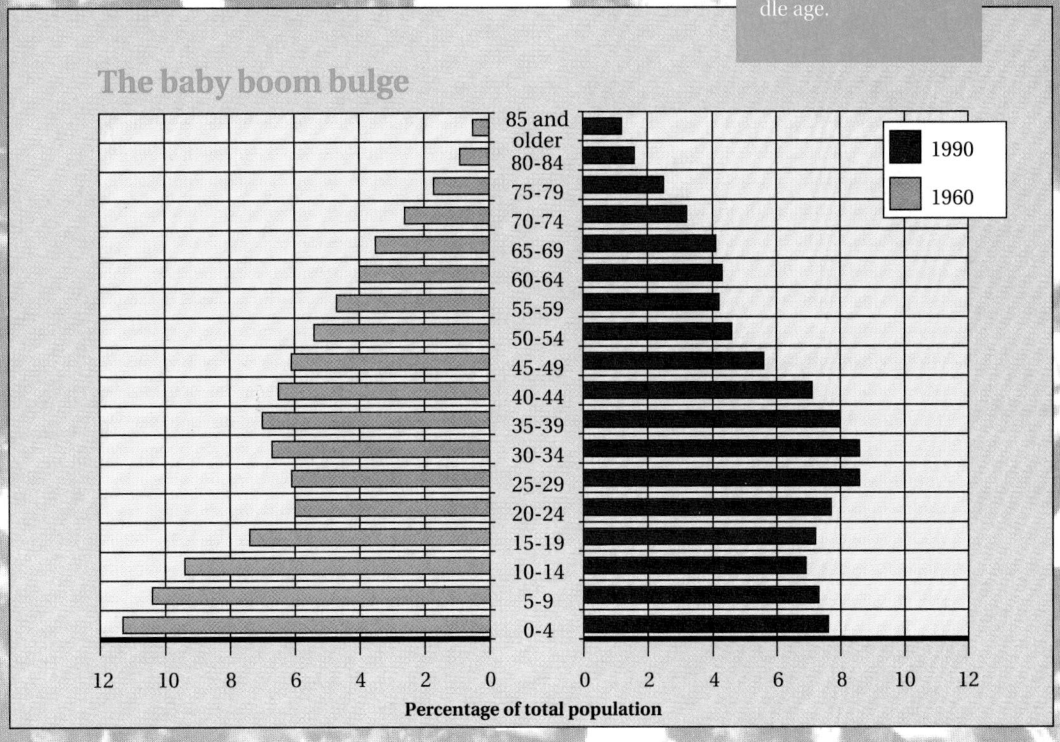

How Americans live

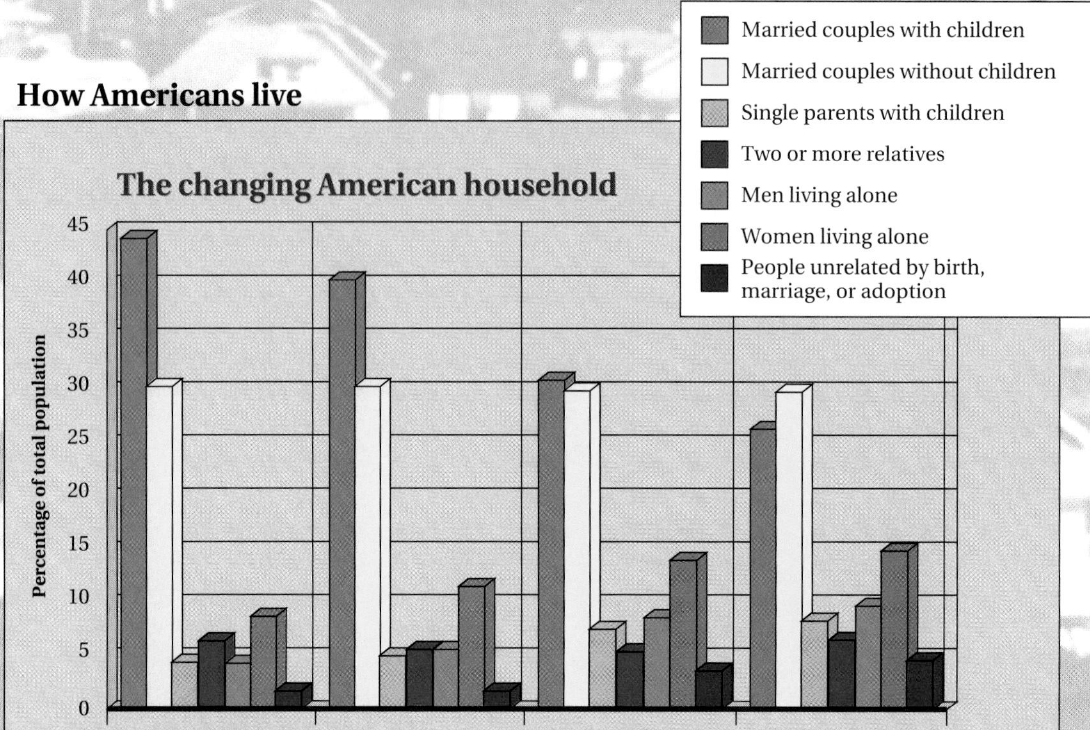

Fewer Americans lived in traditional households–married couples with children–in 1990 than at any time in the past. The most common type of household was a married couple without children or whose children were grown. The number of "nontraditional" households has increased as people marry later, live alone longer, delay having children, and divorce more often.

Marrying later

The average age at which Americans first marry reached its highest level this century in 1990–26.1 years for men, 23.9 years for women. The marriage age has steadily risen since a low in 1956 of 22.5 years for men and 20.1 for women.

The ratio of divorced Americans to married Americans quadrupled from 1960 to 1990. Divorced people who have not remarried made up 8 per cent of the total U.S. population in 1990. More women than men were divorced because men were more likely to remarry.

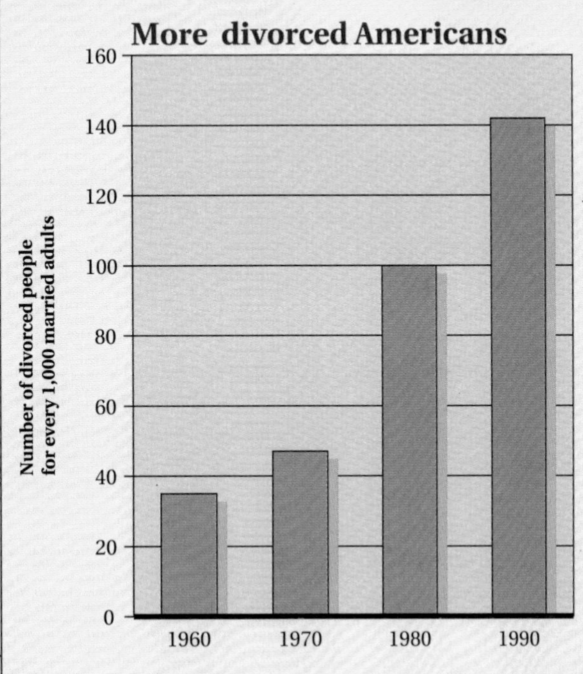

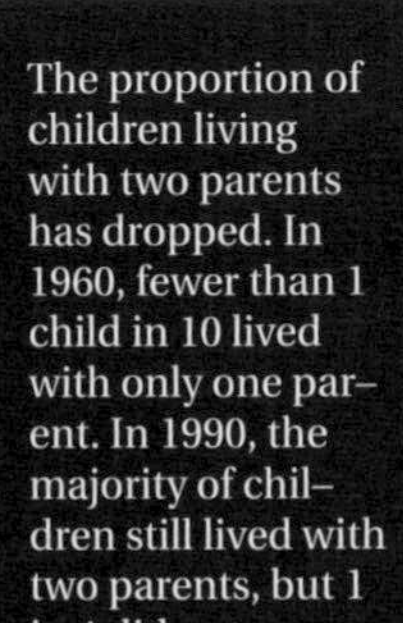

The proportion of children living with two parents has dropped. In 1960, fewer than 1 child in 10 lived with only one parent. In 1990, the majority of children still lived with two parents, but 1 in 4 did not.

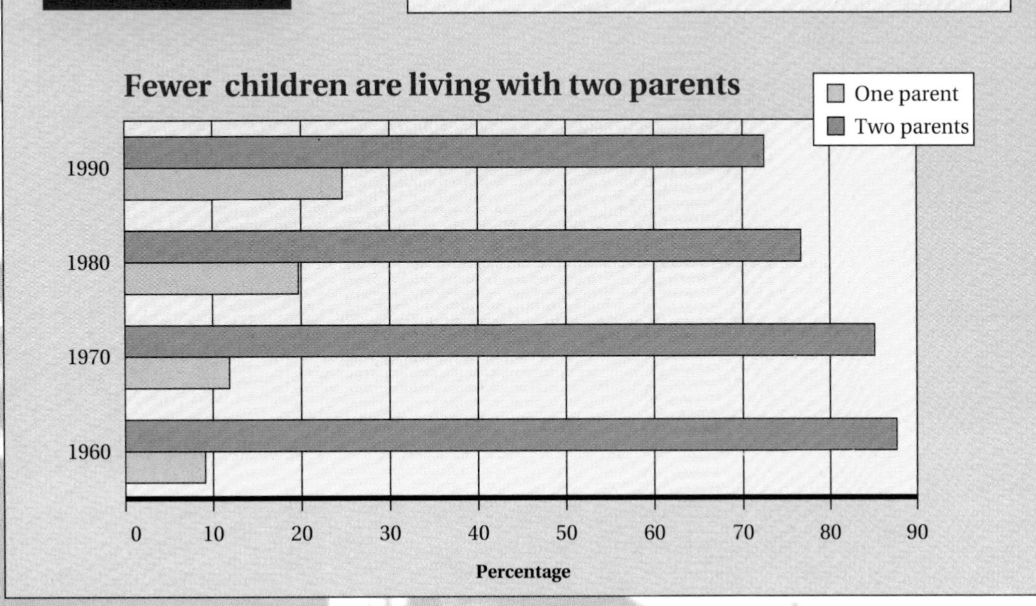

Uses of the census

Congressional representation

The official reason for taking a census, as stipulated by the Constitution of the United States, is to determine the number of seats each state will fill in the House of Representatives. After each census, House seats are *reapportioned* (redistributed) on the basis of population. Because the total number of House seats is fixed at 435, one state's gain means another state's loss. Every state must have at least one representative, however.

After the 1990 census, 13 states lost a total of 19 seats, and 8 states gained those seats. California was the biggest winner, picking up 7 seats for a 52-seat total, the largest number of House seats any state has ever held. New York was the biggest loser, giving up 3 seats.

The Bureau of the Census also provides each state with a block-by-block count of its residents. The states use these counts to make sure that all legislative districts within the state contain an approximately equal number of people. If districts have unequal representation, their boundaries must be redrawn before the 1992 congressional elections.

All states not listed below kept the same number of seats in the House.

States that gained seats:

California	+7
Florida	+4
Texas	+3
Arizona	+1
Georgia	+1
North Carolina	+1
Virginia	+1
Washington	+1

States that lost seats:

New York	-3
Illinois	-2
Michigan	-2
Ohio	-2
Pennsylvania	-2
Iowa	-1
Kansas	-1
Kentucky	-1
Louisiana	-1
Massachusetts	-1
Montana	-1
New Jersey	-1
West Virginia	-1

Other uses for the census

Federal, state, and local governments use census data to assign funds for education, welfare programs, and other services. Plans for schools, housing, transportation routes, and other facilities are based on information in the census. Businesses use the census to target markets for their products or services. Historians trace the growth of the United States by analyzing census data.

Magnified millions of times, 60-atom carbon molecules look like eggs in a crate. The bonds between the atoms form hexagons and pentagons (inset).

Chemistry. The process in nature that produces bones, teeth, sea shells, and other hard tissues was successfully mimicked in the laboratory, chemists reported in January 1991. Despite the importance of this process, known as *biomineralization*, much about its chemistry remains a puzzle.

During biomineralization, *organic polymers*—long, chainlike molecules containing carbon—combine with inorganic substances, such as calcium, to produce a composite material. The organic polymers—similar to those found in plastics—provide a flexible framework for the resulting composite. The inorganic crystals embedded in the composite give it strength.

Mimicking nature. Patricia A. Bianconi, a chemist at Pennsylvania State University in University Park, and her colleagues *synthesized* (created in a laboratory) a composite, achieving a high degree of control over the size, shape, and placement of the inorganic crystals—features that are key to biomineralization in nature. They used a compound called polyethylene oxide as the organic polymer and cadmium chloride as the inorganic component.

Bianconi chose an organic polymer that could draw in inorganic compounds and then bind them tightly. The process yielded a composite that contained cubic crystals of cadmium sulfite with a uniform size.

Because natural composites are strong and fracture resistant, insights into biomineralization promise breakthroughs in materials synthesis. Scientists hope to use the process to make tough, flexible materials with specific magnetic, electronic, or optical properties. Cadmium sulfite, for example, is a semiconductor and might be used in electronic or optical devices.

Little drips. How small can a drop of water be and still act like a drop? According to a computer model developed at the University of Pennsylvania, drops containing fewer than 100 molecules act just like raindrops with a quintillion molecules. Chemists Joseph Hauptman and Michael L. Klein reported in October that the behavior of these microscopic drops depends on the material they are touching. On electrically charged surfaces, the water flattens out. On electrically neutral surfaces, it beads up. The more the water beads up, the greater the angle at which it contacts a surface and the less it wets the material it touches.

The "wettability" of materials interests scientists for various reasons. Wettability governs the application of glues, paints, and other industrial liquids. In addition, wettability is a critical factor in developing polymers that can be moistened for use in such devices as contact lenses and artificial heart valves.

Target practice. Chemists at the University of California in Berkeley announced in April that they had developed a way of helping the body's immune system identify and attack a virus in disguise. Viruses have a variety of strategies for evading the immune system. Some viruses, for example, constantly change their outer protein coats. Other viruses adopt camouflage, covering themselves with molecules commonly found in their host. Peter G. Schultz and Kevan M. Shokat reported that they had managed to paste a molecular target on a piece of an invading virus. Once the molecular target was in place, the immune system could fight back.

The chemists chose *human immunodeficiency virus* (HIV), the virus that causes AIDS, as the invader in one test. Like a "virus of a thousand faces," HIV adopts a variety of disguises to evade detection. But even HIV has features it cannot vary. One such feature scientists call gp120. The immune system cannot find gp120, however, because it is situated deep within a cleft in the virus, beyond the reach of *antibodies* (disease-fighting molecules produced by the immune system).

To solve this problem, the researchers created a three-piece molecule that hooked up with gp120 and that antibodies could home in on. For the first piece of their target, the "paste" that would bind to gp120, the chemists used a proteinlike compound. The second piece was a chain of four linked molecules that can dip into the cleft and tether the molecule to gp120. The third piece was an *antigen,* a molecule or piece of a molecule that the immune system recognizes as foreign and attacks. Because the antigen acts as the actual target, the chemists chose a molecule widely recognized by the immune system, dinitrobenzene.

The combined molecule they built bound to the gp120 and drew to itself antibodies that attack dinitrobenzene. The scientists next planned to test the combined molecules in HIV-infected white blood cells. If effective, such targeting may add to the arsenal of weapons physicians can wield against organisms that adopt disguises.

It computes. A process for synthesizing thousands of related chemical compounds simultaneously was announced by chemists at Affymax Research Institute in Palo Alto, Calif., in February. The process, reported by Stephen P. A. Fodor and his colleagues, borrows techniques developed for the manufacture of computer chips. It could speed up drug studies by rapidly producing new compounds for testing.

Computer chips are made by a process called photolithography. First, a piece of material is coated with a compound that reacts to light. To form a pattern on the reacting surface, light passes through a pattern masked on a screen, much as ink passes through a stencil. This pattern is the electric circuit on the chip.

In the Affymax process, the pattern directs the addition of new chemicals in separate squares on a surface, much like a tiny checkerboard. After chemical synthesis occurs, the compounds can be tested directly on the surface for such properties as how well they bind to antibodies. The Affymax chemists performed a 10-step synthesis that produced more than 1,000 distinct peptides, which form the basis for many important drugs. Peter J. Andrews

In *World Book,* see **Chemistry.**

Chess. Elimination matches to determine who will challenge the overall world champion Garry Kasparov, 28, of the former Soviet Union, began in 1991. At year's end, four grandmaster challengers remained in contention: former world champion Anatoly Karpov, 40, and Artur Yusupov, 31, both of the former Soviet Union; Jan Timman, 40, of the Netherlands; and Nigel Short, 26, of Great Britain. The four were scheduled to play a series of elimination matches in 1992, with the sole surviving challenger to meet Kasparov in a 24-game match to be held in Los Angeles in autumn 1993.

Twenty-year-old Xie Jun of the People's Republic of China became the seventh women's world champion on Nov. 2, 1991. She defeated the 30-year-old reigning champion, Maya Chiburdanidze of the former Soviet Union, in a match held in Manila, the capital of the Philippines. Chiburdanidze had held the women's title for 13 years. Xie Jun was scheduled to meet the survivor of elimination tournaments and matches held throughout 1992 in a championship match, like the overall championship, in Los Angeles in 1993.

U.S. championships. Gata Kamsky, 17, of New York City, won the U.S. Championship in Los Angeles on Aug. 9, 1991. He was the youngest player to win the championship since Bobby Fischer did so at age 14 in 1958. Irina Levitina of Teaneck, N.J., and Esther Epstein of Brookline, Mass., became U.S. women's co-champions in Highland Beach, Fla., on Aug. 25, 1991.

Other tournaments. Kamsky won the World Open, beating out more than 1,200 other hopefuls from around the world, on July 7 in Philadelphia. Alexander Goldin, 26, of Russia, won the New York Open on March 31.

Younger players. The World Student Team Championship, held in Maringa, Brazil, ended on September 13 with a gold medal for the Soviet team. The U.S. team won the silver, while a determined Argentine team took the bronze.

On June 24, Alex Sherzer, 20, of Fallston, Md., won the U.S. Junior Championship, while Vadim Tsemekman, 17, of Southfield, Mich., won the U.S. Junior Open. Both events were held at Illinois Wesleyan University in Bloomington, Ill.

A record-breaking total of more than 2,700 players competed in the national school team championships held throughout the United States each spring. Fuller Elementary School of Tempe, Ariz., won the national elementary school team championship held in Rye, N.Y., from April 26 to 28. Masterman School of Philadelphia won the ninth-grade-and-under championship, while Metcalf Junior High of Burnsville, Minn., won the eighth-grade-and-under championship. Both events were held from April 12 to 14 in Dearborn, Mich. Cleveland Heights School of Cleveland won the high school championship, held from May 3 to 5 in Atlanta, Ga. Al Lawrence

In *World Book,* see **Chess.**

Chicago Mayor Richard M. Daley and his family celebrate Daley's reelection as mayor of Chicago on April 2 with 71 per cent of the vote.

Chicago. Richard M. Daley won reelection as mayor of Chicago on April 2, 1991, with 71 per cent of the vote. Daley easily defeated R. Eugene Pincham, a former judge and the leader of the Harold Washington Party—named for Chicago's first black mayor, who died in 1987. Pincham received 25 per cent of the vote. Republican George Gottlieb got only 4 per cent. By year-end, however, fiscal problems in Chicago's government and schools and a continued increase in violent crime had eroded some of Daley's popularity.

Daley, elected mayor in a special election in April 1989, also had won handily in the Democratic primary held on Feb. 26, 1991. He garnered 63 per cent of the vote compared with 31 per cent for Danny K. Davis, a former City Council member from Chicago's West Side, and 6 per cent for former Mayor Jane M. Byrne.

Budget. On November 20, the City Council approved a $3.24-billion "everybody suffers" budget for 1992 that included $84 million in new taxes. Daley said the taxes were needed to offset the effects of a national recession. He said the city sought to maintain spending on social programs and to pay for wage increases for city workers, due in 1992. Daley also raised property taxes by $25 million, which he had previously promised not to do.

Schools. The city's budget problems were mild compared with those of Chicago's Board of Education, whose members spent much of 1991 trying to avoid a shortfall originally estimated at $315 million for 1991 and $500 million for 1992. On July 3, 1991, Superintendent Ted D. Kimbrough announced plans to close eight elementary and eight high schools, triggering protests that later caused the board to cancel some of the proposed cuts. A threatened teachers' strike in mid-November was averted by the promise of a 3 per cent raise.

Census. On July 15, the United States Bureau of the Census reaffirmed its final count of the city's population for 1990—2,783,726, or 7 per cent below the 1980 total of 3,005,072. City officials claimed the bureau missed 236,000 people, an oversight they said would cost the city nearly $1 billion in federal funds during the 1990's.

Electricity franchise. On October 22, the Daley administration announced a proposed 29-year renewal of the city's electrical service franchise agreement with the Commonwealth Edison Company (ComEd). The agreement ended years of controversy over whether the city should buy ComEd's distribution lines and run its own electrical utility. Initially, the City Council demanded that ComEd abide by Chicago's ambitious quotas for hiring minority and female subcontractors. But under pressure from Daley and ComEd, the council backed down and approved the original agreement on December 11.

Homicides. A lethal mix of drugs, gangs, and hot weather made August the deadliest month in the city's history, with 120 homicides. Murders occurred at the rate of one every 10 hours throughout the year, pushing the annual total to 923.

Corruption trials. The three-year-old Operation Greylord probe of judicial corruption drew to a close on December 30 after producing convictions of 15 former or sitting Cook County judges and about 70 lawyers, court staff, sheriff's deputies, and police officers. On January 9, 10 soybean traders were convicted on corruption charges in the two-year-old probe of futures traders at the Chicago Board of Trade and the Chicago Mercantile Exchange. But the trials of 12 other traders ended with acquittals or hung juries. Former Cook County Judge David J. Shields and Pasquale "Pat" De Leo, a politically connected lawyer, were convicted of bribery on September 24 under Operation Gambat, a federal investigation of organized crime's influence on Chicago politics.

New stadiums. On April 18, the Chicago White Sox played their first game at the new $150-million Comiskey Park. While they were losing 16-0 to the Detroit Tigers, demolition proceeded on old Comiskey Park, which had been baseball's oldest stadium. The Chicago Plan Commission on September 12 approved a proposal by the owners of the Black Hawks hockey team and Bulls basketball team to build an indoor arena on the West Side to replace the 62-year-old Chicago Stadium. John F. McCarron

In ***World Book,*** see **Chicago.**

Children's books. See **Literature for children.**

Chile. Chile's economy benefited in 1991 from the peaceful settlement of labor disputes and the decision by a rebel group to work within the system. These developments helped attract substantial new foreign business investment.

In July and August, respectively, strikes at Chuquicamata, the world's largest open-pit copper mine, and at El Teniente, the world's largest underground copper mine, were settled peacefully. In both cases the government-operated mines made concessions to miners, including bonuses for returning to work.

Rebels disarm. With guarantees of amnesty, rebels of the Manuel Rodríquez Patriot Front laid down their weapons on May 31 and formed a legal political organization. Their action eased fears of a recurrence of the violence that shook the nation in March and April, when unknown assailants killed four political figures, including Jaime Guzman, a prominent senator.

Assassination arrest. On September 23, Chile arrested the former head of its secret police, General Juan Manuel Contreras Sepúlveda, in connection with the 1976 assassination of the former Chilean ambassador to the United States, Orlando Letelier. Letelier died in a car bomb explosion in Washington, D.C. Contreras served as head of Chile's secret police from 1973 to 1977. Nathan A. Haverstock

See also **Latin America** (Facts in brief table). In ***World Book,*** see **Chile.**

China improved its relations with several important nations during 1991. This improvement followed a period of strained international relations which began in June 1989, when Chinese soldiers killed hundreds of pro-democracy demonstrators in Beijing, China's capital. Despite lessening tensions with other nations in 1991, however, the Chinese government continued to jail dissidents. The country also continued to drift economically and politically as its elderly leaders remained divided on basic policies.

Foreign relations. In August, then Japanese Prime Minister Toshiki Kaifu became the first leader of a major industrial country to visit China since 1989. Britain's Prime Minister John Major arrived in China on Sept. 2, 1991. Although he was criticized at home for making the trip, Major argued that the best way to improve China's poor human-rights record was through personal pressure. He asked Chinese Premier Li Peng to look into the cases of jailed dissidents.

China strengthened ties to other countries as well. Foreign Minister Qian Qichen visited eastern and western Europe in February and March. On May 14, Jiang Zemin, the general secretary of China's Communist Party, became the first Chinese party leader to visit Moscow since a 1957 trip made by Mao Zedong, Communist China's founder. Jiang' s visit signaled the restoration of relations between the world's two largest Communist parties, which had been bitterly divided since the early 1960's. But the reconciliation came at a time when Communist Party control and the party itself was disintegrating in the Soviet Union.

The visit came after China had agreed on March 15, 1991, to make "a favorable commodity loan" to the Soviet Union worth $733 million. At the time of Mao's 1957 trip, China was dependent upon Moscow for economic aid. But Moscow abruptly ended aid in 1960 out of fear of Chinese competition for world Communist leadership. By 1991, the Chinese economy was functioning better than the Soviet one, despite China's low standard of living and more than $45 billion in foreign debts. China supplied consumer goods to the Soviet Union and bought some Soviet weapons.

Despite improved relations with the Soviet Union, however, China's leaders remained suspicious of Soviet political reform. They quickly voiced support for the August attempt to overthrow the government of Mikhail S. Gorbachev. When the coup failed, Chinese leaders feared that China might be affected by the Soviet examples of public defiance of authority, and they ordered a tightening of Communist controls and more political indoctrination in their own country.

Relations with the United States were strained in 1991 by trade problems and human rights issues. In July, the U.S. Senate and House of Representatives passed separate bills to require China to meet international standards in human rights and in trading practices in order to continue to receive most-favored-nation trade terms from the United States. But Congress was unable to agree on a single bill by year's end.

President George Bush threatened to veto any bill that denied most-favored-nation trade status to China. However, Bush announced on May 27 that the United States would not sell China certain parts for computers and communications satellites, due to reports that China had exported nuclear technology to Algeria, Pakistan, and other countries.

The United States announced on October 10 that it was investigating Chinese restrictions on importing American products. Largely because of such restrictions, China had a trade advantage of $13 billion with the United States in 1991. China claimed it was moving to correct the imbalance. It also said it would stop the export of goods made in prisons. The United States, which banned the importation of prison-made goods from any country, had protested that China was disguising the origin of such products.

Secretary of State James A. Baker III visited China from November 15 to 17. After their talks with Baker, Chinese leaders agreed to restrict the sale of certain weapons to other countries. The Chinese refused, however, to ease their harsh policies on human rights.

China's neighbors. The Chinese government improved relations with Vietnam in 1991, but some tensions remained. Vietnam's Communist Party leader Do Muoi and Prime Minister Vo Van Kiet visited China in November to end the hostility existing between the two countries since they fought a border war in 1979. North Korean President Kim Il-song toured China in October. He apparently sought aid for his declining economy but was reported not to have gotten any.

Human rights. Most of the trials of students and intellectuals who had taken part in the June 1989 demonstrations were completed in early 1991. The president of the Supreme People's Court, Ren Jianxin, said on April 3 that more than 770 persons had been prosecuted for what was labeled a counter-revolutionary rebellion centered in Beijing. The United States estimated that more than 1,000 Chinese dissidents had been imprisoned. Most of the known sentences were between 2 and 7 years, but some dissidents were given prison terms of 15 years or more.

Chinese leaders allowed human rights organizations from Australia, the United States, and other countries to visit. China assured the organizations that conditions were improving. However, Communist leader Jiang said on May 1 that "we should build a Great Wall of iron" to keep out ideas that might weaken Communist doctrine. On September 13, officials expelled a British journalist who had written about a police crackdown on ethnic Mongolians in a region of Inner Mongolia where the influx of ethnic Chinese had reduced Mongolians to a minority.

Government changes. The annual meeting of China's parliament, the National People's Congress, ended on April 8 with two promotions. Zou Jiahua, the head of the State Planning Commission, was given the title of vice premier. Zhu Rongji, who as mayor of Shanghai was noted for his efforts to liberalize the city's economy, also became a vice premier.

Zhu's promotion was widely attributed to Deng Xiaoping. The 87-year-old Deng remained the key figure among the aged leaders who still dominated Chinese politics in 1991. Deng, a supporter of economic reform, apparently thought of Zhu as a possible successor to the conservative premier, Li Peng.

Economic problems. The elderly leaders could not agree among themselves on important policies. They argued throughout 1991 about the pace and direction of economic reform without giving clear directions to the officials responsible for daily affairs.

On March 25, Premier Li presented to parliament China's eighth 5-year economic development plan and a 10-year "development strategy." He called for some expansion of free enterprise but warned that any attempt to weaken Communist political control would not be permitted. The new programs contained few specific solutions to economic problems, reflecting the unresolved disputes among the leaders over whether to loosen state economic controls in order to encourage individual initiative.

Li said that food output was not increasing as fast as the population, that state-owned factories made many unnecessary goods, and that there had been little economic progress in the previous decade. He also warned, however, against any attempts to move faster in efforts to liberalize the economy.

Nevertheless, there were a few signs of economic progress in 1991. While unemployment grew in densely populated interior areas, such as Sichuan Province, many jobless workers migrated to the southeastern coastal area. In that region, investment from Taiwan, Hong Kong, and ethnic Chinese living abroad created a boom in factories producing export goods.

Higher defense spending was announced by Finance Minister Wang Bingqian. Despite a growing budget deficit and disputes between the central government and the provinces over taxes, military spending rose nearly 12 per cent. This was the second big increase the army had been awarded since it crushed the 1989 demonstrations. The Chinese armed forces were worried about falling further behind Western military technology after seeing outmoded Soviet weapons devastated by modern American and European weapons in the Persian Gulf War.

The heaviest rains in a century in the Yangtze River Basin of central and eastern China in July 1991, caused about 2,300 deaths, destroyed or damaged 9 million homes, and affected 220 million people. Total damage was estimated at $13 billion.

Jiang admitted that the government had neglected to maintain the water control systems, thereby leaving the river basin vulnerable to floods. But officials said farmers had failed to maintain drainage channels since 1978 reforms had ended strict government control of agriculture. They also said that the construction of small factories and other structures on levees and floodways had weakened flood control measures.

A growing drug problem. State Councilor Wang Fang said on June 24, 1991, that a recent spread of narcotics had created the worst situation in China since the early 1950's. He called for a "people's war" against drug addiction.

Tibetan demonstrations. On May 23, China celebrated the 40th anniversary of what it called the peaceful liberation of Tibet. Chinese reports described Tibet as a peaceful and prosperous part of China. However, virtual martial law was imposed by thousands of troops on the Tibetan capital, Lhasa, to prevent any recurrence of the demonstrations for independence that have taken place there in recent years.

The anniversary passed peacefully, but three days later demonstrations broke out simultaneously in three parts of Lhasa. Demonstrators who chanted independence slogans and stoned Chinese-owned stores were quickly suppressed by security forces.

Mao Zedong's widow, Jiang Qing, committed suicide on May 14. Jiang had been blamed for many of the widely hated policies imposed during Mao's feeble old age. Five years after Mao died in 1976, she was sentenced to death for crimes against the state, but the sentence was commuted in 1983 to house arrest for life. Jiang had been suffering from cancer when, at age 77, she hanged herself.

Henry S. Bradsher

See also **Asia** (Facts in brief table); **Taiwan.** In ***World Book,*** see **China.**

City. Few cities in the United States had much to celebrate in 1991. A prolonged recession stretched financial resources even thinner than in years past, hampering efforts to combat drugs and crime, and to provide better education, health care, and affordable housing. In July, the National League of Cities issued its annual survey of fiscal conditions in 525 U.S. cities and towns. The survey found that 61 per cent of the cities surveyed anticipated a budget shortfall in 1991. Twenty-six per cent expected the gap between revenues and expenditures to be 5 per cent or more. Overall, more than 70 per cent of cities had financial conditions in 1991 that were worse than in 1990.

Bankrupt city. Few events better dramatized the plight of the nation's older cities than the bankruptcy of Bridgeport, Conn., filed by the city's mayor, Republican Mary C. Moran, on June 6, 1991. She declared that the city, the largest in the state, would be unable to absorb the impact of lagging local tax revenues and severe cutbacks in state aid without gutting the city work force or more than doubling local property taxes. Bridgeport was the first major city since the Great Depression of the 1930's to initiate a bankruptcy action. In August 1991, however, a federal judge ruled that the city "undoubtedly was in deep financial trouble," but that it was not insolvent and not entitled to bankruptcy-law protection.

Finding funds. A majority of U.S. cities were forced to raise local taxes or fees during 1991. These actions were necessary to offset stagnant local revenues, widespread cutbacks in state aid, and a growing list of responsibilities for local governments. The new responsibilities, such as developing ways to control pollution in wastewater and storm runoffs, were usually mandated by federal and state laws and often were passed with little or no funding assistance.

Growing resentment about these "unfunded mandates" as well as other neglected urban priorities led a number of civic leaders to organize marches that demonstrated their frustration. In August, black activist Jesse Jackson led a march from Bridgeport to Hartford, the capital of Connecticut, to evoke concern for the state's hard-pressed cities. In September, Mayor Kurt L. Schmoke of Baltimore led a 39-mile (63-kilometer) "Save Our Cities" march to Washington, D.C. The march concluded with some 3,000 people gathered outside the U.S. Capitol to show their support for a stronger commitment by Congress to domestic urban needs. The U.S. Conference of Mayors planned another, even larger march on Washington, D.C., for April 1992.

Urban ills. The groundswell for a "save our cities" campaign involved more than redirecting national budget priorities. It arose from the concern among city leaders about the problems of drug abuse and drug-related crime; homelessness and the lack of affordable housing; deteriorating infrastructure, such as roads and bridges; and deficiencies in providing child care, health care, or a way out of poverty. The U.S. Bureau of the Census reported in September 1991 that the number of Americans living in poverty increased from 31.5 million in 1989 to 33.6 million people in 1990.

Crime and gun control. Violent crime continued to soar in many cities, often the result of criminals using high-powered weapons in drug-related activities. But gangs and random violence also contributed to the number of injuries and deaths. Such violence led to a congressional battle over gun control in autumn 1991. As the congressional debate got underway, many city leaders and police were pitted against the gun lobby, headed by the National Rifle Association. Local officials and law enforcement agencies wanted to outlaw semiautomatic assault weapons and to require a seven-day waiting period on handgun sales to allow time for a background check on prospective purchasers. The gun lobby opposed both proposals.

On October 16, the same day as the House of Representatives debated legislation to control assault weapons, a man used two semiautomatic pistols to kill 23 people and wound at least 20 others in a cafeteria in Killeen, Tex. He then took his own life. The next day, the House of Representatives defeated the proposal to ban assault weapons.

Congressional action also was stalled on the so-called *Brady bill,* named after former President Ronald Reagan's press secretary, James Brady. Brady was severely wounded in 1981 during an attempt on the

Flames silhouette a fire fighter on the roof of a house in Oakland, Calif., on October 20, when wildfires killed 25 people and left 5,000 homeless.

President's life. The assailant had an illegally obtained handgun. The Brady bill required a five-day waiting period for handgun purchases. It was included in a massive anticrime bill, the Omnibus Crime Control Act of 1991, that was blocked by a Senate filibuster in November.

Mayoral elections. Violent crime and fiscal problems contributed to the defeat of some prominent mayors in 1991. Richard Hackett, mayor of Memphis for eight years, was defeated on October 3. On November 5, Mayor Moran was defeated in Bridgeport. Mayor Kathryn J. Whitmire lost after serving 10 years as mayor of Houston. In a runoff election on December 7, a businessman, Bob Lanier, won the nonpartisan mayoralty. Mayor John Rousakis lost in Savannah, Ga., after holding office for 21 years, and Mayor John Fedo of Duluth, Minn., was defeated after serving 12 years. San Francisco Mayor Art Agnos lost a runoff election on December 10 against Frank Jordan, the city's former police chief.

Frank L. Rizzo, the "tough cop" and former two-term mayor of Philadelphia, died of a heart attack on July 16. He had won the Republican nomination for mayor in May. His death turned a potentially close race into an easy victory for Democrat Edward G. Rendell, a former city prosecutor. A long-standing local law setting a two-term limit prevented Mayor W. Wilson Goode from seeking reelection. And term limits for municipal officials gained public support in such cities as Phoenix; San Antonio; San Jose; New Orleans;

50 largest cities in the United States

Rank	City	Population*	Per cent change in population since 1980	Unemployment rate†	Mayor‡
1.	**New York City**	7,322,564	+3.5	8.8%	David N. Dinkins (D, 12/93)
2.	**Los Angeles**	3,485,398	+17.4	8.6	Tom Bradley (NP, 6/93)
3.	**Chicago**	2,783,726	-7.4	6.2	Richard M. Daley (D, 5/95)
4.	**Houston**	1,630,553	+2.2	6.0	Bob Lanier (NP, 1/94)
5.	**Philadelphia**	1,585,577	-6.1	6.7	Edward G. Rendell (D, 1/96)
6.	**San Diego**	1,110,549	+26.8	7.0	Maureen F. O'Connor (NP, 12/92)
7.	**Detroit**	1,027,974	-14.6	8.9	Coleman A. Young (NP, 12/93)
8.	**Dallas**	1,006,877	+11.3	6.2	Steve Bartlett (NP, 12/95)
9.	**Phoenix**	983,403	+24.5	4.6	George Miller (D, 12/95)
10.	**San Antonio**	935,933	+19.1	7.0	Nelson W. Wolff (NP, 6/93)
11.	**San Jose**	782,248	+24.3	6.2	Susan Hammer (D, 12/94)
12.	**Indianapolis**	741,952	+4.3	5.0	Stephen Goldsmith (R, 12/95)
13.	**Baltimore**	736,014	-6.4	6.2	Kurt L. Schmoke (D, 12/95)
14.	**San Francisco**	723,959	+6.6	5.1	Frank Jordan (NP, 1/96)
15.	**Jacksonville, Fla.**	672,971	+17.9	7.2	T. Ed Austin (D, 7/95)
16.	**Columbus, Ohio**	632,910	+12.0	4.7	Gregory Lashutka (R, 12/95)
17.	**Milwaukee**	628,088	-1.3	4.3	John O. Norquist (D, 4/92)
18.	**Memphis**	610,337	-5.5	5.6	W. W. Herenton (NP, 12/95)
19.	**Washington, D.C.**	606,900	-4.9	4.4	Sharon Pratt Kelly (D, 1/94)
20.	**Boston**	574,283	+2.0	8.2	Raymond L. Flynn (NP, 12/95)
21.	**Seattle**	516,259	+4.5	4.7	Norman B. Rice (NP, 12/93)
22.	**El Paso**	515,342	+21.2	10.8	William S. Tilney (NP, 4/93)
23.	**Nashville**	510,784	+6.9	4.9	Philip Bredesen (D, 8/95)
24.	**Cleveland**	505,616	-11.9	5.3	Michael R. White (D, 12/93)
25.	**New Orleans**	496,938	-10.9	6.8	Sidney J. Barthelemy (D, 5/94)
26.	**Denver, Colo.**	467,610	-5.1	4.3	Wellington E. Webb (D, 6/95)
27.	**Austin, Tex.**	465,622	+34.6	5.1	Bruce Todd (NP, 6/94)
28.	**Fort Worth, Tex.**	447,619	+16.2	7.0	Kay Granger (NP, 5/93)
29.	**Oklahoma City, Okla.**	444,719	+10.1	5.3	Ronald J. Norick (NP, 4/93)
30.	**Portland, Ore.**	437,319	+18.8	4.7	J. E. (Bud) Clark (NP, 12/93)
31.	**Kansas City, Mo.**	435,146	-2.9	5.6	Emanuel Cleaver (D, 4/95)
32.	**Long Beach, Calif.**	429,433	+18.8	8.6	Ernie E. Kell (NP, 6/94)
33.	**Tucson, Ariz.**	405,390	+22.6	3.6	George Miller (D, 12/95)
34.	**St. Louis, Mo.**	396,685	-12.4	6.7	Vincent C. Schoemehl, Jr. (D, 4/93)
35.	**Charlotte, N.C.**	395,934	+25.5	5.3	Richard Vinroot (R, 11/93)
36.	**Atlanta, Ga.**	394,017	-7.3	5.1	Maynard H. Jackson (D, 1/94)
37.	**Virginia Beach, Va.**	393,069	+49.9	6.2	Meyera E. Oberndorf (NP, 6/92)
38.	**Albuquerque, N. Mex.**	384,736	+15.6	5.6	Louis E. Saavedra (NP, 11/93)
39.	**Oakland, Calif.**	372,242	+9.7	6.1	Elihu Mason Harris (D, 12/94)
40.	**Pittsburgh, Pa.**	369,879	-12.8	5.9	Sophie Masloff (D, 12/93)
41.	**Sacramento, Calif.**	369,365	+34.0	7.1	Anne Rudin (NP, 11/92)
42.	**Minneapolis, Minn.**	368,383	-0.7	4.1	Donald M. Fraser (NP, 12/93)
43.	**Tulsa, Okla.**	367,302	+1.8	5.8	Roger A. Randle (D, 5/94)
44.	**Honolulu, Hawaii**	365,272	+0.1	2.3	Frank F. Fasi (R, 1/93)
45.	**Cincinnati, Ohio**	364,040	-5.5	5.1	Dwight Tillery (D, 11/93)
46.	**Miami, Fla.**	358,548	+3.4	9.3	Xavier L. Suarez (NP, 11/93)
47.	**Fresno, Calif.**	354,202	+62.9	11.0	Karen Humphrey (D, 3/93)
48.	**Omaha, Nebr.**	335,795	+7.0	3.2	P. J. Morgan (NP, 6/93)
49.	**Toledo, Ohio**	332,943	-6.1	9.7	John McHugh (D, 12/93)
50.	**Buffalo, N.Y.**	328,123	-8.3	6.3	James D. Griffin (D, 12/93)

*1990 census (source: U.S. Bureau of the Census).
†July 1991 figures for metropolitan areas (source: U.S. Bureau of Labor Statistics).
‡The letters in parentheses represent the mayor's party, with *D* meaning Democrat, *R* Republican, *I* Independent, and *NP* nonpartisan. The date is when the term of office ends (source: mayors' offices).

Kansas City, Mo.; Jacksonville, Fla.; Oklahoma City, Okla.; Colorado Springs, Colo.; and Wichita, Kans.

Women and minorities made some significant gains in local elections in 1991. Deedee Corradini was elected the first woman mayor in Salt Lake City, Utah, as were Kay Granger in Fort Worth, Tex., and Jan Laverty Jones in Las Vegas, Nev. Emanuel Cleaver was elected the first black mayor in Kansas City, Mo., on March 26, as was Wellington Webb in Denver on June 18 and W. W. Herenton in Memphis on October 3.

Population shifts. When the final 1990 census figures were announced in January 1991, Los Angeles had surged past Chicago, which had been the second most populous city in the United States after New York City, according to 1980 census figures. The 1990 census also found that 6 of the 10 largest U.S. cities were in the South or West. Of these six cities, all except Houston were still growing rapidly. Among the rest of the top 10, New York City registered a 3.5 per cent gain in population, and Chicago, Philadelphia, and Detroit each lost population between 1980 and 1990. See also **Census,** Special Report: **The 1990 Census: An American Self-Portrait.**

Population characteristics of U.S. cities were changing, too, according to an analysis of Census Bureau data by *USA Today* reported in September. The analysis found that minority groups accounted for more than half the total population of 15 of the nation's 28 largest cities. Blacks represented the largest single minority group in 20 of those cities, Hispanics were the largest minority in 6, and Asian and Pacific Islanders in 2—Seattle and San Francisco.

Although the United States became increasingly urbanized during the 1980's, the greatest population growth occurred in suburban areas. According to the census, some places that did not even exist in 1980, such as Santa Clarita and Moreno Valley in California, exploded into major population centers with more than 100,000 residents by 1991.

No census adjustment. The U.S. Department of Commerce announced on July 15 that it would not make a statistical adjustment to the 1990 census figures. The decision came despite a census undercount ranging from 4 million to 6 million people, mostly minority populations in urban areas, according to an April survey by the Census Bureau. New York City, Chicago, and other plaintiffs reactivated their 1988 lawsuit in federal court to force a statistical adjustment. Because census figures are used to distribute certain federal funds, a lower census count would mean less federal money for a city. See **Census.**

Oakland fires. On Oct. 20, 1991, wildfires swept through 1,800 acres (730 hectares) of the Oakland Hills section of Oakland, Calif. The windswept inferno killed 25 people, injured 148 others, and left some 5,000 without homes. It destroyed more than 1,800 homes and 900 apartment units, causing damages estimated as high as $2 billion. This tragedy occurred almost two years to the day after an earthquake leveled

50 largest cities in the world

Rank	City	Population
1.	Mexico City	10,263,275
2.	Seoul, South Korea	9,645,932
3.	Moscow	8,769,000
4.	Tokyo	8,353,674
5.	Bombay, India	8,227,332
6.	Shanghai	8,214,436
7.	Beijing	7,362,425
8.	New York City	7,322,564
9.	São Paulo, Brazil	7,033,529
10.	London	6,767,500
11.	Jakarta, Indonesia	6,761,886
12.	Cairo, Egypt	6,052,836
13.	Baghdad, Iraq	5,908,000
14.	Tianjin, China	5,855,068
15.	Hong Kong	5,756,000
16.	Teheran, Iran	5,734,199
17.	Lima, Peru	5,493,900
18.	Istanbul, Turkey	5,475,982
19.	Karachi, Pakistan	5,208,170
20.	Bangkok, Thailand	5,153,902
21.	Rio de Janeiro, Brazil	5,093,232
22.	Delhi, India	4,884,234
23.	St. Petersburg, Soviet Union	4,295,000
24.	Santiago, Chile	4,225,299
25.	Shenyang, China	4,130,000
26.	Bogotá, Colombia	3,982,941
27.	Pusan, South Korea	3,516,807
28.	Los Angeles	3,485,398
29.	Ho Chi Minh City, Vietnam	3,460,500
30.	Wuhan, China	3,340,000
31.	Calcutta, India	3,305,006
32.	Madras, India	3,276,622
33.	Guangzhou, China	3,220,000
34.	Madrid, Spain	3,123,713
35.	Berlin, Germany	3,062,979
36.	Yokohama, Japan	2,992,644
37.	Sydney, Australia	2,989,070
38.	Lahore, Pakistan	2,952,689
39.	Alexandria, Egypt	2,917,327
40.	Buenos Aires	2,908,001
41.	Rome	2,830,569
42.	Chicago	2,783,726
43.	Chongqing, China	2,730,000
44.	Melbourne, Australia	2,645,484
45.	Pyongyang, North Korea	2,639,448
46.	Taipei, Taiwan	2,637,100
47.	Osaka, Japan	2,636,260
48.	Harbin, China	2,590,000
49.	Hanoi, Vietnam	2,570,905
50.	Chengdu, China	2,540,000

Sources: 1990 census figures for U.S. cities from the U.S. Bureau of the Census; censuses or government estimates for cities of other countries.

Some of the thousands of homeless people in New York City put up tents in an empty lot after being evicted from a municipal park in summer 1991.

the elevated Nimitz Freeway in Oakland on Oct. 17, 1989, killing 42 people.

Storm damage. In March 1991, a freak ice storm hit upstate New York. Broken tree limbs, downed power lines, and impassable streets paralyzed much of Rochester and many surrounding communities for a week or more. Hurricane Bob ripped through New England in August, causing 16 deaths and an estimated $780 million in damage in cities and towns there. Some of the storm's worst damage was on Cape Cod in Massachusetts.

Two more Atlantic storms swept cities and towns along the east coast of the United States in October and November, bringing heavy seas ashore and leaving at least five people dead. The storms caused hundreds of millions of dollars in damage. Among the many houses destroyed or damaged by the October storm was President George Bush's summer home in Kennebunkport, Me. Surging waves as high as the rooftop swept away an entire wall, furniture, and many of the Bush family's mementos.

New baseball cities. Miami, Fla., and Denver were selected in June to become the homes of two new National League baseball teams, the Florida Marlins and the Colorado Rockies. The teams will be ready to play in the 1993 season. The 1991 season set a major league record for attendance at games—56.9 million spectators. Randolph C. Arndt

In *World Book,* see **City.**

Civil rights. A two-year stalemate between President George Bush and Congress over legislation that would make it easier for minorities and women to sue their employers for discrimination ended when Bush signed the Civil Rights Act of 1991 into law on Nov. 21, 1991. The law overturned a series of 1989 rulings by the Supreme Court of the United States. It also allows women, people with handicaps, and religious minorities to collect monetary awards and limited punitive damages for intentional on-the-job discrimination. Previously, only racial minorities could collect punitive damages for intentional discrimination.

Bush, who defeated a similar civil rights bill in 1990, had repeatedly threatened to veto the 1991 version. But Senator John C. Danforth (R., Mo.) drafted a compromise bill acceptable to the President. The Administration had claimed previous forms of the bill would force businesses to set quotas for hiring minorities and women.

The signing of the law also was enveloped in controversy. On November 20, White House Counsel C. Boyden Gray issued a proposed presidential order telling federal agencies to eliminate their requirement for affirmative action programs and such requirements for companies holding federal contracts. These programs were designed to stimulate the hiring and promotion of minorities and women. Amid an uproar by civil rights leaders and some members of Bush's Cabinet, the order was rescinded on November 21.

Thomas nomination. Clarence Thomas, a judge on the U.S. Court of Appeals for the District of Columbia, won Senate confirmation to a seat on the Supreme Court on October 15, despite opposition from many civil rights organizations and allegations of sexual harassment. Thomas was formally seated on November 1 as the second black justice in Supreme Court history and the successor to Justice Thurgood Marshall, who retired effective October 1.

Criticism of Thomas' nomination by civil rights groups focused on his opposition to affirmative-action programs and busing for school desegregation. While heading the Department of Education's Office of Civil Rights from 1981 to 1982 and the Equal Employment Opportunity Commission (EEOC) from 1982 to 1990, Thomas opposed programs that give minorities, as a group, preferences in getting jobs and government contracts. He favored direct help for individual victims of discrimination.

Despite criticism from civil rights groups, Thomas seemed assured of confirmation until a confidential report by the Federal Bureau of Investigation (FBI) to the Senate Judiciary Committee became public. The report detailed allegations of sexual harassment made by Anita F. Hill, a law professor at the University of Oklahoma in Norman, who had worked for Thomas at the Education Department and the EEOC. The Senate Judiciary Committee reconvened and held a dramatic series of hearings to explore the charges in October.

Court rulings. Before Marshall retired, the Supreme Court issued two important civil rights rulings. On March 26, 1991, the court said that a section of the 1964 Civil Rights Act protecting workers from discrimination based on their race, religion, ethnicity, or sex does not apply to Americans working for U.S. companies abroad. Voting 6 to 3, the court said it was not clear that Congress intended to extend the protections of Title VII of the Civil Rights Act beyond U.S. borders, because the law does not specifically mention U.S. workers stationed in other countries. However, Congress overturned the ruling in the Civil Rights Act of 1991.

In two important cases affecting the makeup of state judiciaries, the court on June 20, 1991, ruled that the Voting Rights Act, passed in 1965 and amended in 1982, applies to the election of state judges. The Voting Rights Act bars states and communities from using voting practices or establishing voting-district boundaries that discriminate against minorities. In the first case, the justices voted 6 to 3 in favor of black voters challenging the boundaries of voting districts for the election of judges to the Louisiana Supreme Court. By the same margin, the justices also voted in favor of black and Hispanic voters challenging the at-large election of trial judges in Texas.

Civil rights museum. The National Civil Rights Museum, which memorializes the struggle for racial equality in the 1950's and 1960's, was dedicated on July 4, 1991, in Memphis. The museum is housed in the Lorraine Hotel, where civil-rights leader Martin Luther King, Jr., was assassinated in 1968. At the museum, visitors can view displays on such events as the 1955 bus boycott in Montgomery, Ala.; the integration of the University of Mississippi in University in 1961; and the 1965 voting-rights march from Selma, Ala., to Montgomery.

The "I am a man" display is one of the exhibits at the new National Civil Rights Museum in Memphis, which was dedicated on July 4.

FBI harassment. The FBI on August 23 announced that eight agents had been disciplined for their role in harassing Donald Rochon, a black former agent. Rochon claimed he had received death threats and was subjected to other intimidation while working at the FBI's Omaha and Chicago offices. Under a 1990 settlement, the agency paid Rochon more than $1 million, and he agreed to leave the bureau. FBI officials also agreed to review the bureau's conduct in the matter. In April 1991, FBI Director William S. Sessions had met with black FBI agents to discuss problems concerning minority agents and head off a threatened lawsuit accusing the agency of racial discrimination.

Hate crimes. The Department of Justice in 1991 filed charges against 53 defendants in 30 cases involving hate crimes—crimes motivated by racial, ethnic, or sexual prejudice. Fourteen cases involved members of the Ku Klux Klan or other organized groups. The number of filings in 1991 was down from 1990, when the department filed 35 cases. Of the 1991 cases, 6 resulted in convictions, 36 in plea bargains, and 1 in acquittal. Nine cases were pending at year-end.

Civil rights

Bensonhurst trials. The last three trials stemming from the 1989 killing of Yusuf K. Hawkins in New York City ended in 1991. Hawkins, a black teen-ager, was fatally shot after being surrounded by a white mob when he went to see a used car in the Bensonhurst neighborhood of Brooklyn. Pasquale Raucci, who had been tried on murder as well as a number of lesser charges, was convicted on charges of rioting and illegally carrying a weapon. He was sentenced to three years' probation and 200 hours of community service and fined $500. Two other defendants were found not guilty. Five of the eight men indicted in the racially motivated crime were tried in 1990. One was convicted of murder, three were found guilty on lesser charges, and one was acquitted.

International report. Amnesty International, a London-based human-rights organization, reported on human-rights violations in 141 countries in its 1991 annual report, which covered events in 1990. The group reported that tens of thousands of people were killed or held in secret detention by their governments. But the report also noted a "respect for fundamental human rights" as a driving force behind dramatic political changes in eastern and central Europe. In addition, the group said, the 1990 release of black leader Nelson Mandela and other political prisoners in South Africa "signaled the start of negotiations for change" in that country.

Minority scholarships. The Education Department on December 4 proposed regulations that would ban most college scholarships based strictly on the recipient's race. The announcement came one year after the head of the department's Office of Civil Rights declared that race-based scholarships at institutions receiving federal aid violate the law. That declaration had caused a storm of protest, prompting Secretary of Education Lamar Alexander to conduct a seven-month study of the issue. Alexander said race could be considered in awarding scholarships, but race-specific programs would be allowed only if they were mandated by court order, funded by Congress, or provided through private money.

Bias studies. A study using equally matched pairs of black and white male job-seekers found that hiring discrimination against blacks is "widespread and entrenched." The study, reported on May 14, was conducted by the Urban Institute, a research organization based in Washington, D.C. The researchers found that black male job applicants in Chicago and Washington were three times as likely as whites to experience racial discrimination. A separate study distributed by the Urban Institute in September found that blacks faced bias 59 per cent of the time when they contacted real estate agents to buy a home and 56 per cent of the time when trying to rent. Hispanic home buyers faced discrimination 56 per cent of the time; Hispanic renters, 50 per cent of the time.

Linda P. Campbell and Geoffrey A. Campbell

In *World Book,* see **Civil rights.**

Classical music. Anniversaries brightened the musical scene in 1991, 200 years after the death of composer Wolfgang Amadeus Mozart and the birth of opera composer Giacomo Meyerbeer. For composer Sergei Prokofiev and songwriter Cole Porter, there were 100-year anniversaries of their births, as there were for the founding of New York City's Carnegie Hall and the Chicago Symphony Orchestra. The Metropolitan Opera marked 25 years at Lincoln Center in New York City.

The Mozart celebrations eclipsed all the rest. Philips, the Dutch recording firm, issued its *Complete Mozart Edition*, with more than 800 of his works on 180 compact discs amounting to about 200 hours of music. Two German music publishers brought forth *Mozart: New Edition of the Complete Works*, which contained 23,334 pages of music in 20 volumes.

Lincoln Center presented every Mozart work in 1991. The series began on January 27, Mozart's birthday, with a program by the New York Philharmonic based on one that the composer once offered at the Burgtheater in Vienna, Austria: his *Haffner* Symphony, two piano concertos, four concert arias, a serenade, and selected solo piano music. The Metropolitan Opera staged seven Mozart operas in 1991. The Houston Grand Opera devoted April and May to a five-opera Mozart festival. In San Francisco, there was a five-week Mozart celebration in May and June.

The spring Vienna Festival featured eight Mozart operas. The Barbican Center in London presented a series of 21 programs, each made up of selections from a year of Mozart's life. Mozart's *Requiem* was performed in many places on December 5, the day of Mozart's death, including at St. Stephen's Cathedral in Vienna, where his funeral service took place.

Other anniversaries. Commemorations for Meyerbeer were less lavish. Although he once was famous and respected, his music is now largely ignored. However, his 200th birthday was recognized with revivals of *Les Huguenots* by the Royal Opera of Covent Garden in London and *L'Africaine* by the Deutsche Staatsoper in Berlin, Germany.

For the 100th anniversary of the birth of Prokofiev, there were new productions of his *War and Peace* by the San Francisco Opera and *The Gambler* by Chicago's Lyric Opera. In a series of performances from Boston to Long Beach, Calif., Prokofiev's score for the motion picture *Alexander Nevsky* was performed by a 100-piece orchestra and 150-voice chorus.

Gala concerts in Indianapolis and New York City were among the events honoring the American songwriter Cole Porter. There was also a revival of his musical *Jubilee* by the Indiana University Opera Theater in Bloomington.

The Carnegie Hall centennial celebrations climaxed with a 10-day festival surrounding May 5, the day when, in 1891, Peter Ilich Tchaikovsky conducted the hall's opening night concert. Pianist Van Cliburn played Tchaikovsky's Concerto for Piano and Orchestra

No. 1 and the Cleveland Orchestra performed Antonín Dvorák's Symphony No. 9, *From the New World*, which was premiered in Carnegie Hall in 1893.

Two programs led by retiring music director Sir Georg Solti cast the spotlight on the Chicago Symphony Orchestra and its 100th birthday in April 1991. One program featured a concert version of Verdi's *Otello*, with tenor Luciano Pavarotti singing the title role for the first time. The other program combined Gustav Mahler's Symphony No. 5 with the premiere of Sir Michael Tippett's *Byzantium,* set for soprano and orchestra and based on a poem by William Butler Yeats.

The Metropolitan Opera marked its 25 years of residence at Lincoln Center with a gala performance that was presented on pay-per-view television, rather than on Public Broadcasting Service (PBS) stations. Some wondered whether this ushered in a new era in which major musical events would require television "admission" payments. For many viewers, that would mean fewer opportunities to see performances of classical music. For deficit-beleaguered arts institutions, however, it could mean new and needed revenues.

Important personnel changes occurred in 1991. After 12 seasons, Zubin Mehta stepped down as music director of the New York Philharmonic to be succeeded by Kurt Masur. Claudio Abbado resigned as music director of the Vienna State Opera, following a disagreement with management about the amount of time he spent with the Berlin Philharmonic, his other major directorial responsibility. Solti's 22-year reign in Chicago ended as Daniel Barenboim took over.

Squeezed budgets continued to plague musical organizations. Opera/Columbus in Ohio cut back its season because of a $1.7-million debt. Maxim Shostakovich, who was owed back pay of $100,000, in April resigned as music director of the New Orleans Symphony. He returned in autumn, however, when the symphony came up with the funds to pay him.

Most of the attention at the annual conference of the American Symphony Orchestra League held in Chicago in June was focused on money. Louisville (Ky.) Orchestra board member Carole Birkhead said, "In the 1980's we thought we could do it all: expand our programs and give musicians better salaries and more work. We are having to change our vision."

A general lack of interest in classical music among young people was part of the problem, according to John E. Frohnmayer, chairman of the National Endowment for the Arts. He addressed the conference after having visited the Chopin School on Chicago's West Side. Frohnmayer reported that "Ninety-five per cent of the students have no idea who Chopin was. Five per cent are aware of classical music, five per cent of jazz, and 100 per cent of rap."

Controversial opera. The most talked-about premiere came in March, when *The Death of Klinghoffer* opened in Brussels, Belgium. This work of composer John Adams, librettist Alice Goodman, and director

Violinist Isaac Stern, cellist Yo-Yo Ma, and conductor Zubin Mehta enjoy the applause at Carnegie Hall's 100th anniversary celebration in May.

Grammy Award winners in 1991

Classical Album, Charles Ives, Symphony No. 2, *The Gong on the Hook and Ladder, Central Park in the Dark, The Unanswered Question,* Leonard Bernstein, conductor.

Orchestral Performance, Dimitri Shostakovich, Symphonies No. 1 and No. 7, Chicago Symphony Orchestra, Leonard Bernstein, conductor.

Opera Recording, Richard Wagner, *Das Rheingold,* Metropolitan Opera Orchestra, James Levine, conductor.

Choral Performance, Sir William Walton, *Belshazzar's Feast;* Leonard Bernstein, *Chichester Psalms, Missa Brevis,* Atlanta Symphony Chorus and Orchestra, Robert Shaw, conductor.

Classical Performance, Instrumental Solo with Orchestra, Dimitri Shostakovich, Violin Concerto No. 1; Alexander Glazunov, Violin Concerto in A minor, Itzhak Perlman, violinist, with Israel Philharmonic, Zubin Mehta, conductor.

Classical Performance, Instrumental Solo Without Orchestra, *The Last Recording,* Vladimir Horowitz, pianist.

Chamber Music or Other Small Ensemble Performance, Johannes Brahms, The Three Violin Sonatas, Itzhak Perlman, violinist, and Daniel Barenboim, pianist.

Classical Vocal Performance, *Carreras, Domingo, Pavarotti in Concert,* José Carreras, Placido Domingo, Luciano Pavarotti, tenors.

Contemporary Composition, "Arias and Barcarolles," Leonard Bernstein.

Peter Sellars had its U.S. debut in September 1991 at the Brooklyn Academy of Music in New York City. *Klinghoffer* tells the story of the wheelchair-bound American tourist Leon Klinghoffer, who was murdered by pro-Palestinian terrorists during the 1985 hijacking of the cruise ship *Achille Lauro.*

Some viewers felt that the opera shed too favorable a light on terrorists. Klinghoffer's daughters expressed outrage, saying that the production "appears to us to be anti-Semitic." Librettist Goodman responded by insisting that the opera "does honor to the destiny of the Jewish people."

There was also debate about the work's musical quality. Patrick Smith of *Opera News* called it "the moment when American opera finally has achieved maturity." But Edward Rothstein, in *The New York Times,* wrote that "the text is set in so unmusical a fashion that the surtitles are required to decipher it."

Other operatic premieres included Carlisle Floyd's *The Passion of Jonathan Wade,* by the Houston Grand Opera; John Oliver's *Guacamayo's Old Song and Dance,* by the Canadian Opera in Toronto; and the New Jersey State Opera's premiere of *Frederick Douglass* by Ulysses Kay. Philadelphia's American Music Theater Festival introduced *Frida* by Robert Xavier Rodriguez; Manfred Trojahn's *Enrico* premiered at the Schwetzingen Festival in Germany; and Elizabeth Swados' *Pied Piper* was performed in Orlando, Fla.

There were also premieres of Harrison Birthwistle's *Gawain* at Britain's Royal Opera; Ferenc Farkas' *A Guest Performance in Bolzano* by the Budapest State Opera in Hungary; the much-anticipated but critically berated *Ubu Rex* of Krzysztof Penderecki at the Munich Opera Festival in Germany; Mikis Theodorakis' setting of *Medea* by the Teator Arriaga in Bilbao, Spain; and *Mer de Glace* by Richard Meale at the Australian Opera in Sydney. *The Ghosts of Versailles* by John Corigliano, a work commissioned by the Metropolitan Opera, opened in December.

Symphonic premieres. The Carnegie Hall celebrations included several orchestral commissions, including Alfred Schnittke's Concerto Grosso No. 5, played by the Cleveland Orchestra, and Terry Riley's *Jade Palace Orchestral Dances,* premiered by the St. Louis (Mo.) Symphony. Charles Wuorinen's cantata *Genesis* also premiered in 1991. It was introduced by the San Francisco Symphony Orchestra.

Rock star debut. Much press went to former Beatle Paul McCartney's first sojourn into the realm of classical music. His *Liverpool Oratorio* sought to honor the musician's home town in England. Written in collaboration with composer-conductor Carl Davis, the 97-minute work was given lukewarm reviews by the critics. Nevertheless, it received a standing ovation from the audience that filled the Liverpool Anglican Cathedral for its June premiere. Peter P. Jacobi

In ***World Book,*** see **Classical music; Opera.**

Clinton, William Joseph (1946-), threw his hat into the presidential ring on Oct. 3, 1991, and became the fifth candidate to announce his bid for the Democratic nomination. The five-term governor of Arkansas hoped to appeal to the middle class with statements about recovering the "American Dream."

Born in Hope, Ark., on Aug. 19, 1946, Bill Clinton was raised in a family of modest means. But he went on to attend Georgetown University in Washington, D.C.; Oxford University in England, where he was a Rhodes scholar; and Yale University Law School in New Haven, Conn. Before entering politics, Clinton practiced and taught law.

Clinton served as attorney general in Arkansas from 1977 until 1979, when he was elected governor for the first time. He lost his bid for reelection in 1981 but regained the governorship in 1983 and has held the office since.

As governor, Clinton has been active in formulating education and employment policies both locally and nationally. He cochaired the President's education summit with the nation's governors and headed the Education Commission of the States. He also headed the Democratic Leadership Council from 1990 to 1991 and chaired the National Governors' Association from 1986 to 1987.

Clinton is married to the former Hillary Rodham, and they have a daughter. Lori Fagan

Clothing. See **Fashion.**

Coal. The United States will supply an increasingly large share of the world's coal after the year 2000, the U.S. Department of Energy (DOE) predicted in a report issued on July 1, 1991. The report said that American coal exports, which totaled 106 million short tons (96 million metric tons) in 1990, will more than double to 250 million short tons (227 million metric tons) by 2010. The demand for U.S. coal is expected to increase as inefficient coal mines in Germany, Great Britain, and Poland are closed and as worldwide consumption of coal increases.

Increasing exports and demand for electricity will have a major impact in stimulating the domestic coal industry, according to industry experts. New long-term DOE projections issued on July 19, 1991, suggest that domestic coal production will increase by almost 50 per cent by the year 2010. Production—which exceeded 1 billion short tons (900 million metric tons) for the first time in 1990—will reach 1.5 billion tons (1.4 billion metric tons) per year by 2010, the DOE predicted. Nevertheless, coal production during the first six months of 1991 totaled 496 million short tons (450 million metric tons), a decrease from the 518 million tons (470 million metric tons) produced during the first half of 1990, the DOE said on Sept. 1, 1991.

Safety violations charged. The U.S. Department of Labor on April 4 announced that it would fine 500 mining companies for tampering with devices used to monitor the air inside coal mines for high levels of coal dust. The fines eventually totaled $7 million.

Federal regulations to limit the amount of coal dust permitted inside mines were enacted to prevent black lung disease. This serious condition, which is caused by inhaling coal dust, has affected an estimated 260,000 coal miners. About 4,000 retired miners die of black lung disease each year, according to the federal Mine Safety and Health Administration.

To monitor levels of coal dust, some miners are required to wear small air filters that collect dust samples inside the mines. Mine operators must then ship the filters to government inspectors for testing. The Labor Department accused mine operators of vacuuming the filters or otherwise tampering with them to prevent the accumulation of coal dust. Mining companies denied the charges, claiming that the government sampling devices were faulty.

Research refinery. The DOE on June 18 picked a group of researchers to develop an advanced coal refinery that will transform coal into a variety of other valuable products. DOE will provide up to $15 million to build and operate the experimental refinery near Carterville, Ill. Illinois will provide $3 million to the research group, headed by Kerr-McGee Coal Corporation in Oklahoma City, Okla. Each day, the plant will convert about 24 short tons (22 metric tons) of coal into liquid and solid products that can be used as fuel or as industrial materials. Michael Woods

See also **Energy Supply; Mining.** In ***World Book,*** see **Coal.**

Colombia. In Colombia, a new Constitution adopted in July 1991 raised hopes for an end to rebellion and drug terrorism. The most controversial provision of the new governing document provides that Colombians will not be extradited to foreign nations to stand trial on drug-trafficking charges.

Drug king surrenders. Barely hours after the assembly writing the Constitution approved the ban on extradition on June 19, 41-year-old Pablo Escobar Gaviria, a multibillionaire drug kingpin, surrendered to Colombian authorities to enter a jail of his own design in his hometown of Envigado. Escobar, head of the Medellín drug cartel, is also wanted in the United States on murder and drug-trafficking charges.

In accord with a plea bargain, Escobar agreed to serve three years in return for the Colombian government's guarantee of his safety while in confinement. Opinions in Colombia and abroad were divided on the unique arrangement. Some thought the government had given in to the drug dealers, but Colombia's Nobel laureate writer, Gabriel García Márquez, called the deal "a triumph of intelligence."

Most Colombians agreed with their president, César Gaviria Trujillo, who supported the new Constitution's nonextradition provision. Colombians were hopeful that other drug dealers would follow the example set by Escobar so that Colombia's war against drugs would end. Terrorism by drug dealers had resulted in the deaths of 2,000 Colombians, including more than 300 judges and court functionaries, between 1985 and 1991.

Meanwhile, separate groups of former rebels laid down their guns in January and March to join the political process in return for promises from the government that they would not be prosecuted. One of Colombia's former rebels, Antonio Navarro Wolff, played a leading role in writing the new Constitution and emerged as a possible future presidential candidate. Navarro Wolff led the 1985 storming of Colombia's Supreme Court by guerrillas of the M-19 movement, which left about 100 people dead, including half of the court's 24 justices.

Economic upswing. During the 1980's, despite wars on drugs and guerrillas, Colombia's economy expanded at an annual rate of 4 per cent, the highest figure in Latin America. By late 1991, the country had foreign reserves of $5 billion, enough for a year's worth of imports. During the first half of 1991, $1.1-billion that had been invested abroad was reinvested at home. As an example of this economic strength, Colombia's publishing industry reported export book sales of $80 million in 1990, double the figure of four years earlier. In 1991, Colombia became Latin America's biggest book exporter. Nathan A. Haverstock

See also **Latin America** (Facts in brief table). In ***World Book,*** see **Colombia.**

Colorado. See **State government.**

Common Market. See **Europe.**

Comoros. See **Africa.**

Computer. The United States computer industry saw wide changes in 1991. Significant new products were introduced, including a computer that can read printed handwriting and also accept data entry from a keyboard. Leading computer companies formed new alliances in an effort to strengthen their competitiveness. While the sales of large mainframe computers continued to sag, experts forecast strong growth for small, desktop computers.

Apple and IBM. One of the most dramatic events of the year took place in early July, when archrival hardware manufacturers—International Business Machines Corporation (IBM) of Armonk, N.Y., and Apple Computer, Incorporated, of Cupertino, Calif.—said that they were negotiating a broad alliance to develop new technologies. The results of those negotiations were announced on October 2, when the companies established two subsidiaries. One subsidiary—Kaleida—would create and license multimedia computer technologies (technology that allows a combination of video, still pictures, or animation with text and sound). The other subsidiary—Taligent—would develop an operating system (the basic software that enables computers to process information and use other software), based on object-oriented programming. The new system would allow users to create personalized computer programs by combining different programming elements called *objects.*

Apple and IBM also agreed to develop software for the advanced Reduced Instruction Set Chip (RISC) microprocessor made by the Motorola Corporation of Schaumburg, Ill. Many computer analysts agree that RISC microprocessors will be the basis of the next generation of personal computers and workstations.

Most observers saw the IBM-Apple alliance as a competitive move against the Microsoft Corporation of Redmond, Wash., the largest personal computer software publisher in the world. Microsoft, which publishes MS-DOS, the operating system used with most IBM-compatible personal computers, was once a close partner of IBM's. That relationship soured in July 1991 when Microsoft announced it would abandon IBM's new OS/2 operating system, which Microsoft developed in conjunction with IBM, in favor of Microsoft's Windows operating system, introduced in May 1990. Windows is an addition to MS-DOS that allows users to perform multiple tasks through the use of "windows" on the computer screen and to operate their personal computers by pointing at *icons* (pictures) with a control device, usually a mouse.

Multimedia technology. One of the major causes for the reshuffling of computer company alliances has been the interest in multimedia technology. On Oct. 8, 1991, several companies that had formed the Multimedia Personal Computer (MPC) Marketing Council, a group designed to promote standards for multimedia such as quality of sound and of video images, introduced 60 multimedia software titles from 40 different developers. A week earlier, the Tandy Corporation of Fort Worth, Tex., began shipping the first computers to meet MPC standards.

The least expensive Tandy MPC computer—at a price of $2,779—uses an Intel 80386 microprocessor with an advanced audio board and a CD-ROM (Compact Disc Read-Only Memory) drive. The new Tandy computer uses an MS-DOS 5.0 operating system and Windows 3.0. It can also work with multimedia extensions from Microsoft.

Smaller computing. Shipments of desktop personal computers to U.S. businesses peaked in 1990 at 6 million machines and will shrink to 4.9 million machines by 1993, according to Forrester Research Incorporated of Cambridge, Mass., a computer industry analysis firm. By 1993, sales of laptop and smaller computers, which represented about 19 per cent of the U.S. market in 1991, will grow to 35 per cent of the market. This new class of mobile computers has emerged as the fastest-growing segment in the market. Mobile computers are smaller and lighter than laptop computers and perform most of the functions of a regular computer, but with less memory. Decreasing in size, mobile computers consist of notebook, sub-notebook, palmtop, hand-held computers, and personal organizers. By 1995, one-third of all computers sold in the United States will be mobile computers, according to Forrester Research.

Pen-top computers. An important milestone for the industry came on October 7, when Momenta International of Mountain View, Calif., debuted the first "pen-top" computer that can also accept data entry from a keyboard. The Momenta pen-top allows users to scribble notes on the computer screen in situations where typing would be difficult, such as in business meetings. Special software recognizes printed handwriting and other marks made on the screen with the attached pen.

Although other companies offer pen-based computers, Momenta was the first to offer one that can accept data entry from a keyboard. Momenta claims the new computer is 98 per cent accurate in recognizing printed handwriting. Microsoft and the Go Corporation of Foster City, Calif., were developing operating systems for pen-based computers.

Mainframe computing. The U.S. market for the largest, most powerful computers—mainframes—continued to be sluggish in 1991. In the autumn of 1990, IBM released a new generation of mainframe computers called the Enterprise System/9000. But after initial demand was met, sales were slow. According to estimates by the International Data Corporation (IDC) of Framingham, Mass., revenues for mainframe computers will rise only 1.4 per cent a year through 1996. According to IDC, 1,690 mainframes were shipped in 1986. That number should drop to 1,100 by 1992, the company said. Elliot King

See also **Electronics; Manufacturing.** In ***World Book,*** see **Computer.**

Congo. See **Africa.**

Congress of the United States. Two dramatic happenings in Congress in 1991 captured public attention: a debate over authorizing the nation to wage war in the Middle East and televised Senate hearings on sexual harassment charges against a nominee for the Supreme Court of the United States.

There also were the usual battles between a Republican President and the Democratic majorities in the Senate and House of Representatives. And, true to form, Congress wrapped up much of the work on important measures—civil rights, jobless benefits, highways, banking—in the last few days of the congressional session during a frantic rush toward adjournment on November 27.

Debate on war with Iraq. Some of Congress's most vigorous debates of 1991 involved the situation in the Persian Gulf. When the United Nations (UN) set a January 15 deadline for Iraq to withdraw from Kuwait, which it had seized in August 1990, President George Bush made it clear that he was determined to enforce the ultimatum with military might.

Most congressional Democrats favored reliance on UN-declared economic sanctions to wear down Iraq's resolve. Most Republicans backed a Bush request of January 8 for congressional authorization to use force against Iraq. The President insisted, however, that he did not really need such authorization.

The debate in the Senate and House of Representatives began on January 10 and concluded two days later. Much of the discussion was both emotional and solemn. So many of the members wanted to speak that both chambers met in rare overnight sessions on January 11.

On January 12, the Senate voted 52 to 47 to approve a resolution authorizing the use of force if military action were deemed necessary to oust Iraq from Kuwait. The House vote was 250 to 183. Only two Republican senators and three Republican representatives opposed the resolution. The measure was supported by 10 Democrats in the Senate and 86 in the House. On January 17, the forces of an allied coalition attacked Iraq by air. The war was concluded victoriously in late February with a massive ground assault. See **Persian Gulf,** Special Report: **War in the Persian Gulf.**

Some Republicans in Congress seized the moment to proclaim that Democrats who had voted against war would be punished in the 1992 elections. But by late in the year, the war was a receding memory, and it appeared likely that the continuing economic recession would be the dominant issue in 1992.

Supreme Court nominee debate. Thurgood Marshall, the first black to serve on the U.S. Supreme Court, announced his retirement on June 27, 1991, after 24 years' service. Bush promptly nominated another black jurist, federal appeals court Judge Clarence Thomas, for the vacant Supreme Court seat.

After conducting confirmation hearings, the Senate Judiciary Committee on September 27 voted 7 to 7

Women members of the House of Representatives go to the Senate on October 8 to urge a delay in the vote on the Clarence Thomas nomination.

Members of the United States House of Representatives

The House of Representatives of the second session of the 102nd Congress consisted of 268 Democrats, 166 Republicans, and 1 independent (not including representatives from American Samoa, the District of Columbia, Guam, Puerto Rico and the Virgin Islands), when it convened on Jan. 3, 1992, compared with 267 Democrats, 167 Republicans, and 1 independent when the first session convened. This table shows congressional district, legislator, and party affiliation. Asterisk (*) denotes those who served in the 101st Congress; dagger (†) denotes "at large."

Alabama
1. H. L. Callahan, R.*
2. William L. Dickinson, R.*
3. Glen Browder, D.*
4. Tom Bevill, D.*
5. Bud Cramer, D.
6. Ben Erdreich, D.*
7. Claude Harris, D.*

Alaska
†Donald E. Young, R.*

Arizona
1. John J. Rhodes III, R.*
2. Ed Pastor, D.*
3. Bob Stump, R.*
4. Jon L. Kyl, R.*
5. Jim Kolbe, R.*

Arkansas
1. Bill Alexander, D.*
2. Ray Thornton, D.
3. John P. Hammerschmidt, R.*
4. Beryl F. Anthony, Jr., D.*

California
1. Frank Riggs, R.
2. Wally Herger, R.*
3. Robert T. Matsui, D.*
4. Vic Fazio, D.*
5. Nancy Pelosi, D.*
6. Barbara Boxer, D.*
7. George E. Miller, D.*
8. Ronald V. Dellums, D.*
9. Fortney H. (Peter) Stark, D.*
10. Don Edwards, D.*
11. Tom Lantos, D.*
12. Tom J. Campbell, R.*
13. Norman Y. Mineta. D.*
14. John T. Doolittle, R.
15. Gary A. Condit, D.*
16. Leon E. Panetta, D.*
17. Calvin Dooley, D.
18. Richard H. Lehman, D.*
19. Robert J. Lagomarsino, R.*
20. William M. Thomas, R.*
21. Elton Gallegly, R.*
22. Carlos J. Moorhead, R.*
23. Anthony C. Beilenson, D.*
24. Henry A. Waxman, D.*
25. Edward R. Roybal, D.*
26. Howard L. Berman, D.*
27. Mel Levine, D.*
28. Julian C. Dixon, D.*
29. Maxine Waters, D.
30. Matthew G. Martinez, D.*
31. Mervyn M. Dymally, D.*
32. Glenn M. Anderson, D.*
33. David Dreier, R.*
34. Esteban E. Torres, D.*
35. Jerry Lewis, R.*
36. George E. Brown, Jr., D.*
37. Alfred A. McCandless, R.*
38. Robert K. Dornan, R.*
39. Wiilliam E. Dannemeyer, R.*
40. C. Christopher Cox, R.*
41. William D. Lowery, R.*
42. Dana Rohrabacher, R.*
43. Ronald C. Packard, R.*
44. Randy (Duke) Cunningham, R.
45. Duncan L. Hunter, R.*

Colorado
1. Patricia Schroeder, D.*
2. David E. Skaggs, D.*
3. Ben Nighthorse Campbell, D.*
4. Wayne Allard, R.
5. Joel Hefley, R.*
6. Daniel Schaefer, R.*

Connecticut
1. Barbara B. Kennelly, D.*
2. Samuel Gejdenson, D.*
3. Rosa DeLauro, D.
4. Christopher Shays, R.*
5. Gary Franks, R.
6. Nancy L. Johnson, R.*

Delaware
†Thomas R. Carper, D.*

Florida
1. Earl Hutto, D.*
2. Pete Peterson, D.
3. Charles E. Bennett, D.*
4. Craig T. James, R.*
5. Bill McCollum, R.*
6. Cifford B. Stearns, R.*
7. Sam M. Gibbons, D.*
8. C. W. Bill Young, R.*
9. Michael Bilirakis, R.*
10. Andy Ireland, R.*
11. Jim Bacchus, D.
12. Thomas F. Lewis, R.*
13. Porter J. Goss, R.*
14. Harry A. Johnston II, D.*
15. E. Clay Shaw, Jr., R.*
16. Lawrence J. Smith, D.*
17. William Lehman, D.*
18. Ileana Ros-Lehtinen, R.*
19. Dante B. Fascell, D.*

Georgia
1. Lindsay Thomas, D.*
2. Charles F. Hatcher, D.*
3. Richard B. Ray, D.*
4. Ben Jones, D.*
5. John Lewis, D.*
6. Newt Gingrich, R.*
7. George Darden, D.*
8. J. Roy Rowland, D.*
9. Edgar L. Jenkins, D.*
10. Doug Barnard, Jr., D.*

Hawaii
1. Neil Abercrombie, D.
2. Patsy T. Mink, D.*

Idaho
1. Larry LaRocco, D.
2. Richard H. Stallings, D.*

Illinois
1. Charles A. Hayes, D.*
2. Gus Savage, D.*
3. Marty Russo, D.*
4. George Sangmeister, D.*
5. William O. Lipinski, D.*
6. Henry J. Hyde, R.*
7. Cardiss Collins, D.*
8. Dan Rostenkowski, D.*
9. Sidney R. Yates, D.*
10. John Edward Porter, R.*
11. Frank Annunzio, D.*
12. Philip M. Crane, R.*
13. Harris W. Fawell, R.*
14. J. Dennis Hastert, R.*
15. Thomas W. Ewing, R.
16. John W. Cox, Jr., D
17. Lane A. Evans, D.*
18. Robert H. Michel, R.*
19. Terry L. Bruce, D.*
20. Richard J. Durbin, D.*
21. Jerry F. Costello, D.*
22. Glenn Poshard, D.*

Indiana
1. Peter J. Visclosky, D.*
2. Philip R. Sharp, D*
3. Tim Roemer, D.
4. Jill Long, D.*
5. James Jontz, D.*
6. Danny L. Burton, R.*
7. John T. Myers, R.*
8. Frank McCloskey, D.*
9. Lee H. Hamilton, D.*
10. Andrew Jacobs, Jr., D.*

Iowa
1. Jim Leach, R.*
2. Jim Nussle, R.
3. David R. Nagle, D.*
4. Neal Smith, D.*
5. Jim Ross Lightfoot, R.*
6. Fred Grandy, R.*

Kansas
1. Pat Roberts, R.*
2. James C. Slattery, D.*
3. Jan Meyers, R.*
4. Dan Glickman, D.*
5. Dick Nichols, R.

Kentucky
1. Carroll Hubbard, Jr., D.*
2. William H. Natcher, D.*
3. Romano L. Mazzoli, D.*
4. Jim Bunning, R.*
5. Harold (Hal) Rogers, R.*
6. Larry J. Hopkins, R.*
7. Carl C. (Chris) Perkins, D.*

Louisiana
1. Robert L. Livingston, Jr., R.*
2. William J. Jefferson, D.
3. W. J. (Billy) Tauzin, D.*
4. Jim McCrery, R.*
5. Thomas J. (Jerry) Huckaby, D.*
6. Richard Hugh Baker, R.*
7. James A. (Jimmy) Hayes, D.*
8. Clyde C. Holloway, R.*

Maine
1. Thomas H. Andrews, D.
2. Olympia J. Snowe, R.*

Maryland
1. Wayne T. Gilchrest, R.
2. Helen Delich Bentley, R.*
3. Benjamin L. Cadin, D.*
4. Thomas McMillen, D.*
5. Steny H. Hoyer, D.*
6. Beverly B. Byron, D.*t
7. Kweisi Mfume, D.*
8. Constance A. Morella, R.*

Massachusetts
1. John W. Oliver, D.
2. Richard E. Neal, D.*
3. Joseph D. Early, D.*
4. Barney Frank, D.*
5. Chester G. Atkins, D.*
6. Nicholas Mavroules, D.*
7. Edward J. Markey, D.*
8. Joseph P. Kennedy II, D.*
9. John Joseph Moakley, D.*
10. Gerry E. Studds, D.*
11. Brian J. Donnelly, D.*

Michigan
1. John Conyers, Jr., D.*
2. Carl D. Pursell, R.*
3. Howard E. Wolpe, D.*
4. Frederick S. Upton, R.*
5. Paul B. Henry, R.*
6. Bob Carr, D.*
7. Dale E. Kildee, D.*
8. Bob Traxler, D.*
9. Guy Vander Jagt, R.*
10. Dave Camp, R.
11. Robert W. Davis, R.*
12. David E. Bonior, D.*
13. Barbara-Rose Collins, D.
14. Dennis M. Hertel, D.*
15. William D. Ford, D.*
16. John D. Dingell, D.*
17. Sander M. Levin, D.*
18. William S. Broomfield, R.*

Minnesota
1. Timothy J. Penny, D.*
2. Vin Weber, R.*
3. Jim Ramstad, R.
4. Bruce F. Vento, D.*
5. Martin O. Sabo, D.*
6. Gerry Sikorski, D.*
7. Collin C. Peterson, D.
8. James L. Oberstar, D.*

Mississippi
1. Jamie L. Whitten, D.*
2. Mike Espy, D.*
3. G. V. (Sonny) Montgomery, D.*
4. Mike Parker, D.*
5. Gene Taylor, D.*

Missouri
1. William L. (Bill) Clay, D.*
2. Joan Kelly Horn, D.
3. Richard A. Gephardt, D.*
4. Ike Skelton, D.*
5. Alan D. Wheat, D.*
6. E. Thomas Coleman, R.*
7. Mel Hancock, R.*
8. Bill Emerson, R*
9. Harold L. Volkmer, D.*

Montana
1. Pat Williams, D.*
2. Ron Marlenee, R.*

Nebraska
1. Doug Bereuter, R.*
2. Peter Hoagland, D.*
3. Bill Barrett, R.

Nevada
1. James H. Bilbray, D.*
2. Barbara F. Vucanovich, R.*

New Hampshire
1. Bill Zeliff, R.
2. Dick Swett, D.

New Jersey
1. Robert E. Andrews, D.
2. William J. Hughes, D.*
3. Frank Pallone, Jr., D.*
4. Christopher H. Smith, R.*
5. Marge Roukema, R.*
6. Bernard J. Dwyer, D.*
7. Matthew J. Rinaldo, R.*
8. Robert A. Roe, D.*
9. Robert G. Torricelli, D.*
10. Donald M. Payne, D.*
11. Dean A. Gallo, R.*
12. Richard A. Zimmer, R.
13. H. James Saxton, R.*
14. Frank J. Guarini, D.*

New Mexico
1. Steven H. Schiff, R.*
2. Joe Skeen, R.*
3. William B. Richardson, D.*

New York
1. George J. Hochbrueckner, D.*
2. Thomas J. Downey, D.*
3. Robert J. Mrazek, D.*
4. Norman F. Lent, R.*
5. Raymond J. McGrath, R.*
6. Floyd H. Flake, D.
7. Gary L. Ackerman, D.*
8. James H. Scheuer, D.*
9. Thomas J. Manton, D.*
10. Charles E. Schumer, D.*
11. Edolphus Towns, D.*
12. Major R. Owens, D.*
13. Stephen J. Solarz, D*
14. Susan Molinari, R.*
15. Bill Green, R.*
16. Charles B. Rangel, D.*
17. Ted Weiss, D.*
18. Jose E. Serrano, D.*
19. Eliot L. Engel, D.*
20. Nita M. Lowey, D.*
21. Hamilton Fish, Jr., R.*
22. Benjamin A. Gilman, R.*
23. Michael R. McNulty, D.*
24. Gerald B. Solomon, R.*
25. Sherwood L. Boehlert, R.*
26. David O'B. Martin, R.*
27. James T. Walsh, R.*
28. Matthew F. McHugh, D.*
29. Frank Horton, R.*
30. Louise M. Slaughter, D.*
31. William Paxon, R.*
32. John J. LaFalce, D.*
33. Henry J. Nowak, D.*
34. Amory Houghton, Jr., R.*

North Carolina
1. Walter B. Jones, D.*
2. Tim Valentine, D.*
3. H. Martin Lancaster, D.*
4. David E. Price, D.*
5. Stephen L. Neal, D.*
6. Howard Coble, R.*
7. Charlie Rose. D.*
8. W. G. (Bill) Hefner, D.*
9. J. Alex McMillan III, R.*
10. Cass Ballenger, R.*
11. Charles H. Taylor, R.

North Dakota
†Byron L. Dorgan, D.*

Ohio
1. Charles Luken, D.
2. Willis D. Gradison, Jr., R.*
3. Tony P. Hall, D.*
4. Michael G. Oxley, R.*
5. Paul E. Gillmor, R.*
6. Bob McEwen, R.*
7. David L. Hobson, R.
8. John A. Boehner, R.
9. Marcy Kaptur, D.*
10. Clarence E. Miller, R.*
11. Dennis E. Eckart, D.*
12. John R. Kasich, R.*
13. Donald J. Pease, D.*
14. Thomas C. Sawyer, D.*
15. Chalmers P. Wylie, R.*
16. Ralph Regula, R.*
17. James A. Traficant, Jr., D.*
18. Douglas Applegate, D.*
19. Edward F. Feighan, D.*
20. Mary Rose Oakar, D.*
21. Louis Stokes, D.*

Oklahoma
1. James M. Inhofe, R.*
2. Mike Synar, D.*
3. Bill Brewster, D.
4. Dave McCurdy, D.*
5. Mickey Edwards, R.*
6. Glenn English, D.*

Oregon
1. Les AuCoin, D.*
2. Robert F. Smith, R.*
3. Ron Wyden, D.*
4. Peter A. DeFazio, D.*
5. Mike Kopetski, D.

Pennsylvania
1. Thomas M. Foglietta, D.*
2. Lucien Blackwell, D.
3. Robert A. Borski, Jr., D.*
4. Joseph P. Kolter, D.*
5. Richard T. Schulze, R.*
6. Gus Yatron, D.*
7. W. Curtis Weldon, R.*
8. Peter H. Kostmayer, D*
9. E. G. (Bud) Shuster, R.*
10. Joseph M. McDade, R.*
11. Paul E. Kanjorski, D.*
12. John P. Murtha, D.*
13. Lawrence Coughlin, R.*
14. William J. Coyne, D.*
15. Don Ritter, R.*
16. Robert S. Walker, R.*
17. George W. Gekas, R.*
18. Rick Santorum, R.
19. William F. Goodling, R.
20. Joseph M. Gaydos, D.*
21. Thomas J. Ridge, R.*
22. Austin J. Murphy, D.*
23. William F. Clinger, Jr., R.*

Rhode Island
1. Ronald K. Machtley, R.*
2. John F. Reed, D.

South Carolina
1. Arthur Ravenel, Jr., R.*
2. Floyd Spence, R.*
3. Butler Derrick, D.*
4. Elizabeth J. Patterson, D.*
5. John M. Spratt, Jr., D.*
6. Robert M. (Robin) Tallon, D.*

South Dakota
†Tim Johnson, D.*

Tennessee
1. James H. Quillen, R.*
2. John J. Duncan, Jr., R.*
3. Marilyn Lloyd, D.*
4. James H. Cooper, D.*
5. Bob Clement, D.*
6. Bart Gordon, D.*
7. Donald K. Sundquist, R.*
8. John S. Tanner, D.*
9. Harold E. Ford, D*

Texas
1. Jim Chapman, D.*
2. Charles Wilson, D.*
3. Sam Johnson, R.
4. Ralph M. Hall, D.*
5. John W. Bryant, D.*
6. Joe Barton, R.*
7. Bill Archer, R.*
8. Jack Fields, R.*
9. Jack Brooks, D.*
10. J. J. (Jake) Pickle, D.*
11. Chet Edwards, D.
12. Preston P. (Pete) Geren, D.*
13. Bill Sarpalius, D.*
14. Greg Laughlin, D.*
15. Eligio (Kika) de la Garza, D.*
16. Ronald D. Coleman, D.*
17. Charles W. Stenholm, D.*
18. Craig A. Washington, D.*
19. Larry Combest, R.*
20. Henry B. Gonzalez, D.*
21. Lamar S. Smith, R.*
22. Tom DeLay, R.*
23. Lucian Blackwell, D.
24. Martin Frost, D.*
25. Michael A. Andrews, D.*
26. Richard K. Armey, R.*
27. Solomon P. Ortiz, D.*

Utah
1. James V. Hansen, R.*
2. Wayne Owens, D.*
3. William Orton, D.

Vermont
†Bernard Sanders, ind.

Virginia
1. Herbert H. Batemans, R.*
2. Owen B. Pickett, D.*
3. Thomas J. (Tom) Bliley, Jr., R.*
4. Norman Sisisky, D.*
5. Lewis F. Payne, Jr., D.*
6. James R. Olin, D.*
7. George F. Allen, R.
8. James P. Moran, Jr., D.
9. Frederick C. Boucher, D.*
10. Frank R. Wolf, R.*

Washington
1. John R. Miller, R.*
2. Al Swift, D.*
3. Jolene Unsoeld, D.*
4. Sid Morrison, R.*
5. Thomas S. Foley, D.*
6. Norman D. Dicks, D.*
7. Jim McDermott, D.*
8. Rod Chandler, R.*

West Virginia
1. Alan B. Mollohan, D.*
2. Harley O. Staggers, Jr., D.*
3. Robert E. Wise, Jr., D.*
4. Nick J. Rahall II, D.*

Wisconsin
1. Les Aspin, D.*
2. Scott Klug, R.
3. Steven Gunderson, R.*
4. Gerald D. Kleczka, D.*
5. Jim Moody, D.*
6. Thomas E. Petri, R.*
7. David R. Obey, D.*
8. Toby Roth, R.*
9. F. James Sensenbrenner, Jr., R.*

Wyoming
†Craig Thomas, R.*

Nonvoting representatives
American Samoa
Eni F. H. Faleomavaega, D.*

District of Columbia
Eleanor Holmes Norton, D.

Guam
Ben Blaz, R.*

Puerto Rico
Jaime B. Fuster, D.*

Virgin Islands
Ron de Lugo, D.*

Members of the United States Senate

The Senate of the second session of the 102nd Congress consisted of 57 Democrats and 43 Republicans when it convened on Jan. 3, 1992. Senators shown starting their term in 1991 were elected for the first time in the Nov. 6, 1990, elections, except for John F. Seymour (R., Calif.), who was appointed on Jan. 2, 1991, by Governor-elect Pete Wilson to fill Wilson's Senate seat, and Harris L. Wofford (D., Pa.), who was sworn in on May 9, 1991, to replace Senator John Heinz, who was killed in an airplane crash. Wofford won a special election on Nov. 5, 1991. Others shown ending their current terms in 1997 were reelected to the Senate in the 1990 balloting. The second date in each listing shows when the senator's term expires.

State	Term
Alabama	
Howell T. Heflin, D.	1979-1997
Richard C. Shelby, D.	1987-1993
Alaska	
Theodore F. Stevens, R.	1968-1997
Frank H. Murkowski, R.	1981-1993
Arizona	
Dennis DeConcini, D.	1977-1995
John McCain III, R.	1987-1993
Arkansas	
Dale Bumpers, D.	1975-1993
David H. Pryor, D.	1979-1997
California	
Alan Cranston, D.	1969-1993
John F. Seymour, R.	1991-1993
Colorado	
Timothy E. Wirth, D.	1987-1993
Hank Brown, R.	1991-1997
Connecticut	
Christopher J. Dodd, D.	1981-1993
Joseph Lieberman, D.	1989-1995
Delaware	
William V. Roth, Jr., R.	1971-1995
Joseph R. Biden, Jr., D.	1973-1997
Florida	
Bob Graham, D.	1987-1993
Connie Mack III, R.	1989-1995
Georgia	
Sam Nunn, D.	1972-1997
Wyche Fowler, Jr., D.	1987-1993
Hawaii	
Daniel K. Inouye, D.	1963-1993
Daniel K. Akaka, D.	1990-1995
Idaho	
Steven D. Symms, R.	1981-1993
Larry E. Craig, R.	1991-1997
Illinois	
Alan J. Dixon, D.	1981-1993
Paul Simon, D.	1985-1997
Indiana	
Richard G. Lugar, R.	1977-1995
Dan R. Coats, R.	1989-1997
Iowa	
Charles E. Grassley, R.	1981-1993
Tom Harkin, D.	1985-1997
Kansas	
Robert J. Dole, R.	1969-1993
Nancy Landon Kassebaum, R.	1978-1997
Kentucky	
Wendell H. Ford, D.	1974-1993
Mitch McConnell, R.	1985-1997

State	Term
Louisiana	
J. Bennett Johnston, Jr., D.	1972-1997
John B. Breaux, D.	1987-1993
Maine	
William S. Cohen, R.	1979-1997
George J. Mitchell, D.	1980-1995
Maryland	
Paul S. Sarbanes, D.	1977-1995
Barbara A. Mikulski, D.	1987-1993
Massachusetts	
Edward M. Kennedy, D.	1962-1995
John F. Kerry, D.	1985-1997
Michigan	
Donald W. Riegle, Jr., D.	1976-1995
Carl Levin, D.	1979-1997
Minnesota	
David F. Durenberger, R.	1978-1995
Paul D. Wellstone, D.	1991-1997
Mississippi	
Thad Cochran, R.	1978-1997
Trent Lott, R.	1989-1995
Missouri	
John C. Danforth, R.	1976-1995
Christopher S. (Kit) Bond, R.	1987-1993
Montana	
Max Baucus, D.	1978-1997
Conrad Burns, R.	1989-1995
Nebraska	
J. James Exon, D.	1979-1997
Robert Kerrey, D.	1989-1995
Nevada	
Harry M. Reid, D.	1987-1993
Richard H. Bryan, D.	1989-1995
New Hampshire	
Warren B. Rudman, R.	1980-1993
Robert C. Smith, R.	1991-1997
New Jersey	
Bill Bradley, D.	1979-1997
Frank R. Lautenberg, D.	1982-1995
New Mexico	
Pete V. Domenici, R.	1973-1997
Jeff Bingaman, D.	1983-1995
New York	
Daniel P. Moynihan, D.	1977-1996
Alfonse M. D'Amato, R.	1981-1993
North Carolina	
Jesse A. Helms, R.	1973-1997
Terry Sanford, D.	1986-1993
North Dakota	
Quentin N. Burdick, D.	1960-1995
Kent Conrad, D.	1987-1993

State	Term
Ohio	
John H. Glenn, Jr., D.	1974-1993
Howard M. Metzenbaum, D.	1976-1995
Oklahoma	
David L. Boren, D.	1979-1997
Don Nickles, R.	1981-1993
Oregon	
Mark O. Hatfield, R.	1967-1997
Bob Packwood, R.	1969-1993
Pennsylvania	
Arlen Specter, R.	1981-1993
Harris L. Wofford, D.	1991-1997
Rhode Island	
Claiborne Pell, D.	1961-1997
John H. Chafee, R.	1976-1995
South Carolina	
Strom Thurmond, R.	1956-1997
Ernest F. Hollings, D.	1966-1993
South Dakota	
Larry Pressler, R.	1979-1997
Thomas A. Daschle, D.	1987-1993
Tennessee	
James Sasser, D.	1977-1995
Albert A. Gore, Jr., D.	1985-1997
Texas	
Lloyd M. Bentsen, Jr., D.	1971-1995
Phil Gramm, R.	1985-1997
Utah	
Edwin Jacob Garn, R.	1974-1993
Orrin G. Hatch, R.	1977-1995
Vermont	
Patrick J. Leahy, D.	1975-1993
James M. Jeffords, R.	1989-1995
Virginia	
John W. Warner, R.	1979-1997
Charles S. Robb, D.	1989-1995
Washington	
Brock Adams, D.	1987-1993
Slade Gorton, R.	1989-1995
West Virginia	
Robert C. Byrd, D.	1959-1995
John D. Rockefeller IV, D.	1985-1997
Wisconsin	
Robert W. Kasten, Jr., R.	1981-1993
Herbert Kohl, D.	1989-1995
Wyoming	
Malcolm Wallop, R.	1977-1995
Alan K. Simpson, R.	1979-1997

on the Thomas nomination and referred the matter to the Senate floor without a recommendation. A vote, which Thomas was expected to win easily, was scheduled for October 8. The situation, however, took an unexpected turn. On October 6, it was disclosed, through news "leaks," that the Judiciary Committee had kept quiet about charges that Thomas, while an official in the Administration of President Ronald Reagan, had sexually harassed a subordinate, Anita F. Hill.

The Senate vote on the Thomas nomination was postponed, and on October 11 the Judiciary Committee began three days of televised hearings on the charges against Thomas. Rarely had a political incident claimed such a rapt audience.

Hill, a law professor at the University of Oklahoma in Norman, testified that when she was an assistant to Thomas at the Department of Education and at the Equal Employment Opportunity Commission (EEOC), he repeatedly pestered her with unwanted advances, boasted of his sexual prowess, and related the details of pornographic films. Thomas denied all the accusations. A number of witnesses on both sides of the question also testified. In the end, many people had difficulty deciding which of the two principals, Thomas or Hill, was telling the truth. On October 15, Thomas was confirmed by a vote of 52 to 48, the closest for a Supreme Court nominee in this century. See also **Supreme Court of the United States.**

Congress develops an image problem. Many people who watched the hearings on television were critical of the all-male Senate Judiciary Committee's attempts to come to terms with the problem of sexual harassment. Women, especially, were saying that the committee members had no real comprehension of the issue.

The hearings—coming soon after disclosures that House members owed thousands of dollars to congressional restaurants, routinely bounced checks at the House Bank, and used the House sergeant at arms to fix parking tickets—fueled public discontent with Congress. Many voters were also angry at senators for voting earlier in the year, on July 17, to raise their annual salaries from $101,900 to $125,100 to match the salaries that the House voted itself in 1989. In a move to deflect public criticism, the senators also followed the House's lead in combining the pay hike with a ban on speaking fees.

Civil rights battle. Having failed to do so in 1990, Congress tried again in 1991 to reverse the effects of several Supreme Court rulings that made it more difficult for employees to sue companies for discrimination in their hiring and promotion practices. The House passed an antidiscrimination bill on June 5, but the vote of 273 to 158 was shy of the two-thirds that would be needed to override a Bush veto. Senator John C. Danforth (R., Mo.) and six other Republicans then tried for three weeks to work out a compromise with the Bush Administration. Danforth gave up on June 27, saying further talks would be futile.

House and Senate conferees took on the problem again in September and submitted a compromise bill to the President. But the Bush Administration announced on September 24 that this version of the measure was also unacceptable because, the Administration said, it was "a quota bill" that would make life overly difficult for business owners.

But the political climate changed when former neo-Nazi and Ku Klux Klan grand wizard David E. Duke gained prominence as a Republican candidate for governor in Louisiana. Opposing civil rights legislation, for whatever reason, was suddenly perceived as a dangerous strategy that threatened to make any politician, the President included, look like a racist. On October 24, Danforth and the President agreed to a measure that had been a veto target a day earlier. The Senate passed the bill 93 to 5 on October 30, and the House followed suit, 381 to 38, on November 7.

But the drama was not over. On the evening of November 20, the day before Bush was to sign the bill, White House Counsel C. Boyden Gray circulated a directive widely interpreted as ending federal affirmative-action programs and hiring guidelines benefiting women and minorities. Civil rights leaders claimed that Bush, through the executive order, was trying to undo the legislation. At the signing ceremony on November 21, Bush claimed that he had never seen the directive, and he repudiated Gray's action.

Helping the jobless. Congress and the Administration also disagreed on extending unemployment benefits for victims of the recession. On August 1, the Senate passed by voice vote a bill providing up to 20 additional weeks of benefits for nearly 3 million unemployed people who had exhausted their regular 26 weeks of benefits. The House passed the measure 375 to 45 the next day. Bush signed it on August 17 but refused to declare a fiscal emergency, which would be necessary for the extension to take effect.

On October 1, Congress passed another bill, which included a fiscal emergency declaration. The President vetoed the measure on October 11, saying its $6.4-billion cost would break a 1990 budget agreement between Congress and the Administration. A Senate effort on October 16 to override the veto fell two votes short, 65 to 35.

Later in the month, with his standing in national opinion polls falling and Republicans joining in the cry for a jobless-benefits extension, Bush said he wanted to avoid another veto showdown on the issue. He and congressional leaders reached agreement on a $5.3-billion package on November 13. The House approved the compromise 396 to 30 on November 14, and the Senate did the same, 91 to 2, the next day. Bush immediately signed the bill, which provided from 6 to 20 weeks of additional unemployment benefits.

Abortion counseling. On May 23, 1991, the Supreme Court upheld federal regulations, issued in 1988, prohibiting 4,000 government-funded family planning clinics from providing information to patients about abortion. Congress sought to restore the clinics' right to discuss abortion. On November 6, the House passed a "prochoice" health-funding bill 272 to 156, and the Senate acted, 73 to 24, a day later. Bush, as expected, vetoed the measure on November 19. The House attempted to override the veto but fell 12 votes short.

Anticrime bill defeated. On November 24, Senate and House conferees agreed on a $3-billion anticrime bill. The measure included a provision requiring a five-day waiting period for buying a handgun and extended the federal death penalty to more than 50 crimes, ranging from major drug-trafficking offenses to assassinations. The House passed the legislation, 205 to 203, on November 27, but it was killed by a Republican filibuster in the Senate. Senate Democrats blamed the bill's defeat on fierce lobbying by the National Rifle Association.

Highway and transit legislation. On February 13, Bush proposed a five-year, $105-billion program to upgrade the nation's highways, bridges, and mass transit systems. By the time the Senate and House reached agreement on the measure in late November, it had become a six-year, $151-billion program. The legislation, signed by President Bush on December 18, was expected to help stimulate the sagging economy by providing employment for some 60,000 construction workers and creating as many as 4 million jobs.

Banking reform. Also passed at the end of the 1991 session was a scaled-down version of a Bush plan for banking reform. The measure authorized $70 billion for the nearly broke Federal Deposit Insurance Corporation (FDIC), the agency that guarantees bank deposits against loss, and tightened bank regulation. But Congress rejected Bush's request for legislation authorizing banks to establish branches throughout the nation and to go into the insurance and brokerage businesses.

Ethics issues. On Feb. 27, 1991, the Senate Select Committee on Ethics concluded a 14-month investigation into charges that five of its members had intervened improperly on behalf of California savings and loan executive Charles H. Keating, Jr. The committee said it had found "substantial credible evidence" of ethics violations by Senator Alan Cranston (D., Calif.). It held that the other four members of the so-called Keating Five—Senators Dennis DeConcini (D., Ariz.), Donald W. Riegle, Jr. (D., Mich.), John H. Glenn, Jr. (D., Ohio), and John McCain III (R., Ariz.)—broke no rules but that DeConcini and Riegle had engaged in conduct that "gave the appearance of being improper." The committee said McCain and Glenn had "exercised poor judgment."

In the late 1980's, Keating had allegedly sought the senators' help in thwarting a federal investigation into his handling of the Lincoln Savings & Loan Association of Irvine, Calif. That probe resulted in his being indicted for fraud in 1990. Keating was convicted in December 1991.

On November 19, the committee split 3 to 3 along party lines on recommending that Cranston be censured by the full Senate. Instead it reprimanded him for "repugnant" conduct. Cranston, former Senate Democratic whip, expressed "deep remorse," then denied violating the norms of Senate behavior.

On August 2, the Ethics Committee rebuked Senator Alfonse M. D'Amato (R., N.Y.). It found that D'Amato, who was seeking a second term, had "conducted the business of his office in an improper and inappropriate manner" by letting his brother use it for personal business. But the committee said it had found no evidence that D'Amato had violated any Senate rule or federal law. D'Amato had been under investigation for allegedly using the influence of his office to benefit friends and campaign contributors.

Gray resigns. On September 11, House Democratic Whip William H. Gray III of Pennsylvania left Congress to head the United Negro College Fund. He was succeeded as whip by David E. Bonior of Michigan.

Deaths. Two members of Congress died in 1991. On February 8, Representative Silvio O. Conte (R., Mass.) died after a battle with cancer. And on April 4, Senator John Heinz III (R., Pa.) was killed in the crash of a private plane in Pennsylvania.

Frank Cormier and Margot Cormier

See also **United States, Government of the.** In ***World Book,*** see **Congress of the United States.**

Connecticut. See **State government.**

Conservation. A major environmental battle began taking shape in the United States in May 1991 over the definition of *wetlands* (swamps, marshes, bogs, and other frequently damp ecosystems). On May 14, several federal agencies proposed new criteria to define wetlands, a change that would drastically reduce the amount of land protected from development under U.S. law.

Once dismissed as worthless, wetlands have been recognized as a valuable resource. They help purify water supplies, control flooding, and serve as refuges and breeding grounds for an enormous variety of wildlife. In 1989, the U.S. government broadened the definition of wetlands to include areas that have mucky or peat-based soils, vegetation that thrives in moist areas, or water lying within 18 inches (46 centimeters) of the surface for at least seven straight days during the growing season.

Real estate developers, farmers, and oil and gas companies said the 1989 definition of wetlands was too broad and sought to loosen restrictions. In early August, the Administration of President George Bush proposed a redefinition of wetlands as areas that have standing water for 15 consecutive days or that have surface soil saturated with water for 21 consecutive days during a year. The new proposal also limited vegetation in wetlands to species that grow well in saturated soil, de-emphasizing plants that can exist in either wet or dry ground.

Environmentalists accused President Bush of abandoning his 1988 campaign pledge to allow "no net loss of wetlands." Estimates of the lands that would lose protection as wetlands under the proposed new definition ranged from 10 million acres (4 million hectares) to tens of millions of acres. After a three-month study, government scientists concluded that the redefinition would open nearly half the nation's wetlands to development. In November, Bush Administration officials backed away from the proposed redefinition and stated that any new regulations would uphold the President's campaign pledge. At year-end, the policy change was still under review.

Drilling ban. In late August, the Bush Administration announced that it planned to ban drilling for oil and gas off the northern half of the coast of Washington state. The area is one of the few coastlines in the lower 48 states that remains a wilderness. It includes the Olympic Coast National Marine Sanctuary, a refuge for sea otters and humpback, blue, and gray whales. As proposed, the ban could be repealed in the year 2000, a disappointment to the U.S. senators representing Washington state, who believe the ban should be permanent.

Grand Canyon cleanup. The owners of a giant coal-burning power plant in northern Arizona, 15 miles (24 kilometers) northeast of the Grand Canyon, agreed in August to install costly air pollution control equipment to help reduce smog that often blankets the canyon. The five electric utilities that share ownership of the Navajo Generating Station will install new equipment worth $430 million at the plant between 1997 and 1999. The equipment is designed to reduce the sulfur dioxide generated by the plant's smokestacks from about 70,000 short tons (63,000 metric tons) a year to about 7,000 short tons (6,400 metric tons) a year. The agreement was finalized on September 18.

Everglades. In July, the U.S. government and the state of Florida agreed to protect the Everglades from pollution and resolve a lawsuit that accused Florida of failing to enforce its own environmental laws. The settlement will create a 35,000-acre (14,000-hectare) artificial marsh designed to filter the runoff of chemical fertilizers used in farming. Those chemicals—mostly phosphorus—would otherwise flow into the Everglades National Park and the Loxahatchee National Wildlife Refuge. The phosphorus accumulates in sediment and causes a build-up of algae, which depletes the oxygen supply in the water. As a result, sawgrass, the primary native vegetation in the Everglades, dies out. Cattails and other nonnative plants replace the sawgrass, disrupting the ecosystem and natural wildlife patterns.

Amazon rain forest. Brazilian President Fernando Collor de Mello announced protective measures for the Amazon rain forest in June. He abolished tax subsidies that made the cutting of the forest for ranching

A world globe on Lake Washington near Seattle symbolizes Earth Day celebrations, which were held nationwide on April 22.

or farming highly profitable and allowed foreign governments and private organizations to fund environmental projects. He also dismissed the head of the country's Indian protection agency for failing to enforce measures to protect the endangered Yanomami people, who live in the Amazon rain forest.

In April, the Peruvian government granted permission to Texas Crude Exploration Incorporated of Houston to explore for oil in a 2.5-million-acre (1-million-hectare) tract of Amazon forest. Three-fourths of the site lies in the Pacaya-Samiria National Reserve, Peru's largest Amazonian refuge and habitat for many endangered species, including black and spectacled caymans (relatives of the alligator), Amazonian manatees, pink and gray dolphins, giant South American river turtles, and tiny monkeys called saddleback tamarins. A major outcry from environmentalists in Peru and the United States slowed the project. Peruvian President Alberto Fujimori pledged not to conclude the deal with Texas Crude if scientific evidence indicated that drilling would damage the area's fragile ecosystem.

Black-footed ferrets. The black-footed ferret was returned to wild habitats in 1991. The species was nearly extinct in the United States in the mid-1980's.

The black-footed ferret is a type of weasel once common in the American West. Black-footed ferrets prey on prairie dogs and live in burrows that their prey have vacated. Ranchers and farmers considered prairie dogs pests and began exterminating them in the early 1900's. But as the prairie dogs vanished, so did the ferrets. Years passed without any black-footed ferret sightings, and many scientists thought the species was extinct.

In 1981, a black-footed ferret colony was discovered in Wyoming, but in 1985, a sudden outbreak of canine distemper killed many of the animals. Hoping to launch a breeding program, the Wyoming Fish and Game Department captured the last 18 black-footed ferrets known to exist in 1986. The animals reproduced rapidly, and their population rose to 325 by 1991.

At a September 3 ceremony conducted by John Turner, director of the U.S. Fish and Wildlife Service (FWS), and Wyoming Governor Mike Sullivan, two black-footed ferrets were set free in an area of grassy plains. Eventually, 49 black-footed ferrets were released, all of them wearing radio collars so that biologists can track their movements. Compared with original FWS predictions that 90 per cent of the ferrets would die in the wild, only six of the ferrets were confirmed dead by the end of 1991.

The California condor, America's largest flying land bird, was readied for release into the wild in 1991. With a wingspan up to 10 feet (3 meters) across, these vultures once soared over the Pacific coast from Canada to Mexico and ranged as far east as Florida. As human population spread, condors suffered from habitat loss, hunting, and poisoning. Their numbers plummeted in the mid-1980's, and only 16 California condors remained alive in 1985.

Researchers captured those survivors and sent them to the San Diego Wild Animal Park and the Los Angeles Zoo to start a breeding program. Their population has since grown to 52. At the end of June 1991, researchers sent a San Diego *hatchling* (chick) to Los Angeles to meet another California condor chick and begin the socialization process, the first step toward release. Because condors seem to fare better in small groups, keepers added a pair of Andean condor chicks—South American relatives of the California condor—to the group.

On October 10, researchers took the pioneer birds to the Sespe Condor Sanctuary in the Los Padres National Forest 70 miles (113 kilometers) northwest of Los Angeles. The condors were kept in an artificial cave and a *hacking tower* (a large cage mounted on a tall pole) camouflaged to blend into the forest. The birds' food was dropped into their quarters through a chute. Researchers planned to hold the young condors until they are ready to fly. The greatest concern is that the condors might eat deer killed with lead bullets, which are poisonous, or that they will eat poisoned animal remains that ranchers have set out to kill coyotes. Eugene J. Walter, Jr.

See also **Environmental pollution; Water,** Special Report: **Our Precious Ground Water.** In ***World Book,*** see **Conservation.**

Consumerism. The lingering recession and inflation in the United States continued to inhibit consumer spending in 1991. Retail sales in October 1991 were 2 per cent lower than they were in October 1990, while consumer debt equaled 97 per cent of all disposable income.

Inflation in the United States, as measured by the Consumer Price Index (CPI), was rising at an annual rate of 2.7 per cent as of August 1991, and was 3.8 per cent higher than it had been the previous year. The CPI, which is compiled by the Department of Labor's Bureau of Labor Statistics, is the standard measure of living costs.

Consumer confidence in the economy, as measured by the Consumer Confidence Index, was at a low 72.7 as of September 1991, compared with a rating of 91.5 in 1990. The index measures consumers' confidence in their financial status for the next six months.

Food Labeling. The U.S. Food and Drug Administration in November 1991 proposed changes in the regulation of food labeling. The new rules would require food companies to give the amount of fat, salt, calories, cholesterol, and fiber in almost all foods. According to the proposal, foods labeled as "fresh," "low-cholesterol," and "low-fat" would have to meet stricter standards to avoid misleading consumers.

Banking. Banks came under pressure in 1991 to loosen their credit requirements to help spur the economy. The Administration of President George

Bush said that bank regulators had become increasingly cautious in the wake of the savings and loan failures due to bad loans. This inhibited bankers from making loans.

The U.S. General Accounting Office (GAO) said in early 1991 that bank failures could cost the Federal Deposit Insurance Corporation (FDIC) some $10 billion by the end of 1991. The GAO further predicted that the FDIC would run out of money by the end of 1991.

To prevent future bailouts of the savings and loan industry, the U.S. Congress and the Bush Administration proposed several changes in banking regulations. While Congress did not pass extensive reform measures, some new consumer protections were added to banking laws.

Telecommunications. Increased charges for cable television prompted the Federal Communications Commission in June 1991 to approve a plan to reregulate cable TV charges in communities having fewer than six broadcast stations. Cable rates, which had increased 61 per cent between November 1986 and April 1991, had been deregulated in 1984.

Local telephone companies were allowed to enter the telecommunications market when a federal appeals court in October 1991 lifted restrictions that had prevented them from providing electronic information services. The ruling permits local telephone companies to provide such services as electronic directories, medical information, and information on stocks, sports, and news.

Energy consumption. A bill calling for an increase in the amount of mileage automobiles obtain from a gallon of fuel was introduced in early 1991 by Senator Richard H. Bryan (D., Nev.). The bill calls for the combined city and highway fuel economy of cars to be at least 40 miles (64 kilometers) per gallon (4 liters) by the year 2001. The current standard, known as the Corporate Average Fuel Economy standard, is 27.5 miles (44 kilometers) per gallon. The bill's critics, which include the U.S. National Highway Traffic Safety Administration, say that such a mandate would reduce overall auto safety by forcing manufacturers to produce smaller cars that, in an accident, do not protect passengers as well as large cars do. At year-end, the bill was still pending in Congress.

In the aftermath of the Persian Gulf War, the U.S. Congress and the Bush Administration proposed several energy plans designed to decrease U.S. dependence on foreign oil. The plans variously called for taxes on imported oil, an increase in domestic oil production, and a decrease in consumer demand for oil. The Bush proposals also included faster licensing for nuclear power plants and the opening of 1.5 million acres (607,000 hectares) of the Arctic National Wildlife Refuge in Alaska for oil exploration, which Congress voted down. John W. Merline

See also, **Labor; Bank;** and **Food.** In ***World Book,*** see **Consumerism.**

Costa Rica. See **Latin America.**

Costner, Kevin (1955-), won the Academy of Motion Picture Arts and Sciences Award for best director in March 1991 for *Dances with Wolves* (1990), the first movie the popular actor directed. Costner also starred in the film, which won an Oscar for best picture, as a United States Army lieutenant who is befriended by Sioux Indians.

Kevin Costner was born on Jan. 18, 1955, in Los Angeles. While a marketing student at California State University in Fullerton, Costner also performed with a community theater group. After graduating in 1978, he took a marketing job, which he quit after only 30 days to seek work as an actor in Hollywood.

Costner's first film job—in *Sizzle Beach*, a low-budget movie shot in the late 1970's—left him so dissatisfied that he formed a theater workshop. In the early 1980's, Costner began working in films again. His first significant role was in *Testament* (1983).

Costner was cast as a suicidal man in *The Big Chill* (1983), but his scenes were cut before the movie was released. The director of that film then gave Costner a major role in *Silverado* (1985), which brought him critical and popular notice. Costner became one of Hollywood's top stars with the release of *The Untouchables* (1987). His other film credits include *No Way Out* (1987), *Bull Durham* (1988), *Field of Dreams* (1989), and *Robin Hood: Prince of Thieves* (1991).

Costner married Cindy Silva in 1978. They have two daughters and a son. Barbara A. Mayes

Courts. In the most highly publicized trial of 1991, a jury in West Palm Beach, Fla., on December 11 acquitted William Kennedy Smith of rape and battery. Smith, 31, a nephew of Senator Edward M. Kennedy (D., Mass.), had been charged with raping a young woman at the Kennedy estate in Palm Beach over the Easter weekend.

The identity of Smith's accuser was withheld by most of the news media before and during the trial, and her face was blocked out electronically during television broadcasts of the proceedings. After the trial, she identified herself publicly as Patricia Bowman, 30, of Jupiter, Fla., saying she wanted to help other alleged victims of "date rape."

Abortion issues. Most provisions of a Pennsylvania state abortion law were upheld by a federal appeals court ruling on October 10. The federal court let stand a provision requiring parental consent for abortions for females under age 18 and another requiring all women seeking abortions to have professional counseling first. But it ruled unconstitutional a requirement that women notify their husbands before having an abortion. An appeal of the ruling to the Supreme Court of the United States would be a direct challenge to the 1973 *Roe v. Wade* ruling that made abortions legal.

Operation Rescue, a group of antiabortion activists from around the country, converged on Wichita, Kans., during the summer of 1991 and attempted to shut down several abortion clinics there. On July 23, federal judge Patrick F. Kelly issued a restraining order against the protesters, who then argued before a federal appeals court that the federal judge had no jurisdiction in the matter. The protesters were supported in their legal efforts by the U.S. Department of Justice. Judge Kelly on August 21 ordered the arrest of three Operation Rescue leaders and fined them $10,000 plus $500 a day until they agreed to abide by his injunction against blocking the clinics. On August 23, the appeals court upheld Kelly's injunction. The federal judge then ordered the leaders to leave Wichita. That ended the demonstrations, which had resulted in more than 2,500 arrests for trespassing and civil disobedience during the summer-long protests.

Hate speech or free speech? A ruling that could have widespread repercussions was made on October 12, when a federal judge overturned a University of Wisconsin rule prohibiting "hate speech." The university's Board of Regents had instituted a ban on forms of speech that were considered demeaning to a person's color, creed, disabilities, race, religion, sex, or sexual orientation. The federal court ruled that the university's prohibition was too broad and violated the First Amendment guarantee of free speech. Legal experts predicted that the case would be appealed to the Supreme Court.

Car-seat case. A Miami, Fla., judge on May 3 dismissed a charge of vehicular homicide against a father accused of killing his 3-year-old daughter in a car crash. The charge resulted from the man's failure to comply with a Florida law requiring children under age 4 to be strapped into a safety seat. The judge said the prosecutors had failed to prove that the defendant, Ramiro de Jesus Rodriguez, had shown a "willful or wanton" disregard for his daughter's safety. Rodriguez, 31, a Nicaraguan immigrant, was believed to be the first person charged with homicide under a state law requiring young children to be fastened into a car seat when riding in an automobile.

Noriega on trial. The trial of General Manuel Antonio Noriega, who was deposed as dictator of Panama in January 1990, began on Sept. 5, 1991, in Miami and continued into 1992. Noriega was charged with drug trafficking, money laundering, and racketeering in connection with his alleged dealings with Colombian cocaine smugglers. See **Panama.**

Keating convicted. Charles H. Keating, the former owner of the now-defunct Lincoln Savings and Loan Association of Irvine, Calif., was found guilty of securities fraud on Dec. 4, 1991, in Los Angeles. A California Superior Court jury deliberated for two weeks before convicting Keating on 17 of 18 counts of defrauding small investors by enticing them to buy high-risk, uninsured Lincoln bonds. Sentencing was set for February 1992.

Other noteworthy convictions. Pamela Smart, a 23-year-old New Hampshire high school teacher, was convicted on March 22, 1991, of conspiring to kill her husband. The jury found that Smart had talked one of her students into staging a robbery at her Derry, N.H., condominium in May 1990 and fatally shooting her husband, Gregory. The student, William Flynn, who was 15 at the time of the crime, testified that he and Smart had been having an affair. Smart was sentenced to life in prison with no chance of parole.

A Federal Bureau of Investigation (FBI) tape recording of a 16-year-old girl being stabbed to death resulted in a murder conviction on Oct. 26, 1991, against the girl's parents, Zein Isa and Maria Isa of St. Louis, Mo. The couple, who were immigrants, allegedly were angry at the girl for defying family strictures and demanding to lead an American-style teen-age life. The FBI had bugged the family's apartment, thinking that Zein Isa might be taking part in illegal activities on behalf of the Palestine Liberation Organization. An unattended FBI tape made on Nov. 6, 1989, the night of Tina Isa's death, contained the voices of the parents telling Tina that her life is over and the girl begging for mercy as her father, according to the prosecution, stabbed her six times with a knife.

A jury in New York City on Aug. 19, 1991, found Julio Gonzalez, 37, a Cuban immigrant, guilty of arson and murder for starting a fire at the Happy Land Social Club in New York City on March 25, 1990, in which 87 people died. On Sept. 19, 1991, Gonzalez was sentenced to the maximum term of 25 years to life in prison.

The sixth and last teen-ager charged in a brutal attack on a woman jogger in New York City's Central Park in April 1989 pleaded guilty on Jan. 30, 1991. Stephen Lopez, 16, had been charged with rape, attempted murder, robbery, and several other crimes but, in a plea-bargain agreement, pleaded guilty only to robbery. He was sentenced to 1½ to 4½ years in prison. The other five youths had been convicted on more serious charges in 1990. They received sentences of up to 5 to 15 years in prison.

On March 12, 1991, Pasquale Raucci, 21, was acquitted of murder but convicted on lesser counts in the killing of Yusuf K. Hawkins, 16. Hawkins was shot to death during a confrontation with a mob of youths in Brooklyn, a borough of New York City, on Aug. 23, 1989. Two other defendants, Charles Stressler, 22, and Steven Curreri, 20, were acquitted of all charges on Feb. 7, 1991. Raucci, Stressler, and Curreri were the last of eight defendants to be tried in the Bensonhurst case. The prosecutions resulted in just one murder conviction. See **Civil rights.**

Jim Bakker's sentence reduced. Former television evangelist Jim Bakker, sentenced in 1989 to 45 years in prison for defrauding his followers, got his sentence reduced in 1991. On August 23, a U.S. judge in Charlotte, N.C., cut Bakker's prison term to 18 years, making him eligible for parole in 1995.

David L. Dreier

See also **Crime; Supreme Court of the United States.** In ***World Book,*** see **Court.**

Cresson, Edith (1934-   ), was appointed prime minister of France by President François Mitterrand on May 15, 1991. She succeeded Michel Rocard, who stepped down after three years in office. Cresson, a Socialist, had previously held several cabinet positions.

Cresson was appointed minister of agriculture in 1981, minister of trade in 1983, and minister for European affairs in 1988. In those posts, she gained a reputation for combativeness, known especially for describing Japan's trade policies as a "strategy of conquest." In naming her prime minister, Mitterrand said he wanted someone who could aggressively promote French economic interests in a united Europe. See **France.**

Cresson was born Edith Campion on Jan. 27, 1934, in a Paris suburb. She earned a degree in business and a doctorate in demography from the School of Higher Commercial Studies in Paris. Her political career began in 1965, when she campaigned for Mitterrand in his unsuccessful presidential bid. Remaining active in the Socialist movement, she was elected mayor of Thuré in west-central France in 1973 and mayor of nearby Châtellerault in 1983. From 1979 to 1981, Cresson sat in the European Parliament, an advisory body to the European Community. In 1981, she was elected to the National Assembly, one of France's two houses of parliament, winning reelection in 1986 and 1988. Cresson and her husband, Jacques, an automobile executive, have two daughters. Karin C. Rosenberg

Crime. More than in most years, murder dominated crime headlines during 1991. The arrest in Milwaukee, Wisc., of an alleged killer of at least 17 people was especially startling because of the gruesome fate of the victims. And in a scene that has become numbingly familiar, a gunman burst into a crowd of people—this time at a restaurant in Texas—and committed mayhem with a semiautomatic weapon. Multiple slayings, or arrests for such crimes, in Iowa, Arizona, and elsewhere added to the year's grim litany of homicide.

A ghastly apartment in Milwaukee. On July 22, Milwaukee police officers, led by a man claiming to have narrowly escaped being murdered, knocked on the apartment door of Jeffrey L. Dahmer, a 31-year-old factory laborer. Looking through the apartment, the officers found the dismembered remains of 11 male bodies. According to the police, Dahmer later admitted to those killings and to 6 others as well, stretching over a period of 13 years and back to his boyhood home of Bath, Ohio. Dahmer reportedly told investigators that he picked up most of his victims, almost all of them black men, at bars or shopping malls. At his apartment, he allegedly drugged and killed them, usually by strangulation, and then cut the bodies into pieces.

The investigation of the crimes led to public outrage when it was revealed that police officers had earlier gone to Dahmer's apartment in a black neighborhood. In May, neighbors reported seeing a naked and

Investigators in Killeen, Tex., examine a pickup truck driven through the window of a restaurant on October 16 by a man who fatally shot 23 diners.

bleeding boy outside the building. The investigating officers, however, reportedly accepted Dahmer's explanation that the boy, a Laotian immigrant, was an adult and his homosexual lover. They allowed Dahmer to take the boy back to his apartment. Minutes later, Dahmer reportedly confessed in July, the youth became victim number 12. After Dahmer's arrest, the officers were suspended for failing to make a routine check that would have disclosed a prior conviction for sexual molestation. Dahmer had been convicted in 1989 of sexually molesting the boy's older brother and was still on probation for that offense in 1991.

In January 1992, Dahmer pleaded guilty to 15 murder charges, and his attorneys said that he would claim insanity. If he were ruled insane, Dahmer would be sent to a mental hospital instead of to prison, and he would be eligible to petition for release after just one year of treatment.

Terror at a Texas restaurant. The worst mass shooting in United States history occurred on Oct. 16 , 1991, in Killeen, Tex. As lunchtime patrons at Luby's cafeteria watched in stunned amazement, a man crashed his pickup truck through the front window, stepped out of the cab, and began methodically firing two 9-millimeter semiautomatic pistols. For 10 minutes, until the police arrived, the man fired at the scrambling customers. Then, after being wounded in an exchange with police officers, he pointed a pistol at his head and shot himself. Twenty-three people, including the gunman, lay dead. About 20 others were wounded, and 1 died later at a hospital.

The killer was identified as George J. Hennard, 35, of nearby Belton, Tex., a former merchant marine sailor. People who had known Hennard described him as a troubled, combative loner who harbored a hatred of women. Law enforcement authorities said they were unable to determine Hennard's motive.

Bloody revenge. Less than three weeks after the Texas massacre, a graduate student at the University of Iowa in Iowa City went on a shooting rampage, but one in which the victims were carefully chosen. Gang Lu, 28, who had earned a doctorate in physics in May, shot six people to death on November 1 after losing out to another student in his quest for a prestigious academic award. Armed with a .38-caliber revolver, Lu first killed his rival, Linhua Shan, 27, and three members of the physics and astronomy faculty. Minutes later, he fatally shot a female administrator and severely wounded a receptionist. He then killed himself. The police said that unmailed letters found in Lu's apartment after the killings outlined his murder plans in detail.

Post office shootings. Twice in autumn 1991, fired postal workers killed their former supervisors and other postal employees, according to the police. On October 11, Joseph M. Harris, 35, was captured by a police SWAT (special weapons and tactics) team at the Paterson, N.J., post office after he allegedly shot and killed two mail handlers. Earlier, Harris had gone to the home of his former boss, Carol Ott, stabbed her to death, and fatally shot her boyfriend, police said.

A month later, on November 14, a former postal worker in the Detroit area sought similar vengeance. According to witnesses, Thomas McIlvane, 31, who had been fired from his job as a clerk at the Royal Oak post office, came into the post office with a sawed-off .22-caliber semiautomatic rifle and began shooting at his former supervisors and other employees. After killing three people and wounding six, one of whom died later, McIlvane turned the gun on himself and shot himself in the head. He died the next day in the hospital. The two episodes were the fourth and fifth multiple shootings at U.S. post offices by disgruntled employees since 1986.

Man claims to have killed 60. A Texas drifter, under arrest in Mississippi for the rape and murder of a 10-year-old girl, reportedly told investigators in August that the child was just one victim among many. According to the police, the suspect, Donald Leroy Evans, 34, said that from 1977 to 1986, he killed at least 60 people, mostly women, in about 20 states. That number would be a record for serial murder in the United States. At year-end, the Federal Bureau of Investigation (FBI) was working with state law enforcement officials in an effort to determine whether Evans' story is true.

Two more murders in Gainesville. In Gainesville, Fla., where five college students—all but one of them women—were brutally slain in August 1990, two similar killings occurred in 1991. On June 7, two female University of Florida students were found strangled to death in the apartment they shared. The day after the latest bodies were found, a 29-year-old carpet cleaner, Alan Robert Davis, was arrested for the crime. The police said that Davis admitted killing the two women.

On November 15, Danny H. Rolling, 36, the son of a Louisiana policeman, was indicted for the 1990 Gainesville slayings. While Gainesville investigators compiled evidence against Rolling, he was serving time in nearby Marion County for the September 1990 armed robbery of an Ocala, Fla., supermarket.

Woman charged with highway murders. Another series of Florida murders was apparently solved in January 1991 with the arrest in Daytona Beach, Fla., of 33-year-old Aileen Carol Wuornos. Wuornos was accused of killing as many as seven middle-aged men whose bodies were found beside Interstate Highway 75 in 1989 and 1990. Investigators said the woman evidently killed men who had picked her up along the highway or who had stopped to offer her help. Property belonging to some of the victims was found in Wuornos' possession, the police said.

Violent death amid tranquillity. Nine people at a Thai Buddhist Temple near Phoenix were found slain on August 10. The victims—six priests, two young disciples, and an elderly nun—had all been shot in the head, apparently methodically executed. Investigators first theorized that the murders were an anti-Asian hate crime, but they later concluded that the killers were robbers who had become enraged at finding little worth stealing. In September, four Tucson men were charged with the crime, but they were later released. In late October, three Phoenix-area teen-agers were arrested and charged with the murders.

Poisoned medicine. In March, three residents of the Tacoma, Wash., area were poisoned, two of them fatally, by Sudafed decongestant capsules that had been laced with cyanide. An investigation by the U.S. Food and Drug Administration, which collected all the Sudafed capsules in the state, turned up several more packages with cyanide. The FBI said the tampering was evidently done locally. Nonetheless, the maker of Sudafed, the Burroughs Wellcome Company of Research Triangle Park, N.C., issued a nationwide recall of the drug. At year-end, no one had been arrested for the crime.

Crime up in 1991. The number of violent crimes reported to the police in the United States increased by 5 per cent from 1990 to 1991, the FBI reported in October 1991. The FBI said that in the first six months of 1991, murder was up 5 per cent; rape, 4 per cent; aggravated assault, 2 per cent; and robbery, 9 per cent. The FBI report was based on statistics supplied by 16,000 law enforcement agencies throughout the United States. David L. Dreier

In *World Book,* see **Crime.**

Cuba. The collapse of Communism in the Soviet Union in 1991 brought an end to Soviet assistance to Cuba. Nevertheless, Cuban President Fidel Castro positioned himself and Cuba to survive, if not embrace, a changed world. Addressing members of Cuba's ruling Communist Party on October 12, Castro called Western democracy "complete garbage," indicating that he had no intention of introducing the democratic reforms that had undermined Soviet Communist rule.

On September 19, the Soviet government said that it would withdraw all of its military troops and advisers from Cuba, thus ending a troublesome chapter of the Cold War and leaving Cuba to defend itself. On May 25, the last Cuban soldiers departed from Angola, where they had been supporting a Marxist regime for more than a decade.

Without the support of a superpower, Castro was forced to make peace with his neighbors. In July, he attended a meeting in Mexico where some of his democratically elected peers lectured him about the need for Cuba to adopt a more open political system. In August, he welcomed some 14,000 athletes, journalists, and officials—including 2,000 Americans—to Havana for the Pan American Games, one of the first nonpolitical events in Cuba since Castro came to power in 1959. At a meeting in Mexico on Oct. 23, 1991, Castro asked the leaders of Mexico, Colombia, and Venezuela for help in persuading the United States to lift its trade embargo against Cuba.

Athletes perform opening ceremonies at the Pan American Games. Cuba hosted the games in August 1991 in Havana.

With the end of Soviet assistance, life became harder for Cubans. On June 1, the government cut the daily bread ration in Havana to 3 ounces (85 grams), the equivalent of one small loaf or two rolls. On September 9, cigars and cigarettes joined the expanding list of rationed items, which included everything from food and fuel to paper and shoes. There were cuts in public transportation, and bicycles became a major mode of transportation. Factories had to shorten workdays or close because of the loss of Soviet and East bloc raw materials.

Call for elections. On May 31, a group of Cuban intellectuals issued a declaration calling for democratic reforms. Among the refoms demanded were free, direct election of delegates to Cuba's National Assembly; the elimination of restrictions on emigration; the return of peasant free markets, which provide people a chance to meet food shortages by selling their own produce; and the freeing of political prisoners.

Nuclear safety. Also on May 31, the U.S. government urged Cuba to work with the United Nations International Atomic Energy Agency to guarantee safe completion of a nuclear power plant on Cuba's southern coast. With reduced Soviet assistance, there were fears that Cuba did not have the necessary technicians to finish the job safely. Nathan A. Haverstock

See also **Latin America** (Facts in brief table). In *World Book,* see **Cuba.**

Cyprus. See **Middle East.**

Czechoslovakia. The two political movements that in 1989 had united to end Communist rule peacefully in Czechoslovakia broke into factions in 1991. These two movements were the Civic Forum in the Czech Republic—the party of Czechoslovak President Václav Havel—and Public Against Violence, its ally in the Slovak Republic. In addition, growing separatist demands by the Slovak Republic threatened to break apart the federation that bound the two republics into a single nation in 1918.

In the Czech Republic, disagreements over the speed of economic change split the Civic Forum. One faction sought as fast a departure as possible from the country's centrally run economy. The opposing faction favored a gradual transition to a free-market economy to ease the pain of unemployment and inflation that was expected to accompany economic reform.

In the Slovak Republic, a separatist tide splintered the Public Against Violence movement and revived old tensions between the richer, more industrial Czech lands and the poorer, more agricultural Slovak region. Although Slovakia largely manages its regional affairs, Slovak nationalists complained of "rule from Prague," the nation's capital, referring to Czech dominance in the federal government.

Throughout the year, Slovak demonstrators clamored for a declaration of sovereignty by the republic's government, which would give laws passed by the Slovak legislature precedence over federal laws. Nonetheless, public opinion polls suggested that most Slovaks opposed outright secession. Instead, they preferred a looser federation with more powers granted to the republics.

On July 18, 1991, Czechoslovakia's Federal Assembly (parliament) authorized a nationwide referendum to determine future Czech and Slovak relations. But the two sides failed to set a date for the referendum in talks held in November.

Economic reform. The International Monetary Fund, an agency of the United Nations, in January granted a $1.78-billion loan to ease Czechoslovakia's move to a market economy and reduce the impact of higher petroleum prices following the Persian Gulf War. The federal government, however, repeatedly

Dancers with Feld Ballets/NY perform the premiere in February of choreographer Eliot Feld's *Fauna*, a dance with Oriental motifs, in New York City.

complained of the slow pace of Western aid and investment. Havel warned on June 12 that without adequate Western backing economic reform could be seriously slowed, making political and social unrest in the country likely.

By mid-1991, most industrial sectors showed a marked decline, and unemployment neared 400,000 people. Trade with the West had dropped 18 per cent. In addition, trade with the East suffered from the collapse of the East-bloc trade alliance, Comecon; from German reunification, with the loss of the East German market; and from the slump in the Soviet Union's economy. Eric Bourne

See also **Europe** (Facts in brief table). In ***World Book,*** see **Czechoslovakia.**

Dancing. A major event in dance during 1991 was a spectacular new production of *The Sleeping Beauty* by the New York City Ballet. Because the ballet has been a cornerstone of dance repertories around the world since its premiere in Russia in 1890, a new production normally would not be newsworthy. But City Ballet's reworking remained true to the spirit of Marius Petipa, the French-born choreographer who created the ballet, while bringing a fresh perspective to the dance.

This production, directed by Peter Martins, City Ballet's artistic director, both affirmed and challenged the company's traditions. On the one hand, a restaging of the ballet was a natural project for a company that had been led by the Russian-born choreographer George Balanchine until his death in 1983. Balanchine, who was considered Petipa's artistic heir, had often expressed a wish to stage *The Sleeping Beauty.* On the other hand, restaging the classic ballet ran counter to City Ballet's long-standing policy of presenting only new ballets.

Martins' production dazzled the critics and public alike. It sold out during its two-week run in April 1991 at the New York State Theater at Lincoln Center for the Performing Arts in New York City and drew record crowds in Saratoga Springs, N.Y., in July. Martins' total reworking of some sections of the ballet and updating of others were so flawless that critics said it was difficult to know where Petipa left off and Martins began.

The new production, which cost more than $2.5-million, was also notable for its modern decorative devices. Instead of using a revolving painted backdrop to convey the famous transformation scenes—when the prince journeys through enchanted lands to find the sleeping princess—designer David Mitchell used long sequences of slide projections to convey the journey and the passage of 100 years.

With each of the ballet's soloist roles shared by several dancers, the production also proved the company's depth, thus affirming City Ballet's reputation as the world's strongest exponent of classical ballet.

Company B. Another big success came from modern-dance choreographer Paul Taylor, whose *Company B* was premiered by the Houston Ballet on June 20 at the John F. Kennedy Center for the Performing Arts in Washington, D.C. *Company B,* set to songs recorded by the Andrews Sisters, captured brilliantly the happy-go-lucky quality of the popular vocal group and the songs they made popular in the 1940's. Yet beneath the light-heartedness were glimmers of tragedy, when dancers dressed as World War II soldiers occasionally fell to the ground or were separated from loved ones. Observers were impressed with the ability of Taylor to evoke such happiness and sadness simultaneously.

Company B was the first of six dances commissioned from regional companies in the United States by and for presentation at the Kennedy Center under a project to strengthen American ballet. On October 8, the second production in the project, *The Age of Anxiety* by John Neumeier, was unveiled by Ballet West of Salt Lake City, Utah.

Pennsylvania Ballet woes. One of the six companies participating in the Kennedy Center ballet project nearly collapsed before it could fulfill its commission. On March 11, the Pennsylvania Ballet's board of trustees suspended the company's operations indefinitely because of a $3-million debt.

Artistic director Christopher d'Amboise, however, kept the company in business by securing agreements from all the dancers, musicians, and technical staff to work for free and by mounting a fund-raising campaign. Within two weeks, the company had collected more than $1 million in contributions from the public. That vote of confidence inspired several foundations to make major grants to the company. By July, the Pennsylvania Ballet had raised the $3 million needed to pay off its debts.

Financial problems also plagued many other U.S. troupes in 1991. Programming by the American Ballet Theatre (ABT) was markedly conservative because of budget cuts imposed by its board. The ABT's major productions for 1991 were, basically, recyclings of former productions. The only fresh touches to the company's latest version of *Coppélia* were the new sets and costumes. For *Don Quixote,* the company invited former Bolshoi Ballet star Vladimir Vasiliev to create new choreography. To enliven its longest engagement of the year—an eight-week season at New York City's Metropolitan Opera in spring 1991—the troupe's codirector Jane Hermann invited guest artists to perform. Among them were Carla Fracci, Fernando Bujones, and Sylvie Guillem. On June 12, Cynthia Gregory, the ABT's senior ballerina, retired from the company.

Having survived financially tumultuous times in 1990, the Dance Theatre of Harlem and the Joffrey Ballet limped along in 1991. Both troupes presented new works, though their touring schedules were limited. One of the Joffrey's most promising young choreographers, Edward Stierle, presented a new ballet, *Empyrean Dances,* on March 5 and, three days later, died at age 23 of complications resulting from AIDS.

Modern dance. Following the death of choreographer Martha Graham on April 1, the Martha Graham Dance Company continued to perform on a curtailed basis. On October 8, the company premiered in New York City a fragment of a dance that Graham had been working on at the time of her death, *The Eyes of the Goddess.* The work had been commissioned to celebrate the quincentennial of Christopher Columbus' arrival in the New World.

Merce Cunningham, now the foremost modern dance choreographer in the United States, extended the boundaries of his craft in March with the premiere of *Trackers,* created with the aid of a computer. It was the first presentation of a computer-assisted dance by a major choreographer.

Twyla Tharp, another important modern-dance choreographer, assembled a new company during a four-week residency at Ohio State University in Columbus. On October 4, Tharp and her group of 16 dancers presented two new works.

Imports. Of the many foreign troupes visiting the United States in 1991, none aroused more curiosity than Great Britain's Royal Ballet, which had disappointed audiences on its last U.S. tour in 1983. The British troupe performed in the United States in March and again in July. Although the company had no stand-out dancers, critics were impressed by its improvement. Nancy Goldner

See also **Dancing,** Special Report: **Two Legends of Dance.** In ***World Book,*** see **Ballet; Dancing.**

Two Legends of Dance

By Nancy Goldner

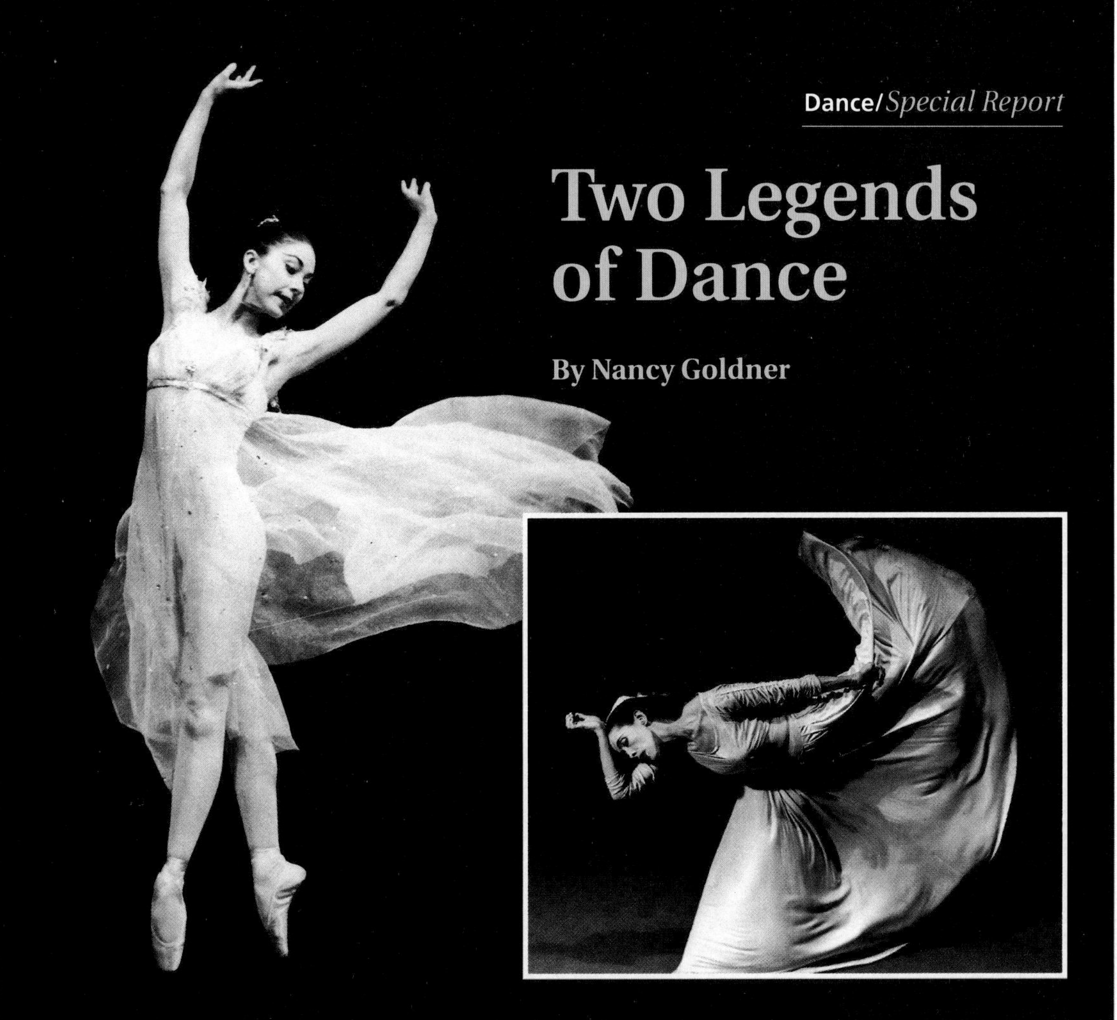

Different styles

Margot Fonteyn, *above left,* strikes a classic ballerina's pose in 1958. Martha Graham, *above,* dances in a 1945 performance of *Letter to the World,* a piece inspired by the life and poetry of Emily Dickinson.

The world was reminded of the vastly different, but equally brilliant, contributions Martha Graham and Dame Margot Fonteyn made to dance in the 1900's when both died in early 1991. Graham was the high priestess of modern dance, while Fonteyn was the ideal ballerina. The two worked together only once, in 1975, when Fonteyn and Rudolf Nureyev performed in *Lucifer,* a dance Graham composed especially for them. Although this was not the first time that the traditionally warring worlds of modern dance and ballet had joined forces, the event was notable because it brought together artists who represented the best of each form.

Graham did not invent American modern dance, but her name came to be synonymous with it. She exemplified modern dance's search for techniques and movements different from those of classical ballet. She was also an extraordinarily productive artist, an inexhaustible source of new ideas in the modern dance movement for over 60 years.

Graham was born on May 11, 1894, in Allegheny, Pa. In 1908, she moved with her family to Santa Barbara, Calif. Her career as a dancer began at age 22, when she joined the Denishawn company, an experimental dance troupe. After performing on the vaudeville circuit with the Denishawn company from 1916 to 1923, Graham began to choreograph her own dances in 1926. Her technique, inspired by her close observation of the different motions and forms that accompany breathing in and out, centered on the contraction and release of the back and torso muscles. The technique is taught today around the world.

Graham's dances had an underlying theme that no earlier choreographer had dared bring to the stage: the complex interior life of individual persons. Whether her heroine was a solitary woman rejected by society, as in *Heretic* (1929), an American frontier woman on her wedding day in *Appalachian Spring* (1944), or a tragic, mythic figure, as in *Clytemnestra* (1958), the dancing always revealed the character's inner self.

Graham dramatized private thoughts and emotions through her own vocabulary of dance movements. She said that she never deliberately set out to create a new way of moving. Rather, she needed to find new movements because she had new subjects to express. Her work created a wave of modern dances designed to reveal psychological states. Today it is almost impossible to see a modern dance that does not bear some sign of her style, with its angular positions and powerfully rhythmic movements.

Graham pioneered her art in the solitude of her studio. Fonteyn's career, in contrast, developed through collaborations with other artists. Born May 18, 1919, in Reigate, England, Fonteyn was only a teen-ager when she began to work with the late English choreographer Sir Frederick Ashton in the many ballets he created for the Royal Ballet and its predecessors, the Vic-Wells and Sadler's Wells companies.

Beginning in 1935, Ashton and Fonteyn forged what is known as the English style of ballet, which is characterized by its grace and elegance. Fonteyn's hallmark style was a deep musicality and a lyrical, curved body line from head to toe. Her special gift was to create an image of perfectly harmonized movements while she danced.

Fonteyn's second great collaborator was Rudolf Nureyev, who defected from the Soviet Union in 1961 at the age of 23. By 1960, Fonteyn had begun to think of retiring, but in 1962 she was reinspired to dance by Nureyev's fiery temperament—the exact opposite of her own—and by his superb Russian training. The two quickly became a legendary partnership, dancing with many companies around the world.

Both Graham and Fonteyn suffered great disappointments. Graham was devastated by the failure of her marriage in 1951 to the dancer Erick Hawkins. Fonteyn's husband, the Panamanian diplomat Roberto Arias, was shot in a 1964 assassination attempt that left him paralyzed from the waist down. He died in 1989. Yet both women remained devoted to their art. Graham did not stop dancing until 1969, when she was 75 years old, and she never stopped choreographing dances. Fonteyn only left the stage in 1981. She then coached dancers in roles she had made famous.

Fonteyn died on Feb. 21, 1991, of cancer in Panama City, Panama, at age 71. Little more than a month later, on April 1, Graham died at age 96 in New York City of complications from pneumonia. When Fonteyn danced in Graham's *Lucifer*, Graham announced that "the war"—between ballet and modern dance—"has ended." In death, Fonteyn and Graham seemed even more perfectly allied: unique artists, to be sure, but ones who had been alike in redefining the technical and aesthetic boundaries of dance.

The author:

Nancy Goldner is the dance critic for *The Philadelphia Inquirer.*

Deaths in 1991 included those listed below, who were Americans unless otherwise indicated.

Abbott, Berenice (1898-Dec. 10), early modern American photographer best known for her black-and-white photographs of New York City in the 1930's.
Abe, Shintaro (1924-May 15), foreign minister of Japan from 1982 to 1986.
Allen, Irwin (1916-Nov. 20), motion-picture producer known for star-studded disaster films, such as *The Poseidon Adventure* (1972) and *The Towering Inferno* (1974).
Anderson, Carl D. (1905-Jan. 11), physicist who discovered two subatomic particles, the positron and the muon, and shared the 1936 Nobel Prize in physics for his discovery of the positron.
Anderson, Thomas F. (1911-Aug. 11), biophysical chemist and geneticist who was among the first to use electron microscopes for the study of viruses.
Appling, Luke (Lucius Benjamin Appling) (1907-Jan. 3), shortstop for the Chicago White Sox from 1930 to 1950; member of the National Baseball Hall of Fame.
Arrau, Claudio (1903-June 9), Chilean-born concert pianist.
Arrupe y Gondra, Pedro (1907-Feb. 5), Spanish-born Roman Catholic priest who headed the Jesuit order from 1965 to 1983.
Arthur, Jean (Gladys Georgianna Greene) (1908-June 19), husky-voiced actress who starred in films of the 1930's and 1940's, including *Mr. Smith Goes to Washington* (1939).
Ashcroft, Dame Peggy (Edith Margaret Emily Hutchinson) (1907-June 14), British actress who began on the stage and then became a star of film and television.
Atwater, Lee (Harvey Leroy Atwater) (1951-March 29), former Republican Party chairman.
Axthelm, Peter M. (1943-Feb. 2), sports columnist and TV sports commentator.
Bacon, Mary (1948?-June 8), jockey and one of the first women to race successfully on the thoroughbred circuit in the 1960's.
Barbie, Klaus (1913-Sept. 25), Nazi war criminal known as the "butcher of Lyon" for directing the torture and execution of Resistance leaders in Lyon, France, during World War II (1939-1945).
Bardeen, John (1908-Jan. 30), physicist who twice won the Nobel Prize in physics, in 1956 for the invention of the transistor and in 1972 for the theory of superconductivity, the ability of some substances to conduct electricity without resistance at extremely low temperatures.
Barghoorn, Frederick C. (1911-Nov. 20), political scientist and expert on the Soviet Union.
Barnet, Charlie (1913-Sept. 4), jazz saxophonist and bandleader.
Barrera, Lazaro Sosa (1924-April 25), Cuban-born horse trainer who trained Affirmed, the 1978 Triple Crown winner.
Baruch, André (1908?-Sept. 15), broadcast announcer and voice of the 1930's radio program "The Shadow."
Bell, Cool Papa (James Bell) (1903-March 7), Negro League outfielder known for his blazing speed on the base paths; member of the National Baseball Hall of Fame.
Bellamy, Ralph Rexford (1904-Nov. 29), veteran character actor who appeared in more than 100 motion pictures and was acclaimed for his stage role as President Franklin D. Roosevelt in *Sunrise at Campobello.*
Berg, Jack (Judah Bergman) (1909-April 22), British lightweight boxing champion from 1934 to 1936 and world junior welterweight champion from 1930 to 1931.
Bergalis, Kimberly (1968-Dec. 8), a victim of AIDS who helped spearhead efforts to have health-care providers tested for AIDS after she contracted AIDS from her dentist.
Bigart, Homer (1907-April 16), Pulitzer Prize-winning reporter for the *New York Herald Tribune* and *The New York Times* from 1929 to 1972.

Charles H. Goren, contract bridge expert.

Floyd B. McKissick, civil rights leader.

Graham Greene, British novelist.

Danny Thomas, entertainer and TV actor.

Bolling, Richard W. (1916-April 21), Democratic representative from Missouri from 1949 to 1983.
Brickhill, Paul (1916-April 23), Australian journalist and novelist who wrote *The Great Escape* (1950).
Brown, Paul (1908-Aug. 5), legendary football coach who founded the Cleveland Browns and Cincinnati Bengals.
Brunet, Pierre (1902-July 27), French-born figure skater who won national and world titles and two Olympic gold medals in the 1920's and 1930's and later became a renowned skating teacher.
Burch, Dean (1927-Aug. 4), chairman of the Federal Communications Commission from 1969 to1974.
Burgess, Smoky (Forest Burgess) (1927-Sept. 15), baseball player who formerly held the major league career record for most pinch hits.
Burleson, Omar T. (1906-May 14), Democratic representative from Texas from 1947 to 1979.
Busch, Niven (1903-Aug. 25), novelist and screenwriter noted for his Westerns.
Capra, Frank (1897-Sept. 3), motion-picture director noted for his populist portrayals of the "little man" battling corruption in *Mr. Deeds Goes to Town* (1936) and *Mr. Smith Goes to Washington* (1939) and for his depiction of small-town life in *It's a Wonderful Life* (1946).
Carter, Gwendolen M. (1906-Feb. 20), Canadian-born political scientist who was a founder of the African Studies Association.
Carter, Sonny (Manley Lanier Carter, Jr.) (1947-April 5), United States astronaut who flew aboard the space shuttle *Discovery* on a military mission in 1984.

Deaths

Isaac Bashevis Singer, Nobel laureate.

Red Grange, legendary football star.

Rudolf Serkin, concert pianist.

Colleen Dewhurst, star of stage and screen.

Caulfield, Joan (1922-June 18), actress who starred in motion pictures in the 1940's and in TV's "My Favorite Husband" in the 1950's.
Chaikin, Sol Chick (1918-April 1), president of the International Ladies' Garment Workers' Union from 1975 to 1986.
Chandler, Happy (Albert Benjamin Chandler) (1898-June 15), Democratic governor of Kentucky from 1935 to 1939, senator from that state from 1939 to 1945, and commissioner of baseball from 1945 to 1950.
Clark, Gene (Harold Eugene Clark) (1941-May 24), singer, songwriter, and musician who helped found the folk-rock group The Byrds in 1964.
Clark, Manning (Charles Manning Hope Clark) (1915-May 23), Australian historian whose six-volume *A History of Australia* (1962-1987) was the first comprehensive history of that continent.
Clark, Steve M. (1960?-found dead Jan. 8), British guitarist for the heavy-metal rock group Def Leppard.
Clayton, Buck (1911-Dec. 8), jazz trumpeter who starred with the Count Basie Band.
Cleveland, James L. (1931-Feb. 9), gospel musician and composer known as the "King of Gospel."
Collins, LeRoy (1909-March 12), Democratic governor of Florida from 1955 to 1961.
Combs, Bert T. (1911?-Dec. 4), former governor of Kentucky who championed civil rights and fiscal reform.
Connolly, Thomas A. (1899-April 18), Roman Catholic archbishop of Seattle from 1951 to 1975.
Conte, Silvio O. (1921-Feb. 8), Republican representative from Massachusetts from 1959 until his death in office.
Cooney, Jimmy "Scoops" (James Edward Cooney) (1894-Aug. 7), former baseball player who made the last recorded unassisted triple play in the National League while playing shortstop for the Chicago Cubs in 1926.
Cooper, John Sherman (1901-Feb. 21), Republican senator from Kentucky from 1946 to 1949, from 1952 to 1955, and from 1956 to 1973.
Coppola, Carmine (1910-April 26), composer of movie scores; father of director Francis Ford Coppola.
Crosby, John Campbell (1912-Sept. 7), novelist and former newspaper columnist.
Curtis, Ken (Curtis Gates) (1916-April 28), singer and actor who played Deputy Festus on TV's "Gunsmoke" from 1963 to 1975.
Dallis, Nicholas P. (1911-July 6), creator of the "Judge Parker," "Rex Morgan," and "Apartment 3-G" comic strips.
Daly, John (1914-Feb. 25), host of the TV game show "What's My Line?" (1950-1967).
Davis, Brad (1949-Sept. 8), actor who starred in *Midnight Express* (1978) and *Chariots of Fire* (1981).
Davis, Miles (1926-Sept. 28), jazz trumpeter and innovator who influenced several generations of jazz musicians and helped establish such styles as cool jazz, hard bop, and modal.
De Castries, Christian Marie Fernand de la Croix (1902-July 30), French brigadier general who commanded French forces at the battle of Dien Bien Phu in Vietnam in 1954; his surrender on May 17 to Viet Minh guerrillas signaled the defeat of French colonialism in Indochina.
Delacorte, George T. (1894-May 4), founder of Dell Publishing Company.
Dewhurst, Colleen (1926-Aug. 22), actress known for her stage roles in the plays of Eugene O'Neill.
Dill, Bobby (Robert E. Dill) (1920-April 16), defenseman for the New York Rangers from 1943 to 1945; member of the U.S. Hockey Hall of Fame.
Dimitrios I (Dimitrios Papadopoulos) (1914-Oct. 2), ecumenical patriarch of Constantinople (Istanbul, Turkey) and spiritual leader of Eastern Orthodox Christians.
Dodd, Ed (1902-May 27), cartoonist who created the "Mark Trail" comic strip.
Donegan, Horace W. B. (1900-Nov. 11), Episcopal bishop of New York known for his involvement in civil rights and women's rights.
Dunnock, Mildred (1901-July 5), actress who was nominated for Academy Awards for her performances in *Death of a Salesman* (1951) and *Baby Doll* (1956).
Durocher, Leo Ernest (1905-Oct. 7), shortstop who became a major league manager and led his teams to three pennants and a world championship and coined the phrase, "Nice guys finish last."
Elliott, Sumner Locke (1917-June 24), novelist and playwright whose work drew upon his experiences growing up in Australia.
Evers, Hoot (Walter A. Evers) (1921-Jan. 25), outfielder for the Detroit Tigers from 1941 to 1952 who later became an executive with the baseball club.
Fairbank, John K. (1907-Sept. 14), historian known for his scholarship on the history and culture of China and an early advocate in the United States of establishing diplomatic relations with the People's Republic of China.
Fender, Clarence L. (1909-March 21), guitar designer who in 1954 introduced the Fender Stratocaster, used by many rock stars and the first electric guitar to be mass-produced.
Ferber, Herbert (1906-Aug. 20), abstract expressionist sculptor.
Finkelstein, Louis (1895-Nov. 29), leader of Conservative Judaism in America and chancellor emeritus of the Jewish Theological Seminary of America.
Fish, Hamilton (1888-Jan. 18), Republican representative from New York from 1920 to 1945; grandson, son, and father of three other congressmen, all also named Hamilton Fish.
FitzGibbon, Theodora (1916-March 25), food writer known for her cookbooks on the food of Ireland.

Fletcher, James C. (1919-Dec. 22), former head of the National Aeronautics and Space Administration, who launched the shuttle program.
Fodor, Eugene (1905-Feb. 18), Hungarian-born author of travel guides.
Fonteyn, Dame Margot (Margaret Hookham) (1919-Feb. 21), ballet dancer often considered the greatest British ballerina of all time. See **Dancing,** Special Report: **Two Legends of Dance.**
Ford, Tennessee Ernie (Ernest Jennings Ford) (1919-Oct. 17), country-and-Western singer and folksy TV host known for his recording of "Sixteen Tons," one of the biggest-selling records ever.
Forsey, Eugene A. (1904-Feb. 20), Canadian constitutional expert who served in Canada's Senate from 1970 to 1979.
Foxx, Redd (John Elroy Sanford) (1922-Oct. 11), comedian and star of the television series "Sanford and Son."
Franciscus, James (1934-July 8), actor who starred in films and the television series "Mr. Novak."
Freeman, Bud (Lawrence Freeman) (1906-March 15), jazz saxophonist.
Friedman, Maurice H. (1903-March 8), physician and medical researcher who developed a pregnancy test known as the *rabbit test.*
Frisch, Max (1911-April 4), Swiss novelist, essayist, and playwright.
Frye, Northrop (1912-Jan. 23), Canadian literary critic noted for his study of myths and symbols in literature.
Gaillard, Slim (Bulee Gaillard) (1916-Feb. 26), jazz pianist, guitarist, and composer known for such hit songs as "Flat Foot Floogie" and "Tutti Frutti."
Gandhi, Rajiv (1944-May 21), prime minister of India from 1984 to 1989.
García Robles, Alfonso (1911-Sept. 2), Mexican diplomat and co-winner of the 1982 Nobel Peace Prize for his efforts to promote peace and disarmament.
Garry, Charles R. (Garabed Robutlay Garabedian) (1909-Aug. 16), attorney who defended leaders of the Black Panther Party and other radical activists during the 1960's.
Getz, Stan (1927-June 6), tenor saxophone great who was an innovator of cool jazz.
Gobel, George (1919-Feb. 24), crew-cut comedian who starred in TV's "The George Gobel Show" (1954-1960).
Goren, Charles H. (1901-April 3), contract bridge expert who developed point-count bidding.
Gowing, Sir Lawrence (1918-Feb. 5), British landscape and portrait painter, knighted in 1982.
Graham, Bill (Wolfgang Grajonca) (1931-Oct. 25), rock music impresario who helped develop the rock concert as a theatrical event.
Graham, Martha (1894-April 1), dancer and choreographer who pioneered in the modern dance movement. See **Dancing,** Special Report: **Two Legends of Dance.**
Grange, Red (Harold Grange) (1903-Jan. 28), lightning-quick running back nicknamed the Galloping Ghost; member of the Professional Football Hall of Fame.
Greene, Graham (1904-April 3), British author whose novels described a world of criminals, mentally disturbed people, and international intrigue.
Guard, Dave (1934?-March 22), a founding member of the Kingston Trio folk music group.
Guthrie, A. B., Jr. (Alfred Bertram Guthrie, Jr.) (1901-April 26), Western novelist whose best-known books include *The Big Sky* (1947) and *The Way West* (1949), which won the 1950 Pulitzer Prize for fiction.
Hall, Kevin Peter (1955?-April 10), 7-foot 2-inch (218-centimeter) actor who starred in TV's "Harry and the Hendersons."
Hannah, John A. (1902-Feb. 23), first chairman of the U.S. Commission on Civil Rights, from 1957 to 1969.
Hatfield, Richard B. (1931-April 26), premier of the Canadian province of New Brunswick from 1970 to 1987.
Head, Howard (1914-March 3), sporting goods manufacturer who invented the oversized Prince tennis racket.

Harry Reasoner, broadcast newsman.

Michael Landon, television actor.

Redd Foxx, comedian and TV actor.

Roger Revelle, noted geologist.

Heidelberger, Michael (1888-June 25), internationally recognized pathologist known as a founding father of modern immunology.
Heinz, H. John, III (1938-April 4), Republican senator from Pennsylvania since 1977 and an heir to the H. J. Heinz food empire.
Hildesheimer, Wolfgang (1916-Aug. 21), German novelist and playwright known for his biography of Austrian composer Wolfgang Amadeus Mozart.
Hill, Sir Austin Bradford (1897-April 18), British epidemiologist who led one of the first research teams that in 1952 established a link between smoking and cancer.
Honda, Soichiro (1906-Aug. 5), founder of Japan's Honda Motor Company.
Husak, Gustav (1913-Nov. 18), former president of Czechoslovakia and leader of its Communist Party until ousted from the party leadership by reformers in 1987 and from the presidency in 1989.
Hyde-White, Wilfrid (1903-May 6), British actor who portrayed Colonel Pickering in the motion picture *My Fair Lady* (1964).
Irving, Robert A. (1913-Sept. 13), musical director of the New York City Ballet from 1958 to 1989.
Irwin, James B. (1930-Aug. 8), former astronaut who walked on the moon during the Apollo 15 mission in 1971.
Jacoby, Jim (1932?-Feb. 8), contract bridge champion and author of a syndicated column on bridge.
Jagger, Dean (1903-Feb. 5), actor who won an Academy Award for his performance as an Air Force officer in the 1949 motion picture *Twelve O'Clock High.*

Sir David Lean, British motion-picture director.

Leo Durocher, baseball manager.

Lee Remick, motion-picture actress.

Tennessee Ernie Ford, country singer.

Jiang Qing (1914-May 14), Chinese political leader and widow of Mao Zedong who was serving a life sentence for her role as leader of the so-called Gang of Four.
Johnson, Bob (1931-Nov. 26), college and professional hockey coach who led the Pittsburgh Penguins to the Stanley Cup in 1991.
Joyce, Eileen (1912-March 25), Australian-born concert pianist.
Kaganovich, Lazar Moyseyevich (1894-July 25), last surviving Bolshevik leader who joined the Communist Party before the Russian Revolution of 1917.
Kane, Peter (Peter Cain), (1918-July 23), British boxer who held the world flyweight title from 1938 to 1943.
Kelso, Louis O. (1913-Feb. 17), lawyer and investment banker who helped pioneer employee stock ownership plans (ESOP's), stock buyouts that enable employees to own the companies where they work.
Kempff, Wilhelm (1895-May 23), German pianist widely respected as an interpreter of Beethoven and Schubert.
Kerr, Sir John (1914-March 24), governor general of Australia from 1974 to 1977.
Kert, Larry (1930-June 5), singer and actor who played Tony in the original Broadway production of *West Side Story* (1957).
Kiker, Douglas (1930?-Aug. 14), broadcast and newspaper journalist.
Kinski, Klaus (Nikolaus Gunthar Nakazynski) (1926-Nov. 23), Polish-born German motion-picture actor best noted for his leading roles in the films of German director Werner Herzog.
Kiviat, Abel (1892-Aug. 24), member of the National Track and Field Hall of Fame, former recordholder in the 1,500-meter run, and a silver medalist in the 1912 Olympics.
Knight, James L. (1909-Feb. 5), newspaper publisher who with his older brother, John, built a family newspaper into the Knight-Ridder media empire comprising several major newspapers, including the *Detroit Free Press*.
Kosinski, Jerzy (1933-May 3), Polish-born novelist who described his experiences in war-torn Eastern Europe in *The Painted Bird* (1965).
Kulp, Nancy (1921-Feb. 3), actress who played the secretary Jane Hathaway on TV's "The Beverly Hillbillies" in the 1960's.
Land, Edwin H. (1909-March 1), inventor of instant photography and founder of the Polaroid Corporation.
Landon, Michael (Eugene Maurice Orowitz) (1936-July 1), actor who starred in two popular television series: "Bonanza" and "Little House on the Prairie."
Lean, Sir David (1908-April 16), British motion-picture director who won Academy Awards as best director for *The Bridge on the River Kwai* (1957) and *Lawrence of Arabia* (1962).
Lefebvre, Marcel (1905-March 25), French Roman Catholic archbishop who led a movement supporting traditional Latin rites and was declared to be excommunicated in 1988 for defying the Vatican reforms.
Le Gallienne, Eva (1899-June 3), British-born actress who was one of the grand figures of the U.S. stage.
Lewis, Sir Arthur (1915-June 15), British economist, born in St. Lucia, West Indies, who in 1979 became the first black to win the Nobel Prize in economics.
Lewis, Herbert A. (1907-Jan. 20), Canadian-born hockey star who played left wing with the Detroit Red Wings from 1928 to 1939 and a member of the Hockey Hall of Fame.
Libonati, Roland V. (1900-May 26), Democratic representative from Illinois from 1957 to 1965.
Liedtke, William C., Jr., (1924-March 1), oilman who helped found Pennzoil Company, serving as its president from 1967 to 1977, when he became chairman and chief executive officer.
Long, Dale (1926-Jan. 27), home-run-hitting catcher for the Pittsburgh Pirates, Chicago Cubs, Washington Senators, and New York Yankees in the 1950's and early 1960's.
Luke, Keye (1904-Jan. 12), Chinese-born actor who played Charlie Chan's number-one son in the detective films of the 1930's and 1940's and the martial arts teacher on TV's "Kung Fu" in the 1970's.
Luria, Salvador E. (1912-Feb. 6), Italian-born biologist and physician who won the 1969 Nobel Prize for physiology or medicine.
Macdonald, James (1906-Feb. 1), Scottish-born sound-effects specialist who provided the voice of Mickey Mouse from 1946 to 1976.
MacMurray, Fred (1908-Nov. 5), motion-picture and television actor who starred in *Double Indemnity* (1944) and in the TV series, "My Three Sons," from 1960 to 1972.
Masaoka, Mike M. (1916-June 26), decorated U.S. combat veteran who campaigned to restore the rights of Japanese Americans following his return home from World War II (1939-1945).
Mason, Belinda (1958-Sept. 9), the first AIDS-infected member of the National Commission on AIDS.
Maxwell, Robert (Jan Ludwig Hoch) (1913-Nov. 5), billionaire owner of an international media empire that included the New York *Daily News* and the London *Daily Mirror*.
McCone, John A. (1902-Feb. 14), chairman of the Atomic Energy Commission from 1958 to 1961 and director of the Central Intelligence Agency from 1961 to 1965.
McIntire, John (1907-Jan. 30), actor who replaced Ward Bond as the wagon master on the TV series "Wagon Train."
McKissick, Floyd B. (1922-April 28), civil rights leader who headed the Congress of Racial Equality in the 1960's.
McMillan, Edwin Mattison (1907-Sept. 7), scientist who shared the Nobel Prize in chemistry in 1951.

McPartland, Jimmy (1907-March 13), jazz cornetist.
Mercury, Freddie (1946-Nov. 24), lead singer for the hard-rock group Queen.
Miles, Lord (Bernard Miles) **(1907-June 14),** the only British actor other than Laurence Olivier to be honored with a life peerage.
Mollenhoff, Clark R. (1921-March 2), newspaperman who won a Pulitzer Prize in 1958 for an exposé of trade union racketeering.
Montalban, Carlos (1903-March 28), Spanish-born actor and dancer who appeared in television commercials for Savarin coffee as El Exigente.
Montand, Yves (Ivo Livi) **(1921-Nov. 9),** Italian-born French actor and singer known for his motion-picture roles over four decades.
Moorman, Charlotte (1933-Nov. 8), cellist and pioneer performance artist.
Motherwell, Robert (1915-July 16), artist who was considered a leading figure in the abstract expressionist movement.
Murray, Arthur (Moses Teichman) **(1895-March 3),** teacher of ballroom dancing.
O'Faolain, Sean (John F. Whelan) **(1900-April 20),** Irish short-story writer.
Olav V (1903-Jan. 17), king of Norway since 1957.
Nemerov, Howard (1920-July 5), former poet laureate of the United States.
Page, Irvine H. (1901-June 10), medical researcher who was among the first to recognize that high blood pressure was a treatable disease.
Page, Ruth (1899-April 7), ballet dancer and teacher.
Panufnik, Sir Andrzej (1914-Oct. 27), composer and conductor who developed a unique contemporary style of music.
Papp, Joseph (Joseph Papirofsky) **(1921-Oct. 31),** theatrical producer who produced *A Chorus Line* (1983), the longest-running musical on Broadway, and *Hair* (1967), and who founded the New York Shakespeare Festival.
Payne, Ethel L. (1912?-May 28), journalist who reported from Washington, D.C., for the *Chicago Defender* and in the 1970's became the first black female commentator on network television.
Penney, Lord William George (1909-March 3), physicist credited with directing the development of Great Britain's first atomic bomb in 1952.
Porter, Sylvia (1913-June 5), financial columnist; long-time member of *The World Book Year Book* Board of Editors.
Rains, Albert M. (1902-March 22), Democratic representative from Alabama from 1945 to 1965.
Ray, Aldo (Aldo DaRe) **(1926-March 27),** actor best-known for playing tough soldiers in such war movies as *Battle Cry* (1955) and *The Naked and the Dead* (1958).
Reasoner, Harry (1923-Aug. 6), television newscaster known for his wry wit as an anchor on "60 Minutes."
Remick, Lee (1937-July 2), actress noted for many stage and screen credits but especially noted for her roles in *The Days of Wine and Roses* (1962) and *Anatomy of a Murder* (1959).
Revelle, Roger (1909-July 15), noted geologist, oceanographer, and population expert who helped develop the geological theory of plate tectonics and was among the first to warn in the 1950's of a possible global warming; former member of the editorial advisory board of World Book's *Science Year*.
Revolta, Johnny (1911?-March 3), Professional Golfers' Association (PGA) champion in 1935.
Richardson, Tony (1928-Nov. 15), British-born motion-picture director known for such films as *Tom Jones* (1963) and *Look Back in Anger* (1959).
Rizzo, Frank L. (1920-July 16), controversial former mayor of Philadelphia.
Robinson, Earl (1910-July 27), composer of songs about the labor movement, including "Joe Hill."
Roddenberry, Gene (1921-Oct. 24), television and motion-picture producer who created the "Star Trek" TV series.
Rogers, Jean (Eleanor Lovegren) **(1916-Feb. 24),** actress who played Dale Arden in the Flash Gordon serials.

Sylvia Porter, financial columnist.

Ruth Page, ballet dancer and teacher.

Miles Davis, jazz trumpeter and innovator.

Frank Capra, motion-picture director.

Roosevelt, James (1907-Aug. 13), former congressman and lobbyist and eldest son of former President Franklin D. Roosevelt.
Ruffin, David (Davis Eli Ruffin) **(1941-June 1),** original member of the Temptations singing group who sang lead vocals on "My Girl" (1965).
Runnels, Pete (James E. Runnels) **(1928-May 20),** infielder for the Washington Senators and the Boston Red Sox; American League batting champion in 1960 and 1962.
Russell, John (1921-Jan. 26), actor, best known in the title role of TV's "The Lawman" (1958-1962).
Sabry, Aly (1920-Aug. 3), Egyptian prime minister from 1964 to 1965.
Schaefer, Jack W. (1907-Jan. 24), author of dozens of Westerns, including the 1949 novel *Shane*.
Schafer, Natalie (1900-April 10), actress who played the millionaire's wife on TV's "Gilligan's Island" (1964-1967).
Schuyler, James M. (1923-April 12), winner of the 1981 Pulitzer Prize for poetry.
Serkin, Rudolf (1903-May 8), concert pianist born in what is now Czechoslovakia; known for his interpretations of the works for piano by Beethoven and Brahms.
Seuss, Dr. (Theodor Seuss Geisel) **(1904-Sept. 24),** author and illustrator of more than 50 children's books known for their tongue-twisting rhymes, alliterations, and fantastic characters. See **Deaths,** Special Report: **Dr. Seuss: Oh, the Places He Took Us!**
Shea, William A. (1907-Oct. 3), attorney who helped win a National League baseball franchise for New York City; Shea Stadium, home of the New York Mets, was named for him.

Fred MacMurray, film and TV actor.

Robert Maxwell, media magnate.

Luke Appling, shortstop for Chicago White Sox.

Yves Montand, Italian-born French actor.

Shoemaker, Vaughn (1902-Aug. 18), cartoonist who created the character John Q. Public.
Siegel, Don (1912-April 20), director of such action pictures as *Dirty Harry* (1971) and *The Shootist* (1976).
Siegmeister, Elie (1909-March 10), composer who combined elements of folk music, jazz, and street songs in his compositions, which included eight symphonies, eight operas, and numerous concertos.
Singer, Isaac Bashevis (1904-July 24), winner of the 1978 Nobel Prize for literature, who wrote in Yiddish about Jewish life in his native Poland and in America.
Smallwood, Joseph R. (1900-Dec. 17), Canadian political leader who served as Newfoundland's premier for 22 years.
Smith, Jabbo (Cladys Smith) (1908-Jan. 16), jazz trumpeter renowned for his improvisations.
Snelling, Richard A. (1927-Aug. 14), former governor of Vermont.
Speck, Richard (1941-Dec. 5), notorious killer imprisoned for life for the murder of eight student nurses in Chicago in 1966.
Staggers, Harley Orrin, Sr., (1907-Aug. 20), Democratic representative from West Virginia from 1949 to 1980.
Stigler, George Joseph (1911-Dec. 1), economist who won the Nobel Prize in economics in 1982.
Tamayo, Rufino (1899-June 24), artist and a major figure in the Mexican Renaissance who was noted for pursuing abstraction at a time when his contemporaries were not.
Thomas, Danny (Muzyad Yakhoob) (1914-Feb. 6), nightclub entertainer who starred in the TV series "Make Room for Daddy" (1953-1964).
Tierney, Gene (1920-Nov. 6), actress best known for her role as Laura in the 1944 motion picture of that name.
Toomey, Regis (1898-Oct. 12), character actor who appeared in more than 200 motion pictures; best known for giving actress Jane Wyman one of the longest onscreen kisses, at 185 seconds.
Towe, Harry L. (1898-Feb. 8), Republican representative from New Jersey from 1943 to 1951.
Tower, John G. (1925-April 5), Republican senator from Texas from 1961 to 1985.
Towns, Forest G. (1914?-April 9), world-champion hurdler who broke several world records and won a gold medal in the 1936 Olympics.
Tryon, Thomas (1926-Sept. 4), motion-picture actor who became a best-selling novelist.
Tsedenbal, Yumjaagiyn (1916-April 20), premier of Mongolia from 1952 to 1984.
Wade, Leigh (1898?-Aug. 31), U.S. pilot who participated in the first round-the-world flight in 1924 and later became a major general in the U.S. Air Force.
Wagner, Friedelind (1918-May 8), German opera director and granddaughter of composer Richard Wagner who fled Nazi Germany following her attacks on Nazi culture.
Wagner, Robert F. (1910-Feb. 12), mayor of New York City from 1954 to 1965.
Walcha, Helmut (1907-Aug. 11), German organist and harpsichordist internationally recognized as a foremost interpreter of the works of Johann Sebastian Bach.
Walters, Bucky (William H. Walters) (1909-April 20), pitching star for the Cincinnati Reds in the 1930's and 1940's and voted Most Valuable Player in the National League in 1939.
Wanglie, Helga (1905-July 4), Minneapolis hospital patient whose husband sued a county hospital that threatened to remove her from life support.
Watson, Phil (Phillipe Henri Watson) (1914-Feb. 1), Canadian-born hockey star who played forward for the New York Rangers from 1935 to 1948.
Werblin, David A. (Sonny) (1910-Nov. 21), former football team owner who signed quarterback Joe Namath to his first professional football contract.
West, Dottie (Dorothy Marie West) (1933?-Sept. 4), country-music singer best known for her 1964 Grammy Award-winning song "Here Comes My Baby" and for her series of duets with Kenny Rogers.
White, Carrie Joyner (1874-Feb. 14), 116-year-old woman named in the *Guinness Book of World Records* as the world's oldest person.
Whitman, Ann C. (1908?-Oct. 15), personal secretary to U.S. President Dwight D. Eisenhower from 1952 to 1960 and chief of staff to Vice President Nelson A. Rockefeller from 1974 to 1977.
Wiggins, Alan A. (1958-Jan. 6), outfielder and second baseman who scored 106 runs and stole 70 bases for the San Diego Padres in 1984, the year the Padres won the National League pennant.
Wilson, Allan C. (1934-July 21), New Zealand-born biochemist who explored molecular genetics in order to study human evolution.
Wilson, Sir Angus (Angus Frank Johnstone-Wilson) (1913-May 31), British author and satirist.
Winter, Jack A. (1909?-Feb. 9), founder of the apparel company that bears his name.
Winters, Bernie (Bernie Weinstein) (1932-May 4), British comedian.
Wolfson, Sir Isaac (1897-June 20), British philanthrophist and chairman of the fifth-largest retail chain—Great Universal Stores—in Great Britain.
Zwicker, Ralph W. (1903?-Aug. 9), Army major general who played a key role in the U.S. Senate's censure of Senator Joseph R. McCarthy (R., Wis.) in 1954, after McCarthy began investigating alleged Communist infiltration of the Army.
Rod Such

Delaware. See **State government.**

Dr. Seuss: Oh, the Places He Took Us!

By Ruth K. MacDonald

Theodor Seuss Geisel, widely and affectionately known as Dr. Seuss, the beloved author and illustrator of children's books, died on Sept. 24, 1991, at his home in La Jolla, Calif. In a career that spanned more than 50 years, Geisel produced 55 books, including publications for adults and a few works written under other pseudonyms. His books have sold more than 200 million copies and have been translated into 20 languages. Geisel's gift lay in his ability to tell a swiftly moving story with high interest, offbeat rhymes, a tight vocabulary, and unique illustrations.

From his first book in 1937, *And to Think That I Saw It on Mulberry Street,* Geisel led children's literature away from instructional, bland stories. His books encouraged readers to treasure wild flights of imagination.

Geisel was born on March 2, 1904, in Springfield, Mass. He graduated

The author:
Ruth K. MacDonald heads the Department of English at Purdue University Calumet in Hammond, Ind., and has written several books on children's literature.

from Dartmouth College in Hanover, N.H., and received an honorary doctorate degree from his alma mater in 1956. He married Helen Marion Palmer in 1927, and they had no children. After the death of his first wife in 1967, he married Audrey Stone Dimond, who survives him.

Before achieving success as an author, Geisel worked as an illustrator for *Life, Vanity Fair,* and *Liberty* magazines. He also produced a number of films, including two documentaries that won him Academy Awards. In addition, he created animated cartoons for television.

Theodor Seuss Geisel (1904-1991) wrote and illustrated books for children. Such works as *The Cat in the Hat, Yertle the Turtle,* and *Horton Hears a Who!* enchanted and gently instructed both young and old.

When Geisel began to write children's stories, he used his middle name, Seuss (also his mother's maiden name), and plunked the Dr. in front. He chose this pseudonym in order to retain the Geisel name for use if he should become a "serious" writer. He never used Geisel.

Geisel's early writing was noteworthy for its imagination and its bold, bouncy illustrations. But the author's greatest achievements in children's literature began when Random House, Incorporated published *The Cat in the Hat* (1957) and a subsequent series of Beginner Books. *The Cat in the Hat* drew upon a word list from a basic reading series for first-graders. Yet the result was far from condescending or simplistic. The naughty cat and his messy friends invade the pages and scatter chaos from left to right. As the confident cat piles up and balances a mountain of household items, a tension also builds up and up until the very last pages, when he cleans up his mess and leaves. The book conveys the message that reading can be as much fun as making messes and breaking rules.

Only 237 different words tell the story of *The Cat in the Hat.* All are easily read and understood by most young readers, yet there is no feeling that the story is restricted by its vocabulary. Geisel repeated this success in *Green Eggs and Ham* (1960), which tells another outlandish story using a mere 53 different words. Some of those words, however, cannot be found in any dictionary—words such as boom-pahs and beezle-nut. A trademark of Geisel's was that he invented new words and strained at the limits of grammatical correctness.

In the 1970's and 1980's, Geisel ventured into more controversial topics in his children's books, including environmental conservation in *The Lorax* (1971) and the nuclear arms race in *The Butter Battle Book* (1984). Although the topics were serious—and sometimes even urgent—the rhymes and pictures remained wildly inventive and ultimately reassuring.

In 1984, Geisel received a Pulitzer Prize for "his contribution. . .to the education and enjoyment of America's children and their parents." In 1980, he won the Laura Ingalls Wilder Award for children's literature but never received the prestigious Caldecott Medal for illustration or the Newbery Medal for story. This may have indicated a reluctance among teachers and librarians to promote strong fantasy, invented words, and a limited illustration style. But Geisel's work never aimed to be "high art."

Geisel's last book, *Oh, The Places You'll Go!* (1990), was written for adults as well as children and was on *The New York Times* best-seller list for over a year. The book is a farewell to his audience and an urging to push forward—to achieve, invent, and imagine worlds beyond our own.

Former Senator Paul E. Tsongas, the first to bid for the 1992 Democratic presidential nomination, campaigns in April in his hometown, Lowell, Mass.

Democratic Party. A Democratic Party in disarray found new life on Nov. 5, 1991, as Pennsylvania voters handed the Administration of Republican President George Bush a major defeat in a special election for the U.S. Senate. Republican Richard L. Thornburgh, a former two-term governor of Pennsylvania who had resigned as United States attorney general to run for the Senate seat, saw a 44-point lead in the polls evaporate as the election approached. He was trounced by his Democratic opponent, Harris L. Wofford.

Wofford had been a political unknown until his appointment to the Senate seat vacated by the death of Republican John Heinz, who was killed in an airplane crash in April 1991. Wofford overwhelmed Thornburgh by hammering on such populist themes as national health insurance and an extension of unemployment benefits for victims of the recession. But Wofford did not attack just Thornburgh. He repeatedly took President Bush to task, asserting that the President was neglecting major problems at home to focus on foreign policy. That message, and Pennsylvania voters' response to it, was enough to cause Bush to postpone from November to December a trip to Australia, Singapore, South Korea, and Japan. The President also began trying to formulate a program to aid the faltering economy.

Democratic leaders were quick to point out that Thornburgh's upset—as evidenced by Bush's abrupt change of travel plans—almost certainly had national implications. Ronald H. Brown, chairman of the Democratic National Committee (DNC), termed the Wofford victory a "wake-up call" for Bush on health care and the economy.

The presidential race takes shape. The revival of Democratic spirits came after months of disarray following the 1991 Persian Gulf War. Bush's ratings in the national polls soared to the 90 per cent level after the crushing allied victory over Iraq in late February. Meanwhile, many Democrats in Congress were criticized for having opposed the use of force to oust Iraq from Kuwait. For a time, no Democrat of national stature seemed willing to step forward to challenge Bush for the presidency in 1992, and some announced that they would not try. In July, Missouri Congressman Richard A. Gephardt, the Democratic leader of the House of Representatives and an unsuccessful presidential aspirant in 1988, said he would not run in 1992. Similar announcements came in August from Senators Albert A. Gore, Jr., of Tennessee and John D. Rockefeller IV of West Virginia.

The only announced candidate in the first half of the year was former Senator Paul E. Tsongas (D., Mass.), who entered the race on April 30. Tsongas had resigned from the Senate in 1985 because he was suffering from cancer.

As the year wore on, the sagging economy, coupled with a growing public perception that the nation's domestic problems were being neglected,

Virginia Governor L. Douglas Wilder campaigns in Portsmouth, N.H., in August but is the first to drop out of the presidential race in January 1992.

brought Bush's popularity down. By late November, his approval rating had fallen to 51 per cent.

Earlier, during late summer and into the fall, a procession of Democratic challengers joined Tsongas: L. Douglas Wilder of Virginia, the first elected black governor of any state; Tom Harkin of Iowa, a two-term senator with a populist message; Senator Robert Kerrey of Nebraska, a former Nebraska governor and Vietnam War hero; Edmund G. (Jerry) Brown, Jr., a former governor of California; and Bill Clinton, five-term governor of Arkansas. (See individual biographies of candidates.)

On November 2, civil rights leader Jesse L. Jackson announced that he would not mount a presidential campaign in 1992. In previous attempts, he had finished third in the 1984 primaries and second in 1988. Jackson said, however, that "it's just a matter of time" before he tries again to become the first black to win a major-party presidential nomination.

For most of the year, Governor Mario M. Cuomo of New York kept fellow Democrats guessing about his intentions for 1992. Cuomo was seen by many in the party as the front-runner should he decide to get into the race, and Bush and some of his advisers reportedly considered him potentially the strongest Democratic candidate. On December 20, Cuomo finally seemed to end the suspense, saying he would not run in 1992.

Reviving liberal values. The renewed confidence of Democrats at the end of 1991 stood in stark contrast to the mood of near-desperation that had prevailed early in the year. In January, a majority of Democrats in Congress found themselves on the losing side in voting against authorizing Bush to take military action against Iraq. Opposition to the use of force was an unpopular position to have taken once the war began, and many Democrats feared that their vote would come back to haunt them.

Divisions among liberal Democrats over the war were evident at a meeting on January 26 of the Coalition for Democratic Values (CDV), a group formed in late 1990. The well-attended session, held in Chantilly, Va., established the CDV as a counter to the more middle-of-the-road Democratic Leadership Council (DLC). But the new group was so preoccupied by events in the Middle East that it could not come to grips with issues central to its stated purpose of reviving the party's liberal and progressive forces.

The DNC, meeting in Washington, D.C., on March 22 and 23, 1991, was unable to find a clear solution to the party's apparent lack of direction. Most speakers agreed that Democrats should emphasize the issues of health care, education, the environment, and the economy. But there was considerable disagreement on what specific programs the party should endorse if it hoped to capture the White House in 1992.

Frank Cormier and Margot Cormier

See also **Elections; Republican Party.** In ***World Book,*** see **Democratic Party.**

Denmark in 1991 forged closer ties with the 12-nation European Community (EC or Common Market). Then, in August, it became one of the first countries to establish diplomatic relations with the newly independent Baltic nations of Estonia, Latvia, and Lithuania, which are near Denmark's borders.

Tamil resettlement. Denmark's government, headed by Prime Minister Poul Schlüter, was shaken in May by a scandal involving past treatment of Tamil refugees from Sri Lanka. Former Justice Minister Erik Ninn-Hansen, who opposed allowing refugees from Sri Lanka to resettle with relatives in Denmark in 1988, had allegedly halted the process under which resettlement was taking place. He was accused of doing so despite advice from government officials that his actions violated Danish law.

Ninn-Hansen denied having done anything improper or illegal. His public statements that other prominent politicians had backed his actions embarrassed the government, especially Schlüter.

Danish attitudes toward the EC, which Denmark joined in 1973, warmed noticeably in 1991. Opinion polls during the year showed that most Danes favored closer economic union of EC member countries, including the introduction of a single currency. In the past, many Danes had opposed such measures, fearing they would take too much power over economic decision-making from the Danish government.

Most Danes remained skeptical, however, about EC

President George Bush escorts Queen Margrethe II of Denmark to a state dinner held at the White House on February 20.

moves toward a common policy on defense and foreign affairs, preferring that the Danish government determine the country's foreign policy. But at an EC summit meeting in the Netherlands in December, Denmark backed plans for EC economic and monetary union as well as plans for closer EC political union.

A key government aim was the preparation of Denmark's economy for the tighter EC economic integration scheduled to take effect after 1992. The Danish government levies high taxes on Danish businesses and individuals and in return provides generous social benefits. Schlüter feared that Denmark's high tax rates could place Danish companies at a competitive disadvantage once the EC abolishes all trade barriers among member countries at the end of 1992. To bring Denmark in line with EC countries that have lower tax rates, Schlüter favored instituting big cuts in personal income tax as well as smaller cuts in sales taxes.

Despite initial hesitation over EC integration, Denmark has acted faster than many other EC members in enacting laws needed to facilitate the free movement of goods and services among EC nations. Such measures should also help Denmark compete with Germany, its powerful neighbor to the south, and help it open new trade markets in the Baltic states and the former Soviet Union. Philip Revzin

See also **Europe** (Facts in brief table), Special Report: **The Rocky Road to European Unity.** In ***World Book,*** see **Denmark.**

Detroit. Detroit Police Chief William L. Hart and former Deputy Police Chief Kenneth Weiner were indicted by a federal grand jury on Feb. 11, 1991, for allegedly embezzling $2.6 million from a secret police fund supposedly set up for financing undercover operations. The indictments grew from an investigation of police corruption in Detroit by the Federal Bureau of Investigation (FBI). According to the FBI, Weiner diverted money from the fund to phony corporations in California. Hart admitted that money from the fund was also used to pay rent on his daughter's home in Beverly Hills, Calif.

Detroit Mayor Coleman A. Young named Police Commander Stanley Knox to replace Hart on February 13. But Mayor Young also accused federal officials of conducting a vendetta against black city officials. On May 22, federal prosecutors charged 11 Detroit police officers and 5 civilians with taking payoffs from FBI agents posing as drug dealers.

In an unrelated case, Weiner on January 15 was convicted of fraud and tax evasion on charges involving a phony investment scheme. Weiner, who was also a former business partner of Young, was sentenced to 10 years in prison on those charges on May 3.

Money and people. Detroit ended the 1990-1991 fiscal year with a $40-million deficit in its $1.9-billion budget. On April 1, the city laid off 502 city employees, including 300 police officers. City officials eliminated another 300 jobs in early autumn.

The population of Detroit in 1990 was 1,027,974, according to final figures released by the United States Bureau of the Census on Jan. 25, 1991. The bureau reported that Detroit's population had dropped by 15 per cent between 1980 and 1990.

Murders. The shooting death of Army Specialist Anthony Riggs in Detroit on March 18, 1991, only 10 days after he had returned to the United States from combat duty in the Persian Gulf War (1991), attracted national attention. At first, the police believed that Riggs was the victim of a random shooting incident. But on March 26, the police arrested Toni Cato Riggs, Riggs's alleged wife, and her brother, Michael Cato, for the killing. The woman (who was not legally married to Riggs, because she had wedded him before her previous marriage had been dissolved) was released on April 29. A judge ruled that prosecutors had failed to produce evidence of her involvement in the murder. Cato was awaiting trial at year-end. The police said he killed Riggs to collect his life insurance.

A former postal clerk killed three people and injured six on November 14 during a shooting rampage at a postal service center in Royal Oak, Mich., about 2 miles (3.2 kilometers) north of Detroit. See **Crime.**

Playing hardball. Officials of the Detroit Tigers baseball team announced in 1991 that the team would begin looking outside Michigan for possible sites for a new open-air baseball stadium. The announcement came after the ball club rejected two sites proposed by officials from Detroit and surrounding Wayne County. Club officials, who contended that Tiger Stadium was too old to salvage, argued that they needed a new stadium to compete financially with other teams. Tigers officials also argued that they could not afford to build a new stadium, which could cost as much as $200 million, without financial help. Some city and county officials charged the Tigers with deliberately sabotaging negotiations over a new stadium so they could leave the state.

Schools. On July 1, 1991, Deborah McGriff, 41, the former deputy superintendent of schools in Milwaukee, became superintendent of the Detroit public school system. McGriff, who had gained a reputation as a reform-minded risk-taker, became Detroit's first woman school superintendent.

McGriff's first major challenge was a court battle over a plan to establish three all-male schools. The Detroit Board of Education on February 26 had approved a plan for setting up these special schools as part of an attempt to deal with the violence and other problems that beset inner-city boys. On August 5, however, the American Civil Liberties Union and the National Organization for Women Legal Defense Fund sued the district, claiming that the schools would discriminate against girls. On August 15, a federal district court judge ordered the district to open the schools as coed facilities. Constance C. Prater

In *World Book,* see **Detroit.**

Dinosaur. See **Paleontology.**

Disasters. The worst natural disaster of 1991 was a devastating typhoon that struck Bangladesh on April 29 and 30. The storm battered heavily populated coastal districts, including the port city of Chittagong, as well as islands in the Bay of Bengal, killing at least 139,000 people.

Disasters that resulted in 25 or more deaths in 1991 include the following:

Aircraft crashes

Feb. 1—Los Angeles. A USAir passenger jetliner collided with a SkyWest commuter plane on a runway. Twenty-two people aboard the USAir jetliner and all 12 aboard the commuter plane were killed.

Feb. 5—Othris Mountains, Greece. A Greek military transport crashed in stormy weather in a mountainous region of Greece, killing all 66 people on board.

March 3—Colorado Springs, Colo. A United Airlines jetliner approaching the airport plunged nose first into a neighborhood park and exploded. No one on the ground was seriously injured, but all 25 people aboard the aircraft died.

March 5—Near Santa Barbara, Venezuela. All 43 people aboard a Venezuelan jetliner died after the plane crashed on an Andean mountain.

March 21—Northern Saudi Arabia. A Saudi transport plane, hindered by smoke from burning oil fields in Kuwait that had been set afire by Iraqi troops in late February, crashed while trying to land, killing 92 Senegalese soldiers and 6 Saudi crew members. The Senegalese troops had been part of the multinational force rushed to Saudi Arabia to defend that country from a possible Iraqi invasion.

March 21—Off San Diego. Two U.S. Navy planes collided in midair over the Pacific Ocean during a training exercise. Twenty-seven crew members died.

March 23—Tashkent, Soviet Union. Thirty-one people died aboard a Soviet jetliner that skidded off a runway and smashed into concrete construction blocks.

March 25—Near Bangalore, India. Twenty-five Indian Air Force trainees and three crew members died in the crash of a military transport plane.

May 26—Near Bangkok, Thailand. An Austrian charter jetliner exploded in midair and crashed into the jungle, killing all 223 people aboard. The plane, a Boeing 767, was bound for Vienna. Austrian officials reported in June that a computer malfunction apparently caused an engine on the jetliner to accidentally switch into reverse.

July 11—Jidda, Saudi Arabia. A DC-8 jetliner carrying Muslim pilgrims home to Nigeria nose-dived and exploded on the tarmac while trying to make an emergency landing shortly after take-off. All 261 people reported on board were killed. The death toll was the 10th highest ever reported for a commercial air disaster.

Aug. 16—Near Imphal, India. An Indian Airlines jet, flying from Calcutta to Imphal, the capital of the state of Manipur, caught fire and crashed 27 miles (43 kilometers) short of its destination, killing all 69 people aboard.

Oct. 5—Jakarta, Indonesia. A military transport plane, carrying airmen who had just take part in an Armed Forces Day ceremony in Jakarta, the capital, crashed into a building shortly after take-off, killing all 132 aboard. A guard in the building was reportedly killed. Witnesses reported that one of the plane's engines caught fire after take-off.

Rural villagers rummage through the wreckage of an Austrian jetliner that exploded in midair near Bangkok, Thailand, in May, killing 223 people.

Disasters

Dec. 22—Near Heidelberg, Germany. A 1942-built DC-3, chartered by a documentary film crew, crashed into a hillside, killing 26 people. Four people survived.

Earthquakes

Feb. 1—Afghanistan and Pakistan. A deadly earthquake killed up to 1,200 people.

April 4-5—Peru. A series of earthquakes caused at least 39 deaths.

April 22—Costa Rica and Panama. An estimated 95 people died in a powerful earthquake.

April 29—Republic of Georgia, Soviet Union. An earthquake killed at least 360 people.

Oct. 20—Uttar Pradesh, India. An earthquake lasting only 45 seconds struck the northern part of Uttar Pradesh state in the Himalayan foothills. The official death toll initiallly was put at 361, but as relief workers combed the countryside, they later estimated up to 1,600 deaths.

Explosions and fires

Feb. 15—Phang-Nga province, Thailand. A truck carrying dynamite overturned and the dynamite exploded, killing at least 171 people who had gathered to look at the accident.

April 9—Istanbul, Turkey. A fire swept through a double-decker tourist bus, claiming 36 lives.

May 8—Kuala Lumpur, Malaysia. An explosion at a fireworks factory ignited fires that destroyed 6 other factories and 50 houses and caused more than 100 deaths.

Sept. 3—Hamlet, N.C. A fire in a chicken-processing plant killed 25 workers, who were reportedly trapped in freezers and behind blocked doors.

Oct. 20—Oakland, Calif. A huge brush fire swept through residential areas of Oakland and neighboring Berkeley and resulted in 25 deaths and the destruction of about 1,800 houses and 900 apartment units. About 5,000 people were left homeless. City officials estimated that damages would amount to between $1.5 billion and $2 billion.

Oct. 31—Pyonggang, North Korea. Up to 80 people were believed killed by an explosion that occurred near the town's railway station.

Landslides and avalanches

Feb. 24—Papua New Guinea. A mud slide wiped out several villages and killed at least 200 people.

May 4—Uzbek Republic, Soviet Union. A landslide caused at least 50 deaths in a mountain village.

June 18—Antofagasta, Chile. Hours of torrential rains triggered a mud slide that claimed at least 116 lives.

Shipwrecks

Jan. 12—Off Newfoundland, Canada. A Singapore-registered cargo ship sank in stormy seas with a crew of 33. There were no signs of survivors.

March 1—Off Malindi, Kenya. A ship carrying Somali refugees struck a reef in the Indian Ocean, causing the deaths of at least 160 passengers.

April 10—Off Leghorn (Livorno), Italy. A car ferry collided with an anchored oil tanker in fog in the Ligurian Sea, killing at least 139 ferry passengers.

May 6—Marañon River, Peru. A ferry crashed into an oil tanker and sank, leaving about 150 passengers missing and feared dead.

Nov. 18—Off Cape Maisí, Cuba. A sailboat carrying possibly as many as 135 Haitian refugees reportedly capsized in high seas, killing all aboard.

Dec. 15—Off Safaga, Egypt. High waves swept a ferry carrying 649 passengers against a reef in the Red Sea. At least 471 people, mostly religious pilgrims, were believed drowned as the ferry sank.

Storms and floods

Jan. 5-6—Great Britain and Ireland. At least 28 people died or were missing at sea in windstorms.

March 10—Near Mulanja, Malawi. Torrential downpours caused flash floods that claimed at least 500 lives.

April 26—Midwestern United States. A series of tornadoes, spawned by a single storm system, caused 25 deaths, including 20 in Kansas.

April 29 and 30—Bangladesh. A typhoon claimed at least 139,000 lives.

May 7—Chhaydana, Bangladesh, near Dhaka. A tornado killed at least 40 people.

Mid-May—Eastern Turkey. At least 30 people perished in flash floods.

June 2—Meghna River, Bangladesh. At least 200 people drowned after some 30 fishing boats sank during a typhoon.

July 9—Yangtze River Basin, China. The Chinese government announced that flooding from a month of rain had left at least 978 people dead. In mid-July, with torrential downpours continuing, the death toll rose to about 1,700 people.

July 28—Bacau, Romania. Heavy rains burst a dam, unleashing floods that killed at least 66 people.

July 30—Mohad, India, near New Delhi. A river swollen from torrential rains burst a dike, and 500 people were reported missing in the resulting flood.

Aug. 1—Nagpur region, India. The Wardha River overflowed its banks, killing about 350 people.

Sept. 27 to 28—Near Osaka, Japan. A typhoon claimed at least 45 lives and injured about 700 people.

Nov. 5—Leyte and Negros islands, Philippines. Flash floods spawned by a tropical storm swept through parts of Negros Island and through villages along two major rivers on the island of Leyte, killing about 6,000 people.

Train wrecks

April 6—Near Manacas, Cuba. A passenger train derailed, killing 55 people in Cuba's worst-ever rail accident.

May 14—Near Shigaraki, Japan. Forty-two people died after a tourist train slammed head-on into another train.

June 8—Sind province, Pakistan. A passenger train crashed into a parked freight train, causing at least 100 deaths.

Nov. 19—Tehuacan, Mexico. A runaway train, abandoned by its crew, killed at least 50 people.

Other disasters

Jan. 13—Near Orkney, South Africa. At least 42 soccer fans were trampled to death after a brawl broke out.

Feb. 13—Chalma, Mexico. At least 41 Ash Wednesday worshipers died after panic broke out when a narrow alleyway leading to a packed church became too congested.

June 3—Mount Unzen, Japan, near Nagasaki. A long-dormant volcano erupted, killing at least 38 people.

June 9 to 16—Luzon Island, Philippines. Eruptions of Mount Pinatubo beginning on June 9 initially caused about 296 deaths, most of them on June 15 and 16. But in the months that followed, flows of volcanic mud, triggered by rainstorms, resulted in mud slides that brought the death toll to more than 700 persons.

Aug. 28—Dogubeyazit, Turkey. A bus failed to negotiate a curve and plunged into a ravine, killing 52 of the 53 people aboard. Rod Such

Djibouti. See **Africa**.

Dog. The Westminster Kennel Club held its 115th annual show on Feb. 11 and 12, 1991, at Madison Square Garden in New York City. More than 2,900 dogs of 140 breeds and varieties entered, and 1,903 dogs competed. Dorothy Welsh of Neilsville, Wis., selected a standard poodle, Champion Whisperwind on a Carousel, as Best-in-Show. The dog is owned by Frederick and Joan Hartsock of Potomac, Md.

The American Kennel Club (AKC) in 1991 reported a total of 1,253,214 dogs registered in 1990, a drop of more than 4,000 from 1989. Cocker spaniels continued to lead the list with a total of 105,642, about 6,000 less than in 1989.

The AKC added in 1991 three new registerable breeds to its list. They were the Chinese crested, the miniature bull terrier, and the Chinese shar-pei. Robert Maxwell of Hauppauge, N.Y., became president of the AKC in September 1991.

Britain's dogs. In Birmingham, England, the 100th Crufts dog show—England's most prestigious dog event—took place in January. The Best-in-Show winner, a clumber spaniel, Show Champion Raycroft Socialite, was owned by Ralph Dunne and defeated nearly 23,000 dogs competing for the title.

Britain decided that tail *docking* (cutting) would become illegal there in July 1993. Roberta Vesley

In *World Book,* see **Dog.**

Dominican Republic. See **Latin America.**

Drought. See **Water; Weather.**

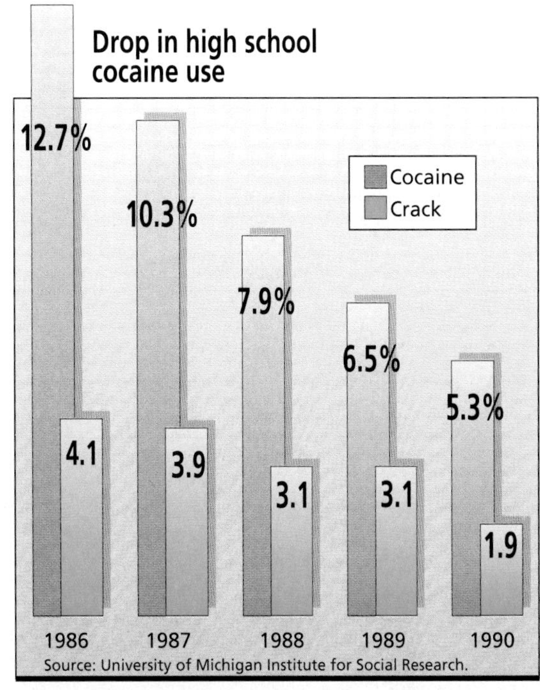

Results of annual surveys of high school seniors show a sharp decline in the percentage of students using cocaine or crack during 1990.

Drug abuse. The percentage of high school seniors in the United States who have used illegal drugs declined to less than 50 per cent in 1990, according to a report by the University of Michigan Institute for Social Research in January 1991. This was the lowest percentage since 1975, when the institute began to gather such information. Although high school drug-use figures were down, the survey did not include high school dropouts, a group thought to have the highest percentage of drug users.

The Michigan survey of 15,676 seniors found that 9. per cent had tried cocaine at some time in their lives. The percentage who had used cocaine within the last year declined to 5.3 per cent of those surveyed in 1990 from 6.5 per cent in 1989. The percentage of seniors using *crack* (a cheap but more potent form of cocaine that is smoked) within the previous year also dropped, to 1.9 per cent in 1990 from 3.1 per cent in 1989. Marijuana use declined as well, to 41 per cent among surveyed seniors in 1990 from 44 per cent in 1989. The report showed almost no reduction in cigarette smoking among high school seniors. The percentage of seniors who said they had ever smoked was about 64 per cent in 1990, compared with about 66 per cent in 1989.

Alcohol use among high school seniors was high, according to the Michigan report. About 90 per cent of the seniors surveyed said that they had tried alcohol, and 57 per cent said they had had at least one drink within the last month. Most disconcerting was the fact that nearly one-third of the students said they had drunk five or more alcoholic beverages on at least one occasion during the two weeks before the survey.

A September report from the United States Centers for Disease Control in Atlanta, Ga., also reported worrisome findings on alcohol use among high school students. That survey of 11,631 students in grades 9 through 12 showed that 59 per cent had had a drink in their lifetime, and 37 per cent had had five or more drinks at one sitting during the preceding month.

Families with alcoholics. Children's exposure to alcoholism in the family has become more common in recent generations, according to a report released by the U.S. National Center for Health Statistics in October 1991. Data from a survey of 43,809 adults in 1988 showed that 21 per cent of those aged 18 to 44 years grew up in a family with an alcoholic. Sixteen per cent of those between the ages of 45 and 64 had had an alcoholic in the family, and 8 per cent of those over age 65 had lived with an alcoholic. The survey also found that nearly 10 per cent of adults have been married to or have had a live-in relationship with an alcoholic or problem drinker.

Anabolic steroids. Possession or sale of anabolic steroids without a prescription became a federal crime in February 1991. Steroids, which are used by some young athletes to build muscles, are known to cause a wide variety of health problems. David C. Lewis

In *World Book,* see **Drug abuse.**

Drugs. Many of the 2 million to 3 million people in the United States with chronic congestive heart failure could benefit from a widely used blood pressure drug, a five-year government study concluded on Aug. 1, 1991. Researchers found that adding the drug, enalapril, to the standard drug treatment for heart failure reduced the risk of death by about 16 per cent and the need for hospitalization by about 33 per cent. The study was organized by the National Heart, Lung, and Blood Institute (NHLBI) in Bethesda, Md.

In chronic heart failure, the heart is unable to pump enough blood to the body's tissues, causing fluid to accumulate in the lungs and other areas. Symptoms include shortness of breath, fatigue, weakness, and swollen legs. It is the leading cause of hospitalization among Americans over age 65, accounting for about 645,000 hospital stays and 40,000 deaths each year. Claude J. Lenfant, director of the NHLBI, estimated that enalapril could prevent 10,000 to 20,000 deaths each year, avoid 100,000 hospitalizations, and save $1 billion in medical costs.

Drug for spinal cord injuries. Researchers at the Shock Trauma Center of the Maryland Institute for Emergency Medical Services in Baltimore and other institutions on June 27 reported that a new drug, GM-1 ganglioside, may help victims of spinal cord injury regain some lost nerve and muscle function. About 10,000 Americans suffer spinal cord injuries each year, often as the result of diving mishaps, gunshots, car crashes, and other accidents. Most victims are young men, aged 24 to 34, who may suffer permanent paralysis that means lifelong confinement to a wheelchair.

GM-1 ganglioside helps damaged nerve cells regenerate. Researchers said that more studies will be needed to confirm the drug's effectiveness.

Help for hepatitis C. The U. S. Food and Drug Administration (FDA) on February 25 approved the first drug for treating hepatitis type C, a viral infection of the liver. About 150,000 Americans become infected with hepatitis C each year, usually after contact with infected blood. Some develop a chronic liver condition that can result in permanent damage to the liver. The drug, alpha interferon, protects patients from such liver damage.

Cancer drugs. The FDA on February 21 approved a genetically engineered drug that can reduce the number of infections in cancer patients who undergo *chemotherapy* (drug treatment). The drug, granulocyte colony stimulating factor (G-CSF), increases the body's production of special infection-fighting white blood cells. Each year, about 225,000 cancer patients face a high risk of life-threatening infections due to certain kinds of chemotherapy that destroy or reduce production of these cells. The FDA said that G-CSF significantly reduces the number of infections, the need for intravenous antibiotics, and the length of hospitalization among chemotherapy patients.

Blood-poisoning drug. Another genetically engineered drug showed promise for combating an infection of the bloodstream that kills up to 100,000 Americans each year, researchers reported on February 14. The condition, *gram-negative bacteremia* or "blood poisoning," results from toxins secreted by bacteria. The new drug, called HA-1A or Centoxin (its brand name), is a protein similar to those produced naturally by the immune system and neutralizes the bacterial toxin. The study, which involved more than three dozen U.S. and European medical centers, found that the drug reduced the death rate in bacteremia patients from 49 per cent to 30 per cent.

Treating chronic fatigue. A small group of patients with chronic fatigue syndrome (CFS) improved dramatically after receiving injections of the experimental drug Ampligen, researchers at Hahnemann University in Philadelphia reported on October 1. CFS is a mysterious ailment that produces profound, lasting fatigue. The cause is unknown. The study included 92 patients, about half of whom were given Ampligen injections twice a week for 24 weeks.

After treatment, patients who received Ampligen scored higher on exercise and psychological tests and in their ability to accomplish daily chores, compared with patients receiving a *placebo* (inactive substance). Researchers said that larger studies would be necessary to verify the findings. Michael Woods

See also **Medicine,** Special Report: **Genetic Medicine: Promise and Perils.** In ***World Book,*** see **Drug.**

Duke, David E. (1950-), stepped away from a losing bid for the governorship of Louisiana in 1991 and entered the race for the United States presidency on December 4. Duke, a Louisiana state representative since 1989, became President George Bush's first challenger for the Republican presidential nomination.

Republicans sought to disassociate themselves from Duke because of his controversial past. He had served as grand wizard of the Knights of the Ku Klux Klan, a white supremacist organization, from 1975 to 1980. In December 1991, Republican officials in Georgia denied Duke a place on the ballot in the state's presidential primary, citing his Klan leadership and his "Nazi past." Duke also founded and was president of the National Association for the Advancement of White People. The candidate, however, denied charges of racism and chalked up his Klan membership to youthful folly.

Duke was born on July 1, 1950, in Tulsa, Okla. He attended Louisiana State University in Baton Rouge, where he earned a bachelor's degree in history. Duke is divorced and has two teen-age daughters.

As a state representative, Duke introduced legislation against affirmative action programs and served on the Health and Welfare Committee and the Judiciary Committee. Political analysts did not expect Duke to take the Republican nomination away from Bush. But they believed he might win enough support to wage an independent campaign for the 1992 presidential election. Lori Fagan

Moscow priests lead a procession in front of St. Basil's Cathedral on January 7, officially celebrating Orthodox Christmas for the first time since 1917.

Eastern Orthodox Churches. Dimitrios I, the 77-year-old ecumenical patriarch of Constantinople (Istanbul, Turkey) and spiritual leader of the world's 300 million Eastern Orthodox Christians, died on Oct. 2, 1991, of a heart attack. On October 22, Metropolitan Bartholomew of Chalcedon was unanimously elected to succeed Dimitrios. The new church leader was installed in Istanbul on November 2 as Patriarch Bartholomew I.

Ecumenical tensions. Orthodox churches attending the World Council of Churches (WCC) meeting in Canberra, Australia, in February charged the WCC with abandoning its stated goal of working toward unity among all the Christian churches of the world. Orthodox representatives met in Geneva, Switzerland, in September to further detail the Orthodox position on this issue and other controversial points, such as how each denomination is represented on the council.

In the United States, Archbishop Iakovos, primate of the Greek Orthodox Church of North and South America, suspended the church's relationship with the National Council of Churches on June 6. The suspension was meant to protest liberal positions taken by some Protestant denominations that belong to the council. The liberal positions in question centered on such issues as legalized abortion and the ordination of homosexuals.

Eastern European issues. Czechoslovakia, Romania, the Soviet Union, and Yugoslavia passed laws in 1991 that restored properties to their Eastern Rite

Roman Catholic churches. Former Communist governments in these countries had outlawed the Eastern Rite Roman Catholic religion in the 1930's and 1940's. Many Catholics then joined Orthodox churches, which took over the Eastern Rite property. Under 1991 laws, the churches were restored to the Eastern Rite Roman Catholics, and the Orthodox were expelled, at times violently, leaving them without places to worship.

The restoration of religious freedom in Albania led the ecumenical patriarch to appoint Bishop Anastasios Yannoulatos as patriarchal exarch of Albania.

Many Roman Catholic and Protestant missionaries from the United States and Europe entered eastern European countries during 1991 to convert the Orthodox to their faiths. Their proselytizing activity, however, was criticized by both Roman Catholic and Protestant authorities.

The Russian Orthodox Church assumed a more public role in 1991. In several Soviet republics, including Ukraine and Moldavia, the church observed January 7 as the official Orthodox Christmas. During Holy Week, the first week of April 1991, Orthodox religious services were televised. In early September, Patriarch Aleksei II, head of the Russian Orthodox Church, openly supported Boris Yeltsin, a reformer and president of the Russian republic, who helped defeat an attempted coup against Soviet President Mikhail S. Gorbachev.

Stanley Samuel Harakas

In *World Book,* see **Eastern Orthodox Churches.**

Economics. The world economy in 1991 grew by only about 1 per cent, the smallest advance in nine years. The slowdown largely reflected a stagnant United States economy, which for the first time since 1982 failed to expand.

The United States in July 1990 had entered a recession that persisted throughout 1991. In a nine-month period ending in June 1991, the United State's *gross national product* (GNP)—the total value of all goods and services produced—fell by 1.2 per cent, after adjusting for inflation. By early summer, the U.S. economy had begun a modest recovery, but it appeared to waver. Calls mounted in Congress for income tax cuts to spur consumer buying. In response, U.S. President George Bush tried to revive an earlier proposal for a lower capital gains tax to help stimulate business. Congress, however, was not receptive to this idea, and congressional action on any type of tax-cut proposal was put off until 1992.

Lower interest rates. In an attempt to bolster the U.S. economy, the Federal Reserve Board (the Fed), which sets monetary policy, reduced its *discount rate*—the interest it charges financial institutions. In five steps during 1991, the Fed cut the discount rate from 6.5 per cent to 3.5 per cent, the lowest level since 1964. The Fed also lowered the *federal funds rate*—the interest rate that banks and other financial institutions charge each other for overnight loans—to 4 per cent. The *prime rate*—the interest banks charge

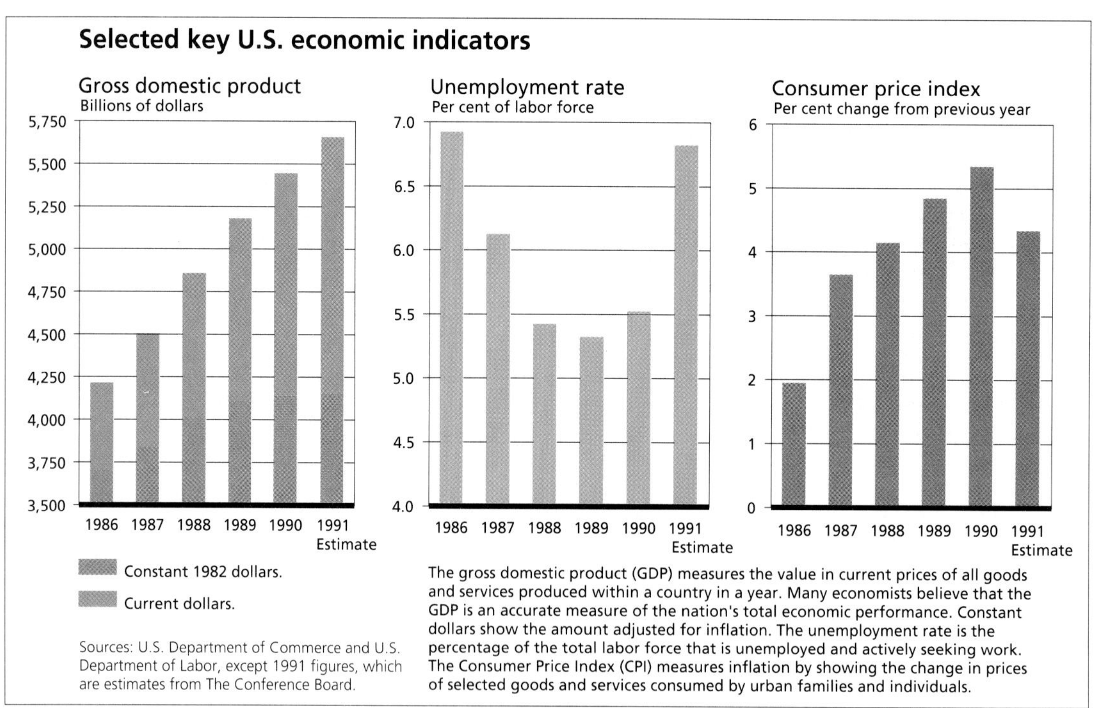

Sources: U.S. Department of Commerce and U.S. Department of Labor, except 1991 figures, which are estimates from The Conference Board.

The gross domestic product (GDP) measures the value in current prices of all goods and services produced within a country in a year. Many economists believe that the GDP is an accurate measure of the nation's total economic performance. Constant dollars show the amount adjusted for inflation. The unemployment rate is the percentage of the total labor force that is unemployed and actively seeking work. The Consumer Price Index (CPI) measures inflation by showing the change in prices of selected goods and services consumed by urban families and individuals.

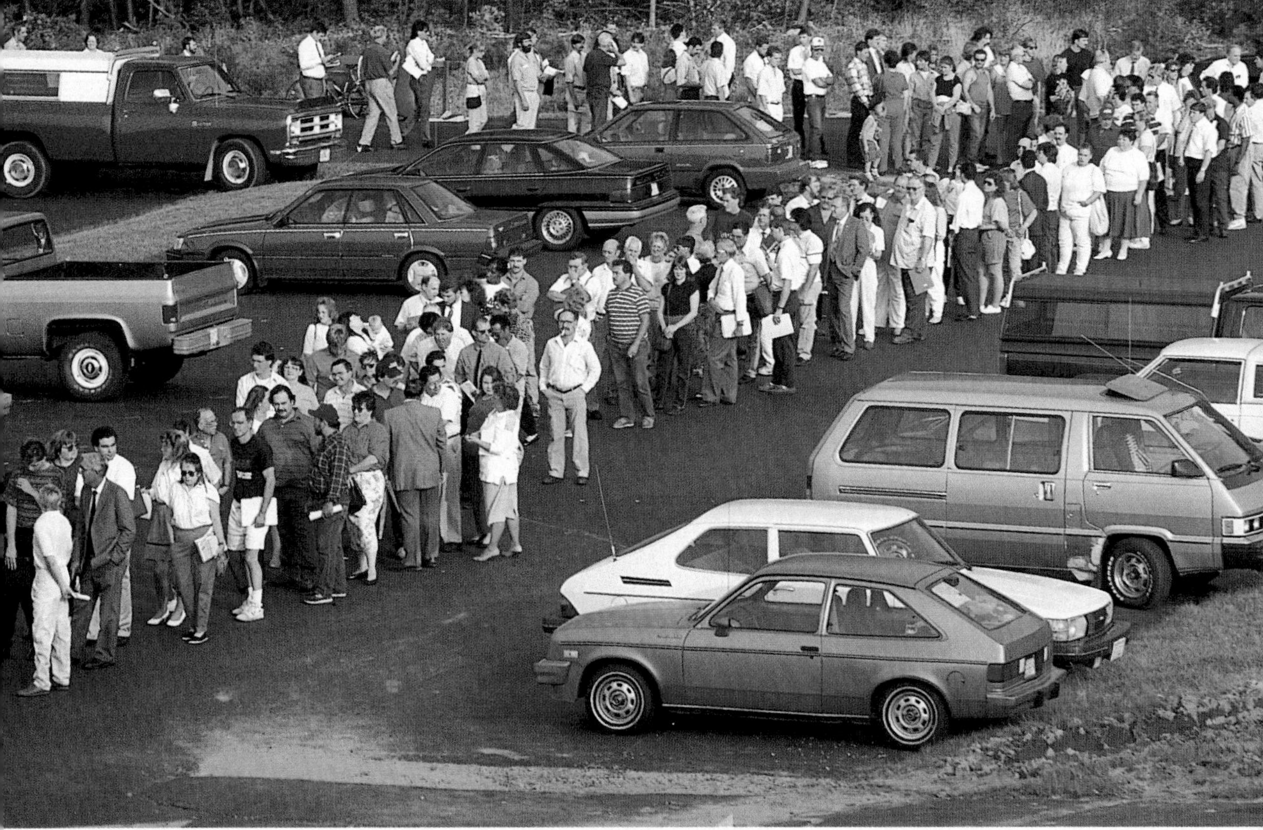

People seeking jobs line up outside a manufacturing firm in New Hampshire in September. The U.S. recession left many jobless in 1991.

their best customers—dropped from 9.5 per cent early in the year to 6.5 per cent by the end of December.

Despite the reduction in interest rates, U.S. retail sales remained flat. Factory orders were uneven, industrial output was down from 1990, and housing starts hit their lowest level since 1945.

The weak economic recovery appeared to reflect many factors. Among them were excessive business and consumer debt, more cautious bank lending, a commercial real estate boom that ran out of steam, tax hikes by many state and local governments, slowing foreign demand for U.S. goods, a cutback in federal defense spending, and relatively high long-term interest rates.

In 1991, private debt in the United States rose at the lowest rate since 1950. Disposable personal income (income left after taxes) failed to keep pace with inflation. Consumer confidence in November fell to its lowest level since the early 1980's, according to The Conference Board, a business research group in New York City.

Job insecurity fed consumer uncertainty, according to economic analysts. In June 1991, the U.S. civilian unemployment rate rose to its highest level in five years—7 per cent. That month, 8.7 million U.S. workers were jobless. By October, about 8.5 million people were still unemployed. This prompted President Bush and Congress to agree in November to extend unemployment benefits for up to 20 additional weeks to an estimated 3 million laid-off workers—a $5.3-billion package. Earlier, Bush had rejected the benefits extension, arguing that it would increase the federal budget deficit.

Worker productivity increased in the United States by about 1 per cent during 1991. Industrial productivity—as measured by output per worker-hour—rose for the first time since 1988, and productivity in the services sector, after stagnating for more than a decade, finally improved.

A record U.S. deficit. The U.S. federal deficit in fiscal 1991 (the 12 months through September 30) soared to a record $268 billion, raising the national debt to $3.6 trillion. The higher deficit reflected a weak economy, which tended to reduce tax receipts, and larger federal outlays to rescue failing banks and savings and loan institutions.

Economists forecast a still bigger budget deficit of about $350 billion for fiscal 1992. This raised doubts about whether a 1990 agreement between President Bush and Congress to balance the budget by fiscal 1995 was a realistic goal.

Inflation in the United States eased a bit in 1991, however. The U.S. inflation rate was estimated at about 4 per cent, as measured by the GNP Implicit Price Deflator, a reflection of prices throughout the economy. The Consumer Price Index, a narrower measure of inflation, rose by about 3 per cent, the lowest rate since 1986.

The Dow. Slowing inflation and falling interest rates helped propel the Dow Jones Industrial Average (the Dow) to a record high of 3,077.15 on October 18, though corporate profits generally declined, and some major businesses posted exceptional losses. On November 15, the Dow fell 120 points, the fifth largest one-day decline in its history. The Dow climbed again in December, closing at a new record of 3,168.83 on December 31.

Major losses. The "Big Three" automakers—General Motors Corporation, Ford Motor Company, and Chrysler Corporation—reported more than $5 billion in combined losses in 1991. Citicorp, the nation's largest bank holding company, reported a near-record $885-million loss in the year's third quarter (July to September), forcing the firm to suspend a common stock dividend for the first time since 1813.

Foreign investors reduced investments in the United States in 1991. In the 12 months through June 1991, new foreign direct investment—investment that represents 10 per cent or more ownership of a property—totaled $20 billion. This was one-third the average annual foreign investment rate in the United States from 1987 to 1989.

The world's slow economic growth reflected not only the U.S. recession but also recessions in Great Britain and Canada. Western Europe's growth generally slowed, but Germany, Europe's biggest economy, still posted a 3 per cent growth rate, despite problems in modernizing eastern Germany's industry. Japan again led the industrial nations in growth with a 4.5 per cent expansion.

The foreign debt of less developed nations remained at about $1.35 trillion in 1991. Major debt relief packages were arranged for Poland and Egypt. The United States and other industrial nations forgave about half the debt of those two nations, which had totaled about $60 billion. The industrial nations also helped Nicaragua pay its debts, enabling it to get new loans from international aid agencies.

Leading industrial nations also offered the former Soviet Union support for its economic reforms in 1991. At an economic summit, held from July 15 to 17 in London, the United States, Canada, France, Germany, Italy, Japan, and Great Britain invited the Soviet Union to form a "special association" with the International Monetary Fund (IMF) and the World Bank, two United Nations lending agencies.

On October 5, the IMF agreed to provide the Soviet Union economic policy advice and technical assistance. On November 5, the Soviet Union and the World Bank signed a similar accord. To further help the Soviets, the seven economic summit nations on November 21 agreed in principle to defer $3.6 billion in Soviet debt repayments in 1992. Richard Lawrence

See also **Bank; International trade; Manufacturing; Stocks and bonds;** and individual country articles. In ***World Book,*** see **Economics.**

Ecuador. See **Latin America.**

Education. President George Bush in April 1991, announced an ambitious but controversial plan for improving the nation's schools. The President's plan, called America 2000, proposed creating, by 1996, 535 "New American Schools" that would offer innovative academic programs. Under the plan, the federal government would grant $1 million each for the schools, while businesses and the community would be expected to contribute other start-up costs as well as continuing operational costs. United States Secretary of Education Lamar Alexander drafted the plan.

To give parents a broader choice of schools for their children, America 2000 urged Congress to approve public funding of private and parochial school tuition. Critics of the "choice" proposal argued that it would undermine the public school system and violate the constitutional provision for the separation of church and state.

The President's plan further called for a national examination system based on new achievement standards in five key subjects: history, geography, math, science, and English. It also proposed report cards for schools that would be based on students' exam performance; financial rewards for outstanding teachers and schools; and job skills training for adults.

By year-end, the national examination and experimental schools projects were underway. But Congress, fearful of possible adverse effects on public education, rejected the proposals for funding private education.

A mixed report on academic gains. Signs in 1991 indicated that the nation's investments in school reform during the 1980's were beginning to pay dividends in some areas. In September, the National Educational Goals Panel, composed of governors, congressional leaders, and officials of the Bush Administration, released an evaluation of U.S. students. The findings were the first of a series of annual report cards on the nation's education system.

The panel's report said the high school graduation rate of 19- and 20-year-olds increased to 83 per cent in 1990 from 81 per cent in 1975. The improvement was greatest among black students, where graduation rates increased to 78 per cent from 66 per cent during the same period. The panel also documented student gains in science and math during the 1980's.

Despite this progress, other evidence suggested that the nation's schools were still underachieving in 1991. The panel report revealed that less than 20 per cent of the nation's 4th- , 8th- , and 12th-graders were competent in math as measured by standardized tests. In June, the federally funded National Assessment of Educational Progress had reported that only half of the nation's 12th-graders understood fractions, decimals, and percentages—math concepts normally introduced in the 7th grade.

National standards. The push to improve the nation's schools sparked support in 1991 for a national curriculum and examination system. In addition to the Bush Administration, influential leaders in labor, business, and education called for national testing as a way of pressuring local educators to raise academic standards.

The sudden popularity of national testing represented a significant shift in the nation's thinking about its schools. National testing would take some decisions on academic standards away from local officials and place them with central authorities.

The classroom environment. Some educators argued in 1991 that many school systems lacked the funding necessary to help students do well on national exams. They argued that national testing would be unfair to students from low-income areas. In his best-selling book, *Savage Inequalities: Children in America's Schools,* social critic Jonathan Kozol recounted in graphic detail the inadequate facilities and often unsafe surroundings of many inner-city schools. The book, which was published in October, contrasts rundown schools in low-income areas with well-equipped schools in other areas.

An October report by the U.S. Centers for Disease Control in Atlanta, Ga., underscored the issue of safety. The report noted that 20 per cent of American high school students sometimes bring a weapon, such as a gun or a knife, to school. Among boys only, the figure was about 33 per cent.

Property taxes. Lawsuits challenging school finance systems that rely on local property taxes were filed in New York, Pennsylvania, and Ohio in 1991. This brought to at least 19 the number of states that have such suits pending in the courts.

A major cause of disparities among schools is the use of property taxes as a source of funding. Communities with low property values are not able to raise much money for schools through property taxes even if they tax themselves at higher percentage rates than the rates charged in affluent communities.

In April, Texas lawmakers passed a bill designed to make funding among schools more equitable. The law required affluent communities to raise their property tax rates to a minimum level set by the state and then share their proceeds with poorer school districts. Like national testing, the step was a blow to local control of education.

AIDS concerns. New York City schools in November became the first in the nation to distribute condoms to high school students on demand. The decision illustrated educators' growing anxiety about teen-age pregnancies and the spread of the AIDS virus. The city's school board voted 4 to 3 to make free condoms available without parental consent in the city's 122 public high schools. Officials of the Roman Catholic Church denounced the measure, and the issue sparked nationwide debate.

Higher education came under siege in 1991 as universities faced scandals regarding misappropriation of research funds and widespread criticism of tuition costs. Hard hit by budget cuts, many public colleges

Rae Ellen McKee, winner of the National Teacher of the Year Award in 1991, shows President Bush educational materials her students use in class.

© Michael Sieron

"She's easily our most successful teacher."

and universities were forced to raise tuitions, reduce enrollment, and cut courses. The average tuition at public colleges rose 12 per cent between 1990 and 1991, the College Board reported in October. The average tuition at a four-year public college for the 1991-1992 academic year was $2,137.

The prestige of the nation's top research universities was badly tarnished in March when a U.S. House subcommittee on energy and commerce held a hearing on allegations that U.S. universities had improperly used federal research funds. Stanford University in Stanford, Calif., was at the center of the scandal. Auditors with the Office of Naval Research charged that Stanford overbilled the government by as much as $200 million between 1980 and 1990 for "indirect" research expenses. These included $184,000 for the depreciation of a yacht and $7,000 for linens used in the university president's house. As a result of the charges, Stanford President Donald Kennedy announced in July 1991 that he would resign in the spring of 1992.

The Massachusetts Institute of Technology in Cambridge, Mass., announced in April 1991 that it would return $731,000 it had received from the federal government for indirect research costs. And Harvard Medical School in Boston declared in April that it would deduct indirect costs of $500,000 from a bill it had submitted for research funding.

In the wake of the investigations, the White House Office of Management and Budget proposed new regulations outlining the types of indirect research items that colleges could include in their charges. The federal government in October also announced that universities will receive less money for research-related expenses in the future.

"Political correctness" on campus became a heated issue in 1991 as writers and political commentators debated whether curriculums and standards of conduct were being ideologically influenced. Critics charged that some campus conduct codes limited free speech, that admissions policies diminished the role of merit, and that curriculums undermined Western traditions by promoting nonwhite, nonmale, and non-Western peoples and ideas. The conservative side of the critique was led by Dinesh D'Souza's *Illiberal Education: The Politics of Race and Sex on Campus.* The book quickly became a best seller after its publication in March.

In October, a U.S. district court struck down a policy of the University of Wisconsin at Madison that banned speech demeaning a person's race, sex, religion, color, creed, disability, sexual orientation, or ancestry. Conservatives had argued that "hate speech" codes such as those sanctioned by the university violated the First Amendment right to free speech. In its ruling, the court agreed.

Racial perspectives scrutinized. The proper response to the growing ethnic and racial diversity of the nation's students also came under scrutiny at the elementary and secondary school levels in 1991. In June, an advisory panel of educators and scholars appointed by New York state's commissioner of education, Thomas Sohol, published a report calling on the state to increase public schools' discussion of nonwhite and non-European peoples in its curriculum. Titled "One Nation, Many Peoples: A Declaration of Cultural Interdependence," the report charged that history classes too often focus on European events and the accomplishments of white males.

In July, the New York State Board of Regents approved a set of recommendations, based on the report, that would increase the range of cultures discussed in New York's schools. The guidelines also noted that history classes should include the perspectives of minority cultures to a greater degree than they have been. For example, information about the Civil War could include the study of journals written by slaves. Critics of the report charged that the recommendations were too extreme. "It is politically and intellectually unwise for us to attack the traditions, customs, and values which attracted immigrants to these shores in the first place," wrote Kenneth Jackson, a historian and member of the panel, in a dissenting statement.

Schools for black males. Several cities, including Detroit and Milwaukee, sought in 1991 to create special schools for black male students. The new schools aimed to lower the dropout rate of inner-city schools and to emphasize African culture and history. Some educators reasoned that schools such as these would help African-American students learn by boosting their self-esteem.

But in August, the American Civil Liberties Union and the National Organization for Women filed a lawsuit saying the schools discriminated against females. A U.S. district court judge ruled that Detroit's three proposed schools for boys violated federal and state laws by denying girls equal educational opportunities. In November, the Detroit Board of Education voted to allow girls to enroll in the schools.

Critics of the proposal argued that all-male schools would undermine the goals of cultural and racial harmony. "We proposed that public school systems be required to respond to the needs of African-American male students without resorting to segregation," said a spokesperson for the National Association for the Advancement of Colored People.

Enrollment. The number of Americans attending U.S. schools and colleges in the fall of 1991 surpassed 60 million, according to U.S. Department of Education estimates. Nearly 47 million students attended elementary and secondary schools, while more than 14 million students were enrolled in colleges and universities. The Department of Education estimated that a total of $414 billion would be spent to educate students during the 1991-1992 school year, an increase of 5.5 per cent from the previous year. Thomas Toch

In ***World Book,*** see **Education.**

Egypt. President Hosni Mubarak's support of the United States-led military coalition against Iraq during the Persian Gulf crisis in 1990 and 1991 earned him a role as a regional power broker. Egypt's ability to reassert its former leadership in the Arab world, however, appeared to depend on Mubarak's commitment to economic reform, his ability to overcome divisions within the Arab world, and on the outcome of Arab-Israeli peace negotiations.

Windfall. During and after the Persian Gulf crisis, Egypt was relieved of nearly half its $50-billion foreign debt. In the fall of 1990, the United States had canceled Egypt's $7.1-billion military debt. In addition, Saudi Arabia, Kuwait, and other Arab states in the lower Persian Gulf had forgiven another $6 billion in Egyptian debt. Under pressure from the U.S. government, a group of 17 creditor nations agreed in May 1991 to cancel half of the $20.2-billion debt Egypt owed them.

Economic problems and austerity. Egyptian officials, however, continued to argue that their country needed new infusions of cash in addition to debt relief. They pointed to some $12 billion in revenue lost during the Persian Gulf crisis because of drops in tourism and fees from the Suez Canal. The economy was also strained by the loss of remittances from 2 million Egyptians who had been working in Kuwait and Iraq but who returned to Egypt during the Persian Gulf crisis. Government spending to support these returning workers, few of whom were able to find employment in Egypt, also rose.

The International Monetary Fund (IMF), an agency of the United Nations, had resisted lending Egypt additional money. IMF officials had argued that Egypt, which had become the fourth largest debtor among developing nations, had a poor debt repayment record. They also argued that Egypt's unwillingness to implement austerity measures—for fear of popular unrest—would inhibit future economic growth.

In April, Egypt finally agreed to the austerity measures in return for debt rescheduling and financial aid. During the next 18 months, Egypt was expected to reduce government subsidies, cut government employment, encourage the sale of government-owned enterprises to private interests, and increase domestic energy prices and sales taxes. In return, Egypt was to be allowed to borrow up to $372 million to offset the negative effects of these social reforms. In July, Western governments offered Egypt $8 billion in development aid over the next two years.

Domestic pressures. As the coalition's air war against Iraq continued in late January and February, Mubarak's support among the Egyptian public waned. On January 24, Mubarak urged Israel not to retaliate against Scud surface-to-surface missile attacks by Iraq, saying that such retaliation would increase sympathy for Iraq among Egyptians.

Peace conference. During 1991, Egypt supported attempts by the United States to organize an Arab-Israeli peace conference. On July 19, Egypt called on Arab states to suspend their 43-year trade boycott of Israel if Israel agreed to halt the construction of settlements in the Israeli-occupied territories. See **Middle East.**

But Mubarak reacted warily to U.S. proposals for regional arms control in the Middle East. Egyptian officials said in July that they would agree to limitations on chemical, biological, and nuclear arms if such limitations applied equally to all Middle Eastern states, including Israel, which is widely believed to possess nuclear weapons. In late June, news accounts reported that an Egyptian-based company, jointly owned by British and Arab interests, was producing a surface-to-surface missile with the assistance of North Korea.

Arab League. Egypt's Foreign Minister, Esmat Abdel Meguid, was elected secretary general of the Arab League on May 15. The election was seen as another sign of Egypt's return to the Arab fold. Egypt had been expelled from the league in 1979 for signing a peace treaty with Israel but was readmitted in 1989.

Ferry disaster. At least 471 people died near Bur Safajah, an Egyptian port on the Red Sea, when a ferry sank after being swept against a reef. Nearly all the victims were Egyptians returning from a visit to Muslim holy sites in Saudi Arabia. Christine Helms

See also **Middle East** (Facts in brief table); **Persian Gulf,** Special Report: **War in the Persian Gulf.** In ***World Book,*** see **Egypt.**

Elections. Elections in the United States in 1991 ended with a controversial flourish on November 16 in Louisiana with the defeat of Republican David E. Duke in the governor's race. Duke, a former Ku Klux Klan leader and Nazi sympathizer, lost to Edwin W. Edwards, a Democrat and three-term former governor whose final years in office were marked by corruption charges. To get into the runoff, Duke defeated incumbent Governor Charles E. (Buddy) Roemer III in an October 18 primary. Roemer, elected as a Democrat, had become a Republican in March.

Other governors' races. In Mississippi, businessman Kirk Fordice won over incumbent Democratic Governor Ray Mabus by attacking welfare programs and racial quotas. In the November 5 election, Fordice became the first Republican governor of Mississippi since the Reconstruction era after the Civil War (1861-1865).

In Kentucky, Democratic Lieutenant Governor Brereton C. Jones won the governorship over Republican U.S. Representative Larry J. Hopkins.

On February 26, Republican J. Fife Symington defeated Democrat Samuel P. (Terry) Goddard in a runoff to become governor of Arizona.

A major Republican upset. In a special U.S. Senate election in Pennsylvania, Richard L. Thornburgh, a former Republican governor of that state, was dealt an unexpected defeat. Thornburgh had resigned as U.S. attorney general in August to run against Harris L. Wofford, a relatively unknown Democrat who had been appointed to fill the seat of Republican Senator John Heinz. Heinz was killed in a plane crash in April.

In congressional elections, Pennsylvania Democrat Lucien Blackwell on November 5 defeated three opponents to succeed U.S. Representative William H. Gray III, who resigned in September. In Virginia, Republican George F. Allen defeated Democrat Kay Slaughter to succeed Slaughter's cousin, retiring Republican Representative D. French Slaughter, Jr.

There were three special elections for the U.S. House of Representatives before November, with Democrats gaining one seat. Democrats in June won the First Congressional District of Massachusetts for the first time since 1893. John W. Oliver narrowly defeated Republican Steven Pierce to succeed Republican Silvio O. Conte, who died February 8. In a May 18 runoff in Texas, Republican State Representative Sam Johnson was elected to succeed Republican U.S. Representative Steve Bartlett, who quit Congress to run successfully for mayor of Dallas. Democrat Ed Pastor was elected on September 24 to succeed retiring Democrat Morris K. Udall in Arizona.

State legislatures. Republicans gained veto-proof majorities in both houses in New Jersey in November and picked up strength in Virginia. In the 40-member Virginia Senate, Republican strength went from 10 seats to 18.

Mayoral elections. In November 5 mayoral elections, Steve Bartlett was elected in nonpartisan balloting in Dallas to succeed Mayor Annette G. Strauss. Democrat Deedee Corradini became Salt Lake City's first female mayor. In Houston, five-term Mayor Kathy Whitmire was defeated, but a runoff was needed to pick a winner. Real estate developer Bob Lanier was elected in Houston's nonpartisan runoff on December 7. Former Police Chief Frank Jordan won in San Francisco's nonpartisan runoff balloting on December 10.

In Baltimore, Democratic Mayor Kurt L. Schmoke was reelected on November 5 over Republican Samuel Culotta. In Boston, Mayor Raymond L. Flynn won a third term over fellow Democrat Edward Doherty. Republican Stephen Goldsmith was elected to succeed four-term Republican Mayor William H. Hudnut III of Indianapolis, defeating Democrat Louis J. Mahern. Democrat Edward G. Rendell won over Republican Joseph M. Egan, Jr., to become mayor of Philadelphia.

Kay Granger was elected on May 4 as the first woman mayor of Fort Worth, Tex. W. W. Herenton of Memphis and Emanuel Cleaver of Kansas City, Mo., became the first black mayors of their cities, on October 3 and March 26, respectively. Richard M. Daley was reelected in Chicago on April 2, and Richard Arrington was reelected mayor of Birmingham, Ala., on October 8. Frank Cormier and Margot Cormier

See also **Congress of the United States; Democratic Party; Duke, David E.; Republican Party; State government.** In ***World Book,*** see **Election; Election campaign.**

Electric power. See **Energy supply.**

Electronics. One of 1991's most remarkable innovations was the Data Discman manufactured by Sony Corporation. The Discman, a virtual portable library that can be read like an electronic book, is about the size of a thick paperback. It reads compact discs (CD's), which can each store 200 megabytes of data or the equivalent of 100,000 pages of text. The list price for the machine is $550, and discs containing various types of reference information cost about $40 each. Information is displayed on a screen.

Television. The nature of television in 1991 began to change as manufacturers introduced new technologies that altered both the look of television and how people interact with it. Thomson Consumer Electronics began marketing in France a forerunner of a high-definition television (HDTV), which can produce a screen image with the clarity of a 35-millimeter slide and costs $7,000. The new wide-screen TV has a screen ratio of 16 inches (40 centimeters) of width per 9 inches (23 centimeters) of height. Traditional TV's have a width-height ratio of 4:3. In November, Japan became the first country to broadcast daily programming for HDTV's.

Philips Electronics N.V. introduced CD-I (Interactive), and Commodore International Limited brought out CDTV in 1991. Both systems transfer digital sound, graphics, and textual information from CD's to a television screen. Available discs include such resources as encyclopedias, museum tours, and sports information.

Both machines list for $1,000 and can also play audio-only CD's.

Camcorders. Home video cameras continued to become even smaller in 1991. Canon and Sony introduced the smallest camcorders yet. The machines are almost palm-sized, weigh about 1.3 pounds (0.6 kilogram), and list for between $1,200 and $1,500. Canon also introduced the first camcorder that is capable of using interchangeable lenses for either video or still photography.

The shape of things to come. Philips said in 1991 that it plans to market a new audio format, the digital compact cassette (DCC), and Matsushita Electric Industrial Company said they would manufacture players for the DCC's. A DCC is a digital tape recording and playback system that promises sound like that derived from a CD. Existing analog tapes can also be played on DCC machines. The companies hope to introduce the products in 1992. When DCC's become available, they are expected to replace digital audiotape as a widespread audio format.

Sony announced plans to market a new audio format in 1992 as well. Sony's creation is a 2.5-inch (6.4-centimeter) Mini Disc (MD), which allows users to record as well as play—something standard CD's have been incapable of doing. The MD format is not compatible with existing CD players. Frank Vizard

See also **Computer; Television.** In ***World Book,*** see **Electronics.**

El Salvador. In the final hours of 1991, President Alfredo Cristiani Burkard and antigovernment rebels reached an agreement in New York City to end El Salvador's 12-year-old civil war. A final agreement was to be signed in Mexico City on Jan. 16, 1992.

Under the United Nations-sponsored plan, rebel and government forces would cease fighting on Feb. 1, 1992. Several important matters remained unresolved as 1992 began, however.

Unresolved issues included how the rebels would give up their weapons and a complete schedule by which the agreement would be carried out. If the two sides were still not in agreement by Jan. 10, 1992, the United Nations was to impose a settlement. The agreement would reform El Salvador's court system, place more emphasis on human rights protections for Salvadorans, and reduce the size of the army. A new national police force would also be established.

Jesuit murder convictions. On Sept. 28, 1991, a Salvadoran court found army Colonel Guillermo Alfredo Benavides Moreno guilty of ordering the killings of six Jesuit priests, their cook, and her daughter in November 1989. The court also found Lieutenant Yusshy René Mendoza Vallecillos guilty of murdering the daughter. Nathan A. Haverstock

See also **Latin America** (Facts in brief table). In ***World Book,*** see **El Salvador.**

Employment. See **Economics; Labor.**

Endangered species. See **Conservation.**

Energy supply. President George Bush on Feb. 20, 1991, proposed a new national energy strategy for the United States. The goals of the master plan included increasing domestic energy production and encouraging conservation without increasing taxes or federal regulation of energy companies. Bush said that by following the plan, the United States could keep oil imports at their current level—about 40 to 45 per cent of total U.S. oil consumption. According to computer projections in Bush's plan, imports, unless checked, would account for 65 per cent of total oil consumption by the year 2010. Bush called for diversifying U.S. sources of foreign oil to prevent interruptions in deliveries because of foreign political upheavals.

The plan also included proposals for increasing energy production from the sun, wind, and other renewable sources; setting energy-efficiency standards for electric lights; streamlining the licensing of new nuclear power plants; and encouraging the use of alternative motor vehicle fuels such as methanol. The plan also proposed opening to oil exploration 1.5 million acres (607,000 hectares) of environmentally sensitive land in Alaska, including parts of the Arctic National Wildlife Refuge.

A number of the plan's provisions came under attack from Democrats in the U.S. Congress and from environmental groups. Some Democrats argued that the plan focused too heavily on increased production at the expense of conservation and renewable energy sources. Environmental groups criticized the proposal to increase oil production in Alaska.

Storing energy. The first commercial compressed air energy storage (CAES) plant in the United States began operation on May 31, 1991, in McIntosh, Ala., about 40 miles (64 kilometers) north of Mobile. The plant, owned by the Alabama Electric Cooperative, was intended to demonstrate new technology for storing energy for use in generating electricity during peak periods of demand. The plant will produce enough electricity to supply 11,000 homes. Energy experts said that CAES plants could help electric utilities meet growing demand for electricity without building expensive new coal-fired or nuclear power plants.

During periods of low demand, the plant uses electricity from a nearby coal-fired generating station to pump air into an underground reservoir, which occupies an area measuring 19 million square feet (1.8 million square meters). During periods of high electricity demand, pressurized air that is released from the reservoir and heated by natural gas or oil spins a turbine generator.

Energy production in the United States during the first half of 1991 totaled about 34 quadrillion British thermal units (Btu's), a decrease of 1 per cent from the same period in 1990, the U.S. Department of Energy (DOE) reported on Sept. 26, 1991. (A Btu is the amount of heat needed to raise the temperature of 1 pound [0.45 kilogram] of water by 1 Fahrenheit degree [0.56 Celsius degree].) Poor economic conditions,

Workers prepare for the restart in May of the Browns Ferry nuclear power plant in Alabama, shut down since 1986 for repair and safety checks.

higher energy prices, and an unusually warm winter contributed to the decline.

Coal accounted for about 32 per cent of total U.S. energy production in 1991; natural gas, 27 per cent; petroleum, 27 per cent; nuclear power, 9 per cent; and hydroelectric power, 5 per cent. Alternative energy sources such as municipal waste, wind, solar, and geothermal sources accounted for less than 1 per cent.

Solar energy. A group of California utilities on August 28 announced plans to build the world's most advanced solar energy plant. The $39-million Solar Two plant will use giant mirrors to focus the sun's rays onto a 300-foot (90-meter) tower. Molten nitrate salt, pumped to the top of the tower, will be heated to more than 1,000 °F (538 °C). The salt, stored in an insulated tank, will then be used to heat water to create steam. The steam will turn a turbine generator like those in conventional electric power stations.

Southern California Edison, the project leader, said construction will begin in 1992 at a site in the Mojave Desert near Barstow, Calif. When completed in 1994, the plant was expected to produce about 10 megawatts of electricity. Officials said the plant is intended to test technology that could be used in much larger solar plants. Southern California Edison already has another experimental solar energy plant, Solar One, on the same site.

Electric car. The Nissan Motor Company, Japan's second largest automaker, on Aug. 26, 1991, announced plans to manufacture an electric car. The car, the Nissan FEV (Future Electric Vehicle), would be powered by nickel-cadmium batteries that could be recharged in about 15 minutes. Nissan said the car would be able to travel about 100 miles (160 kilometers) at 45 miles (72 kilometers) per hour before its batteries need recharging. Nissan did not announce when the four-passenger car would be available.

Fuel cells for vehicles. Los Alamos National Laboratory in New Mexico and General Motors Corporation said on July 1 they would cooperate in developing a fuel cell system suitable for powering passenger cars, vans, and buses. Fuel cells, used to generate electricity on manned spacecraft, combine hydrogen and oxygen in a chemical reaction to produce an electric current and water.

The automobile fuel cell system will operate on methanol, which is easier to handle and store than is hydrogen. Methanol can be produced from natural gas or from abundant domestic energy sources such as coal and decaying yard wastes or other plant material. The system will use a fuel processor to convert methanol into hydrogen, which will be combined with oxygen from the air to produce electricity. Experts said that the fuel cell would produce substantially less air pollution than do gasoline-powered vehicles.

Nuclear energy. The amount of electricity generated with nuclear power in the United States increased by 5 per cent during the first half of 1991 compared with the same period in 1990, the DOE reported on Sept. 26, 1991. Nuclear plants supplied 21.4 per cent of the nation's electricity during the first half of 1991, up from 20.5 per cent in 1990.

Nuclear license extension. The U.S. Nuclear Regulatory Commission (NRC) on June 28, 1991, took the first formal steps toward permitting older nuclear power plants to continue operating after their original 40-year licenses expire. The NRC issued guidelines that would permit utilities to apply for license renewals for periods of up to 20 years. Without the license extension program, dozens of nuclear power plants first licensed in the 1960's would have to begin shutting down beginning in the year 2000. Under the guidelines, utilities seeking to renew a license would have to propose measures for dealing with aging reactor components, such as brittle or corroded pipes.

Yankee Rowe shutdown. Yankee Atomic Electric Company began closing its Yankee Rowe nuclear power station in Massachusetts on Oct. 1, 1991, because of NRC concerns over the safety of the plant's aging components. Yankee Rowe, located about 1 mile (1.6 kilometers) south of the Vermont border, began operating in 1960 and was the oldest commercial nuclear power plant in the United States.

Yankee Atomic officials said they closed the plant only because the NRC was about to order it shut. They insisted that it could continue to operate safely. NRC studies had raised questions about the strength of the plant's reactor vessel, a thick steel chamber that encloses the nuclear reactor. The NRC feared that the vessel, brittle from years of exposure to radiation, might crack and release radioactive material during an accident.

Japanese accident. Japan's plans to expand its nuclear power industry, which generates about 25 per cent of the electricity used in that oil-poor country, suffered a setback in 1991 after an accident raised questions about the safety of some plants. The accident, which occurred on February 9, severely damaged Japan's Mihama nuclear power plant about 220 miles (350 kilometers) west of Tokyo. Although no dangerous amounts of radiation were released, the accident triggered protests against nuclear power.

The Mihama reactor shut down automatically after a pipe broke, releasing 60 short tons (54 metric tons) of radioactive water inside the plant. An investigation showed that the pipe broke because of the improper installation of a device designed to control vibration. Japanese nuclear power officials ordered inspections of 17 other plants with the same type of reactor. Officials found similar defects at the Takahama nuclear plant, 200 miles (320 kilometers) west of Tokyo, and on March 21 ordered the plant closed for repairs.

Reducing oil imports. Three of the largest philanthropic organizations in the United States on January 10 announced plans to establish a foundation that will work to reduce U.S. dependence on imported oil. The organization, called the Energy Foundation, will operate with an initial grant of $20 million from the Rockefeller Foundation, the John D. and Catherine T. MacArthur Foundation, and the Pew Charitable Trusts. The foundation will identify and promote ways of increasing the energy efficiency of buildings, electric lighting, home appliances, and motor vehicles and promote the use of renewable energy sources, such as solar and wind power. Foundation officials predicted that such conservation measures could reduce by up to 50 per cent the amount of imported oil used in the United States yearly.

Reducing greenhouse gases. Energy conservation measures that reduce emissions of carbon dioxide will be crucial in limiting the effects of global warming, according to a report issued by the Office of Technology Assessment (OTA) on February 6. Carbon dioxide, released in the combustion of coal, gasoline, and other fuels, is one of the major *greenhouse gases,* which trap heat in Earth's atmosphere. Many scientists fear that increased levels of the greenhouse gases may cause a rise in atmospheric temperatures, which could lead to widespread crop failure and flooding. The OTA, which advises Congress on energy matters, said that energy conservation could cut carbon dioxide emissions by 30 per cent over the next 25 years.

Michael Woods

In ***World Book***, see **Energy supply.**

Engineering. See **Building and construction.**

England. See **Great Britain.**

Environmental pollution. The most visible environmental devastation in 1991 stemmed from the Persian Gulf War, especially from oil wells set afire in Kuwait. But Kuwait's ecological wounds were not the only major signs of environmental havoc. Scientists reported the worst recorded thinning of the ozone layer in the upper atmosphere above the Antarctic. Scientific studies also documented new health hazards from current levels of air pollution and occupational exposures to radiation.

The gulf war. In January, a United States-led multinational coalition declared war on Iraq for occupying and refusing to leave the neighboring nation of Kuwait. The fighting in this oil-rich region led to major oil spills in the gulf waters. One spill, reportedly caused when the Iraqis opened oil pipelines, dumped an estimated 168 million gallons (636 million liters) of petroleum into the Persian Gulf. Damaged oil production facilities delivered another 126,000 gallons (477,000 liters) of crude oil into the gulf daily. The spills killed 20,000 to 40,000 sea birds and several rare marine mammals known as dugongs. Oil spills threatened not only the gulf's fisheries—some of the most productive on Earth—but also mangrove swamps, coral reefs, and shallow fish-spawning areas.

As Iraqi defenses crumbled, the retreating troops set ablaze more than 600 Kuwaiti oil wells. Some of these continued to burn until early November. The resulting black smoke clouded an area that covered

Fire fighters attempt to shut off one of more than 600 Kuwaiti oil wells that were left burning after the Persian Gulf War.

some 16,000 square miles (41,000 square kilometers).

Initially, some pollution analysts had estimated that up to 10 per cent of the people in southeastern Kuwait might suffer respiratory problems from the pervasive well-fire smoke. However, in its October 25 gulf war update to Congress, the U.S. Environmental Protection Agency (EPA) noted that Kuwaiti hospitals reported no increase in emergency room visits for acute respiratory infections or asthma. See **Persian Gulf,** Special Report: **War in the Persian Gulf.**

Air pollution. On November 20, the EPA reported that more than 74 million people—about one-third of the nation's population—were breathing air that violated at least one federal air pollution standard. According to the EPA, 63 million people live in counties that exceed the smog limit, nearly 22 million people live in counties that exceed the carbon monoxide standard, and almost 19 million people live in areas violating the federal limit for *particulates* (tiny, dust-sized air pollutants that include soot and sulfates). (Because some counties violate more than one air pollutant limit, the total figure remains at about 74 million.)

Such pollutants affect the health of people with and without chronic respiratory problems, several new reports showed. One study reported in March followed 320 nonsmokers for six months. Runny noses, sore throats, head colds, *sinusitis* (infection of the sinuses), and other upper respiratory symptoms occurred most often when *ozone* (a form of oxygen that is a pollutant at ground level) and particulates were highest, researchers with the California Department of Health Services announced in March.

In examining the lungs of 14- to 25-year-old accident victims, researchers at the University of Southern California in Los Angeles found extensive evidence of chronic bronchitis and other forms of subtle but severe lung damage. Pathologist Russell P. Sherwin said that the changes in young human lungs matched those he had observed in the lungs of monkeys exposed to ozone. He attributed at least some of the damage to Los Angeles' smog, which is the worst in the nation, according to the EPA.

Also in March, Joel Schwartz, a senior scientist at the EPA, reported that just 23 per cent of the federal limit for particulates produced toxic effects in humans. He concluded that 60,000 U.S. residents may die annually from particulate pollution at or below federal limits. According to Schwartz's data, the elderly and persons suffering from respiratory disease suffer most from particulate pollution.

Ozone depletion. The same ozone that contributes to smog and lung damage in Earth's lower atmosphere, when present in the *stratosphere* (upper atmosphere), prevents the sun's harmful ultraviolet radiation from reaching Earth's surface. Ultraviolet radiation can cause skin cancer and other problems. The 1991 seasonal thinning of stratospheric ozone over the Antarctic began in the second week of September, a week earlier than usual. Within one month, the thinning produced the most severe ozone "hole" yet recorded, containing only 54 per cent of the ozone considered normal for this time of year.

A United Nations panel of scientists reported for the first time in October that ozone loss above the United States and other middle latitude areas of the globe is taking place during summertime. Scientists had thought that ozone depletion took place only over Earth's poles and middle latitude areas during winter. This finding alarmed many scientists, who feared the decrease in the protective ozone layer during summer could lead to an increase in the incidence of skin cancer. In April, the EPA reported that ozone levels in the stratosphere above the United States decreased by 4 to 5 per cent during the 1980's, three times the 1970's rate. As a result of the increased rate of ozone depletion, the EPA estimated that almost 200,000 additional deaths from skin cancer could occur in the United States during the next 50 years.

Mount Pinatubo. Millions of tons of sulfur dioxide spewed into the atmosphere as a result of the June eruption of Mount Pinatubo, a volcano in the Philippines. Atmospheric scientists, using computer models, predicted that the sulfur dioxide could thin the stratospheric ozone layer, especially in the middle latitudes such as over the United States, by as much as 15 per cent during the winter of 1991-1992. Computer models also suggested that summer 1992 ozone levels may fall 6 to 8 per cent as a result of the eruption, creating the potential for an increase in skin cancer risk.

Radiation. In March, a study of 8,318 men working at Oak Ridge National Laboratory in Tennessee, a federal nuclear research facility, estimated that the risk of dying from cancer rose almost 5 per cent for each 5 *rems* (a measure of the absorbed dose) of *ionizing radiation* the men received between 1943 and 1984. (Ionizing radiation is energetic enough to ionize—knock electrons from—atoms or molecules in human tissue.) This new risk estimate was 10 times higher than previous data on the cancer risk for Japanese atomic bomb survivors had indicated. The study strengthened the evidence linking low doses of radiation to cancer.

Two other studies suggested a possible human cancer link with *nonionizing* radiation associated with low-frequency electromagnetic fields (EMF's), such as those around electric power lines. In March, researchers at Johns Hopkins University in Baltimore reported finding a rate of breast cancer among telephone linemen that was 6.5 times higher than that typical of men in the Unites States as a whole. The cancer victims had been exposed to switches that rapidly turned powerful electrical equipment on and off. In June, the same scientists also announced finding a slightly increased risk of *leukemia* (a form of blood cancer) among telephone linemen working with the same switching equipment.

Lead levels. On February 21, three U.S. agencies announced a national initiative designed to reduce lead exposure in children. The program called for the training of experts to remove lead-based paint from home interiors and from soil and to recycle batteries, which account for about 80 per cent of the lead used in the United States. The nationwide program also was intended to increase enforcement against companies that violate lead standards and to encourage the voluntary phase-out of lead-soldered cans in food packaging.

In May, the EPA revised drinking water standards for lead contamination, lowering the average level of lead allowed in water from 50 parts per billion (ppb) to 5 ppb. The rules also mandated that water suppliers monitor for lead at the customer's faucet. Formerly, lead could be measured anywhere in the water supply system. The EPA estimated that the measures would bring the blood lead level of 600,000 children to within safe levels.

On October 7, however, the U.S. Department of Health and Human Services lowered the level at which children are considered to have lead poisoning. The new limit is 10 micrograms per deciliter (μg/dl) of blood, down from 25 μg/dl. The government's action was based on scientific studies which show that blood lead levels as low as 10 μg/dl can cause mental problems in children and stunt their growth.

Janet Raloff

See also **Conservation.** In ***World Book,*** see **Environmental pollution.**

Equatorial Guinea. See **Africa.**

Crowds gather in Tallinn, Estonia's capital, on August 23, the 52nd anniversary of a Nazi-Soviet pact that deprived Estonia of its independence.

Estonia declared full and immediate independence from the Soviet Union on Aug. 20, 1991, during an unsuccessful coup against Soviet President Mikhail S. Gorbachev. In 1940, during World War II, the Soviet Union had forcibly annexed the three Baltic republics: Estonia, Latvia, and Lithuania. The independence declaration marked the resumption of Estonia's short life as an independent state—from 1918 to 1940—after seven centuries of foreign domination by Germans, Danes, Swedes, and Russians. But popular sentiment for independence had remained strong.

In 1988, Estonia's parliament asserted its right to veto laws passed by the Soviet government, and Estonia thereby became the first Baltic state to take steps toward independence. But Estonia later avoided the confrontations that at times brought Lithuania and Latvia into violent showdowns with the Soviet government. In a referendum held on March 3, 1991, 77.8 per cent of Estonian voters had backed independence, including many ethnic Russians living in Estonia.

Diplomatic recognition swiftly followed Estonia's August proclamation, first by its Scandinavian neighbors and then by the major Western governments, including the United States. Acceptance also came from Boris Yeltsin, president of the Russian republic. On September 6, the Soviet government formally recognized Estonia's independence.

Soviet relations. Following the independence declaration, Estonian Prime Minister Edgar Savisaar raised issues requiring negotiation with the Soviet Union. These included the citizenship status of ethnic Russians, who make up 30 per cent of Estonia's population. Most of the Russians had moved to Estonia after it was annexed by the Soviet Union. Another issue revolved around the presence of some 100,000 Soviet troops, stationed in Estonia since World War II, until their final withdrawal can be completed.

The new country's leaders acknowledged the need for good relations with their Soviet neighbors, politically as well as economically. Complicating the economic situation was the fact that 60 per cent of Baltic exports had traditionally gone to other Soviet republics. Estonia's exports include timber products, dairy products, and oil shales.

Seeking EC assistance. In September 1991, the newly independent Baltic countries sought association with the 12-nation European Community (EC or Common Market) in the hope that full membership in the EC would follow. The EC, however, offered nothing more than its assurances of future economic aid and technical advice on economic restructuring. An EC study released in September estimated that the Baltic countries together would need nearly $3 billion annually in short-term assistance during their transition to market economies. Eric Bourne

See also **Europe** (Facts in brief table); **Union of Soviet Socialist Republics.** In the World Book Supplement section, see **Estonia.**

Ethiopia. After nearly 30 years, Ethiopia's civil war came to an abrupt end in May 1991 as rebels in the provinces of Eritrea and Tigre toppled the military regime of Colonel Mengistu Haile-Mariam. On May 21, Mengistu resigned and fled by plane to Zimbabwe.

The war had begun in 1962 with a secessionist movement in Eritrea against Ethiopia's previous ruler, Emperor Haile Selassie. The revolt was later joined by a separatist movement in Tigre and by several ethnic groups demanding freedom from oppression.

The Soviet Union and the United States helped bring the war to an end. The tottering Soviet state, a long-time supporter of Mengistu's regime, terminated military aid to Ethiopia in 1990. The United States attempted from January to May 1991 to achieve a negotiated settlement between Mengistu and the rebels.

Of greater importance, however, was the ability of the many rebel groups, after years of separate struggle, to coordinate their military strategies. In 1991, the Eritrean People's Liberation Front (EPLF) joined forces with the Ethiopian People's Revolutionary Democratic Front (EPRDF), an umbrella organization of the Tigrean guerrillas and other rebel groups. After Mengistu's ouster, the EPRDF installed its leader, Meles Zenawi, as Ethiopia's acting president.

Although many observers had predicted that chaos would follow a rebel victory, the well-disciplined EPRDF troops maintained order in the capital and quickly mopped up the few pockets of resistance elsewhere. Meles ordered the major officials of the Mengistu regime jailed or placed under house arrest. But lower-ranking officials, bureaucrats, and soldiers were encouraged to remain at their jobs.

Political reform. With peace restored, communities throughout the country in late 1991 began electing local law-enforcement committees to replace Mengistu-appointed councils. The ban on political party activity was lifted for all but Mengistu's Workers Party of Ethiopia. The government invited 25 parties to participate in an EPRDF-convened conference in July aimed at reforming the nation. The conferees voted to establish a free-market economy and a democratic multiparty system. Elections were set for 1993.

One thorny issue remaining at year-end was the secessionist goal of the Eritreans. The charter adopted at the July conference accepted the principle of national self-determination—including the right of secession—but many non-Eritreans wanted to preserve the unity of the Ethiopian state. The EPLF agreed to wait two years before voting on independence.

Foreign policy. On May 24 and 25, the remnants of Mengistu's government allowed an estimated 14,500 Ethiopian Jews to be airlifted to Israel. That humanitarian gesture engendered good relations with Israel, and Meles was expected to try and maintain those ties. J. Gus Liebenow and Beverly B. Liebenow

See also **Africa** (Facts in brief table). In ***World Book,*** see **Ethiopia.**

A rebel fighting Ethiopia's Marxist regime checks a damaged government tank in Addis Ababa, the capital, in May as the rebels neared victory.

Europe

Europe continued to reshape itself in fundamental ways in 1991. The industrialized countries of western Europe increasingly integrated their economies into a powerful trading bloc, while the former Communist countries of eastern Europe struggled to move toward market economies.

The collapse of Communism in the Soviet Union in August allowed the Baltic republics of Estonia, Latvia, and Lithuania to win independence and seek a place in Europe. Eleven of the remaining 12 Soviet republics agreed on December 21 to form a Commonwealth of Independent States at a meeting in Alma Ata, the capital of Kazakhstan, signalling the apparent end of the Soviet Union. Moldavia, which was considering uniting with Romania, joined the commonwealth instead. Only Georgia, which was torn by factional fighting, failed to join the new commonwealth, which was to have its capital in Minsk in Byelorussia.

The spirit of independence among European nationality groups also had tragic consequences in 1991. The Yugoslav republics of Slovenia and Croatia declared their independence in June, and Croatia was soon caught in a bloody civil war with the Yugoslav federal army, which was dominated by Serbs who opposed Croatian independence. See **Yugoslavia,** Special Report: **A Troubled Past Clouds Yugoslavia's Future.**

European defense and security policies came under reevaluation during 1991. Western Europe began rethinking its defense strategy as the threat from the Soviet Union receded—especially after a coup attempt by Soviet hard-liners failed in August—and as both the United States and the Soviet Union announced sweeping reductions in nuclear arms.

The European Community (EC or Common Market) debated whether to add responsibilities for European defense and security to its current economic role. The 12 members of the EC are Belgium, Denmark, France, Germany, Great Britain, Greece, Ireland, Italy, Luxembourg, the Netherlands, Portugal, and Spain. Since 1949, the North Atlantic Treaty Organization (NATO) has provided for the collective defense of western Europe. NATO links all the EC countries except Ireland in a military alliance with the United States, Canada, Iceland, Norway, and Turkey.

France wanted the EC to assume more and more of NATO's role in European defense. Great Britain and other nations favored a continued U.S. military presence in Europe through NATO and opposed any moves to expand Europe's defense role that would undermine close ties to North America. Critics of a common European defense policy argued that Europe

In Riga, Latvia, a crowd marks the collapse of Soviet authority in August by gathering round a fallen statue of V. I. Lenin, founder of the Soviet Union.

THE

Polish Prime Minister Jan K. Bielecki, left, and former German Chancellor Willy Brandt shake hands as their nations sign a friendship treaty in June.

had been deeply divided over participation in the Persian Gulf War and intervention in the Yugoslav civil war. This showed, they said, that Europe was not yet ready to speak with one voice on security issues.

NATO's adversary in the past, the Soviet-led Warsaw Pact, formally agreed to disband at a meeting in Prague, Czechoslovakia, in July. NATO leaders met at a summit in November to discuss the future role of the alliance in light of the Warsaw Pact's termination and the Soviet Union's breakup. At the summit, EC leaders affirmed their support for a continued U.S. military presence in Europe. France and Germany proposed in October that the EC create a multinational, European army. This raised U.S. concern that NATO might be supplanted as the leading force in European defense.

NATO leaders also expressed the concern that the breakup of the Soviet Union could leave hundreds of nuclear weapons inside newly independent republics, whose leaders might not feel bound by treaties signed by the central Soviet government. Many European politicians held their breath at year's end, fearing that economic hardship in the former Soviet Union could lead to violence.

At an EC summit in Maastricht, the Netherlands, in December, European leaders agreed to establish common defense and foreign policies. The agreement on political union was one of two historic treaties—the other covered economic union—that provided for the closer integration of European nations.

Political union. The EC's negotiations on political union remained deadlocked during much of 1991 over the controversial issue of redistributing political power among EC institutions. Great Britain and France favored keeping most decision-making powers in the Council of Ministers, where prime ministers and other high-ranking officials represent member governments and approve EC legislation.

Germany and some smaller EC member nations, on the other hand, favored giving much more political power to the European Parliament, which currently serves mainly as an advisory body. The Parliament is made up of elected representatives from all the member states, based on their population. These representatives are seated by political affiliation, such as conservative or Socialist, rather than by country.

Before the December summit, Germany reluctantly agreed to a compromise that gave the Parliament veto powers over EC laws and projects in only a few areas, including the environment and research. Discussion was to continue through the 1990's on expanding the Parliament's powers, however.

Another stumbling block was the creation of a common labor policy, to which Britain objected. The proposal was finally dropped from the draft treaty, though the other 11 EC members adopted it separately. Britain also insisted that policy decisions on "major" issues be made by a unanimous vote of the Council of Ministers, a condition agreed to by the other EC

Facts in brief on European countries

Country	Population	Government	Monetary unit*	Foreign trade (million U.S.$) Exports†	Imports†
Albania	3,346,000	President Ramiz Alia; Prime Minister Vilson Ahmeti	lek (5.75 = $1)	378	255
Andorra	55,000	The bishop of Urgel, Spain, and the president of France	French franc & Spanish peseta	1	531
Austria	7,486,000	President Kurt Waldheim; Chancellor Franz Vranitzky	schilling (11.50 = $1)	41,881	50,017
Belgium	9,954,000	King Baudouin I; Prime Minister Wilfried Martens	franc (33.63 = $1)	118,295 (includes Luxembourg)	120,067
Bulgaria	9,021,000	President Zhelyu Zhelev; Prime Minister Filip Dimitrov	lev (18.13 = $1)	13,428	13,089
Czechoslovakia	15,749,000	President Václav Havel; Premier Marián Čalfa	koruna (29.01 = $1)	11,882	13,106
Denmark	5,123,000	Queen Margrethe II; Prime Minister Poul Schlüter	krone (6.35 = $1)	35,112	31,766
Estonia	1,595,000	Chairman of the Supreme Council Arnold Rüütel		Not Available	
Finland	4,997,000	President Mauno Koivisto; Prime Minister Esko Aho	markka (4.42 = $1)	26,743	27,110
France	56,578,000	President François Mitterrand; Prime Minister Edith Cresson	franc (5.58 = $1)	209,996	233,163
Germany	77,042,000	President Richard von Weizsäcker; Chancellor Helmut Kohl	mark (1.63 = $1)	359,706	287,661
Great Britain	57,640,000	Queen Elizabeth II; Prime Minister John Major	pound (0.57 = $1)	185,976	224,938
Greece	10,077,000	President Constantinos Karamanlis; Prime Minister Constantinos Mitsotakis	drachma (185.77 = $1)	8,019	19,777
Hungary	10,535,000	President Arpad Goncz; Prime Minister Jozsef Antall	forint (77.72 = $1)	9,707	8,764
Iceland	257,000	President Vigdis Finnbogadóttir; Prime Minister David Oddsson	krona (58.65 = $1)	1,590	1,677
Ireland	3,791,000	President Mary Robinson; Prime Minister Charles Haughey	pound (punt) (0.61 = $1)	23,778	20,716
Italy	57,425,000	President Francesco Cossiga; Prime Minister Giulio Andreotti	lira (1,230.25 = $1)	141,600 (includes San Marino)	143,100
Latvia	2,718,000	President Anatolijs Gorbunovs		Not Available	
Liechtenstein	28,000	Prince Hans Adam I; Prime Minister Hans Brunhart	Swiss franc	no statistics available	
Lithuania	3,742,000	President of the Supreme Council Vytautas Landsbergis		Not Available	
Luxembourg	367,000	Grand Duke Jean; Prime Minister Jacques Santer	franc (33.63 = $1)	118,295 (includes Belgium)	120,067
Malta	356,000	President Vincent Tabone; Prime Minister Eddie Fenech Adami	lira (0.32 = $1)	858	1,505
Monaco	30,000	Prince Rainier III	French franc	no statistics available	
Netherlands	14,852,000	Queen Beatrix; Prime Minister Ruud Lubbers	guilder (1.84 = $1)	131,839	126,195
Norway	4,236,000	King Harald V; Prime Minister Gro Harlem Brundtland	krone (6.42 = $1)	34,072	26,905
Poland	38,793,000	President Lech Walesa	zloty (11,154 = $1)	13,627	8,160
Portugal	10,343,000	President Mário Alberto Soares; Prime Minister Aníbal Cavaço Silva	escudo (145.23 = $1)	16,341	25,057
Romania	23,487,000	President Ion Iliescu; Prime Minister Theodor Stolojan	leu (34.93 = $1)	6,095	9,240
San Marino	23,000	2 captains regent appointed by Grand Council every 6 months	Italian lira	no statistics available	
Spain	39,625,000	King Juan Carlos I; Prime Minister Felipe González Márquez	peseta (103.99 = $1)	55,640	87,694
Sweden	8,334,000	King Carl XVI Gustaf; Prime Minister Carl Bildt	krona (5.98 = $1)	57,423	54,580
Switzerland	6,534,000	President Flavio Cotti	franc (1.44 = $1)	63,884	69,869
Turkey	57,749,000	President Turgut Özal; Prime Minister Suleyman Demirel	lira (5,072.76 = $1)	12,922	21,810
Union of Soviet Socialist Republics	284,900,000	President Mikhail S. Gorbachev‡	ruble (0.57 = $1)	104,177	120,651
Yugoslavia	24,093,000	Vice President Branko Kostic´; Federal Executive Council Vice President Aleksandar Mitrovic´§	dinar (21.23 = $1)	14,312	18,890

*Exchange rates as of Nov. 29, 1991, or latest available data. †Latest available data.

‡Gorbachev resigned on December 25 as the new Commonwealth of Independent States replaced the U.S.S.R.

§Both President Stjepan Mesíc and Premier Ante Markovic´ resigned in December.

leaders. Decisions on less important matters, however, could be reached by a majority of the Council.

Economic and monetary union. The adoption of a treaty on economic and monetary union (EMU) at the December summit marked a further step toward EC economic integration. The treaty extended a 1985 plan to remove most barriers to the free movement of goods, money, people, and services within the EC by the end of 1992—a plan that remained on schedule.

The EMU proposal was even more ambitious: It called for creating a European Central Bank to assume much of the economic policymaking now carried out by national governments. But before an EC nation could become a member of the central bank, certain aspects of its economy—its budget deficit, interest rates, and inflation rate, for example—would have to satisfy tough EC requirements. The bank's chief purpose would be to oversee the creation of a single, noninflationary European currency that would replace the current national currencies, such as the French franc and the German mark, perhaps as early as 1997.

Those in favor of EMU and its single European currency argued that it would produce enormous annual savings by sparing individuals and businesses the need to exchange currencies for transactions outside their own country. Proponents also claimed that EMU would allow a central authority to defend Europe's economic interests against its major competitors, the United States and Japan.

Among EC members, Great Britain had the strongest reservations about EMU, fearing that it would have to yield too much control over its own economy. To win British approval for EMU, EC officials allowed Britain to delay its decision on adopting a common currency. Britain planned to have its Parliament vote on whether the country would enter the EMU.

Expanding Europe's single market. The EC's economic power proved attractive to nonmember European countries in 1991. In October, the seven-nation European Free Trade Association (EFTA) successfully negotiated a combined free-trade zone with the EC. EFTA members—Austria, Finland, Iceland, Liechtenstein, Norway, Sweden, and Switzerland—hoped to participate in the economic benefits that the EC's single market is expected to generate after it takes effect on Jan. 1, 1993. Under the new agreement, that single market will be expanded to include the EFTA nations. As part of the agreement, the EFTA nations, which have a higher average income than the EC nations, pledged about $2.4 billion to a fund to help develop poorer regions of Europe.

Although the pact will give EFTA members many of the EC's trade benefits, EFTA nations will have no vote on EC laws that will affect them. Thus, despite the new agreement, EFTA members Austria and Sweden planned to pursue their applications for EC membership, and Switzerland and Finland were expected to apply soon.

Former Communist-bloc members Czechoslovakia, Hungary, and Poland signed agreements with the EC in November that should make it easier for them to sell their exports within the EC. The three countries all said they would like to join the EC, but their economies and legal systems will not meet the requirements for EC membership for many years.

Trade talks. The EC's economic unity continued to play a major role in international trade talks held under the auspices of the General Agreement on Tariffs and Trade (GATT). These negotiations, begun in 1985, had stumbled in 1990 over disagreements on an agricultural policy: The EC had rejected U.S. demands that it radically reform its system of paying farmers for raising more crops or livestock. The United States, Australia, and other exporters of farm products have complained that the EC farm policy distorted the price of beef, wheat, and other commodities in Europe and gave European farmers an unfair advantage on world markets.

In September 1991, the EC agriculture commissioner made a proposal that could unlock the negotiations. He proposed that the EC replace the current system of paying farmers for how much they produce with a system of direct income supplements not tied to production. By year's end, the proposal had not won approval, however.

In another important trade development, the EC in August decided to continue to protect its automobile industry from foreign competition. An agreement with Japan limits through 1999 the annual sales of Japanese-made cars to 16 per cent of all cars sold within the EC, up from an 11 per cent market share in 1991. After 1999, however, all limits will be removed, unless European carmakers convince their governments that they still need protection.

Some EC countries, including France and Italy, have limited Japanese car sales to less than 3 per cent of all cars sold there. Others, such as the Netherlands, have allowed Japanese manufacturers to sell all the cars they can.

East and West. Western Europe groped during 1991 for ways to aid eastern Europe. Led by Germany, the EC agreed to send the Soviet Union more than $1-billion in food aid to help ease food shortages expected over the harsh Soviet winter.

A new international institution, the European Bank for Reconstruction and Development, was formally inaugurated in London in April 1991 for the purpose of providing loans to eastern Europe. The EC governments owned 51 per cent of the bank, which had more than $12 billion for funding projects to develop free markets and improve telephone systems and technology in eastern Europe and the Soviet Union. Other investors included the United States and Japan.

Hundreds of European companies, especially German and French firms, invested in joint ventures in eastern Europe in 1991 in an effort to exploit potential new markets of consumers hungry for goods. But Western investment arrived far more slowly than east-

As the Soviet Union completes its withdrawal from Czechoslovakia in June, two soldiers carry their bedrolls to a train that took them home.

ern European governments had hoped. Western Europeans also set up business schools in eastern Europe to train young managers in Western management methods. Many eastern European managers had never had to make a profit or calculate the most efficient ways to make their products.

Immigration to western Europe from eastern Europe and the former Soviet Union created major social and political problems. Eastern Europeans flocked to the West, as their economies struggled and tens of thousands of people lost their jobs. Suffering from economic slowdowns and high jobless rates themselves, a number of western European countries moved to limit legal immigration in various ways.

Immigration to western Europe from Turkey and North Africa also created problems during 1991. In France and Belgium, North African immigrants and their children, many of whom had been born in Europe, staged demonstrations and riots to protest what they claimed was discrimination against them in housing and jobs. In Germany, right wing extremists harassed immigrants, at times violently. By espousing anti-immigration policies, right wing groups gained strength in several western European countries with large immigrant communities. Philip Revzin

See also **Europe,** Special Report: **The Rocky Road to European Unity; U.S.S.R.,** Special Report: **Why Communism Failed in the U.S.S.R.;** and the various European country articles. In ***World Book,*** see **Europe.**

Explosion. See **Disasters.**

The Rocky Road to European Unity

By Philip Revzin

The 12-nation European Community's route toward a single, barrier-free market has not been a smooth one, and more problems are likely to stand in the way of economic and political unity.

On the official flag of the European Community, each star in the circle represents a member nation.

In the Europe of the future, driving from Lisbon, Portugal, to Athens, Greece, could be as unrestricted as driving from Los Angeles to New York City. Today, travelers going from one European country to another must stop at the borders and have their passports examined. Future travelers from Portugal, Greece, or any other nation in the European Community (EC) may not have to go through this, because border posts will be gone. Instead of using francs in France, pounds in England, and marks in Germany, future shoppers may spend one kind of money in all the EC countries, just as Americans spend dollars in all the states. Voters may elect a president of Europe.

Such an integrated Europe does not yet exist. Further unification of the 12 EC countries, whose people speak nine languages and use 11 different kinds of money, will be a difficult task. Indeed, during 1991, complications arose, both political and economic, that appeared to cast doubt on the unification process. Nevertheless, Dec. 31, 1992, is the deadline when most of the barriers to the movement of people, goods, money, and services among EC members are scheduled to come down, forming a single market of 340 million people, the largest in the world.

The EC's first step toward a more unified market occurred in February 1986, when member nations signed the Single European Act. In addition to market unification, the act paved the way for such things as future economic and monetary union and political union. Following ratification of the act in 1987 by all members, the EC wrote 276 rules and regulations to implement the act's provisions.

Creating a European community

The idea of a unified Europe has been circulating for centuries. In the past, some people thought that a united Europe was possible because the various nations shared a common civilization. But the EC that was created in the post-World War II (1939-1945) period came about largely in response to economic and political changes caused by the war.

The war had destroyed much of the industrial capacities of the Allied countries of Western Europe. Also, in the immediate postwar period, the Soviet Union threatened the newly won peace by imposing Communist-dominated governments on countries in Eastern Europe. In response to both the necessity of reconstruction and the Soviet threat, Western European nations began to rebuild and integrate their economies, concentrating at first on industries necessary to produce weapons—coal, iron, and steel. Thus, the European Coal and Steel Community (ECSC) was formed on April 18, 1951, when Belgium, France, Italy, Luxembourg, the Netherlands, and West Germany signed the Treaty of Paris to promote mutual production and trade of coal, steel, and iron ore

The success of the ECSC was outstanding. Coal production in the six member nations increased 23 per cent from 1951 to 1955, and iron and steel production rose 145 per cent during the same period. These results led to more ambitious plans for European cooperation. On March 25, 1957, the six members of the ECSC signed the Rome Treaties, establishing two new organizations: the European Economic Community (EEC) and the European Atomic Energy Community (Euratom).

The EEC was formed to promote economic growth and unrestricted movement of *capital* (money or other property used to carry on business) and labor among members. The EEC also mandated common policies for transport and business competition. The perception was that integrating the economies of member nations would lead to political unification.

To promote trade, the EEC established a *customs union,* which regulated trade among EEC members and between the EEC and other nations. All *tariffs* (taxes on traded goods) among EEC members were eliminated by 1968. The customs union agreed to impose one set of tariffs on goods imported from nonmember nations. Thus, each EEC member charged the same duty on a given product imported from a nonmember country.

Glossary

Capital: Money or other property used to carry on business.

Common Agricultural Policy (CAP): The main instrument the European Community uses to carry out its agricultural objectives. CAP consists mainly of price supports.

Customs union: An arrangement formed when nations eliminate tariffs on trade among themselves and agree on a set of tariffs on trade with nonmember nations.

European Currency Unit: A unit of value, not actual currency, used by the European Community to establish exchange rates among member nations.

Exchange rate: The price of one nation's currency in relation to another nation's currency.

Tariffs: Taxes on traded goods.

Value-added tax: A tax imposed on goods and services at each stage of production.

The author:

Philip Revzin is editor of *The Wall Street Journal Europe* and reports on European affairs from Brussels, Belgium.

What is the European Community?

The European Community (EC) is an organization of Western European nations that was founded after World War II (1939-1945) to rebuild national economies that the war destroyed. The EC's success in promoting the economic growth of members attracted other nations to seek membership and led to a gradual expansion from the original 6 nations to 12 nations. By Dec. 31, 1992, trade barriers among EC members are scheduled to come down, creating a single market of 340 million people, the world's largest. Beyond 1992, EC goals include monetary and political unification.

Great Britain

Language: English

Population: 57,537,000

Chief exports: chemicals, aerospace equipment, heavy machinery, petroleum

Currency: pound

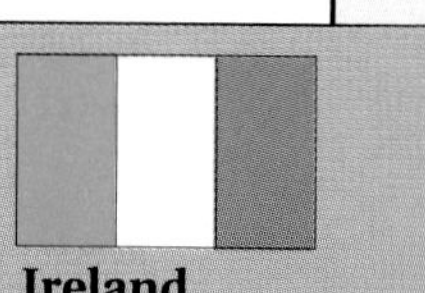

Ireland

Language: English, Gaelic

Population: 3,755,000

Chief exports: chemicals, computers, dairy products, meat, textiles

Currency: Irish pound

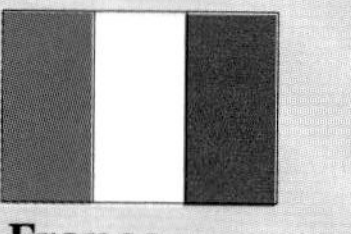

France

Language: French

Population: 56,375,000

Chief exports: chemical products, machinery, electrical equipment, automobiles

Currency: franc

Portugal

Language: Portuguese

Population: 10,314,000

Chief exports: clothing, cork, paper, textiles, wine

Currency: escudo

Spain

Language: Castilian Spanish

Population: 39,479,000

Chief exports: automobiles, citrus fruits, iron and steel, olives, textiles, wine

Currency: peseta

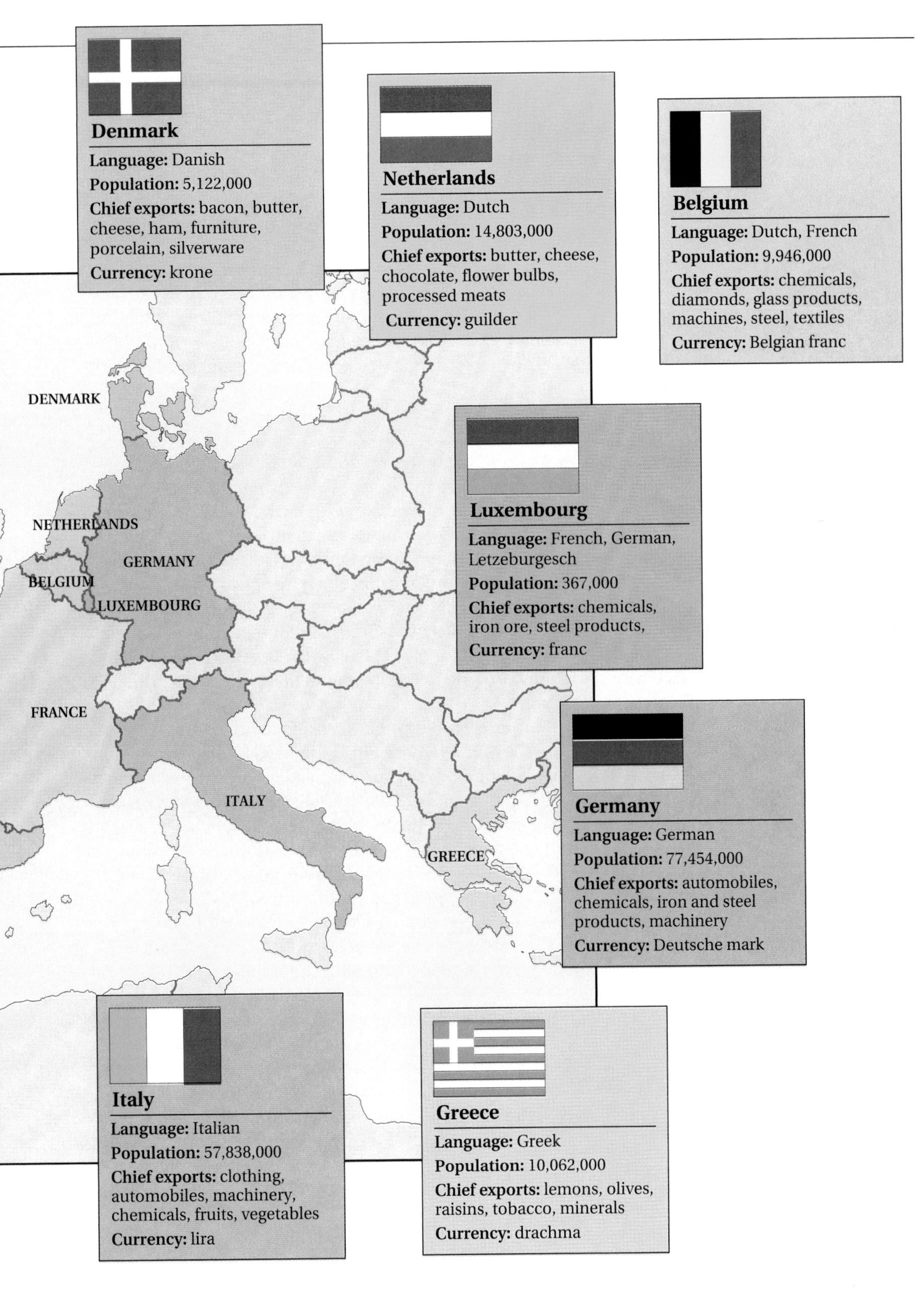
Denmark
Language: Danish
Population: 5,122,000
Chief exports: bacon, butter, cheese, ham, furniture, porcelain, silverware
Currency: krone
Netherlands
Language: Dutch
Population: 14,803,000
Chief exports: butter, cheese, chocolate, flower bulbs, processed meats
Currency: guilder
Belgium
Language: Dutch, French
Population: 9,946,000
Chief exports: chemicals, diamonds, glass products, machines, steel, textiles
Currency: Belgian franc
DENMARK
NETHERLANDS
GERMANY
BELGIUM
LUXEMBOURG
FRANCE
ITALY
GREECE
Luxembourg
Language: French, German, Letzeburgesch
Population: 367,000
Chief exports: chemicals, iron ore, steel products,
Currency: franc
Germany
Language: German
Population: 77,454,000
Chief exports: automobiles, chemicals, iron and steel products, machinery
Currency: Deutsche mark
Italy
Language: Italian
Population: 57,838,000
Chief exports: clothing, automobiles, machinery, chemicals, fruits, vegetables
Currency: lira
Greece
Language: Greek
Population: 10,062,000
Chief exports: lemons, olives, raisins, tobacco, minerals
Currency: drachma

Euratom was formed to bring together nuclear experts and technicians to exchange information on the use of atomic energy for peaceful purposes. Euratom also collected raw material and equipment to construct nuclear power plants to generate electricity in Europe.

In 1967, the ECSC, the EEC, and Euratom merged executive functions to form the Commission of the European Communities, known as the EC. Trade among the members increased greatly, from $6.8 billion in 1958 to $60 billion in 1972, according to EC statistics. This success attracted other European nations to seek EC membership. Great Britain, Ireland, and Denmark joined in 1973, Greece joined in 1981, and Spain and Portugal joined in 1986, bringing to 12 the total number of member nations.

Economic diversity

Expansion, however, brought greater economic diversity to the EC than existed when the organization first formed. The expanded EC had some member nations that were heavily industrialized, while others were largely dependent on agriculture. This diversity has made farming objectives particularly troublesome for the EC to implement. The EC's agricultural objectives include promoting the free movement of agricultural goods and providing a fair standard of living for people engaged in agriculture. The main instrument the EC has used to carry out its agricultural objectives is called the Common Agricultural Policy (CAP), established in 1962, which consists mainly of a price support system that guarantees farmers a set price for their crops.

However, price supports and subsidies have led to problems for the EC, both among members and between the EC and its trading partners elsewhere in the world. For example, large farms receive the most money, because they produce the greatest crop yields. According to a May 1991 report, 80 per cent of the EC farm budget goes to 20 per cent of the farms. Moreover, CAP spending accounts for about two-thirds of the EC's budget—an estimated $39 billion in 1991, up from about $34 billion in 1990. Some experts say that the CAP budget is out of control. Subsidies also have resulted in huge surpluses of such products as butter and wine.

Resolving the EC's subsidies problem is a major concern of many of the 108 countries that have signed the General Agreement on Tariffs and Trade (GATT). Created in 1947, GATT is the world's main international trade agreement. GATT nations include every EC member, as well as the United States and Japan. Disagreement among GATT nations over the EC's agricultural subsidies led to the breakdown of regularly scheduled talks in December 1990. By November 1991, GATT talks had not resumed.

A less troublesome EC mechanism that has encouraged EC members to trade with each other has been the European Monetary System (EMS). It began in 1979 with the full participation of eight of the EC countries (Belgium, Denmark, France, Ireland, Italy, Luxembourg, the Netherlands, and West Germany). The system maintains official prices, called *exchange rates,* of the currencies of its members. The EMS establishes the exchange rate of one nation's currency in relation to another nation's currency by relating both to a unit of value called a European Currency Unit (ECU).

Problems from within
About 200,000 French farmers marched through Paris on September 29 to demonstrate their despair over a 25 per cent drop in agricultural prices that could bankrupt many of them. The farmers also feared that the European Community would reduce subsidies and price supports in its common agricultural policy. Price supports have created huge surpluses by encouraging overproduction of farm products.

(As yet, ECU's do not exist as actual money.) For example, if the French franc were worth 1 ECU and the Dutch guilder were worth 2 ECU's, the official rate for these currencies would be 2 francs to 1 guilder. By the end of 1990, all the EC nations had signed the EMS agreement, but Greece and Portugal remained outside the exchange rate mechanism. They are expected to join when their economies are stronger.

Early on, the EC recognized economic differences among member nations and has attempted to reduce those differences through its aid programs, called structural funds. The funds are used to stimulate investment and create jobs in poor EC regions. EC aid also goes to areas where industrial decline has caused high unemployment and to areas where agriculture has been mechanized and no longer requires a large labor force. This aid accounted for 10 per cent of the 1991 EC budget.

In order to pay for these programs, EC members give the EC a small portion of the customs duties that each member collects on imports from nonmember countries. EC members also give a small portion, currently less than 2 per cent, of their *value-added tax* to the EC. This tax is imposed on goods and services at each stage of production, but usually the cost is passed on to consumers in the form of higher prices. The amount of the tax is determined by the amount of the value that a company adds to the materials and services it buys from other firms.

The administrative system of the EC has four branches. The executive branch, a 17-member Commission headquartered in Brussels, Belgium, carries out provisions of the three treaties that established the EC. The Commission has exclusive power to propose policies and legislation applicable to all member states.

The legislative branch, or Council of Ministers, is also based in Brus-

Problems from without
Imported autos, such as those exhibited at a Japanese car fair in Madrid, Spain, in June, are of great concern to France and Italy, who want to protect their own automobile industries. France wants to count Japanese cars made in Great Britain in its import quota, but Great Britain along with Germany objects. Negotiators are hoping for a transition period to a free car market after 1992.

sels. The council is composed of cabinet members of all 12 EC nations. It adopts laws that are based on proposals submitted by the Commission, but it can reject Commission proposals as well. The council also has authority to ask for proposals from the Commission.

The advisory branch of the EC, the European Parliament, is based in Strasbourg, France. It meets monthly in weeklong sessions to debate Commission proposals and can question both the Commission and the council. Parliament can amend or reject the EC budget, except for agricultural spending, and by a two-thirds vote expel the entire Commission, but it never has done so. The European Parliament has the power to amend or reject certain legislation approved by the council and to approve or reject applications of other nations to join the EC.

The judicial branch, the Court of Justice, sits in Luxembourg. The court decides whether actions of the Commission, the council, member governments, and private organizations comply with EC rules. The court also hears appeals brought to it by EC nations, the Commission, the council, or private citizens. All parties, including the governments of EC members, must abide by the court's decisions.

By autumn of 1991, the Commission had proposed all the necessary new rules to implement the Single European Act, the Council of Ministers had approved most of them, and the 12 national governments were reviewing them. But the most difficult obstacles to European unity await settlement. These include problems ranging from import policy to when to implement a common rate for the value-added tax. Particularly thorny is how to widen the EC market for automobiles imported from Japan. Several EC nations, such as France and Italy, have quotas limiting the number of Japanese-made cars that may be sold in their countries. These rules protect French and Italian automobile manufacturers from Japanese competitors. Many EC nations, however, that do not have automobile industries to protect want to end these limits entirely. Negotiators say that the quotas could be phased out during the 10 years following the 1992 deadline for implementing the Single European Act.

Another problem awaiting solution is how to make the different rates of the value-added tax in each EC nation the same. A member country with a low tax could attract consumers from a high-tax member. All EC nations agreed in June 1991 to keep their basic tax at a minimum of 15 per cent but postponed until some future time any effort to make the rate mandatory. Rates range from a low of 12 per cent in Spain and Luxembourg to a high of 22 per cent in Denmark.

Toward greater unity?

The EC is already looking well beyond the completion of a single market. On Dec. 14, 1990, officials from the 12 member nations began negotiations to draft amendments to the Rome Treaties that would set the stage for economic, monetary, and political union. Experts say these areas will probably be the most difficult to integrate. Economic and monetary union would mean transferring control of most of the 12 members' economic policies to EC institutions, including a new system of central banks, similar to the U.S. Federal Reserve System. This central banking system eventually would administer a single European currency.

Steps toward political union may include formulating a common foreign policy and providing for defense of EC nations against outside attack. But, Great Britain has objected to the idea of political union and an EC defense policy, because it does not want to relinquish control over these areas. The EC's lack of a unified response to the Persian Gulf crisis and its failed attempts to quell the persistent crisis in Yugoslavia during 1991 prompted political analysts to say that political pressures within EC nations once again demonstrated the EC's inability to act as one.

Another issue facing the EC in 1991 and beyond was membership for other European nations. Austria, Cyprus, Malta, Sweden, and Turkey have formally applied for membership. Expansion to include these countries will mean assimilating more economic diversity, a complex process that the EC is currently watching in Germany, as the agricultural East reunites with the industrialized West.

Exporting nations, including the United States and Japan, favor Europe's unity plans. They see great advantages in allowing their goods to have access to a vast, barrier-free market. However, observers say that for the EC to find common ground for a more fully united Europe—economically, monetarily, and politically—it will probably have to travel down a rocky road.

For further reading:

The Politics of 1992: Beyond the Single European Market. Ed. by Colin Crouch and David Marquand. Basil Blackwell, 1991.

Goodman, S. F. *The European Community.* St. Martin, 1991.

Farm and farming. The United States farm economy in 1991 was dominated by purchases made by the former Soviet Union as that country's political structure and economy unraveled. The farm industry was also embroiled in an environmental controversy over federal regulation of wetlands. Despite crop losses from heavy spring rains, drought, and an early freeze, 1991 crops were larger than expected.

Soviet purchases. For 20 years, the Soviet Union has been a major cash customer for U.S. grain, purchasing an average of 12 per cent of U.S. corn and wheat exports. In some years, the Soviets bought as much as one-third of U.S. grain exports. By 1990, however, the Soviets had became dependent on U.S. government guarantees for credit purchases of farm products as well as on direct price subsidies.

On Dec. 12, 1990, U.S. President George Bush authorized $1 billion in agricultural credits to the Soviet Union. During January 1991, however, Soviet troops cracked down on independence movements in Lithuania and Latvia, leaving about 20 people dead. Some members of the U.S. Congress suggested that the United States government withhold the Soviet Union's credits. But Soviet leaders had already used most of the credits before the violence occurred.

On June 11, 1991, after tensions between the Soviet Union and the United States had eased somewhat, President Bush authorized another $1.5 billion in credits, to be distributed gradually through February 1992. The decision to grant the credits was made after an extensive study of whether the Soviet Union, with its deteriorating economy, could repay the credits. "Our current evaluation of, and past experience with, Soviet commitments convinced us that they will fully meet their financial obligations to the United States," U.S. Secretary of Agriculture Edward R. Madigan said.

Concern about Soviet shortages. After an August 1991 coup against Soviet President Mikhail S. Gorbachev failed, the U.S. government released $900-million in unused credits ahead of schedule—$315 million on August 26 and $585 million on October 1. In early October, Madigan traveled to the Soviet Union to assess growing international concerns about Soviet food shortages. In 1991, the Soviet grain crop fell by 26 per cent from the 1990 harvest, and the country's centralized food distribution system broke down.

On Nov. 20, 1991, Bush offered the Soviets another $1.25 billion in credit guarantees for farm products—after securing promises from the leaders of individual republics in the disintegrating Soviet Union that they would take responsibility for repaying the credits if the central government collapsed. The Soviets bought mostly wheat for bread and corn and soybeans for livestock feed.

The Bush Administration also announced that the United States would provide $165 million in direct food aid, finance the construction of a model farm near St. Petersburg (formerly Leningrad), and provide funds for the development of wholesale markets as well as for private farmers in the Armenian, Kazakh, and Uzbek republics. The Administration also announced credit guarantees for food processing and distribution facilities.

Trade talks. Negotiators seeking to reform trade rules under the General Agreement on Tariffs and Trade (GATT) finally began to draft the outline of a possible compromise in late 1991, five years after the round of talks, known as the Uruguay Round, began. The talks had collapsed in December 1990, mainly because of a dispute between the European Community (EC or Common Market) and the United States and other agricultural exporters over the issue of farm subsidies. Rather than abandon the talks, however, Congress authorized the Bush Administration to continue negotiating for two more years.

The extension granted to trade negotiators also gave the Bush Administration a green light to begin talks in June to lower trade barriers with Canada and Mexico under a North American Free-Trade Agreement. The new agreement would expand upon a U.S.-Canada Free-Trade Agreement, which went into effect on Jan. 1, 1989. The first major agricultural dispute under the agreement with Canada was resolved in June 1991 with the elimination of a U.S. duty on imports of Canadian pork products. The United States agreed to repay $18 million in duties collected since September 1989.

Canadian farm bailout. Canadian farmers, under pressure from crop losses in 1990 and low prices for farm products on the world market, staged a series of protests in 1991 to demand government compensation. On October 10, the Canadian government announced a farm bailout worth $800 million Canadian ($700 million U.S.). Farmers welcomed the aid but complained that the amount was too low.

Food labels. The Agriculture Department and the Food and Drug Administration (FDA) on November 6 issued regulations providing for the most sweeping reforms in food labeling in 50 years. The regulations provide guidance for implementing the Nutrition Labeling and Education Act of 1990.

The new labels, scheduled to appear on products in stores in May 1993, were to provide reliable information about the nutritional content of food (see **Food**). The new labeling law did not require the Agriculture Department to change its labels on meat and poultry. However, Agriculture Secretary Madigan directed that meat and poultry labels should be similar to those on other foods regulated by the FDA.

Wetlands debate. The Environmental Protection Agency (EPA), the U.S. Army Corps of Engineers, and other government agencies attempted in 1991 to resolve a controversy over the definition of wetlands subject to federal restrictions on farming, development, and other uses. Farmers and developers had complained about the narrowness of a 1989 definition, which defined wetlands as areas saturated up to

18 inches (46 centimeters) below the soil surface for only 7 days per year.

On Aug. 1, 1991, the Bush Administration proposed to redefine wetlands as areas covered by standing water for 15 days or areas saturated at the soil surface for 21 days during the growing season. Environmentalists attacked the new wetlands definition, charging that the revision would open to farming or various forms of development an estimated 30 to 50 per cent of the wetlands protected under the 1989 definition. The U.S. government continued to collect public comment on the wetlands issue through January 1992. See **Conservation.**

Environmental issues. Proposed restrictions on agricultural practices along the U.S. coasts of the Atlantic and Pacific oceans, the Great Lakes, and the Gulf of Mexico were issued by the EPA in July 1991. The restrictions carry out 1990 amendments to the Coastal Zone Act of 1972. Under the restrictions, coastal states were given until 1994 to develop programs to reduce pollution from erosion, cattle feed lots, dairies, hog and poultry operations, irrigation, and the application of pesticides, manure, and chemical fertilizer. The law represented a key shift in environmental programs for agriculture from a voluntary approach to required practices.

Farmers in the Pacific Northwest expressed concern over a decision by the National Marine Fisheries Service of the Department of Commerce to designate the Snake River sockeye salmon as an endangered species. The agency's decision was announced on Nov. 14, 1991. Two other species of salmon that spawn in the Snake River were also being considered for the endangered list.

Efforts to boost the population of the sockeye salmon in the Snake River could force a lowering of water levels in reservoirs on the Columbia River. Such a move would release more water into the Snake River, which would assist the salmon in their journey to the ocean. Lowering the reservoirs, however, would also reduce the amount of water available to farmers for irrigation.

U.S. production. In 1991, U.S. farmers suffered from weather problems, including severe drought in California, heavy spring rains in the Midwest and the South, summer drought in the eastern Corn Belt, and an early freeze in the Midwest. On November 27, Congress approved $995 million in funds for crop disaster assistance, also holding out the possibility of an additional $755 million in aid. Despite the bad weather in some areas, however, U.S. crops were larger than expected. The corn harvest of 7.49 billion bushels declined by only 6 per cent from the 1990 yield.

Wheat crops fell because of lower yields and because of a new farm program that allows farmers to plant sunflowers and other crops on acreage previously allotted to grain—while still receiving grain subsidies. Wheat farmers harvested 1.98 billion bushels, 28 per cent less than in 1990. The winter wheat crop, the smallest since 1978, was down 32 per cent. Durum wheat for pasta was down 15 per cent, and other spring wheat was off 13 per cent. In contrast, the sunflower harvest rose by 45 per cent.

A researcher pulls rather than shears wool from a sheep treated with a hormone, developed in Australia, that weakens wool fibers just above the skin.

Peanut production rose by a record 37 per cent. Cotton was up 18 per cent; soybeans, 2 per cent; grain sorghum, 1 per cent; and rice, 3 per cent. The oat harvest declined by 32 per cent. Beef production increased by 1 per cent; pork, 4 per cent; and poultry, 5 per cent.

World production. Although global wheat production declined by 7 per cent from 1990's record level, the harvest was still the second largest wheat harvest ever. Rice declined by 2 per cent from a record harvest in 1990. Corn fell slightly and soybeans rose 2 per cent. Cotton production increased by 5 per cent, setting a record. World beef production declined slightly, pork production was stable, and poultry production increased by 4 per cent.

Exports and income. United States farm exports in fiscal year 1991 (Oct. 1, 1990, to Sept. 30, 1991) declined by 6 per cent to $37.5 billion, the first drop in five years. Net farm income declined by 13 per cent to $44 billion, after reaching a record $50.8 billion in 1990. The decline was the result of lower livestock prices, smaller government subsidies, and increases in expenses. Sonja Hillgren

See also **Environmental pollution.** In ***World Book,*** see **Agriculture; Farm and farming.**

A diagonal zipper and flared hemline give an asymmetrical look to Claude Montana's creation, shown in a ready-to-wear collection in Paris in March.

Fashion. Retailers hoped in 1991 that new designer names in fashion design would bring new approaches to invigorate the fashion business. This, in turn, they hoped, would attract new customers during a time when business was sluggish. Some fashion industry executives said the recession had severely affected the business, declaring that the fashion industry had a recession of its own before the rest of the United States felt the economic downturn.

New designer names that surfaced in the 1991 world of fashion belonged to young people in their 30's, such as Gemma Kahng, Todd Oldfield, and Zang Toi. They received the kind of play in stores and magazines traditionally accorded long-established designers, such as Geoffrey Beene, Oscar de la Renta, and Bill Blass. Retailers eagerly promoted the fresh faces, because these new designers will eventually replace the old guard.

By 1991, the well-known and well-established designers were in their 50's and 60's. Geoffrey Beene, regarded by many as the most prestigious designer in New York City, has been the head of his own fashion company for 28 years. James Galanos, whose headquarters is in Los Angeles, has been a fashion leader for 40 years. Valentino celebrated his 30th anniversary in Rome in the spring of the year, and Hubert de Givenchy marked his company's 40th year in business in the autumn of 1991. No one, however, expected these older designers to step aside immediately for the younger crowd.

Focus on jackets. Designers everywhere focused on the jacket as the key to contemporary dressing. Denim jackets and leather biker's styles appealed to younger people. For the sophisticated woman, there were long, gently curved jackets from major designers, such as Giorgio Armani and Karl Lagerfeld of Chanel, as well as less expensive versions without designer labels.

A standard way for women to dress for the office was to wear one of these longer jackets over a skirt that stopped short of the knees. But all kinds of combinations were possible, such as jackets with trousers, leggings, or tights. Jackets with shorts also gained acceptance in some areas for more formal daytime wear, as women wore shorts to offices during the hot summer weather. A more formal alternative to separates was the jacket and dress, adopted by many women, including the U.S. first lady, Barbara Bush.

Casual wear. For women whose lives did not require formal dressing, including most students, T-shirts, sweat shirts, sweat pants, and jeans were the rule. Calvin Klein, Donna Karan, and other major designers introduced special jeans collections to appeal to these women and to those who dressed informally during the weekend. The special weekend-wear category was not limited to basic blue jeans. Designers offered white and black jeans, stone washed, and beige styles. Cutoffs and jackets to match appeared in stores, as did overalls and skirts, both short and long.

Skirt length moved into fashion consciousness again. Since 1988, short skirts were considered the standard, though many women wore their hems at midcalf. Designers everywhere in the fashion world introduced some longer styles into their collections. The consensus among fashion leaders was that long and short hemlines could coexist. Many designers claimed that they already did.

Plaids made a strong fall fashion entry, spurred by Oscar de la Renta's suits, coats, and even furs worked in plaid patterns. They were shown at his Paris debut in March. De la Renta was the first American designer to join the French ready-to-wear shows.

Fashion leadership still remained in the hands of ready-to-wear designers in 1991. But the *couture,* or made-to-order branch of the fashion industry, based in Paris, showed renewed vigor. Designers such as Lagerfeld at Chanel, with his denim and motorcycle jackets, and Claude Montana, who introduced space age looks at the House of Lanvin, revitalized couture fashion during the year. But all the couture houses also had ready-to-wear collections that were less expensive than made-to-order clothes. Ready-to-wear designers also introduced secondary lines, such as Valentino's Oliver, Gianni Versace's Versus, and Emanuel Ungaro's Emanuel, priced lower than their regular collections. These secondary lines tried to lead the way to a wider distribution of clothes by top designers.

Bernadine Morris

In ***World Book,*** see **Clothing; Fashion.**

Finland in April 1991 formed a new government, a four-party coalition led by the Center Party. In elections held on March 17, the Center Party won 55 of the 200 seats in the Eduskunta, Finland's parliament, more than any other political party. The party's leader, 37-year-old Esko Aho, became prime minister. Aho replaced Harri Holkeri of the Conservative Party, who had led a Conservative-Social Democratic Party coalition since 1987.

The Center Party, which draws its support mainly from rural areas, added 15 seats to its previous 40 in the Eduskunta. The election's big losers were the Social Democrats, who went from 56 to 48 seats and left the ruling coalition. This marked the first time since 1962 that they failed to win the largest number of seats. Also losing ground were the Conservatives, who dropped from 53 to 40 seats. Voters seemed to blame the ruling parties for a slump in Finland's economy.

EC membership debated. Soon after the elections, Aho opened public debate about future membership for Finland in the 12-nation European Community (EC or Common Market). Opinion polls showed that most Finns favored joining the EC. Finland was expected to apply for EC membership in 1992, in part because its neighbor Sweden had done so in 1991. Many Finns feared that failure to join the EC could cause Finland to fall behind Sweden economically as Sweden gained access to EC markets.

In June, Aho's government took a major step toward EC membership by linking the value of Finland's currency, the markka, to the European Currency Unit (ECU), a specially created unit of value that links the currency of EC nations. So that the markka did not lose too much value compared to the ECU, the Finnish government needed to restrain spending and bring down the country's high inflation rate. The currency linkage should also help Finland meet the EC's membership requirements should it decide to apply.

Soviet friendship treaty. The collapse of Communism in the Soviet Union in 1991 removed a major obstacle to EC membership for Finland. To preserve its independence after World War II (1939-1945), Finland had signed a friendship treaty in 1948, agreeing to cooperate militarily with the Soviet Union if Germany or its allies attempted to cross Finland to attack the Soviet Union. The treaty also barred Finland from allying itself with any enemies of the Soviet Union, effectively keeping it out of the North Atlantic Treaty Organization, the Western security alliance, and out of the EC. In autumn 1991, the two countries renegotiated the treaty. Provisions about military cooperation were dropped, as were restrictions on Finnish alliances.

Philip Revzin

See also **Europe** (Facts in brief table), Special Report: **The Rocky Road to European Unity.** In ***World Book,*** see **Finland.**

Fire. See **Disasters.**

Flood. See **Disasters.**

Florida. See **State government.**

Food. The United States Food and Drug Administration (FDA) took steps in 1991 to outlaw food labels that falsely suggest a product has a low fat content. For example, cooking oils with labels that picture a heart and claim to be cholesterol free could mislead consumers into thinking the product is low in fat and, therefore, good for the heart, said FDA Commissioner David A. Kessler in May. Other products claiming to be almost fat free but deriving a high percentage of their calories from fat also are deceptive, Kessler said.

The FDA also stepped up enforcement of regulations regarding products labeled as fresh. Officials ordered several companies to remove the word "fresh" from items such as orange juice and tomato sauce that had undergone processing.

Product ingredients. The FDA issued regulations in November that would require food manufacturers to relabel most of their products. The rules were designed to help implement the Nutrition Labeling and Education Act of 1990. The act requires product labels to list all ingredients and the nutrition content of all packaged foods except meat and poultry. The new regulations will force manufacturers to identify more explicitly the ingredients of their foods. This information will be useful not only to health-conscious consumers, but also to those concerned about allergic reactions and about observing religious dietary rules.

In April, the United States Department of Agriculture (USDA) issued its proposals for mandatory nutrition labeling for processed meat and poultry. It recommended that labels list the number of calories and the amount of total fat, saturated fat, cholesterol, protein, and sodium. The proposal said fresh meat and poultry would be exempt from mandatory labeling, but retail outlets would be encouraged to voluntarily post such information. The USDA hoped to coordinate its labeling requirements with those of the FDA and have them take effect by 1993.

Fear of fat. Food manufacturers and fast-food companies responded to America's concern about dietary fat by introducing a host of low-fat and nonfat products throughout 1991. The products included such traditionally fatty items as cakes, "ice cream," hamburgers, chocolate bars, and even Spam. Substitute fats made from oat bran, egg whites, corn starch, pectin (an extract of citrus fruit), or other ingredients entered the market in a variety of forms. But products made with these substitutes did not immediately win over America's taste buds, and makers began competing in earnest to develop fat alternatives that taste like the real thing.

Food safety. Although food safety remained a concern for most people, confidence in the integrity of the U.S. food supply reached an all-time high in 1991. Eighty-two per cent of shoppers surveyed in January by the Food Marketing Institute (FMI) in Washington, D.C., said they were completely or mostly confident about food safety. Spoilage was the main

"...Man, the FDA is really cracking down on food labeling...."

perceived health hazard, but respondents also expressed increased concern about pesticides and other residues.

On May 14, the Safety of Pesticides in Food Act of 1991 was introduced in Congress. It contained a standard for pesticide use that would allegedly pose a negligible risk in raw and processed foods. It also called for rigid regulations for calculating negligible risk. Opponents of the bill, including many in the food industry and some scientists, complained that the act would abolish valuable pesticides and that it failed to establish nationally uniform compliance. Several alternative bills were also introduced.

High levels of lead found in some table wines prompted the FDA in September to suggest a limit on lead levels for all domestic and imported table wines. The agency proposed a limit of 300 parts per billion (ppb) and was conducting further studies to determine the need for banning wines that exceed this amount. Tests had revealed that 3 to 4 per cent of the wines checked exceeded the 300 ppb limit.

Zapping bacteria. The first irradiation facility for food such as poultry, fruits, and vegetables was scheduled to begin operating in Florida by early 1992. Irradiation with gamma rays kills bacteria and prolongs the product's shelf life. An activist group opposed the facility, saying irradiation was a danger to health. But the FDA, the USDA, and the World Health Organization said the process was safe.

Total U.S. food sales were projected to be $1.2-trillion in 1991, according to the U.S. Department of Commerce. Retail sales comprised $410 billion of the total; manufactured items made up $395 billion; and produce totaled $386 billion. Weekly grocery spending per household rose from $74 in January 1990 to $79 in January 1991, according to the FMI survey. Americans spent an estimated 11.8 per cent of their *disposable income* (money left after taxes) on food.

Nutrition pyramid. Secretary of Agriculture Edward R. Madigan in April 1991 postponed indefinitely publication of the "Eating Right Pyramid." The USDA had designed the pyramid to replace the food wheel illustrating the four food groups. The pyramid was designed to help consumers understand nutrition guidelines for maintaining good health. The triangular shape depicts cereals, breads, and grains at the base; fruits and vegetables at the next tier; meat and dairy products near the top; and fats and oils at the top.

Madigan said some people had complained that the pyramid's organization was unclear and that children might not understand it. Other USDA officials said the pyramid was not targeted to children and that the delay was due to strong opposition from the National Cattlemen's Association, the American Meat Institute, and the National Milk Producers Federation. These organizations had criticized the design, saying that it would give consumers the impression that meat and dairy products were bad foods. Bob Gatty

In ***World Book,*** see **Food; Food supply.**

Football.

Football. Professional and college football in the United States crowned new champions in the 1991 season. The New York Giants, who won Super Bowl XXV in January 1991, slipped to an 8-8 record as the Washington Redskins won Super Bowl XXVI in January 1992. The University of Miami in Florida and the University of Washington in Seattle won separate polls and became the unofficial college champions for the 1991 season, succeeding Colorado and Georgia Tech.

Professional. The National Football League's (NFL) 1991 season was good for the Buffalo Bills, who won their conference title, reached the Super Bowl, and featured one of the year's best players in running back Thurman Thomas and the year's best quarterback in Jim Kelly. It was a good season for the Atlanta Falcons, who made the play-offs for the first time since 1982; the Detroit Lions, who made the play-offs for the first time since 1983; and the Dallas Cowboys, who made the play-offs for the first time since 1985. It was good for the players because, according to the National Football League Players Association (NFLPA), the average salary rose 18 per cent to $422,149.

It was a bad season for the health of the sport's two most exciting quarterbacks. Joe Montana of the San Francisco 49ers tore a tendon in his elbow and missed the entire season, and Randall Cunningham of the Philadelphia Eagles tore two knee ligaments in the season opener on Sept. 1, 1991, and did not play again during the season. It was a bad year for television as the popularity of NFL games stagnated and advertising losses reached many millions of dollars.

In the NFL National Conference, the division champions were Washington (14-2), Detroit (12-4), and the New Orleans Saints (11-5). They were joined in the play-offs by three wild-card teams—the Chicago Bears (11-5), Dallas (11-5), and Atlanta (10-6). In the American Conference, the division champions were Buffalo (13-3), the Denver Broncos (12-4), and the Houston Oilers (11-5). The Kansas City Chiefs (10-6), the Los Angeles Raiders (9-7), and the New York Jets (8-8) were wild-card teams in the play-offs.

Washington relied on a vastly improved quarterback in Mark Rypien, an explosive offense, a sound defense, and excellent special teams. The Redskins advanced to the Super Bowl by beating Atlanta, 24-7, on Jan. 4, 1992, and Detroit, 41-10, on January 12. In the American Conference, Buffalo defeated Kansas City, 37-14, on January 5 and Denver, 10-7, on January 12.

Super Bowl. Washington played Buffalo in the Super Bowl on January 26 in the Metrodome in Minneapolis, Minn. Washington won, 37-24, as Rypien, voted the game's Most Valuable Player, threw two touchdown passes.

NFL expansion. On May 22, 1991, the NFL owners voted to expand the league by two teams, which would begin play in 1994. The expansion would be the league's first since 1976, when the Seattle Seahawks and Tampa Bay Buccaneers entered the NFL.

College football's 1991 Heisman Trophy winner, Desmond Howard of the University of Michigan, sprints down the sideline.

Free agency. Players filed a series of antitrust suits against the NFL in 1991. Most of those suits charged that the league illegally bound players to one team and prevented true free agency.

The club owners hoped to reach a collective-bargaining agreement before then. They proposed an eight-year contract that would establish a two-tier, unrestricted free-agency system. Under the owners' plan, a player would become a free agent if he had not been offered at least $300,000 in salary by his fourth season or $1 million by his sixth. The proposal also guaranteed the players a percentage of the clubs' gross income and set up a salary cap for each team and a rookie wage and bonus scale.

Canadian. On Feb. 25, 1991, the Toronto Argonauts were sold for $5 million to Bruce McNall, the owner of the Los Angeles Kings hockey team; Wayne Gretzky, the star of that hockey team; and John Candy, the comedian. The Argonauts signed Raghib (Rocket) Ismail, the former Notre Dame wide receiver and kick returner, who had been expected to be the first choice in the NFL draft.

The Argonauts gave Ismail a four-year contract guaranteeing him $18.5 million. The team attracted large crowds at home and away, and Ismail paid immediate dividends on the field. He led the league in total offense with 2,959 yards and helped the Argonauts win the Eastern Division.

In the Grey Cup championship game on November 24 in Winnipeg, Manitoba, Ismail's 87-yard kickoff return for a fourth quarter touchdown clinched a 36-21 victory over the Calgary Stampeders. The Canadian Football League (CFL) Player of the Year was another U.S. citizen, Doug Flutie, the quarterback for the British Columbia Lions. He passed for 6,619 yards in 18 games, a CFL record.

The World League of American Football, a springtime league created by the NFL, struggled through its first season, which was played from March to June 1991. The new league had six teams (New York City; Birmingham, Ala.; Sacramento, Calif.; San Antonio; Orlando, Fla.; and Raleigh/Durham, N.C.) in the United States. One (Montreal) was in Canada and three (Frankfurt, Germany; London; and Barcelona, Spain) were in Europe. In the World Bowl championship game on June 9 in London, the London Monarchs shut out the Barcelona Dragons, 21-0, on two touchdown passes by Stan Gelbaugh.

Hall of Fame. The Pro Football Hall of Fame added four players and an administrator in July 1991. The players were fullback Earl Campbell (1978-1985), offensive guard John Hannah (1973-1985), kicker Jan Stenerud (1967-1985), and offensive guard/defensive tackle Stan Jones (1954-1966). The Hall of Fame also admitted Texas (Tex) Schramm, general manager and president of the Cowboys from 1960 to 1989.

College. Attempts to determine an official national champion continued to meet obstacles. The National Collegiate Athletic Association (NCAA) rejected proposals to establish play-offs, saying they would extend an already long season.

To rectify the confusion and attain the best bowl match-ups, a tentative coalition was formed by four bowls (Orange, Cotton, Sugar, and Fiesta); five conferences (Big Eight, Atlantic Coast, Southeastern, Southwest, and Big East); and one nonconference team (Notre Dame). Their plan would allow the Orange, Cotton, and Sugar bowls to take their traditional conference champions. Then the member bowl with the highest-ranked team would pick as its opponent the Atlantic Coast Conference (ACC) champion, the Big East champion, or Notre Dame. The other bowls would then pick conference champions or runners-up from the pool.

The coalition planned to start operating in the 1992 season. However, the year-old Blockbuster Bowl in Miami, Fla., shut out of the coalition, offered the ACC and the Big East a reported $4.3 million each for their champions, the highest bowl fee except for the Rose Bowl's $6.5 million. The two conferences and the coalition deferred all decisions to 1992.

Another problem arose when the Federal Trade Commission (FTC) began antitrust proceedings against the College Football Association (CFA), made up of 66 major colleges, and Capital Cities/ABC Incorporated, which owns the ABC television network. The FTC said the five-year, $300-million contract between the CFA and Capital Cities/ABC to televise college football

National Football League final standings

American Conference

Eastern Division	W.	L.	T.	Pct.
Buffalo Bills*	13	3	0	.813
New York Jets*	8	8	0	.500
Miami Dolphins	8	8	0	.500
New England Patriots	6	10	0	.375
Indianapolis Colts	1	15	0	.063
Central Division				
Houston Oilers*	11	5	0	.733
Pittsburgh Steelers	7	9	0	.438
Cleveland Browns	6	10	0	.375
Cincinnati Bengals	3	13	0	.188
Western Division				
Denver Broncos*	12	4	0	.750
Kansas City Chiefs*	10	6	0	.625
Los Angeles Raiders*	9	7	0	.563
Seattle Seahawks	7	9	0	.438
San Diego Chargers	4	12	0	.250

*Made play-off.

National Conference

Eastern Division	W.	L.	T.	Pct.
Washington Redskins*	14	2	0	.875
Dallas Cowboys*	11	5	0	.688
Philadelphia Eagles	10	6	0	.625
New York Giants	8	8	0	.500
Phoenix Cardinals	4	12	0	.250
Central Division				
Detroit Lions*	12	4	0	.750
Chicago Bears*	11	5	0	.688
Minnesota Vikings	8	8	0	.500
Green Bay Packers	4	12	0	.250
Tampa Bay Buccaneers	3	13	0	.188
Western Division				
New Orleans Saints*	11	5	0	.688
Atlanta Falcons*	10	6	0	.625
San Francisco 49ers	10	6	0	.625
Los Angeles Rams	3	13	0	.188

Super Bowl champion—Washington Redskins (defeated Buffalo, 37-24)

Individual statistics (American Conference)

Leading scorers, touchdowns	TD's	Rush	Rec.	Ret.	Pts.
Mark Clayton, Miami	12	0	12	0	72
Thurman Thomas, Buffalo	12	7	5	0	72
Brad Baxter, Jets	11	11	0	0	66
Leroy Hoard, Cleveland	11	2	9	0	66
Kevin Mack, Cleveland	10	8	2	0	60
Allen Pinkett, Houston	10	9	1	0	60
Andre Reed, Buffalo	10	0	10	0	60
Christian Okoye, Kansas City	9	9	0	0	54

Leading scorers, kicking	PAT	FG	Longest	Pts.
Pete Stoyanovich, Miami	28/29	31/37	53	121
Jeff Jaeger, L.A. Raiders	29/30	29/34	53	116
David Treadwell, Denver	31/32	27/36	47	112
Nick Lowery, Kansas City	35/35	25/30	48	110
Scott Norwood, Buffalo	56/58	18/29	52	110
Pat Leahy, New York Jets	30/30	26/37	40	108
John Kasay, Seattle	27/28	25/31	54	102
Gary Anderson, Pittsburgh	31/31	23/33	54	100
Jim Breech, Cincinnati	27/27	23/29	50	96

Leading quarterbacks	Att.	Comp.	Yds.	TD's	Int.
Jim Kelly, Buffalo	474	304	3,844	33	17
Bernie Kosar, Cleveland	494	307	3,487	18	9
Dan Marino, Miami	549	318	3,970	25	13
Dave Krieg, Seattle	285	187	2,080	11	12
Warren Moon, Houston	655	404	4,690	23	21
Steve DeBerg, Kansas City	434	256	2,965	17	14
Neil O'Donnell, Pittsburgh	286	156	1,963	11	7
Ken O'Brien, New York Jets	489	287	3,300	10	11
John Elway, Denver	451	242	3,253	13	12
Jeff George, Indianapolis	485	292	2,910	10	12

Leading receivers	Number caught	Total yards	Avg. gain	TD's
Haywood Jeffires, Houston	100	1,181	11.8	7
Drew Hill, Houston	90	1,109	12.3	4
Marv Cook, New England	82	808	9.9	3
Andre Reed, Buffalo	81	1,113	13.7	10
Al Toon, New York Jets	74	963	13	0
Bill Brooks, Indianapolis	72	888	12.3	4
Mark Duper, Miami	70	1,085	15.5	5
Mark Clayton, Miami	70	1,053	15.0	12
Brian Blades, Seattle	70	1,003	14.3	2
Ernest Givins, Houston	70	996	14.2	5
Rob Moore, New York Jets	70	987	14.1	5

Leading rushers	No.	Yards	Avg.	TD's
Thurman Thomas, Buffalo	288	1,407	4.9	7
Gaston Green, Denver	261	1,037	4.0	4
Christian Okoye, Kansas City	225	1,031	4.6	9
Leonard Russell, New England	266	959	3.6	4
Mark Higgs, Miami	231	905	3.9	4
Marion Butts, San Diego	193	834	4.3	6
Rod Bernstine, San Diego	159	766	4.8	8
John Williams, Seattle	188	741	3.9	4
Harold Green, Cincinnati	158	731	4.6	2

Leading punters	No.	Yards	Avg.	Longest
Reggie Roby, Miami	54	2,466	45.7	64
Jeff Gossett, L.A. Raiders	67	2,961	44.2	61
Greg Montgomery, Houston	48	2,105	43.9	60
Lee Johnson, Cincinnati	64	2,795	43.7	62

Individual statistics (National Conference)

Leading scorers, touchdowns	TD's	Rush	Rec.	Ret.	Pts.
Barry Sanders, Detroit	17	16	1	0	102
Jerry Rice, San Francisco	14	0	14	0	84
Emmitt Smith, Dallas	13	12	1	0	78
Andre Rison, Atlanta	12	0	12	0	72
Michael Haynes, Atlanta	11	0	11	0	66
Gerald Riggs, Washington	11	11	0	0	66
Vince Workman, Green Bay	11	7	4	0	66

Leading scorers, kicking	PAT	FG	Longest	Pts.
Chip Lohmiller, Washington	56/56	31/43	53	149
Ken Willis, Dallas	37/37	27/39	54	118
Morten Andersen, New Orleans	38/38	25/32	60	113
Roger Ruzek, Philadelphia	27/29	28/33	51	111
Eddie Murray, Detroit	40/40	19/28	50	97
Norm Johnson, Atlanta	38/39	19/23	50	95
Mike Cofer, San Francisco	49/50	14/28	50	91
Matt Bahr, N.Y. Giants	24/25	22/29	54	90
Kevin Butler, Chicago	32/34	19/29	50	89

Leading quarterbacks	Att.	Comp.	Yds.	TD's	Int.
Steve Young, San Francisco	279	180	2,517	17	8
Mark Rypien, Washington	421	249	3,564	28	11
Steve Bono, San Francisco	237	141	1,617	11	4
Troy Aikman, Dallas	363	237	2,754	11	10
Jeff Hostetler, N.Y. Giants	285	179	2,032	5	4
Rich Gannon, Minnesota	354	211	2,166	12	6
Chris Miller, Atlanta	413	220	3,103	26	18
Jim McMahon, Philadelphia	311	187	2,239	12	11
Steve Walsh, New Orleans	255	141	1,638	11	6
Bobby Hebert, New Orleans	248	149	1,676	9	8

Leading receivers	Number caught	Total yards	Avg. gain	TD's
Michael Irvin, Dallas	93	1,523	16.4	8
Andre Rison, Atlanta	81	976	12.0	12
Jerry Rice, San Francisco	80	1,206	15.1	14
Cris Carter, Minnesota	72	962	13.4	5
Art Monk, Washington	71	1,049	14.8	8
Gary Clark, Washington	70	1,340	19.1	10
Sterling Sharpe, Green Bay	69	961	13.9	4
Eric Martin, New Orleans	66	803	12.2	4
Henry Ellard, L.A. Rams	64	1,052	16.4	3
John Taylor, San Francisco	64	1,011	15.8	9
Floyd Turner, New Orleans	64	927	14.5	8

Leading rushers	No.	Yards	Avg.	TD's
Emmitt Smith, Dallas	365	1,563	4.3	12
Barry Sanders, Detroit	342	1,548	4.5	16
Rodney Hampton, N.Y. Giants	256	1,059	4.1	10
Earnest Byner, Washington	274	1,048	3.8	5
Herschel Walker, Minnesota	198	825	4.2	10
Reggie Cobb, Tampa Bay	196	752	3.8	7
Neal Anderson, Chicago	210	747	3.6	6
Robert Delpino, L.A. Rams	214	688	3.2	9
Ricky Ervins, Washington	145	680	4.7	3

Leading punters	No.	Yards	Avg.	Longest
Harry Newsome, Minnesota	68	3,095	45.5	65
Rich Camarillo, Phoenix	76	3,445	45.3	60
Tommy Barnhardt, New Orleans	86	3,743	43.5	61
Sean Landeta, N.Y. Giants	64	2,768	43.3	61

The 1991 college football season

College conference champions

Conference	School
Atlantic Coast	Clemson
Big East	Miami (Fla.)
Big Eight	Nebraska—Colorado (tie)
Big Sky	Nevada
Big Ten	Michigan
Big West	Fresno State
Gateway	Northern Iowa
Ivy League	Dartmouth
Mid-American	Bowling Green
Mid-Eastern	North Carolina A&T
Ohio Valley	Eastern Kentucky
Pacific Ten	Washington
Patriot	Holy Cross
Southeastern	Florida
Southern	Appalachian State
Southland	McNeese State
Southwest	Texas A&M
Southwestern	Alabama State
Western Athletic	Brigham Young
Yankee	Delaware—Villanova—New Hampshire (tie)

Major bowl games

Bowl	Winner	Loser
Aloha	Georgia Tech 18	Stanford 17
Amos Alonzo Stagg (Div. III)	Ithaca 34	Dayton 20
Blockbuster	Alabama 30	Colorado 25
Blue-Gray	Gray 20	Blue 12
California	Bowling Green 28	Fresno State 21
Copper	Indiana 24	Baylor 0
Cotton	Florida State 10	Texas A&M 2
East-West Shrine	West 14	East 6
Fiesta	Penn State 42	Tennessee 17
Florida Citrus	California 37	Clemson 13
Freedom	Tulsa 28	San Diego State 17
Gator	Oklahoma 48	Virginia 14
Hall of Fame	Syracuse 24	Ohio State 17
Holiday	Iowa 13	Brigham Young 13
Hula	West 27	East 20
Independence	Georgia 24	Arkansas 15
John Hancock	UCLA 6	Illinois 3
Liberty	Air Force 38	Mississippi State 15
Orange	Miami 22	Nebraska 0
Peach	East Carolina 37	North Carolina St. 34
Rose	Washington 34	Michigan 14
Senior	AFC 13	NFC 10
Sugar	Notre Dame 39	Florida 28
NCAA Div. I-AA	Youngstown State 25	Marshall 17
NCAA Div. II	Pittsburg St. (Kans.) 23	Jacksonville St. (Ala.) 6
NAIA Div. I	Central Arkansas 19	Central State (Ohio) 16
NAIA Div. II	Georgetown (Ky.) 28	Pacific Lutheran 20

All-America team (as picked by AP)

Offense

Quarterback—Ty Detmer, Brigham Young
Running backs—Vaughn Dunbar, Indiana; Marshall Faulk, San Diego State
Wide receivers—Desmond Howard, Michigan; Mario Bailey, Washington
Tight end—Kelly Blackwell, Texas Christian
Center—Jay Leeuwenburg, Colorado
Guards—Jerry Ostroski, Tulsa; Jeb Flesch, Clemson
Tackles—Greg Skrepenak, Michigan; Bob Whitfield, Stanford
All-purpose—Ryan Benjamin, Pacific
Place-kicker—Carlos Huerta, Miami

Defense

Linemen—Steve Emtman, Washington; Santana Dotson, Baylor; Brad Culpepper, Florida; Leroy Smith, Iowa
Linebackers—Robert Jones, East Carolina; Marvin Jones, Florida State; Joe Bowden, Oklahoma
Backs—Kevin Smith, Texas A&M; Terrell Buckley, Florida State; Darryl Williams, Miami; Dale Carter, Tennessee
Punter—Mark Bounds, Texas Tech

Player awards

Heisman Trophy (best player)—Desmond Howard, Michigan
Lombardi Award (best lineman)—Steve Emtman, Washington
Outland Award (best interior lineman)—Steve Emtman, Washington

games was monopolistic. On August 6, a federal administrative judge, James P. Timony, dismissed the suit, saying the FTC lacked jurisdiction.

The college season. The best records among major colleges were achieved by Miami (11-0), Washington (11-0), Florida (10-1), Alabama (10-1), Michigan (10-1), Iowa (10-1), Texas A&M (10-1), and East Carolina (10-1). On Jan. 1, 1992, Miami routed Nebraska, 22-0, in the Orange Bowl in Miami and Washington whipped Michigan, 34-14, in the Rose Bowl in Pasadena, Calif.

The next day, the Associated Press (AP) postseason poll of writers and broadcasters crowned Miami as the national champion. The United Press International board of football experts and the USA Today/CNN board of coaches ranked Washington first, however.

Honors. Desmond Howard, Michigan's wide receiver and kick returner, won the Heisman Trophy as the nation's outstanding player. Steve Emtman, a defensive tackle from Washington, won the Outland Award and the Lombardi Trophy as the outstanding lineman. Howard and Emtman were juniors.

Marshall Faulk, a San Diego State freshman, led the nation in rushing (158.7 yards per game) and scoring (15.56 points per game). Quarterback Ty Detmer of Brigham Young became the all-time NCAA leader in passing yards (15,031) and touchdown passes (121).

Frank Litsky

In *World Book,* see **Football.**

France in 1991 continued to work toward the integration of western Europe in the 12-nation European Community (EC or Common Market). At home, the political scene was dominated by the appointment of Edith Cresson as France's first woman prime minister, by the declining popularity of the Socialist government, and by the increasing unity of conservative opposition parties.

In international affairs, France sought to underscore its role as a leading power by sending about 15,000 soldiers to the Persian Gulf as part of the multinational coalition that drove Iraqi occupying forces from Kuwait. In February, French troops played a key role in the allied sweep across Iraq to encircle Iraqi forces. French warplanes flew hundreds of missions against Iraqi targets during the Persian Gulf War. See **Persian Gulf,** Special Report: **War in the Persian Gulf.**

France's role in the coalition, which was led by the United States, exposed divisions within the Socialist government. French Defense Minister Jean-Pierre Chevènement, an opponent of his country's growing participation in the effort against Iraq, resigned on January 29, shortly after the war began. The French people generally supported the effort to drive Iraq from Kuwait, according to French opinion polls.

Cresson appointment. Edith Cresson, a Socialist who had served in several cabinet posts, was named prime minister in May, replacing Michel Rocard. Rocard stepped down at the request of French President

François Mitterrand, who feared that his Socialist Party would lose control of the National Assembly, the more powerful of the two houses of Parliament, in elections scheduled for June 1993.

In appointing Cresson, Mitterrand said he wanted to give a big push to the French economy before most trade barriers among EC nations fell at the end of 1992. In previous government positions, Cresson had championed policies that helped French business compete against foreign competitors.

The popularity of Cresson's government plummeted following a spate of bad economic news. In June 1991, the jobless rate reached 9.5 per cent of the labor force. Cresson pledged to institute new job-training programs and incentives to encourage small businesses to hire more young people. But it was unlikely that those programs would create many new jobs before the 1993 parliamentary elections.

Immigration—particularly from Algeria, Morocco, and Tunisia—remained an explosive political issue in 1991. In May and June, riots by young people of Arab descent shook several French cities, including Lyon and Paris. The rioting broke out in poor, outlying immigrant neighborhoods, where unemployment was high. The right wing National Front Party, which favors halting the flow of immigration from northern Africa, saw its support rise sharply in cities with large immigrant communities, such as Marseille. Some politicians called for expelling jobless immigrants.

Conservative gains. Opinion polls throughout 1991 showed France's conservative opposition parties making big gains. A poll in June indicated that the conservatives could easily have defeated the Socialists if an election were held then. Paris Mayor Jacques Chirac and former President Valéry Giscard d'Estaing were expected to lead the two main conservative parties in the 1993 elections. Rivalry between them has split the conservative vote in the past. But in 1991, the two men agreed to institute a complicated voting procedure within their parties, which would designate only one of them to run against the Socialist candidate in the next presidential election in 1995.

The Socialists and their smaller allied parties fell 16 seats short of an absolute majority in the 577-member National Assembly. Thus, Cresson had to depend on centrist parties or on the Communist Party to win passage of her government's programs. A long-standing, informal pact with the Communists not to bring down the government in a no-confidence vote was expected to enable the Socialists to remain in office until the 1993 elections. Philip Revzin

See also **Cresson, Edith; Europe** (Facts in brief table), Special Report: **The Rocky Road to European Unity.** In ***World Book,*** see **France.**

Gabon. See **Africa.**

Gambia. See **Africa.**

Gas and gasoline. See **Energy supply; Petroleum and gas.**

Edith Cresson, the first woman prime minister of France, greets members of the press as she arrives at work on May 17, her first day in office.

Gates, Robert (1943-), became director of the United States Central Intelligence Agency (CIA) on Nov. 12, 1991. He succeeded William Webster, who resigned in May. Gates had been nominated by President Ronald Reagan in 1987 for the same post, but he withdrew his name from consideration at that time in the wake of questions surrounding his possible role in the Iran-contra affair. Similar questions arose after his nomination in June 1991. However, the United States Senate, which reviewed Gates's nomination during months of confirmation hearings, decided that Gates was essentially innocent of wrongdoing in connection with the Iran-contra scandal.

Gates was born in Wichita, Kans., and graduated with a B.A. in history from the College of William and Mary in Williamsburg, Va. He received an M.A. in Eastern European history from Indiana University in Bloomington and a Ph.D. in Soviet studies from Georgetown University in Washington, D.C.

Gates was already working for the CIA as an analyst when he graduated from Georgetown. From 1974 to 1979, he was a National Security Council aide at the White House. He returned to the CIA in early 1980 and became deputy director in 1986, a post he held until 1989. Gates then served for two years as deputy national security adviser to President Bush.

Gates and his wife, Rebecca, have two children, Eleanor and Bradley. Douglas Clayton

Genetic engineering. See **Biology**.

Geology. Large eruptions from three volcanoes made headlines in 1991. These, like most of Earth's volcanoes, were located along *subduction zones,* areas where one *tectonic plate* is descending beneath another. (Tectonic plates are huge segments of Earth's outer layers on which the oceans and continents ride.) As a subducting plate plunges beneath another plate, some rock above it melts and pushes up through the overriding plate to form volcanoes.

Mount Unzen in southwestern Japan erupted on June 3 and continued to eject rock, lava, and gas intermittently throughout the summer. The eruptions of the volcano, which was formed because of the subduction of the Pacific Plate beneath the Eurasian Plate, killed at least 38 people.

Mount Pinatubo on Luzon Island in the Philippines also erupted in June. At least 700 people died in the eruptions and in the mud slides that followed. Mount Pinatubo is fed by melting rock from the zone where the Eurasian Plate is sliding beneath the Philippine Plate. The eruption was the fourth largest eruption of the 1900's. See **Philippines.**

Hudson volcano in southern Chile erupted on Aug. 12, 1991. This volcano formed because of the subduction of the Nazca Plate beneath the South American

A thick plume of hot ash rises from Mount Unzen in southern Japan during an eruption in June in which at least 38 people died.

Plate. The ash from the volcano covered 25,000 square miles (64,700 square kilometers) of southern Argentina, creating severe health and economic problems for residents of the region. See **Chile.**

Superplumes. A number of geologic phenomena thought to be unrelated may actually be linked, according to a theory proposed in October 1991. Geologists have long known that during the mid-Cretaceous Period, which lasted from 83 million to 124 million years ago, Earth's climate grew warmer, the sea floor expanded rapidly, and sea levels rose dramatically. Also during this period, much of the world's petroleum reserves were formed from the remains of microorganisms that inhabited the shallow seas that covered much of Earth. In addition, Earth's magnetic field, which in recent years has reversed its orientation about once every 1 million years, did not change for tens of millions of years.

Roger L. Larson, a geologist at the University of Rhode Island in Kingston, proposed that all these geologic effects resulted from the development of one or more superplumes. The superplumes, which were hundreds to thousands of kilometers across, were upwellings of hot rock that rose from the lower *mantle* (the layer between the outer crust and the core).

As the plumes rose, they partially melted. This magma fed volcanoes, both on the land and on the sea floor, that produced huge outpourings of lava. The enormous amounts of lava spewing from the mid-ocean *rifts* (places where two plates are pulling apart) greatly increased the elevation of the sea floor. This reduced the volume of water the oceans could hold, and sea levels rose dramatically.

Climate warming. As the superplume magma reached the surface, it released large amounts of carbon dioxide (CO_2), which had been dissolved in the rock. The higher levels of atmospheric CO_2 warmed Earth's climate. In the CO_2-rich ocean, microorganisms that use that gas to make shells flourished. The rapid production, burial, and decay of their bodies led to the creation of most of the world's oil and gas.

Geologists believe that reversals in Earth's magnetic field result from shifts in the currents of liquid iron and nickel flowing through the outer core. Larson also argued that the rise of the superplumes cooled the upper layers of the outer core, increasing the temperature difference between the upper and lower layers of this region.

Just as hot air tends to move more rapidly into a cool region than it does into a warm region, the material in the hot lower layers of the outer core flowed rapidly into the now-cooler upper layers of the outer core. And like fast-moving rivers, these speedy currents were unlikely to form eddies that could cause the currents to reverse their direction. Therefore, the magnetic poles remained stable for tens of millions of years. Eldridge Moores

In ***World Book,*** see **Geology; Volcano.**

Georgia. See **State government.**

Germany. The joy that accompanied the unification of East and West Germany in 1990 gave way in 1991 to the reality: Raising the living standards of the 17 million former East Germans was going to be costly and difficult. Even so, Germany's economy remained the most dynamic in Europe.

As a postscript to unification, the Bundestag (lower house of parliament) voted in June to make Berlin, Germany's traditional capital, the seat of the united German government. The upper house of parliament, the Bundesrat, voted in July to remain in Bonn, the current capital, for the time being.

The costs of unification. The German government estimated that in 1991 it would spend 80 billion Deutsche marks (about U.S. $50 billion) on welfare and unemployment benefits and on rebuilding dilapidated roads and outdated factories in the five newly established east German states. By October, more than 2.2 million eastern Germans, nearly one-third of the total work force, were unemployed or working less than full-time.

Unification spending had a direct effect on the German economy. Although the economic growth rate remained strong in 1991—about 3 per cent—inflation began to rise, reaching a peak annual rate of 4.4 per cent in August. To support the value of the German currency, interest rates were raised several times during the year. In February, the federal government announced a tax-increase package to help pay for east Germany's economic recovery. This reversal of a pledge not to raise taxes to pay for unification hurt Chancellor Helmut Kohl politically.

Kohl's popularity sank throughout 1991, as the cost of unification affected more and more voters. In May, the main opposition party, the Social Democratic Party (SPD), chose 51-year-old Björn Engholm, prime minister of the state of Schleswig-Holstein, as its new leader. The SPD soon afterward won a majority in June elections in the city-state of Hamburg.

Kohl had been embarrassed earlier when the SPD beat his Christian Democratic Union (CDU) in April elections in the chancellor's home state of Rhineland-Palatinate—the first time the CDU had lost control in that state since the state's formation soon after World War II. As a result of the defeat, the CDU lost its majority in the Bundesrat. But Kohl's position as chancellor remained secure because his coalition partners, the Free Democrats, were not likely to desert him.

Germany's foreign policy concerns focused on instability in eastern Europe. Foreign Minister Hans-Dietrich Genscher strongly supported the declarations of independence in June by the Yugoslav republics of Croatia and Slovenia, and despite objections by the United States, Germany recognized the two states in December. Germany also took part in efforts by the 12-nation European Community (EC or Common Market) to negotiate a cease-fire in Yugoslavia's civil war.

The quick end to the Persian Gulf War came as a relief to Germany. The country had faced internation-

Thousands of Germans march in September to protest the violent attacks by right wing groups against foreigners living in Germany.

al criticism for not giving more support to the United States-led coalition that freed Kuwait from Iraqi occupation in early 1991. Kohl argued that the German Constitution, adopted in 1949, prevented the government from sending soldiers to fight outside Germany. But Germany did provide $5.8 billion in direct aid to the coalition. Kohl pledged to work toward amending the Constitution to permit German troops to participate in United Nations-backed peacekeeping efforts.

Terrorism resurfaced in Germany during 1991. On April 1, Detlev Rohwedder, a government official, was shot dead. Rohwedder had headed the agency in charge of selling off or shutting down former East German state-owned industries. The agency had been criticized by eastern Germans for contributing to high unemployment. Responsibility for the assassination was claimed by the Red Army Faction, a group that carried out terrorist acts during the 1970's and 1980's.

Rohwedder was replaced in his job by Birgit Breuel, who continued selling off East German factories. The process was helped when a German court ruled in April that the government did not have to restore to previous owners property that had been seized by the Soviet Union during its occupation of East Germany from 1945 to 1949. The government had previously agreed to compensate or restore property to those whose property had been seized after 1949 by the Communist government. The court decision removed legal hurdles that had slowed investment in the east.

Violent attacks against foreigners living in Germany flared up in 1991, as refugees continued to flock to the country. Thousands of Germans in many cities joined peaceful marches to protest the growing racial violence. In the first 10 months of 1991, more than 200,000 foreigners arrived in Germany seeking asylum. Many of them had come from eastern Europe and hoped to take advantage of Germany's liberal policy on political asylum. In October, the government decided to open refugee camps. Immigration was to be limited to those fleeing political persecution, excluding those seeking simply to better their economic lot. Decisions were to be reached on a refugee's status within six weeks. Those rejected were to be deported.

Honecker flees. On March 13, Erich Honecker, the long-time Communist leader of East Germany, was secretly flown to Moscow, supposedly for medical treatment. (Honecker had been in a Soviet military hospital in the former East Germany.) Throughout the year, German authorities requested Honecker's extradition so that he could stand trial for manslaughter. Honecker was charged with having given orders to East German border guards to shoot anyone trying to cross from East Berlin to West Berlin. An estimated 200 people had died during Honecker's rule as a result of the shootings. Philip Revzin

See also **Europe** (Facts in brief table), Special Report: **The Rocky Road to European Unity.** In ***World Book,*** see **Germany.**

Ghana. The revitalization of Ghana's gold-mining industry, a rise in exports, and a trade pact with Cuba were among the few bright spots in 1991 in an otherwise declining economy. Inflation, which the government had been taming, rose to 37.7 per cent during the year. Meanwhile, government deficits climbed, and agriculture and manufacturing declined.

A group of Western governments and donor agencies that have been aiding Ghana agreed in May to lend the country another $970 million because of its progress toward restoring civilian government. Earlier, in January, Ghana's military ruler, Jerry John Rawlings, established the National Commission for Democracy to recommend provisions for a new constitution. In midyear, the commission presented a report recommending a multiparty parliamentary system headed by a president, with liberties and human rights guaranteed by courts free of government control. But the commission rejected what Rawlings had called "pure" or "colonial" democracy and advocated giving the military a key role in several national institutions.

On August 26, the Rawlings regime appointed a 260-member Consultative Assembly to consider the commission's recommendations and draw up a constitution. Plans called for the constitution to be put to a public vote in February 1992 and for elections to be held later that year.

J. Gus Liebenow and Beverly B. Liebenow

In ***World Book,*** see **Ghana.**

Golf. Ian Woosnam of Wales, Ian Baker-Finch of Australia, and Payne Stewart and newcomer John Daly of the United States won the 1991 grand-slam tournaments for men. Meg Mallon won two of the four major tournaments for women, and Jack Nicklaus won two of the major tournaments for senior men.

Grand slam. Woosnam captured the year's first major tournament, the Masters, held from April 11 to 14 in Augusta, Ga. He also became the only pro to win on both the American and European tours during the year and led the world rankings for most of the year.

In the Masters, Woosnam, Jose-Maria Olazabal of Spain, and Tom Watson were tied with one hole to go. Then Olazabal bunkered his drive, Watson pushed his drive into the trees, and Woosnam sank a 7-foot (2.13-meter) putt and won with a 72-hole score of 277. Olazabal finished one stroke behind.

In the United States Open from June 12 to 16 in Chaska, Minn., Stewart and Scott Simpson tied after 72 holes at 282, with Fred Couples and Larry Nelson three strokes behind. In a windy 18-hole play-off on June 17, Simpson finished with three consecutive bogeys, and Stewart won with a 75 to Simpson's 77.

In the British Open from July 18 to 21 in Southport, England, Baker-Finch finished the front nine in 29 strokes, equaling the best nine-hole score ever on the final day of play of a major championship. He finished with a 66 for 272 and a two-stroke victory over Mike Harwood of Australia.

In the Professional Golfers' Association (PGA) championship from August 8 to 11 in Carmel, Ind., the 25-year-old Daly, a tour rookie, was the ninth alternate. When he was notified at the last minute that he would play, he drove all night from Memphis, Tenn. His monstrous drives and go-for-broke style made him an instant gallery favorite. His 276 total beat Bruce Lietzke by three strokes and gave Daly his first tour victory.

PGA tour. In the year's 45 tournaments, seven pros won twice, and no one won more than twice. Corey Pavin, one of the seven, led in earnings with $979,430 and was second in scoring with a 69.63 average for 18 holes compared with Couples' 69.59 average. Pavin became the PGA Player of the Year. On October 13, in the Las Vegas Invitational, Chip Beck shot an 18-hole round of 59, equaling Al Geiberger's 1977 tour record over a longer and more difficult course. Beck shot 13 birdies and 5 pars.

Ryder Cup. Twelve pros from the U.S. PGA tour played 12 pros from Europe in the biennial Ryder Cup matches, held from September 27 to 29 on Kiawah Island, S.C. The United States, which lost the cup in 1985 and failed to regain it in 1987 and 1989, got it back this time by winning, 14½ points to 13½. Had Bernhard Langer of Germany sunk a 6-foot (1.83-meter) downhill putt on the last hole, the final score would have been 14-14, and the Europeans would have kept the cup. Instead, the putt slipped by the hole by the width of a golf ball.

Women. In its first season under its new commissioner, Charles S. Mechem, Jr., the Ladies Professional Golf Association (LPGA) staged 37 tournaments carrying $17.4 million in prize money. Mallon and Pat Bradley won four tournaments each, and Bradley's four gave her 30 for her career and automatic entry into the LPGA Hall of Fame. Bradley led in earnings with $763,118 and became the first woman to reach $4-million in career earnings.

Mallon won the Mazda LPGA championship by a stroke on June 30 in Bethesda, Md., and the United States Open by two strokes on July 14 in Fort Worth, Tex. In the other majors, Amy Alcott won the Nabisco Dinah Shore by eight strokes from March 28 to 31 in Rancho Mirage, Calif., and Nancy Scranton won the du Maurier Classic by three strokes from September 12 to 15 in Coquitlam, British Columbia. Mallon and Scranton had never won on the tour before.

Senior men. On the PGA senior tour, Mike Hill won five tournaments and $1,065,657, making him golf's leading money winner for 1991. Lee Trevino and Juan (Chi Chi) Rodriguez won four each, and Nicklaus and George Archer won three each. Nicklaus won the PGA senior championship from April 18 to 21 in Palm Beach Gardens, Fla. He also beat Rodriguez by four strokes in a play-off for the United States Open title from July 25 to 29 in Birmingham, Mich.

Frank Litsky

In ***World Book,*** see **Golf.**

A van bursts into flames after terrorists fired mortars from it at 10 Downing Street, where Prime Minister John Major was in conference on February 7.

Great Britain. Prime Minister John Major struggled in 1991 to establish himself as a competent successor to Margaret Thatcher. Thatcher had dominated the British political scene as prime minister for more than 11 years, until November 1990, when she resigned and Conservative Party members of Parliament elected Major to head the government.

The opposition Labour Party taunted Major as a "gray man" who lacked the charisma of his predecessor. However, as 1991 progressed, Major asserted himself in both international and domestic spheres. Great Britain's participation in the Persian Gulf War, which began on January 17, led to 61 per cent of the British public saying that they were satisfied with Major's performance, according to a January 27 poll. It was the highest rating of any British prime minister since Winston Churchill during World War II (1939-1945).

Major was chairman in 1991 of the Group of Seven (G-7), an organization of seven of the world's major industrialized democracies—Canada, Great Britain, France, Germany, Italy, Japan, and the United States. As G-7 chairman, Major coordinated the West's policies toward the economic plight of the Soviet Union. After the G-7's July summit meeting in London, a liberal British newspaper said Major demonstrated "a sense of command" without trying to "hog the show" as the paper suggested Thatcher might have done.

Britain and the EC. Major also adopted a more open attitude than had Thatcher toward increased integration of the 12 nations of the European Community (EC or Common Market), which includes Great Britain. In a key speech that analysts regarded as signifying a break with Thatcher's policies, Major told an audience in Bonn, Germany, on March 11 that he wanted Britain to be "at the heart of Europe, working with our partners in building the future."

However, Britain's position toward a more unified Europe was a dangerous domestic political issue for Major during 1991. He faced the possibility of a Conservative Party split over Britain's participation in EC negotiations to establish greater political and economic union. The Bruges Group of Conservative members of Parliament, mainly Thatcher supporters, was determined to prevent the British government from giving to a central European authority Britain's right to form its own foreign and economic policies.

At an EC summit meeting held in the Netherlands in December, Major and other British negotiators agreed to the creation of a single European currency by Jan. 1, 1999, and a common monetary policy to be established by a central bank. But Britain also got a concession clause to "opt out" of the currency agreement indefinitely if the British Parliament disapproves of it. Major claimed an even greater victory when, under British pressure, the EC dropped a social provision in the political union treaty that would have called for member nations to give up sovereign rights to set policy on such matters as equal employment rights for men and women and number of hours in the workweek. Political analysts said that eliminating the social provision was crucial to Major's Conservative government. The Conservative Party had succeeded in gradually reducing the power of labor unions in Britain, and the social provision would have negated the party's efforts.

Thatcher continued to criticize the idea of a European superstate while traveling in the United States in June. Her comments drew an immediate, furious reaction from another former prime minister, Edward Heath, who had never forgiven Thatcher for ousting him from the Conservative Party leadership in 1975. In the House of Commons, the lower house of Parliament, Heath said people were "sick and tired" of her anti-European "sneers."

Electoral politics. Speculation on exactly when a general election would be held was one of several domestic issues that dominated British political life during 1991. Under the Constitution, a general election must be held by July 1992, but the prime minister has the power to choose the exact date. Major waited for a politically favorable moment, but after hostilities ended in the Persian Gulf, opinion polls showed Major's popularity waning. Finally on October 1, Major said that he would not call an election before the end of 1991.

On June 28, Thatcher announced that she would not seek reelection when the next general election was called. She would devote her time to establishing the Margaret Thatcher Foundation. Funded by private donations, the foundation would promote free enterprise and a strong national defense. British politicians said Thatcher's retirement from Parliament would help strengthen Major's control of the Conservative Party. They said that her unrestrained, public criticism of Major was a divisive force in British politics.

Poll tax pitched. Early in 1991, Major and his Conservative Party struggled to get rid of the "community charge," generally known as the poll tax. The poll tax went into effect on April 1, 1990, despite anti-tax rallies, including one held in London, attended by 40,000 people on March 31, that became a street war. The poll tax was levied on every individual between ages 18 and 65 to fund local government services. Many people hated the tax because they had to pay more under the poll tax system than under the old property tax system, which it had replaced.

In an attempt to make the poll tax more palatable, Chancellor of the Exchequer Norman S. Lamont announced on March 19, 1991, that the government would cut poll tax bills by 140 pounds (about U.S. $252) per person per year. But the value-added tax (VAT), a tax on most sales and services, would increase from 15 per cent to 17.5 per cent. Taxes on alcohol, gasoline, and tobacco would also rise. Finally, two days later, on March 21, Environment Secretary Michael Heseltine announced the death of the poll tax. It was replaced by a new local tax based on a combination of property values and the number of individuals living in each property.

Conservative election losses. The Conservative Party suffered several election setbacks during 1991. On March 8, they lost the northern rural seat of Ribble Valley in Lancashire to the centrist Liberal Democratic Party in a by-election. Ribble Valley had long been considered a Conservative Party stronghold, staunchly supporting Major. The Conservative Party loss was attributed to anger over the poll tax.

In local council elections on May 2, the Conservatives lost 890 seats, more than twice the number they had expected to lose, but Major called the loss "bearable." On May 16, Conservatives lost Monmouth in Wales to the Labour Party. Analysts blamed the loss on the continuing recession and opposition to government reform of the national health-care system.

Health service reform. The future of the National Health Service (NHS) was the second most controversial domestic political issue of 1991 after the poll tax. The NHS, which was formed in 1948, provides free medical care in Britain. Under government reforms effective in April 1991, the system was split into two parts: medical-care sellers (mainly hospitals) and medical-care buyers (mainly doctors). Doctors serving more than 9,000 patients could control their own budgets, enabling them to buy services from a hospital outside the one under contract in their district. The NHS hospitals could become independent trusts with authority to set their own prices for services. These hospitals would remain part of the NHS system, but they would no longer be under the control of regional health authorities.

The government claimed that reform had cut patient waiting lists, which had lengthened over the years. But the British Medical Association, representing Britain's 78,000 doctors, denied the government's claim that more patients were being treated as a result of reform. Opinion polls showed strong public distrust of the idea and a widespread feeling that it was a prelude to privatization of health care.

Citizen's Charter. On July 22, the Conservative government disclosed its plan, called a Citizen's Charter, to guarantee high-quality public services. Major reportedly played a leading role in drafting the charter, which contained more than 70 legislative proposals ranging from the privatization of the British Rail Corporation to improving communication between schools and parents to setting guaranteed maximum waiting times for inpatient care at hospitals. In another initiative, Major signaled a return to an emphasis on reading, writing, and arithmetic in elementary education, eliminating what he described as the "left wing canker" of trendy theories, low expectations, and poor achievement.

Economic recession. Britain was in a deep recession during 1991. Manufacturing output was 6.5 per cent lower than in 1990, and unemployment rose to 8 per cent of the work force. To combat inflation, interest rates had been raised to 15 per cent in 1989 with devastating effects on industry and on home owners with large mortgages. Figures released in August 1991 showed that a record 36,610 homes were repossessed during the first half of the year, an increase of more than 33 per cent over the number of repossessions in the second half of 1990. The government's strategy was to bring down inflation and interest rates without sparking a consumer and credit boom. By September 1991, inflation fell to 5.5 per cent from its peak of nearly 11 per cent in late 1990.

Hostages freed. John McCarthy, a television news producer, was freed in Beirut, Lebanon, in August 1991, after being held captive for more than five years. Jack Mann, a retired airline pilot held hostage in Beirut since May 1989, was released in September 1991. Terry Waite, an envoy of the Church of England, was freed in Beirut in November, after being held captive since 1987.

The Irish Republican Army (IRA) set off a firebomb at London's National Gallery on Dec. 15, 1991, without causing injuries or damage to the artworks. London police said that the IRA had planted 75 bombs in Britain since December 1. An IRA statement said that disruptions would continue "as long as the British government and its army continue to occupy part of Ireland's national territory." Ian J. Mather

See also **Ireland; Northern Ireland.** In ***World Book,*** see **Great Britain.**

Greece in 1991 struggled to shore up a weak economy that threatened to prevent the country from benefiting fully from the removal of most trade barriers within the 12-nation European Community (EC or Common Market) by the end of 1992.

Economic reforms. Greek Prime Minister Constantinos Mitsotakis, who took office in 1990, sought to implement a program of economic reforms aimed at cutting a huge government budget deficit and at reducing the country's high inflation rate, which neared 20 per cent in 1991. The controversial reforms included cutting government benefits and pensions and selling a number of government-owned companies. Pressure from the Socialist and Communist opposition parties, and even from members of his own conservative New Democratic Party, prevented Mitsotakis from taking effective steps.

Greece came under criticism for the slow pace of economic reform from several international organizations. By year's end, the Greek currency, the drachma, was not yet strong enough to participate fully in the EC's monetary system, which ties national exchange rates to one another. And government subsidies still protected Greek companies and farmers from competition from EC nations that they will face after 1992.

The trial of Andreas Papandreou—Greece's prime minister from 1981 to 1989—opened in Athens in March 1991. Papandreou and three former cabinet members were charged with corruption for aiding a

At a United States naval base on the Greek island of Crete in July, President George Bush thanks Greece for its help during the Persian Gulf War.

scheme to embezzle money from the Bank of Crete and divert it to their own political party, the Panhellenic Socialist Movement (PASOK). Papandreou, who has denied the charges, refused to attend the trial or be represented by a lawyer.

The trial was delayed in April by the death of a defendant, former Justice Minister Agamemnon Koutsogeorgas, who suffered a stroke in the courtroom. It took another turn when a key witness, George Koskotas, former owner of the Bank of Crete, decided to testify. Koskotas, who faced charges of embezzling more than $200 million from the bank, claimed that Papandreou had blackmailed him into joining the scheme.

The Persian Gulf War prompted a series of bombings in January 1991 against the Athens offices of British and United States companies. The Greek terrorists who claimed responsibility said they were protesting the British and American involvement in the war to force Iraqi troops from Kuwait.

Albania's border with Greece opened in January, and more than 15,000 people poured into Greece, most of them Albanians of Greek ancestry. About a third of the immigrants later returned to Albania.

Philip Revzin

See also **Europe** (Facts in brief table), Special Report: **The Rocky Road to European Unity.** In ***World Book,*** see **Greece.**

Grenada. See **Latin America.**

Guatemala. On Jan. 14, 1991, Jorge Serrano Elías, 45, a businessman and adviser to former Guatemalan military governments, was sworn in for a five-year term as the president of Guatemala. Serrano faced an inflation rate of more than 75 per cent, unemployment of more than 40 per cent, and a smoldering guerrilla war that had taken almost 100,000 lives since the 1960's.

Serrano pledged to liberalize trade policies, carry out agrarian reforms, and distribute wealth more fairly. But Serrano was handicapped by the failure of his party, the Solidarity Action Movement, to control a majority of seats in the national legislature and by his reliance on the nation's military to keep him in power. Although the government held talks with rebels from April to July 1991, the military continued to be criticized abroad and at home for its brutality in dealing with the rebels.

In July, high-level members of the previous administration, including a brother of former Guatemalan President Vinicio Cerezo Arévalo, were accused of having taken bribes from the scandal-ridden Bank of Credit and Commerce International (BCCI). The government was investigating whether BCCI bribed government officials to keep quiet about illegal coffee smuggling.

Nathan A. Haverstock.

See also **Latin America** (Facts in brief table). In ***World Book,*** see **Guatemala.**

Guinea. See **Africa.**

Guyana. Guyanese national elections that had been scheduled for Dec. 16, 1991, were postponed until 1992. The postponement occurred when the National Registration Center, dominated by the incumbent People's National Congress (PNC) Party, failed to produce a list of registered voters acceptable to Guyana's opposition parties in time to permit voting in the December elections.

It was the second postponement of national elections in 1991. In accordance with Guyana's Constitution, elections should have been called by May 1991. Opponents of the PNC claimed that the process of voter registration was marked by fraud and excluded large numbers of the nation's ethnic East Indians, most of whom supported 73-year-old Cheddi B. Jagan, the leading candidate to replace President Hugh Desmond Hoyte.

Jagan, an avowed Marxist, was elected prime minister of Guyana (then British Guiana) in 1953, only to have the British remove him from office six months later out of fears he would transform the nation into a Communist dictatorship. Approaching next year's elections, Jagan has styled himself a "Gorbachev before Gorbachev," referring to Mikhail S. Gorbachev, the leader of the Soviet Union, who spurred the Soviet republics' move away from Communism in 1991.

Nathan A. Haverstock

See **Latin America** (Facts in brief table). In ***World Book,*** see **Guyana.**

Haiti. On Sept. 30, 1991, the Haitian military overthrew the nation's first democratically elected head of state, President Jean-Bertrand Aristide. The leader of the coup, Brigadier General Raoul Cedras, seemed unable to control his troops, and as many as 300 people died during sporadic fighting in the streets of Port-au-Prince, the nation's capital, according to diplomatic sources. Aristide, meanwhile, went into exile in Venezuela. See **Aristide, Jean-Bertrand.**

Haiti's National Assembly, reportedly threatened by the nation's police force, voted that the presidency had been "vacated." The 34-nation Organization of American States (OAS) declared the assembly's vote illegal and approved a trade embargo against Haiti on October 8. In defiance of the OAS, Haiti's National Assembly swore in Joseph Nerette, a justice of the Haitian Supreme Court, on October 8 as Haiti's interim president. In explaining the coup, Nerette alleged that Aristide had officially sanctioned violence, increased class tensions, and disregarded constitutional checks and balances. He later promised that Haiti would hold new national elections in January 1992.

Nearly 10,000 refugees fled Haiti after the coup and headed for the United States. Often the refugees were crowded into small boats. At first, the U.S. Coast Guard was under orders to forcibly return the refugees, but a U.S. federal judge ordered a temporary halt to the returns on Nov. 19, 1991. The U.S. government then began housing the refugees at its naval

Haitians riot in the aftermath of the military overthrow of President Jean-Bertrand Aristide on September 30.

base in Guantánamo, Cuba. In December, a U.S. federal appeals court overturned the November ruling and said that the refugees could be returned.

The United States cut off all aid to Haiti following the coup and froze Haitian assets in the United States. Other nations also took action. On October 9, President Bush banned all commercial trade with Haiti effective November 5. Because Haiti depends on the United States for about three-quarters of its trade as well as for most of its foreign investment, the mesure was expected to create pressure for the return of democracy. In expectation of trouble, the United States government withdrew all nonessential diplomatic personnel from Haiti.

On October 4, an OAS delegation went to Haiti where it failed to work out a compromise that would allow Aristide to return to power. On November 15, a second OAS team announced that it had reached a tentative agreement with a broad coalition of Haitian representatives, including interim Prime Minister Jean-Jacques Honorat, that would allow a return of democracy in Haiti. On December 22, Aristide accepted a proposal to allow Haitian Communist Party leader Rene Theodore—a critic of Aristide—to become prime minister, guaranteeing a place for an opposition member in the government.

Nathan A. Haverstock

See also **Latin America** (Facts in brief table). In ***World Book,*** see **Haiti.**

Handicapped. The United States Equal Employment Opportunity Commission (EEOC) on July 25, 1991, issued regulations that businesses must follow to implement many provisions of the Americans with Disabilities Act of 1990. That law, which bans discrimination by private business against people with mental and physical disabilities, was also designed to ensure people with handicaps access to a wide range of services and public facilities. The provisions of the new law were to be phased in over three years, beginning in January 1992.

According to the law, existing retail businesses and public facilities, such as hospitals, museums, and transportation centers, must make structural changes to accommodate people with disabilities unless those changes would be too difficult or expensive. Beginning in January 1993, all new or remodeled businesses must be fully accessible to people with disabilities, including those in wheelchairs.

Under the EEOC regulations, for example, two-thirds of the seating area in restaurants must be accessible to people with disabilities, and at least 5 per cent of the tables must be usable by people in wheelchairs. Theaters and concert halls must provide seating arrangements that allow people with disabilities to sit with nondisabled companions. In addition, the aisles in grocery and in retail stores must be wide enough to accommodate wheelchairs. Hotels with more than five rooms are required to equip at least 5 per cent of the rooms with flashing lights and other visual alarms for people with hearing impairments.

Workers with handicaps. The EEOC regulations also forbid employers to reject job applicants or to dismiss workers with disabilities unless the employers can show a "high probability" that the disabilities would endanger the health and safety of the disabled themselves or their co-workers. Advocates for people with handicaps, however, charged that the "high probability" provision would enable employers to avoid hiring people with physical or mental impairments.

Benefits for children with disabilities. In July 1991, the Social Security Administration began reviewing the claims of more than 500,000 poor, disabled children who had been denied benefits under the Supplemental Security Income program since 1980. The Supreme Court of the United States ordered the review after ruling in 1990 that the government's eligibility standards for children with disabilities were illegal because they were stricter than those for disabled adults. Under the stricter standards, the government approved benefits only for children with certain medical conditions. In contrast, adults with disabilities were also judged on their ability to work. The new standards take into consideration not only a child's medical condition but also the effect of that condition on the child's ability to eat, walk, and perform other daily activities. Barbara A. Mayes

In ***World Book***, see **Handicapped.**

Harkin, Tom (1939-), Democratic senator from Iowa, entered the race for the 1992 Democratic presidential nomination on Sept. 15, 1991. Harkin, an unabashed liberal, attacked President George Bush as a leader who cares only about the rich. He said his campaign would advocate an investment in people and in the nation's domestic needs. See **Democratic Party.**

Thomas Richard Harkin was born on Nov. 19, 1939, in Cumming, Iowa. He attended Iowa State University in Ames on a Navy ROTC scholarship, graduating in 1962 with a bachelor's degree in government and economics. He then served five years in the Navy as a pilot, including a tour of duty in Vietnam.

In 1972, Harkin earned a law degree at Catholic University of America in Washington, D.C. He then returned to Iowa to practice law.

Harkin was elected to the United States House of Representatives in 1974. He spent 10 years in the House, becoming known as a leading supporter of U.S. farmers and a strong advocate of human rights.

In 1984, Harkin was elected to the U.S. Senate. Since 1989, he has been chairman of the Senate's Appropriations Subcommittee on Labor, Health, and Human Services.

Harkin's wife, Ruth, who is also a lawyer, is his most important political adviser. The Harkins have two daughters. David L. Dreier

Harness racing. See **Horse racing.**
Hawaii. See **State government.**

Health and disease. Scientists in 1991 reported numerous discoveries about the roles genes play in various diseases. Genes are segments of a molecule called DNA (*deoxyribonucleic acid*) that contain hereditary information. A human being's estimated 50,000 to 100,000 genes are carried by chromosomes, tiny threadlike structures in cells.

Mental retardation gene. An international scientific team in May announced the discovery of a gene responsible for *fragile X syndrome*, which may cause the most common inherited form of mental retardation. Fragile X syndrome, which is incurable, occurs in about 1 out of every 1,000 males and 1 out of every 2,500 females. (A genetic disorder called *Down's* or *Down syndrome* causes more cases of mental retardation, but it is not transmitted from parents to children in standard hereditary patterns.) The effects of fragile X syndrome may range from mild learning disabilities to severe retardation that leaves victims barely able to function. In some individuals, the genetic defect appears to have little or no effect.

The syndrome's name originates in the frail appearance of the X chromosome in affected people: One piece of the X chromosome dangles by a thread, as if about to break. The X chromosome is one of the two chromosomes that determine an individual's gender. Women have two X chromosomes, and men have one X and one Y chromosome.

In December, French and Australian scientists reported the development of a test that can be used for prenatal diagnosis of the disorder—an accomplishment made possible by the gene's discovery. Scientists said tests also could be used to verify the suspicion that some cases of retardation now attributed to lack of oxygen during birth and other factors actually are caused by fragile X syndrome.

Other genetic discoveries. Researchers in 1991 succeeded in linking genes with several other human diseases. On February 21, British scientists reported discovering a *mutation* (alteration) of a gene that causes one form of *Alzheimer's disease*, a brain disorder marked by progressive memory loss and other symptoms. Also, two groups of scientists on April 4 announced that they had linked liver cancer to a specific human gene. Researchers on July 25 reported isolating the gene responsible for *Marfan's syndrome*, a hereditary disorder that affects the heart, bones, eyes, and other parts of the body. And on August 9, another group of scientists announced identification of a gene believed to trigger development of an inherited form of colon cancer.

Estrogen and heart benefits. Women who take the female hormone estrogen after menopause may reduce their risk of having a heart attack by 40 per cent, according to a September 12 report of the most comprehensive study ever conducted on the topic. The study, directed by Meir J. Stampfer of Harvard Medical School and Brigham and Women's Hospital, both in Boston, monitored the health of 48,470 nurses for 10 years. The nurses all had experienced menopause, the time when menstrual periods cease and a woman no longer is able to become pregnant. The women were taking estrogen to prevent *osteoporosis*, a thinning of the bones, and relieve symptoms of menopause.

Researchers compared the incidence of heart attacks among women who took estrogen to those who did not. The incidence of heart disease in women rises sharply after menopause, when a woman's estrogen levels decline. They concluded that estrogen prescribed after menopause has a powerful effect in preventing coronary heart disease, the leading cause of death among postmenopausal women.

Previous studies showed that estrogen increases the risk of some forms of cancer. The new study concluded that estrogen's benefits in preventing heart attacks outweigh its cancer risks.

Dieting hazard. Millions of Americans who repeatedly lose and regain weight may double their risk of dying from heart disease, researchers warned in a study published on June 27. The study revealed that such weight cycling, popularly known as *yo-yo dieting*, may be just as dangerous as simply remaining obese.

The study monitored the health consequences of weight cycling among 3,130 men and women over a 32-year period. People who experienced the most weight fluctuation had a 25 to 100 per cent higher risk of heart disease, death from heart disease, and death from all causes. Researchers cited several ways in which yo-yo dieting may increase the risk of heart disease. Initial weight loss, they noted, usually involves loss of both fat and muscle tissue. But people regain mainly fat tissue, which accumulates in the abdominal area. Studies have linked abdominal fat to a sharply increased risk of heart disease.

Preventing heart disease. In April, a panel of health experts issued new guidelines for the prevention of heart disease, recommending that all children with a family history of heart attacks have their blood cholesterol levels tested. The recommendations, from the National Cholesterol Education Program (NCEP), noted that *atherosclerosis*, the underlying cause of most heart attacks, begins in childhood. Atherosclerosis clogs critical blood vessels in the heart with cholesterol, fat, and other material, reducing the flow of blood to the heart muscle. Sometimes a blood clot forms over the deposit, blocking the flow of blood, causing a heart attack.

The NCEP panel estimated that about one-fourth of all children have parents or grandparents who developed heart attacks or certain other heart problems at a relatively early age—before age 55—and about 50 per cent of these children will have high blood cholesterol. The panel recommended that family members older than age 2 follow a low-fat, low-cholesterol diet. Michael Woods

See **Medicine,** Special Report: **Genetic Medicine: Promise and Perils.** See also **Biology.** In ***World Book,*** see **Disease; Health.**

Henderson, Rickey (1958-   ), became baseball's leading career base stealer on May 1, 1991, when the Oakland Athletics' outfielder stole his 939th base in a home game against the New York Yankees. Henderson broke Lou Brock's career record. See **Baseball.**

One of eight children, Henderson was born in Chicago. His family moved to Pine Bluff, Ark., and then, when he was 7 years old, to Oakland, Calif. Although he was a high school All-American in football, Henderson also excelled at baseball. The Athletics drafted him in 1976.

Henderson made his major league debut on June 23, 1979. He quickly established himself as a threat on the bases, leading the Athletics with 33 steals in his first year.

During the 1982 season, he stole 130 bases for the Athletics, breaking Brock's single season record of 118. The Athletics traded Henderson to the Yankees in December 1984, but Oakland reacquired him in June 1989.

Henderson was voted the American League Most Valuable Player for 1990 and has been named to the All-Star team 10 times. In 1985, he became the first American League player to hit at least 20 home runs and steal 50 bases in the same season when he hit 24 homers and stole 80 bases.

Henderson and his wife, Pam, have a daughter. They live in Hillsborough, Calif. Mark Dunbar

Hobbies. See **Stamp collecting; Toys and games.**

Hockey. The National Hockey League's (NHL's) 1990-1991 season ended on an improbable note. The Pittsburgh Penguins and the Minnesota North Stars were unlikely opponents in the Stanley Cup finals. The Penguins won the championship, 4 games to 2.

Neither team had been expected to do well in the play-offs. During the regular season, the Penguins managed to win the Patrick Division title. However, their 88 points in the final standings were far fewer than the totals of the other division winners.

The North Stars were even more surprising finalists. During the 1989-1990 season, they were a failing franchise ready to relocate. In 1990-1991, however, they revived under a new owner (Norman Green), general manager (Bobby Clarke), and coach (Bob Gainey). They finished the regular season 12 games under .500, but they improved late in the season.

In reaching the finals, the North Stars eliminated the Chicago Black Hawks, 4 games to 2. They then beat the St. Louis Blues, 4 games to 2, and the Edmonton Oilers, the defending Stanley Cup champions, 4 games to 1. The Penguins defeated the New Jersey Devils (4 games to 3), the Washington Capitals (4 games to 1), and the Boston Bruins (4 games to 2).

The finals were the first between two United States teams since 1981, when the New York Islanders beat the North Stars in five games. This time, the North Stars won two of the first three games and took strong leads in the fourth and fifth games. But the

The Pittsburgh Penguins (in dark uniforms) battled the Minnesota North Stars in the 1991 Stanley Cup finals. The Penguins won the series, 4 games to 2.

Penguins came back to win the fourth game, 5-3, and the fifth game, 6-4. An 8-0 victory in the sixth game sealed the Penguins' first Stanley Cup championship.

Honors. Mario Lemieux, the Penguins' center, was voted the Conn Smythe Trophy recipient as the Most Valuable Player in the play-offs. The regular season's Most Valuable Player was Brett Hull, the St. Louis Blues's right wing, who led the league with 86 goals.

Wayne Gretzky, the Los Angeles Kings's center, received the Art Ross Trophy as the scoring champion (163 points) and the Lady Byng Trophy for sportsmanship. Ed Belfour of the Black Hawks won the Vezina Trophy as the outstanding goalie and the Calder Trophy as the outstanding rookie. The all-star team consisted of Hull, Gretzky, Belfour, defensemen Ray Bourque of the Bruins and Al MacInnis of the Calgary Flames, and left wing Luc Robitaille of the Kings.

Other news. The San Jose Sharks, an NHL expansion team, began play during the 1991-1992 season. For $50 million each, the Ottawa (Canada) Senators and the Tampa Bay (Fla.) Lightning also became NHL franchises. They will start playing during the 1992-1993 season.

Sweden won the world championship, held April 19 through May 4 in Finland, with Canada second, the Soviet Union third, and the United States fourth.

Frank Litsky

In *World Book*, see **Hockey**.

Honduras. See **Latin America**.

National Hockey League standings

Clarence Campbell Conference

James Norris Division	W.	L.	T.	Pts.
Chicago Black Hawks*	49	23	8	106
St. Louis Blues*	47	22	11	105
Detroit Red Wings*	34	38	8	76
Minnesota North Stars*	27	39	14	68
Toronto Maple Leafs	23	46	11	57
Conn Smythe Division				
Los Angeles Kings*	46	24	10	102
Calgary Flames*	46	26	8	100
Edmonton Oilers*	37	37	6	80
Vancouver Canucks*	28	43	9	65
Winnipeg Jets	26	43	11	63

Prince of Wales Conference

Charles F. Adams Division	W.	L.	T.	Pts.
Boston Bruins*	44	24	12	100
Montreal Canadiens*	39	30	11	89
Buffalo Sabres*	31	30	19	81
Hartford Whalers*	31	38	11	73
Quebec Nordiques	16	50	14	46
Lester Patrick Division				
Pittsburgh Penguins*	41	33	6	88
New York Rangers*	36	31	13	85
Washington Capitals*	37	36	7	81
New Jersey Devils*	32	33	15	79
Philadelphia Flyers	33	37	10	76
New York Islanders	25	45	10	60

*Made play-off.

Stanley Cup winner—
Pittsburgh Penguins (defeated Minnesota North Stars, 4 games to 2)

Scoring leaders	Games	Goals	Assists	Pts.
Wayne Gretzky, Los Angeles	78	41	122	163
Brett Hull, St. Louis	78	86	45	131
Adam Oates, St. Louis	61	25	90	115
Mark Recchi, Pittsburgh	78	40	73	113
John Cullen, Pittsburgh/Hartford	78	39	71	110
Joe Sakic, Quebec	80	48	61	109
Steve Yzerman, Detroit	80	51	57	108
Theo Fleury, Calgary	79	51	53	104
Al MacInnis, Calgary	78	28	75	103
Steve Larmer, Chicago	80	44	57	101
Jeremy Roenick, Chicago	79	41	53	94
Ray Bourque, Boston	76	21	73	94

Leading goalies (25 or more games)	Games	Goals against	Avg.
Ed Belfour, Chicago	74	170	2.47
Don Beaupre, Washington	45	113	2.64
Patrick Roy, Montreal	48	128	2.71
Andy Moog, Boston	51	136	2.87
Pete Peeters, Philadelphia	26	61	2.88

Awards

Calder Trophy (best rookie)—Ed Belfour, Chicago
Hart Trophy (most valuable player)—Brett Hull, St. Louis
Lady Byng Trophy (sportsmanship)—Wayne Gretzky, Los Angeles
Masterton Trophy (perseverance, dedication to hockey)—Dave Taylor, Los Angeles
Norris Trophy (best defenseman)—Ray Bourque, Boston
Ross Trophy (leading scorer)—Wayne Gretzky, Los Angeles
Selke Trophy (best defensive forward)—Dirk Graham, Chicago
Smythe Trophy (most valuable player in Stanley Cup)—Mario Lemieux, Pittsburgh
Vezina Trophy (most valuable goalie)—Ed Belfour, Chicago

Major horse races of 1991

Race	Winner	Value to winner
Arlington Million	Tight Spot	$600,000
Belmont Stakes	Hansel	$1,417,480
Breeders' Cup Classic	Black Tie Affair	$1,500,000
Breeders' Cup Distaff	Dance Smartly	$520,000
Breeders' Cup Juvenile	Arazi	$520,000
Breeders' Cup Juvenile Fillies	Pleasant Stage	$520,000
Breeders' Cup Mile	Opening Verse	$520,000
Breeders' Cup Sprint	Sheikh Albadou	$520,000
Breeders' Cup Turf	Miss Alleged	$1,040,000
Budweiser International	Leariva	$450,000
Champion Stakes (England)	Tel Quel	$509,877
Derby Stakes (England)	Generous	$689,943
Hollywood Gold Cup Handicap	Marquetry	$550,000
Irish Derby (Ireland)	Generous	$646,001
Jockey Club Gold Cup	Festin	$510,000
Kentucky Derby	Strike the Gold	$655,800
King George VI and Queen Elizabeth Diamond Stakes (England)	Generous	$537,339
Molson Export Million Stakes	Dance Smartly	$600,000
Pacific Classic	Best Pal	$550,000
Pimlico Special Handicap	Farma Way	$450,000
Preakness Stakes	Hansel	$432,770
Prix de l'Arc de Triomphe (France)	Suave Dancer	$987,000
Rothmans International (Canada)	Sky Classic	$624,750
Santa Anita Handicap	Farma Way	$550,000
Super Derby	Free Spirit's Joy	$600,000
Travers Stakes	Corporate Report	$600,000

Major U.S. harness races of 1991

Race	Winner	Value to winner
Cane Pace	Silky Stallone	$261,595
Hambletonian	Giant Victory	$559,500
Little Brown Jug	Precious Bunny	$228,334
Meadowlands Pace	Precious Bunny	$500,000
Messenger Stakes	Die Laughing	$237,500
Woodrow Wilson	Sportsmaster	$444,500

Sources: *The Blood-Horse* magazine and U.S. Trotting Association.

Horse racing. The struggle to determine America's 1991 thoroughbred Horse of the Year ended in a three-way battle among Black Tie Affair, who won the Breeders' Cup Classic; Arazi, a 2-year-old colt who ran every race except one in France; and Dance Smartly, a 3-year-old filly who won the Canadian triple crown. All won impressively in the season-ending Breeders' Cup races on October 30 in Louisville, Ky.

Thoroughbreds. The seven Breeders' Cup races were expected to decide the Horse of the Year. Instead, the picture became hazier because the richest race, the $3-million Classic, lost strong candidates. They included In Excess, who had won the Metropolitan, Suburban, Whitney, and Woodward; Farma Way, who had won the 10-race American Championship Racing Series; and Hansel, who had won two American Triple-Crown races for 3-year-olds.

In Excess ran in the Breeders' Cup Mile rather than the Classic and finished ninth. Farma Way was withdrawn with an injured ankle. Hansel had already been retired with an injured left foreleg. Without them, Black Tie Affair won the Classic, his sixth consecutive stakes victory.

For the Kentucky-bred Arazi, the Juvenile was his first race outside France, his first on dirt, and his first counterclockwise. With a mighty move, he roared from next to last to a 4¾-length victory. Dance Smartly won the Distaff and became the first filly to reach $3 million in career earnings.

Strike the Gold opens up in the stretch to win the 117th Kentucky Derby on May 4 at Churchill Downs race track in Louisville, Ky.

The 1991 Triple-Crown series began with the Kentucky Derby on May 4 in Louisville. Strike the Gold won by 1¾ lengths, with the favored Hansel finishing 10th. Then Hansel won the remaining two Triple-Crown races—the Preakness by seven lengths on May 18 in Baltimore and the Belmont by a head on June 8 in Elmont, N.Y.

Bill Shoemaker, the retired jockey who had ridden a record 8,833 winners, broke his neck in a car accident on June 8. He was paralyzed after the accident.

Harness. The year's outstanding horse was Precious Bunny, a 3-year-old colt. He won the Adios, Little Brown Jug, the $1-million North American Cup, and the $1-million Meadowlands Pace. His Meadowlands time of 1 minute 49⅘ seconds was the fastest harness mile ever in a night race and only one-fifth of a second slower than Nihilator's 1985 record for the sport's fastest mile in a race. For the year, Precious Bunny recorded 20 victories and three second-place finishes in 23 races. He earned $2.21 million, a record for the sport, and was then retired. Precious Bunny was not nominated for the final Breeders' Cup races on October 25 in Pompano Beach, Fla. John Campbell drove three winners on the final Breeders' Cup program and became the first driver to reach $100 million in career purses. The Breeders' Cup winners included Giant Victory, a 3-year-old trotter who had previously won the Hambletonian. Frank Litsky

In ***World Book,*** see **Harness racing; Horse racing.**

Hospital. In 1991, the American Hospital Association (AHA) reported that in 1990 United States hospitals survived on income from sources other than patient care—for example, from investments and charitable contributions. According to figures released by the AHA, total hospital income was 4.8 per cent greater than expenses in 1990, but revenues from patient care fell short of expenses by 0.2 per cent. Figures for the first half of 1991 were more encouraging: Total profit margins were 5.3 per cent for the second quarter of 1991, and patient-care margins were 0.4 per cent.

Closings. The AHA reported in February 1991 that 63 U.S. hospitals had closed in 1990. The total number of closings for 1980 through 1990 was 761, including 558 community hospitals. Of those, 278 were in urban areas, and 280 were in rural areas.

Rural hospitals. The uncertain fate of many rural hospitals garnered much attention during 1991. In September, the Department of Health and Human Services awarded $23.4 million to 533 small rural hospitals to enable them to convert facilities to new purposes, train workers, and enhance or expand their services. In addition, seven states and 51 rural hospitals received $9.8 million in federal funds to develop new strategies for rural hospital care.

Changes in Medicare and Medicaid payments to hospitals led to sharp debate throughout 1991. In January, the Health Care Financing Administration (HCFA), which oversees Medicare and Medicaid, announced that it would no longer directly repay hospitals for the costs of investing in new or improved facilities or technologies. Then in September, the HCFA announced it would bar states from taking advantage of a quirk in federal law that allowed them to solicit or demand money from hospitals, allocate the funds to Medicaid, and then receive federal matching funds for the Medicaid monies. A December compromise allowed some of the programs to continue, however.

Hospitals and AIDS testing. In 1991, the AHA joined many other health-care organizations in opposing mandatory HIV testing of health-care workers. (HIV is the virus that causes AIDS.) Hospitals cited the cost of testing and the fact that, as of 1991, no health-care worker was known to have transmitted HIV to a patient, with the exception of one Florida dentist.

Living wills. On Dec. 1, 1991, the U.S. Patient Self-Determination Act went into effect. The law required hospitals and other health-care providers to inform patients about state law regarding "living wills" and other documents in which mentally competent patients state under what circumstances they would refuse treatment to prolong life.

Work force. Hospitals remained the largest employers in health care in 1990, according to a 1991 report by the Department of Labor. Nearly 4 million people worked in U.S. hospitals. Emily Ann Friedman

In ***World Book***, see **Hospital.**

Housing. See **Building and construction.**

Houston. Bob Lanier, a real estate developer, was elected mayor of Houston in a Dec. 7, 1991, nonpartisan runoff election. Crime was the dominant issue in the campaign and contributed to the defeat of Mayor Kathryn J. Whitmire after 10 years in office. Whitmire did not even make it to the runoff, finishing a distant third behind Lanier and State Representative Sylvester Turner in the November 5 general election. The runoff campaign was bitter and punctuated by complaints of dirty politics by both candidates. Lanier, the overwhelming favorite of white voters, received 53 per cent of the runoff ballot, defeating Turner's bid to become Houston's first black mayor.

Crime. A series of brutal murders in 1991, some committed by parolees who were freed after serving only a fraction of their sentence, fueled a public perception that crime in Houston may be out of control. Although other cities had higher crime rates, Houston residents were shocked by the steady rise in the local homicide count. By mid-December, the death toll had reached 640, surpassing the total of 617 homicides for all of 1990. During one deadly weekend in September, 16 people were murdered.

The community was also alarmed by the increasing number of juvenile offenders. In one highly publicized case, the police took a 3-year-old girl into custody after she allegedly tried to sell crack cocaine to undercover officers. In another case, a 15-year-old girl was charged in the shooting death of her former boyfriend. The victim, a captain of his high school football team, was shot in the back as he stood in line for breakfast in the school cafeteria. In an effort to reduce the incidence of youth crime, the City Council in October enacted a juvenile curfew making it illegal for anyone under 16 to be on the streets between midnight and 6 a.m.

Transit Plan. In March, the Metropolitan Transit Authority approved plans for a $1.2-billion monorail system to link the downtown area with the city's Galleria business district and suburbs to the west. Despite the backing of Mayor Whitmire and many business leaders, the proposal became an object of widespread public scorn—polls showed that as many as 80 per cent of Houstonians opposed the idea. In October, suburban Republican Representative Tom DeLay prevailed upon his colleagues in Congress to block federal funding for the project, effectively putting it on hold.

The issue of a Houston rail system was expected to remain alive in 1992, however. Lanier said he would support a commuter rail system built along existing freight-train routes.

Republican National Convention. In January, the Republican National Committee selected Houston as the host for the party's 1992 presidential nominating convention. City officials in President George Bush's adopted hometown began almost immediately to make preparations for the event, set for Aug. 17 to 20, 1992, in the Astrodome. To accommodate the Republicans and give them time to refit the stadium, the Houston Astros, the city's professional baseball team, agreed to make a 29-day road trip before and during the convention. That would be the longest scheduled stretch away from a home playing field in modern baseball history.

Zoning. In January 1991, Houston became the last major United States city to adopt a comprehensive zoning ordinance aimed at promoting more orderly growth. Zoning had long been fought by Houston's powerful real estate interests. They argued that the absence of building restrictions had been a key factor in the city's explosive economic growth over the years. The impetus for change came from neighborhood groups fed up with the city's haphazard patterns of development and with commercial encroachment into residential areas. The zoning plan, after being endorsed by Mayor Whitmire, was unanimously adopted by the City Council.

Education. In August, the Houston Independent School District got a new superintendent, Frank Petruzielo, who promised to give individual schools more authority over their operations. Petruzielo, who had been associate superintendent of the Miami, Fla., school system, quickly slashed about 200 jobs from the central administrative staff. Petruzielo succeeded Superintendent Joan Raymond, who departed after district trustees said she was moving too slowly to decentralize the school system. Timothy J. Graham

See also **City**. In ***World Book,*** see **Houston**.

Hungary.

Hungary. Public confidence in the ruling Hungarian Democratic Forum (HDF) and the country's fledgling parliamentary democracy slipped during 1991 despite some notable economic success. Foreign investment helped reduce the country's $20-billion foreign debt by $1.5 billion during the year.

At the same time, living standards declined, and the HDF came under increasing pressure to halt the decline. For most Hungarians, purchasing power fell as a result of hefty price increases under the government's economic reform program. Discontent was fueled by the emergence of a thriving entrepreneurial class making handsome profits. And Hungarians greeted skeptically official predictions that living standards would improve by 1994.

Economic reform made headway, nonetheless. Because of the progress, Hungary in November became one of the first eastern European countries to reach an agreement with the 12-nation European Community (EC or Common Market) giving Hungarian exports preferential treatment within the EC.

By mid-1991, the government had registered more than 5,000 business ventures under joint Hungarian and foreign ownership. They represented more than half the total foreign investment of $1.2 billion in eastern Europe in the previous 12-month period. Germany and Austria topped the list of the investors, followed by Japan and Sweden.

In February, the government launched a four-year plan to stabilize the value of Hungary's currency and make it *convertible* (internationally exchangeable). The plan foreshadowed the nation's transition to a market economy through the rapid sale of state-owned enterprises and through limiting government control over the economy. During the year, several hundred state-run hotel and catering groups and transportation enterprises were auctioned off, with more than 2,000 such businesses still to be sold.

The reform program was drafted to meet the requirements for a three-year loan of $1.6 billion from the International Monetary Fund (IMF), a United Nations agency. Additional IMF aid earmarked for Hungary raised the total amount available to $2.6 billion.

Trade with the Soviet Union, which had totaled $6.5 billion in 1990, was expected to drop by half in 1991. But trade with the West, up 18 per cent in 1990, was expected to jump another 40 per cent in 1991. The EC absorbed nearly half of Hungary's exports during the first nine months of the year.

Compensating former landowners. In April, the Hungarian parliament approved an $800-million fund to compensate landowners whose property had been nationalized by the Communist government after June 1949. Compensation was to take the form of vouchers permitting people to acquire as much as 124 acres (50 hectares) of land as it came up for sale.

Eric Bourne

See also **Europe** (Facts in brief table). In ***World Book,*** see **Hungary**.

Iacobucci, Frank (1937-), chief justice of the Federal Court of Canada, was sworn in as a justice of the Supreme Court of Canada on Jan. 7, 1991. He is the first Italian Canadian to take a seat on the Supreme Court. Prime Minister Brian Mulroney chose Iacobucci to replace Justice Bertha Wilson.

Iacobucci was born in Vancouver, B.C., on June 29, 1937, to Italian immigrant parents. He earned bachelor's degrees in commerce and in law from the University of British Columbia in Vancouver. Cambridge University in England awarded him a master's in laws and a diploma in international law. In 1989, Iacobucci received an honorary doctor of laws from the University of British Columbia and from the University of Toronto in Ontario. He began practicing law in 1964 with a New York City firm and specialized in corporate law. In 1967, he moved to Ontario and took a teaching position at the University of Toronto. From 1967 to 1985, he held several posts at the university, including dean of the faculty of law and provost of the university.

In 1985, Iacobucci was appointed deputy minister of justice and deputy attorney general of Canada. He assumed the responsibilities of chief justice of the Federal Court of Canada in 1988.

While in his 20's, Iacobucci was invited to try out for a professional baseball team. But he decided to pursue a career in law instead. The chief justice is married to the former Nancy E. Eastham and has three children. Lori Fagan

Ice skating. The United States made figure-skating history in 1991 by sweeping all three of the women's medals in the world championships. American men had done that three times in the 1950's, but a sweep had never been achieved by women from any nation.

The world championships, the first since the abolition of compulsory figures, were held from March 12 to 16 in Munich, Germany. The women's field was strong even without the 1990 winner, Jill Trenary of Colorado Springs, Colo., who was recovering from ankle surgery. Midori Ito of Japan, the favorite, crashed into another skater during a warm-up and fell over the boards into a television camera pit.

Nineteen-year-old Kristi Yamaguchi of Fremont, Calif., won after a free-skating program that included seven triples. Tonya Harding of Portland, Ore., the U.S. champion, finished second, and Nancy Kerrigan of Woburn, Mass., was third.

Ito placed fourth and 17-year-old Surya Bonaly of France, the European champion, fifth. Bonaly, a former world junior tumbling champion, barely missed becoming the first woman to land a quadruple jump. In the U.S. championships, held from February 10 to 17 in Minneapolis, Minn., Harding became the first American woman to complete a triple axel.

Kurt Browning of Edmonton, Canada, won the men's world title for the third consecutive year. Viktor Petrenko of the Soviet Union, the European champion, finished second, and Todd Eldredge of Chatham, Mass., the U.S. champion in 1990 and 1991, was third.

Natalia Mishkutienok and Artur Dmitriev of the Soviet Union won the pairs. It was the seventh year in a row that Soviet skaters have won the pairs competition. Isabelle and Paul Duchesnay dethroned Marina Klimova and Sergei Ponomarenko of the Soviet Union in ice dancing, a title won by Soviet skaters during the six preceding years. The Duchesnays, who are sister and brother, were raised in Canada, trained in Germany, coached by a Czechoslovak, and choreographed by a Briton. They skated for France.

Of the 12 world-championship medals, the United States won 5, its most since 1959.

Speed skating. The world speed-skating championships were held in Norway, Germany, and the Netherlands. Two German women, Gunda Kleeman and Monique Garbrecht, won the overall and world sprint titles, respectively. German women also took three of the four World Cup series championships: Garbrecht in the 1,000 meters, Kleeman in the 1,500 meters, and Heike Warnicke in the 3,000-5,000 meters combined.

Among the men, Johann Olav Koss of Norway won the overall championship, and Igor Zhelesovski of the Soviet Union took the sprint competition.

Frank Litsky

In ***World Book***, see **Ice skating.**

Iceland. See **Europe.**

Idaho. See **State government.**

Illinois. See **Chicago; State government.**

Immigration. The United States Department of State arranged a lottery in October 1991 that allowed 40,000 foreigners to win green cards, the document that indicates permanent residency status for immigrants. The first 40,000 applications to arrive at a Virginia post office between October 14 and October 20 qualified for the card. The lottery, held in accordance with stipulations set forth in the Immigration Act of 1990, was the first of four lotteries scheduled to occur yearly through 1994. Citizens of 34 designated countries and territories, most of them in Europe, were eligible to win. The lottery, and its restrictions on eligibility, aimed to diversify the ethnic mix of immigrants entering the United States. Since 1965, when U.S. immigration laws allowed increased migration from Asia and Latin America, the numbers of European immigrants had declined significantly. Under the Immigration Act, the yearly cap on the number of visas granted will rise to 700,000 in 1994.

Cold War list. In late October, President George Bush signed legislation directing the State Department to remove approximately 300,000 names from a secret list of "undesirable" aliens. The list, begun in 1952, barred some foreigners from entering the United States because of their perceived ideas. Names of people thought to be associated with Communism comprised a large portion of the list.

Asian influx. In the 1980's, Asian Americans became the fastest-growing minority group in the

United States, according to a report released on June 11, 1991, by the U.S. Bureau of the Census. During the previous 25 years, the number of Asian-American immigrants had increased from 1 million to 7.3 million, with more than 2 million arriving since 1980.

Immigration law. In May, the U.S. government extended a ban on the entry of foreigners infected with the AIDS virus. Although the director of the U.S. Department of Health and Human Services had suggested lifting the ban, the U.S. Immigration and Naturalization Service supported the ban.

During the Persian Gulf War in January and February 1991, and during the events leading up to it, the U.S. Department of Justice ordered that all persons entering the United States with Iraqi or Kuwaiti passports be photographed and fingerprinted. This unusual action was designed to limit the threat of terrorism. Those with Kuwaiti passports were included because Iraq gained control of blank Kuwaiti passports after seizing Kuwait in August 1990.

To decrease the numbers of Cubans immigrating to the United States, the U.S. government in July 1991 froze the issuance of six-month Cuban tourist visas. State Department officials said Cuban visa applications had tripled from 1990 to 1991, and many Cubans were staying beyond the term allowed.

Frank Cormier and Margot Cormier

In *World Book,* see **Immigration.**

Income tax. See **Taxation.**

India. Former Prime Minister Rajiv Gandhi, the leader of India's largest political party, was assassinated on May 21, 1991, as he campaigned during elections for the lower house of Parliament. Gandhi was the second member of his family to die as a result of political violence. His mother, former Prime Minister Indira Gandhi, was assassinated in office in 1984. A compromise choice to head Gandhi's Congress Party, P. V. Narasimha Rao, became prime minister after the Congress Party won the largest bloc of seats. See **Rao, P. V. Narasimha.**

The elections were called after Gandhi withdrew his Congress Party's support from a minority government led by Chandra Shekhar, a Socialist. Lacking enough parliamentary support to conduct government business, Shekhar resigned on March 6, 1991. President Ramaswamy Iyer Venkataraman dissolved Parliament on March 13 and arranged for elections from May 20 through 26, with different parts of the country scheduled to vote on different days.

The campaign focused on Gandhi's attempt to regain the office of prime minister by securing a parliamentary majority for the Congress Party. The party had dominated Indian politics under two earlier prime ministers, Gandhi's grandfather, Jawaharlal Nehru, and his mother. Gandhi promised free-market reforms to encourage economic growth.

Opposing Gandhi was the Janata Dal Party, led by Vishwanath Pratap Singh, who had succeeded Gandhi

P. V. Narasimha Rao, a long-time ally of the Gandhi family, greets well-wishers after becoming India's new prime minister in June.

as prime minister after the last parliamentary election in November 1989. In November 1990, Singh was succeeded by Shekhar. Singh campaigned against the Hindu caste system that had kept power in the hands of a small elite. Gandhi's other main opponent was the Bharatiya Janata Party (BJP), which proposed the abolition of special rights for religious minorities—especially Muslims, who make up about 11 per cent of India's population—and advocated making India a Hindu state.

Gandhi murdered. After several states had voted on May 20, 1991, Gandhi began a campaign tour of Tamil Nadu, a state in southern India. On the evening of May 21, 1991, he arrived at the small town of Sriperumpudur, 25 miles (40 kilometers) southwest of the state capital, Madras. As Gandhi walked to a platform to speak, a woman bowed in traditional greeting to him, triggering a powerful explosive around her waist. The woman, Gandhi, and 15 other people were killed.

In June, police investigators indicated that the murder was organized by the Liberation Tigers of Tamil Eelam, a Sri Lankan separatist group. Earlier in the decade, Indira Gandhi's government had supported the Tigers' guerrilla warfare efforts to obtain a separate state for the Tamil ethnic minority in Sri Lanka. In July 1987, however, Rajiv Gandhi sent Indian troops to Sri Lanka to help the Sri Lankan government disarm the Tigers. Indian police accused the Tigers of killing Gandhi in revenge for these policies, but Tiger spokesmen denied any responsibility.

In the largest manhunt in India's history, more than 50 people suspected of involvement in the murder were captured or reportedly committed suicide when cornered. The man accused of masterminding the murder, a Tiger specialist in assassinations named Raja Arumainayagam, and six of his accomplices reportedly killed themselves as police closed in on them on Aug. 20, 1991.

Rao chosen. Gandhi had no clearly accepted deputy in the Congress Party at the time of his death. After his assassination, the party's executive group tried to continue the Nehru/Gandhi family tradition and win voter sympathy by electing Gandhi's widow, Sonia, as party president. But Sonia, a Roman Catholic born in Italy, refused the job. While she remained a powerful influence on the party, urging it to remain unified, Congress was forced to turn to a compromise leader, Rao.

Election results. After Gandhi's death, voting was delayed until June 12 and 15 in most areas. There was widespread violence surrounding the elections. Approximately 400 people were killed during the campaign and voting. Various parties used thugs to seize and stuff some ballot boxes while helpless officials looked the other way.

The elections left the Congress Party and its allies 16 seats short of a parliamentary majority, but it was the only party able to form a government. Singh's Janata Dal fell from the 144 seats it held in 1989 to 56 seats. The BJP rose from 86 seats in 1989 to 119, and many observers thought it would have done even better except for the sympathy vote for Congress that came in the wake of Gandhi's death. Rao was sworn in as prime minister on June 21.

Sonia Gandhi (in sunglasses) walks beside the funeral pyre of her husband, Rajiv Gandhi, who was assassinated during national elections in May.

Conflict in Kashmir. For the second year in a row, violence wracked the Srinagar valley region of India's mountainous northern state, Jammu and Kashmir. The valley has a Muslim majority, and militants there sought independence or union with neighboring Pakistan, a Muslim nation. Indian police and

soldiers—most of them Hindus—allegedly used indiscriminate force on occasion to counter or prevent ambushes and other forms of violence, further alienating Muslim residents. On May 8, police opened fire on mourners at a funeral held for earlier police victims, killing at least 14 people. When a sniper murdered a policeman on June 11, police killed an additional 18 people.

Punjab killings. Militants of the Sikh religion in Punjab state continued to wage a terrorist campaign for the state's independence. Terrorism in the Punjab had led to 3,787 deaths during 1990. In 1991, about 5,700 people died in the continuing troubles. Sikh terrorists reportedly killed 3,595 people, and Indian police killed 2,179 of the alleged terrorists. In September, police killed the leaders of two main terrorist groups in separate gun battles, but several other groups continued to operate. On December 26, a group of gunmen, reported to be Sikh separatists, seized a passenger train in the Punjab and shot Hindu passengers, killing 55 and wounding about 70. In the state of Assam, a separatist group called the United Liberation Front of Assam staged a kidnapping and killed three of their hostages.

India's population was estimated at 844 million people in 1991, an increase of 161 million from a decade earlier, according to a census report made public March 25. Henry S. Bradsher

See also **Asia** (Facts in brief table). In ***World Book***, see **India**.

Choctaw Indians in Mississippi campaign against a proposal, defeated in a tribal referendum in April, to permit a toxic-waste dump on tribal land.

Indian, American. Native people in the Canadian province of Ontario have an innate right to self-government "flowing from the Creator and from the First Nations' original occupation of the land," according to a historic agreement signed by Ontario officials and 12 First Nations chiefs on Aug. 6, 1991. With the signing of the accord, known as the Statement of Political Relationship, Ontario became the first government in Canada to recognize the Indians' right to govern their own affairs.

Under the terms of the pact, Ontario pledged to negotiate all issues concerning the Indians on a government-to-government basis with Indian representatives. While praising the agreement, Indian leaders also called on the government to grant them control over their own land and other resources to enable native people to become self-sufficient.

Indian population grows. The number of Americans identifying themselves as Indians rose by more than 38 per cent from 1980 to 1990, according to preliminary results from the 1990 census released in February 1991. The United States Bureau of the Census reported that 1.8 million Americans identified themselves as Native American on the 1990 census form, compared with about 1.4 million in 1980. Between 1970 and 1980, the number of people claiming identity as Indians rose by more than 70 per cent.

The Census Bureau reported that the biggest gains occurred in urban areas and in states with traditionally small Indian populations. For example, the number of Indians in Alabama soared by 117.7 per cent.

Demographers theorized that higher birth rates among Native Americans and improved counting methods by the Census Bureau accounted for part of the increase. The primary reason for the increase, census officials concluded, was that Americans who previously identified themselves as white, black, or Hispanic now say they are American Indian. Some sociologists suggested that a growing acceptance of Native American culture accounted for the shift. This acceptance has encouraged increasing numbers of people with at least some Indian ancestry to acknowledge their Native American identity.

Battlefield renamed. The Custer Battlefield National Monument in Montana, the site of a 1876 fight between Sioux and Cheyenne Indians and U.S. Army troops under the command of General George Armstrong Custer, will be renamed the Little Bighorn Battlefield National Monument under legislation passed by Congress in November. The bill also authorizes the construction of a memorial to the Indian warriors who fought and died in the battle.

Navajo inauguration. Peterson Zah was sworn in as the first elected tribal president of the Navajo Nation on Jan. 15, 1991. Zah, an education consultant and former tribal chairman, was elected to the newly created post in November 1990. Previously, the Navajo's top elected leader was the tribal chairman. The tribe reorganized its government, however, following the 1989 suspension of tribal Chairman Peter MacDonald, who was convicted of bribery, extortion, conspiracy, and ethics charges in October 1990. MacDonald, who was sentenced to nearly six years in prison for the violations, received an additional 450-day jail term in February 1991, after being convicted on other corruption charges.

Chippewa dispute settled. A bitter 17-year legal fight over Chippewa treaty rights in Wisconsin ended in May with the announcement of an accord between state officials and the leaders of six Chippewa bands. The legal battle concerned the rights of the Chippewa under treaties signed with the U.S. government in 1837 and 1842. These treaties gave the Chippewa the right to hunt, fish, and harvest timber forever on the land—roughly the northern third of Wisconsin—which the Chippewa had given to the federal government. The Chippewa's exercise of those rights, however, had triggered angry and sometimes violent protests among whites.

Under the terms of the accord, the Chippewa agreed not to appeal a federal court ruling that denied their right to seek $325 million in damages from the state for having prevented them from exercising their treaty rights. The state, in turn, agreed not to appeal a ruling affirming the Chippewa's right to 50 per cent of the "harvestable natural resources" in northern Wisconsin. Barbara A. Mayes

In ***World Book,*** see **Indian, American.**

Indiana. See **State government.**

Indonesia. Living standards for Indonesia's 186 million people continued to improve in 1991 despite inflation of more than 9 per cent and other economic problems. Industrial growth, primarily on the island of Java, led the expansion of the economy, which has grown by about 20 per cent since 1987. The portion of the population living in poverty continued to drop below the 1987 estimate of 17 per cent.

Economic growth was fueled by export industries that depended on low-wage labor. For example, women working in toy, shoe, or textile factories earned on average the United States equivalent of 58 cents a day. Work stoppages, demonstrations, and strikes for better pay and working conditions increased in 1991. Officials claimed that the average minimum wage had risen since 1989 from 37 per cent of what a single person needed to live to nearly 67 per cent, but even this minimum was not always paid.

Political developments. The government announced on September 7 that parliamentary elections would be held on June 9, 1992. The deadline for nominating candidates was Sept. 16, 1991. President Suharto deleted the names of several candidates on the list submitted by Golkar, his own ruling political organization. These were candidates who had openly criticized Suharto, who has ruled Indonesia since 1966.

Political dissidents from the Group of 50, which included former cabinet ministers and senior military leaders, were allowed to testify before parliament on July 4, 1991. Another group, the Democracy Forum, appealed to the government to loosen controls on politics and communications. The forum, composed of 45 intellectuals, was led by Abdurrahman Wahid, head of the nation's largest Muslim organization. A League for the Restoration of Democracy urged voters "to boycott the 1992 election."

Separatist rebellion. In 1991, the army reportedly brought under control a two-year rebellion in Aceh Province, located on the northern tip of Sumatra Island. Rebels in Aceh were fighting to establish an independent Islamic state. Both sides in the savage guerrilla war were blamed for human rights violations. However, foreign observers were particularly critical of the army.

Trouble in Timor. On February 27, the European Community told the United Nations Commission on Human Rights that Indonesia was guilty of torture and widespread killing in East Timor, a former Portuguese territory that Indonesia annexed in 1976.

On Nov. 12, 1991, army troops fired on mourners at Dili, the capital of East Timor, at the funeral of a youth who had been killed by security forces. Officials said about 50 people were killed in 10 minutes of firing, but local people said from 72 to 100 were killed. Later reports said 60 more youths were killed because they witnessed the massacre. The Indonesian government promised an investigation. Henry S. Bradsher

See also **Asia** (Facts in brief table). In ***World Book,*** see **Indonesia.**

International trade

International trade. World trade in 1991 expanded by less than 1 per cent and remained at about $3.3-trillion. It was the smallest increase since 1982 and reflected a sluggish world economy, turmoil in the Soviet Union, and the effects of the Persian Gulf War.

The United States substantially reduced its foreign trade deficit—the amount of imports not offset by exports—in 1991. The deficit fell from $102 billion in 1990 to about $70 billion, the lowest deficit since 1983. Exports grew by more than 5 per cent in value while imports declined slightly. The improved balance was due mainly to faster economic growth abroad than in the United States. The dollar, an important factor in world trade patterns, rose in value during the first half of 1991, then lost some of its gains in the second half.

The United States made even more progress in improving its international payments balance on current account, a broader measure of U.S. competitiveness, which includes not only merchandise trade but also service transactions, investment earnings, and government military funding. The U.S. international payments deficit, which had totaled $92 billion in 1990, was almost eliminated in 1991. About $40 billion of the improvement, however, was due to a special one-time factor—the contributions of U.S. allies to help the United States pay for the Persian Gulf War.

Japan, with the world's second largest national economy, increased its trade and payments surpluses

United States annual balance of trade in billions of dollars

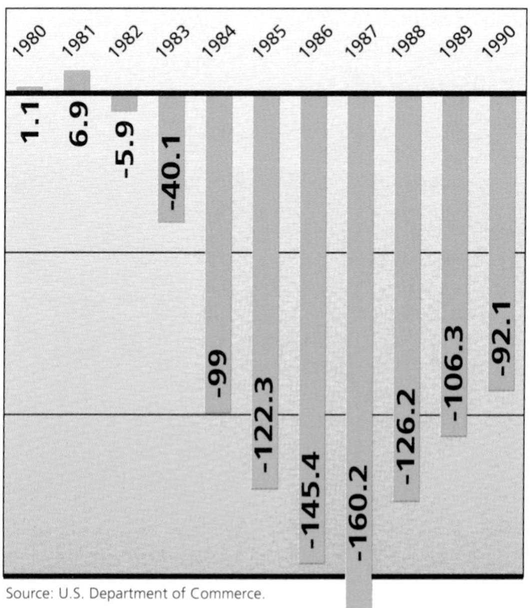

Source: U.S. Department of Commerce.

The U.S. international payments deficit improved in 1990, but the United States imported $92 billion more in goods and services than it exported.

sharply in 1991. The rising surpluses reinforced calls on Japan to open its markets wider to imports.

Japanese-U.S. trade. Friction over trade between the United States and Japan persisted in 1991. The U.S. merchandise trade deficit with Japan remained at more than $40 billion, equivalent to well over half of the total U.S. trade deficit. Several new agreements were signed to reduce the imbalance. The Japanese government pledged to give foreign—in particular, U.S.—firms greater access to Japan's construction, telecommunications, and semiconductor markets. The agreements, however, came only after threats of U.S. trade action against Japan.

GATT talks. The United States and 107 other nations remained unable to conclude comprehensive trade-liberalizing negotiations, known as the Uruguay Round, at the General Agreement on Tariffs and Trade (GATT) in Geneva, Switzerland. The negotiations, begun in 1986, were to lower both tariff and nontariff trade barriers and to improve the protection of intellectual property rights, such as patents and copyrights. By year's end, a compromise on agricultural trade, regarded as a major key to the negotiations, still eluded negotiators.

Regional trade blocs. The prospect of regional trade blocs grew. On Oct. 22, 1991, the 12-nation European Community and the 7-nation European Free Trade Association agreed in principle to integrate their economies. Under the plan, the two groups, with

Romanians line up to buy Levi's jeans, one of many Western products made available to eastern Europeans as trade increased in 1991.

a combined population of more than 380 million people, would by January 1993 dismantle all barriers between them in merchandise and services trade, capital flows, and immigration.

In February 1991, the United States, Canada, and Mexico said they would attempt to form a North American Free Trade Area, building on the existing U.S.-Canada free-trade agreement. The proposed Free Trade Area would embrace nearly 370 million people. Formal negotiations began in August.

Latin-American nations began developing free-trade agreements among themselves. Argentina, Brazil, Paraguay, and Uruguay signed a treaty to establish a common market by 1995. Bolivia, Colombia, Peru, Venezuela, and Ecuador said they would have a free-trade agreement with each other by 1992. Central American nations also began free-trade talks with Mexico and Venezuela.

U.S.-Soviet trade. The United States sought closer trade relations with the former Soviet Union in 1991. President George Bush on November 25 asked Congress to approve a U.S.-Soviet trade agreement that would reduce U.S. tariffs on Soviet goods, assure U.S. firms of Soviet business facilities, and protect U.S. copyrights. Bush signed the legislation in December, but the agreement was not in effect at the end of the year due to turmoil in the Soviet Union.

The U.S. Export-Import Bank, a federal agency, said in February that it would resume financing Soviet purchases of U.S. goods. After that, however, the Soviet Union's credit standing came into question, and by year's end the Export-Import Bank had not issued any credit guarantee covering Soviet trade. The U.S. Commodity Credit Corporation, however, allocated $3.75-billion in credit guarantees for Soviet purchases of U.S. grain and other farm commodities during 1991.

Eastern Europe. The United States announced trade concessions to help eastern European nations earn more foreign exchange. President Bush on July 12 said that the United States would relax its import quotas on eastern European steel, textiles, and dairy products. Bush also declared Czechoslovakia and Bulgaria eligible for duty-free benefits on many of their exports to the United States. On December 4, Bush signed legislation to reduce tariffs sharply on goods from the newly independent nations of Estonia, Latvia, and Lithuania.

U.S.-Chinese disputes. Trade disputes between the United States and China flared in 1991. Both the U.S. Senate and House of Representatives passed legislation to raise tariffs on Chinese goods unless China opened its markets wider to U.S. products, improved its human rights practices, and curtailed its arms shipments abroad. Congress, however, took no further action on the legislation. The Bush Administration threatened trade action against China unless China eased its import restrictions and provided greater protection for U.S. copyrights and patents. China's trade surplus with the United States rose to about $13 billion in 1991—second in size only to Japan's surplus.

South Africa ban lifted. On July 10, the United States lifted most of its economic sanctions against South Africa, after the South African government took steps to end its policies of *apartheid* (racial separation). The sanctions had included an embargo on South African uranium, coal, steel, textiles, sugar, and gold coins. The sanctions also restricted U.S. investment in South Africa. Many U.S. state and local government restrictions on doing business in South Africa remained in force, however.

Trade embargoes. The United States announced two trade embargoes in 1991. One, against Haiti, took effect on November 5 and was in response to the September 30 military overthrow of Jean-Bertrand Aristide, Haiti's first democratically elected president. On December 6, the United States announced that it would impose a trade embargo against Yugoslavia as a result of that nation's continued civil war.

Richard Lawrence

See also **Economics.** In ***World Book,*** see **International trade.**

Iowa. See **State government.**

Iran. Iran's President Ali Akbar Hashemi Rafsanjani called for increased economic and political cooperation with the West and for closer relations with Arab Muslim states in May 1991. Some Middle East analysts argued that Rafsanjani's statement indicated that Iran's moderates had outflanked the country's religious conservatives, who oppose increasing ties with the West. Iran also reportedly helped orchestrate the release of Western hostages held by terrorist groups in Lebanon (see **Middle East**). Although the United States denied any linkage to the hostage issue, U.S. officials agreed in November to pay Iran $278 million in compensation for undelivered military equipment.

During 1991, however, Iran continued to support Islamic fundamentalist groups seeking to establish Islamic states in some North African countries. Iran also was suspected of involvement in the assassinations of exiled Iranian political figures and of people considered to be enemies of Islam.

Economic woes. Iran's weakening economy was reportedly the driving force behind Rafsanjani's call for increased foreign contacts. The demonstrations and bombings that rocked several Iranian cities—including Teheran, Iran's capital—in August were also linked to discontent with worsening economic conditions. During 1991, the cost of heating and cooking fuel jumped by 150 per cent. Iran posted a $4-billion trade deficit for the fiscal year ending in March 1991, despite a record export total of $18 billion.

Iranian officials attributed the country's poor economic performance to reduced oil exports and to destruction and debt resulting from the Iran-Iraq War (1980-1988). In 1991, Iran also sheltered some 2.5 million refugees. Among these were Afghans who had fled the civil war in their country and more than 1 million Kurds who poured into Iran after Iraq suppressed a Kurdish uprising in February and March. At year-end, about 500,000 Kurds remained in Iran.

Economic measures. During 1991, Rafsanjani encouraged the sale of government-owned industries to private interests and worked to attract foreign investment. In an attempt to draw investments by Iranians who had fled the country after the 1979 revolution, Iran's central bank in May lifted travel restrictions on exiles who owed money to the bank. Previously, such exiles, many of whom had worked in banking or commerce, could have been detained on their return to Iran until they paid their debt.

The World Bank, an agency of the United Nations, approved a $250-million earthquake-recovery loan for Iran in March 1991. In 1990, a major earthquake devastated two northwestern provinces, killing an estimated 40,000 people and leaving about 500,000 people homeless. The loan was the first made to Iran by the World Bank since 1974.

Population curbs. In 1991, Iran's population continued to grow at a high rate—4 per cent in some areas. In July, the government announced that beginning in 1992, families that already had three children would not receive benefits for any additional children.

Regional relations. Saudi Arabia and Iran reestablished relations in March 1991. Saudi Arabia had broken off relations in 1988 following a dispute over the number of Iranians allowed to enter Saudi Arabia for the annual *hajj* (pilgrimage) to Mecca, Islam's holiest city. In March 1991, Iran also reopened its embassy in Amman, Jordan, closed in 1981.

Assassinations. Iran's last prime minister before the 1979 revolution, Shahpour Bakhtiar, was found murdered outside Paris in August 1991. Since 1979, some 30 Iranian political exiles have been murdered in Europe. In August and September 1991, French authorities arrested three Iranians allegedly involved in the killing. In October, a French judge issued an arrest warrant for an Iranian official accused of helping the alleged killers obtain French visas.

Violence over British author Salman Rushdie's novel *The Satanic Verses* (1988) occurred in 1991. Ayatollah Ruhollah Khomeini, the founder of the Iranian republic, had imposed the death penalty on Rushdie in 1989, decreeing the book was blasphemous to Islam. On July 3, the Italian translator of Rushdie's novel was attacked in Milan, Italy. On July 12, the book's Japanese translator was murdered in Tokyo. Rushdie remained in hiding in 1991. Christine Helms

See also **Persian Gulf,** Special Report: **War in the Persian Gulf; Middle East** (Facts in brief table). In ***World Book,*** see **Iran.**

Iran-contra affair. Two top figures who had been convicted in the Iran-contra affair, Oliver L. North and John M. Poindexter, won their legal battles in 1991. They succeeded in having all charges against them dropped. Also during the year, federal prosecutors obtained guilty pleas from former Assistant Secretary of State Elliot Abrams and a former official of the Central Intelligence Agency (CIA), Alan D. Fiers, Jr. Two other former CIA officials, Duane R. Clarridge and Clair E. George, were indicted for their alleged participation in the Iran-contra scheme. The operation involved the undercover sale of arms to Iran in 1985 and 1986 during the Administration of President Ronald Reagan and the diversion of profits from those sales to *contra* rebels in Nicaragua.

North convictions thrown out. On Sept. 16, 1991, a federal judge in Washington, D.C., dismissed the charges against North, a former Marine lieutenant colonel and member of the National Security Council (NSC) in the Reagan Administration. North had been convicted in 1990 on three felony counts, including destroying documents.

The federal judge threw out the convictions on the grounds that the Iran-contra independent prosecutor, Lawrence E. Walsh, could not prove that the witnesses who testified against North had not been influenced by North's own testimony at the congressional Iran-contra hearings in 1987. North appeared at those hearings under a grant of immunity, meaning that any incriminating information he presented could not be used against him in court.

Poindexter wins on appeal. The same line of reasoning was used in Poindexter's appeal. In 1990, Poindexter, a retired Navy rear admiral who had served as Reagan's national security adviser, was convicted on five counts of obstruction of justice and lying to Congress. On Nov. 15, 1991, however, the federal appeals court in Washington, D.C., overturned the convictions, ruling that Poindexter's testimony at the 1987 hearings had been unfairly used against him at his trial. Poindexter was the highest-ranking member of the Reagan Administration to have been implicated in the Iran-contra affair.

Guilty pleas. On Oct. 7, 1991, Abrams pleaded guilty to two counts of withholding information from Congress. On November 15, he was sentenced to two years' probation and 100 hours of community service.

Fiers, who had been head of the CIA's Central American Task Force, pleaded guilty on July 9, also to two counts of withholding information from Congress. At year-end, he had not yet been sentenced.

New indictments. George, who was the former head of CIA undercover operations, was indicted on September 6 on 10 counts, including perjury and obstruction of investigations. On November 26, Clarridge, who had directed the CIA's secret operations in Europe, was indicted for perjury and for making false statements about a missile shipment that had been sent to Iran. David L. Dreier

Iraq. An international military coalition, led by the United States, launched a massive bombing campaign against Iraq on Jan. 17, 1991. The attack began less than 17 hours after Iraq's President Saddam Hussein failed to meet a United Nations (UN) deadline for withdrawing his military forces from Kuwait, which Iraq had invaded in August 1990. On Feb. 24, 1991, the United States-led coalition opened a ground war against Iraq. During the fighting, which ended on February 26, an estimated 110,000 Iraqi soldiers and tens of thousands of Iraqi civilians died. According to a UN report released on March 21, Iraq's public works, such as roads and bridges, were bombed into a "pre-industrial" age. See **Persian Gulf,** Special Report: **War in the Persian Gulf.**

Cease-fire terms. The UN approved a permanent cease-fire resolution on April 3. Under the terms of this agreement, Iraq renounced its annexation of Kuwait and released all its prisoners of war. The cease-fire also required Iraq to return all property looted from Kuwait, pay war reparations, and permit the destruction of any nuclear, biological, and chemical weapons as well as any ballistic missiles with a range greater than 90 miles (145 kilometers).

According to the cease-fire, any sales of Iraqi oil were to be conducted under UN supervision, and revenues from the sales were to be used for food and medical supplies. A percentage of the profits from any sales (later set at 30 per cent) were to go for war repa-

A supporter of Iraq's President Saddam Hussein holds up a photograph of the Iraqi leader during a pro-government rally in September.

Iraqi soldiers, carrying white flags and a copy of the Koran, surrender to troops from the United States-led coalition in Kuwait on February 25.

rations. Iraq protested that the provisions of the agreement infringed on its independence.

Postwar uprisings by Shiite Muslims in southern Iraq and by Kurds in northern Iraq in March claimed at least 25,000 lives. Iran lent support to the Shiite Muslim rebels. In addition, defecting Iraqi Army units added to the chaos. The Iraqi Army responded forcefully to the uprisings, heavily damaging holy sites in al-Najaf and Karbala, where rebels had taken refuge.

An international crisis arose when more than 500,000 Kurds fled to Turkey to escape the army. Another 1 million Kurds escaped to Iran. Some 6,700 refugees, mainly children, died in camps along the Turkish-Iraqi border in April and May because of bad weather and poor sanitation. The Kurds accused the United States of encouraging them to rebel and then refusing to support their rebellion.

In mid-April, U.S., French, and British troops established a protected zone for the Kurds in northern Iraq. Most of the refugees had returned to their homes by late May. Coalition forces pulled out of the protected zone in July, leaving behind some 500 UN guards.

Sporadic fighting continued, however, between Iraqi forces and Kurdish rebels. The most serious flare-up occurred in October near Irbil and Sulaimaniya, where Kurdish rebels killed 60 unarmed Iraqi soldiers on October 8. About 50,000 Kurds fled the fighting

there. At year-end, about 500,000 Kurdish refugees remained in Iran.

Kurdish talks. On April 24, Kurdish rebel leaders reported that they and Hussein had agreed in principle to a pact granting greater independence to Iraq's 3.5 million Kurds. The leaders of other Iraqi opposition groups strongly criticized the Kurds for negotiating separately with Hussein. On June 23, Massoud Barzani, the leader of the Kurdish Democratic Party, announced that Hussein had agreed to enact democratic reforms in Iraq and to permit the Kurds to elect their own provincial legislature. But other Kurdish leaders rejected the pact, refusing to sever ties with the West or to abandon their goal of an independent Kurdish state, as Iraq had demanded.

Catastrophic conditions emerged in Iraq during 1991 because of shortages of food and medical supplies and poor sanitation. In May, a team from the Harvard School of Public Health in Cambridge, Mass., predicted that a lack of food and medical care could double the number of Iraqi children under age 5 expected to die in 1991. A July study by the UN's Food and Agriculture Organization also forecast widespread famine and malnutrition.

On August 15, the UN Security Council voted to temporarily lift the trade embargo against Iraq, imposed in August 1990, to permit a one-time sale of oil valued at $1.6 billion for the purchase of food and medical supplies. Iraq, however, refused the offer, contending that UN supervision of the sale and control over the revenues violated its independence.

Consolidating power. While promising political reform, Hussein consolidated his power by frequently shifting cabinet appointments and naming his relatives to key military and intelligence posts. In March 1991, Hussein relinquished the post of prime minister and appointed Sa'doun Hammadi, a Shiite, to the position. In September, however, Hussein fired Hammadi. Also that month, the ruling Baath Party announced that other political parties would be permitted to form only if they were not based on atheism, religion, race, or ethnicity. Christine Helms

See also **Middle East** (Facts in brief table). In the World Book Supplement section, see **Iraq.**

Ireland. The political future of Ireland's Prime Minister Charles J. Haughey seemed uncertain in 1991. The possibility arose that he would be replaced as leader of the Fianna Fáil (Soldiers of Destiny) party, which he has led since 1979. In local elections held on June 27, 1991, Haughey's Fianna Fáil party lost 79 seats and control of the government. Support for the party fell to a 22-year low. Haughey had to form a coalition government with the Progressive Democrats.

Opinion polls taken in autumn of 1991 showed that two-thirds of the voters wanted Haughey to resign. He narrowly beat off a parliamentary vote of no-confidence on October 18, after striking a last-minute deal with the Progressive Democrats over tax reform.

Haughey registered some economic successes in 1991. His economic policies cut inflation in 1991, improved the nation's balance of payments, and reduced levels of government borrowing. But unemployment rose to 20 per cent of the work force. Emigration also continued to rise. In the late 1980's, about 40,000 people were leaving Ireland each year, going mainly to Great Britain, Canada, or the United States. However, there were limited options for stemming emigration because efforts to create more jobs in the public sector would likely cause the national debt to rise even higher.

Business scandals were the most threatening issues to Haughey's government in 1991, though no one suggested he was involved in any of them. Newspapers reported in 1991 that the directors of a state-owned sugar company had used insider information to make 8 million pounds ($10 million U.S.) in profit from company stock transactions before the company was partly privatized in 1990. The directors also reportedly set up large pensions for themselves.

Another scandal, reported in 1991, involved Michael Smurfitt, the chairman of Telecom Eireann, the state telephone company. He bought shares in a company six months before the company made 1.9 million pounds ($5 million U.S.) in profit from the sale of a site for a new Telecom headquarters. On September 24, Telecom's chairman resigned. Haughey ordered a full inquiry into both affairs.

Strained relations developed in 1991 between Haughey and Ireland's first woman president, Mary Robinson, who had been elected in November 1990. Haughey reportedly became jealous of the favorable publicity Robinson received during her frequent public appearances. She won the approval of 85 per cent of the people, according to polls taken in 1991.

Haughey wrote a letter to Robinson in April that was made public. In it, he said that it was constitutional practice for the president to obtain permission from the prime minister before addressing the nation and giving interviews. Robinson chose to ignore the letter.

Ian J. Mather

See also **Northern Ireland.** In ***World Book,*** see **Ireland.**

Irons, Jeremy (1948-), received the Academy of Motion Picture Arts and Sciences Award for best actor in 1991. Irons won the Oscar for his performance as a socialite tried for the attempted murder of his wife in *Reversal of Fortune* (1990).

Jeremy John Irons was born on Sept. 19, 1948, on the Isle of Wight, an island off the southern coast of England. After graduating from secondary school, Irons moved to London, where he took a job as a social worker. Attracted by performing, however, he found work at a theater in Canterbury, England. After attending a theater school for two years, Irons joined the Bristol Old Vic, a repertory company in Bristol, England.

Irons made his London theater debut in 1971 in the rock musical *Godspell.* His work in such stage productions as *Diary of a Madman, Wild Oats,* and *The Rear Column* earned him critical praise.

Irons gained an international reputation in the early 1980's with the release of the movie *The French Lieutenant's Woman* (1981) and the 1982 broadcast in the United States of the television series "Brideshead Revisited." His other motion-picture credits include *Moonlighting* (1982), *Betrayal* (1983), and *Dead Ringers* (1988). Irons made his Broadway debut in 1984 in *The Real Thing,* for which he received an Antoinette Perry (Tony) award for best actor.

Irons married his second wife, actress Sinead Cusack, in 1978. They have two sons. Barbara A. Mayes

Islam proved to be an important factor during the Persian Gulf crisis of 1990-1991 and in the politics of several Muslim countries in 1991. Saudi Arabia and Egypt's leading religious leaders cited Islamic law to justify the presence of foreign, non-Muslim troops in Saudi Arabia, the home of Islam's holy sites and cities, Mecca and Medina. At the same time, Iran's supreme religious leader, Ayatollah Ali Hoseini Khamenei, and Jordanian religious leaders called for a *jihad* (struggle) against foreign intervention.

Support for Saddam. Although Iraq's President Saddam Hussein failed to win support from most Arab political and Muslim leaders during the Persian Gulf crisis, he enjoyed an enormous degree of popular support. Hussein exploited deep-seated political and social issues: the plight of the Palestinians; the failure of Arab governments and societies to deal with poverty, corruption, and the unequal distribution of wealth; and foreign intervention in the Arab world. Hussein sought Islamic support to enhance his image as the champion of the poor and oppressed and to call for a holy war against the United States and those Arab regimes that opposed him.

The sentiment of ordinary citizens in Islamic countries that sent forces to support the United States-led coalition against Iraq often differed from that of their governments. Pro-Hussein and anti-American demonstrations and protest marches occurred in most Islamic nations, even in South Africa's Muslim community. See **Persian Gulf,** Special Report: **War in the Persian Gulf.**

Islam and political liberalization. The Gulf war in 1991 allowed certain Arab governments to slow down or thwart a movement calling for greater political liberalization and democratization. This movement included Islamic organizations and leaders. The governments of Algeria and Tunisia clashed with Islamic movements during 1991. In Algeria, the government canceled scheduled elections in June. In early July, key leaders and more than 3,000 members of Algeria's Islamic Salvation Front (FIS), which had achieved a stunning victory in municipal elections in 1990, were arrested after street battles between police and FIS members. New elections were held on Dec. 24, 1991, and the FIS won 44 per cent of the seats in parliament. The FIS hoped to win a majority in parliament after runoff elections to decide contested seats, which were scheduled for Jan. 16, 1992.

Tunisian President Zine El-Abidine Ben Ali, nervous about the strong performance of Muslim candidates in Tunisia's national elections and the electoral victory of the FIS in neighboring Algeria in 1990, cracked down on the Renaissance Party (formerly the Islamic Tendency Movement). Armed conflict escalated between the government and Muslim activists in May and June 1991, and Ben Ali claimed to have uncovered a fundamentalist plot to overthrow the government of Tunisia.

John L. Esposito

In ***World Book,*** see **Islam.**

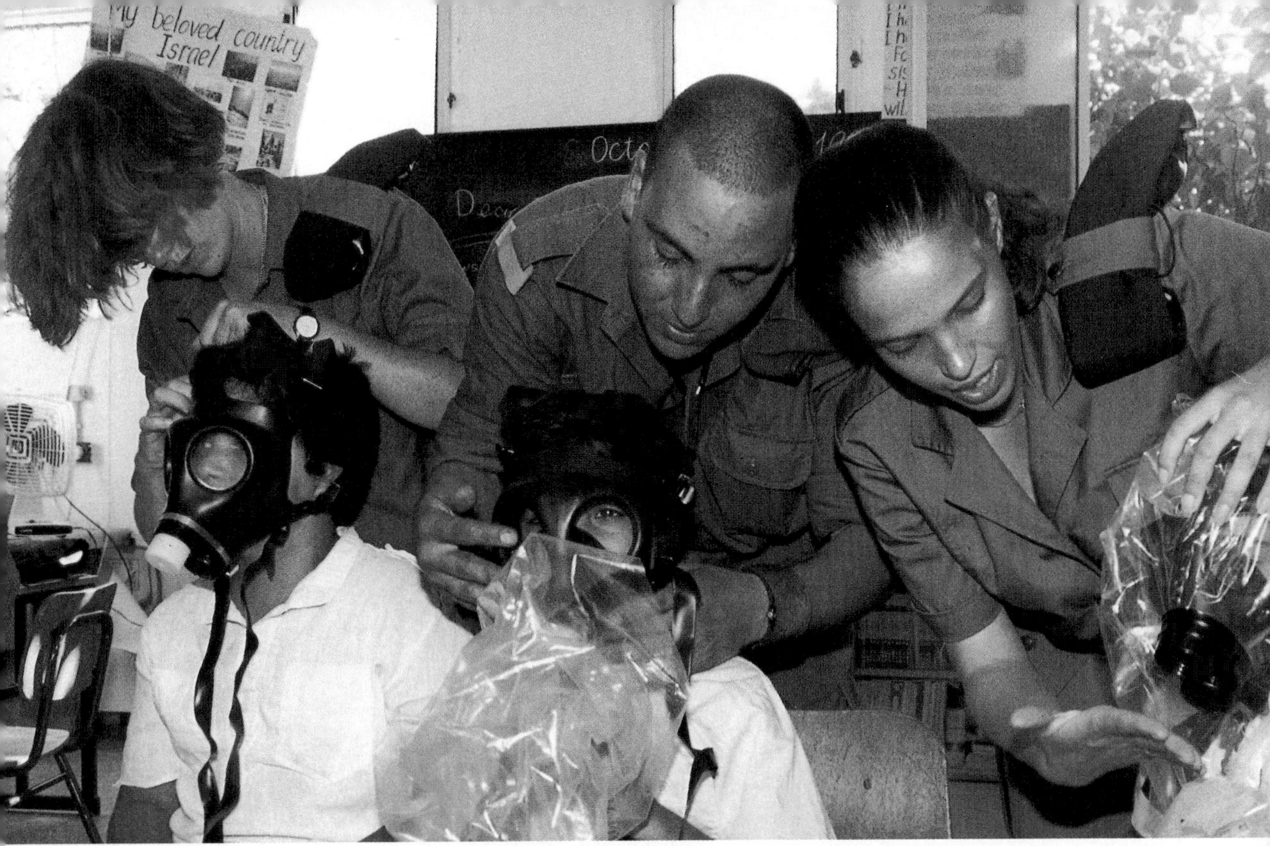

Israeli soldiers fit children with gas masks in preparation for a possible chemical-weapons attack by Iraq during the Persian Gulf War.

Israel. Iraq launched 39 surface-to-surface missiles at Israel in February 1991 during the Persian Gulf War, killing 4 people and injuring 300 others. Despite intense public outrage, Israel's Prime Minister Yitzhak Shamir did not order a military counterattack against Iraq. Iraq's President Saddam Hussein apparently hoped that Israeli retaliation would drive Syria, Egypt, and other Arab states that oppose Israel's control of the occupied territories from the United States-led coalition to expel Iraqi forces from Kuwait.

Immigration. An estimated 175,000 Jewish immigrants, most of them from the Soviet Union, arrived in Israel in 1991, 25,000 fewer than had arrived during 1990, according to the U.S. State Department. Many of the immigrants were professionals who had difficulty finding jobs in Israel's tight labor market. Housing also remained short.

An estimated 14,500 Ethiopian Jews were airlifted to Israel on May 24 and 25, 1991, during a daring evacuation as Ethiopia's government fell to a rebel force. At one point in the operation, 28 planes were in the air at once. The new arrivals joined 12,000 Ethiopian Jews who had immigrated to Israel since 1984.

Settlements. In late March 1991, the U.S. Department of State reported that the Jewish population in the occupied West Bank and Gaza Strip and in the Golan Heights and East Jerusalem had grown by 10 per cent since 1990. In total, some 200,000 Jewish settlers in 200 communities made up 13 per cent of the population of the occupied territories. In March 1991, the Israeli government began to confiscate or bulldoze Arab-owned agricultural land on the West Bank if the Arab families living on the land were unable to prove that they had farmed there for 10 successive years. Israel's continuing settlement of the occupied territories suggested to some Middle East analysts that Israel's foreign policy was being driven as much by economic and immigration pressures as by worries about national security.

U.S. and Soviet relations. Many people in Israel and the United States expected that Israel's restraint during the Persian Gulf War would earn that country additional good will in the United States. In March, the United States provided $650 million in cash to help offset Israel's increased military and civil defense expenses during the Persian Gulf War.

Relations between Israel and the U.S. government grew increasingly strained, however, as Israel accelerated its settlement of the occupied territories and as the two nations disagreed over conditions for holding a Mideast peace conference. In September, Shamir bitterly criticized U.S. President George Bush for asking the U.S. Congress to delay for 120 days Israel's request for early payment of $10 billion in U.S. loan guarantees. The loans were to be used to fund housing construction for Soviet immigrants. The Senate agreed to the delay on October 2. Bush's action was reportedly aimed at encouraging Israeli participation in a Middle

Ethiopians crowd one of 35 aircraft on which an estimated 14,500 Ethiopian Jews were evacuated to Israel within 36 hours on May 24 and 25.

East peace conference. The historic peace conference opened on October 30. See **Middle East.**

Israel and the Soviet Union renewed diplomatic relations on October 18. This was considered a necessary prelude to Soviet co-sponsorship of Arab-Israeli peace negotiations. Relations between the Soviet Union and Israel had been broken after the 1967 Six-Day War.

Violence. Arab attacks on Israelis immediately after the Persian Gulf War claimed at least seven Israeli lives. On October 29, Arab gunmen killed two adults and wounded five children during an assault on a busload of Jewish settlers headed for a rally in Tel Aviv.

There were increasingly violent attacks by Arabs against Arabs in 1991 as a result of the Palestinian uprising. During April and May, 45 Palestinians were killed by other Arabs, 27 more than were killed by the Israeli Army during the same period. Although some of the dead had been accused of collaborating with the Israelis, others reportedly were victims of an increasingly fierce rivalry between the Palestine Liberation Organization (PLO) and Hamas, an Islamic political movement.

Palestinian policy. On Jan. 15, 1991, the Israeli government imposed a strict curfew on all Arab residents of the occupied territories. Palestinians living there were forbidden to leave their homes except to buy food during certain hours. Israeli authorities said

the action was necessary to prevent the Palestinians from rioting in support of Iraq. The curfew was lifted in March.

That month, Israel's Cabinet, angered by Palestinian support of Iraq during the Persian Gulf crisis and attacks on Israelis after the war, voted to continue restrictions on Palestinians. The restrictions limited to 50,000 the number of Palestinians permitted to commute to work in Israel from the occupied territories. This figure was less than half the number allowed before the Persian Gulf War.

In April, Israel released 1,000 of its Palestinian prisoners and announced a tax-incentive program to encourage economic development in the Gaza Strip. On April 30, Israeli authorities reopened Hebron University on the West Bank. The university had been closed since early 1988.

Prisoner release. In September 1991, Israel said it would consider freeing some of its estimated 375 Muslim Shiite prisoners to help secure the release of Western hostages held in Lebanon if it obtained credible information about 7 Israeli soldiers missing in Lebanon. Israel released 51 prisoners on September 11 after receiving accounts of 2 soldiers. On September 12, a Palestinian activist expelled from the West Bank in 1986 was allowed to return in exchange for the body of an Israeli soldier missing since 1983.

Other news. Violent clashes near the Al Aksa Mosque in Jerusalem in October 1990 that resulted in at least 17 Palestinian deaths were triggered by police carelessness, an investigating Israeli judge reported on July 18, 1991. The findings contradicted a 1990 government report which asserted that Palestinians had started the riot. The judge reported that the unrest began when Israeli police accidentally dropped a canister of tear gas that then exploded.

Brigadier General Rami Dotan, the former chief purchasing officer for Israel's air force, pleaded guilty in March 1991 to charges that from 1985 to 1988 he had accepted more than $10 million in illegal payments from U.S. defense contractors. Dotan was sentenced to 13 years in prison. Christine Helms

See **Middle East** (Facts in brief table). In ***World Book,*** see **Israel.**

Italy in 1991 struggled to contend with organized crime and a disorganized government. In addition, a huge influx of poverty-stricken refugees arrived from nearby Albania, Europe's poorest nation.

The war against the Mafia languished because of lax Italian courts and the government's inability to adopt a coherent anticrime policy. The number of people arrested for crimes fell, even though the number of financial, drug-related, and violent crimes continued to climb, particularly in southern Italy where the Mafia is reportedly strongest. Many of those arrested stayed in jail only a short time. For example, Michele Greco, a reputed Mafia boss, was released and then rearrested during the year by judges who could not agree on whether prosecutors had presented enough evidence to charge him with a crime.

Italy's 50th postwar government. Prime Minister Giulio Andreotti, a leader of the Christian Democratic Party, resigned on March 29, after the Socialist Party pulled out of his five-party governing coalition. Italian President Francesco Cossiga asked him to put together a new coalition. On April 11, Andreotti announced the formation of a new government, Italy's 50th since World War II ended in 1945.

Six days later, one member of the coalition, the small Republican Party, withdrew its support, unhappy over the Cabinet assignments the party had received. But Andreotti quickly reached an agreement with the three other coalition members, the Socialist Party, So-

Hundreds of boats clog the Grand Canal in Venice, Italy, in June, as their owners protest a proposed increase in the yearly tax on boats.

cial Democratic Party, and Liberal Party. In August 1991, he won agreement from them not to bring down the government before parliamentary elections scheduled for May 1992.

Election reform. On June 9 and 10, 1991, Italian voters took a first step toward reforming the country's voting system. In a nationwide referendum, 95.6 per cent of those voting approved a proposal to simplify the complex proportional voting system, which in the past had been open to widespread vote fraud. Many Italians believed that the voting procedure weakened the political system by enabling many small political parties to flourish, thus leading to unwieldy coalition governments. Limiting the number of small political parties able to win seats in Parliament was expected to make it easier for the larger parties to either win majority control or to form more stable coalitions.

The Italian economy suffered from a worldwide recession and from a slowdown in tourism following the Persian Gulf War. Political bickering within the government left it unable to do much about Italy's huge budget deficit and other economic problems. The inflation rate of 6.5 per cent was higher than that of most of Italy's partners in the 12-nation European Community (EC or Common Market). Unemployment also remained high, above 11 per cent during 1991. Government efforts to sell some of Italy's many state-owned companies got off to a slow start.

Many Italian business people feared that without widespread privatization and big cuts in government spending Italy would be unprepared for the increased economic integration of EC nations. They worried especially about the ability of Italian businesses to compete following the removal of most EC trade barriers by the end of 1992. Even so, Italy remained solidly behind EC efforts to create a common economic policy.

Communists renamed. Reflecting the decline of Communism in eastern Europe and the Soviet Union, Italy's once-powerful Italian Communist Party in February 1991 renamed itself the Democratic Party of the Left. The party's leader, Achille Occhetto, hoped to replace the current government coalition with a new coalition of left-leaning parties after the 1992 parliamentary elections.

Albanian refugees. More than 20,000 Albanians fleeing hunger and poverty in their country crossed the Adriatic Sea and poured into Italy in March 1991. Italy's slow and disorganized response to the refugees provoked an international outcry. As food shortages worsened in Albania, another wave of refugees arrived in August. By then, the Italian government had mounted a determined effort to repel or send home most of the new arrivals. By year's end, nearly 12,000 Albanians had gone back. Philip Revzin

See also **Europe** (Facts in brief table), Special Report: **The Rocky Road to European Unity.** In ***World Book,*** see **Italy.**

Ivory Coast. See **Africa.**

Jamaica. See **West Indies.**

Japan. Leaders of the ruling Liberal-Democratic Party (LDP) forced Toshiki Kaifu from the prime minister's job despite polls showing that between 55 and 65 per cent of the public supported him. Kiichi Miyazawa became prime minister on Nov. 5, 1991. See **Miyazawa, Kiichi.**

Kaifu had become prime minister in 1989 as a result of a financial scandal, in which numerous politicians were found to have accepted improper payments from the Recruit Company in exchange for political favors. Kaifu was chosen by scandal-tainted LDP leaders, who reportedly saw him as a clean, previously unimportant politician whom they could control while awaiting chances to regain office. During 1990, Kaifu consolidated his position by building up his personal popularity. Throughout Japan, however, he was often seen as carrying out the orders of political bosses who controlled the Diet, Japan's parliament.

During 1991, controversies surrounding the Persian Gulf War and political reform damaged Kaifu's position with the political power brokers, who became determined not to renew his two-year term as party president when it expired October 30. The LDP's parliamentary majority meant that the party's president automatically became prime minister.

Gulf War problems. The Iraqi invasion of Kuwait posed a number of problems for Kaifu. At first, some critics at home and abroad said he was too slow to condemn the August 1990 invasion. Then, in late

Kiichi Miyazawa's honeymoon as Japan's new prime minister in 1991 was over quickly, as trade and other disputes took center stage.

Antinuclear activists in Japan stage demonstrations following a nuclear accident in February at a power plant in Mihama, west of Tokyo.

1990, Kaifu tried unsuccessfully to get opposition parties in Japan's parliament to approve the participation of Japanese troops in a United Nations peacekeeping force in the gulf. Japan finally offered $13 billion to help pay coalition costs, but it would not allow its self-defense forces to take part. These policies were seen in the West and the Arab world as inadequate for a wealthy country dependent upon the Persian Gulf region for more than 70 per cent of its oil. As a result, Kaifu was criticized at home as an ineffective leader.

Kaifu continued in 1991 to seek a parliamentary consensus permitting troops to go abroad for peacekeeping actions. In the past, Japan's Constitution had been interpreted as restricting its soldiers to defending Japan. Although LDP leaders increasingly argued that this limited Japan's role too much in a changing world, the two main opposition parties resisted any change. Parliament adjourned in autumn 1991 without passing a bill that would allow troops to join future UN peacekeeping and disaster relief operations. This was seen as another setback for Kaifu.

Political reforms. Kaifu tried to use his popularity to push through political reforms. His proposals included tighter controls on political donations and redrawing electoral districts for the first time since 1947, a plan that would have changed the pattern of representation in the Diet. The plan was designed to replace constituencies that each elected several Diet members with a system consisting of single-member constituencies.

The executive council of the LDP adopted the plan in June 1991, but party leaders who headed different factions allegedly began to fear it might weaken their power, and opposition parties said it would benefit the LDP. The Diet on September 30 dropped legislation to enact the plan.

Kaifu dropped. Kaifu reacted angrily to the decision by LDP leaders to kill the reforms, hinting that he might dissolve parliament and call a general election on the issue of electoral reform. But on October 1, Kaifu told his Cabinet that all he wanted was to keep reform on the agenda. On October 3, Shin Kanemaru, the leader of the LDP faction that had put Kaifu in power, criticized Kaifu for his failure to carry through on calling an election. The next day, other LDP leaders withdrew their support, forcing Kaifu to abandon hopes of being elected to another term as LDP president and thus remain prime minister. On October 4, Kaifu announced he would not seek reelection.

Miyazawa chosen. Several party leaders who had been tainted by the 1989 financial scandal sought to succeed Kaifu. Kanemaru had been grooming Ichiro Ozawa to become prime minister. Until April 8, Ozawa had been the LDP secretary general, a role in which he acquired a reputation for bullying and high-handedness. He then resigned the party post to accept blame for the defeat on April 7 of the LDP candidate for governor of Tokyo. Soon after resigning, Ozawa suffered a heart attack. When Kaifu was forced out, Kanemaru turned to Ozawa, but he refused to run because of his health.

Kanemaru and former prime minister Noboru Takeshita then interviewed other leaders who wanted to be prime minister. They chose Miyazawa, who led his own small faction of LDP members of the Diet. When another faction endorsed Miyazawa for prime minister, his victory was assured.

Election results. LDP candidates won in 10 of 13 elections for regional governors on April 7, and its candidates for local assemblies won 57 per cent of the seats. But in the race for governor of Tokyo, the LDP suffered an embarrassing defeat. The 80-year-old incumbent, Shunichi Suzuki, was opposed by an LDP candidate—a former television newscaster—who was strongly backed by Ozawa. Suzuki's strong victory reflected voter rejection of Ozawa's maneuvering.

Opposition parties also encountered problems in 1991. The first woman to head a major Japanese political party, Takako Doi, announced on June 21 that she would resign as chairman of the Social Democratic Party, formerly called the Socialist Party. She had led the Socialists to large gains in elections in 1989 for the Diet's upper house and in 1990 for the lower house.

These victories had led to talk that the Social Democratic Party might emerge as the leader of a coalition that would offer an alternative to LDP rule. But Doi was unable to budge her party from opposition to Japan's alliance with the United States and to an expanded role for the self-defense forces. This prevented the Socialists from forming alliances with other parties. Then Doi's party was crushed in the April 7 local elections, losing more than 20 per cent of the seats it had formerly held. Doi was succeeded as Socialist leader by Makoto Tanabe.

Scandals rocked the Tokyo financial world in 1991. Seventeen securities firms admitted making illegal payments worth $1.2 billion to favored clients to cover losses in stock market crashes in 1987 and 1990. Some of the clients were reported to be gangsters.

At the same time, the world's largest securities firm, Nomura Securities Company, was accused of inflating the value of stock in Tokyu Corporation, a railroad company, for the benefit of the former head of an organized crime syndicate. Big banks also admitted making some $5 billion worth of bad loans backed by phony collateral.

As public anger about these improprieties grew and international bankers worried about the soundness of Tokyo financial institutions, Finance Minister Ryutaro Hashimoto announced on October 3 that he would resign. But some Japanese commentators said his resignation should not hide the need for basic reform of the country's financial system, which lacks many of the official regulations that exist in Western countries. Kaifu advocated a watchdog body similar to the U.S. Securities and Exchange Commission.

Foreign relations. U.S. President George Bush met with Kaifu several times in 1991. Despite discussions about how to resolve trade disputes, Japan's trade surplus with the United States caused tensions as it rose again in 1991 after declining for several years. Controversy also surrounded Japan's refusal to allow the importation of U.S. rice.

From April 16 to 19, Soviet President Mikhail S. Gorbachev made the first visit by a Soviet leader to Japan. His talks with Kaifu focused on Japanese demands for the return of the southernmost Kuril Islands seized by the Soviet Union at the end of World War II (1939-1945). No conclusion was reached. This discouraged Japan from providing sizeable aid and investment, which Gorbachev sought. However, on October 8, as the Soviet economy worsened in the wake of the collapse of the Communist Party, the Japanese government announced $500 million in loans for food and medicine and $200 million in other loans.

In a speech in Singapore on May 3, Kaifu expressed "our sincere contrition" for Japanese atrocities during World War II. Nevertheless, conservatives in the Diet prevented passage on December 6—the eve of Japan's attack on Pearl Harbor—of a resolution apologizing for wartime actions.

Volcano and storm damage. In June, volcanic Mount Unzen erupted on the island of Kyushu, killing 38 people. On September 27 and 28, the worst typhoon to hit Japan since 1961 killed more than 45 people. Henry S. Bradsher

See also **Asia** (Facts in brief table). In ***World Book,*** see **Japan.**

U.S. Secretary of State James A. Baker III, left, crosses from Jordan to Israel in May while attempting to organize a Middle East peace conference.

Johnston, Rita (1935-), became the first woman premier in Canada on April 2, 1991. British Columbia's Social Credit Party selected Johnston to serve as the interim premier after a government report said that Premier William N. Vander Zalm had violated conflict-of-interest guidelines. But Johnston's term was short-lived. She had long been politically aligned with Vander Zalm, and though she vowed to demand the highest ethical behavior from her peers, British Columbia's electorate voted her out of office in October.

Johnston was active in the business community before entering politics. She and her husband owned a trailer park, and she managed a finance company.

Johnston began her political career in 1970 when she became alderman for the district municipality of Surrey, B.C. In 1983, she was elected to British Columbia's Legislative Assembly. Shortly thereafter she was appointed parliamentary secretary to the minister of energy, mines, and petroleum resources. She was named minister of municipal affairs and transit in 1986 and two years later was also given jurisdiction over recreation and culture. In 1989, Johnston was appointed British Columbia's minister of transportation and highways and in 1990 was named deputy premier of the province.

Johnston was born to John and Annie Leichert in Melville, Sask., on April 22, 1935. She has been married to George Johnston for 40 years, and they have three children and six grandchildren. Lori Fagan

Jordan. King Hussein I worked during 1991 to repair Jordan's relations with Western countries and with some Persian Gulf states angered by Jordan's pro-Iraq tilt during the Persian Gulf crisis. In doing so, Hussein risked eroding his support among his subjects, whose anti-Western feelings remained strong. In July, he agreed to attend a Middle East peace conference. He argued that refusing to attend the talks, which opened on October 30, would increase Jordan's political and economic isolation. See **Middle East.**

Economic woes. Jordan's economy, heavily dependent on trade with Iraq, was severely damaged by a United Nations (UN) trade embargo imposed on Iraq in August 1990 and by the destruction of Iraq's economy during the 1991 Persian Gulf War. Jordan's *gross national product* (the value of all goods and services produced) fell by about 8 to 12 per cent. Tourism ceased. The number of unemployed, boosted by the 250,000 to 400,000 Jordanian workers who had fled Iraq and Kuwait in 1990, stabilized at about 30 per cent. In 1991, Jordan halted payments on its $8-billion foreign debt as it accrued a monthly deficit of $70 million. Jordan also suffered a fuel shortage. Before the UN sanctions, Iraq had supplied more than 80 per cent of Jordan's energy needs.

U.S. relations. The deaths in January and February of eight Jordanian tanker drivers killed in allied air attacks while transporting Iraqi gasoline to Jordan in apparent violation of the UN embargo aroused a public furor. On February 6, King Hussein denounced the U.S.-led coalition's "savage" war against Iraq as an attempt to assert foreign control over the Middle East.

Angered by Hussein's fiery speech, U.S. President George Bush on February 7 ordered a reappraisal of U.S. aid to Jordan. In March, the U.S. Congress voted to cut $30 million in economic aid and $20 million in military assistance to Jordan. The action authorized Bush to restore the funding if such a move would promote peace in the Mideast. In July, after Jordan agreed to attend the peace conference, the Bush Administration released Jordan's economic aid, then restored military assistance on October 30.

Political changes. Political reforms begun by King Hussein in 1989 continued in 1991. In June, Hussein lifted a ban on political parties that had been in force since 1957. But the government also banned some public demonstrations and publications.

The government also acted to reduce the influence of Jordan's Islamic fundamentalists. In several cabinet reshufflings, fundamentalist ministers opposed to peace negotiations with Israel resigned or were fired. In addition, the government delayed until December the opening of the National Assembly, Jordan's legislature, in which fundamentalists hold the largest bloc of seats. Christine Helms

See also **Middle East** (Facts in brief table); **Persian Gulf,** Special Report: **War in the Persian Gulf.** In ***World Book,*** see **Jordan.**

Judaism. Most of the world's Jews focused their attention on rapidly changing developments in the Soviet Union in 1991 and how those developments would impact on the Jewish community there. The policies of *glasnost* (openness) and *perestroika* (restructuring) renewed and revitalized Jewish religious and cultural life in the former Soviet Union, and these policies also made possible continued Jewish emigration. In 1991, an estimated 142,000 Jews had immigrated to Israel, and thousands were still waiting to leave. Emigration slowed after July 1, but Jewish leaders said that could have been due to uneasiness among potential emigrants brought on by the Persian Gulf War or an economic downturn in Israel.

New religious freedom in the former Soviet Union also meant that many of the more than 2 million Jews remaining there began in 1991 to rebuild Jewish life. In major cities, Orthodox rabbis from Israel and the United States developed new religious and educational programs at historic synagogues. Classes for children and adults were instituted, offering religious education to hundreds of Jews who had never studied their tradition.

Judaism's liberal Reform branch also expanded its outreach to Jews in what had been the Soviet Union during 1991. The first liberal Jewish congregation in the republic of Russia, Congregation Hineni of Moscow, organized in 1989, had grown to more than 1,000 members by the end of 1991. The congregation acquired a building from the Moscow City Council and began converting it to a synagogue.

A symbol of the new visibility of Jewish life in Russia appeared on December 1 when a large menorah was constructed outside the Russian Parliament building in Moscow. The nine-branched candlestick is used for celebrating Hanukkah, the Feast of Lights. The Hanukkah celebration was the first public observance of a Jewish religious ceremony in Russia since 1917.

Most Jews were against the hard-line Communist coup that tried to oust Soviet President Mikhail S. Gorbachev on August 19. One of three citizens slain at the barricades while defending the Russian Parliament on August 20 was a Jewish architect, Ilya Krichevski. Many Soviet Jews hoped that the architect's heroic death would help counter rising anti-Semitism.

Talmud translation. Rabbi Adin Steinsaltz completed publication of the first seven volumes of his new translation of the Talmud in 1991. The Talmud is the ancient foundation of Jewish belief and practice. Steinsaltz teaches at his own academy in Jerusalem, where he also lives. His edition, which eventually will number 25 to 30 volumes, carries the original Aramaic and Hebrew writings followed by an English translation and commentary. Howard A. Berman

See also **Israel.** In ***World Book,*** see **Jews; Judaism.**

Kampuchea. See **Cambodia.**

Kansas. See **State government.**

Kentucky. See **State government.**

Kenya. President Daniel T. arap Moi in 1991 appeared to respond to mounting pressures both at home and abroad for democratic reform in Kenya. On December 2, leaders of the Kenya African National Union (KANU), the only legal political party since 1982, announced that Moi had agreed to allow multiparty politics. But the corruption of Moi's regime, and its dismal record in human rights, raised fears among domestic critics and foreign diplomats that national elections, which had been set for early 1992, would be rigged.

Through most of 1991, the government harassed journalists and censored newspapers, plays, and books. Scores of dissidents—including Kenya's first vice president, Oginga Odinga—were imprisoned without being charged with any crime. Meanwhile, Moi and the other members of his regime continued to accumulate great wealth. Outraged at these excesses, ever-greater numbers of lawyers, journalists, religious leaders, and other private citizens risked jail in demanding reform.

Moi's concessions late in the year were a reaction to an announcement on November 26 by the United States and 11 other donor nations that Moi would receive no further aid until he accepted democratic reforms and curbed government corruption.

J. Gus Liebenow and Beverly B. Liebenow

See also **Africa** (Facts in brief table). In ***World Book,*** see **Kenya.**

Kerrey, Robert (1943-), a relative newcomer to the political arena, announced his candidacy for the Democratic presidential nomination on Sept. 30, 1991. Kerrey was elected a United States senator from Nebraska in November 1988. He was outspoken in his opposition to the Persian Gulf War and to a government bailout of the savings and loan industry.

Joseph Robert Kerrey was born on Aug. 27, 1943, in Lincoln, Nebr. He earned a bachelor's degree in pharmacy at the University of Nebraska at Lincoln in 1966. From 1967 to 1969, he served with the U.S. Navy SEALs in Vietnam, where he sustained a leg injury requiring a below-the-knee amputation. He received the Bronze Star, the Purple Heart, and the Medal of Honor for his military service.

After his discharge from the Navy, Kerrey went into business with his brother-in-law, opening a chain of restaurants and fitness centers, which remain operational. In 1982, with no prior political experience, Kerrey sought and won the Nebraska governor's office against the incumbent. He decided to forego a possible second term as governor to pursue a Senate seat and again defeated the incumbent. Kerrey has served on the Senate Agriculture and Appropriations committees and on subcommittees for veterans affairs, housing and urban development, the treasury, postal service, and general government.

Kerrey is divorced and is the father of two teenage children. Lori Fagan

Korea, North. Two defectors from North Korea, a diplomat and an intelligence officer, said in 1991 that the secretive Communist state was close to completing its first nuclear weapons at a hidden underground plant. North Korean officials in June negotiated an agreement to allow international inspection of its nuclear facilities. But they later balked at signing the agreement, insisting that U.S. nuclear weapons should be withdrawn from South Korea before any inspections were permitted in the north. In December, however, South Korean officials said North Korea had made a new pledge to allow inspections.

The economy deteriorated in 1991, with North Korea suffering food and fuel shortages as the Soviet Union and China cut aid because of their own shortages. Japan, which had promised aid in 1990, froze relations due to the nuclear issue. The north traded coal for rice from South Korea in the first direct trade between the two since 1948.

Other developments. North Korea and South Korea joined the United Nations separately on September 17. The two states on December 13 signed a treaty of reconciliation and nonaggression. In June, North Korea turned over to the United States the remains of 11 Americans killed in the Korean War (1950-1953) and pledged to help look for more than 8,000 missing U.S. soldiers. Henry S. Bradsher

See also **Asia** (Facts in brief table); **Korea, South.** In ***World Book,*** see **Korea.**

Korea, South. The United Nations (UN) admitted both South Korea and North Korea to full memberships on Sept. 17, 1991. The move was a diplomatic triumph for South Korea and a testament to its growing economic power and importance.

South Korea had long tried to join the UN. But Communist North Korea had opposed separate memberships, preferring a single Korean delegation that would be under its influence. The north's allies, the Soviet Union and China, had the power to block a move in the UN to accept South Korea independently.

But South Korea's expanding economy made it a desirable trade partner for China and the Soviet Union. On March 28, the first official Chinese trade representative arrived in the South Korean capital, Seoul. Soviet President Mikhail S. Gorbachev made an overnight visit to South Korea in April. Faced with desertion by its allies, North Korea in May began advocating separate UN memberships for the two Koreas.

Moves toward reunification. Addressing the UN General Assembly on September 24, South Korean President Roh Tae Woo called for reunification of the south and north by stages. Roh (pronounced *Noh*) made the proposal conditional upon North Korea's abandoning its development of nuclear weapons (see **Korea, North**). On December 13, officials from the two Koreas signed a treaty of reconciliation and nonaggression, which was considered an important step toward eventual reunification.

Economic growth at a rate of about 9 per cent in 1991 was overshadowed by a widening trade deficit. From 1985 through 1989, South Korea had exported a greater value of goods than it imported, enabling it to pay off foreign loans. But South Korea's demand for imports grew in 1990 and increased more sharply in 1991. At the same time, South Korea's exports became less competitive abroad as their prices increased due to inflation and other factors.

Local elections. The first local government elections in 30 years were held on March 26. Many of the 4,304 council seats were uncontested, and only 55 per cent of voters took part in the election, the lowest turnout in South Korea's history. Supporters of Roh's government won two-thirds of all seats.

Politics. After years of political fragmentation, South Korea resumed two-party politics in 1991. In 1990, Roh had joined his Democratic Justice Party with two conservative opposition groups to form the Democratic Liberal Party. Outside the governing party was the New Democratic Party of a veteran politician, Kim Dae Jung. On Sept. 10, 1991, Kim Dae Jung merged his party—whose strength was primarily in southwestern Korea—with the Democratic Party based in the southeast. The resulting group, named the Democratic Party, held only 77 of the 298 seats in the National Assembly but was well placed to benefit from widespread popular discontent.

Student protests flared in April and May, in what had become a usual springtime occurrence in

Antigovernment protesters face off against black-garbed South Korean riot police in Seoul on May 18, after weeks of violent demonstrations.

South Korea. The approximately 10 per cent of university students who were considered political radicals made violent displays of their opposition to Roh as well as to the presence of United States defense forces in South Korea. The 1991 demonstrations were the largest since a student uprising in 1987 toppled South Korea's military regime and led to Roh's election.

Police clubbed a student to death during a Seoul demonstration on April 26, 1991, reportedly after a protester's fire bomb had burned a policeman. Roh issued an apology for the death of the student, Kang Kyung Dae, and fired Interior Minister Ahn Eung Mo. But at Kang's funeral on May 14, more than 30,000 students and laborers demanded human-rights improvements, economic changes, and the dismissal of Roh's entire Cabinet. The demonstrations continued on May 18—the 11th anniversary of an uprising in the city of Kwangju that left hundreds of people dead. In the 1991 protest, some office workers and professionals joined students and laborers in demanding Roh's resignation. During the weeks of demonstrations, seven students set themselves ablaze and died.

Prime Minister Ro Jai Bong assumed responsibility for the trouble and resigned on May 22. Roh named a new Cabinet on May 24 with Chung Won Shik, a former education minister, as prime minister. Although the protesters did not approve of the choice, calm returned. Henry S. Bradsher

See also **Asia** (Facts in brief table). In ***World Book,*** see **Korea**.

Kuwait

Kuwait was liberated by a United States-led military force on Feb. 26, 1991, nearly seven months after the oil-rich kingdom had been invaded by Iraq. But that same day, Emir Jabir al-Ahmad al-Jabir Al-Sabah, Kuwait's hereditary leader, declared martial law and prohibited Kuwaitis who had fled the country after the Iraqi invasion from returning to their homeland for three months. The emir contended that such steps were necessary because of chaotic conditions in Kuwait. Government opponents, however, charged the emir with using the crisis to stifle political opposition. The government lifted martial law on June 26.

Iraqi abuses. During and after the war, there were broad-based allegations of human rights violations committed by Iraqi occupation forces. The Iraqis were charged with murdering, torturing, kidnapping, and raping Kuwaiti citizens. The Kuwaiti government alleged that the Iraqis had killed 1,000 people. Independent sources, however, said 300 to 600 Kuwaitis, mostly members of the resistance, had been killed.

Iraqi occupation forces severely damaged Kuwait's water, electrical, and telephone services and vandalized public buildings. The Iraqis also stole more than $100 billion in goods and from $600 million to $700-million in gold from Kuwait's central bank. On August 5, Iraq began returning the gold.

Oil well fires. Kuwaitis also confronted an environmental catastrophe. In late February, retreating Iraqi forces had ignited about 600 oil wells. In addition, more than 100 damaged oil wells gushed out of control. The Kuwaiti government initially reported that extinguishing the fires would take several years. But by November, specially trained crews had capped all the burning or damaged wells.

Because of the damage to its oil industry, Kuwait was forced to import crude-oil products in early 1991. By October, however, Kuwait was exporting 325,000 barrels per day. Before the Iraqi invasion, Kuwait exported 2 million barrels per day.

Public criticism of Kuwait's ruling Sabah family, condemned by opponents as corrupt and undemocratic before the invasion, intensified after the war. Many Kuwaitis, critical of Sabah leadership, demanded a more representative government. Some Kuwaitis alleged that the government had restored basic services to Sabah family members before reestablishing service for other citizens. Intense public anger over the Kuwaiti government's failure to restore basic services quickly enough and the imposition of martial law forced the resignation of Kuwait's Cabinet on March 20. Although the new Cabinet named on April 20 included fewer members of the Sabah family, Sabahs retained all the key posts. The emir also stated he would hold parliamentary elections in October 1992, but opponents remained skeptical.

United States soldiers drive over sand covered with oil from a burning Kuwaiti oil field, one of many set afire by retreating Iraqi forces in February.

Kuwait

Charges against Kuwait. The Kuwaiti government came under severe international criticism because of its harsh treatment of people accused of sympathizing or collaborating with Iraq. In a report issued in September 1991, the human rights organization, Middle East Watch, detailed numerous cases of torture and murder of Kuwaiti residents of foreign descent by Kuwaiti police and soldiers.

The targets of these actions were chiefly Palestinians, Jordanians, and Iraqis living in Kuwait. Other targets included Arab nomads who considered themselves Kuwaitis but who could not prove their citizenship. The Kuwaiti government admitted that there had been some human rights violations shortly after liberation but denied that human rights abuses were widespread.

Collaboration trials. In May, Kuwaiti martial-law tribunals began trying the first of about 450 people accused of collaborating with Iraqi forces. During the first round of trials, defense lawyers complained that some court proceedings, such as failing to provide evidence to support charges against the accused, violated the right of the defendants to a fair trial. Under international pressure, the government on June 24 commuted to life imprisonment all 29 of the death sentences imposed by the tribunals. Christine Helms

See also **Persian Gulf,** Special Report: **War in the Persian Gulf; Middle East** (Facts in brief table). In ***World Book,*** see **Kuwait.**

Labor. The United States economy slipped into its first recession in more than eight years in the first half of 1991. Unemployment averaged just more than a percentage point higher than in 1990 at 6.7 per cent, but there were widespread fears of joblessness. Both blue-collar and white-collar workers faced layoffs. On Dec. 18, 1991, General Motors Corporation announced plans to close 21 plants in the United States and Canada. This would eliminate more than 70,000 jobs. See **Automobile.**

Although the U.S. recession was not as severe as the 1981-1982 downturn, some economists expressed concern about the chances for a strong recovery because of what they called "structural" difficulties. They argued that none of the traditional sources of recovery—government, business, and consumers—were strong enough to spark a recovery because of huge national, state, and local budget deficits and record levels of business and consumer debt. There was also continuing uneasiness about the ability of the United States to compete in international business markets, which raised the possibility of market setbacks and more job losses.

Pay and benefits of all U.S. workers advanced 4.3 per cent, and pay alone 3.8 per cent, in the 12 months that ended in September 1991, according to the Bureau of Labor Statistics (BLS) Employment Cost Index. Pay and benefits rose 4.3 per cent for private industry workers (except private household workers) and 4.1

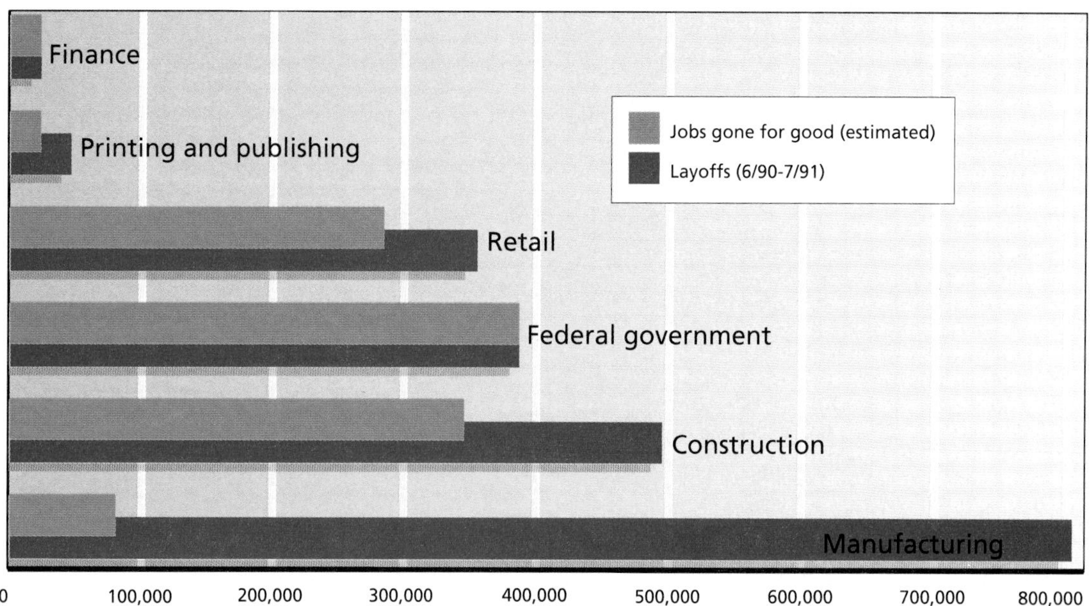

During a 13-month period ending in July 1991, most U.S. job layoffs were in manufacturing and construction, and many jobs were lost for good.

per cent for government workers (except federal). Both white- and blue-collar workers saw 3.9 per cent increases in pay and benefits, but workers in service occupations had the highest pay and benefit increases for the period—5.3 per cent. Generally, increases were slightly higher for all workers in 1991 than in 1990.

New U.S. labor secretary. Lynn M. Martin, a former Illinois congresswoman, became the 21st secretary of labor. She was confirmed by a 94-0 vote of the U.S. Senate and was sworn into office on February 22. Martin succeeded Elizabeth H. Dole, who resigned in autumn of 1990 to take the top spot at the American Red Cross. Martin in 1991 was the only woman running a Cabinet department. See **Martin, Lynn M.**

Job discrimination. According to a Labor Department report issued on Aug. 8, 1991, nine large U.S. companies investigated by the Labor Department rarely placed women or minorities in upper management positions. According to the report, only 6.6 per cent of 4,491 executive level managers with the title of assistant vice president or higher were women and 2.6 per cent were minorities.

In the food and lodging sector, some women managers of the Marriot Corporation won a $3-million sex discrimination settlement from the company on March 1, after challenging the giant chain in court. The company agreed to fill top management positions with women in accord with the proportion of women among qualified applicants.

Labor settlements. Labor negotiations in U.S. communications media continued to be difficult in 1991 as the various media competed for shrinking revenues. The *New York Daily News* and nine unions ended a bitter 15-month dispute on March 20 when the unions agreed to job cutbacks and other concessions with Robert Maxwell, the British publisher who agreed to acquire the paper if there were wage and benefit concessions. The agreement also provided that replacement workers would be let go but union workers who crossed picket lines would be retained. But the future of the newspaper was in doubt following Maxwell's death in November and the disclosure that he left behind massive debts. In December, the *Daily News* filed for bankruptcy.

In metal industries, the United Steelworkers of America on January 3 announced a $415-million settlement with the Continental Can Company on behalf of 3,000 former employees. The agreement, an instance of the growing use of courts and boards to settle labor-management disputes, resulted from a 1989 district court ruling that found Continental Can used a computer system to track employees so that the company could fire them before they became eligible for pension benefits.

The steelworkers' union also came to terms with the USX Corporation in February on a three-year contract involving about 17,500 workers. The new contract boosts wages $1.50 an hour over the life of the contract and restores $1 an hour in wage cuts that workers took during the recession of 1981-1982. The company also agreed to pay workers $2,500 each in the form of a cost-of-living bonus over the life of the contract. The base pay for USX steelworkers is $11.23 an hour.

Changes in the United States labor force

	1990	1991
Total labor force	**126,424,000**	**126,843,000**
Armed forces	1,637,700	1,560,000
Civilian labor force	124,786,300	125,283,000
Total employment	119,550,000	118,276,000
Unemployment	6,874,000	8,412,000
Unemployment rate	5.4%	6.7%
Changes in real earnings of production and nonsupervisory workers (private nonfarm sector)*	3.5%	0.7%
Change in output per employee hour (private nonfarm sector)†	0.6%	0.3%

*Constant (1982) dollars. 1990 change from December 1989 to December 1990; 1991 change from October 1990 to October 1991 (preliminary data).

†Annual rate for 1990; for 1991, change is from third quarter 1990 to third quarter 1991 (preliminary data).

Source: U.S. Bureau of Labor Statistics.

Labor negotiations between 11 railroad unions and 10 major U.S. freight railroads involving more than 200,000 workers entered their third year in 1991. Unions representing the workers agreed on February 12 to a 60-day extension of a "cooling-off" period scheduled to end on February 15. On April 5, the Transportation Communications Union, representing some 50,000 white-collar railroad workers, reached the first agreement with the carriers in the three-year dispute. Later in April, the Signalmen's Union and the Train Dispatchers' Union reached agreement.

The pacts reflected the Jan. 17, 1991, presidential emergency board report that recommended $2,000 signing bonuses and wage increases of 3 per cent in July 1991 and July 1993 and a 4 per cent boost in July 1994. The emergency board also recommended lump-sum payments to workers equal to 3 per cent of their prior-year earnings on July 1, 1992; Jan. 1, 1993 and 1994; and 2 per cent on Jan. 1, 1995. The board also called for negotiated or arbitrated solutions to health care cost disputes.

When the other rail unions and the carriers failed to reach agreement by the April deadline, President George Bush signed legislation on April 18 that halted

Workers in San Antonio, Tex., fearing the loss of U.S. jobs, in April protest a proposed free-trade agreement between the United States and Mexico.

a one-day nationwide rail strike and provided for a new presidential panel with power to impose settlements in the remaining disputes. Unions that had reached agreements could proceed with ratification votes. In mid-July, the new panel imposed the original board's recommendations for settlement.

New Teamsters Union boss. In mid-December, Ron Carey, a 55-year-old reform candidate and president of Teamsters Union local 804 in New York City, won election to a five-year term as the new national Teamsters Union president. He cut his salary from $225,000 to $175,000, vowed to put the union first, and end union corruption. The election was supervised by the federal government to help guarantee honesty.

The Teamsters Union and nationwide trucking companies reached agreement on a three-year labor contract that would provide a guaranteed $1.40 hourly wage increase over the life of the contract. On May 1, the union reported that 68 per cent of its membership voted for the contract.

After the failed 1990 attempt to buy United Airlines, the unions began negotiating with United for new contracts. In early April, the pilots reached an agreement with United and ratified it on May 9. It raised pay to the level of Delta Air Lines pilots, who are reportedly the industry's highest-paid pilots. In March, the independent Allied Pilots Association and American Airlines agreed to a four-year pact that would bring their pay closer to that of Delta pilots.

After 56 years in business, Pan American Airways, a pioneer in international scheduled flights, ceased flight operations on December 4, putting 9,000 employees out of work. Efforts to reorganize the carrier failed as the year ended.

The United Rubber Workers and Bridgestone-Firestone Incorporated announced an agreement on April 22, providing for 18 per cent increases in wages and benefits over the life of the three-year contract. This contract became the basis of wage and benefit settlements with the other two major U.S. tire makers—Goodyear Tire & Rubber Company and Uniroyal/Goodrich Incorporated. The last ratification (Goodyear) occurred at the end of May.

In postal negotiations, an arbitration panel in mid-June imposed a settlement on postal unions representing more than 560,000 workers and the U.S. Postal Service. The three-year pact provided a $351 onetime payment in place of retroactive wage increases, a 1.2 per cent salary increase on June 15, 1.5 per cent increases in November 1991 and 1992, and a 1.6 per cent boost in November 1993. In March, the Postal Mail Handlers Union also agreed to onetime payments in place of general wage increases. The payments would be $900 in the first and second years of the contract and $600 in the third and last year of the contract. The workers would also receive cost-of-living increases.

The General Electric Company, the Union of Electronic Workers, and the United Electrical Workers announced a settlement on July 1, 1991, after five weeks of negotiation. The agreements provided pay increases of 3.5 per cent retroactive to July 1, 1991, and 2.5 per cent on June 29, 1992, and June 28, 1993. The settlements also provided for cost-of-living increases and special wage adjustments for skilled workers.

Union membership in the United States continued to hold steady at just under 17 million in 1991. But continued growth of the labor force dropped the proportion of workers in unions from 16.4 per cent in 1989 to 16.1 per cent in 1990, according to BLS data released on Feb. 6, 1991. Union workers' average weekly pay of $509 remained higher than the average nonunion workers' pay of $390.

Major labor legislation. On February 21, the U.S. Equal Employment Opportunity Commission (EEOC) issued proposed rules on how to enforce the 1990 Americans with Disabilities Act, which made it illegal to discriminate against disabled workers.The act also requires businesses to provide the same level of service to physically and mentally disabled customers as that provided to other customers.

Workers would be affected by new provisions under the act that require restaurant servers either to read menus to blind customers or offer them menus in Braille. Other sections of the act mandate that disabled customers must be able to use pumps at self-service gas stations, or that attendants help them use the pumps. Places of lodging with more than five rooms must also provide special phones that allow deaf or hearing-impaired customers to make calls. On July 25, the EEOC issued a set of final rules for employers to carry out the employment title of the Disabilities Act. Some of the rules were very general, however, so that they could be implemented on a case-by-case basis. The regulations would apply to employers of 25 or more in July 1992 and to those employing 15 or more in July 1994. See **Handicapped.**

President Bush signed a $5.3-billion bill on Nov. 15, 1991, to extend jobless benefits. The signing followed a yearlong dispute between the White House and Congress on the duration of the benefits and how they would be financed. The legislation provided for up to 20 weeks of additional unemployment benefits to workers who had exhausted their regular entitlements under any state's provisions. Bush had vetoed two earlier bills extending unemployment benefits.

On November 21, Bush signed the 1991 Civil Rights Act intended to make it easier for workers to sue for job discrimination. The bill passed the Senate on October 30 and the House of Representatives on November 7. The bill also permitted jury trials, limited awards for compensatory and punitive damages in sex discrimination cases, and extended employment discrimination protections to Americans working for U.S. companies abroad. Robert W. Fisher

See also **Civil Rights; Economics; Manufacturing.** In ***World Book,*** see **Labor force; Labor movement.**

Laos. The ruling Communist party, the Lao People's Revolutionary Party, held its fifth congress from March 27 to 29, 1991. Kaysone Phomvihan, the party leader since 1955, was given the title of party chairman and put "in charge of guiding and correcting the daily work" of party officials. Four leaders were dropped from the party's guiding group, the Politburo. They included a former president of Laos, Prince Souphanouvong, who had been sick since 1987, and Phoumi Vongvichit, who was acting president.

The party congress endorsed continued market-based economic reforms under party control. It also placed less emphasis on ties with Vietnam, which long had dominated Laotian affairs, while indicating interest in establishing closer relations with China, Thailand, and Western nations. Economic troubles in the Soviet Union deprived Laos of its largest source of aid in 1991.

A new Constitution, the first since the Communists came to power in 1975, was unanimously adopted by parliament on Aug. 14, 1991. It said the people's democratic rights "are exercised and insured through" a political system in which the Communist party functions as the "leading organ." On August 15, Phoumi resigned as acting president, and parliament elected Kaysone to replace him. Defense Minister Khamtai Siphandon became premier. Henry S. Bradsher

See also **Asia** (Facts in brief table). In ***World Book,*** see **Laos.**

Latin America

Latin Americans turned to the pursuit of an old dream in 1991—the forging of a regional economic union. Governments that were, with rare exceptions, democratically elected reported progress toward the goal of economic union during the year.

Rush to unify. On February 5, the United States, Canada, and Mexico announced their intention to negotiate a North American Free Trade Agreement to build on one already in effect between the United States and Canada. At a meeting with Mexico's President Carlos Salinas de Gortari on April 7, U.S. President George Bush promised a "head on head" fight, if necessary, with U.S. organized labor to win congressional approval of such a pact. A free-trade agreement would promote commerce by eventually abolishing tariffs on goods traded between participating countries.

On June 12, in Toronto, Canada, trade officials from the three countries agreed on a timetable to create a common market comprising 360 million people that would link the financial fortunes of the United States with its two most important trading partners.

Mercosur. On March 26, the presidents of Argentina, Brazil, Paraguay, and Uruguay signed the Treaty of Asunción in Asunción, Paraguay. The treaty called for a free-trade zone named Mercosur after its Spanish abbreviation. The four nations have a combined population of nearly 200 million and produce about $400 billion worth of goods and services annually. Mercosur's headquarters would rotate among its members every six months. The treaty reduced tariffs 47 per cent among participants beginning in June. The four nations pledged to eliminate all tariffs on trade among themselves by the end of 1995.

On May 6, 1991, the presidents of Brazil and Paraguay dedicated the 18th and final turbine of the massive Itaipú hydroelectric dam located on their common border on the Paraná River. By 1992, the plant will generate 12,600 megawatts, enough to meet about 40 per cent of Brazil's electricity needs or supply much of the power needs elsewhere in the Mercosur region.

Other common markets. Not to be outdone by their neighbors, the presidents of Bolivia, Colombia, Ecuador, Peru, and Venezuela met in Caracas, Venezuela, on May 18, 1991, and agreed to create a free-trade zone by January 1992 and a fully operational common market by 1995. Four of the nations will abolish tariffs on regional trade by Jan. 1, 1992, with Ecuador eliminating half its tariffs by then and the balance six months later.

By mid-1991, the Latin-American economic integra-

A Haitian soldier patrols the streets of Port-au-Prince, Haiti, after a September coup that drew angry protests from many Latin-American leaders.

tion movement seemed to be running at full throttle. On July 17, Mexico, Colombia, and Venezuela approved a free-trade pact to take effect Jan. 1, 1992. Among their reasons for eliminating mutual trade barriers was the desire to allow multinational corporations to take better advantage of the three nations' raw materials and manufacturing capacities.

In Central America, the presidents of Costa Rica, El Salvador, Honduras, Guatemala, Nicaragua, and Panama moved ahead with plans to revive their own regional common market at a meeting held in El Salvador from July 16 to 18, 1991. At that meeting, the Organization of Central American States awarded Panama full membership. In late October, four Central American presidents and the prime minister of Belize opened a regional parliament in Guatemala City aimed at ending regional political violence.

Economy expands. In 1991, for the first time in four years, the overall Latin-American economy expanded during the first six months of the year, according to a September report by the United Nations Economic Commission for Latin America (ECLA). The ECLA estimated that the increase would be 2 per cent for the region for the entire year, with oil-producing Venezuela leading the way with a 6 per cent increase.

Economists attributed the turnaround to the adoption of more traditional economic policies, such as eliminating protectionist measures for key industries and government subsidies on basic products and services. Government policies that formerly called for delaying debt payments were no longer in favor. Neither were radical reforms that sent economies spinning into deep recessions without producing favorable results, even in the long term. Resistance to foreign economic involvement in Latin-American affairs was also vanishing. From Argentina to Mexico, the watchword was privatization—the selling of money-losing state enterprises to entrepreneurs willing to risk their money on making them profitable.

The new mood extended even to the highly protected petroleum industry. In Venezuela, the same president who nationalized foreign-owned oil companies in the 1970's, President Carlos Andrés Pérez, now appealed to them to come back and help boost Venezuela's oil production by 40 per cent by 1995.

In the United States, what were once considered undervalued Latin-American stocks showed impressive gains on the New York Stock Exchange. The Brazil Fund increased in value 150.7 per cent in the first nine months of the year. The Chile Fund grew in value by 115.7 per cent, and the Latin America Investment Fund grew 91.3 per cent in value.

United States trade with Latin America also grew. In the second quarter of 1991, U.S. exports to Latin America reached $15.6 billion—15 per cent of total U.S. exports. These figures represented a healthy rebound to the levels of the 1960's and 1970's before Latin America was hit by the debt crisis and a succession of costly wars and conflicts.

Easing of conflict. Rebels in several Latin-American nations met during 1991 with governments that they have been fighting to overthrow. Talks mediated by the United Nations led to a truce on November 16 between the rebels and the Salvadoran government. There also was progress toward peace in Guatemala, due to mediation by the Roman Catholic Church.

In Suriname, Ronald Venetiaan of the New Front for Democracy Party was sworn in for a five-year term as president on September 16. He replaced a regime that took power after a December 1990 military coup.

In Colombia, former rebels turned in their firearms, took up government offers of amnesty, and became participants in the democratic process. The rebels actually had the swing votes at a June 1991 convention empowered to write a new constitution. Millions of Colombians watched on television as the rebels participated in the convention to form a new constitution.

Several Latin-American nations acted to solve old disputes with their neighbors. On August 14, Guatemala's new president, Jorge Serrano Elías, agreed to Belize's right to political self-determination. Guatemala has long claimed Belize as part of its territory, but Serrano pledged to work out a solution to the problem. In a similar spirit, Peru and Ecuador agreed on August 26 to keep their respective military forces apart within a disputed area of their borders.

Reduced military spending. The democratically elected heads of three countries long under military rule—Argentina, Brazil, and Chile—made headway in reducing military spending and slowing an arms race that peaked in the late 1980's. On Sept. 5, 1991, the foreign ministers of the three nations signed a declaration at Mendoza, Argentina, banning the development, manufacture, and use of chemical weapons, though none of the countries was known to possess these weapons.

Cholera and AIDS. In late January, a cholera outbreak struck northern Peru. In the next eight months, the disease spread to eight other Latin-American countries. Hardest hit was Peru, which by November had reported more than 276,712 cholera cases and 2,664 deaths. By November, Colombia had reported 9,542 cases and 130 deaths. By October, Ecuador had reported 39,154 cases and 606 deaths, according to the Pan American Health Organization (PAHO).

Figures released on June 30 by the PAHO indicated that the Caribbean has one of the most concentrated populations of AIDS cases in the world. For reasons that puzzled researchers, the Central American nation of Honduras was reported to have the highest rate of people infected with the AIDS virus in Latin America.

Other international efforts. The heads of 19 Latin-American nations, Spain, and Portugal met at Guadalajara, Mexico, from July 18 to 19 for an Ibero-American Summit—the first ever. One purpose of the meeting was to discuss ways that Spain and Portugal could help represent Latin-American interests within the European Community.

Facts in brief on Latin-American political units

Country	Population	Government	Monetary unit*	Foreign trade (million U.S.$) Exports†	Imports†
Antigua and Barbuda	82,000	Governor General Sir Wilfred Jacobs; Prime Minister Vere C. Bird	dollar (2.7 = $1)	22	225
Argentina	33,083,000	President Carlos Saúl Menem	austral (9,910.50 = $1)	9,579	4,204
Bahamas	267,000	Governor General Sir Henry Taylor; Prime Minister Lynden O. Pindling	dollar (1.00 = $1)	2,786	3,001
Barbados	265,000	Governor General Dame Nita Barrow; Prime Minister Lloyd Erskine Sandiford	dollar (2.01 = $1)	209	700
Belize	189,000	Governor General Dame Minita E. Gordon; Prime Minister George Price	dollar (2 = $1)	129	211
Bolivia	7,732,000	President Jaime Paz Zamora	boliviano (3.71 = $1)	900	715
Brazil	156,044,000	President Fernando Collor de Mello	cruzeiro (829.15 = $1)	31,408	20,501
Chile	13,585,000	President Patricio Aylwin Azócar	peso (386.89 = $1)	8,580	7,272
Colombia	33,020,000	President César Gaviria Trujillo	peso (693.99 = $1)	5,739	5,010
Costa Rica	3,152,000	President Rafael Angel Calderón Fournier	colón (139.75 = $1)	1,362	1,743
Cuba	10,655,000	President Fidel Castro	peso (1.32 = $1)	5,518	7,579
Dominica	88,000	President Clarence Augustus Seignoret; Prime Minister Eugenia Charles	dollar (2.7 = $1)	45	107
Dominican Republic	7,457,000	President Joaquín Balaguer Ricardo	peso (12.85 = $1)	924	1,964
Ecuador	11,363,000	President Rodrigo Borja Cevallos	sucre (1,252.90 = $1)	2,714	1,862
El Salvador	5,515,000	President Alfredo Cristiani Burkard	colón (8.13 = $1)	412	902
Grenada	85,000	Governor General Sir Paul Scoon; Prime Minister Nicholas Brathwaite	dollar (2.7 = $1)	31	88
Guatemala	9,734,000	President Jorge Serrano Elías	quetzal (5.08 = $1)	1,108	1,654
Guyana	819,000	President Hugh Desmond Hoyte; Prime Minister Hamilton Green	dollar (121.26 = $1)	167	248
Haiti	6,752,000	Interim President Joseph Nerette Interim Prime Minister Jean-Jacques Honorat	gourde (5 = $1)	200	344
Honduras	5,451,000	President Rafael Leonardo Callejas	lempira (5.95 = $1)	869	933
Jamaica	2,593,000	Governor General Howard Cooke Prime Minister Michael Manley	dollar (17.85 = $1)	1,116	1,864
Mexico	85,082,000	President Carlos Salinas de Gortari	peso (3,073 = $1)	22,819	23,633
Nicaragua	4,122,000	President Violeta Barrios de Chamorro	gold córdoba (5 = $1)	300	923
Panama	2,511,000	President Guillermo Endara	balboa (1 = $1)	321	1,489
Paraguay	4,510,000	President Andrés Rodríguez Pedotti	guaraní (1,333 = $1)	1,163	695
Peru	23,399,000	President Alberto Fujimori	new sol (1.03 = $1)	3,274	2,455
Puerto Rico	3,522,000	Governor Rafael Hernández Colón	U.S. dollar	13,200	11,800
St. Christopher and Nevis	48,000	Governor General Clement Athelston Arrindell; Prime Minister Kennedy Alphonse Simmonds	dollar (2.7 = $1)	30	95
St. Lucia	161,000	Governor General Sir Stanislaus James; Prime Minister John Compton	dollar (2.7 = $1)	83	155
St. Vincent and the Grenadines	114,000	Acting Governor General David Jack; Prime Minister James F. Mitchell	dollar (2.7 = $1)	64	87
Suriname	415,000	President Ronald Venetiaan	guilder (1.79 = $1)	301	294
Trinidad and Tobago	1,323,000	President Noor Hassanali; Prime Minister Patrick Manning	dollar (4.26 = $1)	2,049	1,222
Uruguay	3,174,000	President Luis Alberto Lacalle	peso (2,404 = $1)	1,693	1,343
Venezuela	20,683,000	President Carlos Andrés Pérez	bolívar (60.57 = $1)	17,586	6,365

*Exchange rates as of Nov. 29, 1991, or latest available data. †Latest available data.

Latin America

Shortly before the Guadalajara meeting, the newly constituted Group of 100, a group of leading Latin-American men and women, called for a Latin-American ecological alliance to help preserve the region's environment. The group noted the alarming rate at which remaining tropical rain forests are being destroyed, the theat to endangered Latin-American plant and animal species, and fears that Latin America has become a dumping ground for toxic wastes generated by foreign companies.

Government corruption. Drug-related corruption at the highest levels of government made headlines in 1991. A U.S. court for the first time ever tried a former head of state, General Manuel Antonio Noriega of Panama, on drug-trafficking charges. In Argentina, the former appointments secretary to the president was indicted on charges of complicity in a drug-money laundering conspiracy. In Mexico, authorities discovered that a jailed drug dealer was overseeing the operations of a large-scale drug-trafficking operation from his cell, which was complete with a fax machine and telephones.

In Colombia, Pablo Escobar Gaviria, the leader of the Medellín drug cartel, turned himself in for confinement at a luxury prison. It was part of a deal whereby Colombia, by refusing to extradite drug traffickers to the United States to stand trial in U.S. courts, hoped to reduce drug-related violence.

In Peru, former President Alan García Pérez was stripped of the immunity from prosecution normally enjoyed by former heads of state to answer charges that he had stolen $50 million from the nation's treasury with the help of the scandal-ridden Bank of Credit and Commerce International (BCCI), which was implicated in laundering illicit drug profits. In November, Peru's attorney general dismissed the accusation of theft but charged García with using $500,000 in state funds to build three houses.

Iran-contra scandal. Two former U.S. officials pleaded guilty to two misdemeanor charges each of withholding information from Congress in 1986 in connection with illegal arms sales to Iran to raise money for Nicaraguan contra rebels. The officials were Elliott Abrams, former assistant secretary of state for inter-American affairs, and Alan D. Fiers, Jr., former head of the Central Intelligence Agency's Central American Task Force. See also **Iran-contra affair.**

U.S. Hispanic surge. Figures released from the 1990 U.S. census confirmed a continuing sharp rise in the U.S. Hispanic population. According to the census, the U.S. Hispanic population increased by 53 per cent from 1980 to 1990 to 22.4 million people. During that period, California's Hispanic population reached 7.7 million people. This represented a growth rate of nearly 70 per cent, compared with an overall state population growth rate of 25.7 per cent. According to the census, the Hispanic population of California in 1990 exceeded the total population of all but eight U.S. states.

Frictions between fast-growing Hispanic populations and local police forces erupted in violence in 1991 in Los Angeles, New York City, and Washington, D.C. Two days of rioting followed the wounding on May 5 of a Salvadoran immigrant by police in the Mount Pleasant neighborhood of Washington, D.C., where there is a large concentration of Central American immigrants.

Columbus' anniversary. As the world prepared to mark the 500th anniversary in 1992 of Christopher Columbus' arrival in the New World, opinions about his achievement were sharply divided. Critics noted that Columbus' voyages marked the beginning of centuries of oppression for native peoples of the Americas. Others supported the position that his journey was one of the greatest events in world history.

To prepare for the commemoration of Columbus' voyage, the government of the Dominican Republic spent nearly $2 billion beginning in 1988 to restore historic structures and refurbish Santo Domingo. The city claims to be the Western Hemisphere's oldest European settlement. Included in the price was a $50-million "Columbus Memorial Lighthouse," 150 feet (46 meters) high, which will light up the nighttime sky with a cross formed by laser beams.

Nathan A. Haverstock

See also articles on the individual nations. In ***World Book,*** see **Latin America** and articles on the individual nations.

Latvia took advantage of the upheaval surrounding a coup attempt against Soviet President Mikhail S. Gorbachev in August 1991 to declare independence from the Soviet Union. In a nationwide referendum on March 3, nearly three-fourths of Latvia's people had voted for independence. On September 6, following formal Soviet recognition, Latvia's independence became official.

Forging a market economy. Like Lithuania and Estonia, its Baltic neighbors, Latvia faced formidable problems in freeing itself from a strictly Soviet-tied economy and establishing a competitive, free-market economy. Latvia is a small country with few raw materials and little fuel. Nonetheless, its manufactured goods—electronics as well as machine tools and consumer goods—sold well in the Soviet market because of their superiority to goods made in other Soviet republics. But with world markets now open to those republics, Latvia faced an uphill task in maintaining Soviet demand for its products.

Latvia also hoped to preserve the historic role of its ports, which for years handled about half of all Soviet exports. Planners visualized Riga, Latvia's capital and largest port, as a European "Hong Kong"—a flourishing free port in which no import duties are collected. To that end, government officials visited the free ports of Hong Kong and Singapore during the year. Russia, however, reportedly planned to bypass Latvian ports by building a port for heavy cargo elsewhere.

Latvians arrest an officer of the Committee of State Security (KGB), the Soviet secret police, in September, soon after Latvia gained independence.

Attracting foreign investment was another top economic priority. As a first step, the government planned to offer companies launched with foreign capital complete immunity from taxes for four years. Such companies could also take all profits out of Latvia in *hard* (internationally exchangeable) currency. Targeting tourism for development, the government proposed restoring health spas along the Gulf of Riga, which had been popular with wealthy Scandinavians before World War II (1939-1945).

The future citizenship of Latvian residents of non-Latvian ancestry remained a sensitive issue. Non-Latvians—many of them ethnic Russians—made up nearly half the population and formed the majority in Riga. Following the independence declaration, the government pledged that all residents would enjoy full basic rights. But the large Russian minority, which accounted for 34 per cent of the population, feared that only people living in Latvia before 1940—the year of its annexation by the Soviet Union—would receive citizenship in the new Latvian state.

Strong opposition to full citizenship for all residents came from an ethnic Latvian party, the Popular Front. It claimed the policy could lead to an ethnic Russian majority in Latvia. Eric Bourne

See also **Europe** (Facts in brief table); **Union of Soviet Socialist Republics.** In the World Book Supplement section, see **Latvia.**

Law. See **Courts; Supreme Court of the U.S.**

Lebanon. Lebanon's parliament ratified a wide-ranging security pact with Syria on Sept. 16, 1991. The pact, which expands on a cooperation treaty signed by the leaders of the two countries on May 22, calls for mutual cooperation on issues as diverse as military security, intelligence-sharing, efforts to curb drug trafficking, and media affairs. Under the terms of the accord, Syria, which controls about two-thirds of the area in Lebanon, also agreed to withdraw its 40,000 troops to the eastern side of Lebanon's Bekaa Valley as soon as the Lebanese government reestablished its authority over the country or by September 1992, whichever came first. However, 49 of the parliament's 108 legislators were absent for the vote on the pact. The absent legislators argued that the accord would give Syria a free hand to interfere in Lebanese affairs.

Western hostages released. Between August and December 1991, all American and British hostages held in Lebanon were released. In addition, Israel released about 90 of its Lebanese Muslim Shiite prisoners in return for information on three Israeli soldiers missing since the Israeli invasion of Lebanon in June 1982. See **Middle East.**

Disarming militias. The Lebanese Cabinet on March 28, 1991, ordered all militias to turn in their firearms and abandon their military posts as a necessary step to reestablishing the supremacy of Lebanon's army and central government. Among those agreeing to the order were Hezbollah (Party of God), a pro-Iranian group, and Amal, a Muslim Shiite organization, two of the largest militias in Lebanon. In response to the disarmament order, the Palestine Liberation Organization (PLO), which also had troops in Lebanon, announced it would not oppose Lebanese forces, but refused to halt its attacks against Israel and the Israeli-sponsored South Lebanon Army.

Army campaigns. In mid-February, the Lebanese Army—for the first time since 1975—moved into southern Lebanon, a frequent staging site for raids against Israel by the PLO and Lebanese Muslim militias. The army hoped to convince Israeli forces to abandon a narrow strip along Lebanon's southern border with Israel, which Israel had occupied as a security zone since 1985. In late January and early February 1991, just before the Lebanese army moved into southern Lebanon, Israel launched a five-day air campaign against Palestinian positions in the area.

On July 5, Lebanese troops retook PLO strongholds near Sidon, 25 miles (40 kilometers) south of Beirut, after four days of fighting in which 80 people were killed. Although the army was careful not to enter Palestinian refugee camps, it encountered resistance from some of the 6,000 guerrilla fighters of Al Fatah, the PLO's largest mainstream organization, who were based in and around the refugee camps in Tyre and Sidon. A July 4 agreement between the PLO and the Lebanese government forestalled further violence, and Al Fatah agreed to turn over its weapons. Possibly as a concession, the Lebanese government announced on July 4 that job-related restrictions on 400,000 Lebanese Palestinians had been lifted.

Despite sporadic violence, Beirut returned to a semblance of normalcy in 1991. But on December 30, a car bomb exploded, killing at least 20 people and wounding more than 80 others.

Awn flees. Michel Awn (also spelled Aoun), a Christian general who had staged an 11-month rebellion against the Lebanese government in late 1989 and 1990, secretly left Lebanon for exile in France on Aug. 29, 1991, a few hours after Lebanon's parliament approved his departure. Appointed the head of an interim military government in September 1988, Awn had refused to surrender power after the election of Ilyas Hrawi as president in September 1989. Hrawi was elected under a "charter of national reconciliation" that shifted significant political power to Lebanon's Muslims from the country's once-dominant Christian community.

Awn fled to the French Embassy in Beirut in October 1990 after he and his supporters were routed from the presidential palace by Syrian forces and troops loyal to Hrawi's government. Awn's popularity in the army and among Lebanon's Christians prompted parliament to issue him an amnesty, rather than put him on trial. Christine Helms

See also **Persian Gulf,** Special Report: **War in the Persian Gulf; Middle East** (Facts in brief table). In ***World Book,*** see **Lebanon.**

Leno, Jay (1950-), a stand-up comic who appeals to the common person, was chosen in June 1991 to replace retiring Johnny Carson on "The Tonight Show" in May 1992. Leno has served as the permanent guest host of the show since 1988. Executives of the National Broadcasting Company (NBC) said they picked Leno because of his ability to attract younger viewers.

Performing more than 250 times a year in clubs throughout the United States and Canada, Leno peddles humor based on the bizarre aspects of everyday life. He first came to national attention in the early 1980's, when he regularly appeared on "Late Night with David Letterman." In 1986, Leno signed an exclusive contract with NBC and hosted "Showtime Special," "Saturday Night Live," and "Jay Leno's Family Comedy Hour." In 1990, Leno entertained allied troops in Saudi Arabia. He has also appeared in several films and has compiled three books of "ridiculous samplings from America's newspapers."

James Douglas Leno was born in New Rochelle, N.Y., on April 28, 1950, and grew up in a middle-class suburb of Boston. Taking a workmanlike approach to his job, Leno says his philosophy is: "Write joke. Tell joke. Get check."

When he's not on the job, Leno likes to tinker with the antique cars and motorcycles he has collected. Leno lives in Beverly Hills, Calif., with his wife, Mavis Nicholson. Lori Fagan

Lesotho. See **Africa.**

Liberia. Despite the presence of a west African peacekeeping force in Liberia, the civil war that began in December 1989 continued through much of 1991. The two rebel groups that overthrew President Samuel K. Doe in 1990—and after that fought each other and the remnants of Doe's army—agreed to a truce in February 1991. Later in the year, the peacekeeping force arranged a series of cease-fires. Nonetheless, attacks on civilians and property continued. The warring factions reached a new accord in late June, but it was not until September that Charles Taylor, leader of the largest rebel movement, the National Patriotic Front of Liberia (NPFL), agreed to surrender his arms.

Interim president gets to work. Although Taylor's forces controlled 90 per cent of the countryside in 1991 and Taylor insisted that he should head the new government, the brutality of his rebel group led most Liberians to reject his claims to the presidency. Also scorned by the people were Taylor's chief rival in the civil war, Prince Yormie Johnson, and former Vice President Harry Moniba, who asserted that he was Doe's constitutional successor.

At several conferences in 1991, Liberian civilian leaders reaffirmed their overwhelming preference for Amos Sawyer, a popular Liberian author and educator, to serve as interim president. Sawyer, who was installed in that post in November 1990, chaired the drafting of the 1984 Liberian Constitution and was later forced into exile for criticizing Doe.

The Harold Washington Library Center, named for Chicago's former mayor and the largest public library in the United States, opened in October.

Sawyer worked diligently in 1991 to reconcile Liberia's various military, ethnic, and political interests and to prepare the country for elections the following year. In May, he oversaw the establishment of an interim legislative assembly with 40 per cent of the seats allotted to the NPFL. During the year, he also named a presidential Cabinet and, in consultation with Taylor, selected judges for a supreme court. Sawyer said, however, that he would not be a candidate for president in 1992.

Reconstruction. To facilitate the return and resettlement of refugees from the civil war, the interim assembly in June granted amnesty to most combatants. The government began coordinating relief efforts. In Liberia's capital, Monrovia, which was devastated by the fighting in 1990, telephone service, water, electricity, and other basic services had been restored by late 1991. Still, the city continued to bear the scars of war. Along ruined streets, gutted buildings waited to be repaired or torn down.

Funding the reconstruction effort was difficult. Some $27 million in government funds deposited in overseas banks were stolen by members of the Doe regime. Also, private firms were slow in paying taxes and fees. Fortunately, private donors and foreign governments were generous in their offers of help.

J. Gus Liebenow and Beverly B. Liebenow

See also **Africa** (Facts in brief table). In ***World Book,*** see **Liberia.**

Library. A slumping economy and growing resistance to higher taxes compounded the financial problems facing libraries in the United States in 1991. Many libraries, already hard-pressed by soaring costs for reading materials and shrinking support from financially beleaguered local governments, were forced to trim their hours of service and discontinue special services such as literacy programs and bookmobile routes. Some libraries were forced to close. Librarians found the cutbacks particularly troubling because of a rising demand for library services. During economic downturns, people increasingly turn to libraries as an economical means of obtaining reading material and finding information, such as job notices.

New York City, struggling with a $2-billion budget deficit in fiscal year 1992, slashed funding for its public libraries by $25 million, an 18 per cent drop over the libraries' fiscal 1991 allocation. As a result, branch libraries in some parts of the city were able to open only two days a week. Budget cuts also led the Albuquerque (N. Mex.) Public Library to shorten the hours of service at its 12 branches and to cut staff by more than 15 per cent.

Meanwhile, Chicago dedicated the largest public library in the United States. In October, the Chicago Public Library opened the Harold Washington Library Center to house the library's main collection. The $144-million library building also has a 400-seat auditorium and a glass-enclosed winter garden.

Small-town libraries also experienced budget woes. For example, the public library in Gray, Me., reduced its hours from 40 to 16 per week. At least 30 per cent of the public libraries in Massachusetts substantially reduced their hours of service and cut expenditures for books and other materials during 1991.

Funding problems also have taken a toll on school libraries. Library officials in California reported in 1991 that only about 1,000 of California's 7,350 elementary schools had libraries or media centers, a 50 per cent drop over the number of such facilities in 1981.

Promoting libraries. The financial problems plaguing libraries prompted the American Library Association (ALA) to launch a year-long campaign, "Libraries Are Worth It!" The goal of the program is to rally public support for libraries, librarians, and ready access to information. The ALA kicked off the campaign on June 29, 1991, at its 110th annual conference in Atlanta, Ga.

The future role of libraries was the focus of the second White House Conference on Libraries and Information Services, held from July 9 to 13 in Washington, D.C. More than 700 delegates and 1,300 alternates and observers approved 94 resolutions on such topics as intellectual freedom, funding, and the importance of libraries as centers for lifelong learning. A resolution calling for improved library services to children and young adults received the strongest support.

Libraries and the homeless. The clash between the right of library patrons, including homeless people, to have access to information and libraries' interest in maintaining a suitable environment was the focus of a federal court case in 1991. The case concerned a homeless man named Richard Kreimer who had sued the Free Public Library of Morristown, N.J., after being ejected from the library for allegedly disobeying library regulations on patron behavior.

In recent years, growing numbers of homeless people have sought shelter in public libraries. In some cases, however, homeless people have engaged in behavior, such as talking loudly and washing their clothes in drinking fountains, that other library patrons have found disruptive. In response, some libraries have established regulations governing the behavior and personal hygiene of patrons. These regulations have come under attack by legal experts and advocates for the homeless, who have argued that the rules violate the right of all patrons to obtain information under the First Amendment to the Constitution of the United States.

In May, Judge H. Lee Sarokin ruled that the library had violated Kreimer's rights by expelling him for having an offensive body odor. In his ruling, Judge Sarokin determined that the library's regulations were unconstitutional because they were too broad and vague. The judge also ruled that the regulations violated Kreimer's First Amendment rights. The library appealed the decision. Peggy Barber

In *World Book,* see **Library.**

Libyan soldiers, captured during Libyan raids on Chad in 1988, await release in February 1991, before their eventual resettlement in the United States.

Libya was accused in 1991 of involvement in the bombings of two civilian aircraft, in which 441 people died. On November 14, the United States accused two Libyan intelligence officials of building and planting the bomb that exploded aboard Pan American World Airways Flight 103 over Lockerbie, Scotland, in 1988, killing 270 people. A federal grand jury in Washington, D.C., charged Abdel Basset Ali al-Megrahi and Lamen Khalifa Fhimah with conspiracy, the killing of 189 Americans aboard Flight 103, and the destruction of a civil aircraft. According to U.S. investigators, Libya had ordered the Pan American attack in retaliation

for U.S. bombing raids on Libya in 1986. Those raids were reprisals for Libya's alleged involvement in the 1986 bombing of a dance club in Berlin in which two American soldiers died. In early December 1991, Libya announced it would try al-Megrahi and Fhimah under Libyan law.

French action. On October 30, a French judge issued arrest warrants for four Libyans linked to the 1989 bombing of a French airliner over Niger in north-central Africa, in which 171 people were killed. Libya had reportedly ordered that bombing in retaliation for French support for the government of Chad, which defeated Libyan-backed rebels in 1987.

Screwworm flies eradicated. An infestation of a dangerous cattle pest that had established an African beachhead in Libya in 1988 was eradicated in April 1991. The screwworm fly, whose larvae feed on living flesh, was the target of an eradication campaign by the Food and Agriculture Organization (FAO), a United Nations agency. In February, FAO scientists released 40 million sterile male screwworm flies over Libya. The flies mated with native females, who mate only once and then die. Within about 10 generations, the flies had died out. Scientists had been concerned that the spread of the flies would have crippled livestock production in Africa. Christine Helms

See also **Persian Gulf,** Special Report: **War in the Persian Gulf; Africa** (Facts in brief table). In ***World Book,*** see **Libya.**

Liechtenstein. See **Europe.**

Literature. A revival of ambitious, sprawling novels dealing with large themes marked American fiction in 1991. Such novels had grown unfashionable during the 1970's and 1980's, when slender, inward-looking minimalist novels flooded the literary market.

Mark Helprin's 792-page *A Soldier of the Great War* was a sterling example of the new broad-shouldered fiction. In it, an Italian veteran of World War I looks back on the savage fighting with the Austro-Hungarians in the northern mountains of his country, reaching the conclusion that war is an unexplainable part of the human condition, and that soldiers "learn to live in mystery and anger."

An equally ambitious novel was *Harlot's Ghost*, Norman Mailer's voluminous exploration of the murky depths of the Central Intelligence Agency. Harold Brodkey's 835-page *The Runaway Soul* was the noted short story writer's long-awaited, often brilliant first novel about the inner life of an adopted boy.

On only a slightly smaller scale, John Sayles's *Los Gusanos* was a large, great-hearted novel about a family of Cuban exiles living in Miami. Similarly, Amy Tan's *The Kitchen God's Wife* painted on a broad canvas the life of a Chinese matriarch in San Francisco; Anne Roiphe's *The Pursuit of Happiness* was a vivid, five-generation tale of Jewish immigrants; and Norman Rush's National Book Award-winning *Mating* was a sprawling comedy of manners set in Africa.

Other important novels were Robert Coover's *Pinocchio in Venice*; John L'Heureux's *An Honorable Profession*; Charles Portis' *Gringos*; John Barth's *The Last Voyage of Somebody the Sailor*; Denis Johnson's *Resuscitation of a Hanged Man*; Gail Godwin's *Father Melancholy's Daughter*; Stanley Elkin's *The MacGuffin*; Paul Theroux's *Chicago Loop*; the late Isaac Bashevis Singer's *Scum*; Don DeLillo's *Mao II*; Anne Tyler's *Saint Maybe*; Russell Banks's *The Sweet Hereafter*; Carolyn See's *Making History*; Pete Dexter's *Brotherly Love*; and Jane Smiley's *A Thousand Acres*.

Among the year's noteworthy first novels were two by Chinese Americans: Frank Chin's *Donald Duk* and Gish Jen's *Typical American*. The journalist Anna Quindlen contributed *Object Lessons*, an entertaining coming-of-age story. Louis Begley's *Wartime Lies* looked at war through the eyes of a child.

Short stories. Leading collections of short stories were Allan Gurganus' *White People*; Reynolds Price's *The Foreseeable Future*; Marianne Wiggins' *Bet They'll Miss Us When We're Gone*; and Joyce Carol Oates's *Heat and Other Stories*.

Fiction from other countries. Fiction from England included John Le Carré's *The Secret Pilgrim*; V. S. Pritchett's *Complete Collected Stories*; Julian Barnes's *Talking It Over*; and Anita Brookner's *Brief Lives*. The Irish-born writer William Trevor published *Two Lives*, a volume containing two novellas. Two notable Canadian works were Robertson Davies' novel *Murther & Walking Spirits* and Margaret Atwood's short-story collection *Wilderness Tips*.

Other important books written in English were the Australian Thomas Keneally's *Flying Hero Class*; the Trinidad-born Canadian Neil Bissoondath's *On the Eve of Uncertain Tomorrows*; and the South African Nobel laureate Nadine Gordimer's *Jump and Other Stories*.

Translations. From Czechoslovakia came Josef Skvorecky's *The Miracle Game*, Ivan Klima's *Love and Garbage*, and Milan Kundera's *Immortality*. The Polish writer Henryk Sienkiewicz' 1884 novel *With Fire and Sword* was also translated for the first time in 1991. From Israel came Amos Oz's latest novel, *To Know a Woman*.

Biographies. A large number of excellent biographies appeared in 1991. The most eagerly awaited of these was the first volume of John Richardson's projected four-volume *A Life of Picasso*, a richly detailed portrait of the modern artist.

Not far behind in scope and excellence was R. W. B. Lewis' *The Jameses: A Family Narrative*, about the distinguished American clan that included novelist Henry; his brother, the philosopher William; and their sister, the intellectual Alice.

Among the year's other literary biographies were Peter Ackroyd's *Dickens*, a gossipy life of the great English novelist; Jonathan Cott's *Wandering Ghost: The Odyssey of Lafcadio Hearn*, which explored the eccentric life of the almost forgotten writer from Cincinnati who became an authority on Japan in the 1890's; Jeffrey Meyers' *Joseph Conrad*, a synthesis of old and new material on the Polish-born British novelist; Michael Shelden's *Orwell*, about the British novelist and essayist who attacked political injustice and hypocrisy in the modern world; and *Goethe: The Poet and the Age*, the first volume of Nicholas Boyle's biography of the towering German poet, playwright, and novelist.

Diane Wood Middlebrook's *Anne Sexton*, a study of the troubled American poet, was controversial for its use of confidential records made available to the author by the late poet's psychiatrist. *Vladimir Nabokov: The American Years* was the second volume of Brian Boyd's wide-ranging life of the Russian-American novelist. Penelope Niven's *Carl Sandburg* explored the life and influence of the poet from the American Midwest. Michael Holroyd published the third and final volume of his excellent biography of the Irish dramatist *Bernard Shaw*.

Two biographies marked the hundredth anniversary of the birth of Henry Miller, an important American novelist of the 1930's: *Henry Miller: A Life*, by Robert Ferguson, and *The Happiest Man Alive: A Biography of Henry Miller*, by Mary V. Dearborn.

Among the year's performing-arts biographies was one by Eric Lax, *Woody Allen*, about the American comedian and film director. Agnes de Mille's *Martha: The Life and Work of Martha Graham*, was an intimate portrait of the great dancer and choreographer. Graham also revealed much of her fascinating life in the autobiographical *Blood Memory*, which appeared

Nadine Gordimer, a South African novelist who has written about the racial injustices in her native land, won the 1991 Nobel Prize for literature.

shortly after her death in April. See **Dance,** Special Report: **Two Legends of Dance.**

Among biographies of political figures, two books on Richard M. Nixon earned widespread interest. Tom Wicker's *One of Us* explored the former President's domestic political style. The other was the concluding volume of Stephen Ambrose's *Nixon* trilogy, subtitled *Ruin and Recovery, 1973-1990*. Two other widely hailed presidential biographies were Lou Cannon's *President Reagan: The Role of a Lifetime* and Robert Dallek's *Lone Star Rising: Lyndon Johnson and His Times, 1908-1960*.

Other important lives of historical figures were Philip Ziegler's *King Edward VIII*, about the British king who abdicated the throne in 1936 to marry an American divorcee; William S. McFeely's *Frederick Douglass*, on the former slave who became an important author and reformer in the years prior to the American Civil War; Robert V. Remini's *Henry Clay*, which explored the life of the Kentucky politician who was a crucial figure in American politics during the first half of the 1800's; and Robert Conquest's *Stalin*, a biography of the notorious dictator who ruled the Soviet Union from 1924 to 1953.

Autobiographical writings. Among the best literary memoirs was *Patrimony*, novelist Philip Roth's sometimes comic, always moving chronicle of his father's final struggle with a brain tumor. *You've Had Your Time* was the second part of British novelist Anthony Burgess' ongoing "Confessions," a lively, engaging autobiography. *The Bookmaker's Daughter* was Southern author Shirley Abbott's fine reminiscence of life with an itinerant gambler father. *The Journals of John Cheever* reflected the novelist's talent for vivid observation, as well as the alcoholism, marital infidelities, and bisexuality that tormented him privately.

Counsel to the President, by Clark Clifford, told of the Washington lawyer's long career as an adviser to U.S. Presidents. Ironically, it was published at a time when its author was enmeshed in a banking scandal that threatened to destroy his reputation. Another public servant, the former U.S. Surgeon General C. Everett Koop, described his contentious, principled life in medicine and politics in *Koop*.

Fortunate Son was the deeply affecting memoir of Lewis H. Puller, Jr., an American soldier who was terribly maimed during the Vietnam war. *Which Side Are You On?* was Thomas Geoghegan's highly personal, idealistic account of his life as a Chicago labor lawyer. Other fine memoirs included Rick Bass's *Winter: Notes from Montana*, about life in the isolated Yaak Valley of the Montana Rockies, and Lorene Cary's *Black Ice*, which described a young black girl's years at an exclusive boarding school in New Hampshire.

Criticism. David Lehman's *Signs of the Times* explored the literary theory of deconstruction and the controversial career of Paul de Man, one of its leading exponents, who wrote pro-Nazi journalism while living in his native Belgium during World War II (1939-1945). *Odd Jobs* was a fine collection of critical essays, speeches, and other nonfiction writings by the American novelist John Updike.

Contemporary nonfiction. The most significant book on current affairs to appear in 1991 was a Soviet import, *The Truth About Chernobyl*, by Grigori Medvedev. A nuclear energy specialist who was once chief engineer at Chernobyl, Medvedev concluded that the reasons for the explosion at the Soviet nuclear power plant in 1986 lay in human error. He expressed grave doubts that nuclear power can ever be made safe.

Another important book of social commentary was *Bringing Down the Great Wall*, a collection of essays, interviews, and speeches by the Chinese scientist Fang Lizhi. Lizhi's various statements coalesce to form a brilliant personal example of dissent against the Beijing government.

Three influential books explored American social problems. Alex Kotlowitz's *There Are No Children Here* was a harrowing exploration of life in a Chicago public housing project. *Savage Inequalities* was Jonathan Kozol's indictment of the vast disparities in spending for education in rich and poor American school districts. *Reflections of an Affirmative Action Baby*, by Stephen L. Carter, was a first-hand account of a black Yale law professor's troubling experience of racial relations and affirmative action policies in contemporary America.

In *Chain Reaction*, Thomas Byrne Edsall and Mary D. Edsall argued that in the last two decades racial divisions and resentments have come increasingly to dominate American politics. In an equally argumentative book, *Den of Thieves*, James B. Stewart detailed the corruption and scandals that tarnished Wall Street during the 1980's.

Two books on the Iran-contra scandal that occurred during Ronald Reagan's presidency were published in 1991: Theodore Draper's *A Very Thin Line* and the best-selling *Under Fire*, a memoir by Oliver North, who was a central figure in the controversy.

A persuasive muckraking volume was Curt Gentry's *J. Edgar Hoover*, which uncovered abuses of power by the late chief of the Federal Bureau of Investigation. Susan Faludi's *Backlash* examined the strong reaction against feminism by conservatives in the United States during the 1980's. *Three Blind Mice*, by Ken Auletta, explored the recent corporate woes of the three major television networks—ABC, CBS, and NBC.

Travel. Of the year's travel books, William Least Heat-Moon's *PrairyErth* plumbed the history of a single county on the Kansas prairie. Jonathan Raban's *Hunting Mister Heartbreak* told of the English travel writer's search for a place to live in America, ending with his decision to settle in Seattle. The distinguished novelist V. S. Naipaul offered *India: A Million Mutinies Now*, his third book of nonfictional observations on contemporary life in India.

History. Nicholas Lemann's *The Promised Land* was a far-reaching study of the great black migration from the South to the North during the 1900's. *Nature's Metropolis*, by William Cronon, examined the relationship of Chicago to its rural Midwestern surroundings during the 1800's. Philip Greven's *Spare the Child* explored the close links between religion and corporal punishment in America.

Albert Hourani's *A History of the Arab Peoples* was a magisterial narrative that covered 14 centuries of Middle East history. Michael R. Beschloss' *The Crisis Years* looked at the perilous relationship that developed between Soviet Premier Nikita Khrushchev and United States President John F. Kennedy during the period that led to the dangerous Cuban missile crisis of 1962. Paul Johnson's *The Birth of the Modern* was an entertaining social history of the period between 1815 and 1830. Johnson argued that these years marked the beginning of the modern era in both technology and thought.

Science. *In the Palaces of Memory: How We Build the Worlds Inside Our Heads*, by George Johnson, explored the processes of human intelligence. *The Arrow of Time* was Peter Coveney and Roger Highfield's discussion of current knowledge about the nature of time. Daniel C. Dennett's *Consciousness Explained* was a fascinating, detailed examination of the experience of being alive and aware.

Social science. *In Search of Human Nature* was Carl N. Degler's thoughtful chronicle of the changing ways in which social scientists have used the biological

sciences to study differences among races, cultures, and social classes.

Best sellers. Two unusual books on the "men's movement," a male counterpart to feminism, rode high on the best seller list during 1991. They were Robert Bly's *Iron John* and Sam Keen's *Fire in the Belly. Scarlett*, Alexandra Ripley's long awaited sequel to Margaret Mitchell's *Gone with the Wind*, was a critical disaster but a bookstore triumph. Other notable best-selling books were Kitty Kelley's controversial *Nancy Reagan*; lawyer Alan M. Dershowitz' *Chutzpah*; actress Katharine Hepburn's *Me*; minister Robert Fulghum's *Uh-Oh*; Tom Clancy's *The Sum of All Fears*; and Derek Humphry's *Final Exit*, a book that presented an argument in favor of suicide for people suffering from terminal illness.

A controversial paperback best seller was *The Education of Little Tree*, by Forrest Carter. The book was originally presented as the memoir of an orphaned boy who was raised by his Cherokee grandparents. It was later discovered, however, that the book was a hoax, having been written by the late Asa Carter, a segregationist speechwriter for Southern politicians. After the hoax was discovered, some newspapers and magazines moved the book from the nonfiction best seller list to the fiction list.

Henry Kisor

See also **Canadian literature; Literature for children; Poetry.** In ***World Book***, see **Literature.**

Literature for children. Children's books published in 1991 continued to emphasize multicultural and environmental subjects. Picture books and toy books for preschoolers were plentiful, as were educational publications. Fewer books of poetry, fantasy, and folk tales were published. Literature for older children addressed current social problems, growing up, and friendship.

Outstanding books of 1991 included the following:

Picture books. *Nurse Lugton's Curtain* by Virginia Woolf, illustrated by Julie Vivas (Gulliver Bks.). An imaginative tale of a sewing pattern that comes to life while the seamstress sleeps. Ages 7 and up.

The Wretched Stone by Chris Van Allsburg (Houghton Mifflin). A mysterious stone brought on board a ship causes ominous changes. Ages 7 to 10.

Changes by Anthony Browne (Knopf). A boy's father tells him that changes are coming, and the boy's lively imagination goes to work. Ages 5 and up.

The Wing Shop by Elvira Woodruff, illustrated by Stephen Gammell (Holiday House). This highly imaginative tale tells of a boy who flies off on wings to find his old home. Ages 3 to 8.

Trouble Dolls by Jimmy Buffett and Savannah Buffett, illustrated by Lambert Davis (Harcourt Brace Jovanovich). When Lizzy's father is lost, the trouble dolls help her look for him. Ages 6 and up.

Tar Beach by Faith Ringgold (Crown). In a tale that originated in a quilt made by the author, a little girl dreams of flying. Bold, dramatic paintings and quilt design borders decorate the pages. Ages 4 to 8.

Sophie and Lou by Petra Mathers (HarperCollins). Shy Sophie begins to dance and speak to people after a dancing school opens across the street. Ages 4 to 8.

The Thieves' Market by Dennis Haseley, illustrated by Lisa Desimini (HarperCollins). Haunting paintings join a mesmerizing tale of children who go to the thieves' market during the night. Ages 7 to 11.

The Boxing Champion by Roch Carrier, translated by Sheila Fischman, illustrated by Sheldon Cohen (Tundra). A boy who loses in the ring sends away for barbells to make him a champion. Ages 7 to 10.

Piggies by Don and Audrey Wood, illustrated by Don Wood (Harcourt Brace Jovanovich). Fingers become comical pigs with various traits. Ages 3 to 6.

Moonhorse by Mary Pope Osborne, illustrated by S. M. Saelig (Knopf). Haunting, luminous pictures depict a girl riding a horse across the sky. Ages 4 to 7.

Where Does the Trail Lead? by Burton Albert, illustrated by Brian Pinkney (Simon & Schuster). Wonderful scratchboard illustrations and a simple, flowing text tell of a boy's summer explorations. Ages 5 to 8.

Tree of Cranes by Allen Say (Houghton Mifflin). A Japanese boy learns about Christmas from his California-born mother. Beautiful, simple, expressive paintings. Ages 4 to 8.

Hildegard Sings by Thomas Wharton (Farrar, Straus & Giroux). When Hildegard, a budding hippo opera star, loses her voice, extreme measures must be taken. Comical paintings add to the fun. Ages 4 to 8.

The Sea Lion by Ken Kesey, illustrated by Neil Waldman (Viking Children's Books). Because of his crooked back, Eemook is scorned by his people until he saves them from the Sea Lion.

Alpha and the Dirty Baby by Brock Cole (Farrar, Straus & Giroux). Alpha must outwit the imps to regain her parents. Ages 4 to 8.

Wempires by Daniel Pinkwater (Macmillan). A boy who wants to be a vampire entertains three unusual vampires one night. Outrageously silly. Ages 4 to 8.

Appelemando's Dreams by Patricia Polacco (Philomel). A drab town comes to life when Appelemando's colorful dreams begin to stick. Ages 4 to 8.

The Rag Coat by Lauren Mills (Little, Brown). Minna has no coat until the quilting women make one out of scraps, but the other children jeer. Ages 4 to 8.

Classics retold in picture books. *Kashtanka* by Anton Chekhov, translated by Richard Pevear, illustrated by Barry Moser (Putnam). A dog loses her master and finds a new home for a while. Superb paintings. All ages.

Cyclops by Leonard Everett Fisher (Holiday House). Odysseus and his men must outwit the one-eyed giant or die. Highly dramatic paintings. Ages 5 to 8.

Tailypo! retold by Jan Wahl, illustrated by Wil Clay (Henry Holt). After an old man cuts off and eats a creature's tail, the creature keeps showing up at the man's door. Ages 6 to 9.

Illustrations and text from *Black and White* won for David Macaulay the 1991 Caldecott Medal for most distinguished picture book for children.

Hark! A Christmas Sampler by Jane Yolen, illustrated by Tomie DePaola (Putnam). This collection of colorfully illustrated tales, legends, poems, customs, and carols (with music) should delight all ages.

Fiction. *The China Year* by Emily Cheney Neville (HarperCollins). When Henrietta's father teaches in China for a year, she must find her way in a new culture. Ages 12 and up.

Along the Tracks by Tamar Bergman, translated by Michael Swirsky (Houghton Mifflin). Yasha tries to survive after being separated from his mother and sister fleeing the Nazis during World War II. Ages 11 to 14.

Al Capsella and the Watchdogs by J. Clarke (Henry Holt). In this funny story, Al and friends try to escape their parents' watchful eyes. Ages 11 to 14.

Monkey Island by Paula Fox (Orchard Bks.). In this story, a homeless man befriends Clay—whose parents deserted him—and cares for him until Clay becomes desperately ill. Ages 11 to 14.

The Rain Catchers by Jean Thesman (Houghton Mifflin). Grayling has grown up with her grandmother and other women who share her house, but a visit to her mother might change everything. Ages 12 and up.

Anastasia at This Address by Lois Lowry (Houghton Mifflin). Anastasia uses half-truths to answer a personal ad and finds herself getting deeper and deeper into trouble. Ages 10 to 12.

Go Fish by Mary Stolz, illustrated by Pat Cummings (HarperCollins). Thomas goes fishing with his grandfather and learns some valuable lessons. Ages 7 to 11.

Nothing But the Truth: A Documentary Novel by Avi (Orchard Bks). Phillip Malloy hums the national anthem in school, and events escalate. Ages 11 and up.

The Cookcamp by Gary Paulsen (Orchard Bks.). A 5-year-old boy is sent to his grandmother, who is a cook at a wilderness camp for road workers. Ages 10 to 12.

Hide and Seek by Ida Vos, translated by Terese Edelstein and Inez Smidt (Houghton Mifflin). The book reveals the sufferings of a family who hid from the Nazis. Ages 12 and up.

The Man from the Other Side by Uri Orlev, translated by Hillel Halkin (Houghton Mifflin). A boy living in Warsaw during World War II learns about the ghetto, and a secret changes his views. Ages 12 and up.

The Boy and the Samurai by Erik Christian Haugaard (Houghton Mifflin). Saru, an orphan struggling to survive, meets a samurai and helps rescue another samurai's wife. Ages 12 and up.

The Chickenhouse House by Ellen Howard, illustrated by Nancy Oleksa (Atheneum). Alena grows to love the intimacy of a chicken house where her family lives while their new home is being built. Ages 7 to 10.

Wolf by the Ears by Ann Rinaldi (Scholastic). Harriet Hemings, a slave of Thomas Jefferson and said to be his daughter, must decide about her future when she turns 21. Ages 12 and up.

Year of Impossible Goodbyes by Sook Nyul Choi (Houghton Mifflin). In 1945, a Korean family flees Soviet occupation.

Mama, Let's Dance by Patricia Hermes (Little, Brown). When their mother deserts them, three children learn the importance of family. Ages 10 and up.

The Kingdom by the Sea by Robert Westall (Farrar, Straus & Giroux). Henry sees his house bombed during World War II and sets out to survive on his own. Ages 12 and up.

Poetry. *Polaroid and Other Poems of View* by Betsy Hearne, illustrated by Peter Kiar (M. K. McElderry Bks.). Fresh imagery and photos enliven the senses. Ages 12 and up.

A Cup of Starshine by Jill Bennett, illustrated by Graham Percy (Harcourt Brace Jovanovich). Perfect pictures capture each rhyme in this anthology for the young. Ages 2 to 6.

Birds, Beasts and Fishes: A Selection of Animal Poems by Ann Carter, illustrated by Reg Cartwright (Macmillan). A variety of poems with striking paintings make this a fine collection. All ages.

In for Winter, Out for Spring by Arnold Adoff, illustrated by Jerry Pinkney (Harcourt Brace Jovanovich). Adoff captures the seasons and a child's actions in free verse and lovely paintings. Ages 4 to 8.

Mr. Mistoffelees with Mungojerrie and Rumpelteazer by T. S. Eliot, illustrated by Errol Le Cain (Harcourt Brace Jovanovich). Two lively cat poems by the great English poet are accompanied by imaginative, amusing paintings. All ages.

The Lampfish of Twill by Janet Taylor Lisle, illustrated by Wendy Anderson Halperin (Orchard Bks.). Eric, an orphan with a pet seagull, seeks the elusive lampfish on an underseas journey. Ages 10 and up.

The Ballad of the Harp Weaver by Edna St. Vincent Millay, illustrated by Beth Peck (Philomel). Oil paintings complement a haunting poem about a starving child and his mother. Ages 5 and up.

The Adventures of Isabel by Ogden Nash, illustrated by James Marshall (Joy St.). Marshall's zany illustrations augment the poem's hilarity. Ages 4 to 8.

All Join In by Quentin Blake (Little, Brown). Nonsensical songs and riotous illustrations result in an irresistible collection. Ages 4 to 8.

Dragons Dragons by Laura Whipple, illustrated by Eric Carl (Philomel). Mythical creatures in verse are dramatically depicted in collage. All ages.

Fantasy. *Child of the Air* by Grace Chetwin (Bradbury Pr.). Mylanfyndra and her brother discover that they can fly, and a new world with a new language is created in this adventurous tale. Ages 12 and up.

Dragon Cauldron by Laurence Yep (HarperCollins). A sequel to *Dragon of the Lost Sea* and *Dragon Steel,* Thorn and his friends continue their adventures. Ages 12 and up.

Rosemary's Witch by Ann Turner (HarperCollins). Nine-year-old Rosemary and her family have found a perfect house, or have they? Ages 11 and up.

Black Unicorn by Tanith Lee, illustrated by Heather Cooper (Atheneum). Aided by a unicorn, Tanaquil flees her mother's isolated fortress and has many adventures. Ages 12 and up.

The Jewel of Life by Anna Kirwan-Vogel (Harcourt Brace Jovanovich). When Duffy becomes apprenticed to an apothecary, mysteries begin. Ages 10 to 14.

Seven Strange and Ghostly Tales by Brian Jacques (Philomel). A varied collection to frighten and fascinate, with some humorous characters. Ages 8 and up.

Hauntings: Ghosts and Ghouls from Around the World edited by Margaret Hodges, illustrated by David Wenzel (Little, Brown). Sixteen stories offer shivers and wonder. Ages 8 to 12.

Animals, people, places, and things. *Where Food Comes From* by Dorothy Hinshaw Patent, illustrated by William Munoz (Holiday House). Fine color photos and a clear text show how the sun, water, and earth help produce foods. Ages 8 to 12.

Prairie Visions: The Life and Times of Solomon Butcher by Pam Conrad (HarperCollins). Conrad provides fascinating stories from pioneers depicted in Butcher's photography. Ages 11 and up.

The Wright Brothers: How They Invented the Airplane by Russell Freedman (Holiday House). Illustrated with the Wright brothers' photographs, the book describes the pair's exploits. Ages 10 and up.

Animal Amazing: A Casebook of Unsolved Zoological Mysteries by Judith Herbst (Atheneum). Information about animals and their antics will keep animal-loving children engrossed. Ages 10 and up.

Gentle Annie: The True Story of a Civil War Nurse by Mary F. Shura (Scholastic). A portrayal of Anna

Etheridge provides glimpses of Civil War heroism and women who disguised themselves as men in order to fight. Ages 12 and up.

Discovering Dinosaur Babies by Miriam Schlein, illustrated by Margaret Colbert (Four Winds). Fossil finds that impart knowledge about dinosaurs are clearly shown and described. Ages 6 to 10.

Fire & Silk: Flying in a Hot Air Balloon by Neil Johnson (Joy St.). The procedures, joys, and hazards of ballooning are discussed. Gorgeous color photos. Ages 5 and up.

Anno's Math Games No. III by Mitsumasa Anno (Philomel). Mathematical concepts involving shapes and mazes and such are intriguingly presented as games and puzzles. Ages 4 to 8.

Appalachia: The Voices of Sleeping Birds by Cynthia Rylant, illustrated by Barry Moser (Harcourt Brace Jovanovich). A loving view of the region and its people lays stereotypes to rest. Ages 5 and up.

Awards. Jerry Spinelli won the 1991 Newbery Medal for his novel *Maniac Magee.* The medal is given by the American Library Association (ALA) for outstanding children's literature published the previous year. The ALA's Caldecott Medal for "the most distinguished American picture book for children" went to David Macaulay, the illustrator and author of *Black and White.* Marilyn Fain Apseloff

In ***World Book,*** see **Caldecott Medal; Newbery Medal; Literature for children.**

Lithuania, which first tried to secede from the Soviet Union in 1990, saw independence become a reality in 1991. Before that occurred, however, Lithuania stood up to military intimidation as the Soviet government attempted to crush the country's independence movement. The Soviet Union had forcibly annexed Lithuania in 1940, along with its Baltic neighbors, Estonia and Latvia.

Soviet crackdown. In January 1991, the Soviet defense ministry sent special troops into seven republics, including Lithuania, to enforce compliance with the military draft and arrest those who had ignored military call-ups. On January 11, amid escalating tension, the Soviet troops stormed and seized several government buildings in Vilnius, Lithuania's capital. Demonstrators poured into the streets in protest.

On January 13, the Soviet take-over of the radio and television broadcasting station left 13 people dead and more than 100 wounded. Thousands of Lithuanians then came out to defend the parliament against an anticipated assault. At the end of January, the Soviet government announced the withdrawal of the special troops.

The crackdown met with sharp international disapproval. The reaction prompted Soviet President Mikhail S. Gorbachev to disavow responsibility for the shootings by blaming a local army commander for the decision to take action against the demonstrators.

In February, the Soviet leader announced talks with Lithuania and the two other Baltic republics on a package of political, social, and economic issues. But Gorbachev maintained that independence had to proceed through constitutional channels, which meant a lengthy waiting period and the approval of the Soviet parliament.

Lithuanians celebrate their nation's August independence declaration atop a fallen statue of V. I. Lenin, leader of Russia's Communist Revolution.

The Vilnius leadership held a referendum on Lithuania's future on February 9, in defiance of Soviet authorities. An overwhelming majority of the voters backed independence, including many members of Lithuania's ethnic Russian and ethnic Polish minorities. Gorbachev declared the vote illegal.

On August 21, in the wake of an attempted coup against Gorbachev, Lithuania reaffirmed its independence declaration of March 1990. The Soviet Union formally acknowledged the independence of all three Baltic states on Sept. 6, 1991.

The sobering realization of the difficult economic problems ahead followed quickly upon the euphoria over independence. Aside from shipyards and some chemical and textile plants, Lithuania has a small industrial base. Food products constitute the country's principal export. In August, the government introduced rationing because of shortages of nearly all consumer goods.

Government planners anticipated that instability at year's end among other former Soviet republics would have further harmful effects on Lithuania's economy. Until the collapse of the Soviet Union, Lithuania depended almost entirely on imported Soviet energy and traded almost exclusively with Soviet republics. Economic planning was based on Lithuania's continuing to conduct about 80 per cent of its trade with the former Soviet republics, primarily through barter.

Government economists said in October that the nation needed $2 billion in Western aid or investment to set economic reforms in motion. As first steps, the government planned to lift all price controls and sell state properties valued at $3 billion. Eric Bourne

See also **Europe** (Facts in brief table); **Union of Soviet Socialist Republics.** In the World Book Supplement section, see **Lithuania.**

Los Angeles. A sweeping report on the Los Angeles Police Department (LAPD), released on July 9, 1991, concluded that the department had ignored long-standing violent and racist behavior by "a problem group" of officers. The report recommended that the department take steps to end the use of excessive force against crime suspects by police officers. It also called for the resignation of Los Angeles Police Chief Daryl F. Gates as head of the 8,300-member department, a position he had held for 13 years, and urged that future chiefs be limited to two five-year terms.

The report was issued by a 10-member blue-ribbon panel formed to study the LAPD in the wake of the beating on March 3 of a black motorist, Rodney G. King, by four white police officers. The incident, captured on videotape by a bystander and aired on national television, prompted a public outcry over the behavior of the police officers and seemed to give credence to the many allegations of brutality and racism that had been leveled against the LAPD.

The four officers implicated in the beating of King were indicted on March 15. On March 26, they all pleaded not guilty to the charges against them. Their trial was scheduled to begin in February 1992. Gates was briefly suspended in April, and in July he said he would resign in April 1992.

The Los Angeles County Sheriff's Department also came under fire in 1991. On September 10, Sheriff Sherman Block announced that he had formed his own panel of community leaders to advise him on how to implement reforms in his department. Block took that action after an unprecedented public hearing aired a number of grievances against the Sheriff's Department, including charges that deputies were too quick to shoot suspects. In one case cited by critics, deputies allegedly killed a mentally disturbed man with nine bullets to the back.

There had also been allegations of corruption in the sheriff's office. On September 4, federal prosecutors announced that five more members of an elite antinarcotics team, which was disbanded in 1990, had been indicted for pocketing money seized from drug dealers. The federal investigation had resulted in eight convictions in 1990.

Elections. On March 8, Gloria Molina, the daughter of a laborer, was sworn in as the first Hispanic to serve on the Los Angeles County Board of Supervisors in 115 years. The 42-year-old Mexican-American woman, elected on February 19, also became the first-ever female member of the board, which governs a county population of some 9 million.

Molina's election was made possible by a 1988 lawsuit, filed by several civil rights groups, contending that the all-Anglo board had discriminated against Hispanics in redrawing district boundaries in 1981. Hispanics make up about one-third of the county's population. The successful suit led to the drawing of a new and fairer district map.

Demonstrators in Los Angeles in April demand an end to alleged police brutality after several officers were videotaped beating a black motorist.

Los Angeles Police Chief Daryl F. Gates, temporarily suspended from duty for allegedly tolerating police brutality, talks to the press on April 4.

On June 11, 1991, Rita Walters, a former member of the Los Angeles school board, became the first black woman elected to the Los Angeles City Council. Walters won by a razor-thin margin of 76 votes following a count of absentee ballots.

Education. The Los Angeles Unified School District opened its fall term on August 19 with a new calendar that eliminates the traditional summer vacation. For the majority of the district's 625,000 students in kindergarten through 12th grade, classes started almost a month earlier than usual. The students go to school for 90 days, and then get 30 days off.

The district's move to a new school calendar came amid a fiscal crisis that forced the Board of Education to make sharp cuts in its $3.9-billion budget. On September 10, the board voted to increase class sizes in elementary schools, a move that cost more than 800 teachers their jobs.

Nurses' strike. Thousands of nurses at six Los Angeles County hospitals and dozens of medical clinics went on strike October 28 to demand better pay and benefits. The two-day walkout was the first of a series of work stoppages planned for various county departments by the Service Employees International Union. The strike shut down emergency rooms and trauma centers. Victor Merina

In ***World Book,*** see **Los Angeles.**

Louisiana. See **State government.**

Luxembourg. See **Europe.**

Madigan, Edward R. (1936-), was sworn in as United States secretary of agriculture on March 7, 1991. Madigan, an 18-year veteran of the U.S. House of Representatives (R., Ill.), had spent 16 years on the House Agriculture Committee and was considered one of Congress's leading authorities on agriculture. In his new post, Madigan will oversee the implementation of the 1990 farm bill, which sets U.S. agricultural policy through 1995.

Madigan was born on Jan. 13, 1936, in Lincoln, Ill. He grew up there and attended Lincoln College, from which he graduated in 1955 with a degree in business administration. From 1955 to 1973, he owned an automobile-leasing and taxi company in Lincoln.

In 1966, Madigan was elected to the Illinois House of Representatives. He was reelected twice, serving until 1972, when he was elected to Congress.

In addition to serving on the House Agriculture Committee—for eight years as its highest-ranking Republican—Madigan was a long-time member of the Committee on Energy and Commerce. He also served on two House subcommittees: health and the environment, and telecommunications and finance. On the Agriculture Committee, Madigan helped shape the 1985 and 1990 farm bills, making a concerted effort to protect the income of American farmers and expand foreign markets for their products.

Madigan is married to the former Evelyn George. They have three daughters. David L. Dreier

Magazine. The United States magazine industry in 1991 suffered one of the most tumultuous years in its history. Advertising pages registered their steepest decline in two decades, as a nationwide recession forced advertisers to slash budgets. Unable to weather the storm, a number of magazines suspended publication or went out of business entirely.

Economic hard times affected almost all magazine publishers. Even such industry giants as Time Incorporated Magazine Company, Condé Nast Publications Incorporated, and the Hearst Corporation saw their advertising pages and revenues drop sharply.

Family Media Incorporated of New York City became the first large-scale magazine publisher to bow to the recession. After trying for months to sell off its titles, which included *Discover*, *Health*, and *Golf Illustrated*, the company closed down operations in August. With its energies focused on shoring up declining advertising—rather than on editorial quality—Family Media had begun losing readers. In the end, the company found itself unable to borrow sufficient funds to pay its debts and continue publishing. It sold *Discover*, a science monthly, to the Walt Disney Company, but its other six titles ceased publication.

Some magazine categories fared better than others. Magazines that covered the computer industry, for example, posted impressive circulation gains. Magazines aimed at teen-agers, on the other hand, dropped precipitously, with the exception of *Sassy*, a sprightly magazine for teen-age girls. The magazine's rise in subscription sales so cheered *Sassy* publisher, Lang Communications Incorporated of New York City, that in September the company introduced *Dirt*, a magazine for teen-age boys.

A Los Angeles life-style magazine, *Buzz*, epitomized the industry's precariousness. Launched in 1990 by three young entrepreneurs, *Buzz* suspended publication in February 1991 for lack of funding. To everyone's surprise, it was back a few months later thanks to the financial backing of a Thai businessman.

Ms. magazine, on the verge of folding in 1990, scored a comeback. In July 1991, *Ms.* announced the success of a yearlong experiment in publishing without advertisers, raising revenues solely from subscriptions and newsstand sales.

Start-ups. Several companies dared to launch new titles during what magazine publishers called the worst slump in memory. Black Entertainment Television, the first and only cable television service aimed at a black audience, began publication in August of *YSB* (for "Young Sisters and Brothers"), a life-style magazine for black teens.

The year's major new magazine was *Martha Stewart Living*, launched by Time. After testing two trial issues, Time announced in May that *Martha Stewart Living* would become a permanent addition to its publications list. This glossy publication for upscale homemakers was filled with pictures of little girls in organdy dresses hunting Easter eggs and features on how to serve the perfect Christmas dinner.

Condé Nast came out early in 1991 with *Allure*, an oversized magazine about beauty. By September, Condé Nast announced it would cut *Allure's* size to a standard magazine format. Other new magazines of 1991 included *Crime Beat*, *Parent's Digest*, *Family Fun*, and *Soap Opera*.

Shut-downs. The trend, however, was to shut down magazines rather than start them up. Among 1991 casualties were *California* and its two small sister publications, *SF* and *Angeles*. *California*, a cheerful life-style magazine, had been started by *New York Magazine's* founding editor, Clay Felker, in 1976 as *New West*. The magazine became *California* when it changed owners in 1983. The death of these publications underscored the difficulties experienced by many city and regional magazines that depend for advertising revenues on local retailers, businesses especially hard hit by the recession.

Other publications that also folded in 1991 were *Egg*, a year-old publication that focused on New York City's Manhattan social scene; *Memories*, a magazine that looked at old movies and earlier times; *OutWeek*, a publication directed to the gay community; *New England Living*, a regional life-style magazine; and *Museum & Arts Washington*, a publication about the cultural scene in the District of Columbia.

Deirdre Carmody

In ***World Book,*** see **Magazine.**

Mahony, Roger M. Cardinal (1936-   ), was elevated to cardinal of the Roman Catholic Church on June 28, 1991, by Pope John Paul II in Rome. Mahony was ordained a bishop in Fresno, Calif., on March 19, 1975, and the pope appointed him archbishop of Los Angeles on July 16, 1985.

One of twin boys, Mahony was born on Feb. 27, 1936, in Hollywood, Calif. He also has one older brother. Mahony received training for the priesthood at Our Lady Queen of the Angels Seminary in San Fernando, Calif., and at St. John's Seminary College in Camarillo, Calif., where he earned a B.A. degree in 1958. From 1958 to 1964, he continued his education at St. John's Theologate in Camarillo and at Catholic University of America in Washington, D.C.

After ordination as a priest on May 1, 1962, Mahony served the Monterey-Fresno diocese in California, an area of special interest for him because of its large Hispanic community, many of whom are migrant workers. In 1975, then governor of California Edmund G. Brown, Jr., appointed Mahony the first chairman of the California Agricultural Labor Relations Board. The board helped settle disputes between the United Farm Workers of America and California growers.

Mahony is a member of the Pontifical Council for the Pastoral Care of Migrants and Itinerant People, which meets in Vatican City. Carol L. Hanson

Maine. See **State government.**
Malawi. See **Africa.**

Malaysia in 1991 launched a New Development Policy intended to make the nation an economically "fully developed country" by the year 2020. Prime Minister Mahathir bin Mohamad presented the policy on June 17 to replace the New Economic Policy that had guided Malaysia since the 1970's.

The goals of the former policy had been to eradicate poverty and give the nation's ethnic Malay majority a larger economic voice in relation to Malaysia's ethnic Chinese citizens, who had dominated the business arena. The number of people living below the official poverty line fell from 37 per cent in 1973 to 15 per cent in 1987, according to the World Bank, an agency of the United Nations. The percentage of local companies owned by ethnic Malays also rose during that time from 2.4 per cent to 20.3 per cent. The old policy, however, had created ethnic resentment because the government favored Malays over Chinese.

Vision of 2020. On National Day, August 30, Mahathir said that the new policy had laid the foundation for progress. He described progress not only as the creation of more industries and higher income but also as better education, better care for all, and greater regard for the environment and for religion. Throughout 1991, the economy continued its rapid growth, though slowing slightly from the year's 10 per cent gain after adjustment for inflation. However, the nation's increasing imports of consumer goods and machinery created a foreign trade deficit.

Cabinet change. On February 9, Mahathir accepted the resignation of Finance Minister Daim Zainuddin, a businessman who had run the national economy for seven years. The public credited Daim with reducing regulations and taxes, thus freeing the economy to expand. But he was blamed for having been an investor in an illegal fireworks factory that exploded in May 1991, killing 24 people. Education Minister Anwar Ibrahim, widely assumed to be the political heir to the 65-year-old Mahathir, succeeded Daim.

Kelantan and Sabah. After opponents of Mahathir's ruling party won control of two states, Kelantan and Sabah, in October 1990 elections, Mahathir's national government in 1991 exerted pressure on Kelantan by such tactics as delaying government payments. A partnership of a Kelantan Islamic party and the Spirit of '46 party—led by an old foe of Mahathir, Prince Razaleigh Hamzah—won two local by-elections on August 24.

In Sabah, the national government arrested Jeffrey Kitingan, brother of Sabah's chief minister, on May 13 on the suspicion that he was plotting to have Sabah secede from Malaysia. Kitingan called the act political persecution. Henry S. Bradsher

See also **Asia** (Facts in brief table). In ***World Book,*** see **Malaysia.**

Maldives. See **Asia.**
Mali. See **Africa.**
Malta. See **Europe.**

Manitoba. A monthlong nursing strike, the longest such strike in Canada's history, ended Feb. 1, 1991, when Manitoba's 10,500 nurses accepted a two-year contract giving them a salary increase of 14 per cent over two years. The settlement disappointed many nurses, but the provincial government said it could not pay more than $391 million ($346 million U.S.) annually for nursing care.

Manitoba's weak financial position was underlined by the budget, released on April 16. The fiscal plan limited government spending increases to 3.2 per cent, cut programs in 27 departments and agencies, and eliminated 1,000 public service jobs. To hold the province's projected deficit to $324 million ($286 million U.S.), monies were taken from a reserve fund and from provincial lottery revenues.

With 22 per cent of Manitobans under age 25 unemployed and a low level of private investment in the province, Manitoba was suffering the worst economic conditions since the Great Depression of the 1930's. In response, the provincial government passed legislation in June 1991 to impose a one-year salary freeze on 48,000 public service employees.

In July, mosquitoes infested Manitoba. Heavy rains had provided favorable breeding grounds for the insects, and a number of cases of mosquito-transmitted encephalitis were reported. David M. L. Farr

See **Canada,** Special Report: **Canada and Quebec at a Crossroads.** In ***World Book,*** see **Manitoba.**

Manufacturing. The United States economy entered its ninth recession since World War II (1939-1945) in 1990, and the recession continued into 1991. In the second half of 1991, manufacturers played an important role in the nation's attempt to rebound from the recession, but growth in the spring and summer slowed and stalled by autumn.

United States industrial production started 1991 with a 0.5 per cent decline in January and a steep 0.8 per cent plunge in February, the fifth consecutive month of decline. There were big drops in the production of automobiles, steel, and lumber. After a 0.6 per cent drop in March, production finally turned around with a gain of 0.1 per cent in April, according to the Federal Reserve Board, the agency that regulates U.S. banking.

Manufacturing gains continued with a 0.7 per cent increase in U.S. production in May and a 0.8 per cent increase in June. That represented a quarter of a year of increases after two consecutive quarters of decline. After a dramatic 0.7 per cent jump in production in July, there was no change in August as automobile production slipped after five months of gains. In September, manufacturing production rose only 0.1 per cent, was unchanged in October, and declined 0.4 per cent in November, according to the Federal Reserve Board.

With orders slow, U.S. manufacturing plants ran at only 78.8 per cent of capacity in January. That rate of production slipped to 78 per cent of capacity in February (compared with 83 per cent in February 1990) and peaked at 78.7 per cent of capacity in August 1991 before slipping back to 78 per cent of capacity in September as the recovery slowed.

Factory orders. After five consecutive monthly drops, orders to U.S. manufacturers rose 2.1 per cent in April to $230.5 billion, according to the Department of Commerce. A robust 2.9 per cent gain in May was the largest in 12 months. But the high point of the year came in July, with a 6.1 per cent surge in orders to $248 billion. However, August saw a 1.9 per cent drop in factory orders to $243.3 billion, followed in September by a 1.7 per cent drop as previously strong orders for aircraft and parts slowed. Orders rebounded by 1.9 per cent in October to $242.1 billion, still well below July's peak level.

New orders for durable goods (machinery and appliances designed to last three or more years) fell by 0.7 per cent in January to $118.5 billion. Orders for durable goods are an indicator of how much businesses plan to spend on new plants and equipment. Orders for these types of goods sank 8.4 per cent in January. Shipments of completed goods, which reflect current capital spending (spending on new plants and equipment), were also weak, down 0.8 per cent in January. The only area that kept some manufacturers' backlog of orders high was transportation equipment.

Orders for durable goods plunged 6.2 per cent in March to a rate that would have totaled $110.3 billion

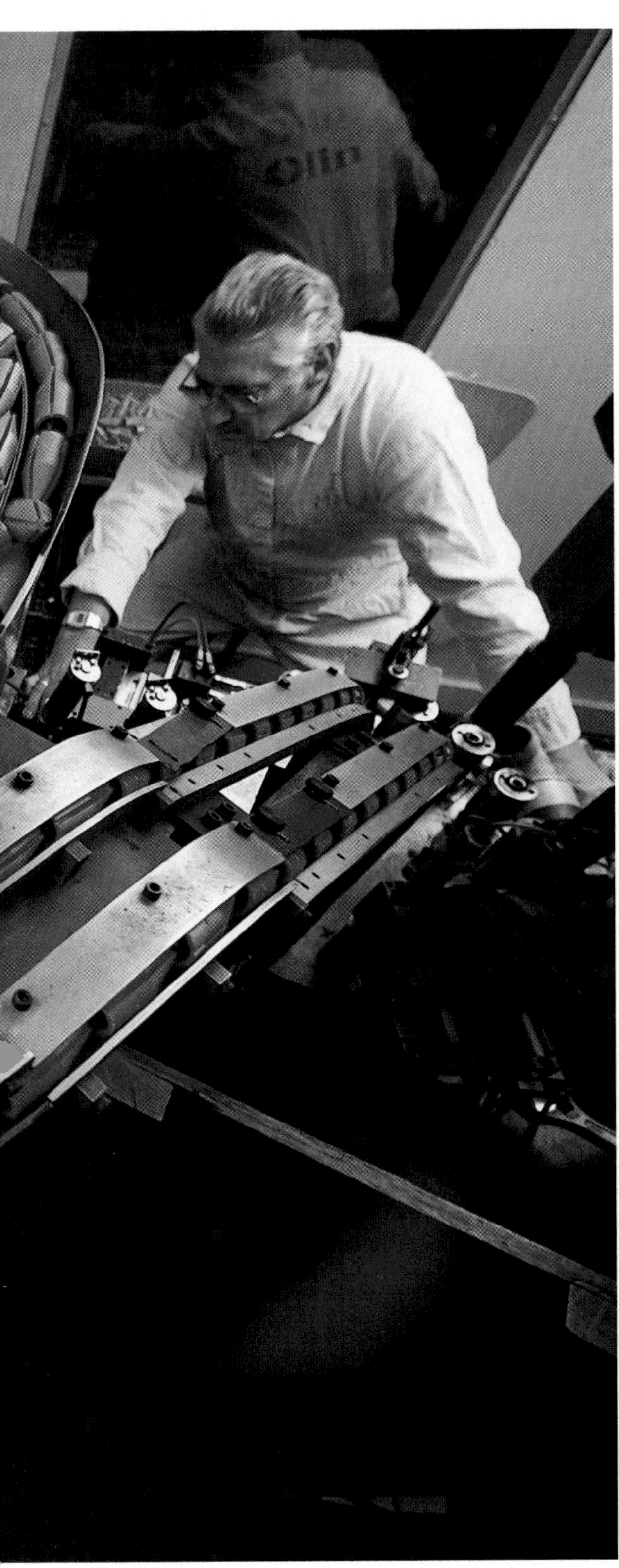

for the entire year—the lowest U.S. order level in more than three years. Shipments of durable goods also fell 2.4 per cent in March to $114.7 billion, the fifth consecutive monthly drop. Once again, businesses showed no desire to invest in new equipment.

But things began to improve in the spring. In April, durable-goods orders rose 2.9 per cent to $115.5 billion, according to the Department of Commerce—the first rise in 1991. In the same month, electronic equipment orders rose 11 per cent, orders for industrial machinery rose 1.2 per cent, and orders for primary metals rose 7.8 per cent. Some of the April increases reflected increased military spending for the Persian Gulf War in January and February.

Shipments of durable goods increased 4.3 per cent in April to $119.4 billion after five straight months of decline. Orders for automobiles rose 5.5 per cent, orders for consumer goods rose 3.2 per cent, orders for machinery and equipment rose 3.7 per cent, orders for computers rose 3.7 per cent, and orders for health-care products rose 6.1 per cent. The backlog of orders remained weak, however, with only aircraft orders amounting to much.

After a 1 per cent decline in June, durable-goods orders skyrocketed in July with a dramatic 11.7 per cent gain, the largest jump since December 1970. Much of the growth came from aircraft and parts orders, but the jump included a 24 per cent gain in transportation orders, a 13 per cent increase in orders for electronic equipment, a 6 per cent jump in primary metals, and a 2 per cent gain in orders for industrial machinery and equipment.

As quickly as optimism and confidence grew in July, orders for durable goods contracted, declining by 4.1 per cent in August to $125.9 billion and by 4.2 per cent in September. September saw the steepest decline in military orders since 1984, a drop from $49.2-billion to $5.5 billion. Production of aircraft, ships, and tanks declined dramatically as not only the Persian Gulf War but also the Cold War against the Soviet Union and Communism ended. At this point in the year, many economists feared that the economic recovery that appeared to have begun in April had stalled. But durable-goods orders bounced back by 3.0 per cent in October to $123.79 billion, led by a rebound in military orders and aircraft.

Capital spending, which has been an important means of leading the United States out of recessions, increased at only a 2.4 per cent rate from January to March 1991. The Commerce Department revised that weak figure downward to a meager 0.5 per cent after surveys in July and August, however. Based on a survey conducted in October and November, the Commerce Department estimated that businesses would spend $530 billion in 1991 on capital equipment,

A worker at a U.S. munitions plant inspects weapons parts in January. Defense plants ran at full capacity in preparation for the Persian Gulf War.

down 0.5 per cent from 1990. But manufacturers actually indicated that their spending on capital equipment would likely drop 3.3 per cent from 1990 levels.

NAPM index. A good indication of the health of U.S. manufacturing is the National Association of Purchasing Management (NAPM) index—a monthly survey of 300 industrial companies. The NAPM index measures manufacturers' factory orders, employment, inventories, and production statistics. A reading of 50 per cent indicates an expanding manufacturing economy. Anything below 50 per cent signifies a shrinking economy. A reading below 44 per cent demonstrates a declining economy, according to economists.

At the start of 1991, the NAPM index stood at 37.7 per cent, close to its lowest levels in the 1981-1982 recession. February's 38.5 per cent reading was the first increase in nine months. March saw a rise to 40.0 per cent, but it was the 10th consecutive month under the 50 per cent expansion measure. In June, however, the index spurted to 50.9 per cent, the first reading above 50 per cent since May 1990. A separate NAPM index that tracks new orders jumped from 50.6 per cent in May 1991 to 59.1 per cent in June, the largest jump since February 1983, when the economy emerged from the previous recession.

Employment. Manufacturers employed more than 19 million Americans in 1990—about 20 per cent of all U.S. workers. That was about the same percentage as in 1965.

Weak orders and production figures meant that manufacturers had to watch payrolls closely in 1991. Producers of automobiles, construction equipment and materials, home appliances, and furniture continued to trim payrolls in 1991 to cut labor costs.

In January, 232,000 U.S. jobs were lost, including 69,000 manufacturing jobs. Many of the more than 2 million jobs lost since the economy entered the recession came from the service sector, however. Many manufacturers had been cutting payrolls since 1989. The U.S. unemployment rate was 6.2 per cent in January 1991 and rose to 7.0 per cent in June, the highest level since October 1986, before settling to 6.8 per cent in October and November 1991.

As orders increased in spring 1991, factories added 25,000 jobs in July and another 42,000 in August. But as orders slowed in the autumn, factories trimmed 31,000 workers in September and 32,000 in October. In November, major companies announced layoffs to cut costs. Computer giant International Business Machines Corporation of Armonk, N.Y., said it would trim 20,000 jobs in 1991 and at least that many in 1992. Construction equipment maker Caterpillar Incorporated of Peoria, Ill., laid off nearly 10,000 workers in 1991 due to the effects of a strike. General Motors in December announced it would close 21 plants, resulting in more than 70,000 lost jobs. Defense cutbacks continued to result in manufacturing job losses.

Ronald Kolgraf

In *World Book,* see **Manufacturing.**

Martin, Lynn M. (1939-), was sworn in as United States secretary of labor on Feb. 22, 1991. She succeeded Elizabeth H. Dole, who resigned to head the American Red Cross. At her confirmation hearings, Martin pledged to work toward tough enforcement of child-labor and worker-safety laws.

From 1981 to 1991, Martin represented the 16th Illinois district in the U.S. House of Representatives. She generally supported the Republican Party on economic and foreign-policy issues. But she opposed President George Bush on several social issues, including her support for abortion rights. Martin gave up her House seat to run unsuccessfully for the U.S. Senate in 1990 against Democratic incumbent Paul Simon.

Martin was born Judith Lynn Morley in Evanston, Ill., a Chicago suburb, on Dec. 26, 1939. After graduating in 1960 from the University of Illinois in Urbana-Champaign, she taught high school economics, government, and English. Her political career began in 1972 when she won a seat on the Winnebago (Ill.) County Board. Before entering national politics, she served in the Illinois legislature from 1977 to 1981.

Martin married federal Judge Harry Leinenweber in 1987. She has two grown daughters from a previous marriage. Karin C. Rosenberg

Maryland. See **State government.**
Massachusetts. See **State government.**
Mauritania. See **Africa.**
Mauritius. See **Africa.**

Medicine. A Michigan doctor helped two women commit suicide on Oct. 23, 1991, refueling a nationwide debate concerning the medical ethics of such action. In a remote cabin in the Detroit area, pathologist Jack Kevorkian attached suicide devices that he had constructed to two women, one with multiple sclerosis and the other with a severe pelvic disorder. Kevorkian's lawyer said the women had pleaded with the doctor for two years to let them use his device.

In June 1990, Kevorkian, for the first time, had assisted a woman with Alzheimer's disease to commit suicide using one of his devices. Kevorkian had been charged with murder in that case, but the charges were dismissed in December 1990.

Some ethicists called Kevorkian's latest actions "immoral, unethical, and very dangerous." Others said the question remains to be answered whether a physician under some circumstances should help a person end his or her life. On Nov. 20, 1991, the Michigan Board of Medicine voted unanimously to suspend Kevorkian's medical license. On December 18, the medical examiner of Oakland County, in which the suicides took place, ruled that the deaths were homicides. The following day, a county prosecutor said he had asked a grand jury to decide in January 1992 whether to bring murder charges against Kevorkian.

On Nov. 5, 1991, voters in the state of Washington rejected a referendum to legalize assisted suicide for the terminally ill.

W. John Martin of the University of Southern California in Los Angeles reported in September that a rare virus could cause chronic fatigue syndrome.

First portable heart device. The world's first fully portable device to assist the heart in pumping blood was implanted in a 52-year-old man by surgeons at the Texas Heart Institute in Houston on May 9, 1991. The device helps a diseased heart pump blood while the patient awaits a heart transplant. The device is implanted in the patient's abdomen, and a tiny motor pumps the blood through tubes attached to the heart. Electricity for the motor travels from a battery pack, strapped under the patient's shoulder, through a wire inserted into the skin. Although the device functioned well, the first recipient died on May 23 from kidney and liver failure and other problems unrelated to the device.

New focus on women. The U.S. Department of Health and Human Services on Feb. 27, 1991, announced a 39-point plan to increase medical research on diseases of special concern to women. On April 19, the National Institutes of Health in Bethesda, Md., announced a 10-year, $500-million study of women's health concerns.

A series of studies published in July in two leading medical journals focused on the differences in medical care and research between men and women that may deprive women of needed treatment. The studies found that women with coronary artery disease were less likely than men to receive certain forms of diagnosis and treatment. Coronary artery disease, the cause of most heart attacks, involves formation of fatty deposits that block blood flow in arteries that nourish heart tissue. The studies found that men with coronary disease were more likely to receive coronary angiography, a key diagnostic test to determine the extent of blockages in the coronary arteries and to help identify patients for surgical treatment. Men also were more likely to be treated with coronary bypass surgery or angioplasty, a procedure in which blockages are opened with a tiny balloon inflated inside the coronary arteries.

Required breast implant information. A regulation issued on September 25 by the U.S. Food and Drug Administration required manufacturers of breast implants to provide risk information associated with these products. Studies show that some implants may rupture and interfere with cancer detection.

High blood pressure in the elderly. Drugs that treat isolated systolic hypertension, a form of high blood pressure found mainly in elderly people, can reduce the risk of heart attacks and stroke, according to a five-year federal study reported on June 25. The study, which was conducted at 16 medical centers in the United States and included almost 4,800 people, found that drug treatment for this condition reduced the incidence of strokes by 36 per cent and heart attacks by 27 per cent. Michael Woods

See also **AIDS; Health and disease; Medicine,** Special Report: **Genetic Medicine: Promise and Perils.** In ***World Book,*** see **Medicine.**

Genetic Medicine: Promise and Perils

By Jerry E. Bishop

Identifying genes that cause disease and developing ways to correct them offers great hope for human health, but critics fear that information about a person's genetic makeup could be misused.

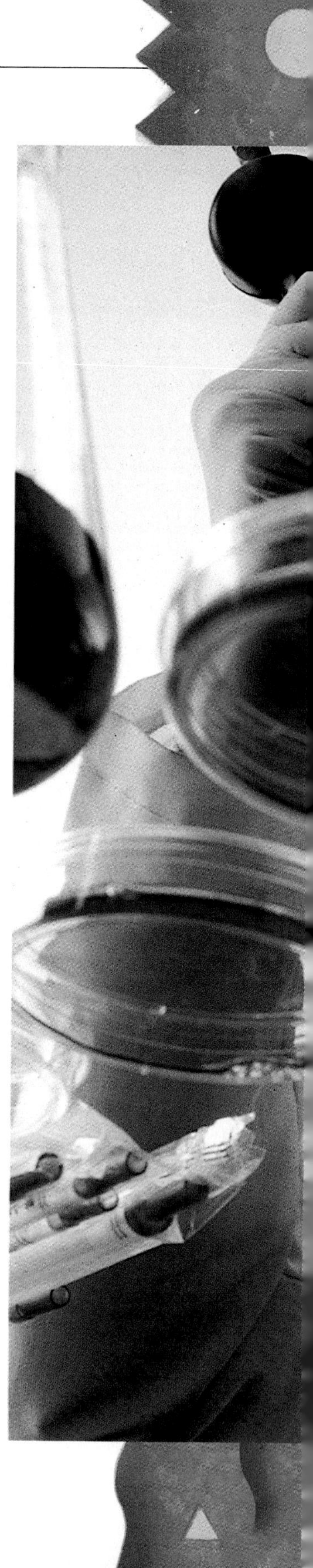

A quiet revolution is reshaping the world of medicine. That revolution, which marks the dawn of a new era in health care, is the result of a new field called *genetic medicine*. Its pioneers are delving into the molecular machinery at the core of human cells and discovering a growing number of genes that underlie many illnesses. These findings are leading to the development of screening tests to identify people whose genes put them at risk of future disease. Investigators are also learning to manipulate patients' genes to treat some inherited disorders, a bold new approach to treatment known as *gene therapy*.

The era of genetic medicine was ushered in by advances in genetics during the previous two decades and especially during the 1980's. In the early 1980's, just as biotechnology companies were astonishing the world by using the methods of genetic engineering to produce insulin, human growth hormone, and other drugs, molecular biologists in the United States made a breakthrough that received little notice at the time. The scientists found ways to locate and identify previously unknown human genes. As a handful of scientists contemplated this development, they realized it had profound implications for human health. They saw that the ability to find faulty genes and replace them with normal ones would dramatically change the diagnosis and treatment of many diseases.

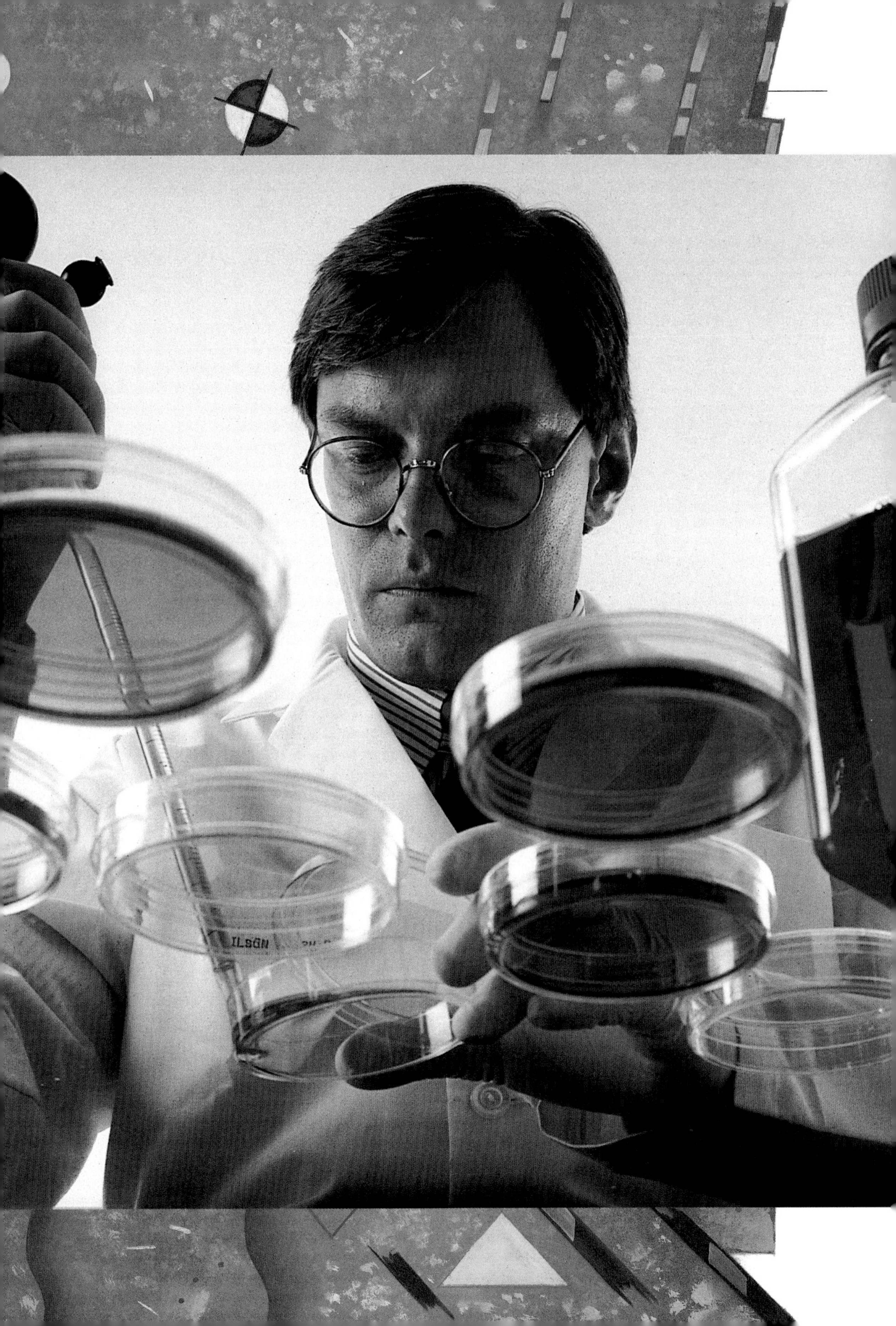

Some people, however—scientists among them—are expressing concerns about how genetic medicine may be used, knowing that it has the potential to alter human society. Is it likely, they ask, that a battery of genetic tests might soon be developed that could uncover everyone's genetic strengths and flaws? And might such information be used by employers, insurance companies, government agencies, schools—indeed, the entire society—to genetically "label" an individual at birth and thereby determine his or her place in society?

There are other questions as well, including one that is bound to stir heated controversy in coming years: How far should gene therapy be taken? Should the correction of genetic disorders be done strictly on a case-by-case basis, or might it someday be acceptable to make genetic alterations that are passed on to future generations?

Glossary

Chromosomes: Tiny structures in the cell nucleus that carry the genes.

DNA (Deoxyribonucleic acid): The molecule of which genes are made.

Gene: The basic unit of heredity; a segment of DNA that carries coded information for the production of a protein.

Genetic predisposition: A genetic makeup that does not cause a disease directly but which increases the likelihood of developing certain diseases, such as heart disease and cancer.

Gene therapy: The insertion of normal genes into cells to correct disorders caused by defective genes.

Hereditary disease: A disorder caused by a genetic defect inherited from one or both parents.

Significant developments in genetic science

That the hopes and fears aroused by the prospect of genetic medicine were about to be realized was evident at the beginning of the 1990's as researchers continued to push back the boundaries of genetic knowledge. Advances in 1990 and 1991 included several important developments:

- Scientists in the United States, Canada, and Europe were ferreting out a growing number of defective genes responsible for inherited diseases, such as muscular dystrophy, a genetic disorder that causes the muscles to deteriorate, and physicians began experimental treatments of children with this fatal disease.
- Researchers at the National Institutes of Health (NIH) in Bethesda, Md., used gene therapy in an experimental attempt to treat a rare disorder of the immune system and one form of cancer.
- U.S. scientists were planning to replace defective genes in children who were born with extremely high levels of *cholesterol* (a fatlike substance) in their blood, which put them at risk for heart attacks before they reached age 12.
- Fertility clinics that specialize in test-tube fertilization were beginning to offer genetic tests of embryos so that a couple could select the healthiest embryo for the pregnancy.

These and other developments are a reflection of how rapidly scientists are expanding their understanding of genes. Genes, of course, are the blueprints for all life, from single-cell bacteria to human beings, flowers, elephants, and whales. Genes passed from parent to offspring determine the offspring's biological nature. The genes ensure that an organism's ability to make the substances and structures necessary to life, such as enzymes, hormones, cell walls, and muscles, are transmitted intact to each succeeding generation. The genes that human beings inherit from their parents influence everything from eye color and height to the ability to learn to read and write and the skill (or lack of it) to hit a baseball.

The author:

Jerry E. Bishop is deputy news editor of *The Wall Street Journal* and author of the book *Genome.*

The word *gene* is derived from the Greek word meaning "to give birth to." Danish botanist Wilhelm Ludvig Johannsen coined the name in 1907 to describe mysterious "hereditary units" that seemed to be passed from parents to children. At the time, scientists knew almost nothing about genes; indeed, the existence of genes could only be inferred by studying patterns of inheritance in successive generations of organisms.

It started with pea plants

Genetics had gotten its start as an established science just a few years earlier, in 1900, when three European botanists rediscovered research reported in 1866 by an Austrian monk, Gregor Johann Mendel. In a series of experiments with pea plants, Mendel found that each trait inherited by a plant, such as the color of its flowers or the smoothness of its seeds, is determined by two "hereditary units." One "unit," he discovered, is inherited from the male parent plant and the other from the female parent plant.

By 1900, biologists had also discovered the microscopic sausage-shaped structures called *chromosomes* that are in the nucleus of every cell. Scientists now know that the genes lie on the chromosomes and that human body cells contain 23 pairs of chromosomes, one of each pair being inherited in the sperm cell of the father and the other inherited in the egg cell of the mother. (These *sex cells*—also known as *germ cells*—in contrast to body cells, contain 23 unpaired chromosomes.) At conception, the single sets of sperm and egg chromosomes match up to form the 23 pairs of chromosomes that will be present in every body cell of the child that develops from the fertilized egg.

The purpose of most genes is to direct the making of proteins. All of the tens of thousands of proteins that carry out the functions of life are the products of particular genes. Researchers had learned by the beginning of the 1940's that genes make proteins, but the question of what a gene was made of and how it worked was still a complete mystery. Then, in 1944, a team of geneticists in the United States discovered that genes are composed of a molecule called *DNA* (deoxyribonucleic acid), found in the nucleus of the cell.

Deciphering the structure of DNA

In 1953, one of the great scientific breakthroughs of the century occurred at Cambridge University in England. Two Cambridge researchers, James D. Watson of the United States and his British colleague, Francis H. C. Crick, discovered the three-dimensional molecular structure of DNA. Watson and Crick showed that a DNA molecule consists of two incredibly long strands linked

What are genes?

Genes, located in the nucleus of cells on tiny structures called *chromosomes*, are segments of a molecule called *DNA* (deoxyribonucleic acid). Each of the 46 chromosomes found in human cells contains a long, coiled stretch of DNA that includes more than 1,000 genes, carrying the instructions for all physical traits and bodily functions. Genes are also the basic units of heredity. Transmitted in the *sex cells* (the male sperm and the female egg), the genes pass characteristics, such as hair color, from parents to offspring.

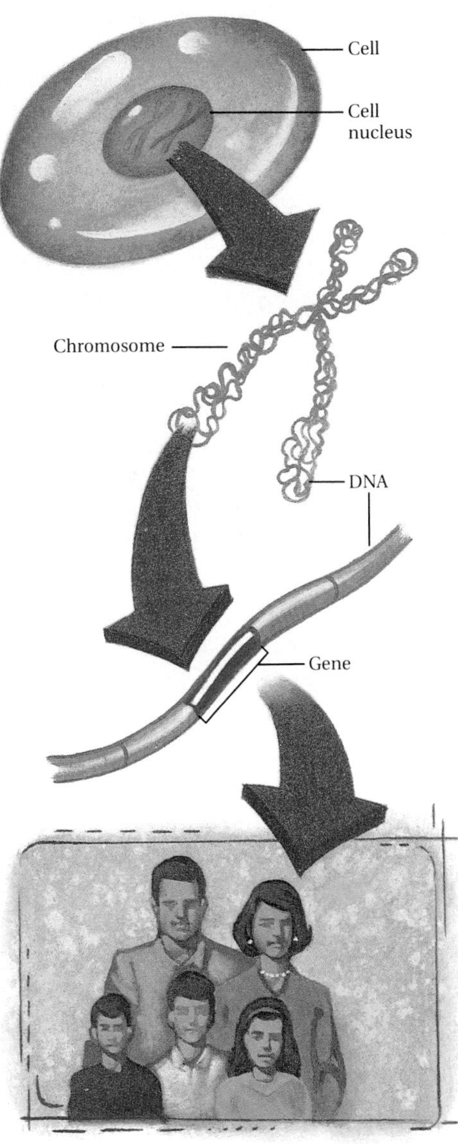

by millions of molecular "rungs" and twisted into the shape of a coiled ladder. A gene, the scientists realized, is simply a segment of the DNA ladder.

As a result of this discovery, a new breed of scientists, called *molecular biologists,* learned how genes produce proteins and found ways of manipulating DNA. They found that they could use certain types of proteins, called restriction enzymes, as chemical scissors to cut the DNA molecule at certain sites. The researchers used these enzymes to snip out selected genes from one organism and splice the genes into the DNA of other organisms. This manipulation of DNA is called *genetic engineering.*

Genetically engineered drugs

Today, using the tools of genetic engineering, biologists are able to transplant human genes into bacteria, yeasts, or other single-celled organisms. These genetically altered microorganisms then make the human protein specified by the inserted human gene. The microorganisms can be grown in vats to produce large quantities of the human protein, which is then purified and used to treat a disorder. The fruits of genetic engineering are beginning to crowd the shelves of pharmacies. Human *insulin* for the treatment of diabetes; *interferon,* a protein that helps the body fight off viruses; *human growth hormone* to treat children threatened with dwarfism; and *tissue plasminogen activator* (t-PA), a drug used to dissolve blood clots in the coronary arteries of heart attack victims, are just a few

How genes can cause disease

Most genes code for the production of a particular protein. This protein aids in carrying out a function in a particular cell, for example, a white blood cell of the immune system.

A normal gene results in the production of a normal protein, which helps a body cell to function properly.

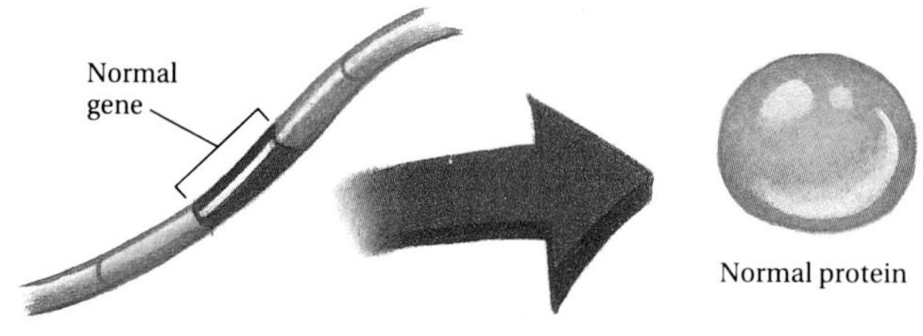

Even a tiny change in one gene results in the production of an abnormal protein, which can cause a malfunction in the cell. Such malfunctions are the underlying causes of all genetic diseases.

Some disorders related to faulty genes

Disorder	Incidence	Cells involved	DNA test available?
Cystic fibrosis	1 in 2,000 whites, 1 in 17,000 blacks	Lung, pancreas cells	Yes, for about 70% of cases
Duchenne muscular dystrophy	1 in 3,300 males	Muscle cells	Yes, for about 70% of cases
Emphysema (inherited tendency)	1 in 3,500	Lung, liver cells	Yes, but not very reliable
Familial hypercholesterolemia	1 in 500	Liver cells	Yes, for about 90% of cases
Hemophilia	1 in 20,000 males	Liver cells	Yes
Severe combined immunodeficiency disease (SCID)	Rare	Bone marrow cells, T lymphocytes	Yes, for some forms, but not all
Thalassemia (inherited anemia)	1 in 600 among certain ethnic groups	Bone marrow cells, red blood cells	Yes
Huntington's disease	1 in 10,000	Brain cells	Yes
Hereditary hypertension	Uncertain	Kidney, adrenal cells	No

of the genetically engineered proteins that have recently become available to patients.

The courts have ruled that genes that are isolated and used to manufacture proteins can be patented. Thus, biotechnology companies are able to obtain the exclusive right to produce and market the gene products they develop. In June 1991, the federal government tried to extend patent protection much further than that. The NIH applied for a U.S. patent on 340 DNA sequences before determining what proteins those sequences were involved with making. The NIH action ignited a worldwide chorus of protests. Many scientists feared that the application, if granted, would result in a willy-nilly rush to patent genes and would severely harm basic research aimed at understanding—and not just profiting from—the discovery of new genes.

Genetic medicine also involves the use of sophisticated tests. DNA tests, often used before birth, can now diagnose many genetic diseases. Some of these hereditary disorders may one day be treated with gene therapy. But the ability to identify faulty genes in a person carries the potential for abuse by employers or insurance companies.

The search for disease genes

Although genetic engineering has been a tremendous medical advance, molecular biologists in the early 1980's made an even more dramatic breakthrough. They discovered ways to find particular genes in human cells, including genes closely linked to hereditary diseases. By the end of the 1980's, they had located or were close on the trail of the genes causing muscular dystrophy; a genetic form of Alzheimer's disease, a brain disorder that causes severe mental decline in many older people; cystic fibro-

Inserting new genes

A major challenge researchers face is how to get new genes into a patient's cells. In some of the first human experiments with gene therapy, researchers in 1991 used a harmless virus carrying a normal gene to replace a defective gene in the white blood cells of patients with a rare disorder of the immune system. A similar approach may be used to insert new genes into patients with other kinds of genetic disorders.

1. Blood is taken from the patient's arm.

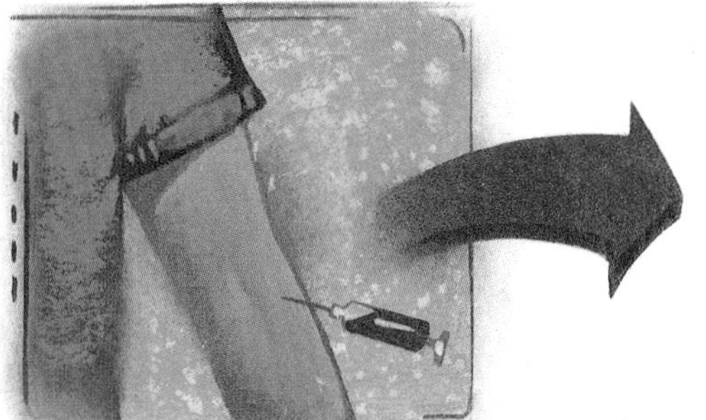

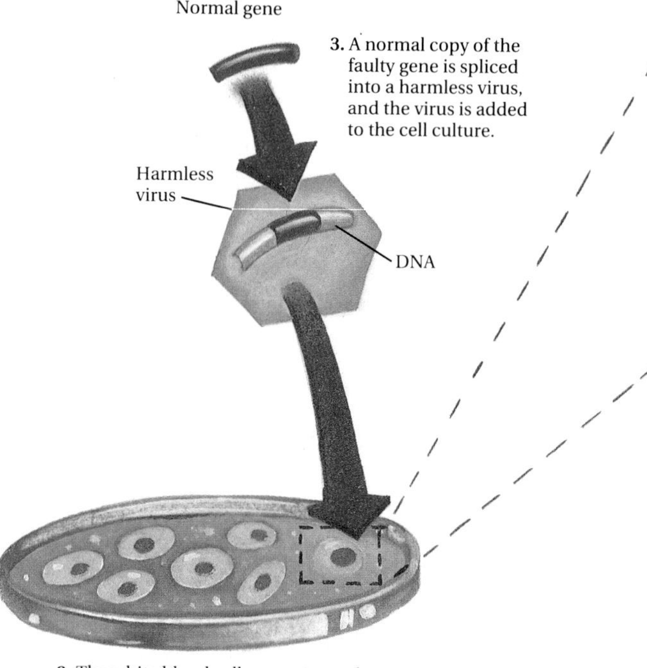

2. The white blood cells are extracted and grown in a laboratory dish.

sis, a deadly lung disease; Huntington's disease, a fatal disorder of the nervous system; and scores of other inherited diseases.

Researchers also began uncovering a different kind of unwanted gene, one that doesn't cause disease but which makes a person more vulnerable to a particular illness. In the case of cancer, for example, scientists have found genes called *tumor-suppressor genes.* The protein products of these genes ordinarily hold cell growth in check so that a cell, even if it is malignant, is unable to multiply and become a tumor. A person with a defective tumor-suppressor gene is more likely to develop cancer sometime in the future than someone with a normal tumor-suppressor gene. Researchers are now trying to track down genes that predispose an individual to heart attacks or certain forms of mental illness and addiction.

Finding the gene is half the battle in conquering a genetic disease. With the gene identified, researchers can study the protein the gene codes for and determine what role that protein plays in the body. If a faulty gene is creating an abnormal protein, supplying the normal protein to the body may be enough to relieve symptoms of the disorder. In 1986, for instance, molecular biologists in Boston and in Toronto, Canada, tracked down the abnormal gene that causes the most common and most rapidly progressing form of muscular dystrophy, a type that affects only boys. The investigators found that the gene in its normal state produces a protein that they

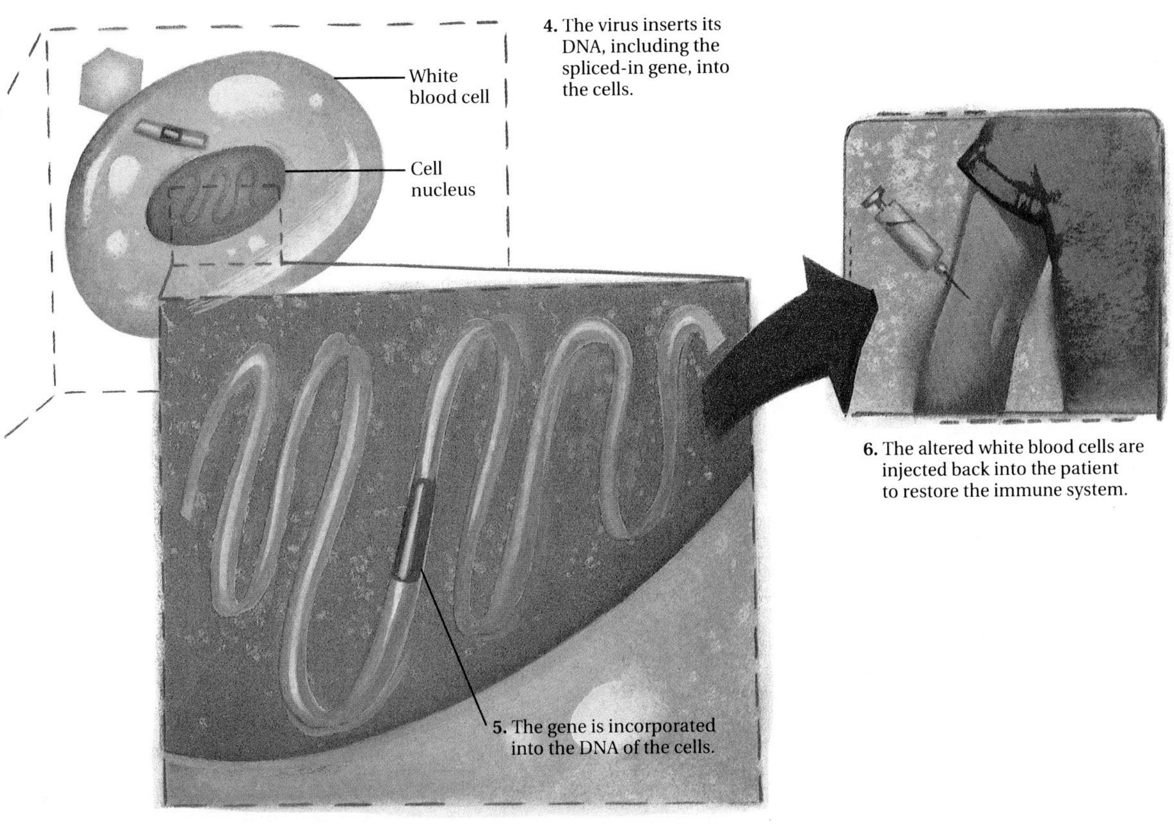

4. The virus inserts its DNA, including the spliced-in gene, into the cells.

5. The gene is incorporated into the DNA of the cells.

6. The altered white blood cells are injected back into the patient to restore the immune system.

dubbed *dystrophin.* That knowledge opened the door to the first attempts ever to treat muscular dystrophy. In May 1991, researchers in Memphis, Tenn., began injecting normal muscle cells into the crippled muscles of boys with muscular dystrophy in hopes that the transplanted cells would begin to supply the missing dystrophin and prevent the breakdown of muscle cells.

Correcting genetic defects

The infant science of gene therapy aims at going a step further by inserting copies of a normal gene into a patient's tissues to take the place of a faulty gene. The first federally approved human experiments to see if a new, normal gene would work in a person with a genetic disease began at the NIH in September 1990. NIH scientists treated two young girls suffering from a rare immune-system disorder called *adenosine deaminase* (ADA) *deficiency.* The condition results from a defect in the gene coding for ADA, an enzyme that enables the immune system to break down certain harmful chemicals. In the absence of ADA, those chemicals accumulate and destroy key cells of the immune system, leaving the patient vulnerable to a host of potentially fatal infections.

The NIH scientists removed about 1 billion white blood cells from each of the girls. White blood cells are important infection-fighting components of the immune system, but because of ADA deficiency the girls' white blood cells were unable to carry out their protective function. In the laboratory, the scientists' treated the cells in the laboratory with a harmless virus containing a spliced-in copy of the normal human ADA gene. The virus incorporated the gene into the DNA of the blood cells. The cells were then infused back into the girls' bloodstreams. In late 1991, the researchers reported that, as a result of the treatment, both girls' immune systems had greatly improved and were producing ADA.

One problem with this approach, however, is that it has to be repeated every few weeks as the genetically altered white blood cells, like all blood cells, die off and are replaced by the body. The NIH scientists hope to get around this shortcoming in treating ADA deficiency by adding new genes to *stem cells*, immature cells in the bone marrow that are the "grandfathers" of all the different kinds of blood cells. A batch of altered stem cells would presumably survive permanently in the bone marrow and pass the new gene on to each new generation of blood cells. Unfortunately, stem cells are difficult to distinguish from mature blood cells, so scientists have not yet been able to isolate them for use in gene therapy.

Other gene therapy experiments

In a similar gene therapy experiment at the NIH, which was begun in January 1991, researchers treated several patients afflicted with *advanced melanoma*, a severe and fatal form of skin cancer that has spread to other parts of the body from the original site. The scientists removed cancer-fighting white blood cells and again used a virus to insert into them a human gene coding for a protein that destroys cancer cells. The genetically altered cells were then injected into the patients in hopes that the cells would deliver a knockout dose of the protein to the patients' tumors.

In late 1991, scientists began planning a gene therapy experiment to treat children born with a defective gene that makes their liver cells incapable of removing cholesterol from the bloodstream. As a result of this genetic flaw, cholesterol in the blood builds up to a level five or six times higher than normal. Children with this inherited disease, called *familial hypercholesterolemia* (FH), are usually stricken with heart attacks before they reach their teen years. Researchers intend to remove some of an FH child's liver cells, insert a normal gene into them, and reimplant them in the child's liver. There, it is hoped, the cells will multiply and begin removing cholesterol from the blood.

Coming: a map of all human genes

For now, gene therapy has its limits. For one thing, it can be used only to treat disorders caused by single genes, and then only if the gene is known. Moreover, the procedures involved are very exacting and so are limited to major medical centers.

When—and whether—the day will come when genetic defects can be treated in a more routine way is uncertain. What seems beyond doubt, however, is that scientists will eventually identify all the human genes that cause or contribute to disease—and every other human gene as well. In 1990, the U.S. government began spending $200 million a year on a project that, in league with similar programs in other countries, is expected to lead to a complete map of all human genes by the year 2005. Because the collection of all DNA in a human cell is known as the *human genome*, the project has been named the Human Genome Initiative. Like a road map that shows the location of every American city and town, the genetic map will list all the estimated 50,000 to 100,000 human genes and give their positions on the chromosomes. By the end of 1991, scientists involved in this international effort had found and mapped almost 2,500 genes, and they were discovering and mapping new genes at the rate of almost 1 a day.

Testing for faulty genes

Inherent in mapping a gene is the ability to test for the gene. Some such tests have already been developed and are used to identify people who are "silent carriers" of defective genes that do not adversely affect them

Gene therapy and future generations

The insertion of a new gene into a person's blood cells or other body cells affects only that individual. Any children that person may later have will not inherit the gene. But a gene added to the *sex cells* (male sperm or female eggs) would be inherited by offspring and would be passed on to future generations. Thus, inserting new genes into sex cells could prevent children from inheriting a deadly disorder. But the idea of using a form of gene therapy that would alter future generations is a highly controversial one.

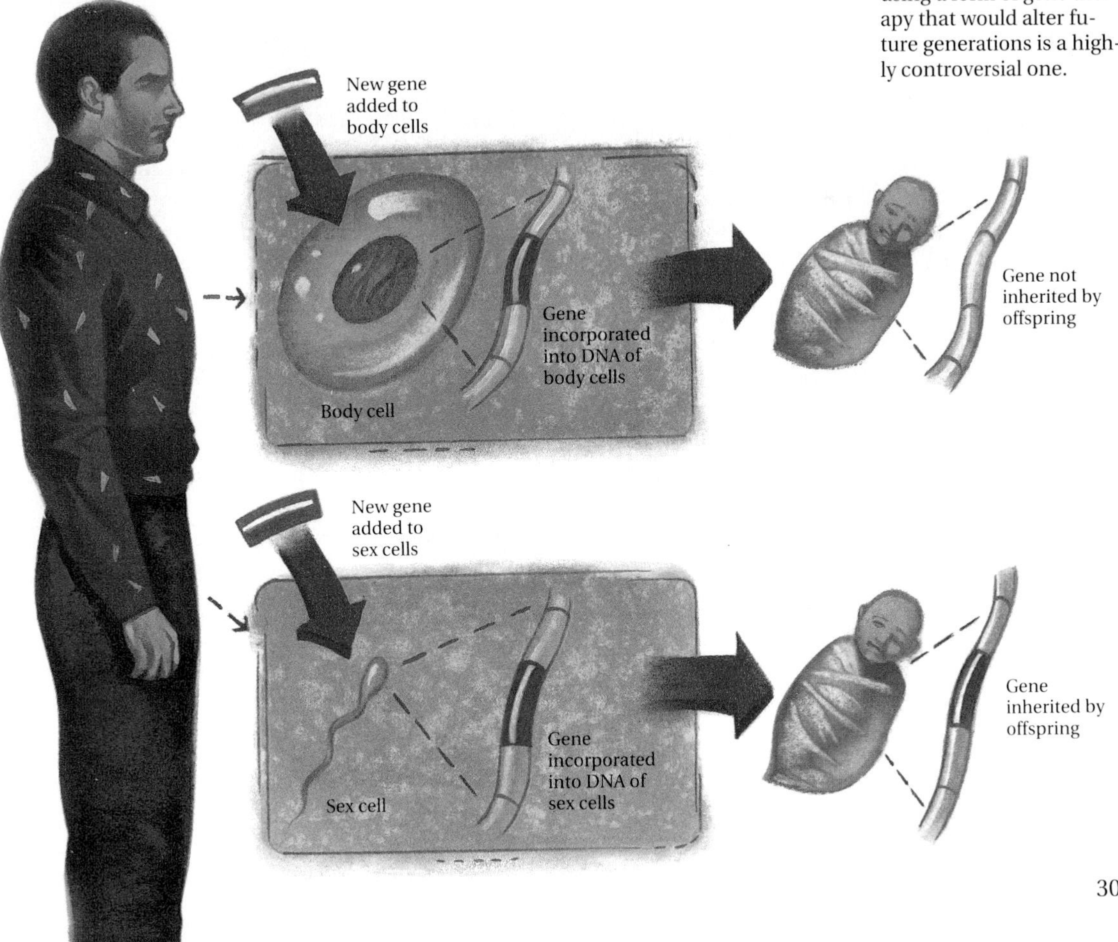

but that might endanger their children. The cells of silent carriers contain single copies of abnormal genes that must be present in a "double dose" to cause disease. Such is the case with cystic fibrosis. If a man and woman who are planning to marry discover they are both silent carriers of the cystic fibrosis gene, they know there is a 25 per cent chance that any child they have will inherit the faulty gene from both of them and develop the disease.

Genetic screening tests can be used to analyze DNA samples taken from newborn babies and even from unborn fetuses to find out whether they have inherited various disease-causing genes. In the future, as even more is known about genes and their effect on health, young couples may be able to have their newborn babies tested for the genes that predispose the child to future heart attacks, cancer, and even mental illness. If a baby is found to be carrying any such genes, the parents can help the child minimize his or her risk. A child at risk of developing heart disease, for instance, could be guided to eating a low-fat diet and getting regular exercise. Likewise, a child whose genes show a vulnerability to cancer could be instructed to avoid environments where there is a high risk of exposure to cancer-causing substances .

Potential social hazards of genetic testing

But the same genetic tests that forewarn us of health risks are also threatening to pose difficult new social problems. Despite the fact that a person with a genetic predisposition to a disease may never develop that condition, there are already hints that the "genetically handicapped" may face various forms of discrimination. Many insurance companies have already stated that when detailed genetic testing becomes widely used, they will want to know an applicant's genetic profile before selling that person life insurance. If the analysis discloses the presence of genes associated with early cancer, heart disease, or any other life-threatening illness, the company might either refuse to sell the person life insurance or charge a higher premium than is paid by someone without those potentially harmful genetic tendencies.

Future employment decisions may also be influenced by genetic testing. A chemical company, for example, might be wary of letting a person with a genetic predisposition for cancer work around chemicals that can cause cancer. An airline would be unlikely to hire a pilot who is at risk for an early heart attack. And a corporate board of directors, pondering candidates for the company presidency, would think twice about appointing someone whose genetic profile reveals a vulnerability to alcoholism, depression, or Alzheimer's disease.

Some sociologists worry that genetically based discrimination may eventually lead to a "biological underclass." And early on, medical geneticist Arno G. Motulsky of the University of Washington in Seattle warned that genetic tests might one day determine a person's "niche in society." The possibility of such scenarios, however, will most likely prompt society to adopt safeguards against the misuse of genetic information. The courts, the U.S. Congress, and state legislatures may step in to assert that people have a right of privacy with regard to their genetic makeup. Lawmakers may also decree that discrimination based on genetics—just like discrimination based on race or sex—is illegal.

Altering humanity's genetic library

As genetic knowledge advances, we may acquire the ability to rid ourselves of the genetic defects that cause so much human suffering. In theory, that might be done by altering the genes of sex cells, creating changes that people would pass on to their descendants. Making changes in sex cells is extremely controversial, however, and some critics say it should never be done. They argue that making permanent changes in the human genetic "library" could lead to problems, such as the accidental development of undesirable new traits, that we have no way of foreseeing.

But there is another way to eliminate defective genes: the selection of genetically superior embryos from test-tube fertilizations. Although this option, too, is apt to provoke controversy, it was already being done on a limited scale at some fertility clinics in the United States and Europe at the start of the 1990's. The basic procedure offered at these clinics—long available to couples who are unable to conceive naturally—involves taking several eggs from the woman and fertilizing them in a laboratory dish with the husband's sperm. The clinics are now broadening their services to include genetic tests for cystic fibrosis, muscular dystrophy, and other genetic diseases for couples who are at risk of having a child with a genetic disorder. The tests are conducted a day or so after laboratory fertilization, when each new embryo is a microscopic clump of eight cells. Only an embryo that is free of detectable genetic defects is implanted in the woman's womb to produce a pregnancy.

When the gene mapping project is completed, it should be possible to test embryos for a legion of faulty genes. But gene mappers predict that the options open to prospective parents by that time will go far beyond screening for hereditary defects. People may then be making choices about their future children that are unheard of today, selecting perhaps the height, eye and hair color, athletic and musical ability, and even intelligence of each child. At that point, the human race, for better or worse, will have gained mastery of its genetic destiny.

For further reading:

Bishop, Jerry E., and Waldholz, Michael. *Genome.* Simon & Schuster Trade Books, 1991.

Murrell, J. C., and Roberts, L. M., editors. *Understanding Genetic Engineering.* Prentice Hall, 1989.

Suzuki, David, and Knudson, Peter. *Genethics: The Clash Between the New Genetics and Human Values.* Harvard University Press, 1990.

Verma, Inder M. "Gene Therapy." *Scientific American,* November 1990.

Weinberg, Robert A. "The Dark Side of the Genome Project." *Technology Review,* April 1991.

Mental health. Post-traumatic stress disorder (PTSD) may occur far more often than previously believed, psychologists reported in March 1991. PTSD features a variety of symptoms, including recurring nightmares and memories of a traumatic event, difficulty concentrating, emotional detachment from loved ones, and extreme suspicion of other people. Experts previously believed that PTSD occurred mainly among small numbers of people, such as combat veterans and victims of natural disasters. But researchers from the Henry Ford Hospital in Detroit found that about 9 per cent of a sample of 1,007 young adults had developed PTSD sometime in their lives.

Researchers found that nearly 40 per cent of the subjects had experienced events considered "stressors" for PTSD. Such events, which can trigger an episode of the condition, include a serious injury or accident, rape or other form of physical assault, observing a serious injury or death, and receiving news of the sudden death of a friend or loved one. The study indicated that about 24 per cent of people who experience such events may develop PTSD.

Participants in the study were aged 21 to 30, making PTSD one of the most common psychiatric disorders in that age group. Young adults living in urban areas may experience PTSD more often than any other psychiatric disorder except phobias, clinical depression, and drug or alcohol dependence, the study concluded.

Warm parents. Hugs, kisses, cuddling, and other expressions of warmth by parents play a key role in helping children develop into psychologically healthy adults, a 36-year study concluded in April. The study, led by psychologist Carol Franz of Boston University, was the first to examine the long-term influence of parental warmth on social adjustment of children.

Researchers at Harvard University in Cambridge, Mass., began the study in 1951 by selecting 379 mothers and their kindergarten-aged children in the Boston area. They interviewed the mothers to gather information on parenting practices and the children's social behavior. Kindergarten teachers also were asked to rate each child's social development.

In 1987, Franz and her colleagues questioned 94 people from the original sample of children and examined their social accomplishments and psychological well-being. Children of affectionate parents were better able to sustain long and happy marriages, raise children, and be involved with friends, recreational, and social activities. The study concluded that warm parenting has more influence on adult social adjustment than any other parental or childhood factor.

Insanity committal law nullified. The Supreme Court of Canada on May 2, 1991, nullified the country's automatic confinement law, which specified mandatory commitment to a mental hospital for anyone found not guilty of a crime by reason of insanity. In ruling that the law violated the Canadian Charter of Rights and Freedoms, Canada's bill of rights, the court said that it sometimes meant indefinite confinement of people who were under treatment and no longer posed any danger to society.

Stress and the common cold. Strong new evidence of a link between mental and physical health was reported on August 29 by researchers who found that people under emotional stress have an increased risk of catching a cold. Sheldon Cohen, a psychologist at Carnegie-Mellon University in Pittsburgh, Pa., who codirected the study, said it was the first scientific evidence linking stress and an infectious disease.

In the study of 420 healthy men and women, researchers calculated a stress level for each volunteer by asking about stressful events in the person's life, such as a death in the family or changing jobs. Then they gave 394 of the volunteers nose drops containing one of five different common cold viruses. The remaining 26 received nose drops with no viruses at all.

The researchers tested the volunteers for the presence of cold viruses or *antibodies* (disease-fighting proteins) produced by the body to battle the infection and found that stress increased the chances of becoming infected with any of the five viruses. People with the highest stress levels faced the highest risk of infection. Compared with the group with the lowest stress, they had twice the risk of developing cold symptoms and more than five times the risk of becoming infected with a cold virus. Michael Woods

See also **Psychology.** In ***World Book,*** see **Mental illness.**

Mexico. Mexico's highly centralized government in 1991 continued to emphasize economic modernization and closer ties with the United States. The success of free-market policies, including selling government-owned businesses to private business owners, translated into a healthy credit rating. In the two years that ended in November 1991, the Mexican government sold more than $4.4 billion in government bonds to investors in international markets.

Free trade. Mexico debated the pros and cons of joining a proposed North American Free Trade Agreement with the United States, Mexico's most important trading partner, and Canada. Beginning on April 7, following a meeting with U.S. President George Bush in Houston, Mexico's President Carlos Salinas de Gortari toured seven cities in the United States and Canada in an effort to convince business leaders of the benefits of free trade with Mexico. The proposed trade agreement would lead to the eventual abolition of tariffs on goods traded among the three nations. Many foreign companies with operations in Mexico were already positioning themselves to take advantage of an enlarged free market for goods they produced in Mexico. Volkswagen of Mexico quietly embarked on a $1-billion expansion program to double the production of its plant at Puebla.

Elections. Mexicans showed that they approve of their country's leadership on Aug. 18, 1991. The ruling Institutional Revolutionary Party of 43-year-old Presi-

Thick smog in Mexico City hides the skyline from view. To help relieve the problem, the government closed a major oil refinery in the city in March.

dent Salinas won 290 of 300 directly elected seats in the Chamber of Deputies and all but one of the 32 seats in the Senate. The Mexican government, anxious to ease lingering doubts over the 1988 presidential election, when there were widespread complaints of fraud, voided election results on Aug. 30, 1991, in the state of Guanajuato and called for new elections as a result of fraud allegations there. The government also ordered a new election in the state of San Luis Potosí following the resignation on October 9 of recently elected Governor Fausto Zapata, who was unable to persuade voters that he had been fairly elected.

Economic confidence. Mexico's strengthened economy earned praise at home and abroad. On September 9, U.S. Secretary of State James A. Baker III called Mexico "a model for countries both in this hemisphere and other countries around the world."

In a dramatic domestic show of confidence in the government's economic policies, Mexican investors paid the government $3.2 billion on August 27 for a controlling interest in a previously state-run bank, the Banco Nacional de Mexico, and $2.5 billion on October 28 for the Bancomer bank. The transactions were reportedly the largest cash payments for banks in any nation. The sales were part of a program that has resulted in the closing or sale of more than 1,150 government-owned enterprises to private entrepreneurs.

Mexico City pollution. Responding to environmental concerns, President Salinas shut down a giant oil refinery north of Mexico City on March 18. The refinery had been one of the major air polluters in Mexico City. Experts estimated that the closing of the state-run refinery would cost Mexico $500 million and reduce the country's oil production by 100,000 barrels a day. For his bold initiative, Salinas won the United Earth Prize on June 5—an award created by a descendant of the founder of the Nobel Prizes, the Swedish inventor Alfred Nobel.

Drug corruption. On May 17, a drug trafficker took over the prison in which he was jailed at Matamoros in northern Mexico. Eighteen prisoners were killed in the take-over. The prisoner, Oliverio Chávez Araujo, said he feared that Mexican drug enforcement officers had offered to pay members of a rival drug gang in the prison to kill him. Chávez surrendered on May 30, and as part of the surrender agreement, the Mexican government offered to protect him from the drug agents he claimed were trying to kill him.

Chávez had allegedly been operating an extensive drug trafficking network since 1989 from his suite of cells, which was reportedly equipped with cellular phones and a fax machine. In the wake of these revelations, the government arrested two top jail officials and dismissed the country's attorney general.

Nathan A. Haverstock

See also **Latin America** (Facts in brief table). In *World Book,* see **Mexico.**

Michigan. See **State government.**

Middle East

The Persian Gulf War, fought by a United States-led coalition to liberate Kuwait from Iraqi occupation in January and February 1991, had important political effects on the Middle East during the year. The collapse of Arab unity before the war opened the door to historic peace negotiations between Israel and its Arab neighbors. The ordeal of Western hostages held in Lebanon finally ended in December.

But these hopeful signs were offset by sobering facts. Hard-line positions maintained by Israel and its Arab neighbors severely limited progress during the first and second phases of the Middle East peace conference, held in October in Madrid, Spain, and in December in Washington, D.C., respectively. Many Arab states continued to deal with popular demands for democratic reform by reshuffling cabinets, altering election procedures, and declaring martial law, as well as by arresting and torturing political opponents.

After the war, many Mideast nations also stepped up their purchases of military equipment. Some, in particular Algeria and Iran, had reportedly purchased or were seeking to purchase nuclear technology and information that some experts claimed could be used to produce nuclear weapons. In addition, Kuwait and other Persian Gulf states confronted environmental damage resulting from Kuwaiti oil-well fires set by departing Iraqi forces and from several large oil spills in the gulf, also blamed on Iraq.

War's aftermath. The war against Iraq produced mixed results. The U.S.-led coalition ousted Iraqi forces from Kuwait and seriously damaged Iraq's ground forces, perceived by many in the coalition as a threat to regional security.

The war also largely destroyed Iraq's weapons arsenal. Under an April 3 cease-fire agreement, Iraq said it would allow inspectors from the United Nations (UN) and the International Atomic Energy Agency, an organization that promotes the peaceful use of nuclear energy, to search for and destroy its facilities for producing chemical, biological, and nuclear weapons. In September, UN weapons inspectors reported that Iraq's technical ability to produce weapons of mass destruction had been greater than Iraq had revealed and Western experts had believed.

Despite Iraq's military loss, President Saddam Hussein remained in power. Some Western governments had hoped the Iraqi Army would overthrow Hussein. But some Middle East experts argued that the allies' devastating air war and ground attack had left the army too weak for this action. The allied force lost 340 troops in the fighting, compared with an estimated

Arab and Israeli delegates listen to opening statements at the Middle East peace conference, which began on October 30 in Madrid, Spain.

John McCarthy, a British journalist kidnapped by Lebanese Shiite Muslims in 1986, waves to a welcoming crowd after his release on Aug. 8, 1991.

110,000 Iraqi troops and tens of thousands of civilians. In addition, postwar uprisings by Iraq's Shiites and Kurds threatened to fragment Iraq and intensify regional instability. Kurdish guerrilla separatists in Turkey also stepped up their activity. See **Iraq; Persian Gulf,** Special Report: **War in the Persian Gulf.**

PLO setbacks. The Palestinian Liberation Organization (PLO) and its leader, Yasir Arafat, were severely weakened in the aftermath of the Persian Gulf War. The PLO's support for Saddam Hussein angered coalition members, including Saudi Arabia and other gulf states, which reportedly withdrew their financial support from the PLO. In January, Salah Khalaf, Arafat's chief aide, was assassinated in Tunisia. In July, the Lebanese Army forced PLO fighters out of southern Lebanon.

Organizing a peace conference. U.S. President George Bush and Soviet President Mikhail S. Gorbachev opened the Middle East peace conference in Madrid on October 30. For the first time since the founding of Israel in 1948, delegates from Israel and its four Arab neighbors—Egypt, Jordan, Syria, and Lebanon—sat together at a negotiating table.

The United States, concerned about the ongoing potential for war in the Middle East and the increasing number of weapons of mass destruction in the region, had begun pressing for comprehensive negotiations between Israel and its Arab neighbors soon after the war ended. No longer bound by Arab unity, Arab states saw political and economic benefits in attending a peace conference.

The Madrid meeting marked what was hoped to be the first phase of a three-phase peace process. The first phase was intended as a general meeting between Israel and its Arab neighbors. The second phase was to consist of *bilateral* (one-on-one) meetings between Israel and each of the Arab states. It was hoped that the second phase would lead to peace settlements with Syria, Jordan, and Lebanon. (Israel and Egypt signed a peace treaty in 1979.) The final phase was to be a meeting of all interested Middle Eastern states to address issues of arms control, water supplies, economic development, and other problems.

Obstacles. Three of the main obstacles U.S. Secretary of State James A. Baker III faced while organizing the conference were the role of the UN, the status of the Israeli-occupied territories, and Palestinian representation at the talks. Syria, which seeks to regain the Golan Heights—captured by Israel in 1967—demanded that the conference be held under UN sponsorship because UN Resolution 242 calls for the return of Israeli-occupied territories in exchange for Arab recognition of Israel's "right to secure and recognized borders." But Israel's current government, which opposes trading land for peace, opposed a major role for the UN. The two sides finally agreed to allow the United States and the Soviet Union to cosponsor the talks, at which the UN would have an observer.

The second obstacle—the status of the occupied

territories—became more critical during 1991 as Israel accelerated its building of settlements there. Israel's Prime Minister Yitzhak Shamir had said in April that Israel was willing, in principle, to attend a peace conference, though there were many unresolved problems. On July 16, the leaders of seven industrialized nations called on Arab states to suspend their 43-year economic boycott of Israel in exchange for an agreement by Israel to freeze settlement construction.

By July 21, Syria, Jordan, Egypt, and Lebanon had announced their willingness to suspend the boycott and declared their willingness to attend the first phase of the talks. The only Arab holdout to the conference was the PLO, which continued to insist on being the Palestinian people's sole legitimate representative at any talks. The PLO also continued to oppose any bilateral agreements between Israel and individual Arab states.

In July, however, Shamir rejected any link between Israeli settlements in the occupied territories and the Arab boycott. Although the issue of the settlements remained unresolved, the agreement by Arab states to attend a peace conference increased pressure on Israel to formally agree to come to the negotiating table.

United States officials used the settlement issue to exert pressure on Israel to agree to the talks. The U.S. Senate on October 2 approved President's Bush's request to delay for 120 days approval of an Israeli request for early payment of $10 billion in loan guarantees to help fund housing for Soviet immigrants.

A third main hurdle was the issue of Palestinian representation at the conference. Shamir said on August 1 that Israel was willing to attend an Arab-Israeli peace conference but would not negotiate with members of the PLO, which Israel considers a terrorist organization. On September 28, the Palestine National Council, the PLO's governing body, endorsed Palestinian participation in the peace conference. The action essentially gave PLO assent to the formation of a Palestinian delegation not closely associated with the the PLO leadership.

On October 18, Palestinian leaders in Israel and the occupied territories formed a delegation acceptable to Israel and agreed to talk first about a period of limited self-rule before negotiating the final status of the occupied territories. Finally, the Palestinian representatives agreed to join the Jordanian delegation.

After providing written assurances on the procedures and form of the conference, the United States and the Soviet Union issued formal invitations. On October 20, Israel's Cabinet voted to attend the talks.

The conference opens. Many analysts doubted that the conference, which was punctuated by personal insults and bitter accusations, broke any psychological barriers. Baker openly scolded Israeli and Arab representatives—who refused to shake hands—for not dealing with the "human dimension" of their problem. During three days of meetings, the delegates

American correspondent Terry A. Anderson, the last U.S. hostage in Lebanon to be freed, greets journalists after his release on December 4.

merely set forth their historical positions rather than address their current problems.

On November 3, at the end of the Madrid meeting, delegates met to determine the location of the second phase of the conference. The Jordanian-Palestinian team won praise from the Israeli delegates for agreeing to continue their talks. The Syrian, Lebanese, and Israeli representatives, however, were unable to agree on a site for the next meeting. Israel pressed for the Middle East, and the Arabs argued for Europe or the United States. The talks remained stalled until the United States invited all parties to Washington, D.C., on December 4. Arab delegates turned up at the meeting. Israel did not, insisting that it needed until December 9 to prepare.

Talks collapse. Although all parties were present in Washington on December 10, the talks between Israeli and Palestinian delegates failed over the issue of whether the Israelis would meet separately with the Palestinians. Israeli and Syrian delegates met, but their talks remained deadlocked.

Zionism resolution repealed. On December 16, the UN General Assembly repealed a 1975 resolution equating Zionism—a movement supporting the establishment of a Jewish state in Palestine—with racism.

Opposition to peace talks. The peace talks did not meet with universal approval in the Middle East. Thousands of Lebanese and Iranians—opposed to any negotiations with Israel and, in fact, to the existence

Facts in brief on Middle Eastern countries

Country	Population	Government	Monetary unit*	Foreign trade (million U.S.$) Exports†	Imports†
Bahrain	547,000	Amir Isa bin Salman Al-Khalifa; Prime Minister Khalifa bin Salman Al-Khalifa	dinar (0.38 = $1)	2,689	2,866
Cyprus	714,000	President George Vassiliou (Turkish Republic of Nothern Cyprus: Acting President Rauf R. Denktaş)	pound (0.46 = $1)	956	2,565
Egypt	56,506,000	President Hosni Mubarak; Prime Minister Atef Sedky	pound (3.33 = $1)	2,582	9,202
Iran	59,601,000	Leader of the Islamic Revolution Ali Hoseini Khamenei; President Ali Akbar Hashemi Rafsanjani	rial (1,400 = $1)	12,300	12,000
Iraq	18,048,000	President Saddam Hussein	dinar (0.31 = $1)	12,500	10,200
Israel	4,713,000	President Chaim Herzog; Prime Minister Yitzhak Shamir	shekel (2.33 = $1)	11,576	15,104
Jordan	3,510,000	King Hussein I; Prime Minister Tahir al-Masri	dinar (0.68 = $1)	922	2,603
Kuwait	2,096,000	Amir Jabir al-Ahmad al-Jabir al-Sabah; Prime Minister & Crown Prince Sad al-Abdallah al-Salim al-Sabah	dinar (0.29 = $1)	11,476	6,303
Lebanon	3,088,000	Prime Minister Omar Karami; President Ilyas Harawi	pound (879.50 = $1)	1,000	1,500
Oman	1,568,000	Sultan Qaboos bin Said Al-Said	rial (0.39 = $1)	3,933	2,255
Qatar	451,000	Amir and Prime Minister Khalifa bin Hamad Al-Thani	riyal (3.64 = $1)	3,541	1,139
Saudi Arabia	15,234,000	King & Prime Minister Fahd bin Abd al-Aziz Al-Saud	riyal (3.75 = $1)	28,369	21,153
Sudan	26,672,000	Prime Minister Umar Hasan Ahmad al-Bashir	pound (15.00 = $1)	509	1,060
Syria	13,397,000	President Hafez al-Assad; Prime Minister Mahmud Zubi	pound (21 = $1)	4,062	2,526
Turkey	57,749,000	President Turgut Özal; Prime Minister Suleyman Demirel	lira (5,072.76 = $1)	12,922	21,810
United Arab Emirates	1,660,000	President Zayid bin Sultan Al-Nuhayyan; Prime Minister Maktum bin Rashid Al-Maktum	dirham (3.67 = $1)	15,837	6,422
Yemen	11,199,000	President Ali Abdallah Salih; Prime Minister Haydar Abu Bakr al-Attas	rial (12.10 = $1)	935	1,898

*Exchange rates as of Nov. 29,1991, or latest available data. †Latest available data.

of the Jewish state—demonstrated against the conference. Palestinians at odds themselves over the talks, staged protests and battled one another.

Hostages freed. The ordeal of U.S. hostages held in Lebanon ended on December 4, with the release of Terry A. Anderson, a news correspondent who had been kidnapped in 1985. Nine other Western hostages—five of them American—were released between August and December 1991. One Italian, believed to be dead, and two German hostages remained in captivity at year-end.

Many analysts attributed the release of the hostages to an eagerness by Syria and Iran to end their political isolation. With the collapse of Iraq in the Persian Gulf War, the two countries saw an opportunity to reassert their leadership in the Middle East. But their support for Lebanese kidnappers remained an obstacle to that leadership as well as to the development of political and economic ties with the West.

Hopes that Western hostages in Lebanon might finally be released first arose on August 8 when British hostage John McCarthy was freed. McCarthy carried a letter to UN Secretary General Javier Peréz de Cuéllar from a pro-Iranian Shiite Muslim group. The letter suggested that all Western hostages might be freed if Israel would release its estimated 375 Lebanese Shiite prisoners. Israel responded favorably to the suggestion, indicating it would be willing to do so if it received information about seven Israeli servicemen missing in Lebanon. Iran also said it was time to end the hostage crisis. The release three days later of American hostage Edward Austin Tracy and a Frenchman kidnapped on August 8 were seen as positive signs.

After UN mediation, two more hostages, American Jesse Turner and Briton Jack Mann, were released on September 24 and on October 21, respectively. On November 18, Lebanese captors released Briton Terry Waite and American Thomas Sutherland. The remaining three American hostages—Joseph Cicippio, Alann Steen, and Anderson—were freed during the first week of December.

Also between August and December, Israel released 91 Arab prisoners and the bodies of 9 Arab guerrillas and allowed an exiled Palestinian activist to return to the West Bank. During this period, Israel received information on three of its missing servicemen.

BCCI scandal. A scandal surrounding the Bank of Credit and Commerce International (BCCI) severely embarrassed many members of ruling families in the Middle East who had financial links with the BCCI or its activities. The 1991 collapse of the bank, which had branches in 70 countries, also pointed out the instability of Mideast banking institutions. At year-end, law enforcement agencies on several continents were investigating charges of bribery, kickbacks, fraud, and money-laundering by the BCCI. Christine Helms

See also articles on the various Middle Eastern countries. In ***World Book,*** see **Middle East** and individual Middle Eastern country articles.

Mining. An Alaskan zinc mine that began full operations in 1991 will double the United States production of this key industrial metal, the U.S. Bureau of Mines predicted in July. The Red Dog Mine, located in the De Long Mountains about 300 miles (480 kilometers) southwest of Barrow, is one of the largest zinc mines in the world. It will produce about 2.1 million short tons (1.9 million metric tons) of zinc ore each year, enough ore to supply about two-thirds of U.S. domestic needs for zinc. Experts believe that the amount of zinc ore deposited at the Red Dog site is large enough to keep the mine in operation for 50 years.

Developing the mine took 15 years and $450 million. A mill at the mine site will convert the ore into zinc concentrate. The concentrate will be shipped to other nations for processing because the United States no longer has any zinc smelters to convert zinc concentrate into pure metal.

Copper output. The United States produced a record 1.8 million short tons (1.6 million metric tons) of copper in 1990, almost overtaking Chile as the world's leading producer of the metal, the Bureau of Mines reported in August 1991. The 1990 copper output surpassed the previous U.S. record set in 1973. Copper production in the United States has increased partly because of the availability of better, less expensive technology for extracting the metal.

Disaster-rescue vehicle. Australian engineers in February 1991 announced that they had developed the world's first remotely controlled emergency rescue vehicle for mine disasters. The eight-wheeled vehicle was designed to travel over debris and through flooded mine shafts, collecting data on explosive gases and other conditions that would help rescuers plan efforts to reach trapped miners.

Named the *Numbat*, the vehicle was developed at the request of the Australian mining industry after a 1986 disaster in which 12 people were trapped in a coal mine. Because rescuers were unable to reach the miners, all 12 died.

Video cameras on the *Numbat* transmit images via a fiber-optic cable to workers on the surface, who use remote control devices to guide the vehicle through mine tunnels. The *Numbat* is also equipped with an ultrasonic sensor capable of "seeing" through mine shafts filled with dust or smoke from explosions or fires. Chemical sensors mounted inside an explosion-proof enclosure continuously monitor air inside the mine for poisonous or explosive gases that could endanger rescuers. *Numbat*'s developers said the vehicle could have life-saving applications in other accidents and natural disasters where explosions and cave-ins are hazards. Michael Woods

See also **Coal; Petroleum and gas.** In ***World Book,*** see **Mining.**

Minnesota. See **State government.**
Mississippi. See **State government.**
Missouri. See **State government.**

Miyazawa, Kiichi (1919-), became prime minister of Japan on Nov. 5, 1991, nine days after he was elected head of the majority Liberal-Democratic Party (LDP). For several decades, Miyazawa has been an important shaper of Japanese economic and foreign policy. Some of his recent statements suggest that he would now like Japan to play a more influential role in global political affairs.

Miyazawa is fluent in English and professes a great fondness for the United States. However, he has also occasionally criticized the United States for what he considers unwise economic policies. Recently he has said that the two countries should work harder to resolve their trade disputes.

Miyazawa was born in Tokyo on Oct. 8, 1919, and graduated from Tokyo Imperial University with a law degree in 1941. He became an official in wartime Japan's Ministry of Finance in 1942. In 1949, he was made private secretary to the Minister of Finance, Hayato Ikeda. From 1953 to 1965, he served in the House of Councillors, which is the upper house of Japan's parliament, the Diet. In 1967, he was elected to the House of Representatives, the Diet's lower house. He has headed Japan's ministries of finance, international trade and industry, and foreign affairs.

Miyazawa is married and has two grown children.
Douglas Clayton

Mongolia. See **Asia**.
Montana. See **State government**.

Montreal. Canada's recession hit the Montreal business community hard during 1991. More than 10,000 business executives in Montreal's downtown area lost their jobs. In the industrial sector, unemployment increased from 9.4 per cent in January to 12 per cent in November. In areas such as Montreal East and Pointe St. Charles, where school dropout rates are high, unemployment was as great as 40 per cent among people under age 25.

Office vacancy rates soared. Montreal had the third highest rate of vacant offices of all Canadian cities in 1991. Only Toronto, Ont., and Calgary, Alta., fared worse. Montreal's vacancy rate rose to 14.8 per cent in 1991 from 12.6 per cent in 1990. Industry experts estimated that the office space will not be completely rented for at least 10 to 12 years.

The recession also affected one of the city's largest shelters for the homeless. Dernier Recours (Last Hope) was forced to close its doors in the summer of 1991 because of a lack of funds. Scores of homeless people and their advocates set up camps outside the shelter. Police cleared away the camps and the shelter remained closed.

The budget, released in early November, for the Montreal Urban Community, which includes both the city and its suburbs, exceeded $1 billion ($884 million U.S.) for the 1991-1992 fiscal year and was the largest budget on record. Montreal's lawmakers set the budget at $1.14 billion ($1 billion U.S.), an expansion of 17.5 per cent in one year. They blamed massive cuts in provincial subsidies as the reason for the dramatic increase. The lawmakers expected higher property taxes and transit fares to pay for the budget increase.

Mayor Jean Doré encountered criticism in 1991 for his plans to spend $340,000 ($300,000 U.S.) on a new window for his office and tens of thousands of dollars on porcelain dog toilets for Montreal's West End neighborhood. Doré also produced ire when he denied raises to civil servants but increased his salary by $5,000, boosting his annual pay to $107,000 ($94,600 U.S.). After a candidate whom Doré strongly supported in a by-election placed fourth out of four, the mayor publicly declared that he was "humiliated."

A strike by the city's maintenance workers in November threatened to paralyze Montreal just as the first snow of the 1991-1992 winter season began to fall. But after only 25 minutes off the job, the workers decided to accept the city's offer. This ended several months of rotating strikes, which had affected garbage collection and other city services, and even led to vandalism.

Police problems. On July 3, 1991, a member of the Montreal police tactical team shot and killed a young black man, Marcellus Francois, in what was called a clear case of mistaken identity. The police were tracking another young black man involved in a murder case when they shot the unarmed Francois. The incident prompted strong protests that led to outbreaks of rioting and other types of public disorder.

This was the third controversial police killing of a black citizen within a period of a few months. The Montreal police force has about 4,400 members, of whom only 24 are black. The police department and city have said they are trying to add more blacks to the police force.

The Olympic Stadium in Montreal was closed on Sept. 13, 1991, when a concrete girder weighing 56 short tons (51 metric tons) tore away from its brackets and crashed down onto a concourse roof. Montreal's professional baseball franchise, the Expos, had to play the remainder of their home games on the road. Earlier in the summer, high winds had torn off part of the stadium's roof. Since its opening in 1976, when Montreal hosted the Olympic Games, the $1-billion stadium has needed regular repairs, costing millions of dollars in construction bills and lost revenues. The stadium was expected to be reopened in time for an automobile show in January 1992.

Population. Since 1986, Montreal has lost 96,519 citizens to other parts of Canada, and most of the people who left were young professionals with families, according to Statistics Canada. Of those who left, 61,150 were between the ages of 25 and 44 and they took 17,782 children with them. In 1990, about 8,200 young professionals moved away from Montreal and the province of Quebec. Kendal Windeyer

See **Canada,** Special Report: **Canada and Quebec at a Crossroads.** In ***World Book,*** see **Montreal.**

Morocco. King Hassan II celebrated 30 years of rule in February 1991. While the king won praise for his political skill, he also was criticized for his failure to increase popular participation in government and for the government's poor record on human rights.

Morocco's national debt of about $22 billion in 1991 was one of the highest in the Arab world relative to population. The country also continued to suffer from high unemployment, inflation, rising food costs, and poor working and living conditions. In addition, Morocco suffered a dramatic loss of tourism because of the Persian Gulf crisis. The tourist industry, one of the country's most important foreign-exchange earners, had brought in $1.5 billion yearly and employed an estimated 300,000 people.

Persian Gulf crisis. In February, Hassan toned down his initial support for the United States-led coalition against Iraq after learning of the extensive damage resulting from the allied bombing. Many Moroccans called for the return of the 1,500 troops Hassan had sent to Saudi Arabia. Hassan defended his action with assertions that the Moroccan force had been deployed strictly to protect Saudi oil facilities.

Human rights. Nearly 1,000 Moroccans were allegedly jailed after hurried trials in late 1990 and early 1991, according to a March 1991 report by Amnesty International, the human rights organization based in London. The trials grew out of December 1990 riots arising from public frustration with economic conditions. More than 100 Moroccans were believed to have been killed. Amnesty International reported that about 850 people, many of whom were forced to confess, had been given 15-year prison sentences. At least 85 people were reportedly tried together. The Amnesty International report also stated that about 100 people had received prison terms for publicly demonstrating in support of Iraq. On February 3, however, the government allowed at least 300,000 pro-Iraqi demonstrators to march through Rabat, the capital.

In August, Hassan pardoned about 40 political prisoners. In September, the government released Abraham Serfaty, a prominent dissident, who was expelled to France after 17 years in detention in Morocco. Serfaty leads a group that advocates independence for Western Sahara.

Western Sahara. A United Nations-supervised cease-fire between Moroccan forces and the Polisario Front guerrillas in Western Sahara went into effect on September 7. The government and the Polisario Front, which has been fighting for Saharan independence since 1976, agreed to the cease-fire in preparation for a referendum scheduled for January 1992. The vote was called to decide whether the phosphate-rich Western Sahara becomes a province of Morocco or gains its independence. Christine Helms

See also **Persian Gulf,** Special Report: **War in the Persian Gulf; Africa** (Facts in brief table); **Middle East.** In ***World Book,*** see **Morocco.**

Motion pictures.

Motion pictures. The motion picture industry in 1991 experienced a year that was chaotic both creatively and commercially. Many of the most profitable movies were not released until the end of the year. Some of 1991's most favorable reviews alighted on director Ridley Scott's *Thelma and Louise,* which also garnered much media attention. Starring Geena Davis and Susan Sarandon, *Thelma and Louise* told of the plight of two Arkansas women running from legal entanglements and domestic oppression. Some critics felt it mixed comedy and tragedy more deftly than any film since the 1967 landmark *Bonnie and Clyde.* Some moviegoers, however, accused the film of condoning "male bashing."

Among the most eagerly awaited films of 1991 was Oliver Stone's *JFK.* The movie starred Kevin Costner as former New Orleans District Attorney James Garrison, who challenged the Warren Commission's findings regarding the assassination of former President John F. Kennedy. Stone kept the script a secret before the film's release. But word leaked out that the movie proposed that Kennedy was assassinated because he planned to withdraw troops from Vietnam, which, supposedly, may have wrecked the national economy.

Disappointments peppered the 1991 film year, too. Robert Benton's movie version of E. L. Doctorow's *Billy Bathgate* featured Dustin Hoffman as the mobster Dutch Schultz. The movie looked elegant, but the acting was lifeless. Mark Rydell's *For the Boys* with Bette

Beauty and the Beast, a musical adaptation of the classic fairy tale, won critical acclaim in 1991 and was Disney's 30th full-length, animated film.

Academy Award winners in 1991

Best Picture, *Dances with Wolves.*
Best Actor, Jeremy Irons, *Reversal of Fortune.*
Best Actress, Kathy Bates, *Misery.*
Best Supporting Actor, Joe Pesci, *GoodFellas.*
Best Supporting Actress, Whoopi Goldberg, *Ghost.*
Best Director, Kevin Costner, *Dances with Wolves.*
Best Original Screenplay, Bruce Joel Rubin, *Ghost.*
Best Screenplay Adaptation, Michael Blake, *Dances with Wolves.*
Best Cinematography, Dean Semler, *Dances with Wolves.*
Best Film Editing, Neil Travis, *Dances with Wolves.*
Best Original Score, John Barry, *Dances with Wolves.*
Best Original Song, Stephen Sondheim, "Sooner or Later (I Always Get My Man)" from *Dick Tracy.*
Best Foreign-Language Film, *Journey of Hope* (Switzerland).
Best Art Direction, Richard Sylbert, *Dick Tracy.*
Best Costume Design, Franca Squarciapino, *Cyrano de Bergerac.*
Best Sound, Russell Williams II, Jeffrey Perkins, Bill W. Benton, and Greg Watkins, *Dances with Wolves.*
Best Sound Effects Editing, Cecelia Hall and George Watters II, *The Hunt for Red October.*
Best Makeup, John Caglione, Jr., and Doug Drexler, *Dick Tracy.*
Best Animated Short Film, *Creature Comforts.*
Best Live-Action Short Film, *The Lunch Date.*
Best Feature Documentary, *American Dream.*
Best Short Subject Documentary, *Days of Waiting.*

Midler turned into what some critics called an overproduced musical drama.

Critics' choice. Joel and Ethan Coen's *Barton Fink,* a dark and cerebral comedy about a young writer who sells out to Hollywood, won three top film awards, including the Golden Palm Award, at the 44th Cannes International Film Festival in May. Spike Lee's *Jungle Fever* was well received at the festival and won an award in the best supporting actor category.

Terry Gilliam's fantasy romance *The Fisher King* received positive reviews for its direction and the acting of Robin Williams and Jeff Bridges. Critics also praised Jodie Foster's directing debut, *Little Man Tate.* Gus Van Sant's *My Own Private Idaho,* which featured teen idols River Phoenix and Keanu Reeves as male hustlers in Portland, Ore., was favorably reviewed, though it was not as highly praised as Van Sant's 1989 film, *Drugstore Cowboy.*

Critics raved about John Sayles's *City of Hope,* a searing story of moral and municipal decay in contemporary urban society. Audiences, however, apparently deemed it to be too depressing. *Rambling Rose,* Martha Coolidge's film of a young girl's impact on a genteel Southern family, was noted for the superb acting of Robert Duvall, Diane Ladd, Laura Dern, and Lukas Haas.

Bruce Beresford followed his 1989 commercial hit, *Driving Miss Daisy,* with the beautifully photographed *Black Robe.* The film offers a graphic and often brutal account of the hardships endured by a Jesuit priest in the 1800's who tries to convert Canadian Indians. Peter Greenaway, whose *The Cook, The Thief, His Wife & Her Lover* was both praised and scorned in 1990, once again ignited controversy with another film, *Prospero's Books.* The film was a variation of William Shakespeare's *The Tempest.*

Thrillers. Two of 1991's most prominent films featured memorable, if despicable, villains. Anthony Hopkins' droll but frightening performance as Hannibal Lecter in Jonathan Demme's *The Silence of the Lambs* became an instant addition to film folklore. The imprisoned cannibalistic psychiatrist collaborates with an FBI trainee, played by Jodie Foster, to entrap a serial killer. Even more terrifying, though slightly less sophisticated, was Robert De Niro's character of Max Cady, the self-appointed "avenging angel" in Martin Scorsese's remake of *Cape Fear.*

Summertime shows. Economically, 1991 had the fourth-best summer on record. Summer movie releases had projected gross earnings of $1.65 billion—but still lower than the $1.86 billion earnings for the summer of 1990. The all-time summer record was attained with 1989's earnings of $2.04 billion.

Moviemakers released three major hits at the beginning of the summer of 1991. They were: *Terminator 2: Judgment Day,* with Arnold Schwarzenegger portraying a protector rather than a destroyer; *Robin Hood: Prince of Thieves,* with Kevin Costner as the prince of Sherwood Forest; and *City Slickers,* with Billy Crystal combating a midlife crisis by joining a cattle drive. The last half of the summer season brought forth no major blockbusters, but there were a few flops. Among the box-office failures showcasing major stars were: *Hudson Hawk* with Bruce Willis; *Dying Young* with Julia Roberts; and *Regarding Henry* with Harrison Ford.

In September, 33 films opened, the fewest releases during that month since 1981. The peak year for September releases was 1967, when filmmakers introduced 65 new movies.

At year's end, several films generated high hopes for box-office success. Barbra Streisand presented her long-awaited version of Pat Conroy's best seller *The Prince of Tides,* an emotional drama of a strife-torn family starring Streisand and Nick Nolte. Steven Spielberg ushered in *Hook,* a revival of the Peter Pan story, starring Dustin Hoffman as the nasty Captain Hook, Robin Williams as an adult Peter Pan, and Julia Roberts as the fairy Tinker Bell. Barry Levinson lined up with *Bugsy,* starring Warren Beatty as Bugsy Siegel, the gangster who built Las Vegas, Nev.

Animation. The Walt Disney Company in November released a lavish musical production of *Beauty and the Beast.* Economists predicted that it would be the first animated feature film to break $100 million in gross domestic earnings. *Beauty and the Beast* won glowing reviews and again showed how animation could ascend to great heights.

Bette Midler and James Caan star in *For the Boys,* a 1991 film that received mixed reviews and failed to attract its target audience, those over age 30.

Steven Spielberg also released an animated film, *An American Tail: Fievel Goes West.* But it was not as successful as Disney's *Beauty and the Beast.*

Universal Pictures announced its plans for a full-length feature film based on Casper the Friendly Ghost. In 1990, the studio acquired a 20 per cent stake in Harvey Comics Entertainment, which owns the rights to the Casper character. The studio also planned a short feature with Baby Huey, another Harvey character. Paramount Pictures planned to return to animation after a 35-year hiatus, with a romantic musical to be released in December 1992.

Japan earned approximately $20 million in 1991 for exporting animated cartoons, while Germany also was a popular source of animated features. However, neither the Japanese nor German animated films were generally shown in the United States.

Musical biographies promised to be another upcoming movie trend. Oliver Stone's *The Doors* met with mixed critical and audience response. Biographies of such musical legends as Bobby Darin, Bob Marley, and Otis Redding were reportedly in various stages of preparation in 1991.

Black filmmakers continued to make inroads in Hollywood and released a number of notable films in 1991. Directors who presented new works included Mario Van Peebles with *New Jack City,* Charles Lane with *True Identity,* Robert Townsend with *The Five Heartbeats,* John Singleton with *Boyz N the Hood,* Doug McHenry with *House Party 2,* Joseph B. Vasquez with *Hangin' With the Homeboys,* Charles Burnett with *To Sleep With Anger,* Bill Duke with *A Rage in Harlem,* and Matty Rich with *Straight Out of Brooklyn.*

Unfortunately, two of the most critically acclaimed films of the group, *To Sleep With Anger* and *A Rage in Harlem,* did poorly at the box office. And *New Jack City* and *Boyz N the Hood* were greeted with violence in some urban areas. Ironically, the latter film contained a pacifist message.

Foreign films released in the United States during 1991 did not achieve the popularity of some previous imports. But Luc Bresson's *La Femme Nikita;* Agnieszka Holland's *Europa, Europa;* Zhang Yimou's *Ju Dou;* and Giuseppe Tornatore's *Everybody's Fine* made strong showings.

As with domestic releases, there were high expectations for films that opened at the year's end. These included Claude Chabrol's version of Gustave Flaubert's *Madame Bovary* with Isabelle Huppert; Akira Kurosawa's *Rhapsody in August,* featuring Richard Gere in a significant supporting role; and Pedro Almodovar's *High Heels,* which broke national records in Spain and followed the director's past success, *Women on the Verge of a Nervous Breakdown.*

International. Audiences throughout the world continued to turn to big-scale Hollywood blockbusters rather than to art films. *Terminator 2: Judgment Day* and *Robin Hood: Prince of Thieves* were international smash hits. Even *Hudson Hawk,* a notorious flop in the United States, performed well in other countries. Art films found audiences in France, Italy, and Sweden but lost followers in Germany, Spain, and Denmark.

Film production was generally on the upswing internationally, though British releases were at their lowest rate since 1981. The fall of the Berlin Wall made Berlin a choice site for film locations. Three major German films went into production during 1991.

The Library of Congress again added 25 films to its National Film Registry. Under the National Film Preservation Act of 1988, the selections represent films that are "culturally, historically, or aesthetically significant." The films chosen in 1991 were *The Battle of San Pietro* (1945), *The Blood of Jesus* (1941), *Chinatown* (1974), *City Lights* (1931), *David Holzman's Diary* (1968), *Frankenstein* (1931), *Gertie the Dinosaur* (1909), *Gigi* (1958), *Greed* (1924), *High School* (1968), *I Am a Fugitive From a Chain Gang* (1932), *The Italian* (1915), *King Kong* (1933), *Lawrence of Arabia* (1962), *The Magnificent Ambersons* (1942), *My Darling Clementine* (1946), *Out of the Past* (1947), *A Place in the Sun* (1952), *The Poor Little Rich Girl* (1917), *The Prisoner of Zenda* (1937), *Shadow of a Doubt* (1943), *Sherlock, Jr.* (1924), *Tevye, the Milkman* (1939), *Trouble in Paradise* (1932), and *2001: A Space Odyssey* (1968).

Philip Wuntch

See also **Bates, Kathy; Costner, Kevin; Irons, Jeremy; Roberts, Julia.** In ***World Book,*** see **Motion picture.**

Mozambique. See **Africa.**

Mulroney, Brian (1939-). Popular approval of Canadian Prime Minister Brian Mulroney and the Progressive Conservative (PC) Party that he leads ebbed to its lowest point ever in 1991. Results of a Gallup Poll released at the end of August showed that only 12 per cent of decided voters supported the party, and 78 per cent were unhappy with Mulroney.

Mulroney made tough decisions in 1991, including changing the positions of 23 of his 39 Cabinet members. In September, he mediated a Cabinet consensus on constitutional reform proposals. Mulroney realized that his unpopularity might work against the proposals and wisely asked a minister to promote them.

Mulroney also recognized that Canada would benefit from participating in free-trade blocs with other nations. Accordingly, he directed Canada into free-trade negotiations with the United States and Mexico.

In October, Mulroney's name was placed on a list of those being considered for secretary-general of the United Nations. But Mulroney, citing his commitment to solving Canada's unity problem, asked that his name be withdrawn. David M. L. Farr

See **Canada,** Special Report: **Canada and Quebec at a Crossroads.** In ***World Book,*** see **Mulroney, Brian.**

Music. See **Classical music; Popular music.**

Myanmar. See **Burma.**

Namibia. See **Africa.**

Nebraska. See **State government.**

Nepal. See **Asia.**

Netherlands. During the last half of 1991, the Netherlands held the presidency of the Council of Ministers, the policymaking body of the 12-nation European Community (EC or Common Market). The EC presidency, which rotates among member nations every six months, gave the Netherlands responsibility for drafting major treaties on future EC economic and political union. Members of the council signed the treaties at an EC summit meeting held in Maastricht, the Netherlands, on December 9 and 10.

European role. The Netherlands favored giving much greater power in shaping EC policies to the European Parliament, the EC's advisory branch. The Dutch proposed, for example, giving the Parliament veto power over laws passed by the council—laws that the Parliament now can only amend. But at early negotiations in September, some members of the council rejected a Dutch plan to give the Parliament a greater say about foreign policies and defense policies.

Because the Netherlands held the EC presidency, the nation also played a major part in EC efforts to halt the civil war in Yugoslavia, which met with little success. After a series of cease-fires failed to hold, the Dutch supported plans to impose sanctions against Yugoslavia in November.

The coalition government led by Prime Minister Ruud Lubbers, the popular head of the Christian Democratic Appeal, struggled to cut the country's large budget deficit. The government, to which the Labor

Party also belonged, proposed a new tax on dividends, but it still needed to cut social welfare programs.

Many observers thought Lubbers might seek the job of president of the European Commission, the EC's executive branch. The post is currently held by Jacques Delors of France, whose term expires at the end of 1992. Should Lubbers get the job, as many Europeans anticipated, the Netherlands would almost certainly face new elections in 1992 to select his replacement as prime minister.

Following the collapse of Communism in the Soviet Union, the Netherlands rethought its position on European defense. Lubbers remained a strong backer of close defense ties with the United States through the North Atlantic Treaty Organization (NATO), the Western security alliance to which the Netherlands belongs. Lubbers also favored increased European cooperation on defense within the Western European Union, an organization of nine EC members.

Van Gogh theft. On April 14, 1991, thieves stole 20 paintings by the Dutch artist Vincent van Gogh, valued at $200 million, from the Van Gogh Museum in Amsterdam. The paintings were recovered from an abandoned getaway car at a nearby railroad station within an hour after their theft. Philip Revzin

See also **Europe** (Facts in brief table) and Special Report: **The Rocky Road to European Unity.** In ***World Book,*** see **Netherlands.**

Nevada. See **State government.**

New Brunswick. The Liberal Party retained power after elections on Sept. 23, 1991. The party, which was led by Premier Frank J. McKenna, had held all 58 legislative seats since 1987. In the September elections, the Liberals captured 46 seats and won just less than half of the province's popular vote. The two-year-old Confederation of Regions Party (CoR) won 8 seats and 20 per cent of the vote. The Progressive Conservatives, who had governed New Brunswick for 17 years before 1987, regained three legislative seats, and the New Democratic Party gained one.

The CoR had campaigned against New Brunswick's law sanctioning both English and French as its official languages. The CoR advocated English as the only official language. New Brunswick is the only province that uses English and French as official languages.

McKenna, a strong supporter of an economic union among Canada's three small Atlantic provinces—New Brunswick, Nova Scotia, and Prince Edward Island—convened a June 17 meeting of the Cabinet members of all three provinces. The group decided to create a common securities commission and to remove barriers to the movement of transport trucks within their region. David M. L. Farr

See **Canada,** Special Report: **Canada and Quebec at a Crossroads.** In ***World Book,*** see **New Brunswick.**

New Hampshire. See **State government.**

New Jersey. See **State government.**

New Mexico. See **State government.**

New York City. The restructuring of New York City's government, mandated by a 1989 reform of the city charter, was completed in late 1991. On Nov. 5, New York City residents elected representatives to a new, expanded 51-member City Council. Twenty-two, or about 40 per cent, of the new council's members were from minority backgrounds. That figure, however, still did not accurately reflect the city's racial mix. The 1990 census showed that blacks and Hispanics constituted a majority of New York's population for the first time in the city's history.

The election completed the changes specified by the 1989 charter revisions. The reform measure called for expansion of the City Council from 35 members to 51, new land-use rules, and elimination of the Board of Estimate as the city's principal policymaking body. The board had been the power base of the five borough presidents. Their power was greatly reduced by the charter reform, which transferred the board's authority to the City Council.

Red ink. New York City's financial problems, which were approaching crisis proportions in 1990, continued in 1991 despite a hiring freeze and spending cuts. On November 5, Mayor David N. Dinkins said that because of inadequate tax revenues, the city's $26-billion budget for fiscal 1992 (July 1, 1991, to June 30, 1992) contained a $200-million deficit. The mayor said that unless further action was taken, the deficit would grow to $7 billion by fiscal 1997. To prevent such a fiscal catastrophe, Dinkins announced a new four-year financial plan, which included the elimination of 16,300 municipal jobs.

Subway crash. On August 28, a subway train on the busy Lexington Avenue line derailed and smashed through more than a dozen metal beams as it approached the 14th Street station. Five people were killed and about 200 injured. It was the worst New York City subway accident since 1928.

The motorman, Robert Ray, 38, was unhurt and walked away from the scene. The police said Ray admitted that he had been drinking, and a laboratory test found a high level of alcohol in his blood. On September 3, Ray was indicted on five counts of second-degree murder.

More people on welfare. In one sign of the stagnant national and local economy, the number of New Yorkers on welfare rose to 955,000 in September, and city officials predicted the number would climb to 1 million in 1992. The growth of the welfare rolls—up from 887,000 in 1990—included a significant jump in the number of single men on public assistance. Many of these men were homeless.

Restoring the city. On Sept. 24, 1991, New York Governor Mario M. Cuomo detailed a $7-billion rebuilding plan for the city. The proposed public-works program calls for constructing a light-rail link between LaGuardia and Kennedy airports, finishing the 63rd Street subway tunnel between the boroughs of Manhattan and Queens, and renovating two train sta-

The wreckage of a New York City subway car—part of a train that crashed on August 28, killing five people—blocks the tracks at the 14th Street station.

tions—Grand Central Terminal and Pennsylvania Station. The plan also includes the future construction, with both public and private funds, of a large residential and office complex on the Queens waterfront and another on the Upper West Side of Manhattan.

Fighting AIDS. In an effort to slow the spread of AIDS and other sexually transmitted diseases, a controversial "condom-on-demand" program was begun in 16 city high schools on November 26. The Board of Education planned to make free condoms available to all of the 260,000 students in the city's 120 public high schools by the end of 1992.

Traffic death sparks rioting. Blacks in Crown Heights, a mixed black and Hasidic Jewish area in Brooklyn, rioted for four days in August 1991 after an Orthodox Jewish driver struck and killed a 7-year-old Guyanese immigrant, Gavin Cato, on the evening of August 19. The car, driven by Yosef Lifsh, went out of control and jumped a curb. Later that night, a visiting Hasidic scholar from Australia, Yankel Rosenbaum, 29, was stabbed to death on a Crown Heights street by a roving gang of black youths in apparent reprisal.

On August 27, a Brooklyn grand jury indicted a black youth for the murder of Rosenbaum. Black leaders in New York City demanded that Lifsh be indicted for vehicular homicide, but a grand jury ruled on September 5 that he was not criminally liable for Cato's death. Owen Moritz

See also **City**. In ***World Book***, see **New York City**.

New York. See **State government**.

New Zealand sent transport aircraft and a medical team to the Persian Gulf region once war began in January 1991. After Iraq's defeat, New Zealand personnel joined United Nations (UN) inspection teams that supervised the destruction of Iraq's chemical weapons and its facilities for developing nuclear weapons under the terms of the UN's permanent cease-fire resolution for the Persian Gulf War. Several New Zealanders were among the UN inspectors who were detained for four days in September by Iraqi soldiers.

Improved U.S. relations. Significant steps to improve relations between New Zealand and the United States were taken in 1991. Relations had been hampered since 1985, when New Zealand banned nuclear-powered and nuclear-armed ships from entering its ports. In response, the United States said in 1986 that it would no longer guarantee New Zealand's security under a defense agreement signed in 1951 by the United States, New Zealand, and Australia.

In September 1991, U.S. President George Bush and New Zealand Prime Minister James B. Bolger met at the United Nations in New York City to discuss the nuclear ban issue. In October, New Zealand diplomats hinted that visits by U.S. nuclear-powered warships may resume in the future if the United States eliminates nuclear weapons from much of its fleet and if New Zealand amends its law to permit entry of nuclear-propelled vessels.

Budget. The National Party's political fortunes slumped after July, when Finance Minister Ruth Richardson presented the administration's first budget. It cut welfare and health spending and froze benefits in an attempt to reduce the mounting budget deficit. The new budget predicted a deficit of $NZ 1.7 billion (about $970 million U.S.) for 1991-1992.

Under the new welfare program, individuals earning more than $NZ 17,280 ($9,800 U.S.) would have to contribute to payments for doctor's bills, prescriptions, and hospital stays. It raised the age for eligibility for welfare programs for single mothers from 16 to 18 and the age for pensions from 60 to 65. The cuts drew widespread criticism, particularly among people over age 55.

Falling inflation. The administration's economic policy succeeded in dropping inflation from 4.1 per cent in 1990 to 2.4 per cent by the end of September 1991. It was the lowest rate among member nations of the Organization for Economic Cooperation and Development, which comprises 24 countries from Western Europe, North America, and the Pacific area.

Rising unemployment. Almost 224,000 people among New Zealand's 3.4 million population were out of work or on government work plans at the end of August, compared with 200,000 in August 1990. The largest loss of jobs was in the manufacturing sector, but sheep and beef farmers registered their worst year ever. Gavin Ellis

See also **Asia** (Facts in brief table). In ***World Book,*** see **New Zealand.**

Newfoundland. The Canadian recession, poor fishing conditions, and a drastic reduction in anticipated federal funding resulted in Newfoundland's harshest budget cuts since the province joined the Dominion of Canada in 1949. The budget, which was released on March 7, 1991, eliminated 2,600 public sector jobs and closed 360 hospital beds. Finance Minister Hubert Kitchen said the measures were necessary to reduce the province's projected deficit from $200 million ($177 million U.S.) to $53.8 million ($47.5 million U.S.) for the 1991-1992 fiscal year. The minister also announced that he was freezing the salaries of all 35,000 provincial employees for the next fiscal year. With unemployment at 18 per cent, Newfoundland's economy could not generate the revenue needed to maintain the previous level of government services.

A reenactment of the probable first landing by Europeans in North America occurred on Aug. 2, 1991, at L'Anse-aux-Meadows, on the northern tip of Newfoundland. A graceful replica of a Viking ship of the 900's, the 79-foot- (24-meter-) long *Gaia,* sailed amid towering icebergs to repeat the voyage of Norse explorer Leif Ericson that many historians believe took place almost 1,000 years ago. The replica ship, which carried a crew of 10, took 2½ months to make the hazardous North Atlantic crossing from Norway.

David M. L. Farr

See **Canada,** Special Report: **Canada and Quebec at a Crossroads.** In ***World Book,*** see **Newfoundland.**

Newsmakers of 1991 included the following:

Zachary Taylor. He's been dead for more than 140 years, but Taylor, 12th President of the United States, was making news again in 1991—as the possible victim of an assassination plot. On June 17, Taylor's remains were removed from the limestone crypt in Louisville, Ky., where he and his wife, Margaret, were entombed. County and federal officials authorized the exhumation at the request of a Florida author, Clara Rising, who was researching a book on Taylor.

Rising suspected that "Old Rough and Ready," whose sudden fatal illness in July 1850 was attributed to an intestinal inflammation, had actually been poisoned with arsenic, which would have produced much the same symptoms. Although he was a Southern slaveowner, Taylor opposed the extension of slavery to new states in the West, a stance that had outraged many of his fellow Southerners. But despite making some serious political enemies, Taylor apparently died of natural causes. Laboratory analyses of his tissues failed to support Rising's theory of murder in the White House. The tests detected only a tiny trace of arsenic, far less than a lethal amount, that could have come from innocent sources in the environment.

Center of attention. After every U.S. census, some American town is proclaimed the center of population for the United States, the point at which the country would balance like a teeter-totter if it were a

Waving good-by on September 26, eight "Biospherians" enter Biosphere II, an enclosed environment in Arizona, for a two-year ecology experiment.

flat, rigid map and every U.S. resident weighed the same. After reviewing its 1990 head count, the Bureau of the Census in September 1991 bestowed this distinction on Steelville, Mo., a community of 1,465 people about 65 miles (105 kilometers) southwest of St. Louis. Steelville residents observed the occasion by dedicating a monument and marker at the precise population center—a spot in the nearby Mark Twain National Forest.

A knighthood for Schwarzkopf. There was plenty of room on General H. Norman Schwarzkopf's broad chest for another medal, and on May 20 he got a dandy. At a private ceremony at MacDill Air Force Base in Tampa, Fla., Great Britain's Queen Elizabeth II bestowed an honorary knighthood on Schwarzkopf and presented him with a crimson-ribboned medallion. The four-star general, commander of allied forces in the Persian Gulf War (1991), was the 58th American since World War II (1939-1945) to become an honorary knight of the realm.

Sphere trek. As excited as if they were embarking on the starship *Enterprise,* eight volunteers entered an artificial world in the Arizona desert on Sept. 26, 1991, for a much-publicized experiment in ecological harmony. Clad in futuristic dark-blue uniforms, the four men and four women passed through the airlock of Biosphere II, a glass and steel habitat that covers 3.15 acres (1.27 hectares), and closed it behind them. Sealed off from the outside world, the "Biospherians" will live for two years with 3,800 species of plants and animals, eating only food they grow themselves. The point of the endeavor is to recreate the conditions of "Biosphere I"—planet Earth—on a small scale, thereby gaining knowledge that might be used in future space colonies or applied to solving Earth's environmental problems. Although many scientists have criticized the project as being more showmanship than research, Biosphere II's creators contended that the experiment will produce findings of scientific value.

The project suffered its first mishap a few days into the experiment. On October 11, Biospherian Jane Poynter, 29, of Surrey, England, had to be taken to Tucson for surgery on her hand after she cut off the tip of a finger while using a rice-threshing machine. Poynter, manager of Biosphere's agricultural systems, was back with the group by the end of the day.

Lost Squadron stays lost. While hunting for sunken Spanish galleons off the eastern coast of Florida in May, the operators of the submersible exploration vessel *Deep See* came upon something else entirely. There, sitting on the seabed in 750 feet (230 meters) of water, were five U.S. Navy Avenger torpedo bombers from the 1940's. The planes looked like they might be the famous "Lost Squadron," a group of five Avengers from the naval air station at Fort Lauderdale, Fla., whose pilots became disoriented, ran out of fuel, and ditched into the sea on Dec. 5, 1945, while making a routine training flight over the Atlantic Ocean. Neither the planes nor their 14 crew members were ever seen again after that day.

The disappearance of the squadron and of other planes and ships in the same general area fed the legend of the so-called Bermuda Triangle, a region that is bounded by Miami, Bermuda, and Puerto Rico, where unknown dangers supposedly lurk. *Deep See*'s discovery apparently laid the mystery of the Lost Patrol to rest, but in June the Navy said the planes sighted on the bottom were not the same ones that vanished in 1945. The mystery of the Bermuda Triangle lives on.

Take the money and run. Ivana Trump, former wife of developer Donald J. Trump, decided in March 1991 that $14 million plus a 45-room Connecticut mansion plus an apartment in New York City would have to do. When she and Donald decided to divorce in 1990, Ivana Trump contested the prenuptial contract under which she was to receive $10 million and the Connecticut digs if they split up. That may have seemed like small potatoes at the time, with Trump's fortune estimated at $5 billion. But since then, Donald Trump has been skirting bankruptcy. Ivana's lawyers said that in light of the changed circumstances, she had decided to accept the $14-million offer.

A most unusual pregnancy. On October 12, Arlette Schweitzer, 42, of Aberdeen, S.D., gave birth to twins. The remarkable part of this story is that the babies—a boy and a girl, born five weeks prematurely—are her grandchildren. Schweitzer's daughter, Christa Uchytil of Sioux City, Iowa, was born without a uterus. To enable Christa and her husband, Kevin, to become parents, Schweitzer "lent" them her womb. Doctors at the University of Minnesota in Minneapolis implanted eggs from the daughter's ovaries, fertilized in the laboratory with her husband's sperm, into Schweitzer's womb. "You do what you can for your children because you love them," Schweitzer said. She was the first surrogate mother in the United States to give birth to her own grandchildren.

Contested card. In April 1990, 13-year-old Bryan Wrzesinski of Addison, Ill., bought a 1968 Nolan Ryan baseball card at a nearby Chicago-area sports memorabilia store for $12. When the store's owner, Joe Irmen, learned of the purchase, he was not pleased. The rare rookie-year card, sold by an inexperienced clerk, had been priced at $1,200. Irmen sued, demanding that Wrzesinski either return the card or pay the $1,188 balance, but the boy held his ground. Finally, in April 1991, the two agreed to auction the card and donate the proceeds to charity. In June, the card sold for $5,000.

Honus and Mantle fetch big bucks. The auction price of the Nolan Ryan card paled in comparison with the amounts bidders paid for other rare baseball cards in 1991. At a New York City auction in March, a 1952 Mickey Mantle card that had been valued at $12,000 to $15,000 went for $49,500. But the center of attention at that sale was a circa-1910 card featuring Pittsburgh Pirates star Honus Wagner. Another star, hockey player Wayne Gretzky, paid a record $451,000 for the mint-condition card.

A birthday party for democracy. As Communism sinks into the ashheap of history, what could be more appropriate than a celebration of democracy, one of history's oldest political systems? In September 1991, Greece marked the 2,500th anniversary of an uprising in Athens that led to the founding, in 508 B.C., of the world's first democratic state. The weekend celebration also honored Cleisthenes, the Athenian statesman who led the rebellion and then took the lead in establishing a form of government that centuries later would be adopted around the world.

NOW celebrates a quarter century. The National Organization for Women observed its 25th anniversary in 1991. At NOW's annual convention in New York City in July, Executive Vice President Patricia Ireland, a Miami lawyer, stood in for President Molly Yard, who was recovering from a stroke. Looking ahead to December, when she would succeed Yard as head of the 250,000-member organization, Ireland pledged to carry on the struggle for abortion rights and to focus public attention on domestic violence against women.

Row, row your boat—across the Pacific. "If I had known it would be like this, I never would have tried," said a soaked and battered Gerard d'Aboville, 46, upon becoming the first person to row solo across the North Pacific Ocean. The French mariner arrived in

Flanked by two cosmonauts, British chemist Helen Sharman, winner of a seat on a Soviet space flight, prepares in May to embark for the *Mir* space station.

Gerard d'Aboville of France stands in his custom-built boat in Ilwaco, Wash., on November 21 after rowing solo across the Pacific Ocean from Japan.

Ilwaco, Wash., on November 21 after a 134-day journey from Japan in a custom-built 26-foot (8-meter) rowboat. During the harrowing 6,300-mile (10,140-kilometer) crossing, d'Aboville encountered gale-force winds and waves as high as a four-story building. His boat overturned nearly 40 times, including a near-fatal capsizing on the night before he reached the coast of Washington state.

In 1982-1983, British adventurer Peter Bird rowed solo from San Francisco to Australia. But d'Aboville's voyage was considered a more difficult achievement because of treacherous weather and currents along the route he followed.

Liz does it again. Actress Elizabeth Taylor got married on Oct. 6, 1991—for the eighth time. The groom, who became husband number seven (Taylor was married twice to actor Richard Burton) was Larry Fortensky, 39, a California construction worker. The two had met in the late 1980's at the Betty Ford Center for drug and alcohol rehabilitation in Rancho Mirage, Calif., where Fortensky was receiving treatment after a drunk-driving conviction.

The wedding took place at Neverland Valley, a 1,700-acre (690-hectare) estate at Los Olivos, Calif., owned by rock star Michael Jackson. The $1-million extravaganza featured acres of flowers, miles of white ribbons, and violinists flown in from Venice. Some 200 guests attended, including former President Gerald R. Ford; his wife, Betty Ford; and a crowd of Hollywood celebrities. Liz, in a $30,000 yellow gown, was reported to be teary-eyed but radiant as she exchanged vows with Fortensky. Jackson, wearing a tuxedo and a silver sock, gave the bride away.

The luckiest person you've ever seen. That's how Jill Shields of Euclid, Ohio, describes herself, and few would disagree. Shields, a 31-year-old investment banker and amateur skydiver, survived a fall of 10,500 feet (3,200 meters) from an airplane on May 19, when both of her parachutes became tangled and failed to open. Her two skydiving companions fully expected to find her dead. But, to their astonishment Shields, who had plowed into a mucky patch of swamp, was not only alive but conscious. The woman was rushed by helicopter to a Cleveland hospital, where doctors ascertained that her injuries, though painful, were relatively minor—a fractured pelvis and three broken vertebrae. She required no surgery and was on her way home after 12 days. Shields said that despite her brush with death, she would probably continue skydiving.

Mammoth profits. The disintegrating Soviet Union has been having a host of economic woes lately, but in 1991, the Russian republic was sitting on buried treasure of immense value. Scattered throughout the permafrost in Russia's northern climes are the frozen remains of an estimated 10 million mammoths, Ice Age ancestors of today's elephants. Mammoth tusks used to sell for about $3 a pound (0.45 kilogram), but when a worldwide ban on elephant ivory took effect in January 1990, the price of mammoth ivory—on which there are no trade restrictions—began to climb. In 1991, mammoth ivory was going for $300 to $1,000 a pound, depending on the quality. At that price, the mammoth tusks waiting to be dug up would have a value of about $1 trillion.

Temporary reprieve for the Crayola Eight. In August 1990, Binney & Smith of Easton, Pa., makers of Crayola crayons, retired eight colors, including gray-blue and orange-red, that had fallen out of favor with kids. In the following months, the company received several thousand calls and letters protesting the decision. In October 1991, Binney & Smith announced that the crayons would make a short-term comeback as part of a commemorative box of 10 old favorites. The 10-pack was offered as a premium with the standard 64-crayon set and could not be purchased separately.

Wisconsin capital smothered with cheese! It was "like a giant lava flow," to quote a spokesperson for the Madison, Wis., fire department, which for several days in early May was up to its boottops in melted cheese and butter. The greasy mass oozed onto city streets as fire fighters combated a blaze in a complex of food warehouses. The fire destroyed thousands of tons of dairy products and other surplus food that had been stockpiled by the federal government.

Mickey and Kermit patch things up. Before he died unexpectedly of pneumonia in 1990, puppeteer Jim Henson agreed to sell the Walt Disney Company the rights to his Muppet characters for $150 million. But after Henson's death, the deal went sour when Disney and Henson Associates, Incorporated, butted heads over the purchase price and licensing arrangements. The Henson company filed a lawsuit against Disney in April 1991, and the folks at the Magic Kingdom quickly responded with a countersuit. With bitter accusations flying, both sides were in danger of losing their warm, cuddly image. But all ended well. Before the month was out, the two companies reached a settlement for an undisclosed amount of money.

Unknown front-runner. The nationally syndicated *Miami Herald* humor columnist Dave Barry, mounting a tongue-in-cheek campaign for the 1992 Democratic presidential nomination, received a spot of bad news in May 1991. Although Barry had proclaimed himself the front-runner in the race, 4 out of 5 Florida voters polled had no idea who he was, and only 2 per cent identified him as a humorist. Undaunted, Barry said he would press on to victory.

The sack for Sacks. Oliver Sacks, the British-born neurologist whose book *Awakenings* was made into a motion picture in 1990, was laid off from New York City's Bronx Psychiatric Hospital in February 1991. A member of the hospital's staff since 1967, Sacks was among 1,280 people on the New York state mental health payroll to lose their jobs in budget cuts in 1991. *Awakenings* is Sacks's account of his work with patients suffering from a brain disorder that had put them into a sleeplike state. David L. Dreier

Newspaper companies in the United States struggled through their toughest year in four decades during 1991. Advertising revenue and circulation, in a slump since 1989, fell even further in 1991. Several large and historic newspapers did not survive.

In Little Rock, the 172-year-old *Arkansas Gazette,* an early advocate for civil rights in the South, was bought by its competitor, the *Arkansas Democrat,* in October and promptly shut down. Despite ownership by the Gannett Company, Incorporated, the largest U.S. newspaper chain, the *Gazette* could not survive both the economic downturn and a costly newspaper war with the family-owned *Democrat.* On December 9, the *Dallas Times Herald* stopped publishing, leaving only 15 U.S. cities with two competing papers under separate ownership.

P.M. blues. The poor U.S. economy and changing American life styles spelled the end for a number of afternoon newspapers. Almost two-thirds of the nation's approximately 1,600 daily newspapers appear in the evening. In cities with morning and afternoon papers, the evening paper almost always suffers first. Because increasing numbers of Americans work at 9-to-5 office jobs—rather than at factory jobs, from 7 a.m. to 3:30 p.m.—they have more time in the morning to read a newspaper and less time in the evening.

The afternoon *Shreveport* (La.) *Journal* shut down after 96 years on March 31. The owners of the *San Diego Tribune* announced in September 1991 that they would stop publishing the afternoon paper in early 1992 and would combine it with the morning *San Diego Union.* And the owners of the afternoon *Richmond* (Va.) *News Leader* said that paper would be folded into the morning *Richmond Times-Dispatch* in June 1992. The 149-year-old *State-Times* in Baton Rouge, La., shut down on Oct. 2, 1991, after its circulation had fallen to barely half its mid-1970's level. In Charleston, S.C., *The Evening Post* closed its doors on Sept. 30, 1991. *The Journal Star* in Peoria, Ill., planned to stop publishing an afternoon edition in 1992.

Other newspaper closings in 1991 included *The National,* the first all-sports daily newspaper in the United States. Launched on Jan. 30, 1990, *The National* closed on June 12, 1991, after losing more than $100 million. Its owners blamed the closing on the difficulty of distributing a nationwide newspaper that must include late-breaking sports scores.

Maxwell dies. British publisher Robert Maxwell died suddenly in November, leaving behind enormous debts that forced the *New York Daily News* to declare bankruptcy in December. Maxwell had bought the *Daily News* on March 13, after a crippling 139-day strike by nine unions. By the time of the sale, the *Daily News* was losing $700,000 a day, and circulation had fallen by half. The paper's owner actually paid Maxwell $60 million to buy the paper and its $100 million in debts. The unions had also agreed to substantial cutbacks to keep the paper going. Mark Fitzgerald

In ***World Book,*** see **Newspaper.**

Nicaraguan President Violeta Barrios de Chamorro acknowledges cheers from a joint session of the United States Congress in April.

Nicaragua. Old rivalries surfaced in Nicaragua during 1991, evidence that the wounds of civil war were far from healed. On April 25, the first anniversary of President Violeta Barrios de Chamorro's assumption of office, expectations were gloomy that democracy would succeed where the former Sandinista regime had failed. The gross national product (the value of all goods and services produced) had plunged 5.7 per cent below its dismal performance during the final year of Sandinista rule. An inflation rate of 13,000 per cent had cut deep into people's pocketbooks, and unemployment stood at more than 40 per cent.

To seek relief, Chamorro visited United States President George Bush on April 17. He assured her that he would help rally international support for Nicaragua's democratic government and speed the delivery of $541 million in promised U.S. assistance, of which only $207 million had reached Nicaragua. On July 8, Germany announced that it would provide Nicaragua with about $140 million in aid in 1991. In early September, 17 nations, including the United States and Japan, helped Nicaragua pay off $320 million in loans from the World Bank and the Inter-American Bank. On September 19, the International Monetary Fund, an agency of the United Nations, announced it would issue a standby loan of $56 million to Nicaragua.

Contras rearming. The settling of Nicaragua's international obligations took place amid ominous domestic developments, including the reappearance of armed *contra* (rebel) resistance. The U.S.-backed contras had waged a guerrilla war to topple the Sandinista regime, but they laid down their arms when Chamarro took office in April 1990. Contra dissatisfaction stemmed from the fact that Chamorro maintained Umberto Ortega—brother of the former Sandinista president—as chief of the army. Also, former contras claimed that the government backed out of pledges to supply land and tools to about 5,000 contra veterans. By August 1991, there were reports of increasing clashes near the Honduran border between contras and government troops.

The Sandinistas were angered by legislative proposals to repeal two laws passed hurriedly in their final months in power. The laws gave Sandinista followers large amounts of property. Armed Sandinistas occupied Managua's city hall and a radio station on June 18 to protest the possible loss of the property giveaways. Former Sandinista President Daniel Ortega Saavedra supported the giveways and said on June 19 that their loss could mean a return to civil war.

On November 9, Sandinistas went on a rampage in Managua, the Nicaraguan capital, destroying the Managua city hall, two radio stations, and dozens of cars and trucks. The Sandinistas were angry at the destruction of a Sandinista monument.

Nathan A. Haverstock

See also **Latin America** (Facts in brief table). In ***World Book,*** see **Nicaragua.**

Niger. See **Africa.**

Nigeria. The military regime of President Ibrahim Babangida proceeded with plans in 1991 to return Nigeria to civilian rule in October 1992. To stimulate local civilian political activity, Babangida in August and September 1991 raised the number of district councils from about 450 to 589. And in a move aimed at easing potentially explosive tensions in the federal states, the government in August increased the number of states from 21 to 30, thereby breaking up several large ethnic groups.

National legislative and presidential elections were scheduled for 1992. Only two political parties were authorized: the Social Democratic Party (SDP), which is mostly Christian, and the National Republican Convention (NRC), dominated by Muslims. Over much protest, the government rejected the secret ballot in favor of "open voting," in which voters line up in front of photos of the candidates they favor.

Religious conflict. Ethnic rivalry continued during 1991, but more than ever it was rooted in religious differences. Major riots, including ones in the states of Bauchi in April and Kano in October, broke out when Shiite Muslims attacked Christian minorities in the north and burned churches, houses, and vehicles. Hundreds of people died in the violence.

Nigeria's Muslim extremists want all life to be governed by the Koran, the holy book of Islam. They were encouraged in 1986 when Babangida, who is a Muslim, secretly aligned Nigeria with the 46-member Organization of the Islamic Conference (OIC), an international body that promotes unity among Islamic countries. To reduce religious tensions, Babangida in August 1991 suspended Nigeria's membership in the OIC.

Education. In early 1991, Education Minister Aliu Babatunde Fafunwa launched a program encouraging the use of several indigenous languages in elementary schools. Although the plan was supposed to emphasize Nigeria's cultural diversity and to facilitate literacy at all levels, it came in for severe criticism. Some critics, pointing out that Nigeria has some 250 native languages, said it would be divisive to promote just a few of them. Others said the move would hinder Nigerians' use of English—the nation's official language.

Health. A major cholera epidemic in Nigeria had killed more than 2,000 people by late 1991. More than 20,000 others had been ill with the disease.

The government has long refused to acknowledge the problem of AIDS in Nigeria, and fewer than 100 cases of the disease had been officially reported by 1991. Health experts said, however, that thousands of Nigerians have AIDS. In October, the government launched a major AIDS educational program.

On November 27, Nigeria sealed its borders and ordered people to stay home as the government undertook the first nationwide census since 1973.

J. Gus Liebenow and Beverly B. Liebenow

See also **Africa** (Facts in brief table). In ***World Book,*** see **Nigeria.**

Nobel Prizes in peace, literature, economics, and the sciences were awarded in 1991 by the Norwegian Storting (parliament) in Oslo and by the Royal Swedish Academy of Sciences, the Karolinska Institute, and the Swedish Academy of Literature in Stockholm, Sweden. The value of each prize in 1991 was about $1 million in United States currency.

The peace prize was awarded to Aung San Suu Kyi (pronounced Soo Chee) of Burma (also known as Myanmar). Since 1988, Suu Kyi has been the leader of the National League of Democracy, the main opposition party to Burma's military dictatorship. In July of 1989, she was placed under house arrest in Rangoon, the capital of Burma, as a result of her criticisms of the dictatorship. By year-end, it was possible that Suu Kyi had still not been told that she had won the peace prize.

Suu Kyi was born in Rangoon on June 19, 1945. She spent most of the years between the mid-1960's and 1988 living in England. In April 1988, she returned to Rangoon and joined the opposition movement. Since she was placed under house arrest, the government has said she can leave the country whenever she wishes. Suu Kyi has refused to leave, however, until the government frees all political prisoners, grants political power to civilians, and allows her to speak on television and radio to the nation.

The literature prize went to Nadine Gordimer, a South African novelist whose writings are concerned

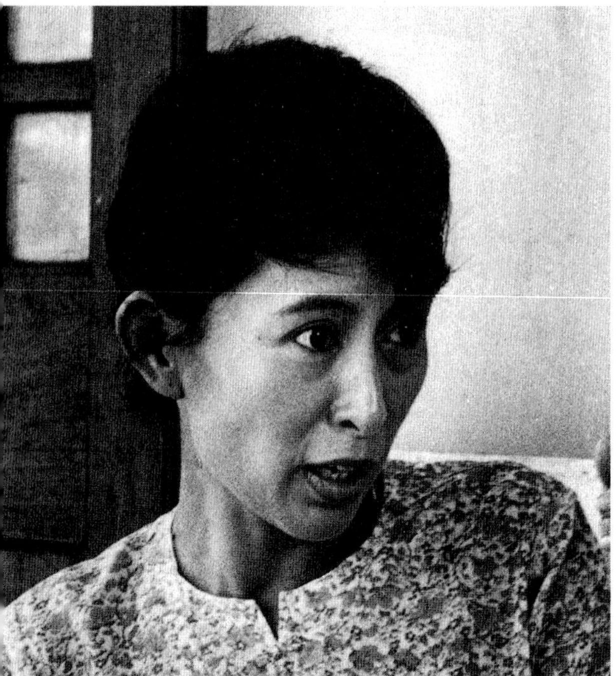

Aung San Suu Kyi, the nonviolent leader of the democratic opposition movement in Burma, received the Nobel Peace Prize in October.

with the political and personal consequences of *apartheid*, the system of racial segregation that was enforced by law in South Africa until 1991, when apartheid laws were repealed. Gordimer has been a critic of racial injustice in South Africa for decades.

Gordimer's best-known novels include *Burger's Daughter* (1979) and *July's People* (1981). Her works mix political themes with modern, often difficult, literary techniques. The Nobel Committee praised "her continual involvement on behalf of literature and free speech in a police state where censorship and persecution of books and people exist."

The economics prize was given to Ronald H. Coase, a British-born professor emeritus at the University of Chicago Law School. Coase's work has focused on the costs of business transactions and on the structures of modern business firms. Economists and legal scholars have described Coase as one of the most influential shapers of modern economic theory.

Coase's articles are famous for their clarity and wide-ranging implications. In one, "The Theory of the Firm," Coase described companies as networks of stable contractual relationships between persons who possess different skills. In another influential article, "The Problem of Social Cost," Coase suggested that contending parties—whether firms or individuals—are likely to resolve their conflicts most efficiently by bargaining with each other. Government regulations, Coase suggested, often lead to more costly solutions.

The physics prize went to Pierre-Gilles de Gennes of France for his research on liquid crystals, polymers, magnetic systems, and superconductors. Much of de Gennes's work has focused on the way molecules in these complex substances move between states of *order* (where the molecules are arranged in a regular pattern) and *disorder* (where there is no pattern). De Gennes has developed mathematical formulas to describe these transitions—called *phase transitions*.

De Gennes has said that all his research is prompted by the search for solutions to practical problems. His work on liquid crystals, for example, has led to innovations in the construction of display systems for laptop computers and digital watches.

The chemistry prize was awarded to Switzerland's Richard R. Ernst for his work on a method for analyzing the structure of chemical compounds. That method, known as *nuclear magnetic resonance spectroscopy*, was first developed during the 1940's.

The Nobel Committee noted that Ernst's research during the 1960's and 1970's contributed greatly to heightening the precision of nuclear magnetic resonance spectroscopy. The improvements devised by Ernst in the late 1970's, for example, have made it possible for scientists to study molecules that consist of thousands of atoms. Nuclear magnetic resonance provides scientists with an invaluable tool for chemical research and the development of new drugs.

The physiology or medicine prize was shared

Ronald H. Coase, winner of the 1991 Nobel Prize for economics, has influenced a generation of economists, legal theorists, and business leaders.

Pierre-Gilles de Gennes was awarded the 1991 Nobel Prize in physics for his research on the molecular behavior of various chemical systems.

by two German scientists, Erwin Neher and Bert Sakmann. Their research made possible a greater understanding of the way in which *ions* (positively or negatively charged atoms) flow in and out of cells. Using a technique that they developed called the *patch clamp*, Neher and Sakmann were able to discover *ion channels*, protein molecules in cell membranes that control the passage of ions. The patch clamp technique also makes it possible to measure the way in which ion channels change shape while regulating the flow of ions in and out of the cell.

In its statement honoring the two scientists, the Nobel Committee said their work on ion channels had "revolutionized modern biology." Their research is expected to help scientists better understand diseases related to ion channel defects, such as cystic fibrosis.

1990 winners of Nobel Prizes were Mikhail S. Gorbachev, president of the Soviet Union, for peace; Mexican poet and essayist Octavio Paz for literature; Americans Harry M. Markowitz, Merton H. Miller, and William Sharpe, for economics; Canadian-born Richard E. Taylor and Americans Jerome I. Friedman and Henry W. Kendall for physics; Elias James Corey of the United States for chemistry; and U.S. transplant specialists Joseph E. Murray and E. Donnall Thomas for physiology or medicine. Douglas Clayton

In ***World Book***, see **Nobel Prizes**.

North Carolina. See **State government**.

North Dakota. See **State government**.

Northern Ireland. The first phase of negotiations aimed at returning self-government to Northern Ireland began in Belfast on June 17, 1991. But the talks were called off on July 3 by British Secretary of State for Northern Ireland Peter Brooke in order to prevent a political crisis.

In the first phase, four major political parties were supposed to agree on a form of regional government for Northern Ireland, which has been run largely from London since 1972. The second phase of talks would be between the Republic of Ireland and Northern Ireland. A third phase between the British and Irish governments has been ongoing.

Leaders of the Ulster Unionists and the Democratic Unionists, representing most of the Protestants of Northern Ireland—who want to remain in the United Kingdom—reportedly agreed to participate in the talks in order to end the 1985 Anglo-Irish Agreement. That agreement gave the Republic of Ireland a say in Northern Ireland affairs. But Unionist leaders threatened to walk out of the talks on July 8, 1991, unless a July 16 meeting between Great Britain and the Republic of Ireland—part of the third phase of talks—was postponed. Brooke headed off the walkout by announcing to the British House of Commons, the lower house of Parliament, that the talks were over, but that they could resume "in due course."

IRA terrorism. On February 7, three mortar shells were fired from a parked van on 10 Downing Street in London, the British prime minister's official residence. Two shells overshot the target, but one shell exploded in the garden, cracking the bulletproof window of the cabinet room, where Prime Minister John Major and 14 senior government members were meeting. No one was seriously hurt. The IRA claimed responsibility.

On February 18, the IRA set off bombs at two London railroad stations. One, at Victoria Station, exploded at the height of the morning rush hour, killing one man and injuring 40 others. Another bomb was set off at Paddington railroad station, damaging the building without causing injury. Analysts speculated that these attacks on civilians could indicate a power shift within the IRA. In December, an IRA bombing disrupted commuter service in London.

The "Birmingham Six," men who had been imprisoned for life after being convicted of planting bombs that killed 21 people in Birmingham, England, in 1974, were freed on March 14, 1991. Testimony given at a Court of Appeal hearing stated that police notebook entries on alleged confessions had been altered. This case was the third in British courts since 1989 in which people convicted of terrorist attacks claimed by the IRA were set free because of charges of misconduct by police and prosecutors. Home Secretary Kenneth Baker announced on March 14 that a royal commission would conduct a two-year study of the British criminal justice system. Ian J. Mather

See also **Ireland.** In ***World Book,*** see **Northern Ireland.**

Northwest Territories. Canada drew up a tentative agreement on Dec. 16, 1991, to give the *Inuit* (Eskimo) people political control over a 770,000-square-mile (2-million-square-kilometer) area in the Northwest Territories, as well as exclusive ownership of 135,000 square miles (350,000 square kilometers). The plan would give the Inuit authority over half of the land in the current territory—or one-fifth of Canada's total land area. The pact heralds the first change in Canada's borders since 1949. The Inuit plan to name their new region *Nunavut,* meaning "our land."

Another land-claim settlement with native peoples in the Northwest Territories was reached on July 13. The Canadian government granted the Gwich'in Indians of the extreme northern area of the Mackenzie Delta title to some 8,600 square miles (22,275 square kilometers) of land straddling the Northwest and Yukon territories. Although the Gwich'in now live in the Northwest Territories, they still use the Yukon—their original homeland—for hunting, trapping, and fishing. The settlement also provides a cash award of $75 million ($66 million U.S.) over 15 years, representing about $40,000 ($35,000 U.S.) for each member of the tribe. The deal grants more economic advantages to the Gwich'in than the benefits that were set forth in a proposed 1990 agreement. David M. L. Farr

See also, **Canada,** Special Report: **Canada and Quebec at a Crossroads.** In ***World Book,*** see **Northwest Territories.**

Norway in 1991 debated whether to apply for membership in the 12-nation European Community (EC or Common Market). Prime Minister Gro Harlem Brundtland of the Labor Party tried to rally nationwide support for a decision to join, but opinion polls showed that the country remained divided. A previous move to join the EC had been narrowly rejected in a nationwide referendum in 1972.

The EC debate. Pressure on Norway to join the EC mounted after Sweden applied for EC membership in 1991 and Finland was expected to do so soon. Nearby Denmark joined the EC in 1973. In October 1991, the seven-member European Free Trade Association, to which Norway does belong, negotiated with the EC an enlarged free-trade zone, known as the European Economic Area. Many Norwegians hoped that their nation would thereby reap most of the benefits of EC membership without actually joining.

In a move to establish closer EC ties in late 1990, Norway had linked its currency, the krone, to the European Currency Unit, a specially created unit of value that links the currency of EC nations. By doing so, Norway committed itself to following the interest rates and other monetary policies of the leading EC nations, such as Germany and France.

Pro-EC Norwegians, including Brundtland, argued that Norway could not remain aloof from the club that links the prosperous European nations. They added that independence for the nearby Baltic states

King Harald V appears before the *Storting* (parliament) with his wife, Queen Sonja, and formally assumes the throne of Norway on January 21.

of Estonia, Latvia, and Lithuania made it even more urgent that Norway join EC members in shaping economic policies, including decisions on how best to help these newly independent countries make the transition to free-market economic systems.

Anti-EC campaigners feared domination within the EC by a powerful Germany. They further argued that some of Norway's revenues from petroleum and natural gas would be diverted to poorer EC nations, such as Portugal and Greece. The anti-EC faction also opposed changing Norwegian laws that prevent foreigners from owning businesses or property in Norway without government permission. Such restrictions are not permitted under EC rules.

New leaders. Norway's Conservative Party elected Kaci Kullmann Five as its new leader in April 1991. She replaced Jan P. Syse, who had headed the previous coalition government, which fell from power in October 1990. Five hoped to topple Brundtland from the prime minister's office in parliamentary elections scheduled for 1993. A former minister of trade and shipping, Five favored EC membership. Norway's small but influential Center Party also chose a woman, Anne Enger Lahnstein, as its new leader.

King Olav V, Norway's monarch since 1957, died on Jan. 17, 1991. His son, who became King Harald V, succeeded him on the throne. Philip Revzin

See also **Europe** (Facts in brief table). In ***World Book,*** see **Norway.**

Nova Scotia. The province gained its 21st premier on Feb. 26, 1991. Donald Cameron, a former dairy farmer and minister of industry, succeeded interim premier Roger S. Bacon. Cameron was elected to the post at a Progressive Conservative Party (PC) convention on February 9. Bacon had been named premier after John Buchanan, Nova Scotia's premier for 12 years, stepped down amid scandal in 1990.

On Feb. 21, 1991, Roland Thornhill, the man Cameron narrowly defeated for the party leadership, was charged with 17 counts of fraud stemming from 1979 banking transactions. Thornhill resigned his Cabinet position but remained in the legislature as an independent. Most of the charges were later dismissed.

The PC's held a one-seat majority in the legislature. It narrowly won a crucial vote of confidence on a $4.7-billion ($4.1 billion U.S.) austerity budget. The budget called for a two-year salary freeze for 44,000 civil servants and teachers and reduced coverage for senior citizens' prescriptions. In spite of drastic spending cuts in social programs, the province's operating deficit was expected to rise 44 per cent, to $191.8 million ($170 million U.S.) for fiscal 1991-1992.

David M. L. Farr

See **Canada,** Special Report: **Canada and Quebec at a Crossroads.** See also, **Cameron, Donald.** In ***World Book,*** see **Nova Scotia.**

Nuclear energy. See **Energy supply.**

Nutrition. See **Food.**

Ocean. In an effort to obstruct allied forces during the Persian Gulf War, Iraq allegedly opened Kuwaiti oil tankers, pipelines, and wells in January 1991 and flooded the Persian Gulf with crude oil. Scientists could not determine the exact amount of oil released by Iraqi troops, but a United States government report in April estimated that 168 million gallons (636 million liters) had flowed into gulf waters, making it the largest oil spill in history. In May, some 126,000 gallons (477,000 liters) per day were still pouring into the gulf from sabotaged oil-storage facilities.

The oil spread about 250 miles (400 kilometers) down the coastline of Kuwait and Saudi Arabia. This area is an important region for migrating birds. The spill destroyed or damaged numerous coral reefs, seagrass beds, and mangrove swamps that house and nourish many varieties of sea life. Cleanup efforts were slowed by limited funding, bureaucratic tangles, and a lack of experienced workers.

Coral reefs. A group of oceanographers, climatologists, ecologists, and other environmental experts sponsored by the U.S. National Science Foundation (NSF) reported in June 1991 that increased water temperatures appear to be associated with a type of coral reef deterioration known as *bleaching.* Bleaching occurs when reefs discharge the algae that reside in and nourish the coral. The coral turns white, stops growing, and becomes weakened.

Coral reefs, which support a unique and fragile underwater ecosystem, have been bleaching for at least 75 years. But, since the early 1980's, bleachings have been more intense and widespread. Although reefs normally rebound within a year, scientists are concerned that the repeated bleachings may destroy the reefs beyond rejuvenation.

The NSF study was organized in response to a 1990 report suggesting that global warming caused an increase in ocean temperatures, which resulted in the bleachings. Corals can bleach when water temperatures rise just a couple of degrees for a few days. But the NSF could not discount other possible causes of the bleachings, such as increased salt content, pollution, disease, and damage from boats and swimmers.

Global warming. An international group of oceanographers conducted a transocean experiment in January 1991 to test the possibility of using underwater sound to detect global warming. The researchers sent a loud hum from underwater devices in waters off the coast of Heard Island in the southern Indian Ocean to 21 listening posts scattered throughout the world. By measuring the time it takes for the sounds to reach these posts—and combining that information with knowledge about how the speed of sound increases as water warms—the researchers hope to determine over time whether the oceans are warming. Because deep ocean temperatures fluctuate very little under normal conditions, the scientists believe that if such changes are regularly found, they could indicate a general warming of the planet.

Ohio

Hazardous waste. A U.S. government study began in 1991 to determine the possible risks to marine life from nuclear and other hazardous waste dumped into the Pacific Ocean from 1946 to 1970. Researchers from the National Oceanic and Atmospheric Administration (NOAA) estimated that some 47,000 barrels of waste were dumped in the Gulf of the Farallones, about 27 miles (43 kilometers) west of San Francisco. The barrels contain mercury and plutonium.

The gulf is home to the Farallones National Marine Sanctuary, a sea and island habitat abundant with birds, whales, porpoises, seals, and sea lions. The waters also support one of the largest fishing industries on the West Coast.

Scientists do not know exactly how much radioactive material is submerged or whether it presents an immediate threat to the area. But images made with sound waves have recently shown that the barrels have decayed somewhat. The NOAA study will try to determine the extent of the corrosion, whether radioactive material is leaking from the barrels, and how to safely remove or contain the waste. A marine geologist from the U.S. Geological Survey is studying the stability of the area's sea floor, which is about 50 miles from the San Andreas fault. Arthur G. Alexiou

In ***World Book,*** see **Ocean.**

Ohio. See **State government.**
Oklahoma. See **State government.**
Old age. See **Social security.**

Olympic Games. On Sept. 18, 1991, Robert H. Helmick, president of the United States Olympic Committee (USOC), resigned in the wake of news reports that he accepted more than $275,000 in 1990 and 1991 for consulting work from clients with business interests in the Olympics. The USOC elected William J. Hybl, a corporate executive from Colorado Springs, Colo., to replace Helmick and finish his term.

Helmick denied any conflict of interest in the affair, and the USOC executive committee cleared him of wrongdoing. An independent report issued in November was highly critical of Helmick's behavior as USOC president, however. In the wake of that report, Helmick resigned in December from the International Olympic Committee (IOC), of which he had also been a member.

In October 1991, the USOC said it would test a program to raise money through 15 state lotteries during 1992. USOC officials said lotteries could raise as much as $26 million by 1996. The USOC has raised most of its money from corporate donations and the sale of television rights to broadcast the Olympics.

On June 15, 1991, the IOC awarded the 1998 Winter Olympics to Nagano, Japan. Nagano won over Salt Lake City, Utah, on the final ballot. The other candidates were Ostersund, Sweden; Aosta, Italy; and Jaca, Spain. Frank Litsky

In ***World Book,*** see **Olympic Games.**

Oman. See **Middle East.**

About 2,000 representatives of business and industry on June 27 protest the economic policies of Ontario's Socialist Premier Robert K. Rae.

Ontario. The recession that began in Canada in April 1990 hit Ontario hard as nearly 226,000 people in the province lost their jobs. This number represented three-fourths of all jobs lost in Canada during this time period. Ontario's unemployment rate climbed from 5.3 per cent at the beginning of the recession to 10.2 per cent in June 1991.

Ontario's governing New Democratic Party, under the leadership of Socialist Premier Robert K. Rae, embarked on expenditures designed to stimulate economic activity. The government unveiled a $52.76-billion ($46.65-billion U.S.) budget on April 29, 1991, that included a deficit of $9.7 billion ($8.6 billion U.S.). The shortfall was three times larger than any provincial budget deficit in Canada's history. Overall spending was predicted to increase 13.4 per cent, while revenues were to decrease 1 per cent to $43 billion ($38-billion U.S.), the first decline in more than 40 years.

Provincial Treasurer Floyd Laughren announced tax increases of $670 million ($592 million U.S.), most of which targeted cigarettes, gasoline, alcohol, and individuals with incomes greater than $84,000 ($74,000 U.S.). He announced tax cuts for people on low incomes and extra funds for welfare programs, affordable housing, and businesses hurt by the recession.

New policies. The legislative session ended on June 27, with the government having introduced 88 bills. A bill passed on November 25 restricted Sunday shopping. The bill was sent to a legislative committee for further study. A rent-control measure stipulated that rents be tied to the inflation rate, and it allowed an additional increase of 2 per cent each year to pay for capital improvements.

The government abandoned Rae's 1990 campaign promise to bring in a system of government-administered automobile insurance. Economists estimated that such a move would require $1.4 billion ($1.2 billion U.S.) in starting costs, and that 5,600 jobs in the private sector would be lost.

On Aug. 6, 1991, Rae signed a historic agreement at a meeting in Thunder Bay with 12 First Nations chiefs who represented Ontario's 170,000 to 200,000 native peoples. The agreement, the first of its type in Canada, recognized native peoples' right to self-government. It ended the paternalistic relationship between the government and Indians and promised more direct negotiations. Although the agreement will bring no immediate material benefits to Ontario's native peoples, native leaders hailed it as a major political advance. David M. L. Farr

See **Canada,** Special Report: **Canada and Quebec at a Crossroads.** In ***World Book,*** see **Ontario.**

Opera. See **Classical music.**

Oregon. See **State government.**

Pacific Islands. Among the most significant events in the Pacific Islands during 1991 were the failure of the Papua New Guinea government to end a rebellion on Bougainville and the delay of elections in Fiji. There were also political tensions in Vanuatu.

Papua New Guinea's government was unable in 1991 to end a rebellion on the island of Bougainville that began in 1988, when armed militants and traditional landowners demanded that a copper mine at Panguna on Bougainville be closed and that $12 billion be paid to Bougainville residents for environmental damage caused by mining operations. In May 1990, the rebels had declared Bougainville independent.

On Jan. 24, 1991, the government and the rebels signed the "Honiara Declaration," agreeing to refrain from the use of weapons and to invite a multinational peacekeeping force to the island. But the rebels soon repudiated parts of the declaration, and the government did not expedite its efforts to arrange for a multinational force to go to Bougainville. Although the government lifted its blockade of goods and services to the island, only small quantities of supplies reached the 160,000 inhabitants during the year. Many people died because of inadequate medical services. Each side blamed the other for the situation and for a breakdown in peace talks. Meanwhile, some fighting continued on the island.

Papua New Guinea Governor General Sir Serei Eri resigned on October 1. He had been governor general

Facts in brief on Pacific Island countries

Country	Population	Government	Monetary unit*	Foreign trade (million U.S.$) Exports†	Imports†
Australia	17,116,000	Governor General Bill Hayden; Prime Minister Robert Hawke	dollar (1.27 = $1)	39,628	38,800
Fiji	767,000	President Ratu Sir Penaia Ganilau; Prime Minister Ratu Sir Kamisese Mara	dollar (1.47 = $1)	234	735
Kiribati	72,000	President Teatao Teannaki	Australian dollar	5	22
Nauru	9,000	President Bernard Dowiyogo	Australian dollar	93	73
New Zealand	3,430,000	Governor General Dame Catherine Tizard; Prime Minister James B. Bolger	dollar (1.78 = $1)	9,435	9,489
Papua New Guinea	4,217,000	Governor General Sir Wiwa Korowi; Prime Minister Rabbie Namaliu	kina (0.95 = $1)	1,281	1,335
Solomon Islands	351,000	Governor General Sir George Lepping; Prime Minister Solomon Mamaloni	dollar (2.75 = $1)	75	114
Tonga	99,000	King Taufa'ahau Tupou IV; Prime Minister Baron Vaea	pa'anga (1.27 = $1)	9	57
Tuvalu	9,000	Governor General Tupua Leupena; Prime Minister Bikenibeu Paeniu	Australian dollar	1	3
Vanuatu	156,000	President Fred Timakata; Prime Minister Maxime Carlot	vatu (109.60 = $1)	20	71
Western Samoa	173,000	Head of State Malietoa Tanumafili II; Prime Minister Tofilau Eti Alesana	tala (2.41 = $1)	12	67

*Exchange rates as of Nov. 29, 1991, or latest available data. †Latest available data.

since January 1990. That same day, Deputy Prime Minister Edward Ramu Diro resigned from Parliament. Diro was leader of the People's Action Party, second largest partner in the nation's coalition government. Both resignations arose from a ruling by a Leadership Tribunal on Sept. 27, 1991, that Diro was guilty of 81 out of 96 charges of misconduct and corruption.

The tribunal recommended that Governor General Sir Serei dismiss Diro from his government posts and his parliamentary seat and bar him from office for three years. Under Papua New Guinea's Constitution, only the governor general is empowered to remove a member of Parliament from his seat, and the governor general must accept the tribunal's advice. However, Sir Serei, a former president of the People's Action Party and a friend of Diro's, refused to accept the tribunal's decision and was forced to resign. In November, Parliament appointed the Minister for Minerals and Energy, Sir Wiwa Korowi, governor general.

On July 18, Parliament passed a law to take effect in mid-1992 that will give greater stability to a newly elected national government. The new law forbids a motion of no-confidence against a government for the first 18 months of its term, instead of 6 months.

Fiji. The interim government of Fiji, in authority since two military coups ousted the government and revoked the Constitution in 1987, announced in May 1991 that it was delaying general elections until mid-1992 so that new political boundaries could be drawn. Under a new Constitution, effective since July 1990, Parliament has a 70-seat House of Representatives and a 34-member Senate of Chiefs. In the House of Representatives, 37 seats are reserved for native Fijians, 27 for Fiji-Indians, 5 for other ethnic groups, and 1 for the outlying island of Rotuma. In the general elections, voters will choose candidates from separate ballots, according to ethnic groups. The president will appoint members to the Senate of Chiefs. The position of prime minister is reserved for native Fijians.

The new Constitution was drawn up with the support of the military to assure that native Fijians would control the government. Almost half of Fiji's population of 767,000 are Fiji-Indians, descendants of people brought to Fiji from India as laborers. Since the coups in 1987, the Fiji-Indian population has been steadily declining as families leave the country.

Major General Sitiveni Rabuka, former commander of the Fiji military forces and leader of the coups, resigned from the army in August 1991 and accepted appointment as joint deputy prime minister and minister for home affairs in the interim government. He said he would run for Parliament as leader of the newly formed Fijian Political Party. Prime Minister Ratu Sir Kamisese Mara said that he would not contest the election and would retire in May 1992.

Vanuatu's government was preoccupied during 1991 with Prime Minister Walter Lini's struggle to cling to power. Lini, leader of the Vanuaaku Party, has held office since Vanuatu's independence from Great Britain and France in 1980. But he has been under pressure to step down because of ill health. In August 1991, after Lini dismissed many Cabinet members, government workers, and some of his close advisers, the party chose as its new leader Donald Kalpokas, one of the dismissed ministers. But Lini refused to resign. In the December 2 general election, Lini ran as leader of a breakaway group, the National United Party, which won 10 seats, but no party won enough seats to form a government. Lini's party formed a coalition government with the Union of Moderate Parties, and its leader, Maxime Carlot, was elected prime minister.

Western Samoa in April 1991 held its first general election that permitted all eligible adults to vote. Tofilau Eti Alesana was reelected prime minister. Previously, only *matai* (heads of extended families) could vote, a restriction in effect since 1962, when Western Samoa ceased to be a United Nations Trust Territory administered by New Zealand. A 1990 *plebiscite* (direct vote by qualified voters) approved the expansion of voting rights.

New United Nations members. The Federated States of Micronesia and the republic of the Marshall Islands were admitted to the United Nations General Assembly in September 1991. Stuart Inder

In ***World Book,*** see **Pacific Islands.**

Painting. See **Art.**

Prime Minister Nawaz Sharif of Pakistan finished his first full year in office in 1991 amid charges of widespread corruption in his government.

Pakistan. The Islamic Democratic Alliance (IDA) that had come to power in a disputed 1990 election consolidated its power in 1991 under Prime Minister Nawaz Sharif. In 25 national and provincial by-elections held on Jan. 10, 1991, the IDA won 19 of 25 seats, and in provincial assembly selection of national senators on March 14, it won 24 of 46 seats. The Pakistan People's Party, led by former Prime Minister Benazir Bhutto, failed to regain any of the power it had lost during the preceding year.

Scandal charges. Bhutto had been ousted from the prime minister's job in August 1990 by President Ghulam Ishaq Khan on charges of corruption. This led to the November 1990 elections. Bhutto struck back in 1991 by publicizing charges against Sharif. One of Sharif's former political advisers supported Bhutto's claim that the IDA had stolen the 1990 elections. In addition, an auditor's report said millions of dollars had been misappropriated or embezzled by government departments in Punjab Province in 1989 when Sharif headed the provincial government there.

Economic policies. Sharif, the first businessman to become Pakistan's prime minister, adopted several important measures to reform Pakistan's economy in 1991. In April, he worked out an agreement on dividing federal taxes and other resources among the central government and the provinces. He also began to reduce official regulation of the economy and to sell government-owned companies. Sharif hoped to stimulate Pakistan's stagnant economy through privatization and by attracting foreign investment.

Despite some progress in this effort, the program ran into trouble. Labor unrest and numerous bank robberies, bomb attacks, and other violence, as well as new taxes, discouraged investment.

Foreign and military affairs. There was speculation in early summer that another military coup would soon occur, continuing Pakistan's long history of army seizures of the government. The talk centered around General Mirza Aslam Beg, who had been publicly critical of several government policies. When his term as army chief of staff ended on August 17, however, Beg quietly yielded his post to General Asif Nawaz.

Earlier in the year, Beg had objected to Pakistan's support of the American-led alliance that defeated Iraq in the Persian Gulf War. Popular support for Iraq was widespread in Pakistan, but Sharif stuck with the alliance. After the war, which ended in February, the Administration of United States President George Bush tried to get the U.S. Congress to relax its ban on aid to Pakistan. The ban had been imposed because of Pakistan's efforts to produce nuclear weapons. In September, when relations between the United States and Pakistan remained cool, President Ishaq Khan visited Iran to propose a confederacy of 43 Islamic states.

Henry S. Bradsher

See also **Asia** (Facts in brief table). In ***World Book,*** see **Pakistan.**

Paleontology. The development of complex life forms more than 500 million years ago was more sudden and widespread than scientists had believed. That conclusion was reported in May 1991 by paleontologists L. Ramskold of the Swedish Museum of Natural History in Stockholm and Hou Xianguang of the Nanjing Institute of Geology and Paleontology in China.

Ramskold and Xianguang based their conclusion on an analysis of a spectacular collection of diverse marine fossils found in China in 1984. These fossils, which include examples of sponges, trilobites, and worms, date from about 520 million to 530 million years ago, the beginning of the Cambrian Period. Before the Cambrian Period, which began about 540 million years ago, life forms consisted mainly of soft-bodied organisms, such as algae and primitive worms.

The paleontologists found that many of the species discovered in China resemble those unearthed in the Burgess Shale, a fossil bed in the Canadian Rockies that had been the main source of information about early Cambrian life forms. The similarity between the two groups of fossils suggests that the explosion of life during the early Cambrian Period occurred over a shorter period and over a wider area than scientists had believed.

A deadly ancient June. A study of the remains of an ancient lily pond found in Wyoming has provided more support for the theory that a mass extinction 65 million years ago occurred suddenly and as the result of a meteorite collision with Earth. Among the creatures that died out in this extinction at the end of the Cretaceous Period were many marine organisms and the last of the dinosaurs. In a study published in August 1991, geologist Jack Wolfe of the United States Geological Survey in Denver also reported that the impact probably occurred in early June. Some scientists, however, expressed skepticism that Wolfe could pinpoint the time of the impact so precisely.

According to the impact theory, the collision of one or more meteorites with Earth injected huge amounts of dust into the atmosphere. This triggered a series of environmental disasters, including a dramatic cooling of Earth's climate.

While examining the fossilized remains of the ancestors of modern water lilies dating from the end of the Cretaceous Period, Wolfe discovered a distinctive pattern of wrinkles in the leaves. Wolfe was able to re-create this pattern in modern water lily leaves by freezing them. Wolfe concluded from this that the ancient leaves had been rapidly chilled and frozen.

In addition, Wolfe reported finding evidence that the ancient plants had flowered just before they froze. Because modern water lilies of this type flower in early summer, Wolfe concluded that the destruction of the ancient plants probably occurred in early June. Wolfe also reported that a second impact may have occurred shortly after the first. Carlton E. Brett

In *World Book,* see **Dinosaurs; Paleontology.**

Complex life forms arose more suddenly than believed, according to a May study of 520-million-year-old marine fossils, including this arthropod fossil.

Manuel Antonio Noriega's daughter, middle, and wife, right, arrive at the trial of the former Panamanian ruler in Miami, Fla., in September.

Panama. Beginning on Sept. 5, 1991, jurors in a Miami, Fla., courtroom listened to tales of secret meetings involving drug kingpins, suitcases full of new $100 bills, and high-level Panamanian government officials. The occasion was the trial of General Manuel Antonio Noriega nearly four years after he was indicted in the United States on drug trafficking charges and almost two years after U.S. troops invaded Panama.

Noriega faced 10 counts of drug trafficking, money laundering, and racketeering. United States government prosecutors were anxious to win their case against Noriega in order to justify the extraordinary expense to taxpayers that went into bringing him to trial. Prosecutors called to the witness stand nearly half of the 16 defendants named in the original 1988 indictment against Noriega. The defendants who were called had previously pleaded guilty to a variety of drug and racketeering charges and agreed to testify against Noriega in return for reduced sentences.

In defending Noriega, his lawyers drew on U.S. government documents that showed the U.S. Central Intelligence Agency, the U.S. Drug Enforcement Administration, and other agencies had paid Noriega at least $320,000 for his help in curtailing illegal drug shipments into the United States, funneling firearms to U.S.-supported Nicaraguan *contra* rebels, and providing intelligence on the Communist government of Cuba. Noriega's lawyers claimed that he had actually received about $11 million from the U.S. government.

Drug smuggling up. Despite the U.S. government's attempts to crush the cocaine trade in Panama, the Panamanian Coast Guard reported in August that cocaine was still being smuggled out of the country. Panamanian law enforcement officials reported in August that the average monthly seizures of cocaine in Panama had risen to nearly 1,900 pounds (860 kilograms) in 1991 compared with 730 pounds (330 kilograms) per month in 1990.

Antidrug measures. In an attempt to stem the flow of cocaine, Panama and the United States agreed on March 18, 1991, to operate joint patrols of Panamanian coastal waters. On April 11, the two nations also signed a treaty providing U.S. officials with access to Panamanian banking records in order to help stop possible drug trafficking and money laundering.

Government shakeup. Weakening economic conditions and personal animosities led to a split in April 1991 within the fragile ruling coalition that had governed Panama since the U.S. invasion. In an unusual twist, Noriega's old party—the Democratic Revolutionary Party—controlled the swing votes in Panama's legislature after the split in the coalition.

Nathan A. Haverstock

See also **Latin America** (Facts in brief table). In ***World Book,*** see **Panama.**

Papua New Guinea. See **Asia; Pacific Islands.**

Paraguay. See **Latin America.**

Pennsylvania. See **Philadelphia; State government.**

War in the Persian Gulf

By William R. Cormier

Using massive air strikes and surprise movements by troops on the ground, an international military force spearheaded by the United States drove Iraqi invaders from the oil-rich nation of Kuwait.

The missiles and bombs began falling on their targets in and around Baghdad, Iraq's capital, at about 3 a.m. on Jan. 17, 1991 (about 7 p.m. January 16, Eastern Standard Time). As the tracer fire from Iraqi antiaircraft batteries streaked the moonless sky, hundreds of allied warplanes swept over the city, dropping their deadly cargo. Tomahawk cruise missiles launched from United States warships in the Persian Gulf and Red Sea and laser-guided *smart* bombs fired from combat aircraft zeroed in on missile-launching sites, airfields, weapons plants, bridges, electric generating plants, and other key targets in Iraq and Iraqi-occupied Kuwait.

The thunderous air attack was the opening salvo in Operation Desert Storm, an international, United States-led effort to drive invading Iraqi forces from the Arab nation of Kuwait. The attack began less than 17 hours after the expiration of a United Nations (UN) deadline for an Iraqi pullout from Kuwait, which Iraq had overrun on Aug. 2, 1990.

Superior firepower, detailed knowledge of enemy positions, control of the skies over Iraq and Kuwait, and a superior ground battle plan provided the keys to the international coalition's victory. Forty-two days of air bombardment and a 100-hour ground war smashed what had been the largest army in the Middle East in one of the most lopsided victories in modern military history. Although an estimated 110,000 Iraqi soldiers and tens of thousands of Iraqi civilians died in the Persian Gulf War, the con-

flict resulted in only 340 allied deaths in combat, 148 of them American.

The political outcome of the war was much less decisive, however. Iraq's President Saddam Hussein not only survived Iraq's military defeat but also remained powerful enough to quash two postwar civil uprisings. Freed from its destructive occupation by Iraq, Kuwait struggled to rebuild its economy amid an enormous ecological disaster—hundreds of burning oil wells set alight by fleeing Iraqi troops. On returning home, Kuwait's exiled monarchy was also confronted by a reinvigorated political opposition demanding a more democratic government and by charges of human rights abuses. The closer relationship between the United States and Arab nations forged during the war, however, may have improved long-term prospects for peace in the region. A Middle East peace conference to address the long-standing conflict between Israel and its Arab neighbors began on October 30 in Madrid, Spain. See **Middle East**.

Preceding pages: Iraqi vehicles lie burnt and wrecked along the main highway linking Kuwait and Iraq after a fierce attack by allied warplanes on Feb. 26, 1991. An estimated 10,000 Iraqi troops attempting to flee Kuwait were killed along what became known as the *highway of death.*

The background to the war

Saddam Hussein had shocked the world when his forces stormed across Iraq's border with Kuwait and seized that oil-rich desert kingdom in August 1990. Although Hussein had threatened military action against Kuwait less than three weeks earlier and had massed tens of thousands of troops along their common border, few observers in the United States or the Middle East believed he would actually attack.

The invasion was the climax of an increasingly bitter dispute between Iraq and Kuwait over oil, money, and land. Together, the two countries have known oil reserves of about 194.5 billion barrels. In combination with Saudi Arabia's estimated 257.5 billion barrels, they control 45 per cent of the world's known petroleum reserves. By seizing Kuwait's oil wells and threatening Saudi Arabia, Hussein had gambled that he could increase his oil profits and significantly enhance his power both within the Middle East and among the nations of the world.

In the wake of a ruinous eight-year war with neighboring Iran, which ended in 1988, Iraq needed money—both to rebuild and to repay an international debt of at least $50 billion. Before the invasion of Kuwait, Iraq earned more than 95 per cent of its revenues from the sale of oil. But Iraq's oil earnings had fallen—the result, Hussein charged, of overproduction by Kuwait and the United Arab Emirates (U.A.E.), which had increased world oil supplies, driving down prices. Since the late 1980's, Kuwait and the U.A.E. had failed to abide by production quotas set by the Organization of Petroleum Exporting Countries (OPEC), the international oil cartel. As a result of lower oil prices, Hussein estimated, Iraq had lost $14 billion in oil revenues. In July 1990, Iraq's Foreign Minister Tariq Aziz released a letter detailing Iraq's complaints against Kuwait, including accusations that Kuwait had stolen $2.4 billion worth of oil from an oil field that straddles the Iraq-Kuwait border.

The author:

William R. Cormier works on the international desk of the Associated Press in New York City.

Like other Iraqi leaders before him, Hussein also had designs on the Kuwaiti islands of Bubiyan and Warba in the northern Persian Gulf, off Iraq's southern border. Iraq has only one major port—al-Basrah—and one outlet to the gulf—the Shatt al Arab waterway—which forms its eastern border with Iran. Control of the two islands would have given Hussein easier access to the gulf.

Finally, Hussein demanded that Kuwait and the other Persian Gulf States write off some $30 billion in loans that they had made to Iraq during the Iran-Iraq War. Hussein, whose attack on Iran started the Iran-Iraq War, argued that Iraq's military efforts against Iran had limited the ability of Iran's Islamic fundamentalist government to foment antigovernment activity in other Arab countries.

In mid-July, Hussein threatened military action against Kuwait and the U.A.E. unless they cut their oil output. The two countries quickly agreed to abide by their OPEC production quotas. In addition, OPEC voted to raise the price of oil by $3 per barrel, to $21 per barrel. But in a meeting held on August 1 in Saudi Arabia, Kuwaiti and Iraqi officials failed to resolve their differences. On August 2, Hussein's tanks rolled into Kuwait.

The build-up to war

Iraq's occupation of Kuwait sparked a rush of diplomatic activity. On August 3, the UN Security Council condemned the attack and demanded that Iraq withdraw its forces. That same day, the United States and the Soviet Union, both of whom had supplied Iraq with weapons in the past, jointly urged all nations to halt arms shipments to Iraq. On August 4, the European Community, consisting of 12 European nations, banned all oil imports from Iraq and Kuwait. On August 6, the Security Council clamped economic sanctions on Iraq, cutting off all trade with that country, except for certain humanitarian items such as medical supplies and food.

The invasion also triggered a military response. On August 7, U.S. President George Bush announced that he was immediately dispatching U.S. jet fighters, paratroopers, and armored forces to Saudi Arabia to discourage an Iraqi attack on that country. Then, on August 22, Bush ordered the mobilization of U.S. military reserve units, the first such call-up for a foreign crisis since 1968, when they were sent to serve in Vietnam. On Aug. 25, 1990, the Security Council authorized U.S.-led naval forces in the Middle East to take military action to enforce the trade embargo against Iraq. Scores of countries sent or pledged military forces to the U.S.-led effort, dubbed Operation Desert Shield.

The Arab League, an organization of 20 Middle Eastern and African nations and the Palestine Liberation Organization (PLO), also condemned Iraq's attack on Kuwait and on August 10 voted in favor of a resolution to send troops to Saudi Arabia. Many Arab states, however, including some of those voting against Iraq, said that the invasion was an Arab problem that required an Arab solution. Many Arabs also expressed grave concern over the deployment of non-Islamic military forces in Saudi Arabia, which controls two of Islam's holiest sites—Mecca and Medina. In most Arab countries, there were demonstrations against U.S. intervention.

Hussein became increasingly belligerent and defiant in the face of his diplomatic and military isolation. On August 8, Iraq annexed Kuwait. In mid-August, Hussein announced that the estimated 9,000 North American, European, and Australian civilians living and working in Iraq and

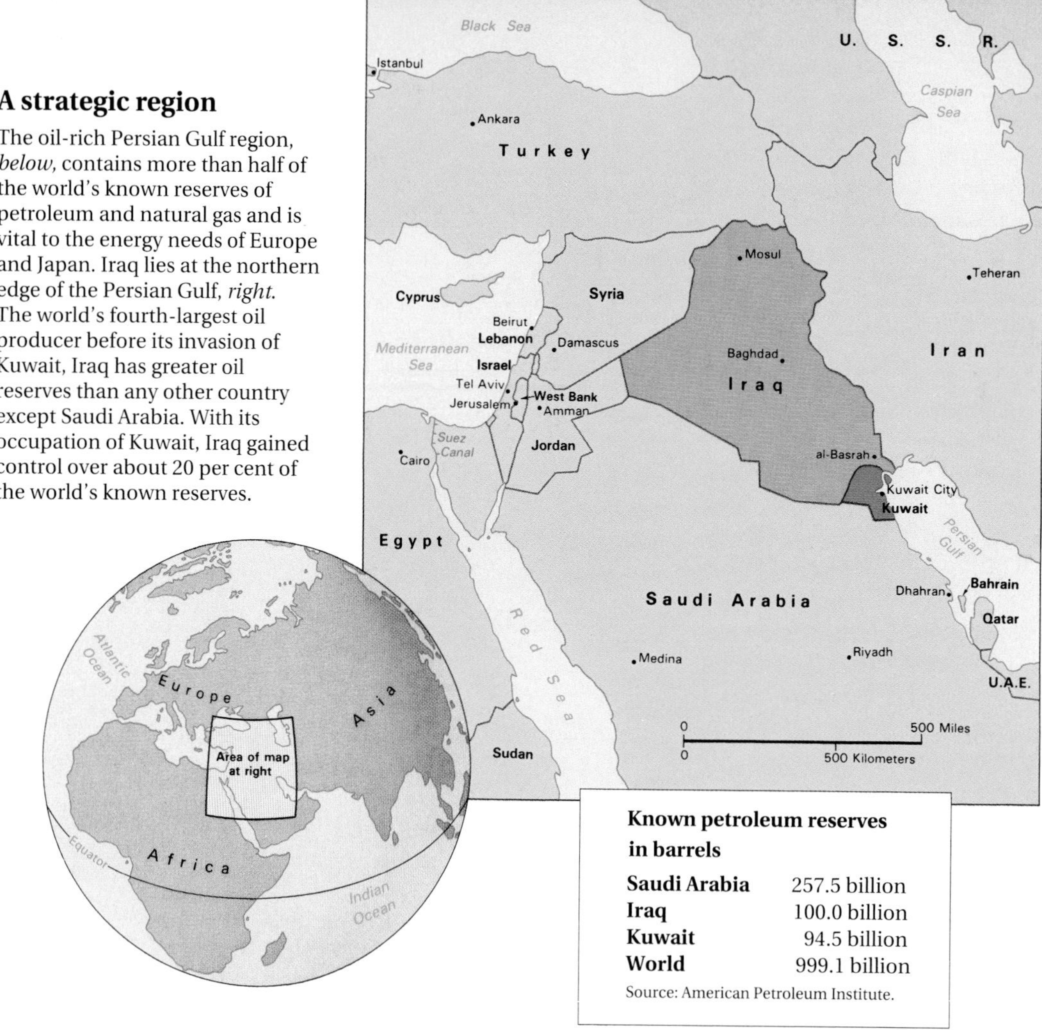

A strategic region

The oil-rich Persian Gulf region, *below,* contains more than half of the world's known reserves of petroleum and natural gas and is vital to the energy needs of Europe and Japan. Iraq lies at the northern edge of the Persian Gulf, *right.* The world's fourth-largest oil producer before its invasion of Kuwait, Iraq has greater oil reserves than any other country except Saudi Arabia. With its occupation of Kuwait, Iraq gained control over about 20 per cent of the world's known reserves.

Known petroleum reserves in barrels

Saudi Arabia	257.5 billion
Iraq	100.0 billion
Kuwait	94.5 billion
World	999.1 billion

Source: American Petroleum Institute.

Kuwait were hostages. Many of the hostages were moved to strategic military or industrial sites within Iraq and Kuwait to serve as "human shields" to discourage allied attack. By December 6, however, Hussein had permitted all foreign hostages to leave Iraq and Kuwait.

Meanwhile, Iraq's ruling Revolutionary Command Council urged Iraqi citizens to prepare for "the mother of all battles." Hussein campaigned for—and won—considerable popular Arab support by insisting that any sanctions imposed on him because of his invasion of Kuwait should also be applied to Israel for occupying the West Bank and Gaza Strip after the 1967 Six-Day War. Hussein also insisted that any solution to the crisis should address the Palestinian issue, and he demanded that the oil-rich states of the Persian Gulf share more of their wealth with less fortunate Arab countries.

At the same time, Hussein poured more forces into Kuwait. By October 1990, about 300,000 Iraqi soldiers were massed along Kuwait's southern border with Saudi Arabia and along Kuwait's gulf coast, according to Secretary of Defense Richard B. Cheney's official report on the war released to the U.S. Congress in September 1991. The troops, dug in behind minefields and heavily fortified walls of sand, were backed by artillery and armored units. Behind the front-line soldiers, many of whom were reportedly poorly supplied civilian recruits, were the infantry and armored divisions of the Republican Guards, the well-trained elite of Hussein's army.

The nature of the allied effort shifted from a defensive to a potentially offensive operation in early November, when Bush announced that he would nearly double the number of U.S. troops in Saudi Arabia, which then totaled 230,000. The likelihood of war grew even greater on November 29 when the UN Security Council authorized the use of military force to eject Iraqi troops from Kuwait if Iraq failed to withdraw by Jan. 15, 1991. By January, an estimated 500,000 Iraqi soldiers faced 467,000 allied combat ground troops, including 320,000 U.S. Army and Marine ground soldiers.

While preparations for war were underway, diplomats continued negotiations for a peaceful solution to the crisis. But a last-ditch meeting between U.S. Secretary of State James A. Baker III and Iraq's Tariq Aziz on January 9 in Switzerland ended in a stalemate. Several other diplomatic initiatives during the following week, including several Arab attempts, also fizzled.

On January 10, the U.S. Senate and House of Representatives began three days of impassioned debate over a resolution authorizing Bush to use force to drive Iraq from Kuwait. Despite pleas by some members of Congress that Bush give economic sanctions more time to take effect, both houses, by narrow margins, approved the resolution on January 12.

Throughout the conflict, public opinion polls reported that the overwhelming majority of Americans approved of the U.S. actions. The minority of Americans who opposed the conflict staged antiwar protests in New York City, Chicago, and other U.S. cities.

The air war begins

The war began on January 17 with allied air and missile attacks on Iraq and Iraqi positions in Kuwait. Fighter planes and fighter-bombers from the United States, Great Britain, Kuwait, Saudi Arabia, and other coalition nations pounded missile launchers; plants believed to manufacture nuclear, chemical, biological, and conventional weapons; military communications centers; ammunition dumps; and other key Iraqi defense installations. Targets also included oil refineries and pipelines, strategic bridges and roads, rail lines, and the electric power system. Iraqi ground forces and armored units also came under air attack. During the war, the allies flew more than 110,000 combat *sorties* (individual

Members of the Coalition

The following countries supplied military forces or combat support forces to the allied effort in the Persian Gulf War.*

Afghanistan
Argentina
Australia
Bahrain
Bangladesh
Belgium
Canada
Czechoslovakia
Denmark
Egypt
France
Germany
Great Britain
Greece
Honduras
Hungary
Italy
Korea, Republic of
Kuwait
Morocco
Netherlands
Niger
Norway
New Zealand
Oman
Pakistan
Poland
Portugal
Qatar
Saudi Arabia
Senegal
Sierra Leone
Singapore
Spain
Sweden
Syria
Turkey
United Arab Emirates
United States

Source: United States Department of Defense.

*Japan, though not a member of the coalition, contributed economic assistance to the allied effort.

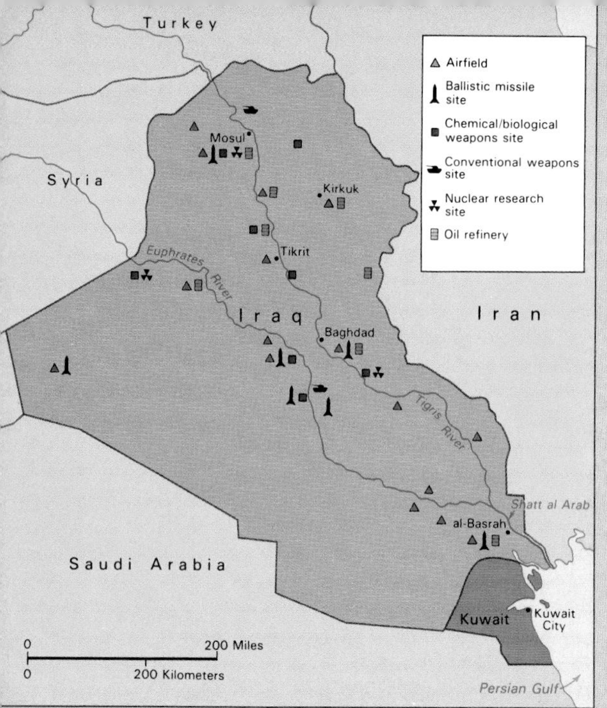

The air war

The air war was launched by the allied forces on Jan. 17, 1991. Targets included Iraqi troop concentrations and key Iraqi military and industrial facilities. During the air war, an estimated 88,500 short tons (80,300 metric tons) of bombs fell on Iraq and Kuwait.

The allies relied on many high-tech weapons, including warplanes and missiles designed to avoid radar detection. The shape of the F-117A Stealth fighter, *left,* and the materials used in its construction deflect radar waves. The Tomahawk cruise missile, *above,* flies at very low altitudes to escape detection by ground-based radar systems.

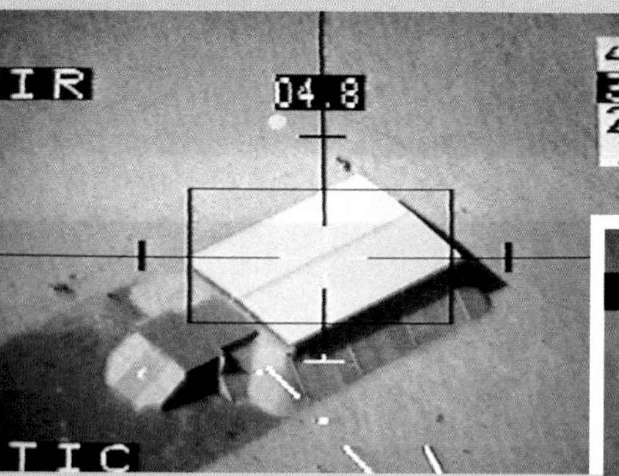

Infrared photographs from a camera mounted on a Jaguar fighter-bomber record the targeting, *above,* of an Iraqi ammunition depot and its destruction, *right,* by a laser-guided *smart* missile.

Two Patriot antimissile missiles streak through the night sky over Tel Aviv, one of Israel's largest cities, to intercept incoming Iraqi missiles, known as *Scuds.* U.S. soldiers operated the Patriot batteries. Iraq's Scud attacks on Israel during the Gulf War killed 4 people and injured 300 others.

Iraqis inspect the wreckage of a building in Baghdad, Iraq's capital, destroyed by allied bombs in mid-February. Allied bombardment during the war severely crippled Iraq's electrical power and telecommunications systems and destroyed thousands of homes and many of the country's bridges and roads.

bombing missions), including 8,000 sorties during the first week alone.

Although Iraq shot down 36 allied aircraft, according to Cheney's report, there was very little resistance from Iraq's 550-plane air force. As a result, the allies quickly seized control of the skies over Iraq and Kuwait. At first, some military analysts speculated that Hussein was reserving his air force for an expected ground war. But, mysteriously, most of his planes sat out the war in heavily fortified bunkers. During the second week of the air war, scores of Iraqi planes fled to Iran, where they were grounded for the duration of the war.

The war gave officials of the U.S. Department of Defense the chance to test and showcase a number of high-cost, high-tech weapons. Among these weapons was the Tomahawk cruise missile. The stubby-winged missiles, which cost about $1.3 million each, fly at extremely low altitudes to escape radar detection. Another high-tech, high-profile weapon was the $106-million F-117A Stealth fighter, designed to slip into enemy territory without appearing on enemy radar screens. The plane has a sharp-angled shape and covering of special graphite compounds that both absorb and deflect the radio waves used in radar systems.

In addition to conventional bombs, Stealth fighters and other allied warplanes carried *smart* bombs, which are bombs guided to their target by *lasers* (narrow, intense beams of light), *infrared* (heat) rays, or television cameras. One well publicized videotape recording by a TV camera in a Stealth fighter showed the devastating impact of a smart bomb on Iraqi Air Force headquarters in Baghdad. Following a laser beam locked onto the rooftop opening of the building's air shaft, the 2,000-pound (900-kilogram) bomb hurtled down the shaft and then exploded, collapsing the building. Reports issued in late spring and summer 1991 by Defense Department and independent military analysts, however, suggested that some of the high-tech weapons had not performed as well during the war as U.S. military officials had reported.

Scud retaliation

Although allied warplanes roamed Iraqi air space almost at will, Iraq was far from submissive. Less than 24 hours into the air war, Iraq began launching *Scud* missiles at Israel. These were Soviet-made *surface-to-surface* missiles (missiles launched from the ground or the sea to attack targets on the surface). The Scud attacks failed to provoke Israel into counterattacking. Israeli involvement in the war, Hussein evidently hoped, would transform the conflict into a fight between Iraq and Israel and the United States and so drive Syria, Egypt, and other Arab states that oppose Israel from the coalition.

The Scud attacks were especially terrifying because of fears that Hussein might arm the missiles with chemical warheads. But, for unknown reasons, Hussein, who used chemical weapons to kill thousands of Kurds in northern Iraq in 1988, did not use chemical weapons in the war.

Nevertheless, the Scuds took their toll. The 39 Scud missiles that fell on Israel in 18 separate attacks killed 4 people and injured nearly 300 others. And on Feb. 25, 1991, a Scud slammed into a U.S. military barracks in

A United States military vehicle rolls past a burning Iraqi tank destroyed by shelling during the rapid advance by allied ground forces across the desert to liberate Iraqi-occupied Kuwait.

Saudi Arabia, killing 28 soldiers and injuring 97 others.

Earlier, on February 15, hopes for a peaceful end to the crisis rose dramatically when Hussein made a conditional offer to withdraw from Kuwait. But Bush quickly dismissed the proposal as a "cruel hoax" because he said it was too weighted down by conditions. Bush also rejected as "inadequate" a peace plan offered by Iraq and the Soviet Union on February 21. On February 22, Bush issued another ultimatum to Iraq: Accept all UN resolutions unconditionally by noon on February 23 or prepare for a huge ground assault.

The ground war

The climax of the conflict was a lightning 100-hour ground war. The allies' battle plan was based on a two-part deception, disclosed at a press briefing on February 27 by U.S. General H. Norman Schwarzkopf, Jr., commander of the allied forces in the Persian Gulf.

The first ruse was convincing Hussein that the allies planned to launch an amphibious attack on Kuwait's eastern coast. To that end, the allies stationed a considerable number of naval vessels in the Persian Gulf off the coast of Kuwait. In addition, 18,000 U.S. Marines stationed on ships in the gulf conducted several amphibious maneuvers, apparently in preparation for such an assault. To defend against a beach landing, the Iraqis

The ground war

The ground war, which lasted for 100 hours, began on Feb. 24, 1991. The allies' battle plan was based on a two-part deception.

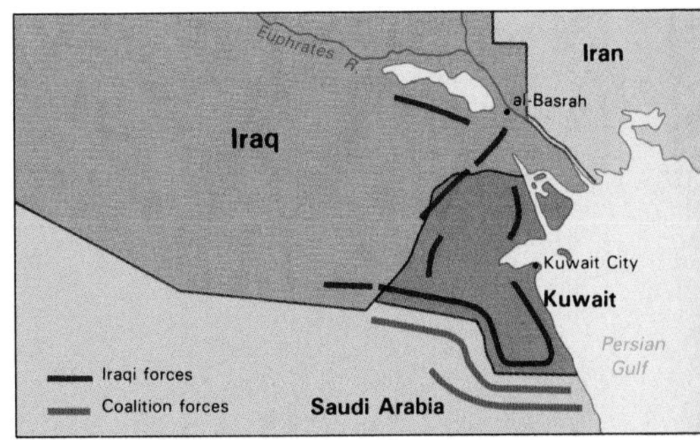

Allied troops were first deployed along the Saudi-Kuwaiti border in an attempt to make Iraq believe that the allies would attack northward into Kuwait.

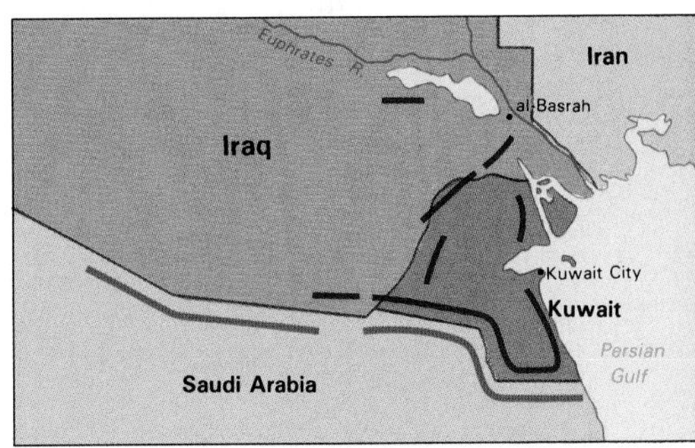

The allies then shifted 1,500 tanks, more than 150,000 troops, and tons of supplies to the west after eliminating Iraq's surveillance capability by grounding its air force.

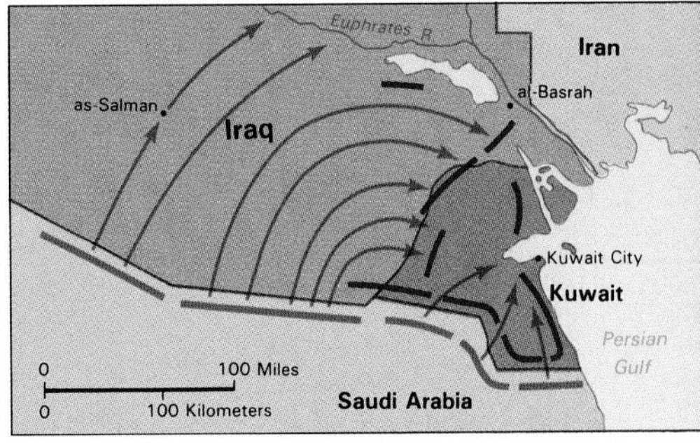

On February 24, while some allied troops attacked through southern Kuwait, the main force pushed into southern Iraq, then wheeled east to attack the Iraqis' flank.

Important dates in the Gulf crisis

☆ ☆ ☆ ☆ ☆ ☆ ☆ ☆

Aug. 2, 1990—Iraq invades Kuwait.

August 3—The United Nations (UN) Security Council condemns Iraq's move into Kuwait and demands that Iraq withdraw its forces immediately.

August 6—The Security Council prohibits all trade with Iraq and Kuwait except for humanitarian items.

August 6-7—United States President George Bush sends U.S. military forces to Saudi Arabia to discourage an Iraqi invasion of that country.

August 8—Iraq annexes Kuwait.

August 10—The Arab League votes to send troops to Saudi Arabia.

August 13-14—Iraq says the approximately 9,000 North Americans, Europeans, and Australians in Iraq and Kuwait may not leave until hostilities end.

August 25—The Security Council authorizes allied naval forces to take military action to enforce the trade embargo against Iraq.

August 28—Iraq's President Saddam Hussein declares that all foreign women and children may leave Iraq and Kuwait.

November 8—President Bush announces that the United States will nearly double the number of its military forces in the Persian Gulf.

November 29—The Security Council authorizes the use of military force to eject Iraq from Kuwait unless Iraq withdraws its forces by Jan. 15, 1991.

December 6—Hussein announces all remaining foreign hostages in Iraq and Kuwait are free to leave.

Jan. 9, 1991—U.S. Secretary of State James A. Baker III and Iraq's Foreign Minister Tariq Aziz meet in Switzerland but fail to resolve the crisis.

January 12—The U.S. Congress authorizes President Bush to use force to end Iraq's occupation of Kuwait.

January 15—The UN deadline for Iraq's withdrawal from Kuwait expires with Hussein's forces still entrenched in that country.

January 17—The allies launch an air war against Iraq and Kuwait. Iraq fires eight Scud surface-to-surface missiles against Israel.

January 26—Tens of thousands of people in Washington, D.C., rally against the war in the largest of many antiwar protests held in U.S. cities during January.

February 15—Hussein makes a conditional offer to withdraw from Kuwait. The allies reject the offer.

February 24—The allies launch a ground war against Iraq and Kuwait.

February 25—A Scud missile hits a U.S. Army barracks in Saudi Arabia, killing 28 people.

February 26—Allied troops enter the city of Kuwait.

February 27—President Bush announces a temporary cease-fire.

April 3—The Security Council approves the terms of a permanent cease-fire.

April 6—Iraq accepts the terms of the UN cease-fire.

April 11—The Security Council officially declares an end to the Persian Gulf War.

massed about 6 of their 42 army divisions along the Kuwaiti coast and brought in artillery and armored units from Iraq's southern border with Saudi Arabia. The allies also tricked Hussein into believing that the thrust of the main allied ground assault would be northward from Saudi Arabia into Kuwait. In this belief, Hussein had deployed additional Iraqi infantry divisions and most of his artillery and armored units along the Saudi-Kuwaiti border.

Surprise maneuver

In reality, the allies planned a flanking maneuver—one in which allied forces would attack along Iraq's lightly defended southern border with Saudi Arabia. Three weeks before the scheduled start of the ground war, Schwarzkopf began to move more than 1,500 allied tanks and 150,000 U.S., British, and French troops as well as tens of thousands of tons of fuel, water, spare parts, and other supplies from 150 to 200 miles (240 to 320 kilometers) to the west. Hussein, whose air force was grounded and who had no access to spy satellites, was blind to the maneuver.

The invasion began just before dawn on February 24. U.S. Marines and Saudi, Kuwaiti, and other Arab troops smashed through Iraqi defenses in southern Kuwait, feigning the start of a frontal invasion. To the west, however, allied armored units and airborne troops rushed into Iraq in three main forces. Their goal was not only to attack Hussein's forces in southern Iraq but also to cut off any avenue of escape into northern Iraq.

The first force, made up of American and British armored units, drove north into Iraq and then wheeled eastward to attack the tanks and troops of the Republican Guard in southern Iraq and northern Kuwait. To the left of the first force, the U.S. airborne troops of the second force launched an air assault deep into central Iraq, establishing a forward fuel and supply station. From there, these airborne troops rushed north toward the Euphrates River to block the Iraqis' escape route. Finally, the third force, made up of U.S. airborne troops and French armored units, pushed into western Iraq to guard the allies' far left flank.

Iraqi troops, hungry, demoralized by weeks of ferocious air attacks, and, often, deserted by their commanders, surrendered in droves. Within the first two days, the allies took more than 30,000 Iraqi prisoners.

Hussein's final defeat came in several fierce tank clashes in southern Iraq on February 27 and 28. In the largest tank battle since World War II (1939-1945), hundreds of U.S. tanks, light armored vehicles, and attack helicopters reportedly destroyed 200 Iraqi tanks. According to U.S. military reports, no allied tanks were destroyed.

The allies also routed Iraqi forces fleeing from the city of Kuwait, Kuwait's capital, along the main highway to al-Basrah on February 26. Without air protection, the Iraqis, their bumper-to-bumper vehicles creating a huge traffic jam, were defenseless against allied air and tank bombardment. An estimated 10,000 Iraqis died on what became known as the *highway of death.*

Advancing U.S. and Arab troops paused on reaching the outskirts of Kuwait's capital on February 26 to allow Saudi and Kuwaiti fighters to re-

After the war

At the end of the war, Iraq and Kuwait confronted political turmoil and the massive task of rebuilding, while Americans celebrated a military victory.

A ticker tape parade in New York City on June 10 was one of many staged in cities across the United States to welcome American troops returning from the Middle East.

An inferno of fire and dense black smoke rises from 1 of the more than 730 oil wells in Kuwait set afire or damaged by retreating Iraqi troops in February. The smoke cloud from the blazes covered 26,000 square miles (67,300 square kilometers).

Kurdish refugees mob a bread truck at a camp in Turkey. More than 1.5 million Kurds fled to Iraq's borders with Turkey and Iran in April after a Kurdish uprising against the Iraqi government collapsed.

claim it. Hours later, U.S. troops were wildly welcomed by jubilant Kuwaitis.

In a televised address on February 27, Bush ordered a cease-fire, reporting that the allies had met their military objectives. The next day, Iraq announced it would end hostilities. On April 3, the UN Security Council formally approved the terms for a permanent cease-fire. The Council ordered Iraq to revoke its annexation of Kuwait, accept liability for war damages, and disclose all stocks of chemical and nuclear weapons. Iraq reluctantly agreed to the terms on April 6.

Aftermath of the war

The war's end signaled the start of two insurrections inside Iraq. In early March, Shiite Muslims in southern Iraq, who violently opposed Hussein, launched a rebellion in and around al-Basrah. Although Shiite Muslims comprise the majority in Iraq, the government is dominated by members of the Sunni Muslim sect. In northern Iraq, tens of thousands of Kurdish guerrillas, who have been fighting for independence for decades, began a separate uprising. Hussein crushed both rebellions within a month at an estimated loss of 20,000 lives.

More than 1.5 million Kurds, fearful of reprisals by Hussein's army and pressured by the Kurdish rebel underground, fled to Iraq's northern borders with Iran and Turkey. President Bush, responding to intense public pressure, ordered U.S. soldiers into northern Iraq in April to protect the Kurds and to distribute food and other supplies. The allies also temporarily established a Kurdish refuge within Iraq and set up refugee camps. Most of the Kurds returned to their homes over the next three months.

Kuwait, while rejoicing in victory, faced the huge task of reconstructing a country ravaged by occupation and war. The country struggled to put out hundreds of oil well fires set by retreating Iraqi troops. The United States also accused Iraq of spilling at least 168 million gallons (636 million liters) of Kuwaiti oil into the Persian Gulf, adding to the region's ecological woes. Although all the oil well fires had been extinguished by November, unexploded shells and mines continued to pose a danger, and damaged buildings, shops, and hotels stood in need of repair.

Politically, Kuwait's exiled rulers returned to an emboldened opposition clamoring for democratic reform, including parliamentary elections. Kuwait also found itself the target of international criticism for the harsh treatment, including trials, deportations, and killings, of the country's Palestinians, who were accused of sympathizing or collaborating with the Iraqi invaders.

Meanwhile, in the United States, returning troops were welcomed by parades and congratulatory speeches. For many Americans, haunted by the defeats and painful memories of the Vietnam War, the allies' success in the Persian Gulf excited a wave of pride in U.S. military forces. It remained uncertain, however, whether the victory of the international coalition would contribute to increased stability in the Middle East or whether the war would ultimately prove to be just another conflict waged on a milleniums-old battleground.

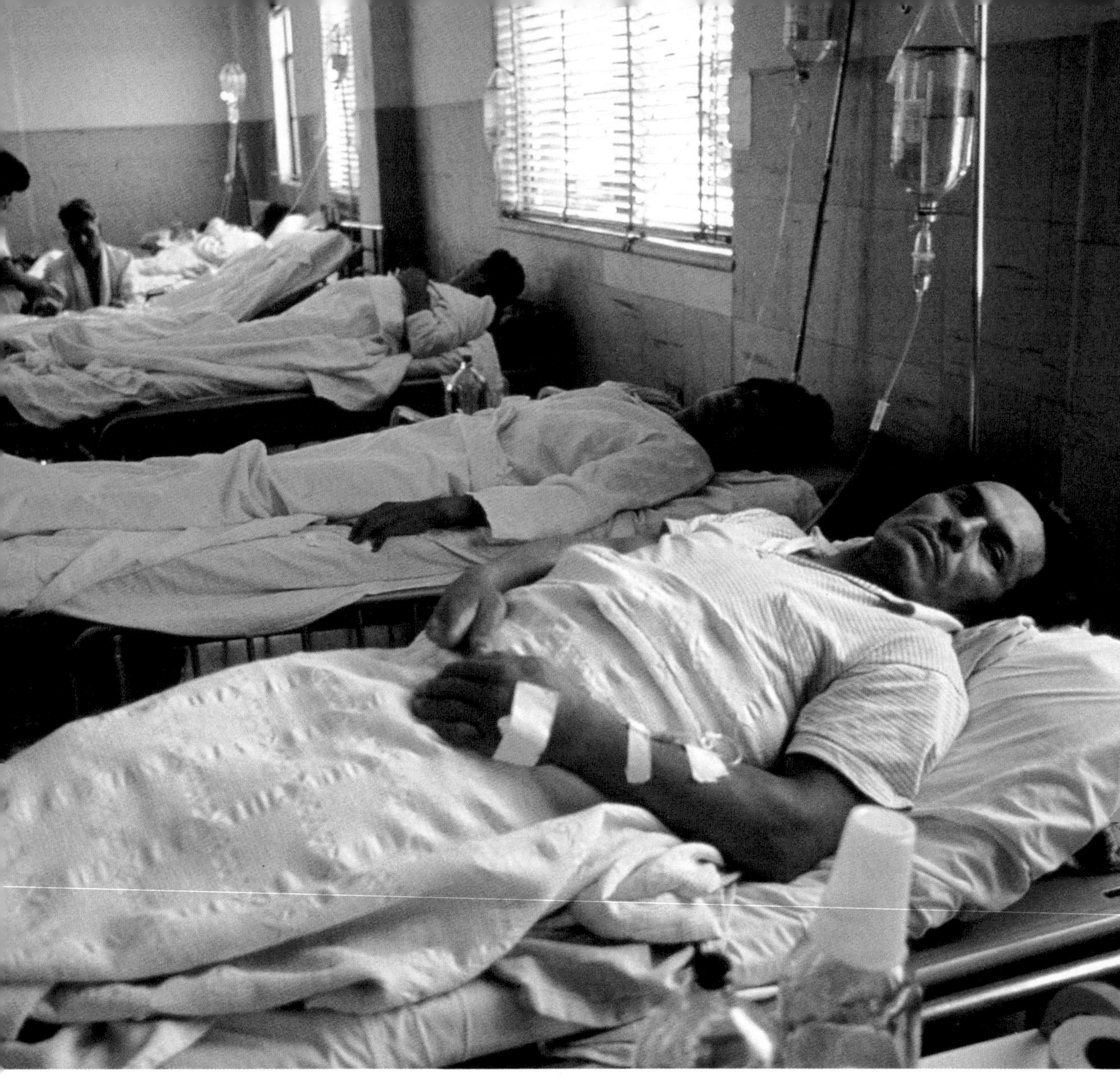

Cholera patients crowd a hospital in Lima, Peru, in February. Cholera struck more than 275,000 people and killed at least 2,664 in Peru in 1991.

Peru. A cholera outbreak began in northern Peru in late January 1991. By November, the outbreak had reached epidemic proportions, with doctors reporting more than 275,000 cases and 2,664 deaths, according to the Pan American Health Organization.

Former president indicted. On July 29, former Peruvian President Alan García Pérez, once highly popular with many Peruvians for refusing to make payments on the nation's huge foreign debt, was indicted in New York City for banking fraud. The indictment charged that García, who was president of Peru from 1985 to 1990, looted the nation's banks of as much as $50 million while he was in office with the help of the scandal-ridden International Bank of Credit and Commerce (BCCI). Two of García's top financial officials were also charged with taking millions of dollars in bribes to place Peru's reserves with BCCI.

Military assistance. On Aug. 6, 1991, the United States said it would send military trainers to help Peru overcome drug traffickers and a costly guerrilla war. The new assistance, coupled with $34.9 million in military aid, was meant to weaken an alliance between drug traffickers and Maoist guerrillas belonging to the Shining Path movement. These guerrillas controlled most of Peru's mountainous Upper Huallaga Valley, which produces much of the hemisphere's coca leaf—the raw material for cocaine. The U.S. decision followed the bloodiest month of Peru's 11-year-old guerrilla war in June, when an average of 18 people were killed each day.

But the U.S. Congress stalled the delivery of U.S. military assistance to Peru because many members were angry about continued allegations of brutality by Peru's military. A report released by a human rights team of the Organization of American States in October expressed similar concerns. Suspicions about the military arose after hooded gunmen killed 16 people and wounded 4 more at a chicken barbecue in a poor neighborhood of Lima, the capital, on November 3. Although the government blamed the killings on guerrillas, many suspected the military was involved.

Fight against inflation. Despite the chaotic condition of Peru's economy, President Alberto Fujimori, unlike his predecessors, refused to create more inflation by allowing Peru's central bank to print new money. From an inflation rate of thousands of percentage points, Fujimori reduced inflation to about 150 per cent during his first year in office. Impressed with his performance, the United States and Japan promised in early June to provide Peru with $750 million to help pay off international loans. Returning to Lima from an official visit to Washington, D.C., on September 21, Fujimori carried an estimated $2.5 billion in additional financial commitments from United States and other international sources.

Nathan A. Haverstock

See also **Latin America** (Facts in brief table). In ***World Book,*** see **Peru.**

Pet. See **Cat; Dog.**

Petroleum and gas. The world's petroleum industry was affected by a series of political and economic crises throughout 1991. An attempted military coup in August in the Soviet Union, the world's largest oil producer, sent oil prices sharply higher for a few days. On January 17, the Persian Gulf crisis, triggered by Iraq's invasion of Kuwait in August 1990, erupted into a war that was fought amid some of the world's richest oil fields. See **Persian Gulf,** Special Report: **War in the Persian Gulf.**

Although the war lasted only six weeks, Iraq suffered enormous casualties, and its economy, infrastructure, and oil facilities were severely damaged. In addition, before fleeing from Kuwait in February 1991, Iraqi troops sabotaged Kuwait's oil fields, leaving more than 700 oil wells on fire or gushing out of control. The Iraqis also allegedly dumped millions of gallons of Kuwaiti oil into the Persian Gulf. However, despite the damage to Iraq's and Kuwait's oil industries and a United Nations (UN) embargo that kept 4 million barrels per day (bpd) of Iraqi and Kuwaiti petroleum off the market, world oil supplies remained ample in 1991. Oil prices remained stable for much of the year.

OPEC production. Most members of the Organization of Petroleum Exporting Countries (OPEC), the international oil cartel, produced at near-capacity for much of 1991. OPEC's oil output ranged from 23 million to 24 million bpd for the year. This total nearly equaled OPEC output levels before the beginning of the Persian Gulf crisis.

Although there was a danger that an extremely cold winter could tighten up oil supplies, several of OPEC's leading member nations warned in late 1991 that an oil glut could return by spring of 1992 if oil exporting countries continued to produce at near-capacity. The oil ministers of Algeria, Nigeria, and Indonesia were among those calling on oil exporting countries to again consider instituting voluntary cutbacks in production to make room for Iraqi and Kuwaiti oil, once those two countries had resumed exporting oil in quantity.

OPEC had suspended its voluntary curbs in August 1990 after Iraq invaded Kuwait. Some countries, including Saudi Arabia, Venezuela, and the United Arab Emirates, greatly expanded production to help offset the loss of Iraqi and Kuwaiti oil. Having spent vast sums to finance their expansions, however, these countries were reluctant to lower their output to previous levels. Saudi Arabia, OPEC's leading producer, had expanded production from 5.4 million bpd to 8.5 million, for example.

At an OPEC meeting held in Geneva, Switzerland, in September 1991, Saudi Arabian representatives announced that their government considered 8.5 million bpd Saudi Arabia's share of the world oil market, no matter what Iraq and Kuwait were able to produce. Despite opposition from some members, the organization agreed to a Saudi Arabian plan to increase the total OPEC oil production to 23.6 million bpd, more than 1 million bpd higher than the group's production ceiling in 1990.

Iraqi production. Osama A. R. Al-Hiti, Iraq's oil minister, said in September 1991 that Iraq was then producing up to 400,000 bpd. Before the Persian Gulf crisis began, Iraq had produced 3.2 million bpd. On August 15, the UN Security Council voted to temporarily lift its trade embargo against Iraq to permit that country to sell $1.6 billion in oil for emergency purchases of food and medicine. Iraq refused, arguing that UN supervision of the oil sale would infringe on its independence.

Kuwaiti production. Soon after the liberation of Kuwait by U.S.-led coalition forces in February, teams of oil-well fire fighters began arriving in that country from around the world. Despite predictions that extinguishing or capping the damaged wells would take several years, the teams finished their work in early November. Kuwait's oil production, which had been 1.5 million bpd in August 1990, passed 400,000 bpd by November 1991.

Oil demand. During 1991, world demand for petroleum was relatively flat, averaging about 66.1 million bpd. This figure was only slightly higher than the sluggish pace set in 1990. The run-up in prices after the invasion of Kuwait and the effects of the economic recession that began in the United States and some other industrial countries in the second half of

1990 had caused world petroleum consumption to decline. The United States had the biggest drop—as much as 7 per cent—in early 1991. By autumn, as the recession began to show some signs of lifting, world demand for petroleum began to rise again.

The International Energy Agency (IEA), an organization of 21 oil-importing countries, estimated in December that world petroleum demand would be up by as much as 500,000 bpd during the first three months of 1992. According to the IEA's estimates, oil demand in Europe would be flat in the early months of 1992. However, worldwide demand would rise sharply because of anticipated increases in oil use in the United States and in Canada. The estimated gains for North American oil demand for the first half of 1992 were based mainly on an anticipated rebound in the national economies of the United States and Canada.

Some oil industry analysts, however, questioned whether the IEA was being too optimistic about the predicted extent of economic recovery, particularly in the United States. If oil demand did not rebound as expected and if OPEC members failed to cut back production, additional supplies coming out of Iraq and Kuwait in 1992 could contribute to a new oil surplus.

Oil prices, which had remained steady at about $20 per barrel for the first half of 1991, began to rise slightly at midyear, reaching about $24 per barrel before declining in the fall. In the wake of Iraq's invasion of Kuwait, petroleum prices had surged, peaking at more than $40 a barrel in October 1990. By early 1991, the cost of a barrel of oil hovered around $30. Oil industry analysts widely assumed prices would escalate sharply, perhaps passing the 1990 high, if war broke out in the Persian Gulf region. To prevent a jump in oil prices, the U.S. government and the IEA prepared to release emergency crude oil stocks if needed.

In early 1991, however, refineries were humming at capacity, and higher prices had throttled back oil demand. As a result, by January 17, when the air war against Iraq began, supplies actually exceeded demand. Although oil prices surged immediately after the Persian Gulf War began—by $6 a barrel—they fell by $10 a barrel within hours, the biggest one-day drop ever. The plunge came after the huge successes of the first coalition air attacks revealed that Iraq lacked the punch to destroy Saudi Arabia's oil fields, as it had threatened.

The upturn in oil prices at midyear was sparked in part by a turnaround in the sluggish demand for petroleum. However, the market was also jittery because of fears that supplies might become tight if the winter turned extremely cold. Analysts also worried about possible shortages of some types of crude oil and fuels if oil output by the Soviet Union continued to decline. By late 1991, Soviet oil exports had fallen to slightly under 2 million bpd—a one-third decline from 1990 production—because of the political and economic upheaval in that country.

But even as crude oil prices rose, some fuel prices fell. In the United States, the pump prices of gasoline fell to as little as $1.13 per gallon in some areas, a historic low after accounting for inflation.

Crude oil production in the United States remained flat during 1991. The United States produced an average of 7.4 million bpd during the year, about the same as in 1990. Crude oil imports fell, averaging 5.8 million bpd during the first 10 months of 1991, compared with 5.96 million during the same period in 1990, but were rising slightly again toward year end.

Domestic natural gas production rose slightly in 1991. The United States produced 13.084 trillion cubic feet (373.8 billion cubic meters) of gas during the first nine months of 1991, compared with 13.072 trillion cubic feet (373.5 billion cubic meters) in 1990. About 1.195 trillion cubic feet (34.1 billion cubic meters) was imported during the period, up from the 1.095 trillion cubic feet (31.3 billion cubic meters) imported in 1990.

Natural gas prices plummeted in 1991 because of excess supplies. Some producers were charging only about $1 per 1,000 cubic feet before the approach of winter brought higher prices. That was the lowest price for natural gas in the field since the late 1970's and contributed to a major slump in U.S. drilling. By late 1991, only about 800 U.S. drilling rigs were working, compared with as many as 4,500 in late 1981.

James Tanner

In *World Book,* see **Gas; Gasoline; Petroleum.**

Philadelphia. On Nov. 5, 1991, Edward G. Rendell, a former district attorney, was elected mayor of Philadelphia. Rendell, a Democrat, won in a 2 to 1 landslide. One of his major pledges was to return Philadelphia, which had been reeling from budgetary woes in recent years, to a state of financial health.

The mayoral race had taken an unexpected turn on July 16, 1991, with the death of the Republican nominee, Frank L. Rizzo. Rizzo, 70, a former Philadelphia mayor (1971-1979), died of a heart attack at his downtown campaign headquarters. After Rizzo's death, the city's Republican leaders chose Joseph M. Egan, a developer and former deputy director of commerce for the city as the party's candidate to oppose Rendell. The incumbent mayor, Democrat W. Wilson Goode, was completing his second four-year term in 1991 and was not eligible for reelection.

The city's political scene was further disrupted during the year by the loss of two prominent Pennsylvania members of Congress: Republican Senator John H. Heinz III, who died in a plane crash, and Democratic Representative William H. (Bill) Gray III, who resigned to become the United Negro College Fund's president.

Heinz died on April 4 when his private plane collided with a helicopter just outside Philadelphia. The crash triggered a fiery explosion that rained debris over an elementary school playground. The two pilots of Heinz's plane, the two pilots of the helicopter, and two first-grade girls on the ground were also killed.

A blaze at the One Meridian Plaza office building on February 23 and 24—the worst high-rise fire in Philadelphia history—killed three fire fighters.

Heinz, heir to the H. J. Heinz food company fortune, first won election to the Senate in 1976. He was considered the most popular politician in Pennsylvania at the time of his death.

Congressman Gray resigned from the House of Representatives on September 11. He was the third-ranking Democrat in the House, the highest-ranking black member of Congress, and one of the most influential figures in Philadelphia.

City financial crunch. After seven months of negotiations between the cash-starved city and Pennsylvania government officials, the state on June 5 established a board to monitor the city's treasury. The board announced plans to sell millions of dollars in bonds on the city's behalf. The city needed the backing of the board to help close a deficit of about $210-million. Additional money will come from receipts of a 1 per cent city sales tax that took effect in September 1991. The tax is charged in addition to the state's 6 per cent sales tax.

Skyscraper fire. Three fire fighters were killed and 17 injured on February 23 and 24 in the worst skyscraper fire in the city's history. Investigators reported that the fire started when oil-soaked rags, left behind by a cleaning crew on the 22nd floor of the 38-story One Meridian Plaza office building, ignited by spontaneous combustion. About 200 fire fighters from 35 stations fought the blaze, which raged for almost 19 hours before being brought under control.

The three fire fighters who died had radioed for

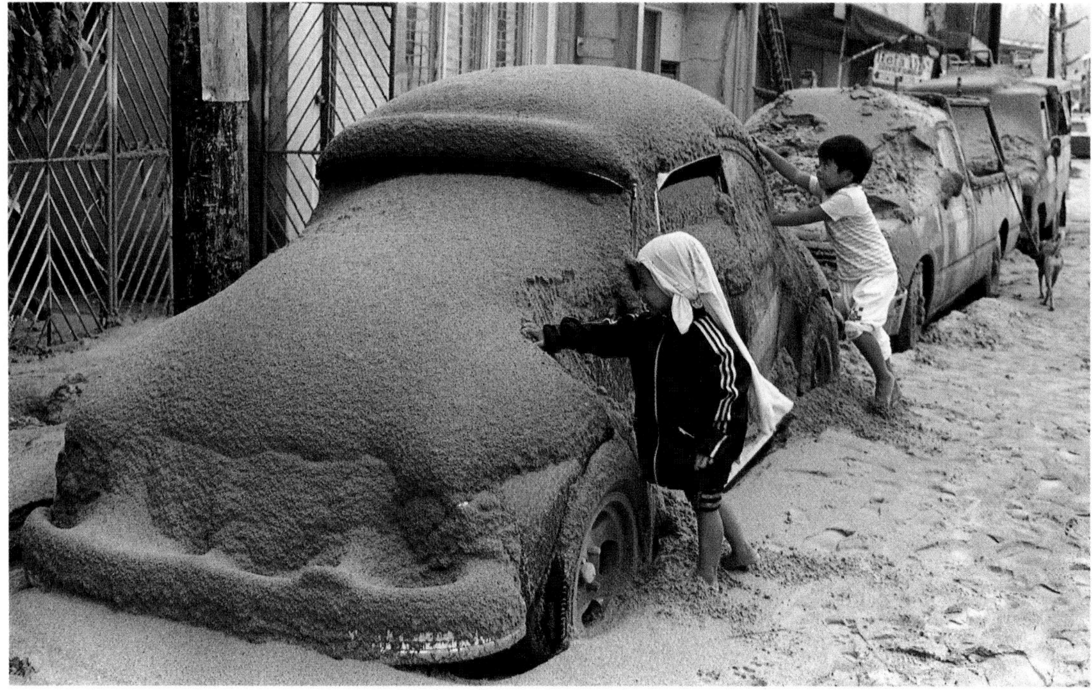

Filipino children scrape at a blanket of ash covering a car on the island of Luzon after Mount Pinatubo erupted in June, devastating a wide area.

help about midnight on Saturday, saying their portable air supply was running out. When a rescue team reached the men on the 28th floor, they were already dead. None of the building's major safety systems—including the pipelines for upper-floor hoses—worked during the blaze.

Roads around the building were closed until June, when crews finished work to certify that the building was still structurally intact. The building sat vacant at year's end while the owners debated whether to restore or demolish it.

Ballet saves itself. The board of the Pennsylvania Ballet, the city's major dance company, announced on March 11 that the 27-year-old troupe would fold for financial reasons. The board said the company was facing a large deficit and did not have the $2.5 million needed to finish the 1991 performance season, which normally runs through July, or a commissioned work for the Kennedy Center in Washington, D.C.

Christopher d'Amboise, the ballet's artistic director, immediately launched a campaign to save the ballet and, within two weeks, the troupe had collected $1.2-million. Much of the money was donated during a scheduled program that the dancers, musicians, and technical staff staged without pay. The ballet began its new season in October on a sound financial footing after securing matching grants for the money it had collected. Howard S. Shapiro

See also **City; Dance.** In ***World Book,*** see **Philadelphia.**

Philippines. Flash floods on Nov. 5, 1991, left about 6,000 people dead on the central Philippine islands of Leyte and Negros (see **Disasters**). A less deadly disaster but one with more repercussions occurred in June, when Mount Pinatubo, a volcano 55 miles (89 kilometers) northwest of the capital, Manila, erupted.

The volcanic eruption initially caused about 300 deaths, devastated a wide area, set back the economy, and affected relations with the United States. On June 12, the volcano, dormant for 600 years, began blasting ash high into the air and sending lava down its slopes. Areas up to 12 miles (19 kilometers) from the crater were buried under several feet of ash. As the eruptions subsided in July, officials said that 108,000 homes had been destroyed or damaged. Nearly 1.2 million people were affected, with about 650,000 losing their livelihoods. By November, the death toll had risen to more than 700 due to continuing slides of volcanic mud and other debris. Still other Filipinos died after reaching refugee camps.

President Corazon C. Aquino appealed for foreign aid to repair the damages and for foreign jobs to help displaced workers. The economy had been in trouble before the eruption, however. The economic growth rate in 1991 was less than 1 per cent and the unemployment rate was 15.1 per cent.

U.S. bases dispute. The economy also faced a loss of some 80,000 jobs and up to $1 billion of income per year because of the closure of United States military facilities. In early June, the Philippines had asked the United States to pay $825 million a year in rent for the continued use of the facilities for seven years. The United States offered $360 million a year for 10 to 12 years, supplemented by military personnel spending money at local businesses.

Then, the eruption of Mount Pinatubo threatened the two most important U.S. bases. Clark Air Base, the key U.S. air facility in the western Pacific, was buried under ash from the volcano 10 miles (16 kilometers) away. The United States decided to abandon the base as unusable, though officials wanted to keep Subic Bay Naval Station, the largest U.S. naval base abroad, 25 miles (40 kilometers) southwest of Pinatubo.

The two nations signed a treaty on August 27 to extend U.S. use of Subic Bay for at least 10 years for a rental payment of at least $203 million a year. The United States also promised trade and economic benefits that, with the rent, could total $3.5 billion over the decade. But nationalists in the Philippine Senate argued that the Philippines, a former U.S. possession, could not be truly independent until every U.S. base was gone. On September 16, the Philippine Senate voted 12 to 11 to reject the treaty.

With public opinion polls showing strong support for a continued American presence, Aquino used the threat of a public vote on the treaty to negotiate a compromise with senators on October 2. The compromise gave the United States three years to leave Subic Bay, without having to pay rent. Some observers speculated that this would enable officials to reopen the issue after national elections in May 1992, when different senators might accept a treaty.

Election preparations heated up as Aquino repeated her refusal to seek another presidential term. The nation's largest political party chose Ramon Mitra, speaker of the lower house of parliament, as its presidential candidate for the May 1992 voting. Marcelo Fernan resigned as chief justice and also sought the presidency, and others considered entering the race.

Rebels arrested. On February 6, the police arrested two leaders of two rebel military groups that had staged unsuccessful coup attempts. Police also captured the intelligence and communications chiefs of the Communist guerrillas' New People's Army (NPA) in July. On August 5, they caught the NPA's military commander, Romulo Kintanar, and his wife when the two went to a hospital seeking treatment after having had cosmetic surgery to disguise their identities.

Imelda Marcos returns. Aquino allowed Imelda Marcos, the widow of former president Ferdinand E. Marcos, to return from exile on November 4 but refused to let her bring her husband's body home for burial. Imelda Marcos was charged with illegal possession of government money. She pleaded not guilty in December. Henry S. Bradsher

See also **Asia** (Facts in brief table). In ***World Book,*** see **Philippines.**

Imelda Marcos speaks to well-wishers in Manila on November 4, when she returned to the Philippines after almost six years in exile.

Physics. One of chemistry's most fascinating molecules, a carbon molecule in the shape of a soccer ball, became a plaything for physicists in April 1991. At that time, a team of researchers at AT&T Bell Laboratories announced that the molecules, popularly known as buckyballs, can be made *superconducting* (able to conduct electricity without resistance).

The structure of buckyballs. In a buckyball, 60 carbon atoms are arranged at the corners of a 32-sided solid consisting of 20 hexagons and 12 pentagons. These 60-atom carbon molecules are formally known as *buckminsterfullerenes* because they resemble the geodesic domes popularized by the architect R. Buckminster Fuller.

Each of the carbon atoms in a buckyball is linked to three neighboring atoms. But because carbon atoms form four chemical bonds, one of the links is a double bond. This extra bond can easily attach itself to an atom of another element, providing a framework on which to build additional, potentially useful molecules. Researchers have suggested, for example, that a buckyball holding a hard outer shell of fluorine atoms would act as a sort of miniature ball bearing and thus make a superb lubricant.

Buckyball conductors. When buckyballs are packed to form crystals, space remains between the molecules—just as space is left when any round objects are stacked. Normally, these crystals conduct electricity poorly: All the electrons are tightly bound to the carbon atoms, unable to move along and carry an electric charge. But by adding potassium atoms—which have a single, loosely bound outer electron—the Bell researchers produced a good conductor. The potassium atoms slipped into the empty spaces, leaving their outer electrons free to conduct electricity.

The researchers then tried cooling the buckyball-potassium compound. At -427 °F. (-255 °C), the crystals lost all electrical resistance and became superconductors. Whether this new material offers any practical advantages over other superconductors remained to be seen. But the discovery again showed that superconductivity can occur in a wide variety of materials.

A heavy neutrino? No subatomic particle has posed more scientific mysteries than the elusive neutrino, which comes as close to nothing as a particle can get. There are three varieties of neutrino, and all interact so feebly with matter that they can pass right through Earth with only a small chance of being absorbed or deflected. Neutrinos, however, play a crucial role in radioactivity on Earth and in the nuclear reactions that power the sun and other stars.

Physicists have never been able to show that neutrinos had any mass. But in 1991, four new experiments reported evidence that about 1 per cent of the neutrinos released in a common form of radioactivity called *beta decay* have a mass about $\frac{1}{30}$ the mass of an electron. These experiments support a controversial result first observed by physicist John Simpson at the University of Guelph in Canada in 1985.

In beta decay, energy is released in the form of an electron and a neutrino. But only the electron can be easily observed and its energy measured. The rest of the energy is assumed to go to the neutrino. Simpson's team observed that the number of electrons emitted suddenly dropped by about 1 per cent, with an energy just below the highest possible electron energy. The missing electrons, Simpson believes, had to give up this much energy to the mass of the neutrino.

One of the four confirming experiments was a new measurement by Simpson's team, but the others were performed in Great Britain, California, and Yugoslavia. A fifth experiment at the California Institute of Technology (Caltech) in Pasadena failed to observe the effect. The final verdict was not yet in, however. The Caltech experiment, as well as five others performed soon after Simpson's 1985 experiment, measured the electron energy with a device called a *magnetic spectrometer* and failed to confirm his result. All the confirming experiments used purely electronic devices. It is possible that electronic devices somehow produce the effect or that magnetic devices mask it.

The reported mass was much higher than theoretical physicists expected. Predictions for the mass of neutrinos range from a thousand times smaller than the measured value to a million times smaller. So, if upheld, Simpson's discovery will have an impact that far outweighs the neutrino. Robert H. March

In ***World Book,*** see **Neutrino; Physics.**

Poetry. The most important book of American poetry to appear in 1991 was John Ashbery's *Flow Chart.* In the opinion of many readers, Ashbery is America's greatest living poet. For others, his poetry is distressingly obscure and difficult. Yet even Ashbery's most devoted fans must have been baffled by parts of *Flow Chart,* a long poem about its own making, interlacing elements from the poet's life, travels, and reflections on art. On every page, however, there was language that was both enchanting and mysterious.

Vastly different from Ashbery's abstract work was Philip Levine's *What Work Is,* his latest set of conversational poems about life in the gritty, assembly-line Detroit of his youth. The opening lines of the title poem are typical of the direct, plain-spoken flavor of Levine's book: "We stand in the rain in a long line waiting at Ford Highland Park. For work." A similarly urgent social conscience could be found in Jorie Graham's *Region of Unlikeness,* a series of meandering poems about the burdens of history.

Dark poetry and light. Death is an important theme in the poetry of William Bronk, as the titles of his latest collections indicate: *Death Is the Place, Life Supports,* and *Living Instead.* His short meditations resemble Japanese haikus. "Boiled Down," reads in its entirety: "It's not about us/It's what we're about."

Allen Grossman's *The Ether Dome: And Other Poems,* is a collection of visionary, funny, and oratorical pieces. One typically witty poem begins, "And the sun—that clumsy arsonist—has fled/The burning factories of the dawn (a double agent with an absolute device,/Ambiguous instructions and a suspicious limp)/Who was at noon, according to police reports, far to the south."

In *Becoming Light: Poems, New and Selected,* Erica Jong also offered a collection of witty, often satiric poems. Although best known for her novels on women and sex, Jong started out as a poet. This volume collects all of her best verse, much of it similar in subject matter to that of Jong's novels. The poem "Ritratto" opens in a characteristically frank and ironic way: "He was a two-bit Petrarchist who lounged/Near the Uffizi in the ochre afternoons/Surveying the girls."

In *Dark Verses and Light,* Tom Disch turns even his most disturbing poems into marvels of wit and invention. Similarly, *The Burnt Pages,* by the British-born poet John Ash, dazzles with its wonderful imaginings, as in "The Ungrateful Citizens," where the poet leans back in his desk chair and daydreams that he is in Naples. Perhaps the most delightful book of the year was *More Opposites,* Richard Wilbur's playful and ingenious collection of light verse.

Other books of poetry published in 1991 included Linda Pastan's largely autobiographical *Heroes in Disguise;* Andrew Hudgin's dark *The Never-Ending;* Mary Kinzie's wide-ranging *Autumn Eros;* Ai's *Fate;* Norman Dubie's *Radio Sky;* Eric Pankey's *Apocrypha;* Daniel Halpern's wistful *Foreign Neon;* and Cynthia Macdonald's energetic *Living Wills.*

Controversy. In May, businessman and poet Dana Gioia contributed an argumentative essay to the *Atlantic Monthly* magazine that stirred up controversy among poets and critics around the United States. Gioia criticized his contemporaries for their academic interests, writing-program sensibilities, and self-absorbed poetry. Poets around the United States sent in a great number of letters to the *Atlantic* to counter Gioia's claims. A collection of Gioia's own poetry, The *Gods of Winter,* also appeared in 1991. It contained the extremely affecting "Planting a Sequoia," about the death of Gioia's young son.

Anthologies. The most comprehensive survey of emerging poets published in 1991 was the hefty anthology *New American Poets of the '90s,* edited by Jack Myers and Roger Weingarten. The finest guide to the year in poetry was *The Best American Poetry, 1991,* the latest installment in an annual series under the general direction of David Lehman, with a different guest editor each year. The guest editor for 1991 was Mark Strand, who also retired as poet laureate of the United States.

Poet laureate. A naturalized Russian émigré, Joseph Brodsky, was named the new poet laureate of the United States on May 10, 1991. One of Brodsky's first acts in office was to attend a memorial reading for the beloved former laureate Howard Nemerov, who died in 1991 of cancer. Michael Dirda

In *World Book,* see **Poetry**.

Joseph Brodsky, a Soviet-born poet who won the Nobel Prize for literature in 1987, was named the fifth poet laureate of the United States in 1991.

Poland had a difficult year in 1991. The living standards of many Poles continued to slide and political divisions splintered the Solidarity movement, which had toppled the Communist government in 1989.

Parliamentary elections. In elections held on Oct. 27, 1991, there was low voter turnout, and no party came close to achieving a majority. In all, 29 parties won seats in the 460-member *Sejm* (lower house of parliament). The Democratic Union, a Solidarity splinter party, received the most votes to take 62 seats in the Sejm, only 2 seats more than the Alliance of the Democratic Left—the renamed Communist Party.

Poland's President Lech Walesa had earlier sought to change the election laws to prevent such a fragmented parliament. But the Sejm, then still dominated by Communists, rejected his proposals. When no clear winner emerged from the October election, Walesa offered to fill the position of prime minister himself. But his offer was coolly received as the Democratic Union tried to form a coalition.

Political tension had increased during the year between the parliament and the trade unions (including Solidarity) on the one hand and Walesa, who seemed increasingly dictatorial, on the other. Walesa, Solidarity's founder, often came into conflict with his former associates. In May, Solidarity staged a national protest day against government actions to limit pay hikes without placing similar curbs on prices. Political uncertainty mounted in September when Walesa

Poland's President Lech Walesa greets Pope John Paul II in June, on the pope's first visit to his native Poland since the fall of its Communist government.

sought special powers to bypass parliament and enact economic laws by decree.

Recession and industrial unrest threatened government efforts to integrate Poland with Western market economies. By late summer, almost 2 million people were unemployed. Although shops were better stocked with basic goods and luxuries, few people could afford them. To many Poles, the "shock therapy" designed to move Poland rapidly toward a market economy seemed to have benefited only a handful of entrepreneurs while hardship prevailed for the rest.

Foreign aid. In February, the International Monetary Fund, a United Nations agency, approved a $2-billion loan for Poland. In March, the United States and other creditors waived part of Poland's foreign debt. But Poland lagged behind neighboring Hungary and Czechoslovakia in securing foreign investment. The situation improved in June, however, after the government announced plans to sell a fourth of Poland's state-owned industries, involving some 400 firms. Through the distribution of vouchers, every adult citizen was to receive a share. During the year, Walesa repeatedly criticized western European countries and the United States for adopting a "wait and see" attitude toward Poland and for not making their markets more accessible to Polish exports. Eric Bourne

See also **Europe** (Facts in brief table). In ***World Book,*** see **Poland.**

Pollution. See **Environmental pollution.**

Popular music. A new method for ranking top-selling country and popular music albums was used for the first time in charts appearing in the May 25, 1991, issue of *Billboard,* a major recording industry magazine. The chart rankings were based on actual retail store sales using sales data obtained directly from cash registers via computerized bar-code scanners. The new system reportedly provides greater speed and accuracy in ranking the most popular music releases. Previously, chart positions were determined by telephone or fax reports of best-selling titles from a cross-section of record retailers across the United States. But this process was not based on actual sales counts, and it was open to honest mistakes as well as record company manipulation.

The new system made a striking impact. Many new albums reached the number-one spot in the first week of release. Some record companies complained that the system used an inadequate sampling of retail outlets, because chain music stores in malls were heavily represented. But *Billboard* said that eventually more stores and music departments will be added to the system, giving greater representation to smaller independent stores. These stores are more likely to stock recordings by new and developing artists that are not often carried in depth by the big retail chains and department stores.

Responding to the Persian Gulf War, rock musicians Yoko Ono, Sean Lennon, and Lenny Kravitz adapted John Lennon's antiwar song "Give Peace a Chance." The song, recorded by a number of artists listed as the Peace Choir, was released on January 15, the United Nations' deadline for Iraq to pull out from Kuwait. On February 10 in Los Angeles, nearly 100 celebrities recorded "Voices That Care" to express support for allied troops. Proceeds from the recording went to the American Red Cross Gulf Crisis Fund and United Service Organizations.

Concert casualties. Three teen-age fans were crushed to death on January 18 during an AC/DC concert at the Salt Palace arena in Salt Lake City, Utah. The crowd had surged forward toward the stage as the concert began, trampling and suffocating the young fans. Subsequently, the company that managed the arena suspended *festival seating,* a practice of either removing chairs from the front of a concert facility so that fans can stand near the stage or making the area unreserved seating.

On July 2, 60 people were injured during an hour-long melee at a Guns N' Roses concert at Riverport Amphitheater in a suburb of St. Louis, Mo. Violence began after lead singer Axl Rose dived off the stage to confront a fan with a camera. After security guards lifted Rose back onto the stage, he stomped off, and the fans began ripping out seats and damaging the stage and sound equipment. Damage to the theater was estimated at $200,000.

Recession. Music retailers blamed economic recession and few blockbuster hits for declining business in

A crowd estimated at 750,000 people hear Paul Simon perform a nationally televised free concert in New York City's Central Park on August 15.

1991. According to the Recording Industry Association of America, a trade group, shipments of prerecorded music and music videos dropped 11 per cent during the first six months of 1991 over the same period in 1990—from 424 million units to 377 million units.

Million-dollar deals. Singer Michael Jackson signed an unprecedented multimedia partnership with Sony Software Corporation in March 1991 that was valued in potential sales from music, films, and entertainment software at $1 billion. His sister Janet Jackson that same month signed an album contract said to be worth over $50 million. Mötley Crüe and Aerosmith signed album deals for $35 million and $24 million, respectively.

Rock music sales rose in the last half of 1991. Part of the resurgence was due to two albums by Guns N' Roses—*Use Your Illusion I* and *Use Your Illusion II.* The albums, released simultaneously at midnight on September 17 in stores across the United States, sold an estimated 1.5 million copies during the first week. The albums also made history by debuting at the top two positions of *Billboard*'s 200 Top Albums chart for the week ending September 22.

Other rock groups showing strong sales in 1991 were Skid Row, Metallica, Van Halen, Queensryche, Extreme, R.E.M., U2, Nirvana, and Firehouse. Strong solo rockers included Tom Petty, Bonnie Raitt, Bob Seger, John Cougar Mellencamp, Prince, and Bryan Adams, whose huge hit "(Everything I Do) I Do It For You" topped the singles charts for eight weeks and sold more than 3 million copies.

Concerts. "The Simple Truth," a charity concert to benefit Kurdish refugees, played to a sellout crowd at London's Wembley Arena on May 12. The concert combined live performances at the arena with satellite telecasts from concert halls in Europe, Japan, and the United States. An estimated 300 million viewers watched the five-hour concert starring Rod Stewart, Sting, and Sinéad O'Connor, among others. Viewers were asked to donate to the International Committee of the Red Cross to aid Iraq's Kurdish refugees.

In New York City's Central Park, Paul Simon performed a nationally televised free concert on August 15 before a crowd estimated at nearly 750,000. And at Moscow's Tushino Airfield on September 28, "Monsters of Rock," a free concert, drew from 150,000 to more than 500,000, depending on the estimate, to hear AC/DC, Metallica, the Black Crowes, and Pantera. On November 3, the Grateful Dead and Santana, among others, performed before a crowd of 300,000 at San Francisco's Golden Gate Park in memory of concert promoter William Graham, who died in a helicopter crash on October 25.

Boxed compact disc sets released in 1991 honored many of the most important names in popular music. The largest set contained nine discs, *The Complete Stax/Volt Singles, 1959-1968,* which included all the classic rhythm and blues hits by Otis Redding; Sam

Grammy Award winners in 1991

Record of the Year, "Another Day in Paradise," Phil Collins.

Album of the Year, *Back on the Block,* Quincy Jones.

Song of the Year, "From a Distance," Julie Gold.

New Artist, Mariah Carey.

Pop Vocal Performance, Female, "Vision of Love," Mariah Carey.

Pop Vocal Performance, Male, "Oh Pretty Woman," Roy Orbison.

Pop Performance by a Duo or Group with Vocal, "All My Life," Linda Ronstadt with Aaron Neville.

Pop Instrumental Performance, "Twin Peaks Theme," Angelo Badalamenti.

Rock Vocal Performance, Female, "Black Velvet," Alannah Myles.

Rock Vocal Performance, Male, "Bad Love," Eric Clapton.

Rock Performance by a Duo or Group with Vocal, "Janie's Got a Gun," Aerosmith.

Rock Instrumental Performance, "D-FW," Vaughan Brothers.

Hard Rock Performance, *Time's Up,* Living Colour.

Metal Performance, "Stone Cold Crazy," Metallica.

Alternative Music Performance, *I Do Not Want What I Haven't Got,* Sinéad O'Connor.

Rhythm-and-Blues Vocal Performance, Female, *Compositions,* Anita Baker.

Rhythm-and-Blues Vocal Performance, Male, "Here and Now," Luther Vandross.

Rhythm-and-Blues Performance by a Duo or Group with Vocal, "I'll Be Good to You," Ray Charles and Chaka Khan.

Rhythm-and-Blues Song, "U Can't Touch This," James Miller and M. C. Hammer.

Rap Solo Performance, "U Can't Touch This," M. C. Hammer.

Rap Performance by a Duo or Group, "Back on the Block," Ice-T, Melle Mel, Big Daddy Kane, and Kool Moe Dee.

New-Age Performance, *Mark Isham,* Mark Isham.

Jazz Fusion Performance, *Birdland,* Quincy Jones.

Jazz Vocal Performance, Female, "All That Jazz," Ella Fitzgerald.

Jazz Vocal Performance, Male, *We Are in Love,* Harry Connick, Jr.

Jazz Instrumental Performance, Soloist, *The Legendary Oscar Peterson Trio Live at the Blue Note,* Oscar Peterson.

Jazz Instrumental Performance, Group, *The Legendary Oscar Peterson Trio Live at the Blue Note,* Oscar Peterson Trio.

Jazz Instrumental Performance, Big Band, "Basie's Bag," Count Basie Orchestra.

Country Vocal Performance, Female, "Where've You Been," Kathy Mattea.

Country Vocal Performance, Male, "When I Call Your Name," Vince Gill.

Country Performance by a Duo or Group with Vocal, *Pickin' on Nashville,* Kentucky Headhunters.

Country Vocal Collaboration, "Poor Boy Blues," Chet Atkins and Mark Knopfler.

Country Instrumental Performance, "So Soft, Your Goodbye," Chet Atkins and Mark Knopfler.

Bluegrass Recording, "I've Got That Old Feeling," Alison Krauss.

Country Song, "Where've You Been," Jon Vezner and Don Henry.

Music Video, Short Form, "Opposites Attract," Paula Abdul.

Music Video, Long Form, "Please Hammer Don't Hurt 'Em, the Movie," M. C. Hammer.

& Dave; and Booker T. & The MGs. Other popular music sets featured songs of Barbra Streisand; James Brown; Crosby, Stills & Nash; Patsy Cline; The Monkees; Tony Bennett; Billie Holiday; Ray Charles; Bob Dylan; and Yes. A four-disc set, *Phil Spector Back to Mono (1958-1969),* featured the output of Phil Spector, one of rock music's most significant producers.

Country music continued to climb in popularity, led by Garth Brooks, whose third album, *Ropin' the Wind,* was the first country album ever to debut at number one. His music video "The Thunder Rolls" was banned on two country video stations for its adulterous plot and violent ending. Holly Dunn pulled her single and video "Maybe I Mean Yes" from playlists as a result of criticism that the song encouraged date rape. New artists Mike Reid, Diamond Rio, and Trisha Yearwood all enjoyed chart-topping debut singles. Mother-daughter duo The Judds quit performing as a team because of mother Naomi Judd's chronic hepatitis. Willie Nelson issued *Who'll Buy My Memories? The IRS Tapes* as a means of paying off a big tax debt.

Tragically, seven members of Reba McEntire's band were killed on March 16, when their private plane crashed in California near the Mexican border. Her road manager and two pilots were also killed.

Rap. M. C. Hammer changed his name to Hammer in 1991. Vanilla Ice, Ice Cube, and Ice-T each had motion picture roles in 1991. Controversial rap groups N.W.A and Public Enemy had top-selling albums. The popularity of Jamaican star Shabba Ranks represented the inroads reggae-rap has made in the United States.

Mainstream artists. Mariah Carey and Paula Abdul followed up their hugely successful debut albums with successful second albums. in 1991. Natalie Cole's album *Unforgettable* was a tribute to her father Nat (King) Cole's legacy. The album sold more than 3 million copies. Rhythm-and-blues artist Luther Vandross solidified his crossover to the pop charts with his album *Power of Love.* Wilson Phillips, Roxette, and Michael Bolton stayed front-runners among established artists. Christian artist Amy Grant had a number-one secular hit with "Baby Baby."

Dance music. C&C Music Factory stepped over the boundaries between rock and dance with the hit album *Gonna Make You Sweat.* "Gypsy Woman," Crystal Waters' song about a homeless person, was another big dance crossover. Madonna's 1991 *Truth or Dare* was a full-length documentary of her "Blond Ambition" tour of 1990.

Jazz. New York City's Lincoln Center for the Performing Arts instituted a jazz department in 1991 headed by trumpeter Wynton Marsalis. Dutch jazz saxophonist Candy Dulfer had a pop debut hit single and album. Harry Connick, Jr., continued his jazz album chart-topping success with the big band sound in *Blue Light, Red Light.* Jim Bessman

See also **Popular music,** Special Report: **The Flap over Rap.** In ***World Book,*** see **Country music; Jazz; Popular music.**

The Flap over Rap

By Alan Light

While debates about the controversial and uncensored lyrics of some rappers continue to flare up, the music is becoming more popular than ever.

Few forms of entertainment have aroused such passion and engendered such controversy as rap music. Critics have frequently charged that the music encourages violence, racism, and hatred of women. Some also maintain that rap isn't music at all, since the vocals are not sung and the accompaniment usually is not played on musical instruments. On the other hand, supporters of rap believe that it is the most vital and significant popular music being produced today. Certainly, it is the music that matters most to millions of young listeners, while it calls up concern and even alarm in the minds of a great many parents.

The author:
Alan Light writes about rap and rock music for *Rolling Stone* magazine.

Rap may be new to many listeners, but its roots run deep. African story rhymes, bebop rhythms, and street corner rhyming games played by inner city black youth all have a part in making up rap music. The basic rap sound consists of a vocalist or group of vocalists reciting lyrics in the form of simple rhymes. The background sound is provided not by musicians, but by a disk jockey with two or more turntables. Playing sounds from records on these turntables and rapidly switching back and forth between them produces the loud, distinctive background noise that accompanies the vocalist.

Early rappers

People who follow the rap music scene generally agree that rap first appeared in New York City's South Bronx in the late 1970's. Kool Herc, a disk jockey from Jamaica, is most often credited with having created rap's basic sound. Herc would set up two or more turntables and mix several records together, switching back and forth between isolated, propulsive beats.

In the earliest live rap music, vocalists chanted rhymes over this turntable-produced "cutting and scratching." The music became one part of an emerging black American cultural phenomenon called "hip-hop," which included break dancing and graffiti art. Rap proved to be the most lasting of hip-hop's components.

Rap's first hit single, "Rapper's Delight," was made by a group called the Sugar Hill Gang in 1980. Soon rap records from performers such as Kurtis Blow and Grandmaster Flash were being released regularly. Although rap was initially built on turntable manipulations, most of these early recordings featured a live band playing musical figures based on disco beats.

Since its earliest days, rap has been controversial. Rap often speaks directly to and for a young black audience, and just as often the message has been in the form of graphic, some would say obscene, language. The early black male rappers wore outrageous costumes and their lyrics were filled with fantasies and sexual boasting, glorifying urban outlaws.

In 1982, Grandmaster Flash released "The Message," a single containing a harrowing portrayal of inner city despair. This moved rap in the direction of social commentary, as did *Run-D.M.C.*, a rap album by a trio of the same name.

The first rap hits

Public Enemy, *preceding page*, is one of rap's most controversial groups. Their recordings mix radical politics with portraits of black urban life.

Then in the summer of 1986 came the first hit album by a rap group, *Raising Hell*, by Run-D.M.C. It included a remake of the rock group Aerosmith's 1977 hit single, "Walk This Way." Run-D.M.C.'s crisp, aggressive delivery made the song appeal to teen-agers nationwide, and it climbed to number four on the pop music charts. Propelled by the single, the *Raising Hell* album sold 3 million copies. Rap had arrived in middle America.

Rap's place in the mainstream was confirmed in 1987, when the Beastie Boys, three white ex-punk rockers, released *Licensed to Ill*, which sold even more copies than *Raising Hell*. The Beastie Boys album also introduced the new sound of "sampling" to a mass audience. Sampling is the term for new technology that made it possible to replace the old "cutting

Rap branches out

Hammer, *left*, brings rap into the mainstream with his popular recordings and television commercials. Queen Latifah, *above*, is one of several women rappers who responded to rap's frequent sexism with feminist messages and pride.

and scratching" techniques on turntables with the more precise, computerized isolation of sections from records. These bits of music were then reconstructed into new patterns, and sampling rapidly became the dominant way of creating rap's background sound.

During the late 1980's, rap continued to diversify in terms of its performers and its themes, and this increased its appeal to a broader audience. Philadelphia's D.J. Jazzy Jeff and the Fresh Prince brought a lighthearted pop attitude to rap, scoring big with their 1988 smash single "Parents Just Don't Understand." On the other end of the spectrum, Boogie Down Productions, a group from New York City's South Bronx, performed "gangsta rap," which focused on the hard realities of violence and rage in contemporary urban life.

In response to the criticism that rap lyrics were demeaning to women at best and, at worst, encouraged violence against women, there appeared in the late 1980's a wave of black women rappers. Perhaps the most prominent of these was Queen Latifah. Her album *All Hail the Queen* heralded a new era of strong, outspoken female rappers intent upon striking back at rap's frequent tendencies toward *misogyny* (hatred of women) and sexism. Even Boogie Down Productions by 1989 was leading a "Stop the Violence" movement after its disk jockey, Scott LaRock, was shot dead while trying to stop a street fight.

Rap heads in two directions

Ironically, as rap was becoming more mainstream, it also became more controversial. For example, Ice-T, a rapper from Los Angeles, presented in his rhyming lyrics realistic, detailed depictions of gang life. Then, beginning with their album *Yo! Bum Rush the Show* (1987), Public Enemy, rappers from Hempstead, N.Y., began replacing sexual boasting and humor with radical politics. Their second album, *It Takes a Nation of Millions to*

Hold Us Back (1988), remains one of rap's most influential recordings, a blazing amalgam of dense noise, black nationalist sloganeering, and street analysis. In Public Enemy's wake came a number of explicitly political rap groups, many of whom endorsed the black nationalist teachings of the former Black Panthers and Louis Farrakhan, leader of the Nation of Islam.

Controversy and profits

In 1989, a scandal erupted following anti-Semitic remarks made by Public Enemy's "Minister of Information," Professor Griff. The group temporarily disbanded, but reunited shortly thereafter and dismissed Griff. By 1990, controversy had overshadowed the music as a nationwide debate flared up about whether or not it is appropriate for rap musicians to use the uncensored language of the street. There was widespread outrage when the Los Angeles group N.W.A released their *Straight Outta Compton* album. The group claimed that their graphic inner-city portraits were simply reports from the urban front lines. Many of their critics, however, said that the lyrics were glamorizing criminal behavior, hatred of women, and random violence.

Rap's biggest controversy of 1990 centered around the obscenity trial of 2 Live Crew, a Miami rap group, and its album of locker-room sex rhymes called *As Nasty As They Wanna Be.* On June 6, a federal judge in Fort Lauderdale, Fla., ruled that the lyrics were obscene. Many record stores withdrew the album, but Charles Freeman, a Fort Lauderdale record store owner, continued to offer the album and was arrested after selling one. Members of 2 Live Crew were arrested on June 10 for performing songs from the album in a Hollywood, Fla., nightclub. In October, Freeman was found guilty and fined $1,000. A jury acquitted 2 Live Crew, however, reportedly because the evidence, a recording of the performance, was difficult to understand.

In 1991, rap continued to spread from the margins to the mainstream of the popular music world. While some rap performers retained an angry, rebellious image, others gladly accommodated themselves to the more moderate tastes of the mass market. The result was a bewilderingly diverse rap scene, extending from the militant theatrics of Public Enemy to the prime-time rap of Hammer (formerly M. C. Hammer).

Sales of all kinds of rap albums continued to climb throughout 1990 and 1991. Hammer's innocuous dance-rap album *Please Hammer Don't Hurt 'Em* sold 10 million copies. The simple rhymes of white rapper Vanilla Ice sold another 8 million albums. Even the brutal, often misogynistic *Efil4zaggin* by N.W.A in June 1991 entered *Billboard* magazine's pop charts at number two and hit number one the following week. Public Enemy's *Apocalypse 91: The Enemy Strikes Black,* released in September 1991, enjoyed similarly spectacular sales. Given these sales statistics, those who like rap and those who don't can probably agree on one thing: Whether at its most commercially palatable or at its hard-core, outrageous edge—for good or for ill—rap has become a vivid, influential part of contemporary American popular music.

Population. In 1991, the population of the world reached 5.4 billion and was growing faster than ever before, with 250,000 babies being born every day. When the United Nations Fund for Population Activities released these statistics in May, it also reported that estimates of future population growth may have to be revised significantly. Experts had predicted that the population would level off at about 10.2 billion in the year 2075—that is, the birth rate would equal the death rate. But new projections say that the population could reach 10 billion by 2050, and continue to increase for 100 years, peaking at 11.6 billion.

About 95 per cent of population growth occurs in developing countries, where total population has more than doubled since 1950, from 1.7 billion to 4.1-billion. Population growth in these nations has occurred despite a dramatic reduction in births per woman after the 1960's. Since then, the number of women choosing to use birth control has expanded from 10 per cent to 51 per cent.

The population in industrialized nations grew from 832 million in 1950 to 1.2 billion in 1990. In 1991, the Soviet Union, with about 285 million people, ranked third in population behind China, which had more than 1 billion people, and India, with about 844 million people. The United States ranked fourth with 253 million people. Lori Fagan

See also **Census** and **Census Supplement.** In ***World Book,*** see **Population.**

Portugal in 1991 affirmed its commitment to political stability. In January, voters reelected Mário Alberto Soares, a former member of the Portuguese Socialist Party, to a second term as president. (Soares had given up party ties after his 1986 election victory.) In October, the Social Democratic Party led by Prime Minister Aníbal Cavaço Silva won a majority of seats in parliament. It was the second time Cavaço Silva received an *absolute majority*—more than half the votes cast. His first majority, in 1987, had given Portugal its first stable, democratic government in years. A series of unstable coalitions had followed the overthrow of Portugal's military dictatorship in 1974.

Impressive election victories. Soares won reelection in 1991 with an impressive 70.4 per cent of the vote. Because of his cooperation with the Social Democrats, they did not run a candidate against him.

The parliamentary victory of Cavaço Silva's Social Democrats gave them 50.4 per cent of the vote and 132 seats in the 230-member parliament. The main opposition, the Socialist Party, won just under 30 per cent of the vote and claimed 70 seats in parliament. The once-powerful Portuguese Communist Party fared poorly, winning less than 10 per cent of the vote.

Cavaço Silva rode to victory in parliament on the strength of the economy, which has benefited from Portugal's membership in the 12-nation European Community (EC or Common Market). Since joining the EC in 1986, Portugal has expanded its trade with EC members and received considerable EC financial assistance. Such assistance helped Portuguese farmers by raising the prices they received for their products and helped the government rebuild roads and make other needed improvements.

Portugal's economy grew at a rate of nearly 3 per cent in 1991, though the country's economic growth had exceeded 5 per cent in the late 1980's. Portugal's inflation rate, which topped 12 per cent in 1991, remained among the highest in Europe.

After his election, Cavaço Silva pledged to continue selling state-owned companies to private investors and to make the economy more competitive by decreasing government regulation. These actions were intended to strengthen Portugal's economy by the time a single market takes effect within the EC at the end of 1992. As the EC moved toward greater economic integration, Portugal also needed to cut its high budget deficit and support the value of its currency, the escudo, against stronger EC currencies.

The removal of trade barriers within the EC will prevent Portugal from imposing high tariffs or quotas on imports to protect its textile, fishing, and farming industries from competition. Increased competition from Spain and other EC countries could threaten the market for Portuguese exports. Philip Revzin

See also **Europe** (Facts in brief table), Special Report: **The Rocky Road to European Unity.** In ***World Book,*** see **Portugal.**

Postal Service, United States. The Postal Rate Commission recommended on Jan. 4, 1991, that the price of a first-class United States stamp be raised from 25 cents to 29 cents. The U.S. Postal Service's Board of Governors had sought an increase to 30 cents but on January 22 accepted the recommendation of the independent five-member commission. (The 11-member board can set its own rate, but only by a unanimous vote.) The new 29-cent rate—along with other postage hikes—took effect on February 3. The increases were expected to raise Postal Service revenues by an additional $6.2 billion annually.

On July 2, the board reversed its January vote and unanimously rejected the new rate schedule—which nonetheless remained in effect. The board once again asked the commission for a 30-cent first-class rate. Postmaster General Anthony M. Frank told a U.S. Senate subcommittee that the extra penny was needed to help offset an expected $900-million drop in revenue due to the recession.

On October 4, the Postal Rate Commission again turned down the 30-cent rate. It proposed instead a package of other rate hikes, including higher rates for third-class mail, also known as *junk mail,* that would raise the Postal Service's income by $333 million a year. The issue moved back to the Board of Governors, which could accept the commission's proposals or impose the 30-cent rate. On November 5, the board voted to keep the price of a first-class stamp at 29 cents.

Stamp printing. In a drive to cut costs, the Postal Service in 1991 experimented with having some of its stamps printed privately. All stamps were once printed by the Department of the Treasury.

A number of members of Congress were outraged during the year when the Postal Service had some stamps printed in Canada. Collectors fumed about one new stamp that lost its ink when they soaked it off envelopes. An issue honoring author William Saroyan was printed on paper that could not be perforated, so 160 million stamps had to be destroyed. Another 300 million stamps, these honoring Hubert H. Humphrey, were printed with biographical information on the margin of each sheet of stamps that cited inaccurate dates for Humphrey's tenure as Vice President. The stamps were scheduled for the shredder when Frank canceled the destruction order in response to complaints from Congress that reprinting all the stamps would cost $580,000.

New contract for postal workers. On June 12, an arbitration panel in Washington, D.C., approved a four-year labor agreement that granted cost-of-living increases to postal workers. It gave the Postal Service long-sought authority to hire part-time workers.

Frank Cormier and Margot Cormier

In ***World Book,*** see **Post office; Postal Service, United States.**

President of the United States. See **Bush, George H. W.; United States, Government of the.**

Prince Edward Island. Exporters of one of the province's major agricultural products, potatoes, suffered a severe setback when food inspectors found a virus called *PVY-n* on seed potatoes in January 1991. The United States imposed a partial ban on imports of potatoes from the island because the virus, though harmless to humans, can kill tobacco, tomato, and pepper plants. The ban was eased in February, but some 27,000 short tons (25,000 metric tons) of marketable potatoes had to be dumped for compost. The Canadian government compensated the potato growers for their loss. To make sure the virus would be wiped out, the government prohibited the general population from growing potatoes in home gardens during 1991.

The province's Liberal Party government, headed by Premier Joseph A. Ghiz, brought in an austerity budget on April 9, 1991. The plan raised personal income taxes by 2.5 per cent to 59 per cent of the federal income tax rate. Sales taxes for nonprescription drugs also were imposed. The increase made the tax rate one of the highest in Canada. Despite these measures, the Ghiz government won a by-election in April, giving it 30 of the legislature's 32 seats. The Progressive Conservative Party held the remaining two seats. David M. L. Farr

See **Canada,** Special Report: **Canada and Quebec at a Crossroads.** In ***World Book,*** see **Prince Edward Island.**

Prison. The number of inmates in state and federal prisons in the United States reached a record 804,524 by June 1991, according to the U.S. Department of Justice's Bureau of Justice Statistics (BJS). However, the growth from June 1990 to June 1991 was the lowest annual percentage increase since 1984, according to the BJS. The number of women held in U.S. prisons increased by 4.5 per cent to 46,230. The number of incarcerated men grew by 3.9 per cent to 758,294.

Drug crimes. The percentage of inmates held in federal prisons for drug possession or trafficking offenses more than doubled since 1989, according to a 1991 BJS report. And those in federal prisons for drug-related offenses accounts for 53 per cent of the federal prison population—32,614 out of 61,536.

Inmates and AIDS. People infected with the virus that causes AIDS are more likely to be found in prison than in any other United States public institutions except hospitals, the National Commission on AIDS reported on March 28, 1991. Infected inmates account for 2 to 6 per cent of the U.S. prison population. In contrast, some experts estimate that just one-tenth of 1 per cent of the entire U.S. population carries the virus. The commission, however, said there was "negligible transmission" of the disease within prisons.

Alternatives to incarceration. Four out of five Americans favor community correctional programs over prison terms for nonviolent offenders, according to a 1991 survey sponsored by the International

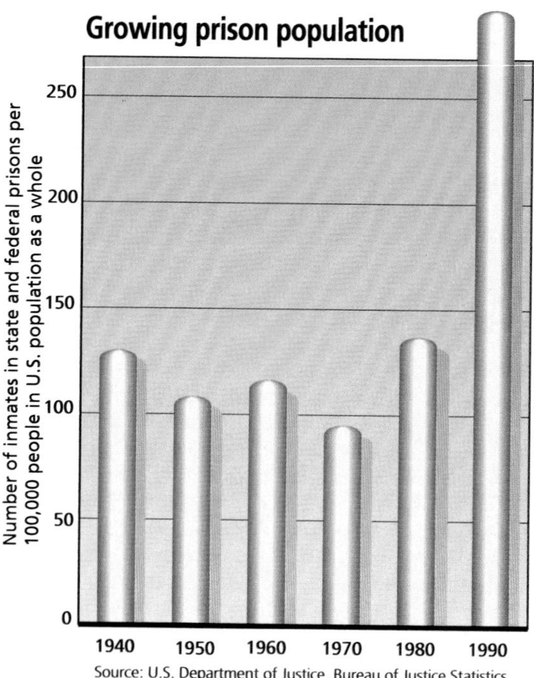

The number of inmates held in state and federal prisons in the United States jumped dramatically in 1990 to an all-time high of 771,243.

Prisoners at the Talladega, Ala., federal prison display their grievances during a 10-day take-over in August that ended when hostages were rescued.

Association of Residential and Community Alternatives. Such programs require offenders to hold a job, perform community service, repay their victims, and receive counseling.

Cuban uprising. On August 21, 121 Cuban prisoners at the Talladega Federal Correctional Institution in Alabama seized 10 hostages and began a 10-day takeover of their cell block. The inmates, 32 of whom were to be deported to Cuba on August 22, demanded an end to U.S. deportations of Cuban prisoners. The inmates were among some 125,000 Cubans who had come to the United States during a massive boatlift in 1980. The 1991 uprising came to an end when federal agents stormed the facility. No one was seriously hurt.

Prison conditions. The Supreme Court of the United States ruled in June 1991 that conditions such as overcrowding and unsanitary and unsafe surroundings do not violate prisoners' constitutional rights unless "deliberate indifference" by prison authorities can be proven. The 5 to 4 decision may make it more difficult for inmates to prove that poor prison conditions constitute cruel and unusual punishment.

Executions. The number of inmates executed in the United States in 1991 totaled 14 as of December 16. All were men. Inmates awaiting execution numbered close to 2,500. Jennifer A. Nichols

See also **Crime; Supreme Court of the United States.** In ***World Book,*** see **Prison.**

Prizes. See **Nobel Prizes; Pulitzer Prizes.**

Protestantism. Highly evangelistic movements of Protestants, mainly from the United States, during 1991 hurried to convert to their faith people in the Soviet Union. This is an area of the world where there are few Protestants. A law passed in the Soviet Union in October 1990 promising freedom of conscience and prohibiting government interference in religious matters had helped revive religious interest among Soviet people. The collapse of Communism in 1991 also enabled Soviet people to practice religion openly. In September, the Russian Bible Society distributed free Bibles in the lobby of the parliament building of the Russian republic, and Soviet television showed delegates rushing to leave the legislative session before it adjourned to tear open boxes of Bibles.

But so hurried and zealous were some of the evangelical movements from the West and from within the Soviet Union that some Soviet citizens complained of being exploited. Tensions between the evangelical Protestants and other religious organizations in the Soviet Union also grew.

An official with the office of the Patriarch of the Russian Orthodox Church in Moscow said in October that he was opposed to the aggressive style of evangelicals, not to their work. He stated that they should be working with the Orthodox, not around them.

Also in October, a spokesperson for the National Council of Churches in New York City said that importing a different Christian religion into the Soviet Union

Wearing a miter, Anglican Bishop George L. Carey enters Canterbury Cathedral in England on April 19 to become the cathedral's 103rd archbishop.

was inappropriate, because Christian churches already existed there.

During a conference in Budapest, Hungary, in September, evangelical leaders from eastern Europe also expressed their concern about "too much evangelism" from the West. Representatives to the conference said that the Orthodox churches in two Soviet republics, Georgia and Russia, opposed evangelical movements, because Orthodoxy was trying to become recognized as the national church in these republics.

The Persian Gulf War divided Protestant denominations from one another and divided members within a sect. Before the war began in January, bishops of the Episcopal and the United Methodist churches and the Evangelical Lutheran Church in America urged negotiations between the United States and Iraq. President George Bush, an Episcopalian, consulted independent Protestant leaders, including evangelist Billy Graham and television pastor Robert Schuller.

Once the air war began and during the brief land war, the majority of Protestants supported U.S. military action against Iraq. After the war was over, Protestant churches again spoke for actions other than massive military approaches to international problems. Thousands of churches held "welcome home" ceremonies for returning troops and offered prayers of thanksgiving for their safety.

Intimate issues. The most intimate aspects of life dominated discussions at the conventions of major Protestant denominations during 1991. The delegates debated issues such as abortion, birth control, gender relations, the family, and homosexuality. The churches were torn between traditionalists, who argued that the Bible had clear and simple answers to these questions, and liberals who wanted to reinterpret theological aspects of these issues in the light of new scientific and biological studies of human beings, modern emphasis on individual freedom, and a "sexual revolution" that brought about relaxed standards of sexual behavior.

Presbyterian convention. Heated debates occurred before and during the June convention of the General Assembly of the Presbyterian Church (U.S.A.) held in Baltimore. A special committee authorized by the Presbyterian Church to study sexual issues wanted the general assembly to authorize a two-year churchwide review of its report, which had been released in February. Instead, the general assembly rejected the 200-page majority report as being a radical breach with the Biblical, Protestant, and Presbyterian pasts.

The report advocated a church policy to receive gays and lesbians as full church members and to open ordination to all qualified Presbyterian candidates regardless of their sexual orientation. Also, celibacy should not be a requirement for ordination to the ministry, the report said. Critics at the general assembly contended that the report provided a license for an "anything goes" way of life.

General assembly delegates adopted a treatise that reaffirmed the traditional position of the Presbyterian Church against sexual relations outside of marriage. A different group, the Theology and Worship Ministry Unit, was authorized to study and report on sexual issues for the next Presbyterian general assembly scheduled for 1992.

Episcopalians, during a July 1991 meeting of the denomination's governing body in Phoenix, debated the issue of whether to ordain homosexuals without demanding that they live celibate lives. A resolution that had been passed in 1979 opposed ordination of gays and lesbians; however, actual decisions in these cases were left to the local bishops. A lesbian who had publicly declared her relationship with another woman was ordained an Episcopal priest in Washington, D.C., in June 1991.

The Episcopal convention in July 1991 passed a resolution that stated, "Physical sexual expression is appropriate only within the lifelong, monogamous 'union of husband and wife.'" But the resolution also stated that the church would try "to reconcile the discontinuity between this teaching and the experience of many members of this body." The Episcopal convention rejected a proposal permitting the ordination of sexually active homosexuals, but it also rejected a proposal to censure bishops who ordained sexually active homosexuals. Bishops and other representatives were commissioned to hold further discussions about issues involving sexuality and prepare a "pastoral teaching" before the next Episcopal convention, which is scheduled to be held in 1994.

A United Methodist Church special committee also took up the issue of homosexuality. After a four-day meeting in August, the committee could not agree on whether homosexual practice is "incompatible with Christian teaching." After three years of work, the committee issued two versions of its report, identical except for a sentence asking members to delete from social policy a condemnation of homosexuality. A majority of committee members endorsed removal of the condemnation, but a minority held to a version asking for retention of the condemnation.

Protestantism

Abortion dilemma. The Evangelical Lutheran Church in America (ELCA) issued its first statement on abortion during the denomination's convention in Orlando, Fla., in summer 1991. The statement said, "The strong Christian presumption is to preserve and protect life. Abortion ought to be an option only of last resort." The statement was not in favor of laws prohibiting abortion. However, it urged ELCA members to continue debating the issue, recognizing that the church was deeply divided over the abortion question. The statement said that language "should neither obscure the moral seriousness of the decision faced by the woman nor hide the moral value of the newly conceived life." A church staff member said that the statement would help form ELCA public positions on abortion, but it was not binding on members' consciences.

Baptist fundamentalists reelected Morris H. Chapman to the presidency of the Southern Baptist Convention during its June convention in Atlanta, Ga. With nearly 15 million members, the convention is the largest Protestant denomination in the United States. Chapman was unopposed in the election. The election marked 12 successive years that fundamentalists have held the post.

Dissident Baptists, mainly moderates, objected to the fundamentalist insistence that the Bible is literally true. About 6,000 moderates, meeting in Atlanta in May, elected John H. Hewett to lead a new organization called the Cooperative Baptist Fellowship. The fellowship will allow members to carry on activities independent of fundamentalist control, without breaking away from the Southern Baptist Convention. Attendees voted to ask local congregations to support the new fellowship.

New archbishop of Canterbury. On April 19, Bishop George L. Carey was installed as archbishop of Canterbury, spiritual head of the Church of England and 70 million Anglicans worldwide. He succeeded Robert A. K. Runcie, who retired.

Denominational survey. The City University of New York Graduate Center in April released the results of a poll it conducted that was reported to be the largest survey ever of religious affiliations in the United States. The survey reported that 86.5 per cent of the 113,000 people contacted called themselves Christian, 1.8 per cent claimed Judaism, 0.5 per cent said they were Muslim, and less than 0.5 per cent said they were Buddhist. However, estimates by Jewish and Islamic organizations put their memberships at higher figures than did the university's survey.

Church membership. The 1991 edition of the *Yearbook of American and Canadian Churches* revealed that church membership in 1989 grew by 1.5 per cent over 1988. The population grew by 0.9 per cent during the same period. Martin E. Marty

See also **Eastern Orthodox Churches; Islam; Judaism; Religion; Roman Catholic Church.** In ***World Book,*** see **Protestantism.**

Psychology.

High levels of psychological stress substantially increase a person's chances of catching a cold, according to a study published in August 1991. The investigation found a link between mental stress and the functioning of the body's immune system, said psychologist Sheldon Cohen of Carnegie-Mellon University in Pittsburgh, Pa.

Cohen's research team asked 420 healthy British volunteers to answer a questionnaire concerning major stressful events experienced in the year before the study; the ability to cope with daily demands; and the frequency of such emotions as depression, anger, and irritation. Using data from the questionnaires, the investigators divided the volunteers into four groups, representing lowest to highest levels of stress. Then, 394 of the volunteers received nasal drops containing one of five cold-causing viruses. The remaining 26 received noninfectious drops containing salt. Nasal-wash samples were examined for the presence of cold viruses. During the following week, 325 virus-exposed people became infected, and 148 of these developed sneezing, watery eyes, and other symptoms of a cold. No one taking salt drops developed cold symptoms.

The volunteers who reported the most psychological stress ran twice the risk of developing cold symptoms and more than five times the risk of becoming infected with a cold virus without actually developing any symptoms. This pattern remained when the researchers considered other influences on immune function, including age, allergies, and diet. Personality traits reported by the volunteers also had no effect on the link between stress and colds.

Adolescent self-esteem. Adolescent girls report much sharper drops in their feelings of self-worth and self-esteem than boys, according to a survey released in January by the American Association of University Women in Washington, D.C. The sharpest decline in self-esteem for both sexes occurred when the young people began junior high. Girls responding to the survey also reported less enthusiasm for mathematics and science, less confidence in academic abilities, and fewer aspirations to professional careers than their male counterparts. The survey polled 2,400 girls and 600 boys, ages 9 years to 16 years, who attend 36 public elementary and high schools in the United States.

White and Hispanic girls reported feeling low self-esteem in a number of areas, including their appearance, confidence, family relationships, and talents. More than half the black girls surveyed reported high levels of self-esteem, apparently because of strong family and community support, survey directors said.

However, another study of 128 youngsters in junior high, published in February and directed by psychologist Barton J. Hirsch of Northwestern University in Evanston, Ill., identified comparable levels of self-esteem in both boys and girls. About two-thirds of the students, who were questioned as they reached sixth, seventh, and eighth grades, displayed strong self-esteem, healthy psychological adjustment, and good school grades. The remaining one-third of the students either suffered from a long history of low self-esteem and poor school achievement or began junior high with strong self-esteem that rapidly plunged to very low levels.

Filling in the blanks. Evidence presented in April suggests that the human brain automatically fills a blind spot in the eye's field of vision with visual information from the area immediately surrounding this spot. Each of our eyes contains a small blind spot, a point on the retina where the optic nerve enters the eye. This area is insensitive to light.

The new findings contradict a long-standing theory that the brain simply ignores visual blind spots. Psychologists Vilayanur S. Ramachandran of the University of California in San Diego and Richard L. Gregory of the University of Bristol in England showed volunteers a computer screen displaying designs with sections that were deleted to imitate blind spots. One test indicated that the brain fills in color and texture information. Volunteers watched a pink background with twinkling black dots and a small gray square with black dots moving horizontally across it. When volunteers focused their eyes just to the right or left of the square, those areas fell within their blind spots. Within seconds, they reported that the surrounding pink replaced the gray. Then, the twinkling dots replaced the moving dots. Bruce Bower

In ***World Book,*** see **Psychology.**

Public health. The American Red Cross on May 19, 1991, announced a $100-million program to overhaul its blood bank system in an effort to improve the safety of its blood supplies. Red Cross officials said there had been incidents in which regional centers distributed tainted blood to hospitals or failed to follow adequate safety precautions. Blood collection centers are required to test for viruses that cause AIDS, hepatitis, and other infectious diseases transmissible through infected blood.

The Red Cross provides half of all blood for transfusions in the United States. The new program requires the temporary, sequential closing of its 53 regional blood centers over a two-year period. At each center, employees will be retrained in new collecting, handling, and testing procedures. Also, each regional blood center will be connected to a new computer network linking the entire Red Cross system. The network will replace 10 different computer systems used in the past. Red Cross officials said that the lack of a single computer system made it difficult to enforce uniform standards and monitor procedures at all the regional centers.

Obesity. Efforts to encourage the U.S. public to maintain proper body weight through exercise and good nutrition have had little effect, according to a study reported in July by the U.S. Centers for Disease Control (CDC) in Atlanta, Ga. The CDC found that Americans are just as likely to be obese in 1991 as they were in the early 1960's. (The criterion for clinical obesity is being 20 per cent heavier than desired weight appropriate for the person's age, sex, and height.)

The study found that about 24 per cent of American men and 27 per cent of American women were significantly overweight and that obesity continues to be an especially serious problem among poor people and minority groups. For example, about 25 per cent of white women in the study were obese compared with 44 per cent of black women. Obesity is a risk factor for heart disease, diabetes, and certain forms of cancer.

Hepatitis B vaccine. A CDC advisory panel in March 1991 recommended adding hepatitis B to the list of vaccines routinely administered to children in the United States. The list, known as the standard pediatric immunization schedule, now includes immunization against diphtheria, tetanus, pertussis, rubella, rubeola, mumps, and polio. Hepatitis B is an increasingly common viral disease of the liver. The CDC estimates that about 200,000 to 300,000 cases occur each year in the United States, an increase of about 30 per cent since 1979. Hepatitis B is spread by infected blood and by contact through sexual intercourse and can lead to serious liver disorders, including liver cancer.

Rubella cases rising. In February 1991, the CDC reported an increase in German measles (rubella) and in birth defects related to the viral disease. German measles is a mild childhood disease that usually causes only a rash, joint aches, and low fever. But women who catch rubella early in pregnancy, risk miscarriage or bearing a child with serious birth defects, collectively known as congenital rubella syndrome (CRS). CRS may cause deafness, heart malformation, impaired vision, or mental retardation. The CDC reported there were 1,093 cases of rubella in 1990, the most since 1982, and 11 confirmed cases of CRS, the most since 1986. The number of cases was still far below the millions reported before a measles vaccine was developed in the late 1960's. Health officials recommended that physicians and clinics increase their emphasis on immunization.

Cholera epidemic. At least 275,000 people in Peru were infected with cholera and 2,664 Peruvians died of the disease during the first 11 months of 1991, the Pan American Health Organization reported in November. Cholera is a contagious intestinal disease that causes severe diarrhea and vomiting. Without treatment, it can kill a person in as few as 10 hours. Cholera is spread by contaminated water and food.

The epidemic, the first in South America since 1895, began in Peru in January, and in February, it spread northward to neighboring Ecuador, striking nearly 32,000 people and killing 500, according to the CDC report. In March, cholera moved still farther north to Colombia, infecting 4,300 people and killing 76, the CDC said. Michael Woods

See also **AIDS.** In ***World Book,*** see **German measles; Public health.**

Puerto Rico. On Dec. 8, 1991, Puerto Ricans defeated by a 55 to 45 per cent margin a referendum that was supported by those who would like to see the island continue as a commonwealth of the United States in any future vote on Puerto Rico's political status. The vote was seen as a setback for Puerto Rican Governor Rafael Hernández Colón, leader of the incumbent Popular Democratic Party, who campaigned vigorously for the measure's passage. The vote was seen a victory for the New Progressive Party, which favors U.S. statehood for Puerto Rico.

The vote, though not legally binding, capped a year in which the question of whether Puerto Rico would become a U.S. state topped the island's political agenda. On February 27, a U.S. Senate committee failed to pass a measure that would have allowed Puerto Ricans to vote as early as 1992 on three alternatives for the island's political status: statehood, independence, or a continuation of commonwealth status. As commonwealth residents, Puerto Ricans have some, but not all, of the benefits of U.S. citizenship.

On April 5, Governor Colón signed a law making Spanish the island's official language, superseding a law that gave English an equal status. Political analysts saw the law as retaliation for the U.S. Senate's February failure to allow Puerto Ricans to vote on their political future. Nathan A. Haverstock

See also **Latin America** (Facts in brief table). In ***World Book,*** see **Puerto Rico.**

Pulitzer Prizes in journalism, letters, music, and drama were awarded in April 1991 by Columbia University in New York City on the recommendation of the Pulitzer Prize Board.

Awards for letters and the arts. John Updike won his second Pulitzer Prize for fiction for *Rabbit at Rest.* Neil Simon won the drama prize for *Lost in Yonkers.* The prize for poetry went to Mona Van Duyn, for a collection titled *Near Changes.* The award for biography was given to Steven Naifeh and Gregory White Smith, for *Jackson Pollock: An American Saga.* The recipients for general nonfiction were Bert Hölldobler and Edward O. Wilson for *The Ants.* The history award went to Laurel Thatcher Ulrich for *A Midwife's Tale: The Life of Martha Ballard, Based on Her Diary, 1785-1812.* The prize for music was awarded to Shulamit Ran for *Symphony.*

Journalism awards. The public service award in journalism went to *The Des Moines* (Iowa) *Register* for a series of articles by Jane Schorer on a rape victim. Awards for international reporting went to Serge Schmemann of *The New York Times* for his reports on the reunification of Germany and to Caryle Murphy of *The Washington Post* for articles filed from Kuwait during the Iraqi invasion of Aug. 2, 1990. Jim Hoagland, also of *The Washington Post,* won the commentary award for columns on events leading up to the Persian Gulf War and on the political problems of Soviet President Mikhail S. Gorbachev.

Other journalism awards: National reporting, Marjie Lundstrom and Rochelle Sharpe of the Gannett News Service, for a series on child abuse deaths. Beat reporting, Natalie Angier, *The New York Times,* for articles on scientific topics. Editorial writing, Ron Casey, Harold Jackson, and Joey Kennedy, *The Birmingham* (Ala.) *News,* for editorials on inequalities in Alabama's tax system. Investigative reporting, Joseph T. Hallinan and Susan M. Headden, *The Indianapolis Star,* for a series on medical malpractice suits. Feature writing, Sheryl James, *The St. Petersburg* (Fla.) *Times,* for a story on a mother who abandoned her baby.

Explanatory reporting, Susan C. Faludi, *The Wall Street Journal,* for an article on employees who lost their jobs due to the leveraged buyout of Safeway Stores, Incorporated. Criticism, David Shaw, *The Los Angeles Times,* for a series criticizing his newspaper and others for coverage of a case involving alleged child abuse at the McMartin Pre-School in Manhattan Beach, Calif. Spot News, *The Miami* (Fla.) *Herald,* for articles on a religious cult leader who was accused of ordering several murders.

Feature photography, William Snyder, *The Dallas Morning News,* for pictures of poor children in Romania. Spot news photography, Greg Marinovich, The Associated Press, for photos of a murder committed in South Africa. Editorial cartoon, Jim Borgman, *The Cincinnati* (Ohio) *Enquirer.* Douglas Clayton

In ***World Book,*** see **Pulitzer Prizes.**

Edward O. Wilson shared the 1991 Pulitzer Prize for general nonfiction with Bert Hölldobler for their comprehensive survey, *The Ants.*

Quayle, Dan (1947-), 44th Vice President of the United States, became a focus of national debate in May 1991 when President George Bush suffered from an irregular heartbeat caused by a thyroid condition. This precipitated fresh talk about Quayle's fitness for the presidency. During the year, Bush insisted that he had no intention of dropping Quayle as his 1992 running mate, and Quayle's participation in an October 30 campaign fund-raising kickoff in Houston seemed to erase any doubts about his status.

Quayle sought to bolster his image during the year by working diligently as chairman of the President's Council on Competitiveness, a group that seeks ways to improve the global standing of U.S. industry. He particularly favored a council-approved plan to reduce the legal expenses of American business by placing curbs on civil suits. When Quayle attended the American Bar Association's annual convention in Atlanta, Ga., in August to promote the measure, he received a chilly reception.

The Vice President continued to travel abroad extensively in 1991 as Bush's representative. Besides visiting India, Japan, and several European countries, he made his eighth trip in 30 months to Latin America, stopping in Venezuela, Argentina, Brazil, and Haiti.

In April, the Quayles reported paying $24,558 in U.S. income taxes on a 1990 adjusted income of $121,126. Frank Cormier and Margot Cormier

In ***World Book***, see **Quayle, Dan.**

Quebec. The province's political parties debated in 1991 the issue of whether Quebec should seek independence from Canada. The Parti Québécois (PQ) was committed to independence but divided on how to achieve it. At a convention in Quebec City in January, party members agreed to a plan that included drafting a constitution for a sovereign Quebec, negotiating with the federal government on sharing assets and debts, and holding a popular vote on sovereignty.

Politics. On August 12, the PQ won its first by-election ever when Jean Filion captured a legislative seat from the governing Liberal Party. This brought to 30 the number of seats held by the PQ.

The Liberals, holding 90 seats in the legislature, were divided on the extent to which Quebec should assert its autonomy. The party officially maintained a federalist position and sought better terms for Quebec. In January, it released a report called *A Quebec Free to Choose,* which called for a radical transfer of federal powers to Quebec. Premier Robert Bourassa supported the report but also stressed the economic benefits of Quebec remaining within Canada. He said that if Quebec and Canada could not agree on constitutional reforms and Quebec became independent, he expected the two countries to enter into an economic pact similar to that of the European Community.

In June, the Quebec legislature passed a bill calling for a popular vote on sovereignty to be held by October 1992 if Canada does not offer acceptable changes in the Constitution. However, Quebec's government would not be bound to abide by the results of the referendum.

Hydropower stirs conflict. Bourassa was frustrated throughout 1991 in his efforts to push forward a massive hydroelectric project that would divert five rivers and flood 1,700 square miles (4,400 square kilometers) of land in the James Bay area at the southern end of Hudson Bay. Known as the Great Whale project, it stirred bitter disputes between Quebec's utility company, Hydro-Québec, and 15,000 Cree Indians and *Inuit* (Eskimos) living in the James Bay area. The Indians claimed that an earlier hydro project at James Bay had damaged their way of life. In June, the Quebec government bowed to Cree pressure and canceled public hearings on the project's environmental impact.

On August 27, Bourassa announced that construction of the Great Whale project would be delayed for one year and that the deadline for signing a proposed contract with the New York Power Authority had been extended until Nov. 30, 1992. The Cree hailed this as a sign that the project was dying. In September 1991, a federal judge ruled that the Canadian government must undertake an environmental impact study of the project. The ruling could sink the scheme because federal requirements are stricter than provincial regulations. David M. L. Farr

See **Canada,** Special Report: **Canada and Quebec at a Crossroads.** In ***World Book,*** see **Quebec.**

Railroad. Despite the economic recession in 1991, railroad revenues in the United States were similar to revenues in 1990. Analysts said in October 1991 that the industry's downturn may be ending. They said that aggressive cost-cutting measures, such as reducing the size of train crews, and increased shipments of grain accounted for modest gains in earnings. Traffic decreased, however, posting 844.2 billion *ton-miles* through the first 10 months of 1991, a 1.8 per cent drop over the same period in 1990. (A ton-mile is 1 short ton of freight carried a distance of 1 mile.)

Freight railroads in the United States moved more than 15,000 carloads of military equipment and supplies to U.S. ports for shipment to the Persian Gulf between August 1990 and January 1991. Military cargo included ammunition, hospital supplies, armored personnel carriers, M-1 tanks, and food supplies.

Spring strike. On April 17, railroad unions representing 235,000 workers in the United States struck the nation's freight railroads over wages, work rules, and health benefits. Some passenger service was also affected. It was the first nationwide strike since 1982. But the next day, April 18, 1991, the U.S. Congress approved and President George Bush signed legislation to settle the dispute and order the railworkers back to work. The legislation called for a special three-member panel appointed by the President to impose a settlement on both the unions and the railroads if the two sides could not agree on issues within a 65-day

Germany's new intercity passenger trains, introduced on May 29, can travel up to 250 miles (400 kilometers) per hour and carry up to 750 riders.

period. The panel imposed a settlement on July 18 that gave railroad management flexibility to cut the size of train crews and awarded union members a modest pay increase.

Accidents. According to preliminary figures from the Federal Railroad Administration, accidents, injuries, and deaths for the first seven months of 1991 were down compared with the same period in 1990. As of July 31, 1991, there had been 2,647 accidents at rail-highway grade crossings, 1,067 injuries, and 291 deaths.

President Bush signed legislation in late October that required transport workers to submit to mandatory testing for alcohol as part of a drug-testing program that went into effect for most railroad and aviation workers in 1990.

Lobbying efforts by railroads against trucking companies' increased use of longer and heavier trucks continued in 1991. Of concern were double- and triple-trailers with total lengths of more than 100 feet (30 meters) and weights possibly greater than 135,000 pounds (61,000 kilograms). The current federal limit is 80,000 pounds (36,000 kilograms). A provision in the $151-billion transportation reauthorization would keep truck weight restrictions in each state at the level they were on June 1, 1991. As of that date, only 15 states allowed trucks with triple trailers equaling 84 feet (26 meters) in length. Kathy Keeney

In *World Book,* see **Railroad.**

Rao, P. V. Narasimha (1921-), became India's ninth prime minister following national elections in May and June. Rao is the leader of the Congress Party, which has governed India for most of the years since the nation gained independence in 1947. The party, which was out of power from 1989 to 1991, made a dramatic comeback in the 1991 elections, apparently due to a surge of sympathy following the assassination of its former chief, Rajiv Gandhi, in May.

A very well-educated man, Rao is a linguist and scholar of considerable standing. He is a poet, writer of fiction, and translator, and has been credited with knowing as many as 12 languages. He was chief minister of Andhra Pradesh, a state in southern India, from 1971 to 1973. As a Congress Party stalwart, he has headed India's ministries of Foreign Affairs, Defense, Home Affairs, and Human Resource Development.

Despite his experience in these ministries, Rao has never been regarded as a forceful presence in Indian politics. In June, many experts predicted that he would be a weak, transitional prime minister. However, in the weeks following his election, Rao effectively consolidated his position within the Congress Party and relegated his main political rivals to positions of lesser power. A further sign of his increasing power came during by-elections in November, when Rao won his seat in Parliament by a landslide vote.

Rao, a widower, is the father of eight children.
Douglas Clayton

Religion. The collapse of Communist rule in the Soviet Union and ongoing political changes in eastern Europe continued to have an impact on religion. Albania, Bulgaria, Czechoslovakia, Hungary, Poland, and Romania relaxed restrictions on religion. Albania, officially atheist since 1967, established diplomatic relations with Vatican City in September 1991.

Jesuit murders. In September, a jury in El Salvador convicted a military officer and an enlisted man of murder in the 1989 deaths of six Jesuit priests, their cook, and her daughter. The officer was the highest-ranking military official ever convicted of killing a civilian in El Salvador. The jury acquitted seven others, and some critics charged that the government failed to pursue evidence that top-ranking military officials were involved.

Dead Sea Scrolls. In September 1991, the Huntington Library in San Marino, Calif., announced that its master set of photographic negatives of the Dead Sea Scrolls was available to any qualified researcher. The Dead Sea Scrolls contain the oldest known manuscripts of all the books of the Old Testament except Esther. The scrolls date from about 200 B.C. to A.D. 50. Fewer than half of these scrolls have been published. Many Biblical scholars expressed great enthusiasm over the release of the scrolls, which were termed the archaeological find of the century when they were discovered in the late 1940's and early 1950's in caves near the Dead Sea in what is now the Israeli-occupied West Bank.

A group of scholars with exclusive publishing rights to the scrolls had been criticized over the years for the delay in publishing their translations. This group has maintained that the unpublished portion consists of fragments yet to be pieced together, a painstaking process. Nevertheless, the Israeli Antiquities Authority, a government agency supervising the scroll project, announced on October 27 that Biblical scholars could view unpublished fragments providing they promised not to publish complete texts of these writings.

Ecumenical dialogues. The Roman Catholic Church continued scholarly ecumenical dialogues with two major Protestant bodies in 1991. On January 24, the Second Anglican-Roman Catholic International Commission issued a report of its understanding of the Christian church as a whole and how it functions. The report not only recognized the "affinity" between the Anglican and Roman Catholic churches but also admitted to differences both in the historical origins of the two churches and in recent developments within each body. A Roman Catholic-Methodist dialogue in April resulted in a statement that said a mutual recognition of ministry would require a resolution of fundamental differences between these churches.

The Episcopal Church and the Evangelical Lutheran Church in America announced in January that they had reached an accord to bring their churches into a union just short of a merger. The "Concordat of Agreement" would make their clergy interchange-

Religious groups with 150,000 or more members in the United States*

African Methodist Episcopal Church	2,210,000
African Methodist Episcopal Zion Church	1,200,000
American Baptist Association	250,000
American Baptist Churches in the U.S.A.	1,535,971
Antiochian Orthodox Christian Archdiocese of North America	350,000
Armenian Apostolic Church of America	150,000
Armenian Church of America, Diocese of the	450,000
Assemblies of God	2,181,502
Baptist Bible Fellowship, International	1,405,900
Baptist Missionary Association of America	229,166
Christian and Missionary Alliance	279,207
Christian Church (Disciples of Christ)	1,039,692
Christian Churches and Churches of Christ	1,070,616
Christian Methodist Episcopal Church	718,922
Christian Reformed Church in North America	226,163
Church of God (Anderson, Ind.)	205,884
Church of God (Cleveland, Tenn.)	620,393
Church of God in Christ	3,709,661
Church of God in Christ, International	200,000
Church of Jesus Christ of Latter-day Saints	4,267,000
Church of the Nazarene	573,834
Churches of Christ	1,683,346
Conservative Baptist Association of America	210,000
Coptic Orthodox Church	165,000
Episcopal Church	2,446,050
Evangelical Free Church of America	165,000
Evangelical Lutheran Church in America	5,240,739
Free Will Baptists	197,206
General Association of Regular Baptist Churches	168,068
Greek Orthodox Archdiocese of North and South America	1,950,000
International Church of the Foursquare Gospel	199,385
International Council of Community Churches	250,000
Jehovah's Witnesses	858,367
Jews	5,981,000
Liberty Baptist Fellowship	180,000
Lutheran Church—Missouri Synod	2,602,849
National Baptist Convention of America	2,668,799
National Baptist Convention, U.S.A., Inc.	5,500,000
National Primitive Baptist Convention	250,000
Orthodox Church in America	1,000,000
Polish National Catholic Church	282,411
Presbyterian Church in America	223,935
Presbyterian Church (U.S.A.)	3,788,009
Progressive National Baptist Convention, Inc.	521,692
Reformed Church in America	326,850
Reorganized Church of Jesus Christ of Latter Day Saints	189,524
Roman Catholic Church	58,568,015
Salvation Army	445,566
Seventh-day Adventist Church	717,446
Southern Baptist Convention	15,038,409
Unitarian Universalist Association	191,543
United Church of Christ	1,599,212
United Methodist Church	8,904,824
United Pentecostal Church, International	500,000
Wisconsin Evangelical Lutheran Synod	420,039

*A majority of the figures are for the years 1990 and 1991. Includes only groups with at least 150,000 members within the United States itself.
Source: National Council of the Churches of Christ in the U.S.A., *Yearbook of American and Canadian Churches* for 1992.

Huntington Library officials in San Marino, Calif., examine a negative of the Dead Sea Scrolls, which the library opened to researchers in September.

able, and members could receive sacraments, including Communion, in either denomination. The two Protestant groups have been studying the possibility of close union for more than 20 years. Both denominations will study and discuss the concordat on a churchwide basis. Their governing bodies were not likely to vote on it until their meetings in 1994 and 1995. Nevertheless, Edmond L. Browning, the presiding bishop of the Episcopal Church, called the proposal "a historic agreement."

The American Bible Society celebrated its 175th anniversary by introducing a new translation of the Bible that emphasizes ease of listening, according to the scholar who headed the translation team. This translation reportedly has the tone of ordinary conversation. The society has distributed 5.8 billion Bibles, Testaments, and portions of Scripture "without doctrinal note or comment, and without profit" since it was founded in 1816.

New World Council president. For the first time, the World Council of Churches at its meeting in Canberra, Australia, in February 1991 elected a black American to one of its eight presidencies. Bishop Vinton Anderson of the African Methodist Episcopal Church will be the council's North American representative. Owen F. Campion

See also **Eastern Orthodox Churches; Islam; Judaism; Protestantism; Roman Catholic Church.** In ***World Book,*** see **Religion.**

Republican Party. The elections of Nov. 5, 1991, provided three notable bright spots for the Republican Party (GOP)—in Mississippi, New Jersey, and Virginia. But one race, for a United States Senate seat from Pennsylvania, resulted in a stunning defeat with national implications. Also part of the year's political mix was a major embarrassment for the national party in Louisiana, where a former Ku Klux Klan leader and Nazi sympathizer became the Republican nominee for governor, prompting President George Bush to say that his choice was the Democrat.

The Republican National Committee (RNC) had a change of leadership in early 1991. On January 25, RNC Chairman Lee Atwater, battling inoperable brain cancer, resigned and was succeeded by Clayton K. Yeutter. The new chairman, who had been serving as secretary of agriculture until his appointment, had little practical political experience. Atwater, 40, who had been the mastermind of Bush's controversial 1988 presidential campaign, died on March 29.

On the day of Yeutter's installation as RNC chairman, Edward J. Rollins, Jr., resigned as cochairman of the National Republican Congressional Committee. Earlier, there had been speculation that Rollins would leave the Republican Congressional Committee. He had reportedly infuriated Bush by urging GOP candidates in 1990 to distance themselves from the President on tax and budget issues. Rollins was succeeded by E. Spencer Abraham, a top political aide to Vice

President Dan Quayle and a former chairman of the Michigan Republican organization.

Houston to host 1992 convention. On Jan. 8, 1991, Republican officials selected Houston's Astrodome as the site of the 1992 Republican National Convention. Houston was chosen over San Diego and New Orleans. The convention was scheduled to be held from August 17 to 20, a month after Democrats hold their convention in New York City.

On April 17, 1991, Yeutter said he hoped convention delegates would retain a strict antiabortion position in the GOP platform. Before his death, Atwater had been trying to steer the party toward a "big tent" philosophy that would accommodate differing views on the touchy issue. On October 8, Quayle met with reporters and said he favored retaining the antiabortion plank. But he advocated amending the wording to emphasize that prochoice advocates were welcome under the "big tent."

A major upset in Pennsylvania. For President Bush, the Republican defeat in the Pennsylvania Senate race cut close to home. The GOP candidate was former two-term Pennsylvania Governor Richard L. Thornburgh, who resigned as U.S. attorney general in August. Thornburgh had a 44-point lead in the opinion polls over his obscure Democratic opponent, Harris Wofford. Wofford had been appointed by Pennsylvania Governor Robert P. Casey to fill the Senate seat vacated by the death of Republican John Heinz, who was killed in a plane crash in April.

At first, Thornburgh was considered a sure bet to win the election, but Wofford refused to give up. He appealed to Pennsylvania voters with a call for national health insurance and government action to revive the nation's slumping economy. On election day, Wofford stunned Thornburgh, winning by 10 percentage points. He also stunned Bush, who quickly began talking about possible action on health insurance, tax cuts, and other measures espoused by Wofford.

GOP victories in November may have owed much to a "throw-the-rascals-out" mood among voters. In New Jersey, Republicans gained veto-proof majorities in both houses of the legislature. New Jersey voters were evidently retaliating for recent tax hikes passed by the legislature at the urging of Democratic Governor James J. Florio.

Virginia voters, it seemed, simply wanted to turn incumbents out of office. Republicans in that state boosted their standing from 10 seats to 18 in the 40-member Senate. The GOP also picked up strength in the Virginia House of Delegates and in many local contests.

The other good news for Republicans came from Mississippi, where Democratic Governor Ray Maybus lost his reelection bid to GOP businessman Kirk Fordice, the first Republican elected governor of that state since the Reconstruction era after the Civil War (1861-1865). Fordice tapped into white middle-class anger with attacks on welfare and racial quotas.

Spotlight on Louisiana. The GOP banner in a November 16 runoff election for Louisiana governor was carried by State Representative David Duke, a former neo-Nazi and grand wizard of the Ku Klux Klan, who said he had renounced those past ties. Duke lost to former Democratic Governor Edwin W. Edwards, receiving 39 per cent of the vote to Edwards' 61 per cent. But Duke's campaign had struck a chord among white Louisianians, 55 per cent of whom voted for him. It was the black vote that gave Edwards such a decisive victory. See also **Elections; Duke, David.**

Bush's popularity declines. Bush, whose poll ratings topped 90 per cent after the end of the Persian Gulf War in early 1991, lost political strength slowly but steadily during the rest of the year. A national poll in October found that, for the first time, fewer than 50 per cent of respondents were inclined to vote for Bush's reelection. In December, conservative commentator Patrick Buchanan declared he would challenge Bush for the Republican presidential nomination. See also **Bush, George Herbert Walker.**

On October 11, Bush authorized the formation of a campaign committee to be called "Bush-Quayle '92." He and the Vice President kicked off their campaign at a fund-raiser in Houston on October 30.

Frank Cormier and Margot Cormier

See also **Buchanan, Patrick; Democratic Party.** In ***World Book***, see **Republican Party.**

Rhode Island. See **State government.**

Roberts, Julia (1967-), solidified her position in 1991 as one of Hollywood's hottest new movie stars. Following up her 1990 Academy Award nomination as best supporting actress for her performance as Sally Field's dying daughter in *Steel Magnolias* (1989), Roberts in 1991 received a best-actress nomination for her portrayal of a winsome prostitute in the smash film *Pretty Woman* (1990). Both those performances brought her Golden Globe Awards from the Hollywood Foreign Press Association.

Roberts was born on Oct. 28, 1967, in Smyrna, Ga. Her parents ran a regional-theater workshop in nearby Atlanta. Although that venture failed, it ignited a love of performing in the four Roberts children, three of whom decided to pursue careers as actors. One of them, Eric Roberts, has been a well-known motion-picture and television actor since the late 1970's.

Julia Roberts made her movie debut in 1986 in the film *Blood Red*, in which she had a small part. After other minor roles in *Satisfaction* (1988) and the TV movie *Baja Oklahoma*, she attracted critical attention as a Portuguese-American pizza-parlor waitress, Daisy, in the 1988 picture *Mystic Pizza*.

Roberts' other film credits include leading roles in *Flatliners* (1990), *Sleeping with the Enemy* (1991), and *Dying Young* (1991). In late 1991, she starred as the fairy Tinker Bell in Steven Spielberg's film *Hook*. Based on the play *Peter Pan*, that movie also starred Dustin Hoffman and Robin Williams. David L. Dreier

Roman Catholic Church. As Communism crumbled in the former Soviet Union during 1991, Roman Catholicism began to reemerge as a religious force. The Vatican appointed 10 bishops for the Ukraine on January 16, virtually reconstituting the Catholic hierarchy in that republic. Some of these appointments had actually been made earlier in secret. On March 30, Myroslav Cardinal Lubachivsky returned to his Ukrainian diocese of Lvov after a 45-year exile.

The Vatican also appointed Bishop Tadeusz Kondrusiewicz as archbishop of Moscow on April 13. With his appointment, Bishop Kondrusiewicz became the highest Roman Catholic official to function publicly in the Soviet Union for generations.

On August 23, Pope John Paul II wired President Mikhail S. Gorbachev the message that the attempt to overthrow the Soviet leader had been an occasion of "intense apprehension." The pope said he thanked God for Gorbachev's safe return.

Pope in Poland. Pope John Paul II visited Poland twice in 1991. His June visit was his first since Poland's Communist government fell in 1989. During this visit, he spoke out frequently against abortion in Poland. Estimates of the number of abortions performed in Poland each year vary from 500,000 to 1 million. The pope also called for spiritual renewal among Polish Catholics and for a new crusade against the secularism of western Europe. Church leaders said that the pope wants the Catholic church in Poland to lead in spreading the Gospel among the nations of eastern Europe since the failure of Communism.

Upon his return to Poland in August 1991, Pope John Paul II led the World Day of Youth, an event sponsored by the Vatican to inspire young Catholics to remain faithful to their religion. The celebration, on August 14, drew a crowd of 1 million young people from all over Europe to the Jasna Gora Monastery to hear the pope speak. The monastery houses Poland's most sacred icon, the Black Madonna.

Also while in eastern Europe in August, Pope John Paul II visited Hungary, where he again spoke of spiritual rebirth in this traditionally Catholic country. In Budapest, he praised scientists, artists, and writers, who had been persecuted by successive Communist regimes.

Albania initiated diplomatic relations with the Holy See on September 7. Albania had dealt harshly with Catholics while the nation was under repressive Stalinist-type governments until Communism's grip began loosening in the mid-1980's.

Pope in Brazil. Pope John Paul II visited Brazil, the nation with the largest Roman Catholic population in the world, in October 1991. During his 10-day visit, the pope urged Brazilian Catholics to crusade against fundamentalist Protestant groups, whose influence has spread in many places in the world and particularly in Latin America. Brazilian bishops said that the Roman Catholic Church in Brazil loses as many as 600,000 people each year to fundamentalist and evangelical sects. The bishops said that about 25 per cent of Brazil's 150 million people are non-Catholic, where once the Roman Catholic Church was virtually without competition.

Gulf war concerns. Tensions in the Persian Gulf region concerned Pope John Paul II in 1991. Although the pope condemned the outrage of Iraq's invasion and occupation of Kuwait, he warned in a January 12 address to foreign diplomats that a war in the Persian Gulf would represent "a decline for all humanity."

From the time of Iraq's invasion of Kuwait in August 1990 to the cease-fire in February 1991, Pope John Paul II issued more than 50 appeals for peace. He appealed directly to both Iraqi President Saddam Hussein and United States President George Bush to do everything possible to prevent an outbreak of violence. When the bombing of Iraq began on January 17, the pope viewed the event with "grief." He allowed the *apostolic pro-nuncio* (Vatican ambassador) to Iraq, Archbishop Marian Oles, to remain in Baghdad during the bombings for diplomatic and charitable purposes. After President Bush ordered the cease-fire on February 27, the pope expressed his relief, calling the war an "adventure with no return."

Most Roman Catholic clergy and theologians also voiced disapproval of the war, including Archbishop John Roach of the St. Paul-Minneapolis, Minn., archdiocese. He deplored the fact that the war was enflaming already existing animosities among Christians, Jews, and Muslims in the Middle East. In Latin America, 30 Roman Catholic theologians denounced the war as morally "unjustifiable."

The war damaged one of the oldest Roman Catholic churches in Iraq, as well as the two Roman Catholic churches in Kuwait.

Major encyclicals. Pope John Paul II issued two major *encyclicals* (papal messages) in 1991, stating the church's position on missionary activity and on the importance of market economies. *The Church's Missionary Mandate,* a 153-page document on evangelization published on January 22, was the result of five years' work. In it, the pope urged Catholics to teach their faith in places where Christianity had grown weak. Aides to the pope said that he was particularly concerned about former Christian areas of Africa and the Middle East, where Islam was rapidly supplanting Christianity, and about southern Europe, where migration has brought in many Muslims.

On May 2, the pope issued *The Hundredth Year* to mark the 100th anniversary of *On the Condition of Workers,* an encyclical issued by Pope Leo XIII in 1891 in defense of private property and against socialism. The 1891 encyclical is considered a landmark in Catholic social teaching in the modern industrial era. Several popes have commemorated various anniversaries of this encyclical with ones of their own. In his encyclical, Pope John Paul II reaffirmed Pope Leo's statements about human dignity and the need for justice in the marketplace and in industry. Pope John Paul II

Pope John Paul II processes down the streets of Funchal on Portugal's Madeira Island, where he said Mass for 50,000 people on May 12.

said that "the free market is the most efficient instrument for utilizing resources and effectively responding to needs." But he also said conditions in many workplaces were worse in 1991 than they were in 1891.

Abortion issue. Church leaders continued to assert Catholic moral opposition to abortion. In March 1991, James Cardinal Hickey of Washington, D.C., strongly criticized the decision of Georgetown University, a Catholic university in Washington, D.C., to fund a student group that considers abortion a right. The archdiocese of Boston barred Massachusetts Lieutenant Governor Paul Celucci, who is pro-choice, from speaking to graduates of the Catholic high school he attended in Boston. Many Catholic bishops, clergy, and lay leaders supported Operation Rescue, a militant campaign in which abortion opponents demonstrated at abortion clinics and sought to prevent people from entering the facilities.

New cardinals. Pope John Paul II appointed Archbishop Anthony J. Bevilacqua of Philadelphia and Archbishop Roger M. Mahony of Los Angeles as cardinals on May 29, 1991, along with 21 other bishops from around the world. See also **Bevilacqua, Anthony J. Cardinal; Mahony, Roger M. Cardinal.**

The pope announced that Bishop Ignatius Gong Pin Mei of Shanghai was actually appointed a cardinal in secret in 1979, while serving a life sentence in a Chinese prison for not disavowing his loyalty to the Vatican. The Chinese prelate was released in 1985, after 30 years in prison, and is now living in the United States.

Among the other new cardinals, Archbishop Alexandru Todea of Romania and Bishop Jan Chryzostom Korec of Czechoslovakia also spent years in prison in their homelands for their religious activities.

Archbishop dies. Archbishop Marcel Lefebvre died on March 25, 1991, in Martigny, Switzerland. He had caused a schism in the Roman Catholic Church, the first since 1870, when he defied Pope John Paul II by consecrating four bishops to help him preserve religious practices, such as the Latin Mass, rejected after the ecumenical council Vatican II. He also deplored the church's decision to hold dialogues with Protestants, Muslims, and Jews. Pope John Paul II declared the archbishop to be excommunicated in June 1988. The archbishop, nevertheless, claimed thousands of loyal followers. A Vatican statement, issued on the day Archbishop Lefebvre died, said that the pope had hoped up to the last moment for a conciliatory gesture from Lefebvre, but none came.

Laetare Medal. On March 9, 1991, the University of Notre Dame in Notre Dame, Ind., announced former Representative Corinne C. (Lindy) Boggs (D., La.) was the recipient of its annual Laetare Medal. The medal is annually conferred upon an outstanding Catholic American. Owen F. Campion

See also **Religion.** In ***World Book,*** see **Roman Catholic Church.**

Romania. Political uncertainty mounted and unrest spread as Romania struggled toward a market economy in 1991. A change of government led to a coalition composed mainly of non-Communist independents.

Violent riots led by coal miners forced the National Salvation Front (NSF) government of Prime Minister Petre Roman to resign on September 26. The NSF came to power following the overthrow of Romania's Communist dictator Nicolae Ceausescu in 1989. The miners were protesting hardships inflicted by economic reforms, which included hefty price hikes.

The parliament on Oct. 16, 1991, confirmed Roman's successor, former Finance Minister Theodor Stolojan, who had resigned six months earlier, claiming the government was implementing his reforms too slowly. The day before, Stolojan named a Cabinet of nine independents like himself, seven members of the NSF, three members of the National Liberal Party, and one each from two smaller groups. Romania's Liberal Party thereby entered the government for the first time since the Communists took power in 1947.

The new Cabinet was generally viewed as a caretaker government until parliamentary elections scheduled for 1992. But the change in government did not affect the position of President Ion Iliescu, a former high-ranking Communist, whose resignation was repeatedly demanded by the opposition during 1991.

Roman's government had made a bold start on economic reform by lifting government subsidies on food and other goods and letting prices rise. The reforms brought more goods into stores but at prices few people could afford—a pattern common in eastern Europe. In March, an NSF congress overwhelmingly supported the continuation of market reforms. But further price hikes and a drop in purchasing power triggered a wave of strikes.

Although 3 million pensioners lived below the poverty level, Roman resisted pressures to slow economic reform. The government announced in August, however, that wages, pensions, and welfare payments would automatically increase to cover 40 per cent of the inflation rate.

Human rights. The opposition had attacked Roman's Cabinet as "Communists in disguise" during the year, and journalists protested government pressure exerted on the media. The United States Helsinki Watch Committee, a human-rights group, also criticized Romania's slow progress on human rights. On November 6, the parliament adopted a new constitution that guaranteed civil liberties and established a multiparty political system. Voters approved the constitution in a nationwide referendum on December 8.

Eric Bourne

See also **Europe** (Facts in brief table). In ***World Book,*** see **Romania.**

Rowing. See **Sports.**

Russia. See **Union of Soviet Socialist Republics.**

Rwanda. See **Africa.**

Safety. The United States Department of Health and Human Services (HHS) in October 1991 revised its recommendations for treating children exposed to lead. Blood lead levels that are less than half of what the agency had formerly considered safe should prompt concern and possible intervention, according to a report issued by HHS Secretary Louis W. Sullivan. The HHS cut the "threshold of concern" from 25 to 10 micrograms of lead per deciliter of whole blood. However, even this level may cause some neurological problems, according to the report. The revised exposure levels followed the announcement in February 1991 of an HHS plan to eliminate childhood lead poisoning in the next 20 years. Lead poisoning is one of the most common health problems, affecting 3 million to 4 million U.S. children under age 6.

Nonfatal accidents. About 41 million Americans suffer economic loss from nonfatal injuries each year, according to a major study requested by the U.S. Congress and released in April 1991. The study, conducted by the Rand Corporation, a nonprofit research center in Santa Monica, Calif., surveyed 26,000 households. Based on the survey's findings, researchers estimated that accidents affect one-sixth of the population annually and cost the economy about $176 billion in medical expenses and lost productivity.

The report noted that children and teen-agers had the greatest risk of accidental injury, and people over age 65 had the lowest risk. About 30 per cent of accidents occurred while people were engaged in leisure activities; 25 per cent happened as they performed household chores; 25 per cent took place at work or on the way to work; and 20 per cent occurred at other times. Falls caused about 40 per cent of all mishaps. Toys, sports equipment, tools, or other products were involved in 30 per cent of all accidents. Motor vehicle accidents accounted for 20 per cent, and other causes were implicated in the remaining 20 per cent. Most accidents were minor, and only 10 per cent were considered permanently disabling or life-threatening.

Avoiding electric shocks. The U.S. Consumer Product Safety Commission (CPSC) on May 21 recommended household use of an inexpensive device that protects consumers from potentially fatal electric shocks. Called ground-fault circuit-interrupters (GFCIs), the devices constantly monitor the electricity in a circuit. If the amount of electricity flowing from the circuit differs at all from the amount returning, the GFCI instantly shuts off the current.

The CPSC noted that homes and apartments constructed since 1973 were required to have GFCIs built into some electrical receptacles. But it said that millions of residences still lack the devices. The consumer can install the product easily by plugging it into a wall outlet and then plugging the electrical appliance into the GFCI.

Safety helmets. Laws that require all motorcycle riders to wear safety helmets can save 350 to 700 lives every year, according to a study released by the U.S. General Accounting Office (GAO) in July 1991. About 55 per cent of the 3,238 motorcycle riders who died in traffic accidents in 1990 were not wearing helmets, the study noted. Riders without helmets also were at risk for suffering serious head injuries.

As of May 1991, 24 states and the District of Columbia required all motorcycle riders to wear helmets. Twenty-three other states had limited laws, requiring only some riders, such as young people, to wear helmets, while the states of Colorado, Illinois, and Iowa had no requirements.

The CPSC on July 31 rejected a request from 34 health and safety groups to require bicycle helmet manufacturers to meet mandatory safety standards. The groups argued that some helmets are improperly designed and may come off during a crash. The CPSC replied that the evidence was not sufficient to show that helmets on the market fail to protect bike riders.

The largest fine ever collected by the U.S. Occupational Safety and Health Administration came out of the pockets of the Arco Chemical Company in January 1991. Arco, the owner of a petrochemical plant near Houston, was fined $3.48 million for "willful" breaches of federal safety regulations that led to an explosion at the plant that killed 17 people in 1990.

Michael Woods

See also **Aviation; Consumerism; Food.** In ***World Book,*** see **Safety.**

Sailing. See **Boating.**

San Diego. A San Diego Police Department report released in May 1991 called for a complete restructuring of the department. The report recommended cutting the layers of authority between patrol officers and top administrators and doing away with military-type titles such as sergeant and lieutenant. The study was commissioned in response to citizen outrage over long-standing problems with the department, including frequent allegations of police brutality, complaints that officers were too quick to use their guns against suspects, and rumors of widespread corruption.

In a probe that began in 1990 and continued during 1991, a law enforcement task force was investigating at least five current and former police officers for various offenses. The investigators were looking into charges that the officers had been stealing and reselling drugs seized in raids or keeping them for their own use, falsifying documents, and having sexual relations with prostitutes who were police informants. The task force was also examining whether the officers might have been involved in the murders of some of the 44 prostitutes who disappeared or were found dead in the San Diego area in the 1980's.

Utility merger voted down. After nearly three years of heated debate, the California Public Utilities Commission voted on May 8, 1991, to reject a proposed merger between two large utility companies, the San Diego Gas & Electric Company and the Southern California Edison Corporation. The commission voted 5 to 0 against the proposal on the grounds that it would adversely affect competition and that the two utilities had failed to prove that such a merger would result in lower rates for consumers.

Polls showed that the majority of San Diegans were strongly opposed to the merger, fearing that the move would lead to rate increases, lost jobs, and harm to the environment. The joining of the two companies would have created the country's largest investor-owned utility. Neither utility appealed the commission's decision.

Population explosion. A report released in early 1991 by the United States Bureau of the Census, disclosed that the population of San Diego County had swelled to about 2.5 million, making it the fourth largest county in the nation. The county's population increased by 34.2 per cent between 1980 and 1990, one of the highest growth rates recorded in the United States. See **Census Supplement.**

The year in sports. There were some high points and some disappointments for San Diego sports fans during 1991. Sailing enthusiasts were thrilled by the International America's Cup Class World Championship in May. A racing syndicate from Italy won the eight-day competition, which featured the debut of a new class of yachts, the International America's Cup Class. The championship was a prelude to the America's Cup yacht race, to be held at San Diego in 1992.

San Diego got some bad sports news in March 1991. The city had made a bid for the 1993 Super

Bowl, which the National Football League (NFL) had decided to relocate from Phoenix, Ariz. But San Diego lost out to the Los Angeles area when NFL officials announced that the game will be played at the Rose Bowl in Pasadena. San Diego was host to the Super Bowl in 1988, the only time the championship game has been played there.

The recession. Throughout 1990, the San Diego area seemed virtually untouched by the national recession. But statistics released by the state of California in March 1991 showed that San Diego County had experienced a net loss of 2,500 jobs since March 1990. The drop marked the first time since 1983 that the county had lost more jobs than it gained over a one-year period.

Drought relief. In late February 1991, just one month before mandatory water rationing was due to take effect, San Diego was hit with heavy downpours. The rains came again in August, making that month one of the wettest in the city's history. The rainfall was not enough to make up for five consecutive years of drought, but it kept the mandatory water restrictions from going into effect. In March, San Diego Mayor Maureen F. O'Connor was publicly embarrassed about disclosures that she and her husband had used more than twice as much water at their home as she had reported earlier in the year.

Sharon K. Gillenwater

In ***World Book,*** see **San Diego.**

Saskatchewan voters on Oct. 21, 1991, ousted the ruling Progressive Conservative Party (PC) led by Tory Premier Grant Devine. They voted in the New Democratic Party (NDP) led by Roy Romanow, a middle-of-the-road leader who promised fiscal responsibility. The NDP won 55 legislative seats.The PC, in office since 1982, lost 22 of its 32 legislative seats. The Liberal Party won 24 per cent of the popular vote but captured only 1 seat. The total number of house seats expanded in 1991 from 64 to 66.

Devine's government was burdened by two unpopular measures. The first sought to decentralize the civil service by moving 1,500 employees from Regina, the capital, to rural communities. The other proposed merging the provincial sales tax with the federal goods and services tax (GST) in 1992. In 1991, the PC had already expanded the base of the provincial tax to include many items in the GST. The NDP filibustered during the sales tax debate for 135 hours, and in June, Devine abruptly adjourned the legislative session, leaving 13 bills and the budget unresolved.

Devine had tried to improve his election chances by creating new jobs in Saskatchewan. He also persuaded the federal government to move the head office of the Farm Credit Corporation to Regina.

David M. L. Farr

See also **Canada,** Special Report: **Canada and Quebec at a Crossroads.** In ***World Book,*** see **Canada; Saskatchewan.**

Saudi Arabia, which hosted more than 400,000 allied troops during the Persian Gulf War in early 1991, claimed victory when Kuwait was liberated from Iraqi occupation on February 26 (see **Persian Gulf,** Special Report: **War in the Persian Gulf**). Several months later, however, the rewards of victory were less clear.

Financial drain. The $64 billion Saudi Arabia spent on war-related expenses drained its treasury. The government reportedly had an estimated budget deficit of $50 billion for 1990 and 1991, despite oil revenues of more than $30 billion in 1991. In May, Saudi Arabia obtained a loan for $4.5 billion from foreign banks. This was the first such loan Saudi Arabia had asked for in 20 years.

In addition to supporting Kuwaiti refugees and increasing defense-related outlays, the Saudis spent heavily to boost oil production from 5 million to more than 8 million barrels per day. The increase was intended to offset the loss on the world market of Iraqi and Kuwaiti oil, which was embargoed by the United Nations in August 1990.

During late 1990 and 1991, a number of countries received Saudi grants and loans as compensation for war-related expenses and as a reward for their support during the Persian Gulf crisis. The Saudis gave more than $4 billion to Syria, Egypt, and Turkey. The Soviet Union received a $1.5-billion loan. Another $13.5 billion was promised to the United States to help pay the cost of the war.

Public reaction to the war was mixed. Saudis themselves suffered relatively little war-related damage, though some Saudis privately criticized the allied destruction of Iraq. The social unrest in Kuwait after its liberation, however, worried Saudis, who feared the consequences of rapid political and social change in the region.

After the war, the government found itself torn between calls for political and social liberalization and a resurgence of Islamic conservatism. In April, 43 prominent Saudis published a letter calling for the establishment of national and municipal consultative councils. On August 5, the government announced several cabinet changes, but, despite repeated promises, failed to establish a consultative council.

The country's religious police, who are responsible for enforcing strict Islamic social codes, became more zealous after the war. In addition, on June 8, seven people were beheaded under Islamic law in the first publicly announced executions since July 1990. Tapes advocating fundamentalist positions also became increasingly popular.

U.S. relations. After the war, some U.S. officials hoped that Saudi Arabia would become an important Middle East ally. The U.S. Department of Defense hoped to stockpile enough military equipment for at least one division in Saudi Arabia. The Saudis, however, were reluctant to allow a U.S. military presence large enough to be considered a U.S. base. Following the war, King Fahd reportedly counseled the United

Saudi King Fahd, right, and U.S. Gen. H. Norman Schwarzkopf, Jr., allied commander in the Persian Gulf, review troops in Saudi Arabia in January.

States against further interference in Iraq's affairs and pressed for the speedy withdrawal of U.S. forces from the Mideast.

Peace conference. After the war, the Saudis came under U.S. pressure to assist attempts to organize a peace conference between Israel and its Arab neighbors. On July 20, 1991, Saudi officials announced their willingness to end their participation in the 43-year Arab boycott against Israel if Israel agreed to halt its expansion of settlements in Israeli-occupied territories. The Saudis also financed Arab delegations to the conference, which opened on October 30 in Madrid, Spain.

Environmental damage. A huge oil slick that fouled the Persian Gulf and severely damaged Saudi Arabia's gulf shoreline in late January was traced to a damaged Kuwaiti pumping station. The U.S.-led coalition assailed Iraq for deliberately releasing the oil. Iraq insisted that allied bombs had damaged the station. An international effort to clean up the shoreline and save the region's wildlife began immediately.

Plane crashes. A Saudi plane crash on March 21 claimed the lives of 92 Senegalese coalition soldiers and 6 Saudi crewmen. On July 11, 261 people, mostly Nigerian Muslim pilgrims, died when their plane crashed outside Jidda. Christine Helms

See also **Middle East** (Facts in brief table). In ***World Book,*** see **Saudi Arabia.**

School. See **Education.**

Schwarzkopf, H. Norman, Jr. (1934-), commanded the allied forces that freed Kuwait from a seven-month occupation by Iraq during the Persian Gulf War in early 1991 (see **Persian Gulf** Special Report: **War in the Persian Gulf**). General Schwarzkopf retired from the military on August 31.

Schwarzkopf was born on Aug. 22, 1934, in Trenton, N.J. In 1952, he entered the United States Military Academy at West Point, N.Y., where he was on the wrestling and football teams. He graduated in 1956, ranking 43rd in a class of 480.

Schwarzkopf served two tours of duty during the Vietnam War (1957-1975), attaining the rank of battalion commander. He became a general in 1983 and led U.S. ground forces in the attack on the Caribbean island of Grenada in October of that year. In November 1988, he became commander in chief of the U.S. Central Command, the group in charge of coordinating U.S. military action in the Middle East.

During the allied ground offensive, from February 24 to 28, Schwarzkopf used a battle plan based on deception, which was credited for the quick victory over Iraq. The deception involved the appearance of a major attack on Kuwait from the south, while the main allied forces attacked the Iraqis from the west.

Schwarzkopf, nicknamed "Stormin' Norman," enjoys country music, hunting, and magic tricks. He married the former Brenda Holsinger in 1968. They have three children. Mark Dunbar

Seles, Monica (1973-), Yugoslavia's teen-aged tennis wonder, won three of the four grand slam events in women's tennis during 1991, becoming the sport's top-ranked player in March. At 17 years and 3 months, she was the youngest tennis player—male or female—ever to achieve the number-one ranking.

Seles' first grand slam victory of the year came in January, over Jana Novotna of Czechoslovakia in the Australian Open. In June, Seles defeated Arantxa Sánchez Vicario of Spain to win her second consecutive French Open. In September, Seles overwhelmed the American tennis veteran Martina Navratilova at the United States Open. See **Tennis.**

Despite these impressive achievements, Seles drew even more attention for the one tournament at which she failed to appear. Just days before Wimbledon began in June, Seles withdrew without any explanation. Weeks later, she attributed her absence from the All-England Championship to a case of shin splints. The no-show cost Seles the top ranking, which was regained by Germany's Steffi Graf. But Seles reclaimed the number-one spot after winning the U.S. Open.

Seles was born on Dec. 2, 1973, in Novi Sad, Yugoslavia. She began playing tennis at age 9 and was coached by her father. Seles moved to Florida with her family in 1986 and turned professional in 1988. A left-hander, Seles plays from the baseline, grunting loudly as she blasts her opponents with powerful two-handed ground strokes. Karin C. Rosenberg

Senegal. In response to mounting criticism, President Abdou Diouf on April 7, 1991, announced several reforms. He named a veteran politician, Habib Thiam, to the newly restored post of prime minister in an effort to improve relations between his office and the National Assembly. He also appointed key opponents of his Socialist Party to a coalition Cabinet. The reforms were in part a response to Diouf's failed economic policies. To stimulate economic development, the government in August lowered prices on oil, electricity, and cement.

Another source of discord was the failure of the military to suppress a secessionist movement in the southern province of Casamance. Compounding the problem were international reports that the army was abusing and torturing prisoners and civilians in that province. In a surprise move, Diouf on May 29 announced a cease-fire agreement with the rebels, released political prisoners, and began to improve conditions in Casamance.

Senegal took steps during the year to end a virtual state of war with Mauritania that began after a minor border incident in April 1989 escalated into riots and mass deportations of each other's citizens. On July 18, 1991, the foreign ministers of both nations met to begin the restoration of diplomatic ties.

J. Gus Liebenow and Beverly B. Liebenow

See also **Africa** (Facts in brief table). In ***World Book,*** see **Senegal.**

Shaw, Bernard (1940-), television anchorman for Cable News Network (CNN), provided the only live, continuous account with two other CNN reporters of the first bombing of Baghdad, Iraq, on Jan. 17, 1991. From the window of his ninth floor hotel room, Shaw described explosions in the predawn sky as the United States and its allies began the air war against Iraq. Special telephone lines transmitted the reporters' voices and the sounds of battle, picked up by a microphone hanging from the window. No video transmission was possible during the initial bombing. See **Persian Gulf,** Special Report: **War in the Persian Gulf.**

Shaw has covered several major events for CNN since joining the network in 1980, including the 1988 Moscow summit meeting between then President Ronald Reagan and Soviet President Mikhail S. Gorbachev. He also covered the 1989 student demonstrations in Tiananmen Square in Beijing.

Shaw was born in Chicago on May 22, 1940. From 1963 to 1967, he studied history at the University of Illinois at Chicago, but did not graduate. From 1971 to 1977, he was a Washington, D.C., correspondent for CBS News. He received the 1990 ACE Award for Best News Anchor from the Academy of Cable Excellence.

Shaw and his wife, Linda, live in Tacoma Park, Md., with their two children. Carol L. Hanson

Sierra Leone. See **Africa.**

Singapore. See **Asia.**

Skating. See **Hockey; Ice skating; Sports.**

Skiing. Austrian and Swiss skiers won most of the honors in the 1991 Alpine events of the World Ski Championships and World Cup races.

In the world championships, the Austrians and the Swiss won 8 of the 10 gold medals and 17 of the 30 total medals. In the World Cup series, the overall champions were 27-year-old Marc Girardelli of Luxembourg among the men and, for the second consecutive year, 21-year-old Petra Kronberger of Austria among the women.

World championships. The biennial championships were held from January 22 to February 3 in Saalbach-Hinterglemm, Austria. Stefan Eberharter, a 21-year-old Austrian competing in his first world championship, won the men's super giant slalom and the combined. Girardelli won the slalom, Franz Heinzer of Switzerland took the downhill, and Rudolf Nierlich of Austria repeated in the giant slalom.

Petra Kronberger won the women's downhill, Vreni Schneider of Switzerland the slalom, Chantal Bournissen of Switzerland the combined, and Pernilla Wiberg of Sweden the giant slalom. Ulrike Maier of Austria retained her 1989 title in the super giant slalom. The best finish by an American or Canadian man or woman was fifth place in the women's giant slalom by Eva Twardokens of Santa Cruz, Calif.

World Cup. The World Cup series was held from November 1990 to March 1991 in Europe, the United States, Canada, and Japan. Girardelli won his fourth

Marc Girardelli of Luxembourg races in Aspen, Colo., on his way to winning the men's overall title in the 1991 World Cup championships.

men's overall title, matching the record of Gustavo Thoeni of Italy and Pirmin Zurbriggen of Switzerland. This time Girardelli totaled 242 points to 222 for second-place finisher Alberto Tomba of Italy. Tomba might have won except for an incident in March at Lake Louise in Canada, where he was charged with knocking down a recreational skier and swinging his poles at a female lift attendant. When the resort manager revoked Tomba's lift pass, Tomba was unable to compete in that day's super giant slalom.

The men's season champions were Heinzer in downhill and super giant slalom, Girardelli in slalom, and Tomba in giant slalom. The women's season titles went to Kronberger in slalom, Schneider in giant slalom, Bournissen in downhill, and Carole Merle of France in super giant slalom.

The only American victory came when Julie Parisien of Auburn, Me., won a women's giant slalom race in Waterville Valley, N.H. No American had won a World Cup race since Tamara McKinney in 1987.

Nordic. In the world Nordic championships, held from February 8 to 17 in Val di Fiemme, Italy, Elena Valbe of the Soviet Union won three gold medals and one silver in women's cross-country. Gunde Svan of Sweden took one gold and three silver in men's cross-country. Valbe and Vladimir Smirnov, also of the Soviet Union, won the season-long World Cup titles.

Frank Litsky

In ***World Book***, see **Skiing**.

Soccer. The United States National Team acquired a new coach in 1991. It promptly won a major tournament, an important step in preparing for the 1994 World Cup competition in the United States. Former coach Bob Gansler resigned on March 23, 1991.

The new leaders of the United States Soccer Federation, the national governing body, on March 27 named 46-year-old Bora Milutinovic of Yugoslavia as the new coach. He had coached the 1986 Mexican and 1990 Costa Rican World Cup teams.

The federation created the CONCACAF Gold Cup tournament in Los Angeles. CONCACAF stands for the Confederation of North, Central American, and Caribbean Association Football, the regional governing body. In the Gold Cup semifinals, the U.S. team upset Mexico, 2-0. In the final on July 7, the United States defeated Honduras, 4-3, on penalty kicks.

Large crowds attended games involving the U.S. team. Attendance exceeded 35,000 in Denver; 51,000 in Foxboro, Mass.; 33,000 in New Haven, Conn.; and 41,000 in Chicago. All of those cities were potential sites for 1994 World Cup games.

U.S. women take world title. The U.S women's soccer team won the Women's World Soccer Championship on Nov. 30, 1991, with a 2-1 victory over Finland in Guangzhou (Canton), China. It was the first world championship in soccer for the United States. Michelle Akers-Stahl scored both goals for the United States in the championship game.

Professional league. The United States in 1991 still lacked a major professional outdoor league. Its most important league was the Major Soccer League (MSL), formerly the Major Indoor Soccer League. However, it still played a scaled-down game indoors.

In the 1990-1991 season, the San Diego Sockers won the indoor title for the fourth consecutive year. But the team lost $750,000 for the season, and its owners suspended operations.

Other competitions. In the major European competitions, Red Star of Belgrade won the European Champions' Cup, and Manchester United of England won the European Cup Winner's Cup. Internazionale of Milan won the Union of European Football Association Cup. In England, Arsenal won the English League's first division, and Tottenham won the Football Association's (VEFA) Cup. Sheffield Wednesday took the English League Cup. In South America, Argentina won the Nations' Champion Cup, and Colo Colo of Chile was the club champion.

Argentina played without Diego Maradona, the world's most celebrated player. When he tested positive for drugs on March 29, the Italian Soccer Federation suspended him for 15 months. The 30-year-old Maradona was arrested twice for possession of cocaine—in April in Buenos Aires, Argentina, and in June in Naples, Italy. An Italian court gave him a 14-month suspended sentence. Frank Litsky

In ***World Book,*** see **Soccer.**

Social security benefits were to increase by 3.7 per cent as of Jan. 1, 1992, under the annual cost-of-living adjustment program. At the same time, the maximum wage subject to the social security payroll tax rose from $53,400 to $55,500. The benefit increase, based on the Consumer Price Index, was the smallest in five years. The raise boosted the average social security check by $22 a month, to $629 from $607.

Congressional help was enlisted by the United States Social Security Administration (SSA) in February 1991 to obtain an extra $100 million from the Office of Management and Budget (OMB). SSA officials said the money was urgently needed to keep administrative operations running at an acceptable level.

Twenty-five senators and 32 members of the House of Representatives wrote to OMB Director Richard G. Darman to demand release of the money from a contingency fund Congress had set up to meet emergency needs of the retirement program. Darman released the money on March 15. The SSA spends more than $4 billion of its $263-billion annual budget to administer social security benefits.

Proposed tax cut killed. On April 24, 1991, the U.S. Senate voted 60 to 38 to reject a plan to reduce the social security tax on annual wages less than $53,400. Senator Daniel Patrick Moynihan (D., N.Y.) sponsored the proposal, which would have decreased taxes from 6.2 per cent to 5.2 per cent over a five-year period. Moynihan argued that the tax was being wrongly used to reduce the federal deficit. President George Bush strongly opposed the plan and said it would "bankrupt the social security system."

Medicare issues. On May 31, the federal Health Care Financing Administration (HCFA) announced plans to drastically revise Medicare reimbursement for physicians' services. According to provisions set forth in 1989 by Congress, Medicare was to establish a new fee schedule whereby physicians would be reimbursed on the basis of the "relative value" of the procedures they performed, rather than the customary rates they charged patients. The aim of the new fee schedule was to balance payments among physicians by increasing the amount of money allowed for primary care providers, such as family and general practitioners, and reducing amounts permitted for specialists, such as surgeons and cardiologists.

However, the new fee schedule proposed by HCFA also included "volume performance standards" that would have reduced physician payments rather than simply narrowing the gap between primary care providers and specialists. Facing opposition from the American Medical Association and other physician groups, HCFA officials decided in August to add $6.9-billion to the fee schedule, which was to take effect Jan. 1, 1992. With the revision, HCFA expects Medicare payments to doctors to total $191 billion over the next five years. Frank Cormier and Margot Cormier

In ***World Book,*** see **Social security.**

Somalia. President Mohamed Siad Barre, who came to power in a military coup in 1969, was ousted by rebel forces on Jan. 27, 1991. Barre fled into exile in Kenya but returned later in the year. At year-end, he was reported to be under house arrest.

Africa Watch, a human-rights monitoring group, reported in 1990 that about 50,000 Somalis had been killed in combat or at the hands of Barre's security forces since June 1988, when the rebels first took up arms against Barre's rule, which had become increasingly abusive in the two years before his overthrow.

The rebel forces that overthrew Barre were a loose coalition of at least six guerrilla organizations, each based upon a different *clan* (a group of related families). In the south, the uprising was led by the United Somali Congress (USC) and the Somali Patriotic Front (SPF). Over the objections of the other clan rebel forces, who were not consulted in advance, those two organizations installed a USC leader, Ali Mahdi Mohamed, as provisional president of Somalia.

To placate the other members of the coalition, Mohamed in late July carried out an earlier pledge to convene a national conference to draw up a new constitution. The six major rebel groups were represented, and the conference was monitored by observers from 20 countries and international political organizations. The conferees produced a document guaranteeing a multiparty system, free elections, respect for human rights, and a market economy. President Mohamed was given two more years to govern before having to stand for election.

Continued strife. The defeat of Barre did not end the civil war. Many pro-Barre troops continued to fight on for several months, and rebels within the coalition fought the USC.

An even greater threat was posed by the principal rebel group in the north, the Somali National Movement (SNM), which sought independence for the northern region, known as British Somaliland before it was incorporated into the new nation of Somalia in 1960. In May, the SNM declared an independent Somaliland Republic, and the SNM leader, Abduraham Ahmed Ali, was named interim president. The move went unopposed for the time being because the USC lacked the military power to stop it.

A second coup? Late in the year, Somalia faced the prospect of a second change of leadership. In September, General Mohamed Farah Aideed, the chairman of the USC and an archrival of Mohamed, made a bid for power, and in November he launched an attack on Mogadishu, the capital. At year-end, it was uncertain which of the two would emerge victorious. But whoever wins, Somalia faces a bleak future. It is one of the poorest countries in Africa, and the war has left its economy and public services in shambles.

J. Gus Liebenow and Beverly B. Liebenow

See also **Africa** (Facts in brief table). In ***World Book,*** see **Somalia.**

South Africa. At a national convention held in Johannesburg on Dec. 20 and 21, 1991, representatives of some 20 racial, ethnic, and political groups gathered to lay the groundwork for a new constitution for South Africa in 1992. The goal is to give South Africa's 30 million blacks equality with the nation's 5 million whites. The convention was just one of several important steps taken during the year to dismantle *apartheid* (racial separation) in South Africa.

South Africa's State President Frederik Willem de Klerk continued to take the lead in proposing significant reforms. At the opening of Parliament on Feb. 1, 1991, de Klerk boldly recommended dropping one of the key pillars of apartheid, the Population Registration Act of 1950. This law required each South African to be classified as either European (white), African (black), Asian, or Colored (mixed race). On June 17, 1991, Parliament repealed the registration act by a large majority.

Less than two weeks before, on June 5, South Africa's Parliament had overturned another foundation of apartheid, the Group Areas Act of 1950, which segregated urban residents by race. That act's enforcement over 40 years had resulted in the arrests of some 17 million blacks for curfew violations. Also revoked on June 5, 1991, were several acts that had reserved 87 per cent of South Africa's land for the white minority. Additional reforms adopted in midyear ended or eased other oppressive policies.

Zulus brandishing traditional weapons rally near Johannesburg in March. Through much of 1991, the Zulus fought with black rivals in South Africa.

Political fragmentation. The division between whites and blacks in South Africa was paralleled in 1991 by splits within the various racial groups. President de Klerk's National Party did not have the support of the more liberal Democratic Party for a plan that he unveiled in September for giving voting rights to blacks. Democratic Party members said that the proposal was aimed mainly at protecting the political power of whites. The proapartheid Conservative Party attempted to thwart all the reform measures that were proposed during the year. And the even more obstructionist neo-Nazi Afrikaner Resistance Movement resorted to vigilante tactics and street violence in its attempts to stop reform.

Black political groups also had their share of disagreements, with some black leaders refusing to follow Nelson Mandela. Mandela, who in early July replaced the ailing Oliver Tambo as president of the African National Congress (ANC), the oldest and the largest of the black antiapartheid organizations, sought during 1991 to cooperate with the de Klerk government.

Mandela's biggest problem was the ANC's relationship with the Inkatha Freedom Party, a political organization based on the Zulu ethnic group. The ANC and Inkatha had been bitter rivals for years, engaging in frequent bloody battles that continued into 1991. ANC leaders had long charged that the Zulus received preferential treatment from the government. That suspicion was confirmed in July when the government admitted that two of its ministers had secretly funneled money to Inkatha.

On September 14, Mandela and Inkatha's leader, Chief Mangosuthu Gatsha Buthelezi, signed an agreement with the government. The pact set up special police and judicial units to quickly investigate and defuse violence between black groups.

Sanctions lifted. The United States and a number of other nations ended their economic sanctions against South Africa in 1991 as the apartheid situation improved. In addition, the International Olympic Committee in July lifted a 21-year-old ban on South African participation in the Olympic Games.

Winnie Mandela convicted. On May 13, Winnie Mandela, the wife of Nelson Mandela, was convicted of kidnapping for her part in the December 1988 abduction and beating of four black youths at her home in the black township of Soweto. One of the young men was later murdered. Mandela was sentenced to six years in prison. She was freed while her conviction was being appealed.

J. Gus Liebenow and Beverly B. Liebenow.

See also **Africa** (Facts in brief table). In ***World Book,*** see **South Africa.**

South America. See **Latin America.**
South Carolina. See **State government.**
South Dakota. See **State government.**
Soviet Union. See **Union of Soviet Socialist Republics.**

Space exploration. The National Aeronautics and Space Administration (NASA) flew six successful space shuttle missions during 1991 and unveiled its newest shuttle, *Endeavor*. Completed in April, *Endeavor* replaced *Challenger*, which was destroyed in an explosion soon after liftoff in January 1986.

Emergency spacewalk. The shuttle *Atlantis* rocketed into orbit on April 5, 1991, carrying five astronauts and the 17-ton (15-metric-ton) *Gamma Ray Observatory* (*GRO*). The *GRO* was designed to survey the galaxy and beyond for gamma rays, a high-energy form of radiation emitted by exploding stars, quasars, black holes, and other astronomical objects. (Later, NASA changed the name of the *GRO* to the *Compton Observatory*, in honor of Arthur H. Compton, a Nobel-prize winning American physicist.)

During an attempt to launch the *GRO* from the shuttle cargo bay, an antenna on the observatory became stuck, and two astronauts had to make an emergency spacewalk to free it. The attempt was successful, and the observatory was placed in Earth orbit on April 7. During a later, scheduled spacewalk, the crew tested maneuvering devices planned for use in constructing a space station. The mission ended on April 11, as *Atlantis* landed at Edwards Air Force Base in California.

SDI test. On April 28, *Discovery* took off on a military mission. Most of this eight-day flight was devoted to testing instruments and collecting data for the Strategic Defense Initiative (SDI), a space-based missile defense system also known as "Star Wars." The astronauts launched and retrieved a small satellite that contained sensors for detecting exhaust plumes from enemy missiles. The mission ended when the seven-man crew landed at Cape Canaveral, Fla., on May 6.

Medical experiments. On June 5, after two postponements, *Columbia* carried a crew of four men and three women, plus 29 rats and more than 2,000 jellyfish, into orbit. For the next nine days, the crew, three of whom were physicians, conducted medical tests on the animals and on themselves. It was the most detailed examination of the effects of weightlessness on humans ever conducted in space. The flight ended with a landing at Edwards Air Force Base on June 14.

To obtain additional information about the biological effects of prolonged spaceflight, NASA extended an *Atlantis* mission launched on August 2 from five days to nine days. The primary goal of the flight was to release a *Tracking and Data Relay Satellite*, which forms part of a space communications system that relays data and commands between spacecraft and a ground station. *Atlantis* returned on August 11.

Other shuttle flights. *Discovery* went into orbit again on September 12, carrying a 7-ton (6-metric-ton) *Upper Atmosphere Research Satellite* (*UARS*) and a five-man crew. Once launched, *UARS* began measuring the effects of air pollution on Earth's upper atmosphere and gathering information to help meteorologists predict global weather changes. Bad weather forced the cancellation of a scheduled Florida landing, so *Discovery* set down in California on September 17.

On November 24, *Atlantis* took off on a military mission, the last shuttle flight of the year. When one of the shuttle's three navigational units failed, the planned 10-day flight was shortened, with *Atlantis* returning to Edwards Air Force Base on December 1.

Asteroid flyby. The first close-up picture of an asteroid was taken by the *Galileo* spacecraft on October 29. *Galileo*, which had been launched from *Atlantis* on Oct. 18, 1989, encountered the 8-mile (13-kilometer)-long asteroid on its way to a 1995 rendezvous with Jupiter.

Galileo's umbrella-shaped antenna, needed for optimum communications with Earth as *Galileo* orbits Jupiter, failed to unfurl completely when ground technicians commanded it to open on April 11, 1991, however. Attempts to open the antenna in May and August also failed.

U.S. space-program plans. In April 1991, the National Space Council, a NASA oversight panel, announced that NASA and the Department of Defense would develop a new unmanned booster that might replace the shuttle for some uses. In March, NASA had announced plans to simplify the design of the planned

Opposite: Atlantis launches the *Gamma Ray Observatory* (inset top) on April 5. Astronauts free a stuck antenna on the observatory (inset bottom).

USA
NASA
United States
Atlantis

Freedom space station. Although a House of Representatives subcommittee recommended no funding for *Freedom* in 1992, Congress allocated $2 billion for the station in a $14.3-billion NASA budget.

Soviet space stations. While the United States planned to launch the first elements of its space station in 1996, the abandoned Soviet space station, *Salyut 7*, fell to Earth. The 43-ton (39-metric-ton) station, which had been launched in 1982 and abandoned in 1986, broke up as it fell into Earth's atmosphere on Feb 7, 1991. Some debris fell in southern Argentina and the Atlantic Ocean.

Meanwhile, the Soviets struggled to fund their present station, *Mir*, which had been in orbit since February 1986. Starting in 1990, Soviet officials began accepting paying passengers aboard *Mir*. In May 1991, commercial sponsors spent an undisclosed sum to put the first Briton in space—biologist Helen Sharman. Then, in October, Austria reportedly paid $7 million to make engineer Franz Viehboeck the first Austrian in space.

In August, cosmonaut Anatoly Artsebarsky conducted an experiment paid for by the Coca-Cola Company. While aboard *Mir*, he drank Coca-Cola from a special pressurized can as an instrument measured the separation of gas and liquid inside the can of carbonated beverage.

International cooperation. A U.S. astronaut was to fly on a long-duration mission aboard *Mir* under a cooperative agreement between the United States and the Soviet Union, which was signed on July 31. The agreement had called for a cosmonaut to fly on a U.S. shuttle mission, and for the two nations to cooperate in monitoring the environment from space.

Such cooperation took place in August when a U.S. instrument to map the ozone layer above Antarctica went into orbit aboard a Soviet weather satellite. The device, called the *Total Ozone Mapping Spectrometer*, reached orbit on August 15.

On August 29, the Soviets launched India's second remote-sensing satellite. The United States tried to launch a Japanese communications satellite on April 18, but the booster rocket tumbled out of control and had to be destroyed. NASA had better luck on August 29, when a U.S. telescope for measuring X rays emitted by solar flares was successfully launched by a Japanese M-3S2 rocket from Kagoshima Space Center.

The European Space Agency (ESA) on January 16 launched Italian and European-Community communications satellites aboard an Ariane rocket. ESA also put a large Canadian communications satellite into orbit on April 4. However, an antenna on the Canadian satellite failed to deploy, rendering the craft useless. A sister satellite was successfully launched on September 9. Another Ariane roared into space on July 16, sending Europe's first *Earth Remote Sensing* satellite into orbit. William J. Cromie

See also **Astronomy.** In ***World Book***, see **Space travel.**

Spain

Spain in 1991 prepared for the removal of most trade barriers within the 12-nation European Community (EC or Common Market) by the end of 1992. In April 1991, the Spanish government removed the last remaining restrictions on moving currency in or out of Spain, permitting Spaniards to open foreign bank accounts and freely transfer money abroad. Spain also tied its currency, the peseta, more closely to other EC currencies. This meant that Spain had to pursue anti-inflationary economic policies similar to those of Germany and France.

The Spanish economy slowed down in 1991, along with economies in the rest of Europe. Even so, Spain's growth rate outpaced the European average, because the government continued to spend large amounts on such projects as building roads and dams and improving the country's railroads and telephone system. Spanish consumers also spent freely. An anticipated growth rate of 3 or 4 per cent in 1991, however, still fell below the 5 per cent average that Spain had experienced during much of the 1980's.

Spanish banks and other large companies merged to create bigger companies that would be more competitive in the EC's coming single market. Banks, for example, gained nationwide networks through mergers. The cost of employing Spanish workers, once well below that of other European countries, began to rise in 1991. But Spain still remained an attractive location for foreign-owned factories.

The Socialist Workers' Party government, headed by Prime Minister Felipe González Márquez, supported EC plans for greater economic and political unity. Despite strong public opposition to the Persian Gulf War, Spain joined its EC partners in helping to enforce a naval embargo against Iraq. The quick end to the war helped defuse antigovernment sentiment.

Feuding within the Socialist Workers' Party, especially between moderates and leftists, cost the party popularity with voters. In local elections held in May, the party lost control of the cities of Seville and Valencia. But an even bigger loser was the Union of the Democratic Center, which performed so badly that its founder, former Prime Minister Adolfo Suárez González, resigned as party leader after the elections. The conservative Popular Alliance, led by José Maria Aznar, did well in the elections, especially in Madrid, and showed it could prove a strong challenger to the Socialist Workers' Party in the next national elections, which were scheduled for 1993.

A wave of immigrants, especially from northern Africa, caused a political stir during 1991. Many of them had entered Spain illegally, drawn by its economic boom. Some parties questioned Spain's ability to provide jobs and welfare benefits for the estimated 170,000 immigrants who lived in the country illegally.

Philip Revzin

See also **Europe** (Facts in brief table); **Spain,** Special Report: **Spain Takes Center Stage in 1992.** In ***World Book,*** see **Spain.**

Spain Takes Center Stage in 1992

By Anne Spiselman

Spain hopes for new prestige in Europe and around the world in 1992 as the nation hosts not only the largest—and last—world's fair of the 1900's but also the Summer Olympics.

Much of the world's attention will focus on Spain in 1992. Spain will host Expo '92, the largest and last world's fair of the 20th century, in Seville from April 20 to October 12, and the 1992 Summer Olympics, from July 25 to August 9, in Barcelona. To prepare for the 18 million to 19 million visitors these two events are expected to attract, Spain has begun vast building campaigns in both cities and their surrounding regions.

The Spanish government made plans to spend more than $10 billion on construction projects at the Expo site and surrounding area, plus $6.33 billion on new construction, renovations, and other preparations for the Olympics. These investments were designed with the future in mind. Spain hopes that the year's events will help bring long-term economic benefits and worldwide prestige as the nation tries to assume a higher profile within the European Community (EC). See **Europe,** Special Report: **The Rocky Road to European Unity.**

These hopes are especially relevant to Expo '92, which promises to transform not only Seville, but also Andalusia, the southern region of which the city is the capital and traditionally one of Spain's poorest areas.

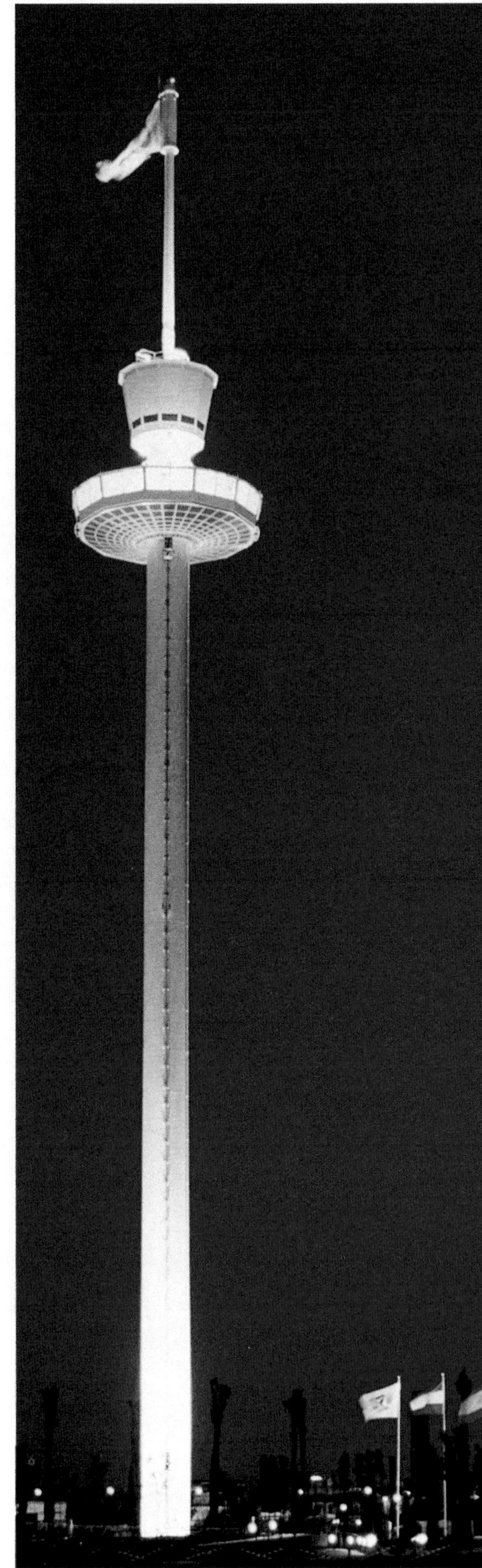

Olympic Stadium in the Montjuïc area of Barcelona, *above*, will showcase some of the world's best athletes during the 1992 Summer Olympics. An observation tower overlooks the 1992 world's fair site in Seville, *previous page*. About 18 million visitors are expected to visit the fair.

The author:

Anne Spiselman is a free-lance writer who has traveled widely in Spain.

Improvements in transportation alone, completed or underway by late 1991, include airport expansions, new highways and roads in Seville, 40 miles (64 kilometers) of new roads outside the city, a new central railroad station, a high-speed train to Madrid, the capital, and several bridges across the Guadalquivir River to the Expo site on the island of La Cartuja. Hotels have been constructed, and palaces and monuments have been restored. Seville, the setting of famous operas such as *The Barber of Seville* and *Carmen*, finally got its first opera house, the Teatro de la Maestranza, in May 1991.

Seville is an appropriate choice for Expo '92 because of its connection with Christopher Columbus and the celebration of the 500th anniversary of his voyage to America. The explorer planned some of his voyages while staying at the Santa María de las Cuevas (St. Mary of the Caves) Carthusian monastery, which has been restored to be a centerpiece of the fair. During the 1400's and 1500's, Seville had a royal monopoly on trade with the New World, resulting in a brief Golden Age for the city.

With the broad theme, "The Age of Discoveries: 1492 to 1992," Expo '92 will build on Columbus' voyage by examining the continuing worldwide importance of his accomplishment. Visitors can explore the results of the spirit of exploration on a "Route of Discovery"—a walking tour that highlights many of humanity's greatest scientific achievements.

The route starts on the grounds of the Pavilion of the Fifteenth Century in the Santa María de las Cuevas monastery. Here visitors can experience the world of 1492 through audio-visual shows, art exhibits, and other displays. Near the Fifteenth Century Pavilion is the Pavilion of Discoveries, where visitors will see exhibits representing some of the most important geographic and scientific discoveries since the 1400's. The Pavilion of Navigation will allow visitors to explore the advances in ocean navigation that made some of the world's greatest geographic discoveries possible. The route concludes at the Pavilion of the Future along the Discovery Waterway, a canal that flows into a lake surrounded by the main Spanish pavilion, plus 17 separate pavilions representing the nation's governmental regions. Nearby will be pavilions of more than 100 countries, representing every continent, as well as the buildings of various international organizations and corporations.

Almost a quarter of the 538-acre (218-hectare) Expo site is devoted to gardens, parks, and plazas, including about 350,000 trees and plants from around the world. Designed to keep people cool in the intense summer heat, these areas will offer musicians, acrobats, puppeteers, and other entertainers. A total of 55,000 concerts, plays, operas, *zarzuelas* (Spanish operettas), and other performances are scheduled during Expo '92 in facilities ranging from a 7,000-seat open-air auditorium to 300-seat theaters.

Activities at Expo '92 will continue until 4 a.m., with dancing and fireworks nightly. In a first for a world's fair, the festivities will be broadcast worldwide. After Expo '92 closes, the site will become an academic, scientific, and technological research complex.

Barcelona will probably experience fewer benefits as a result of hosting the Olympics. Barcelona is already a favorite with tourists. The city offers museums, an old Gothic Quarter, and *ramblas* (wide streets lined with shops and restaurants). Modern architecture, especially the unfinished Holy Family Church and other fanciful works by Spanish architect Antonio Gaudí, also draws visitors. The Summer Olympics will run for 16 days and are expected to attract about 500,000 people to this capital of the region of Catalonia.

Preparations for the Olympics have included the construction of a new international air terminal, numerous hotels, and roads. The Montjuic area of the city, the site of about a dozen Olympic events, has received most of the attention. About $7 million went into remodeling the 60,000-seat Olympic Stadium. Other buildings, such as a 15,000-seat arena for volleyball and gymnastics and a 7,500-seat swimming arena, have also been readied. The National Palace, which overlooks the entrance to Olympic Stadium, was also restored. The palace houses the Catalonian Museum of Art, which has one of Spain's finest art collections.

In the northwest section of the city, near Barcelona University, private sports clubs and arenas, such as the 120,000-seat Camp Nou Stadium, are being remodeled to accommodate equestrian competitions, soccer, and judo. In the working class Vall d'Hebron district, construction of new facilities for archery and tennis have begun near the Municipal Velodrome, built in 1984 for the World Track Cycling Championships. The Parc de Mar area, an industrial zone dating from the 1800's, is being converted to modern housing for the 15,000 Olympic athletes.

When the Olympic Games are over, this housing will be sold as private residences. Many Barceloneans hope this will restore a long-neglected neighborhood—the birthplace of the Spanish industrial revolution—and spur more development.

Kim Zmeskal performs on the way to winning the first ever U.S. women's all-around title at the World Gymnastics Championships in September.

Sports. The rapid international political changes of 1991 affected the sports world. New teams arose when their nations gained independence, and other traditionally powerful national teams lost strength due to political changes in their countries.

South Africa repealed its restrictive racial laws of apartheid (racial separation) on June 17, and the International Olympic Committee (IOC), which had expelled South Africa in 1970, welcomed it back on July 9, 1991. However, rival federations governing several sports within South Africa had difficulty merging. It was therefore unclear whether South Africa would compete in the 1992 Winter and Summer Olympics. These multiple federations prevented South Africa from entering the 1991 world track and field championships. However, South Africa did compete in the World Gymnastics Championships in September.

Europe. The IOC recognized the Baltic republics of Latvia, Lithuania, and Estonia after they declared independence from the Soviet Union in 1991.

Following the 1990 reunification of West Germany and East Germany, united German teams competed in 1991 world championships. However, in the track and field and swimming championships, the united teams won fewer medals than had the East Germans.

Because of political unrest in Yugoslavia, Goran Ivanisevic and Goran Prpic, both Croatians and both ranked in the world top 20, refused to play for Yugoslavia in the Davis Cup tennis semifinals. Two lower-ranked Serbs replaced them, and Yugoslavia lost to France on September 22.

International competition. The Pan American Games were held from August 2 to 18 in Havana, Cuba. Cuba led the United States, 140 to 130, in gold medals, though the United States led Cuba in total medals, 352 to 265. Athletes from North, South, and Central America, as well as the Caribbean, competed in 26 sports. Many elite athletes from the United States bypassed the games in favor of the world outdoor championships in track and field held in Tokyo in late August, and the World Gymnastics Championships in Indianapolis in mid-September.

The World University Games held from July 14 to 21 in Sheffield, England, attracted 5,500 athletes from 111 nations. The leaders in gold medals were the United States with 29, China with 20, and the Soviet Union with 15. In total medals, the United States won 76, the Soviet Union 51, and China 48.

In the Winter World University Games from March 2 to 10 in Sapporo, Japan, the Japanese won 14 gold medals and the Soviets 6. Japan won 32 total medals, the Soviet Union 22, and the United States 12.

NCAA. The National Collegiate Athletic Association, the major governing body for college sports, continued its program to reform college sports. It cut athletic scholarships by 10 per cent in all sports, reduced coaching staffs, eliminated athletic dormitories, made seasons shorter for all sports except football, decreased the number of recruiting contacts, and limited practice time to 20 hours per week. The NCAA Council and the NCAA Presidents Commission supported proposals to raise academic standards for athletes.

Little League world series. Four teams from the United States and four foreign teams competed from August 20 to 24 in the Little League world series in Williamsport, Pa. The Tai Chung Chinese Taipei team defeated the San Ramon Valley team from Danville, Calif., in the final by a score of 11-0 on August 24.

Awards. On March 12, John Smith became the first wrestler to win the James E. Sullivan Award as the outstanding amateur athlete in the United States since the Amateur Athletic Union created the award in 1930. Smith was the first American to win four consecutive world wrestling championships. Finalists for the Sullivan Award included Mike Barrowman from swimming, Raghib (Rocket) Ismail from football, Bonnie Blair from speed skating, and Jill Trenary from figure skating. The U.S. Olympic Committee named Smith as its Sportsman of the Year and Lynn Jennings of Newmarket, N.H., the world cross-country champion, as its Sportswoman of the Year.

Among the winners in 1991 were:

Cycling. Miguel Indurain of Spain led the last 10 days and won the Tour de France, which ended on July 28 in Paris. Greg LeMond of Wayzata, Minn., winner in 1989 and 1990, had a viral infection and finished seventh. Gianni Bugno of Italy finished second, but Bugno later won the world road-racing championship.

Diving. Chinese divers gained four of the six world championships held from Jan. 3 to 13, 1991, in Perth, Australia. Gao Min of China won both women's springboard titles. The other Chinese winners were 12-year-old Fu Mingixia off the women's platform and 14-year-old Sun Shuwei off the men's platform. Kent Ferguson of Boca Raton, Fla., won the men's three-meter, his first international title.

Fencing. Of the 10 titles in the world championships held from June 13 to 22 in Budapest, Hungary, the Soviet Union and Hungary won three each and Italy won two.

Gymnastics. The Soviet Union won both team titles, and Grigory Misutin of the Soviet Union won the men's all-around title in the world championships held from September 6 to I5 in Indianapolis. Fifteen-year-old Kim Zmeskal of Houston upset the Soviet defender, Svetlana Boguinskaya, to win the women's all-around, the first U.S. gymnast to do so.

Rowing. Germany won 7 of the 22 men's, women's, and lightweight titles in the world championships held from August 20 to 25 in Vienna, Austria. The eight-oared winners were the German heavyweight men, the Italian lightweight men, and the Canadian women. The University of Pennsylvania men won the U.S. college and Eastern sprint titles.

Wrestling. The United States won three gold medals and three silver medals at the world freestyle championships held from October 3 to 6 in Varna, Bulgaria. The United States won two silver medals in the world Greco-Roman championships held from September 27 to 30, also in Varna. The U.S. gold medal winners were John Smith of Stillwater, Okla., at 136.5 pounds (62 kilograms); Zeke Jones of Bloomsburg, Pa., at 114.5 pounds (52 kilograms); and Kevin Jackson of Ames, Iowa, at 180.5 pounds (82 kilograms).

Other champions

Archery, world freestyle champions: men, Simon Fairweather, Australia; women, Soo Nyung Kim, South Korea.
Badminton, world champions: men, Jianhua Zhao, China; women, Jiuhong Tang, China.
Biathlon, world champions: men's 10-kilometer, Marc Kirchner, Germany; men's 20-kilometer, Marc Kirchner; women's 7.5-kilometer, Grete Ingeborg Nykkelmo, Norway; women's 15-kilometer, Petra Schaaf, Germany.
Billiards, world three-cushion champion: Raymond Ceulemans, Belgium.
Bobsledding, world champions: two-man, Rudi Lochner, Germany; four-man, Wolfgang Hoppe, Germany.
Canoeing, world champions: men's 500-meter canoe, Mikhail Slivinsky, Soviet Union; men's 500-meter kayak, Renn Chrichlow, Canada; women's 500-meter kayak, Katrin Borchert, Germany; men's 10,000-meter kayak, Greg Barton, Bellingham, Wash.
Court tennis, world champion: Wayne Davies, New York City.
Cross-country, world champions: men, Khalid Skah, Morocco; women, Lynn Jennings, Newmarket, N.H.
Curling, world champions: men, David Smith, Scotland; women, Dordi Nordby, Norway.
Equestrian, World Cup champions: jumping, Jon Whitaker, Great Britain; dressage, Kyra Kyrklund, Finland.
Field hockey, men's Champions Trophy champion: Germany.
Handball, world four-wall champions: men, Pancho Monreal, Mexico; women, Anna Engele, St. Paul, Minn.
Horseshoe pitching, world champions: men, Walter Ray Williams, Jr., Stockton, Calif.; women, Tari Powell, Rantoul, Ill.
Judo, world heavyweight champions: men, Sergei Kosorotov, Soviet Union; women, Ji-Yoon Moon, South Korea.
Lacrosse, U.S. college champions: men, North Carolina; women, Virginia.
Luge, world champions: men, Arnold Huber, Italy; women, Susi Erdmann, Germany.
Modern pentathlon, world champions: men, Arkad Skrzypassek, Poland; women, Eva Fjedllerup, Denmark.
Motorcycle racing, world 500-cc champion: Wayne Rainey, Downey, Calif.
Parachute jumping, world paraski champions: men, Roman Pogacar, Yugoslavia; women, Claudia Gratzel, Czechoslovakia.
Platform tennis, U.S. doubles champions: Rich Maier, Scarsdale, N.Y., and Steve Baird, Harrison, N.Y.
Racquetball, U.S. champions: men, Andy Roberts, Memphis, Tenn.; women, Michelle Gilman, Ontario, Ore.
Racquets, world champion: James Male, Great Britain.
Rhythmic gymnastics, world all-around champion: Oksana, Skalinda, Soviet Union.
Rodeo, world all-around champion: Ty Murray, Stephenville, Tex.
Rugby, World Cup champions: men, Australia; women, United States.
Shooting, World Cup smallbore rifle three-position champions: men, Jean-Pierre Amat, France; women, Valentina Cherkasova, Soviet Union.
Softball, U.S. fast-pitch champions: men, Guanella Brothers, Rohnert Park, Calif.; women, Raybestos Brakettes, Stratford, Conn.
Surfing, OP pro champions: men, Barton Lynch, Australia; women, Frieda Samba, Flagler Beach, Fla.
Synchronized swimming, world solo champion: Sylvie Frechette, Montreal, Canada.
Table tennis, world champions: men, Jorgen Persson, Sweden; women, Deng Yaping, China.
Tae kwon do, U.S. heavyweight champions: men, Scott Miranti, Bozeman, Mont.; women, Lynette Love, Detroit.
Triathlon, Ironman champions: men, Mark Allen, Cardiff, Calif.; women, Paula Newby-Fraser, Encinitas, Calif.
Volleyball, World Cup champions: men, Soviet Union; women, Cuba.
Water polo, world champions: men, Yugoslavia; women, the Netherlands.
Water skiing, world overall champions: men, Patrice Martin, France; women, Karen Neville, Australia.
Weightlifting, world superheavyweight champion: Alexander Kurlovich, Soviet Union.

Frank Litsky

See also articles on the various sports. In ***World Book,*** see articles on the sports.

Sri Lanka went through a constitutional crisis in 1991. On August 28, the opposition Sri Lanka Freedom Party (SLFP) submitted a petition to the speaker of Parliament calling for the impeachment of President Ranasinghe Premadasa. The SLFP claimed that the petition was signed by a majority of the 225 Parliament members, including 47 members of Premadasa's United National Party (UNP).

Parliament suspended. On August 30, Premadasa suspended Parliament to prevent an impeachment vote. On September 3, he claimed that 116 of the 125 UNP members of Parliament had signed a resolution rejecting his impeachment. Some names appeared on both the resolution and the original petition. So the speaker ruled on October 7 that some signatures on the petition were invalid, and impeachment proceedings were dropped.

One impeachment charge was that Premadasa had ordered the army to arm a guerrilla group, the Liberation Tigers of Tamil Eelam, which has been fighting to create a separate state for Sri Lanka's Tamil ethnic minority. Starting in 1987, India, at the request of Sri Lanka's government, had sent troops to fight the Tigers. Before the Indian Army left in March 1990, it created a separate Tamil force to oppose the Tigers. On Sept. 23, 1991, the Sri Lankan defense ministry confirmed that it had helped the Tigers crush the Indian-armed force at a time when the government was having peace talks with the Tigers. The impeachment petition called this treason, since weapons given to the Tigers were turned on the Sri Lankan Army.

Battles with Tigers. On February 17, a Tiger ambush killed 44 Sri Lankan soldiers, the highest losses suffered by the army in one incident in almost a decade of civil war. After three soldiers were killed by a land mine on June 12, the army reportedly killed more than 100 nearby civilians. On July 10, about 5,000 Tigers began a siege of the army camp at Elephant Pass, which controlled the only road to the Tiger-dominated northern peninsula of Sri Lanka. The army landed an 8,000-man relief force on the coast. For 24 days, it fought the bloodiest battle of the civil war. On August 11, the government declared victory, claiming that 2,552 Tigers and 178 soldiers had been killed.

Terrorist bombings in the capital, Colombo, were blamed on the Tigers. On March 2, the minister of state for defense, Ranjan Wijeratne, and 28 others—mostly bystanders—were killed in an explosion. The defense ministry's headquarters was wrecked, and 22 people were killed in another bombing on June 21. The Tigers were also blamed for the murder of former Indian Prime Minister Rajiv Gandhi. See **India.**

More than 75 per cent of Sri Lanka's eligible voters turned out on May 11 for local government elections held everywhere except in the Tiger-dominated northeast. The UNP won control of 190 of Sri Lanka's local authorities. Henry S. Bradsher

See also **Asia** (Facts in brief table). In ***World Book,*** see **Sri Lanka.**

State government. Budget problems preoccupied many state legislatures and governors in the United States in 1991. Still, some states made progress on education reforms and health-care initiatives.

Taxes and finance. States had a bleak fiscal year, as budget gaps forced many state governments to cut spending or raise revenues. The recession continued to hit the Northeast the hardest, but even California confronted a $14-billion deficit.

Demands for spending on welfare and unemployment benefits increased at the same time as the shaky economy hurt state revenue collections. Higher expenditures threw state budgets further out of kilter.

Hikes in personal income taxes and sales taxes in 35 states were expected to bring in an additional $15-billion in the 1992 fiscal year. Increases in California, Connecticut, Pennsylvania, and Texas accounted for almost three-fourths of that amount. California's $7.3-billion tax hike was the nation's largest.

Connecticut in August 1991 adopted a new income tax as it struggled to avoid a projected $2.3-billion deficit. Governor Lowell P. Weicker, Jr., an independent, had earlier vetoed three budgets passed by the Democratic legislature that would have boosted the sales tax instead. Only nine states remained without a personal income tax following Connecticut's action.

Along with raising revenues, states also cut previously enacted budgets by some $7.5 billion. A dozen states laid off workers, and more than half the states froze hiring or made cuts in state programs. Nearly 15,000 state workers lost their jobs between January and July, according to one survey. Seven states shut down government offices for several days, giving state workers time off without pay.

More states turned to gambling in 1991 as a painless way to raise revenues. Texas voters in November approved ending a ban on a state lottery. Louisiana introduced a lottery in September. Georgia planned to vote on a lottery in November 1992. Lotteries in more than 30 states generated more than $20 billion during 1990. Iowa and Illinois launched gambling aboard Mississippi riverboats in the summer of 1991. Similar cruises were slated to start in 1992 in Louisiana and Mississippi.

Education. A Texas court upheld a new school financing plan passed by the Texas legislature in April 1991. The state had been ordered by the court to equalize per-student spending in rich and poor school districts. Despite a similar court order in August 1991, Tennessee legislators failed to approve a package of education and tax reforms proposed by Governor Ned Ray McWherter. See **Education.**

The Oregon legislature enacted a plan to better prepare students for jobs and college. By the 10th grade, students must demonstrate mastery of basic academic skills. The plan also expanded Head Start programs for preschoolers and called for grouping children in kindergarten through third grade by ability rather than age. Minnesota allowed state-certified educators to open their own schools, supported by state funds.

The Illinois legislature in 1991 amended a state law decentralizing the Chicago school system. The Illinois Supreme Court had ruled the law unconstitutional because it gave greater weight to parents than to other community residents in voting for members of parent-community-teacher councils. The councils were established to give parents greater control over the schools. The new law gives equal weight to parents and other community members. See **Chicago.**

Despite budget problems, California retained most of its education budget. It also approved an $89-million program to extend preschool programs to an additional 21,000 four-year-olds and to expand school health and other support services, counseling in early grades, and academic testing services.

Health. Among the fastest-growing state expenses was Medicaid, a joint federal-state program that provides health coverage to some low-income and disabled people. Medicaid spending grew by more than 20 per cent during 1991. The states together contributed $40 billion to Medicaid during the year.

More than 30 states registered alarm over a federal rule, issued in September, which would deny them billions of dollars in federal Medicaid reimbursement. States have been raising nearly $5 billion a year in donations and special taxes from hospitals, nursing homes, and other health agencies to help pay for Medicaid programs. Federal matching for these funds was to end as of October 1992. See **Hospital.**

Oregon worked on an ambitious plan to extend basic health care to the needy through changes in its Medicaid program. The state listed health-care procedures in order of priority. By eliminating coverage for certain low-priority procedures, Oregon hoped to provide checkups, preventive care, and basic care to most of its poorest citizens. The so-called rationing plan required the approval of the federal government.

Massachusetts delayed the scheduled 1992 implementation of a universal health-care plan, which requires most employers to offer their employees health coverage. The postponement resulted from concern over the plan's high cost.

Five states in 1991 passed family-leave laws that allow workers to take time off without pay to care for newly born or adopted children as well as sick parents, children, or spouses. New family-leave laws in California, Maine, and Oregon apply to both public and private sector workers, while laws in Florida and Hawaii cover only state workers.

Elections. In 1991, two incumbent governors lost reelection bids, and one defeat set the stage for a runoff election that drew national attention. In Louisiana, Charles E. (Buddy) Roemer III, who had switched from the Democratic to Republican Party in March, came in a distant third in the October primary. Elected on a promise to clean up government, Roemer had

Democrat Ann W. Richards gives her inaugural address as governor of Texas in front of the State Capitol in Austin on January 15.

Selected statistics on state governments

State	Resident population*	Governor†	Legislature† House (D)	House (R)	Senate (D)	Senate (R)	State tax revenue‡	Tax revenue per capita‡	Public school expenditures per pupil§
Alabama	4,062,608	Guy Hunt (R)	82	23	28	7	$ 3,820,000,000	$ 950	$3,310
Alaska	551,947	Walter J. Hickel (I)	24	16	10	10	1,546,000,000	2,810	7,250
Arizona	3,677,985	J. Fife Symington (R)	27	33	17	13	4,377,000,000	1,190	4,130
Arkansas	2,362,239	Bill Clinton (D)	91	9	31	4	2,261,000,000	960	3,270
California	29,839,250	Pete Wilson (R)	47	33	25	13#	43,419,000,000	1,460	4,650
Colorado	3,307,912	Roy Romer (D)	27	38	12	23	3,069,000,000	930	4,580
Connecticut	3,295,699	Lowell P. Weicker, Jr. (I)	89	62	20	16	5,268,000,000	1,600	7,880
Delaware	688,696	Michael N. Castle (R)	17	24	15	6	1,130,000,000	1,700	5,840
Florida	13,003,362	Lawton Chiles (D)	74	46	22	18	13,289,000,000	1,030	5,050
Georgia	6.508.419	Zell Miller (D)	145	35	45	11	7,078,000,000	1,090	4,470
Hawaii	1,115,274	John Waihee (D)	45	6	22	3	2,335,000,000	2,110	4,620
Idaho	1,011,986	Cecil D. Andrus (D)	28	56	21	21	1,139,000,000	1,130	3,200
Illinois	11,466,682	Jim Edgar (R)	72	46	31	28	12,891,000,000	1,130	4,790
Indiana	5,564,228	Evan Bayh (D)	52	48	24	26	6,102,000,000	1,100	4,110
Iowa	2,787,424	Terry E. Branstad (R)	55	45	28	21**	3,313,000,000	1,190	4,640
Kansas	2,485,600	Joan Finney (D)	63	62	18	22	2,669,000,000	1,080	4,850
Kentucky	3,698,969	Brereton C. Jones (D)	68	32	27	11	4,261,000,000	1,160	3,790
Louisiana	4,238,216	Edwin W. Edwards (D)	89	15††	35	4	4,087,000,000	970	3,840
Maine	1,233,223	John R. McKernan, Jr. (R)	97	54	22	13	1,561,000,000	1,270	5,550
Maryland	4,798,622	William Donald Schaefer (D)	116	25	38	9	6,450,000,000	1,350	5,860
Massachusetts	6,029,051	William F. Weld (R)	119	38‡‡	23	18**	9,369,000,000	1,560	6,170
Michigan	9,328,784	John Engler (R)	61	49	18	20	11,343,000,000	1,220	5,050
Minnesota	4,387,029	Arne H. Carlson (R)	79	55	46	21	6,819,000,000	1,560	5,030
Mississippi	2,586,443	Kirk Fordice (R)	98	23††	43	9	2,396,000,000	930	3,120
Missouri	5,137,804	John Ashcroft (R)	98	64**	23	11	4,939,000,000	970	4,230
Montana	803,655	Stan Stephens (R)	61	39	29	21	858,000,000	1070	4,470
Nebraska	1,584,617	E. Benjamin Nelson (D)	unicameral (49 nonpartisan)				1,513,000,000	960	3,870
Nevada	1,206,152	Bob Miller (D)	22	19**	11	10	1,583,000,000	1,320	4,490
New Hampshire	1,113,915	Judd Gregg (R)	124	268§§	11	13	595,000,000	540	5,100
New Jersey	7,748,634	James J. Florio (D)	22	58	13	27	10,434,000,000	1,350	8,440
New Mexico	1,521,779	Bruce King (D)	49	21	26	16	2,014,000,000	1,330	4,140
New York	18,044,505	Mario M. Cuomo (D)	95	55	26	35	28,615,000,000	1,590	7,920
North Carolina	6,657,630	James G. Martin (R)	81	39	36	14	7,865,000,000	1,190	4,370
North Dakota	641,364	George A. Sinner (D)	48	58	27	26	677,000,000	1,060	3,570
Ohio	10,887,325	George V. Voinovich (R)	61	38	12	21	11,436,000,000	1,050	5,200
Oklahoma	3,157,604	David Walters (D)	68	33	37	11	3,477,000,000	1,110	3,440
Oregon	2,853,733	Barbara Roberts (D)	28	32	10	20	2,786,000,000	980	5,050
Pennsylvania	11,924,710	Robert P. Casey (D)	107	96	24	26	13,220,000,000	1,110	6,110
Rhode Island	1,005,984	Bruce Sundlun (D)	89	11	45	5	1,233,000,000	1,230	6,430
South Carolina	3,505,707	Carroll A. Campbell, Jr. (R)	77	42##	34	12	3,934,000,000	1,130	3,730
South Dakota	699,999	George S. Mickelson (R)	25	45	17	18	500,000,000	720	3,730
Tennessee	4,896,641	Ned Ray McWherter (D)	57	42	20	13	4,245,000,000	870	3,320
Texas	17,059,805	Ann W. Richards (D)	93	57	22	9	14,717,000,000	870	4,060
Utah	1,727,784	Norman H. Bangerter (R)	31	44	9	10	1,768,000,000	1,030	2,720
Vermont	564,964	Howard Dean (D)	73	75#	15	15	666,000,000	1,180	5,420
Virginia	6,216,568	L. Douglas Wilder (D)	58	41††	22	18	6,600,000,000	1,070	5,150
Washington	4,887,941	Booth Gardner (D)	58	40	24	25	7,423,000,000	1,530	4,590
West Virginia	1,801,625	Gaston Caperton (D)	74	26	33	1	2,230,000,000	1,240	4,510
Wisconsin	4,906,745	Tommy G. Thompson (R)	58	39***	19	14	6,558,000,000	1,340	5,710
Wyoming	455,975	Mike Sullivan (D)	22	42	10	20	612,000,000	1,350	5,380

*1990 Census (source: U.S. Bureau of the Census).
†As of January 1992 (source: state government officials).
‡1990 figures (source: U.S. Bureau of the Census).
§1989-1990 figures for elementary and secondary students in average daily attendance (source: National Education Association).
#Two independents.
**One vacancy at time of publication.
††One independent.
‡‡One independent; two vacancies at time of publication.
§§Two independents; six vacancies at time of publication.
##One independent; four vacancies at time of publication.
***Two vacancies at time of publication.

run into trouble getting his proposals through the Legislature, and voters had defeated his tax proposals. The November runoff pitted former Louisiana Governor Edwin W. Edwards, a Democrat who had previously been indicted and acquitted on corruption charges, against an even more controversial figure, Republican State Representative David Duke, a former Ku Klux Klan leader and Nazi sympathizer. Although Duke was soundly defeated, he won 55 per cent of the white vote and in December declared his candidacy for the presidential nomination. See **Duke, David E.**

Incumbent Mississippi Governor Ray Mabus, who had also been elected on a promise of reform, lost in November to Kirk Fordice. Like Roemer, Mabus had met resistance from the Legislature. In January 1992, Fordice was to become Mississippi's first Republican governor in more than 100 years.

Kentucky's Lieutenant Governor Brereton C. Jones led a Democratic sweep of state offices in November 1991. He succeeded Democratic Governor Wallace G. Wilkinson, who could not succeed himself.

New Jersey voters ousted the Democratic majority in the state legislature and gave the Republicans control for the first time in 20 years. Many observers considered the vote a referendum on Democratic Governor James J. Florio. He and the Democratic legislature had enraged voters in 1990 by passing a $2.8-billion tax increase to cover a budget deficit and to make spending among rich and poor school districts more equal. Republicans campaigned on a promise to roll back some $600 million in tax hikes in 1992.

Voters in Washington state turned down a proposal to limit the terms of state and federal legislators. Under the proposed limit, Thomas S. Foley, Speaker of the U.S. House of Representatives, would have lost his congressional seat in 1994. Colorado and Oklahoma, however, adopted term limits in 1990. More states were expected to vote on the issue in 1992. The California Supreme Court upheld a 1990 ballot measure to limit the terms of state officeholders.

Two other governors took office in 1991. In Arizona, Republican J. Fife Symington III won a February 26 runoff against Samuel Pearson Goddard. In Vermont, Democratic Lieutenant Governor Howard Dean succeeded to the governorship after the death of Republican Governor Richard A. Snelling in August.

Political scandals shook Arizona and South Carolina in 1991. Seven legislators were forced out of office in Arizona following a police sting operation. Undercover agents offered money in return for votes on "legislation" that the agents had invented for the operation. In South Carolina, the Federal Bureau of Investigation (FBI) uncovered evidence of vote buying and drug violations that resulted in indictments against nearly 30 legislators, officials, and lobbyists. Both states passed campaign reform laws following the scandals. Elaine S. Knapp

See also **Elections.** In ***World Book,*** see **State government** and the articles on the individual states.

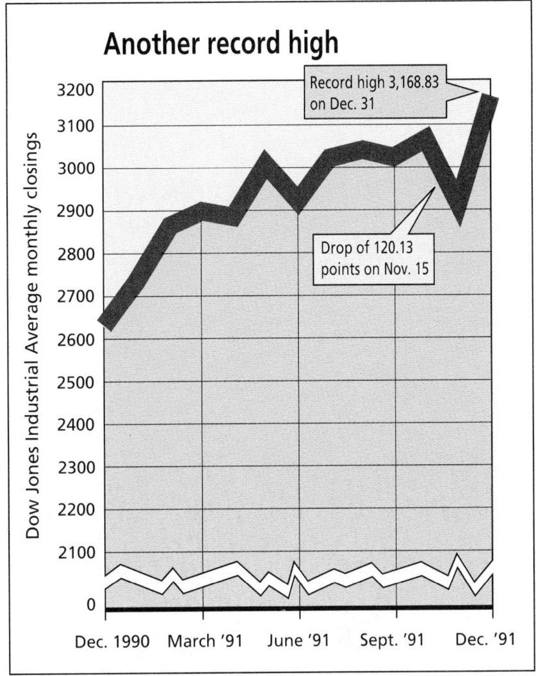

The Dow Jones Industrial Average—the best-known stock market index—ended 1991 with a record high, after its fifth worst one-day loss.

Stocks and bonds. During much of 1991, financial markets in the United States rode a high from the Persian Gulf War that ended in February. Prior to the outbreak of the war, however, stock and bond markets and consumer confidence were at a low. The U.S. economy had entered a recession in July 1990 after eight years of expansion, and the country was jittery about the looming war in the Middle East.

Highs and lows. When allied forces began bombing Iraq on Jan. 17, 1991, oil prices collapsed and financial markets around the world soared. Within weeks, it seemed that the U.S. economy was recovering. Markets remained high for most of the year, barely blinking at the failed August coup in the Soviet Union and the admission by Salomon Brothers Incorporated, also in August, that the firm had cheated in bidding during U.S. Treasury bond auctions.

But by late November, it was clear that the economic recovery was faltering. Repeated drops in short-term interest rates had failed to spark growth. Although the Dow Jones Industrial Average (the Dow) reached record highs in early autumn, it finally reacted to the continuing bad economic news in mid-November, when the Dow plunged 120 points, its fifth worst one-day loss ever. A Christmas rally, sparked by lower interest rates, pushed the stock market to record highs by year-end.

The Dow began 1991 at 2,633.66 and reached a record high of 3,168.83 on December 31, posting a gain of 20 per cent. The Standard & Poor's 500 Composite Index, considered by many economists to be a more comprehensive indicator than the Dow, opened 1991 at 330.22. It ended the year at 417.09.

The best performing U.S. stock market in 1991 was made up of over-the-counter stocks, generally stocks of smaller and younger companies than those in the other averages. The National Association of Securities Dealers Automated Quotations (NASDAQ) composite index, a measure of smaller stocks, soared 57 percent in 1991, beginning the year at 373.84 and ending at 586.34.

International stock markets did not mirror U.S. markets in 1991. They reacted more to developments in their home countries. The Australia All-Ordinaries Index gained the most for the year. It started the year at 1,279.80 and rose nearly 29 per cent to close the year at 1,651.40.

In Great Britain, the London Financial Times-Stock Exchange Index of 100 stocks posted a gain of 16 per cent, beginning the year at 2,143.50 and ending at 2,493.10. In Canada, the Toronto Stock Exchange Index rose about 8 per cent, beginning the year at 3,256.70 and ending at 3,512.36.

The Nikkei Index of 225 large Japanese companies was the only major world index to post a loss for 1991, continuing a slide that began in 1990. The Nikkei began 1991 at 23,848.71 and ended the year down 4 per cent, at 22,983.77.

The U.S. bond market. The yield on 30-year U.S. Treasury bonds ended the year about where it began, at just under 8 per cent. Long-term rates stubbornly refused to budge much during the year, despite the Federal Reserve Board's (the Fed) aggressive lowering of short-term rates. The Fed cut the discount rate—the interest rate it charges member banks for loans—five times in 1991, to 3.5 per cent from 6.5 per cent.

Junk bonds. The market for junk bonds staged a solid recovery during 1991. At the beginning of the year, junk bond yields were around 19 per cent, a spread of 11 per cent above the yield for 10-year Treasury bonds, a rate that reflected the high risk of junk bonds. By year-end, that spread had dropped to 7 per cent.

Scandal at Salomon Brothers. In August 1991, a scandal rocked the U.S. Treasury securities market. Salomon Brothers, a large New York City financial trading firm, admitted that it had submitted bids in clients' names without their permission in an attempt to purchase more than the allowed percentage of security issues at some Treasury market auctions. The firm's top three executives were forced to resign, and the firm's top two Treasury market traders were fired. As a result of the scandal, the U.S. Department of the Treasury announced in September that securities traders making bids on behalf of clients must submit written requests from the clients. Pat Widder

In ***World Book,*** see **Bond; Investment; Stock; Capital.**

Sudan. The problems of Sudan, wracked by famine, drought, a bankrupt economy, and civil war, mounted during 1991. Villages were deserted as water supplies failed and farmers sold their belongings.

More than 8 million Sudanese faced starvation by the beginning of the year. Some relief agencies, fearful of the possibility of violence because of Prime Minister Umar Hasan Ahmad al-Bashir's anti-Western stance during the Persian Gulf crisis, had suspended work in Sudan. In addition, despite warnings of famine by relief agencies, Bashir in 1989 had halted a United Nations (UN) food relief program, accusing Western nations of using reports of a famine to undermine his regime. In March 1991, Bashir yielded to world pressure and restarted the UN relief program.

Political unrest intensified after several Persian Gulf countries cut financial aid to Sudan because of Bashir's support for Iraq during the Persian Gulf crisis. In March, the government imposed a new penal code based on Islamic law in northern Sudan. The imposition of Islamic law has been a key issue in the ongoing civil war between northern Sudanese, who are predominantly Muslim, and southern Sudanese, who practice Christianity or local religions. In April, Bashir announced the release of all political prisoners to ease political unrest. Christine Helms

See also **Persian Gulf,** Special Report: **War in the Persian Gulf; Middle East** (Facts in brief table). In ***World Book,*** see **Sudan.**

Sununu, John H. (1939-), embattled chief of staff to President George Bush, resigned in December 1991. Sununu had taken the spotlight in April amid criticism that he had abused the privileges of office. The criticism followed disclosures that Sununu had made a number of flights aboard United States Air Force jets on personal and Republican Party business. Under White House rules, Sununu paid only a fraction of the cost of those trips, while taxpayers underwrote the remainder. See **Bush, George Herbert Walker.**

John Henry Sununu was born on July 2, 1939, in Havana, Cuba, where his parents were visiting. He received a Ph.D. in mechanical engineering from the Massachusetts Institute of Technology in Cambridge in 1966. Before entering politics, Sununu headed his own engineering firm and served as associate dean at the Tufts University College of Engineering in Medford, Mass. In 1982, Sununu was elected to the first of three two-year terms as governor of New Hampshire.

In 1988, Sununu won the gratitude of George Bush by helping engineer a Bush victory in the New Hampshire presidential primary—a victory that helped revive Bush's flagging presidential campaign. Sununu campaigned vigorously for Bush and soon after the election was named White House chief of staff. In that position, he controlled access to the President and supervised the development of White House policies.

Sununu married Nancy Hayes in 1958. They have eight children. Karin C. Rosenberg

Supreme Court of the United States. During its 1990-1991 term, the Supreme Court of the United States put new restrictions on the rights of criminal defendants, particularly death row inmates, and set the stage for a confrontation in Congress over abortion counseling at health clinics receiving federal tax money. But the most significant event of the term took place on the last day of the court session, June 27, when Justice Thurgood Marshall announced his retirement after 24 years. Marshall, the nation's premier civil rights lawyer when President Lyndon B. Johnson appointed him to the Supreme Court in 1967, was the court's first black justice. See **Supreme Court of the United States,** Special Report: **A Champion of Civil Rights Retires.**

A controversial nominee. On July 1, President George Bush nominated another black jurist, federal appeals court Judge Clarence Thomas, to succeed Marshall. Thomas, 43, had headed civil rights enforcement at the U.S. Department of Education and chaired the Equal Employment Opportunity Commission (EEOC) for eight years before Bush appointed him to the appeals court in Washington, D.C., in 1990. Thomas, an outspoken conservative, was opposed by many liberals and civil rights groups. After extensive confirmation hearings, the Senate Judiciary Committee on September 27 split 7 to 7 on whether to endorse Thomas. The committee referred the nomination to the Senate with no recommendation.

In early October, as the Senate was preparing to vote on the matter, an unexpected development cast a new light on the nomination. The press received a leaked report that a University of Oklahoma law professor, Anita F. Hill, had informed the Senate Judiciary Committee that Thomas had sexually harassed her in the early 1980's when she was his assistant at the Education Department and at the EEOC.

In response to public pressure, the Judiciary Committee on October 11 convened special televised hearings that riveted the nation's attention for three days. In her testimony, Hill asserted that Thomas had pestered her for dates, described pornographic motion pictures to her, and boasted in graphic detail of his sexual prowess. Thomas vehemently denied Hill's allegations and said he was being made the victim of a "high-tech lynching" organized by liberal opponents of his nomination. The committee also questioned other witnesses, some supporting Hill's version of events and others backing Thomas.

On October 15, the Thomas nomination was finally put to a vote by the Senate. He was confirmed 52 to 48, one of the closest margins ever received by a Supreme Court nominee. Eleven Democrats and 41 of the Senate's 43 Republicans voted in favor of confirmation. Thomas was formally seated on November 1.

Abortion counseling. On May 23, the court voted 5 to 4 to uphold rules prohibiting counselors at family-planning clinics funded by the federal government from discussing abortion with patients or referring them to physicians who perform abortions. The restrictions, adopted by the Department of Health and Human Services (HHS) in 1988, changed a long-standing policy of allowing abortion counseling at federally financed clinics, which serve mostly poor women.

Supreme Court nominee Clarence Thomas, testifing before the Senate Judiciary Committee in October, denies that he sexually harassed a former employee.

The court's ruling sparked a fight between the Bush Administration and Congress that lasted into late autumn 1991. In November, both the House and Senate approved a bill to block the HHS rules from taking effect for a year. The President, however, vetoed the measure on November 19, and the House fell 12 votes short of overriding the veto.

Murder trial sentencing. In one of the term's most controversial decisions, the court ruled 6 to 3 on June 27 that juries may consider evidence about a murder victim and the victim's family when deciding whether to sentence the killer to death. The decision, which recognized a growing national movement on behalf of victims' rights, overturned two recent Supreme Court rulings that prevented prosecutors from introducing information about a murder victim when arguing for the death penalty. The high court made its ruling in an appeal brought by a Tennessee man, Pervis T. Payne, who was convicted in 1988 of killing a woman and her 2-year-old daughter. Payne received the death sentence after the jury was told the crime had devastated the dead woman's 3-year-old son.

Criminal defendants' rights. On June 24, the Supreme Court curtailed the right of state-prison in-

University of Oklahoma professor Anita F. Hill, who charged Clarence Thomas with sexual harassment, tells the media on October 8 of her plans to testify.

mates to challenge the constitutionality of their convictions and sentences in federal court. The 6 to 3 ruling, which swept aside a landmark 1963 high court decision guaranteeing that right in most instances, was the second decision of the term to restrict the avenues of appeal for death row inmates. On April 16, 1991, in another 6 to 3 ruling, the court said inmates must raise all their claims about violations of their constitutional rights in one federal appeal. Repeated appeals, which inmates frequently file, now will be accepted only in limited circumstances, the court said.

A defendant's right to a fair trial is not automatically violated when prosecutors introduce in court a confession that the police coerced from the defendant, the court ruled, 5 to 4, on March 26. The court said the fact that a confession was not made voluntarily is unimportant if other evidence in a case is sufficient to convict the defendant. And on June 27, the court ruled, 5 to 4, that sentencing people who were caught with large amounts of drugs to life in prison without parole does not violate the Eighth Amendment ban on "cruel and unusual punishment."

Women in the workplace. In a major victory for working women, the court ruled on March 20 that companies cannot exclude women from hazardous jobs in order to protect their reproductive health. In its 6 to 3 ruling, the court declared that both the Civil Rights Act of 1964 and the Pregnancy Discrimination Act of 1978 prohibit employers from discriminating against women on the basis of their capacity to become pregnant.

School desegregation. A 5 to 3 Supreme Court vote on January 15 opened the way for public school districts to end the court-ordered busing of students. The high court ruled that school districts may terminate busing if they can show that they have taken all possible steps to eliminate the effects of past segregation. Under the ruling, a district can regain control of its schools from federal courts by showing that the local school board is protecting the rights of all students and a return to discriminatory practices is unlikely.

Voting rights. In a pair of 6 to 3 decisions in cases from Texas and Louisiana, the court said on June 20 that the U.S. Voting Rights Act applies to election of state judges. The act, which Congress passed in 1965 and amended in 1982, bars states and communities from using voting practices or establishing voting-district boundaries that discriminate against minorities.

Jury selection. In two decisions in 1991, the court reinforced the principle that people cannot be excluded from sitting on juries on the basis of their race. In 1986, the court had said such exclusions violate the Constitution's guarantee of equal protection under the law. That decision, however, appeared to apply only to cases involving black jurors and black defendants. On April 1, 1991, the court in its 7 to 2 ruling made clear that this principle applies regardless of the race of the defendant or of the excluded jurors. The case in question involved a white man, Larry J. Powers of Ohio, who was convicted of murdering two white people. The prosecutors in that case were allowed to exclude seven potential jurors who were black. The court expanded its ruling again on June 3. In a 6 to 3 decision, it said that racially based juror exclusions are impermissible in civil trials as well as in criminal cases.

No limit on punitive damages. The court on March 4 declined to place limits on the amount of punitive damages awarded to plaintiffs in civil cases. Punitive damages are fines that a guilty defendant must pay to a plaintiff as a form of punishment. In its 7 to 1 ruling, the court said that while some juries may "run wild" and award plaintiffs huge amounts in personal-injury cases and business disputes, the method states use to assess punitive damages is constitutional.

Freedom of the press. The court ruled 7 to 2 on June 20 that inaccuracies in quoted statements attributed to a public figure—even quotes that are deliberate alterations—are not libelous if the essence of what the person actually said has not been changed. On June 24, the court ruled, 5 to 4, that news organizations can be sued for revealing the names of sources who had been promised confidentiality.

Linda P. Campbell and Geoffrey A. Campbell

See also **Courts.** In ***World Book,*** see **Supreme Court of the United States.**

Surgery. See **Medicine.**
Suriname. See **Latin America.**
Swaziland. See **Africa.**

A Champion of Civil Rights Retires

By Geoffrey A. Campbell and Linda P. Campbell

Thurgood Marshall, center, celebrates with other civil rights lawyers in front of the Supreme Court following their landmark victory in *Brown v. Board of Education* in 1954.

On June 27, 1991, Justice Thurgood Marshall announced his retirement from the Supreme Court of the United States. The next morning, he said he hoped people would remember him as a man who "did what he could with what he had." Future generations are likely to agree that what Marshall had was an uncommon gift for combining shrewd legal reasoning with a passion for human rights. What he did was work for 58 years to reform American society, first as a civil rights lawyer, then as U.S. solicitor general, and finally as the first black Supreme Court justice.

When President Lyndon B. Johnson nominated him to the high court in 1967, Marshall was already the nation's leading civil rights lawyer. His most famous cases challenged racial injustice in the public schools. In the late 1930's, Marshall and his assistants at the NAACP Legal Defense and Educational Fund began filing lawsuits to improve schools for black children in Southern cities. Soon they directly challenged segregated schools. Separate schools, they argued, were inherently unequal and denied black students their rights to equal protection under the law. In 1954, Marshall won the landmark case of *Brown v. Board of Education of Topeka*, convincing the Supreme Court that public schools segregated by law violate the equal protection clause of the U.S. Constitution's 14th Amendment.

Marshall also won court rulings giving blacks voting rights, breaking down racial housing barriers, and integrating interstate buses. "He really helped to transform the law and the country," said William L. Taylor, a civil rights lawyer who worked with Marshall at the Legal Defense Fund. Taylor said Marshall helped "rid the country of the formalized caste system carried out through the segregation laws in border and Southern states."

Marshall's efforts to transform American society were prompted by his own experience of racial injustice. The great-grandson of a slave, he was born in 1908 to a Baltimore teacher and a Pullman-car waiter. Marshall attended Lincoln University in Pennsylvania, a school for black students, and earned his law degree from all-black Howard University in Washington, D.C. While working on cases throughout the South, he was forced to stay at the homes of local black lawyers since most hotels were for whites only. Once he was arrested when police falsely accused him of drunken driving. His life was threatened several times.

Considering these obstacles, Marshall's achievements are all the more remarkable. He won 29 of the 32 cases he argued before the Supreme Court. Then, from 1961 to 1965, Marshall was a judge on the 2nd U.S. Circuit Court of Appeals in New York. From 1965 to 1967, he argued cases before the Supreme Court as U.S. solicitor general, the federal government's main courtroom lawyer. In 1967, Marshall's nomination to the high court was approved by a vote of 69 to 11.

The Supreme Court that Marshall joined in 1967 had been expanding individual rights through a series of rulings on racial segregation, press freedom, and protections for criminal defendants. Marshall fit in well with the spirit of that court. But in the early 1970's, the court began a conservative shift, reversing or moderating many of the earlier liberal rulings, and Marshall was soon writing more dissenting opinions. With the retirement of Justice William J. Brennan, Jr., in 1990, Marshall became the Supreme Court's sole remaining liberal justice.

Lawyers who worked for Marshall say that he encouraged the other justices to consider the impact of their decisions. "He made sure the justices understood there were real live people who were going to be affected," said law professor Susan Low Bloch of Georgetown University in Washington, D.C., who clerked for Marshall from 1976 to 1977.

In his dissents, Marshall spoke out for equal justice and stood up for poor people. In one typical dissent, written in 1973, he objected when the court upheld a Texas public school finance system that left some districts very wealthy and others with meager funds. "I, for one, am unsatisfied with the hope for an ultimate 'political' solution sometime in the indefinite future," he wrote, "while, in the meantime, countless children unjustifiably receive inferior educations that may affect their hearts and minds in a way unlikely ever to be undone."

Legal scholars compare Marshall to earlier Supreme Court justices, such as Oliver Wendell Holmes, Jr., and Louis D. Brandeis, who issued powerful dissenting opinions during the early 1900's, particularly in the area of individual rights. Their viewpoints later were reflected in law. Now with Marshall's departure, the court has lost one of its most outspoken recent dissenters. Like Holmes and Brandeis, he will be remembered both for his dissents and for his lasting influence on American life.

The authors:

Geoffrey A. Campbell is a staff reporter for the *Bond Buyer*. Linda P. Campbell is National Legal Affairs Correspondent for the *Chicago Tribune*.

Sweden. Dramatic political change came to Sweden in 1991 when a minority conservative government took power in October, replacing a Socialist government. The new government pledged to cut the country's high income tax rates, reform the generous but costly welfare system, and take long-neutral Sweden into the 12-nation European Community (EC or Common Market) as quickly as possible.

In elections held on September 15, the Social Democratic Party suffered a humiliating defeat. The party won only 137 seats in the 349-member Riksdag (parliament), down from its previous 156 seats. The party's leader, Ingvar Carlsson, resigned as Sweden's prime minister the next day. The Social Democrats had ruled Sweden for all but 6 of the last 59 years.

The election's biggest winner was the Moderate Party, whose leader, 42-year-old Carl Bildt, became prime minister on October 4. Bildt formed a four-party coalition government. It was composed of his own Moderate Party with 80 seats in the Riksdag, the Liberal Party with 34 seats, the Center Party with 31 seats, and the Christian Democratic Party with 26 seats. The coalition fell five votes short of a majority in the Riksdag. To pass laws, the coalition must rely on votes or abstentions by New Democracy, a newly formed conservative party that holds 25 seats in the Riksdag. Bildt declined to take New Democracy into his government because he disagreed with some of the party's proposals, including reducing the prices of alcoholic beverages.

Changes ahead. Bildt announced that during his three-year term he planned to sell some of Sweden's state-owned industries and some of its state services, such as day care, and cut tax rates on businesses to make them more competitive abroad. His proposals for lessening the role of the government in Swedish life moved further and faster than similar plans advanced early in 1991 by Carlsson.

Bildt also pledged that he would reorient Sweden's foreign policy toward the West. Previous Swedish governments had opposed the Vietnam War (1957-1975) and championed Cuba's Communist government, but Bildt planned to stop Swedish aid to Cuba.

EC application. Sweden in July 1991 applied to join the European Community. The application followed years of debate within the country, which focused mainly on whether EC membership would require Sweden to give up its long-standing political neutrality and lose some control over economic decision-making. But the collapse of Communism in eastern Europe and the Soviet Union rendered the neutrality argument largely irrelevant. Moreover, Swedish business people argued that the country risked becoming isolated and falling behind the rest of Europe economically if it remained outside the EC.

Philip Revzin

See also **Europe** (Facts in brief table) and Special Report: **The Rocky Road to European Unity.** In ***World Book,*** see **Sweden.**

Swimming. The United States and a surprising group of swimmers from Hungary won the most titles in the 1991 world championships. Germany and the Soviet Union did not do as well as expected, though the Soviets rebounded in August in the European championships.

The world championships in Perth, Australia, from January 7 to 13, saw the United States win 13 gold medals to Hungary's 5. The United States, with 23, and the unified German team, with 20, won the most total medals.

Winners among American men included Mike Barrowman in the 200-meter breaststroke; Melvin Stewart in the 200-meter butterfly; Matt Biondi in the 100-meter freestyle; Tom Jager in the 50-meter freestyle; and Jeff Rouse in the 100-meter backstroke. Barrowman's time of 2 minutes 11.23 seconds set a world record. Stewart's time of 1 minute 55.69 seconds also set a world record. Barrowman lowered his mark to 2:10.60 on August 13 at the U.S. National Swimming Championships in Ft. Lauderdale, Fla.

Among the American women, Janet Evans won the freestyle at 400 meters and 800 meters, and Nicole Haislett won the 100-meter freestyle. Summer Sanders won the 200-meter butterfly.

Hungarian world champions. Tamas Darnyi of Hungary set two world records in the men's individual medleys in Perth (1 minute 59.36 seconds for 200 meters and 4 minutes 12.36 seconds for 400 meters). Darnyi's teammate Norbert Rozsa broke the men's 100-meter breaststroke world record with a time of 1 minute 1.45 seconds, which he lowered on August 20 to 1 minute 1.29 seconds.

Hungary's Krisztina Egerszegi also won the women's 100-meter and 200-meter backstroke. In the European championships in Athens, Greece, from August 17 to 25, the 17-year-old Egerszegi set world backstroke records of 1 minute 0.31 second for 100 meters and 2 minutes 6.62 seconds for 200 meters.

Men's champions in Perth also included Martin Zubero of Spain in the 200-meter backstroke and Anthony Nesty of Suriname in the 100-meter butterfly. The two were teammates at the University of Florida in Gainesville.

Other world records. Germany's Joerg Hoffmann set a world record at the world championships in the 1,500-meter freestyle with 14 minutes 50.36 seconds. At the Pan Pacific Championships, held from August 22 to 25 in Edmonton, Canada, Rouse bettered the 100-meter backstroke record in 53.93 seconds, and Kieren Perkins of Australia broke the 800-meter freestyle record in 7 minutes 47.85 seconds. Zubero set two world records in the 200-meter backstroke—1:57.30 on August 13 and 1:56.57 on November 23.

Other competitions. The United States won 26 of 34 gold medals in the Pan Pacific Championships and 24 of 32 gold medals in the Pan American Games, held in August in Havana, Cuba.

Frank Litsky

In ***World Book,*** see **Swimming.**

Switzerland wavered over joining the 12-nation European Community (EC or Common Market) during much of 1991. Business and government support for joining strengthened. But Swiss voters in June rejected the adoption of a value-added tax, a kind of national sales tax, that would have brought the country's tax system more in line with those of EC members.

In addition to its tax structure, Switzerland would probably have to change some of its banking laws, which keep bank accounts secret, to join the EC. Moreover, EC membership would make it more difficult for Switzerland to maintain its policy of strict military neutrality. In December, EC leaders agreed to develop a common defense policy.

In October, the European Free Trade Association, to which Switzerland belongs, agreed to join with the EC in forming an enlarged free-trade zone to take effect at the end of 1992. This would bring Switzerland many of the economic benefits of EC membership.

Right wing, anti-immigration parties made gains in parliamentary elections in October 1991. Despite losing seats, however, a four-party coalition that has governed Switzerland since 1959 remained in power.

Switzerland celebrated the 700th anniversary of its founding in 1991. This prompted many Swiss politicians to point out that the Swiss system of self-governing states under a weak central government could prove a useful model for Europe. Philip Revzin

See also **Europe.** In ***World Book,*** see **Switzerland.**

Syria. Syria's President Hafez al-Assad reentered mainstream Arab politics by sending troops to aid the United States-led coalition that drove Iraq from Kuwait in early 1991. The Syrian leader also repaired his battered relations with Western countries by participating in the Middle East peace conference sponsored by the United States and the Soviet Union in Madrid, Spain, in late October and early November. During the 1980's, Syria's diplomatic relations had suffered because of its support for Iran in the Iran-Iraq War (1980-1988), its backing of terrorist groups, and its involvement in Lebanon's civil war.

In siding with the coalition, Assad reaped a range of economic and political rewards. For example, Syria received from $2 billion to $3 billion in badly needed aid from Saudi Arabia and other Persian Gulf states that opposed Iraq.

Some Middle East experts argued, however, that Assad's new-found image of moderation was a temporary convenience. They pointed out that while international attention was diverted by the Persian Gulf crisis, Syria consolidated its position in Lebanon (see **Lebanon**). In addition, half the money donated by the Gulf states reportedly was used to purchase long-range missiles. Western governments also criticized Syria for its support of terrorism and its unwillingness to halt drug trafficking by its troops in Lebanon.

Mideast peace conference. On July 18, 1991, Syria reversed its long-standing opposition to nego-

Syria's President Assad and U.S. Secretary of State James A. Baker III meet in Damascus in April to discuss the terms of a Mideast peace conference.

tiations with Israel and agreed to a U.S. proposal for a Middle East peace conference. Syria thus became the second Arab country, after Egypt, to agree to enter into direct talks with Israel without preconditions. The first round of talks opened on October 30. However, the Syrians expressed reluctance to continue with the talks unless Israel indicated some willingness to return the Golan Heights, which Israel had captured from Syria in 1967 and had annexed in 1981. See **Middle East.**

Some Middle East analysts theorized that Assad's willingness to participate in the conference stemmed in part from a reappraisal of Syria's position in the wake of the collapse of the Soviet Union as a world power. In the past, the Soviet Union was Syria's major arms supplier.

Terrorism. In May 1991, the U.S. Department of State listed Syria as a state sponsor of terrorism in its annual report on international terrorism. The report accused Syria of providing financial support to and refuge for a number of terrorist groups. Countries on the State Department list are ineligible for U.S. aid and liable to trade sanctions. To improve U.S. relations, Assad permitted Syrian officials to hold an unprecedented meeting with a U.S. counterterrorism team in late July. Christine Helms

See also **Persian Gulf,** Special Report: **War in the Persian Gulf; Middle East** (Facts in brief table). In ***World Book,*** see **Syria.**

Taiwan. Independence from mainland China was the main political issue in Taiwan in late 1991. Ever since Taiwan's ruling party, the Kuomintang (KMT), was driven from mainland China by the Communists in 1949, both sides had insisted that Taiwan was still a part of China and that the two would eventually be reunited. However, Taiwan's growing prosperity and recent democratic reforms caused some of its politicians to question the desirability of reestablishing ties to the mainland.

On Sept. 7 and 8, 1991, the opposition Democratic Progressive Party (DPP) proposed that Taiwan seek a separate United Nations (UN) membership. In 1971, the Communist People's Republic of China had taken over China's UN seat, which Taiwan had held since 1945 under the name of the Republic of China. Since then, Taiwan has debated whether to seek UN membership under a name other than China.

China's opposition. Communists on the mainland denounced any UN membership application for Taiwan and revived old hints of a military attack on Taiwan if it sought independence. Undeterred, the DPP on October 13 called for the creation of a Republic of Taiwan, subject to a popular referendum. President Li Teng-hui called this "a rash and irresponsible" move, and the government arrested 11 members of groups that had long advocated independence.

National Assembly elections in December centered on the issue of independence. The elections also provided the first popular choice for most National Assembly seats, which had been held by elderly KMT members who received life terms to the Assembly in elections held in 1947.

Campaigning on a platform of "reform, stability, and prosperity," the KMT won 71 per cent of the votes. The DPP won only 24 per cent and minor parties won 5 per cent. The result was a rejection of independence calls and a mandate for continued cautious change by President Li.

Emergency rule ended. The elections for the seats of the old KMT Assembly members were part of a more widespread effort to liberalize Taiwan's authoritarian political system. On April 30, Li formally ended a "period of Communist rebellion" declared in 1948, which had permitted emergency rule in Taiwan. Technically, however, a state of war with the mainland continued, despite $7 billion in trade in 1991 between the two countries and expanding Taiwanese investment in the People's Republic of China.

The economy recovered quickly in 1991 from a stock market crash and other problems in 1990 that had cut economic growth to just 5.1 per cent—low by Taiwan's booming standards. As exports rose 14 per cent in 1991, annual economic growth neared 7 per cent. Henry S. Bradsher

See also **Asia** (Facts in brief table); **China.** In ***World Book,*** see **Taiwan.**

Tanzania. See **Africa.**

Taxation. Conservative Republicans caught President George Bush and the Congress of the United States off guard in November 1991 when they proposed tax cuts designed to lift the U.S. economy out of the recession that began in 1990.

Pushed by House Republican Whip Newt Gingrich of Georgia, the proposals included reducing capital gains taxes from 28 per cent to 19.6 per cent, repealing the 10 per cent luxury tax on big-ticket items, and allowing withdrawals from individual retirement accounts (IRA's) without tax penalty.

Bush initially resisted a tax-cut package, saying he would deal with tax policy when Congress returned in January 1992. Then, just before Congress adjourned on Nov. 27, 1991, Bush declared: "I want the package passed, and I want to see it done fast." House Speaker Thomas S. Foley (D., Wash.) insisted that the President state clearly whether he wished Congress to reconvene in December and pass a tax-cut bill. Bush did not press the matter further, knowing that the Democratic-controlled Congress would scrap Republican tax-cut proposals and pass its own package if called back into session in December.

The House Ways and Means Committee responded by holding December hearings on tax policy. The committee examined numerous Democratic tax-cut proposals aimed at helping the middle class. Ways and Means Chairman Dan Rostenkowski (D., Ill.) unveiled one of these proposals, which would provide an estimated 90 million households with refundable tax credits of $200 to $400 a year for the next two years. The hearings gave Democrats a forum for attacking the Administration's economic policies.

Social security taxes. For the second straight year, the Senate killed a proposal by Senator Daniel P. Moynihan (D., N.Y.) to cut social security payroll taxes. Moynihan complained that much of the social security tax was being improperly used to reduce the federal budget deficit. His proposal would have reduced the payroll tax paid by individuals from 6.2 per cent to 5.2 per cent over five years, netting the average worker a five-year savings of $2,300.

Senate Democratic Leader George J. Mitchell of Maine backed the Moynihan plan. It was opposed by Senator Lloyd M. Bentsen, Jr. (D., Tex.), who argued that it would increase the deficit and undermine faith in the social security system. The Senate rejected the bill by a 60 to 38 vote on April 24.

Military tax break. On January 21, Bush signed an executive order designating the Persian Gulf region a combat area. This exempted service personnel stationed there from paying federal income tax on their military pay. On January 24, Congress passed legislation that made these tax breaks retroactive to Iraq's invasion of Kuwait on Aug. 2, 1990.

Frank Cormier and Margot Cormier

See also **State government.** In ***World Book,*** see **Taxation.**

Television. On the evening of Jan. 16, 1991, more Americans were watching a single television broadcast than they had at any other time in history. Hours before, a United States-led international coalition had started bombing Iraq, and President George Bush, in a televised speech that night, confirmed to the American people the beginning of the Persian Gulf War. Almost 80 per cent of all households were tuned in to Bush's announcement. Although a greater percentage of Americans had watched the televised funeral of former President John F. Kennedy, the total number of people watching Bush was greater than the number who had viewed the funeral.

War news. America and the world derived much of their information about the war from television reports, and Turner Broadcasting's Cable News Network (CNN) was at the forefront of the reporting. When allied bombs first struck Baghdad, CNN was the only network able to maintain communications with its correspondents there. Bombs had destroyed the Iraqi telephone exchange in the first few minutes of fighting. But months before the fighting started, CNN had installed a special telephone wire that bypassed the Iraqi telecommunications system and sent a signal to a satellite relay in Amman, Jordan. This hookup allowed CNN correspondents to broadcast an uncensored blow-by-blow account of the war's first 16 hours.

Correspondents Bernard Shaw, John Holliman, and Peter Arnett provided the live reports. Shaw and Holliman left Baghdad within a few days, but Arnett stayed behind, reporting for CNN—and receiving criticism from some in the United States, who said his censored reports simply relayed Iraqi propaganda. Although CNN's ratings soared during the early days of the war, the American Broadcasting Companies (ABC) subsequently became the network of choice for U.S. viewers. Its daily newscast with anchorman Peter Jennings led the ratings for news programs for the remainder of the year.

The television networks provided electrifying pictures of Iraqi Scud-missile damage in Israel, but found their coverage limited by Iraqi and U.S. military officials. CBS correspondent Robert Simon and his crew were captured by Iraqi troops when they attempted to cover the fighting without an official U.S. military escort. Most of the memorable war pictures shown on TV were from videotapes taken by military planes. They showed laser-guided "smart" bombs and missiles striking targets with amazing precision.

Other news events in 1991 drew large television audiences. In October, cable stations such as CNN and C-SPAN provided continuous coverage of Senate hearings investigating sexual harassment charges against U.S. Supreme Court nominee Clarence Thomas. Anita Hill, a law professor and former colleague of Thomas' brought the charges. See **Thomas, Clarence.** In December, the Florida rape trial of William Kennedy Smith also received broad network and cable coverage.

Emmy Award winners in 1991

Comedy

Best Series: "Cheers"
Lead Actress: Kirstie Alley, "Cheers"
Lead Actor: Burt Reynolds, "Evening Shade"
Supporting Actress: Bebe Neuwirth, "Cheers"
Supporting Actor: Jonathan Winters, "Davis Rules"

Drama

Best Series: "L.A. Law"
Lead Actress: Patricia Wettig, "thirtysomething"
Lead Actor: James Earl Jones, "Gabriel's Fire"
Supporting Actress: Madge Sinclair, "Gabriel's Fire"
Supporting Actor: Timothy Busfield, "thirtysomething"

Other awards

Drama or Comedy Miniseries or Special: *Separate But Equal*
Variety, Music, or Comedy Program: *The 63rd Annual Academy Awards*
Lead Actress in a Miniseries or Special: Lynn Whitfield, The *Josephine Baker Story*
Lead Actor in a Miniseries or Special: Sir John Gielgud, *Masterpiece Theater: Summer's Lease*
Supporting Actress in a Miniseries or Special: Ruby Dee, *Hallmark Hall of Fame: Decoration Day*
Supporting Actor in a Miniseries or Special: James Earl Jones, *Heatwave*

Network finances. The millions of dollars that the war coverage cost the major networks—in correspondents' expenses and equipment, as well as in lost advertising—could not have come at a worse time. The U.S. economic recession had hit hard at all advertising-supported media. At the same time, the three major networks—ABC, the National Broadcasting Company (NBC), and CBS Inc.—continued to lose viewers to cable channels, independent stations, the Fox network, and the videocassette industry. All three networks laid off employees during the year.

The ratings race. For the sixth straight year, NBC led the Nielsen ratings race for the 1990-1991 television season, which ran from the fall of 1990 to April 1991. NBC's audience, however, had dwindled from the previous season. ABC came in a close second, and CBS followed on the heels of ABC.

By September 1991, 5 of the 10 most-watched shows belonged to CBS, and the network ranked first in the ratings. Its Monday night lineup, consisting of "Evening Shade," "Major Dad," "Murphy Brown," "Designing Women," and "Northern Exposure," was the strongest ratings night on television.

The highest rated of the new shows was ABC's "Home Improvement," starring stand-up comic Tim Allen. "Step by Step," featuring well-known actors Suzanne Somers and Patrick Duffy, attracted a fairly large audience on Friday nights.

The Fox network made strong ratings gains when it started new episodes of the high school drama "Beverly Hills, 90210" during the summer. The show quickly attracted a large teen-age audience. Fox's addition of the comedy "Roc," starring Broadway veteran Charles Dutton, to Sunday night, and "Drexell's Class," starring Dabney Coleman, to Thursday night also helped boost ratings. "The Simpsons" and "Married . . . with Children" remained Fox's most popular shows.

Out with the old. Among the cancellations in the spring were three of ABC's critically acclaimed dramas: "thirtysomething," "China Beach," and "Twin Peaks." NBC pulled the plug on "Shannon's Deal," and CBS ended "Dallas" after 14 seasons. Replacing these programs were comparatively inexpensive reality-oriented shows, such as ABC's "FBI: The Untold Stories" and NBC's "The Adventures of Mark and Brian."

In June, Johnny Carson announced that he would leave "The Tonight Show" in May 1992. NBC announced that comedian Jay Leno would replace him.

NBC again failed to produce a successful news hour in prime time. "Real Life with Jane Pauley" and "Exposé," which ran on Friday nights, were canceled in October. Adding to NBC's troubles is the probable ending of "The Cosby Show" after the 1991-1992 season. Star Bill Cosby planed to sell a new version of the old Groucho Marx show "You Bet Your Life," and he was not expected to renew his NBC contract.

The ratings of NBC's "Today" show increased when Katherine Couric replaced Deborah Norville as the

On "Northern Exposure," Rob Morrow plays dyed-in-the-wool New Yorker Joel Fleischman, who is out of his element as a physician in Alaska.

Top-rated U.S. television series

The following were the most-watched television series for the 31-week regular season—Sept. 17, 1990, through April 14, 1991—as determined by Nielsen Media Research.

1. "Cheers" (NBC)
2. "60 Minutes" (CBS)
3. "Roseanne" (ABC)
4. "A Different World" (NBC)
5. "The Cosby Show" (NBC)
6. "NFL Monday Night Football" (ABC)
7. "America's Funniest Home Videos" (ABC)
8. "Murphy Brown" (CBS)
9. (tie) "America's Funniest People" (ABC)
"Designing Women" (CBS)
"Empty Nest" (NBC)
12. "The Golden Girls" (NBC)
13. "Murder, She Wrote" (CBS)
14. "Unsolved Mysteries" (NBC)
15. "Full House" (ABC)
16. "Family Matters" (ABC)
17. (tie) "Coach" (ABC)
"Matlock" (NBC)
19. "In the Heat of the Night" (NBC)
20. "Major Dad" (CBS)
21. (tie) "CBS Sunday Movie" (CBS)
"Doogie Howser, M.D." (ABC)
"L.A. Law" (NBC)
"Who's the Boss?" (ABC)
25. "Grand" (NBC)

show's co-host. However, ABC's "Good Morning America" remained the most popular morning program.

For the first time in 10 years, Brandon Tartikoff did not oversee NBC's new programming. The long-time NBC executive had relinquished his title of entertainment chairman to assistant Warren Littlefield in 1990, but Tartikoff remained in charge of the programming division. In the spring of 1991, he left NBC to become chairman of Paramount Pictures.

In with the new. Plenty of half-hour comedies were introduced for the 1991-1992 television season. Redd Foxx returned to prime time in the CBS comedy "The Royal Family." The show looked promising, but Foxx died in October, and the program's future was uncertain. Proven stars James Garner, in "Man of the People," and Robert Guillaume, in "Pacific Station," failed to attract an audience on Sunday nights and were among the first shows NBC removed from its schedule.

"Reasonable Doubts," a courtroom drama, starred Mark Harmon and deaf actress Marlee Matlin, who had won the 1987 Academy Award for best actress for her work in *Children of a Lesser God.* A new cable channel called Court TV covered real-life courtroom trials all day, every day, including the Smith trial.

The season's most critically acclaimed new shows were CBS's "Brooklyn Bridge," a comedy-drama created by Gary David Goldberg, about growing up in Brooklyn in 1956; NBC's "I'll Fly Away," a drama created by Joshua Brand and John Falsey, set amid racial tensions in a small Southern town in the late 1950's; NBC's "Eerie, Indiana," a fantasy-comedy about life in a fictional town as seen through the fervent imagination of a 13-year-old; and Fox's "Roc," a comedy about the family of a hard-working garbageman in Baltimore. Critics also praised "Dinosaurs," which ABC introduced in April and brought back in autumn. The show's puppetlike characters were created by Jim Henson Productions.

Television regulations. In June 1991, the Federal Communications Commission (FCC) reinstated regulations governing charges for cable television. However, the ruling only applied to cable operators who competed with less than six broadcast television stations or one multichannel service. Since cable providers in large cities usually face this amount of competition, they were unaffected by the ruling, and only those cable providers in small towns and rural areas faced possible rate adjustments.

In October 1991, a federal appeals court ruled that local telephone companies could enter the television market. The ruling permits local phone companies to provide a variety of informational services, such as electronic directories, and medical, stock market, and sports information. Michael Hill

See **Persian Gulf,** Special Report: **War in the Persian Gulf.** See also, **Leno, Jay; Shaw, Bernard.** In ***World Book,*** see **Television.**

Tennessee. See **State government.**

Jimmy Connors displays his seemingly timeless energy at the U.S. Open in New York City where, at age 39, he reached the semifinals in September.

Tennis. Monica Seles, a 17-year-old Yugoslav living in Florida, was the most successful and most controversial player in 1991. Stefan Edberg of Sweden and Boris Becker of Germany won major titles among the men, and 20-year-old Jim Courier of Dade City, Fla., joined them as a grand-slam winner.

Seles won three of the four grand-slam titles—the Australian, French, and United States Opens. On November 24, in New York City, she won her second straight Virginia Slims Championships final. During the year, she played in 16 tournaments, winning 10.

Seles became the youngest player to be ranked first in the world and the youngest to win $1 million in a year. Her earnings of $2,457,758 broke Martina Navratilova's 1984 women's record of $2,173,556.

Seles drew her greatest attention for the grand-slam tournament she did not play, the Wimbledon championships in England. She withdrew three days before the June 24 start, citing an injury in a minor but unspecified accident. She later said she was suffering from shin splints and a slight stress fracture of the left leg. The Women's Tennis Association (WTA) fined Seles $6,000 for the late withdrawal. A week after Wimbledon, when she played in an exhibition tournament in Mahwah, N.J., for a $300,000 appearance fee, the WTA fined her $20,000 because of a conflict with a nearby tour event.

Seles, citing the injured leg, withdrew from the Federation Cup, the women's equivalent of the Davis

Cup. Spain, led by Arantxa Sánchez Vicario, won the cup by defeating the United States, 2-1, in the final on July 28 in Nottingham, England.

Women. In the grand-slam finals, Seles defeated Jana Novotna of Czechoslovakia, 5-7, 6-3, 6-1, in the Australian Open on January 26 in Melbourne, Australia; Sánchez Vicario, by 6-3, 6-4 in the French Open on June 8 in Paris; and Navratilova, by 7-6, 6-1 in the United States Open on September 7 in New York City.

On July 6 at Wimbledon, Steffi Graf of Germany won her third title by beating Gabriela Sabatini of Argentina, 6-4, 3-6, 8-6. Otherwise, it was a troubled year on and off the court for Graf, who lost her first place in the computer rankings to Seles in March. In the French Open semifinals, Graf suffered the worst loss of her career—6-0, 6-2—to Sánchez Vicario.

At age 35, Navratilova broke the retired Chris Evert's career record of 1,309 tournament victories and tied her record of 157 singles titles. At age 15, Jennifer Capriati defeated Seles, Sabatini, and Navratilova, became the youngest Wimbledon semifinalist ever, and climbed to sixth place among the women.

Men. The grand-slam tournaments produced four winners. In the Australian Open final on January 27, Becker defeated Ivan Lendl of Greenwich, Conn., and Czechoslovakia, the two-time defender, 1-6, 6-4, 6-4, 6-4. On June 9, in the French Open, Courier downed Andre Agassi of Las Vegas, Nev., 3-6, 6-4, 2-6, 6-1, 6-4, in the first all-American final in 37 years.

In Wimbledon's first-ever all-German final, Michael Stich defeated Becker, 6-4, 7-6, 6-4, on July 7. On September 8, in the United States Open, a year after Edberg was eliminated in the first round, he routed Courier in the final, 6-2, 6-4, 6-0.

The hero in the United States Open was Jimmy Connors, at age 39, making a comeback with a surgically repaired wrist. He was ranked so low that he needed a wild-card invitation to get into the tournament. Connors defeated Patrick McEnroe (John's younger brother) in five sets, Aaron Krickstein in five sets, and Paul Haarhuis of the Netherlands in four sets. That put Connors into the semifinals, where he lost quietly to Courier, 6-3, 6-3, 6-2. The two-week run raised Connors' world ranking from 174th to 66th.

Edberg and Becker alternated as the year's top-ranked player. Courier rose to second, the highest ranking for an American since John McEnroe held that rank in 1986.

Davis Cup. From Nov. 29 to Dec. 1, 1991, on an indoor carpet in Lyon, France, the French team beat the United States and won the Davis Cup championship for men for the first time since 1932. Henri Leconte and Guy Forget led the French to a 3-1 victory, each defeating Pete Sampras of Rancho Palos Verdes, Calif. Two weeks earlier, Sampras won the Association of Tennis Professionals Tour World Championship.

Frank Litsky

See also **Seles, Monica.** In ***World Book,*** see **Tennis.**

Texas. See **State government.**

Thailand. Thailand's armed forces quietly ousted a civilian government on Feb. 23, 1991. It was the ninth successful military coup in 17 attempts since 1932.

Prime Minister Chatchai Chunhawan (sometimes spelled Chatichai Choonhavan) was arrested by soldiers as he was going to see King Bhumibol Adulyadej about the appointment of a new deputy defense minister whom military commanders did not like. The armed forces' supreme commander, General Sunthorn Kongsompong, announced that Thailand would be ruled by a National Peacekeeping Council (NPC). The NPC accused Chatchai of corruption and trying to establish a "parliamentary dictatorship."

The NPC's strongman was General Suchinda Kraprayoon. On March 3, 1991, the NPC named a respected former diplomat and businessman, Anan Panyarachun, as interim prime minister, and he assembled a cabinet of experienced civilian experts, diplomats, and businessmen. This reassured important foreign investors. The government lifted martial law in most parts of Thailand on May 3.

Elections promised. On February 24, Suchinda announced that elections would be held in six months. This deadline was later extended to March 1992. On March 15, 1991, the NPC also appointed a national legislative assembly and proposed a new Constitution, which was formally approved on December 9. Several political parties criticized the Constitution as being undemocratic and favoring military influence.

Supporters of Suchinda established a Justice Unity Party. Suchinda indicated that he might eventually seek the prime minister's job. His predecessor as army chief of staff, Chaovalit Yongchaiyut, led his own political party and also expressed interest in the job.

Several reforms were made by Anan's government. It cut some government subsidies and introduced a value-added tax. It also restructured the civil service to reduce political interference. An economic development plan was made public on September 9. The plan called for a growth rate of 8.2 per cent a year for the gross national product—the value of all goods and services produced—through 1996, down from the annual average of 10.5 per cent since 1987.

The plan acknowledged, however, a growing gap between rich and poor. It noted that Bangkok, Thailand's capital, has become more prosperous due to the recent rapid increase in industrialization there. But in rural areas, particularly in the northeast, many people remain impoverished and illiterate. Critics said the new plan favored the urban middle class.

Foreign relations. Thailand's relations with its neighbors improved in 1991. In March, Suchinda agreed with Laos on a withdrawal of both countries' troops from a disputed northern border area. Thailand also helped arrange the Cambodian peace agreement, which was intended to end Cambodia's long civil war.

Henry S. Bradsher

See also **Asia** (Facts in brief table). In ***World Book,*** see **Thailand.**

Theater. The leadership of major United States theaters underwent a number of changes in 1991. One of the year's saddest and most dramatic events was the death of producer Joseph Papp on October 31.

In 1954, Papp had founded the New York Shakespeare Festival, the largest nonprofit theater institution in the United States. The Shakespeare festival, which has staged free productions of plays by William Shakespeare in New York City's Central Park every summer since 1957, moved into its permanent headquarters at the Public Theater in 1966. As producer of the Public Theater, Papp presented the premiere of numerous legendary shows, including the rock musical *Hair* and *A Chorus Line*, which became Broadway's longest-running musical.

A genius for spotting talent, Papp championed such playwrights as John Guare, David Hare, Caryl Churchill, Miguel Piñero, Ntozake Shange, Wallace Shawn, and David Henry Hwang. Papp also helped launch the careers of actors George C. Scott, James Earl Jones, Colleen Dewhurst, Meryl Streep, Raul Julia, and Kevin Kline, among others. A frequent crusader for social causes, Papp was a forerunner in *nontraditional casting*—casting nonwhite actors in Shakespearean productions and other classical plays.

New directions. In August 1991, JoAnne Akalaitis, Papp's artistic associate, succeeded Papp as director of the Shakespeare Festival. Lincoln Center Theater also had a change in command. Gregory Mosher, who had been running the theater with producer Bernard Gersten since 1985, decided to return to his previous career as an independent director. Chosen to replace him was André Bishop. In recent years, Bishop, as artistic director of Playwrights Horizons, an off-Broadway theater, had produced a string of successful plays and musicals, including *Driving Miss Daisy, The Heidi Chronicles,* and *Sunday in the Park with George,* each of which won a Pulitzer Prize.

Major theaters outside New York City also changed hands. Zelda Fichandler retired from the Arena Stage, the theater in Washington, D.C., that she had helped create in 1950.

Lloyd Richards retired as the head of the Yale Repertory Theater in New Haven, Conn. He was replaced by Stan Wojewodski, Jr., the artistic director of Baltimore's Center Stage. San Francisco's American Conservatory Theatre, which was badly damaged in a 1989 earthquake, experienced more turmoil this year when its artistic director resigned and its founder, William Ball, committed suicide.

Broadway musicals. In recent years, Broadway has been dominated by huge, multimillion-dollar musicals that have succeeded despite a generally dismal financial climate, and 1991 was no exception. The biggest hit of the year was *The Will Rogers Follies,* which paid homage to vaudeville shows of the early 1900's with their endearing animal acts and scantily clad dancing girls. Keith Carradine starred as writer and folk hero Will Rogers, who coined the expression, "I never met a man I didn't like."

Another major new production was *The Secret Garden*, adapted by Marsha Norman and Lucy Simon from Frances Hodgson Burnett's 1911 classic novel. Eleven-year-old Daisy Eagan, who played the starring role of a young girl coping with the death of her parents, won an Antoinette Perry (Tony) Award for best featured actress in a musical.

Miss Saigon, the London hit by Alain Boublil and Claude-Michel Schönberg, the authors of *Les Misérables*, finally arrived on Broadway in April 1991. Loosely inspired by the Giacomo Puccini opera *Madama Butterfly*, the musical portrays the romance between a U.S. soldier and a Vietnamese prostitute who meet just before the fall of Saigon in April 1975. Preceded by months of controversy over the casting of a white actor in the starring role of a Eurasian pimp, the show's opening was something of an anticlimax. But the reviews were respectful, and the musical settled in for a long run to sold-out houses.

Nick and Nora, based on the "Thin Man" movies of the 1930's, opened in December 1991 after a long and troubled tryout period. It received poor reviews and closed after playing only nine performances.

Comedies. Neil Simon has always been a popular playwright, but few of his comedies have won as much critical praise as *Lost in Yonkers*, which opened in March. It gathered a Pulitzer Prize for drama, a Tony Award for best play, and the Drama Desk Award

Tony Award winners in 1991

Best Play, *Lost in Yonkers,* Neil Simon.

Best Musical, *The Will Rogers Follies.*

Best Revival, *Fiddler on the Roof.*

Leading Actor in a Play, Nigel Hawthorne, *Shadowlands.*

Leading Actress in a Play, Mercedes Ruehl, *Lost in Yonkers.*

Leading Actor in a Musical, Jonathan Pryce, *Miss Saigon.*

Leading Actress in a Musical, Lea Salonga, *Miss Saigon.*

Featured Actor in a Play, Kevin Spacey, *Lost in Yonkers.*

Featured Actress in a Play, Irene Worth, *Lost in Yonkers.*

Featured Actor in a Musical, Hinton Battle, *Miss Saigon.*

Featured Actress in a Musical, Daisy Eagan, *The Secret Garden.*

Direction of a Play, Jerry Zaks, *Six Degrees of Separation.*

Direction of a Musical, Tommy Tune, *The Will Rogers Follies.*

Book of a Musical, Marsha Norman, *The Secret Garden.*

Original Musical Score, Cy Coleman, Betty Comden, and Adolph Green, *The Will Rogers Follies.*

Scenic Design, Heidi Landesman, *The Secret Garden.*

Costumes, Willa Kim, *The Will Rogers Follies.*

Lighting, Jules Fisher, *The Will Rogers Follies.*

Choreography, Tommy Tune, *The Will Rogers Follies.*

Regional Theater, Yale Repertory Theater.

Actress Lea Salonga, center, plays a Vietnamese prostitute whose love affair with an American soldier is doomed by war in the musical *Miss Saigon*.

for best new play. Exceptional performances by Irene Worth as a crusty, hard-hearted mother and by Mercedes Ruehl as the daughter struggling for her independence accounted for much of the play's appeal.

Another major hit was Brian Friel's *Dancing at Lughnasa*, which originated at the Abbey Theatre in Dublin, Ireland, and became a hit in London before moving to New York City with most of its Irish cast. The play's focus on a country priest and five penniless sisters caused critics to compare it favorably to dramas by Russian playwright Anton Chekhov.

Nicol Williamson starred in *I Hate Hamlet*, a short-lived comedy about a group of actors haunted by the ghost of actor John Barrymore. Television star and comedienne Tracey Ullman opened in *The Big Love*, based on Florence Aadland's memoir of her 15-year-old daughter's love affair with actor Errol Flynn. The one-character play got lukewarm reviews and closed after a short run.

Lincoln Center Theater mounted the premiere of *Mule Bone*, a recently rediscovered 1930 collaboration between American poet Langston Hughes and novelist Zora Neale Hurston. The play held more interest as a literary curiosity than as a theater piece, however.

Cutting prices. A consortium of producers called the Broadway Alliance attempted to fill some of the many vacant theaters on Broadway with serious plays at low ticket prices. Seats were to sell for no more than $24. The results were mixed. Steve Tesich's *The Speed of Darkness* was badly received, while Timberlake Wertenbaker's *Our Country's Good* earned positive reviews but closed after a short run.

The Roundabout Theater Company, known for producing modern classics off-Broadway, moved to a Broadway theater and opened with a successful revival of Harold Pinter's 1965 drama, *The Homecoming*. One of the strangest productions on Broadway in years was *La Bête*, a comedy in verse by David Hirson, modeled on Molière's 1666 satire, *The Misanthrope*. The surreal, lavishly designed sets and costumes were spectacular, but the play closed quickly, losing more than $1 million.

Off-Broadway. Playwrights Horizons in New York City did sellout business with *Assassins*, a macabre revue by Stephen Sondheim and John Weidman, and had a long-running hit with *The Substance of Fire*, Jon Robin Baitz's drama about a publisher suffering a nervous breakdown. Terrence McNally enjoyed his third hit in a row at the Manhattan Theater Club with *Lips Together, Teeth Apart*, a comedy about New Yorkers on vacation. Solo performer John Leguziamo won instant acclaim for *Mambo Mouth*, his spoof of Latin stereotypes. Sam Shepard's play *States of Shock* was considered a remarkably weak effort by one of the best U.S. playwrights.

Regional theaters. The Hartford (Conn.) Stage Company emerged in 1991 as one of the most prestigious U.S. theaters. It sent several acclaimed productions to New York City, including *Marvin's Room* by Chicago playwright Scott McPherson. In addition, the company won rave reviews for its double-billed production of *March of the Falsettos* and *Falsettoland*, two related one-act musicals by William Finn.

Plays about AIDS made a significant impact in 1991. Tony Kushner's seven-hour epic *Angels in America* premiered at San Francisco's Eureka Theater. The Arena Stage produced Cheryl West's *Before It Hits Home*, which dramatizes the effect of AIDS on a black family.

Popular film and television director James L. Brooks made his debut as a stage director with *Brooklyn Laundry*, which starred Glenn Close and Laura Dern. The comedy, by Lisa-Maria Radano, premiered at the Serendipity Theater in Los Angeles. Writer and director Frank Galati, whose adaptation of John Steinbeck's novel *The Grapes of Wrath* (1939) won the 1990 Tony Award for best play, created a stage adaptation of Anne Tyler's 1977 novel, *Earthly Possessions*, at Chicago's Steppenwolf Theatre Company.

Nontraditional casting proliferated in the United States in 1991. Black actors took leading roles in productions of *Death of a Salesman* at the Guthrie Theater in Minneapolis, Minn.; *The Visit* at Chicago's Goodman Theater; *The Great Gatsby* at Chicago's Wisdom Bridge Theatre; and *Iphigenia* at Boston's Huntington Stage Company. Don Shewey

In ***World Book*,** see **Theater.**

Thomas, Clarence (1948-), became an associate justice of the Supreme Court of the United States on Oct. 18, 1991. He replaced Justice Thurgood Marshall.

Thomas' nomination was opposed by several civil rights groups, who criticized his opposition to affirmative action and hiring quotas for minorities and women. In the final weeks of the Senate confirmation process, his nomination was bitterly debated after charges that Thomas had sexually harassed a former assistant came to light. The Senate finally confirmed Thomas by a vote of 52 to 48.

Thomas, who is black, was born on June 23, 1948, in Pin Point, Ga. He was raised by his grandparents in Savannah, Ga., and graduated from Holy Cross College in Worcester, Mass. In 1974, he received his law degree from Yale University in New Haven, Conn.

Thomas served as an assistant attorney general of Missouri from 1974 to 1977. After two years as a legal counsel at Monsanto Company in St. Louis, Mo., he became a legislative aide to Senator John Danforth (R., Mo.). From 1981 to 1982, Thomas was assistant secretary for civil rights in the U.S. Department of Education. He was then named chairman of the Equal Employment Opportunity Commission, a position he held until 1989. That year he became a judge on the U.S. Court of Appeals for the District of Columbia.

Thomas has been married twice. He has one child, a son, from his first marriage. Douglas Clayton

Togo. See **Africa.**

Toronto. June Rowlands was elected the first woman mayor of Toronto on Nov. 12, 1991. Rowlands, a member of the Liberal Party, captured 60 per cent of the vote.

Arthur Eggleton, the popular 47-year-old politician who had served as Toronto's mayor since 1980, had announced on May 1, 1991, that he was retiring from politics. The ensuing battle among several candidates vying for the mayoral seat dominated Toronto's news stories until election day.

Eggleton's sudden and unanticipated withdrawal focused public attention on Jack Layton, a member of the City Council who represented a downtown ward. Layton belonged to the socialist New Democratic Party (NDP) and quickly became the candidate favored to win the election.

Observers expected that conservatives and liberals would coalesce around one opposition candidate to stop Layton. Instead, three major candidates jumped into the race. Betty Disero, a 34-year-old City Council member, also from the Liberal Party, was of Italian ancestry and hoped to appeal to the city's many immigrants. Rowlands, 67, was a former city councilor who had served a three-year term as chair of the Metro Toronto Police Services Board. Susan Fish, 46, a Progressive Conservative Party member, was a former councilor, had been a member of the Ontario legislature, and had served as a cabinet minister. Fish presented herself as the candidate of "the moderate middle," who could speak to both sides of the polarized city council.

The four candidates began a grueling round of speeches, public debates, and "all candidates meetings," which are a tradition in Toronto politics. By the end of September, Disero and Fish were lagging in the polls. Disero dropped out of the race on October 1, and Fish ended her campaign on October 18. Fish had waited until one week after nominations closed so that her name would remain on the ballots even though she was no longer a candidate.

By election day, the city had become polarized between Rowlands on the right and Layton on the left. Both candidates were struggling to attract the undecided voters in the middle. Stressing law and order, fiscal responsibility, and economic revival, Rowlands won the election by capturing 113,993 votes. Despite a strong NDP organization, Layton won only 54,044 votes, or about 35 per cent.

Despite Layton's mayoral loss, members of the NDP retained a foothold in local politics. They kept the six seats they had had in the City Council.

Most incumbents returned. Elsewhere in the 1991 elections, Metropolitan Toronto Chairman Alan Tonks retained his position *by acclamation* (having faced no opposition). Nine of the 28 members of the Metropolitan Council also were returned to their seats without opposition. All of the mayors of the five municipalities that make up Metro Toronto were reelected. However, major changes took place in the city of

York, Metro Toronto's second smallest municipality, where a record 56 per cent of the voters turned out to replace six of the eight members of the York Council.

The York election had been affected by charges of corruption against two Council members. Through media stories, voters had learned of plans to sell a city swimming pool to a condominium developer. The developer and a member of his firm, as well as two members of the York Council, were charged with municipal corruption on October 31, midway through the election campaign. A member of the Metropolitan Council and an employee of a United States waste-disposal company were also charged. The two York aldermen facing charges, Anthony Mandarano and James Fera, were among those defeated at the polls.

SkyDome under new management. SkyDome, home of the city's professional baseball team, the Toronto Blue Jays, came under new management in November 1991. The provincial government, which had assumed responsibility for the $356-million ($315-million U.S.) debt of the 56,000-seat domed stadium, struck a deal to turn over management of the facility to a private company. A committee appointed by Premier Robert Rae negotiated with members of the consortium that promotes the dome to take over its operation and assume most of its debt.

David Lewis Stein

See **Canada,** Special Report: **Canada and Quebec at a Crossroads.** In ***World Book,*** see **Toronto.**

Toys and games. Retail toy sales in the United States for 1991 registered only a 3 per cent rise over 1990 sales. Industry analysts blamed the Persian Gulf War, the economic recession, and high unemployment for shoppers' unwillingness to spend money. Video games were one of the few exceptions to flat sales of toys and games in 1991, as they were in 1990.

One of 1991's best-selling items was the new Super Nintendo Entertainment System manufactured by Nintendo of America, Incorporated, of Redmond, Wash. Super NES, as it is called, is a 16-bit video game system that reportedly provides sharper colors, clearer sound, and faster action than the older 8-bit systems. In October, Nintendo forecast that total retail sales of its hardware, software, and accessories would reach $4-billion in 1991, which was 18 per cent above the company's 1990 sales of $3.6 billion. The 16-bit market had been dominated by the Genesis game system from Sega of America Incorporated of South San Francisco, Calif. Genesis first rolled out in 1989.

The Persian Gulf War spurred quick development of some military toys, in contrast to the drop in popularity of toy guns and other war toys experienced during U.S. participation in the Vietnam War (1957-1975). The Scud missile used by Iraq during the Persian Gulf War inspired International Hobby Corporation of Philadelphia to introduce a missile and missile-launcher model kit with the same name. Trading card producer Topps Company Inc. of Brooklyn, a borough of New York City, published a Desert Storm Collector Series of stickers and trading cards depicting U.S. military officers, weapons, and hardware. Other companies rushed to produce novelty items bearing the likeness of Iraq's President Saddam Hussein, such as golfballs and punching bags. But many of these items disappeared from stores shortly after the war ended.

Summer fads. Exceptionally warm spring and summer weather in many parts of the United States helped boost the popularity of some outdoor fad items, which, in turn, helped offset the toy sales drought. Super Soaker from Larami Corporation of Philadelphia hit the stores with a splash of popularity that caught many store owners by surprise. Super Soaker is a semiautomatic water pistol that holds two quarts (1.9 liters) of water. It reportedly can shoot up to 1,000 times without a refill and can hit targets almost 60 feet (18 meters) away.

Super Grip Ball, an outdoor game manufactured by Mantae America, Incorporated, of Walnut, Calif., was made for two players. The game consists of two components—one Velcro-covered ball about the size of a tennis ball and two Velcro-covered disks with strap handles. The disks function like a baseball catcher's mitt. The self-sticking Velcro on both components makes the ball easy to catch.

Environmental themes mushroomed throughout the toy industry in 1991. Pollution/Solution and Save the World games and Animals of the Rain Forest stuffed toys were among a growing list of items focusing on ecological topics. Toyland troops joining the fight to save Earth included characters from comics, motion pictures, and television, as many large and small manufacturers unveiled new action heroes for the 1990's.

The Swamp Thing line from Kenner Products Company of Cincinnati, Ohio, was modeled after elements in a syndicated television series. In the series, the hero, biochemist Dr. Alec Holland, becomes a plantlike creature because of a toxic accident. He battles an environment-wrecking mad scientist. The toy line included action figures, a Swamp Thing Swamp Trap, and a Bayou Blaster Villain Vehicle. Also based on a television show, the Toxic Crusaders line from Playmates Toys Incorporated of La Mirada, Calif., featured Toxie, the leader of a band of troubadors who fight crime, corruption, and planetary polluters.

Captain Planet and the Planeteers are the stars of a popular syndicated animated series that depicts the adventures of a modern superhero. He and his mortal helpers teach the world about good ecological habits, such as recycling, and fight those who pollute Earth. The toy line from Tiger Electronics Incorporated of Vernon Hills, Ill., featured Planeteers from Africa, Asia, South America, the former Soviet Union, and the United States.

Some old favorites also enlisted in the ecological wars. G.I. Joe, produced by Hasbro Inc. of Pawtucket, R.I., appeared as G.I. Joe Eco-Warrior. His "mission" was to stop the evil Cobra's contamination of the biosphere. Tyco Toys of Mount Laurel, N.J., updated its laboratory sets to include a complete environmental laboratory, called Chemcraft Ecology Science Lab, with 10 ecological experiments, such as testing for acid rain. Kenner's Care Bears stuffed toys were redesigned to include special graphics on their tummy patches that bear environmental themes, such as recycling.

Crayon Power of Jersey City, N.J., used the company name on one of its coloring books that contained pictures of a rain forest and suggested ways for children to help save rain forests. The Dayton Hudson chain of department stores in Minneapolis, Minn., donated a portion of the sale price of its own holiday teddy bear, Twigs, to an organization that replants trees in the national forests of the United States.

Realistic dolls. Mattel Toys of El Segundo, Calif., debuted a line of black fashion dolls named Shani that was based on African-American culture. The dolls reflected the physical diversity of black women. The dolls were available in three skin tones and had different facial features. They wore fashions inspired by black culture throughout the world.

Doll marketer Cathy Meredig of Woodbury, Minn., created the Happy to Be Me doll, the first product of her High Self-Esteem Toys Corporation, because she wanted to offer a doll with realistic body proportions, such as larger waists. Diane P. Cardinale

In ***World Book,*** see **Doll; Game; Toy.**

Track and field. A stunning track and field performance was given in 1991 by Mike Powell, a long jumper from Alta Loma, Calif., who shattered the oldest world record. In the 100-meter dash, Carl Lewis of Houston lost the world record and then regained it. This occurred during the world outdoor championships held August 24 to September 1 in Tokyo.

On August 30, on the fifth of the six rounds of the men's long jump final, Powell soared 29 feet 4½ inches (8.95 meters). Lewis, with two jumps over 29 feet (8.84 meters), finished second at 29 feet 2¾ inches (8.91 meters). The record by the 27-year-old Powell ended Lewis' streak of 65 consecutive long jump victories since 1981. Powell's record also ended Bob Beamon's reign of 23 years as the world recordholder with his celebrated 1968 Olympic jump of 29 feet 2½ inches (8.90 meters) in Mexico City.

Also during the Tokyo championships, Lewis and Leroy Burrell met in the world 100-meter final. They were teammates and had trained together. Earlier, on June 14, at the USA/Mobil national outdoor championships in New York City, Burrell had barely defeated Lewis and had bettered Lewis' previous world record of 9.92 seconds with a 9.90 effort. Lewis finished second in 9.93 seconds. Then, in the world championships in Tokyo, Burrell led with 10 meters to go. But Lewis, seven weeks past his 30th birthday, shot by and set a world record of 9.86 seconds. Burrell was a close second in 9.88 seconds.

Carl Lewis (1136) sets a world record of 9.86 seconds in the 100 meters on August 25 at the world track and field championships in Tokyo.

Pole vault. On March 15, Sergei Bubka of the Soviet Union became the first person to pole-vault 20 feet (6.10 meters) when he reached that height at an international indoor meet in San Sebastian, Spain. On August 5, he equaled that vault at an outdoor meet in Malmö, Sweden, becoming the first person to pole-vault 20 feet outdoors. In 1991, Bubka shattered the world pole vault record four times indoors and three times outdoors, reaching 20 feet 1 inch (6.12 meters) indoors on March 23 in Grenoble, France.

Other stars. Dan O'Brien of Moscow, Ida., won the decathlon in the USA/Mobil championships with 8,844 points and the world championships with 8,812 points, an American record. In May, Seppo Raty of Finland, using a new type of javelin that stayed in the air longer, set a men's world record of 301 feet 9 inches (91.98 meters) and 318 feet 1 inch (96.96 meters) in June. Noureddine Morceli of Algeria won the men's 1,500-meter indoor world championship in 3 minutes 41.57 seconds in March in Seville, Spain, and the world championships outdoors in 3 minutes 32.84 seconds.

Among the women, Katrin Krabbe of Germany won the world championships outdoors at 100 meters (10.99 seconds) and 200 meters (22.09 seconds). In each final, Merlene Ottey of Jamaica, who had not lost an outdoor race in two years, finished third. Jackie Joyner-Kersee of Newport Beach, Calif., captured the world long jump title in Tokyo with her leap of 24 feet 1/4 inch (7.32 meters). But an injured hamstring

Long jumper Mike Powell of the United States breaks the oldest track and field record on August 30, leaping 29 feet 4 1/2 inches in Tokyo.

World outdoor track and field records established in 1991

Men

Event	Holder	Country	Where set	Date	Record
4 x 100 meters	Andre Cason Leroy Burrell Dennis Mitchell Carl Lewis	U.S.A.	Tokyo	Sept. 1	0:37.50
Long jump	Mike Powell	U.S.A.	Tokyo	Aug. 30	29 ft. 4 1/2 inches (8.95 m)
100 meters	Carl Lewis	U.S.A.	Tokyo	Aug. 25	0:09.86
20,000 meters	Arturo Barrios	Mexico	La Fleche, Portugal	March 31	56:55.6
Pole vault	Sergei Bubka	Soviet Union	Malmö, Sweden	Aug. 5	20 ft. (6.10 m)
1 hour	Arturo Barrios	Mexico	La Fleche, Portugal	March 30	23,076 yards (21,101 m)
Javelin throw	Seppo Raty	Finland	Punkalaidun, Finland	June 3	318 ft. 1 inch (96.96 m)

Women

Event	Holder	Country	Where set	Date	Record
Triple jump	Inessa Kravets	Soviet Union	Moscow	June 10	49 ft. 3/4 inch (14.95 m)

knocked her out of the heptathlon, in which she had a big lead after three of the seven events.

World championships. In the outdoor championships, the Soviet Union won 28 medals (9 gold, 9 silver, and 10 bronze); the United States, 26 (10-8-8); Germany, 17 (5-4-8); Kenya, 8 (4-3-1); and Great Britain, 7 (2-2-3). Joyner-Kersee was the only American woman to win a gold medal in Tokyo.

The U.S. men's winners were Powell, Lewis, O'Brien, and Michael Johnson in the 200 meters (20.01 seconds). The 400-meter relay team was anchored by Lewis (37.50 seconds, a world record). The U.S. gold medal winners also included Antonio Pettigrew in the 400 meters (44.57 seconds) and Greg Foster in the 110-meter hurdles (13.06 seconds). Charles Austin of San Marcos, Tex., won the high jump with a leap of 7 feet 9¾ inches (2.38 meters), and Kenny Harrison of Emeryville, Calif., won the triple jump with a jump of 58 feet 4 inches (17.78 meters).

In the indoor championships, the Soviet Union won 16 medals (7 gold, 6 silver, and 3 bronze); Germany, 9 (6-1-2); and the United States, 7 (4-1-2). The U.S. winners included Andre Cason in the 60-meter dash (6.54 seconds) and Foster in the 60-meter hurdles (7.45 seconds). Hollis Conway set a U.S. record and won the high jump with a leap of 7 feet 10½ inches (2.40 meters). Diane Dixon won the women's 400 meters in 50.64 seconds, also a U.S. record. Frank Litsky

In *World Book,* see **Track and field.**

Transit. President George Bush signed major highway and mass transit legislation in 1991, after months of controversy and delay. The President, the United States Senate, and the House of Representatives each had somewhat different proposals for the reauthorization bill. But finally, on December 18, President Bush signed the Intermodal Surface Transportation Efficiency Act of 1991. Over its six-year life, this bill authorizes expenditures of $151 billion and designates $31.5 billion for mass transit systems. But there is flexibility in how state and local governments may use the $119 billion authorized for highways, so that up to $64.8 billion may be used for mass transit.

Fatal accident. A New York City motorman was indicted on second-degree murder charges on September 3 stemming from the August 28 derailment of the subway train he was operating. Five riders died and more than 200 people were injured when the 10-car train smashed into a pillar near the Union Square station. New York City police alleged that the motorman told them he had been drinking heavily for at least 12 hours before operating the train. The accident prompted U.S. Secretary of Transportation Samuel K. Skinner to urge Congress on August 28 to expand mandatory drug testing to include urban mass transit workers. President Bush signed such a bill into law on October 28. See **New York City.**

Clean air was another key issue for the transit industry in 1991. Many buses were modified to burn compressed natural gas, a cleaner burning fuel than gasoline. Los Angeles ordered 250 engines that burn methanol for installation in city buses to reduce pollution. Both Los Angeles and Oakland, Calif., studied electric trolleybuses as a means of reducing pollution along the most heavily traveled bus routes. Los Angeles may convert 10 of its busiest bus routes to the electric trolleybus.

California rapid transit. Contracts were awarded in April for the second phase of a subway from downtown Los Angeles to San Fernando Valley suburbs, and work continued on a second light rapid transit (LRT) line from Norwalk to El Segundo-Los Angeles International Airport. An LRT line uses electrically powered cars that run on tracks. On September 16, the San Francisco Bay Area Rapid Transit District (BART) began an expansion to Dublin and West Pittsburg in the East Bay and to the San Francisco airport in the West Bay.

After several years of delay, Santa Clara County completed its LRT in San Jose in April by extending the line south to Santa Teresa and Almaden. Weekday ridership doubled to 25,000 trips, inspiring plans for an extension, including a possible connection with BART.

In the Rockies, Denver approved construction of a downtown LRT in July, which city transit officials expected to expand eastward to a new international airport under construction. In Dallas, after years of indecision, construction on the new LRT system of the Dallas Area Rapid Transit finally got underway in August and will include a subway portion beneath the North Central Freeway.

In the South, New Orleans was well along on the complete renovation of the St. Charles streetcar line by the end of 1991. Memphis started construction of a downtown *circulator trolley,* so-named because the route circles the business district. The trolley line will use vintage cars from Portugal and Australia, which will link the Mid-America Pyramid convention center with the National Civil Rights Museum. In Miami, Fla., the downtown people mover was expanded to link more of the city's central business district with the rapid transit system.

In the East, the Washington, D.C., Metrorail system opened five new stations on three lines in May and June. By December, construction reached the halfway point in Baltimore on a new subway from Charles Center, an area of ongoing redevelopment, to Johns Hopkins Hospital. A new central LRT line in Baltimore was scheduled to open in April 1992, in time to transport fans to the first Baltimore Orioles' baseball game at the team's new stadium. The commuter Virginia Railway Express also will open in 1992.

Transit ridership dropped slightly in 1991—from 9.2 billion trips in 1990 to less than 9 billion trips—perhaps due to the continuing economic recession.

George M. Smerk

In *World Book,* see **Bus; Electric railroad; Subway; Transportation.**

Trinidad and Tobago. See **Latin America.**

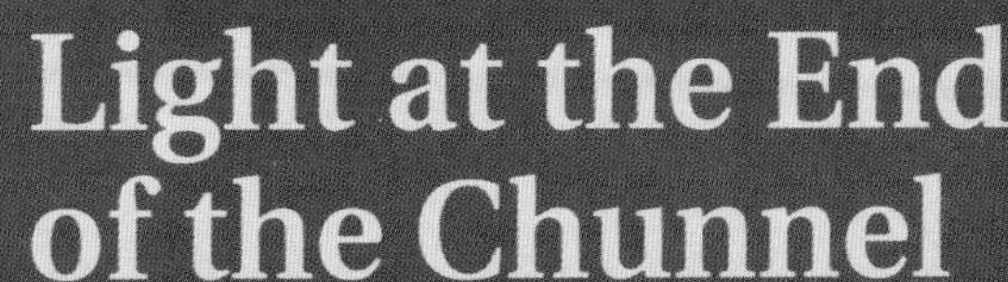

Light at the End of the Chunnel

By Laura van Dam

Work is well along on a railway tunnel under the English Channel that will, when it opens in 1993, physically link Great Britain and the European continent for the first time in history.

Throughout most of history, a trip between England and the European continent meant crossing the rough waters of the English Channel by boat. Periodically, someone envisioned constructing a tunnel under the channel to permit travelers to make the trip by train or carriage, and a French engineer's proposal for a tunnel in the mid-1800's aroused the interest of Great Britain's Queen Victoria. Alluding to the problem of seasickness, the queen reportedly said that if the Frenchman could carry out his scheme, he would have the blessing of "all the ladies of England."

The English ladies of Victoria's time never got a tunnel, but their wish is coming true for the travelers of the 1990's and beyond. In 1991, workers were well on their way to finishing a 31-mile (50-kilometer) tunnel system between England and France, the longest underwater tunnel in the world. The Channel Tunnel, or Chunnel, will enable train riders to cover the 240 miles (386 kilometers) between London and Paris in just over three hours. That trip now takes twice as long and requires transferring to a ferryboat or hovercraft for the channel crossing. Traveling between London and Paris by way of the Chunnel could be just as quick, and even cheaper, than taking a plane, given the time that air travelers spend going to and from airports.

The construction of the Channel Tunnel has been a monumental undertaking. Consider the labor involved in excavating several million tons of rock and muck from three tunnels 31 miles long—two train tunnels flanking a smaller tunnel for service vehicles. The digging of the tunnels was completed in mid-1991, and if all goes well, the Chunnel will open for business on June 15, 1993, though long-distance passenger trains designed to use the tunnel may not be ready until 1994.

The project got going in earnest in 1985, when the French and British governments invited competitive proposals for the construction of a privately financed tunnel under the channel. To many ears, the idea must have sounded like yet another improbable dream. For more than 200 years, the various proposals for a channel tunnel had come to nothing. The French plan that captured Queen Victoria's imagination was followed in the 1880's by a British initiative. That one was actually begun, and tunnelers advanced about 8,000 feet (2,400 meters). But under pressure from the British military, who were losing sleep over the possibility that a tunnel might be used by invading armies from the continent, the government terminated the project. Still, the dream persisted, and by the mid-1950's sentiment was building for another go at it. In 1973, the British and French governments announced plans for a tunnel, and the next year engineers on both sides of the channel made trial borings. Once again, however, the British government pulled the plug. This time the issue was money—specifically, not enough of it.

In the 1980's, the group that submitted the winning proposal in the 1985 competition, a banking consortium named Eurotunnel, raised the necessary funding, and it appeared that the Channel Tunnel would at last get built. Construction began in England near the end of 1987 and in France in early 1988. Still, money continued to be a sticking point. Starting in late 1989, Eurotunnel changed its estimate for the project several

The author:

Laura van Dam is a senior editor at *Technology Review* magazine.

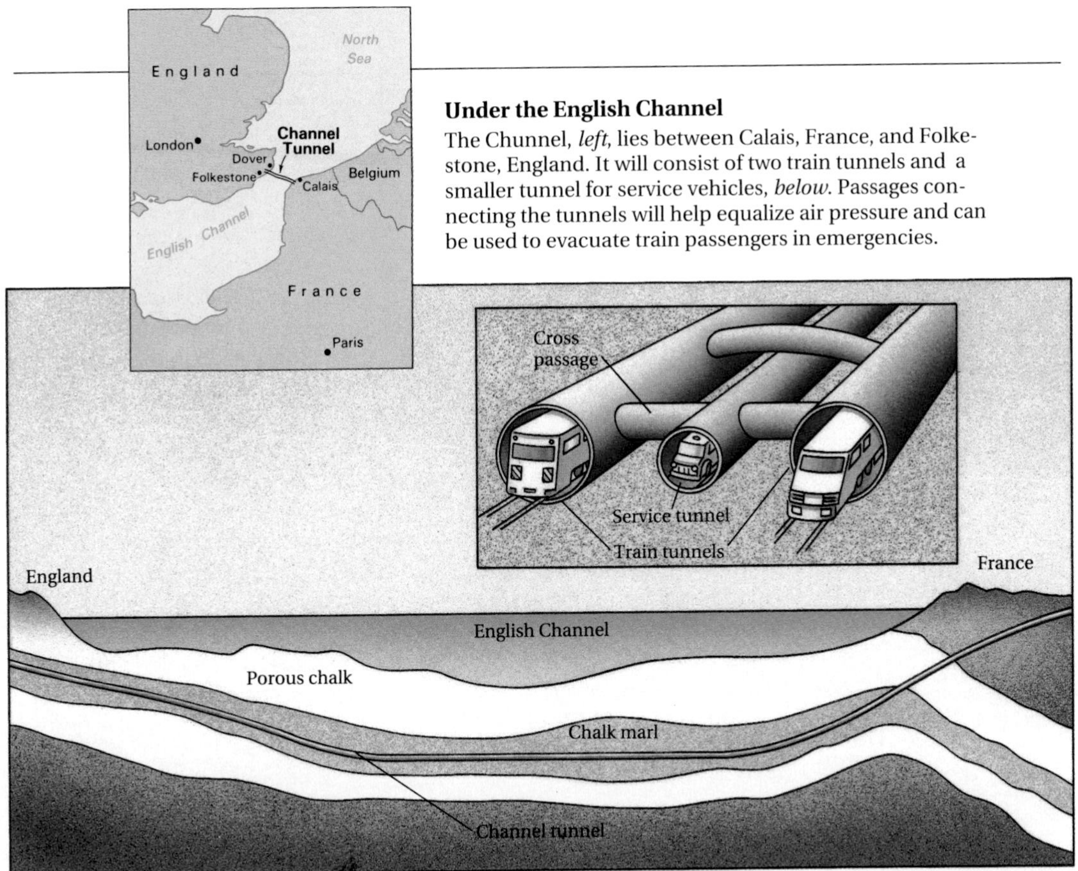

Under the English Channel

The Chunnel, *left*, lies between Calais, France, and Folkestone, England. It will consist of two train tunnels and a smaller tunnel for service vehicles, *below*. Passages connecting the tunnels will help equalize air pressure and can be used to evacuate train passengers in emergencies.

The tunnel was bored through a layer of soft, watertight limestone called chalk marl, *above*. Near the French coast, the chalk marl folds downward, and workers had to dig through porous, water-saturated chalk.

times, finally setting the price tag at a staggering $14.9 billion. For a while, it looked as though money would run out. At last, in October 1990, the consortium bankers agreed to invest up to $3.9 billion more in the endeavor, and the sale of Eurotunnel stock raised additional funds.

The escalating costs stemmed partly from delays, when workers on both sides of the channel ran into technical problems. The French diggers, as expected, encountered wet conditions near the French coast. There, the layer of watertight *chalk marl*—a type of limestone—through which most of the tunnel was dug folds down and workers had to bore through porous chalk. But the British excavators, digging through chalk marl all the way, also had to deal with serious water seepage along part of the route. The tunnel boring machines, known as *moles*, that were used for the excavating work also presented some difficulties. Because of their huge size, these machines had to be assembled at the work site. On the British side, this operation took longer than expected. Assembly of the French moles went as planned, though one machine had design problems that had to be ironed out.

The tunneling machines were mechanical monsters that gnawed their way through the soft, gray chalk marl at an average pace of about 100 feet (30 meters) a day. At the head of each mole was a huge circular head powered by electric motors and equipped with tungsten picks and cutting disks. As the head slowly rotated, it ground away the rock and deposited the debris onto a conveyor belt for disposal. Powerful rams inside the machine and retractable grippers at the side propelled the mole forward after each few feet of rock had been excavated.

Just behind the mole, workers lined the tunnel with segments of precast concrete or cast iron and sealed them against water leaks with a cement mixture called grout. And in back of them, the rock and muck carried rearward by the conveyor belt was dumped into railcars to be transported out of the tunnel. In all, the machinery used to dig and line the tunnel extended for more than 325 yards (300 meters).

Laser beams, aimed along the surveyed route of the tunnel, kept the digging on course. Each beam was aimed at a screen on the back of a mole. As the machine moved forward, microprocessors monitored the position of the laser beam on the screen and relayed needed course corrections to the mole operator. So accurate was this system that the two halves of the service tunnel were only 4 inches (10 centimeters) out of alignment horizontally and 18 inches (46 centimeters) vertically when the diggers met at midchannel. The rail tunnel excavations met precisely.

With digging completed, the Chunnel builders turned to the task of finishing passenger terminals and installing tracks and power lines for the

Workers stand in the front end of a tunneling machine, or *mole*, being assembled at the entrance to the Chunnel on the French side of the English Channel.

electric trains that will use the tunnel. They also began setting up cooling, ventilation, lighting, and safety systems.

When the Chunnel goes into service, travelers will have the option of taking two kinds of trains: regular passenger trains or shuttle trains that carry automobiles and buses. The passenger trains will connect many cities in Europe and Great Britain. The shuttles will run between the two coastal sites where the tunnel originates—near Folkestone, England, and Calais, France—taking on vehicles at special terminals.

Within the tunnel, trains will travel up to 100 miles (160 kilometers) per hour), completing the trip under the channel in about 35 minutes. Passenger trains entering from France, where trains will be able to streak along at more than 185 miles (298 kilometers) per hour, will have to slow down, and they will have to reduce their speed even more when they hit England. In Great Britain, trains run no faster than 60 miles (96 kilometers) per hour. British Rail, the national railway system, has expressed interest in building a high-speed train line that could reduce travel time between Folkestone and London by up to 30 minutes. People in Britain, however, concerned about costs and about impact on the environment, tend to be far less enthused than other Europeans about superfast trains. Thus, British Rail's proposal has met stiff resistance from the public and some members of the British Parliament.

But the prospect of express trains rocketing across the landscape is not all that bothers many Britons about the Chunnel project. The construction of the first physical link between England and the rest of Europe in 8,000 years—there was a natural land bridge before that time—is having a profound effect on the nation. Many people feel uneasy about losing their island status. Others worry that the tunnel will make it easier for Europeans from the continent to come over and find jobs. And some wonder: Will the Chunnel be a magnet for bomb-wielding terrorists? Could rabid animals from France travel through the tunnel and spread rabies in England, which is free of the disease?

In contrast, many people in France seem to look favorably upon the Chunnel, viewing it as a symbol of economic advancement. Perhaps that attitude will become more prevalent among Britons as people get used to having a "corridor to the continent." In January 1991, the European Commission, a group of government ministers, announced plans for a system of high-speed rail lines throughout western Europe that will be completed after the turn of the century. Because of the Chunnel, Great Britain will be an integral part of that network.

For further reading:

Gannon, Robert. "Journey Down the World's Longest Underwater Tunnel." *Popular Science*, June 1990.

Guterl, Fred, and Ruthen, Russell. "Chunnel Vision." *Scientific American*, January 1991.

Jones, Bronwen, editor. *The Tunnel, the Channel and Beyond*. Prentice Hall, 1987.

Van Dam, Laura. "The Big Dig." *Technology Review*, October 1990.

Tsongas, Paul (1941-), a former United States senator from Massachusetts, became the first declared candidate for the 1992 Democratic presidential nomination on April 30, 1991. Often described as a "pro-business liberal," Tsongas has argued for a stronger government role in stimulating economic growth and helping businesses develop new technology.

Paul Efthemios Tsongas was born on Feb. 14, 1941, in Lowell, Mass. After receiving a Bachelor of Arts degree in 1962 from Dartmouth College in Hanover, N.H., he earned a law degree from Yale University Law School in New Haven, Conn.

From 1962 to 1968, Tsongas worked for the Peace Corps in Ethiopia and the West Indies. He was elected city councilor in Lowell in 1968, a position he held until 1972, when he won election as county commissioner in Middlesex County. From 1969 to 1971, he also served as deputy assistant attorney general for Massachusetts. In 1974, he was elected to the first of two terms in the U.S. House of Representatives. In 1978, he won election to the U.S. Senate.

Tsongas decided not to run for a second term in the Senate after discovering in 1983 that he had cancer, for which he underwent a successful bone marrow transplant. He joined a private law firm in 1985. In 1989, he was appointed chairman of the Massachusetts Board of Regents of Higher Education.

Tsongas and his wife, Nicola, a lawyer, have three daughters. Barbara A. Mayes

Tunisia. The Persian Gulf crisis in 1991 aggravated Tunisia's economic and political problems and strained its ties with the West and with other Arab governments. In 1990, President Zine El-Abidine Ben Ali had condemned Iraq's August 2 invasion of Kuwait. Many members of the United States-led coalition against Iraq were among Tunisia's most important trading partners. Beset by high unemployment and rising inflation, Tunisia also relied on some coalition members for financial aid. Finally, the government wanted to protect the country's budding tourist industry, an increasingly important source of revenue.

Pro-Iraq sentiment among the Tunisian public, however, became so strong that government officials decided to risk Western anger by criticizing the deployment of coalition troops in Saudi Arabia and the extensive damage to Iraq caused by coalition bombing. Some Middle East analysts suggested that by criticizing the coalition, the government also may have hoped to curb the rising popularity of Islamic fundamentalists. The fundamentalists, who in the 1980's had received financial aid from Saudi Arabia—a foe of Iraq's in the Persian Gulf War—were slow to capitalize on public sympathy for Iraq.

Fundamentalist plot charged. Violent clashes between the government and Islamic fundamentalists that began in September 1990 continued into 1991. On February 17, fundamentalists firebombed an office of the ruling Democratic Constitutional Rally (DCR) in Tunis, Tunisia's capital, killing a guard. As tensions escalated, the government on March 29 banned a university student group and clamped down on groups and activities affiliated with the Renaissance Party, an Islamic fundamentalist party. The police also raided the University of Tunis, a fundamentalist stronghold, and drafted hundreds of students into the army. Unrest at the university continued, however, and at least two students died on May 8, when police fired on protesters.

Many Tunisians criticized Ben Ali's tactics in dealing with the students. But the government won some support in May when officials displayed weapons allegedly captured from fundamentalists. Officials charged that the weapons were evidence of a fundamentalist plot to overthrow the government and establish an Islamic republic. Some 300 people were arrested.

Fears of a fundamentalist take-over and financial and political privileges granted to opposition politicians temporarily muted calls for democratic reforms. On September 28, Ben Ali discharged nine DCR members of parliament and offered opposition politicians the opportunity to run unopposed for the seats in elections scheduled for October 13. But the opposition refused, citing the DCR's control of Tunisia's political institutions and media. Christine Helms

See also **Persian Gulf,** Special Report: **War in the Persian Gulf; Africa** (Facts in brief table). In ***World Book,*** see **Tunisia.**

Turkey. President Turgut Özal in early 1991 offered political support to the United States-led military coalition against Iraq despite overwhelming opposition from Turkey's public, its military establishment, and many of its politicians. Özal had also supported a United Nations (UN) trade embargo imposed on Iraq because of its invasion of Kuwait in August 1990.

In aligning Turkey with the coalition, Özal hoped to boost Turkey's standing in the West at a time when his country's strategic importance as part of the Western defense against the Soviet Union was declining. Özal also hoped his actions would earn Turkey good will from the European Community (EC or Common Market). In 1989, the EC had delayed action on Turkey's application for membership until 1993.

Gulf war military support. On Jan. 17, 1991, Turkey's parliament agreed to allow the United States to use the Turkish military base at Incirlik on the Mediterranean coast to launch air strikes against Iraq during the Persian Gulf War. Turkey also permitted the coalition to station troops at Silopi near the Turkish-Iraqi border to protect Iraqi Kurds, who had fled to the area after the Iraqi Army crushed a Kurdish rebellion in March.

Kurdish problems. In April, some Western governments criticized Turkey for what they said was its slowness in opening its borders to fleeing Iraqi Kurds and for its allegedly harsh treatment of the refugees. An estimated 500,000 Kurds fled to the Turkish-Iraqi

Kurdish refugees from Iraq grab for bread in April at a makeshift camp at the Turkish border, where they had fled after a failed uprising in Iraq.

border after the war. Turkey's government reacted angrily to the charges, noting that it had spent at least $50 million on direct aid to the refugees. In addition, in early 1991, Turkey was supporting an estimated 27,000 Kurds who had fled Iraq in 1988.

During 1991, Kurdish guerrillas in Turkey, fighting for an independent Kurdish state, stepped up their attacks on Turkish forces. In July, at least 15 Turkish soldiers were killed and 122 injured in Diyarbakir in southeast Turkey. Most of Turkey's 12 million Kurds—about 20 per cent of the population—live in the mountainous southeast. Beginning in August, Turkey's air force attacked camps reportedly belonging to the separatist Kurdish Workers' Party and located 6 miles (10 kilometers) inside Iraq. Turkish officials claimed that Turkey's Kurds were receiving aid from the Kurds in Iraq. Some analysts, however, argued that the raids were meant to disguise the fact that Turkish Kurds are becoming a militant, effective force.

Turkey's economic crisis worsened during the Persian Gulf crisis as the country incurred an estimated $7 billion in war-related costs. That amount included earnings lost from exports, tourism, contracts, and fees for shipping Iraqi oil. In August 1990, in order to comply with the UN trade embargo, Turkey had shut down two pipelines that carried Iraqi oil across its territory. By November 1991, the inflation rate had climbed to 70 per cent, Turkey's foreign debt was $44-billion, and the budget deficit was $6 billion.

In an effort to offset some of Turkey's war-related debts, the United States increased Turkey's foreign aid package by $300 million. Part of the funds were to help buy 80 F-16 U.S. fighter planes. Although Turkey also received additional assistance from other countries in the coalition, the amount did not fully compensate Turkey for its shortfall.

Election losses. Deteriorating economic conditions, Özal's pro-Western tilt during the Persian Gulf crisis, and charges of corruption and favoritism to Özal's relatives contributed to the defeat of Özal's ruling Motherland Party in parliamentary elections held on October 20. Candidates from the conservative True Path Party won 180 out of 450 seats. Suleyman Demirel, the head of that party, became prime minister for the seventh time.

Terrorist attacks. Islamic fundamentalists continued their attacks on government and Western targets in Turkey in 1991. Dev-Sol, a left wing group, claimed responsibility for a spate of bombings in major Turkish cities, including Ankara, the capital. Lieutenant General Hulusi Sayin, a Turkish government adviser, was assassinated on January 30, reportedly by radical Kurds.

Christine Helms

See also **Middle East** (Facts in brief table); **Persian Gulf**, Special Report: **War in the Persian Gulf.** In ***World Book,*** see **Turkey.**

Uganda. See **Africa.**

Unemployment. See **Economics; Labor.**

Union of Soviet Socialist Republics

The Soviet Union officially ceased to exist as a political entity on Dec. 25, 1991. That day, Soviet President Mikhail S. Gorbachev resigned, after six years in power. And the Soviet red flag, with its hammer standing for the workers and its sickle for the peasants, was lowered from the Kremlin in Moscow, which had been the center of the Soviet government. Taking the place of the defunct union was a new association—the Commonwealth of Independent States—made up of 11 of the 15 former Soviet republics.

The commonwealth was formally established on December 21, with the signing of an agreement by the presidents of the 11 former Soviet republics in Alma-Ata, the capital of Kazakhstan. Georgia was the only remaining republic not to affiliate with the commonwealth by year's end. In September, the three Baltic republics—Estonia, Latvia, and Lithuania—had become independent, sovereign states, and they chose not to seek a commonwealth link.

The collapse of the Soviet Union had occurred rapidly in the wake of a failed coup against Gorbachev in August. One Soviet republic after another had declared independence from the union, culminating in the dissolution of the multinational Communist state that had been born out of the 1917 Russian Revolution led by Vladimir I. Lenin.

The coup attempt began on Monday, Aug. 19, 1991, while Gorbachev was vacationing in the Crimea, on the coast of the Black Sea. In the early morning hours, an eight-member junta declared a state of emergency. Gorbachev's isolated seaside villa was ringed by troops from the Soviet secret police (KGB) and all communications to it were cut.

The junta, which called itself the State Committee for the State of Emergency, was headed by the man Gorbachev had appointed as his deputy: Vice President Gennady I. Yanayev. Other members included KGB chief Vladimir A. Kryuchkov and the interior and defense ministers, Boris K. Pugo and Dimitry T. Yazov. Yanayev had taken over as president, the official Soviet news agency Tass said, "because of Gorbachev's inability to perform his duties for health reasons."

The timing of the coup made clear the plotters' purpose: Gorbachev had been due back in Moscow to sign a treaty on August 20 that delegated significant aspects of the central government's authority to the Soviet republics. The leaders of the coup were Communist hard-liners, opposed to any loosening of central control. As their first decree, they asserted that

A Russian tricolor flag—about to replace the Soviet red flag—is unfurled in Moscow's Red Square after a failed coup by Communist hard-liners in August.

Tanks approach a barrricade of trolley cars protecting the Russian republic's parliament building on the night of August 20 during the attempted coup.

the Soviet Constitution took precedence over the constitutions of individual republics.

By the second day, August 20, it became evident that the coup was ill planned and foundering. Aside from isolating Gorbachev and his family, the emergency committee had accomplished little. Several hours had elapsed on August 19 before the first tanks rolled into the center of Moscow. By that time, thousands of Muscovites had arrived at the Russian parliament building, where they cheered Boris N. Yeltsin, who had been elected president of the Russian republic in June. Yeltsin denounced the plotters and called for a general strike. The failure to muzzle Yeltsin was but one example of the ineptitude of the coup leaders.

Even a crackdown on the media was incomplete. Only a few radio and TV stations were silenced, while others continued broadcasting. Newspapers that the junta had supposedly suppressed brought out emergency issues. After the tanks arrived, defiant civilian protesters caused tank crews to lose their nerve.

Surprisingly little violence occurred, despite the presence of tanks. On the night of August 20, however, a *Molotov cocktail* (gasoline grenade) set fire to a tank near the Russian parliament. Soldiers opened fire, killing three people.

By August 21, it was clear that the coup was crumbling. Divisions became apparent among members of

the emergency committee, and on the afternoon of August 21, the Executive Committee of the Supreme Soviet of the U.S.S.R. (parliament) reinstated Gorbachev as president. A visibly shaken Gorbachev flew back to Moscow on August 22.

Yanayev and 12 other suspected coup leaders were then indicted on charges of treason. One conspirator, Pugo, committed suicide before he could be arrested. The plotters clearly had not anticipated opposition to their actions. But opposition came not only from the people but also, reportedly, from some units of the armed forces and the KGB.

Aftermath of the coup. Dramatic events had already begun to unfold by the time Gorbachev returned to power. The three Baltic republics—Estonia, Latvia, and Lithuania—on August 20 and 21 had claimed the independence they first declared in 1990. Many of the remaining 12 republics also took advantage of the political uncertainty following the coup to assert their intention of becoming independent.

Blame for the coup fell largely on the Communist Party. The party finally collapsed in late August, as one republic after another closed down party headquarters and requisitioned party property and newspapers. In the Russian republic, Yeltsin banned the party and its widespread *cells* (small units) in the key institutions and at all workplaces from which it had wielded all-encompassing power. See **U.S.S.R.,** Special Report: **Why Communism Failed in the U.S.S.R.**

On August 24, Gorbachev resigned as the general secretary of the Communist Party and disbanded the party's Central Committee. The Supreme Soviet fell into line on August 29 and indefinitely suspended all party activities on Soviet soil. Under a new head, the KGB was purged and its authority greatly reduced. The dissolution of the Communist Party removed the last barrier to dissolving the Soviet Union itself.

The republics take charge. Ironically, the failed coup speeded the very change—power to the republics—that the coup leaders had most wanted to block. On September 5, the Congress of People's Deputies, the country's highest legislative body, approved Gorbachev's plan to transfer power from the central government to the republics. Under the plan, the central government would have only those powers granted to it by the republics, presumably including authority over defense and internal security.

A transitional government was set up to run the country until the transfer of power was completed. This interim government included a State Council, comprised of Gorbachev and the leaders of the republics. As its first act, the new State Council recognized the independence of Estonia, Latvia, and Lithuania on September 6.

For the rest of the year, Gorbachev fought frantically to hold the unraveling Soviet Union together. On October 19, he succeeded in getting 8 of the remaining 12 republics to sign a treaty on economic union. The treaty aimed at setting up a central bank, a common currency, and a free-trade zone. Fearing domination by Russia—by far the largest and wealthiest of the republics—Azerbaijan, Georgia, Moldavia (renamed Moldova) and Ukraine at first rejected the accord. But after the United States threatened to withhold aid, Ukraine and Moldova agreed to the treaty in November. The agreement, however, did little to stem the Soviet Union's impending breakup.

Gorbachev's hopes for salvaging the union received a sharp setback on November 25, when the State Council rejected his long-delayed plan for a looser political union. The independence-minded republics, by then, mistrusted any control from the center.

The next blow came on December 1 when voters in Ukraine—the most populous and wealthiest of the re-

The Breakup of the Soviet Union

The Soviet Union, which was born in the Russian Revolution of 1917, came to an end in 1991. In September, the Baltic republics—Estonia, Latvia, and Lithuania—gained independence. In December, 11 of the 12 remaining republics formed a Commonwealth of Independent States. Only Georgia did not join. Independence movements kindled strong nationalist feelings in the former republics. Each of them has a different dominant nationality group, and most of them have substantial ethnic minorities as well.

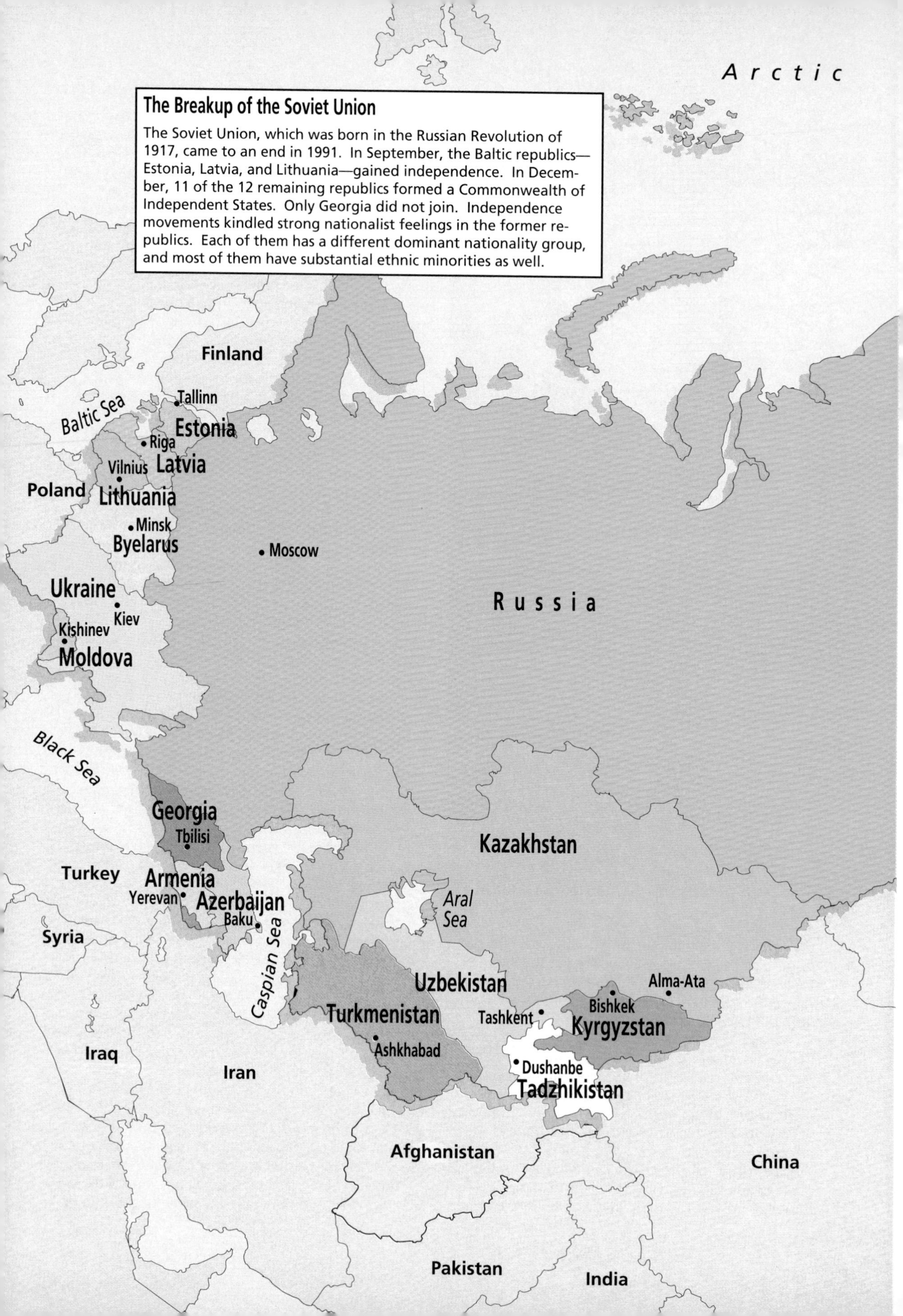

Arctic
Finland
Baltic Sea
Tallinn
Estonia
Riga
Latvia
Vilnius
Poland
Lithuania
Minsk
Byelarus
Moscow
Ukraine
Kiev
Kishinev
Moldova
Russia
Black Sea
Georgia
Tbilisi
Kazakhstan
Turkey
Armenia
Yerevan
Azerbaijan
Baku
Aral Sea
Syria
Caspian Sea
Uzbekistan
Alma-Ata
Bishkek
Tashkent
Turkmenistan
Kyrgyzstan
Ashkhabad
Iraq
Iran
Dushanbe
Tadzhikistan
Afghanistan
China
Pakistan
India

Commonwealth of Independent States

Armenia
Population 3,580,000. Major ethnic group: Armenians 93%.

Azerbaijan
Population 7,145,600. Major ethnic groups: Azerbaijanis 78%, Russians 8%, Armenians 8%.

Byelarus
Population 10,259,000. Major ethnic groups: Byelarusians 78%, Russians 13%.

Kazakhstan
Population 16,690,300. Major ethnic groups: Kazakhs 42%, Russians 38%, Ukrainians 5%.

Kyrgyzstan
Population 4,372,000. Major ethnic groups: Kyrgyz 52%, Russians 21.5%, Uzbeks 13%.

Moldova
Population 4,341,000. Major ethnic groups: Moldovans 64%, Ukrainians 14%, Russians 13%.

Russia
Population 147,386,000. Major ethnic group: Russians 83%.

Tadzhikistan
Population 5,112,000. Major ethnic groups: Tadzhiks 59%, Uzbeks 23%, Russians 10%.

Turkmenistan
Population 3,621,700. Major ethnic groups: Turkmen 68%, Russians 13%, Uzbeks 8.5%.

Ukraine
Population 51,704,000. Major ethnic groups: Ukrainians 71%, Russians 20%, Byelarusians 8%.

Uzbekistan
Population 20,322,000. Major ethnic groups: Uzbeks 69%, Russians 11%.

Unaffiliated former republics

Estonia
Population 1,573,000. Major ethnic groups: Estonians 61.5%, Russians 30%.

Georgia
Population 5,449,000. Major ethnic groups: Georgians 69%, Armenians 9%, Russians 7%, Azerbaijanis 5%.

Latvia
Population 2,681,000. Major ethnic groups: Latvians 52%, Russians 34%.

Lithuania
Population 3,690,000. Major ethnic groups: Lithuanians 80%, Russians 9%, Poles 8%.

Source: *Europa World Year Book 1991.*

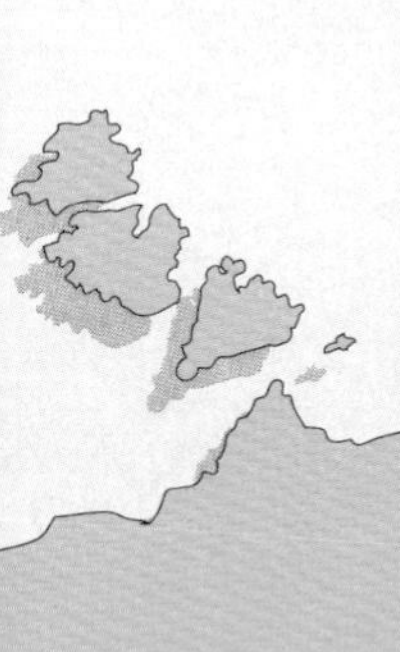

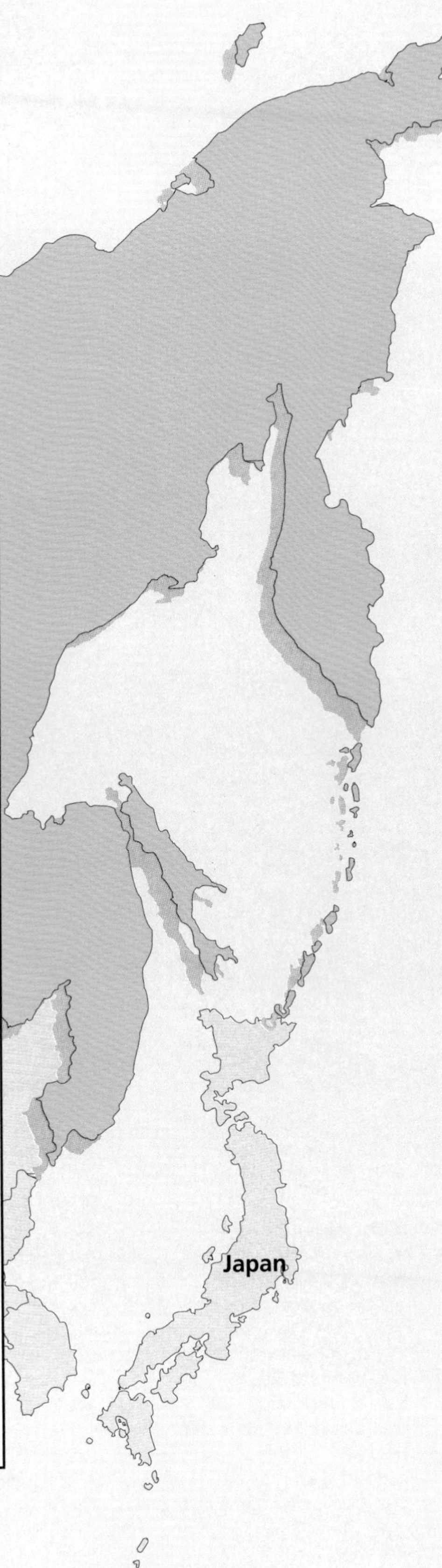

Russian President Boris Yeltsin, his hand raised in the victory signal, defies the coup leaders and rallies a Moscow crowd in protest.

publics after Russia—chose independence by a 9-to-1 majority. Both Yeltsin and Leonid M. Kravchuk, president of Ukraine, recognized that their two republics would benefit economically from continued association. They hastily worked out a proposal.

An independent commonwealth. On December 8, the leaders of Russia, Byelarus (formerly Byelorussia), and Ukraine agreed to form a Commonwealth of Independent States. Together, the three republics held about three-fourths of the Soviet population and produced about three-fourths of its farm products and two-thirds of its consumer goods. The capital of the new commonwealth was to be Minsk in Byelarus, thus ending all association with the former Soviet capital, Moscow. The three commonwealth partners quickly invited the other Soviet republics to join them. On December 21, Armenia, Azerbaijan, and Moldova joined the five Central Asian republics—Kazakhstan, Kyrgyzstan (formerly Kirghiz), Tadzhikistan, Turkmenistan, and Uzbekistan—in agreeing to become part of the commonwealth.

Exactly how the commonwealth would be organized and what powers it would have remained unresolved at year's end. At a December 30 meeting, the commonwealth leaders scrapped an earlier plan for a unified military command and agreed that the states could form armies. And although all states in the com-

monwealth were to be equal, many observers found it difficult to see how the smaller states could avoid domination by the large and powerful Russian state.

Assertions of Russian dominance were not hard to find. In November, Yeltsin had declared Russia's control over all natural resources in its territory. They included about nine-tenths of the Soviet Union's petroleum and about two-thirds of its gold. Later that month, after the central government found itself near bankruptcy, Yeltsin announced that Russia would pay the salaries of government employees. After the commonwealth was proclaimed, Yeltsin moved quickly to take control of what remained of the central Soviet government, including the Kremlin.

Some U.S. officials, including Secretary of State

James A. Baker III, questioned how long the commonwealth would last. The United States, however, moved quickly to establish diplomatic relations with Russia and several other commonwealth states.

Violence in Georgia. As the central government collapsed, violence flared in Tbilisi, the capital of Georgia, where opponents of President Zviad K. Gamsakhurdia tried to force him from office. Gamsakhurdia had been elected by a large majority in May. But after taking office, he came under increasing criticism for stifling dissent and following dictatorial policies. On Jan. 6, 1992, Gamsakhurdia fled to Armenia.

The Soviet economy all but collapsed in 1991. Production statistics showed a precipitous decline in all major sectors. Agriculture was hit especially hard, following a severe drought in eastern Siberia and Kazakhstan and flooding in Ukraine. The grain harvest fell by 26 per cent from 1990's near-record harvest. By the end of 1991, the production of many essential consumer goods had virtually stopped. Rationing of basic foods began in Moscow in November.

Inflation ran at about 250 per cent for the year, as the central Soviet government kept printing money to pay its bills. In July, the government acknowledged the phenomenon of unemployment for the first time by registering the jobless and offering them benefits.

Some American experts thought that the Soviet Union's breakup would facilitate economic reform, though others anticipated chaos. Yeltsin demanded, and the Russian parliament on November 1 granted, special economic powers enabling him to bypass government bureaucracies and issue decrees to speed reform. His economic reform program called for the lifting of price controls on Jan. 2, 1992, and the rapid sale of state-owned farmland and factories. The Russian government predicted that prices would triple, but some estimates ran much higher. Other commonwealth states, fearing that the skyrocketing prices would draw goods from their republics into Russia, planned to free prices, too. Yeltsin acknowledged that living standards had to fall for at least six months.

Nuclear arsenal. Also worrisome was the control of an estimated 27,000 nuclear weapons scattered among four former Soviet republics: Russia, Ukraine, Byelarus, and Kazakhstan. Although the commonwealth members agreed to place the weapons under a joint command, details had still to be worked out.

Yeltsin had insisted that the arms would be concentrated in Russia under the joint control of the four states that previously had them. But Kazakhstan objected to turning its weapons over to Russia. Ukraine, still recovering from the disastrous 1986 explosion at its Chernobyl nuclear power plant, and Byelarus declared their intention of becoming nuclear-free zones.

The leaders of the four commonwealth states with nuclear arms did assure Secretary of State Baker in mid-December 1991 that they would carry out arms reductions agreed to earlier in the year by Gorbachev and U.S. President George Bush. The agreements in-

A tired Mikhail Gorbachev, followed by his wife and granddaughter, arrives in Moscow on August 22, president again after the coup collapsed.

cluded a Strategic Arms Reduction Treaty (START), signed on July 31 after years of negotiations, and later proposals to eliminate short-range weapons and reduce the strength of armed forces. Baker offered the former republics financial and technical assistance in dismantling their nuclear weapons. See **Armed forces.**

Assistance from abroad. The United States and other Western nations generally held back on loans and credits during the year. On August 29, the United States and Great Britain agreed on a six-point plan to implement existing food credits, accelerate humanitarian aid, and expand technical assistance directly to the Soviet republics. But they did not offer direct financial support. On October 8, the 12-nation European Community (EC or Common Market) agreed to increase food aid as part of a $7.5-billion package, dependent on matching contributions from the United States, Japan, and Canada. On November 20, Bush pledged $1.5 billion to the Soviet republics in food aid. See **Farm and farming.**

As an alternative to cash support, the Russians suggested "assets for technology" exchanges as a means of stimulating their economy. For example, obsolete technology made Soviet production of petroleum inefficient, a Russian official told a group of Western business leaders in September. Western technology, he said, would raise the output of oil, natural gas, and timber and yield ample rewards for investors.

Debt repayment also became an issue, especially after some republics indicated they would not take over the Soviet foreign debt. In November, the Group of Seven—the seven leading industrialized nations—offered $1 billion in new loans and agreed to defer repayment on outstanding loans in return for an agreement by the republics to assume joint responsibility for the Soviet debt. But finding *hard* (internationally exchangeable) currency with which to repay the debt would not be easy. Hard-currency earnings from exports plummeted after the August coup.

A new Soviet foreign policy emerged on two troublesome issues in yet another sequel to the failed August coup. One issue involved a long-standing territorial dispute with Japan over the southernmost Kuril Islands in the Pacific Ocean. In September, both Gorbachev and Yeltsin signaled that they were ready to acknowledge Japan's claim to the islands, which the Soviet Union has occupied since the end of World War II in 1945. Ending the dispute would open the way for economic aid from Japan.

The other issue concerned the Soviet military presence in Cuba, a 30-year irritant in Soviet-U.S. relations. In September 1991, Gorbachev told Secretary of State Baker that the withdrawal of Soviet troops from Cuba would begin soon. The first withdrawals had been made as the year ended. Eric Bourne

See also **Europe** (Facts in brief table); **Estonia; Latvia; Lithuania.** In the World Book Supplement section, see **Estonia; Latvia; Lithuania.**

Why Communism Failed in the U.S.S.R.

By Robert V. Daniels

After ruling the Soviet Union for 74 years, the Communist party proved to be beyond reform and, despite a last-ditch coup attempt by party stalwarts, lost power.

The once all-powerful Communist system in the Soviet Union collapsed suddenly in the wake of a coup attempt in August 1991. But it was not just the failure of the coup that brought about the demise of the Communist Party. Looking back, we can see that the downfall of Communism was likely sooner or later because of the nature of its beginnings in the Revolution of 1917.

Like the French Revolution of the late 1700's, the Russian Revolution began with a moderate democratic phase under a provisional government that was set up after the overthrow of Czar Nicholas II in March 1917. But then came an extremist phase. The Bolsheviks under Vladimir I. Lenin seized power in November 1917 and fought a victorious civil war against all opponents to assure their one-party rule. The Bolsheviks—renamed Communists in 1918—believed fanatically in the dictatorship of the *proletariat* (the industrial working class). They envisioned a classless society of socialism with an ultimate transition to communism. Then there would be no more government and everyone would be equal, according to their revolutionary ideology called Marxism-Leninism.

However, no revolution has ever stuck to such a radical ideal. When Joseph Stalin took control of the Communist Party after Lenin's death in 1924, he set up a postrevolutionary dictatorship to build up the power of the country. Stalin exerted control through the Communist Party and the secret police. He gave orders to the top party council, the Politburo, which passed them down through the chain of command. As in an army, ordinary party members who worked in the government, industry, agriculture, and the media were only supposed to see that these orders were carried out.

During his five-year plans of the 1920's and 1930's, Stalin expanded Soviet industry by placing the entire economy under strict central planning and control. He ended private farming and forced peasants onto collective farms. When they resisted, he seized their crops or sent them into exile in Siberia. Harsh conditions and widespread starvation killed millions. He forced millions of other people into labor camps. He uprooted entire villages of ethnic minorities, transplanting them to other regions in the Soviet Union.

In the mid-1930's, Stalin began a program of terror called the Great Purge. Some Soviet scholars estimate that as many as 20 million people may have been killed. Most high Soviet officials and generals were executed and replaced by younger people more loyal to Stalin. All independent thinking was wiped out. By 1939, the start of World War II, no political opposition to Stalin remained.

Along with preserving his own power, Stalin's main objective was to build the industrial base for military power. This meant severe shortages for consumers. On the other hand, it meant that the Soviet Union had the might to throw back the Germans in World War II (1939-1945). Nevertheless, a system that ruled in this manner could not go on forever. When a postrevolutionary dictatorship fails to meet the needs of the country, it is sooner or later overthrown by people who want to go back to the ideals of the original moderate phase of the revolution and start over. This is what happened in the Soviet Union between 1985 and 1991.

Glossary

Bolsheviks: The political party of V. I. Lenin that seized control of the Russian government after the fall of the czar in 1917 and renamed the Communist Party in 1918.

Glasnost: *Openness,* a policy begun in 1985 to increase freedom of expression in the Soviet Union.

Great Purge: Joseph Stalin's program of terror in the 1930's to eliminate his political opposition.

Perestroika: *Restructuring,* a 1985 policy to reform the Soviet political and economic systems.

Preceding page: Ukrainians demanding independence from the Soviet Union display a defaced poster of V. I. Lenin during a rally in Kiev, the capital, on Sept. 15, 1991.

The author:

Robert V. Daniels is professor emeritus of history at the University of Vermont in Burlington. He is the author of numerous books on Communism in the Soviet Union.

The fall of the czar

Rebellious Russian soldiers burn symbols of the monarchy during the March 1917 revolution that overthrew Czar Nicholas II. The monarchy was succeeded by a weak provisional government, which Lenin and his Bolsheviks ousted in November, thus beginning 74 years of Communist rule.

Meanwhile, after Stalin died on March 5, 1953, Nikita S. Khrushchev took over as head of the Communist Party. He openly denounced Stalin's tyranny and relaxed political control over writers, artists, and scholars. He shifted government planning targets to produce more clothing, food, and other consumer goods, areas neglected under Stalin. Gains were slow, however, and Khrushchev was overthrown by a conspiracy of high-ranking Communists in 1964.

At the same time, high party and government officials were enjoying special privileges, such as secret stores and country houses called *dachas.* Under Leonid Brezhnev, who headed the Communist Party from 1964 to 1982, bribery and corruption became common. Party members stole supplies from factories while ordinary citizens stood in long lines at the stores for the most basic necessities and waited years to buy a car or get an apartment. Nevertheless, the Communist Party continued to justify its methods by proclaiming through the media that it was working on "the transition to communism." Brezhnev reestablished many of Stalin's rigid cultural and economic policies, and the party again suppressed all public criticism. Soviet successes in manufacturing missiles and putting satellites into orbit were supposed to show the superiority of the Communist system.

By the 1970's, it was becoming more difficult to achieve economic progress through the Stalinist or "neo-Stalinist" system and at the same time keep up with the West in high technology and advanced weapons. People had neither enough incentive to work hard nor freedom to take the initiative. To obtain technology and extra grain from the West, Brezhnev eased tensions in a policy that became known as *détente.* But friendly relations with the West, along with short-wave radio, also brought in Western ideas. The more people learned about political freedom and the standard of living in the West, the more dissatisfied they became. Eventually, almost no one took the official Marxist-Leninist ideology seriously.

In 1985, as the Stalinist generation of leaders grew old and died away, reformers of all stripes rallied around a new leader, Mikhail S. Gorbachev. He hoped, at first, to reinvigorate the party and get the country moving again through discipline and incentives. This was called *perestroika* (restructuring). Conservative party bureaucrats, however, balked at his plans, and Gorbachev decided to get around them in two ways. First, he established the policy of *glasnost* (openness), which freed the press and the public to criticize the bureaucrats. Second, he democratized the party and the government through genuine elections.

In March 1989, Gorbachev conducted the first contested elections in Soviet history. Soviet voters elected delegates to a newly created Congress of People's Deputies and a new Supreme Soviet (parliament). When many non-Communists won in the elections and reformers challenged conservatives within the Communist Party, the one-party monopoly came to an end. Frank discussions in the popular media about Soviet history and Stalin's crimes destroyed whatever sense of legitimacy the party still had. Finally, in March 1990, free elections were held in all the Soviet republics, and non-Communist political organizations of every hue sprang up. In addition, non-Russian separatists in many republics of the Soviet Union, such as Estonia, Latvia, and Lithuania, took advantage of the new democracy to call for national independence.

Important Soviet leaders

Leaders of the Soviet Communist Party were the most powerful people in the Soviet Union until March 1990, when the government created the office of president of the U.S.S.R. and elected Mikhail S. Gorbachev as the first president.

Joseph Stalin, dictator of the Soviet Union from 1929 until his death in 1953, was responsible for the imprisonment and deaths of millions of Soviet citizens.

Nikita S. Khrushchev became head of the Communist Party in 1953. He exposed Stalin's crimes and improved relations with the West, but was ousted in 1964.

Leonid I. Brezhnev headed the party from 1964 until his death in 1982. He eased tensions with the West, but reinstituted rigid, centrally controlled economic policies.

Mikhail S. Gorbachev won control of the party in 1985. This first party head not trained by Stalin instituted rapid political and economic change, which led to unrest.

Guns or Goods

A parade of tanks through Moscow in 1987, *below,* to celebrate the 70th anniversary of the Russian Revolution, was one of many such public displays of military might. The centrally planned economy placed heavy emphasis on military spending. This and other economic problems caused frequent shortages of consumer goods. By 1991, Soviet citizens faced daily shortages of basic food items and had to stand in long lines at state-run stores, *right.*

These steps alarmed not only the old Stalinists but also many of the younger party officials who had originally supported Gorbachev but who now feared the loss of their power and privileges. The party divided into three factions: Conservatives, led by the party's Second Secretary Yegor Ligachev, wanted to limit reform to increased discipline and efficiency. Moderate reformers, including Politburo member Alexander Yakovlev and Foreign Minister Eduard Shevardnadze, feared the conservatives and advocated step-by-step reform. And radicals, exemplified by Boris Yeltsin, Moscow party secretary from 1985 to 1987 and president of the Russian Republic in 1990, wanted to democratize the government quickly and decentralize the economy.

Fearing that the conservatives had enough power through the party, the secret police, and the army to overthrow him as they had Khrushchev in 1964, Gorbachev maneuvered between them and the radicals. He alternately pushed for reform and then withdrew partway. He persuaded the party congress in July 1990 to reorganize the Politburo so that it would confine itself to the party's organizational affairs and no longer function as the supreme policymaking body for the government. However, Gorbachev's tactics alienated almost everyone, particularly when in autumn 1990 he abandoned the so-called "500 Days" plan to reform the economy on free-market lines and replaced most top reformist officials with conservatives. There was open talk of a military coup, with the conservatives urging one and the reformers fearing it. Shevardnadze resigned from the government in December 1990 to dramatize his warning of a coup.

By the spring of 1991, industrial and agricultural production were falling and the stores were empty. Gorbachev changed his tack once again. He sought an economic accord with the reformers, abolished the "leading role" guaranteed to the Communist Party under the old Constitution, and prepared a new union treaty to replace the Soviet Union with a loose confederation of republics. He persuaded the Communist Party Central Committee to accept a new program that dropped the old Marxist-Leninist ideology altogether.

All of this was too much for the Communist conservatives. In June, they tried to get the Supreme Soviet to transfer most of Gorbachev's presidential powers to the conservative prime minister, Valentin Pavlov. Failing in this, they struck at Gorbachev personally in the coup of August 19, putting him under house arrest, telling the country he was too ill to rule, and announcing emergency measures to restore order.

But the coup failed, and with its failure the remaining authority of the Communist Party vanished. When Gorbachev returned to Moscow after his brief captivity, he hoped at first that the party could still be reformed. Then, evidently, he realized that the party no longer had any standing with the Soviet people. On Aug. 24, 1991, Gorbachev resigned as Communist Party general secretary and dissolved the party's Central Committee. He then persuaded the Congress of People's Deputies to dissolve itself in favor of a new parliament with limited power over the republics. Most of the republics banned Communist activities and seized party property.

Although the authority of the Communist Party seemed to have faded beyond any hope of revival, this did not automatically guarantee democracy in the former Soviet republics. For one thing, local Communist officials still remained in positions of governmental power or headed factories and collective farms in many districts. Die-hard Communists and Russian nationalists, opposing the breakup of the Soviet Union, reopened the formerly Communist newspapers. Some popularly elected leaders assumed dictatorial powers and suppressed opposition organizations and small minority nationalities. By the end of 1991, democratic institutions were still in danger, and the future of the Soviet Union seemed as uncertain as it had in 1917.

For further reading:

Daniels, Robert V. *Russia: The Roots of Confrontation.* Harvard University Press, 1985.

The Transformation of Socialism: Perestroika and Reform in the Soviet Union and China. Ed. by Mel Gurtov. Westview, 1990.

United Nations. On Dec. 21, 1991, 11 former republics of the Soviet Union declared themselves the Commonwealth of Independent States and agreed that Russia would take over the Soviet Union's permanent United Nations (UN) Security Council seat. Of the new commonwealth states, Byelarus (formerly Byelorussia) and Ukraine were already members of the UN General Assembly. The commonwealth planned to campaign for the other states to acquire UN seats as well. See **Union of Soviet Socialist Republics.**

The membership of the 15-nation Security Council was set to change beginning Jan. 1, 1992, when the two-year terms of 5 of the 10 nonpermanent members expired. As a result, Cuba, Ivory Coast, Romania, Yemen, and Zaire were to be replaced by Cape Verde, Hungary, Japan, Morocco, and Venezuela. Ecuador, Austria, Belgium, India, and Zimbabwe remained in the Council in 1992 along with the permanent member nations of the United States, Russia, China, France, and Great Britain.

The Persian Gulf War between Iraq and an international coalition force led by the United States dominated the agenda of the UN Security Council early in 1991. The Council gave Iraq a deadline of January 15 to withdraw its troops from Kuwait or face punitive action. In a last-minute diplomatic maneuver, UN Secretary-General Javier Pérez de Cuéllar went to Baghdad, the capital of Iraq, on January 12 to persuade Iraqi President Saddam Hussein to remove his troops from Kuwait. But Hussein was unmovable.

On January 17, an air war began with allied air forces bombing military targets in Iraq. The combined allied troops, numbering more than 400,000, were based in Saudi Arabia and on battleships in the Persian Gulf. On February 7, Pérez de Cuéllar reported to the Council that the bombing was widespread in Iraq, and that civilian casualties appeared to number in the thousands. UN agencies such as the High Commissioner for Refugees and the International Labor Organization reported that more than 2 million foreigners who had been working in Iraq and Kuwait had fled those countries because of the war.

On February 24, allied forces launched a ground-war offensive. On February 27, Iraq informed the UN Security Council that it would abide by 12 resolutions the Council had mandated for Iraq after Iraqi troops had invaded Kuwait in August. The resolutions included stipulations that Iraq immediately and unconditionally withdraw from Kuwait and release any foreigners being held in Iraq and Kuwait.

On March 2, the Council adopted resolution 686, which reaffirmed the 12 prior resolutions. Resolution 686 also demanded that Iraq revoke its annexation of Kuwait; accept liability for damage, loss, or injury to Kuwait or to third-party individuals or corporations in Kuwait; and return all properties seized from Kuwait.

After the fighting ceased, Pérez de Cuéllar sent Undersecretary-General Martti Ahtisaari to lead a UN team to Iraq in March to assess the war damages and the need for humanitarian assistance. The team reported that the war had had "near-apocalyptic" effects on the Iraqi economy. It also said the country's infrastructure, including roads and bridges, had been reduced to a "preindustrial age."

The Estonian delegation, newly admitted to the United Nations, listens to opening speeches of the General Assembly's 46th session on September 17.

The longest resolution the Council had ever been known to approve was adopted on April 3. Composed of more than 4,000 words, resolution 687 set specific conditions for a permanent cease-fire in the Persian Gulf War. It passed with a vote of 12 to 1. Cuba voted against it, and Ecuador and Yemen abstained. The resolution said that Iraq must recognize Kuwait's border, make reparations to Kuwait, and return to Kuwait any property Iraq had stolen from it. The resolution further demanded that Iraq submit to the elimination of all its biological and chemical weapons as well as its ballistic missiles having a range of more than 90 miles (145 kilometers). It also required Iraq to halt development of nuclear weapons and destroy facilities for the manufacture of nuclear weapons. Iraq accepted the terms of the resolution on April 6, and the war was formally ended. On April 9, the Security Council approved the establishment of a UN peacekeeping force to monitor the cease-fire.

After the war ended, some 1.5 million Iraqi civilians, most of whom were Kurds, fled their country for Iran or Turkey. Alarmed by the magnitude of the exodus, several UN agencies participated in a massive program for humanitarian assistance to the refugees. Re-

Vytautas Landsbergis, president of the Supreme Council in newly independent Lithuania, is welcomed to the United Nations on September 17.

lief officials said caring for the refugees for three months would require $500 million.

The 46th session of the UN General Assembly opened on September 17 with the election to the UN presidency of Saudi Arabia's UN representative Samir Shihabi. The Assembly began its work with a sense of renewed prestige following the Security Council's handling of the Persian Gulf War. Delegates to the Assembly proposed changes that would strengthen the UN system in dealing with the world economy, social problems, and human rights.

The Assembly admitted seven new members: North Korea and South Korea; the Marshall Islands; the Federated States of Micronesia; and the Baltic states of Lithuania, Estonia, and Latvia, which were newly independent from the Soviet Union. The admission of these nations increased the UN membership to a total of 166 countries.

Continuing problems in Iraq demanded the Council's immediate attention. In the face of reports of impending famine in Iraq, the Security Council on September 19 approved a measure allowing Iraq to export $1.6-billion worth of oil. The measure was designed as an exception to the trade sanctions that had been imposed on Iraq in 1990 as a result of its invasion of Kuwait. Proceeds from the oil exports were to be administered by the UN and used to purchase food, medicine, and other essentials for Iraqi civilians. The revenues were also to pay for war damages, to compensate for losses suffered by migrant workers, and to defray costs incurred for weapons destruction. But the Iraqi government rejected the measure and called it an insult to its sovereignty.

On September 8, Iraq, in violation of the cease-fire agreement, barred UN inspectors from using their own helicopters to search for Iraqi weapons facilities. Iraq later relented and allowed the helicopter flights with some conditions imposed. But on September 23, Iraqi authorities detained 44 UN inspectors for four days after the inspectors had discovered thousands of confidential documents showing that Iraq had a nuclear weapons program. Under strong pressure from the Council, Iraq released the inspectors after being provided with an inventory of the documents.

Cambodia. On October 31, the Security Council unanimously adopted a resolution giving its "full support" for an agreement to settle the Cambodian conflict. The agreement had been signed by 19 nations on October 23 in Paris. The agreement ended a civil war that had raged in Cambodia since 1978. After the October 1991 settlement, the UN helped administer part of the Cambodian government during a transition period. The peace settlement also called for the UN to monitor the cease-fire among Cambodia's four warring factions and to organize general elections for a new, sovereign, and neutral government.

One day after the endorsement by the Council, Pérez de Cuéllar announced a plan to send a 268-member UN mission to Cambodia. This group was to supervise the cease-fire and prepare for the arrival in early 1992 of a massive UN peacekeeping force. That force, the UN Transitional Authority in Cambodia, was to consist of thousands of military and civilian personnel to register the population and organize elections to be held in early 1993.

Referendum in Western Sahara. The Security Council on April 29, 1991, decided that the United Nations would arrange a popular vote on independence for Western Sahara, which had been under Moroccan rule since 1975. The Council voted to send a coalition of as many as 3,000 people, including some 1,700 military troops, to oversee the election.

El Salvador. On Dec 31, 1991, just as he was relinquishing his post as UN Secretary-General, Pérez de Cuéllar orchestrated a peace pact between El Salvador's government and guerrilla rebels. The treaty was to bring an end to fighting between the factions and terminate the civil war that has plagued the country since 1979.

The accord called for a final settlement to be signed on Jan. 16, 1992, and for a formal cease-fire to become effective February 1. The UN was given the authority to decide any remaining points of the settlement that the El Salvador government and the rebels had not agreed upon by the signing date.

The release of Western hostages, many of whom had been held in the Middle East for many years, was orchestrated by UN representatives in 1991.

On August 8, hostage John McCarthy was released from captivity in Lebanon to deliver a message to Pérez de Cuéllar. The kidnappers demanded an exchange of Western hostages for some 375 Arabs being held in Israel.

Pérez de Cuéllar sent his special assistant for hostage affairs, Giandomenico Picco, to the Middle East to negotiate freedom for Western hostages. Between August and December, 10 hostages were freed. The bodies of two other hostages who were killed in captivity were also released. Two Germans were still being held at year-end.

Israel relinquished 91 Arab hostages during the same time period. Before freeing any others, Israel wanted information on four Israeli soldiers still missing in Lebanon.

Zionism resolution repealed. The General Assembly on December 16 voted to repeal a 1975 resolution that said "Zionism is a form of racism and racial discrimination." Zionism is the movement that established a Jewish state in Palestine, the historical homeland of the Jews. Zionism seeks to promote the state of Israel.

United States President George Bush in September 1991 had addressed the United Nations and requested that the General Assembly revoke the organization's Zionism statement. An overwhelming majority, 111 nations, voted to support the repeal. Most of the 25 nations voting against the repeal were Arab countries in the Middle East, where conflict with Israel has been severe and long-standing.

Secretary-general. On November 21, the Security Council nominated Egypt's Deputy Prime Minister Boutros Ghali to succeed Pérez de Cuéllar as the next secretary-general of the United Nations. Of the 15-member Security Council, 11 members voted for Ghali, and 4 abstained. Ghali's term was set to begin on Jan. 1, 1992, and end on Dec. 31, 1996.

Six Africans were nominated for the position by the Organization of African Unity. Ghali and Zimbabwe's Finance Minister Bernard Chidzero were the leading candidates. Ghali's Egypt, though considered a Middle Eastern country, is part of Africa and ranks as Africa's second largest nation in population. A number of countries supported placing an African in the secretary-general post because no African had ever served in that position. Four Westerners, including Canadian Prime Minister Brian Mulroney, had also been suggested for the leadership.

On Dec. 3, 1991, the 69-year-old Ghali took the oath of allegiance in a formal ceremony in the UN General Assembly. Ghali had served as Egypt's foreign minister from 1977 to 1991 and had held several other important positions in his government. He also had been a professor of international law, and he speaks English and French fluently. J. Tuyet Nguyen

See also **Cambodia; Iraq; Israel; Middle East; Persian Gulf,** Special Report: **War in the Persian Gulf.** In ***World Book,*** see **United Nations.**

United States, Government of the. All three branches of the U.S. government in 1991 were looking ahead to the presidential campaign in 1992. President George Bush and Congress were set to wrestle over controversial issues bypassed in 1991, including taxes, crime, and health care financing. The Supreme Court of the United States was faced with having to make a definitive ruling on the abortion issue. Prochoice activists hoped the court would decide the issue before the November 1992 elections, reasoning that any ruling limiting women's right to an abortion would bolster efforts to defeat antiabortion candidates running for state or national office.

Bush spent most of 1991 dealing with foreign policy and offering assurances that the U.S. economy was climbing out of recession. Then came the November 1991 elections, and Bush and fellow Republicans were stunned by the outcome of a race for a U.S. Senate seat from Pennsylvania. An obscure Democrat, Harris L. Wofford, scored a decisive upset victory over the Republican candidate, former Attorney General Richard L. Thornburgh, who had served two terms as governor of Pennsylvania. Wofford made health care reform and the ailing economy winning issues.

Voter discontent. Seeing Thornburgh's defeat as a warning that voters were in an angry mood, Bush said he would be ready to consider health care reform and economic issues in 1992. But he declined to rush things. He resisted calls from fellow Republicans to urge Congress to pass economy-stimulating tax cuts before adjourning its 1991 session. Earlier, in October, Congress took some action on its own in response to the recession, passing a bill to extend unemployment benefits. Bush vetoed the legislation on October 11, saying it would cost too much. After Thornburgh's election defeat in November, however, Bush signed the measure in a slightly different form.

Economic concerns. The government made several moves in an effort to lift the economy out of recession. On October 8, Bush announced a series of steps to ease bank regulation in an effort to spur lending. On November 12, he suggested that banks lower the interest rates charged to credit card users. The next day, Senator Alfonse M. D'Amato (R., N.Y.) introduced legislation to mandate a ceiling on such rates. The Senate passed the bill later in the day, 74 to 19, and the House of Representatives seemed sure to follow. But on November 15, the Dow Jones Industrial Average (the Dow), a leading index of stock prices, plunged 120 points. Many bankers and stock market analysts blamed D'Amato's bill, which threatened to bite into the profits earned by banks on credit cards, for the sudden downturn. House Speaker Thomas S. Foley (D., Wash.) quickly promised that the measure would be set aside for further study.

The Federal Reserve Board (the Fed) reduced the *discount rate* (the rate at which it lends money to banks) several times during the year. In December, it dropped the discount rate to 3.5 per cent, the lowest rate since the 1960's. This led to a lowering of interest rates that banks charge customers. See **Economics.**

An economic proposal of sweeping potential was launched on February 5, when Bush joined the leaders of Mexico and Canada in announcing plans for a North American free-trade pact. The agreement would link the economies of the three countries into one huge, unified market. In April, Congress gave Bush two years in which to negotiate the treaty.

Growing deficit. Overhanging much of what the federal government did, and did not do, in 1991 was the budget deficit, which reached a record high of $268.7 billion in the 1991 fiscal year, which ended on September 30. Representative Leon E. Panetta (D., Calif.), chairman of the House Budget Committee, said, "The numbers confirm our worst fears that the deficit remains out of control at the very time when we need resources in order to strengthen the economy." The Office of Management and Budget said the fiscal 1992 deficit would be an estimated $348 billion. The Congressional Budget Office was even more pessimistic, predicting a shortfall of $362 billion.

The Department of Defense felt the budget pinch throughout the year. On January 7, Secretary of Defense Richard B. Cheney killed a research and development program for an A-12 Stealth attack plane for the Navy. Production of the plane was running 18 months behind schedule, and development costs had soared to more than $6.5 billion.

On July 10, Bush approved an independent commission's recommendation to close 34 military bases in the United States and shrink 48 others by 1997. The move, which was approved by Congress, was expected to save $1.5 billion a year after the costs of closing or scaling down the bases are paid.

In November, Congress passed a $291-billion defense bill that would boost spending on the Strategic Defense Initiative (SDI) antimissile program, known popularly as "Star Wars," to $4.15 billion from $2.9-billion. Bush had sought $5.15 billion. Although the program had been a favorite target of congressional Democrats, they decided in a change of heart that a limited version of SDI might be useful in defending against small-scale missile launches, such as by terrorists or Third World countries.

Congress also clipped the wings of the B-2 Stealth bomber. A new study cast doubt on the radar-evading capabilities of the bomber, which had already cost more than $30 billion. Congress on October 31 voted to keep the production line open but refused to vote funds for more than the 15 planes that had already been ordered.

In May, Bush appointed General Colin L. Powell to a second two-year term as chairman of the Joint Chiefs of Staff. Powell became a popular hero after the stunning victory of U.S. forces and allies in the 1991 Persian Gulf War against Iraq. See also **Persian Gulf,** Special Report: **War in the Persian Gulf.**

Federal spending

United States budget for fiscal 1991*

	Billions of dollars
National defense	272.5
International affairs	16.2
General science, space, technology	15.9
Energy	1.8
Natural resources and environment	18.7
Agriculture	14.9
Commerce and housing credit	75.6
Transportation	31.5
Community and regional development	7.4
Education, training, employment, and social services	41.5
Health	71.2
Social security	269.0
Medicare	104.5
Income security	171.2
Veterans' benefits and services	31.3
Administration of justice	12.3
General government	11.4
Interest	195.0
Undistributed offsetting receipts	–39.4
Total budget outlays	**1,322.5**

*Oct. 1, 1990, to Sept. 30, 1991.

Source: U.S. Department of the Treasury.

U.S. income and outlays

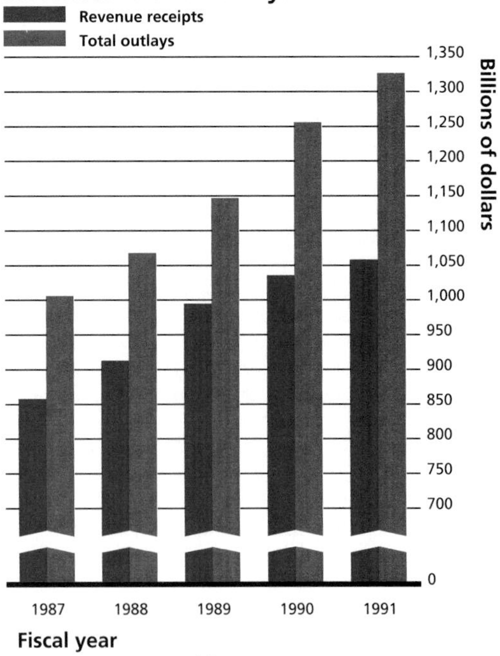

Source: U.S. Department of the Treasury.

Defense-contracting scandal. Prosecutions in the three-year-old Defense Department weapons-procurement scandal continued in 1991. The highest-ranking target of the probe, former Assistant Navy Secretary Melvin R. Paisley, was sentenced on October 18 to four years in prison and fined $50,000 for his role in illegally awarding $1 billion in defense contracts in return for large kickbacks. On September 6, a fine of $190 million was levied against the Unisys Corporation. Unisys had pleaded guilty to conspiracy and bribery.

An embarrassed U.S. Navy announced on October 17 that it had wrongly accused sailor Clayton M. Hartwig of deliberately causing a 1989 gun turret blast aboard the battleship *Iowa* that killed Hartwig and 46 others. Admiral Frank B. Kelso, chief of naval operations, apologized to Hartwig's family and said the cause of the explosion might never be known. See also **Armed forces.**

NASA. Budget pressures forced the National Aeronautics and Space Administration (NASA) in 1991 to scale back plans for an orbiting space station. Congress provided about $2 billion for the project, estimated to cost $30 billion by the year 2000.

In May, NASA disclosed that the space shuttle *Columbia* had been put in jeopardy by making repeated flights with a cracked temperature sensor that could have caused engine failure had it come loose. The problem was solved before the shuttle's next flight, on June 5.

Financial bailouts. Federal efforts to clean up catastrophic losses by savings institutions and banks continued in 1991, at great cost. In March, House and Senate conferees produced compromise legislation to provide the Resolution Trust Corporation (RTC), the agency created to bail out failed savings and loan associations, with an additional $78 billion. The Senate passed the bill on March 19, and the House approved it two days later.

On June 26, Secretary of the Treasury Nicholas F. Brady gave a Senate subcommittee a "conservative" estimate that the RTC would need at least $180 billion for the coming year. The Administration later sought an additional $80 billion for the RTC, but in November Congress provided just $25 billion. See also **Bank.**

On October 16, L. William Seidman resigned as chairman of the Federal Deposit Insurance Corporation, the agency that guarantees bank deposits against loss, and as head of the RTC. Seidman had headed the FDIC for six years.

The Democratic majority on the Senate Banking Committee on November 6 rejected the nomination of Robert L. Clarke to a second six-year term as comptroller of the currency. Committee Chairman Donald W. Riegle, Jr. (D., Mich.), contended that Clarke, as chief bank regulator, had permitted reckless lending.

Alan Greenspan, chairman of the Fed, was named to a second four-year term on July 10. Senate action on the nomination was delayed until 1992.

Iran-contra prosecutions. Special Prosecutor Lawrence E. Walsh obtained guilty pleas from two officials in 1991, even as two others were freed of all charges. The cases involved the secret government arms sales to Iran in the mid-1980's, with profits used to support *contra* rebels fighting the then Marxist government in Nicaragua.

On September 16, a federal judge dismissed all charges against retired Marine Lieutenant Colonel Oliver L. North, who was a central Iran-contra figure as an aide to former President Ronald Reagan. The judge ruled that North's conviction in 1989 was invalid because information he presented at congressional Iran-contra hearings in 1987 under a guarantee of immunity may have been used against him at his trial.

For the same reason, a U.S. Court of Appeals on November 15 reversed the 1990 conviction of retired Navy Rear Admiral John M. Poindexter. Poindexter, who had been Reagan's national security adviser, was the highest-ranking official of the Reagan Administration to be implicated in the Iran-contra scandal.

Meanwhile, Walsh obtained guilty pleas from two former high officials of the Reagan Administration. On July 9, Alan D. Fiers, Jr., who had headed the CIA's Central American Task Force, pleaded guilty to two misdemeanor counts of unlawfully withholding information from Congress. And on October 7, former Assistant Secretary of State Elliott Abrams pleaded guilty, like Fiers, to two counts of withholding information from Congress.

On September 6, Walsh obtained the indictment of Clair E. George, former chief of the CIA's covert operations, on 10 felony counts of lying and obstructing investigations. Duane R. (Dewey) Clarridge, another former CIA official, was indicted November 26 on seven felony counts of perjury concerning secret arms shipments to Iran in 1987. See also **Iran-contra affair.**

New CIA director. Robert Gates, a White House aide for national security affairs, was nominated by Bush to become the new director of the Central Intelligence Agency (CIA). After nearly six months of debate in the Senate, Gates was confirmed by a vote of 64 to 31 on November 5. See **Gates, Robert.**

Cabinet changes. There were several changes in the Bush Cabinet in 1991. Clayton K. Yeutter resigned as secretary of agriculture in January to become chairman of the Republican National Committee. He was succeeded by Representative Edward R. Madigan of Illinois, senior Republican on the House Agriculture Committee. Attorney General Thornburgh resigned to run for the Senate in Pennsylvania. His successor was William P. Barr, his deputy. In December, Secretary of Transportation Samuel K. Skinner resigned to become Bush's White House chief of staff, replacing John H. Sununu. See **Barr, William P.; Madigan, Edward R.; Cabinet, United States; Sununu, John H.**

Courts. On June 27, Thurgood Marshall retired as an associate justice of the Supreme Court. Marshall, who had served on the court for 24 years, was suc-

Selected agencies and bureaus of the U.S. government*

Executive Office of the President
President, George Bush
Vice President, Dan Quayle
White House Chief of Staff, Samuel K. Skinner
Presidential Press Secretary, Martin Fitzwater
Assistant to the President for National Security Affairs, Brent Scowcroft
Assistant to the President for Science and Technology, D. Allan Bromley
Council of Economic Advisers—Michael J. Boskin, Chairman
Office of Management and Budget—Richard G. Darman, Director
Office of National Drug Control Policy—Bob Martinez, Director
U.S. Trade Representative, Carla A. Hills

Department of Agriculture
Secretary of Agriculture, Edward R. Madigan

Department of Commerce
Secretary of Commerce, Robert A. Mosbacher
Bureau of Economic Analysis—Allan H. Youn, Director
Bureau of the Census—Barbara E. Bryant, Director

Department of Defense
Secretary of Defense, Richard B. Cheney
Secretary of the Air Force, Donald B. Rice
Secretary of the Army, Michael P. W. Stone
Secretary of the Navy, H. Lawrence Garrett III
Joint Chiefs of Staff—
General Colin L. Powell, Chairman
General Merrill A. McPeak, Chief of Staff, Air Force
General Gordon R. Sullivan, Chief of Staff, Army
Admiral Frank B. Kelso II, Chief of Naval Operations
General Carl E. Mundy, Commandant , Marine Corps

Department of Education
Secretary of Education, Lamar Alexander

Department of Energy
Secretary of Energy, James D. Watkins

Department of Health and Human Services
Secretary of Health and Human Services, Louis W. Sullivan
Public Health Service—James O. Mason, Assistant Secretary
Centers for Disease Control—William L. Roper, Director
Food and Drug Administration—David A. Kessler, Commissioner
National Institutes of Health—Bernadine P. Healy, Director
Surgeon General of the United States Antonia C. Novello
Social Security Administration—Gwendolyn S. King, Commissioner

Department of Housing and Urban Development
Secretary of Housing and Urban Development, Jack F. Kemp

Department of the Interior
Secretary of the Interior, Manuel Lujan, Jr.

Department of Justice
Attorney General, William P. Barr
Bureau of Prisons—J. Michael Quinlan, Director
Drug Enforcement Administration—Robert C. Bonner, Administrator
Federal Bureau of Investigation—William S. Sessions, Director
Immigration and Naturalization Service—Gene McNary, Commissioner
Solicitor General, Kenneth W. Starr

Department of Labor
Secretary of Labor, Lynn M. Martin

Department of State
Secretary of State, James A. Baker III
U.S. Representative to the United Nations, Thomas R. Pickering

Department of Transportation
Acting Secretary of Transportation, James B. Busey IV
Federal Aviation Administration—Barry L. Harris, Acting Administrator
U.S. Coast Guard—William J. Kime, Commandant

*As of Dec. 31, 1991.

Department of the Treasury
Secretary of the Treasury, Nicholas F. Brady
Internal Revenue Service—Fred T. Goldberg, Jr., Commissioner
Treasurer of the United States, Catalina Vasquez Villalpando
U.S. Secret Service—John R. Simpson, Director
Office of Thrift Supervision—T. Timothy Ryan, Jr., Director

Department of Veterans Affairs
Secretary of Veterans Affairs, Edward J. Derwinski

Supreme Court of the United States
Chief Justice of the United States, William H. Rehnquist
Associate Justices
Byron R. White
Harry A. Blackmun
John Paul Stevens
Sandra Day O'Connor
Antonin Scalia
Anthony M. Kennedy
David H. Souter
Clarence Thomas

Congressional officials
President of the Senate pro tempore, Robert C. Byrd
Senate Majority Leader, George J. Mitchell
Senate Minority Leader, Robert J. Dole
Speaker of the House, Thomas S. Foley
House Majority Leader, Richard A. Gephardt
House Minority Leader, Robert H. Michel
Congressional Budget Office—Robert D. Reischauer, Director
General Accounting Office—Charles A. Bowsher, Comptroller General of the United States
Library of Congress—James H. Billington, Librarian of Congress
Office of Technology Assessment—John H. Gibbons, Director

Independent agencies
ACTION—Jane A. Kenny, Director
Agency for International Development—Ronald W. Roskens, Administrator
Central Intelligence Agency—Robert M. Gates, Director
Commission on Civil Rights—Arthur A. Fletcher, Chairman
Commission of Fine Arts—J. Carter Brown, Chairman
Consumer Product Safety Commission—Jacqueline Jones-Smith, Chairman
Environmental Protection Agency—William K. Reilly, Administrator
Equal Employment Opportunity Commission—Evan J. Kemp, Jr., Chairman
Federal Communications Commission—Alfred C. Sikes, Chairman
Federal Deposit Insurance Corporation—William Taylor, Chairman
Federal Election Commission—John W. McGarry, Chairman
Federal Emergency Management Agency—Wallace E. Stickney, Director
Federal Reserve System Board of Governors—Alan Greenspan, Chairman
Federal Trade Commission—Janet D. Steiger, Chairman
General Services Administration—Richard G. Austin, Administrator
Interestate Commrce Commission—Edward J. Philbin, Chairman
National Aeronautics and Space Administration—Richard H. Truly, Administrator
National Endowment for the Arts—John E. Frohnmayer, Chairman
National Endowment for the Humanities—Lynne V. Cheney, Chairman
National Labor Relations Board—James M. Stephens, Chairman
National Railroad Passenger Corporation (Amtrak)—W. Graham Claytor, Jr., Chairman
National Science Foundation—Walter E. Massey, Director
National Transportation Safety Board—James L. Kolstad, Chairman
Nuclear Regulatory Commission—Ivan Selin, Chairman
Peace Corps—Elaine L. Chao, Director
Securities and Exchange Commission—Richard C. Breeden, Chairman
Selective Service System—Robert William Gambino, Director
Small Business Administration—Patricia F. Saiki, Administrator
Smithsonian Institution—Robert McC. Adams, Secretary
U.S. Arms Control and Disarmament Agency—Ronald f. Lehman II, Director
U.S. Information Agency—Henry E. Catto, Director
U.S. Postal Service—Anthony M. Frank, Postmaster General

ceeded by federal appeals court Judge Clarence Thomas. The Thomas nomination was surrounded by controversy. In October, televised Senate Judiciary Committee hearings were held to investigate charges of sexual harassment brought against him by a former employee. See **Thomas, Clarence; Supreme Court of the United States,** Special Report: **A Champion of Civil Rights Retires.**

Bush's nomination of U.S. District Judge Kenneth L. Ryskamp to be a judge on the 11th Circuit Court of Appeals was rejected on April 11 by the Senate Judiciary Committee. Committee Democrats cited Ryskamp's alleged insensitivity to civil rights in turning back the nomination.

On June 29, U.S. District Judge Robert F. Collins of New Orleans was indicted on charges of bribery for fixing a drug case. Collins, the first federal judge to be found guilty of taking a bribe, was sentenced on September 6 to a prison term of 6 years and 10 months.

Frank Cormier and Margot Cormier

See also **Bush, George H. W.; Congress of the United States.** In ***World Book,*** see **United States, Government of the.**

Uruguay. See **Latin America.**
Utah. See **State government.**
Vanuatu. See **Pacific Islands.**
Venezuela. See **Latin America.**
Vermont. See **State government.**
Vice President of the U.S. See **Quayle, Dan.**

Vietnam experienced a change in leadership during 1991. Nguyen Van Linh resigned as general secretary of the ruling Communist Party due to old age and poor health. He was succeeded on June 27 by Do Muoi, the prime minister. On August 9, Vo Van Kiet replaced Do Muoi as prime minister.

At Vietnam's Seventh Communist Party Congress, held from June 24 to 27, discussion focused on the cautious economic reforms of recent years. Party leaders endorsed further efforts to liberalize the nation's economy, while also asserting that Vietnam should remain a one-party, Communist state.

The 1,176 congress delegates named a new executive committee, or Politburo, of 13 men. The new party leader, Do Muoi, has generally been regarded as a political and economic conservative. However, since the late 1980's, he has advocated the creation of market incentives to stimulate Vietnam's economy. Vo Van Kiet, 69 years old, has been one of Vietnam's leading proponents of economic and political reform.

Economic problems. Radical changes in the former Soviet Union threatened Vietnam's economy in 1991. In 1990, the Soviets failed to deliver all the oil and fertilizer that they had earlier promised Vietnam. On Jan. 31, 1991, the Soviets announced that Vietnam would henceforth have to pay for goods that it previously had received as aid. The Soviets also said that by 1994, the 50,000 Vietnamese nationals working in the Soviet Union would have to return to Vietnam.

Do Muoi responded to the diminishing assistance from the Soviet Union by stating his desire for improved economic and diplomatic relations with the United States. The United States, in turn, announced that lifting its ban on trade with Vietnam would be contingent upon a peace settlement in Cambodia, which Vietnam had invaded in 1978. On Oct. 23, 1991, a Cambodian peace agreement was signed by the four main Cambodian factions, the United States, Vietnam, and 16 other nations. Secretary of State James A. Baker III said on the same day that the United States was prepared to open talks on establishing normal relations with Vietnam.

Missing soldiers. In 1991, there were intensified demands in the United States for a full inquiry into the status of American servicemen missing in Indochina since the Vietnam War (1957-1975). The Vietnamese government on April 20 agreed to allow a U.S. office to be established in the capital, Hanoi, to coordinate efforts to account for the missing soldiers.

Returning refugees. On October 2, the Vietnamese government tentatively agreed to the forced return of as many as 100,000 Vietnamese refugees who have been living for years in refugee camps in other Southeast Asian countries.

Henry S. Bradsher

See also **Asia** (Facts in brief table); **Cambodia.** In ***World Book,*** see **Vietnam.**

Virginia. See **State government.**
Vital statistics. See **Census; Population.**

Washington, D.C. Sharon Pratt Dixon, a Democrat and former utility company executive, was sworn in as Washington's mayor on Jan. 2, 1991. Dixon, 46, was the third person to be elected to that post since the District obtained home rule from Congress in 1974. She also became the first native Washingtonian to serve as the city's mayor and the first black woman elected to run a large city in the United States.

Dixon was elected with 86 per cent of the vote in November 1990, after three-term Mayor Marion S. Barry, Jr., who had been convicted of cocaine possession, decided not to run again. The mayoral race was Dixon's first bid for elective government office. In her inaugural address, she promised to "clean house," to pare down the city government bureaucracy, and to deal with the District's serious financial problems.

Sworn in the same day were a new City Council chairman, Democrat John A. Wilson; six other council members; the city's first "shadow senators," Democrats Jesse L. Jackson and Florence Pendleton; and its first "shadow representative," Democrat Charles J. Moreland. The "shadow legislators" are actually lobbyists, elected to promote statehood for Washington, D.C., in Congress.

Shrinking the payroll. The City Council supported Dixon in her efforts to cut the size of the municipal bureaucracy, authorizing her in July 1991 to fire as many as 2,000 midlevel managers. In her first round of job-cutting in October 1991, the mayor discharged

Tensions between blacks and Hispanics in Washington, D.C., erupted into rioting in May after a black police officer shot a Hispanic suspect.

more than 300 employees and eliminated nearly 300 unfilled positions.

Money woes. The staff reductions were part of an effort to eliminate a projected budget deficit of $300 million. The $3.29-billion budget for fiscal 1992, approved by the City Council on April 9, 1991, included a freeze, or small cuts, in funding for schools, the police, and other city departments and activities. Congress helped out in September by approving a $200-million increase in the federal payment to the District, raising it to $630.5 million for fiscal 1992.

Barry goes to prison. Former Mayor Barry entered the federal prison in Petersburg, Va., on Oct. 26, 1991, to serve a six-month term for his August 1990 conviction for cocaine possession. In July 1991, the U.S. Court of Appeals in Washington, D.C., upheld Barry's conviction but granted him a resentencing, ruling that U.S. District Court Judge Thomas Penfield Jackson had not precisely stated his reasoning for the original sentence, handed down in October 1990. But in September 1991, Jackson gave Barry the same sentence: six months' imprisonment, a $5,000 fine, and a monthly bill for the cost of his incarceration.

Racial violence. Riots broke out in a largely Hispanic neighborhood in Washington on May 5. The violence began after a Hispanic man was shot and wounded by a black female police officer whom he had allegedly threatened with a knife. That night, crowds of youths threw rocks and bottles at the police, set several police cars on fire, and looted stores.

On May 6, Mayor Dixon declared a state of emergency and imposed a curfew. Rioting erupted again that night and spread to adjacent areas, with many black youths taking part in the violence and looting.

The disturbances were a reminder of the racial tensions in the city. The District government is predominantly black, and Washington's Hispanic population—about 5 per cent of the D.C. population—complains that it is underrepresented and ignored.

Assault on assault weapons. Gun manufacturers and sellers were made liable for deaths and injuries in Washington, D.C., inflicted by assault weapons under an ordinance approved by District voters on November 5. The new law, reportedly the first of its kind in the United States, allows shooting victims and their families to sue for damages in civil court.

Murder capital. Washington preserved its title as America's murder capital in 1991. Statistics reported in August by the Federal Bureau of Investigation showed that the District once again had the highest homicide rate of any large U.S. city: 732 murders per 100,000 population. For the fourth straight year, the District set a new homicide record, with the number of killings rising from 483 in 1990 to 489 in 1991.

Mayor Dixon weds. Mayor Dixon married businessman James R. Kelly III on December 7, becoming Sharon Pratt Kelly. Sandra Evans

See also **City.** In ***World Book,*** see **Washington, D.C.**

Washington. See **State government.**

Water. The first phase of the Great Man-Made River, a huge project for bringing water from beneath the Sahara Desert to Libya's coast was unveiled by Libyan leader Muammar Muhammad al-Qadhafi on Aug. 28, 1991. Despite its name, the project is actually a 1,250-mile- (2,000-kilometer-) long pipeline. It is designed to carry 523 million gallons (2 billion liters) of water per day from wells that tap *aquifers* (water-bearing layers of porous rock) beneath the desert. The pipeline extends to Libya's coastal cities of Sirte and Benghazi. These areas had obtained most of their drinking water from wells, which had become increasingly salty.

The Great Man-Made River was designed primarily by British and American engineers and built by South Koreans. It is one of the world's largest civil-engineering projects, and planners expect to expand it even further with four more phases.

In phase II, a western pipeline now under construction will bring well water from an aquifer in west-central Libya to the coast near Tripoli. Most of this water will be used for crop irrigation. This will boost agricultural output, make the country self-sufficient in food production, and help decrease Libya's economic reliance on revenues from its oil industry. The project was criticized by the London-based Economist Intelligence Unit for its costliness, which so far has totaled more than $14 billion.

Desalinization. Threats to the availability of drinking water in Saudi Arabia and California in 1991 focused unprecedented attention on *desalinization,* a process that turns salty water into fresh water. In January, seawater desalinization plants in Saudi Arabia were threatened by crude oil gushing into the Persian Gulf from Kuwaiti oil tankers, pipelines, and wells damaged during the Persian Gulf War. Although oil containment *booms* (floating barriers) were in place to protect the desalination plants, no one knew if they could stave off the millions of gallons of oil released into the gulf.

As a precautionary measure, the Saudi authorities closed a plant in Safaniya on the northern coast after the oil slick had polluted a desalinization plant in Kuwait. Fortunately, gulf currents pushed the slick away from the coast, and the Saudi plants were not contaminated.

Three desalinization plants, at Jubail, Al Khubar, and Al Khafi, provide more than one-third of Saudi Arabia's drinking water. The Jubail plant is the largest in the world, producing 270 million gallons (1 billion liters) per day of fresh water for the Saudi capital of Riyadh.

The Saudi desalinization plants produce fresh water through a process called *multistage flash distillation.* This procedure involves collecting and boiling seawater, then allowing the salt-free steam to condense into pure water. The salt water that does not boil away is pumped into a second chamber with lowered air pressure. This causes it to boil again so that more steam can be gathered. The process is repeated up to 40 times for each batch of water. Although multistage flash distillation uses a lot of energy, it is the principal desalinization process used throughout the world, especially in the oil-rich, desert nations of the Middle East and North Africa.

The first U.S. plant to permanently provide desalinized seawater for residential use began operating in June 1991. The new plant, located on Santa Catalina Island off the coast of southern California, can produce 132,000 gallons of water per day.

Another plant, being constructed in Santa Barbara, Calif., was scheduled to open by March 1992 and will produce about 2.7 million gallons (10 million liters) of fresh water per day. The facility will be the largest in the United States for the municipal use of seawater. Most other desalinization facilities in the United States are used only for brackish water, which has about one-tenth the salt that seawater contains.

Unlike the Saudi plants, the California facilities produce fresh water from seawater through a process called *reverse osmosis.* This procedure involves forcing seawater under pressure through a membrane that filters out suspended and dissolved substances, including salts. Reverse osmosis requires less energy than the multi-stage flash distillation process, and it yields more fresh water per gallon of seawater. However, plants using this process are smaller and produce less fresh water overall. Iris Priestaf

In ***World Book,*** see **Water.**

Our Precious Ground Water

By Stanley N. Davis

Natural underground reservoirs of water, which provide drinking water for millions of people and irrigation for many farms, are threatened by overuse and by pollution from many sources.

The Popo Agie River in central Wyoming flows into an underground limestone cavern to become ground water. Most ground water, however, originates as rain or snow.

In 1991, a pattern of drought stretched like an ominous shadow over the western and north-central United States and south-central Canada. For most of California, Nevada, Colorado, North Dakota, southern Manitoba, and parts of adjacent states and provinces, 1991 was the fifth year of below-normal rainfall and the third year of severe water shortages. In some areas, *dry farming* (growing crops in semiarid regions without irrigation) became impossible. Lack of natural pasture forced the sale of livestock. Large water distribution systems, such as the California State Water Project, were forced to cut as much as 90 per cent of deliveries to some cities. Certain agricultural interests were cut off entirely from their customary sources of irrigation water. Large reservoirs stood almost empty with sun-baked floors exposed as stark evidence of the regional disaster.

Despite this calamity, many regions in California were fortunate to have large volumes of ground water stored beneath the land surface. Ground water is an important resource for both urban and farming areas. For example, a single deepwater well in the Central Valley of California will yield, in many areas, more than 2 million gallons (7.5 million liters) each day. This is more than enough to supply domestic water to 10,000 people or to irrigate a square mile of farmland.

But ground water is more than just a California resource, and its use is not restricted to times of drought. It exists everywhere beneath Earth's surface. For everything from drinking water to street cleaning, millions of people rely on ground water every day. Yet, as population grows, this valuable resource is under increasing risk from contamination and overuse.

Roughly half the people in the United States—124 million people—rely on ground water for drinking and home use. In addition to homeowners and farmers, municipal water systems and industries also use ground water. Of the approximately 340 billion gallons (1.3 trillion liters) of water used each day in the United States, about 22 per cent—75 billion gallons (280 billion liters)—comes from ground water, according to the United States Geological Survey, headquartered in Reston, Va. Two-thirds of this ground water is used to irrigate farms, mostly in the Great Plains and other Western states.

As miraculous as fresh, cool water gushing from a deep well may seem, the water originates and moves in response to well-understood laws of nature. To ignore or misinterpret these laws will greatly compound the problems of managing this precious resource. Wells can go dry if too much water is taken out of the ground. Chemicals dumped on the land surface may find their way into underground water and render the water unfit for use for many decades. Money can literally be thrown down a hole in trying to obtain large supplies of well water where none exists. Even when huge amounts of water are found, poorly constructed wells may collapse creating water shortages and considerable financial loss.

The source and location of ground water

Most ground water originates as rain or melted snow. As water reaches the ground, it can run over the surface into lakes and rivers, evaporate, be absorbed by the roots of plants and trees, or enter layers of earth below the surface called *aquifers.* Ground water collects in cracks, small holes (pores), and other spaces within and between the layers of material that make up aquifers.

Ground water normally has a constant temperature and chemical makeup. It may contain dissolved minerals and organic particles, but it rarely contains disease-causing bacteria. For this reason, ground water is usually acceptable for most uses with little treatment.

In general, ground water can be encountered at depths of from 20 to 400 feet (6 to 120 meters) over the United States, Canada, and most regions of the world. Often, water wells must be much deeper, however, because the first ground water encountered may not flow easily into the wells. Some aquifers may be several thousand feet below the surface. For

The author:

Stanley N. Davis is a professor emeritus of hydrology at the Department of Hydrology and Water Resources at the University of Arizona in Tucson.

Glossary

Ground water: Water that is stored naturally below Earth's surface. Most ground water originates as rain or snow and seeps into the ground.

Aquifer: A layer of material such as rock beneath the ground where ground water collects.

Overdraft: Using more water from an aquifer than can be naturally restored from rain or snow runoff.

Confining bed: A layer of rock that separates aquifers.

Porous rock: Rock with many small *pores* (holes) that allow it to hold water.

Permeable rock: Rock that allows water to pass easily through it.

Saltwater intrusion: The entrance of seawater into a fresh water aquifer.

example, some freshwater aquifers in south-central Texas are more than 5,000 feet (1,500 meters) deep. The deepest widely used aquifers are in east-central Australia and are more than 6,000 feet (1,800 meters) deep.

Although an immense amount of ground water exists, not all of it can be used. Ground water left over from ancient ocean water may lie very far below the surface and thus be too costly to extract. It may also be ancient ocean water that was trapped in pores at the time the rocks were formed. Thus, the water could be too salty for human use.

The U.S. Geological Survey divides the lower 48 states into 26 main aquifer regions. Aquifer regions are usually made up of many smaller aquifer systems with similar characteristics. Among the most important aquifer regions in the United States are the Atlantic and Gulf Coastal Plains region, the High Plains region, the Florida Peninsula region, the California Central Valley region, and the Northwest Volcanic Rocks region. The Coastal Plains region extends from Long Island in New York state down the East Coast and west along the Gulf Coast. The High Plains region, sometimes called the Ogallala region, extends from South Dakota to Texas. The Florida Peninsula region lies beneath Florida, Georgia, and parts of Alabama and South Carolina. The Central California Valley region is in central California, and the Northwest Volcanic Rocks region lies under parts of Washington, Oregon, and Idaho. An important aquifer system in this region is the Columbia Plateau system.

Aquifers in the United States are most commonly made of gravel, sand, sandstone, limestone, or *basalt* (volcanic rock). The High Plains aquifer region, for example, is mostly sand, gravel, and silt. The Columbia Plateau system contains a large amount of basalt. Much of the Atlantic and Gulf Coastal Plains region, on the other hand, is made of thick layers of sand and clay, along with minor amounts of limestone.

Ground water in motion

Ground water is always in motion due to the force of gravity and the pressure of new water entering the ground from above. Once below the surface, water spreads out and moves toward areas of discharge—lakes, rivers, springs, oceans, or wells. The rate at which water moves through an aquifer depends on the type of rock in the aquifer. Water is able to move through rock for the same reason that rocks can hold water in the first place—the numerous pores that occur naturally in the rock, as well as the spaces between rocks, such as cracks and fissures that form as a result of geological activity.

Hydrologists are concerned with two qualities possessed by aquifers, *permeability* (the ease with which water can pass through) and *porosity* (the ability to store water). Rock such as sandstone with many pores is said to be *porous* and has the ability to hold large volumes of water. It also has good permeability. Clay has numerous pores, but its permeability is low. This is because the pores in clay are microscopic and restrict water passage. Hard, dense rock such as granite or slate, on the other hand, may have both a low porosity and a low permeability. The majority of aquifers in the United States are formed by sand and gravel, and if we could look

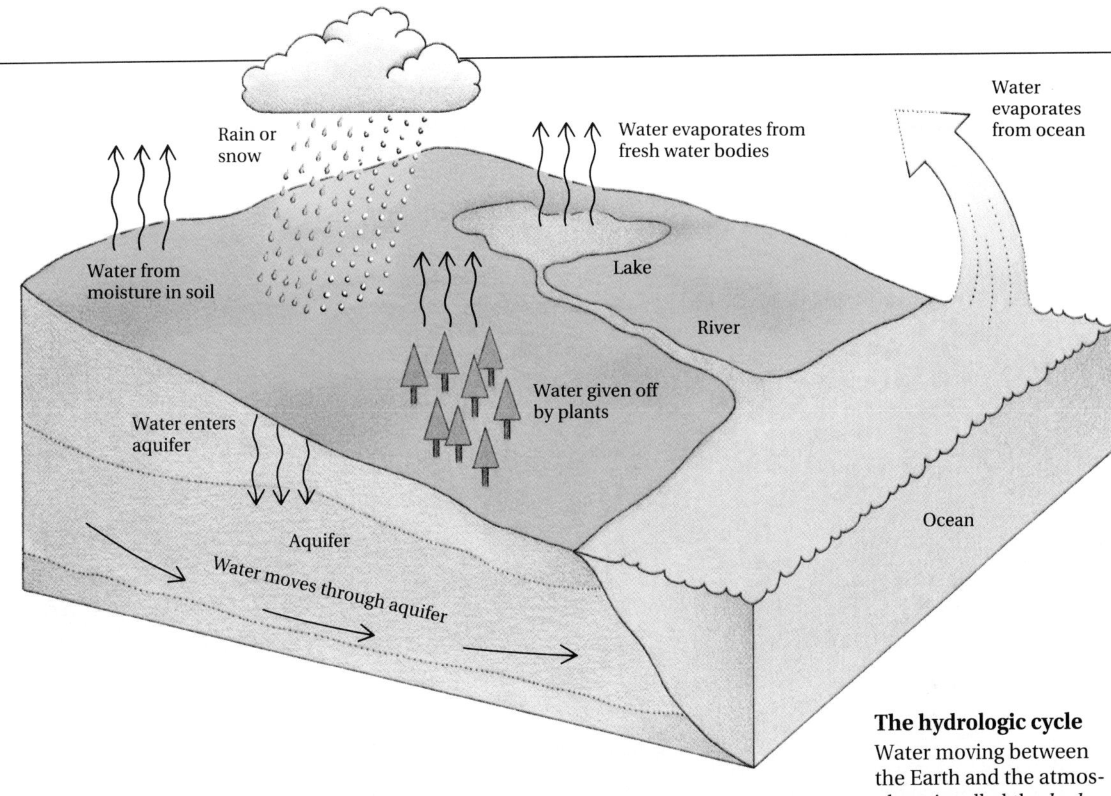

The hydrologic cycle
Water moving between the Earth and the atmosphere is called the *hydrologic cycle.* The sun's heat causes surface water to evaporate. Plants release water through *transpiration.* Evaporation and transpiration produce water vapor, which forms clouds. Water in the form of rain or snow then falls back to Earth. Some of this water seeps down to the aquifers and becomes ground water. It moves slowly through aquifers and ultimately empties into lakes, rivers, or the ocean to repeat the cycle.

inside them they would appear similar to a cross section of a gravel pit or a large pile of dense sand saturated with water.

Even in an aquifer with highly permeable rock, however, water moves relatively slowly underground. The rate at which ground water flows ranges from 0.03 foot (0.9 centimeter) per year to more than 1,000 feet (300 meters) per day. In many areas of the United States, water may take 30 to 50 years to pass through the ground and emerge again into lakes or streams. In deep aquifers, this process may take thousands of years.

Most ground water is extracted by means of wells. Wells pump water through pipes inserted far enough into the ground to reach an aquifer. In areas where aquifers are close to the surface, land owners sometimes dig wells with shovels and picks. But because most aquifers are too deep to reach by digging, wells are most often drilled or driven into the ground with more sophisticated equipment.

There are about 14 million water wells in the United States, according to the National Water Well Association in Dublin, Ohio. In rural areas, about 95 per cent of drinking water comes from wells on private property. As with private users, many cities and towns also obtain ground water from wells.

Pollution of ground water

Aquifers in nearly every area of the United States are susceptible to pollution. Most at risk are shallow aquifers, which pollutants can reach more easily than they can deeper layers of rock. Shallow aquifers are also the most commonly used for water supplies.

Abundant aquifers, abundant pollution

Some major ground water regions in the United States include the High Plains aquifer region in the Great Plains, the Atlantic and Gulf Coastal Plains region stretching from Texas up to New York, the Florida Peninsula region, and the region of Northwest Volcanic Rocks, which includes the Columbia Plateau system. About 124 million people—half the U.S. population—rely on ground water. Although ground water is plentiful, so are the threats to it. Pesticides, toxic wastes, landfills, and overuse continue to threaten ground water supplies. The U.S. Environmental Protection Agency is working with states to protect ground water supplies.

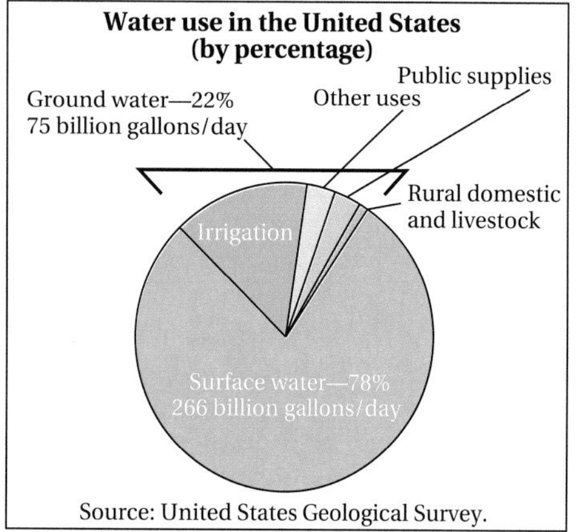

Americans use about 75 billion gallons (280 billion liters) of ground water per day—22 per cent of the nation's total daily water use. Most ground water—about 50 billion gallons (190 billion liters) per day—is used for irrigation.

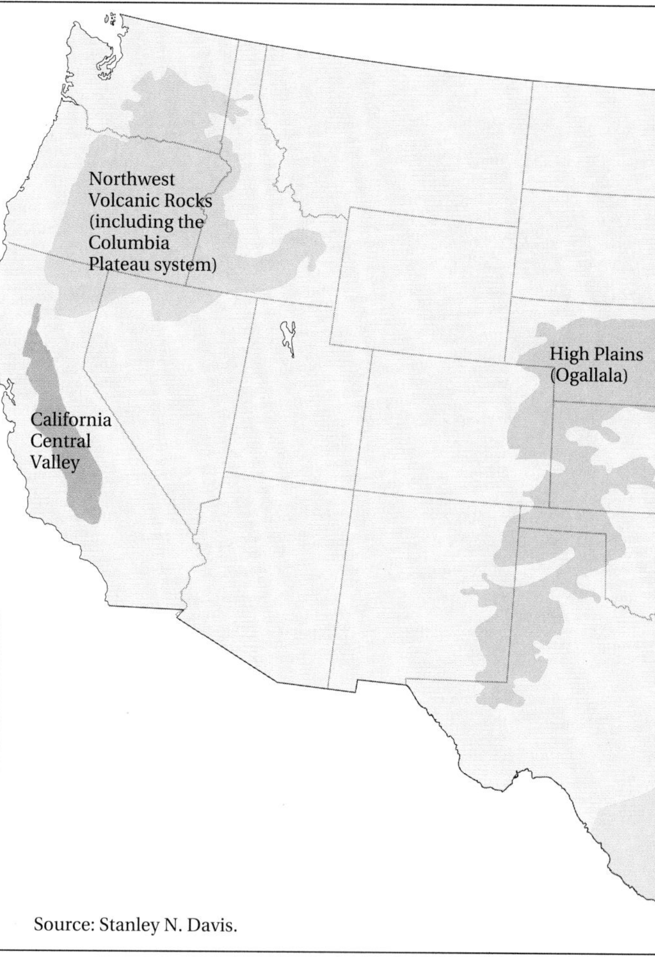

Drums containing petroleum refinery waste leak into water in Butler County, Pennsylvania. Thousands of toxic waste dumps across the United States threaten aquifers. Poisonous chemicals can leak from containers and into the ground, contaminating aquifers.

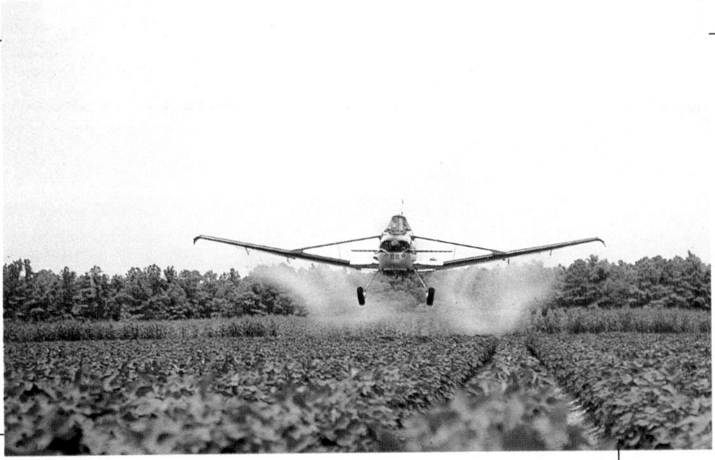

A plane sprays pesticide on cotton in the Southeastern United States, *left.* The heavy use of pesticides sometimes contaminates aquifers when these chemicals are washed into the soil. Landfills, *below,* can also be a threat to ground water. Dangerous chemicals that form when garbage decomposes can be carried into aquifers by rain water seeping down through the ground.

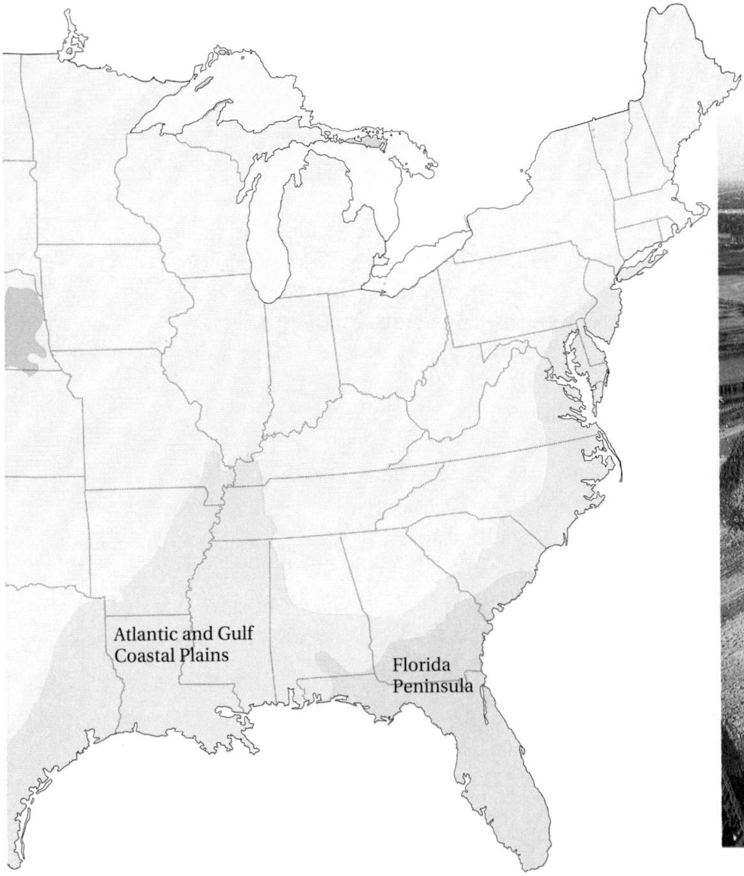

Atlantic and Gulf
Coastal Plains
Florida
Peninsula

Part per million

Salt
Grain
of Salt
Water
10 oz.
(300 ml)

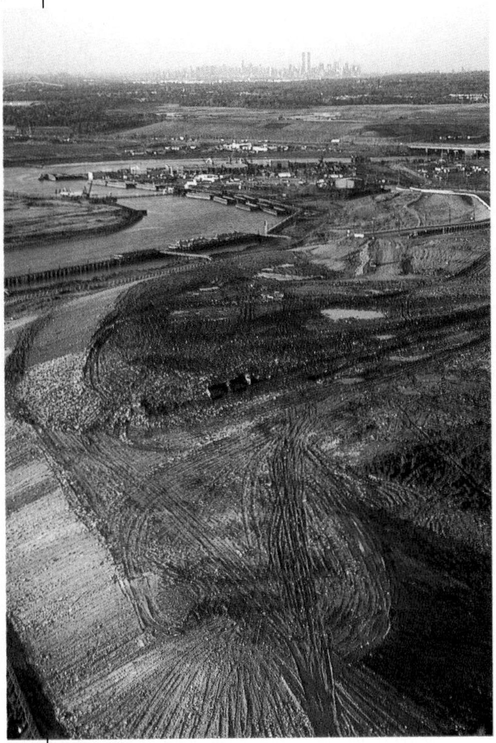

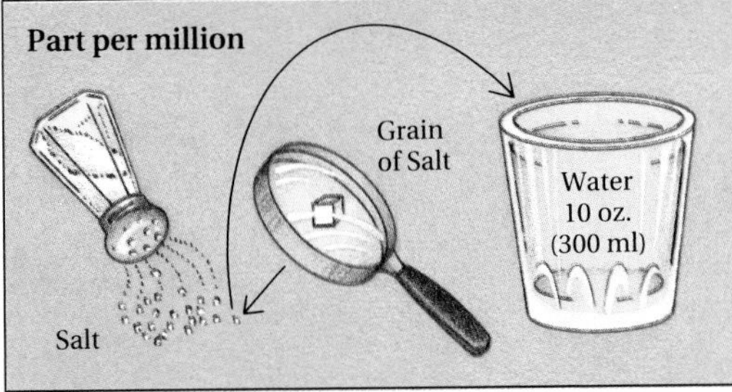

Even the slightest trace of some poisonous chemicals can pollute a large body of water such as an aquifer. United States government regulations do not permit even one thousandth part per million of certain chemicals in drinking water. One part per million is equal to one grain of salt dissolved in a 10-ounce (300-milliliter) glass of distilled water.

The most common threats to ground water are pesticides and nitrate fertilizers used in farming, toxic chemicals produced by industry, hazardous liquids leaking from underground storage tanks, and water that becomes contaminated after seeping through garbage in landfills. Other sources of contamination include runoff from roads where salt has been used for ice removal, sewage plants, septic tanks, and abandoned wells used as dumping sites to inject toxic wastes into the subsurface. Rain and snowmelt trickling through stockpiles of coal also will react with minerals in the coal to form sulfuric acid, which can then seep into the ground and become a serious contaminant. Many modern coal-storage areas attempt to intercept this water and neutralize it before it seeps into the ground. However, contaminants from older storage areas do not go away quickly once they get underground. So, despite improved practices, coal storage problems will remain a little-noticed source of contamination.

Pesticides and aquifers

But even a seemingly pristine pasture may be the source of serious contamination to underlying ground water because of pesticides and fertilizers. Pesticides are chemicals used widely in agriculture to kill weeds and insects that are harmful to crops. Nitrates, in addition to being used as fertilizers, are found in manure from cattle feed lots and in the overflow from septic tanks. Without pesticides, most farmers would lose some, if not all, of their crops to disease and insects. Often, pesticides and nitrates remain in the soil and pose little threat. However, in areas of heavy farming, these chemicals may find their way into aquifers as rain. Irrigation water also can wash the chemicals into the soil and streams. As a result, pesticides and nitrates have been found in drinking-water wells in several states, forcing some states to take preventive steps.

Some states, including California and Iowa, have instituted restrictions on the use of some pesticides in areas that contain shallow aquifers. In 1980, the New York State Department of Environmental Regulation prohibited the use of the pesticide *aldicarb* after regulators discovered unsafe levels of the chemical in the ground water of Long Island. New York also banned the pesticide *oxamyl* in 1983 in Long Island for the same reason.

In a survey of 1,347 private and public drinking water wells across the United States, the U.S. Environmental Protection Agency (EPA) reported in November 1990 that 10.5 per cent of the public wells (those that serve 25 people or more) contained detectable levels of one or more pesticides compared with 4.2 per cent of the private wells tested. The EPA used the survey findings to estimate that 60,000 private wells and 750 public water wells in the United States contain unsafe levels of pesticides.

Landfills can represent a threat to aquifers because the garbage in them *decomposes* (breaks down). Waste such as paper, packaging material, plant cuttings, and other wet organic trash can produce harmful chemicals and gases that can enter water as it moves through a landfill. Organic material can produce carbon dioxide as it decomposes. When it mixes with water, carbon dioxide will form *carbonic acid*, which can alter metals such as copper that are often found in landfills. These metals can

Consequences of ground water loss

Withdrawing ground water faster than it can be replaced can have destructive consequences. In Winter Park, Fla., a sinkhole appeared in May 1981 due to excessive ground water withdrawal, *above.* At Edwards Air Force Base in California, a *fissure* (deep crack) opened in the ground in April 1991, *left,* due to loss of ground water. In Baytown, Tex., a well foundation is exposed due to land that sank as a result of too much ground water withdrawal, *below.*

then dissolve in water. Water that passes through landfills can become as black as ink from absorbing such contaminants and, as it seeps into the ground, may pollute aquifers.

Hazardous waste dangers

Dumping of hazardous chemicals is a major threat to aquifers. Due to carelessness and ignorance, some companies and individuals in the United States have dumped thousands of tons of cancer-causing chemicals such as *trichloroethylene* (TCE), used in cleaning metals, and *polychlorinated biphenyls* (PCB's) into landfills and ponds. These chemicals can leak into the ground. The EPA has identified 1,300 *Superfund sites*—top-priority locations where such dumping poses a threat to public health. The EPA says there may be as many as 30,000 more of these dump sites across the country. Of the 1,300 Superfund sites, 70 per cent may be causing ground water problems, according to the EPA. Since 1980, the EPA has spent $7.5 billion cleaning Superfund sites, and most estimates say that the effort will require at least $300 billion more.

Underground storage tanks, used to hold gasoline and other fuels at service stations, commercial and industrial buildings, and farms, are one of the most common potential threats to aquifers. These tanks can leak, spilling fuel and other chemicals into nearby aquifers. According to the EPA, there are 1.4 million fuel and chemical storage tanks underground in the United States, and at least 140,000 of them may be leaking. The smallest trace of oil or gasoline in ground water produces a terrible odor and taste, and large amounts can pose a fire hazard if the contaminated water is pumped out of the ground.

In addition to the threat from contamination, ground water supplies are also threatened by continued overuse. In some areas of the United States, ground water is used faster than it can be resupplied by rain or runoff from snow. In the Great Plains and other Western states, where rainfall is sparse, the *natural recharge* (resupply of water) of aquifers is infrequent. In these areas, wells almost always pump water that has taken thousands of years to collect.

The threat of overdraft

Pumping water faster than it is recharged is called *overdraft* of an aquifer. Although overdraft is most common in desert regions, it may happen anywhere ground water is used heavily. Overdraft reduces water for emergencies such as drought or fire, lowers water levels in wells, and may require the deepening of existing wells. In areas with limestone aquifers such as Florida, overdraft may cause the ground surface to cave in, forming *sinkholes.* In other areas, land may subside over a wide area as underground water levels fall. This can cause subsidence of the land surface and in some places deep fractures and rifts. Overdraft may also drain off the best quality water, leaving only deeper, saltier water.

During the recent drought in the West, farmers in California relied more heavily than usual on ground water for irrigation. In some areas of

Protecting our ground water

Scientists collect samples of ground water to test them for contamination, *left.* Because the main source of contamination in polluted aquifers can be difficult to find and remove, scientists are developing advanced ways to clean polluted aquifers, *below left.* One new method uses special microbes, *below right,* that break down pesticides and other pollutants in aquifers into harmless components.

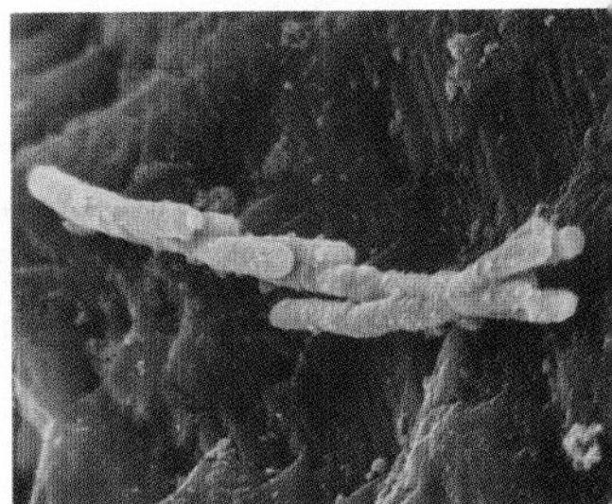

heavy pumping, land has subsided 5 to 6 feet (1.5 to 1.8 meters) since 1986. And in the southern part of California's Central Valley, land has subsided as much as 30 feet (9 meters) since the 1930's as a result of ground water extraction. About 9.8 million acres (3.9 million hectares) in the United States—roughly a fifth of the nation's irrigated land—is watered by overdrafted aquifers. In its southern portions, the High Plains aquifer system has been drained of as much as one-fourth of its water.

In coastal areas, where freshwater aquifers meet underground salt water, overdraft may allow the salt water to enter these aquifers. This is called *saltwater intrusion.* Saltwater intrusion into freshwater aquifers has been very troublesome in Florida and California, sometimes ruining the drinking water of whole communities.

The importance of keeping ground water free of contamination is becoming clearer to hydrologists, who realize that ground water is far more difficult to clean than surface water once it has been polluted. For example, a New Jersey township spent $10 million over six years, beginning in

1978, to clean a contaminated water well by pumping out the water and treating it. But pollution in the returned water rose to levels twice as high as before because the subsurface zone from which the toxic chemicals emanated had not been found and the concentrated chemicals removed.

Even if the main source of pollution can be located, pumping contaminated water from aquifers and treating it may never remove all the pollution. For example, Air Force officials at a base in Michigan discovered that a supply line to an underground storage tank containing TCE had burst, contaminating an aquifer that supplied drinking water to the entire base. The Air Force asked the U.S. Geological Survey to design a system to pump the contaminated water out, clean it, and pump it back into the ground. After more than 10 years of pumping and treating the water, there were still traces of TCE in it.

Cleaning contaminated aquifers

Several modern developments have greatly aided the control of groundwater contamination. First, scientists use powerful computer programs to predict future paths of the migration of contaminants and then the consequences of different proposed remedial actions. This helps them plan what action to take. Second, various strains of bacteria have been found useful in attacking organic contaminants. Some of these bacteria are already in the soil and the deeper subsurface, and scientists can stimulate their growth by injecting harmless chemicals such as methane. In other cases, scientists inject cultured, harmless bacteria into the subsurface to "eat" the contaminants. Third, new types of substances have been developed that can be injected or placed in deep trenches to form barriers to the migration of contaminants.

Finally, researchers are developing new methods of extracting contaminants by using air. Many of the most troublesome contaminants are organic chemicals that will move into surrounding air. Passing air through contaminated ground water will extract the chemicals in an air stream. The air is then pumped out into the atmosphere. Similarly, ground water can be pumped out by bubbling air through the water. The air carries away the contaminants, and the clean water can be used.

Other methods are used to prevent contaminants from seeping into ground water in the first place. One method involves covering solid waste with impermeable clay or plastic to keep surface water from seeping into the waste. Impermeable layers of material can also be placed under the waste to intercept contaminants before they enter ground water. In addition, wells can be drilled to extract contaminated water.

Government cleanup efforts

Although ground water experts recognized and publicized problems of pollution even before the 1900's, meaningful legislation for aquifer protection was slow to develop. The EPA, the federal regulatory agency most involved with ground water contamination, was not even created until 1970. The initial Clean Water Act was not passed until 1972, and the Resource Conservation and Recovery Act (RCRA) was not enacted until 1976. These and other legislative acts along with a number of amendments and resulting federal regulations provide the framework for both effective ground water protection in the future as well as correction of many past problems of water contamination. Many common sense regulations, which should have been instituted decades ago, are now in force. For example, it is illegal to inject hazardous wastes into aquifers that provide drinking water. Disposal sites for hazardous wastes must be designed so as to prevent leakage of the wastes into drinking water. Furthermore, monitoring wells must be installed to ensure that waste is not escaping. Regulations also require that past waste-handling methods that resulted in ground water pollution must be corrected and remedial action taken.

Due to its continued concern over ground water contamination, the EPA in 1984 established a comprehensive national ground water protection strategy that encouraged states to determine which aquifers were most at risk from contamination and to monitor them. But the program was not mandatory. In May 1991, the EPA launched a new effort to establish more effective nationwide legislation to protect ground water. The new strategy is designed to help every state pass thorough ground water protection laws by 1994.

At present, the United States is spending more than $50 billion per year on problems of water contamination. More than half of this amount is spent on problems related to ground water. The EPA estimates that the total cost of water contamination may reach $75 billion per year by the year 2000. Such enormous amounts of money raise numerous questions about the basic regulations that are driving this effort. As commendable as cleaning up every speck of contamination might be, how much is really needed, or as a nation, how much can we really afford? Most certainly, the dual public concern about environmental protection—balanced against the wise use of financial resources—will be a central issue of public debate well into the next century.

For more information:

Organizations that offer information about ground water and ground water protection include:

The Environmental Protection Agency, Office of Ground Water and Drinking Water, U.S. EPA, WH 550G, 401 M St. SW, Washington, DC 20460.

The National Water Well Association, 6375 Riverside Dr., Dublin, OH 43017.

The U.S. Geological Survey, Books and Open-File Reports Section, Federal Center, Box 25425, Denver, CO 80225.

Residents of Scituate, Mass., survey damage to a beachfront home caused by a severe storm that lashed the U.S. East Coast in late October.

Weather. For the lower 48 states in the United States, 1991 was one of the warmest years in recent history. Continuing a trend that began in the 1970's, above-normal temperatures prevailed during eight of the first nine months of the year, with the highest above-normal temperatures occurring in the eastern half of the nation. Much of this area, particularly from Oklahoma to Pennsylvania, suffered from moderate drought. The Southeastern states, which had experienced drought conditions in recent years, had large amounts of rainfall, especially the areas bordering the Gulf of Mexico.

Floods. In Texas, heavy rains during December caused flash floods that killled at least 15 people. Rivers in eastern and southeastern Texas rose to record levels and left thousands of people homeless.

On Nov. 5, 1991, heavy rains caused flash flooding on the Philippine island of Leyte, killing about 6,000 people. Hardest hit was the city of Ormoc, where at least 3,000 people died. Philippine relief agencies estimated 20,000 people were homeless as a result of the flooding.

Drought in California. For the first time in 96 years, California endured its fifth successive year with serious shortages of rain. The state normally receives nearly all its rainfall during the winter months, but from Oct. 1, 1990, through Feb. 28, 1991, less than 50 per cent of normal precipitation fell statewide, making this the third driest such period on record. Total water reservoir storage fell from 60 per cent of capacity to 48 per cent at the end of February, and snow in the Sierra Nevada mountains was only 14 per cent of normal levels.

At the end of February, a series of Pacific Ocean storms brought large amounts of rain to most parts of the state. A March record of 12.3 inches (31.2 centimeters) of rain fell at Santa Barbara, where the reservoir had previously dropped to 15 per cent of capacity. Sierra Nevada snow levels increased to 75 per cent of normal, and total reservoir capacity increased to 57 per cent of capacity across the state. Despite these improvements, California entered the summer with dangerously depleted water supplies.

A persistent *anticyclone* (an area of high pressure around which winds blow in a clockwise manner in the Northern Hemisphere) hung over the Western United States during the last half of September and the first three weeks of October 1991, bringing hot, dry winds to California and other Western states. Partly as a result of the dry conditions created by the winds, many forest fires developed from Washington to California. The worst of these fires began in the hills above Oakland, Calif., on October 20. This fire killed at least 25 people and destroyed more than 1,800 houses, 900 apartment units and other property valued at more than $1.5 billion.

Deadly tornadoes. The number of tornadoes recorded in the first half of 1991 by the U.S. National Severe Storm Forecast Center was a record. According to the center, there were 945 tornadoes in the first six months of 1991, 111 more than the previous record set in 1990 for the first six months of the year.

The deadliest outbreak of tornadoes occurred on April 26, 1991. Forty-two tornadoes—32 in Kansas and 10 in Oklahoma—caused extensive damage. One tornado thundered through Clearwater and Haysville on the south side of Wichita, Kans., wrecking 200 homes before destroying a trailer park in Andover, Kans. The tornadoes killed 25 people, including 20 in Kansas, and injured hundreds more.

Hurricanes. Although Atlantic hurricanes in 1991 were infrequent by historical standards, two made headlines. From August 16 to 17, a low pressure area developed rapidly east of the Bahamas, and on August 18 it reached hurricane force. The eye of this storm, named Hurricane Bob, passed about 40 miles (64 kilometers) east of Cape Hatteras, N.C., and moved inland across Rhode Island. Passing near Providence, R.I., and directly over Boston, the storm set low pressure records at both cities and produced wind gusts of up to 125 miles (200 kilometers) per hour. Bob then dumped 7.8 inches (19.8 centimeters) of rain on Portland, Me., contributing to that city's wettest month ever. Insurance losses as a result of Hurricane Bob totaled $780 million, the second highest figure behind Hurricane Hugo's toll of $2.1 billion in 1989. Total losses from Bob were estimated at more than $1 billion.

A second Atlantic hurricane, Grace, formed about

200 miles (320 kilometers) east of Cape Hatteras on October 28. It continued northward until a severe winter storm absorbed it the next day. The winter storm, which developed rapidly south of Nova Scotia, moved slowly southeastward creating high winds along the coast as far south as North Carolina. The storm created tides up to 10 feet (3 meters) above normal and waves up to 20 feet (6.1 meters) high. Thousands of people were evacuated from coastal dwellings in Long Island, New Jersey, and Connecticut.

Devastation in Bangladesh. One of the worst disasters in history occurred early on the morning of April 30 when a tropical cyclone moved over low-lying coastal areas of Bangladesh. At least 139,000 people died as a result of the storm. Property damage was estimated to exceed $1.4 billion. More than 10 million persons, about one-tenth of the nation's population, were left homeless. The storm developed in the southern Bay of Bengal on about April 25, intensifying rapidly as it moved north. When the storm hit land on April 29 and 30, it brought winds of 140 to 150 miles (225 to 240 kilometers) per hour and a 20-foot tidal wave that carried ocean water miles inland over heavily populated areas. A similar storm that struck in 1970 had killed about 266,000 people in East Pakistan, which later became Bangladesh.

The warmest year. Based on global surface temperature recordings, 1990 was the warmest year since temperature recordings began on a wide scale in the 1860's. This was reported in January 1991 by scientists from the British Meteorological Office and the National Aeronautics and Space Administration's Goddard Institute for Space Studies in New York City. Although the scientists did not say the temperature record was the result of global climate warming, this report fueled speculation among atmospheric scientists about whether "greenhouse" gases such as carbon dioxide, methane, and water vapor could cause Earth's climate to warm. These gases trap heat in Earth's atmosphere that would otherwise escape into space.

Although greenhouse gases occur naturally, human activity such as the burning of fossil fuels and the destruction of large tracts of tropical rain forests increase levels of greenhouse gases in the atmosphere. Some computer climate models predict a slow warming of Earth's climate by the late 2000's as a result of the expected increase of greenhouse gases, but even the best computer models are imprecise. For this reason, it is not clear how much effect—if any—human activities have had on global climate. The decade of the 1930's was accompanied by another spectacular warming at least as great as that which occurred in the 1980's, and this temperature rise occurred before there was any large increase in the abundance of greenhouse gases. In 1991, atmospheric scientists continued to study this important question.

Alfred K. Blackadar

In *World Book,* see **Weather.**

Weightlifting. See **Sports.**

Welfare. The United States Bureau of the Census reported in September 1991 that the number of people living in poverty in the United States increased for the first time since 1983. People living below the poverty line increased to 33.6 million in 1990 from 31.5 million in 1989, according to the report. The poverty line in 1990 for a family of three was $10,419. The threshold for a single person was $6,652. The 1990 poverty rate rose to 13.5 per cent of the population from 12.8 per cent in 1989.

Median household income also declined. The median household income dropped for the first time since 1982, to $29,943 in 1990 from $30,468 in 1989. The median is the point at which half of all households have higher incomes and half have lower.

In August 1991, the number of people receiving food stamps jumped to an all-time high, according to the U.S. Department of Agriculture. The number of Americans receiving food stamps totaled 23.6 million, which was an increase of more than 3 million since August 1990.

Michigan cuts welfare. On Oct. 1, 1991, Michigan cut its general assistance program, and 90,000 people deemed fit to work lost financial support from the state. Those in favor of eliminating the $247-million program said the move would force people to get jobs and not rely on welfare. But others said it would create insurmountable hardships for many people, such as the elderly, those with mental health problems, and those who had no job skills.

Children's issues. Health and Human Services (HHS) Secretary Louis W. Sullivan announced on April 15 a major consolidation of federal programs providing services to children. The new agency, called the Administration for Children and Families, combined the Family Support Administration, the Office of Human Development Services, and the $553-million Maternal and Child Health Block Grant program. The new agency also oversees the major welfare program, Aid to Families with Dependent Children, as well as Head Start and programs dealing with child abuse, family breakup, and training for mothers. A budget of $27-million was allocated for the agency, and HHS Assistant Secretary Jo Anne B. Barnhart was appointed head of the organization.

On Feb. 11, 1991, the U.S. government released regulations that would allow as many as 37,000 children with severe disabilities to receive benefits. See **Handicapped.**

One out of eight children under age 12 suffers from hunger, according to a March 1991 report from the Food Research and Action Center in Washington, D.C. The private, nonprofit organization surveyed 2,335 low-income U.S. households from 1989 to 1990 and concluded that 5.5 million children do not have enough to eat, and 6 million more are at risk for going hungry.

Frank Cormier and Margot Cormier

See **Census,** Special Report: **The 1990 Census: An American Self-Portrait.** In *World Book,* see **Welfare.**

West Indies. Leaders of 13 Caribbean nations met from July 1 to 4, 1991, at Basseterre in St. Christopher (commonly called St. Kitts) to review their progress toward creating a fully integrated common market by 1994. At the meeting, President Carlos Andrés Pérez of Venezuela said that his country will provide the Caribbean nations with preferential access to its markets for five years as a means of stimulating trade. The nations were worried by their impending loss of preferential access to European markets for crops such as bananas when the European Community (EC or Common Market) becomes fully integrated in 1993. See **Europe,** Special Report: **The Rocky Road to European Unity.**

Haiti sanctions. On October 8, the Organization of American States (OAS), which includes eight West Indian nations, imposed economic sanctions against Haiti in response to the September 30 military overthrow of the freely elected government of Jean-Bertrand Aristide. The sanctions include the freezing of Haitian assets in all 34 OAS nations. See **Haiti.**

The OAS sent nine representatives to Haiti from October 4 to 6 in order to seek a compromise with coup leaders that would allow Aristide to return to power. The OAS team failed to reach a compromise to allow Aristide to return as head of the government, but it organized further talks between Aristide and representatives of the Haitian Parliament.

On December 22, the OAS announced that Aristide had agreed to the appointment of one of his critics—Haitian Communist Party leader Rene Theodore—as prime minister. Opponents of Aristide had demanded that an opposition prime minister be appointed, and the agreement could allow a resolution of the crisis, according to the OAS.

Trinidad and Tobago elections. On December 16, Patrick Manning, a geologist, was elected prime minister of Trinidad and Tobago. Manning's People's National Movement Party also won 26 of 36 seats in the nation's Parliament.

Manning promised to reverse some of the austerity measures that had been put in place by incumbent Prime Minister Arthur Napoleon Raymond Robinson. Many attributed an attempted coup in Trinidad and Tobago in July 1990 to resentment toward the austerity measures, which cut government wages and eliminated many government jobs.

Grenada pardon. On August 14, Prime Minister Nicholas Braithwaite lifted the death sentences of 14 people convicted for the 1983 killing of Prime Minister Maurice Bishop and 10 others during an attempted coup. The coup attempt had touched off a United States invasion of the island. Not all Grenadans were happy about the lifting of the death sentences, which Braithwaite justified in the name of "national unity."

Nathan A. Haverstock

See also **Latin America** (Facts in brief table). In ***World Book,*** see **West Indies.**

West Virginia. See **State government.**

Wilder, L. Douglas (1931-), governor of Virginia, announced on Sept. 12, 1991, that he would seek the Democratic presidential nomination in 1992. But in a surprise move on Jan. 8, 1992, Wilder dropped out of the race. He said that he found he could not conduct a presidential campaign and give proper attention to governing Virginia.

Lawrence Douglas Wilder was born on Jan. 17, 1931, in Richmond, Va. He graduated from Virginia Union University in Richmond in 1951, served in the United States Army in 1952 and 1953 and fought in the Korean War (1950-1953), earning a Bronze Star for bravery. In 1959, he earned a law degree at the Howard University School of Law in Washington, D.C.

In 1959, Wilder returned to Richmond and became a successful trial lawyer. He entered politics in 1969, becoming the first black elected to the Virginia Senate since 1877 in the Reconstruction era. In 1985, he was elected Virginia's lieutenant governor. In 1989, Wilder became the first black elected governor of any state and was elected as a supporter of abortion rights.

Wilder's political stance is essentially middle-of-the-road. He said he would try to attract the support of moderate white voters in 1992.

Wilder has been divorced since 1978. He has three grown children. David L. Dreier

Wisconsin. See **State government.**

Wyoming. See **State government.**

Yemen. See **Middle East.**

Yugoslavia was torn apart by a bloody civil war during 1991, after a year of escalating violence between the country's two largest nationality groups, Serbs and Croats. Yugoslavia's breakup had struck many observers as inevitable after the death in 1980 of Josip Broz Tito, the Communist leader who had held together the multinational Yugoslav federation of six republics. As 1991 ended, it was clear that Tito's federation was gone for good. The war had cost thousands of lives, left hundreds of thousands homeless, and ruined an economy that had once been the only prosperous one in Communist Eastern Europe.

Animosity among the republics grew worse early in 1991, as Croatia and Slovenia—the two most Westernized republics—moved toward secession. Both republics had ousted their Communist governments in parliamentary elections in 1990, as democratic movements swept across Eastern Europe. Voters in these republics favored a loose confederation of independent states in place of Yugoslavia's federal government. But leaders in Serbia, the largest and most populous republic, wanted to maintain centralized federal control. Elections in 1990 had kept Serbia's hard-line Communists (renamed Socialists) in power.

Heightening tensions was Serbia's refusal in May 1991 to allow a Croat, Stjepan Mesić, to take his constitutional turn as head of Yugoslavia's federal presidency. Since Tito's death, Yugoslavia had had a collective presidency comprising representatives from the

Smoke rises over the old walled city of Dubrovnik in Croatia, after the federal army bombed it during the civil war that gripped Yugoslavia in 1991.

six republics and two provinces. The head of this presidency rotated annually among members. (Mesić finally took office on June 30 but resigned in December.)

The fighting begins. On June 25, Slovenia and Croatia declared themselves independent. Serbia's leaders ordered federal troops to preserve central control over the two breakaway republics. Slovenia, the first republic to come under attack, put up strong resistance. After less than two weeks of fighting, federal forces withdrew. A truce between Slovenia and the Yugoslav government was reached on July 7.

The federal army then switched its operations to Croatia, where Serbs made up nearly 12 per cent of the population. Many Serbs in Croatia had already declared their opposition to living under independent Croat rule and taken up arms. Serbia's President Slobodan Milošević said he would accept Yugoslavia's breakup only if borders between republics were redrawn to bring Serb-inhabited areas within one state.

Full-scale warfare raged through the summer and autumn in eastern Croatia, where Serb militias joined federal forces in battling Croatian troops. The Croatian city of Vukovar, with its large Serb population, fell to the federal army on November 17 after an 86-day siege. Federal forces also moved westward in autumn to blockade Croatian ports along the Adriatic Sea. The old walled city of Dubrovnik, considered to be a European cultural treasure, came under heavy shelling.

On December 20, Federal Executive Council President (premier) Ante Marković, a Croat, stepped down after refusing to approve a federal budget of which four-fifths was earmarked for the war effort. All semblance of a central government was gone, and only two republics, Serbia and Montenegro, had not declared independence.

In December, both Macedonia and the republic of Bosnia and Hercegovina—with its mixed population of Muslims, Serbs, and Croats—formally announced they would seek independence. The announcements were spurred by a decision of the 12-nation European Community (EC or Common Market) to extend recognition by Jan. 15, 1992, to any independence-minded Yugoslav republic that met certain conditions, including stable borders and respect for minority rights. On Dec. 23, 1991, Germany recognized Croatia and Slovenia.

Peace efforts. Leaders of the EC worked tirelessly to bring about a lasting cease-fire in Yugoslavia and in September launched a peace conference. But by year's end, numerous cease-fires had failed to hold, and the federal army held control of about a third of Croatia. The United Nations (UN) also sought to settle the crisis but refused to send a peacekeeping force until the fighting had stopped. On Jan. 1, 1992, UN negotiator Cyrus Vance announced that both sides had accepted a UN peacekeeping plan. Eric Bourne

See also **Yugoslavia,** Special Report: **A Troubled Past Clouds Yugoslavia's Future.** In ***World Book,*** see **Yugoslavia.**

A Troubled Past Clouds Yugoslavia's Future

By David Lawday

Bitter ethnic conflicts that threatened to tear Yugoslavia apart in 1991 are rooted deep in that troubled region's past.

A Croat guardsman takes aim at a Serb position in the warfare that followed declarations of independence by the Yugoslav republics of Croatia and Slovenia in June.

Yugoslavia, a relatively young European country, may not have been built to last. It assumed its most recent form—a federation of six republics—after World War II (1939-1945). But that federation was inherently unstable, as volatile as the political past of the Balkan region it covers. The federation had been held together by the ruling Communist Party. After the party lost control, long-simmering ethnic animosities came to a boil. In 1991, four republics either declared independence from the federation or planned to do so. Subsequent fighting between the republic of Croatia and federal forces pitched Yugoslavia into civil war. The violence was yet another chapter in the region's turbulent history.

Yugoslavia, which means Land of the South Slavs, came into being at the end of World War I. It arose in 1918 from the ruins of two defeated empires—Austria-Hungary and the Ottoman (Turkish) Empire. Croatia and Slovenia, Yugoslavia's two northwestern republics, once formed part of Austria-Hungary. The Ottoman Turks long ruled the four southern republics: Serbia, Bosnia and Hercegovina, Montenegro, and Macedonia.

The frontiers of these republics roughly follow the traditional boundaries of Yugoslavia's six largest Slavic nationality groups. Today, these groups, in order of population, are Serbs, Croats, Bosnian Muslims, Slovenes, Macedonians, and Montenegrins. But no republic is peopled by just one ethnic group. Pockets of Serbs are found in Croatia and Bosnia, for example, and Muslims live in Serbia and Montenegro. In addition, Yugoslavia has sizable non-Slavic ethnic minorities, including Albanians, Bulgarians, Greeks, Gypsies, Hungarians, Italians, and Turks. In all, a dozen or so nationalities spill over the borders of Yugoslavia's republics.

Each of Yugoslavia's nationalities, nevertheless, has retained a sense of cultural identity. Croatia and Slovenia, ruled by the Habsburg monarchy of Austria-Hungary until 1918, are more Western than the republics to the east and south, regions formerly under Turkish rule. Croats and Slovenes, moreover, are predominantly Roman Catholic. In contrast, many Bosnians are Muslim, and most Serbs, Montenegrins, and Macedonians are Eastern Orthodox. Reflecting the East-West cultural split, the most commonly spoken language in Yugoslavia, Serbo-Croatian, has two different written forms: Serbian is written in the Cyrillic alphabet and Croatian in the Roman alphabet. Slovenian, the main language spoken in Slovenia, also uses the Roman alphabet, while Macedonian uses Cyrillic.

The fragmentation of the Balkan peninsula—shared by Yugoslavia, Greece, Bulgaria, and Albania—along ethnic lines has made the term *Balkanization* an equivalent for division into many small, often hostile units. During the late 1800's, independence movements gained strength among the many Balkan nationality groups. At the same time, rivalries intensified among European powers, which sought to retain their influence in the region. The Balkans became known as the "Powder Keg of Europe" because turmoil there kept threatening to ignite a major European war. In 1914, the assassination of Austrian Archduke Francis Ferdinand by a Serb patriot in Sarajevo, Bosnia, triggered World War I.

After the war, the Allied victors pressed the South Slavs together in a single country: the Kingdom of the Serbs, Croats, and Slovenes (named after the country's three largest nationalities). From the outset, Serbia viewed itself as the dominant partner: Serbia had already existed as an independent country, having won independence from the Turks in 1878. The Serbs, moreover, had fought on the side of the victorious Allies in World War I. King Alexander I of Serbia's ruling dynasty took power in the newly formed country, which he renamed Yugoslavia in 1929.

Unification did not bring unity. Alexander's dictatorial rule ended with his assassination in 1934, reportedly by the *Ustaše*, a Croatian separatist group. Hostility between Serbs and Croats continued after Alexander's son Peter succeeded him as king.

Yugoslavia broke apart following its invasion by German and Italian forces in April 1941. During World War II, Yugoslavia was divided among

The author:

David Lawday is Europe correspondent for *U.S. News & World Report.*

An ethnic mosaic

Yugoslavia (meaning Land of the South Slavs) is made up of six republics, each with a different Slavic ethnic majority. Yugoslavia's largest non-Slavic nationalities occupy two provinces within the republic of Serbia. Religious differences further splinter the country.

several occupying powers. Croatia and part of Bosnia and Hercegovina became an "independent" pro-German state under the Ustaše. For the rest of the war, Yugoslav guerrillas called *Partisans* struggled to drive out occupation troops and bring down the Ustaše. The Partisans were led by Josip Broz Tito, then secretary-general of Yugoslavia's Communist Party.

The federation of six republics that took shape after World War II was nailed together by Tito, who remained the country's Communist leader until his death in 1980. Although Tito had received his political training in Moscow, he broke with Soviet dictator Joseph Stalin in 1948. Tito thereafter managed to keep the Soviet Union at arm's length as he took Yugoslavia on an independent Communist path that gave its people some sense of shared nationhood.

The federation began to unravel after Tito's death, however, as economic problems fueled resentment of the central government. The Communist Party's countrywide clamp on power loosened in 1990, when democratic movements swept across eastern Europe and four of Yugoslavia's six republics elected non-Communist governments. (Hard-liners remained in power in Serbia and Montenegro.) Communism had kept rivalries among nationality groups under control, but the collapse of the Communist system pried apart the centrally run federation.

On June 25, 1991, Yugoslavia's most prosperous and most democratized republics—Slovenia and Croatia—declared their independence from the federation. The breakaway republics wanted a new, looser confederation of independent states in place of the centralized federation, which they felt Serb conservatives dominated. Serbia, on the other hand, favored a strong central government to hold Tito's multinational federation together. Serbia's nationalist leader, Slobodan Milošević, said he would accept the federation's breakup only if Serb-inhabited areas, especially those in Croatia, were incorporated into Serbia. Under its own nationalist chief, Franjo Tudjman, Croatia resisted Serbian expansion. The Milošević regime had already asserted Serbia's authority over the *autonomous* (self-governing) Yugoslavian provinces of Kosovo and Vojvodina.

Fanning the flames of ethnic hatred were tragic memories from World War II. The memories revolved around the wartime Croatian puppet state under the Ustaše, which put to death huge numbers of Serbs. Partisan guerrillas, many of them Serbs, killed large numbers of Croats in revenge.

A dangerous catalyst in the conflict was the Yugoslav federal army, commanded by Communist hard-liners, most of whom were Serbs. The army also sided with the Serbs because Milošević announced his intention of keeping the Yugoslav federation together. Without the federation, the federal army had no reason to exist.

In Slovenia, the federal army put up only brief resistance to the secession attempt. Of Yugoslavia's six republics, only Slovenia could be considered ethnically homogeneous, and the army seemed willing to let it go.

In Croatia, however, some 4 million Croats had nearly 600,000 Serbs in their midst. These Serb "exiles" reacted against Croatia's campaign to secede from Yugoslavia by creating defiant autonomous zones within the breakaway republic. From these strongholds, Serb insurgents began the advance on Croatian territory that meant civil war. Milošević encouraged the Serb insurgents. Acting on his claims that Serb lives were endangered, federal forces went to war in Croatia.

Among the republics, only the smallest—Montenegro—backed Serbia's actions. The two remaining republics—Bosnia and Hercegovina in the middle of the country and impoverished Macedonia in the far south—were as wary of Serbian aims as were the breakaway northern republics. Both voted in autumn in favor of independence.

By year's end, the outcome of the Yugoslav crisis was uncertain. A peace conference launched in September had failed to impose a lasting cease-fire. The Yugoslav people could only hope that their memories of the past would not condemn them to repeat it in the future.

Yukon Territory. New negotiations in 1991 between the Canadian federal and territorial governments and the Yukon's 14 bands of Indians involved land rights and self-government. By year's end, four bands expected to sign contracts specifying their land rights. Bands also were negotiating the transfer of powers—such as those pertaining to health and social services, education, and the administration of justice.

Rights to oil and gas reserves beneath the Beaufort Sea, located north of the Yukon and Alaska, came to the fore as issues in 1991. In May, the Yukon and the neighboring Northwest Territories agreed on a border dividing the waters off their coasts and on regulations governing offshore drilling for oil and gas. However, maritime boundary disputes arose between Canada and the United States. Canada claimed that the land boundary between the Yukon and Alaska should be extended through the Beaufort Sea and into the Arctic Ocean. But the United States contended that the boundary should be drawn in a northeasterly direction to reflect the curve of the coast.

Canada and the United States in 1991 also debated issues involving the development of the oil and gas industry in the Alaskan breeding grounds of the Porcupine caribou herd. The caribou, named after a Yukon river, migrate between Alaska and Canada and are an important source of food and clothing for some 9,000 native people there. David M. L. Farr

In ***World Book,*** see **Yukon Territory.**

Zaire. President Mobutu Sese Seko in 1991 faced the greatest challenge ever posed to his rule. Although Mobutu, Zaire's ruler since 1965, had promised in 1990 to allow multiparty democracy in Zaire, he used many tactics in 1991 to keep from making good on that pledge. As a result, he was challenged throughout the year, often violently, by the political opposition. In addition, rioting and looting in September by angry soldiers brought the nation close to chaos. Mobutu made a few apparent concessions while at the same time maneuvering to hold onto power.

Mobutu's opponents had long decried his regime's corruption and human-rights abuses, but it was mostly the nation's staggering economy and soaring prices that brought things to a head in 1991. Zaire is potentially one of Africa's most prosperous countries, with large deposits of uranium, diamonds, copper, and other valuable resources. In 1991, however, its economy was in shambles—the result of gross mismanagement, lower world prices for copper, a huge foreign debt, and the withdrawal of aid by the United States and other donor nations.

Strike, violence lead to "reforms." The protests against Mobutu's government began in February with a three-day strike called by union leaders, students, political organizers, and other dissatisfied factions. The groups arrayed against Mobutu demanded multiparty democracy, a new popularly drafted constitution, and presidential and parliamentary elections. In the ensuing months, the demonstrations and strikes intensified in their frequency and violence.

Mobutu appeared to accept reform by permitting press freedom. But he refused to allow a coalition of about 150 opposition parties, known popularly as the Sacred Union, use of the state media.

Mobutu agreed in September to share power with a prime minister and a coalition cabinet. That concession came in the wake of the military rioting, which had to be put down by troops flown in from France and Belgium. Mobutu insisted, however, that several key ministries be headed by persons loyal to him. In late September, Mobutu named a bitter rival, Etienne Tshisekedi, as prime minister but dismissed him within three weeks, an action that led to renewed rioting.

National conference collapses. Representatives of more than 200 political groups gathered in Kinshasa, the capital, on August 7 for a national conference to write a new constitution and prepare the country for elections. Mobutu, however, packed the membership with his supporters and controlled the agenda. Sessions were frequently interrupted by riots and demonstrations, and once by troops with machine guns who surrounded the meeting hall. On August 15, the government suspended the conference.

J. Gus Liebenow and Beverly B. Liebenow

See also **Africa** (Facts in brief table). In ***World Book,*** see **Zaire.**

Zambia. See **Africa.**

Ziaur Rahman, Khaleda (1945-), became the first woman prime minister of Bangladesh following parliamentary elections in February 1991. She is head of the Bangladesh Nationalist Party (BNP), which leads a coalition government. See **Bangladesh.**

Known as Khaleda Zia, the new prime minister entered the political arena following the assassination of her husband, President Ziaur Rahman, who was the leader of Bangladesh from 1975 until his death in 1981. Prior to joining the BNP in 1982, she had had no direct political experience. She was born in 1945 in Dinajpur, a small city in the northwest part of what is now Bangladesh (then part of India). There she received the equivalent of a high school education. A housewife up to the time of her husband's assassination, Zia has two sons, who are 23 and 18.

Zia was appointed senior vice chairman of the BNP in 1983 and became the party's acting chairman in 1984. In 1990, Zia joined forces with Sheik Hasina Wazed, now her main political rival, to form an opposition movement that finally forced President Hussain Mohammad Ershad out of office on Dec. 6, 1990.

Zia supported Bangladesh's recent return to a parliamentary system of government, with power vested in the legislature and prime minister, rather than in an autocratic president like General Ershad. She favors free-market reforms, including privatizing many public-sector enterprises. Douglas Clayton

Zimbabwe. See **Africa.**

Zoology. Zoologists announced the discovery of a new whale species in February 1991. James G. Mead of the Smithsonian Institution in Washington, D.C., and Koen Van Waerebeck of the Peruvian Center for Cetalogic Studies in Lima, Peru, made the announcement based on studies of 10 whale specimens found since 1972. The new species, a gray whale with the scientific name *Mesoplodon peruvianus,* lives in the Pacific Ocean off the coast of Peru. The whale grows to 12 feet (3.7 meters) in length and has a dolphinlike snout.

Eye on the sky. Lizards use a third "eye" on top of their heads to determine the position of the sun and find their way home, two biologists reported in August 1991. Barbara Ellis-Quinn and Carol Simon of the City University of New York studied Yarrow's spiny lizards in Arizona and found that they have a crude eye consisting of a cornea, lens, and retina on top of their heads.

The biologists covered this eye, then released the lizards 160 yards (150 meters) from their homes. Only 8 of 40 lizards with their third eye covered found their way back, compared with 24 of 40 released the same distance away with their third eye uncovered.

Mingling bees. As they spread north from South America, Africanized honey bees known as killer bees have been mating with European bees along the way, entomologists reported in July. Thomas E. Rinderer, a bee specialist with the United States Department of Agriculture in Baton Rouge, La., and his fellow scientists compared the genetic makeup and appearance of bees in 163 hives in the Yucatán Peninsula in Mexico—a region where both Africanized and European bees are found.

The researchers discovered that almost one-third of the bees from the Yucatán contained genes from Africanized queens. Rinderer suggested that this mixing of genes of both species could make the undesirable aspects of Africanized bees less of a menace to U.S. farmers and beekeepers.

Sibling rivalry. A team of researchers from the University of California at Berkeley discovered in 1991 that sibling rivalry among infant spotted hyenas is often fatal. In May, psychologist Laurence G. Frank and his colleagues filmed five litters of spotted hyenas in a laboratory for a month.

The researchers reported that the young hyenas attacked each other within an hour of birth, with the attacks most likely to occur between litter mates of the same sex. Studies of hyenas in the wild have noted that among infant spotted hyena twins collected from dens, one twin is often near death from wounds on the back and neck. But because infant spotted hyenas rarely emerge from their dens, direct observation of their early behavior is difficult. Frank's laboratory observations determined that the deadly wounds were likely the result of sibling rivalry.

Elizabeth Pennisi

In ***World Book,*** see **Zoology.**

Zoos and aquariums in the United States experienced many blessed events in 1991, but among the biggest were the births one week apart of two beluga whale calves at the New York Aquarium in Brooklyn, a borough of New York City, during August. The calves, both male, were the first belugas to survive infancy in captivity in U.S. aquariums. Each calf at birth weighed between 170 and 180 pounds (77 to 82 kilograms) and was 4 to 5 feet (1 to 1.5 meters) in length. They had different mothers, but the same 20-year-old, 2,000-pound (900-kilogram) father. Their births provide a unique opportunity for scientists to study the social behavior and communication of this small whale species.

Grand opening. Tennesseans strolled through the gates of the Nashville Zoo for the first time on May 17, during grand opening celebrations. The new park exhibits more than 500 animals representing 115 species. One section of the 135-acre (55-hectare) animal park duplicates an African savanna, complete with zebras and antelopes, such as eland and gemsbok. Visitors can climb the stairs of a 14-foot (4-meter) observation tower for an eye-to-eye view of giraffes. The Valley of the Cats is home to tigers, clouded leopards, cougars, Canadian lynx, and caracals, cousins of the lynx from Asia and Africa. The reptile house features 60 displays of snakes, turtles, and lizards.

Happy anniversary. On January 5, the San Diego Zoo celebrated its 75th anniversary with the arrival of four koalas, a gift from the Australian government. Other zoos from around the world also sent presents, among them Rothschild's peacock pheasants from Hong Kong; Siberian weasels from St. Petersburg (formerly Leningrad) in the former Soviet Union; and mishmi takins (large, shaggy, goatlike mammals from the mountains of central Asia) from Berlin, Germany. As part of the yearlong celebration, the zoo opened Gorilla Tropics, 2½ acres (1 hectare) of hilly habitat for lowland gorillas.

Primate popularity. The Pittsburgh (Pa.) Zoo premiered its Tropical Forest on April 11. The 5-acre (2-hectare) exhibit takes visitors on a worldwide "tour" to meet endangered primates, the highest order of mammals. The tour begins with ring-tailed and red ruffed lemurs of Madagascar. White-faced sakis and spider monkeys represent South America, and orangutans and white-cheeked gibbons live in the section depicting Southeast Asia. The tour concludes with species native to Africa, including lowland gorillas, black-and-white colobus monkeys, and mandrills (forest-dwelling baboons). Part of the mandrill habitat was *clear-cut* (all the trees cut down) and burned, illustrating human impact on the world's forests and wildlife.

The Cheyenne Mountain Zoo in Colorado Springs, Colo., opened Primate World on June 30. The new facility houses lion-tailed macaques, colobus monkeys, two guenon species, golden lion tamarins, orangutans, and lowland gorillas. The gorilla display covers

Beluga whales interact with staff members of Chicago's Oceanarium, the John G. Shedd Aquarium's new indoor marine habitat that opened in April.

nearly an acre (0.5 hectare) and provides multiple viewing spots for visitors.

Polar ponds and coral reefs. In May, two exhibits opened in Minnesota that represent climatic extremes. The Lake Superior Zoological Society of Duluth welcomed visitors to a new, multispecies exhibit that suits Duluth's cool, natural climate. Polar Shores contains large, open-air ponds and streams that are home to polar bears, penguins, harbor seals, and river otters.

The Minnesota Zoological Gardens outside Minneapolis-St. Paul opened its new Coral Reef Sharks tank, where visitors can view several shark species commonly found in tropical waters. Through underwater viewing windows, visitors can come nose-to-nose with bonnethead, nurse, lagoon, and black- and white-tipped sharks. Butterfly fish, damselfish, snappers, and other tropical species mingle among rose, staghorn, elkhorn, and brain corals.

Florida added two major aquatic exhibits during 1991. The first of these was at Lowry Park Zoo in Tampa, where Florida Aquatics opened on January 5. The exhibit is devoted to the Caribbean *manatee* (sea cow), a popular but highly endangered native species. Many are killed by powerboats, and many others bear scars from boat propellers. The new exhibit contains a hospital and rehabilitation pools to treat manatees that are injured or become sick in the wild.

Sea World of Florida in Orlando invited visitors to see the Terrors of the Deep on June 1. The public descends into a 45,000-square-foot (4,200-square-meter) acrylic tunnel, the world's largest, where they are surrounded by some of the sea's most awesome predators. Along the submerged walkway, visitors encounter scorpionfish and lionfish, whose poisonous spines can inflict painful wounds; deadly sea snakes (aquatic cobras); and sleek, snaggle-toothed barracudas. Huge groupers, toothy moray eels, and purple-mouthed eels swim amid naturalistic coral reefs, rocks, and caves. Artificially created waves and currents heighten the drama. The climax, after descending 16 feet (4.8 meters) below the water's surface, is the opportunity to view sand tiger, bull, brown, and nurse sharks from an acrylic-encased people mover.

Whales, seals, and dolphins greeted Chicagoans at the John G. Shedd Aquarium when the Oceanarium opened on April 27. Two 9-foot (2.7-meter) beluga whales, harbor seals, and Pacific white-sided dolphins are the major attractions in the 2.6-million-gallon (9.8-million-liter) tank, the world's largest indoor marine mammal habitat. Windows 33 feet (10 meters) high rise above the tank, creating the illusion that the water inside extends outside into Lake Michigan. Visitors also find Magellanic, gentoo, and rockhopper penguins clustered along Penguin Shore, a replica of the Falkland Islands near the Antarctic.

Eugene J. Walter, Jr.

In ***World Book,*** see **Zoo.**

Dictionary Supplement

...Artificial reality ■ bungee cord ■ la-la ■ rad...

A list of new words added to the 1992 edition of ***The World Book Dictionary*** because they have been used enough to become a permanent part of our ever-changing language.

A a

Af|ro|cen|tric (af′rō sen′trik) *adj.* regarding Africa as the source and center of African-American culture: *Bethel is proudly Afrocentric—a bright mural of African faces is painted over the altar* (Time).

artificial life, lifelike organisms created and existing in a computer: *They are creating a field called artificial life, mixing the impulses of biology with the tools of computation* (New York Times).

artificial reality, an environment created by computer graphics that appears three-dimensional and real: *Artificial reality . . . relies on the techniques of interactive computer graphics to create the illusion of navigating* (Time).

attack politics, a political campaign that attacks the character or reputation of an opponent rather than political issues: *The Helms-Gantt race . . . provides a stark commentary on both the effectiveness—and the hollow core—of the attack politics of the 1990's* (New York Times Magazine).

B b

Baby Bell, any of the regional telephone companies originally a part of the national American Telephone and Telegraph Company.

blad|er (blā′dər) *n.* a person who skates using blades: *"Every weekend it's a battle between the cyclists and the bladers"* (Time).

boarder baby, *U.S.* an infant or young child who is kept indefinitely in a hospital because the parents are not able or legally permitted to assume custody: *A good example of a boarder baby would be a child born addicted to drugs as a result of* [*the*] *mother's addiction* (New York Times).

boom box, a large portable radio, often combined with a cassette player; ghetto blaster: *Advertising trucks equipped with monstrous boom boxes are cruising East German towns blaring rock music interspersed with advertising blurbs* (Time).

bungee cord, an elastic cord with hooks at both ends, used to hold bulky items in place, as on top of a car or a bike rack.

C c

call-out (kôl′out), *n.* a summons into service or for some special duty or purpose: *an emergency crew's response to a call-out; a call-out of the National Guard.*

catalytic antibody, an enzyme that is designed to speed chemical reactions in certain substances in an organism: *Scientists have designed many catalytic antibodies known also as abzymes* (Science News).

collateral damage, the killing of civilians or damaging of nonmilitary structures in the course of conducting bombing raids or other military operations: *Avoidance of collateral damage means "trying not to kill civilians"* (New York Times Magazine).

crack baby, a baby born with various disabilities or deformities caused by the mother's use of crack-cocaine while pregnant: *The most widely cited estimate—*[*of*] *fetally exposed babies (or "crack-babies"), born per year—is much too high* (Washington Post).

D d

dance|hall (dans′hôl′, däns′-) *n.* dance music that is an electronic mixture of various popular music styles accompanied by talking or rapping to the rhythm of the music: *Historically,* [*Jamaican*] *dancehall can be viewed as the antecedent to American rap* (Rolling Stone). —**dance′-hall′**, *adj.*

date rape, the act of having forced sexual intercourse with a female while on a social date: *The popular term is the narrower "date rape," which suggests an ugly ending to a raucous night on the town* (Time).

dis (dis), *v.t.,* **dissed**, **dis|sing**. *Slang.* to show disrespect; scorn: *We hope that you guys don't dis us for it* (New York Magazine).

DJ-ing, (dē jā′ing) *n.* talking over or with a recording, in time to the beat of the music: *The guys who spin the songs would rap on top of the rhythm, which we call DJ-ing* (Rolling Stone).

E e

e|co-safe (ē′kō sāf′), *adj.,* **-saf|er**, **-safest**. ecologically safe; not likely to damage the environment: *Eco-safe products for the home—biodegradable garbage bags, toilet paper and dishwashing soap, dioxin-free baby wipes and water-conservation kits* (Rolling Stone).

e-mail (ē′māl′), *n.,* or **E mail**, communications sent by computer; electronic mail.

eye candy, something or someone pleasing to look at: *But most actresses are accessories, used for supportive warmth or eye candy* (Vanity Fair).

F f

faux (fō), *adj.* fake; imitation: *In Cleveland a plagiarism suit between two* faux *Elvises resulted in the defendant's singing "Burnin' Love" in an actual courtroom* (Spy Magazine). [< F *faux* fake]

fetal alcohol syndrome, a group of physical and mental defects in a newborn, including retardation, resulting from the consumption of too much alcohol by the mother during pregnancy: *French researchers first identified what has come to be called the "fetal alcohol syndrome" (malformations and behavioral damage)* (New Scientist).

G g

glass ceiling, an intangible barrier that prevents a person's advancement to higher executive positions: *In climbing the corporate ladder they* [*women*] *collide with a "glass ceiling" of subtle discrimination* (New York Times).

good cop, bad cop, **1** a technique of interrogating suspects by a team of two police officers in which one officer is friendly and easygoing and the other is combative and easily angered. **2** any partnership where one person is friendly and relaxed and the other tense and difficult: *"There are many partnerships in Hollywood where it's 'good cop, bad cop,' " says one studio executive* (Spy Magazine).

good-cop, bad-cop (gu̇d′kop bad′-kop), *adj.* having both good and bad qualities or characteristics; opposite: *It's a good-cop, bad-cop story of psychological subtlety* (Time).

green consuming, the use of products that do not damage the environment: *Although "green consuming" in the supermarket has largely been a matter of what to avoid rather than what to buy, this is changing* (Philadelphia Inquirer). —**green consumer**.

Green Party, a European political movement that represents environmental interests: *These organizations, often known as Green Parties, have had a growing influence on environmental policies in Western Europe* (Alan McGowan).

H h

happy camper, someone who is well-behaved and contented with his or her situation: *"She's a happy camper. She's a doll." Tamba . . . threw her trunk above her head like a lady flinging open a parasol* (New Yorker).

hard dock, a joining of orbiting spacecraft by mechanical coupling: *Finally, they . . .* [*carried*] *out a dramatic series of maneuvers—and achieved a hard dock* (Newsweek).

hard-dock (härd′dok′), *v.i.* to join orbiting spacecraft with a mechanical coupling, as by a lock or other mechanism: *The crew finally hard-docked late the first night by hot-wiring the retract mechanism of the docking probe* (Science News).

hate crime, a crime usually committed by a group against an individual and motivated by prejudice: *Human-rights activists say San Diego's racial attacks are a microcosm of hate crimes flaring nationally* (Time).

hot button, a matter of immediate interest or concern: *Graphics and bright colors highlight stories on baby-boomer "hot buttons," such as the environment, divorce, personal finance, etc.* (Wall Street Journal).

human shield, **1** any person or group of people who acts as a shield against some danger. **2** a person or group of people, including civilians, prisoners of war, or other noncombatants held hostage at a location of strategic military importance to protect it from enemy attack: *If, by vowing to deploy the POWs as human shields, . . . Saddam aimed to curtail the allied aerial campaign, the plan backfired* (Time). —**hu′man-shield**, *adj.*

Pronunciation Key: hat, āge, cãre, fär; let, ēqual, tėrm; it, īce; hot, ōpen, ôrder; oil, out; cup, pu̇t, rüle; child; long; thin; ᴛʜen; zh, measure; ə represents **a** in about, **e** in taken, **i** in pencil, **o** in lemon, **u** in circus.

L l

lake effect, the effect of a large inland lake on weather systems passing over it: *But there's a positive side to Superior too. Thanks to the lake effect, temperatures even in mid-winter average between 15 and 30 degrees* (Lands' End Catalog).

la-la (lä′lä′), *adj.* divorced from reality; unreal; dreamy: [*Easterners*] *think this is la-la land out here . . . in Southern California. They probably think we're doing this interview in a Jacuzzi* (Vanity Fair).

M m

mainstream smoke, tobacco smoke inhaled by a smoker: *Mainstream smoke, but not sidestream, has been linked to cancers of the mouth, throat, voice box . . . kidney and pancreas* (Sunday Times).

med|i|gap (med′ə gap′), *n.* a policy of supplemental health insurance that provides coverage of some or all medical, hospital, and other costs of health care not provided by Medicare and Medicaid: *Revised medigap policies were required this year . . . About 22 million of 33 million Medicare beneficiaries have supplemental insurance* (New York Times).

mercy killer, a person who commits a mercy killing: *Judges and juries across the country have been remarkably lenient on family members who become mercy killers* (Time).

met|al|head (met′əl hed′), *n.* a person who is a devotee of heavy-metal music: *"I was under the impression he was a metalhead. He does like heavy metal. But he's unusually well read. He was reading Shakespeare"* (New York Times).

music video, a videotape recording of a visual display accompanying a popular song; video.

N n

negative cam|paign|ing (kam pā′ning), the political tactic of campaigning against an opponent's character instead of for particular positions on certain issues: *"If there hadn't been negative campaigning, no one would have had anything to talk about," says* [*a*] *political scientist* (Time).

notebook computer, a portable computer that is about the size of a notebook: *The company describes both models as "notebook" computers . . . . Judged as lightweight laptops, though, the new . . . models are very impressive* (New York Times).

nut|ball (nut′bôl′), *n.* an odd, eccentric, or slightly crazy person: *She's a nutball, a crazy, difficult—she's got the director's migraine rep* (Vanity Fair).

P p

Pa|tri|ot (pā′trē ət), *n.* a surface-to-air, computer-guided missile.

peace dividend, the financial benefit expected to be derived from a decrease in military spending as a result of an improvement in international relations, especially with the U.S.S.R.: *The fact that the peace dividend is largely illusory is not likely to quell congressional debate on how to spend it* (The Nation).

phone bank, a group of telephones connected to the same number used to canvass voters, survey consumers, or raise money for some cause or institution: *Senator Bentsen's organization and his phone banks and his campaign pushed the turnout way up* (Atlantic).

politically correct, socially acceptable within a certain group: *These detractors see books added to reading lists because they are "politically correct"—because they portray, for example, a strong woman battling a sexist society—while books of proven merit are condemned . . .* [*as*] *"politically incorrect"* (New York Times Magazine).

poster boy, a person who is the perfect example of something; symbol: *With the release of government documents spelling out the conflict-of-interest allegations . . . Neil Bush replaced Charles Keating as the S&L poster boy* (Time).

Q q

quality time, time spent exclusively with a child or as a family: *Publicity whiz Suzanne Eagle puts a spin on quality time by working out while walking the baby* (Vanity Fair).

R r

rad² (rad), *adj. Slang.* terrific; fantastic; radical.

re|cla|ma (rə klä′mə), *n.* a request or appeal to reconsider a decision, proposed action, or policy: *Margaret Thatcher, wrote . . . Schlesinger . . . in 1986, "appeared at Camp David to deliver a reclama on Reykjavik"* (New York Times Magazine).

Ro|lo|dex (rō′lō deks′), *n.* a person's list of acquaintances, friends, and valued associates: *Right in the middle of the head, just underneath the hairline is the location of a person's Rolodex* (Washington Post). [< *Rolodex,* trademark for a personal directory]

S s

share|ware (shãr′wãr′), *n.* computer software available free from other users or at very low cost from producers or vendors: *It is perfectly legal, and even encouraged, to distribute copies of shareware and public-domain programs. Not so with other software* (Sunday Times).

side|stream smoke (sīd′strēm), *n.* tobacco smoke emitted into the air by smoldering cigarettes, cigars, and pipes.

smoke and mirrors, manipulation, or an obscuring of fact to achieve some desired result; deception: *He promised decisive action. But when he unveiled his "plan," it was all smoke and mirrors* (New York Times).

soft dock, a joining of two spacecraft without a mechanical coupling: *The two spacecraft joined in a "soft dock" in which they touched but could not be locked together* (New York Times).

soft-dock (sôft′dok′), *v.i.* to join orbiting spacecraft without a mechanical coupling, as by a lock or other device.

T t

track|ball (trak′bôl′), *n.* a device to control a cursor or other image on a computer display screen: *A trackball has the ball on top, where you move it with your fingers* (Sunday Times).

triple A, artillery used against attacking aircraft: *Artillery in the war on Iraq also appears in an abbreviation used by airmen: viewers heard debriefing pilots say* triple A . . . *which means "antiaircraft artillery"* (New York Times Magazine).

V v

virtual reality, **1** an environment created by computer graphics that appears three-dimensional and real and through which the computer operator can move by using special equipment: *I was sitting in a room crowded with strangers, but within the space of my virtual reality, I was totally alone* (Time). **2** of or relating to virtual reality: *He can make whole virtual-reality "worlds" in less than two hours* (Time).

voice mail, a system for communication by telephone that records messages electronically for later retrieval by subscribers who dial a central computer to get the messages stored under a subscriber's identification number: *Hyatt Hotels Corp . . . using technology to upgrade service . . . begins installing voice mail* (Wall Street Journal).

von Wil|le|brand factor (wil′ə brand, vil′-), a protein found in the walls of blood vessels and plasma which binds with a substance in blood platelets to begin the process of blood clotting.

W w

wedge issue, an issue that divides or distinguishes points of view: *The White House is preparing "wedge" issues to sharply distinguish Republicans from Democrats* (Time).

white bread, *n. Informal.* a member of affluent white society or the society and its values: *But part that hippie hair and he's white bread, no matter how you slice him* (Vanity Fair).

Y y

yin and yang, people or things totally different from each other; opposites: *"They were like two book ends; they were like yin and yang. They were alter egos"* (Vanity Fair).

yin-yang (yin′yang′), *adj.* made up of opposites; contrasting: *a cast and crew that's half Hollywood, half Baltimore, a yin-yang crowd that's given to vegetarian lasagna and peanut M&M's* [*a candy*] (Vanity Fair).

Z z

zap|per (zap′ər), *n.* **1** a remote control for a television set or a videocassette player: *The people of America are armed with the zapper, the . . . remote-control program annihilator* (Details). **2** a person who uses a remote control for a television set.

World Book Supplement

...Estonia ■ Jazz ■ Iraq ■ Latvia ■ Lithuania...

To help ***World Book*** owners keep their encyclopedias up to date, the following articles are reprinted from the 1992 edition of the encyclopedia.

483 **Estonia**
486 **Iraq**
493 **Jazz**
500 **Latvia**
503 **Lithuania**
506 **Races, Human**

Tass from Sovfoto

Tallinn is the capital and largest city of Estonia. The city has many beautiful churches, castles, and other structures that were built from the 1200's to the 1500's.

Estonia, *eh STOH nee uh,* is a European nation that regained its independence in 1991, after more than 50 years of forced annexation to the Soviet Union. Estonia lies on the Baltic Sea in northern Europe. It had been independent from 1918 until 1940, when the Soviet Union occupied it and made it one of the 15 republics of the Soviet Union.

Estonia covers 17,413 square miles (45,100 square kilometers) and has a population of 1,595,000. Tallinn is the capital and largest city. Other major cities include Tartu and Kohtla-Järve. The country's name in Estonian, the official language, is *Eesti Vabariik* (Republic of Estonia).

Facts in brief

Capital: Tallinn.
Official language: Estonian.
Official name: Eesti Vabariik (Republic of Estonia).
Area: 17,413 sq. mi. (45,100 km²). *Greatest distances*—north-south, 150 mi. (240 km); east-west, 230 mi. (370 km). *Coastline*—481 mi. (774 km).
Elevation: *Highest*—Munamagi, 1,043 ft. (318 m). *Lowest*—sea level along the coast.
Population: *Estimated 1992 population*—1,595,000; density, 92 persons per sq. mi. (35 per km²); distribution, 72 per cent urban, 28 per cent rural. *1989 census*—1,572,916. *Estimated 1997 population*—1,633,000.
Chief products: *Agriculture*—barley, beef cattle, butter, chickens, eggs, hogs, milk, rye. *Manufacturing*—machinery, petrochemicals, food products, textiles.

Estonia's manufacturing and mining industries are the country's leading employers. About 70 per cent of Estonia's people live in cities or in towns.

Through the centuries, Germans, Danes, Swedes, Poles, and Russians controlled Estonia. But the Estonians kept an independent spirit, and they continue to treasure their own culture and language.

Government. Estonia is governed by a chief executive and a legislative body called the Supreme Council. The council has 105 members. A constitutional assembly has been formed to write a constitution.

People. Estonia went through great social and eco-

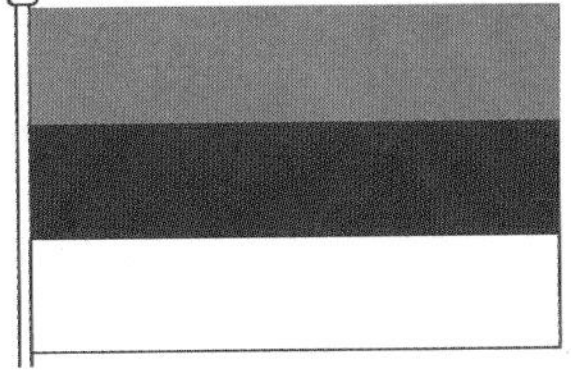

The Flag Research Center

Symbols of Estonia. Estonia's flag has three horizontal stripes. The blue stripe at the top of the flag represents the sky. The middle stripe of black stands for the land. The white stripe at the bottom symbolizes hope in the future. The Estonian coat of arms features three blue lions on a golden shield.

nomic changes during the period of Soviet rule. Estonians, a people related to the Finns, formed about 90 per cent of the population in 1940, when Soviet troops occupied the country. Today, only about 60 per cent of the people are Estonians. Hundreds of thousands of Russians settled in Estonia while the country was under Soviet control. Estonia also has a few thousand Byelorussians, Finns, Jews, and Ukrainians. Estonians speak the Estonian language, which is closely related to Finnish.

Estonia has seven colleges and universities. The oldest and best known is Tartu University, which was founded in 1632.

About 80 per cent of the people in Estonia are Lutherans, and almost 20 per cent belong to one of the Eastern Orthodox Churches. From 1940 until the late 1980's, the Soviet government restricted religious freedom in Estonia. But in the late 1980's, it ended its restrictions.

Almost two-thirds of the Estonians farmed the land and lived in rural villages until the Soviets industrialized the area. Today, most of the people of Estonia work in factories or mines and live in apartments in cities or towns.

Many Estonians have colorful traditional costumes, which they wear on festive occasions. Folk songs have a long tradition in Estonia. A huge song festival is held every five years in Tallinn. It attracts thousands of singers and hundreds of thousands of visitors.

Land and climate. Estonia consists chiefly of a low plain. Farmland covers about 40 per cent of Estonia, forests another 30 per cent, and swamps 20 per cent. Lake Peipus and the Narva River form much of Estonia's eastern boundary.

Estonia has a total of 481 miles (774 kilometers) of coastline on the Baltic Sea and on the Gulf of Finland and the Gulf of Riga. The sandy western coast is a favorite resort area. About a tenth of Estonia consists of Baltic islands, the largest of which is Saaremaa Island.

François Gohier, Explorer

Traditional Estonian costumes are bright and colorful. The Estonian woman shown above is wearing a costume that includes an embroidered blouse and hat.

Estonia has a surprisingly mild climate for an area so far north. Sea winds help keep the weather from becoming very cold or hot. Temperatures average from about 19 °F to 28 °F (−7 °C to −2 °C) in January to 61 °F to 64 °F (16 °C to 18 °C) in July. An average of 19 to 23 inches (48 to 58 centimeters) of rain falls annually in Estonia.

Economy. During the period when the Soviets controlled Estonia, they prohibited private factories and farms and established government-controlled enterprises. The Soviets created economic plans under which industrial development was emphasized. Estonia experi-

Estonia

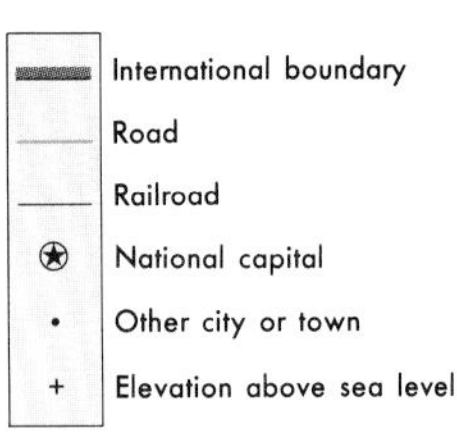

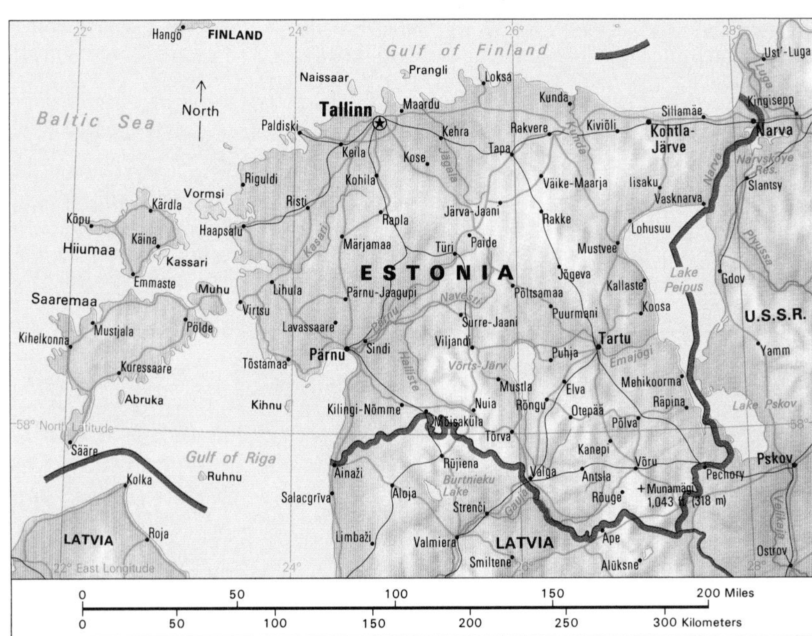

WORLD BOOK map

© Gary Matoso, Contact Press

Estonians celebrated independence in September 1991, when the Soviet Union recognized Estonia as an independent nation. Estonia had been part of the Soviet Union since 1940, when the Soviets forcibly made it a Soviet republic.

enced much industrial development under Soviet rule. Although its economy was advanced by Soviet standards, there were widespread complaints about the shortages and poor quality of consumer goods and services. Economic development brought many Soviet immigrants to work in Estonia. Industrial pollution became a major problem.

During the 1980's, large numbers of Estonians called for greater control of their economy and reduced Soviet influence. Since 1988, numerous new private and cooperative firms have been established in Estonia.

Manufacturing and mining account for about 75 per cent of Estonia's economic output. Oil shale is used extensively as fuel for electrical power plants. It is also refined into petrochemicals. Estonia also manufactures chemical fertilizer, construction materials, agricultural machinery, processed foods, and textiles. Tallinn is an important center for fashion and design.

Agriculture and fishing provide about 20 per cent of Estonia's economic output. The chief farm products include milk, butter, eggs, beef, pork, poultry, potatoes, rye, and barley. Commercial fishing is also an important economic activity.

History. People lived in what is now Estonia by 7000 B.C. The ancestors of the Estonians settled there several thousand years ago. They formed several independent states headed by elected elders.

During the early 1200's, the Teutonic Knights, an organization of German crusaders, converted the Estonians to Christianity by force. They took control of southern Estonia, and Danish forces conquered the north. The Danes sold their Estonian holdings to the Teutonic Knights in 1324. By the 1500's, German nobles owned much of Estonia's land and controlled thousands of Estonian *serfs.* Serfs worked on the estates of the nobles.

In 1561, Sweden took over northern Estonia, and Poland conquered the southern part. Sweden controlled all of Estonia from 1625 to 1721, when the area fell to Russia (the name for the Soviet Union before 1922). But German nobles kept estates in Estonia until 1919.

The serfs were freed in 1816, but most of the land remained in the hands of German nobles. In 1868, former serfs gained the right to buy land. Some became successful landowners and educated their children well. Others found industrial employment in cities.

A national revival begun in the mid-1800's led to the establishment of Estonia as an independent country. Independence was proclaimed on Feb. 24, 1918. Russia recognized Estonia's independence in 1920. The Estonian constitution established a democratic form of government. In 1919, the government took over the country's large estates and began distributing the land to thousands of Estonian citizens.

In 1939, Germany and the Soviet Union agreed secretly to take over a number of east European countries between themselves. The Soviet Union established military bases in Estonia. Soviet forces occupied Estonia in June 1940. In August, the Soviets forcibly made Estonia part of the Soviet Union. Germany occupied Estonia in 1941, during World War II, but the Soviet Union regained control of Estonia in 1944. Most Estonians opposed Soviet rule, and tens of thousands of people were deported to Siberia in 1941 (before the German occupation). Large numbers of Estonians were also deported to Siberia in 1949. About 100,000 Estonians fled to Western countries after the Soviet take-over.

After the end of World War II in 1945, movements against Soviet control appeared periodically. A strong guerrilla resistance against the Soviets lasted for several years after the war. A movement to promote human rights began in the 1960's. During the late 1980's, a new wave of Estonian nationalism appeared, fueled in part by Soviet leader Mikhail Gorbachev's call for greater openness of expression in the Soviet Union. Most Estonians demanded greater control over the republic's government and economy, and many demanded complete independence from the Soviet Union.

In 1990, the Estonian parliament declared the 1940 Soviet annexation illegal and Soviet rule in Estonia invalid. The parliament called for the restoration of Estonian independence through a gradual separation from the Soviet Union. The Soviet Union called this action illegal. In August 1991, several conservative Communist officials failed in an attempt to overthrow Gorbachev and take over the Soviet central government. During the upheaval that followed the failed coup, the Estonian parliament declared immediate independence. In September, the Soviet government recognized Estonia's independence. Tõnu Parming

© Filip Horvat, Saba

Baghdad is Iraq's capital and one of the largest cities in the Middle East. Some parts of Baghdad feature modern buildings, *above.* Others have narrow, dusty streets and colorful bazaars. The photograph above was taken before the 1991 Persian Gulf War, which damaged much of the city.

Iraq

Iraq, *ih RAHK* or *ih RAK,* is an Arab country at the head of the Persian Gulf in southwestern Asia. The country is bordered by Turkey, Iran, Kuwait, Saudi Arabia, Jordan, and Syria. Baghdad is Iraq's capital and largest city.

The world's first known civilization and other early cultures developed along the Tigris and Euphrates rivers in what is now Iraq. The ancient Greeks called part of Iraq and the surrounding region *Mesopotamia* (between rivers) because it lay between the Tigris and Euphrates rivers. For thousands of years, civilizations there have depended on controlling flooding from the two rivers and on using their waters for irrigation.

Iraq became part of the Arab Empire in the A.D. 600's and absorbed Arab Muslim culture. Today, about 75 per cent of Iraq's people are Arabs. Iraq also has a large Kurdish population that has struggled on and off for self-government for many years.

Iraq's economy depends heavily on the export of oil. Income produced by the oil industry has improved living conditions for Iraq's people.

Michel Le Gall, the contributor of this article, is Associate Professor of Middle Eastern History at St. Olaf College.

In the 1980's and the early 1990's, President Saddam Hussein and other leaders of the ruling Baath Party involved Iraq in two wars that had devastating effects on the country. Iraq fought a war with Iran from 1980 to 1988, when a cease-fire was declared. In 1990, Iraq invaded and occupied neighboring Kuwait. The United Nations (UN) condemned the invasion and imposed a

Facts in brief

Capital: Baghdad.
Official language: Arabic.
Official name: Al-Jumhuriya Al-Iraqiya (Republic of Iraq).
Area: 169,235 sq. mi. (438,317 km²). *Greatest distances*—north-south, 530 mi. (853 km); east-west, 495 mi. (797 km). *Coastline*—40 mi. (64 km).
Elevation: *Highest*—about 11,840 ft. (3,609 m) in Zagros Mountains. *Lowest*—sea level.
Population: *Estimated 1990 population (prior to Persian Gulf War)*—18,048,000; density, 107 persons per sq. mi. (41 persons per km²); distribution, 74 per cent urban, 26 per cent rural. *1987 census*—16,278,316.
Chief products: *Agriculture*—barley, dates, grapes, rice, tomatoes, and wheat. *Mining*—petroleum. *Manufacturing*—building materials, chemicals, flour, iron and steel, leather goods, petroleum refining, textiles.
National anthem: "Al-Salam Al-Jumhuri" ("Salute to the Republic").
Money: *Basic unit*—dinar. For its price in U.S. dollars see **Money** (table: Exchange rates).

trade embargo on Iraq. A coalition of 39 nations, including the United States and Canada, opposed the invasion and sent forces to the region. In early 1991, they defeated Iraq in the Persian Gulf War.

Government

National government. Although Iraq's Constitution of 1970 states that Iraq is a republic, the country actually functions as a dictatorship. President Saddam Hussein and other leaders of the ruling Baath Party control all branches of the government. The Baath Party eliminated most of its political opponents when it took power in 1968. Since then, the government has restricted the political activity of anyone not belonging to the party or to allied parties. The government has done this partly through its secret police organization.

In September 1991, the government issued a law permitting the formation of opposition political parties. But restrictions in the law will probably prevent any significant challenge to the Baath Party's domination.

According to the Constitution, a president heads the Republic of Iraq and is commander of its armed forces. The president is elected to an indefinite term of office by the Revolutionary Command Council (RCC), which is made up of about 10 top officials of the Baath Party. The president chairs the RCC, and the RCC determines government policy. A Council of Ministers appointed by the president carries out government operations.

Iraq's legislature, the National Assembly, has 250 members. Adults over the age of 18 elect Assembly members to four-year terms. But the Baath Party controls elections through a government-appointed commission that determines who may run for the Assembly. In theory, the Assembly is authorized to either approve or reject RCC proposals. But in practice, the Assembly always approves such proposals.

Local government. Iraq has 18 provinces. The president appoints a governor for each province and a mayor for each Iraqi city. Three Kurdish provinces had limited self-rule as the Kurdish Autonomous Region from 1974 until 1991, when local government was suspended during the Persian Gulf War.

Courts. Iraq's judicial system consists of civil and religious courts and special security courts. Civil courts handle cases of civil, commercial, and criminal law. The religious courts deal primarily with family issues, such as divorce and inheritance. Special security courts prosecute individuals accused of crimes against the state. The president appoints members of the judiciary.

Armed forces. Iraq's armed forces consist of a large army and a smaller air force and navy. Before the Persian Gulf War, the Iraqi army was one of the largest in the world, with an estimated 955,000 troops. All men aged 18 and over must serve in Iraq's military for a period lasting from 21 to 24 months.

People

Population and ancestry. Iraq has about 18 million people. The country's population growth rate of about 3.5 per cent a year is one of the highest in the world. About three-fourths of Iraq's people live in a fertile plain that extends from Baghdad south along the Tigris and Euphrates rivers. This area has many of the largest cities and towns of Iraq.

Arabs make up about 75 per cent of Iraq's population. Approximately 20 per cent of the country's people belong to Iraq's largest ethnic minority, the Kurds. Other ethnic groups in Iraq include Armenians, Assyrians, Turkomans, and Yazidis.

Language. Iraq's official language is Arabic, which is spoken throughout the country. Kurdish, the language of the Kurds, is official in Kurdish areas.

City life. About 70 per cent of Iraq's people live in cities. The number of people living in urban areas has increased dramatically since the 1940's as a result of migration from rural areas. Many people have moved to the cities in search of work. Others fled rural villages and southern Iraqi cities that were heavily damaged in the 1980's during Iraq's war with Iran. Overflowing urban populations have resulted in severe unemployment and housing shortages in some cities.

Wealthy city dwellers work in business and government. Many of them live in the suburbs. People at middle-income levels earn a living as office workers, craftworkers, and owners of small businesses. Many of them reside in apartment buildings in the cities. A large number of laborers and factory and oil workers commute to jobs in Iraq's cities from homes in nearby villages.

Clothing styles vary in Iraq's cities. Middle-class and wealthy people generally wear Western-style clothing. Most laborers prefer traditional clothes. For men, these garments include long cotton gowns and jackets. Traditional dress for women consists of a long, concealing

Iraq's flag was adopted in 1991. The Arabic inscription on the white stripe means "God is great."

The coat of arms, adopted in 1965, has an eagle resembling a sculpture in the castle of Saladin, an Arab warrior.

Iraq lies in southwestern Asia. It is bordered by Turkey, Iran, the Persian Gulf, Kuwait, Saudi Arabia, Jordan, and Syria.

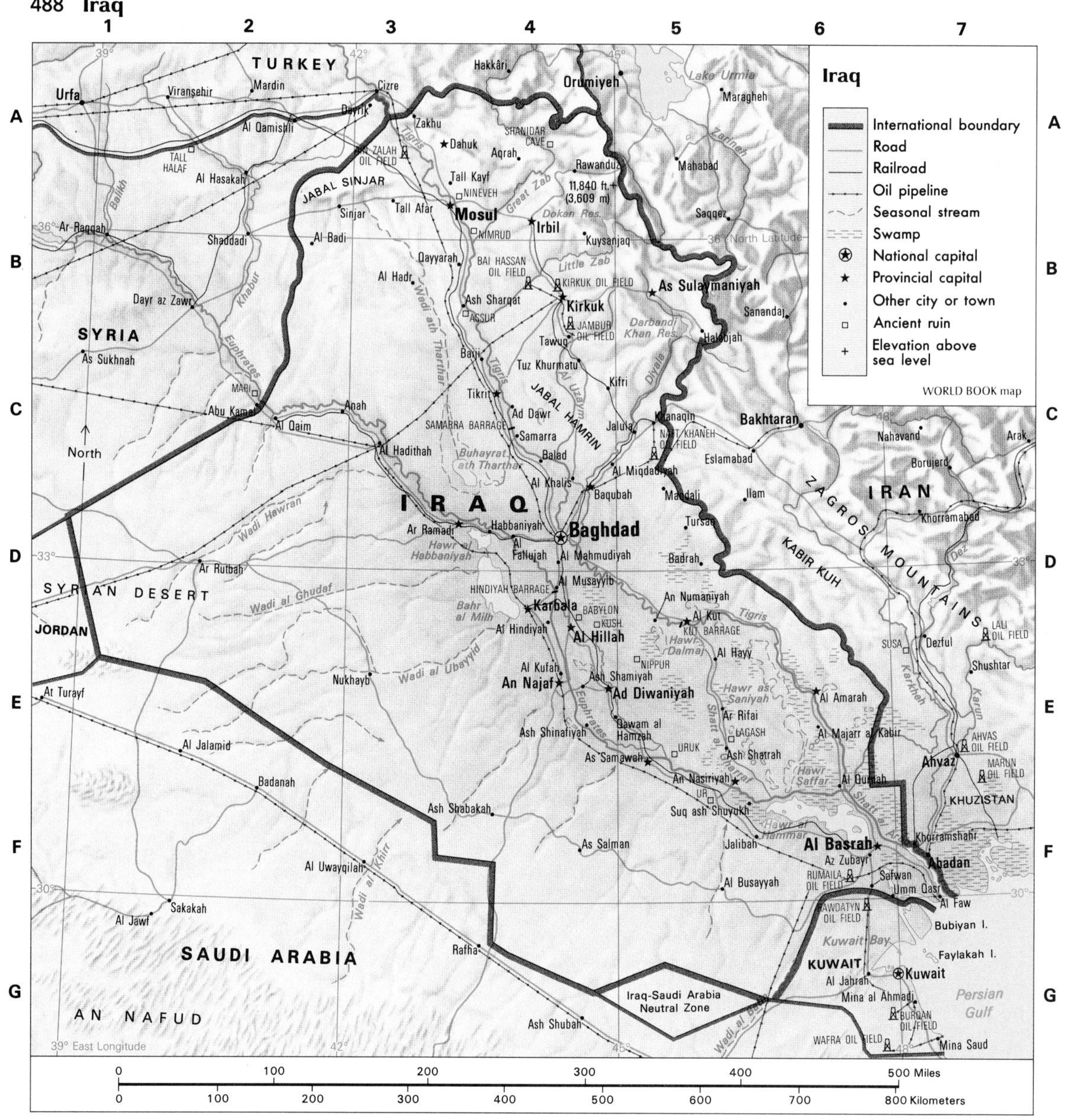

Iraq map index

Cities and towns

Abu al Khasib* ....12,681. .F 7
Abu Ghurayb ....10,554. .D 4
Ad Dawr ....C 4
Ad Diwaniyah ....239,000. .E 5
Al Amarah ......164,000. .E 6
Al Badi ....B 3
Al Basrah ....678,000. .F 6
Al Busayyah ....F 6
Al Fallujah ......174,000. .F 7
Al Faw ....27,000. .F 7
Al Hadithah ....6,849. .C 3
Al Hadr ....B 3
Al Harithah ....9,267. .F 6
Al Hayy ....41,000. .E 5
Al Hillah ....279,000. .D 4
Al Hindiyah ......41,000. .D 4
Al Khalis ....35,000. .C 4
Al Kufah ....30,531. .E 4
Al Kut ....141,000. .D 5
Al Mahmudiyah ....10,656. .D 4
Al Majarr al Kabir ....8,971. .E 6
Al Miqdadiyah ....31,000. .C 5
Al Musayyib .....39,000. .D 4
Al Qaim ....C 2
Al Qasim ....7,436. .E 5
Al Qurnah ....4,988. .F 6
An Najaf ....423,000. .E 4
An Nasiriyah ....191,000. .F 5
An Numaniyah ....29,000. .D 5
Anah ....5,620. .C 3
Aqrah ....8,671. .A 4
Ar Ramadi ......174,000. .D 3
Ar Rifai ....7,551. .E 5
Ar Rumaythah* ....10,433. .E 5
Ar Rutbah ....D 2
As Salman ....F 5
As Samawah .....77,000. .E 5
As Sulaymaniyah ......394,000. .B 5
Ash Shabakah ....F 4
Ash Shamiyah ......32,000. .E 6
Ash Sharqat ....B 4
Ash Shatrah ......46,000. .E 6
Ash Shinafiyah ......6,476. .E 4
Az Zubayr ....70,000. .D 4
Badrah ....D 5
Baghdad ......5,908,000. .D 4
Baiji ....7,042. .C 4
Balad ....34,000. .C 4
Baqubah ....165,000. .D 5
Dahuk ....42,000. .A 3
Habbaniyah ......48,000. .D 4
Halabjah ....11,250. .B 5
Irbil ....479,000. .B 4
Jalibah ....F 5
Jalula ....31,000. .C 5
Karbala ....237,000. .D 4
Khanaqin ....58,000. .C 5
Kifri ....8,267. .C 5
Kirkuk ....404,000. .B 4
Kuysanjaq ....10,379. .B 4
Mandali ....10,951. .D 5
Mosul ....748,000. .B 4
Nukhayb ....E 3
Qawam al Hamzah ....10,817. .E 5
Qayyarah ....B 3
Rawanduz ....5,411. .A 4
Safwan ....F 7
Samarra ....78,000. .C 4
Shatt al Arab* ....13,558. .F 6
Sinjar ....7,984. .B 3
Suq ash Shuyukh ....41,000. .F 5
Tall Afar ....104,000. .B 3
Tall Kayf ....7,381. .A 4
Tawuq ....B 4
Tikrit ....9,863. .C 4
Tursaq ....D 5
Tuz Khurmatu ......35,000. .C 4
Umm Qasr ....F 7
Zakhu ....36,000. .A 3

Physical features

Buhayrat ath Tharthar (lake) ....C 4
Euphrates River ....E 4
Great Zab River ....B 4
Hawr al Habbaniyah (lake) ......D 4
Hawr al Hammar (lake) ....F 6
Hawr as Saniyah (lake) ....E 6
Hindiyah Barrage ....D 4
Kut Barrage ....E 5
Little Zab River ....B 4
Nineveh (ruins) ....B 4
Persian Gulf ....G 7
Samarra Barrage ....C 3
Shatt al Arab River ....F 6
Syrian Desert ....D 1
Tigris River ....C 4
Wadi al Ubayyid (river) ....E 3

*Does not appear on map; key shows general location.

Sources: 1991 estimates from the Center for International Research of the Bureau of the Census for largest cities; latest available census (1965) for other places.

gown and a scarf that covers much of the head.

Rural life. About 30 per cent of Iraq's population lives in the countryside. Many of these people are villagers who farm for a living. Most farmers lease land from the government through companies that are largely government-owned. Herders form a small part of rural society. Bedouin *nomads* (wanderers) herd camels, goats, and sheep in western Iraq. Some Kurds graze livestock in northern Iraq.

Buildings in the rural areas of southern and central Iraq are made of dried mud and brick. In the north, villagers build stone houses.

Clothing in the countryside is traditional. Arab men wear gowns and checkered headdresses. Women dress in long black robes, and some veil their faces. Kurdish men wear shirts and baggy trousers with sashes. Kurdish women wear trousers but cover them with a dress.

Food and drink. Iraqis eat a varied diet that includes vegetables, rice, flat bread, meat, fish, and dates. Bread and rice are the main foods at many meals. Grilled lamb, chicken, and fish are popular. *Sanbusak,* a traditional Iraqi dish, consists of moon-shaped dough stuffed with cheese or meat. Popular beverages in Iraq include tea, coffee, and fruit juices.

Religion. About 95 per cent of Iraq's people are Muslims. More than half of the country's Muslims are Shiites (members of the Shiah branch of Islam). The other Muslims belong to the Sunni sect. Most Arabs living southeast of Baghdad are Shiites. Central and southwestern Iraq is a mixture of Sunni and Shiite Arab populations. The Kurds are Sunnis. Christians and other groups make up about 5 per cent of the Iraqi population. Most high-ranking members of Iraq's ruling Baath Party are Arab Sunni Muslims. Many Shiites resent the Sunni monopoly on governmental power.

Education. Children in Iraq must attend school until the age of 12. About 40 per cent of them continue their education in vocational or secondary schools. About 14 per cent of Iraqi adults from the ages of 20 to 24 attend colleges or universities. Iraq has universities in Al Basrah, Baghdad, Ibril, Mosul, and Tikrit. A higher percentage of men than women attend colleges in Iraq.

About 55 per cent of Iraq's adult population can read and write. The percentage is increasing as a result of government literacy programs.

The land

Iraq has four major land regions: (1) the northern plain, (2) the southern plain, (3) the mountains, and (4) the desert.

The northern plain, a region of dry, rolling land, lies between the Tigris and Euphrates rivers north of the city of Samarra. The highest hills in the area rise about 1,000 feet (300 meters) above sea level. There are a small number of farming villages in the northern plain.

The southern plain begins near Samarra and extends southeast to the Persian Gulf. It includes the fertile delta between the Tigris and Euphrates rivers, where a large number of Iraq's people live. The Tigris and Euphrates meet at the town of Al Qurnah and form the Shatt al Arab river, which empties into the gulf. Some of Iraq's major oil fields are located between the Shatt al Arab and the border with Kuwait.

Complex dam and irrigation systems control the flow of water in the southern plain. This control of water has increased agricultural productivity and allowed for more permanent human settlement, especially north of Al Kut. Much of the region south of Al Kut is swampland, due to frequent flooding and poor drainage.

The mountains of northeast Iraq are part of a range that is called the Zagros in Iran and the Taurus in Turkey. The mountains rise to more than 10,000 feet (3,000 meters) near Iraq's borders with Iran and Turkey. Kurds live in the region's foothills and valleys. Valuable oil fields lie near the cities of Mosul and Kirkuk.

The desert covers southwestern and western Iraq. Most of this region of limestone hills and sand dunes is part of the Syrian Desert, which stretches into Syria, Jordan, and Saudi Arabia. Scattered throughout the desert are *wadis*—valleys that are dry most of the year but become rivers after a rain.

Climate

Iraq's climate ranges from moderate in the north to semitropical in the east and southeast. The west and southwest have a desert climate—warm or hot days and much cooler nights. Summer high temperatures average more than 100 °F (38 °C) throughout much of Iraq. Winter low temperatures may drop to around 35 °F (2 °C) in the desert and in the north.

In general, little rain falls in Iraq. Average annual precipitation ranges from 5 inches (13 centimeters) of rain in the desert to 15 inches (38 centimeters) of rain and snow in the northern mountains. Most of the precipitation falls between November and April.

Economy

The export of oil has played a vital role in Iraq's economy since the 1950's. The government, which owns or controls most sectors of the economy, has used some of Iraq's oil income to improve living conditions in the country and to develop the agricultural sector. Iraq has tried to become less dependent on oil exports by expanding the rest of its industrial sector.

During the 1970's, Iraq's economy prospered under state control. But both the war with Iran and the Persian Gulf War greatly damaged the economy. Trade routes were disrupted, ports were closed, and factories were destroyed. In addition, the UN trade embargo of August 1990 halted all oil exports from Iraq.

Industry, which includes mining, manufacturing, and construction, accounts for 38 per cent of Iraq's gross domestic product (GDP). The GDP is the total value of all goods and services produced within a country in a year. Mining, manufacturing, and construction employ 33 per cent of Iraq's workers.

Oil is the chief mineral resource of Iraq. Iraq was once the second-largest producer of oil in the Middle East. In the early 1980's, the oil industry accounted for about 60 per cent of the country's GDP. But war damaged many of the country's oil reservoirs, pipelines, and refineries and interfered with the oil trade. Iraq's major oil fields are located in southern Iraq near the Kuwait border, and west of the city of Kirkuk in the north. Other natural resources mined in Iraq include phosphates, sulfur, and natural gas.

Until Iraq's refineries were damaged in the Persian Gulf War, the country's largest manufacturing industry

Superstock

Dry grazing land covers much of the northern plain of Iraq. The northern plain lies between the Tigris and Euphrates rivers north of the city of Samarra.

was oil refining and petrochemical production. Several of Iraq's chemical and oil plants are located near the cities of Al Basrah, Baiji, and Kirkuk. Other factories in Iraq process farm products or make such goods as cloth, soap, and beverages.

Service industries account for 46 per cent of Iraq's GDP. About 55 per cent of the country's workers have jobs in the service sector. The government employs about 25 per cent of the work force. Other major service industries in Iraq include banking and real estate.

Agriculture. Iraq was importing about 70 per cent of its food before the 1990 UN trade embargo. Agriculture accounts for 16 per cent of the GDP and employs about 12 per cent of Iraq's work force. The government has invested heavily in agriculture. But poor organization and a lack of labor and private investment have hampered growth. Major crops harvested in Iraq include barley, dates, grapes, rice, tomatoes, and wheat. Many farmers lease their land from the government.

Energy sources. Oil and natural gas are the main sources of energy in Iraq. Until the 1991 Persian Gulf War, electricity was available throughout most of the country.

Foreign trade. Before the 1990 UN trade embargo, oil accounted for most of Iraq's exports. Iraq's major imports included military weapons.

Transportation and communication. A government-owned airline links Baghdad with other major cities in Iraq and the Middle East and in Europe. Roads and railways connect Iraq's largest cities to one another. The country's largest port is Umm Qasr on the Persian Gulf. The shipping facilities at Al Basrah, once a major port, have been closed since Iraq's war with Iran. A large number of Iraqis depend on public transportation because they cannot afford automobiles. Over shorter distances in the cities, many people use bicycles. In the countryside, people often use buses, donkeys, and camels for transportation.

Six daily newspapers—four in Arabic, one in Kurdish, and one in English—are published in Iraq. About 1 out of every 15 Iraqis owns a television set. Many more people have radios. The government controls all radio and TV broadcasting that originates in Iraq, but Iraqis can pick up radio broadcasts from other countries.

History

Early days. The world's first known civilization developed in Sumer, now southeastern Iraq, about 3500 B.C. Sumer was part of Mesopotamia, an area that included most of present-day Iraq and parts of Syria and Turkey. Other ancient civilizations, including Assyria and Babylonia, flourished along the Tigris and Euphrates rivers between about 3500 and 539 B.C.

In 539 B.C., the Persians conquered Mesopotamia. Greek and Macedonian armies under Alexander the Great took the area from the Persians in 331 B.C. Greek rule continued until the Parthians, from Turkestan, took control in 126 B.C. Except for brief periods of Roman rule, the Parthians controlled Mesopotamia until A.D. 227. That year, the Persian Sassanid *dynasty* (family of rulers) seized Mesopotamia. The Sassanids ruled the region for about 400 years.

Arab rule. The birth of Islam in the A.D. 600's inspired Arab Muslims to conquer the Sassanids in 637. The Arabs brought the Arabic language and the new Islamic religion to Mesopotamia. In 752, the ruling Abbasid dynasty established the new capital of the Arab Empire near the small village of Baghdad. Under the Abbasids, Arab civilization reached great heights. By 800, Baghdad had grown into a city of more than 1 million people and had become a world center of trade and culture.

In 1258, Mongols from central Asia invaded Mesopotamia and destroyed the Arab Empire. The Mongols neglected Mesopotamia, and the region deteriorated culturally and economically under their rule.

Ottoman control. Ottoman Turks from central Asia seized Mesopotamia in 1534 and made it part of their empire. By the late 1600's, Ottoman control had weakened, and Arab leaders began to dominate local politics within Mesopotamia.

During the 1700's and 1800's, the Ottoman Empire declined in power and size in the face of new, strong nations that developed in Europe. Great Britain became involved in the Persian Gulf in the 1800's to protect its trade routes with India, which was then under British rule. By World War I (1914-1918), Britain had become interested in Mesopotamia's oil resources.

British rule. British troops took Mesopotamia from the Ottoman Turks during World War I. In 1920, the League of Nations, a forerunner to the United Nations, gave Britain a *mandate* (order to rule) over the area. The British set up a new government in Mesopotamia in 1921. They renamed the country Iraq and chose an Arab prince as King Faisal I.

During the 1920's, British advisers retained positions in the Iraqi government, and the British controlled Iraq's army, foreign policy, finances, and oil resources. Some Iraqis opposed British involvement, and a movement for independence developed.

Independence. Under pressure from Iraq's independence movement, Great Britain signed a treaty with Iraq in 1930. In the treaty, Britain promised military protection and eventual independence for Iraq. In return, Iraq promised Britain continued use of British air bases in Iraq. It also agreed to use foreign advisers from Britain only. The British mandate over Iraq ended in 1932, and Iraq became an independent nation.

In the 1930's, Iraq's politicians disagreed over the alliance with Great Britain. King Faisal worked to balance the interests of Iraq's political factions and to unify the country's various ethnic and religious groups. Faisal died in 1933. His son Ghazi became king. Ghazi was a weak ruler, and tribal and ethnic rebellions broke out. In 1936, anti-British groups in the army took control of the government, though Ghazi officially was still king. Ghazi died in an automobile accident in 1939. His 3-year-old son, Faisal II, became king, but the boy's uncle, Prince Abdul Ilah, ruled for him.

In 1940 and 1941, during World War II, Iraqi government leaders and army officers sought an alliance with the Axis powers—Germany, Italy, and Japan—in an attempt to end British influence in Iraq. Britain attempted to use Iraq as a military base under the provisions of the 1930 treaty, and an armed conflict broke out. The British defeated the Iraqi army in 1941, and the pro-Axis leaders left the country.

Iraq declared war on the Axis in 1943. Inflation and supply shortages brought on by World War II transformed Iraq's society and economy. A wide economic gap developed between the rich and poor. Many blamed the government for their economic situation.

Iraq helped found the Arab League, an association of Arab nations, in 1945. In 1948, Iraq joined other members of the league in a war against the newly created nation of Israel. The defeat of the Arabs touched off demonstrations in Iraq and other Arab countries.

The 1950's. In 1950 and 1952, the government of Iraq signed new agreements with foreign oil companies. The 1952 agreement gave Iraq 50 per cent of the profits from oil drilled there. As a result of these agreements, Iraq's oil revenues rose dramatically. The government used some of this money to build hospitals, irrigation projects, roads, and schools. But the increased amount of money coming into Iraq also caused serious inflation.

Important dates in Iraq

3500 B.C. The world's first known civilization developed in Mesopotamia, now Iraq.

539 B.C. The Persians conquered Mesopotamia.

331 B.C. Alexander the Great seized Mesopotamia.

A.D. 227 The Sassanid dynasty of Persia conquered Mesopotamia.

637 Arab Muslims overthrew the Sassanids.

1258 The Mongols invaded Mesopotamia.

1534 Ottoman Turks seized Mesopotamia.

1920 The League of Nations gave Britain a *mandate* (order to rule) over Mesopotamia.

1932 The British mandate ended, and Iraq became independent.

1958 Army officers overthrew the Iraqi government and declared the country a republic.

1968 The Baath Party took control of Iraq's government.

1973 The Iraqi government completed its take-over of foreign oil companies in Iraq.

1980 Iraq declared war on Iran.

1988 Iraq and Iran agreed to a cease-fire.

1990 Iraq invaded Kuwait.

1991 A coalition of 39 nations, including the United States and Canada, defeated Iraq in the Persian Gulf War.

Faisal II took full power in 1953 at the age of 18. During the 1950's, opposition to the monarchy grew steadily. Many Iraqis wanted a voice in government, and others felt that they had not benefited enough from the country's oil profits.

In addition, a large number of Iraqis opposed the government's ties to the West. In particular, they objected to the Baghdad Pact—a British-supported mutual defense agreement the Iraqi government signed with Iran, Pakistan, and Turkey in 1955. Many Iraqis also felt that the government's ties with the West went against the political movement called *Pan-Arabism.* Advocates of Pan-Arabism believed that Arab countries should strive for political unity and be free of outside influence. In 1958, army officers overthrew the government and declared Iraq a republic. The rebels killed King Faisal and Prince Abdul Ilah.

The republic. The army officers set up a three-man Sovereignty Council consisting of a Shiite Arab, a Kurd, and a Sunni Arab. The council issued a temporary constitution giving a cabinet the power to rule by decree with the council's approval. General Abdul Karim Kassem (also spelled Qasim), who led the revolution, became Iraq's premier. He reversed Iraq's pro-West policy and accepted both economic and military aid from Communist countries. Kassem set up land reform programs aimed at narrowing the gap between rich and poor. He also worked to develop industry in Iraq.

In 1961, Kurdish leaders asked Kassem to give the Kurds complete *autonomy* (self-government) within Iraq and a share of the revenues from oil fields in northern Iraq. Kassem rejected the plan. In response, the Kurds revolted. A cease-fire was finally declared in 1964.

In 1963, army officers and members of the Baath Party assassinated Kassem. The Baath Party took control of the country and named Abdul Salam Arif president and Ahmed Hasan al-Bakr prime minister. Both were army officers. Later that year, Arif used the military to take over the government. Arif died in 1966, and his brother, Abdul Rahman Arif, became president.

Al-Bakr overthrew Arif in 1968 and reestablished Baath control. The Baath Party quickly began to dominate all aspects of Iraqi politics. Party leaders wrote a new constitution in 1970 that institutionalized the party's control of the government. Al-Bakr supported further socialist economic reform and stronger ties with the Soviet Union. During al-Bakr's presidency, Saddam Hussein, who held important party and government posts, gained influence within the government.

In 1973, the Iraqi government completed a take-over of foreign oil companies in the country. After oil prices increased later that year, Iraq made huge profits.

In 1970, al-Bakr signed an agreement with the Kurds ending eight years of on-and-off fighting. In the agreement, the government promised that beginning in 1974 the Kurds would have self-rule and several positions in the government. New fighting erupted in 1974, after the Kurds objected to revisions in the agreement. The revised agreement established limited autonomy for the Kurds in the Kurdish Autonomous Region in northern Iraq. Government forces had largely defeated the Kurds by March 1975, when a cease-fire was declared. But fighting between Kurds and government forces has continued since then.

Oliver Rebbot, Woodfin Camp, Inc.

Iraqi soldiers drive past government officials, including President Saddam Hussein, *arm upraised.* Before the 1991 Persian Gulf War, Iraq had the fourth-largest army in the world.

Al-Bakr resigned the presidency in 1979. Saddam Hussein succeeded him as president.

War with Iran. In September 1980, Iraq invaded Iran, and war broke out between the two countries. The war resulted in part from boundary disputes, from Iran's support for the rebellious Kurds, and from the efforts of Shiite leaders in Iran to incite rebellion in Iraq's Shiite population. In addition, Iraqi leaders believed Iran had become somewhat unstable as a result of its 1979 revolution. They felt Iran's weakened position offered Iraq an opportunity to increase its power in the region.

The war lasted eight years. An estimated 150,000 Iraqi soldiers died, and Iranian air attacks on major cities wounded and killed many of Iraq's civilians. The war also severely damaged Iraq's economy. Bombs damaged oil facilities in southern Iraq, and trade through the Persian Gulf was disrupted. Iraq and Iran finally agreed on a cease-fire in August 1988.

During the war with Iran, Iraq's Kurds supported Iran against the Iraqi government. In 1987 and 1988, the Iraqi government lashed out against the Kurds. The army released poison gas in Kurdish villages, killing thousands of people. There also were reports that the army destroyed several Kurdish towns and that the inhabitants fled to Turkey and Iran.

Tom Stoddart, Katz Pictures from Woodfin Camp, Inc.

Kurdish refugees fled their homes in Iraq in 1991. Many Kurds sought safety in Turkey, Iran, or Iraq's mountains after Iraqi troops put down a Kurdish rebellion that year.

The Persian Gulf War. In August 1990, Iraqi forces invaded and occupied Kuwait. Before the invasion, Hussein had accused Kuwait of violating oil production limits set by the Organization of Petroleum Exporting Countries (OPEC), thus lowering the worldwide price of oil. In addition, Iraq and Kuwait had disagreed over territory and over Iraq's multibillion dollar debt to Kuwait. The UN called for Iraq to withdraw from Kuwait and passed a resolution stating that all nations should stop trading with Iraq, except for food and medical supplies under certain circumstances. A coalition of 39 countries, including the United States and Canada, opposed the invasion and sent military forces to the Persian Gulf region. A number of coalition members stationed troops in Saudi Arabia to defend that country against a possible Iraqi invasion.

In November 1990, the UN Security Council approved the use of force to remove Iraqi troops from Kuwait if they did not leave by Jan. 15, 1991. Iraq refused to withdraw, and war broke out between the allied forces and Iraq early on January 17 Baghdad time (January 16 U.S. time). The United States and its allies bombed Iraqi military targets in Iraq and Kuwait. Iraq launched missiles against Saudi Arabia and Israel. On February 24 (February 23 in the United States), allied land forces began moving into Iraq and Kuwait. They defeated the Iraqi army after 100 hours of fighting. On February 27 U.S. time (February 28 in the war area), U.S. President George Bush declared a halt to all allied military operations.

The Persian Gulf War had a devastating effect on Iraq. An estimated 100,000 Iraqi soldiers were killed in the war, and thousands of civilians also died. Allied air raids destroyed roads, bridges, factories, and oil industry facilities and disrupted electric, telephone, and water service. Diseases spread through contaminated drinking water because water purification and sewage treatment facilities could not operate without electricity. In addition, the trade embargo caused serious economic problems in Iraq.

Recent developments. In March 1991, Kurdish and Shiite uprisings broke out. By April, government troops had put down the rebellions, and refugees flooded across the borders into Iran and Turkey. Allied forces transported supplies to the refugees and set up a safety zone in northern Iraq to protect the Kurds. The UN helped administer the safety zone. The last allied troops left the region in mid-July. The Kurds began negotiations with Hussein for greater Kurdish self-rule in Iraq.

Iraq accepted the terms of a formal cease-fire agreement on April 6. On April 11, the UN Security Council officially declared an end to the war. In the cease-fire agreement, Iraq promised to pay Kuwait for war damages. Iraq also agreed to the destruction of all its biological and chemical weapons, its facilities for producing such weapons, and any facilities or materials it might have for producing nuclear weapons. After the formal cease-fire, the UN continued the embargo to pressure Iraq to carry out its agreements.

In September 1991, under the terms of the cease-fire agreement, the UN Security Council sent a team of experts to Iraq to assess Iraq's ability to produce nuclear weapons. The team found evidence that Iraq's program to develop such weapons was much more advanced than had previously been believed. Michel Le Gall

© David Redfern, Retna

The Count Basie Band

© John Bellissimo, LGI

The Modern Jazz Quartet

© Gary Gershoff, Retna

Pianist Marcus Roberts

Jazz is a popular kind of music that originated in America. It may be performed by a large group called a big band, *top;* a small group called a combo, *above left;* or a soloist, *above right.*

Jazz

Jazz is a kind of music that has often been called the only art form to originate in the United States. The history of jazz began in the late 1800's. The music grew from a combination of influences, including black American music, African rhythms, American band traditions and instruments, and European harmonies and forms. Much of the best jazz is still written and performed in the United States. But musicians from many other countries are making major contributions to jazz. Jazz was actually widely appreciated as an important art form in Europe before it gained such recognition in the United States.

One of the key elements of jazz is *improvisation*—the ability to create new music spontaneously. This skill is the distinguishing characteristic of the genuine jazz musician. Improvisation raises the role of the soloist from just a performer and reproducer of others' ideas to a composer as well. And it gives jazz a fresh excitement at each performance.

The contributor of this article is Frank Tirro, Professor of Music at Yale University and the author of Jazz: A History.

Another important element of jazz is *syncopation.* To syncopate their music, jazz musicians take patterns that are even and regular and break them up, make them uneven, and put accents in unexpected places.

The earliest jazz was performed by black Americans who had little or no training in Western music. These musicians drew on a strong musical culture from black life. As jazz grew in popularity, its sound was influenced by musicians with formal training and classical backgrounds. During its history, jazz has absorbed influences from the folk and classical music of Africa, Asia, and other parts of the world. The development of instruments with new and different characteristics has also influenced the sound of jazz.

The sound of jazz

Jazz may be performed by a single musician, by a small group of musicians called a *combo,* or by a *big band* of 10 or more pieces. A combo is divided into two sections: a solo front line of melody instruments and a back line of accompanying instruments called a *rhythm section.* The typical front line consists of one to five brass and reed instruments. The rhythm section usually consists of piano, bass, drums, and sometimes an acoustic or electric guitar. The front-line instruments perform most of the solos. These instruments may also play together as ensembles. A big band consists of reed, brass, and rhythm sections.

The rhythm section in a combo or big band maintains the steady beat and decorates the rhythm with syncopated patterns. It also provides the formal structure to support solo improvisations. The drums keep the beat steady and add interesting rhythm patterns and syncopations. The piano—or sometimes a guitar—plays the chords or harmonies of the composition in a rhythmic manner. The bass outlines the harmonies by sounding the *roots,* or bottom pitches, of the chords, on the strong beats of each measure. Any of the rhythm instruments, especially the piano, may also solo during a performance.

The brass. The principal brass instruments of jazz are the trumpet, the cornet, and the slide trombone. But the French horn, the valve trombone, the baritone horn, the flügelhorn, and even electronic trumpets have been used in jazz performances.

The cornet and trumpet are melody instruments of identical range. But the cornet is usually considered more mellow and the trumpet more brassy. Most jazz performers today use the trumpet. The slide trombone blends with the trumpet. The typical brass section of a big band consists of four or five trumpets and three trombones.

Jazz trumpeters and trombonists frequently use objects called *mutes* to alter or vary the sound of their instrument. The player plugs the mute into the *bell* (flared end) of the instrument or holds it close to the opening of the bell.

The reeds. The clarinet and saxophone are the principal reed instruments of jazz. The flute, though technically a woodwind, is often classified as a reed in jazz. It is used especially as a solo instrument.

Both the clarinet and saxophone families range from soprano to bass. Only the soprano clarinet has been universally used in jazz. In early jazz, it was an equal member of the front line with the trumpet or cornet and the trombone. The clarinet eventually gave way to the saxophone, which is capable of much greater volume. Four members of the saxophone family—the soprano, alto, tenor, and baritone saxophones—are regularly employed in jazz. A typical reed section in a big band is made up of one or two alto saxophones, two tenors, and a baritone. Musicians often "double" by playing two or more reed instruments, such as an alto saxophone and a tenor saxophone, during a performance.

Duncan P. Schiedt

A traditional jazz band consists of a *front line* of a trumpet, trombone, and clarinet or saxophone, and a *rhythm section* of drums, a bass, a piano, and often a guitar or banjo. Jelly Roll Morton, *at the piano,* led this 1920's jazz group.

Drums of various types were familiar to black Americans dating back to the days of slavery. These early percussion instruments played a vital role in the development of jazz.

As jazz grew, the drum set evolved until one drummer could play more than one percussion instrument at the same time. The invention of a foot-operated bass-drum pedal and pedal-operated cymbals freed the drummer's hands to play other percussion instruments, such as snare drums, tom-toms, cowbells, and wood blocks. Another important invention was a wire brush that the drummer used in place of a drumstick or mallet to produce a more delicate sound on drums and cymbals. Today, a jazz drummer may use electronic percussion instruments that can create an almost infinite variety of sounds and reproduce them accurately at virtually any volume.

The piano. Since the earliest days of jazz, the piano has served both as a solo instrument and as an ensemble instrument that performs as part of the rhythm section. Today, other keyboard instruments, including electronic organs, electric pianos, and synthesizers controlled by a keyboard, may substitute for pianos.

The guitar, like the piano, is capable of playing both chords and melodies. In the early days of jazz, these two instruments, along with the banjo, were often substituted for one another. Later, however, the guitar and banjo were most often used in the rhythm section in addition to the piano. The banjo eventually disappeared from almost all later forms of jazz. Jazz musicians have used the acoustic guitar in ensembles and as a solo instrument since jazz's earliest days. The electric guitar emerged in jazz in the late 1930's to add sustained tones, greater volume, and a new assortment of sounds and effects to jazz.

The bass plays the roots of the harmonies. The musician normally plucks a string bass. The rhythm section may substitute a brass bass, such as a tuba or Sousaphone. When an electronic organ is used, the organist can play the bass part with foot pedals on the instrument. Electric bass guitars have been incorporated into some jazz ensembles, primarily those that play a "fusion" of jazz and rock music.

Other instruments. Nearly every Western musical instrument and many non-Western instruments have been used in jazz at one time or another. The *vibraphone,* an instrument similar to the xylophone, and the violin deserve special mention. The vibraphone has been especially popular in combos. The violin has had only a few notable soloists in jazz, possibly because its volume could not match the power of the trumpet or trombone in ensemble. But throughout jazz history there have been some violinists who have skillfully adapted this basically classical music instrument to jazz. Modern amplification and sound manipulation devices have given the violin new and exciting possibilities as a jazz instrument.

The history of jazz

The roots of jazz. The folk songs and plantation dance music of black Americans contributed much to early jazz. These forms of music occurred throughout the Southern United States during the late 1800's.

Ragtime, a musical style that influenced early jazz, emerged from the St. Louis, Mo., area in the late 1890's. It quickly became the most popular music style in the United States. Ragtime was an energetic and syncopated variety of music, primarily for the piano, that emphasized formal composition.

The blues is a form of music that has always been an important part of jazz. The blues was especially widespread in the American South. Its mournful scale and simple repeated harmonies helped shape the character of jazz. Jazz instrumentalists have long exploited the blues as a vehicle for improvisation.

Early jazz. Fully developed jazz music probably originated in New Orleans at the beginning of the 1900's. New Orleans style jazz emerged from the city's own musical traditions of band music for black funeral processions and street parades. Today, this type of jazz is sometimes called classic jazz, traditional jazz, or Dixieland jazz. New Orleans was the musical home of the first notable players and composers of jazz, including cornetists Buddy Bolden and King Oliver, cornetist and trumpeter Louis Armstrong, saxophonist and clarinetist Sidney Bechet, and pianist Jelly Roll Morton.

Jazz soon spread from New Orleans to other parts of the country. Fate Marable led a New Orleans band that played on riverboats traveling up and down the Mississippi River. King Oliver migrated to Chicago, and Jelly Roll Morton performed throughout the United States. Five white musicians formed a band in New Orleans, played in Chicago, and traveled to New York City, calling themselves the Original Dixieland Jass Band (the spelling was soon changed to "Jazz"). This group made the earliest jazz phonograph recordings in 1917. Mamie Smith recorded "Crazy Blues" in 1920, and recordings of ragtime, blues, and jazz of various kinds soon popularized the music to a large and eager public.

The 1920's have been called *the golden age of jazz* or *the jazz age.* Commercial radio stations, which first appeared in the 1920's, featured live performances by the growing number of jazz musicians. New Orleans, Memphis, St. Louis, Kansas City, Chicago, Detroit, and New York City were all important centers of jazz.

A group of Midwest youths, many from Chicago's Austin High School, developed a type of improvisation and arrangement that became known as "Chicago style" jazz. These musicians included trumpeters Jimmy McPartland and Muggsy Spanier; cornetist Bix Beiderbecke; clarinetists Frank Teschemacher, Pee Wee Russell, Mezz Mezzrow, and Benny Goodman; saxophonists Frankie Trumbauer and Bud Freeman; drummers Dave Tough, George Wettling, and Gene Krupa; and guitarist Eddie Condon. They played harmonically inventive music, and the technical ability of some of the players, especially Goodman, was at a higher level than that of many earlier performers.

In New York City, James P. Johnson popularized a new musical style from ragtime called *stride piano.* In stride piano, the left hand plays alternating single notes and chords that move up and down the scale while the right hand plays solo melodies, accompanying rhythms, and interesting chordal passages. Johnson strongly influenced other jazz pianists, notably Count Basie, Duke Ellington, Art Tatum, Fats Waller, and Teddy Wilson.

From the collection of Dr. Edmond Souchon

Bix Beiderbecke, *second from right,* was one of the first famous jazz musicians. Beiderbecke, a cornet player, made some of the earliest important jazz recordings with a group called the Wolverines, *above,* in a warehouse recording studio in 1924.

Fletcher Henderson was the first major figure in big band jazz. In 1923, he became the first leader to organize a jazz band into sections of brass, reed, and rhythm instruments. His arranger, Don Redman, was the first to master the technique of scoring music for big bands. Various Henderson bands of the 1920's and 1930's included such great jazz instrumentalists as Louis Armstrong and saxophonists Benny Carter and Coleman Hawkins.

Armstrong made some of his most famous recordings with his own Hot Five and Hot Seven combos from 1925 to 1928. These recordings rank among the masterpieces of jazz, along with his duo recordings of the same period with pianist Earl "Fatha" Hines. Armstrong also became the first well-known male jazz singer, and

UPI/Bettmann

Duke Ellington, *at the piano,* has been called the single most significant person in the history of jazz. He led a band almost continuously from the early 1920's until his death in 1974.

Down Beat Magazine

Benny Goodman, *third from left,* was a leading bandleader and clarinet player of the swing era. He also formed several notable small groups. This sextet included two musicians who were pioneers on their instruments—vibraphonist Lionel Hampton and electric guitarist Charlie Christian. Goodman was one of the first white musicians to integrate his band.

popularized *scat singing*—that is, wordless syllables sung in an instrumental manner.

During the late 1920's and early 1930's, jazz advanced from relatively simple music played by performers who often could not read music to a more complex and sophisticated form. Among the musicians who brought about this change were saxophonists Benny Carter, Coleman Hawkins, and Johnny Hodges; the team of violinist Joe Venuti and guitarist Eddie Lang; and pianist Art Tatum. Many people consider Tatum the most inspired and technically gifted improviser in jazz history.

The swing era flourished from the mid-1930's to the mid-1940's. In 1932, Duke Ellington recorded his composition "It Don't Mean a Thing If It Ain't Got That Swing." "Swing" was soon adopted as the name of the newest style of jazz. Swing emphasizes four beats to the bar. Big bands dominated the swing era, especially those of Count Basie, Benny Goodman, and Duke Ellington.

Benny Goodman became known as the "King of Swing." Starting in 1934, Goodman's bands and combos brought swing to nationwide audiences through ballroom performances, recordings, and radio broadcasts. Goodman was the first white bandleader to feature black and white musicians playing together in public performances. In 1936, he introduced two great black soloists—pianist Teddy Wilson and vibraphonist Lionel Hampton. Until then, racial segregation had held back the progress of jazz and of black musicians in particular. In 1938, Goodman and his band, and several guest musicians, performed a famous concert at Carnegie Hall in New York City. Their performance was one of the first by jazz musicians in a concert hall setting.

Other major bands of the swing era included those led by Benny Carter, Bob Crosby, Jimmy Dorsey, Tommy Dorsey, Woody Herman, Earl Hines, Andy Kirk, Jimmie Lunceford, Glenn Miller, Artie Shaw, Chick Webb, and, toward the end of the period, Stan Kenton. The bands in Kansas City, Mo., especially the Count Basie band, had a distinctive swing style. These bands relied on the 12-bar blues form and *riff* backgrounds, which consisted of repeated simple melodies. They depended less heavily on written arrangements, allowing more leeway for rhythmic drive and for extended solo improvisations.

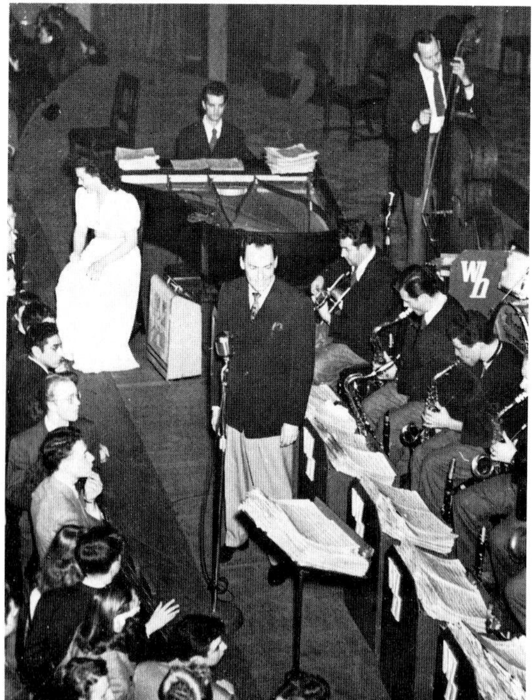

Down Beat Magazine

Woody Herman was a popular bandleader for more than 40 years. Many musicians who joined his band later became noted soloists with their own groups. One of the most famous was tenor saxophonist Stan Getz, seated next to the guitar player.

Boogie-woogie was another jazz form that became popular during the 1930's. Chiefly a piano style, it used eight beats to the bar instead of four. Boogie-woogie featured the traditional blues pattern for most themes. The music had an intense quality that created excitement through the repetition of a single phrase. Albert Ammons, Pete Johnson, Meade Lux Lewis, and Pinetop Smith were among its most important artists.

Jazz vocalists came into prominence during the swing era, many singing with big bands. Many fine jazz singers emphasized popular songs. These singers included Mildred Bailey, Ella Fitzgerald, Billie Holiday, Nat "King" Cole, Carmen McRae, and Sarah Vaughan. Blues singing at its best can be heard in recordings by Jimmy Rushing, Jack Teagarden, Joe Turner, and Dinah Washington. In addition to singing, Nat "King" Cole was a superb jazz pianist and Jack Teagarden was a great jazz trombonist.

Duncan P. Schiedt

Bebop revolutionized jazz in the 1940's. Alto saxophonist Charlie Parker, *left,* was a leader in the movement. He teamed with trumpeter Miles Davis, *right,* in an important bebop combo.

Bebop. In the early 1940's, a group of young musicians began experimenting with more complicated chord patterns and melodic ideas in a combo setting. The group included trumpeter Dizzy Gillespie, alto saxophonist Charlie Parker, pianists Bud Powell and Thelonious Monk, and drummers Kenny Clarke and Max Roach. The style they developed became known as *bebop* or *bop.*

Most bop musicians had an exceptional technique. They played long, dazzling phrases with many notes, difficult intervals, unexpected breaks, and unusual turns in melodic direction. On slower tunes, they displayed a keen ear for subtle changes of harmony. Only extremely skilled musicians were able to play bebop well, and only sophisticated listeners at first appreciated it.

In bebop performances, musicians usually played an intricate melody, followed with long periods of solo improvisation, and restated the theme at the end. The bassist presented the basic beat for the group by plucking a steady, moving bass line. The drummer elaborated the beat with sticks or brushes on cymbals, snare drum, and tom-tom. The bass drum was reserved for unexpected accents called "bombs." The pianist inserted complex chords at irregular intervals to suggest, rather than state, the complete harmonies of the piece.

Hard bop. Bebop was followed in the 1950's by *hard bop,* or *funky,* jazz. This form emphasized some of the traditional values of jazz derived from gospel and blues music, including rhythmic drive, uninhibited tone and volume, and freedom from restricting arrangements. The hard bop leaders were drummer Art Blakey and pianist Horace Silver. Blakey led a combo called the Jazz Messengers from the mid-1950's until his death in 1990. The Jazz Messengers served as a training ground for many of the greatest soloists in jazz history. Trumpeter Clifford Brown and drummer Max Roach were coleaders of another outstanding hard bop combo.

Cool jazz originated in the works of such musicians as tenor saxophonist Lester Young, who starred with Count Basie, and guitarist Charlie Christian, who played with Benny Goodman. In the late 1930's and early 1940's, these musicians made changes in the sound and style of jazz improvisation. For example, they softened the tones of their instruments, used syncopation more subtly, and played with a more even beat.

In 1948, tenor saxophonist Stan Getz recorded a slow, romantic solo of Ralph Burns's composition "Early Autumn" with the Woody Herman band. This work profoundly influenced many younger musicians. In 1949 and 1950, a group of young musicians that included trumpeter Miles Davis, alto saxophonist Lee Konitz, baritone saxophonist Gerry Mulligan, and arranger Gil Evans recorded several new compositions. These recordings emphasized a lagging beat, soft instrumental sounds, and unusual orchestrations that included the first successful use of the French horn and the tuba in modern jazz. The recordings, with Davis as leader, were later released as "The Birth of the Cool."

During the 1950's, many combos became identified with the cool movement. Some of the most successful combos were the Gerry Mulligan Quartet, the Modern Jazz Quartet, and the Dave Brubeck Quartet.

The spread of jazz. In the 1940's and 1950's, the sophisticated forms of bebop and cool jazz began to gain wide acceptance among intellectuals and college students. Jazz concerts became popular. Groups of jazz stars made a series of international tours called Jazz at the Philharmonic. The international growth of jazz resulted in many successful overseas tours by U.S. bands and combos.

The introduction of the $33\frac{1}{3}$ rpm long-playing (LP) record, which was first produced commercially in 1948, also helped spread the popularity of jazz. For 30 years, jazz recordings had been limited to 78 rpm records that

Culver

Louis Armstrong was probably the most popular jazz artist in history. The trumpeter and singer appeared in several motion pictures, including the 1950 film *High Society, above.*

Culver

Dave Brubeck, a classically trained pianist, led one of the most popular jazz quartets of the 1950's. The combo featured the lyrical solos of alto saxophonist Paul Desmond.

restricted performances to about 3 minutes in length. The LP allowed recorded performances to run many minutes. The LP also permitted a number of shorter performances to be issued on a single record.

During the 1950's, musicians in other countries began to improve greatly as jazz performers as they were exposed to performances by American musicians through recordings and concerts. Sweden, France, Germany, Japan, and other countries developed players and composers whose work compared favorably with that of the leading Americans. The first foreign jazz musicians to influence Americans were Belgian-born guitarist Django Reinhardt in the late 1930's, and George Shearing, a blind, English-born pianist who immigrated to the United States in 1947.

In 1954, the first large American jazz festival was held at Newport, R.I. Since then, annual festivals also have been held in Monterey, Calif.; New York City; Chicago; Nice, France; Montreux, Switzerland; Warsaw, Poland; Berlin, Germany; and many other locations throughout the world. These festivals have featured almost all of the most popular jazz musicians and have introduced many extended concert works by Duke Ellington, Billy Strayhorn, John Lewis, and others.

The U.S. government began to use jazz as an instrument of international good will in 1956. The U.S. Department of State sponsored tours of the Near and Middle East and Latin America by a big band led by Dizzy Gillespie. In 1962, Benny Goodman toured the Soviet Union as part of a cultural exchange program.

New directions. Beginning in the 1950's, jazz became even more experimental. Jazz music began to feature nontraditional instruments, such as French horn and bass flute. Jazz musicians began to take an interest in non-Western music, especially the *modes* (different arrangements of scales), melodic forms, and instruments of Africa, India, and the Far East.

In the late 1950's, John Lewis, musical director of the Modern Jazz Quartet, worked with classical musician and composer Gunther Schuller to write and play orchestral works that combined elements of modern jazz and classical concert music. Stan Kenton also played this so-called *third stream music* when he toured the United States with a 40-piece orchestra.

Also during this period, pianist George Russell developed a jazz theory of modes. In 1959, the Miles Davis combo, with pianist Bill Evans and saxophonists John Coltrane and Cannonball Adderley, recorded compositions and improvised solos based on modes rather than on patterns of chords.

In 1960, saxophonist Ornette Coleman reshaped the thinking of younger jazz musicians when he recorded the album *Free Jazz* with a double quartet. In this recording, Coleman discarded harmony, melody, and regular rhythms. He substituted unstructured improvisation played *atonally* (in no definite key). Pianist Cecil Taylor and bassist Charles Mingus conducted similar atonal experiments.

In the 1960's, the influence of the music of India entered jazz through the adaptations of John Coltrane. Jazz musicians also began to use more unusual meters, such as $\frac{5}{4}$, $\frac{7}{4}$ and $\frac{9}{8}$.

Fusion. In the 1970's, many musicians blended jazz and rock music into *fusion jazz.* Fusion combined the melodic and improvisational aspects of jazz with the rhythms and instruments of rock. Electronic music played an important part in fusion. Jazz pianists began exploring the increased sound potential of synthesizers. Horn and string players began to use electronics to intensify, distort, or multiply their sounds. Many well-known jazz musicians gained new popularity by playing fusion. Some of the best-known fusion musicians were guitarist George Benson, trumpeters Donald Byrd and

© John Bellissimo, LGI

Fusion, a form of jazz with rock rhythms, became popular in the 1970's. Miles Davis, *third from right,* who earlier pioneered in bebop and cool jazz, has led several successful fusion combos.

Miles Davis, pianist Herbie Hancock, and two combos, Weather Report and the Mahavishnu Orchestra.

At the same time, many veteran jazz musicians retained their popularity by leading groups that played in the swing, bebop, and cool styles. These leaders included Stan Getz, Dizzy Gillespie, Woody Herman, Gerry Mulligan, and Oscar Peterson.

The late 1900's. During the 1980's, several young jazz musicians returned to *mainstream* jazz, which includes elements of the swing, cool, and bebop styles. The most widely acclaimed young musician of the 1980's was trumpeter Wynton Marsalis, a performer of both jazz and classical music. Marsalis plays with brilliant technique and tone. He and his brother, saxophonist Branford Marsalis, have led excellent hard bop combos.

Many young musicians continued to forge ahead with fusion groups. Two of the most widely respected fusion artists are the brothers trumpeter Randy Brecker and saxophonist Michael Brecker. Jane Ira Bloom displays a mastery of the soprano saxophone and the synthesizer.

In the 1980's, some so-called *New Wave* musicians adopted *minimalism,* a style that often repeats simple patterns for long periods of time. Trombonist George Lewis has experimented with combinations of free jazz, synthesized sound, African rhythms, and unusual horn techniques. Another trombonist of dazzling technique is Ray Anderson. Bebop, rock, popular, free, and various mixtures are all blended in his recordings. One group, the World Saxophone Quartet, omitted the rhythm section while preserving most of the other traditional rhythmic, harmonic, and melodic elements of jazz.

Today, jazz continues to feature a variety of styles. Most experimental jazz is being produced by a few of the older masters. Miles Davis involves himself as much with the studio production of synthesized, mixed, and spliced sounds as with his trumpet playing. The Art Ensemble of Chicago blends free jazz, African costumes and makeup, exotic instruments, and surprise techniques into theatrical musical events. Ornette Coleman's group, Prime Time, mixes free and fusion jazz in new and interesting ways.

© Paul Merideth, TSW/Click/Chicago

Jazz festivals, such as this one in Chicago, draw huge audiences. Such festivals have helped to spread the popularity of jazz both within the United States and internationally.

Electronics technology is gaining a greater role in jazz music. Such young jazz composers as Michael Daugherty are demonstrating that live musicians can interact creatively with computer-generated sound.

By the early 1990's, a new generation of young jazz musicians had emerged, inspired by the commercial and artistic success of Wynton Marsalis. Young musicians who have gained critical praise include saxophonists Scott Hamilton and Christopher Hollyday, pianist Marcus Roberts, trumpeters Philip Harper and Roy Hargrove, trombonist Dan Barrett, and guitarist Howard Alden. Frank Tirro

Related articles in *World Book* include:

Biographies

Armstrong, Louis
Basie, Count
Beiderbecke, Bix
Brubeck, Dave
Christian, Charlie
Cole, Nat "King"
Coltrane, John
Davis, Miles
Ellington, Duke
Fitzgerald, Ella
Getz, Stan
Gillespie, Dizzy
Goodman, Benny
Hampton, Lionel
Handy, W. C.
Hawkins, Coleman
Henderson, Fletcher
Herman, Woody
Hines, Earl
Holiday, Billie
Joplin, Scott
Kenton, Stan
Krupa, Gene
Lewis, John A.
Miller, Glenn
Monk, Thelonious
Parker, Charlie
Peterson, Oscar
Previn, André
Smith, Bessie
Tatum, Art
Teagarden, Jack
Waller, Fats
Whiteman, Paul
Young, Lester W.

Other related articles

Blues
New Orleans (picture: Preservation Hall)
Ragtime
Rock music
Synthesizer
United States (The arts)
Vibraphone

Outline

I. The sound of jazz
A. The brass
B. The reeds
C. Drums
D. The piano
E. The guitar
F. The bass
G. Other instruments

II. The history of jazz
A. The roots of jazz
B. Early jazz
C. The 1920's
D. The swing era
E. Bebop
F. Hard bop
G. Cool jazz
H. The spread of jazz
I. New directions
J. Fusion
K. The late 1900's

Additional resources

Balliett, Whitney. *Sound of Surprise: 46 Pieces on Jazz.* Da Capo, 1978. First published in 1959. *American Musicians: Fifty-Six Portraits in Jazz.* Oxford, 1986.

Case, Brian, and Britt, Stan. *The Harmony Illustrated Encyclopedia of Jazz.* 3rd ed. Harmony Bks., 1987.

Davis, Francis. *Outcats: Jazz Composers, Instrumentalists, and Singers.* Oxford, 1990.

Feather, Leonard. *The Encyclopedia of Jazz.* Da Capo, 1984. First published in 1960. *The Encyclopedia of Jazz in the Sixties.* Horizon Pr., 1986. First published in 1966.

Feather, Leonard, and Gitler, Ira G. *The Encyclopedia of Jazz in the Seventies.* Horizon Pr., 1987. First published in 1976.

Schuller, Gunther. *Early Jazz: Its Roots and Musical Development.* Oxford, 1968. *The Swing Era: The Development of Jazz, 1930-1945.* Oxford, 1989.

Shapiro, Nat, and Hentoff, Nat. *Hear Me Talkin' to Ya.* Dover, 1966. First published in 1955. Also suitable for younger readers. An oral history of jazz.

Latvia, *LAT vee uh,* is a European nation that regained its independence in 1991, after more than 50 years of forced annexation to the Soviet Union. Latvia lies on the eastern shore of the Baltic Sea. It had been independent from 1918 to 1940, when the Soviet Union occupied it and made it one of the 15 republics of the Soviet Union.

Latvia covers 24,595 square miles (63,700 square kilometers) and has a population of about 2,718,000. Riga is Latvia's capital and largest city. The country's name in Latvian, the official language, is *Latvijas Republika* (Republic of Latvia).

Government. At the time it regained its independence, Latvia had not yet established its permanent form of government. Its present government, described here, is considered transitional. Latvia has a parliament called the Supreme Council. The parliament's 201 members are elected by the people. The members of parliament choose a chairperson, who serves as the nation's president. They also choose a prime minister, who heads the Council of Ministers. The council carries out the functions of government. The prime minister selects the council members, subject to parliament's approval.

The people. About 52 per cent of the people of Latvia are Latvians, also called *Letts.* They are ethnically related to the Lithuanians and have their own culture and language. Russians, who speak the Russian language, make up about 34 per cent of the population of Latvia. Byelorussians make up about 5 per cent of Latvia's population, Poles and Ukrainians each account for about 3 per cent, and Lithuanians and Jews together account for about 2 per cent. Most Jews who lived in Latvia during World War II (1939-1945) were killed by the Nazis.

The influence of the Latvians in their own country declined after the Soviet take-over in 1940. Previously, Latvians had made up about 75 per cent of the population.

The Flag Research Center

Symbols of Latvia. The Latvian flag dates back to the 1200's, when it served as a banner in battle for one of the original Latvian tribes. The symbols on Latvia's coat of arms—a rising sun, a red lion, and a silver *griffin* (mythological creature)—stand for the three original provinces of Latvia.

But many thousands were killed or driven from Latvia during World War II or sent to Siberia after the war. Others escaped to the West. Some Latvians were kept out of Latvia by the Russians. Thousands of Russians migrated into Latvia after World War II.

The Latvian language is one of the oldest in Europe. It is related to Sanskrit, a language of ancient India. After the Soviet take-over, all Latvians had to learn Russian, which the Soviets made the official language of Latvia. During most of the period that Latvia was under Soviet control, Russian was spoken as the first language in many government and business offices. It was also the primary language of most newspapers and TV programs. However, in 1989, Latvian again became the land's official language. Since then, Latvian has been the first language in government and business offices, and in much of the media.

About 70 per cent of the Latvian people live in urban areas. Many of the city dwellers have apartments in buildings constructed after World War II. Thousands of people moved from rural areas to the cities to work in

Tass from Sovfoto

Riga, Latvia, lies on the Western Dvina River, south of the Gulf of Riga. It is the capital and largest city of Latvia. Riga is also an important shipping and industrial center.

Facts in brief

Capital: Riga.
Official language: Latvian.
Official name: Latvijas Republika (Republic of Latvia).
Area: 24,595 sq. mi. (63,700 km^2). *Greatest distances*—north-south, 170 mi. (270 km); east-west, 280 mi. (450 km). *Coastline*—293 mi. (472 km).
Elevation: *Highest*—Gaizina (mountain), 1,020 ft. (311 m). *Lowest*—sea level along the coast.
Population: *Estimated 1992 population*—2,718,000; density, 111 persons per sq. mi. (43 per km^2); distribution, 71 per cent urban, 29 per cent rural. *1989 census*—2,680,029. *Estimated 1997 population*—2,782,000.
Chief products: *Agriculture*—barley, flax, oats, potatoes, rye. *Manufacturing*—electrical equipment, machinery, primary metals, food products, transportation equipment.

various industries. Many of Latvia's rural people work on dairy and cattle farms.

Latvians generally wear Western-style clothing, but many wear colorful national costumes during holiday festivals. Latvians have a rich tradition of folklore, especially folk songs. Choral singing is popular, and the people take part in a number of annual song festivals. Latvians enjoy ballet, drama, and opera and participate in a variety of sports, including basketball and soccer.

From 1940 to 1988, the Soviet Union restricted religion in Latvia by permitting religious services but no religious teaching. The Soviet Union also discouraged the people from going to church. For example, church attendance barred people from good educational and job opportunities. In 1988, most restrictions on religion in Latvia were ended. In 1990, the Soviet Union ended all its religious restrictions. Most of the people of Latvia belong to the Lutheran, Roman Catholic, or Russian Orthodox churches.

Almost all the people of Latvia can read and write. Latvia has 10 universities, the largest of which is the Latvian State University in Riga.

Land and climate. Latvia, Estonia, and Lithuania are often called the Baltic States. They make up a region that forms part of the large coastal plain of northern Europe. Latvia consists chiefly of low hills and shallow valleys. It has many small lakes and swamps. Forests cover about 40 per cent of the land.

Latvia's chief river is the Western Dvina (Daugava in Latvian). It flows northwest from Byelorussia through central Latvia and empties into the Gulf of Riga. Latvia has about 293 miles (472 kilometers) of coastline. Many of its beaches are popular resort areas.

Temperatures in Latvia range from about 19 °F to 27 °F (−7 °C to −3 °C) in January to 61 °F to 64 °F (16 °C to 18 °C) in July. Latvia receives from 20 to 31 inches (51 to 80 centimeters) of rain annually.

Economy. Manufacturing makes up about three-fourths of the value of production in Latvia. Latvia's chief industries produce electronic equipment, household appliances, machinery, and processed foods and metals. Latvia produces some buses, railroad cars, and steel, which is used in manufacturing agricultural machinery. It also has a large fishing fleet. Heavy industrial development has caused major pollution of lakes, rivers, and the Baltic Sea. Riga is Latvia's main industrial center. Other centers of manufacturing in Latvia include Daugavpils, Kuldīga, Liepāja, Limbaži, and Rēzekne.

Agriculture accounts for less than a fifth of the value of production in Latvia. Farm products include barley, flax, oats, potatoes, and rye. Many farmers work on dairy and cattle farms. From 1940 to the late 1980's, the Soviet government owned most of Latvia's farms. In the late 1980's, the government began to allow people to start private farms and businesses. Today, most farms are privately owned.

History. People lived in what is now Latvia as early as 7000 or 8000 B.C. They were forced out about the time of Christ by invaders who became the ancestors of the Latvians. In time, these people established trade with

Latvia

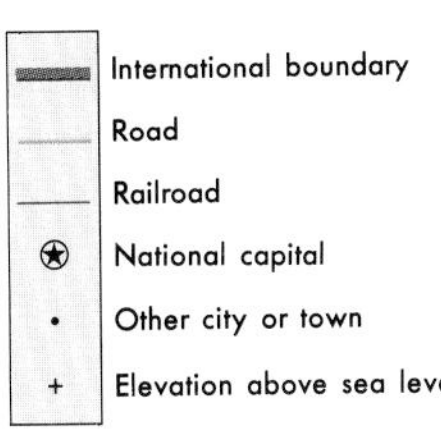

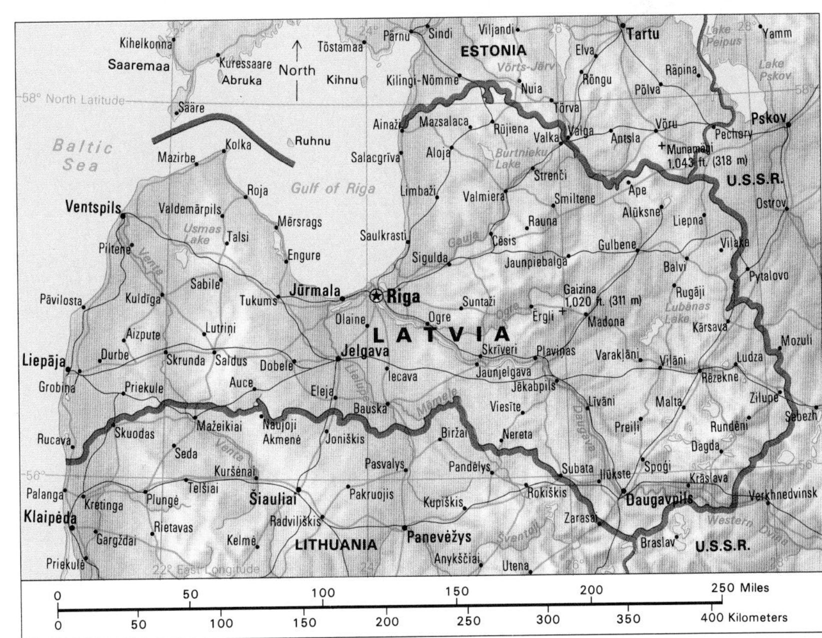

WORLD BOOK map

Arabs, Estonians, Lithuanians, Romans, and other groups, and developed their own language and culture.

The Vikings raided Latvia during the A.D. 800's, and Russian forces attacked Latvia several times in the 900's. The Teutonic Knights, an organization of German crusaders, invaded Latvia during the 1200's. War between the Latvians and the Knights lasted until the late 1200's, when the Latvians surrendered.

For over 200 years, the Knights governed Latvia as part of a larger state called Livonia. But by 1562, most of Latvia had come under the rule of Poland and Lithuania. A German-ruled duchy was also set up there. Sweden conquered northern Latvia in 1621, and Russia took control of this area in 1710. By 1800, Russia ruled all of Latvia. But German merchants and landowners in Latvia continued to hold much political power.

During the late 1800's, the Latvians began to organize an independence movement. This movement became stronger in the early 1900's as Russian and German authority declined in Latvia. On Nov. 18, 1918, just after the end of World War I, Latvia proclaimed itself independent. Russia and Germany tried to keep control of the new nation, but they finally recognized Latvia's independence in 1920.

In 1922, Latvia adopted a constitution that established a democratic form of government. The new democratic government passed land reform laws that broke up the large estates owned by a few wealthy people. The government divided this land into small farms and distributed the farms among the people. In 1936, during the Great Depression, Latvian democracy suffered a setback. The president seized power and reduced the role of parliament and the rights of the nation's political parties.

In 1939, shortly before World War II began, the Soviet Union and Germany agreed secretly to divide much of eastern Europe between themselves. The Soviet Union then forced Latvia to sign a treaty under which the Soviets built military bases in Latvia. Soviet troops occupied Latvia in June 1940, and Latvian Communists took over the government. In August, the Soviets made Latvia part of the Soviet Union. German forces invaded Latvia in 1941. They occupied Latvia until 1944, when Soviet troops recaptured it. Many Latvians tried to prevent the Soviets from taking over their country again. But the Soviets killed or deported those who opposed them.

Life in Latvia changed greatly under the Soviets. The Soviet Union established a powerful Communist government and took control of all industry and land. The Communist Party became Latvia's only legal political party. In addition, a growing number of Russian immigrants reduced the influence of the Latvian culture and language. Continuing Russian immigration threatened to make the Latvians a minority in their own land.

Through the years, Latvians expressed their national spirit and opposition to Soviet rule. Latvian nationalism became especially strong during the mid-1980's, when Soviet leader Mikhail Gorbachev began calling for greater openness of expression in the Soviet Union. In 1988, Latvian reformers established the Popular Front—or People's Front—a large non-Communist organization. The Popular Front sought to gain for Latvia the rights to govern itself and to manage its own economy. Most members of the Latvian non-Communist associations sought complete independence from the Soviet Union.

Large numbers of Latvians showed their support for the aims of the Popular Front by holding demonstrations and by electing Popular Front representatives to the Soviet parliament created in 1989. In the late 1980's, the government of the republic agreed to restore the national Latvian flag and anthem—which had been banned—and allowed freedom to the press and to religious groups. It also changed the official language of the republic from Russian to Latvian.

In late December 1989, Latvia's parliament voted to end the Communist Party's monopoly on power. A multiparty political system was established in January 1990. In February, the parliament condemned the 1940 Soviet take-over of Latvia. New parliamentary elections were held in March. Candidates who favored independence from the Soviet Union won a two-thirds majority of the parliamentary seats. On May 4, 1990, the parliament declared the restoration of Latvian independence and called for a gradual separation from the Soviet Union. The Soviet government called the declaration illegal. In January 1991, commandos of the Soviet Interior Ministry raided the headquarters of the Latvian Interior Ministry, killing four people. In August 1991, several conservative Communist officials failed in an attempt to overthrow Gorbachev and take over the Soviet central government. During the upheaval that followed the failed coup, the Latvian parliament declared immediate independence. In September, the Soviet government recognized Latvia's independence. V. Stanley Vardys

© Peter Stone, Black Star

Latvia gained independence from the Soviet Union in September 1991. Shortly before independence, workers in Riga removed a public statue of Soviet hero Lenin from its pedestal. They then dismantled the pedestal, *above.*

Lithuania, *LIH thoo AY nee uh,* is a European nation that regained its independence in 1991, after more than 50 years of forced annexation to the Soviet Union. Lithuania lies on the eastern shore of the Baltic Sea. It had been independent from 1918 to 1940, when the Soviet Union occupied it and made it one of the 15 republics of the Soviet Union.

Lithuania covers 25,174 square miles (65,200 square kilometers) and has a population of about 3,742,000. Vilnius is the capital and largest city. The country's name in Lithuanian, the official language, is Lietuvos Respublika (Republic of Lithuania).

Government. At the time it regained its independence, Lithuania had not yet established a permanent form of government. Thus its present government, described here, is considered transitional. Lithuania's head of state is the president of the Supreme Council, which is the country's parliament. The president and the 141 members of the council are elected to five-year terms. The prime minister is the head of government. The president appoints the prime minister, with the council's approval. The prime minister, with the parliament's approval, appoints a group of ministers to carry out government functions.

People. About 80 per cent of the people of Lithuania are Lithuanians, a nationality group that has its own customs and language. About 9 per cent of the population are Russians, and a somewhat smaller number are Poles. Byelorussians make up about 2 per cent of the population, and Ukrainians make up about 1 per cent. Less than 1 per cent of the people are Jews. Before World War II (1939-1945), about 8 per cent of Lithuania's population were Jews, but the Nazis killed most of them during the war.

Facts in brief

Capital: Vilnius.
Official language: Lithuanian.
Official name: Lietuvos Respublika (Republic of Lithuania).
Area: 25,174 sq. mi. (65,200 km²). *Greatest distances*—north-south, 175 mi. (280 km); east-west, 235 mi. (375 km).
Elevation: *Highest*—Juozapines (hill), 958 ft. (292 m). *Lowest*—sea level along the coast.
Population: *Estimated 1992 population*—3,742,000; density, 177 persons per sq. mi. (57 per km²); distribution, 68 per cent urban, 32 per cent rural. *1989 census*—3,689,779. *Estimated 1997 population*—3,831,000.
Chief products: *Agriculture*—beef cattle, dairy products, hogs. *Manufacturing*—chemicals, fabricated metal products, electrical equipment, machinery, food products, petroleum products.

The Flag Research Center

Symbols of Lithuania. Lithuania's flag has three horizontal stripes. The yellow stripe stands for fields of ripening grain. The green stripe represents Lithuania's evergreen forests. The red stripe symbolizes the blood shed for freedom. Lithuania's coat of arms features a knight on a white horse.

About 90 per cent of the Lithuanians are Roman Catholics. Most of the rest of the Lithuanians belong to the Lutheran Church or another Protestant denomination. Lithuania's culture developed under Roman Catholic influence, and Catholic traditions remain part of the people's lives.

Under Soviet rule, the government made the practice of many of the old Lithuanian customs very difficult. For example, Soviet laws forbade religious instruction, religious publications, and charity work. The Soviet government also discouraged church attendance. For example, people who attended church were kept from good educational and job opportunities. In 1988, the Soviet restrictions on religion in Lithuania were ended.

Lithuania was a rural society until the Soviet conquest. About three-fourths of its people lived in rural villages. The Soviet government ended the traditional Lithuanian style of life by industrializing the country. The government took away private land and combined small farms into large state-owned farms. It built many factories, and large numbers of people moved from rural areas into cities to work in these factories. Today, more than two-thirds of the people live in urban areas.

Lithuanians wear clothing similar to that worn in Western countries. But they cherish their decorative national costumes and wear them on festive occasions.

TASS from Sovfoto

Vilnius, the capital and largest city of Lithuania, lies along the Neris River. The city is a major cultural and industrial center. It is famous for its many old churches, some of which date from the 1400's. Modern high-rise buildings stand among the older structures.

Lithuanian children are required to attend school from the age of 6 to 17. Lithuania has 16 universities and colleges. The State University in Vilnius was established in 1579.

Land and climate. Most of Lithuania consists of flat or gently sloping land. The highest elevations are in the southeast. The land dips down to central lowlands and rises slightly in the west. White sand dunes along the seacoast provide a popular resort area. The dunes are especially attractive on a long strip of land that separates a lagoon from the Baltic Sea.

The country has about 3,000 small lakes and hundreds of rivers. The lakes cover about $1\frac{1}{2}$ per cent of Lithuania. The longest and largest river is the Neman (called Nemunas in Lithuanian). It begins in Byelorussia, which lies to the southeast, and drains most of Lithuania during its course to the Baltic.

Lithuania has no large, important mineral deposits. Its natural resources include clays and sands, iron ore, gypsum, limestone, peat, dolomite, amber, and small amounts of oil. Forests cover about a fourth of the land.

In January, the coldest month in Lithuania, the temperature averages from about 27 °F (−3 °C) on the seacoast to 21 °F (−6 °C) in the east. In July, the hottest month, temperatures average 61 °F (16 °C) near the sea and 64 °F (18 °C) in the east.

Economy. During the period of Soviet control, the government built many factories in Lithuania. In 1940, Lithuania had little industry. Today, about two-thirds of the economic product is industrial.

Lithuanian industry emphasizes chemical production, construction, electronics, food processing, machinery manufacture, metalworking, and oil refining. The country produces large numbers of metal-cutting lathes and electric motors used in appliances. Towns in southern and eastern Lithuania have many appliance factories. Most of Lithuania's food processing and chemical industries are in towns in central and northern Lithuania. Kaunas, Klaipėda, Vilnius, Šiauliai, and Panevėžys are Lithuania's major industrial centers. Klaipėda has large shipyards. Lithuania also has a large fishing fleet.

Lithuanian agriculture specializes in dairy and meat production. Agriculture accounts for about a fourth of the country's economic output.

Under Soviet rule, the government owned most of Lithuania's businesses, factories, and farmland. But in the late 1980's, it began to allow private businesses. In 1990, it began to allow private ownership of farmland. The government of independent Lithuania supports free enterprise and is attempting to establish a free market economy.

History. People lived in the region that is now Lithuania about 8000 B.C. Groups that were the ancestors of the Lithuanian people lived in the region at the time of Christ.

In the A.D. 100's, the Roman historian Tacitus made the first historical mention of the people who lived near the Baltic Sea. He reported that they sold amber to the Romans. Near the end of the 1100's, the Lithuanian peoples united into a single nation. The first great ruler of Lithuania was Mindaugas, who became king in 1251. Mindaugas was assassinated by nobles in 1263.

In the 1200's, the people fought a group of German crusaders called the Teutonic Knights, who tried to conquer Lithuania. Lithuania expanded its boundaries in the 1300's. In time, it extended nearly to Moscow in the east and to the Black Sea in the south. In 1386, Grand Duke Jagiełło (Jogaila in Lithuanian) united Lithuania with Poland. At first, this union was a confederation of two states ruled mostly by the same king. They were made a single state in 1569.

The Lithuanian-Polish government collapsed in the 1700's, and in 1795, Lithuania came under the rule of the czar of Russia (the name for the Soviet Union before 1922). The people rebelled against Russian rule in 1831 and again in 1863 but failed to win independence. The

Lithuania

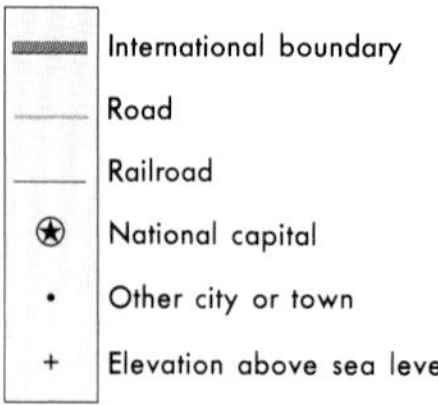

WORLD BOOK map

czar tried to increase Russian influence in Lithuania. He prohibited books printed in Lithuanian and closed Lithuanian schools. But the people continued to educate their children and kept the national culture alive as well. Many Lithuanians emigrated to the United States during this period and also during later periods.

The movement for an independent Lithuania became organized in the 1880's. In 1905, a conference of elected representatives of Lithuania demanded self-government for their people within the Russian state. The Russians rejected this demand. During World War I (1914-1918), German troops occupied Lithuania. On Feb. 16, 1918, Lithuania became the first of the Baltic States to declare its independence from Russia and Germany. Lithuania established a democratic system of government in which the parliament had power over the president. A land-reform program broke up large estates and distributed land among the poor. The government also set up an educational system.

Fighting continued in Lithuania after World War I ended. Russia attempted to take over the country. The Lithuanians defeated the Russians, and a peace treaty was signed in 1920. Poland occupied Vilnius in 1920, and held the city until 1939. In 1926, a group of military officers and civilian politicians seized power in Lithuania. Antanas Smetona became president. He gradually took over more and more of the authority that the president had shared with the parliament.

In March 1939, Germany seized part of Lithuania. A combination of Lithuanian political parties tried to restore democracy, but failed. Later in 1939, Germany and the Soviet Union reached agreements that gave the Soviet Union control of the Baltic region. The Soviet government then built some military bases in Lithuania.

In 1940, during World War II, the Soviet Union occupied all of Lithuania and made it a Soviet republic with a Communist government. After the Germans invaded the Soviet Union in 1941, the Lithuanians revolted against their Soviet rulers and established their own government. But the Germans suppressed the government. They conquered the country and occupied it until 1944, when the Soviet Union again took over Lithuania. From 1944 to 1952, Lithuanian guerrillas fought the Soviet Union. Thousands of the guerrillas were killed in the fighting. The Soviet government also sent about 350,000 Lithuanians to labor camps in Siberia for their political beliefs or as punishment for resisting Soviet rule.

In 1972, many Lithuanian students and young workers demonstrated against the Soviet government, and several people burned themselves to death in protest. Lithuanians continued to express their opposition to Soviet rule, particularly after the mid-1980's, when Soviet leader Mikhail Gorbachev began calling for more openness in Soviet society. In 1988, Lithuanian intellectuals established the Sajūdis, a non-Communist movement that sought to give Lithuania complete control of its economy, citizenship requirements, education, and cultural development. It also sought to clean up Lithuania's rivers and lakes, and the Baltic Sea shores, all of which had been severely damaged by pollution from industries. Most members of this and similar movements sought total independence and separation from the Soviet Union. Lithuanians supported these goals by staging public demonstrations. They also elected representatives who supported their movement to the Soviet parliament that was created in 1989.

In 1989, Lithuania's parliament expressed a commitment to full independence. It declared that laws adopted by the Soviet parliament in Moscow were invalid in Lithuania unless approved by the Lithuanian parliament. The government declared Lithuanian the official language. It also allowed freedom of religion and the press.

On Dec. 7, 1989, the Lithuanian parliament abolished the monopoly of power that the Communist Party had held since 1940. It established a multiparty political system. Parliamentary elections were held in February 1990, and pro-independence candidates won more than 90 per cent of the parliamentary seats. On March 11, the new parliament declared an immediate restoration of Lithuania's independence as a nation. The Soviet Union demanded a recall of the declaration. But the Lithuanians refused. In response, the Soviet Union applied economic pressure. It cut off all of its shipments of oil, medical supplies, and many other goods to Lithuania. In June—under pressure from Western nations—the Soviet Union and Lithuania held a series of talks that led to an agreement. Under the agreement, the Soviets restored shipments of raw materials and other goods to Lithuania. In turn, the Lithuanians agreed to suspend their declaration of independence temporarily if negotiations with the Soviets took place. But in January 1991, Soviet forces moved into Lithuania to crack down on the freely elected government and the independence movement. The forces killed 14 people and injured 700 others.

In August 1991, several conservative Soviet Communist officials failed in an attempt to overthrow Gorbachev and take over the Soviet central government. During the upheaval that followed this failed coup, Lithuania pressed vigorously for recognition of its independence. In September, the Soviet government recognized Lithuania's independence. V. Stanley Vardys

© Ricki Rosen, SABA

Lithuanians celebrated independence in September 1991, when the Soviet Union recognized Lithuania as an independent nation. Lithuania had been under Soviet rule for more than 50 years.

© Michal Heron, Woodfin Camp, Inc.

Human beings resemble one another in many essential ways. However, people also differ from one another. The youngsters in this photo exhibit variations in skin color and hair color. Today, most experts avoid classifying people into races based on such variable physical characteristics.

Human races

Races, Human. All human beings are descended from people who lived hundreds of thousands of years ago. Thus, we all share a common ancestry. This means that all people living today are related to one another. But even though we are all related, we do not all look alike. Our bodies have different sizes and shapes, our skins have varying shades, our eyes differ in color and shape, our lips and noses have different shapes, and our hair has different colors and textures.

Most anthropologists believe that human beings originated in Africa and gradually spread throughout the world (see **Prehistoric people** [How prehistoric human beings developed]). They have observed that groups of people who have lived in certain parts of the world for many thousands of years tend to differ from groups living in other parts of the world. Living in regions with differing environments is one reason human beings have developed different appearances. For example, people whose ancestors lived for many generations in northern parts of the world—such as northern Europe or northern Japan—tend to have light-colored skin. People who come from places near the equator, such as central Africa or southern India, tend to have dark-colored skin. People who come from places between those two environmental extremes tend to have medium-colored skin. For information on how skin colors result from adaptations to the environment, see the *Climatic adaptations* section of this article.

Alan Swedlund, the contributor of this article, is Chairman of the Department of Anthropology at the University of Massachusetts at Amherst.

In some instances, we observe that certain physical traits tend to cluster in a group. For example, we might associate blond hair, blue eyes, and fair skin with people from Denmark, Norway, and Sweden. We also might associate red hair, green eyes, and a freckled complexion with people from Ireland. However, many people in these four countries actually have brown hair, brown eyes, and light brown skin. This example shows some of the problems facing human biologists who attempt to classify human beings into races.

Biologists define a race as a subdivision of a plant or animal *species.* The members of the same species resemble one another in many essential ways. Most importantly, they can breed with one another and produce fertile offspring. Members of different species usually cannot interbreed and produce fertile offspring. Grizzly bears and black bears, for example, are closely related North American bears. Despite their similarities, grizzly bears and black bears do not interbreed. Therefore, they belong to different species.

Many plant and animal species can be subdivided

into groups that differ from one another. These groups have been called *races, subspecies, natural populations, breeds,* or *varieties.* Among grizzly bears, for instance, biologists observe distinct physical differences from region to region. They group grizzly bears into subspecies based on these differences.

All living human beings belong to the subspecies *Homo sapiens sapiens.* But like those of the grizzly bear, human populations differ from one region to another. Scholars have used these differences to classify people into various races. They have devised racial categories for human beings according to such physical characteristics as the color of the skin, the color and texture of the hair, and the shape of the eyes.

But some people assigned to the same race—and even some members of the same family—have widely differing features. Over the years, scientists have disagreed over how many races of human beings can be devised, and over which individuals belong to what race. For this reason, many anthropologists and biologists have come to believe that the assignment of a racial label to any group of people is arbitrary and thus open to argument.

For many years, most scholars believed that "pure" races of human beings existed some time in the prehistoric past. According to these scholars, the "pure" human races developed in complete isolation from one another, and the members of each race exhibited physical characteristics that the members of other races did not possess.

Today, however, most *physical anthropologists* (scientists who study the physical differences and prehistoric development of human beings) doubt that "pure" races ever existed. They point out that people have probably always taken mates from outside their own population as well as from within. They also note that as transportation and communication have become easier, populations have blended more and more. For these reasons, the biological definition of race does not describe human populations well. Most anthropologists now avoid classifying people into races. Instead, they try to learn more about human diversity by studying how human traits vary throughout the world.

Despite the lack of a scientifically valid racial classification system, people generally consider those who "look different" from themselves to be members of a different race. As a result, the concept of race remains important in a sociological sense. Societies continue to divide their members into "races"—though the criteria and labels used may vary from society to society.

The idea of race has often been misunderstood, and the term has sometimes been misused on purpose. The biological concept of race has often been confused with culture, language, nationality, or religion. Differences in physical appearance have led some people to mistakenly conclude that members of different groups are born with differences in intelligence, talents, and moral standards. Race has also been a major basis of *discrimination*—that is, the treatment of other groups as inferior to one's own group. For more information, see the *World Book* articles on **Minority group, Racism,** and **Segregation.**

This article describes some racial classification systems that have been used over the years and discusses alternative approaches to the study of human variation. It also describes how the physical characteristics of human beings change, and it discusses the social significance of race.

Systems of racial classification

Physical differences among human beings have long been recognized, and many of these differences have been used throughout history as bases of racial classification. Obvious physical characteristics, such as size, build, skin color, eye form, hair form, and nose shape, were the main criteria of early classifications of race, with skin color considered most important.

Since the beginning of recorded history, scholars have classified human beings in different ways, and the number of categories recognized by each system varied. The development of racial classification systems was influenced by three important theories: (1) the three-race theory, (2) evolutionary theory, and (3) the geographical-race theory.

The three-race theory. Ancient Egyptians, Greeks, and Romans knew about dark-skinned, curly-haired peoples that lived in Africa. They also knew about the so-called "yellowish-skinned" peoples of Asia, most of whom had folds of skin that extended from their eyelids over the inner corners of their eyes. Limited knowledge of the peoples of the world at this time suggested the existence of three races—European, or "white"; African, or "black"; and Asian, or "yellow." These groups eventually became known as Caucasoid, Negroid, and Mongoloid, respectively. For many years, scholars attempted to classify all human populations in terms of these three races, or some variation of the three. They believed that all people belonged to one of a limited number of racial types. They also believed that the traits of each race were fixed and unchanging.

The major period of European overseas exploration, which began in the late 1400's, provided increased contacts with peoples of different cultures. By the 1800's, it became evident that much of the world's population did not easily fit into the three-race system. For example, as Europeans came into contact with more and more Asian peoples, they realized that the skin of the people they had classified as Mongoloids was not really yellow, but that it varied from very dark to very light brown. They also discovered that the *epicanthic fold*—the inner eyefold thought to characterize Mongoloids—was rare in some Asian populations but present in some of the native peoples of southern Africa and North America. Lip form and hair form were also found to vary across the traditional racial groupings.

Evolutionary theory. The view that human beings could be classified into races based on fixed physical characteristics began to change dramatically as biologists came to accept the theory of evolution. During the early 1800's, most biologists believed that all plant and animal species remained the same from generation to generation. However, geologists found fossils of animals and plants that were not the same as living species, thus providing evidence that species were not fixed.

Even though scientists could now see that species could change, they did not know how evolution worked. It was the idea of *natural selection* as the mechanism for evolution that helped scientists understand how organ-

The geographical-race theory

Geographical races were believed to exist because of the isolation created by oceans, mountains, and deserts. This map shows the races that were recognized by one popular classification system.

WORLD BOOK map

isms could change over many generations. This idea, set forth by the British naturalist Charles R. Darwin in his book *The Origin of Species* (1859), states that populations of organisms can change over generations as they adapt to their physical environment. This new understanding of the processes of evolution through natural selection, when applied to human populations, showed that many of the supposedly "fixed" traits that had been used to identify races were actually adaptations that had evolved over time in response to environmental conditions.

Scientists saw that widely separated groups could develop similar characteristics as a result of adapting to similar environments, even if they shared no recent ancestral relationship. For example, the Quechua, a people who live in the Andes Mountains of South America, and the Sherpas, a people of the Himalaya in Asia, are only remotely related. However, they have many similar physical characteristics as a result of prolonged adaptation to living in their high mountain environments.

As they came to understand evolutionary theory, experts began to see the difficulty of trying to use adaptable traits to fit people into just a few major races. Physical anthropologists began to search for *nonadaptive,* or *neutral,* traits—that is, physical characteristics that would persist even if a population moved to a different environment. They viewed race as something fixed and unchanging and wanted to discover traits that were also unchanging. Anthropologists compared many traits and physiological processes of people living in different environments, including blood groups and rates of respiration, circulation, and metabolism. These comparisons are discussed later in this article, in the section on *How human populations develop and change.*

The geographical-race theory. In an effort to reconcile the theory of evolution with the observed variations among the world's populations, some anthropologists developed a new system of racial classification during the 1950's. They divided human beings into large categories called *geographical races.* These races were collections of populations that exhibited similar characteristics. One popular classification system recognized nine geographical races: (1) African, (2) American Indian, (3) Asian, (4) Australian, (5) European, (6) Indian, (7) Melanesian, (8) Micronesian, and (9) Polynesian.

In general, the geographical races extended throughout major continental areas and large island chains. But they did not correspond exactly to the continents. For example, the European geographical race included populations throughout Europe, in the Middle East, and north of the Sahara in Africa. It also included descendants of these populations in other parts of the world, such as the "whites" of North America and Australia.

Geographical races were believed to exist because of the isolation caused by such natural barriers as oceans, mountains, and deserts. The idea was that these barriers separated groups of people for many thousands of years, allowing the populations to evolve in different directions. India, for example, is partly isolated from the rest of Asia by the Himalaya. According to the geographical-race theory, this isolation permitted the Indian geographical race to develop separately from the Asian geographical race.

Anthropologists used the term *local races* to describe distinct subcategories of geographical races. Some local races had millions of members. For example, the Northwest European local race included the populations of Scandinavia, Germany, Belgium, Luxembourg, the Netherlands, Great Britain, and Ireland. It also included peoples who emigrated—or whose ancestors emigrated—from those areas. Local races containing much smaller numbers of people included the Lapps of extreme northern Europe and the Basques, who live in the mountains between France and Spain.

Some anthropologists used the term *microraces* to describe the subpopulations that existed within local races. But microraces—and even local races—could not always be clearly defined. Within a given geographic

The problem of skin color in racial classification

According to the geographical-race theory, the individuals in the top row of photos would belong to the European race. The individuals in the bottom row would belong to the African race. But skin color varies widely within each racial group. In addition, the skin of the Kuwaiti man—who would be assigned to the European geographical race—is about the same color as that of the woman from southern Chad, who would be assigned to the African geographical race.

© Gerard, Photo Researchers
Woman from Norway

© Blaine Harrington, The Stock Market
Woman from Germany

© David Hundley, The Stock Market
Man from Kuwait

© Jacques Jangoux from Peter Arnold
Woman from southern Chad

© Martha Cooper from Peter Arnold
Woman from Kenya

© Gerd Ludwig, Woodfin Camp, Inc.
Woman from Togo

area, the members of different subpopulations often intermarried, so the physical features used to define these groups blended together.

This expanded, detailed classification system represented a major change in the view of human races. The geographical-race system took into account the theory of evolution as well as heredity, recognizing that populations are shaped by their environment. However, many anthropologists believed it did not eliminate the problems of the older systems. Because members of different races could possess the same physical characteristics, the racial criteria could not be clearly identified.

Alternatives to racial classification

In the past, scholars based racial classifications on clusters of physical characteristics that supposedly represented the "typical" member of that race. But many of the individuals categorized in a particular race did not reflect all the characteristics attributed to that race. In addition, the scholars who constructed classification systems did not always agree on which traits—or how many—should be considered.

To see the problems involved in defining races by means of "typical" characteristics, consider skin color. A pigment called *melanin* determines skin color. Dark skin contains more melanin than light skin does. Skin color has been used as a major classifying characteristic in all racial systems. For example, a light brown skin color was considered "typical" for the members of the European geographical race. But some members of the race had skin that was far lighter than the "typical" color, and others had skin that was much darker. Similarly, the members of the African geographical race "typically" had brownish-black skin. But again, many individuals classified in this race had skin that was lighter than the "typical" shade, and many others had skin that was darker.

To further confuse matters, some of the darker-skinned members of the European geographical race had skin as dark as some of the lighter-skinned members of the African geographical race. In view of these complications, it has become extremely difficult to assign people to a race based solely on skin color.

Increasing the number of identifying traits only added more problems. The shape and fullness of the lips, for example, varied widely among people who were considered members of the same race. Furthermore, lip shape demonstrated the same kind of overlap among members of supposedly different races as did skin color.

These problems have led many anthropologists to conclude that classification based on physical characteristics is not scientifically valid and serves no useful purpose. They find the study of human variation to be more productive than the assignment of racial labels. As a result, they have adopted alternate approaches to traditional systems of racial classification. Chief among these alternatives are (1) the clinal approach and (2) the population approach.

The clinal approach. The geographical distribution of a physical characteristic can be shown on a map by zones called *clines.* Clines are formed by drawing lines to connect points of the same or similar frequency. For example, in the case of skin color, each cline includes locations at which populations demonstrate the same average skin color. As variations from dark to light are plotted on a map, certain distribution patterns begin to emerge. A clinal distribution does not associate specific traits with traditional racial categories, nor does it associate different traits with one another. For example, skin color and blood type would be plotted on separate maps and show different patterns of distribution.

The clinal approach has been used extensively to examine the worldwide distribution of blood types. Scientists classify human blood into groups according to proteins on the membranes of the red blood cells. The presence or absence of these proteins is determined by heredity. Studies show differences in the frequencies of some blood groups throughout the world.

The best-known blood-group system is the ABO system. In this system, type O is the most common, followed by types A, B, and AB. Other systems used in comparing blood-group frequencies include the Kell, Kidd, Lutheran, MNS, P, and Rh systems. See **Blood** (Blood groups).

Clines of blood-type distribution help anthropologists consider possible explanations for the geographic variations they observe. For instance, clinal mapping shows that central Asia has the lowest frequencies of type O blood. One possible explanation for this has to do with the deadly epidemic disease bubonic plague—a disease that has long been present in central Asia. The surface proteins that characterize type O red blood cells resemble the surface proteins found on the infectious bacteria that cause bubonic plague. Normally, the body can produce disease-fighting chemicals that recognize and attack cells that carry the bubonic-plague surface proteins. But if a person has type O blood, the body is less likely to make these disease-fighting substances because they would damage its own red blood cells. During a plague epidemic, central Asians with type O blood would have been at greater risk of dying from the disease than were those with other blood types. Over the centuries, this disadvantage could have led to the comparatively low frequency of type O blood in central Asia. Differences in dietary habits among people living in different regions could also explain the clinal distribution of ABO blood groups.

The population approach is used to study patterns of variation among human populations. Anthropologists define a population as a group of similar people who are more likely to mate with one another than with outsiders. Anthropologists using the population approach investigate clusters of physical traits but make no assumptions about race on the basis of those clusters. Instead, they see each population as the product of a unique set of circumstances, including adaptation, genetic change, isolation, and history of migration. These

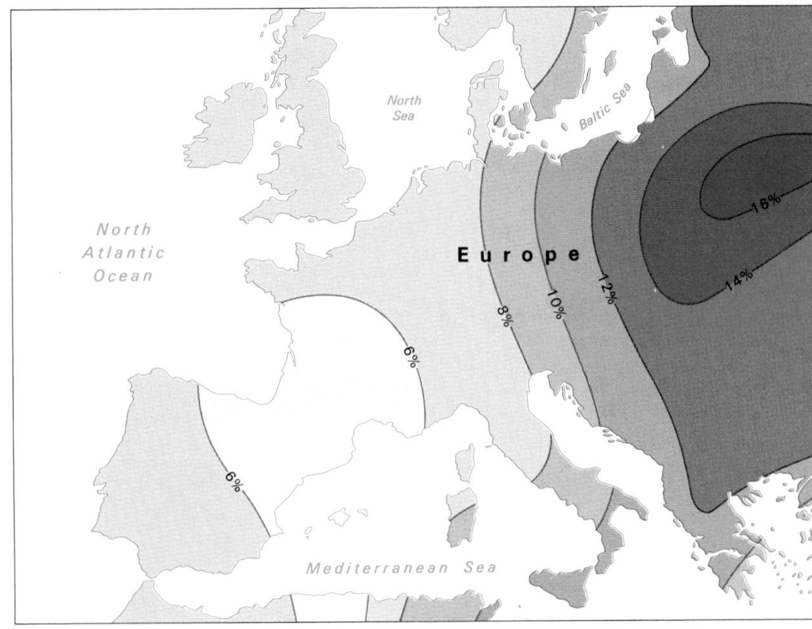

A clinal map shows the geographical distribution of a physical characteristic. Zones called *clines* indicate where the trait occurs with similar frequency. This map shows the distribution of a trait called the *B allele* in the ABO system of blood classification. People with the B allele have type B or type AB blood. It is more common in eastern Europe than in western Europe.

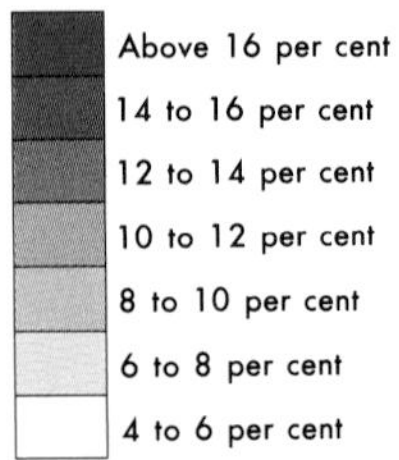

WORLD BOOK map

researchers then attempt to explain the similarities and differences among the populations. They do not try to fit the populations into racial categories.

The population approach assumes that groups of people who have lived in similar environments for a long period will demonstrate similar adaptations. This can happen even if the location of these similar environments is far apart. For example, populations living at very high altitudes must adjust to extreme conditions. Temperatures can get extremely hot during the day and very cold at night. Also, the air pressure is so low that less oxygen is available, making breathing more difficult. Throughout the world, populations living at high altitudes show specific traits in response to similar environmental conditions. For instance, their lungs can hold more air than those of people at lower altitudes, enabling them to inhale more oxygen with each breath.

How human populations develop and change

The characteristics studied by physical anthropologists—such as eye color, nose shape, blood type, body height, and susceptibility to genetic diseases—are determined by both heredity and the environment. The inherited aspects of a trait are determined by tiny biochemical structures in cells, called *genes.* Genes contain chemical instructions for the formation of hereditary characteristics. Children inherit half their genes from their father and half from their mother. The underlying genetic makeup of a trait is called the *genotype.* The actual appearance of the trait is called the *phenotype.* The phenotype results from the environment as well as from heredity.

Members of the same population of human beings tend to have more genes in common than do members of different populations. Closely related populations also share more genes than do distantly related groups, just as cousins have more genes in common than do members of different families. All the genes in a population are called the group's *gene pool.* The degree to which a gene is present in a population is called the *gene frequency.* For more information on how characteristics are inherited, see **Heredity; Cell; Gene.**

Scientists have shown that the gene pools of human populations can change over time. The presence of some genes increases, while the presence of other genes declines. As gene frequencies change, the frequencies of physical characteristics in a population may also change. Such changes can result from a number of different factors, including (1) natural selection, (2) mutation, (3) genetic drift, (4) the founder effect, and (5) migration and gene flow.

Natural selection is the process that enables some organisms or individuals to live and reproduce while others do not survive. Those who reproduce pass their genetic characteristics on to their offspring. Natural selection is the force that drives Darwinian evolution. For example, certain individuals within a population might possess a genetic characteristic that provides resistance to a local disease. As a result, those individuals tend to survive longer and to produce more offspring than the other members of the population. Moreover, their children who inherit the favorable characteristic will likewise tend to live longer and leave more descendants. Over time, individuals who possess the favorable trait will tend to outnumber those who do not, and the gene frequencies of the population will have changed.

As a result of natural selection, a population that lives in a certain area for many generations tends to exhibit distinctive genetic traits or clusters of traits. Scientists have demonstrated that differences in skin color, body build, and many other physical characteristics represent adaptations to different environmental factors. See **Natural selection.**

Climatic adaptations. The genetic makeup of populations may change over time to adjust to climate. For example, dark and light skin and eye color represent adaptations to different amounts of sunlight. The color of our skin, hair, and eyes is determined by the pigment melanin. The amount of melanin in the skin, hair, and eyes can differ greatly from one person to another. Large amounts of melanin in the skin help protect it from sunburn and reduce the risk of skin cancer. Dark pigment in the eyes improves vision in bright sunlight. Therefore, dark skin and dark eyes represent adaptations of people whose ancestors have lived for many generations in sunny climates.

Sunlight also affects skin color in another way. Our bodies need vitamin D to help us absorb calcium. The absorption of sunlight enables our bodies to make vitamin D. In climates with long winter nights, it can be difficult for our bodies to absorb the sunlight needed to make enough vitamin D. People whose ancestors have lived in these climates for generations have adapted to reduced sunlight by developing light-colored skin that will absorb the little sunlight that is available. Therefore, skin colors in humans result from adaptations to the environments in which our ancestors have lived.

Human populations also differ in response to cold. Among Eskimos (also called *Inuit*), for instance, the body maintains a high temperature by burning large amounts of fat and protein. It also keeps large amounts of blood flowing to the arms, legs, fingers, and toes, to prevent frostbite. The Australian Aborigines, who live in a generally warm climate but traditionally slept in below-freezing temperatures with little clothing or shelter, have adapted to cold in a different way. The temperature in their legs and feet drops during sleep, and they burn less energy. But their bodies maintain warmth in the trunk, where the vital organs are.

The Australian Aborigines and the Eskimos of the Arctic have both adapted to cold. The Aborigines have a limited food supply. They have no extra food to burn for body heat when the temperature drops. Instead, their adaptation enables them to save body energy. But this method would not work in the Arctic, where the climate is cold day and night. The Eskimos are adapted to extreme cold—temperatures as low as −40 °F to −60 °F (−40 °C to −51 °C). Their adaptation depends on the availability of food to supply energy and body heat.

Susceptibility to genetic diseases. Many of the diseases that afflict human beings have some genetic basis. Human populations differ in the frequency of the genes that cause certain genetic diseases and disorders. For this reason, a number of genetic diseases are distributed differently throughout the world and affect some populations more than they do others. The fact that certain populations are plagued by particular genetic diseases can be explained in terms of natural selection.

The frequency of a hereditary blood disorder called *sickle cell anemia* varies widely in different populations. Individuals who inherit the sickling gene from both parents suffer from sickle cell anemia. Most cases of this disease are fatal. *Carriers*—people who inherit the defective gene from only one parent—may have almost no problems or experience only mild symptoms. But they can transmit the abnormal gene to their children. See **Sickle cell anemia.**

Scientists have found that carriers of the sickling gene have a higher resistance than noncarriers to *malaria,* a dangerous disease transmitted by certain mosquitoes. Sickle cell anemia is a rare disorder, but it occurs more often among populations of western Africa, the Middle East, southern Europe, and the Caribbean, most of whom live in areas threatened by malaria. Thus, the sickling gene—despite its negative effects—represents an important advantage for people in these areas.

Another genetic disease, *cystic fibrosis,* is more common among European populations and their descendants than among other populations. This rare and incurable disease affects the lungs and other organs. Like sickle cell anemia, cystic fibrosis results from the inheritance of a disease-causing gene from both parents. Carriers of the gene do not contract cystic fibrosis, but they can pass it on to their offspring. Medical geneticists have found that carriers are more resistant than other individuals to *tuberculosis,* an infectious disease affecting the lungs. Tuberculosis swept through Europe from the 1700's to the early 1900's. Carriers of the cystic fibrosis gene would have been more likely to survive these epidemics, which could explain the relatively high frequency of the cystic fibrosis gene in these populations. See **Cystic fibrosis.**

Mutation. A mutation is a change in genetic material. A changed gene often produces a different inherited trait that can be passed on to future generations. Mutations result from a chemical change in *DNA* (deoxyribonucleic acid), the chief chemical compound of genes. Mutations may also result from a change in the number or arrangement of *chromosomes,* the threadlike structures that contain the genes. Scientists know of many agents that can cause mutations, such as certain types of radiation, chemical treatments, and heat, but they cannot tell in advance which genes or chromosomes will mutate or how the trait controlled by that gene or chromosome will change.

Many mutations are harmful, causing mental or physical disorders. But other mutations are neutral, and some are favorable. A favorable mutation may provide the raw material for natural selection by making a person better suited to the environment. For example, a mutation that enhances the body's ability to make vitamin D from sunlight would be advantageous to a person living in the Far North, where the earth receives less sunlight. Such beneficial genes will increase in frequency from generation to generation. On the other hand, individuals possessing harmful mutations may be selected against, so the trait will not tend to increase in a population. In this way, mutation sometimes works together with natural selection to produce changes in gene frequencies. See **Mutation; Heredity** (Heredity and change); **Nucleic acid.**

Genetic drift refers to chance fluctuations in the gene frequencies of a population from generation to generation. The genes of each generation represent only a sample of the previous generation's gene pool. As a result, the gene frequencies of each generation of individuals tend to vary randomly within the limitations of the preceding generation's gene pool. The smaller the population, the stronger the impact of these fluctuations is likely to be. Such changes are not likely to have much effect in very large populations, but they can lead to significant genetic changes in small populations.

The founder effect. When a small number of people from a large population establish a new population in a different place, it is unlikely that the founders represent the full range of diversity in their parent population's gene pool. When these founders produce offspring, a smaller, more limited gene pool is created. This phenomenon is called the *founder effect.* In future generations, the members of a population influenced by the founder effect are likely to resemble one another more closely than they do the members of the larger, more diverse parent population.

The founder effect may explain the increased incidence of certain traits or diseases in a population. For example, a hereditary brain disorder called *Tay-Sachs disease* occurs mainly among Jewish children of eastern European ancestry. People with one Tay-Sachs gene do not have the disease but may transmit the gene to their children. Children who inherit the gene from both parents have the disease. The Jews of eastern Europe made up a small population with a limited gene pool, so the incidence of the disease remains higher among their descendants than in other populations. See **Tay-Sachs disease.**

A similar limitation on a population's gene pool may occur if the genes of one person or family in a small population are passed to a large number of offspring. For example, if one man in a small, isolated group married several women and fathered many children, his genes would appear in future generations with more frequency than would the genes of other members of the population.

Migration and gene flow. When migration occurs between separate populations, new genes or combinations of genes are likely to be introduced into each group through interbreeding. As a result, the gene pool of each group comes to include genes from the gene pools of the other populations. In this manner, migration may cause the gene frequencies of populations to change over time. In modern times, easy access to transportation has greatly increased gene flow.

Since earliest times, people have moved from one place to another and have chosen mates from other groups. The greatest amount of gene flow occurs between populations that live next to one another. Mixture may also occur as a result of various cultural practices. Throughout history, such practices as exploration, colonization, bride capture, and enslavement have brought individuals of various genetic makeups together. The result in many cases has been change in the gene frequencies of the populations affected by these practices.

The social significance of race

As we have seen, most physical anthropologists have abandoned the idea of classifying human beings into biological races. In many societies, however, people continue to identify themselves and others as members of a particular race, often based on skin color. Thus, whatever its shortcomings on a biological basis, racial classification remains an important sociological factor. Social scientists must recognize the way a society defines racial categories if they hope to understand human behavior. It would, for instance, be difficult to analyze American society without taking into account the commonly used division of that society into "white," "black," "Hispanic," and other races. Yet these categories themselves reveal problems with the concept of race. "White" and "black" represent categories traditionally used to identify biological races. But "Hispanic" refers to the language group of Spanish-speaking people, not to any one biological group. Unfortunately, many social distinctions between races result from racial prejudice and misunderstanding.

Race and ethnic or national identity. The biological concept of race is sometimes confused with the idea of ethnicity or nationality. People identify themselves as members of certain ethnic or national groups based on certain geographical, cultural, or religious characteristics. However, these identifications are not based on physical differences. For instance, people sometimes incorrectly speak of the "Arab race," the "German race," the "Irish race," or the "Jewish race." But these labels refer to ethnicity or nationality and have nothing to do with the biological concept of race.

Race and discrimination. History includes many episodes in which the members of one group of people deemed themselves superior to another group. Such beliefs were long used to rationalize the enslavement and persecution of people viewed as inferior. For example, the ancient Romans viewed the Germanic tribes as a "race" of barbarians who were barely human. Europeans who settled in America claimed superiority over the American Indians to justify their expansion into the New World. In the 1930's, the leaders of Nazi Germany preached that Germans belonged to the "superior Aryan race," and that Jews and all other non-Aryan peoples were inferior.

Experts have not discovered any scientific basis for such claims of superiority. But many people still view other groups in terms of *stereotypes.* That is, they have oversimplified, preconceived, and generalized beliefs about the members of these groups. At various times, for example, certain groups have been described as dirty, dishonest, sly, humorless, or dull. These judgments have often been confused with racial traits, though they have nothing to do with the biological concept of race. Many such judgments have nothing to do with culture either, but only with the opinions or prejudices of those who make them. Discrimination can result from these stereotypes. As a result of these beliefs, members of minority groups in many societies have fewer educational and job opportunities than do members of the majority group.

The belief that some groups are more intelligent than others has been used to justify discrimination. Scientists have shown that a person's intelligence is partly inherited and partly determined by the environment. The use of intelligence to compare groups of people is extremely difficult, because few such comparisons can be considered equal. A better-educated group, for example, will score higher on tests that measure education. Groups that value mathematical skills or technical ability will do better on tests involving such skills and knowledge.

Many experts believe it is impossible to design an intelligence test that is not influenced by a person's experiences. Nevertheless, scientists are trying to develop *culture-fair* or *culture-free* tests that reduce the effects of cultural differences on test scores.

The differences among human beings make the world a fascinating place in which to live. But when people focus on these differences, they often fail to appreciate how similar all human beings are. Most of the distinctions people make between themselves and others have much more to do with culture than with biology.

Alan Swedlund

Related articles. See the separate ***World Book*** articles listed under "People" at the end of Africa and Asia. See also:

Adaptation
Africa (People)
Aleuts
Asia (People)
Australia (The Aborigines)
Black Americans
Dyaks
Eskimo
Europe (People)
Evolution
Heredity
Indian, American
Latin America (People)
Maoris
North America (People)
Pacific Islands (People)
Prehistoric people
Racism

Outline

I. Systems of racial classification
- A. The three-race theory
- B. Evolutionary theory
- C. The geographical-race theory

II. Alternatives to racial classification
- A. The clinal approach
- B. The population approach

III. How human populations develop and change
- A. Natural selection
- B. Mutation
- C. Genetic drift
- D. The founder effect
- E. Migration and gene flow

IV. The social significance of race
- A. Race and ethnic or national identity
- B. Race and discrimination

Questions

How do mutations lead to changes in human populations?
Why might the disease cystic fibrosis affect mainly members of European populations and their descendants?
Why do most physical anthropologists doubt that "pure" races ever existed?
Why were natural barriers considered important in the geographical-races theory?
What are difficulties in using intelligence as a basis for comparing groups of people?
What is a *nonadaptive* trait?
How can large amounts of melanin be helpful under some conditions and harmful under others?
What is natural selection? How does it cause human populations to change?
How do anthropologists use clines to study human variations?
How does a race differ from a species?

Additional resources

Klass, Morton, and Hellman, Hal. *The Kinds of Mankind: An Introduction to Race and Racism.* Lippincott, 1971.

Kottak, Conrad P. *Anthropology: The Exploration of Human Diversity.* 5th ed. McGraw, 1991.

Lewontin, Richard C. *Human Diversity.* Scientific Am. Bks., 1982.

Molnar, Stephen. *Human Variation: Races, Types, and Ethnic Groups.* 2nd ed. Prentice-Hall, 1983.

Census Supplement

...Atlanta ■ Boston ■ Chicago...

This section lists official population figures according to the 1990 census of the United States conducted by the U.S. Bureau of the Census. The following pages give population totals for metropolitan areas, counties, and cities. The states are arranged in alphabetical order, and each community is listed alphabetically under the state in which it is located. This supplement is presented as a special service to owners of **The World Book Encyclopedia.**

Alabama ■ population 4,062,608

Metropolitan areas

Anniston 116,034
Birmingham 907,810
Columbus (Ga.) 243,072 (196,212 in Ga.; 46,860 in Ala.)
Decatur 131,556
Dothan 130,964
Florence 131,327
Gadsden 99,840
Huntsville 238,912
Mobile 476,923
Montgomery 292,517
Tuscaloosa 150,522

Counties

Autauga 34,222
Baldwin 98,280
Barbour 25,417
Bibb 16,576
Blount 39,248
Bullock 11,042
Butler 21,892
Calhoun 116,034
Chambers 36,876
Cherokee 19,543
Chilton 32,458
Choctaw 16,018
Clarke 27,240
Clay 13,252
Cleburne 12,730
Coffee 40,240
Colbert 51,666
Conecuh 14,054
Coosa 11,063
Covington 36,478
Crenshaw 13,635
Cullman 67,613
Dale 49,633
Dallas 48,130
De Kalb 54,651
Elmore 49,210
Escambia 35,518
Etowah 99,840
Fayette 17,962
Franklin 27,814
Geneva 23,647
Greene 10,153
Hale 15,498
Henry 15,374
Houston 81,331
Jackson 47,796
Jefferson 651,525
Lamar 15,715
Lauderdale 79,661
Lawrence 31,513
Lee 87,146
Limestone 54,135
Lowndes 12,658
Macon 24,928
Madison 238,912
Marengo 23,084
Marion 29,830
Marshall 70,832
Mobile 378,643
Monroe 23,968
Montgomery 209,085
Morgan 100,043
Perry 12,759
Pickens 20,699
Pike 27,595
Randolph 19,881
Russell 46,860
St. Clair 50,009
Shelby 99,358
Sumter 16,174
Talladega 74,107
Tallapoosa 38,826
Tuscaloosa 150,522
Walker 67,670
Washington 16,694
Wilcox 13,568
Winston 22,053

Cities and towns

Abbeville 3,173
Adamsville 4,161
Addison 626
Akron 468
Alabaster 14,732
Albertville 14,507
Alexander City 14,917
Aliceville 3,009
Allgood 464
Altoona 960
Andalusia 9,269
Anderson 339
Anniston 26,623
Arab 6,321
Ardmore 1,090
Argo 930
Ariton 743
Arley 338
Ashford 1,926
Ashland 2,034
Ashville 1,494
Athens 16,901
Atmore 8,046
Attalla 6,859
Auburn 33,830
Autaugaville 681
Avon 462
Babbie 576
Baileyton 352
Bay Minette 7,168
Bayou La Batre 2,456
Bear Creek 913
Beatrice 454
Beaverton 319
Belk 255
Berry 1,218
Bessemer 33,497
Birmingham 265,968
Blountsville 1,527
Blue Mountain 221
Blue Ridge 1,151
Boaz 6,928
Boligee 268
Branchville 370
Brantley 1,015
Brent 2,776
Brewton 5,885
Bridgeport 2,936
Brighton 4,518
Brilliant 751
Brookside 1,365
Brookwood 658
Brundidge 2,472
Butler 1,872
Bynum 1,917
Cahaba Heights 4,778
Calera 2,136
Camden 2,414
Camp Hill 1,415
Carbon Hill 2,115
Carolina 201
Carrollton 1,170
Castleberry 669
Cedar Bluff 1,174
Center Point 22,658
Centre 2,893
Centreville 2,508
Chatom 1,094
Chelsea 1,329
Cherokee 1,479
Chickasaw 6,649
Childersburg 4,579
Citronelle 3,671
Clanton 7,669
Clayhatchee 411
Clayton 1,564
Cleveland 739
Clio 1,365
Coffee Springs 294
Coffeeville 431
Collinsville 1,429
Colony 298
Columbia 922
Columbiana 2,968
Coosada 912
Cordova 2,623
Cottonwood 1,385
Courtland 803
Cowarts 1,400
Creola 1,896
Crossville 1,350
Cuba 390
Cullman 13,367
Dadeville 3,276
Daleville 5,117
Daphne 11,290
Dauphin Island 824
Daviston 261
Decatur 48,761
Demopolis 7,512
Detroit 291
Dora 2,214
Dothan 53,589
Double Springs 1,138
Douglas 474
Dozier 483
Dutton 243
East Brewton 2,579
Eclectic 1,087
Elba 4,011
Elberta 458
Eldridge 225
Elkmont 389
Enterprise 20,123
Epes 267
Eufaula 13,220
Eutaw 2,281
Eva 438
Evergreen 3,911
Excel 571
Fairfield 12,200
Fairhope 8,485
Fairview 383
Falkville 1,337
Fayette 4,909
Five Points 200
Flint City 1,033
Flomaton 1,811
Florala 2,075
Florence 36,426
Foley 4,937
Forestdale 10,395
Forkland 667
Fort Deposit 1,240
Fort McClellan 4,128
Fort Payne 11,838
Fort Rucker 7,593
Frisco City 1,581
Fulton 384
Fultondale 6,400
Fyffe 1,094
Gadsden 42,523
Gainesville 449
Gantt 265
Garden City 578
Gardendale 9,251
Geiger 270
Geneva 4,681
Georgiana 1,933
Geraldine 801
Gilbertown 235
Glen Allen 350
Glencoe 4,670
Glenwood 208
Good Hope 1,700
Goodwater 1,840
Gordo 1,918
Gordon 493
Goshen 302
Grand Bay 3,383
Grant 638
Graysville 2,241
Greensboro 3,047
Greenville 7,492
Grimes 443
Grove Hill 1,551
Guin 2,464
Gulf Shores 3,261
Guntersville 7,038
Gurley 1,007
Gu-Win 243
Hackleburg 1,161
Haleyville 4,452
Hamilton 5,787
Hammondville 420
Hanceville 2,246
Harpersville 772
Hartford 2,448
Hartselle 10,795
Harvest 1,922
Hayden 385
Hayneville 969
Hazel Green 2,208
Headland 3,266
Heflin 2,906
Helena 3,918
Henagar 1,934
Highland Lake 304
Hillsboro 587
Hobson City 794
Hodges 272
Hokes Bluff 3,739
Holly Pond 602
Hollywood 916
Holt 4,125
Homewood 22,922
Hoover 39,788
Hueytown 15,280
Huguley 3,161
Huntsville 159,789
Hurtsboro 707
Ider 671
Inverness 2,528
Irondale 9,454
Jackson 5,819
Jacksons Gap 789
Jacksonville 10,283
Jasper 13,553
Jemison 1,898
Kansas 230
Kennedy 523
Killen 1,047
Kimberly 1,096
Kinsey 1,679
Kinston 595
Ladonia 2,905
Lafayette 3,151
Lake Purdy 1,840
Lanett 8,985
Langston 207
Leeds 9,946
Leesburg 218
Leighton 988
Level Plains 1,473
Lexington 821
Lincoln 2,941
Linden 2,548
Lineville 2,394
Lipscomb 2,892
Lisman 481
Littleville 925
Livingston 3,530
Loachapoka 259
Lockhart 484
Locust Fork 342
Louisville 728
Loxley 1,161
Luverne 2,555
Lynn 611
Madison 14,904
Madrid 211
Malvern 570
Maplesville 725
Margaret 616
Marion 4,211
Maytown 651
McIntosh 250
McKenzie 464
Meadowbrook 4,621
Mentone 474
Meridianville 2,852
Midfield 5,559
Midland City 1,819
Midway 455
Mignon 1,548
Millbrook 6,050
Millport 1,203
Millry 781
Minor 3,313
Mobile 196,278
Monroeville 6,993
Montevallo 4,239
Montgomery 187,106
Moody 4,921
Moores Mill 3,362
Morris 1,136
Mosses 1,072
Moulton 3,248
Moundville 1,348
Mount Vernon 902
Mountain Brook 19,810
Mountainboro 261
Mulga 261
Muscle Shoals 9,611
Napier Field 462
Nauvoo 240
Nectar 238
New Brockton 1,184
New Hope 2,248
New Market 1,094
New Site 669
Newbern 222
Newton 1,580
Newville 531
North Courtland 973
Northport 17,366
Notasulga 979
Oak Grove 436
Oakman 846
Odenville 796
Ohatchee 1,042
Oneonta 4,844
Opelika 22,122
Opp 6,985
Orange Beach 2,253
Orrville 234
Owens Cross Roads 695
Oxford 9,362
Ozark 12,922
Paint Rock 214
Parrish 1,433
Pelham 9,765
Pell City 8,118
Pennington 302
Phenix City 25,312
Phil Campbell 1,317
Piedmont 5,288
Pinckard 618
Pine Apple 365
Pine Hill 481
Pine Ridge 227
Pinson (-Clay-Chalkville) 10,987
Pisgah 652
Pleasant Grove 8,458
Poarch Creek Reservation 212
Point Clear 2,125
Powell 762
Prattville 19,587
Priceville 1,323
Prichard 34,311
Providence 307
Ragland 1,807
Rainbow City 7,673
Rainsville 3,875
Ranburne 447
Red Bay 3,451
Red Level 588
Redstone Arsenal 4,909
Reece City 657
Reform 2,105
Repton 293
River Falls 710
Riverside 1,004
Roanoke 6,362
Robertsdale 2,401
Rockford 461
Rogersville 1,125
Russellville 7,812
Rutledge 473
St. Florian 388
Saks 11,138
Samson 2,190
Sand Rock 438
Sanford 282
Saraland 11,751
Sardis 1,301
Satsuma 5,194
Scottsboro 13,786
Section 777
Selma 23,755
Selmont (-West Selmont) 3,823
Sheffield 10,380
Shiloh 252
Shorter 461
Silas 245
Silverhill 556
Sipsey 568
Skyline 740
Slocomb 1,906
Smiths 3,456
Smoke Rise 1,367
Snead 632
Somerville 211
South Vinemont 543
Southside 5,580
Spanish Fort 3,732
Springville 1,910
Steele 1,046
Stevenson 2,046
Sulligent 1,886
Sumiton 2,604
Summerdale 559
Susan Moore 658
Sweet Water 243
Sylacauga 12,520
Sylvan Springs 1,470
Sylvania 932
Talladega 18,175
Tallassee 5,112
Tarrant 8,046
Taylor 1,352
Theodore 6,509
Thomaston 497
Thomasville 4,301
Thorsby 1,465
Tillmans Corner 17,988
Town Creek 1,379
Toxey 211
Trafford 739
Triana 499
Trinity 1,380
Troy 13,051
Trussville 8,266
Tuscaloosa 77,759
Tuscumbia 8,413
Tuskegee 12,257
Underwood (-Petersville) 3,092
Union 321
Union Springs 3,975
Uniontown 1,730
Valley 8,173
Valley Head 577
Vance 248
Vernon 2,247
Vestavia Hills 19,749
Vina 356
Vincent 1,767
Vredenburgh 313
Wadley 517
Waldo 309
Walnut Grove 717
Warrior 3,280
Waterloo 250
Weaver 2,715
Webb 1,039
Wedowee 796
West Blocton 1,468
West End (-Cobbtown) 4,034
West Jefferson 388
West Point 257
Weston 384
Wetumpka 4,670
White Hall 814
Wilmer 494
Wilsonville 1,185
Wilton 602
Winfield 3,689
Woodville 687
Yellow Bluff 245
York 3,160

Alaska ■ population 551,947

Metropolitan area

Anchorage 226,338

Boroughs

Aleutians East 2,464
Anchorage 226,338
Bristol Bay 1,410
Denali 1,750
Fairbanks North Star 77,720
Haines 2,117
Juneau 26,751
Kenai Peninsula 40,802
Ketchikan Gateway 13,828
Kodiak Island 13,309
Lake and Peninsula 1,668
Matanuska-Susitna 39,683
North Slope 5,979
Northwest Arctic 6,113
Sitka 8,588

Cities and towns

Adak Station 4,633
Akhiok 77
Akiachak 481
Akiak 285
Akutan 589
Alakanuk 544
Aleknagik 185
Allakaket 170
Ambler 311
Anaktuvuk Pass 259
Anchor Point 866
Anchorage 226,338
Anderson 628
Angoon 638
Aniak 540
Annette 43
Anvik 82
Arctic Village 96
Atka 73
Atkasook 216
Atmautluak 258
Barrow 3,469
Beaver 103
Bethel 4,674
Big Delta 400
Big Lake 1,477
Birch Creek 42
Buckland 318
Butte 2,039
Cantwell 147
Central 52
Chalkyitsik 90
Chefornak 320
Chevak 598
Chickaloon 145
Chignik 188
Chignik Lagoon 53
Chignik Lake 133
Chistochina 60
Chitina 49
Chuathbaluk 97
Circle 73
Clam Gulch 79
Clarks Point 60
Coffman Cove 186
Cohoe 508
Cold Bay 148
College 11,249
Cooper Landing 243
Copper Center 449
Cordova 2,110
Craig 1,260
Crooked Creek 106
Deadhorse 26
Deering 157
Delta Junction 652
Dillingham 2,017
Diomede 178
Dot Lake 70
Eagle 168
Eagle Village 35
Edna Bay 86
Eek 254
Egegik 122
Eielson AFB 5,251
Ekwok 77
Elfin Cove 57
Elim 264
Emmonak 642
English Bay 158
Ester 147
Evansville 33
Eyak 172
Fairbanks 30,843
False Pass 68
Fort Greely 1,147
Fort Yukon 580
Fox 275
Fritz Creek 1,426
Gakona 25
Galena 833
Gambell 525
Glennallen 451
Golovin 127
Goodnews Bay 241
Grayling 208
Gulkana 103
Gustavus 258
Haines 1,238
Halibut Cove 78
Harding Lake 27
Healy 487
Healy Lake 47
Hollis 111
Holy Cross 277
Homer 3,660
Hoonah 795
Hooper Bay 845
Hope 161
Houston 697
Hughes 54
Huslia 207
Hydaburg 384
Hyder 99
Igiugig 33
Iliamna 94
Ivanof Bay 35
Jakolof Bay 28
Juneau 26,751
Kachemak 365
Kake 700
Kaktovik 224
Kalifonsky 285
Kaltag 240
Karluk 71

Alaska (continued)

Kasaan 54
Kasilof 383
Kenai 6,327
Ketchikan 8,263
Kiana 385
King Cove 451
King Salmon 696
Kipnuk 470
Kivalina 317
Klawock 722
Klukwan 129
Kobuk 69
Kodiak 6,365
Kodiak Station 2,025
Kokhonak 152
Koliganek 181
Kongiganak 294
Kotlik 461
Kotzebue 2,751
Koyuk 231
Koyukuk 126
Kupreanof 23
Kwethluk 558
Kwigillingok 278
Larsen Bay 147
Levelock 105
Lime Village 42
Lower Kalskag 291
Manley Hot Springs 96
Manokotak 385
McGrath 528
McKinley Park 171
Mekoryuk 177
Mentasta Lake 96
Metlakatla 1,407
Minto 218
Moose Creek 610
Moose Pass 81
Mountain Village 674
Naknek 575
Napakiak 318
Napaskiak 328
Nelson Lagoon 83
Nenana 393
New Stuyahok 391
Newhalen 160
Newtok 207
Nightmute 153
Nikiski 2,743
Nikolai 109
Nikolski 35
Ninilchik 456
Noatak 333
Nome 3,500
Nondalton 178
Noorvik 531
North Pole 1,456
Northway 123
Northway Village 113
Nuiqsut 354
Nulato 359
Old Harbor 284
Oscarville 57
Ouzinkie 209
Palmer 2,866
Paxson 30
Pedro Bay 42
Pelican 222
Perryville 108
Petersburg 3,207
Pilot Point 53
Pilot Station 463
Pitkas Point 135
Platinum 64
Point Baker 39
Point Hope 639
Point Lay 139
Port Alexander 119
Port Clarence 26
Port Graham 166
Port Heiden 119
Port Lions 222
Prudhoe Bay 47
Quinhagak 501
Rampart 68
Red Devil 53
Ruby 170
Russian Mission 246
St. George 138
St. Marys 441
St. Michael 295
St. Paul 763
Salamatof 999
Salcha 354
Sand Point 878
Savoonga 519
Saxman 369
Scammon Bay 343
Selawik 596
Seldovia 316
Seward 2,699
Shageluk 139
Shaktoolik 178
Sheldon Point 109
Shishmaref 456
Shungnak 223
Sitka 8,588
Skagway 692
Slana 63
Sleetmute 106
Soldotna 3,482
South Naknek 136
Stebbins 400
Sterling 3,802
Stevens Village 102
Stony River 51
Sutton 308
Takotna 38
Talkeetna 250
Tanacross 106
Tanana 345
Tatitlek 119
Tazlina 247
Telida 11
Teller 151
Tenakee Springs 94
Tetlin 87
Thorne Bay 569
Togiak 613
Tok 935
Toksook Bay 420
Tonsina 38
Tuluksak 358
Tununak 316
Twin Hills 66
Two Rivers 453
Tyonek 154
Ugashik 7
Unalakleet 714
Unalaska 3,089
Upper Kalskag 172
Valdez 4,068
Venetie 182
Wainwright 492
Wales 161
Wasilla 4,028
White Mountain 180
Whittier 243
Willow 285
Wiseman 33
Wrangell 2,479
Yakutat 534

Arizona ■ population 3,677,985

Metropolitan areas

Phoenix 2,122,101
Tucson 666,880

Counties

Apache 61,591
Cochise 97,624
Coconino 96,591
Gila 40,216
Graham 26,554
Greenlee 8,008
La Paz 13,844
Maricopa 2,122,101
Mohave 93,497
Navajo 77,658
Pima 666,880
Pinal 116,379
Santa Cruz 29,676
Yavapai 107,714
Yuma 106,895

Cities and towns

Ajo 2,919
Ak Chin 353
Apache Junction 18,100
Avondale 16,169
Bagdad 1,858
Benson 3,824
Bisbee 6,288
Black Canyon City 1,811
Buckeye 5,038
Bullhead City [-Riveira] 21,951
Bylas 1,219
Cameron 493
Camp Verde 6,243
Casa Grande 19,082
Catalina 4,864
Cave Creek 2,925
Central Heights [-Midland City] 2,969
Chandler 90,533
Chinle 5,059
Chino Valley 4,837
Chuichu 330
Cibecue 1,254
Clarkdale 2,144
Claypool 1,942
Clifton 2,840
Colorado City 2,426
Coolidge 6,927
Cornville 2,089
Cottonwood 5,918
Dennehotso 616
Dewey [-Humboldt] 3,640
Douglas 12,822
Dudleyville 1,356
Duncan 662
Eagar 4,025
Ehrenberg 1,226
El Mirage 5,001
Eloy 7,211
Flagstaff 45,857
Florence 7,510
Fort Defiance 4,489
Fountain Hills 10,030
Fredonia 1,207
Ganado 1,257
Gila Bend 1,747
Gilbert 29,188
Glendale 148,134
Globe 6,062
Goodyear 6,258
Grand Canyon Village 1,499
Greasewood 196
Green Valley 13,231
Guadalupe 5,458
Hayden 909
Heber 1,581
Holbrook 4,686
Hotevilla 869
Huachuca City 1,782
Jerome 403
Kaibito 641
Kayenta 4,372
Keams Canyon 393
Kearny 2,262
Kingman 12,722
Komatke 1,116
Lake Havasu City 24,363
Lake Montezuma 1,841
Leupp 857
Litchfield Park 3,303
Lukachukai 113
Luke AFB 4,371
Mammoth 1,845
Many Farms 1,294
Marana 2,187
McNary 355
Mesa 288,091
Miami 2,018
Moenkopi 924
Morenci 1,799
Nogales 19,489
Oracle 3,043
Oro Valley 6,670
Page 6,598
Paradise Valley 11,671
Parker 2,897
Patagonia 888
Payson 8,377
Peach Springs 787
Peoria 50,618
Peridot 957
Phoenix 983,403
Pima 1,725
Pinetop [-Lakeside] 2,422
Piñon 468
Pirtleville 1,364
Pisinimo 341
Polacca 1,108
Prescott 26,455
Prescott Valley 8,858
Quartzsite 1,876
Queen Creek 2,667
Rough Rock 523
Sacaton 1,452
Safford 7,359
St. David 1,468
St. Johns 3,294
St. Michaels 1,119
San Carlos 2,918
San Luis 4,212
San Manuel 4,009
Scottsdale 130,069
Sedona 7,720
Sells 2,750
Shongopovi 730
Shonto 710
Show Low 5,019
Sierra Vista 32,983
Snowflake 3,679
Somerton 5,282
South Tucson 5,093
Springerville 1,802
Sun City 38,126
Sun City West 15,997
Sun Lakes 6,578
Supai 423
Superior 3,468
Surprise 7,122
Swift Trail Junction 1,203
Taylor 2,418
Teec Nos Pos 317
Tempe 141,865
Thatcher 3,763
Three Points 2,175
Tolleson 4,434
Tombstone 1,220
Tuba City 7,323
Tucson 405,390
Tucson Estates 2,662
Wellton 1,066
Whiteriver 3,775
Wickenburg 4,515
Willcox 3,122
Williams 2,532
Window Rock 3,306
Winkelman 676
Winslow 8,190
Youngtown 2,542
Yuma 54,923

Arkansas ■ population 2,362,239

Metropolitan areas

Fayetteville-Springdale 113,409
Fort Smith 175,911 (142,083 in Ark.; 33,828 in Okla.)
Little Rock 513,117
Memphis (Tenn.) 981,747 (863,898 in Tenn.; 49,939 in Ark.; 67,910 in Miss.)
Pine Bluff 85,487
(Tex.) 120,132 (81,665 in Tex.; 38,467 in Ark.)

Counties

Arkansas 21,653
Ashley 24,319
Baxter 31,186
Benton 97,499
Boone 28,297
Bradley 11,793
Calhoun 5,826
Carroll 18,654
Chicot 15,713
Clark 21,437
Clay 18,107
Cleburne 19,411
Cleveland 7,781
Columbia 25,691
Conway 19,151
Craighead 68,956
Crawford 42,493
Crittenden 49,939
Cross 19,225
Dallas 9,614
Desha 16,798
Drew 17,369
Faulkner 60,006
Franklin 14,897
Fulton 10,037
Garland 73,397
Grant 13,948
Greene 31,804
Hempstead 21,621
Hot Spring 26,115
Howard 13,569
Independence 31,192
Izard 11,364
Jackson 18,944
Jefferson 85,487
Johnson 18,221
Lafayette 9,643
Lawrence 17,457
Lee 13,053
Lincoln 13,690
Little River 13,966
Logan 20,557
Lonoke 39,268
Madison 11,618
Marion 12,001
Miller 38,467
Mississippi 57,525
Monroe 11,333
Montgomery 7,841
Nevada 10,101
Newton 7,666
Ouachita 30,574
Perry 7,969
Phillips 28,838
Pike 10,086
Poinsett 24,664
Polk 17,347
Pope 45,883
Prairie 9,518
Pulaski 349,660
Randolph 16,558
St. Francis 28,497
Saline 64,183
Scott 10,205
Searcy 7,841
Sebastian 99,590
Sevier 13,637
Sharp 14,109
Stone 9,775
Union 46,719
Van Buren 14,008
Washington 113,409
White 54,676
Woodruff 9,520
Yell 17,759

Cities and towns

Alexander 201
Alma 2,959
Almyra 311
Alpena 319
Altheimer 972
Altus 433
Amity 526
Arkadelphia 10,014
Arkansas City 523
Ash Flat 667
Ashdown 5,150
Atkins 2,834
Aubrey 204
Augusta 2,759
Austin 235
Avoca 269
Bald Knob 2,653
Barling 4,078
Batesville 9,187
Bauxite 412
Bay 1,660
Bearden 1,021
Beebe 4,455
Bella Vista 9,083
Bellefonte 361
Belleville 390
Benton 18,177
Bentonville 11,257
Bergman 324
Berryville 3,212
Bethel Heights 281
Bigelow 340
Biggers 337
Black Oak 277
Black Rock 736
Blevins 253
Bluff City 227
Blytheville 22,906
Bonanza 520
Bono 1,220
Booneville 3,804
Bradford 874
Bradley 585
Branch 299
Brinkley 4,234
Brookland 919
Bryant 5,269
Buckner 325
Bull Shoals 1,534
Cabot 8,319
Caddo Valley 389
Caldwell 334
Calico Rock 938
Calion 558
Camden 14,380
Cammack Village 828
Campbell Station 247
Caraway 1,178
Carlisle 2,253
Carthage 452
Casa 200
Cash 214
Caulksville 224
Cave City 1,503
Cave Springs 465
Centerton 491
Central City 419
Charleston 2,128
Cherokee Village [-Hidden Valley] 4,416
Cherry Valley 659
Chidester 412
Clarendon 2,072
Clarksville 5,833
Clinton 2,213
Coal Hill 912
College City 339
Colt 334
Concord 262
Conway 26,481
Corning 3,323
Cotter 867
Cotton Plant 1,150
Cove 346
Crawfordsville 617
Crossett 6,282
Cushman 428
Damascus 246
Danville 1,585
Dardanelle 3,722
Decatur 918
Delight 311
Dell 258
Denning 206
De Queen 4,633
Dermott 4,715
Des Arc 2,001
De Valls Bluff 702
De Witt 3,553
Diamond City 601
Diaz 1,363
Dierks 1,263
Dover 1,055
Dumas 5,520
Dyer 502
Dyess 466
Earle 3,393
East Camden 783
Edmondson 286
Elaine 846
El Dorado 23,146
Elkins 692
Elm Springs 893
Emerson 317
Emmet 446
England 3,351
Eudora 3,155
Eureka Springs 1,900
Evening Shade 328
Farmington 1,322
Fayetteville 42,099
Fisher 245
Flippin 1,006
Fordyce 4,729
Foreman 1,267
Forrest City 13,364
Fort Smith 72,798
Fouke 634
Franklin 205
Fredonia 484
Fulton 269
Garfield 308
Garland 415
Gassville 1,167
Gentry 1,726
Gillett 883
Gillham 210
Gilmore 331
Glenwood 1,354
Goshen 589
Gosnell 3,783
Gould 1,470
Grady 586
Grannis 507
Gravel Ridge 3,846
Gravette 1,412
Green Forest 2,050
Greenbrier 2,130
Greenland 757
Greenway 212
Greenwood 3,984
Greers Ferry 724
Griffithville 237
Grubbs 528
Gurdon 2,199
Guy 241
Hackett 490
Hamburg 3,098
Hampton 1,562
Hardy 538
Harrell 258
Harrisburg 1,943
Harrison 9,922
Hartford 721
Hartman 498
Haskell 1,342
Hatfield 414
Havana 358
Haynes 268
Hazen 1,668
Heber Springs 5,628
Hector 478
Helena 7,491
Hermitage 639
Hickory Ridge 436
Higginson 255
Holly Grove 675
Hope 9,643
Horatio 793
Horseshoe Bend 2,239
Hot Springs 32,462
Hot Springs Village 6,361
Hoxie 2,676
Hughes 1,810
Humnoke 311
Humphrey 743
Huntington 715
Huntsville 1,605
Huttig 831
Imboden 616
Jacksonport 264
Jacksonville 29,101
Jasper 332
Jericho 210
Johnson 599
Joiner 645
Jonesboro 46,535
Judsonia 1,915
Junction City 674
Keiser 805

Kensett 1,741
Kibler 931
Kingsland 395
Knobel 317
Knoxville 239
Lafe 315
Lake City 1,833
Lake Hamilton 1,331
Lake View 526
Lake Village 2,791
Lakeview 485
Lamar 768
Lavaca 1,253
Leachville 1,743
Lead Hill 283
Leola 476
Lepanto 2,033
Leslie 446
Letona 218
Lewisville 1,424
Lexa 295
Lincoln 1,460
Little Flock 944
Little Rock 175,795
Lockesburg 608
London 825
Lonoke 4,022
Lowell 1,224
Luxora 1,338
Lynn 299
Madison 1,263
Magazine 799
Magnolia 11,151
Malvern 9,256
Mammoth Spring 1,097
Manila 2,635
Mansfield 1,018
Marianna 5,910
Marion 4,391
Marked Tree 3,100
Marmaduke 1,164
Marshall 1,318
Marvell 1,545
Mayflower 1,415
Maynard 354
McCrory 1,971
McDougal 208
McGehee 4,997
McNeil 686
McRae 669
Melbourne 1,562
Mena 5,475
Menifee 355
Midland 220
Mineral Springs 1,004
Mitchellville 513
Monette 1,115
Monticello 8,116
Montrose 528
Moro 287
Morrilton 6,551
Mount Ida 775
Mount Pleasant 422
Mountain Home 9,027
Mountain Pine 866
Mountain View 2,439
Mountainburg 488
Mulberry 1,448
Murfreesboro 1,542
Nashville 4,639
Newark 1,159
Newport 7,459
Norfork 394
Norman 382
Norphlet 706
North Crossett 3,358
North Little Rock 61,741
Oak Grove 231
Oak Grove Heights 513
Ogden 264
Oil Trough 208
O'Kean 250
Ola 1,090
Omaha 207
Oppelo 643
Osceola 8,930
Oxford 562
Ozark 3,330
Palestine 711
Pangburn 630
Paragould 18,540
Paris 3,674
Parkdale 393
Parkers
[-Iron Springs] 3,611
Parkin 1,847
Patterson 445
Pea Ridge 1,620
Perry 228
Perrytown 248
Perryville 1,141
Piggott 3,777
Pine Bluff 57,140
Pineville 220
Piney 2,500
Plainview 685
Pleasant Plains 256
Plumerville 832
Pocahontas 6,151
Pollard 229
Portia 521
Portland 560
Pottsville 984
Poyen 303
Prairie Grove 1,761
Prattsville 251
Prescott 3,673
Quitman 632
Ravenden 330
Rector 2,268
Redfield 1,082
Reed 355
Reyno 467
Rison 1,258
Rockport 388
Rockwell 2,514
Rogers 24,692
Rondo 283
Rosston 262
Russellville 21,260
St. Francis 201
Salem 1,474
Salem 2,950
Salesville 374
Scranton 218
Searcy 15,180
Shannon Hills 1,755
Sheridan 3,098
Sherwood 18,893
Shirley 363
Sidney 271
Siloam Springs 8,151
Smackover 2,232
Sparkman 553
Springdale 29,941
Stamps 2,478
Star City 2,138
Stephens 1,137
Strawberry 273
Strong 624
Stuttgart 10,420
Subiaco 538
Sulphur Rock 356
Sulphur Springs 523
Summit 480
Sunset 571
Swifton 830
Tafton
[-Wrightsville] 1,062
Taylor 621
Texarkana 22,631
Thornton 502
Tillar 221
Tollette 316
Tontitown 460
Traskwood 488
Trumann 6,304
Tuckerman 2,020
Tull 313
Tupelo 208
Turrell 988
Tyronza 858
Valley Springs 200
Van Buren 14,979
Vilonia 1,133
Viola 320
Wabbaseka 332
Waldo 1,495
Waldron 3,024
Walnut Ridge 4,388
Ward 1,269
Warren 6,455
Watson 282
Weiner 655
West Crossett 2,019
West Fork 1,607
West Helena 9,695
West Memphis 28,259
Western
Grove 415
Wheatley 413
White Hall 3,849
Wickes 570
Widener 381
Wilmar 637
Wilmot 1,047
Wilson 1,068
Wilton 449
Winchester 239
Winslow 342
Winthrop 227
Wooster 414
Wynne 8,187
Yellville 1,181

California ■ population 29,839,250

Metropolitan areas

Anaheim-
Santa Ana 2,410,556
Bakersfield 543,477
Chico 182,120
Fresno 667,490
Los Angeles-
Long Beach 8,863,164
Merced 178,403
Modesto 370,522
Oakland 2,082,914
Oxnard-Ventura 669,016
Redding 147,036
Riverside-
San Bernardino 2,588,793
Sacramento 1,481,102
Salinas-Seaside-
Monterey 355,660
San Diego 2,498,016
San Francisco 1,603,678
San Jose 1,497,577
Santa Barbara-Santa
Maria-Lompoc 369,608
Santa Cruz 229,734
Santa Rosa-
Petaluma 388,222
Stockton 480,628
Vallejo-Fairfield-
Napa 451,186
Visalia-Tulare-
Porterville 311,921
Yuba City 106,895

Counties

Alameda 1,279,182
Alpine 1,113
Amador 30,039
Butte 182,120
Calaveras 31,998
Colusa 16,275
Contra Costa 803,732
Del Norte 23,460
El Dorado 125,995
Fresno 667,490
Glenn 24,798
Humboldt 119,118
Imperial 109,303
Inyo 18,281
Kern 543,477
Kings 101,469
Lake 50,631
Lassen 27,598
Los Angeles 8,863,164
Madera 88,090
Marin 230,096
Mariposa 14,302
Mendocino 80,345
Merced 178,403
Modoc 9,678
Mono 9,956
Monterey 335,660
Napa 110,765
Nevada 78,510
Orange 2,410,556
Placer 172,796
Plumas 19,739
Riverside 1,170,413
Sacramento 1,041,219
San Benito 36,697
San
Bernardino 1,418,380
San Diego 2,498,016
San Francisco 723,959
San Joaquin 480,628
San Luis Obispo 217,162
San Mateo 649,623
Santa Barbara 369,608
Santa Clara 1,497,577
Santa Cruz 229,734
Shasta 147,036
Sierra 3,318
Siskiyou 43,531
Solano 340,421
Sonoma 388,222
Stanislaus 370,522
Sutter 64,415
Tehama 49,625
Trinity 13,063
Tulare 311,921
Tuolumne 48,456
Ventura 669,016
Yolo 141,092
Yuba 58,228

Cities and towns

Adelanto 8,517
Agoura Hills 20,390
Alameda 76,459
Alamo 12,277
Albany 16,327
Alhambra 82,106
Alondra Park 12,215
Alpine 9,695
Alta Sierra 5,709
Altadena 42,658
Alturas 3,231
American Canyon 7,706
Anaheim 266,406
Anderson 8,299
Angels 2,409
Angwin 3,503
Antioch 62,195
Apple Valley 46,079
Aptos 9,061
Arbuckle 1,912
Arcadia 48,290
Arcata 15,197
Arden [-Arcade] 92,040
Armona 3,122
Arnold 3,788
Arroyo Grande 14,378
Artesia 15,464
Arvin 9,286
Ashland 16,590
Atascadero 23,138
Atherton 7,163
Atwater 22,282
Auburn 10,592
August 6,376
Avalon 2,918
Avenal 9,770
Avocado Heights 14,232
Azusa 41,333
Bakersfield 174,820
Baldwin Park 69,330
Banning 20,570
Barstow 21,472
Bayview
[-Montalvin] 3,988
Baywood
[-Los Osos] 14,377
Beale AFB 6,912
Beaumont 9,685
Bell 34,365
Bell Gardens 42,355
Bellflower 61,815
Belmont 24,127
Belvedere 2,147
Ben Lomond 7,884
Benicia 24,437
Berkeley 102,724
Bethel Island 2,115
Beverly Hills 31,971
Big Bear 4,920
Big Bear Lake 5,351
Big Pine 1,158
Biggs 1,581
Bishop 3,475
Bloomington 15,116
Blue Lake 1,235
Blythe 8,428
Bodfish 1,283
Bolinas 1,098
Bonadelle Ranchos
[-Madera
Ranchos] 5,705
Bonita 12,542
Boron 2,101
Borrego Springs 2,244
Bostonia 13,670
Boulder Creek 6,725
Boyes Hot Springs 5,973
Brawley 18,923
Brea 32,873
Brentwood 7,563
Brisbane 2,952
Buellton 3,506
Buena Park 68,784
Burbank 93,643
Burbank 4,902
Burlingame 26,801
Burney 3,423
Buttonwillow 1,301
Calexico 18,633
California City 5,955
Calimesa 4,647
Calipatria 2,690
Calistoga 4,468
Camarillo 52,303
Cambria 5,382
Cameron Park 11,897
Camp Pendleton
North 10,373
Camp Pendleton
South 11,299
Campbell 36,048
Canyon Lake 7,938
Capitola 10,171
Carlsbad 63,126
Carmel-by-
the-Sea 4,239
Carmel Valley 4,407
Carmichael 48,702
Carpinteria 13,747
Carson 83,995
Caruthers 1,603
Casa de Oro [-Mount
Helix] 30,727
Castro Valley 48,619
Castroville 5,272
Cathedral City 30,085
Cayucos 2,960
Central Valley 4,340
Ceres 26,314
Cerritos 53,240
Charter Oak 8,858
Cherry Valley 5,945
Cherryland 11,088
Chester 2,082
Chico 40,079
Chino 59,682
Chino Hills 27,608
Chowchilla 5,930
Chula Vista 135,163
Citrus 9,481
Citrus Heights 107,439
Claremont 32,503
Clayton 7,317
Clearlake
Highlands 11,804
Clearlake Oaks 2,419
Cloverdale 4,924
Clovis 50,323
Coachella 16,896
Coalinga 8,212
Colton 40,213
Colusa 4,934
Commerce 12,135
Compton 90,454
Concord 111,348
Corcoran 13,364
Corning 5,870
Corona 76,095
Coronado 26,540
Corte Madera 8,272
Costa Mesa 96,357
Cotati 5,714
Cottonwood 1,747
Country Club 9,325
Covelo 1,057
Covina 43,207
Crescent City 4,380
Crescent North 3,853
Crestline 8,594
Cucamonga 101,409
Cudahy 22,817
Culver City 38,793
Cupertino 40,263
Cutler 4,450
Cutten 1,516
Cypress 42,655
Daly City 92,311
Dana Point 31,896
Danville 31,306
Davis 46,209
Deer Park 1,825
Del Aire 8,040
Delano 22,762
Delhi 3,280
Del Mar 4,860
Del Monte Forest 5,069
Del Rey Oaks 1,661
Denair 3,693
Desert Hot
Springs 11,668
Desert View
Highlands 2,154
Diamond Bar 53,672
Diamond Springs 2,872
Dinuba 12,743
Discovery Bay 5,351
Dixon 10,401
Dos Palos 4,196
Downey 91,444
Duarte 20,688
Dublin 23,229
Dunsmuir 2,129
Durham 4,784
Earlimart 5,881
East Blythe 1,511
East Compton 7,967
East Hemet 17,611
East La Mirada 9,367
East
Los Angeles 126,379
East Palo Alto 23,451
East Pasadena 5,910
East Porterville 5,790
East San Gabriel 12,736
Easton 1,877
Edwards AFB 7,423
El Cajon 88,693
El Centro 31,384
El Cerrito 22,869
El Cerrito 4,490
El Dorado Hills 6,395
El Granada 4,426
Elk Grove 17,483
El Monte 106,209
El Rio 6,419
El Segundo 15,223
El Sobrante 9,852
El Toro 62,685
El Toro Station 6,869
El Verano 3,498
Emeryville 5,740
Encinitas 55,386
Escalon 4,437
Escondido 108,635
Esparto 1,487
Eureka 27,025
Exeter 7,276
Fair Oaks 26,867
Fairfax 6,931
Fairfield 77,211
Fallbrook 22,095
Farmersville 6,235
Felton 5,350
Ferndale 1,331
Fetters Hot Springs
[-Agua Caliente] 2,024
Fillmore 11,992
Firebaugh 4,429
Florence
[-Graham] 57,147
Florin 24,330
Folsom 29,802
Fontana 87,535
Foothill Farms 17,135
Ford City 3,781
Fort Bragg 6,078
Fortuna 8,788
Foster City 28,176
Fountain Valley 53,691
Fowler 3,208
Frazier Park 2,201
Freedom 8,361
Fremont 173,339
Fresno 354,202
Fullerton 114,144
Galt 8,889
Garden Acres 8,547
Garden Grove 143,050
Gardena 49,847
George AFB 5,085
Gilroy 31,487
Glen Avon 12,663
Glen Ellen 1,191
Glendale 180,038
Glendora 47,828
Gonzales 4,660
Grand Terrace 10,946
Grass Valley 9,048
Graton 1,409
Greenacres 7,379
Greenfield 7,464
Greenville 1,396
Gridley 4,631
Grover City 11,656
Guadalupe 5,479
Guerneville 1,966
Gustine 3,931
Hacienda
Heights 52,354
Half Moon Bay 8,886
Hamilton City 1,811
Hanford 30,897
Hawaiian
Gardens 13,639
Hawthorne 71,349
Hayfork 2,605
Hayward 111,498
Healdsburg 9,469
Heber 2,566
Hemet 36,094
Hercules 16,829
Hermosa Beach 18,219
Hesperia 50,418
Hidden Hills 1,729
Highland 34,439
Hillmar [-Irwin] 3,392
Hillsborough 10,667
Hollister 19,212
Holtville 4,820
Home Garden 1,549
Home Gardens 7,780
Homeland 3,312
Hughson 3,259
Huntington
Beach 181,519
Huntington Park 56,065
Huron 4,766
Idyllwild
[-Pine Cove] 2,853
Imperial 4,113
Imperial Beach 26,512
Indian Wells 2,647
Indio 36,793
Inglewood 109,602
Ione 6,516
Irvine 110,330
Irwindale 1,050
Isla Vista 20,395
Ivanhoe 3,293
Jackson 3,545
Jamestown 2,178
Jamul 2,258
Joshua Tree 3,898
Julian 1,284
Kelseyville 2,861
Kensington 4,974
Kentfield 6,030
Kerman 5,448
Kernville 1,656
Kettleman City 1,411
King City 7,634
Kings Beach 2,796
Kingsburg 7,205
La Canada
Flintridge 19,378
La Crescenta
[-Montrose] 16,968
Ladera Heights 6,316
Lafayette 23,501
Laguna Beach 23,170
Laguna Hills 46,731
Laguna Niguel 44,400
Lagunitas
[-Forest Knolls] 1,821
La Habra 51,266
La Habra Heights 6,226
Lake Arrowhead 6,539
Lake Elsinore 18,285
Lake Isabella 3,323
Lakeland Village 5,159
Lakeport 4,390
Lakeside 39,412
Lakewood 73,557
La Mesa 52,931
La Mirada 40,452
Lamont 11,517
Lancaster 97,291
La Palma 15,392
La Puente 36,955
La Quinta 11,215
La Riviera 10,986
Larkfield [-Wikiup] 6,779
Larkspur 11,070
Las Lomas 2,127
Lathrop 6,841
Laton 1,415
La Verne 30,897
Lawndale 27,331
Laytonville 1,133
Lemon Grove 23,984
Lemoore 13,622
Lennox 22,757
Lenwood 3,190
Lincoln 7,248
Lincoln Village 4,236

California (continued)

Linda 13,033
Lindsay 8,338
Live Oak 4,320
Live Oak 15,212
Livermore 56,741
Livingston 7,317
Lockeford 2,722
Lodi 51,874
Loma Linda 17,400
Lomita 19,382
Lompoc 37,649
London 1,638
Lone Pine 1,818
Long Beach 429,433
Loomis 5,705
Los Alamitos 11,676
Los Altos 26,303
Los Altos Hills 7,514
Los Angeles 3,485,398
Los Banos 14,519
Los Serranos 7,099
Los Gatos 27,357
Los Molinos 1,709
Lower Lake 1,217
Loyalton 931
Lucas Valley [-Marinwood] 5,982
Lucerne 2,011
Lynwood 61,945
Madera 29,281
Madera Acres 5,245
Magalia 8,987
Mammoth Lakes 4,785
Manhattan Beach 32,063
Manteca 40,773
March AFB 5,523
Marina 26,436
Marina Del Ray 7,431
Mariposa 1,152
Martinez 31,808
Marysville 12,324
Mather AFB 4,885
Mayflower Village 4,978
Maywood 27,850
McCloud 1,555
McFarland 7,005
McKinleyville 10,749
Meadow Vista 3,067
Mecca 1,966
Meiners Oaks 3,329
Mendota 6,821
Menlo Park 28,040
Mentone 5,675
Merced 56,216
Mill Valley 13,038
Millbrae 20,412
Milpitas 50,686
Mira Loma 15,786
Mira Monte 7,744
Mission Hills 3,112
Mission Viejo 72,820
Modesto 164,730
Mojave 3,763
Mono Vista 2,599
Monrovia 35,761
Montague 1,415
Montara 2,552
Montclair 28,434
Monte Rio 1,058
Monte Sereno 3,287
Montebello 59,564
Monterey 31,954
Monterey Park 60,738
Moorpark 25,494
Moraga 15,852
Moreno Valley 118,779
Morgan Hill 23,928
Morongo Valley 1,544
Morro Bay 9,664
Moss Beach 3,002
Mount Shasta 3,460
Mountain View 67,460
Mountain View Acres 2,469
Murphys 1,517
Murrieta Hot Springs 1,938
Muscoy 7,541
Myrtletown 4,413
Napa 61,842
National City 54,249
Nebo Center 1,459
Needles 5,191
Nevada City 2,855
Newark 37,861
Newman 4,151
Newport Beach 66,643
Niland 1,183
Nipomo 7,109
Norco 23,302
North Auburn 10,301
North Edwards 1,259
North Fair Oaks 13,912
North Highlands 42,105
Norwalk 94,279
Novato 47,585
Oak View 3,606
Oakdale 11,961
Oakhurst 2,602
Oakland 372,242
Oakley 18,374
Oceano 6,169
Oceanside 128,398
Oildale 26,553
Ojai 7,613
Olivehurst 9,738
Ontario 133,179
Opal Cliffs 5,940
Orange 110,658
Orange Cove 5,604
Orangevale 26,266
Orinda 16,642
Orland 5,052
Orosi 5,486
Oroville 11,960
Oxnard 142,216
Pacheco 3,325
Pacific Grove 16,117
Pacifica 37,670
Pajaro 3,332
Palermo 5,260
Palm Desert 23,252
Palm Springs 40,181
Palmdale 68,842
Palmdale East 3,052
Palo Alto 55,900
Palos Verdes Estates 13,512
Paradise 25,408
Paramount 47,669
Parksdale 1,911
Parkway [-South Sacramento] 31,903
Parkwood 1,659
Parlier 7,938
Pasadena 131,591
Paso Robles 18,583
Patterson 8,626
Pedley 8,869
Penn Valley 1,242
Perris 21,460
Petaluma 43,184
Pico Rivera 59,177
Piedmont 10,602
Pine Hills 2,947
Pinole 17,460
Piru 1,157
Pismo Beach 7,669
Pittsburg 47,564
Pixley 2,457
Placentia 41,259
Placerville 8,355
Planada 3,531
Pleasant Hill 31,585
Pleasanton 50,553
Point Dume 2,809
Pollock Pines 4,291
Pomona 131,723
Poplar [-Cotton Center] 1,901
Port Hueneme 20,319
Porterville 29,563
Portola 2,193
Portola Valley 4,194
Poway 43,516
Prunedale 7,393
Quartz Hill 9,626
Quincy [-East Quincy] 4,271
Rainbow 2,006
Ramona 13,040
Rancho Cordova 48,731
Rancho Mirage 9,778
Rancho Palos Verdes 41,659
Rancho Rinconada 4,206
Rancho San Diego 6,977
Red Bluff 12,363
Redding 66,462
Redlands 60,394
Redondo Beach 60,167
Redway 1,212
Redwood City 66,072
Reedley 15,791
Rialto 72,388
Richgrove 1,899
Richmond 87,425
Ridgecrest 27,725
Rio Del Mar 8,919
Rio Dell 3,012
Rio Linda 9,481
Rio Vista 3,316
Ripon 7,455
Riverbank 8,547
Riverdale 1,980
Riverside 226,505
Rocklin 19,033
Rodeo 7,589
Rohnert Park 36,326
Rolling Hills 1,871
Rolling Hills Estates 7,789
Romoland 2,319
Rosamond 7,430
Roseland 8,779
Rosemead 51,638
Rosemont 22,851
Rosedale 4,673
Roseville 44,685
Ross 2,123
Rossmoor 9,893
Rowland Heights 42,647
Rubidoux 24,367
Running Springs 4,195
Sacramento 369,365
St. Helena 4,990
Salida 4,499
Salinas 108,777
San Andreas 2,115
San Anselmo 11,743
San Bernardino 164,164
San Bruno 38,961
San Carlos 26,167
San Clemente 41,100
San Diego 1,110,549
San Diego Country Estates 77,000
San Dimas 32,397
San Fernando 22,580
San Francisco 723,959
San Gabriel 37,120
San Jacinto 16,210
San Joaquin 2,311
San Jose 782,248
San Juan Bautista 1,570
San Juan Capistrano 26,183
San Leandro 68,223
San Lorenzo 19,987
San Luis Obispo 41,958
San Marcos 38,974
San Marino 12,959
San Martin 1,713
San Mateo 85,486
San Pablo 25,158
San Rafael 48,404
San Ramon 35,303
Sanger 16,839
Santa Ana 293,742
Santa Barbara 85,571
Santa Clara 93,613
Santa Clarita 110,642
Santa Cruz 49,040
Santa Fe Springs 15,520
Santa Maria 61,284
Santa Monica 86,905
Santa Paula 25,062
Santa Rosa 113,313
Santa Ynez 4,200
Santee 52,902
Saratoga 28,061
Sausalito 7,152
Scotts Valley 8,615
Seal Beach 25,098
Searles Valley 2,740
Seaside 38,901
Sebastopol 7,004
Sedco Hills 3,008
Seely 1,228
Selma 14,757
Shafter 8,409
Shingle Springs 2,049
Sierra Madre 10,762
Signal Hill 8,371
Simi Valley 100,217
Solana Beach 12,962
Soledad 7,146
Solvang 4,741
Sonoma 8,121
Sonora 4,153
Soquel 9,188
South El Monte 20,850
South Gate 86,284
South Lake Tahoe 21,586
South Oroville 7,463
South Pasadena 23,936
South San Francisco 54,312
South San Gabriel 7,700
South San Jose Hills 17,814
South Taft 2,170
South Whittier 49,514
South Yuba City 8,816
Spring Valley 55,331
Stanford 18,097
Stanton 30,491
Stockton 210,943
Strathmore 2,353
Suisun City 22,686
Sun City 14,930
Sunnyside [-Tahoe City] 1,643
Sunnyvale 117,229
Susanville 7,279
Sutter 2,606
Sutter Creek 1,835
Taft 5,902
Taft Heights 2,050
Tamalpias [-Homestead Valley] 9,601
Tara Hills 4,998
Tehachapi 5,791
Temecula 27,099
Temple City 31,100
Terra Bella 2,740
Thermalito 5,646
Thousand Oaks 104,352
Thousand Palms 4,122
Tiburon 7,532
Tierra Buena 2,878
Tipton 1,383
Torrance 133,107
Tracy 33,558
Truckee 3,484
Tulare 33,249
Tuolumne 1,686
Turlock 42,198
Tustin 50,689
Tustin Foothills 24,358
Twain Harte 2,170
Twentynine Palms 11,821
Twentynine Palms Base 10,606
Twin Lakes 5,379
Ukiah 14,599
Union City 53,762
Upland 63,374
Vacaville 71,479
Valinda 18,735
Valle Vista 8,751
Vallejo 109,199
Valley Center 1,711
Vandenburg AFB 9,846
Vandenberg Village 5,971
Ventura (San Buenaventura) 92,575
Victorville 40,674
View Park [-Windsor Hills] 11,769
Villa Park 6,299
Vincent 13,713
Vine Hill 3,214
Visalia 75,636
Vista 71,872
Walnut 29,105
Walnut Creek 60,569
Walnut Park 14,722
Wasco 12,412
Waterford 4,771
Watsonville 31,099
Weaverville 3,370
Weed 3,062
Weed Patch 1,892
West Athens 8,859
West Carson 20,143
West Compton 5,451
West Covina 96,086
West Hollywood 36,118
West Menlo Park 3,959
West Pittsburg 17,453
West Puente Valley 20,254
West Sacramento 28,898
West Whittier [-Los Nietos] 24,164
Westlake Village 7,455
Westminster 78,118
Westmont 31,044
Westmorland 1,380
Westwood 2,017
Wheatland 1,631
Whittier 77,671
Wildomar 10,411
Williams 2,297
Willits 5,027
Willowbrook 32,772
Willows 5,988
Windsor 13,371
Winters 4,639
Winton 7,559
Wofford Heights 2,270
Woodacre 1,478
Woodbridge 3,456
Woodcrest 7,796
Woodlake 5,678
Woodland 39,802
Woodside 5,035
Woodville 1,557
Wrightwood 3,308
Yorba Linda 52,422
Yountville 3,259
Yreka 6,948
Yuba City 27,437
Yucaipa 32,824
Yucca Valley 13,701

Colorado ■ population 3,307,912

Metropolitan areas

Boulder-Longmont 225,339
Colorado Springs 397,014
Denver 1,622,980
Fort Collins-Loveland 186,136
Greeley 131,821
Pueblo 123,051

Counties

Adams 265,038
Alamosa 13,617
Arapahoe 391,511
Archuleta 5,345
Baca 4,556
Bent 5,048
Boulder 225,339
Chaffee 12,684
Cheyenne 2,397
Clear Creek 7,619
Conejos 7,453
Costilla 3,190
Crowley 3,946
Custer 1,926
Delta 20,980
Denver 467,610
Dolores 1,504
Douglas 60,391
Eagle 21,928
Elbert 9,646
El Paso 397,014
Fremont 32,273
Garfield 29,974
Gilpin 3,070
Grand 7,966
Gunnison 10,273
Hinsdale 467
Huerfano 6,009
Jackson 1,605
Jefferson 438,430
Kiowa 1,688
Kit Carson 7,140
Lake 6,007
La Plata 32,284
Larimer 186,136
Las Animas 13,765
Lincoln 4,529
Logan 17,567
Mesa 93,145
Mineral 558
Moffat 11,357
Montezuma 18,672
Montrose 24,423
Morgan 21,939
Otero 20,185
Ouray 2,295
Park 7,174
Phillips 4,189
Pitkin 12,661
Prowers 13,347
Pueblo 123,051
Rio Blanco 5,972
Rio Grande 10,770
Routt 14,088
Saguache 4,619
San Juan 745
San Miguel 3,653
Sedgwick 2,690
Summit 12,881
Teller 12,468
Washington 4,812
Weld 131,821
Yuma 8,954

Cities and towns

Aguilar 520
Akron 1,599
Alamosa 7,579
Alamosa East 1,389
Antonito 875
Applewood 11,069
Arriba 220
Arvada 89,235
Aspen 5,049
Ault 1,107
Aurora 222,103
Avon 1,798
Basalt 1,128
Bayfield 1,090
Bennett 1,757
Berthoud 2,990
Black Forest 8,143
Black Hawk 227
Blanca 272
Blue River 440
Boone 341
Boulder 83,312
Bow Mar 854
Breckenridge 1,285
Brighton 14,203
Broomfield 24,638
Brush 4,165
Buena Vista 1,752
Burlington 2,941
Byers 1,065
Calhan 562
Campion 1,692
Canon City 12,687
Carbondale 3,004
Castle Rock 8,708
Castlewood 24,392
Cedaredge 1,380
Center 1,963
Central City 335
Cheraw 265
Cherry Hills Village 5,245
Cheyenne Wells 1,128
Cimarron Hills 11,160
Clifton 12,671
Collbran 228
Colorado City 1,149
Colorado Springs 281,140
Columbine 23,969
Columbine Valley 1,071
Commerce City 16,466
Cortez 7,284
Craig 8,091
Crawford 221
Creede 362
Crested Butte 878
Cripple Creek 584
Crowley 225
Dacono 2,228
De Beque 257
Deer Trail 476
Del Norte 1,674
Delta 3,789
Denver 467,610
Dillon 553
Dinosaur 324
Dolores 866
Dove Creek 643
Durango 12,430
Eads 780
Eagle 1,580
Eaton 1,959
Eckley 211
Edgewater 4,613
Elizabeth 818
Empire 401
Englewood 29,387
Erie 1,258
Estes Park 3,184
Evans 5,877
Evergreen 7,582
Fairplay 387
Federal Heights 9,342
Firestone 1,358
Flagler 564
Fleming 344
Florence 2,990
Fort Carson 11,309
Fort Collins 87,758
Fort Lupton 5,159
Fort Morgan 9,068
Fountain 9,984
Fowler 1,154
Fraser 575
Frederick 988
Frisco 1,601
Fruita 4,045
Fruitvale 5,222
Gateway 7,510
Georgetown 891
Gilcrest 1,084
Glendale 2,453
Glenwood Springs 6,561
Golden 13,116
Granada 513
Granby 966
Grand Junction 29,034
Grand Lake 259
Greeley 60,536
Green Mountain Falls 663
Greenwood Village 7,589
Gunbarrel 9,388
Gunnison 4,636
Gypsum 1,750
Haxtun 952
Hayden 1,444
Holly 877
Holyoke 1,931
Hot Sulphur Springs 347
Hotchkiss 744
Hudson 918
Hugo 660
Idaho Springs 1,834
Ignacio 720
Jamestown 251
Johnstown 1,579
Julesburg 1,295
Keenesburg 570
Ken Caryl 24,391
Kersey 980
Kiowa 275
Kit Carson 305
Kremmling 1,166
Lafayette 14,548
La Jara 725
La Junta 7,637
Lake City 223
Lakewood 126,481
Lamar 8,343
Larkspur 232
La Salle 1,783
Las Animas 2,481
La Veta 726
Leadville 2,629
Leadville North 1,757
Limon 1,831
Lincoln Park 3,728
Littleton 33,685
Lochbuie 1,168
Log Lane Village 667
Longmont 51,555
Louisville 12,361
Loveland 37,352
Lyons 1,227
Manassa 988
Mancos 842
Manitou Springs 4,535
Manzanola 437
Mead 456
Meeker 2,098
Merino 238
Milliken 1,605
Minturn 1,066
Monte Vista 4,324
Montrose 8,854
Monument 1,020
Morrison 465

Mount Crested Butte 264
Mountain View 550
Naturita 434
Nederland 1,099
New Castle 679
Niwot 2,666
Northglenn 27,195
Norwood 429
Nucla 656
Nunn 324
Oak Creek 673
Olathe 1,263
Olney Springs 340
Orchard City 2,218
Orchard Mesa 5,977
Ordway 1,025
Otis 451
Ouray 644
Ovid 349
Pagosa Springs 1,207
Palisade 1,871
Palmer Lake 1,480
Paonia 1,403
Parachute 658
Parker 5,450
Penrose 2,235
Pierce 823
Platteville 1,515
Poncha Springs 244
Pueblo 98,640
Rangely 2,278
Red Cliff 297
Ridgway 423
Rifle 4,636
Rockvale 321
Rocky Ford 4,162
Romeo 341
Saguache 584
Salida 4,737
San Luis 800
Sanford 750
Security (-Widefield) 23,822
Sheridan 4,976
Sherrelwood 16,636
Silt 1,095
Silver Cliff 322
Silverthorne 1,768
Silverton 716
Simla 481
Snowmass Village 1,449
Southglenn 43,087
Springfield 1,475
Steamboat Springs 6,695
Sterling 10,362
Stratmoor 5,854
Stratton 649
Sugar City 252
Superior 255
Swink 584
Telluride 1,309
Thornton 55,031
Towaoc 700
Trinidad 8,580
United States Air Force Academy 9,062
Vail 3,659
Victor 258
Walden 890
Walsenburg 3,300
Walsh 692
Welby 10,218
Wellington 1,340
Westcliffe 312
Westminster 74,625
Westminster East 5,197
Wheat Ridge 29,419
Wiggins 499
Wiley 406
Williamsburg 253
Windsor 5,062
Winter Park 528
Woodland Park 4,610
Woodmoor 3,858
Wray 1,998
Yampa 317
Yuma 2,719

Connecticut ■ population 3,295,669

Metropolitan areas

Bridgeport-Milford 443,722
Bristol 79,488
Danbury 187,867
Hartford 767,841
Middletown 90,320
New Britain 148,188
New Haven-Meriden 530,180
New London-Norwich 266,819 (238,341 in Conn.; 28,478 in R.I.)
Norwalk 127,378
Stamford 202,557
Waterbury 221,629

Counties

Fairfield 827,645
Hartford 851,783
Litchfield 174,092
Middlesex 143,196
New Haven 804,219
New London 254,957
Tolland 128,699
Windham 102,525

Cities, towns, and boroughs

Andover 2,540
Ansonia 18,403
Ashford 3,765
Avon 13,937
Bantam 757
Barkhamsted 3,369
Beacon Falls 5,083
Berlin 16,787
Bethany 4,608
Bethel 8,835 ▲17,541
Bethlehem 1,976 ▲3,071
Bloomfield 19,483
Bolton 4,575
Bozrah 2,297
Branford 5,688 ▲27,603
Bridgeport 141,686
Bridgewater 1,654
Bristol 60,640
Broad Brook 3,585
Brookfield 14,113
Brooklyn 6,681
Burlington 7,026
Canaan 1,194 ▲1,057
Canterbury 4,467
Canton 8,268
Chaplin 2,048
Cheshire 5,759 ▲25,684
Chester 1,563 ▲3,417
Clinton 3,439 ▲12,767
Colchester 3,212 ▲10,980
Colebrook 1,365
Collinsville 2,591
Columbia 4,510
Conning Towers-Nautilus Park 10,013
Cornwall 1,414
Coventry 10,063
Cromwell 12,286
Crystal Lake 1,175
Danbury 65,585
Danielson 4,441
Darien 18,196
Deep River 2,520 ▲4,332
Derby 12,199
Durham 2,650 ▲5,732
East Brooklyn 1,481
East Granby 4,302
East Haddam 6,676
East Hampton 2,167 ▲10,428
East Hartford 50,452
East Haven 26,144
East Lyme 15,340
East Windsor 10,081
Eastford 1,314
Easton 6,303
Ellington 11,197
Enfield 45,532
Essex 2,500 ▲5,904
Fairfield 53,418
Farmington 20,608
Franklin 1,810
Georgetown 1,694
Glastonbury 7,082 ▲27,901
Goshen 2,329
Granby 9,369
Greenwich 58,441
Griswold 10,384
Groton 9,837 ▲45,144
Guilford 2,588 ▲19,848
Haddam 6,769
Hamden 52,434
Hampton 1,578
Hartford 139,739
Hartland 1,866
Harwinton 5,228
Hebron 7,079
Higganum 1,692
Jewett City 3,349
Kensington 8,306
Kent 2,918
Killingly 15,889
Killingworth 4,814
Lake Pocotopaug 3,029
Lebanon 6,041
Ledyard 14,913
Lisbon 3,790
Litchfield 1,378 ▲8,365
Lyme 1,949
Madison 2,139 ▲15,485
Manchester 51,618
Mansfield 21,103
Marlborough 5,535
Meriden 59,479
Middlebury 6,145
Middlefield 3,925
Middletown 42,762
Milford 48,168 ▲49,938
Monroe 16,896
Montville 16,673
Moodus 1,170
Moosup 3,289
Morris 2,039
Mystic 2,618
Naugatuck 30,625
New Britain 75,491
New Canaan 17,864
New Fairfield 12,911
New Hartford 1,269 ▲5,769
New Haven 130,474
New London 28,540
New Milford 5,775 ▲23,629
New Preston 1,217
Newington 29,208
Newtown 1,800 ▲20,779
Niantic 3,048
Norfolk 2,060
North Branford 12,996
North Canaan 3,284
North Granby 1,455
North Grosvenor Dale 1,705
North Haven 22,249
North Stonington 4,884
Norwalk 78,331
Norwich 37,391
Oakville 8,741
Old Lyme 6,535
Old Saybrook 1,820 ▲9,552
Orange 12,830
Oxford 8,685
Pawcatuck 5,289
Plainfield 2,856 ▲14,363
Plainville 17,392
Plymouth 11,822
Pomfret 3,102
Poquonock Bridge 2,770
Portland 5,645 ▲8,418
Preston 5,006
Prospect 7,775
Putnam 6,835 ▲9,031
Quinebaug 1,031
Redding 7,927
Ridgefield 6,363 ▲20,919
Rocky Hill 16,554
Roxbury 1,825
Salem 3,310
Salisbury 4,090
Saybrook Manor 1,073
Scotland 1,215
Seymour 14,288
Sharon 2,928
Shelton 35,418
Sherman 2,809
Sherwood Manor 6,357
Simsbury 5,577 ▲22,023
Somers 9,108
South Coventry 1,257
South Windham 1,644
South Windsor 22,090
South Woodstock 1,112
Southbury 15,818
Southington 38,518
Southwood Acres 8,963
Sprague 3,008
Stafford 11,091
Stafford Springs 4,100
Stamford 108,056
Sterling 2,357
Stonington 1,100 ▲16,919
Storrs 12,198
Stratford 49,389
Suffield 11,427
Tariffville 1,477
Terryville 5,426
Thomaston 6,947
Thompson 8,668
Thompsonville 8,458
Tolland 11,001
Torrington 33,687
Trumbull 32,016
Union 612
Vernon 29,841
Voluntown 2,113
Wallingford 17,827 ▲40,822
Warren 1,226
Washington 3,905
Waterbury 108,961
Waterford 17,930
Watertown 20,456
Wauregan 1,079
Weatogue 2,521
West Hartford 60,110
West Haven 54,021
West Mystic 3,595
West Simsbury 2,149
Westbrook 2,060 ▲5,414
Weston 8,648
Westport 24,407
Wethersfield 25,651
Willimantic 14,746
Willington 5,979
Wilton 15,989
Winchester Center 11,524
Windham 22,039
Windsor 27,817
Windsor Locks 12,358
Winsted 8,254
Wolcott 13,700
Woodbridge 7,924
Woodbury 1,212 ▲8,131
Woodmont 1,770
Woodstock 6,008

▲ Entire township, including rural area.

Delaware ■ population 668,696

Metropolitan area

Wilmington 578,587 (441,946 in Del.; 65,294 in N.J.; 71,347 in Md.)

Counties

Kent 110,993
New Castle 441,946
Sussex 113,229

Cities and towns

Arden 477
Ardencroft 282
Ardentown 325
Bellefonte 1,243
Bethany Beach 326
Bethel 178
Blades 834
Bowers 179
Bridgeville 1,210
Brookside 15,307
Camden 1,899
Cheswold 321
Claymont 9,800
Clayton 1,163
Dagsboro 398
Delaware City 1,682
Delmar 962
Dewey Beach 204
Dover 27,630
Dover Base Housing 4,376
Edgemoor 5,853
Ellendale 313
Elsmere 5,935
Farmington 122
Felton 683
Fenwick Island 186
Frankford 591
Frederica 761
Georgetown 3,732
Greenwood 578
Harrington 2,311
Hartly 107
Henlopen Acres 107
Highland Acres 3,151
Houston 487
Kent Acres 1,807
Kenton 232
Laurel 3,226
Leipsic 236
Lewes 2,295
Little Creek 167
Magnolia 211
Middletown 3,834
Milford 6,040
Millsboro 1,643
Millville 206
Milton 1,417
New Castle 4,837
Newark 25,098
Newport 1,240
Ocean View 606
Odessa 303
Rehoboth Beach 1,234
Rodney Village 1,745
Seaford 5,689
Selbyville 1,335
Slaughter Beach 114
Smyrna 5,231
South Bethany 148
Stanton 5,028
Talleyville 6,346
Townsend 322
Viola 153
Wilmington 71,529
Wilmington Manor 8,568
Woodside 140
Woodside East 1,655
Wyoming 977

Florida ■ population 13,003,362

Metropolitan areas

Bradenton 211,707
Daytona Beach 370,712
Fort Lauderdale-Hollywood-Pompano Beach 1,255,488
Fort Myers-Cape Coral 335,113
Fort Pierce 251,071
Fort Walton Beach 143,776
Gainesville 204,111
Jacksonville 906,727
Lakeland-Winter Haven 405,382
Melbourne-Titusville-Palm Bay 398,978
Miami-Hialeah 1,937,094
Naples 152,099
Ocala 194,833
Orlando 1,072,748
Panama City 126,994
Pensacola 344,406
Sarasota 277,776
Tallahassee 233,598
Tampa-St. Petersburg-Clearwater 2,067,959
West Palm Beach-Boca Raton-Delray Beach 863,518

Counties

Alachua 181,596
Baker 18,486
Bay 126,994
Bradford 22,515
Brevard 398,978
Broward 1,255,488
Calhoun 11,011
Charlotte 110,975
Citrus 93,515
Clay 105,986
Collier 152,099
Columbia 42,613
Dade 1,937,094
De Soto 23,865
Dixie 10,585
Duval 672,971
Escambia 262,798
Flagler 28,701
Franklin 8,967
Gadsden 41,105
Gilchrist 9,667
Glades 7,591
Gulf 11,504
Hamilton 10,930
Hardee 19,499
Hendry 25,773
Hernando 101,115
Highlands 68,432
Hillsborough 834,054
Holmes 15,778
Indian River 90,208
Jackson 41,375
Jefferson 11,296
Lafayette 5,578
Lake 152,104
Lee 335,113
Leon 192,493
Levy 25,923
Liberty 5,569
Madison 16,569
Manatee 211,707
Marion 194,833
Martin 100,900
Monroe 78,024
Nassau 43,941
Okaloosa 143,776
Okeechobee 29,627
Orange 677,491
Osceola 107,728
Palm Beach 863,518
Pasco 281,131
Pinellas 851,659
Polk 405,382
Putnam 65,070
St. Johns 83,829
St. Lucie 150,171
Santa Rosa 81,608
Sarasota 277,776
Seminole 287,529
Sumter 31,577
Suwannee 26,780
Taylor 17,111
Union 10,252
Volusia 370,712
Wakulla 14,202
Walton 27,760
Washington 16,919

Cities, towns, and villages

Alachua 4,529
Altamonte Springs 34,879
Andover 6,251
Anna Maria 1,744
Apalachicola 2,602
Apollo Beach 6,025
Apopka 13,512
Arcadia 6,488
Archer 1,372
Asbury Lake 2,072
Astor 1,273
Atlantic Beach 11,636
Atlantis 1,653
Auburndale 8,858
Aventura 14,914
Avon Park 8,042
Azalea Park 8,926
Babson Park 1,125
Bagdad 1,457
Bal Harbour 3,045
Baldwin 1,450
Bartow 14,716
Baskin 3,834
Bassville Park 2,752
Bay Harbor Islands 4,703
Bay Hill 5,346
Bay Pines 4,171
Bayonet Point 21,860
Bayshore Gardens 17,062
Beacon Square 6,265
Bee Ridge 6,406
Bellair (-Meadowbrook Terrace) 15,606
Belle Glade 16,177
Belle Isle 5,272
Belleair 3,968

Florida (continued)

Belleair Beach 2,070
Belleair Bluffs 2,128
Belleview 2,666
Bellview 19,386
Beverly Hills 6,163
Big Coppitt 2,388
Big Pine Key 4,206
Biscayne Park 3,068
Bithlo 4,834
Bloomingdale 13,912
Blountstown 2,404
Boca Del Mar 17,754
Boca Raton 61,492
Bonifay 2,612
Bonita Springs 13,600
Bowling Green 1,836
Boynton Beach 46,194
Bradenton 43,779
Bradenton Beach 1,657
Brandon 57,985
Brent 21,624
Bristol 937
Broadview (-Pompano Park) 5,230
Broadview Park 6,109
Bronson 875
Brookridge 2,805
Brooksville 7,440
Browardale 6,257
Brownsville 15,607
Buena Ventura Lakes 14,148
Bunche Park 4,388
Bunnell 1,873
Bushnell 1,998
Callaway 12,253
Campbell 3,884
Cape Canaveral 8,014
Cape Coral 74,991
Carol City 53,331
Carrabelle 1,200
Carrollwood 7,195
Carrollwood Village 15,051
Casselberry 18,911
Cedar Grove 1,479
Century 1,989
Century Village 8,363
Charlotte Harbor 3,327
Charlotte Park 2,225
Chattahoochee 4,382
Chiefland 1,917
Chipley 3,866
Citrus Springs 2,213
Clearwater 98,784
Clermont 6,910
Cleveland 2,896
Clewiston 6,085
Cocoa 17,722
Cocoa Beach 12,123
Cocoa West 6,160
Coconut Creek 27,485
Collier Manor (-Cresthaven) 7,322
Combee Settlement 5,463
Conway 13,159
Cooper City 20,791
Coral Gables 40,091
Coral Springs 79,443
Coral Terrace 23,255
Cortez 4,509
Country Club 3,408
Crescent Beach 1,081
Crescent City 1,859
Crestview 9,886
Crooked Lake Park 1,575
Cross City 2,041
Crystal Lake 5,300
Crystal River 4,044
Cudjoe Key 1,714
Cutler 16,201
Cutler Ridge 21,268
Cypress Gardens 9,188
Cypress Lake 10,491
Dade City 5,633
Dade City North 3,058
Dania 13,024
Davenport 1,529
Davie 47,217
Daytona Beach 61,921
Daytona Beach Shores 2,335
De Bary 7,176
Deerfield Beach 46,325
De Funiak Springs 5,120
De Land 16,491
De Land Southwest 1,249
De Leon Springs 1,481
Delray Beach 47,181
Del Rio 8,248
Deltona 50,828
Desoto Lakes 2,807
Destin 8,080
Doctor Phillips 7,963
Dover 2,606
Dundee 2,335
Dunedin 34,012
Dunnellon 1,624
Eagle Lake 1,758
East Lake (-Orient Park) 6,171
East Naples 22,951
East Palatka 1,989
Eastpoint 1,577
Eatonville 2,170
Edgewater 15,337
Edgewood 1,062
Eglin AFB 8,347
Egypt Lake 14,580
Ellers 12,356
Ellenton 2,573
El Portal 2,457
Englewood 15,025
Ensley 16,362
Estero 3,177
Eustis 12,967
Fairview Shores 13,192
Fellsmere 2,179
Fern Park 8,294
Fernandina Beach 8,765
Ferry Pass 26,301
Flagler Beach 3,820
Floral City 2,609
Florida City 5,806
Florida Ridge 12,218
Forest City 10,638
Fort Lauderdale 149,377
Fort Meade 4,976
Fort Myers 45,206
Fort Myers Beach 9,284
Fort Myers Shores 5,460
Fort Pierce 36,830
Fort Pierce North 5,833
Fort Pierce South 5,320
Fort Walton Beach 21,471
Frostproof 2,808
Fruit Cove 5,904
Fruitland Park 2,754
Fruitville 9,808
Fussels Corner 3,840
Gainesville 84,770
Gibsonia 5,168
Gibsonton 7,706
Gifford 6,278
Gladeview 15,637
Glencoe 2,282
Glenvar Heights 14,823
Golden Gate 14,148
Golden Glades 25,474
Goldenrod 12,362
Gonzalez 7,669
Goulding 4,159
Goulds 7,284
Graceville 2,675
Greater Northdale 16,318
Green Cove Springs 4,497
Greenacres City 18,683
Gretna 1,981
Grove City 2,374
Groveland 2,300
Gulf Breeze 5,530
Gulf Gate Estates 11,622
Gulfport 11,727
Haines City 11,683
Hallandale 30,996
Hammocks 10,897
Hamptons at Boca Raton 11,686
Harbor Bluffs 2,659
Harbour Heights 2,523
Harlem 2,826
Havana 1,654
Hawthorne 1,305
Hernando 2,103
Hernando Beach 1,767
Hialeah 188,004
Hialeah Gardens 7,713
High Springs 3,144
Highland Beach 3,209
Highland City 1,919
Hiland Park 3,865
Hilliard 1,751
Hillsboro Beach 1,748
Hobe Sound 11,507
Holden Heights 4,387
Holiday 19,360
Holly Hill 11,141
Hollywood 121,697
Hollywood Reservation 1,394
Holmes Beach 4,810
Homestead 26,866
Homestead AFB 5,153
Homosassa 2,113
Homosassa Springs 6,271
Hudson 7,344
Hutchinson Island South 3,893
Immokalee 14,120
Indialantic 2,844
Indian Harbor Beach 6,933
Indian River Estates 4,858
Indian River Shores 2,278
Indian Rocks Beach 3,963
Indian Shores 1,405
Indiantown 4,794
Inglis 1,241
Interlachen 1,160
Inverness 5,797
Inwood 6,824
Iona 9,565
Islamorada 1,220
Ives Estates 13,531
Jacksonville 672,971
Jacksonville Beach 17,839
Jan Phyl Village 5,308
Jasmine Estates 17,136
Jasper 2,099
Jensen Beach 9,884
June Park 4,080
Juno Beach 2,121
Jupiter 24,986
Kathleen 2,743
Kendale Lakes 48,524
Kendall 87,271
Kendall Green 3,815
Kenneth City 4,462
Kensington Park 3,026
Key Biscayne 8,854
Key Largo 11,336
Key West 24,832
Keystone Heights 1,315
Kings Point 12,422
Kissimmee 30,050
La Belle 2,703
Lacoochee 2,072
Lady Lake 8,071
Laguna Beach 1,876
Lake Alfred 3,622
Lake Buena Vista 1,776
Lake Butler 2,116
Lake City 10,005
Lake Clarke Shores 3,364
Lake Hamilton 1,128
Lake Helen 2,344
Lake Lorraine 6,779
Lake Lucerne 9,478
Lake Magdalene 15,973
Lake Mary 5,929
Lake Panasoffkee 2,705
Lake Park 6,704
Lake Placid 1,158
Lake Wales 9,670
Lake Worth 28,564
Lakeland 70,576
Lakeland Highlands 9,972
Lakeside 29,137
Lakewood Park 7,211
Land O'Lakes 7,892
Lantana 8,392
Largo 65,674
Lauderdale-by-the-Sea 2,990
Lauderdale Lakes 27,341
Lauderhill 49,708
Laurel 8,245
Lealman 21,748
Lecanto 1,243
Leesburg 14,903
Lehigh Acres 13,611
Leisure City 19,379
Lely 3,014
Lighthouse Point 10,378
Lindgren Acres 22,290
Live Oak 6,332
Lockhart 11,636
Longboat Key 5,937
Longwood 13,316
Loughman 1,214
Lower Grand Lagoon 3,329
Lutz 10,552
Lynn Haven 9,298
Macclenny 3,966
Madeira Beach 4,225
Madison 3,345
Maitland 9,110
Malabar 1,977
Mango 8,700
Mangonia Park 1,453
Marathon 8,857
Marco 9,493
Margate 42,985
Marianna 6,292
Mary Esther 4,139
Mascotte 1,761
Mayo 917
Medulla 3,977
Melbourne 59,646
Melbourne Beach 3,021
Melrose Park 6,477
Memphis 6,760
Merritt Island 32,886
Miami 358,548
Miami Beach 92,639
Miami Gardens (-Utopia-Carver) 7,448
Miami Lakes 12,750
Miami Shores 10,084
Miami Springs 13,268
Micco 8,757
Middleburg 6,223
Milton 7,216
Mims 9,412
Minneola 1,515
Miramar 40,663
Molino 1,207
Monticello 2,573
Moore Haven 1,432
Mount Dora 7,196
Mulberry 2,988
Myrtle Grove 17,402
Naples 19,505
Naples Manor 4,574
Naples Park 8,002
Naranja 5,790
Nassau Village (-Ratliff) 4,047
Neptune Beach 6,816
New Port Richey 14,044
New Port Richey East 9,683
New Smyrna Beach 16,543
Newberry 1,644
Niceville 10,507
Nokomis 3,448
Norland 22,109
North Andrews Gardens 9,002
North Bay Village 5,383
North Fort Myers 30,027
North Lauderdale 26,506
North Miami 49,998
North Miami Beach 35,359
North Naples 13,422
North Palm Beach 11,343
North Port 11,973
North River Shores 3,250
North Sarasota 6,702
Oak Ridge 15,388
Oakland Park 26,326
Oakland Park 1,743
Ocala 42,045
Ocean City 5,422
Ocean Ridge 1,570
Ocoee 12,778
Ojus 15,519
Okeechobee 4,943
Oldsmar 8,361
Olympia Heights 37,792
Opa-locka 15,283
Opa-locka North 6,568
Orange City 5,347
Orange Park 9,488
Orlando 164,693
Orlovista 5,990
Ormond Beach 29,721
Ormond-by-the-Sea 8,157
Osprey 2,597
Oviedo 11,114
Pace 6,277
Page Park (-Pine Manor) 5,116
Pahokee 6,822
Palatka 10,201
Palm Bay 62,632
Palm Beach 9,814
Palm Beach Gardens 22,965
Palm Beach Shores 1,040
Palm City 3,925
Palm Coast 14,287
Palm Harbor 50,256
Palm River (-Clair Mel) 13,691
Palm Springs 9,763
Palm Springs North 5,300
Palm Valley 9,960
Palmetto 9,268
Palmetto Estates 12,293
Panama City 34,378
Panama City Beach 4,051
Parker 4,598
Parkland 3,558
Pembroke Park 4,933
Pembroke Pines 65,452
Pensacola 58,165
Perrine 15,576
Perry 7,151
Pierson 2,988
Pine Castle 8,276
Pine Hills 35,322
Pinellas Park 43,426
Pinewood 15,518
Placid Lakes 2,045
Plant City 22,754
Plantation 66,692
Plantation 1,885
Plantation Key 4,405
Poinciana Place 3,618
Polk City 1,439
Pompano Beach 72,411
Pompano Beach Highlands 17,915
Port Charlotte 41,535
Port Orange 35,317
Port Richey 2,523
Port St. Joe 4,044
Port St. John 8,933
Port St. Lucie 55,866
Port St. Lucie (-River Park) 4,874
Port Salerno 7,786
Pretty Bayou 3,839
Princeton 7,073
Punta Gorda 10,747
Punta Rassa 1,493
Quincy 7,444
Redington Beach 1,626
Redington Shores 2,366
Richmond Heights 8,583
Ridge Manor 1,947
Ridge Wood Heights 4,851
Riverland 5,376
Riverview 6,478
Riviera Beach 27,639
Rockledge 16,023
Roseland 1,379
Rotonda 3,576
Royal Palm Beach 14,589
Ruskin 6,046
Safety Harbor 15,124
St. Augustine 11,692
St. Augustine Beach 3,657
St. Augustine Shores 4,411
St. Augustine South 4,218
St. Cloud 12,453
St. James City 1,904
St. Leo 1,009
St. Petersburg 238,629
St. Petersburg Beach 9,200
Samoset 3,119
Samsula (-Spruce Creek) 3,404
San Carlos Park 11,785
Sandalfoot Cove 14,214
Sanford 32,387
Sanibel 5,468
Sarasota 50,961
Sarasota Springs 16,088
Satellite Beach 9,889
Sawgrass 2,999
Scott Lake 14,588
Sebastian 10,205
Sebring 8,900
Seffner 5,371
Seminole 9,251
Sewall's Point 1,588
Sharpes 3,348
Siesta Key 7,772
Silver Springs Shores 6,421
Sky Lake 6,202
Sneads 1,746
Solana 1,128
South Apopka 6,360
South Bay 3,558
South Beach 2,754
South Bradenton 20,398
South Daytona 12,482
South Gate Ridge 5,924
South Miami 10,404
South Miami Heights 30,030
South Palm Beach 1,480
South Pasadena 5,644
South Patrick Shores 10,249
South Sarasota 5,298
South Venice 11,951
Southgate 7,324
Spring Hill 31,117
Springfield 8,715
Starke 5,226
Stock Island 3,613
Stuart 11,936
Sugarmill Woods 4,073
Sun City Center 8,326
Suncoast Estates 4,483
Sunny Isles 11,772
Sunrise 64,407
Sunset 15,810
Surfside 4,108
Sweetwater 13,909
Sylvan Shores 2,155
Tallahassee 124,773
Tamarac 44,822
Tamiami 33,845
Tampa 280,015
Tangelo Park 2,663
Tarpon Springs 17,906
Tavares 7,383
Tavernier 2,433
Taylor Creek 4,081
Temple Terrace 16,444
Tequesta 4,499
Tice 3,971
Titusville 39,394
Town 'n' Country 60,946
Treasure Island 7,266
Trenton 1,287
Tyndall AFB 4,318
Umatilla 2,350
Union Park 6,890
University West 23,760
Upper Grand Lagoon 7,855
Valparaiso 4,672
Vamo 3,325
Venice 16,922
Venice Gardens 7,701
Vero Beach 17,350
Vero Beach South 16,973
Villas 9,898
Wabasso 1,145
Wahneta 4,024
Waldo 1,017
Warm Mineral Springs 4,041
Warrington 16,040
Washington Park 6,930
Watertown 3,340
Wauchula 3,253
Waverly 2,071
Wekiva Springs 23,026
Wellington 20,670
West Bradenton 4,528
West De Land 3,389
West Little River 33,575
West Melbourne 8,399
West Miami 5,727
West Palm Beach 67,643
West Pensacola 22,107
Westchester 29,883
Westview 9,668
Westwood Lakes 11,522
Wewahitchka 1,779
White City 4,645
Whitfield Estates 3,152
Wildwood 3,421
Williamsburg 3,093
Williston 2,179
Willow Oak 4,017
Wilton Manors 11,804
Wimauma 2,932
Windermere 1,371
Winston 9,118
Winter Garden 9,745
Winter Haven 24,725
Winter Park 22,242
Winter Springs 22,151
Woodville 2,760
Wright 18,945
Yalaha 1,168
Yulee 6,915
Zephyrhills 8,220
Zephyrhills North 2,320
Zephyrhills South 2,514
Zephyrhills West 4,249
Zolfo Springs 1,219

Georgia ■ population 6,508,419

Metropolitan areas

Albany 112,561
Athens 156,267
Atlanta 2,833,511
Augusta 396,809
(275,869 in Ga.; 120,940 in S.C.)
(Tenn.) 433,210
(319,259 in Tenn.; 113,951 in Ga.)
Columbus 243,072
(196,212 in Ga.; 46,860) in Ala.)
Macon-Warner Robbins 281,103
Savannah 242,622

Counties

Appling 15,744
Atkinson 6,213
Bacon 9,566
Baker 3,615
Baldwin 39,530
Banks 10,308
Barrow 29,721
Bartow 55,911
Ben Hill 16,245
Berrien 14,153
Bibb 149,967
Bleckley 10,430
Brantley 11,077
Brooks 15,398
Bryan 15,438
Bulloch 43,125
Burke 20,579
Butts 15,326
Calhoun 5,013
Camden 30,167
Candler 7,744
Carroll 71,422
Catoosa 42,464
Charlton 8,496
Chatham 216,935
Chattahoochee 16,934
Chattooga 22,242
Cherokee 90,204
Clarke 87,594
Clay 3,364
Clayton 182,052
Clinch 6,160
Cobb 447,745
Coffee 29,592
Colquitt 36,645

Columbia 66,031
Cook 13,456
Coweta 53,853
Crawford 8,991
Crisp 20,011
Dade 13,147
Dawson 9,429
Decatur 25,511
DeKalb 545,837
Dodge 17,607
Dooly 9,901
Dougherty 96,311
Douglas 71,120
Early 11,854
Echols 2,334
Effingham 25,687
Elbert 18,949
Emanuel 20,546
Evans 8,724
Fannin 15,992
Fayette 62,415
Floyd 81,251
Forsyth 44,083
Franklin 16,650
Fulton 648,951
Gilmer 13,368
Glascock 2,357
Glynn 62,496
Gordon 35,072
Grady 20,279
Greene 11,793
Gwinnett 352,910
Habersham 27,621
Hall 95,428
Hancock 8,908
Haralson 21,966
Harris 17,788
Hart 19,712
Heard 8,628
Henry 58,741
Houston 89,208
Irwin 8,649
Jackson 30,005
Jasper 8,453
Jeff Davis 12,032
Jefferson 17,408
Jenkins 8,247
Johnson 8,329
Jones 20,739
Lamar 13,038
Lanier 5,531
Laurens 39,988
Lee 16,250
Liberty 52,745
Lincoln 7,442
Long 6,202
Lowndes 75,981
Lumpkin 14,573
Macon 13,114
Madison 21,050
Marion 5,590
McDuffie 20,119
McIntosh 8,634
Meriwether 22,411
Miller 6,280
Mitchell 20,275
Monroe 17,113
Montgomery 7,163
Morgan 12,883
Murray 26,147
Muscogee 179,278
Newton 41,808
Oconee 17,618
Oglethorpe 9,763
Paulding 41,611
Peach 21,189
Pickens 14,432
Pierce 13,328
Pike 10,224
Polk 33,815
Pulaski 8,108
Putnam 14,137
Quitman 2,209
Rabun 11,648
Randolph 8,023
Richmond 189,719
Rockdale 54,091
Schley 3,588
Screven 13,842
Seminole 9,010
Spalding 54,457
Stephens 23,257
Stewart 5,654
Sumter 30,228
Talbot 6,524
Taliaferro 1,915
Tattnall 17,722
Taylor 7,642
Telfair 11,000
Terrell 10,653
Thomas 38,986
Tift 34,998
Toombs 24,072
Towns 6,754
Treutlen 5,994
Troup 55,536
Turner 8,703
Twiggs 9,806
Union 11,993
Upson 26,300
Walker 58,340
Walton 38,586
Ware 35,471
Warren 6,078
Washington 19,112
Wayne 22,356
Webster 2,263
Wheeler 4,903
White 13,006
Whitfield 72,462
Wilcox 7,008
Wilkes 10,597
Wilkinson 10,228
Worth 19,745

Cities, towns, and villages

Abbeville 907
Acworth 4,519
Adairsville 2,131
Adel 5,093
Adrian 615
Ailey 579
Alamo 855
Alapaha 812
Albany 78,122
Allenhurst 594
Allentown 273
Alma 3,663
Alpharetta 13,002
Alto 651
Ambrose 288
Americus 16,512
Andersonville 277
Arabi 433
Aragon 902
Arcade 697
Argyle 206
Arlington 1,513
Arnoldsville 275
Ashburn 4,827
Athens 45,734
Atlanta 394,017
Attapulgus 380
Auburn 3,139
Augusta 44,639
Austell 4,173
Avera 215
Avondale Estates 2,209
Baconton 623
Bainbridge 10,712
Baldwin 1,439
Ball Ground 905
Barnesville 905
Bartow 292
Barwick 385
Baxley 3,841
Belvedere Park 18,089
Berkeley Lake 791
Berlin 480
Bethlehem 348
Bibb City 597
Blackshear 3,263
Blacksville 1,112
Blairsville 564
Blakely 5,595
Bloomingdale 2,271
Blue Ridge 1,336
Blythe 300
Bogart 1,018
Boston 1,395
Bostwick 307
Bowdon 1,981
Bowersville 311
Bowman 791
Braselton 418
Braswell 247
Bremen 4,356
Brinson 238
Bronwood 513
Brooklet 1,013
Brooks 328
Broxton 1,211
Brunswick 16,433
Buchanan 1,009
Buena Vista 1,472
Buford 8,771
Butler 1,673
Byromville 452
Byron 2,276
Cadwell 458
Cairo 9,035
Calhoun 7,135
Camak 220
Camilla 5,008
Candler [-McAfee] 29,491
Canon 737
Canton 4,817
Carl 263
Carlton 282
Carnesville 514
Carrollton 16,029
Cartersville 12,035
Cave Spring 950
Cecil 376
Cedartown 7,978
Centerville 3,251
Centralhatchee 301
Chamblee 7,668
Chatsworth 2,865
Chauncey 312
Chester 1,072
Chickamauga 2,149
Clarkesville 1,151
Clarkston 5,385
Claxton 2,464
Clayton 1,613
Clermont 402
Cleveland 1,653
Climax 226
Cobbtown 338
Cochran 4,390
Cohutta 529
Colbert 443
College Park 20,457
Collins 528
Colquitt 1,991
Columbus 178,681
Comer 939
Commerce 4,108
Concord 211
Conley 5,528
Conyers 7,380
Coolidge 610
Cordele 10,321
Cornelia 3,219
Covington 10,026
Crawford 694
Crawfordville 577
Culloden 242
Cumming 2,828
Cusseta 1,107
Cuthbert 3,730
Dacula 2,217
Dahlonega 3,086
Dallas 2,810
Dalton 21,761
Damascus 290
Danielsville 318
Danville 480
Darien 1,783
Davisboro 407
Dawson 5,295
Dawsonville 467
Dearing 547
Decatur 17,336
Deenwood 2,055
Demorest 1,088
Denton 335
De Soto 258
Dexter 475
Dock Junction 7,094
Doerun 899
Donalsonville 2,761
Doraville 7,626
Douglas 10,464
Douglasville 11,635
Druid Hills 12,174
Dublin 16,312
Dudley 430
Duluth 9,029
Dunwoody 26,302
East Boundary 3,271
East Dublin 2,524
East Ellijay 303
East Newnan 1,173
East Point 34,402
Eastman 5,153
Eatonton 4,737
Edison 1,182
Elberton 5,682
Ellaville 1,724
Ellenton 227
Ellijay 1,178
Emerson 1,201
Enigma 611
Ephesus 324
Eton 315
Euharlee 850
Evans 13,713
Experiment 3,762
Fair Oaks 6,996
Fairburn 4,013
Fairmount 657
Fairview 6,444
Fayetteville 5,827
Fitzgerald 8,612
Flemington 279
Flovilla 602
Flowery Branch 1,251
Folkston 2,285
Forest Park 16,925
Forsyth 4,268
Fort Benning 14,617
Fort Gaines 1,248
Fort Gordon 9,140
Fort Oglethorpe 5,880
Fort Stewart 13,774
Fort Valley 8,198
Franklin 876
Franklin Springs 475
Funston 248
Gainesville 17,885
Gainesville Cotton Mills 1,329
Garden City 7,410
Garfield 255
Georgetown 913
Georgetown 5,554
Gibson 679
Glennville 3,676
Glenwood 881
Gordon 2,468
Grantville 1,180
Gray 2,189
Grayson 529
Greensboro 2,860
Greenville 1,167
Gresham Park 9,000
Griffin 21,347
Grovetown 3,596
Gum Branch 291
Guyton 740
Hagan 787
Hahira 1,353
Hamilton 454
Hampton 2,694
Hapeville 5,483
Harlem 2,199
Harrison 414
Hartwell 4,555
Hawkinsville 3,527
Hazlehurst 4,202
Helen 300
Helena 1,256
Hephzibah 2,466
Hiawassee 547
Higgston 274
Hilltonia 402
Hinesville 21,603
Hiram 1,389
Hoboken 440
Hogansville 2,976
Holly Springs 2,406
Homeland 981
Homer 742
Homerville 2,560
Hoschton 642
Ideal 554
Ila 297
Indian Springs 1,273
Iron City 503
Irwinton 641
Isle of Hope [-Dutch Island] 2,637
Ivey 1,053
Jackson 4,076
Jasper 1,772
Jefferson 2,763
Jeffersonville 1,545
Jenkinsburg 213
Jesup 8,958
Jonesboro 3,635
Kennesaw 8,936
Keysville 284
Kingsland 4,699
Kingston 616
Kite 297
La Fayette 6,313
La Grange 25,597
Lake City 2,733
Lake Park 500
Lakeland 2,467
Lakeview 5,237
Lakeview Estates 1,477
Lavonia 1,840
Lawrenceville 16,848
Leary 701
Leesburg 1,452
Lenox 783
Leslie 445
Lexington 230
Lilburn 9,301
Lincolnton 1,476
Lindale 4,187
Linwood 342
Lithia Springs 11,403
Lithonia 2,448
Locust Grove 1,681
Loganville 3,180
Lookout Mountain 1,636
Louisville 2,429
Lovejoy 754
Ludowici 1,291
Lula 1,018
Lumber City 1,429
Lumpkin 1,250
Luthersville 741
Lyerly 493
Lyons 4,502
Mableton 25,725
Macon 106,612
Madison 3,483
Manchester 4,104
Mansfield 341
Marietta 44,129
Marshallville 1,457
Martin 243
Martinez 33,731
Maysville 728
McCaysville 1,065
McDonough 2,929
McIntyre 552
McRae 3,007
Meansville 250
Meigs 1,120
Menlo 538
Metter 3,707
Midville 620
Midway 863
Midway [-Hardwick] 4,910
Milan 1,056
Milledgeville 17,727
Millen 3,808
Milner 321
Molena 439
Monroe 9,759
Montezuma 4,506
Montgomery 4,327
Monticello 2,289
Moody AFB 1,288
Moreland 366
Morgan 252
Morganton 295
Morrow 5,168
Morven 536
Moultrie 14,865
Mount Airy 543
Mount Vernon 1,914
Mount Zion 511
Mountain City 784
Mountain Park 554
Mountain Park 11,025
Nahunta 1,049
Nashville 4,782
Nelson 486
Newborn 404
Newington 319
Newnan 12,497
Newton 703
Nicholls 1,003
Nicholson 535
Norcross 5,947
Norman Park 711
North Atlanta 27,812
North Decatur 13,936
North Druid Hills 14,170
North High Shoals 268
Norwood 238
Oak Park 269
Oakwood 1,464
Ochlocknee 588
Ocilla 3,182
Oconee 234
Odum 388
Oglethorpe 1,302
Oliver 242
Omega 912
Orchard Hill 239
Oxford 1,945
Palmetto 2,612
Panthersville 9,874
Pavo 774
Peachtree City 19,027
Pearson 1,714
Pelham 3,869
Pembroke 1,503
Pendergrass 298
Perry 9,452
Phillipsburg 1,044
Pine Lake 810
Pine Mountain 875
Pinehurst 388
Pineview 594
Pitts 214
Plains 716
Plainville 231
Pooler 4,453
Port Wentworth 4,012
Portal 522
Porterdale 1,278
Poulan 962
Powder Springs 6,893
Preston 388
Pulaski 264
Putney 3,108
Quitman 5,292
Ray City 603
Redan 24,376
Reidsville 2,469
Remerton 463
Rentz 364
Resaca 410
Reynolds 1,166
Rhine 466
Riceboro 745
Richland 1,668
Richmond Hill 2,934
Rincon 2,697
Ringgold 1,675
Riverdale 9,359
Roberta 939
Robins AFB 3,092
Rochelle 1,510
Rockmart 3,356
Rome 30,326
Roopville 248
Rossville 3,601
Roswell 47,923
Royston 2,758
Russell 871
Rutledge 659
St. Marys 8,187
St. Simons Island 12,026
Sale City 324
Sandersville 6,290
Sandy Springs 67,842
Sardis 1,116
Sasser 335
Savannah 137,560
Scotland 244
Scottdale 8,636
Screven 819
Senoia 956
Shannon 1,703
Sharpsburg 224
Shellman 1,162
Shiloh 329
Siloam 329
Skidaway Island 4,495
Smithville 804
Smyrna 30,981
Snellville 12,084
Social Circle 2,755
Soperton 2,797
South Augusta 55,998
Sparks 1,205
Sparta 1,710
Springfield 1,415
Stapleton 330
Statesboro 15,854
Statham 1,360
Stillmore 615
Stockbridge 3,359
Stone Mountain 6,494
Sugar Hill 4,557
Summerville 5,025
Sumner 209
Sunny Side 215
Sunnyside 1,506
Surrency 253
Suwanee 2,412
Swainsboro 7,361
Sycamore 417
Sylvania 2,871
Sylvester 5,702
Talbotton 1,046
Tallapoosa 2,805
Taylorsville 269
Temple 1,870
Tennille 1,552
Thomaston 9,127
Thomasville 17,457
Thomson 6,862
Thunderbolt 2,786
Tifton 14,215
Tiger 301
Tignall 711
Toccoa 8,266
Toomsboro 617
Trenton 1,994
Trion 1,661
Tucker 25,781
Tunnel Hill 970
Twin City 1,466
Ty Ty 579
Tybee Island 2,842
Tyrone 2,724
Unadilla 1,620
Union City 8,375
Union Point 1,753
Unionville 2,710
Uvalda 561
Valdosta 39,806
Varnell 358
Vidalia 11,078
Vienna 2,708
Villa Rica 6,542
Vinings 7,417
Waco 461
Wadley 2,473
Waleska 700
Walnut Grove 458
Walthourville 2,024
Warm Springs 407
Warner Robins 43,726
Warrenton 2,056
Warwick 501
Washington 4,279
Watkinsville 1,600
Waverly Hall 769
Waycross 16,410
Waynesboro 5,701
West Augusta 27,637
West Point 3,571
Westside 2,180
Whigham 605
White 542
White Plains 286
Whitesburg 643
Willacoochee 1,205
Williamson 295
Wilmington Island 11,230
Winder 7,373
Winterville 876
Woodbine 1,212
Woodbury 1,429
Woodland 552
Woodstock 4,361
Woodville 415
Wrens 2,414
Wrightsville 2,331
Yatesville 409
Young Harris 604
Zebulon 1,035

Hawaii ■ population 1,115,274

Metropolitan area

- Honolulu 836,231

Counties

- Hawaii 120,317
- Honolulu 836,231
- Kalawao 130
- Kauai 51,177
- Maui 100,374

Islands

- Hawaii 120,317
- Kahoolawe (no pop.)
- Kauai 50,947
- Lanai 2,426
- Maui 54,492
- Molokai 6,035
- Niihau 230
- Oahu (including outlying islands) 836,231

Cities, towns, and villages

- Ahuimanu 8,387
- Aiea 8,906
- Anahola 1,181
- Barbers Point Housing 2,218
- Captain Cook 2,595
- Eleele 1,489
- Ewa Beach 14,315
- Haleiwa 2,442
- Haliimaile 841
- Hana 683
- Hanalei 461
- Hanamaulu 3,611
- Hanapepe 1,395
- Hauula 3,479
- Hawi 924
- Heeia 5,010
- Hickam Housing 6,553
- Hilo 37,808
- Holualoa 3,834
- Honokaa 2,186
- Honolulu 365,272
- Honomu 532
- Iroquois Point 4,188
- Kaaawa 1,138
- Kaanapali 579
- Kahaluu 3,068
- Kahuku 2,063
- Kahului 16,889
- Kailua 9,126
- Kailua 36,818
- Kalaheo 3,592
- Kalihiwai 435
- Kaneohe 35,448
- Kapaa 8,149
- Kapaau 1,083
- Kaumakani 803
- Kaunakakai 2,658
- Keaau 1,584
- Kealakekua 1,453
- Kekaha 3,506
- Kihei 11,107
- Kilauea 1,685
- Koloa 1,791
- Kualapuu 1,661
- Kukuihaele 316
- Kurtistown 910
- Lahaina 9,073
- Laie 5,577
- Lanai City 2,400
- Laupahoehoe 508
- Lawai 1,787
- Lihue 5,536
- Maili 6,059
- Makaha 7,990
- Makakilo City 9,828
- Makawao 5,405
- Maunaloa 405
- Maunawili 4,847
- Mililani Town 29,359
- Mokuleia 1,776
- Mountain View 3,075
- Naalehu 1,027
- Nanakuli 9,575
- Napili-Honokowai 4,332
- Paauilo 620
- Pahala 1,520
- Pahoa 1,027
- Paia 2,091
- Papaikou 1,634
- Paukaa 495
- Pearl City 30,993
- Pepeekeo 1,813
- Poipu 975
- Princeville 1,244
- Puhi 1,210
- Pukalani 5,879
- Pupukea 4,111
- Schofield Barracks 19,597
- Volcano 1,516
- Wahiawa 17,386
- Waialua 3,943
- Waianae 8,758
- Waikane 717
- Waikapu 729
- Wailua 2,018
- Wailuku 10,688
- Waimanalo 3,508
- Waimanalo Beach 4,185
- Wainaku 1,243
- Waipahu 31,435
- Waipio Acres 5,304
- Whitmore Village 3,373

Idaho ■ population 1,011,986

Metropolitan area

- Boise 205,775

Counties

- Ada 205,775
- Adams 3,254
- Bannock 66,026
- Bear Lake 6,084
- Benewah 7,937
- Bingham 37,583
- Blaine 13,552
- Boise 3,509
- Bonner 26,622
- Bonneville 72,207
- Boundary 8,332
- Butte 2,918
- Camas 727
- Canyon 90,076
- Caribou 6,963
- Cassia 19,532
- Clark 762
- Clearwater 8,505
- Custer 4,133
- Elmore 21,205
- Franklin 9,232
- Fremont 10,937
- Gem 11,844
- Gooding 11,633
- Idaho 13,783
- Jefferson 16,543
- Jerome 15,138
- Kootenai 69,795
- Latah 30,617
- Lemhi 6,899
- Lewis 3,516
- Lincoln 3,308
- Madison 23,674
- Minidoka 19,361
- Nez Perce 33,754
- Oneida 3,492
- Owyhee 8,392
- Payette 16,434
- Power 7,086
- Shoshone 13,931
- Teton 3,439
- Twin Falls 53,580
- Valley 6,109
- Washington 8,550

Cities and towns

- Aberdeen 1,406
- Acequia 106
- Albion 305
- American Falls 3,757
- Ammon 5,002
- Arco 1,016
- Arimo 311
- Ashton 1,114
- Athol 346
- Atomic City 25
- Bancroft 393
- Basalt 407
- Bellevue 1,275
- Blackfoot 9,646
- Bliss 185
- Bloomington 197
- Boise 125,738
- Bonners Ferry 2,193
- Bovill 256
- Buhl 3,516
- Burley 8,702
- Butte City 59
- Caldwell 18,400
- Cambridge 374
- Cascade 877
- Castleford 179
- Challis 1,073
- Chatcolet 72
- Chubbuck 7,791
- Clark Fork 448
- Clayton 26
- Clifton 228
- Coeur d'Alene 24,563
- Cottonwood 822
- Council 831
- Craigmont 542
- Crouch 75
- Culdesac 280
- Dalton Gardens 1,951
- Dayton 357
- Deary 529
- Declo 279
- Dietrich 127
- Donnelly 135
- Dover 294
- Downey 626
- Driggs 846
- Drummond 37
- Dubois 420
- Eagle 3,327
- East Hope 215
- Eden 314
- Elk River 149
- Emmett 4,601
- Fairfield 371
- Ferdinand 135
- Fernan Lake 170
- Filer 1,511
- Firth 429
- Fort Hall 2,681
- Franklin 478
- Fruitland 2,400
- Garden City 6,369
- Genesee 725
- Georgetown 558
- Glenns Ferry 1,304
- Gooding 2,820
- Grace 973
- Grand View 330
- Grangeville 3,226
- Greenleaf 648
- Hagerman 600
- Hailey 3,687
- Hamer 79
- Hansen 848
- Harrison 226
- Hauser 380
- Hayden 3,744
- Hayden Lake 338
- Hazelton 394
- Heyburn 2,714
- Hollister 144
- Homedale 1,963
- Hope 99
- Horseshoe Bend 643
- Huetter 82
- Idaho City 322
- Idaho Falls 43,929
- Inkom 769
- Iona 1,049
- Irwin 108
- Island Park 159
- Jerome 6,529
- Juliaetta 488
- Kamiah 1,157
- Kellogg 2,591
- Kendrick 325
- Ketchum 2,523
- Kimberly 2,367
- Kooskia 692
- Kootenai 327
- Kuna 1,955
- Lapwai 932
- Lava Hot Springs 420
- Leadore 74
- Lewiston 28,082
- Lewisville 471
- Lost River 29
- Mackay 574
- Malad City 1,946
- Malta 171
- Marsing 798
- McCall 2,005
- McCammon 722
- Melba 252
- Menan 601
- Meridian 9,596
- Middleton 1,851
- Midvale 110
- Minidoka 67
- Montpelier 2,656
- Moore 190
- Moscow 18,519
- Mountain Home 7,913
- Mountain Home AFB 5,936
- Moyie Springs 415
- Mud Lake 179
- Mullan 821
- Murtaugh 134
- Nampa 28,365
- New Meadows 534
- New Plymouth 1,313
- Newdale 377
- Nezperce 453
- Notus 380
- Oakley 635
- Oldtown 151
- Onaway 203
- Orofino 2,868
- Osburn 1,579
- Oxford 44
- Paris 581
- Parker 288
- Parma 1,597
- Paul 901
- Payette 5,592
- Peck 160
- Pierce 746
- Pinehurst 1,722
- Placerville 14
- Plummer 804
- Pocatello 46,080
- Ponderay 449
- Post Falls 7,349
- Potlatch 790
- Preston 3,710
- Priest River 1,560
- Rathdrum 2,000
- Reubens 46
- Rexburg 14,302
- Richfield 383
- Rigby 2,681
- Riggins 443
- Ririe 596
- Roberts 557
- Rockland 264
- Rupert 5,455
- St. Anthony 3,010
- St. Charles 189
- St. Maries 2,442
- Salmon 2,941
- Sandpoint 5,203
- Shelley 3,536
- Shoshone 1,249
- Smelterville 464
- Soda Springs 3,111
- Spencer 11
- Spirit Lake 790
- Stanley 71
- State Line 26
- Stites 204
- Sugar City 1,275
- Sun Valley 938
- Swan Valley 141
- Tensed 90
- Teton 570
- Tetonia 132
- Troy 699
- Twin Falls 27,591
- Ucon 895
- Victor 292
- Wallace 1,010
- Wardner 246
- Warm River 9
- Weippe 532
- Weiser 4,571
- Wendell 1,963
- Weston 390
- White Bird 108
- Wilder 1,232
- Winchester 262
- Worley 182

Illinois ■ population 11,466,682

Metropolitan areas

- Aurora-Elgin 356,884
- Bloomington-Normal 129,180
- Champaign-Urbana-Rantoul 173,025
- Chicago 6,069,974
- Davenport (Ia.)-Rock Island-Moline 350,861 (199,882 in Ill.; 150,979 in Ia.)
- Decatur 117,206
- Joliet 389,650
- Kankakee 96,255
- Lake County 516,418
- Peoria 339,172
- Rockford 283,719
- St. Louis (Mo.) 2,449,760 (1,860,765 in Mo.; 588,995 in Ill.)
- Springfield 189,550

Counties

- Adams 66,090
- Alexander 10,626
- Bond 14,991
- Boone 30,806
- Brown 5,836
- Bureau 35,688
- Calhoun 5,322
- Carroll 16,805
- Cass 13,437
- Champaign 173,025
- Christian 34,418
- Clark 15,921
- Clay 14,460
- Clinton 33,944
- Coles 51,644
- Cook 5,105,067
- Crawford 19,464
- Cumberland 10,670
- De Kalb 77,932
- De Witt 16,516
- Douglas 19,464
- Du Page 781,666
- Edgar 19,595
- Edwards 7,440
- Effingham 31,704
- Fayette 20,893
- Ford 14,275
- Franklin 40,319
- Fulton 38,080
- Gallatin 6,909
- Greene 15,317
- Grundy 32,337
- Hamilton 8,499
- Hancock 21,373
- Hardin 5,189
- Henderson 8,096
- Henry 51,159
- Iroquois 30,787
- Jackson 61,067
- Jasper 10,609
- Jefferson 37,020
- Jersey 20,539
- Jo Daviess 21,821
- Johnson 11,347
- Kane 317,471
- Kankakee 96,255
- Kendall 39,413
- Knox 56,393
- Lake 516,418
- La Salle 106,913
- Lawrence 15,972
- Lee 34,392
- Livingston 39,301
- Logan 30,798
- Macon 117,206
- Macoupin 47,679
- Madison 249,238
- Marion 41,561
- Marshall 12,846
- Mason 16,269
- Massac 14,752
- McDonough 35,244
- McHenry 183,241
- McLean 129,180
- Menard 11,164
- Mercer 17,290
- Monroe 22,422
- Montgomery 30,728
- Morgan 36,397
- Moultrie 13,930
- Ogle 45,957
- Peoria 182,827
- Perry 21,412
- Piatt 15,548
- Pike 17,577
- Pope 4,373
- Pulaski 7,523
- Putnam 5,730
- Randolph 34,583
- Richland 16,545
- Rock Island 148,723
- St. Clair 262,852
- Saline 26,551
- Sangamon 178,386
- Schuyler 7,498
- Scott 5,644
- Shelby 22,261
- Stark 6,534
- Stephenson 48,052
- Tazewell 123,692
- Union 17,619
- Vermilion 88,257
- Wabash 13,111
- Warren 19,181
- Washington 14,965
- Wayne 17,241
- White 16,522
- Whiteside 60,186
- Will 357,313
- Williamson 57,733
- Winnebago 252,913
- Woodford 32,653

Cities, towns, and villages

- Abingdon 3,597
- Addison 32,058
- Albany 835
- Albers 700
- Albion 2,116
- Aledo 3,681
- Alexis 908
- Algonquin 11,663
- Alhambra 709
- Allendale 476
- Alorton 2,960
- Alpha 753
- Alsip 18,227
- Altamont 2,296
- Alton 32,905
- Altona 559
- Amboy 2,377
- Andalusia 1,052
- Andover 579
- Anna 4,805
- Annawan 802
- Antioch 6,105
- Apple River 414
- Arcola 2,678
- Argenta 940
- Arlington Heights 75,460
- Aroma Park 690
- Arthur 2,112
- Ashkum 650
- Ashland 1,257
- Ashley 583
- Ashmore 800
- Ashton 1,042
- Assumption 1,244
- Astoria 1,205
- Athens 1,404
- Atkinson 950
- Atlanta 1,616
- Atwood 1,253
- Auburn 3,724
- Augusta 614
- Aurora 99,581
- Ava 674
- Aviston 924
- Avon 957
- Bannockburn 1,388
- Barrington 9,504
- Barrington Hills 4,202
- Barry 1,391
- Bartlett 19,373
- Bartonville 5,643
- Batavia 17,076
- Beardstown 5,270
- Beckemeyer 1,070
- Bedford Park 566
- Beecher 2,032
- Belgium 511
- Belleville 42,785
- Bellevue 1,491
- Bellwood 20,241
- Belvidere 15,958
- Bement 1,668
- Benld 1,604
- Bensenville 17,767
- Benton 7,216
- Berkeley 5,137
- Berwyn 45,246
- Bethalto 9,507
- Bethany 1,369
- Blandinsville 762
- Bloomingdale 16,614
- Bloomington 51,972
- Blue Island 21,203
- Blue Mound 1,161
- Bluffs 774
- Bluford 747
- Bolingbrook 40,843
- Boulder Hill 8,894
- Bourbonnais 13,934
- Braceville 587
- Bradford 678
- Bradley 10,792
- Braidwood 3,584
- Breese 3,567
- Bridgeport 2,118
- Bridgeview 14,402
- Brighton 2,270
- Brimfield 797
- Broadview 8,713
- Brookfield 18,876
- Brooklyn 1,144
- Brookport 1,070
- Brownstown 668
- Buckley 557
- Buda 563
- Buffalo Grove 36,427
- Bunker Hill 1,722
- Burbank 27,600
- Burnham 3,916
- Burr Ridge 7,669
- Bushnell 3,288
- Byron 2,284
- Cahokia 17,550
- Cairo 4,846
- Calumet City 37,840
- Calumet Park 8,418
- Cambria 1,230
- Cambridge 2,124
- Camp Point 1,230
- Canton 13,922
- Capron 682
- Carbon Cliff 1,492
- Carbondale 27,033
- Carlinville 5,416
- Carlyle 3,474
- Carmi 5,564
- Carol Stream 31,716
- Carpentersville 23,049
- Carriers Mills 1,991
- Carrollton 2,507
- Carterville 3,630
- Carthage 2,657
- Cary 10,043
- Casey 2,914
- Caseyville 4,419
- Catlin 2,173
- Cedarville 751
- Central City 1,390
- Centralia 14,274
- Centreville 7,489
- Cerro Gordo 1,436
- Chadwick 557
- Champaign 63,502
- Chandlerville 689
- Channahon 4,266
- Channel Lake 1,660

Chapin 632
Charleston 20,398
Chatham 6,074
Chatsworth 1,186
Chebanse 1,082
Chenoa 1,732
Cherry 487
Cherry Valley 1,615
Chester 8,194
Chicago 2,783,726
Chicago Heights 33,072
Chicago Ridge 13,643
Chillicothe 5,959
Chrisman 1,136
Christopher 2,774
Cicero 67,436
Cisne 645
Cissna Park 805
Clarendon Hills 6,994
Clay City 929
Clayton 726
Clifton 1,347
Clinton 7,437
Coal City 3,907
Coal Valley 2,683
Cobden 1,090
Coffeen 736
Colchester 1,645
Colfax 854
Collinsville 22,446
Colona 2,237
Columbia 5,524
Cordova 638
Cornell 556
Cortland 963
Coulterville 984
Country Club Hills 15,431
Countryside 5,716
Cowden 599
Crainville 1,019
Creal Springs 791
Crescent City 541
Crest Hill 10,643
Crestwood 10,823
Crete 6,773
Creve Coeur 5,938
Crossville 805
Crystal Lake 24,512
Cuba 1,440
Cullom 568
Dakota 549
Dallas City 1,037
Dalton City 573
Dalzell 587
Danforth 457
Danvers 981
Danville 33,828
Darien 18,341
Davis 541
Decatur 83,885
Deer Creek 630
Deer Park 2,887
Deerfield 17,327
De Kalb 34,925
Delavan 1,642
De Pue 1,729
De Soto 1,500
Des Plaines 53,223
Diamond 1,077
Dieterich 568
Divernon 1,178
Dixmoor 3,647
Dixon 15,144
Dolton 23,930
Dongola 728
Downers Grove 46,858
Downs 620
Dunlap 851
Dupo 3,164
Du Quoin 6,697
Durand 1,100
Dwight 4,230
Earlville 1,435
East Alton 7,063
East Cape Girardeau 451
East Carondelet 630
East Dubuque 1,914
East Dundee 2,721
East Galesburg 813
East Hazel Crest 1,570
East Moline 20,147
East Peoria 21,378
East St. Louis 40,944
Edgewood 502
Edinburg 982
Edwardsville 14,579
Effingham 11,851
Elburn 1,275
Eldorado 4,536
Elgin 77,010
Elizabeth 641
Elizabethtown 427
Elk Grove Village 33,429
Elkville 958
Elmhurst 42,029
Elmwood 1,841
Elmwood Park 23,206
El Paso 2,499
Elsah 851
Elwood 951
Energy 1,106
Enfield 683
Equality 748
Erie 1,572
Eureka 4,435
Evanston 73,233
Evansville 844
Evergreen Park 20,874

Fairbury 3,643
Fairfield 5,439
Fairmont City 2,140
Fairmount 678
Fairview 510
Fairview Heights 14,351
Farina 575
Farmer City 2,114
Farmersville 698
Farmington 2,535
Findlay 787
Fisher 1,526
Fithian 512
Flanagan 987
Flora 5,054
Flossmoor 8,651
Ford Heights 4,259
Forest Lake 1,371
Forest Park 14,918
Forest View 743
Forrest 1,124
Forreston 1,361
Forsyth 1,275
Fox Lake 7,478
Fox Lake Hills 2,681
Fox River Grove 3,551
Fox River Valley Gardens 665
Frankfort 7,180
Franklin 634
Franklin Grove 968
Franklin Park 18,485
Freeburg 3,115
Freeport 25,840
Fulton 3,698
Gages Lake 8,349
Galatia 983
Galena 3,647
Galesburg 33,530
Galva 2,742
Gardner 1,237
Geneseo 5,990
Geneva 12,617
Genoa 3,083
Georgetown 3,678
Germantown 1,167
Gibson City 3,396
Gifford 845
Gillespie 3,645
Gilman 1,816
Girard 2,164
Glasford 1,115
Glen Carbon 7,731
Glen Ellyn 24,944
Glencoe 8,499
Glendale Heights 27,973
Glenview 37,093
Glenwood 9,289
Golconda 823
Golden 565
Goreville 872
Grafton 918
Grand Ridge 560
Grand Tower 775
Grandview 1,647
Granite City 32,862
Grant Park 1,024
Granville 1,407
Grayslake 7,388
Grayville 2,043
Green Oaks 2,101
Green Rock 2,615
Green Valley 745
Greenfield 1,162
Greenup 1,616
Greenview 848
Greenville 4,806
Gridley 1,304
Griggsville 1,218
Gurnee 13,701
Hamilton 3,281
Hammond 527
Hampshire 1,843
Hampton 1,601
Hanna City 1,205
Hanover 908
Hanover Park 32,895
Hardin 1,071
Harrisburg 9,289
Harristown 1,319
Hartford 1,676
Harvard 5,975
Harvey 29,771
Harwood Heights 7,680
Havana 3,610
Hawthorn Woods 4,423
Hazel Crest 13,334
Hebron 809
Hennepin 669
Henry 2,591
Herrin 10,857
Herscher 1,278
Heyworth 1,627
Hickory Hills 13,021
Highland 7,525
Highland Park 30,575
Highwood 5,331
Hillcrest 828
Hillsboro 4,400
Hillsdale 489
Hillside 7,672
Hinckley 1,682
Hinsdale 16,029
Hodgkins 1,963
Hoffman Estates 46,561
Holiday Hills 807
Homer 1,264
Hometown 4,769
Homewood 19,278
Hoopeston 5,871

Hopedale 805
Hoyleton 508
Hudson 1,006
Hull 514
Huntley 2,453
Hurst 842
Hutsonville 622
Illiopolis 934
Indian Head Park 3,503
Industry 571
Inverness 6,503
Ipava 483
Irving 516
Irvington 827
Island Lake 4,449
Itasca 6,947
Jacksonville 19,324
Jerome 1,206
Jerseyville 7,382
Johnston City 3,706
Joliet 76,836
Jonesboro 1,728
Justice 11,137
Kankakee 27,575
Kansas 887
Karnak 581
Keithsburg 747
Kenilworth 2,402
Kewanee 12,969
Kildeer 2,257
Kincaid 1,353
Kingston 562
Kinmundy 879
Kirkland 1,011
Kirkwood 884
Knoxville 3,243
Lacon 1,986
Ladd 1,283
La Grange 15,362
La Grange Park 12,861
La Harpe 1,407
Lake Barrington 3,855
Lake Bluff 5,513
Lake Catherine 1,515
Lake Forest 17,836
Lake in the Hills 5,866
Lake of the Woods 2,748
Lake Villa 2,857
Lake Zurich 14,947
Lakemoor 1,322
Lakewood 1,609
La Moille 654
Lanark 1,382
Lansing 28,086
La Salle 9,717
Latham 482
Lawrenceville 4,897
Leaf River 546
Lebanon 3,688
Leland 862
Leland Grove 1,679
Lemont 7,348
Lena 2,605
Le Roy 2,777
Lewistown 2,572
Lexington 1,809
Liberty 541
Libertyville 19,174
Lincoln 15,418
Lincolnshire 4,931
Lincolnwood 11,365
Lindenhurst 8,038
Lisle 19,512
Litchfield 6,883
Livingston 928
Loami 802
Lockport 9,401
Lomax 473
Lombard 39,408
London Mills 485
Long Grove 4,740
Long Lake 2,888
Lostant 510
Louisville 1,098
Loves Park 15,462
Lovington 1,143
Lyndon 615
Lynwood 6,535
Lyons 9,828
Mackinaw 1,331
Macomb 19,952
Macon 1,282
Madison 4,629
Mahomet 3,103
Malta 865
Manhattan 2,059
Manito 1,711
Mansfield 929
Manteno 3,488
Maple Park 641
Marengo 4,768
Marine 972
Marion 14,545
Marissa 2,375
Markham 13,136
Maroa 1,602
Marquette Heights 3,077
Marseilles 4,811
Marshall 3,555
Martinsville 1,161
Maryville 2,576
Mascoutah 5,511
Mason City 2,323
Matherville 708
Matteson 11,378
Mattoon 18,441
Maywood 27,139
Mazon 764

McCullom Lake 1,033
McHenry 16,177
McLean 797
McLeansboro 2,677
Melrose Park 20,859
Mendon 854
Mendota 7,018
Meredosia 1,134
Merrionette Park 2,065
Metamora 2,520
Metropolis 6,734
Midlothian 14,372
Milan 5,831
Milford 1,512
Milledgeville 1,076
Millstadt 2,566
Minier 1,155
Minonk 1,982
Minooka 2,561
Mokena 6,128
Moline 43,202
Momence 2,968
Monee 1,044
Monmouth 9,489
Montgomery 4,267
Monticello 4,549
Morris 10,270
Morrison 4,363
Morrisonville 1,113
Morton 13,799
Morton Grove 22,408
Mound City 765
Mounds 1,407
Mount Auburn 544
Mount Carmel 8,287
Mount Carroll 1,726
Mount Morris 2,919
Mount Olive 2,126
Mount Prospect 53,170
Mount Pulaski 1,610
Mount Sterling 1,922
Mount Vernon 16,988
Mount Zion 4,522
Moweaqua 1,785
Mulberry Grove 660
Mundelein 21,215
Murphysboro 9,176
Murrayville 673
Naperville 85,351
Naplate 609
Nashville 3,202
Nauvoo 1,108
Neoga 1,678
Neponset 529
New Athens 2,010
New Baden 2,602
New Berlin 797
New Boston 620
New Haven 459
New Lenox 9,627
Newark 840
Newman 960
Newton 3,154
Niantic 647
Niles 28,284
Noble 756
Nokomis 2,534
Normal 40,023
Norridge 14,459
Norris City 1,341
North Aurora 5,940
North Barrington 1,787
North Chicago 34,978
North Pekin 1,556
North Riverside 6,005
North Utica 848
Northbrook 32,308
Northfield 4,635
Northlake 12,505
Norwood 495
Oak Brook 9,178
Oak Forest 26,203
Oak Grove 626
Oak Lawn 56,182
Oak Park 53,648
Oakbrook Terrace 1,907
Oakland 996
Oakwood 1,533
Oakwood Hills 1,498
Oblong 1,616
Odell 1,030
Odin 1,150
O'Fallon 16,073
Ogden 671
Oglesby 3,619
Ohio 426
Okawville 1,274
Olney 8,664
Olympia Fields 4,248
Onarga 1,281
Oneida 723
Oquawka 1,442
Orangeville 451
Oreana 847
Oregon 3,891
Orion 1,821
Orland Hills 5,510
Orland Park 35,720
Oswego 3,876
Ottawa 17,451
Palatine 39,253
Palestine 1,619
Palmyra 722
Palos Heights 11,478
Palos Hills 17,803
Palos Park 4,199
Pana 5,796
Panama 294

Paris 8,987
Park City 4,677
Park Forest 24,656
Park Ridge 36,175
Patoka 656
Paw Paw 791
Pawnee 2,384
Paxton 4,289
Payson 1,114
Pearl City 670
Pecatonica 1,760
Pekin 32,254
Peoria 113,504
Peoria Heights 6,930
Peotone 2,947
Percy 925
Peru 9,302
Pesotum 558
Petersburg 2,261
Philo 1,028
Phoenix 2,217
Pierron 554
Pinckneyville 3,372
Piper City 760
Pistakee Highlands 3,848
Pittsburg 602
Pittsfield 4,231
Plainfield 4,557
Plano 5,104
Pleasant Hill 1,030
Pleasant Plains 701
Plymouth 521
Pocahontas 837
Polo 2,514
Pontiac 11,428
Pontoon Beach 4,013
Poplar Grove 743
Port Byron 1,002
Posen 4,226
Potomac 753
Prairie City 497
Prairie du Rocher 540
Prairie Grove 654
Princeton 7,197
Princeville 1,421
Prophetstown 1,749
Prospect Heights 15,239
Quincy 39,681
Ramsey 963
Rankin 619
Rantoul 17,212
Rapids City 932
Raymond 820
Red Bud 2,918
Reynolds 583
Richmond 1,016
Richton Park 10,523
Ridge Farm 939
Ridgway 1,103
River Forest 11,669
River Grove 9,961
Riverdale 13,671
Riverside 8,774
Riverton 2,638
Riverwoods 2,868
Roanoke 1,910
Robbins 7,498
Robinson 6,740
Rochelle 8,769
Rochester 2,676
Rock Falls 9,654
Rock Island 40,552
Rockdale 1,709
Rockford 139,426
Rockton 2,928
Rolling Meadows 22,591
Rome 1,902
Romeoville 14,074
Roodhouse 2,139
Roscoe 2,079
Roselle 20,819
Rosemont 3,995
Roseville 1,151
Rosewood Heights 4,821
Rosiclare 1,378
Rossville 1,334
Round Lake 3,550
Round Lake Beach 16,434
Round Lake Heights 1,251
Round Lake Park 4,045
Roxana 1,562
Royalton 1,191
Rushville 3,229
St. Anne 1,153
St. Charles 22,501
St. David 603
St. Elmo 1,473
St. Francisville 851
St. Jacob 752
St. Joseph 2,052
St. Libory 525
Salem 7,470
San Jose 519
Sandoval 1,535
Sandwich 5,567
Sauk Village 9,926
Savanna 3,819
Savoy 2,674
Saybrook 767
Schaumburg 68,586
Schiller Park 11,189
Schram City 692
Scott Air Force Base 7,245
Seneca 1,878

Sesser 2,087
Shabbona 897
Shannon 887
Shawneetown 1,575
Sheffield 951
Shelbyville 4,943
Sheldon 1,109
Sheridan 1,288
Sherman 2,080
Sherrard 697
Shiloh 2,655
Shipman 624
Shorewood 6,264
Sidell 584
Sidney 1,027
Silvis 6,926
Skokie 59,432
Sleepy Hollow 3,241
Smithton 1,587
Somonauk 1,263
Sorento 596
South Barrington 2,937
South Beloit 4,072
South Chicago Heights 3,597
South Elgin 7,474
South Holland 22,105
South Jacksonville 3,187
South Pekin 1,184
South Roxana 1,961
South Wilmington 698
Southern View 1,906
Sparland 412
Sparta 4,853
Spring Grove 1,066
Spring Valley 5,246
Springfield 105,227
Stanford 620
Staunton 4,806
Steeleville 2,059
Steger 8,584
Sterling 15,132
Stewardson 660
Stickney 5,678
Stillman Valley 848
Stockton 1,871
Stone Park 4,383
Stonington 1,006
Streamwood 30,987
Streator 14,121
Stronghurst 799
Sugar Grove 2,005
Sullivan 4,354
Summit 9,971
Sumner 1,083
Sunnyside 1,529
Swansea 8,201
Sycamore 9,708
Tallula 598
Tamaroa 780
Tamms 748
Tampico 833
Taylor Springs 670
Taylorville 11,133
Teutopolis 1,417
Thayer 730
Thomasboro 1,250
Thompsonville 602
Thomson 538
Thornton 2,778
Tilden 919
Tilton 2,729
Tinley Park 37,121
Tiskilwa 830
Toledo 1,199
Tolono 2,605
Toluca 1,315
Tonica 715
Toulon 1,328
Tovey 533
Towanda 856
Tower Hill 601
Tower Lakes 1,333
Tremont 2,088
Trenton 2,481
Troy 6,046
Tuscola 4,155
Ullin 402
Union 542
University Park 6,204
Urbana 36,344
Valier 708
Valmeyer 897
Vandalia 6,114
Venetian Village 3,133
Venice 3,571
Vermont 806
Vernon Hills 15,319
Vienna 1,446
Villa Grove 2,734
Villa Park 22,253
Viola 964
Virden 3,635
Virginia 1,767
Wadsworth 1,826
Walnut 1,463
Wamac 1,501
Wapella 608
Warren 1,550
Warrensburg 1,274
Warrenville 11,333
Warsaw 1,882
Washburn 1,075
Washington 10,099
Washington Park 7,431
Wataga 879
Waterloo 5,072
Waterman 1,074
Watseka 5,424
Watson 646

Illinois (continued)

Wauconda 6,294
Waukegan 69,392
Waverly 1,402
Wayne 1,541
Wayne City 1,099
Waynesville 440
Wenona 950
West Chicago 14,796
West City 747
West Dundee 3,728
West Frankfort 8,526
West Peoria 5,314
West Salem 1,042
Westchester 17,301
Western Springs 11,984
Westfield 676
Westmont 21,228
Westville 3,387
Wheaton 51,464
Wheeling 29,911
White Hall 2,814
Williamsfield 571
Williamsville 1,140
Willisville 577
Willow Springs 4,509
Willowbrook 8,598
Wilmette 26,690
Wilmington 4,743
Wilsonville 609
Winchester 1,769
Windsor 1,143
Windsor 774
Winfield 7,096
Winnebago 1,840
Winnetka 12,174
Winthrop Harbor 6,240
Witt 866
Wonder Lake 6,664
Wood Dale 12,425
Wood River 11,490
Woodhull 808
Woodridge 26,256
Woodstock 14,353
Worden 896
Worth 11,208
Wyanet 1,017
Wyoming 1,462
Yates City 760
Yorkville 3,925
Zeigler 1,746
Zion 19,775

Indiana ■ population 5,564,228

Metropolitan areas

Anderson 130,669
Bloomington 108,978
Cincinnati (O.) .... 1,452,645 (1,130,324 in O.; 283,486 in Ky.; 38,835 in Ind.)
Elkhart-Goshen 156,198
Evansville .... 278,990 (235,946 in Ind.; 43,044 in Ky.)
Fort Wayne 363,811
Gary-Hammond 604,526
Indianapolis 1,249,822
Kokomo 96,946
Lafayette-West Lafayette 130,598
Louisville (Ky.) .... 952,626 (770,591 in Ky.; 182,071 in Ind.)
Muncie 119,659
South Bend-Mishawaka 247,052
Terre Haute 130,812

Counties

Adams 31,095
Allen 300,836
Bartholomew 63,657
Benton 9,441
Blackford 14,067
Boone 38,147
Brown 14,080
Carroll 18,809
Cass 38,413
Clark 87,777
Clay 24,705
Clinton 30,974
Crawford 9,914
Daviess 27,533
Dearborn 38,835
Decatur 23,645
DeKalb 35,324
Delaware 119,659
Dubois 36,616
Elkhart 156,198
Fayette 26,015
Floyd 64,404
Fountain 17,808
Franklin 19,580
Fulton 18,840
Gibson 31,913
Grant 74,169
Greene 30,410
Hamilton 108,936
Hancock 45,527
Harrison 29,890
Hendricks 75,717
Henry 48,139
Howard 80,827
Huntington 35,427
Jackson 37,730
Jasper 24,960
Jay 21,512
Jefferson 29,797
Jennings 23,661
Johnson 88,109
Knox 39,884
Kosciusko 65,294
Lagrange 29,477
Lake 475,594
La Porte 107,066
Lawrence 42,836
Madison 130,669
Marion 797,159
Marshall 42,182
Martin 10,369
Miami 36,897
Monroe 108,978
Montgomery 34,436
Morgan 55,920
Newton 13,551
Noble 37,877
Ohio 5,315
Orange 18,409
Owen 17,281
Parke 15,410
Perry 19,107
Pike 12,509
Porter 128,932
Posey 25,968
Pulaski 12,643
Putnam 30,315
Randolph 27,148
Ripley 24,616
Rush 18,129
St. Joseph 247,052
Scott 20,991
Shelby 40,307
Spencer 19,490
Starke 22,747
Steuben 27,446
Sullivan 18,993
Switzerland 7,738
Tippecanoe 130,598
Tipton 16,119
Union 6,976
Vanderburgh 165,058
Vermillion 16,773
Vigo 106,107
Wabash 35,069
Warren 8,176
Warrick 44,920
Washington 23,717
Wayne 71,951
Wells 25,948
White 23,265
Whitley 27,651

Cities and towns

Advance 520
Akron 1,001
Albany 2,357
Albion 1,823
Alexandria 5,709
Ambia 249
Amboy 370
Amo 380
Anderson 59,459
Andrews 1,118
Angola 5,824
Arcadia 1,468
Argos 1,642
Ashley 767
Atlanta 703
Attica 3,457
Auburn 9,379
Aurora 3,825
Austin 4,310
Avilla 1,366
Bainbridge 682
Bargersville 1,681
Batesville 4,720
Battle Ground 806
Bedford 13,817
Beech Grove 13,383
Berne 3,559
Beverly Shores 622
Bicknell 3,357
Birdseye 472
Bloomfield 2,592
Bloomingdale 341
Bloomington 60,633
Bluffton 9,020
Boonville 6,724
Borden (New Providence) 270
Boswell 767
Bourbon 1,672
Brazil 7,640
Bremen 4,725
Bright 3,945
Bristol 1,133
Brook 899
Brooklyn 1,162
Brookston 1,804
Brookville 2,529
Brownsburg 7,628
Brownstown 2,872
Bruceville 471
Bryant 273
Bunker Hill 1,010
Burket 200
Burlington 568
Burnettsville 401
Burns Harbor 788
Butler 2,601
Cadiz 202
Cambridge City 2,091
Camden 607
Campbellsburg 606
Cannelton 1,786
Carbon 350
Carlisle 613
Carmel 25,380
Carthage 887
Cayuga 1,083
Cedar Grove 246
Cedar Lake 8,885
Center Point 278
Centerville 2,398
Chalmers 525
Chandler 3,099
Charlestown 5,889
Chesterfield 2,730
Chesterton 9,124
Chrisney 511
Churubusco 1,781
Cicero 3,268
Clarks Hill 716
Clarksville 19,833
Clay City 929
Claypool 411
Clayton 610
Clear Lake 272
Clermont 1,678
Clifford 308
Clinton 5,040
Cloverdale 1,681
Coatesville 469
Colfax 727
Collegeville 993
Columbia City 5,706
Columbus 31,802
Connersville 15,550
Converse 1,144
Corunna 241
Corydon 2,661
Covington 2,747
Crane 216
Crawfordsville 13,584
Cromwell 520
Crothersville 1,687
Crown Point 17,728
Culver 1,404
Cumberland 4,557
Cynthiana 669
Dale 1,553
Daleville 1,681
Dana 612
Danville 4,345
Darlington 740
Darmstadt 1,346
Dayton 996
Decatur 8,644
Decker 281
Delphi 2,531
DeMotte 2,482
Denver 504
Dillsboro 1,200
Dublin 805
Dugger 936
Dune Acres 263
Dunkirk 2,739
Dunlap 5,705
Dunreith 205
Dupont 391
Dyer 10,923
Earl Park 443
East Chicago 33,892
East Germantown 372
Eaton 1,614
Edgewood 2,057
Edinburgh 4,536
Edwardsport 380
Elberfeld 635
Elizabethtown 495
Elkhart 43,627
Ellettsville 3,275
Elnora 679
Elwood 9,494
English 614
Etna Green 578
Evansville 126,272
Fairland 1,348
Fairmount 3,130
Fairview Park 1,446
Farmersburg 1,159
Farmland 1,412
Ferdinand 2,318
Fillmore 497
Fishers 7,508
Flora 2,179
Fort Branch 2,447
Fort Wayne 173,072
Fortville 2,690
Fountain City 766
Fowler 2,333
Fowlerton 306
Francesville 969
Francisco 560
Frankfort 14,754
Franklin 12,907
Frankton 1,736
Fremont 1,407
French Lick 2,087
Fulton 371
Galena 1,231
Galveston 1,609
Garrett 5,349
Gary 116,646
Gas City 6,296
Gaston 979
Geneva 1,280
Gentryville 277
Georgetown 2,092
Glenwood 285
Goodland 1,033
Goshen 23,797
Gosport 764
Grabill 751
Grandview 761
Granger 20,241
Greencastle 8,984
Greendale 3,881
Greenfield 11,657
Greensboro 204
Greensburg 9,286
Greens Fork 416
Greentown 2,172
Greenville 508
Greenwood 26,265
Griffith 17,916
Grissom Air Force Base 4,271
Hagerstown 1,835
Hamilton 684
Hamlet 789
Hammond 84,236
Hanover 3,610
Hardinsburg 322
Harmony 645
Hartford City 6,960
Hartsville 391
Haubstadt 1,455
Hazleton 357
Hebron 3,183
Highland 23,696
Hillsboro 499
Hobart 21,822
Holland 675
Holton 451
Homecroft 758
Hope 2,171
Hudson 438
Huntertown 1,330
Huntingburg 5,242
Huntington 16,389
Hymera 771
Indian Heights 3,669
Indianapolis 731,327
Ingalls 889
Jamestown 764
Jasonville 2,200
Jasper 10,030
Jeffersonville 21,841
Jonesboro 2,073
Jonesville 221
Kempton 362
Kendallville 7,773
Kennard 382
Kentland 1,798
Kewanna 542
Kingman 561
Kingsbury 258
Kingsford Heights 1,486
Kirklin 707
Knightstown 2,048
Knightsville 740
Knox 3,705
Kokomo 44,962
Koontz Lake 1,615
Kouts 1,603
La Crosse 677
Ladoga 1,124
Lafayette 43,764
La Fontaine 909
Lagrange 2,382
Lagro 496
Lake Hart 213
Lake Station 13,899
Lakeville 655
Lanesville 512
La Paz 562
Lapel 1,742
La Porte 21,507
Larwill 219
Laurel 544
Lawrence 26,763
Lawrenceburg 4,375
Leavenworth 320
Lebanon 12,059
Leesburg 584
Lewisville 437
Liberty 2,051
Ligonier 3,443
Linden 718
Linton 5,814
Lizton 410
Logansport 16,812
Long Beach 2,044
Loogootee 2,884
Losantville 253
Lowell 6,430
Lynn 1,183
Lynnville 640
Lyons 753
Macy 218
Madison 12,006
Marengo 856
Marion 32,618
Markle 1,208
Markleville 412
Marshall 379
Martinsville 11,677
Matthews 571
McCordsville 684
Mecca 331
Medaryville 689
Medora 805
Mellott 222
Mentone 912
Meridian Hills 1,728
Merom 257
Merrillville 27,257
Mexico 1,003
Michiana Shores 378
Michigan City 33,822
Michigantown 472
Middlebury 2,004
Middletown 2,333
Milan 1,529
Milford 1,388
Millersburg 854
Milltown 917
Milton 634
Mishawaka 42,608
Mitchell 4,669
Modoc 218
Monon 1,585
Monroe 788
Monroe City 538
Monroeville 1,232
Monterey 230
Montezuma 1,134
Montgomery 351
Monticello 5,237
Montpelier 1,880
Mooreland 465
Moores Hill 649
Mooresville 5,541
Morgantown 978
Morocco 1,044
Morristown 980
Mount Summit 238
Mount Vernon 7,217
Mulberry 1,262
Muncie 71,035
Munster 19,949
Napoleon 238
Nappanee 5,510
Nashville 873
New Albany 36,322
New Carlisle 1,446
New Castle 17,753
New Chicago 2,066
New Harmony 846
New Haven 9,320
New Market 614
New Palestine 671
New Paris 1,007
New Pekin 1,095
New Richmond 312
New Ross 331
New Whiteland 4,097
Newberry 207
Newburgh 2,880
Newpoint 296
Newport 627
Newtown 243
Noblesville 17,655
North Judson 1,582
North Liberty 1,366
North Manchester 6,383
North Salem 499
North Terre Haute 4,331
North Vernon 5,311
North Webster 881
Oak Park 5,630
Oakland City 2,810
Oaktown 655
Odon 1,475
Ogden Dunes 1,499
Oldenburg 715
Oolitic 1,424
Orestes 458
Orland 361
Orleans 2,083
Osceola 1,999
Osgood 1,688
Ossian 2,428
Otterbein 1,291
Owensville 1,053
Oxford 1,273
Palmyra 621
Paoli 3,542
Paragon 515
Parker City 1,323
Patoka 704
Pendleton 2,309
Pennville 637
Perrysville 443
Peru 12,843
Petersburg 2,449
Pierceton 1,030
Pittsboro 815
Plainfield 10,433
Plainville 444
Plymouth 8,303
Poneto 236
Portage 29,060
Porter 3,118
Portland 6,483
Poseyville 1,089
Pottawattomie Park 281
Princes Lakes 1,055
Princeton 8,127
Redkey 1,383
Remington 1,247
Rensselaer 5,045
Reynolds 528
Richmond 38,705
Ridgeville 808
Riley 232
Rising Sun 2,311
Roachdale 902
Roann 447
Roanoke 1,018
Rochester 5,969
Rockport 2,315
Rockville 2,706
Rocky Ripple 751
Rome City 1,138
Rosedale 783
Roseland 706
Rossville 1,175
Royal Center 859
Rushville 5,533
Russellville 336
Russiaville 988
St. Joe 452
St. John 4,921
St. Leon 493
St. Paul 1,032
Salem 5,619
Sandborn 455
Santa Claus 927
Saratoga 266
Schererville 19,926
Schneider 310
Scottsburg 5,334
Seelyville 1,090
Sellersburg 5,745
Selma 800
Seymour 15,576
Shadeland 1,674
Shamrock Lakes 207
Sharpsville 769
Shelburn 1,147
Shelbyville 15,336
Sheridan 2,046
Shipshewana 524
Shirley 817
Shoals 853
Silver Lake 528
Simonton Lake 3,554
Somerville 223
South Bend 105,511
South Haven 6,112
South Whitley 1,482
Southport 1,969
Speedway 13,092
Spencer 2,609
Spiceland 757
Spring Grove 420
Spring Lake 216
Staunton 592
Stilesville 298
Stinesville 204
Straughn 318
Sullivan 4,663
Sulphur Springs 257
Summitville 1,010
Sunman 623
Swayzee 1,059
Sweetser 924
Switz City 257
Syracuse 2,729
Taylorsville 1,044
Tell City 8,088
Tennyson 267
Terre Haute 57,483
Thorntown 1,506
Tipton 4,751
Topeka 912
Town of Pines 789
Trafalgar 531
Trail Creek 2,463
Tri-Lakes 3,299
Troy 465
Union City 3,612
Uniondale 289
Universal 392
Upland 3,295
Utica 411
Valparaiso 24,414
Van Buren 934
Veedersburg 2,192
Vernon 370
Versailles 1,791
Vevay 1,393
Vincennes 19,859
Wabash 12,127
Wakarusa 1,667
Walkerton 2,061
Walton 1,053
Wanatah 852
Warren 1,185
Warren Park 1,763
Warsaw 10,968
Washington 10,838
Waterloo 2,040
Waveland 474
Waynetown 911
West Baden Springs 675

West College Corner 686
West Harrison 318
West Lafayette 25,907
West Lebanon 760
West Terre Haute 2,495
Westfield 3,304
Westport 1,478
Westville 5,255
Wheatfield 621
Wheatland 439
Whiteland 2,446
Whitestown 476
Whiting 5,155
Wilkinson 446
Williams Creek 425
Williamsport 1,798
Winamac 2,262
Winchester 5,095
Windfall City 779
Wingate 275
Winona Lake 4,053
Winslow 875
Wolcott 886
Wolcottville 879
Woodburn 1,321
Worthington 1,473
Wynnedale 269
Yorktown 4,106
Zionsville 5,281

Iowa ■ population 2,787,424

Metropolitan areas

Cedar Rapids 168,767
Davenport-Rock Island (Ill.)-Moline (Ill.) 350,861 (199,882 in Ill.; 150,979 in Ia.)
Des Moines 392,928
Dubuque 86,403
Iowa City 96,119
Omaha (Nebr.) 618,262 (535,634 in Nebr.; 82,628 in Ia.)
Sioux City 115,018 (98,276 in Ia.; 16,742 in Nebr.)
Waterloo-Cedar Falls 146,611

Counties

Adair 8,409
Adams 4,866
Allamakee 13,855
Appanoose 13,743
Audubon 7,334
Benton 22,429
Black Hawk 123,798
Boone 25,186
Bremer 22,813
Buchanan 20,844
Buena Vista 19,965
Butler 15,731
Calhoun 11,508
Carroll 21,423
Cass 15,128
Cedar 17,381
Cerro Gordo 46,733
Cherokee 14,098
Chickasaw 13,295
Clarke 8,287
Clay 17,585
Clayton 19,054
Clinton 51,040
Crawford 16,775
Dallas 29,755
Davis 8,312
Decatur 8,338
Delaware 18,035
Des Moines 42,614
Dickinson 14,909
Dubuque 86,403
Emmet 11,569
Fayette 21,843
Floyd 17,058
Franklin 11,364
Fremont 8,226
Greene 10,045
Grundy 12,029
Guthrie 10,935
Hamilton 16,071
Hancock 12,638
Hardin 19,094
Harrison 14,730
Henry 19,226
Howard 9,809
Humboldt 10,756
Ida 8,365
Iowa 14,630
Jackson 19,950
Jasper 34,795
Jefferson 16,310
Johnson 96,119
Jones 19,444
Keokuk 11,624
Kossuth 18,591
Lee 38,687
Linn 168,767
Louisa 11,592
Lucas 9,070
Lyon 11,952
Madison 12,483
Mahaska 21,522
Marion 30,001
Marshall 38,276
Mills 13,202
Mitchell 10,928
Monona 10,034
Monroe 8,114
Montgomery 12,076
Muscatine 39,907
O'Brien 15,444
Osceola 7,267
Page 16,870
Palo Alto 10,669
Plymouth 23,388
Pocahontas 9,525
Polk 327,140
Pottawattamie 82,628
Poweshiek 19,033
Ringgold 5,420
Sac 12,324
Scott 150,979
Shelby 13,230
Sioux 29,903
Story 74,252
Tama 17,419
Taylor 7,114
Union 12,750
Van Buren 7,676
Wapello 35,687
Warren 36,033
Washington 19,612
Wayne 7,067
Webster 40,342
Winnebago 12,122
Winneshiek 20,847
Woodbury 98,276
Worth 7,991
Wright 14,269

Cities and towns

Ackley 1,696
Adair 894
Adel 3,304
Afton 953
Agency 616
Ainsworth 506
Akron 1,450
Albert City 779
Albia 3,870
Albion 585
Alburnett 456
Alden 855
Algona 6,015
Alleman 340
Allerton 599
Allison 1,000
Alta 1,820
Alta Vista 246
Alton 1,063
Altoona 7,191
Alvord 204
Ames 47,198
Anamosa 5,100
Andrew 319
Anita 1,068
Ankeny 18,482
Anthon 638
Aplington 1,034
Arcadia 485
Arlington 465
Armstrong 1,025
Arnolds Park 953
Arthur 272
Asbury 2,013
Ashton 462
Atalissa 357
Atkins 637
Atlantic 7,432
Auburn 283
Audubon 2,524
Aurelia 1,034
Avoca 1,497
Badger 569
Bagley 303
Bancroft 857
Barnes City 221
Batavia 520
Battle Creek 818
Baxter 938
Bayard 511
Beacon 509
Bedford 1,528
Belle Plaine 2,834
Bellevue 2,239
Belmond 2,500
Bennett 395
Bertram 201
Bettendorf 28,132
Birmingham 386
Blairsburg 269
Blairstown 672
Blakesburg 333
Blencoe 250
Blockton 213
Bloomfield 2,580
Blue Grass 1,214
Bode 335
Bonaparte 465
Bondurant 1,584
Boone 12,392
Boxholm 214
Boyden 651
Braddyville 219
Brandon 320
Breda 467
Bridgewater 209
Brighton 684
Britt 2,133
Bronson 209
Brooklyn 1,439
Buffalo 1,260
Buffalo Center 1,081
Burlington 27,208
Burt 575
Bussey 494
Calamus 379
Callender 384
Calmar 1,026
Camanche 4,436
Cambridge 714
Cantril 262
Carlisle 3,241
Carroll 9,579
Carson 705
Carter Lake 3,200
Cascade 1,812
Casey 441
Cedar Falls 34,298
Cedar Rapids 108,751
Center Point 1,693
Centerville 5,936
Central City 1,063
Chariton 4,616
Charles City 7,878
Charlotte 359
Charter Oak 497
Chelsea 336
Cherokee 6,026
Churdan 423
Cincinnati 363
Clarence 936
Clarinda 5,104
Clarion 2,703
Clarksville 1,382
Clear Lake 8,183
Clearfield 417
Cleghorn 275
Clermont 523
Clinton 29,201
Clive 7,462
Clutier 219
Coggon 645
Coin 278
Colesburg 439
Colfax 2,462
College Springs 230
Collins 455
Colo 771
Columbus City 328
Columbus Junction 1,616
Conesville 334
Conrad 964
Coon Rapids 1,266
Coralville 10,347
Corning 1,806
Correctionville 897
Corwith 354
Corydon 1,675
Coulter 252
Council Bluffs 54,315
Crawfordsville 265
Cresco 3,669
Creston 7,911
Crystal Lake 266
Cumberland 295
Cushing 220
Dakota City 1,024
Dallas Center 1,454
Danbury 430
Danville 926
Davenport 95,333
Davis City 257
Dayton 818
Decorah 8,063
Dedham 264
Deep River 345
Defiance 312
Delhi 485
Delmar 517
Deloit 296
Delta 409
Denison 6,604
Denver 1,600
Des Moines 193,187
De Soto 1,033
De Witt 4,514
Dexter 628
Diagonal 298
Dickens 214
Dike 875
Dixon 202
Donahue 316
Donnellson 940
Doon 476
Dow City 439
Dows 660
Dubuque 57,546
Dumont 705
Duncombe 488
Dunkerton 746
Dunlap 1,251
Durant 1,549
Dyersville 3,703
Dysart 1,230
Eagle Grove 3,671
Earlham 1,157
Earling 466
Earlville 822
Early 649
Eddyville 1,010
Edgewood 776
Elberon 203
Eldon 1,070
Eldora 3,038
Eldridge 3,378
Elgin 637
Elk Horn 672
Elk Run Heights 1,088
Elkader 1,510
Elkhart 388
Elliott 399
Ellsworth 451
Elma 653
Ely 517
Emerson 476
Emmetsburg 3,940
Epworth 1,297
Essex 916
Estherville 6,720
Evansdale 4,638
Everly 706
Exira 955
Fairbank 1,018
Fairfax 780
Fairfield 9,768
Farley 1,354
Farmersburg 291
Farmington 655
Farnhamville 414
Farragut 498
Fayette 1,317
Fenton 346
Fertile 382
Floyd 359
Fonda 731
Fontanelle 712
Forest City 4,430
Fort Atkinson 367
Fort Dodge 25,894
Fort Madison 11,618
Fostoria 205
Fredericksburg 1,011
Fredonia 201
Fremont 701
Fruitland 511
Galva 398
Garden Grove 229
Garnavillo 727
Garner 2,916
Garrison 320
Garwin 533
George 1,066
Gilbert 796
Gilbertville 748
Gilman 586
Gilmore City 560
Gladbrook 881
Glenwood 4,571
Glidden 1,099
Goldfield 710
Goodell 201
Goose Lake 221
Gowrie 1,028
Graettinger 813
Grafton 282
Grand Junction 808
Grand Mound 619
Grandview 514
Granger 624
Granville 298
Gravity 218
Greeley 263
Greene 1,142
Greenfield 2,074
Grimes 2,653
Grinnell 8,902
Griswold 1,049
Grundy Center 2,491
Guthrie Center 1,614
Guttenberg 2,257
Halbur 215
Hamburg 1,248
Hampton 4,133
Hancock 201
Harcourt 306
Harlan 5,148
Harpers Ferry 284
Hartford 768
Hartley 1,632
Harvey 235
Havelock 217
Hawarden 2,439
Hawkeye 460
Hazleton 733
Hedrick 810
Henderson 206
Hiawatha 4,986
Hills 662
Hinton 697
Holland 215
Holstein 1,449
Holy Cross 304
Hopkinton 695
Hornick 222
Hospers 643
Hubbard 814
Hudson 2,037
Hull 1,724
Humboldt 4,438
Humeston 553
Huxley 2,047
Ida Grove 2,357
Independence 5,972
Indianola 11,340
Inwood 824
Ionia 304
Iowa City 59,738
Iowa Falls 5,424
Ireton 597
Irwin 394
Jamaica 232
Janesville 822
Jefferson 4,292
Jesup 2,121
Jewell 1,106
Johnston 4,702
Joice 245
Kalona 1,942
Kamrar 203
Kanawha 763
Kellerton 314
Kelley 246
Kellogg 626
Kensett 298
Keokuk 12,451
Keosauqua 1,020
Keota 1,000
Keswick 284
Keystone 568
Kimballton 289
Kingsley 1,129
Kiron 301
Klemme 587
Knoxville 8,232
Lacona 357
Ladora 308
Lake City 1,841
Lake Mills 2,143
Lake Park 996
Lake View 1,303
Lakeside 522
Lakota 281
Lambs Grove 212
Lamoni 2,319
Lamont 471
La Motte 219
Lansing 1,007
La Porte City 2,128
Larchwood 739
Latimer 430
Laurel 271
Laurens 1,550
Lawler 517
Lawton 482
Le Claire 2,734
Le Grand 854
Lehigh 536
Leland 311
Le Mars 8,454
Lenox 1,303
Leon 2,047
Lester 257
Letts 390
Lewis 433
Libertyville 264
Lidderdale 202
Lime Springs 438
Linden 201
Lineville 289
Lisbon 1,452
Liscomb 258
Little Rock 493
Little Sioux 205
Livermore 436
Lockridge 270
Logan 1,401
Lohrville 453
Lone Tree 979
Long Grove 605
Lorimor 377
Lost Nation 467
Lovilia 551
Low Moor 280
Lowden 726
Lucas 224
Lu Verne 328
Luxemburg 257
Lynnville 393
Lytton 320
Macedonia 262
Madrid 2,395
Magnolia 204
Malcom 447
Mallard 360
Malvern 1,210
Manchester 5,137
Manilla 898
Manly 1,349
Manning 1,484
Manson 1,844
Mapleton 1,294
Maquoketa 6,111
Marathon 320
Marble Rock 361
Marcus 1,171
Marengo 2,270
Marion 20,403
Marquette 479
Marshalltown 25,178
Martelle 290
Martensdale 491
Mason City 29,040
Massena 372
Maurice 243
Maxwell 788
Maynard 513
McCallsburg 292
McCausland 308
McGregor 797
Mechanicsville 1,012
Mediapolis 1,637
Melbourne 669
Melcher-Dallas 1,302
Melvin 250
Menlo 356
Merrill 729
Meservey 292
Middletown 386
Miles 409
Milford 2,170
Milo 864
Milton 506
Minburn 346
Minden 498
Mingo 252
Missouri Valley 2,888
Mitchellville 1,670
Modale 289
Mondamin 403
Monona 1,520
Monroe 1,739
Montezuma 1,651
Monticello 3,522
Montour 312
Montrose 957
Moorhead 259
Moorland 209
Moravia 679
Morning Sun 841
Moulton 613
Mount Ayr 1,796
Mount Pleasant 8,027
Mount Vernon 3,657
Moville 1,306
Murray 731
Muscatine 22,881
Mystic 545
Nashua 1,476
Neola 894
Nevada 6,009
New Albin 534
New Hampton 3,660
New Hartford 683
New London 1,922
New Market 454
New Providence 240
New Sharon 1,136
New Vienna 376
New Virginia 433
Newell 1,089
Newhall 854
Newton 14,789
Nichols 366
Nora Springs 1,505
North English 944
North Liberty 2,926
Northwood 1,940
Norwalk 5,726
Norway 583
Oakland 1,496
Oakville 442
Ocheyedan 539
Odebolt 1,158
Oelwein 6,493
Ogden 1,909
Okoboji 775
Olds 205
Olin 663
Ollie 207
Onawa 2,936
Onslow 216
Orange City 4,940
Orient 376
Orleans 560
Osage 3,439
Osceola 4,164
Oskaloosa 10,632
Ossian 810
Otho 529
Ottumwa 24,488
Oxford 663
Oxford Junction 581
Pacific Junction 548
Packwood 208
Palmer 230
Palo 514
Panama 201
Panora 1,100
Park View 2,192
Parkersburg 1,804
Parnell 209
Paton 255
Paullina 1,134
Pella 9,270
Perry 6,652
Persia 312
Peterson 390

Iowa (continued)

Pierson 341
Pisgah 268
Plainfield 455
Pleasant Hill 3,671
Pleasantville 1,536
Plymouth 453
Pocahontas 2,085
Polk City 1,908
Pomeroy 762
Portsmouth 209
Postville 1,472
Prairie City 1,360
Prairieburg 213
Prescott 287
Preston 1,025
Primghar 950
Princeton 806
Protivin 305
Pulaski 221
Quasqueton 579
Quimby 334
Radcliffe 574
Rake 238
Randolph 243
Raymond 619
Readlyn 773
Red Oak 6,264
Redfield 883
Reinbeck 1,605
Rembrandt 229
Remsen 1,513
Renwick 287
Rhodes 272
Riceville 827
Richland 522
Ridgeway 295
Ringsted 481
Rippey 275
Riverdale 433
Riverside 824
Riverton 333
Robins 875
Rock Rapids 2,601
Rock Valley 2,540
Rockford 863
Rockwell 1,008
Rockwell City 1,981
Roland 1,035
Rolfe 721
Rowley 272
Royal 466
Rudd 429
Runnells 306
Russell 531
Ruthven 707
Ryan 382
Sabula 710
Sac City 2,492
Sageville 288
St. Ansgar 1,063
St. Charles 537
Salem 453
Salix 367
Sanborn 1,345
Saylorville 2,709
Schaller 768
Schleswig 851
Scranton 583
Sergeant Bluff 2,772
Seymour 869
Sheffield 1,174
Shelby 637
Sheldahl 315
Sheldon 4,937
Shell Rock 1,385
Shellsburg 765
Shenandoah 5,572
Shueyville 223
Sibley 2,815
Sidney 1,253
Sigourney 2,111
Silver City 252
Sioux Center 5,074
Sioux City 80,505
Sioux Rapids 761
Slater 1,268
Sloan 938
Smithland 235
Soldier 205
Solon 1,050
South English 224
Spencer 11,066
Spillville 387
Spirit Lake 3,871
Springville 1,068
Stacyville 481
Stanhope 447
Stanton 692
Stanwood 646
State Center 1,248
Steamboat Rock 335
Stockport 260
Storm Lake 8,769
Story City 2,959
Stratford 715
Strawberry Point 1,357
Stuart 1,522
Sully 841
Sumner 2,078
Sutherland 714
Swea City 634
Swisher 645
Tabor 957
Tama 2,697
Templeton 321
Terril 383
Thompson 498
Thor 205
Thornton 431
Thurman 239
Tiffin 460
Tipton 2,998
Titonka 612
Toledo 2,380
Traer 1,552
Treynor 897
Tripoli 1,188
Truro 391
Underwood 515
Union 448
University Heights 1,042
University Park 604
Urbana 595
Urbandale 23,500
Ute 395
Vail 388
Van Horne 695
Van Meter 751
Van Wert 249
Ventura 590
Victor 966
Villisca 1,332
Vinton 5,103
Volga 306
Wadena 236
Wahpeton 484
Walcott 1,356
Walford 303
Walker 673
Wall Lake 875
Walnut 857
Wapello 2,013
Washington 7,074
Washta 284
Waterloo 66,467
Waucoma 277
Waukee 2,512
Waukon 4,019
Waverly 8,539
Wayland 838
Webster City 7,894
Wellman 1,085
Wellsburg 682
Wesley 444
West Bend 862
West Branch 1,908
West Burlington 3,083
West Des Moines 31,702
West Liberty 2,935
West Okoboji 263
West Point 1,079
West Union 2,490
Westgate 207
Westside 348
What Cheer 762
Wheatland 723
Whiting 683
Whittemore 535
Williams 368
Williamsburg 2,174
Wilton 2,577
Windsor Heights 5,190
Winfield 1,051
Winterset 4,196
Winthrop 742
Woden 259
Woodbine 1,500
Woodburn 240
Woodward 1,197
Woolstock 212
Worthington 439
Wyoming 659
Yale 220
Zearing 614

Kansas ■ population 2,485,600

Metropolitan areas

Kansas City 1,566,280 (604,884 in Kans., 961,396 in Mo.)
Lawrence 81,798
Topeka 160,976
Wichita 485,270

Counties

Allen 14,638
Anderson 7,803
Atchison 16,932
Barber 5,874
Barton 29,382
Bourbon 14,966
Brown 11,128
Butler 50,580
Chase 3,021
Chautauqua 4,407
Cherokee 21,374
Cheyenne 3,243
Clark 2,418
Clay 9,158
Cloud 11,023
Coffey 8,404
Comanche 2,313
Cowley 36,915
Crawford 35,568
Decatur 4,021
Dickinson 18,958
Doniphan 8,134
Douglas 81,798
Edwards 3,787
Elk 3,327
Ellis 26,004
Ellsworth 6,586
Finney 33,070
Ford 27,463
Franklin 21,994
Geary 30,453
Gove 3,231
Graham 3,543
Grant 7,159
Gray 5,396
Greeley 1,774
Greenwood 7,847
Hamilton 2,388
Harper 7,124
Harvey 31,028
Haskell 3,886
Hodgeman 2,177
Jackson 11,525
Jefferson 15,905
Jewell 4,251
Johnson 355,054
Kearny 4,027
Kingman 8,292
Kiowa 3,660
Labette 23,693
Lane 2,375
Leavenworth 64,371
Lincoln 3,653
Linn 8,254
Logan 3,081
Lyon 34,732
Marion 12,888
Marshall 11,705
McPherson 27,268
Meade 4,247
Miami 23,466
Mitchell 7,203
Montgomery 38,816
Morris 6,198
Morton 3,480
Nemaha 10,446
Neosho 17,035
Ness 4,033
Norton 5,947
Osage 15,248
Osborne 4,867
Ottawa 5,634
Pawnee 7,555
Phillips 6,590
Pottawatomie 16,128
Pratt 9,702
Rawlins 3,404
Reno 62,389
Republic 6,482
Rice 10,610
Riley 67,139
Rooks 6,039
Rush 3,842
Russell 7,835
Saline 49,301
Scott 5,289
Sedgwick 403,662
Seward 18,743
Shawnee 160,976
Sheridan 3,043
Sherman 6,926
Smith 5,078
Stafford 5,365
Stanton 2,333
Stevens 5,048
Sumner 25,841
Thomas 8,258
Trego 3,694
Wabaunsee 6,603
Wallace 1,821
Washington 7,073
Wichita 2,758
Wilson 10,289
Woodson 4,116
Wyandotte 161,993

Cities

Abilene 6,242
Agra 322
Albert 229
Alma 871
Almena 423
Alta Vista 477
Altamont 1,048
Altoona 456
Americus 891
Andale 566
Andover 4,047
Anthony 2,516
Arcadia 338
Argonia 529
Arkansas City 12,762
Arlington 457
Arma 1,542
Ashland 1,032
Assaria 387
Atchison 10,656
Atlanta 232
Attica 716
Atwood 1,388
Auburn 908
Augusta 7,876
Axtell 432
Baldwin City 2,961
Basehor 1,591
Baxter Springs 4,351
Bazine 373
Beattie 221
Bel Aire 3,695
Belle Plaine 1,649
Belleville 2,517
Beloit 4,066
Belvue 207
Bennington 568
Bentley 360
Benton 669
Bird City 467
Bison 252
Blue Mound 251
Blue Rapids 1,131
Bonner Springs 6,413
Brewster 296
Bronson 343
Brookville 226
Bucklin 710
Buffalo 293
Buhler 1,277
Burden 518
Burdett 248
Burlingame 1,074
Burlington 2,735
Burns 226
Burr Oak 278
Burrton 866
Bushton 341
Caldwell 1,351
Camp Forsyth 1,967
Caney 2,062
Canton 794
Carbondale 1,526
Cawker City 588
Cedar Vale 760
Centralia 452
Chanute 9,488
Chapman 1,264
Chase 577
Cheney 1,560
Cherokee 651
Cherryvale 2,464
Chetopa 1,357
Cimarron 1,626
Claflin 678
Clay Center 4,613
Clearwater 1,875
Clifton 561
Clyde 793
Coffeyville 12,917
Colby 5,396
Coldwater 939
Colony 447
Columbus 3,268
Colwich 1,091
Concordia 6,167
Conway Springs 1,384
Copeland 290
Cottonwood Falls 889
Council Grove 2,228
Countryside 312
Courtland 343
Cuba 242
Cunningham 535
Dearing 428
Deerfield 677
Delphos 494
Denison 225
Derby 14,699
De Soto 2,291
Dexter 320
Dighton 1,361
Dodge City 21,129
Douglass 1,722
Downs 1,119
Dwight 365
Eastborough 896
Easton 405
Edgerton 1,244
Edna 438
Edwardsville 3,979
Effingham 540
El Dorado 11,504
Elk City 334
Elkhart 2,318
Ellinwood 2,329
Ellis 1,814
Ellsworth 2,294
Elwood 1,079
Emporia 25,512
Enterprise 865
Erie 1,276
Eskridge 518
Eudora 3,006
Eureka 2,974
Everest 310
Fairview 306
Fairway 4,173
Florence 636
Ford 247
Fort Scott 8,362
Fowler 571
Frankfort 927
Fredonia 2,599
Frontenac 2,588
Galena 3,308
Galva 651
Garden City 24,097
Garden Plain 731
Gardner 3,191
Garfield 236
Garnett 3,210
Gas 505
Geneseo 382
Geuda Springs 219
Girard 2,794
Glasco 556
Glen Elder 448
Goddard 1,804
Goessel 506
Goodland 4,983
Gorham 284
Grainfield 357
Grandview Plaza 1,233
Great Bend 15,427
Greeley 339
Greenleaf 353
Greensburg 1,792
Grenola 256
Gridley 356
Grinnell 348
Gypsum 365
Halstead 2,015
Hamilton 301
Hanover 696
Hanston 326
Harper 1,735
Hartford 541
Harveyville 267
Haven 1,198
Haviland 624
Hays 17,767
Haysville 8,364
Herington 2,685
Hesston 3,012
Hiawatha 3,603
Highland 942
Hill City 1,835
Hillsboro 2,704
Hoisington 3,182
Holcomb 1,400
Holton 3,196
Holyrood 492
Hope 404
Horton 1,885
Howard 815
Hoxie 1,342
Hoyt 489
Hugoton 3,179
Humboldt 2,178
Hutchinson 39,308
Independence 9,942
Ingalls 301
Inman 1,035
Iola 6,351
Jamestown 325
Jetmore 850
Jewell 529
Johnson City 1,348
Junction City 20,604
Kanopolis 605
Kanorado 276
Kansas City 149,767
Kechi 517
Kensington 553
Kingman 3,196
Kinsley 1,875
Kiowa 1,160
Kirwin 269
Kismet 421
La Crosse 1,427
La Cygne 1,066
La Harpe 650
Lake Quivira 983
Lakin 2,060
Lancaster 299
Lane 247
Lansing 7,120
Larned 4,490
Lawrence 65,608
Leavenworth 38,495
Leawood 19,693
Lebanon 364
Lebo 835
Lecompton 619
Lenexa 34,034
Lenora 329
Leon 707
Leonardville 374
Leoti 1,738
Le Roy 568
Lewis 451
Liberal 16,573
Lincoln 1,381
Lindsborg 3,076
Linn 472
Linwood 409
Little River 496
Logan 633
Longton 389
Louisburg 1,964
Louisville 215
Lucas 452
Luray 261
Lyndon 964
Lyons 3,688
Macksville 488
Madison 845
Maize 1,520
Manhattan 37,712
Mankato 1,037
Maple Hill 406
Marion 1,906
Marquette 593
Marysville 3,359
Mayetta 267
McCracken 231
McCune 462
McFarland 224
McLouth 719
McPherson 12,422
Meade 1,526
Medicine Lodge 2,453
Melvern 423
Meriden 622
Merriam 11,821
Milford 384
Miltonvale 484
Minneapolis 1,983
Minneola 705
Mission 9,504
Mission Hills 3,446
Moline 473
Montezuma 838
Moran 551
Morland 234
Morrill 299
Moscow 252
Mound City 789
Mound Valley 405
Moundridge 1,531
Mount Hope 805
Mulberry 555
Mullinville 289
Mulvane 4,674
Natoma 392
Neodesha 2,837
Neosho Rapids 235
Ness City 1,724
New Strawn 428
Newton 16,700
Nickerson 1,137
North Newton 1,262
Norton 3,017
Nortonville 643
Norwich 455
Oakley 2,045
Oberlin 2,197
Offerle 228
Ogden 1,494
Olathe 63,352
Olpe 431
Onaga 761
Osage City 2,689
Osawatomie 4,590
Osborne 1,778
Oskaloosa 1,074
Oswego 1,870
Otis 385
Ottawa 10,667
Overbrook 920
Overland Park 111,790
Oxford 1,143
Ozawkie 403
Palco 295
Paola 4,698
Park City 5,050
Parker 256
Parsons 11,924
Partridge 213
Pawnee Rock 367
Peabody 1,349
Perry 881
Peru 206
Phillipsburg 2,828
Pittsburg 17,775
Plains 957
Plainville 2,173
Pleasanton 1,231
Pomona 835
Potwin 448
Prairie Village 23,186
Pratt 6,687
Prescott 301
Pretty Prairie 601
Princeton 275
Protection 625
Quenemo 369
Quinter 945
Ransom 386
Rantoul 200
Reading 264
Richmond 528
Riley 804
Robinson 268
Roeland Park 7,706
Rolla 387
Rose Hill 2,399
Rossville 1,052
Russell 4,781
Sabetha 2,341
St. Francis 1,495
St. George 397
St. John 1,357
St. Marys 1,791
St. Paul 687

Salina 42,303
Satanta 1,073
Scammon 466
Scandia 421
Scott City 3,785
Scranton 674
Sedan 1,306
Sedgwick 1,438
Selden 248
Seneca 2,027
Severy 357
Sharon 256
Sharon Springs 872
Shawnee 37,993
Silver Lake 1,390
Smith Center 2,016
Solomon 939
South Haven 420
South Hutchinson 2,444
Spearville 716
Spring Hill 2,191
Stafford 1,344
Sterling 2,115
Stockton 1,507
Strong City 617
Sublette 1,378
Sylvan Grove 321
Sylvia 308
Syracuse 1,606
Tescott 317
Thayer 435
Tipton 267
Tonganoxie 2,347
Topeka 119,883
Toronto 317
Towanda 1,289
Tribune 918
Troy 1,073
Turon 393
Tyro 243
Udall 824
Ulysses 5,474
Uniontown 290
Utica 208
Valley Center 3,624
Valley Falls 1,253
Victoria 1,157
WaKeeney 2,161
Wakefield 900
Walnut 214
Walton 226
Wamego 3,706
Washington 1,304
Waterville 601
Wathena 1,160
Waverly 618
Weir 730
Wellington 8,411
Wellsville 1,563
West Mineral 226
Westmoreland 541
Westwood 1,772
Westwood Hills 383
Wetmore 284
White City 533
White Cloud 255
Whitewater 683
Whiting 213
Wichita 304,011
Williamsburg 261
Wilson 834
Winchester 613
Winfield 11,931
Yates Center 1,815

Kentucky ■ population 3,698,969

Metropolitan areas

Cincinnati (O.) 1,452,645 (1,130,324 in O.; 283,486 in Ky.; 38,835 in Ind.)
Clarksville (Tenn.)-Hopkinsville 169,439 (100,498 in Tenn.; 68,941 in Ky.)
Evansville (Ind.) 278,990 (235,946 in Ind.; 43,044 in Ky.)
Huntington (W. Va.)-Ashland 312,529 (138,463 in W. Va.; 112,232 in Ky.; 61,864 in O.)
Lexington-Fayette 348,428
Louisville 952,662 (770,591 in Ky.; 182,071 in Ind.)
Owensboro 87,189

Counties

Adair 15,360
Allen 14,628
Anderson 14,571
Ballard 7,902
Barren 34,001
Bath 9,692
Bell 31,506
Boone 57,589
Bourbon 19,236
Boyd 51,150
Boyle 25,641
Bracken 7,766
Breathitt 15,703
Breckinridge 16,312
Bullitt 47,567
Butler 11,245
Caldwell 13,232
Calloway 30,735
Campbell 83,866
Carlisle 5,238
Carroll 9,292
Carter 24,340
Casey 14,211
Christian 68,941
Clark 29,496
Clay 21,746
Clinton 9,135
Crittenden 9,196
Cumberland 6,784
Daviess 87,189
Edmonson 10,357
Elliott 6,455
Estill 14,614
Fayette 225,366
Fleming 12,292
Floyd 43,586
Franklin 43,781
Fulton 8,271
Gallatin 5,393
Garrard 11,579
Grant 15,737
Graves 33,550
Grayson 21,050
Green 10,371
Greenup 36,742
Hancock 7,864
Hardin 89,240
Harlan 36,574
Harrison 16,248
Hart 14,890
Henderson 43,044
Henry 12,823
Hickman 5,566
Hopkins 46,126
Jackson 11,955
Jefferson 664,937
Jessamine 30,508
Johnson 23,248
Kenton 142,031
Knott 17,906
Knox 29,676
Larue 11,679
Laurel 43,438
Lawrence 13,998
Lee 7,422
Leslie 13,642
Letcher 27,000
Lewis 13,029
Lincoln 20,045
Livingston 9,062
Logan 24,416
Lyon 6,624
Madison 62,879
Magoffin 15,603
Marion 9,628
Marshall 57,508
Martin 13,077
Mason 16,499
McCracken 27,205
McCreary 12,526
McLean 16,666
Meade 24,170
Menifee 5,092
Mercer 19,148
Metcalfe 8,963
Monroe 11,401
Montgomery 19,561
Morgan 11,648
Muhlenberg 31,318
Nelson 29,710
Nicholas 6,725
Ohio 21,105
Oldham 33,263
Owen 9,035
Owsley 5,036
Pendleton 12,036
Perry 30,283
Pike 72,583
Powell 11,686
Pulaski 49,489
Robertson 2,124
Rockcastle 14,803
Rowan 20,353
Russell 14,716
Scott 23,867
Shelby 24,824
Simpson 15,145
Spencer 6,801
Taylor 21,146
Todd 10,940
Trigg 10,361
Trimble 6,090
Union 16,557
Warren 76,673
Washington 10,441
Wayne 17,468
Webster 13,955
Whitley 33,326
Wolfe 6,503
Woodford 19,955

Cities

Adairville 906
Albany 2,062
Alexandria 5,592
Allen 229
Allensville 218
Anchorage 2,082
Annville 470
Arlington 449
Ashland 23,622
Auburn 1,273
Audubon Park 1,520
Augusta 1,336
Bancroft 582
Barbourmeade 1,402
Barbourville 3,658
Bardstown 6,801
Bardwell 819
Barlow 706
Beattyville 1,131
Beaver Dam 2,904
Bedford 761
Beechwood Village 1,263
Bellefonte 838
Bellemeade 927
Bellevue 6,997
Bellewood 329
Benham 717
Benton 3,899
Berea 9,126
Berry 240
Blaine 271
Bloomfield 845
Blue Ridge Manor 565
Bonnieville 300
Booneville 232
Bowling Green 40,641
Brandenburg 1,857
Breckinridge Center 2,375
Bremen 267
Briarwood 658
Broadfields 273
Brodhead 1,140
Bromley 1,137
Brooks 2,464
Brooksville 670
Brownsboro Farm 670
Brownsboro Village 361
Brownsville 897
Buechel 7,081
Burgin 1,009
Burkesville 1,815
Burlington 6,070
Burnside 695
Butler 625
Cadiz 2,148
Calhoun 854
Calvert City 2,531
Camargo 1,022
Campbellsburg 604
Campbellsville 9,577
Campton 484
Caneyville 549
Carlisle 1,639
Carrollton 3,715
Catlettsburg 2,231
Cave City 1,953
Centertown 383
Central City 4,979
Cherrywood Village 340
Clarkson 611
Clay 1,173
Clay City 1,258
Clinton 1,547
Cloverport 1,207
Coal Run 262
Cold Spring 2,880
Columbia 3,845
Columbus 252
Corbin 7,419
Corydon 790
Covington 43,264
Crab Orchard 825
Creekside 323
Crescent Park 364
Crescent Springs 2,179
Crestview 356
Crestview Hills 2,546
Crestwood 1,435
Crittenden 731
Crofton 699
Crossgate 261
Cumberland 3,112
Cynthiana 6,497
Danville 12,420
Dawson Springs 3,129
Dayton 6,576
Dixon 552
Douglass Hills 5,549
Dover 297
Drakesboro 565
Druid Hills 305
Dry Ridge 1,601
Earlington 1,833
Eddyville 1,889
Edgewood 8,143
Edmonton 1,477
Elizabethtown 18,167
Elkhorn City 813
Elkton 1,789
Elsmere 6,847
Eminence 2,055
Erlanger 15,979
Eubank 354
Evarts 1,063
Fairdale 6,563
Fairmeade 280
Falmouth 2,378
Ferguson 934
Fern Creek 16,406
Fincastle 838
Flatwoods 7,799
Fleming-Neon 759
Flemingsburg 3,071
Florence 18,624
Fordsville 522
Forest Hills 454
Fort Campbell North 18,861
Fort Knox 21,495
Fort Mitchell 7,438
Fort Thomas 16,032
Fort Wright 6,570
Fountain Run 259
Frankfort 25,968
Franklin 7,607
Fredonia 490
Frenchburg 625
Fulton 3,078
Gamaliel 462
Georgetown 11,414
Germantown 213
Ghent 365
Glasgow 12,351
Glencoe 257
Glenview Hills 353
Goose Creek 321
Grand Rivers 351
Graymoor-Devondale 2,911
Grayson 3,510
Greensburg 1,990
Green Spring 768
Greenup 1,158
Greenville 4,689
Guthrie 1,504
Hanson 450
Hardin 595
Hardinsburg 1,906
Harlan 2,686
Harrodsburg 7,335
Hartford 2,532
Hawesville 998
Hazard 5,416
Hazel 460
Henderson 25,945
Hickman 2,689
Highland Heights 4,223
Highview 14,814
Hillview 6,119
Hindman 798
Hiseville 220
Hodgenville 2,721
Hollow Creek 991
Hollyvilla 649
Hopkinsville 29,809
Horse Cave 2,284
Houston Acres 496
Hurstbourne Acres 1,072
Hustonville 313
Hyden 375
Independence 10,444
Indian Hills 1,074
Indian Hills Cherokee Section 1,005
Inez 511
Irvine 2,836
Irvington 1,180
Island 446
Jackson 2,466
Jamestown 1,641
Jeffersontown 23,221
Jeffersonville 1,854
Jenkins 2,751
Junction City 1,983
Keeneland 393
Kenton Vale 358
Kevil 337
Kingsley 399
Kuttawa 535
La Center 1,040
La Grange 3,853
Lakeside Park 3,131
Lakeview Heights 252
Lancaster 3,421
Langdon Place 874
Latonia Lakes 410
Lawrenceburg 5,911
Lebanon 5,695
Lebanon Junction 1,741
Leitchfield 4,965
Lewisburg 772
Lewisport 1,778
Lexington 225,366
Liberty 1,937
Livermore 1,534
Livingston 241
London 5,757
Lone Oak 465
Loretto 820
Louisa 1,990
Louisville 269,063
Loyall 1,100
Ludlow 4,736
Lynch 1,166
Lyndon 8,037
Lynnview 1,017
Mackville 200
Madisonville 16,200
Manchester 1,634
Marion 3,320
Martin 694
Mayfield 9,935
Maysville 7,169
McHenry 414
McKee 870
McRoberts 1,101
Meadow Vale 798
Meadowview Estates 259
Melbourne 660
Middlesboro 11,328
Middletown 5,016
Midway 1,290
Millersburg 937
Milton 563
Minor Lane Heights 1,675
Monticello 5,357
Moorland 467
Morehead 8,357
Morganfield 3,776
Morgantown 2,284
Mortons Gap 987
Mount Olivet 384
Mount Sterling 5,362
Mount Vernon 2,654
Mount Washington 5,226
Muldraugh 1,376
Munfordville 1,556
Murray 14,439
Nebo 227
New Castle 893
New Haven 796
Newburg 21,647
Newport 18,871
Nicholasville 13,603
Norbourne Estates 461
North Corbin 1,601
North Middletown 602
Northfield 898
Nortonville 1,209
Norwood 372
Oak Grove 2,863
Oakland 202
Okolona 18,902
Old Brownsboro Place 348
Olive Hill 1,809
Orchard Grass Hills 1,058
Owensboro 53,549
Owenton 1,306
Owingsville 1,491
Paducah 27,256
Paintsville 4,354
Paris 8,730
Park City 549
Park Hills 3,321
Parkway Village 707
Pembroke 6401
Perryville 815
Pewee Valley 1,283
Phelps 1,298
Pikeville 6,324
Pine Knot 1,549
Pineville 2,198
Pioneer Village 1,130
Plantation 830
Pleasure Ridge Park 25,131
Pleasureville 761
Plum Springs 361
Powderly 748
Prestonsburg 3,558
Prestonville 205
Princeton 6,940
Prospect 2,788
Providence 4,123
Raceland 2,256
Radcliff 19,772
Ravenna 804
Reidland 4,054
Richlawn 435
Richmond 21,155
Riverwood 506
Robinswood 250
Rockport 385
Rolling Fields 593
Rolling Hills 1,135
Russell 4,014
Russell Springs 2,363
Russellville 7,454
Ryland Heights 279
Sacramento 563
Sadieville 255
St. Charles 316
St. Matthews 15,800
St. Regis Park 1,756
Salem 770
Salt Lick 342
Salyersville 1,917
Sanders 231
Sandy Hook 548
Science Hill 628
Scottsville 4,278
Sebree 1,510
Seneca Gardens 684
Sharpsburg 315
Shelbyville 6,238
Shepherdsville 4,805
Shively 15,535
Silver Grove 1,102
Simpsonville 907
Slaughters 235
Smithland 384
Smiths Grove 703
Somerset 10,733
Sonora 295
South Carrollton 202
South Park View 214
South Shore 1,318
Southgate 3,266
Springfield 2,875
Springlee 451
Stamping Ground 698
Stanford 2,686
Stanton 2,795
Stearns 1,550
Strathmoor Gardens 300
Strathmoor Manor 391
Strathmoor Village 361
Sturgis 2,184
Taylor Mill 5,530
Taylorsville 774
Tompkinsville 2,861
Trenton 378
Union 1,001
Uniontown 1,008
Upton 719
Valley Station 22,840
Vanceburg 1,713
Van Lear 1,050
Versailles 7,269
Vicco 244
Villa Hills 7,739
Vine Grove 3,586
Wallins Creek 261
Walton 2,034
Warfield 364
Warsaw 1,202
Washington 795
Water Valley 321
Waverly 345
Wayland 359
Wellington 593
West Buechel 1,587
West Liberty 1,887
West Point 1,216
Westwood 734
Westwood 5,300
Wheatcroft 206
Wheelwright 721
Whipps Millgate 454
White Plains 598
Whitesburg 1,636
Whitesville 682
Whitley City 1,133
Wickliffe 851
Wilder 691
Wildwood 266
Williamsburg 5,493
Williamstown 3,023
Willisburg 223
Wilmore 4,215
Winchester 15,799
Winding Falls 657
Windy Hills 2,452
Wingo 568
Woodburn 343
Woodland Hills 714
Woodlawn 308
Woodlawn (-Oakdale) 4,954
Woodlawn Park 1,099
Worthington 1,751
Wurtland 1,221

Louisiana ■ population 4,238,216

Metropolitan areas

Alexandria 131,556
Baton Rouge 528,264
Houma-Thibodaux 182,842
Lafayette 208,740
Lake Charles 168,134
Monroe 142,191
New Orleans 1,238,816
Shreveport 334,341

Parishes (Counties)

Acadia 55,882
Allen 21,226
Ascension 58,214
Assumption 22,753
Avoyelles 39,159
Beauregard 30,083
Bienville 15,979
Bossier 86,088
Caddo 248,253
Calcasieu 168,134
Caldwell 9,810
Cameron 9,260
Catahoula 11,065
Claiborne 17,405
Concordia 20,828
De Soto 25,346
East Baton Rouge 380,105
East Carroll 9,709
East Feliciana 19,211
Evangeline 33,274
Franklin 22,387
Grant 17,526
Iberia 68,297
Iberville 31,049
Jackson 15,705
Jefferson 448,306
Jefferson Davis 30,722
Lafayette 164,762
Lafourche 85,860
La Salle 13,662
Lincoln 41,745
Livingston 70,526
Madison 12,463
Morehouse 31,938
Natchitoches 36,689
Orleans 496,938
Ouachita 142,191
Plaquemines 25,575
Pointe Coupee 22,540
Rapides 131,556
Red River 9,387
Richland 20,629
Sabine 22,646
St. Bernard 66,631
St. Charles 42,437
St. Helena 9,874
St. James 20,879
St. John the Baptist 39,996
St. Landry 80,331
St. Martin 43,978
St. Mary 58,086
St. Tammany 144,508
Tangipahoa 85,709
Tensas 7,103
Terrebonne 96,982
Union 20,690
Vermilion 50,055
Vernon 61,961
Washington 43,185
Webster 41,989
West Baton Rouge 19,419
West Carroll 12,093
West Feliciana 12,915
Winn 16,269

Cities, towns, and villages

Abbeville 11,187
Abita Springs 1,296
Addis 1,222
Albany 645
Alexandria 49,188
Amelia 2,447
Amite 4,236
Anacoco 823
Angie 235
Arabi 8,787
Arcadia 3,079
Arnaudville 1,444
Ashland 289
Athens 278
Avondale 5,813
Baker 13,233
Baldwin 2,379
Ball 3,305
Barataria 1,160
Basile 1,808
Baskin 243
Bastrop 13,916
Baton Rouge 219,531
Bayou Cane 15,876
Bayou Vista 4,733
Belcher 249
Belle Chasse 8,512
Benton 2,047
Bernice 1,543
Berwick 4,375
Bienville 316
Blanchard 1,175
Bogalusa 14,280
Bonita 265
Bossier City 52,721
Bourg 2,702
Boutte 2,702
Boyce 1,361
Breaux Bridge 6,515
Bridge City 8,327
Broadmoor 3,218
Broussard 3,213
Brownsville [-Bawcomville] 7,397
Brusly 1,824
Bunkie 5,044
Buras [-Triumph] 3,702
Calvin 207
Cameron 2,041
Campti 929
Cankton 323
Carencro 5,429
Carlyss 3,305
Carville 1,108
Cecilia 1,374
Chackbay 2,276
Chalmette 31,860
Charenton 1,584
Chataignier 281
Chatham 617
Chauvin 3,375
Cheneyville 1,005
Choudrant 557
Church Point 4,677
Claiborne 8,300
Clarence 577
Clarks 650
Clayton 917
Clinton 1,904
Colfax 1,696
Collinston 375
Columbia 386
Converse 436
Cotton Valley 1,130
Cottonport 2,600
Coushatta 1,845
Covington 7,691
Crowley 13,983
Cullen 1,642
Cut Off 5,325
Delcambre 1,978
Delhi 3,169
Delta 234
Denham Springs 8,381
De Quincy 3,474
De Ridder 9,868
Des Allemands 2,504
Destrehan 8,031
Deville 1,113
Dixie Inn 347
Dodson 350
Donaldsonville 7,949
Doyline 884
Dry Prong 380
Dubach 843
Dubberly 253
Dulac 3,273
Duson 1,465
East Hodge 421
Eastwood 2,987
Edgard 2,753
Edgefield 207
Elizabeth 414
Elton 1,277
Empire 2,654
Epps 541
Erath 2,428
Estelle 14,091
Estherwood 745
Eunice 11,162
Evergreen 283
Farmerville 3,334
Fenton 265
Ferriday 4,111
Fisher 277
Florien 626
Folsom 469
Fordoche 869
Forest 263
Forest Hill 408
Fort Polk North 3,819
Fort Polk South 10,911
Franklin 9,004
Franklinton 4,007
French Settlement 829
Galliano 4,294
Garyville 3,181
Georgetown 273
Gibsland 1,224
Gilbert 704
Gilliam 202
Glenmora 1,686
Golden Meadow 2,049
Goldonna 417
Gonzales 7,003
Grambling 5,484
Gramercy 2,412
Grand Cane 233
Grand Coteau 1,118
Grand Isle 1,455
Gray 4,260
Grayson 529
Greensburg 583
Greenwood 2,092
Gretna 17,208
Grosse Tete 541
Gueydan 1,611
Hackberry 1,664
Hahnville 2,599
Hall Summit 227
Hamburg
Hammond 15,871
Harahan 9,927
Harrisonburg 453
Harvey 21,222
Haughton 1,664
Haynesville 2,854
Heflin 253
Henderson 1,543
Hessmer 578
Hodge 562
Homer 4,152
Hornbeck 427
Hosston 417
Houma 30,495
Ida 250
Independence 1,632
Iota 1,256
Iowa 2,588
Jackson 3,891
Jean Lafitte 1,469
Jeanerette 6,205
Jefferson 14,521
Jena 2,626
Jennings 11,305
Jonesboro 4,305
Jonesville 2,720
Junction City 749
Kaplan 4,535
Keatchie 277
Kenner 72,033
Kentwood 2,468
Kilbourne 409
Killian 721
Kinder 2,246
Krotz Springs 1,285
Labadieville 1,821
Lacombe 6,523
Lafayette 94,440
Lafitte 1,507
Lake Arthur 3,194
Lake Charles 70,580
Lake Providence 5,380
Laplace 24,194
Larose 5,772
Lecompte 1,592
Leesville 7,638
Leonville 825
Livingston 999
Livonia 970
Lockport 2,503
Logansport 1,390
Lone Star 1,367
Loreauville 860
Lucky 342
Luling 2,803
Lutcher 3,907
Madisonville 659
Mamou 3,483
Mandeville 7,083
Mangham 598
Mansfield 5,389
Mansura 1,601
Many 3,112
Maringouin 1,149
Marion 775
Marksville 5,526
Marrero 36,671
Martin 545
Mathews 3,009
Maurice 432
McNary 248
Melville 1,562
Mer Rouge 586
Meraux 8,849
Mermentau 760
Merryville 1,235
Metairie 149,428
Mimosa Park 4,516
Minden 13,661
Monroe 54,909
Montegut 1,784
Montgomery 645
Montpelier 247
Mooringsport 873
Moreauville 919
Morgan City 14,531
Morganza 759
Morse 782
Moss Bluff 8,039
Napoleonville 802
Natalbany 1,289
Natchez 434
Natchitoches 16,609
New Iberia 31,828
New Orleans 496,938
New Roads 5,303
New Sarpy 2,946
Newellton 1,576
Newllano 2,660
Noble 225
Norco 3,385
North Hodge 477
Norwood 317
Oak Grove 2,126
Oakdale 6,832
Oberlin 1,808
Oil City 1,282
Olla 1,410
Opelousas 18,151
Paincourtville 1,550
Palmetto 229
Parks 400
Patterson 4,736
Pearl River 1,507
Pierre Part 3,053
Pine Prairie 713
Pineville 12,251
Plain Dealing 1,074
Plaquemine 7,186
Pleasant Hill 824
Pollock 330
Ponchatoula 5,425
Port Allen 6,277
Port Barre 2,144
Port Sulphur 3,523
Port Vincent 446
Poydras 4,029
Provencal 538
Raceland 5,564
Rayne 8,502
Rayville 4,411
Reserve 8,847
Richmond 447
Richwood 1,253
Ridgecrest 804
Ringgold 1,856
River Ridge 14,800
Rodessa 294
Rosedale 807
Roseland 1,093
Rosepine 1,135
Ruston 20,027
St. Francisville 1,700
St. Joseph 1,517
St. Martinville 7,137
St. Rose 6,259
Saline 272
Sarepta 886
Schriever 4,958
Scott 4,912
Shreveport 198,525
Sibley 997
Sicily Island 421
Simmesport 2,092
Simpson 536
Simsboro 634
Slaughter 827
Slidell 24,124
Sorrento 1,119
South Mansfield 407
Springfield 439
Springhill 5,668
Sterlington 1,140
Stonewall 1,266
Sulphur 20,125
Sun 429
Sunset 2,201
Supreme 1,020
Swartz 3,698
Tallulah 8,526
Tangipahoa 569
Terrytown 23,787
Thibodaux 14,035
Tickfaw 565
Timberlane 12,614
Tullos 427
Turkey Creek 283
Urania 782
Varnado 236
Vidalia 4,953
Vienna 404
Ville Platte 9,037
Vinton 3,154
Violet 8,574
Vivian 4,156
Waggaman 9,405
Walker 3,727
Washington 1,253
Waterproof 1,080
Welsh 3,299
West Ferriday 1,632
West Monroe 14,096
Westlake 5,007
Westwego 11,218
White Castle 2,102
Wilson 707
Winnfield 6,138
Winnsboro 5,755
Wisner 1,153
Woodworth 754
Youngsville 1,195
Zachary 9,036
Zwolle 1,779

Maine ■ population 1,233,223

Metropolitan areas

Bangor 88,745
Lewiston-Auburn 88,141
Portland 215,281
Rochester (N.H.) 223,578
(174,642 in N.H.; 48,936 in Me.)

Counties

Androscoggin 105,259
Aroostook 86,936
Cumberland 243,135
Franklin 29,008
Hancock 46,948
Kennebec 115,904
Knox 36,310
Lincoln 30,357
Oxford 52,602
Penobscot 146,601
Piscataquis 18,653
Sagadahoc 33,535
Somerset 49,767
Waldo 33,018
Washington 35,308
York 164,587

Cities and towns

Abbot 677
Acton 1,727
Addison 1,114
Albion 1,736
Alexander 478
Alfred 2,238
Allagash 359
Alna 571
Alton 771
Amherst 226
Andover 953
Anson 2,382
Appleton 1,069
Argyle 202
Arrowsic 498
Arundel 2,669
Ashland 1,542
Athens 897
Atkinson 332
Auburn 24,309
Augusta 21,325
Avon 559
Baileyville 2,031
Baldwin 1,219
Bangor 33,181
Bar Harbor 2,768
▲4,443
Baring 275
Bath 9,799
Beals 667
Belfast 6,355
Belgrade 2,375
Belmont 652
Benton 2,312
Berwick 5,995
Bethel 2,329
Biddeford 20,710
Bingham 1,071
▲1,230
Blaine 784
Blue Hill 1,941
Boothbay 2,648
Boothbay Harbor 1,267
▲2,347
Bowdoin 2,207
Bowdoinham 2,192
Bradford 1,103
Bradley 1,136
Bremen 674
Brewer 9,021
Bridgewater 647
Bridgton 2,195
▲4,307
Bristol 2,326
Brooklin 785
Brooks 900
Brooksville 760
Brownfield 1,034
Brownville 1,506
Brunswick 14,683
▲20,906
Brunswick Station 1,829
Buckfield 1,566
Bucksport 2,989
▲4,825
Burlington 360
Burnham 961
Buxton 6,494
Calais 3,963
Cambridge 490
Camden 4,022
▲5,060
Canaan 1,636
Canton 951
Cape Elizabeth 8,854
Cape Neddick 2,193
Caribou 9,415
Carmel 1,906
Carrabassett Valley 325
Carthage 458
Cary 235
Casco 3,018
Castine 1,161
Castle Hill 449
Caswell 2,743
Central Somerset 289
Chapman 422
Charleston 1,187
Charlotte 271
Chelsea 2,497
Cherryfield 1,183
Chester 442
Chesterville 1,012
China 3,713
Chisholm 1,653
Clifton 607
Clinton 1,485
▲3,332
Columbia 437
Columbia Falls 552
Connor 468
Corinna 2,196
Corinth 2,177
Cornish 1,178
Cornville 1,008
Crystal 303
Cumberland 5,836
Cumberland Center 1,890
Cushing 988
Cutler 779
Damariscotta 1,811
Damariscotta-Newcastle 1,567
Danforth 710
Dayton 1,197
Dedham 1,229
Deer Isle 1,829
Denmark 855
Dennysville 355
Detroit 751
Dexter 2,650
▲4,419
Dixfield 1,300
▲2,574
Dixmont 1,007
Dover-Foxcroft 3,077
▲4,657
Dresden 1,332
Durham 2,842
Dyer Brook 243
Eagle Lake 942
East Central Washington 661
East Machias 1,218
East Millinocket 2,075
▲2,166
Eastbrook 289
Easton 1,291
Eastport 1,965
Eddington 1,947
Edgecomb 993
Eliot 5,329
Ellsworth 5,975
Embden 659
Enfield 1,476
Etna 977
Eustis 616
Exeter 937
Fairfield 2,794
▲6,718
Falmouth 7,610
Falmouth Forside 1,708
Farmingdale 2,070
▲2,918
Farmington 4,197
▲7,436
Fayette 855
Fort Fairfield 1,729
▲3,998
Fort Kent 2,123
▲4,268
Frankfort 1,020
Franklin 1,141
Freedom 593
Freeport 1,829
▲6,905
Frenchville 1,338
Friendship 1,099
Fryeburg 1,580
▲2,968
Gardiner 6,746
Garland 1,064
Georgetown 914
Gilead 204
Glenburn 3,198
Gorham 3,618
▲11,856
Gouldsboro 1,986
Grand Isle 558
Gray 5,904
Greenbush 1,309
Greene 3,661
Greenfield 267

Greenville 1,601 ▲1,884
Greenwood 689
Guilford 1,082 ▲1,710
Hallowell 2,534
Hamlin 204
Hampden 3,895 ▲5,974
Hancock 1,757
Hanover 272
Harmony 838
Harpswell 5,012
Harrington 893
Harrison 1,951
Hartford 722
Hartland 1,038 ▲1,806
Haynesville 243
Hebron 878
Hermon 3,755
Hersey 691
Hiram 1,260
Hodgdon 1,257
Holden 2,952
Hollis 3,573
Hope 1,017
Houlton 5,627 ▲6,613
Howland 1,304 ▲1,435
Hudson 1,048
Industry 685
Island Falls 897
Islesboro 579
Jackman 920
Jackson 415
Jay 5,080
Jefferson 2,111
Jonesboro 585
Jonesport 1,525
Kenduskeag 1,234
Kennebunk 4,206 ▲8,004
Kennebunkport 1,100 ▲3,356
Kingfield 1,114
Kingman 246
Kittery 5,151 ▲9,372
Kittery Point 1,093
Knox 681
Lagrange 557
Lamoine 1,311
Lebanon 4,263
Lee 832
Leeds 1,669
Levant 1,627
Lewiston 39,757
Liberty 790
Limerick 1,688
Limestone 1,245 ▲9,922
Limington 2,796
Lincoln 3,399 ▲5,587
Lincolnville 1,809
Linneus 810
Lisbon 9,457
Lisbon Falls 4,674
Litchfield 2,650
Little Falls-South Windham 1,715
Littleton 956
Livermore 1,950
Livermore Falls 1,935 ▲3,455
Loring Air Force Base 7,829
Lovell 888
Lowell 267
Lubec 1,853
Ludlow 430
Lyman 3,390
Machias 1,773 ▲2,569
Machiasport 1,166
Madawaska 3,653 ▲4,803
Madison 2,956 ▲4,725
Manchester 2,099
Mapleton 1,853
Mariaville 270
Mars Hill 1,760
Mars Hill-Blaine 1,717
Marshfield 461
Masardis 305
Mattawamkeag 830
Mechanic Falls 2,388 ▲2,919
Medway 1,922
Mercer 593
Merrill 296
Mexico 2,302 ▲3,344
Milbridge 1,305
Milford 2,228 ▲2,884
Millinocket 6,922 ▲6,956
Milo 2,129 ▲2,600
Minot 1,664
Monmouth 3,353
Monroe 802
Monson 744
Monticello 872
Montville 877
Moose River 233
Morrill 644
Moscow 608
Mount Chase 254
Mount Desert 1,899
Mount Vernon 1,362
Naples 2,860
New Canada 253
New Gloucester 3,916
New Limerick 524
New Portland 789
New Sharon 1,175
New Sweden 715
New Vineyard 661
Newburgh 1,317
Newcastle 1,538
Newfield 1,042
Newport 1,843 ▲3,036
Newry 316
Nobleboro 1,455
Norridgewock 1,496 ▲3,105
North Berwick 1,568 ▲3,793
North Haven 332
North Penobscot 403
North Washington 496
North Windham 4,077
North Yarmouth 2,429
Northeast Piscataquis 218
Northeast Somerset 377
Northport 1,201
Norway 3,023 ▲4,754
Oakfield 846
Oakland 3,510 ▲5,595
Ogunquit 974
Old Orchard Beach 7,789
Old Town 8,317
Orland 1,805
Orono 9,789 ▲10,573
Orrington 3,309
Otis 355
Otisfield 1,136
Owls Head 1,574
Oxford 1,284 ▲3,705
Palermo 1,021
Palmyra 1,867
Paris 4,492
Parkman 790
Parsonfield 1,472
Passadumkeag 428
Passamaquoddy Indian Township Indian Reservation 617
Passamaquoddy Pleasant Point Indian Reservation 572
Patten 1,256
Pembroke 852
Penobscot 1,131
Penobscot Indian Island Indian Reservation 476
Perham 395
Perry 758
Peru 1,541
Phillips 1,148
Phippsburg 1,815
Pittsfield 3,222 ▲4,190
Pittston 2,444
Plymouth 1,152
Poland 4,342
Portage Lake 445
Porter 1,301
Portland 64,358
Pownal 1,262
Prentiss 245
Presque Isle 10,550
Princeton 973
Prospect 542
Randolph 1,949
Rangeley 1,063
Raymond 3,311
Readfield 2,033
Reed 296
Richmond 1,775 ▲3,072
Ripley 445
Robbinston 495
Rockland 7,972
Rockport 2,854
Rome 758
Roque Bluffs 234
Roxbury 437
Rumford 5,419 ▲7,078
Sabattus 3,696
Saco 15,181
St. Agatha 919
St. Albans 1,724
St. Francis 683
St. George 2,261
St. John 274
Sanford 10,296 ▲20,463
Sangerville 1,398
Scarborough 2,586 ▲12,518
Searsmont 938
Searsport 1,151 ▲2,603
Sebago 1,259
Sebec 554
Sedgwick 905
Shapleigh 1,911
Sherman 1,027
Shirley 271
Sidney 2,593
Skowhegan 6,990 ▲8,725
Smithfield 865
Smyrna 378
Solon 916
Somerville 458
Sorrento 295
South Aroostook 404
South Berwick 5,877
South Bristol 825
South Eliot 3,112
South Oxford 455
South Paris 2,320
South Portland 23,163
South Sanford 3,929
South Thomaston 1,227
Southeast Piscataquis 247
Southport 645
Southwest Harbor 1,952
Springfield 406
Springvale 3,542
Square Lake 564
Stacyville 480
Standish 7,678
Starks 508
Stetson 847
Steuben 1,084
Stockholm 286
Stockton Springs 1,383
Stoneham 224
Stonington 1,252
Stow 283
Strong 1,217
Sullivan 1,118
Sumner 761
Surry 1,004
Swans Island 348
Swanville 1,130
Sweden 222
Temple 560
Thomaston 2,445 ▲3,306
Thorndike 702
Topsfield 235
Topsham 6,147 ▲8,746
Tremont 1,324
Trenton 1,060
Troy 802
Turner 4,315
Union 1,989
Unity 1,817
Van Buren 2,759 ▲3,045
Vanceboro 201
Vassalboro 3,679
Veazie 1,633
Verona 515
Vienna 417
Vinalhaven 1,072
Wade 243
Waldo 626
Waldoboro 1,420 ▲4,601
Wales 1,223
Wallagrass 582
Waltham 276
Warren 3,192
Washburn 1,880
Washington 1,185
Waterboro 4,510
Waterford 1,299
Waterville 17,173
Wayne 1,029
Weld 430
Wellington 270
Wells 7,778
West Bath 1,716
West Gardiner 2,531
West Paris 1,514
Westbrook 16,121
Westfield 589
Weston 207
Westport 663
Whitefield 1,935
Whiting 407
Whitneyville 241
Wilton 2,453 ▲4,242
Windham 13,020
Windsor 1,895
Winn 479
Winslow 5,436 ▲7,997
Winter Harbor 1,157
Winterport 1,274 ▲3,175
Winterville 217
Winthrop 2,819 ▲5,968
Wiscasset 1,233 ▲3,339
Woodland 1,402
Woodland 1,287
Woodstock 1,194
Woodville 215
Woolwich 2,570
Yarmouth 3,338 ▲7,862
York 9,818
York Harbor 2,555

▲ Entire township, including rural area.

Maryland ■ population 4,798,622

Metropolitan areas

Baltimore 2,382,172
Cumberland 101,643 (74,946 in Md.; 26,697 in W. Va.)
Hagerstown 121,393
Washington, D.C. 3,923,574 (1,789,029 in Md.; 1,527,645 in Va.; 606,900 in D.C.)
Wilmington (Del.) 578,587 (441,946 in Del.; 65,294 in N.J.; 71,347 in Md.)

Counties

Allegany 74,946
Anne Arundel 427,239
Baltimore 692,134
Calvert 51,372
Caroline 27,035
Carroll 123,372
Cecil 71,347
Charles 101,154
Dorchester 30,236
Frederick 150,208
Garrett 28,138
Harford 182,132
Howard 187,328
Kent 17,842
Montgomery 757,027
Prince Georges 729,268
Queen Annes 33,953
St. Marys 75,974
Somerset 23,440
Talbot 30,549
Washington 121,393
Wicomico 74,339
Worcester 35,028

Cities, towns, and villages

Aberdeen 13,087
Aberdeen Proving Ground 5,267
Accident 349
Accokeek 4,477
Adelphi 13,524
Andrews Air Force Base 10,228
Annapolis 33,187
Arbutus 19,750
Arden on the Severn 2,427
Arnold 20,261
Ashton-Sandy Spring 3,092
Aspen Hill 45,494
Baltimore 736,014
Barton 530
Bel Air 8,860
Bel Air North 14,880
Bel Air South 26,421
Beltsville 14,476
Berlin 2,616
Berwyn Heights 2,952
Bethesda 62,936
Betterton 360
Bladensburg 8,064
Boonsboro 2,445
Bowie 37,589
Braddock Heights 4,778
Brandywine 1,406
Brentwood 3,005
Bridgeport 2,702
Brooklyn Park 10,987
Brunswick 5,117
Bryans Road 3,809
Burtonsville 5,853
Cabin John [-Brookmont] 5,341
California 7,626
Calvert Beach [-Long Beach] 1,728
Calverton 12,046
Cambridge 11,514
Camp Springs 16,392
Cape St. Claire 7,878
Capitol Heights 3,633
Carmody Hills [-Pepper Mill Village] 4,815
Carney 25,578
Catonsville 35,233
Cecilton 489
Centreville 2,097
Charlestown 578
Charlotte Hall 1,992
Chesapeake Beach 2,403
Chesapeake City 735
Chestertown 4,005
Cheverly 6,023
Chevy Chase 8,559
Chevy Chase 2,675
Chillum 31,309
Church Hill 481
Clear Spring 415
Clinton 19,987
Clover Hill 2,823
Cloverly 7,904
Cockeysville 18,668
Colesville 18,819
College Park 21,927
Colmar Manor 1,249
Columbia 75,883
Coral Hills 11,032
Cottage City 1,236
Cresaptown [-Bel Air] 4,586
Crisfield 2,880
Crofton 12,781
Cumberland 23,706
Damascus 9,817
Deale 4,151
Deer Park 419
Delmar 1,430
Denton 2,977
Discovery [-Spring Garden] 2,443
District Heights 6,704
Dodge Park 4,842
Dundalk 65,800
East Riverdale 14,187
Easton 9,372
Edgemere 9,226
Edgewood 23,903
Edmonston 851
Eldersburg 9,720
Elkton 9,073
Ellicott City 41,396
Emmitsburg 1,688
Essex 40,872
Fairland 19,828
Fairmount Heights 1,238
Fallston 5,730
Federalsburg 2,365
Ferndale 16,355
Forest Heights 2,859
Forestville 16,731
Fort Meade 12,509
Fort Ritchie 1,249
Frederick 40,148
Friendly 9,028
Friendsville 577
Frostburg 8,075
Fruitland 3,511
Funkstown 1,136
Gaithersburg 39,542
Galena 324
Garrett Park 884
Germantown 41,145
Glen Burnie 37,305
Glen Echo 234
Glenarden 5,025
Glenn Dale 9,689
Goddard 4,576
Golden Beach 2,944
Grantsville 505
Grasonville 2,439
Green Haven 14,416
Green Valley 9,424
Greenbelt 21,096
Greensboro 1,441
Hagerstown 35,445
Halfway 8,873
Hampstead 2,608
Hampton 4,926
Hancock 1,926
Havre de Grace 8,952
Hebron 665
Herald Harbor 1,707
Hillandale 10,318
Hillcrest Heights 17,136
Hillsmere Shores 3,321
Hughesville 1,319
Hurlock 1,706
Hyattsville 13,864
Indian Head 3,531
Jarrettsville 2,148
Jessup 6,537
Joppatowne 11,084
Keedysville 464
Kensington 1,713
Kentland 7,967
Kettering 9,901
Kingstown 1,660
Kingsville 3,550
Kitzmiller 275
Lake Shore 13,269
Landover 5,052
Landover Hills 2,074
Langley Park 17,474
Lanham [-Seabrook] 16,792
Lansdowne [-Baltimore Highlands] 15,509
La Plata 5,841
Largo 9,475
Laurel 19,438
La Vale 4,694
Lawsonia 1,326
Laytonsville 248
Leonardtown 1,475
Lexington Park 9,943
Linthicum 7,547
Loch Lynn Heights 461
Lochearn 25,240
Lonaconing 1,122
Londontowne 6,992
Lutherville [-Timonium] 16,442
Manchester 2,810
Marbury 1,244
Mardela Springs 360
Marlow Heights 5,885
Maryland City 6,813
Mayo 2,537
Mays Chapel 10,132
Middle River 24,616
Middletown 1,834
Midland 574
Milford Mill 22,547
Millington 409
Montgomery Village 32,315
Morningside 930
Mount Airy 3,730
Mount Rainier 7,954
Mountain Lake Park 1,938
Myersville 464
Naval Academy 5,420
New Carrollton 12,002
New Market 328
New Windsor 757
North Beach 1,173
North Bethesda 29,656
North Brentwood 512
North East 1,913
North Kensington 8,607
North Laurel 15,008
Oakland 1,741
Oakland 2,078
Ocean City 5,146
Odenton 12,833
Olney 23,019
Overlea 12,137
Owings-Mills 9,474
Oxford 699
Oxon Hill [-Glassmanor] 35,794
Palmer Park 7,019
Parkville 31,617
Parole 10,054
Pasadena 10,012
Perry Hall 22,723
Perryman 2,160
Perryville 2,456
Pikesville 24,815
Pittsville 602
Pleasant Hills 2,591
Pocomoke City 3,922
Poolesville 3,796
Port Deposit 685
Potomac 45,634
Potomac Heights 1,524
Preston 437
Prince Frederick 1,885
Princess Anne 1,666
Pumphrey 5,483
Queen Anne 250
Queenstown 453
Randallstown 26,277
Redland 16,145
Reisterstown 19,314
Ridgely 1,034
Rising Sun 1,263
Riva 3,438
Riverdale 5,185
Riviera Beach 11,376
Rock Hall 1,584
Rockville 44,835
Rosedale 18,703
Rosemont 256
Rossville 9,492
St. Charles 28,717
St. Michaels 1,301
Salisbury 20,592
Savage [-Guilford] 9,669
Seat Pleasant 5,359
Secretary 528
Selby-on-the-Bay 3,101
Severn 24,499
Severna Park 25,879
Shady Side 4,107
Sharpsburg 659
Sharptown 609
Silver Spring 76,046
Smithsburg 1,221

Maryland (continued)

Snow Hill 2,217
Somerset 993
South Gate 27,564
South Kensington 8,777
South Laurel 18,591
Stevensville 1,862
Suitland [-Silver Hill] 35,111
Sykesville 2,303
Takoma Park 16,700
Taneytown 3,695
Temple Hills 6,865
Thurmont 3,398
Towson 49,445
Trappe 974
Union Bridge 910
University Park 2,243
Upper Marlboro 745
Vienna 264
Waldorf 15,058
Walker Mill 10,920
Walkersville 4,145
Washington Grove 434
Westernport 2,454
Westminster 13,068
Westminster South 4,284
Wheaton [-Clenmont] 53,720
White Marsh 8,183
White Oak 18,671
White Plains 3,560
Willards 708
Williamsport 2,103
Woodlawn 32,907
Woodlawn 5,329
Woodsboro 513

Massachusetts ■ population 6,029,051

Metropolitan areas

Boston 2,870,669
Brockton 189,478
Fall River 157,272 (139,621 in Mass.; 17,651 in R.I.)
Fitchburg-Leominster 102,797
Lawrence-Haverhill 393,516 (283,828 in Mass.; 109,688 in N.H.)
Lowell 273,067 (263,659 in Mass.; 9,408 in N.H.)
New Bedford 175,641
Pawtucket-Woonsocket (R.I.)-Attleboro 329,384 (227,131 in R.I.; 102,253 in Mass.)
Pittsfield 79,250
Salem-Gloucester 264,356
Springfield 529,519
Worcester 436,905

Counties

Barnstable 186,605
Berkshire 139,352
Bristol 506,325
Dukes 11,639
Essex 670,080
Franklin 70,092
Hampden 456,310
Hampshire 146,568
Middlesex 1,398,468
Nantucket 6,012
Norfolk 60,087
Plymouth 435,276
Suffolk 663,906
Worcester 709,705

Cities and towns

Abington 13,817
Acton 17,872
Acushnet 9,554
Adams 6,356
▲9,445
Agawam 27,323
Alford 418
Amesbury 12,109
▲14,997
Amherst 17,824
▲35,228
Andover 8,242
▲29,151
Arlington 44,630
Ashburnham 5,433
Ashby 2,717
Ashfield 1,715
Ashland 12,066
Athol 8,732
▲11,451
Attleboro 38,383
Auburn 15,005
Avon 4,558
Ayer 2,889
▲6,871
Baldwinsville 1,795
Barnstable 2,790
▲40,949
Barre 1,094
▲4,546
Becket 1,481
Bedford 12,996
Belchertown 2,339
▲10,579
Bellingham 4,535
▲14,877
Belmont 24,720
Berkley 4,237
Berlin 2,293
Bernardston 2,048
Beverly 38,195
Billerica 37,609
Blackstone 8,023
Blandford 1,187
Bolton 3,134
Bondsville 1,992
Boston 574,283
Bourne 1,284
▲16,064
Boxborough 3,343
Boxford 2,072
▲6,266
Boylston 3,517
Braintree 33,836
Brewster 1,818
▲8,440
Bridgewater 7,242
▲21,249
Brimfield 3,001
Brockton 92,788
Brookfield 2,968
Brookline 54,718
Buckland 1,928
Burlington 23,302
Buzzards Bay 3,250
Cambridge 95,802
Canton 18,530
Carlisle 4,333
Carver 10,590
Centerville 9,190
Charlemont 1,249
Charlton 9,576
Chatham 1,916
▲6,579
Chelmsford 32,383
Chelsea 28,710
Cheshire 3,479
Chester 1,280
Chesterfield 1,048
Chicopee 56,632
Chilmark 650
Clarksburg 1,745
Clinton 13,222
Cochituate 6,046
Cohasset 7,075
Colrain 1,757
Concord 17,076
Conway 1,529
Cordaville 1,530
Cotuit 2,364
Cummington 785
Dalton 7,155
Danvers 24,174
Dartmouth 27,244
Dedham 23,782
Deerfield 5,018
Dennis 13,864
Dennis Port 2,775
Dighton 5,631
Douglas 5,438
Dover 2,163
▲4,915
Dracut 25,594
Dudley 9,540
Dunstable 2,236
Duxbury 1,637
▲13,895
East Bridgewater 11,104
East Brookfield 1,396
▲2,033
East Dennis 2,584
East Douglas 1,945
East Falmouth 5,577
East Harwich 3,828
East Longmeadow 13,367
East Pepperell 2,296
Eastham 4,462
Easthampton 15,537
Easton 19,807
Edgartown 3,062
Egremont 1,229
Erving 1,372
Essex 1,507
▲3,260
Everett 35,701
Fairhaven 16,132
Fall River 92,703
Falmouth 4,047
▲27,960
Fiskdale 2,189
Fitchburg 41,194
Florida 742
Forestdale 2,833
Fort Devens 8,973
Foxborough 5,706
▲14,637
Framingham 64,989
Franklin 9,965
▲22,095
Freetown 8,522
Gardner 20,125
Gay Head 201
Georgetown 6,384
Gill 1,583
Gloucester 28,716
Goshen 830
Grafton 13,035
Granby 1,327
▲5,565
Granville 1,403
Great Barrington 2,810
▲7,725
Green Harbor [-Cedar Crest] 2,205
Greenfield 14,016
▲18,666
Groton 1,044
▲7,511
Groveland 5,214
Hadley 4,231
Halifax 6,526
Hamilton 7,280
Hampden 4,709
Hancock 628
Hanover 11,912
Hanson 2,188
▲9,028
Hardwick 2,385
Harvard 12,329
Harwich 10,275
Harwich Port 1,742
Hatfield 1,234
▲3,184
Haverhill 51,418
Hawley 317
Heath 716
Hingham 5,454
▲19,821
Hinsdale 1,959
Holbrook 11,041
Holden 14,628
Holland 2,185
Holliston 12,926
Holyoke 43,704
Hopedale 3,961
▲5,666
Hopkinton 2,305
▲9,191
Housatonic 1,184
Hubbardston 2,797
Hudson 14,267
▲17,233
Hull 10,466
Huntington 1,987
Hyannis 14,120
Ipswich 4,132
▲11,873
Kingston 4,774
▲9,045
Lakeville 7,785
Lancaster 6,661
Lanesborough 3,032
Lawrence 70,207
Lee 2,020
▲5,849
Leicester 10,191
Lenox 1,687
▲5,069
Leominster 38,145
Leverett 1,785
Lexington 28,974
Leyden 662
Lincoln 7,666
Littleton 7,051
Littleton Common 2,867
Longmeadow 15,467
Lowell 103,439
Ludlow 18,820
Lunenburg 1,694
▲9,117
Lynn 81,245
Lynnfield 11,274
Malden 53,884
Manchester 5,286
Mansfield 7,170
▲16,568
Marblehead 19,971
Marion 4,496
Marlborough 31,813
Marshfield 4,002
▲21,531
Marshfield Hills 2,201
Mashpee 7,884
Mattapoisett 2,949
▲5,850
Maynard 10,325
Medfield 5,985
▲10,531
Medford 57,407
Medway 9,931
Melrose 28,150
Mendon 4,010
Merrimac 5,166
Methuen 39,990
Middleborough 6,837
▲17,867
Middlefield 392
Middleton 4,921
Milford 23,339
▲25,355
Millbury 12,228
Millers Falls 1,084
Millis 7,613
Millis [-Clicquot] 4,081
Millville 2,236
Milton 25,725
Monson 7,776
Montague 8,316
Monterey 805
Montgomery 759
Monument Beach 1,842
Nahant 3,828
Nantucket 3,069
▲6,012
Natick 30,510
Needham 27,557
New Bedford 99,922
New Braintree 881
New Marlborough 1,240
New Salem 802
Newbury 5,623
Newburyport 16,317
Newton 82,585
Norfolk 9,270
North Adams 16,797
North Amherst 6,239
North Andover 22,792
North Attleborough 25,038
North Brookfield 2,635
▲4,708
North Eastham 1,570
North Pembroke 2,485
North Plymouth 3,450
North Reading 12,002
North Scituate 4,891
Northampton 29,289
Northborough 5,761
▲11,929
Northbridge 13,371
Northfield 1,322
▲2,838
Norton 14,265
Norwell 9,279
Norwood 28,700
Oak Bluffs 2,804
Oakham 1,503
Ocean Bluff [-Brant Rock] 4,541
Ocean Grove 3,169
Onset 1,461
Orange 3,791
▲7,312
Orleans 1,699
▲5,838
Osterville 2,911
Otis 1,073
Oxford 5,969
▲12,588
Palmer 4,069
▲12,054
Paxton 4,047
Peabody 47,039
Pelham 1,373
Pembroke 14,544
Pepperell 2,350
▲10,098
Peru 779
Petersham 1,131
Phillipston 1,485
Pinehurst 6,614
Pittsfield 48,622
Plainfield 571
Plainville 6,871
Plymouth 7,258
▲45,608
Plympton 2,384
Pocasset 2,756
Princeton 3,189
Provincetown 3,374
▲3,561
Quincy 84,985
Randolph 30,093
Raynham 3,709
▲9,867
Reading 22,539
Rehoboth 8,656
Revere 42,786
Richmond 1,677
Rochester 3,921
Rockland 16,123
Rockport 7,482
Rowe 378
Rowley 1,144
▲4,452
Royalston 1,147
Russell 1,594
Rutland 2,145
▲4,936
Sagamore 2,589
Salem 38,091
Salisbury 3,729
▲6,882
Sandisfield 667
Sandwich 2,998
▲15,489
Saugus 25,549
Savoy 634
Scituate 5,180
▲16,786
Seekonk 13,046
Sharon 5,893
▲15,517
Sheffield 2,910
Shelburne 2,012
Shelburne Falls 1,996
Sherborn 3,989
Shirley 1,559
▲6,118
Shrewsbury 24,146
Shutesbury 1,561
Somerset 17,655
Somerville 76,210
South Amherst 5,053
South Ashburnham 1,110
South Deerfield 1,906
South Duxbury 3,017
South Hadley 16,685
South Lancaster 1,772
South Yarmouth 10,358
Southampton 4,478
Southborough 6,628
Southbridge 13,631
▲17,816
Southwick 7,667
Spencer 6,306
▲11,645
Springfield 156,983
Sterling 6,481
Stockbridge 2,408
Stoneham 22,203
Stoughton 26,777
Stow 5,328
Sturbridge 2,093
▲7,775
Sudbury 14,358
Sunderland 3,399
Sutton 6,824
Swampscott 13,650
Swansea 15,411
Taunton 49,832
Teaticket 1,856
Templeton 6,438
Tewksbury 27,266
Three Rivers 3,006
Tisbury 3,120
Tolland 289
Topsfield 2,711
▲5,754
Townsend 1,164
▲8,496
Truro 1,573
Turners Falls 4,731
Tyngsborough 8,642
Tyringham 369
Upton 4,677
Upton [-West Upton] 2,347
Uxbridge 10,415
Vineyard Haven 1,762
Wakefield 24,825
Wales 1,566
Walpole 5,495
▲20,212
Waltham 57,878
Ware 6,533
▲9,808
Wareham 19,232
Warren 1,516
▲4,437
Warwick 740
Washington 615
Watertown 33,284
Wayland 11,874
Webster 11,849
▲16,196
Wellesley 26,615
Wellfleet 2,493
Wendell 899
Wenham 4,212
West Barnstable 1,508
West Boylston 6,611
West Bridgewater 6,389
West Brookfield 1,419
▲3,532
West Chatham 1,504
West Concord 5,761
West Dennis 2,307
West Falmouth 1,752
West Newbury 3,421
West Springfield 27,537
West Stockbridge 1,483
West Tisbury 1,704
West Wareham 2,059
West Yarmouth 5,409
Westborough 3,917
▲14,133
Westfield 38,372
Westford 16,392
Westhampton 1,327
Westminster 6,191
Weston 10,200
Westport 13,852
Westwood 12,557
Weymouth 54,063
Whately 1,375
Whitinsville 5,639
Whitman 13,240
Wilbraham 3,352
▲12,635
Williamsburg 2,515
Williamstown 4,791
▲8,220
Wilmington 17,651
Winchendon 4,316
▲8,805
Winchester 20,267
Windsor 770
Winthrop 18,127
Woburn 35,943
Worcester 169,759
Worthington 1,156
Wrentham 9,006
Yarmouth 21,174
Yarmouth Port 4,271

▲ Entire township, including rural area.

Michigan ■ population 9,328,784

Metropolitan areas

Ann Arbor 282,937
Battle Creek 135,982
Benton Harbor 161,378
Detroit 4,382,299
Flint 430,459
Grand Rapids 688,399
Jackson 149,756
Kalamazoo 223,411
Lansing-East Lansing 432,674
Muskegon 158,983
Saginaw-Bay City-Midland 399,320

Counties

Alcona 10,145
Alger 8,972
Allegan 90,509
Alpena 30,605
Antrim 18,185
Arenac 14,931
Baraga 7,954
Barry 50,057
Bay 111,723
Benzie 12,200
Berrien 161,378
Branch 41,502
Calhoun 135,982
Cass 49,477
Charlevoix 21,468
Cheboygan 21,398
Chippewa 34,604
Clare 24,952
Clinton 57,883
Crawford 12,260
Delta 37,780
Dickinson 26,831
Eaton 92,879
Emmet 25,040
Genesee 430,459
Gladwin 21,896
Gogebic 18,052
Grand Traverse 64,273
Gratiot 38,982
Hillsdale 43,431
Houghton 35,446
Huron 34,951
Ingham 281,912
Ionia 57,024
Iosco 30,209
Iron 13,175
Isabella 54,624
Jackson 149,756
Kalamazoo 223,411
Kalkaska 13,497
Kent 500,631
Keweenaw 1,701
Lake 8,583

Lapeer 74,768
Leelanau 16,527
Lenawee 91,476
Livingston 115,645
Luce 5,763
Mackinac 10,674
Macomb 717,400
Manistee 21,265
Marquette 70,887
Mason 25,537
Mecosta 37,308
Menominee 24,920
Midland 75,651
Missaukee 12,147
Monroe 133,600
Montcalm 53,059
Montmorency 8,936
Muskegon 158,983
Newaygo 38,202
Oakland 1,083,592
Oceana 22,454
Ogemaw 18,681
Ontonagon 8,854
Osceola 20,146
Oscoda 7,842
Otsego 17,957
Ottawa 187,768
Presque Isle 13,743
Roscommon 19,776
Saginaw 211,946
St. Clair 145,607
St. Joseph 58,913
Sanilac 39,928
Schoolcraft 8,302
Shiawassee 69,770
Tuscola 55,498
Van Buren 70,060
Washtenaw 282,937
Wayne 2,111,687
Wexford 26,360

Cities, towns, and villages

Addison 632
Adrian 22,097
Akron 421
Alanson 677
Albion 10,066
Algonac 4,551
Allegan 4,547
Allen 201
Allen Park 31,092
Alma 9,034
Almont 2,354
Alpena 11,354
Alpha 219
Anchorville 3,202
Ann Arbor 109,592
Applegate 297
Argentine 1,907
Armada 1,548
Ashley 518
Athens 990
Auburn 1,855
Au Gres 838
Augusta 927
Au Sable 1,542
Bad Axe 3,484
Baldwin 821
Bancroft 599
Bangor 1,922
Baraga 1,231
Barnes Lake [-Millers Lake] 1,304
Baroda 657
Barryton 393
Barton Hills 320
Battle Creek 53,540
Bay City 38,936
Bear Lake 339
Beaverton 1,150
Beecher 14,465
Beechwood 2,676
Belding 5,969
Bellaire 1,104
Belleville 3,270
Bellevue 1,401
Benton Harbor 12,818
Benton Heights 5,465
Benzonia 449
Berkley 16,960
Berrien Springs 1,927
Bessemer 2,272
Beulah 421
Beverly Hills 10,610
Big Rapids 12,603
Bingham Farms 1,001
Birch Run 992
Birmingham 19,997
Blissfield 3,172
Bloomfield Hills 4,288
Bloomingdale 503
Boyne City 3,478
Boyne Falls 369
Breckenridge 1,301
Breedsville 213
Bridgeport 8,569
Bridgman 2,140
Brighton 5,686
Britton 694
Bronson 2,342
Brooklyn 1,027
Brown City 1,244
Brownlee Park 2,536
Buchanan 4,992
Buckley 402
Burlington 294
Burr Oak 882
Burt 1,169
Burton 27,617
Byron 573
Cadillac 10,104
Caledonia 885
Calumet 818
Camden 482
Capac 1,583
Carleton 2,770
Caro 4,054
Carrollton 6,521
Carson City 1,158
Carsonville 583
Caseville 857
Casnovia 376
Caspian 1,031
Cass City 2,276
Cassopolis 1,822
Cedar Springs 2,600
Cement City 493
Center Line 9,026
Central Lake 954
Centreville 1,516
Charlevoix 3,116
Charlotte 8,083
Chatham 268
Cheboygan 4,999
Chelsea 3,772
Chesaning 2,567
Clare 3,021
Clarkston 1,005
Clarksville 360
Clawson 13,874
Clayton 384
Clifford 354
Climax 677
Clinton 2,475
Clio 2,629
Coldwater 9,607
Coleman 1,237
Coloma 1,679
Colon 1,224
Columbiaville 934
Comstock Park 6,530
Concord 944
Constantine 2,032
Coopersville 3,421
Copemish 222
Corunna 3,091
Croswell 2,174
Crystal Falls 1,922
Custer 312
Cutlerville 11,228
Daggett 260
Dansville 437
Davison 5,693
Dearborn 89,286
Dearborn Heights 60,838
Decatur 1,760
Deckerville 1,015
Deerfield 922
De Tour Village 407
Detroit 1,027,974
Detroit Beach 2,113
DeWitt 3,964
Dexter 1,497
Dimondale 1,247
Douglas 1,040
Dowagiac 6,409
Dryden 628
Dundee 2,664
Durand 4,283
East Detroit 35,283
East Grand Rapids 10,807
East Jordan 2,240
East Lake 473
East Lansing 50,677
East Tawas 2,887
Eastwood 6,340
Eaton Rapids 4,695
Eau Claire 494
Ecorse 12,180
Edmore 1,126
Edwardsburg 1,142
Elberta 478
Elk Rapids 1,626
Elkton 958
Ellsworth 418
Elsie 957
Emmett 297
Empire 355
Escanaba 13,659
Essexville 4,088
Estral Beach 430
Evart 1,744
Fair Haven 1,505
Fair Plain 8,051
Fairgrove 592
Farmington 10,132
Farmington Hills 74,652
Farwell 851
Fennville 1,023
Fenton 8,444
Ferndale 25,084
Ferrysburg 2,919
Fife Lake 394
Flat Rock 7,290
Flint 140,761
Flushing 8,542
Fowler 912
Fowlerville 2,648
Frankenmuth 4,408
Frankfort 1,546
Franklin 2,626
Fraser 13,899
Freeland 1,421
Freeport 458
Fremont 3,875
Fruitport 1,090
Gaastra 376
Gagetown 337
Gaines 427
Galesburg 1,863
Galien 596
Garden 268
Garden City 31,846
Gaylord 3,256
Gibraltar 4,297
Gladstone 4,565
Gladwin 2,682
Gobles 769
Goodrich 916
Grand Blanc 7,760
Grand Haven 11,951
Grand Ledge 7,579
Grand Rapids 189,126
Grandville 15,624
Grant 764
Grass Lake 903
Grayling 1,944
Greenville 8,101
Grosse Ile 9,781
Grosse Pointe 5,681
Grosse Pointe Farms 10,092
Grosse Pointe Park 12,857
Grosse Pointe Shores 2,955
Grosse Pointe Woods 17,715
Gwinn 2,370
Hamtramck 18,372
Hancock 4,547
Hanover 481
Harbor Beach 2,089
Harbor Springs 1,540
Harper Woods 14,903
Harrison 1,835
Harrisville 470
Hart 1,942
Hartford 2,341
Harvey 1,377
Haslett 10,230
Hastings 6,549
Hazel Park 20,051
Hemlock 1,601
Hersey 354
Hesperia 846
Highland Park 20,121
Hillman 643
Hillsdale 8,170
Holland 30,745
Holly 5,595
Holt 11,744
Homer 1,758
Honor 292
Hopkins 546
Houghton 7,498
Houghton Lake 3,353
Howard City 1,351
Howell 8,184
Hubbardston 404
Hubbell 1,174
Hudson 2,580
Hudsonville 6,170
Huntington Woods 6,419
Imlay City 2,921
Inkster 30,772
Ionia 5,935
Iron Mountain 8,525
Iron River 2,095
Ironwood 6,849
Ishpeming 7,200
Ithaca 3,009
Jackson 37,446
Jenison 17,882
Jonesville 2,283
Kalamazoo 80,277
Kaleva 484
Kalkaska 1,952
Keego Harbor 2,932
Kent City 899
Kentwood 37,826
Kinde 473
Kingsford 5,480
Kingsley 738
Kingston 439
K I Sawyer AFB 6,577
Laingsburg 1,148
Lake Angelus 328
Lake Ann 217
Lake City 858
Lake Fenton 4,091
Lake Linden 1,203
Lake Michigan Beach 1,694
Lake Odessa 2,256
Lake Orion 3,057
Lakeview 1,108
Lakewood Club 659
Lambertville 7,860
L'Anse 2,151
Lansing 127,321
Lapeer 7,759
Lathrup Village 4,329
Laurium 2,268
Lawrence 915
Lawton 1,685
Lennon 534
Leonard 357
LeRoy 251
Leslie 1,872
Level Park [-Oak Park] 3,502
Lexington 779
Lincoln 337
Lincoln Park 41,832
Linden 2,415
Litchfield 1,317
Livonia 100,850
Lowell 3,983
Ludington 8,507
Luna Pier 1,507
Luther 343
Lyons 824
Mackinac Island 469
Mackinaw City 875
Madison Heights 32,196
Mancelona 1,370
Manchester 1,753
Manistee 6,734
Manistique 3,456
Manitou Beach [-Devils Lake] 2,061
Manton 1,161
Maple Rapids 680
Marcellus 1,193
Marine City 4,556
Marion 807
Marlette 1,924
Marquette 21,977
Marshall 6,891
Martin 462
Marysville 8,515
Mason 6,768
Mattawan 2,456
Maybee 500
Mayville 1,010
McBain 692
McBrides 236
Mecosta 393
Melvindale 11,216
Memphis 1,221
Mendon 920
Menominee 9,398
Merrill 755
Mesick 406
Metamora 447
Michigan Center 4,863
Middleville 1,966
Midland 38,053
Milan 4,040
Milford 5,511
Millersburg 250
Millington 1,114
Minden City 233
Mineral Hills 200
Mio 1,886
Monroe 22,902
Montague 2,276
Montogmery 388
Montrose 1,811
Morenci 2,342
Morley 528
Morrice 630
Mount Clemens 18,405
Mount Morris 3,292
Mount Pleasant 23,285
Muir 667
Mulliken 590
Munising 2,783
Muskegon 40,283
Muskegon Heights 13,176
Napoleon 1,332
Nashville 1,654
Negaunee 4,741
New Baltimore 5,798
New Buffalo 2,317
New Era 520
New Haven 2,331
New Lothrop 596
Newaygo 1,336
Newberry 1,873
Niles 12,458
North Adams 512
North Branch 1,023
North Muskegon 3,919
Northport 605
Northview 13,712
Northville 6,226
Norton Shores 21,755
Norway 2,910
Novi 32,998
Oak Park 30,462
Oakley 362
Okemos 20,216
Olivet 1,604
Omer 385
Onaway 1,039
Onekama 515
Onsted 801
Ontonagon 2,040
Orchard Lake Village 2,286
Ortonville 1,252
Oscoda 1,061
Ossineke 1,091
Otisville 724
Otsego 3,937
Otter Lake 474
Ovid 1,442
Owendale 285
Owosso 16,322
Oxford 2,929
Parchment 1,958
Parma 809
Paw Paw 3,169
Paw Paw Lake 3,782
Pearl Beach 3,394
Peck 558
Pellston 583
Pentwater 1,050
Perrinton 393
Perry 2,163
Petersburg 1,201
Petoskey 6,056
Pewamo 520
Pierson 207
Pigeon 1,207
Pinckney 1,603
Pinconning 1,291
Plainwell 4,057
Pleasant Ridge 2,775
Plymouth 9,560
Pontiac 71,166
Port Austin 815
Port Hope 313
Port Huron 33,694
Port Sanilac 656
Portage 41,042
Portland 3,889
Posen 263
Potterville 1,523
Powers 271
Prescott 314
Prudenville 1,513
Quincy 1,680
Quinnesec 1,254
Ravenna 919
Reading 1,127
Reed City 2,379
Reese 1,414
Richland 465
Richmond 4,141
River Rouge 11,314
Riverview 13,894
Rochester 7,130
Rockford 3,750
Rockwood 3,141
Rogers City 3,642
Romeo 3,520
Romulus 22,897
Roosevelt Park 3,885
Roscommon 858
Rose City 686
Rosebush 333
Roseville 51,412
Rothbury 407
Royal Oak 65,410
Saginaw 69,512
St. Charles 2,144
St. Clair 5,116
St. Clair Shores 68,107
St. Helen 2,390
St. Ignace 2,568
St. Johns 7,284
St. Joseph 9,214
St. Louis 3,828
Saline 6,660
Sand Lake 456
Sandusky 2,403
Sanford 889
Saranac 1,461
Saugatuck 954
Sault Ste. Marie 14,689
Schoolcraft 1,517
Scottville 1,287
Sebewaing 1,923
Shelby 1,871
Shepherd 1,413
Sheridan 730
Sherwood 320
Shoreham 737
South Haven 5,563
South Lyon 5,857
South Monroe 5,266
South Range 745
South Rockwood 1,221
Southfield 75,728
Southgate 30,771
Sparlingville 1,974
Sparta 3,968
Spring Arbor 2,010
Spring Lake 2,537
Springfield 5,582
Springport 707
Stambaugh 1,281
Standish 1,377
Stanton 1,504
Stephenson 904
Sterling 520
Sterling Heights 117,810
Stevensville 1,230
Stockbridge 1,202
Stony Point 1,598
Sturgis 10,130
Sunfield 610
Suttons Bay 561
Swartz Creek 4,851
Sylvan Lake 1,884
Tawas City 2,009
Taylor 70,811
Tecumseh 7,462
Tekonsha 722
Temperance 6,542
Thompsonville 416
Three Oaks 1,786
Three Rivers 7,413
Traverse City 15,155
Trenton 20,586
Trowbridge Park 1,831
Troy 72,884
Tustin 236
Twin Lake 1,328
Ubly 821
Union City 1,767
Unionville 590
Utica 5,081
Vandalia 357
Vanderbilt 605
Vandercook Lake 4,642
Vassar 2,559
Vermontville 776
Vernon 913
Vicksburg 2,216
Wakefield 2,318
Waldron 581
Walker 17,279
Walkerville 262
Walled Lake 6,278
Warren 144,864
Waterford 66,692
Watervliet 1,867
Waverly 15,614
Wayland 2,751
Wayne 19,899
Webberville 1,698
Weidman 696
West Branch 1,914
Westland 84,724
Westphalia 780
Westwood 8,957
White Cloud 1,147
White Pigeon 1,458
Whitehall 3,027
Whitmore Lake 3,251
Whittemore 463
Williamston 2,922
Wixom 8,550
Wolf Lake 4,110
Wolverine 283
Wolverine Lake 4,727
Woodhaven 11,631
Woodland 466
Woodland Beach 2,309
Wurtsmith AFB 5,080
Wyandotte 30,938
Wyoming 63,891
Yale 1,977
Ypsilanti 24,846
Zeeland 5,417
Zilwaukee 1,850

Minnesota ■ population 4,387,029

Metropolitan areas

Duluth 239,971 (198,213 in Minn.; 41,758 in Wis.)
Fargo (N. Dak.)-Moorehead 153,296 (102,874 in N. Dak.; 50,422 in Minn.)
Minneapolis-St. Paul 2,464,124 (2,413,873 in Minn.; 50,251 in Wis.)
Rochester 106,470
St. Cloud 190,921

Counties

Aitkin 12,425
Anoka 243,641
Becker 27,881
Beltrami 34,384
Benton 30,185
Big Stone 6,285
Blue Earth 54,044
Brown 26,984
Carlton 29,259
Carver 47,915
Cass 21,791
Chippewa 13,228
Chisago 30,521
Clay 50,422
Clearwater 8,309
Cook 3,868
Cottonwood 12,694
Crow Wing 44,249
Dakota 275,227
Dodge 15,731
Douglas 28,674
Faribault 16,937
Fillmore 20,777
Freeborn 33,060
Goodhue 40,690
Grant 6,246
Hennepin 1,032,431
Houston 18,497
Hubbard 14,939
Isanti 25,921
Itasca 40,861
Jackson 11,677
Kanabec 12,802
Kandiyohi 38,761
Kittson 5,767
Koochiching 16,299
Lac qui Parle 8,924
Lake 10,415

Minnesota (continued)

Lake of the Woods 4,076
Le Sueur 23,239
Lincoln 6,890
Lyon 24,789
Mahnomen 5,044
Marshall 10,993
Martin 22,914
McLeod 32,030
Meeker 20,846
Mille Lacs 18,670
Morrison 29,604
Mower 37,385
Murray 9,660
Nicollet 28,076
Nobles 20,098
Norman 7,975
Olmsted 106,470
Otter Tail 50,714
Pennington 13,306
Pine 21,264
Pipestone 10,491
Polk 32,498
Pope 10,745
Ramsey 485,765
Red Lake 4,525
Redwood 17,254
Renville 17,673
Rice 49,183
Rock 9,806
Roseau 15,026
St. Louis 198,213
Scott 57,846
Sherburne 41,945
Sibley 14,366
Stearns 118,791
Steele 30,729
Stevens 10,634
Swift 10,724
Todd 23,363
Traverse 4,463
Wabasha 19,744
Wadena 13,154
Waseca 18,079
Washington 145,896
Watonwan 11,682
Wilkin 7,516
Winona 47,828
Wright 68,710
Yellow Medicine 11,684

Cities

Ada 1,708
Adams 756
Adrian 1,141
Afton 2,645
Aitkin 1,698
Akeley 393
Albany 1,548
Albert Lea 18,310
Albertville 1,251
Alden 623
Alexandria 7,838
Altura 349
Alvarado 356
Amboy 517
Andover 15,216
Annandale 2,054
Anoka 17,192
Apple Valley 34,598
Appleton 1,552
Arden Hills 9,199
Argyle 636
Arlington 1,886
Ashby 469
Askov 343
Atwater 1,053
Audubon 411
Aurora 1,965
Austin 21,907
Avon 970
Babbitt 1,562
Backus 240
Badger 381
Bagley 1,388
Balaton 737
Barnesville 2,066
Barnum 482
Barrett 350
Battle Lake 698
Baudette 1,146
Baxter 3,695
Bayport 3,200
Beardsley 297
Beaver Creek 249
Becker 902
Belgrade 700
Belle Plaine 3,149
Bellingham 247
Belview 383
Bemidji 11,245
Benson 3,235
Bertha 507
Bethel 394
Big Falls 341
Big Lake 3,113
Bigelow 232
Bigfork 384
Birchwood Village 1,042
Bird Island 1,326
Biwabik 1,097
Blackduck 718
Blaine 38,975
Blooming Prairie 2,043
Bloomington 86,335
Blue Earth 3,745
Bovey 662
Bowlus 260
Boyd 251
Braham 1,139
Brainerd 12,353
Branch 2,400
Brandon 441
Breckenridge 3,708
Breezy Point 432
Brewster 532
Bricelyn 426
Brooklyn Center 28,887
Brooklyn Park 56,381
Brooten 589
Browerville 782
Browns Valley 804
Brownsdale 695
Brownsville 415
Brownton 781
Buckman 201
Buffalo 6,856
Buffalo Lake 734
Buhl 915
Burnsville 51,288
Butterfield 509
Byron 2,441
Caledonia 2,846
Callaway 212
Calumet 382
Cambridge 5,094
Campbell 233
Canby 1,826
Cannon Falls 3,232
Canton 362
Carlos 361
Carlton 923
Carver 744
Cass Lake 923
Center City 451
Centerville 1,633
Ceylon 461
Champlin 16,849
Chandler 316
Chanhassen 11,732
Chaska 11,339
Chatfield 2,226
Chisago City 2,009
Chisholm 5,290
Chokio 521
Circle Pines 4,704
Clara City 1,307
Claremont 530
Clarissa 637
Clarkfield 924
Clarks Grove 675
Clear Lake 315
Clearbrook 560
Clearwater 597
Cleveland 699
Climax 264
Clinton 574
Cloquet 10,885
Cokato 2,180
Cold Spring 2,459
Coleraine 1,041
Cologne 563
Columbia Heights 18,910
Comfrey 433
Cook 680
Coon Rapids 52,978
Corcoran 5,199
Cosmos 610
Cottage Grove 22,935
Cottonwood 982
Courtland 412
Cromwell 221
Crookston 8,119
Crosby 2,073
Crosslake 1,132
Crystal 23,788
Currie 303
Cyrus 328
Dakota 360
Dalton 234
Danube 562
Darwin 252
Dassel 1,082
Dawson 1,626
Dayton 4,443
Deephaven 3,653
Deer Creek 303
Deer River 838
Deerwood 524
Delano 2,709
Delavan 245
Dellwood 887
Detroit Lakes 6,635
Dexter 303
Dilworth 2,562
Dodge Center 1,954
Donnelly 221
Dover 416
Duluth 85,493
Dundas 473
Eagan 47,409
Eagle Bend 524
Eagle Lake 1,703
East Bethel 8,050
East Grand Forks 8,658
East Gull Lake 687
Easton 229
Echo 304
Eden Prairie 39,311
Eden Valley 732
Edgerton 1,106
Edina 46,070
Eitzen 221
Elba 220
Elbow Lake 1,186
Elgin 733
Elk River 11,143
Elko 223
Ellendale 549
Ellsworth 580
Elmore 709
Elrosa 205
Ely 3,968
Elysian 445
Emily 613
Emmons 439
Erskine 422
Evansville 566
Eveleth 4,064
Excelsior 2,367
Eyota 1,448
Fairfax 1,276
Fairmont 11,265
Falcon Heights 5,380
Faribault 17,085
Farmington 5,940
Felton 211
Fergus Falls 12,362
Fertile 853
Fifty Lakes 299
Finlayson 242
Fisher 413
Flensburg 213
Floodwood 574
Foley 1,854
Forest Lake 5,833
Foreston 354
Fosston 1,529
Fountain 327
Franklin 441
Frazee 1,176
Freeborn 301
Freeport 556
Fridley 28,335
Frost 236
Fulda 1,212
Garfield 203
Gary 200
Gaylord 1,935
Gem Lake 439
Geneva 444
Ghent 316
Gibbon 712
Gilbert 1,934
Glencoe 4,648
Glenville 778
Glenwood 2,573
Glyndon 862
Golden Valley 20,971
Gonvick 302
Good Thunder 561
Goodhue 533
Goodview 2,878
Graceville 671
Granada 374
Grand Marais 1,171
Grand Meadow 967
Grand Rapids 7,976
Granite Falls 3,083
Green Isle 239
Greenbush 800
Greenfield 1,450
Greenwald 209
Greenwood 614
Grey Eagle 353
Grove City 547
Grygla 220
Hackensack 245
Hallock 1,304
Halstad 611
Ham Lake 8,924
Hamburg 492
Hammond 205
Hampton 363
Hancock 723
Hanley Falls 246
Hanover 787
Hanska 443
Hardwick 234
Harmony 1,081
Harris 843
Hartland 270
Hastings 15,445
Hawley 1,655
Hayfield 1,283
Hayward 246
Hector 1,145
Henderson 746
Hendricks 684
Hendrum 309
Henning 738
Herman 485
Hermantown 6,761
Heron Lake 730
Hewitt 269
Hibbing 18,046
Hill City 469
Hills 607
Hilltop 749
Hinckley 946
Hitterdal 242
Hoffman 576
Hokah 687
Holdingford 561
Holland 216
Hollandale 289
Hopkins 16,534
Houston 1,013
Howard Lake 1,343
Hoyt Lakes 2,348
Hugo 4,417
Hutchinson 11,523
Independence 2,822
International Falls 8,325
Inver Grove Heights 22,477
Ironton 553
Isanti 1,228
Isle 566
Ivanhoe 751
Jackson 3,559
Janesville 1,969
Jasper 599
Jeffers 443
Jenkins 262
Jordan 2,909
Kandiyohi 506
Karlstad 881
Kasota 655
Kasson 3,514
Keewatin 1,118
Kelliher 348
Kellogg 423
Kennedy 337
Kensington 295
Kenyon 1,552
Kerkhoven 732
Kiester 606
Kimball 690
Kinney 257
La Crescent 4,311
Lafayette 462
Lake Benton 693
Lake Bronson 272
Lake City 4,391
Lake Crystal 2,084
Lake Elmo 5,903
Lake Lillian 229
Lake Park 638
Lake St. Croix Beach 1,078
Lake Shore 693
Lake Wilson 319
Lakefield 1,679
Lakeland 2,000
Lakeland Shores 291
Lakeville 24,854
Lamberton 972
Lancaster 342
Landfall Village 685
Lanesboro 858
La Prairie 438
Lauderdale 2,700
Le Center 2,006
Le Roy 904
Lester Prairie 1,180
Le Sueur 3,714
Lewiston 1,298
Lewisville 255
Lexington 2,279
Lilydale 506
Lindstrom 2,461
Lino Lakes 8,807
Lismore 248
Litchfield 6,041
Little Canada 8,971
Little Falls 7,232
Littlefork 838
Long Beach 204
Long Lake 1,984
Long Prairie 2,786
Longville 224
Lonsdale 1,252
Loretto 404
Lowry 233
Lucan 235
Luverne 4,382
Lyle 504
Lynd 287
Mabel 745
Madelia 2,237
Madison 1,951
Madison Lake 643
Mahnomen 1,154
Mahtomedi 5,569
Mankato 31,477
Mantorville 874
Maple Grove 38,736
Maple Lake 1,394
Maple Plain 2,005
Mapleton 1,526
Mapleview 206
Maplewood 30,954
Marble 618
Marietta 211
Marine on St. Croix 602
Marshall 12,023
Mayer 471
Maynard 419
Mazeppa 722
McGregor 376
McIntosh 665
Medford 733
Medicine Lake 385
Medina 3,096
Melrose 2,561
Menahga 1,076
Mendota Heights 9,431
Middle River 285
Milaca 2,182
Milan 353
Milroy 297
Minneapolis 368,383
Minneota 1,417
Minnesota City 258
Minnesota Lake 681
Minnetonka 48,370
Minnetonka Beach 573
Minnetrista 3,439
Montevideo 5,499
Montgomery 2,399
Monticello 4,941
Montrose 1,008
Moorhead 32,295
Moose Lake 1,206
Mora 2,905
Morgan 965
Morris 5,613
Morristown 784
Morton 448
Motley 441
Mound 9,634
Mounds View 12,541
Mountain Iron 3,362
Mountain Lake 1,906
Murdock 282
Nashwauk 1,026
Nerstrand 210
Nevis 375
New Auburn 363
New Brighton 22,207
New Germany 353
New Hope 21,853
New London 971
New Market 227
New Munich 314
New Prague 3,569
New Richland 1,237
New Ulm 13,132
New York Mills 940
Newfolden 345
Newport 3,720
Nicollet 795
Nisswa 1,391
North Branch 1,867
North Mankato 10,164
North Oaks 3,386
North Redwood 203
North St. Paul 12,376
Northfield 14,684
Northome 283
Northrop 276
Norwood 1,351
Oak Park Heights 3,486
Oakdale 18,374
Ogilvie 510
Okabena 223
Oklee 441
Olivia 2,623
Onamia 676
Orono 7,285
Oronoco 727
Orr 265
Ortonville 2,205
Osakis 1,256
Oslo 362
Osseo 2,704
Ostrander 276
Ottertail 313
Owatonna 19,386
Park Rapids 2,863
Parkers Prairie 956
Paynesville 2,275
Pelican Rapids 1,886
Pemberton 228
Pennock 476
Pequot Lakes 843
Perham 2,075
Peterson 259
Pierz 1,014
Pillager 306
Pine City 2,613
Pine Island 2,125
Pine River 871
Pine Springs 436
Pipestone 4,554
Plainview 2,768
Plato 355
Plummer 277
Plymouth 50,889
Porter 210
Preston 1,530
Princeton 3,719
Prinsburg 502
Prior Lake 11,482
Proctor 2,974
Racine 288
Ramsey 12,408
Randall 571
Randolph 331
Raymond 668
Red Lake Falls 1,481
Red Wing 15,134
Redwood Falls 4,859
Remer 342
Renville 1,315
Rice 610
Richfield 35,710
Richmond 965
Robbinsdale 14,396
Rochester 70,745
Rock Creek 1,040
Rockford 2,665
Rockville 579
Rogers 698
Rollingstone 697
Rose Creek 363
Roseau 2,396
Rosemount 8,622
Roseville 33,485
Rothsay 443
Round Lake 463
Royalton 802
Rush City 1,497
Rushford 1,485
Rushford Village 705
Rushmore 381
Russell 394
Ruthton 328
Sabin 495
Sacred Heart 603
St. Anthony 7,727
St. Bonifacius 1,180
St. Charles 2,642
St. Clair 633
St. Cloud 48,812
St. Francis 2,538
St. Hilaire 298
St. James 4,364
St. Joseph 3,294
St. Louis Park 43,787
St. Martin 274
St. Marys Point 339
St. Michael 2,506
St. Paul 272,235
St. Paul Park 4,965
St. Peter 9,421
St. Stephen 607
Sanborn 459
Sandstone 2,057
Sartell 5,393
Sauk Centre 3,581
Sauk Rapids 7,825
Savage 9,906
Scanlon 878
Sebeka 662
Shafer 368
Shakopee 11,739
Shelly 225
Sherburn 1,105
Shoreview 24,587
Shorewood 5,917
Silver Bay 1,894
Silver Lake 764
Skyline 272
Slayton 2,147
Sleepy Eye 3,694
South St. Paul 20,197
Spicer 1,020
Spring Grove 1,153
Spring Lake Park 6,532
Spring Park 1,571
Spring Valley 2,461
Springfield 2,173
Stacy 1,081
Staples 2,754
Starbuck 1,143
Stephen 707
Stewart 566
Stewartville 4,520
Stillwater 13,882
Stockton 529
Storden 283
Sturgeon Lake 230
Sunfish Lake 413
Swanville 324
Taconite 310
Taylors Falls 694
Thief River Falls 8,010
Tonka Bay 1,472
Tower 502
Tracy 2,059
Trimont 745
Truman 1,292
Twin Valley 821
Two Harbors 3,651
Tyler 1,257
Ulen 547
Underwood 284
Upsala 371
Utica 220
Vadnais Heights 11,041
Vergas 287
Vermillion 510
Verndale 560
Vernon Center 339
Vesta 302
Victoria 2,354
Villard 247
Virginia 9,410
Wabasha 2,384
Wabasso 684
Waconia 3,498
Wadena 4,131
Waite Park 5,020
Waldorf 243
Walker 950
Walnut Grove 625
Wanamingo 847
Warren 1,813
Warroad 1,679
Waseca 8,385
Watertown 2,408
Waterville 1,771
Watkins 849
Watson 211
Waubun 330
Waverly 600
Wayzata 3,806
Welcome 790
Wells 2,465
West Concord 871
West St. Paul 19,248
Westbrook 853
Wheaton 1,615
White Bear Lake 24,704
White Earth 319
Willernie 584
Williams 212

Willmar 17,531
Willow River 284
Wilmont 351
Windom 4,283
Winnebago 1,565
Winona 25,399
Winsted 1,581
Winthrop 1,279
Wood Lake 406
Woodbury 20,075
Woodland 496
Worthington 9,977
Wrenshall 296
Wykoff 493
Wyoming 2,142
Young America 1,354
Zimmerman 1,350
Zumbro Falls 237
Zumbrota 2,312

Mississippi ■ population 2,586,443

Metropolitan areas

Biloxi-Gulfport 197,125
Jackson 395,396
Memphis (Tenn.) 981,747
(863,898 in Tenn.; 49,939 in Ark.; 67,910 in Miss.)
Pascagoula 115,243

Counties

Adams 35,356
Alcorn 31,722
Amite 13,328
Attala 18,481
Benton 8,046
Bolivar 41,875
Calhoun 14,908
Carroll 9,237
Chickasaw 18,085
Choctaw 9,071
Claiborne 11,370
Clarke 17,313
Clay 21,120
Coahoma 31,665
Copiah 27,592
Covington 16,527
De Soto 67,910
Forrest 68,314
Franklin 8,377
George 16,673
Greene 10,220
Grenada 21,555
Hancock 31,760
Harrison 165,365
Hinds 254,441
Holmes 21,604
Humphreys 12,034
Issaquena 1,909
Itawamba 20,017
Jackson 115,243
Jasper 17,114
Jefferson 8,653
Jefferson Davis 14,051
Jones 62,031
Kemper 10,356
Lafayette 31,826
Lamar 30,424
Lauderdale 75,555
Lawrence 12,458
Leake 18,436
Lee 65,581
Leflore 37,341
Lincoln 30,278
Lowndes 59,308
Madison 53,794
Marion 25,544
Marshall 30,361
Monroe 36,582
Montgomery 12,388
Neshoba 24,800
Newton 20,291
Noxubee 12,604
Oktibbeha 38,375
Panola 29,996
Pearl River 38,714
Perry 10,865
Pike 36,882
Pontotoc 22,237
Prentiss 23,278
Quitman 10,490
Rankin 87,161
Scott 24,137
Sharkey 7,066
Simpson 23,953
Smith 14,798
Stone 10,750
Sunflower 32,867
Tallahatchie 15,210
Tate 21,432
Tippah 19,523
Tishomingo 17,683
Tunica 8,164
Union 22,085
Walthall 14,352
Warren 47,880
Washington 67,935
Wayne 19,517
Webster 10,222
Wilkinson 9,678
Winston 19,433
Yalobusha 12,033
Yazoo 25,506

Cities, towns, and villages

Abbeville 399
Aberdeen 6,837
Ackerman 1,573
Algoma 420
Amory 7,093
Anguilla 883
Arcola 564
Artesia 484
Ashland 490
Baldwyn 3,204
Bassfield 249
Batesville 6,403
Bay St. Louis 8,063
Bay Springs 1,729
Beaumont 1,054
Beauregard 206
Belmont 1,554
Belzoni 2,536
Benoit 641
Bentonia 390
Beulah 460
Biloxi 46,319
Blue Mountain 667
Bogue Chitto 689
Bolton 637
Booneville 7,955
Boyle 651
Brandon 11,077
Brookhaven 10,243
Brooksville 1,098
Bruce 2,127
Bude 969
Burnsville 949
Byhalia 955
Caledonia 821
Calhoun City 1,838
Canton 10,062
Carrollton 221
Carthage 3,819
Cary 392
Centreville 1,771
Charleston 2,328
Chunky 292
Clarksdale 19,717
Cleveland 15,384
Clinton 21,847
Coahoma 254
Coffeeville 825
Coldwater 1,502
Collins 2,541
Collinsville 1,364
Columbia 6,815
Columbus 23,799
Columbus AFB Base 2,890
Como 1,387
Conehatta 925
Corinth 11,820
Courtland 329
Crawford 668
Crenshaw 978
Crosby 465
Crowder 758
Cruger 548
Crystal Springs 5,643
Decatur 1,248
De Kalb 1,073
Derma 959
Diamond Head 2,661
D'Iberville 6,566
D'Lo 421
Drew 2,349
Duck Hill 586
Dumas 407
Duncan 416
Durant 2,838
Ecru 696
Edwards 1,279
Ellisville 3,634
Enterprise 477
Escatawpa 3,902
Ethel 454
Eupora 2,145
Falkner 232
Fayette 1,853
Flora 1,482
Florence 1,831
Flowood 2,860
Forest 5,060
French Camp 320
Friars Point 1,334
Fulton 3,387
Gautier 10,088
Georgetown 332
Gloster 1,323
Golden 202
Goodman 1,256
Greenville 45,226
Greenwood 18,906
Grenada 10,864
Gulf Hills 5,004
Gulfport 40,775
Gunnison 611
Guntown 692
Hatley 529
Hattiesburg 41,882
Hazlehurst 4,221
Heidelberg 981
Hernando 3,125
Hickory 493
Hickory Flat 535
Hollandale 3,576
Holly Springs 7,261
Horn Lake 9,069
Houston 3,903
Indianola 11,809
Inverness 1,174
Isola 732
Itta Bena 2,377
Iuka 3,122
Jackson 196,637
Jonestown 1,467
Jumpertown 438
Kilmichael 826
Kiln 1,262
Kosciusko 6,986
Kossuth 245
Lake 369
Lambert 1,131
Laurel 18,827
Leakesville 1,129
Leland 6,366
Lexington 2,227
Liberty 624
Long Beach 15,804
Louin 289
Louise 343
Louisville 7,169
Lucedale 2,592
Lula 224
Lumberton 2,121
Lyman 1,117
Lynchburg 2,071
Lyon 446
Maben 752
Macon 2,256
Madison 7,471
Magee 3,607
Magnolia 2,245
Mantachie 651
Marietta 287
Marion 1,359
Marks 1,758
Mathiston 818
Mayersville 329
McComb 11,591
McLain 536
Meadville 453
Mendenhall 2,463
Meridian 41,036
Meridian Station 2,503
Merigold 572
Metcalfe 1,092
Mize 312
Monticello 1,755
Moorhead 2,417
Morton 3,212
Moss Point 17,837
Mound Bayou 2,222
Mount Olive 914
Myrtle 358
Natchez 19,460
Nellieburg 1,208
Nettleton 2,462
New Albany 6,775
New Augusta 668
Newhebron 373
Newton 3,701
North Carrollton 578
North Gulfport 4,966
Noxapater 441
Oakland 553
Ocean Springs 14,658
Okolona 3,267
Olive Branch 3,567
Orange Grove 15,676
Osyka 483
Oxford 9,984
Pace 354
Pachuta 268
Pascagoula 25,899
Pass Christian 5,557
Pearl 19,588
Pearlington 1,603
Pelahatchie 1,553
Petal 7,883
Philadelphia 6,758
Picayune 10,633
Pickens 1,285
Pittsboro 277
Plantersville 1,046
Pontotoc 4,570
Poplarville 2,561
Port Gibson 1,810
Potts Camp 483
Prentiss 1,487
Puckett 294
Purvis 2,140
Quitman 2,736
Raleigh 1,291
Raymond 2,275
Renova 636
Richland 4,014
Richton 1,034
Ridgeland 11,714
Rienzi 339
Ripley 5,371
Rolling Fork 2,444
Rosedale 2,595
Roxie 568
Ruleville 3,245
Saltillo 1,782
Sandersville 853
Sardis 2,128
Schlater 404
Scooba 541
Sebastopol 281
Seminary 231
Senatobia 4,772
Shannon 1,419
Shaw 2,349
Shelby 2,806
Sherman 528
Shubuta 577
Shuqualak 570
Sidon 596
Silver City 348
Sledge 577
Smithville 871
Soso 366
Southaven 17,949
Starkville 18,458
State Line 395
Stonewall 1,148
Summit 1,566
Sumner 368
Sumrall 903
Sunflower 729
Taylor 288
Taylorsville 1,412
Tchula 2,186
Terry 613
Thaxton 431
Tishomingo 332
Tremont 342
Tunica 1,175
Tupelo 30,685
Tutwiler 1,391
Tylertown 1,938
Union 1,875
Utica 1,033
Vaiden 789
Vancleave 3,214
Vardaman 920
Verona 2,893
Vicksburg 20,908
Walnut 523
Walnut Grove 389
Water Valley 3,610
Waveland 5,369
Waynesboro 5,143
Webb 605
Weir 525
Wesson 1,510
West Point 8,489
Wiggins 3,185
Winona 5,705
Winstonville 277
Woodville 1,393
Yazoo City 12,427

Missouri ■ population 5,137,804

Metropolitan areas

Columbia 112,379
Joplin 134,910
Kansas City 1,566,280
(961,396 in Mo., 604,884 in Kansas.)
St. Joseph 83,083
St. Louis 2,449,760
(1,860,765 in Mo., 588,995 in Ill.)
Springfield 240,593

Counties

Adair 24,577
Andrew 14,632
Atchison 7,457
Audrain 23,599
Barry 27,547
Barton 11,312
Bates 15,025
Benton 13,859
Bollinger 10,619
Boone 112,379
Buchanan 83,083
Butler 38,765
Caldwell 8,380
Callaway 32,809
Camden 27,495
Cape Girardeau 61,633
Carroll 10,748
Carter 5,515
Cass 63,808
Cedar 12,093
Chariton 9,202
Christian 32,644
Clark 7,457
Clay 153,411
Clinton 16,595
Cole 63,579
Cooper 14,835
Crawford 19,173
Dade 7,449
Dallas 12,646
Daviess 7,865
De Kalb 9,967
Dent 13,702
Douglas 11,876
Dunklin 33,112
Franklin 80,603
Gasconade 14,006
Gentry 6,848
Greene 207,949
Grundy 10,536
Harrison 8,469
Henry 20,044
Hickory 7,335
Holt 6,034
Howard 9,631
Howell 31,447
Iron 10,726
Jackson 633,232
Jasper 90,465
Jefferson 171,380
Johnson 42,514
Knox 4,482
Laclede 27,158
Lafayette 31,107
Lawrence 30,236
Lewis 10,233
Lincoln 28,892
Linn 13,885
Livingston 14,592
Macon 15,345
Madison 11,127
Maries 7,976
Marion 27,682
McDonald 16,938
Mercer 3,723
Miller 20,700
Mississippi 14,442
Moniteau 12,298
Monroe 9,104
Montgomery 11,355
Morgan 15,574
New Madrid 20,928
Newton 44,445
Nodaway 21,709
Oregon 9,470
Osage 12,018
Ozark 8,598
Pemiscot 21,921
Perry 16,648
Pettis 35,437
Phelps 35,248
Pike 15,969
Platte 57,867
Polk 21,826
Pulaski 41,307
Putnam 5,079
Ralls 8,476
Randolph 24,370
Ray 21,971
Reynolds 6,661
Ripley 12,303
St. Charles 212,907
St. Clair 8,457
St. Francois 48,904
St. Louis 993,529
Ste. Genevieve 16,037
Saline 23,523
Schuyler 4,236
Scotland 4,822
Scott 39,376
Shannon 7,613
Shelby 6,942
Stoddard 28,895
Stone 19,078
Sullivan 6,326
Taney 25,561
Texas 21,476
Vernon 19,041
Warren 19,534
Washington 20,380
Wayne 11,543
Webster 23,753
Worth 2,440
Wright 16,758

Cities, towns, and villages

Adrian 1,582
Advance 1,139
Afton 21,106
Agency 642
Airport Drive 818
Alba 465
Albany 1,958
Alexandria 341
Alma 446
Altenburg 307
Alton 692
Amazonia 257
Amoret 212
Amsterdam 237
Anderson 1,432
Annapolis 363
Anniston 288
Appleton City 1,280
Arbyrd 597
Arcadia 609
Archie 799
Armstrong 310
Arnold 18,828
Asbury 220
Ash Grove 1,128
Ashland 1,252
Atlanta 411
Augusta 263
Aurora 6,459
Auxvasse 821
Ava 2,938
Avondale 550
Bakersfield 292
Ballwin 21,816
Barnard 234
Barnett 215
Battlefield 1,526
Bell City 469
Bella Villa 708
Belle 1,218
Bellefontaine Neighbors 10,922
Bellerive 238
Bellflower 413
Bel-Nor 2,935
Bel-Ridge 3,199
Belton 18,150
Benton 575
Berger 247
Berkeley 12,450
Bernie 1,847
Bertrand 692
Bethany 3,005
Beverly Hills 660
Bevier 643
Billings 989
Birch Tree 599
Birmingham 222
Bismarck 1,579
Black Jack 6,128
Blackburn 308
Blackwater 221
Bland 651
Blodgett 202
Bloomfield 1,800
Bloomsdale 353
Blue Springs 40,153
Bogard 228
Bolckow 253
Bolivar 6,845
Bonne Terre 3,871
Boonville 7,095
Bosworth 334
Bourbon 1,188
Bowling Green 2,976
Branson 3,706
Brashear 318
Braymer 886
Breckenridge 418
Breckenridge Hills 5,404
Brentwood 8,150
Bridgeton 17,779
Bronaugh 211
Brookfield 4,888
Brookline 283
Browning 331
Brunswick 1,074
Bucklin 616
Buckner 2,873
Buffalo 2,414
Bunceton 341
Bunker 390
Burlington Junction 634
Butler 4,099
Butterfield 248
Cabool 2,006
Cainsville 387
Cairo 282
Calhoun 450
California 3,465
Callao 332

Missouri (continued)

Calverton Park 1,404
Camden 238
Camden Point 373
Camdenton 2,561
Cameron 4,831
Campbell 2,165
Canalou 319
Canton 2,623
Cape Girardeau 34,438
Cardwell 792
Carl Junction 4,123
Carrollton 4,406
Carterville 2,013
Carthage 10,747
Caruthersville 7,389
Cassville 2,371
Cedar Hill 1,966
Cedar Hill Lakes 227
Center 552
Centertown 356
Centerview 214
Centralia 3,414
Chaffee 3,059
Chamois 449
Charlack 1,388
Charleston 5,085
Chilhowee 335
Chillicothe 8,804
Clarence 1,026
Clark 257
Clarksburg 358
Clarksdale 287
Clarkson Valley 2,508
Clarksville 480
Clarkton 1,113
Claycomo 1,668
Clayton 13,874
Cleveland 506
Clever 580
Clinton 8,703
Cobalt City 254
Cole Camp 1,054
Columbia 69,101
Conception Junction 236
Concord 19,859
Concordia 2,160
Conway 629
Cool Valley 1,407
Cooter 451
Corder 485
Cottleville 2,936
Country Club 1,755
Country Club Hills 1,316
Cowgill 257
Craig 346
Crane 1,218
Creighton 289
Crestwood 11,234
Creve Coeur 12,304
Crocker 1,077
Crystal City 4,088
Crystal Lake Park 506
Cuba 2,537
Curryville 261
Dadeville 220
Dearborn 480
Deepwater 441
De Kalb 222
Dellwood 5,245
Delta 450
Desloge 4,150
De Soto 5,993
Des Peres 8,395
Dexter 7,559
Diamond 775
Diggins 258
Dixon 1,585
Doniphan 1,713
Doolittle 599
Downing 359
Drexel 936
Dudley 271
Duenweg 940
Duquesne 1,229
Eagleville 275
East Lynne 289
East Prairie 3,416
Easton 232
Edgar Springs 215
Edgerton 565
Edina 1,283
Edmundson 1,111
Eldon 4,419
El Dorado Springs 3,830
Ellington 994
Ellisville 7,545
Ellsinore 405
Elsberry 1,898
Elvins 1,391
Eminence 582
Eolia 389
Essex 531
Esther 1,071
Eureka 4,683
Everton 325
Ewing 463
Excelsior Springs 10,354
Exeter 597
Fair Grove 919
Fair Play 442
Fairfax 699
Fairview 298
Farber 418
Farley 217
Farmington 11,598
Fayette 2,888
Fenton 3,346
Ferguson 22,286
Ferrelview 338
Festus 8,105
Fidelity 235
Fillmore 256
Fisk 422
Flat River 4,823
Flinthill 229
Flordell Hills 950
Florissant 51,206
Foley 209
Fordland 523
Forest City 380
Forsyth 1,175
Fort Leonard Wood 15,863
Frankford 396
Fredericktown 3,950
Freeburg 446
Freeman 480
Frontenac 3,374
Fulton 10,033
Gainesville 659
Galena 401
Gallatin 1,864
Galt 296
Garden City 1,225
Gasconade 253
Gerald 888
Gideon 1,104
Gilliam 212
Gilman City 393
Gladstone 26,243
Glasgow 1,295
Glen Echo Park 304
Glenaire 597
Glendale 5,945
Golden City 794
Goodman 1,094
Gordonville 345
Gower 1,249
Graham 204
Grain Valley 1,898
Granby 1,945
Grandin 233
Grandview 24,967
Grant City 998
Grantwood 904
Green City 671
Green Ridge 452
Greencastle 254
Greendale 426
Greenfield 1,416
Greentop 425
Greenville 437
Greenwood 1,505
Hale 480
Hallsville 917
Hamilton 1,737
Hanley Hills 2,325
Hannibal 18,004
Hardin 598
Harrisonville 7,683
Hartville 495
Hawk Point 472
Hayti 3,280
Hayti Heights 893
Haywood City 263
Hazelwood 15,324
Henrietta 412
Herculaneum 2,263
Hermann 2,754
Hermitage 512
Higbee 639
Higginsville 4,693
High Hill 204
Hillsboro 1,625
Hillsdale 1,948
Holcomb 531
Holden 2,389
Holland 237
Hollister 2,628
Holt 311
Holts Summit 2,292
Homestown 230
Hopkins 575
Hornersville 629
Houston 2,118
Houston Lake 303
Houstonia 283
Howardville 440
Humansville 1,084
Hume 287
Hunnewell 219
Huntleigh 392
Huntsville 1,567
Hurdland 212
Iberia 650
Independence 112,301
Iron Gates 309
Irondale 474
Ironton 1,539
Jackson 9,256
Jamesport 570
Jamestown 298
Jasper 994
Jefferson City 35,481
Jennings 15,905
Jerico Springs 247
Jonesburg 630
Joplin 40,961
Josephville 445
Junction City 326
Kahoka 2,195
Kansas City 435,146
Kearney 1,790
Kelso 526
Kennett 10,941
Keytesville 564
Kidder 241
Kimberling City 1,590
King City 986
Kingston 279
Kingsville 279
Kinloch 2,702
Kirksville 17,152
Kirkwood 27,291
Knob Noster 2,261
Knox City 262
La Belle 655
Laclede 410
Laddonia 581
Ladue 8,847
La Grange 1,102
Lake Lotawana 2,141
Lake Mykee Town 257
Lake Ozark 681
Lake St. Louis 7,400
Lake Tapawingo 761
Lake Waukomis 1,027
Lake Winnebago 741
Lakeland 351
Lakeshire 1,467
Lamar 4,168
La Monte 995
Lanagan 501
Lancaster 785
La Plata 1,401
Laredo 205
Lathrop 1,794
Lawson 1,876
Leadington 201
Leadwood 1,247
Leasburg 289
Leawood 736
Lebanon 9,983
Lees Summit 46,418
Leeton 632
Lemay 18,005
Levasy 279
Lewistown 453
Lexington 4,860
Liberal 684
Liberty 20,459
Licking 1,328
Lilbourn 1,378
Lincoln 874
Linn 1,148
Linn Creek 232
Linneus 364
Lockwood 1,041
Lone Jack 392
Louisiana 3,967
Lowry City 723
Macks Creek 272
Macon 5,571
Madison 518
Maitland 338
Malden 5,123
Malta Bend 289
Manchester 6,542
Mansfield 1,429
Maplewood 9,962
Marble Hill 1,447
Marceline 2,645
Marionville 1,920
Marlborough 1,949
Marquand 278
Marshall 12,711
Marshfield 4,374
Marston 691
Marthasville 674
Martinsburg 337
Maryland Heights 25,407
Maryville 10,663
Matthews 614
Maysville 1,176
Mayview 279
Meadville 360
Memphis 2,094
Mendon 207
Mercer 297
Meta 249
Mexico 11,290
Middletown 217
Milan 1,767
Mill Spring 252
Miller 753
Mindenmines 346
Miner 1,218
Mineral Point 384
Missouri City 348
Moberly 12,839
Moline Acres 2,710
Monett 6,529
Monroe City 2,701
Montgomery City 2,281
Montrose 440
Morehouse 1,068
Morley 683
Morrisville 293
Moscow Mills 924
Mound City 1,273
Mount Vernon 3,726
Mountain Grove 4,182
Mountain View 2,036
Murphy 9,342
Napoleon 233
Naylor 642
Neelyville 381
Neosho 9,254
Nevada 8,597
New Bloomfield 480
New Cambria 223
New Florence 801
New Franklin 1,107
New Hampton 320
New Haven 1,757
New London 988
New Madrid 3,350
New Melle 486
Newburg 589
Newtonia 204
Niangua 459
Nixa 4,707
Noel 1,169
Norborne 856
Normandy 4,480
North Kansas City 4,130
Northmoor 441
Northwoods 5,106
Norwood 449
Norwood Court 888
Novinger 542
Oak Grove 402
Oak Grove 4,565
Oak Ridge 202
Oakland 1,593
Oakview 351
Oakwood 212
Oakwood Park 213
Odessa 3,695
O'Fallon 18,695
Old Monroe 242
Olivette 7,573
Olympian Village 752
Oran 1,164
Oregon 935
Oronogo 595
Orrick 935
Osage Beach 2,599
Osborn 400
Osceola 755
Otterville 507
Overland 17,987
Owensville 2,325
Ozark 4,243
Pacific 4,350
Pagedale 3,771
Palmyra 3,371
Paris 1,486
Parkdale 212
Parkville 2,402
Parkway 277
Parma 995
Pasadena Hills 1,165
Pasadena Park 532
Pattonsburg 414
Peculiar 1,777
Perry 711
Perryville 6,933
Pevely 2,831
Piedmont 2,166
Pierce City 1,382
Pilot Grove 714
Pilot Knob 783
Pine Lawn 5,092
Pineville 580
Platte City 2,947
Platte Woods 427
Plattsburg 2,248
Pleasant Hill 3,827
Pleasant Hope 360
Pleasant Valley 2,731
Polo 539
Poplar Bluff 16,996
Portage Des Sioux 503
Portageville 3,401
Potosi 2,683
Prairie Home 215
Princeton 1,021
Purcell 359
Purdin 217
Purdy 977
Puxico 819
Queen City 704
Qulin 384
Ravenwood 409
Raymondville 425
Raymore 5,592
Raytown 30,601
Redings Mill 204
Reeds Spring 411
Republic 6,292
Rich Hill 1,317
Richland 2,029
Richmond 5,738
Richmond Heights 10,448
Ridgeway 379
Risco 434
Rivermines 459
Riverside 3,010
Riverview 3,242
Rocheport 255
Rock Hill 5,217
Rockaway Beach 275
Rock Port 1,438
Rogersville 995
Rolla 14,090
Rosebud 380
Rushville 306
Russellville 869
Saginaw 384
St. Ann 14,489
St. Charles 54,555
St. Clair 3,917
St. Elizabeth 257
St. George 1,270
St. James 3,256
St. John 7,466
St. Joseph 71,852
St. Louis 396,685
St. Martins 717
St. Marys 461
St. Paul 1,192
St. Peters 45,779
St. Robert 1,730
St. Thomas 263
Ste. Genevieve 4,411
Salem 4,486
Salisbury 1,881
Sappington 10,917
Sarcoxie 1,330
Savannah 4,352
Schell City 292
Scott City 4,292
Sedalia 19,800
Seligman 593
Senath 1,622
Seneca 1,885
Seymour 1,636
Shelbina 2,172
Shelbyville 582
Sheldon 464
Shoal Creek Drive 296
Shrewsbury 6,416
Sibley 367
Sikeston 17,641
Silver Creek 513
Skidmore 404
Slater 2,186
Smithton 532
Smithville 2,525
South West City 600
Spanish Lake 20,322
Sparta 751
Spickard 326
Springfield 140,494
Stanberry 1,310
Steele 2,395
Steelville 1,465
Stewartsville 732
Stockton 1,579
Stotts City 235
Stoutland 207
Stover 964
Strafford 1,166
Sturgeon 838
Sugar Creek 3,982
Sullivan 5,661
Summersville 571
Sunset Hills 4,915
Sweet Springs 1,595
Sycamore Hills 667
Taneyville 279
Taos 802
Tarkio 2,243
Thayer 1,996
Theodosia 235
Tipton 2,026
Town and Country 9,519
Tracy 287
Trenton 6,129
Trimble 405
Troy 3,811
Truesdale 285
Twin Oaks 506
Union 5,909
Union Star 432
Unionville 1,989
University City 40,087
Uplands Park 499
Urbana 350
Urich 498
Valley Park 4,165
Van Buren 893
Vandalia 2,683
Velda 1,597
Velda Village Hills 1,315
Verona 546
Versailles 2,365
Viburnum 743
Vienna 611
Vinita Park 2,001
Vinita Terrace 338
Walker 283
Walnut Grove 549
Wardell 325
Wardsville 513
Warrensburg 15,244
Warrenton 3,564
Warsaw 1,696
Warson Woods 2,049
Washburn 362
Washington 10,704
Waverly 837
Wayland 391
Waynesville 3,207
Weatherby Lake 1,613
Weaubleau 436
Webb City 7,449
Webster Groves 22,987
Wellington 779
Wellston 3,612
Wellsville 1,430
Wentzville 5,088
West Plains 8,913
Weston 1,528
Westphalia 287
Westwood 309
Wheatland 363
Wheaton 637
Wheeling 284
Whiteman AFB 4,174
Wilbur Park 522
Willard 2,177
Williamsville 391
Willow Springs 2,038
Wilson City 210
Winchester 1,678
Windsor 3,044
Winfield 672
Winona 1,081
Winston 251
Woods Heights 708
Woodson Terrace 4,362
Wright City 1,250
Wyaconda 347
Wyatt 376

Montana ■ population 803,655

Metropolitan areas

Billings 113,419
Great Falls 77,691

Counties

Beaverhead 8,424
Big Horn 11,337
Blaine 6,728
Broadwater 3,318
Carbon 8,080
Carter 1,503
Cascade 77,691
Chouteau 5,452
Custer 11,697
Daniels 2,266
Dawson 9,505
Deer Lodge 10,278
Fallon 3,103
Fergus 12,083
Flathead 59,218
Gallatin 50,463
Garfield 1,589
Glacier 12,121
Golden Valley 912
Granite 2,548
Hill 17,654
Jefferson 7,939
Judith Basin 2,282
Lake 21,041
Lewis and Clark 47,495
Liberty 2,295
Lincoln 17,481
Madison 5,989
McCone 2,276
Meagher 1,819
Mineral 3,315
Missoula 78,687
Musselshell 4,106
Park 14,562
Petroleum 519
Phillips 5,163
Pondera 6,433
Powder River 2,090
Powell 6,620
Prairie 1,383
Ravalli 25,010
Richland 10,716
Roosevelt 10,999
Rosebud 10,505
Sanders 8,669
Sheridan 4,732
Silver Bow 33,941
Stillwater 6,536
Sweet Grass 3,154
Teton 6,271
Toole 5,046
Treasure 874
Valley 8,239
Wheatland 2,246
Wibaux 1,191
Yellowstone 113,419
Yellowstone National Park 52

Cities and towns

Alberton 354
Anaconda 10,278
Arlee 489
Ashland 484
Bainville 165
Baker 1,818
Bearcreek 37

Belgrade 3,411
Belt 571
Big Sandy 740
Big Timber 1,557
Billings 81,151
Boulder 1,316
Bozeman 22,660
Bridger 692
Broadus 572
Broadview 133
Brockton 365
Browning 1,170
Busby 409
Butte 33,941
Cascade 729
Charlo 358
Chester 942
Chinook 1,512
Choteau 1,741
Circle 805
Clyde Park 282
Colstrip 3,035
Columbia Falls 2,942
Columbus 1,573
Conrad 2,891
Crow Agency 1,446
Culbertson 796
Cut Bank 3,329
Darby 625
Deer Lodge 3,378
Denton 350
Dillon 3,991
Dodson 137
Drummond 264
Dutton 392
East Glacier Park 326
East Helena 1,538
Ekalaka 439
Ennis 773
Eureka 1,043
Fairfield 660
Fairview 869
Flaxville 88
Forsyth 2,178
Fort Benton 1,660
Fort Peck 325
Frazer 403
Froid 195
Fromberg 370
Geraldine 299
Glasgow 3,572
Glendive 4,802
Grass Range 159
Great Falls 55,097
Hamilton 2,737
Hardin 2,940
Harlem 882
Harlowton 1,049
Havre 10,201
Hays 333
Heart Butte 499
Helena 24,569
Hingham 181
Hobson 226
Hot Springs 411
Hysham 361
Ismay 19
Joliet 522
Jordan 494
Judith Gap 133
Kalispell 11,917
Kevin 185
Lame Deer 1,918
Laurel 5,686
Lavina 151
Lewistown 6,051
Libby 2,532
Lima 265
Livingston 6,701
Lodge Grass 517
Malstrom AFB 5,938
Malta 2,340
Manhattan 1,034
Medicine Lake 357
Melstone 166
Miles City 8,461
Missoula 42,918
Moore 211
Nashua 375
Neihart 53
Opheim 145
Outlook 109
Pablo 1,298
Philipsburg 925
Plains 992
Plentywood 2,136
Plevna 140
Polson 3,283
Poplar 881
Pryor 654
Red Lodge 1,958
Rexford 132
Richey 259
Ronan 1,547
Roundup 1,808
Ryegate 260
Saco 261
St. Ignatius 778
Scobey 1,154
Shelby 2,763
Sheridan 652
Sidney 5,217
Stanford 529
Stevensville 1,221
Sunburst 437
Superior 881
Terry 659
Thompson Falls 1,319
Three Forks 1,203
Townsend 1,635
Troy 953
Twin Bridges 374
Valier 519
Virginia City 142
Walkerville 605
West Yellowstone 913
Westby 253
White Sulphur Springs 963
Whitefish 4,368
Whitehall 1,067
Wibaux 628
Winifred 150
Winnett 188
Wolf Point 2,880

Nebraska ■ population 1,584,617

Metropolitan areas

Lincoln 213,641
Omaha 618,262 (535,634 in Neb.; 82,628 in Ia.)
Sioux City (Ia.) 115,018 (98,276 in Ia.; 16,742 in Nebr.)

Counties

Adams 29,625
Antelope 7,965
Arthur 462
Banner 852
Blaine 675
Boone 6,667
Box Butte 13,130
Boyd 2,835
Brown 3,657
Buffalo 37,447
Burt 7,868
Butler 8,601
Cass 21,318
Cedar 10,131
Chase 4,381
Cherry 6,307
Cheyenne 9,494
Clay 7,123
Colfax 9,139
Cuming 10,117
Custer 12,270
Dakota 16,742
Dawes 9,021
Dawson 19,940
Deuel 2,237
Dixon 6,143
Dodge 34,500
Douglas 416,444
Dundy 2,582
Fillmore 7,103
Franklin 3,938
Frontier 3,101
Furnas 5,553
Gage 22,794
Garden 2,460
Garfield 2,141
Gosper 1,928
Grant 769
Greeley 3,006
Hall 48,925
Hamilton 8,862
Harlan 3,810
Hayes 1,222
Hitchcock 3,750
Holt 12,599
Hooker 793
Howard 6,055
Jefferson 8,759
Johnson 4,673
Kearney 6,629
Keith 8,584
Keya Paha 1,029
Kimball 4,108
Knox 9,534
Lancaster 213,641
Lincoln 32,508
Logan 878
Loup 683
Madison 32,655
McPherson 546
Merrick 8,042
Morrill 5,423
Nance 4,275
Nemaha 7,980
Nuckolls 5,786
Otoe 14,252
Pawnee 3,317
Perkins 3,367
Phelps 9,715
Pierce 7,827
Platte 29,820
Polk 5,675
Red Willow 11,705
Richardson 9,937
Rock 2,019
Saline 12,715
Sarpy 102,583
Saunders 18,285
Scotts Bluff 36,025
Seward 15,450
Sheridan 6,750
Sherman 3,718
Sioux 1,549
Stanton 6,244
Thayer 6,635
Thomas 851
Thurston 6,936
Valley 5,169
Washington 16,607
Wayne 9,364
Webster 4,279
Wheeler 948
York 14,428

Cities and villages

Adams 472
Ainsworth 1,870
Albion 1,916
Alda 540
Alexandria 224
Allen 331
Alliance 9,765
Alma 1,226
Amherst 231
Ansley 555
Arapahoe 1,001
Arcadia 385
Arlington 1,178
Arnold 679
Ashland 2,136
Atkinson 1,380
Auburn 3,443
Aurora 3,810
Avoca 254
Axtell 707
Bancroft 494
Bartley 339
Bassett 739
Battle Creek 997
Bayard 1,196
Beatrice 12,354
Beaver City 707
Beaver Crossing 448
Beemer 672
Bellevue 30,982
Bellwood 395
Benedict 230
Benkelman 1,193
Bennet 544
Bennington 866
Bertrand 708
Big Springs 495
Bladen 280
Blair 6,860
Bloomfield 1,181
Blue Hill 810
Blue Springs 431
Boys Town 794
Bradshaw 330
Brady 331
Brainard 326
Bridgeport 1,581
Broken Bow 3,778
Brule 411
Bruning 332
Burwell 1,278
Butte 452
Cairo 733
Callaway 539
Cambridge 1,107
Campbell 432
Carroll 237
Cedar Bluffs 591
Cedar Creek 334
Cedar Rapids 396
Central City 2,868
Ceresco 825
Chadron 5,588
Chambers 341
Chapman 292
Chappell 979
Chester 351
Clarks 379
Clarkson 699
Clatonia 296
Clay Center 825
Clearwater 401
Coleridge 596
Columbus 19,480
Cook 333
Cortland 393
Cozad 3,823
Craig 228
Crawford 1,115
Creighton 1,223
Creston 220
Crete 4,841
Crofton 820
Culbertson 795
Curtis 791
Dakota City 1,470
Dalton 282
Dannebrog 324
Davenport 383
David City 2,522
Decatur 641
Deshler 892
De Witt 598
Diller 298
Dix 229
Dodge 693
Doniphan 736
Dorchester 614
Duncan 387
Dwight 227
Eagle 1,047
Edgar 600
Elgin 731
Elkhorn 1,398
Elm Creek 852
Elmwood 584
Elwood 679
Emerson 791
Eustis 452
Ewing 449
Exeter 661
Fairbury 4,335
Fairfield 458
Fairmont 708
Falls City 4,769
Firth 471
Fort Calhoun 648
Franklin 1,112
Fremont 23,680
Friend 1,111
Fullerton 1,452
Garland 247
Geneva 2,310
Genoa 1,082
Gering 7,946
Gibbon 1,525
Giltner 367
Glenville (Glenvil) 304
Gordon 1,803
Gothenburg 3,232
Grand Island 39,386
Grant 1,239
Greeley 562
Greenwood 531
Gresham 253
Gretna 2,249
Guide Rock 290
Hadar 291
Hallam 309
Hampton 432
Harrison 291
Hartington 1,583
Harvard 976
Hastings 22,837
Hay Springs 693
Hebron 1,765
Hemingford 953
Henderson 999
Hershey 579
Hickman 1,081
Hildreth 364
Holdrege 5,671
Homer 553
Hooper 850
Hoskins 307
Howells 615
Humboldt 1,003
Humphrey 741
Hyannis 210
Imperial 2,007
Indianola 672
Johnson 323
Juniata 811
Kearney 24,396
Kenesaw 818
Kennard 371
Kimball 2,574
Laurel 981
La Vista 9,840
Lawrence 323
Leigh 447
Lewellen 307
Lexington 6,601
Lincoln 191,972
Lindsay 321
Lodgepole 368
Long Pine 396
Loomis 376
Louisville 998
Loup City 1,104
Lyman 452
Lynch 296
Lyons 1,144
Madison 2,135
Marquette 211
Maxwell 285
Maywood 313
McCook 8,112
McCool Junction 372
Mead 513
Meadow Grove 332
Merna 377
Milford 1,886
Milligan 328
Minden 2,749
Mitchell 1,743
Morrill 974
Mullen 554
Murdock 267
Murray 418
Nebraska City 6,547
Neligh 1,742
Nelson 627
Newcastle 271
Newman Grove 787
Niobrara 376
Norfolk 21,476
North Bend 1,249
North Loup 361
North Platte 22,605
Oakdale 362
Oakland 1,279
Odell 291
Offutt AFB 10,883
Ogallala 5,095
Omaha 335,795
O'Neill 3,852
Orchard 439
Ord 2,481
Orleans 490
Osceola 879
Oshkosh 986
Osmond 774
Overton 547
Oxford 949
Palisade 381
Palmer 753
Palmyra 545
Panama 207
Papillion 10,372
Pawnee City 1,008
Paxton 536
Pender 1,208
Peru 1,110
Petersburg 388
Phillips 316
Pierce 1,615
Pilger 361
Plainview 1,333
Platte Center 387
Plattsmouth 6,412
Pleasanton 372
Plymouth 455
Polk 345
Ponca 877
Potter 388
Ralston 6,236
Randolph 983
Ravenna 1,317
Red Cloud 1,204
Rising City 341
Rushville 1,127
St. Edward 822
St. Paul 2,009
Santee 365
Sargent 710
Schuyler 4,052
Scotia 318
Scottsbluff 13,711
Scribner 950
Seward 5,634
Shelby 690
Shelton 954
Shickley 360
Sidney 5,959
Silver Creek 625
Snyder 280
South Sioux City 9,677
Spalding 592
Spencer 536
Springfield 1,426
Springview 304
Stanton 1,549
Staplehurst 281
Stapleton 299
Sterling 451
Stratton 427
Stromsburg 1,241
Stuart 650
Superior 2,397
Sutherland 1,032
Sutton 1,353
Syracuse 1,646
Table Rock 308
Talmage 246
Tecumseh 1,702
Tekamah 1,852
Terrytown 656
Thedford 243
Tilden 895
Trenton 656
Trumbull 225
Uehling 273
Ulysses 256
Unadilla 294
Union 299
Utica 718
Valentine 2,826
Valley 1,775
Valparaiso 481
Verdigre 607
Verdon 242
Waco 211
Wahoo 3,681
Wakefield 1,082
Wallace 308
Walthill 747
Waterloo 479
Wauneta 675
Wausa 598
Waverly 1,869
Wayne 5,142
Weeping Water 1,008
West Point 3,250
Western 264
Weston 299
Wilber 1,527
Wilcox 349
Winnebago 705
Winside 434
Wisner 1,253
Wolbach 280
Wood River 1,156
Wymore 1,611
Wynot 213
York 7,884
Yutan 626

Nevada ■ population 1,206,152

Metropolitan areas

Las Vegas 741,459
Reno 254,667

Counties

Carson City 40,443
Churchill 17,938
Clark 741,459
Douglas 27,637
Elko 33,530
Esmeralda 1,344
Eureka 1,547
Humboldt 12,844
Lander 6,266
Lincoln 3,775
Lyon 20,001
Mineral 6,475
Nye 17,781
Pershing 4,336
Storey 2,526
Washoe 254,667
White Pine 9,264

Cities and towns

Battle Mountain 3,542
Beatty 1,623
Boulder City 12,567
Caliente 1,111
Carlin 2,220
Carson City 40,443
Dayton 2,217
East Las Vegas 11,087
Elko 14,736
Ely 4,756
Fallon 6,438
Fallon Station 1,092
Fernley 5,164
Gabbs 667
Gardnerville 2,177
Gardnerville Ranchos 7,455
Hawthorne 4,162
Henderson 64,942
Incline Village [-Crystal Bay] 7,119
Indian Springs 1,164
Kingsbury 2,238
Las Vegas 258,295
Lovelock 2,069
McDermitt 373
McGill 1,258
Mesquite 1,871
Minden 1,441
Nellis AFB 8,377

Nevada (continued)

New Washoe City 2,875
North Las Vegas 47,707
Owyhee 908
Pahrump 7,424
Paradise 124,682
Reno 133,850
Schurz 617
Silver Springs 2,253
Sparks 53,367
Stateline 1,379
Sun Valley 11,391
Sunrise Manor 95,362
Tonopah 3,616
Wadsworth 640
Wells 1,256
Winchester 23,365
Winnemucca 6,134
Yerington 2,367
Zephyr Cove [-Round Hill Village] 1,434

New Hampshire ■ population 1,113,915

Metropolitan areas

Lawrence-Haverhill (Mass.) 393,516 (283,828 in Mass.; 109,688 in N.H.)
Lowell (Mass.) 273,067 (263,659 in Mass.; 9,408 in N.H.)
Manchester 147,809
Nashua 180,557
Portsmouth-Dover-Rochester 223,578 (174,642 in N.H.; 48,936 in Me.)

Counties

Belknap 49,216
Carroll 35,410
Cheshire 70,121
Coos 34,828
Grafton 74,929
Hillsborough 336,073
Merrimack 120,005
Rockingham 245,845
Strafford 104,233
Sullivan 38,592

Cities and towns

Acworth 776
Albany 536
Alexandria 1,190
Allenstown 4,649
Alstead 1,721
Alton 3,286
Amherst 9,068
Andover 1,883
Antrim 1,325 ▲2360
Ashland 1,915
Atkinson 5,188
Auburn 4,085
Barnstead 3,100
Barrington 6,164
Bartlett 2,290
Bath 784
Bedford 12,563
Belmont 5,796
Bennington 1,236
Benton 330
Berlin 11,824
Bethlehem 2,033
Boscawen 3,586
Bow 5,500
Bradford 1,405
Brentwood 2,590
Bridgewater 796
Bristol 1,483 ▲2,537
Brookfield 518
Brookline 2,410
Campton 2,377
Canaan 3,045
Candia 3,557
Canterbury 1,687
Carroll 528
Center Harbor 996
Charlestown 1,173 ▲4,630
Chatham 268
Chester 2,691
Chesterfield 3,112
Chichester 1,942
Claremont 13,902
Clarksville 232
Colebrook 2,444
Columbia 661
Concord 36,006
Contoocook 1,334
Conway 1,604 ▲7,940
Cornish 1,659
Croydon 627
Dalton 827
Danbury 881
Danville 2,534
Deerfield 3,124
Deering 1,707
Derry 20,446 ▲29,603
Dorchester 392
Dover 25,042
Dublin 1,474
Dummer 327
Dunbarton 1,759
Durham 9,236 ▲11,818
East Kingston 1,352
East Merrimack 3,656
Easton 223
Eaton 362
Effingham 941
Enfield 1,560 ▲3,979
Epping 1,384 ▲5,162
Epsom 3,591
Errol 292
Exeter 9,556 ▲12,481
Farmington 3,567 ▲5,739
Fitzwilliam 2,011
Francestown 1,217
Franconia 811
Franklin 8,304
Freedom 935
Fremont 2,576
Gilford 5,867
Gilmanton 2,609
Gilsum 745
Goffstown 14,621
Gorham 1,910 ▲3,173
Goshen 742
Grafton 923
Grantham 1,247
Greenfield 1,519
Greenland 2,768
Greenville 1,135 ▲2,231
Groton 318
Groveton 1,255
Hampstead 6,732
Hampton 7,989 ▲12,278
Hampton Falls 1,503
Hancock 1,604
Hanover 6,538 ▲9,212
Harrisville 981
Haverhill 4,164
Hebron 386
Henniker 1,693 ▲4,151
Hill 814
Hillsborough 1,826 ▲4,498
Hinsdale 1,718 ▲3,936
Holderness 1,694
Hollis 5,705
Hooksett 2,573 ▲8,767
Hopkinton 4,806
Hudson 7,626 ▲19,530
Jackson 678
Jaffrey 2,558 ▲5,361
Jefferson 965
Keene 22,430
Kensington 1,631
Kingston 5,591
Laconia 15,743
Lancaster 1,859 ▲3,522
Landaff 350
Langdon 580
Lebanon 12,183
Lee 3,729
Lempster 947
Lincoln 1,229
Lisbon 1,246 ▲1,664
Litchfield 5,516
Littleton 4,633 ▲5,827
Londonderry 10,114 ▲19,781
Loudon 4,114
Lyman 388
Lyme 1,496
Lyndeborough 1,294
Madbury 1,404
Madison 1,704
Manchester 99,567
Marlborough 1,211 ▲1,927
Marlow 650
Mason 1,212
Meredith 1,654 ▲4,837
Merrimack 22,156
Middleton 1,183
Milan 1,295
Milford 8,015 ▲11,795
Milton 3,691
Monroe 746
Mont Vernon 1,812
Moultonborough 2,956
Nashua 79,662
Nelson 535
New Boston 3,214
New Castle 840
New Durham 1,974
New Hampton 1,606
New Ipswich 4,014
New London 3,180
Newbury 1,347
Newfields 888
Newington 990
Newmarket 4,917 ▲7,157
Newport 3,772 ▲6,110
Newton 3,473
North Conway 2,032
North Hampton 3,637
Northfield 4,263
Northumberland 2,492
Northwood 3,124
Nottingham 2,939
Orange 237
Orford 1,008
Ossipee 3,309
Pelham 9,408
Pembroke 6,561
Peterborough 2,685 ▲5,239
Piermont 624
Pinardville 4,654
Pittsburg 901
Pittsfield 1,717 ▲3,701
Plainfield 2,056
Plaistow 7,316
Plymouth 3,967 ▲5,811
Portsmouth 25,925
Randolph 371
Raymond 2,516 ▲8,713
Richmond 877
Rindge 4,941
Rochester 26,630
Rollinsford 2,645
Roxbury 248
Rumney 1,446
Rye 4,612
Salem 25,746
Salisbury 1,061
Sanbornton 2,136
Sandown 4,060
Sandwich 1,066
Seabrook 6,503
Sharon 299
Shelburne 437
Somersworth 11,249
South Hampton 740
South Hooksett 3,638
Springfield 788
Stark 518
Stewartstown 1,048
Stoddard 622
Strafford 2,965
Stratford 927
Stratham 4,955
Sugar Hill 464
Sullivan 706
Sunapee 2,559
Suncook 5,214
Surry 667
Sutton 1,457
Swanzey 6,236
Tamworth 2,165
Temple 1,194
Thornton 1,505
Tilton 3,240
Tilton-Northfield 3,081
Troy 2,097
Tuftonboro 1,842
Unity 1,341
Wakefield 3,057
Walpole 3,210
Warner 2,250
Warren 820
Washington 628
Weare 6,193
Webster 1,405
Wentworth 630
West Swanzey 1,055
Westmoreland 1,596
Whitefield 1,041 ▲1,909
Wilmot 935
Wilton 1,165 ▲3,122
Winchester 1,735 ▲4,038
Windham 9,000
Wolfeboro 2,783 ▲4,807
Woodstock 1,167
Woodsville 1,122

▲ Entire township, including rural area.

New Jersey ■ population 7,748,634

Metropolitan areas

Allentown-Bethlehem-Easton, Pa. 686,688 (595,081 in Pa.; 91,607 in N.J.)
Atlantic City 319,416
Bergen-Passaic 1,278,440
Jersey City 553,099
Middlesex-Somerset-Hunterdon 1,019,835
Monmouth-Ocean 986,327
Newark 1,824,321
Philadelphia, Pa. 4,856,881 (3,728,909 in Pa.; 1,127,972 in N.J.)
Trenton 325,824
Vineland-Millville-Bridgeton 138,053
Wilmington, Del. 578,587 (441,946 in Del.; 65,294 in N.J.; 71,347 in Md.)

Counties

Atlantic 224,327
Bergen 825,380
Burlington 395,066
Camden 502,824
Cape May 95,089
Cumberland 138,053
Essex 778,206
Gloucester 230,082
Hudson 553,099
Hunterdon 107,776
Mercer 325,824
Middlesex 671,780
Monmouth 553,124
Morris 421,353
Ocean 433,203
Passaic 453,060
Salem 65,294
Somerset 240,279
Sussex 130,943
Union 493,819
Warren 91,607

Cities, towns, townships, boroughs, and villages

Aberdeen 17,038
Absecon 7,298
Alexandria 3,594
Allamuchy 3,484
Allendale 5,900
Allenhurst 759
Allentown 1,828
Alloway 1,371 ▲2,795
Alpha 2,530
Alpine 1,716
Andover 700 ▲5,438
Annandale 1,074
Asbury Park 16,799
Atlantic City 37,986
Atlantic Highlands 4,629
Audubon 9,205
Audubon Park 1,150
Avalon 1,809
Avenel 15,504
Avon-by-the-Sea 2,165
Barnegat 1,160 ▲12,235
Barnegat Light 675
Barrington 6,774
Bass River 1,580
Bay Head 1,226
Bayonne 61,444
Beach Haven 1,475
Beach Haven West 4,237
Beachwood 9,324
Bedminster 7,086
Belleville 34,213
Bellmawr 12,603
Belmar 5,877
Belvidere 2,669
Bergenfield 24,458
Berkeley 37,319
Berkeley Heights 11,980
Berlin 5,672 ▲5,466
Bernards 17,199
Bernardsville 6,597
Bethlehem 3,104
Beverly 2,973
Blackwood 5,120
Blairstown 5,331
Bloomfield 45,061
Bloomingdale 7,530
Bloomsbury 890
Bogota 7,824
Boonton 8,343 ▲3,566
Bordentown 7,683
Bordentown 4,341
Bound Brook 9,487
Bradley Beach 4,475
Branchville 851
Brass Castle 1,419
Brick 66,473
Bridgeton 18,942
Bridgewater 32,509
Brielle 4,406
Brigantine 11,354
Brooklawn 1,805
Browns Mills 11,429
Budd Lake 7,272
Buena 4,441
Buena Vista 7,655
Burlington 9,835 ▲12,454
Butler 7,392
Byram 8,048
Caldwell 7,549
Califon 1,073
Camden 87,492
Cape May 4,668
Cape May Court House 4,426
Cape May Point 248
Carlstadt 5,510
Carneys Point 7,686 ▲8,443
Carteret 19,025
Cedar Glen Lakes 1,611
Cedar Grove 12,053
Chatham 8,007 ▲9,361
Cherry Hill 69,348
Chesilhurst 1,526
Chester 5,958
Chester 1,214
Chesterfield 5,152
Cinnaminson 14,583
Clark 14,629
Clayton 6,155
Clementon 5,601
Cliffside Park 20,393
Clifton 71,742
Clinton 10,816
Clinton 2,054
Closter 8,094
Collings Lakes 2,046
Collingswood 15,289
Colonia 18,238
Colts Neck 8,559
Commercial 5,026
Corbin City 412
Country Lake Estates 4,492
Cranbury 2,500
Crandon Lakes 1,177
Cranford 22,633
Cresskill 7,558
Crestwood Village 8,030
Dayton 4,321
Deal 1,179
Deerfield 2,933
Delanco 3,316
Delaware 4,512
Delran 13,178
Demarest 4,800
Dennis 5,574
Denville 13,812
Deptford 24,137
Dover 76,371
Dover 15,115
Downe 1,702
Dumont 17,187
Dunellen 6,528
Eagleswood 1,476
East Amwell 4,332
East Brunswick 43,548
East Freehold 3,842
East Greenwich 5,258
East Hanover 9,926
East Newark 2,157
East Orange 73,552
East Rutherford 7,902
East Windsor 22,353
Eastampton 4,962
Eatontown 13,800
Edgewater 5,001
Edgewater Park 8,388
Edison 88,680
Egg Harbor 24,544
Egg Harbor City 4,583
Elizabeth 110,002
Elk 3,806
Elmer 1,571
Elmwood Park 17,623
Elsinboro 1,170
Elwood [-Magnolia] 1,487
Emerson 6,930
Englewood 24,850
Englewood Cliffs 5,634
Englishtown 1,268
Erma 2,045
Essex Fells 2,139
Estell Manor 1,404
Evesham 35,309
Ewing 34,185
Fair Haven 5,270
Fair Lawn 30,548
Fairfield 5,699
Fairfield 7,615
Fairton 1,359
Fairview 10,733
Fanwood 7,115
Far Hills 657
Farmingdale 1,462
Fieldsboro 579
Flemington 4,047
Florence 10,266
Florence [-Roebling] 8,564
Florham Park 8,521
Folsom 2,181
Fords 14,392
Forked River 4,243
Fort Lee 31,997
Frankford 5,114
Franklin 2,404
Franklin 2,851
Franklin 42,780
Franklin 14,482
Franklin 4,977
Franklin Lakes 9,873
Fredon 2,763
Freehold 24,710
Freehold 10,742
Frelinghuysen 1,779
Frenchtown 1,528
Galloway 23,330
Garfield 26,727
Garwood 4,227
Gibbsboro 2,383
Gibbstown 3,902
Gilford Park 8,668
Glassboro 15,614
Glen Gardner 1,665
Glen Ridge 7,076
Glen Rock 10,883
Glendora 5,201
Gloucester 53,797
Gloucester City 12,649
Green 2,709
Green Brook 4,460
Greenwich 1,899
Greenwich 5,102
Greenwich 911
Guttenberg 8,268
Hackensack 37,049
Hackettstown 8,120
Haddon 14,837
Haddon Heights 7,860
Haddonfield 11,628
Hainesport 3,249
Haledon 6,951
Hamburg 2,566
Hamilton 86,553
Hamilton 16,012
Hammonton 12,208
Hampton 4,438
Hampton 1,515
Hanover 11,538
Harding 3,640
Hardwick 1,235
Hardyston 5,275
Harmony 2,653
Harrington Park 4,623
Harrison 4,715
Harrison 13,425
Harvey Cedars 362
Hasbrouck Heights 11,488

Haworth 3,384
Hawthorne 17,084
Hazlet 21,976
Helmetta 1,211
High Bridge 3,886
Highland Lakes 4,550
Highland Park 13,279
Highlands 4,849
Hightstown 5,126
Hillsborough 28,808
Hillsdale 9,750
Hillside 21,044
Hi-Nella 1,045
Hoboken 33,397
Ho-Ho-Kus 3,935
Holiday City [-Berkeley] 14,293
Holland 4,892
Holmdel 11,532
Hopatcong 15,586
Hope 1,719
Hopewell 11,590
Hopewell 4,215
Hopewell 1,968
Howell 38,987
Independence 3,940
Interlaken 910
Irvington 61,018
Island Heights 1,470
Jackson 33,233
Jamesburg 5,294
Jefferson 17,825
Jersey City 228,537
Keansburg 11,069
Kearny 34,874
Kendall Park 7,127
Kenilworth 7,574
Keyport 7,586
Kingwood 3,325
Kinnelon 8,470
Knowlton 2,543
Lacey 22,141
Lafayette 1,902
Lake Mohawk 8,930
Lake Telemark 1,121
Lakehurst 3,078
Lakewood 26,095 ▲45,048
Lambertville 3,927
Laurel Springs 2,341
Laurence Harbor 6,361
Lavallette 2,299
Lawnside 2,841
Lawrence 25,787
Lawrence 2,433
Lawrenceville 6,446
Lebanon 5,679
Lebanon 1,036
Leisuretowne 2,552
Leonardo 3,788
Leonia 8,365
Liberty 2,493
Lincoln Park 10,978
Lincroft 6,193
Linden 36,701
Lindenwold 18,734
Linwood 6,866
Little Egg Harbor 13,333
Little Falls 11,294
Little Ferry 9,989
Little Silver 5,721
Livingston 26,609
Loch Arbour 380
Lodi 22,355
Logan 5,147
Long Beach 3,407
Long Branch 28,658
Long Valley 1,744
Longport 1,224
Lopatcong 5,052
Lower 20,820
Lower Alloways Creek 1,858
Lumberton 6,705
Lyndhurst 18,262
Madison 15,850
Madison Park 7,490
Magnolia 4,861
Mahwah 17,905
Manahawkin 1,594
Manalapan 26,716
Manasquan 5,369
Manchester 35,976
Mannington 1,693
Mansfield 3,874
Mansfield 7,154
Mantoloking 334
Mantua 10,074
Manville 10,567
Maple Shade 19,211
Maplewood 21,652
Margate City 8,431
Marlboro 27,974
Marlton 10,228
Matawan 9,270
Maurice River 6,648
Mays Landing 2,090
Maywood 9,473
McGuire AFB 7,580
Medford 20,526
Medford Lakes 4,462
Mendham 4,537
Mendham 4,890
Mercerville [-Hamilton Square] 26,873
Merchantville 4,095
Metuchen 12,804
Middle 14,771
Middlesex 13,055
Middletown 68,183
Midland Park 7,047
Milford 1,273
Millburn 18,630
Millstone 5,069
Millstone 450
Milltown 6,968
Millville 25,992
Mine Hill 3,333
Monmouth Beach 3,303
Monmouth Junction 1,570
Monroe 22,255
Monroe 26,703
Montague 2,832
Montclair 37,729
Montgomery 9,612
Montvale 6,946
Montville 15,600
Moonachie 2,817
Moorestown 16,116
Moorestown [-Lenola] 13,242
Morris 19,952
Morris Plains 5,219
Morristown 16,189
Mount Arlington 3,630
Mount Ephraim 4,517
Mount Holly 10,639
Mount Laurel 30,270
Mount Olive 21,282
Mountain Lakes 3,847
Mountainside 6,657
Mullica 5,896
Mullica Hill 1,117
Mystic Islands 7,400
National Park 3,413
Neptune 28,148
Neptune City 4,997
Netcong 3,311
New Brunswick 41,711
New Egypt 2,327
New Hanover 9,546
New Milford 15,990
New Providence 11,439
Newark 275,221
Newfield 1,592
Newton 7,521
North Arlington 13,790
North Beach Haven 2,413
North Bergen 48,414
North Brunswick 31,287
North Caldwell 6,706
North Cape May 3,574
North Haledon 7,987
North Hanover 9,994
North Plainfield 18,820
North Wildwood 5,017
Northfield 7,305
Northvale 4,563
Norwood 4,858
Nutley 27,099
Oakhurst 4,130
Oakland 11,997
Oaklyn 4,430
Ocean 25,058
Ocean 5,416
Ocean Acres 5,587
Ocean City 15,512
Ocean Gate 2,078
Oceanport 6,146
Ogdensburg 2,722
Old Bridge 22,151 ▲56,475
Old Tappan 4,254
Oldmans 1,683
Oradell 8,024
Orange 29,925
Oxford 1,790
Palisades Park 14,536
Palmyra 7,056
Paramus 25,067
Park Ridge 8,102
Parsippany-Troy Hills 48,478
Passaic 7,826
Passaic 58,041
Paterson 140,891
Paulsboro 6,577
Peapack [and Gladstone] 2,111
Pemberton 1,367 ▲31,342
Pemberton Heights 2,941
Pennington 2,537
Penns Grove 5,228
Pennsauken 34,738
Pennsville 12,218 ▲13,794
Pequannock 12,844
Perth Amboy 41,967
Phillipsburg 15,757
Pilesgrove 3,250
Pine Beach 1,954
Pine Hill 9,854
Piscataway 47,089
Pitman 9,365
Pittsgrove 8,121
Plainfield 46,567
Plainsboro 14,213
Pleasant Plains 2,577
Pleasantville 16,027
Plumsted 6,005
Pohatcong 3,591
Point Pleasant 18,177
Point Pleasant Beach 5,112
Pomona 2,624
Pompton Lakes 10,539
Port Monmouth 3,558
Port Norris 1,701
Port Reading 3,977
Port Republic 992
Presidential Lakes Estates 2,450
Princeton 12,016 ▲13,198
Princeton Junction 2,362
Princeton North 4,386
Prospect Park 5,053
Quinton 2,511
Rahway 25,325
Ramblewood 6,181
Ramsey 13,228
Randolph 19,974
Raritan 15,616
Raritan 5,798
Readington 13,400
Red Bank 10,636
Ridgefield 9,996
Ridgefield Park 12,454
Ridgewood 24,152
Ringwood 12,623
Rio Grande 2,505
River Edge 10,603
River Vale 9,410
Riverdale 2,370
Riverside 7,974
Riverton 2,775
Robertsville 9,841
Rochelle Park 5,587
Rockaway 19,572
Rockaway 6,243
Rockleigh 270
Rocky Hill 693
Roosevelt 884
Roseland 4,847
Roselle 20,314
Roselle Park 12,805
Rosenhayn 1,053
Roxbury 20,429
Rumson 6,701
Runnemede 9,042
Rutherford 17,790
Saddle Brook 13,296
Saddle River 2,950
Salem 6,883
Sandyston 1,732
Sayreville 34,986
Scotch Plains 21,160
Sea Bright 1,693
Sea Girt 2,099
Sea Isle City 2,692
Seabrook Farms 1,457
Seaside Heights 2,366
Seaside Park 1,871
Secaucus 14,061
Sewaren 2,569
Shamong 5,765
Shiloh 408
Ship Bottom 1,352
Shrewsbury 1,098
Shrewsbury 3,096
Silverton 9,175
Somerdale 5,440
Somers Point 11,216
Somerset 22,070
Somerville 11,632
South Amboy 7,863
South Belmar 1,482
South Bound Brook 4,185
South Brunswick 25,792
South Hackensack 2,106
South Harrison 1,919
South Orange 16,390
South Plainfield 20,489
South River 13,692
South Toms River 3,869
Southampton 10,202
Sparta 15,157
Spotswood 7,983
Spring Lake 3,499
Spring Lake Heights 5,341
Springfield 3,028
Springfield 13,420
Stafford 13,325
Stanhope 3,393
Stillwater 4,253
Stockton 629
Stone Harbor 1,025
Stow Creek 1,437
Stratford 7,614
Strathmore 7,060
Succasunna [-Kenvil] 11,781
Summit 19,757
Surf City 1,375
Sussex 2,201
Swedesboro 2,024
Tabernacle 7,360
Teaneck 37,825
Tenafly 13,326
Tewksbury 4,803
Tinton Falls 12,361
Toms River 7,524
Totowa 10,177
Trenton 88,675
Tuckerton 3,048
Turnersville 3,843
Twin Rivers 7,715
Union 5,078
Union 50,024
Union Beach 6,156
Union City 58,012
Upper 10,681
Upper Deerfield 6,927
Upper Freehold 3,277
Upper Pittsgrove 3,140
Upper Saddle River 7,198
Ventnor City 11,005
Vernon 21,211
Verona 13,597
Victory Gardens 1,314
Villas 8,136
Vineland 54,780
Voorhees 24,559
Waldwick 9,757
Wall 20,244
Wallington 10,828
Wanamassa 4,530
Wanaque 9,711
Wantage 9,487
Waretown 1,283
Warren 10,830
Washington 9,245
Washington 5,367
Washington 15,592
Washington 5,815
Washington 41,960
Washington 805
Washington 6,474
Watchung 5,110
Waterford 10,940
Wayne 47,025
Weehawken 12,385
Wenonah 2,331
West Amwell 2,251
West Belmar 2,498
West Caldwell 10,422
West Cape May 1,026
West Deptford 19,380
West Freehold 11,166
West Long Branch 7,690
West Milford 25,430
West New York 38,125
West Orange 39,103
West Paterson 10,982
West Wildwood 453
West Windsor 16,021
Westampton 6,004
Westfield 28,870
Westville 4,573
Westwood 10,446
Weymouth 1,957
Wharton 5,405
White 3,603
White Horse 9,397
White House Station 1,287
White Meadow Lake 8,002
Whitesboro [-Burleigh] 2,080
Wildwood 4,484
Wildwood Crest 3,631
Williamstown 10,891
Willingboro 36,291
Winfield 1,576
Winslow 30,087
Wood-Ridge 7,506
Woodbine 2,678
Woodbridge 17,434 ▲93,086
Woodbury 10,904
Woodbury Heights 3,392
Woodcliff Lake 5,303
Woodland 2,063
Woodlynne 2,547
Woodstown 3,154
Woolwich 1,459
Wrightstown 3,843
Wyckoff 15,372
Yardville [Groveville] 9,248
Yorketown 6,313

▲ Entire township, including rural area.

New Mexico ■ population 1,521,779

Metropolitan areas

Albuquerque 480,577
Las Cruces 135,510
Santa Fe 117,043

Counties

Bernalillo 480,577
Catron 2,563
Chaves 57,849
Cibola 23,794
Colfax 12,925
Curry 42,207
De Baca 2,252
Doña Ana 135,510
Eddy 48,605
Grant 27,676
Guadalupe 4,156
Harding 987
Hidalgo 5,958
Lea 55,765
Lincoln 12,219
Los Alamos 18,115
Luna 18,110
McKinley 60,686
Mora 4,264
Otero 51,928
Quay 10,823
Rio Arriba 34,365
Roosevelt 16,702
San Juan 63,319
San Miguel 91,605
Sandoval 25,743
Santa Fe 98,928
Sierra 9,912
Socorro 14,764
Taos 23,118
Torrance 10,285
Union 4,124
Valencia 45,235

Cities, towns, and villages

Agua Fria 3,717
Alamogordo 27,596
Albuquerque 384,736
Alcalde 308
Anthony 5,160
Artesia 10,610
Aztec 5,479
Bayard 2,598
Belen 6,547
Bernalillo 5,960
Black Rock 858
Bloomfield 5,214
Bosque Farms 3,791
Cannon AFB 3,312
Capitan 842
Carlsbad 24,952
Carlsbad North 1,167
Carrizozo 1,075
Causey 57
Central 1,835
Chama 1,048
Chamisal 272
Chimayo 2,789
Cimarron 774
Clayton 2,484
Cloudcroft 636
Clovis 30,954
Cochiti Pueblo 1,342
Columbus 641
Corona 215
Corrales 5,453
Crownpoint 2,108
Cuba 760
Cuyamungue 329
Deming 10,970
Des Moines 168
Dexter 898
Doña Ana 1,202
Dora 167
Dulce 2,438
Eagle Nest 189
Elida 201
Encino 131
Española 8,389
Estancia 792
Eunice 2,676
Farmington 33,997
Flora Vista 1,021
Floyd 117
Folsom 71
Fort Sumner 1,269
Gallup 19,154
Grady 110
Grants 8,626
Grenville 24
Hagerman 961
Hatch 1,136
Hobbs 29,115
Holloman AFB 5,891
Hope 101
House 85
Hurley 1,534
Isleta Pueblo 1,703
Jal 2,156
Jemez Pueblo 1,301
Jemez Springs 413
Kirtland 3,552
La Cienega 1,066
Laguna 434
Lake Arthur 336
La Luz 1,625
Las Cruces 62,126
Las Vegas 14,753
Logan 870
Lordsburg 2,951
Los Alamos 11,455
Los Lunas 6,013
Los Ranchos de Albuquerque 3,955
Loving 1,243
Lovington 9,322
Magdalena 861
Maxwell 247
Melrose 662
Mescalero 1,159
Mesilla 1,975
Mesita 627
Mexican Springs 242
Milan 1,911
Moriarty 1,399
Mosquero 164
Mountainair 926
Nambe 1,246
Naschitti 323
Newcomb 388
North Valley 12,507
Paguate 492
Paradise Hills 5,513
Pecos 1,012
Peña Blanca 300
Peñasco 648
Peralta 3,182
Placitas 1,611
Portales 10,690
Questa 1,707
Ranchos de Taos 1,779
Raton 7,372
Red River 387
Reserve 319
Rio Communities 3,233
Rio Rancho 32,505
Roswell 44,654
Roy 362
Ruidoso 4,600
Ruidoso Downs 920
San Felipe Pueblo 1,557
San Ildefonso 447
San Jon 277
San Juan Pueblo 5,209
San Ysidro 233
Sandia 6,742
Sandia Pueblo 3,971
Santa Ana Pueblo 476
Santa Clara 10,193
Santa Cruz 2,504
Santa Fe 55,859
Santa Rosa 2,263
Santo Domingo Pueblo 2,866
Shiprock 7,687
Silver City 10,683
Socorro 8,159
South Valley 35,701
Springer 1,262
Sunland Park [-Meadow Vista] 8,179
Taos 4,065
Taos Pueblo 1,187
Tatum 768
Tesuque 1,490
Texico 966
Tijeras 340
Tohatchi 661
Tome [-Adelino] 1,695
Truth or Consequences 6,221
Tucumcari 6,831
Tularosa 2,615
University Park 4,520
Vaughn 633
Virden 108
Wagon Mound 319
White Rock 6,192
White Sands 2,616
Willard 183
Williamsburg 456
Zuni Pueblo 5,857

New York ■ population 18,044,505

Metropolitan areas

Albany-Schenectady-Troy 874,304
Binghamton 264,497
Buffalo 968,532
Elmira 95,195
Glens Falls 118,539
Nassau-Suffolk 2,609,212
New York City 8,546,846
Niagara Falls 220,756
Orange County 307,647
Poughkeepsie 259,462
Rochester 1,002,410
Syracuse 659,864
Utica-Rome 316,633

Counties

Albany 292,594
Allegany 50,470
Bronx 1,203,789
Broome 212,160
Cattaraugus 84,234
Cayuga 82,313
Chautauqua 141,895
Chemung 95,195
Chenango 51,768
Clinton 85,969
Columbia 62,982
Cortland 48,963
Delaware 47,225
Dutchess 259,462
Erie 968,532
Essex 37,152
Franklin 46,540
Fulton 54,191
Genesee 60,060
Greene 44,739
Hamilton 5,279
Herkimer 65,797
Jefferson 110,943
Kings 2,300,664
Lewis 26,796
Livingston 62,372
Madison 69,120
Monroe 713,968
Montgomery 51,981
Nassau 1,287,348
New York 1,487,536
Niagara 220,756
Oneida 250,836
Onondaga 468,973
Ontario 95,101
Orange 307,647
Orleans 41,846
Oswego 121,771
Otsego 60,517
Putnam 83,941
Queens 1,951,598
Rensselaer 154,429
Richmond 378,977
Rockland 265,475
St. Lawrence 111,974
Saratoga 181,276
Schenectady 149,285
Schoharie 31,859
Schuyler 18,662
Seneca 33,683
Steuben 99,088
Suffolk 1,321,864
Sullivan 69,277
Tioga 52,337
Tompkins 94,097
Ulster 165,304
Warren 59,209
Washington 59,330
Wayne 89,123
Westchester 874,866
Wyoming 42,507
Yates 22,810

Cities and villages

Adams 1,753
Addison 1,842
Afton 838
Akron 2,906
Albany 101,082
Albertson 5,166
Albion 5,863
Alden 2,457
Alexander 445
Alexandria Bay 1,194
Alfred 4,559
Allegany 1,980
Almond 458
Altamont 1,519
Altmar 336
Amityville 9,286
Amsterdam 20,714
Andes 292
Andover 1,125
Angelica 963
Angola 2,231
Antwerp 739
Apalachin 1,208
Arcade 2,081
Ardsley 4,272
Argyle 295
Arkport 770
Arlington 11,948
Asharoken 807
Athens 1,708
Atlantic Beach 1,933
Attica 2,630
Auburn 31,258
Aurora 687
Avoca 1,033
Avon 2,995
Babylon 12,249
Bainbridge 1,550
Baldwin 22,719
Baldwinsville 6,591
Ballston Spa 4,937
Balmville 2,963
Barker 569
Barneveld 272
Batavia 16,310
Bath 5,801
Baxter Estates 961
Bay Shore 21,279
Bayport 7,702
Bayville 7,193
Beacon 13,243
Bedford 1,828
Belle Terre 839
Bellerose 1,101
Bellmore 16,438
Bellport 2,572
Belmont 1,006
Bemus Point 383
Bergen 1,103
Bethpage 15,761
Big Flats 2,658
Binghamton 53,008
Black River 1,349
Blasdell 2,900
Bloomingburg 316
Bloomingdale 9,556
Bohemia 9,556
Bolivar 1,261
Boonville 2,220
Brentwood 45,218
Brewerton 2,954
Brewster 1,566
Briarcliff Manor 7,070
Bridgewater 537
Brighton 34,455
Brightwaters 3,265
Brinckerhoff 2,756
Broadalbin 1,397
Brockport 8,749
Brocton 1,387
Bronx 1,203,789
Bronxville 6,028
Brookhaven 3,118
Brooklyn 2,300,664
Brookville 3,716
Brownville 1,138
Brushton 522
Buchanan 1,970
Buffalo 328,123
Burdett 372
Burke 209
Caledonia 2,262
Calverton 4,759
Cambridge 1,906
Camden 2,552
Camillus 1,150
Canajoharie 2,278
Canandaigua 10,725
Canaseraga 684
Canastota 4,673
Candor 869
Canisteo 2,421
Canton 6,379
Cape Vincent 683
Carle Place 5,107
Carmel 4,800
Carthage 4,344
Cassadaga 768
Castile 1,078
Castleton-on-Hudson 1,491
Castorland 292
Cato 581
Catskill 4,690
Cattaraugus 1,100
Cayuga 556
Cayuga Heights 3,457
Cazenovia 3,007
Cedarhurst 5,716
Celoron 1,232
Center Moriches 5,987
Centereach 26,720
Centerport 5,333
Central Islip 26,028
Central Square 1,671
Centre Island 439
Champlain 1,273
Chateaugay 845
Chatham 1,920
Chaumont 593
Cheektowaga 84,387
Cherry Creek 539
Cherry Valley 617
Chester 3,270
Chittenango 4,734
Churchville 1,731
Clayton 2,160
Clayville 463
Cleveland 784
Clifton Springs 2,175
Clinton 2,238
Clyde 2,409
Cobleskill 5,268
Cohocton 859
Cohoes 16,825
Cold Brook 310
Cold Spring 1,998
Cold Spring Harbor 4,789
Colonie 8,019
Commack 36,124
Congers 8,003
Constableville 307
Cooperstown 2,180
Copenhagen 876
Copiague 20,769
Coram 30,111
Corfu 755
Corinth 2,760
Corning 11,938
Cornwall on Hudson 3,093
Cortland 19,801
Coxsackie 2,789
Croghan 664
Croton-on-Hudson 7,018
Crown Heights 3,200
Cuba 1,690
Cutchogue 2,627
Dannemora 4,005
Dansville 5,002
Deer Park 28,840
Deferiet 293
Delanson 361
Delevan 1,214
Delhi 3,064
Delmar 8,360
Depew 17,673
Deposit 1,936
DeRuyter 568
De Witt 8,244
Dexter 1,030
Dix Hills 25,849
Dobbs Ferry 9,940
Dolgeville 2,452
Dresden 339
Dryden 1,908
Dundee 1,588
Dunkirk 13,989
Earlville 883
East Aurora 6,647
East Bloomfield 541
East Farmingdale 4,510
East Glenville 6,518
East Hampton 1,402
East Hills 6,746
East Islip 14,325
East Massapequa 19,550
East Meadow 36,909
East Middletown 4,974
East Moriches 4,021
East Northport 20,411
East Patchogue 20,195
East Quogue 4,372
East Randolph 629
East Rochester 6,932
East Rockaway 10,152
East Syracuse 3,343
East Williston 2,515
Eastchester 18,537
Eden 3,088
Edwards 487
Elba 703
Elbridge 1,219
Ellenville 4,243
Ellicottville 513
Elmira 33,724
Elmira Heights 4,359
Elmont 28,612
Elmsford 3,938
Elwood 10,916
Endicott 13,531
Endwell 12,602
Esperance 324
Evans Mills 661
Fabius 310
Fair Haven 895
Fairmount 12,266
Fairport 5,943
Fairview 4,811
Falconer 2,653
Farmingdale 8,022
Farmingdale 14,842
Farnham 427
Fayetteville 4,248
Fillmore 455
Firthcliffe 4,427
Fishkill 1,957
Flanders 3,231
Fleischmanns 351
Floral Park 15,947
Florida 2,497
Flower Hill 4,490
Fonda 1,007
Forestville 738
Fort Ann 419
Fort Edward 3,561
Fort Johnson 615
Fort Plain 2,416
Fort Salonga 9,176
Frankfort 2,693
Franklin 409
Franklin Square 28,205
Franklinville 1,739
Fredonia 10,436
Freeport 39,894
Freeville 437
Frewsburg 1,817
Fulton 12,929
Fultonville 748
Gainesville 340
Garden City 21,686
Garden City Park 7,437
Gardnertown 4,209
Gates [-North Gates] 14,995
Geneseo 7,187
Geneva 14,143
Gilbertsville 388
Glen Cove 24,149
Glen Park 527
Glens Falls 15,023
Glens Falls North 7,978
Gloversville 16,656
Goldens Bridge 1,589
Goshen 5,255
Gouverneur 4,604
Gowanda 2,901
Grand View-on-Hudson 271
Granville 2,646
Great Neck 8,745
Great Neck Estates 2,790
Great Neck Plaza 5,897
Greece 15,632
Green Island 2,490
Greene 1,812
Greenlawn 13,208
Greenport 2,070
Greenville 9,528
Greenwich 1,961
Greenwood Lake 3,208
Groton 2,398
Hagaman 1,377
Hamburg 10,442
Hamilton 3,790
Hammondsport 929
Hampton Bays 7,893
Hancock 1,330
Hannibal 613
Harriman 2,288
Harris Hill 4,577
Harrison 23,308
Harrisville 703
Hartsdale 9,587
Hastings-on-Hudson 8,000
Hauppauge 19,750
Haverstraw 9,438
Haviland 3,605
Hawthorne 4,764
Head of the Harbor 1,354
Hempstead 49,453
Herkimer 7,945
Hermon 407
Herricks 4,097
Heuvelton 771
Hewlett 6,620
Hewlett Bay Park 440
Hewlett Harbor 1,193
Hewlett Neck 547
Hicksville 40,174
Highland 4,492
Highland Falls 3,937
Hillburn 892
Hillcrest 6,447
Hilton 5,216
Hobart 385
Holbrook 25,273
Holcomb 790
Holland Patent 411
Holley 1,890
Holtsville 14,972
Homer 3,476
Honeoye Falls 2,340
Hoosick Falls 3,490
Hornell 9,877
Horseheads 6,802
Horseheads North 3,003
Houghton 1,740
Hudson 8,034
Hudson Falls 7,651
Hunter 429
Huntington 18,243
Huntington Bay 1,521
Huntington Station 28,247
Hurley 4,644
Ilion 8,888
Interlaken 680
Inwood 7,767
Irondequoit 52,322
Irvington 6,348
Island Park 4,860
Islip 18,924
Islip Terrace 5,530
Ithaca 29,541
Jamestown 34,681
Jamestown West 2,633
Jefferson Valley [-Yorktown] 14,118
Jeffersonville 484
Jericho 13,141
Johnson City 16,890
Johnstown 9,058
Jordan 1,325
Keeseville 1,854
Kenmore 17,180
Kensington 1,104
Kinderhook 1,293
Kings Park 17,773
Kings Point 4,843
Kingston 23,095
Kiryas Joel 7,437
Lackawanna 20,585
Lacona 593
Lake Carmel 8,489
Lake Erie Beach 4,509
Lake George 933
Lake Grove 9,612
Lake Katrine 1,998
Lake Placid 2,485
Lake Ronkonkoma 18,997
Lake Success 2,484
Lakeview 5,476
Lakewood 3,564
Lancaster 11,940
Lansing 3,281
Larchmont 6,181
Latham 10,131
Lattingtown 1,859
Laurel Hollow 1,748
Laurens 293
Lawrence 6,513
Leicester 405
Le Roy 4,974
Levittown 53,286
Lewiston 3,048
Liberty 4,128
Lima 2,165
Limestone 459
Lincoln Park 2,457
Lindenhurst 26,879
Lisle 361
Little Falls 5,829
Little Valley 1,188
Liverpool 2,624
Livingston Manor 1,482
Livonia 1,434
Lloyd Harbor 3,343
Lockport 24,426
Lodi 364
Long Beach 33,510
Loudonville 10,822
Lowville 3,632
Lynbrook 19,208
Lyncourt 4,516
Lyndonville 953
Lyons 4,280
Lyons Falls 698
Macedon 1,400
Madison 316
Mahopac 7,755
Malone 6,777
Malverne 9,054
Mamaroneck 17,325
Manchester 1,598
Manhasset 7,718
Manhattan 1,487,536
Manlius 4,764
Manorhaven 5,672
Mannsville 444
Marathon 1,107
Marcellus 1,840
Margaretville 639
Marlboro 2,200
Massapequa 22,018
Massapequa Park 18,044
Massena 11,719
Mastic 13,778
Mastic Beach 10,293
Matinecock 872
Mattituck 3,902
Mattydale 6,418
Maybrook 2,802
Mayfield 817
Mayville 1,636
McGraw 1,074
Mechanicville 5,249
Medford 21,274
Medina 6,686
Melrose Park 2,091
Melville 12,586
Menands 4,333
Meridian 351
Merrick 23,042
Mexico 1,555
Middle Island 7,848
Middleburgh 1,436
Middleport 1,876
Middletown 24,160
Middleville 624
Milford 462
Mill Neck 977
Millbrook 1,339
Miller Place 9,315
Millerton 884
Millport 342
Mineola 18,994
Mineville [-Witherbee] 1,740
Minoa 3,745
Mohawk 2,986
Monroe 6,672
Monsey 13,986
Montauk 3,001
Montgomery 2,696
Monticello 6,597
Montour Falls 1,845
Mooers 467
Moravia 1,559
Morris 642
Morrisonville 1,742
Morristown 490
Morrisville 2,732
Mount Kisco 9,108
Mount Morris 3,102
Mount Sinai 8,023
Mount Vernon 67,153
Munnsville 438
Munsey Park 2,692
Muttontown 3,024
Myers Corner 5,599
Nanuet 14,065
Naples 1,237
Nassau 1,254
Nelliston 569
Nelsonville 585
Nesconset 10,712
New Berlin 1,220
New Cassel 10,257
New City 33,673
New Hartford 2,111
New Hyde Park 9,728
New Paltz 5,463
New Rochelle 67,265
New Square 2,605
New Windsor 8,898
New York City 7,322,564
New York Mills 3,534
Newark 9,849
Newark Valley 1,082
Newburgh 26,454
Newfane 3,001
Newport 676
Niagara Falls 61,840
Nichols 573
Niskayuna 4,942
Nissequogue 1,620
Norfolk 1,412
North Amityville 13,849
North Babylon 18,081
North Bay Shore 12,799
North Bellmore 19,707
North Bellport 8,182
North Collins 1,335
North Great River 3,964
North Haven 713
North Hills 3,453
North Hornell 822
North Lindenhurst 10,563
North Massapequa 19,365
North Merrick 12,113
North New Hyde Park 14,359
North Patchogue 7,374
North Syracuse 7,363
North Tarrytown 8,152
North Tonawanda 34,989
North Valley Stream 14,574
North Wantagh 12,276
Northport 7,572
Northville 1,180
Norwich 7,613
Norwood 1,841
Noyack 2,059
Nunda 1,347
Nyack 6,558
Oakdale 7,875
Oakfield 1,818
Oceanside 32,423
Odessa 986
Ogdensburg 13,521
Olcott 1,432
Old Bethpage 5,610
Old Brookville 1,823
Old Field 765
Old Westbury 3,897
Olean 16,946
Oneida 10,850
Oneida Castle 671
Oneonta 13,954
Orange Lake 5,196
Orchard Park 3,280
Oriskany 1,450
Oriskany Falls 795
Ossining 22,582
Oswego 19,195
Otego 1,068
Otisville 1,078
Ovid 660
Owego 4,442
Oxford 1,738
Oyster Bay 6,687
Oyster Bay Cove 2,109
Painted Post 1,950
Palatine Bridge 520
Palmyra 3,566
Panama 468
Parish 473
Patchogue 11,060
Pawling 1,974
Pearl River 15,314
Peekskill 19,536
Pelham 6,413
Pelham Manor 5,443
Penn Yan 5,248
Perry 4,219
Perrysburg 404
Peru 1,565
Phelps 1,978
Philadelphia 1,478
Philmont 1,623
Phoenix 2,435
Piermont 2,163
Pike 384
Pine Bush 1,445
Pittsford 1,488
Plainedge 8,739
Plainview 26,207
Plandome 1,347
Plandome Heights 852
Plandome Manor 790
Plattsburgh 21,255
Plattsburgh AFB 5,483
Pleasantville 6,592
Poland 444
Pomona 2,611
Poquott 770
Port Byron 1,359
Port Chester 24,728
Port Dickinson 1,785
Port Ewen 3,444
Port Henry 1,263
Port Jefferson 7,455
Port Jefferson Station 7,232
Port Jervis 9,060

Port Leyden 723
Port Washington .. 15,387
Port Washington
North 2,736
Portville 1,040
Potsdam 10,251
Poughkeepsie 28,844
Prospect 312
Pulaski 2,525
Queens 1,951,598
Quogue 898
Randolph 1,298
Ransomville 1,542
Ravena 3,547
Red Creek 566
Red Hook 1,794
Red Oaks Mill 4,906
Remsen 518
Rensselaer 8,255
Rensselaer Falls 316
Rhinebeck 2,725
Richburg 494
Richfield Springs ... 1,565
Richmondville 843
Ridge 11,734
Ripley 1,189
Riverhead 8,814
Riverside 585
Rochester 231,636
Rockville Centre .. 24,727
Rocky Point 8,596
Roessleville 10,753
Rome 44,350
Ronkonkoma 20,391
Roosevelt 15,030
Rosendale 1,284
Roslyn 1,965
Roslyn Estates 1,184
Roslyn Harbor 1,114
Roslyn Heights 6,405
Rotterdam 21,228
Round Lake 765
Rouses Point 2,377
Rushville 609
Russell Gardens 1,027
Rye 14,936
Sackets Harbor 1,313
Saddle Rock 832
Sag Harbor 2,134
St. James 12,703
St. Johnsville 1,825
Salamanca 6,566
Salem 958
Sands Point 2,477
Sandy Creek 793
Saranac Lake 5,377
Saratoga Springs .. 25,001
Saugerties 3,915
Saugerties South ... 2,346
Savona 974
Sayville 16,550
Scarsdale 16,987
Schaghticoke 794
Schenectady 65,566
Schenevus 513
Schoharie 1,045
Schuylerville 1,364
Scotchtown 8,765
Scotia 7,359
Scottsville 1,912
Sea Cliff 5,054
Seaford 15,597
Selden 20,608
Seneca Falls 7,370
Setauket
[-East Setauket] .. 13,634
Sharon Springs 543
Sherburne 1,531
Sherman 694
Sherrill 2,864
Shirley 22,936
Shoreham 540
Shortsville 1,485
Sidney 4,720
Silver Creek 2,927
Silver Springs 852
Sinclairville 708
Skaneateles 2,724
Sloan 3,830
Sloatsburg 3,035
Smithtown 25,638
Smyrna 211
Sodus 1,904
Sodus Point 1,190
Solvay 6,717
Sound Beach 9,102
South Corning 1,025
South Dayton 601
South Fallsburg 2,115
South Farm-
ingdale 15,377
South Floral Park ... 1,478
South Glens Falls ... 3,506
South Hill 5,423
South Huntington .. 9,624
South Lockport 7,112
South Nyack 3,352
South Valley
Stream 5,328
Southampton 3,980
Southold 5,192
Southport 7,753
Spackenhill 4,660
Speculator 400
Spencer 815
Spencerport 3,606
Spring Valley 21,802
Springs 4,355
Springville 4,310
Stamford 1,211
Staten Island 378,977
Stewart Manor 2,002
Stillwater 1,531
Stony Brook 13,726
Stony Point 10,587
Stottville 1,369
Suffern 11,055
Sylvan Beach 1,119
Syosset 18,967
Syracuse 163,860
Tannersville 465
Tappan 6,867
Tarrytown 10,739
Theresa 889
Thomaston 2,612
Thornwood 7,025
Ticonderoga 2,770
Tivoli 1,035
Tonawanda 17,284
Town Line 2,721
Troy 54,269
Trumansburg 1,611
Tuckahoe 6,302
Tully 911
Tupper Lake 4,087
Turin 295
Tuxedo Park 706
Unadilla 1,265
Union Springs 1,142
Uniondale 20,328
Unionville 548
Upper Brookville ... 1,453
Upper Nyack 2,084
Utica 68,637
Valatie 1,487
Vales Gate 3,014
Valley Cottage 9,007
Valley Falls 527
Valley Stream 33,946
Van Etten 552
Vernon 1,274
Victor 2,308
Victory 581
Village of the
Branch 1,669
Viola 4,504
Voorheesville 3,225
Waddington 944
Walden 5,836
Wallkill 2,125
Walton 3,326
Wampsville 501
Wantagh 18,567
Wappingers Falls ... 4,605
Warrensburg 3,204
Warsaw 3,830
Warwick 5,984
Washingtonville 4,906
Waterford 2,370
Waterloo 5,116
Watertown 29,429
Waterville 1,664
Watervliet 11,061
Watkins Glen 2,207
Waverly 4,787
Wayland 1,976
Webster 5,464
Weedsport 1,996
Wellsburg 617
Wellsville 5,241
West Babylon 42,410
West Bay Shore 4,907
West Carthage 2,166
West Elmira 5,218
West End 1,825
West Glens Falls 5,964
West Haverstraw ... 9,183
West Hempstead .. 17,689
West Hills 5,849
West Islip 28,419
West Nyack 3,437
West Point 8,024
West Sayville 4,680
West Seneca 47,866
West Winfield 871
Westbury 13,060
Westfield 3,451
Westhampton 2,129
Westhampton
Beach 1,571
Westmere 6,750
Westport 539
Westvale 5,952
White Plains 48,718
Whitehall 3,071
Whitesboro 4,195
Whitney Point 1,054
Williamsville 5,583
Williston Park 7,516
Wilson 1,307
Windsor 1,051
Wolcott 1,544
Woodmere 15,578
Woodridge 783
Woodsburgh 1,190
Wurtsboro 1,048
Wyandanch 8,950
Wyoming 478
Yonkers 188,082
Yorktown Heights .. 7,690
Yorkville 2,972
Youngstown 2,075

North Carolina ■ population 6,657,630

Metropolitan areas

Asheville 174,821
Burlington 108,213
Charlotte- Gastonia-Rock
Hill 1,162,093
(1,030,596 in N.C.;
131,497 in S.C.)
Fayetteville 274,566
Greensboro-Winston-
Salem-High Point
.... 942,091
Hickory-
Morganton 221,700
Jacksonville 149,838
Raleigh-Durham
.... 735,480
Wilmington 120,284

Counties

Alamance 108,213
Alexander 27,544
Alleghany 9,590
Anson 23,474
Ashe 22,209
Avery 14,867
Beaufort 42,283
Bertie 20,388
Bladen 28,663
Brunswick 50,985
Buncombe 174,821
Burke 75,744
Cabarrus 98,935
Caldwell 70,709
Camden 5,904
Carteret 52,556
Caswell 20,693
Catawba 118,412
Chatham 38,759
Cherokee 20,170
Chowan 13,506
Clay 7,155
Cleveland 84,714
Columbus 49,587
Craven 81,613
Cumberland 274,566
Currituck 13,736
Dare 22,746
Davidson 126,677
Davie 27,859
Duplin 39,995
Durham 181,835
Edgecombe 56,558
Forsyth 265,878
Franklin 36,414
Gaston 175,093
Gates 9,305
Graham 7,196
Granville 38,345
Greene 15,384
Guilford 347,420
Halifax 55,516
Harnett 67,822
Haywood 46,942
Henderson 69,285
Hertford 22,523
Hoke 22,856
Hyde 5,411
Iredell 92,931
Jackson 26,846
Johnston 81,306
Jones 9,414
Lee 41,374
Lenoir 57,274
Lincoln 50,319
Macon 23,499
Madison 16,953
Martin 25,078
McDowell 35,681
Mecklenburg 511,433
Mitchell 14,433
Montgomery 23,346
Moore 59,013
Nash 76,677
New Hanover 120,283
Northampton 20,798
Onslow 148,838
Orange 93,851
Pamlico 11,372
Pasquotank 31,298
Pender 28,855
Perquimans 10,447
Person 30,180
Pitt 107,924
Polk 14,416
Randolph 106,546
Richmond 44,518
Robeson 105,179
Rockingham 86,064
Rowan 110,605
Rutherford 56,918
Sampson 47,297
Scotland 33,754
Stanly 51,765
Stokes 37,223
Surry 61,704
Swain 11,268
Transylvania 25,520
Tyrrell 3,856
Union 84,211
Vance 38,892
Wake 423,380
Warren 17,265
Washington 13,997
Watauga 36,952
Wayne 104,666
Wilkes 59,393
Wilson 66,061
Yadkin 30,488
Yancey 15,419

Cities, towns, and villages

Aberdeen 2,700
Ahoskie 4,391
Alamance 258
Albemarle 14,939
Alexander Mills 662
Alliance 583
Andrews 2,551
Angier 2,235
Ansonville 614
Apex 4,968
Arapahoe 430
Archdale 6,913
Arlington 795
Asheboro 16,362
Asheville 61,607
Askewville 201
Atkinson 275
Atlantic Beach 1,938
Aulander 1,209
Aurora 654
Ayden 4,740
Badin 1,481
Bailey 553
Bakersville 332
Balfour 1,118
Banner Elk 933
Barker Heights 1,137
Battleboro 447
Bayboro 733
Beaufort 3,808
Belhaven 2,269
Belmont 8,434
Belwood 631
Benson 2,810
Bent Creek 1,487
Bessemer City 4,698
Bethel 1,842
Beulaville 933
Biltmore Forest 1,327
Biscoe 1,484
Black Creek 615
Black Mountain 5,418
Bladenboro 1,821
Blowing Rock 1,257
Boger City 1,373
Boiling Springs 2,445
Boiling Spring
Lakes 1,650
Bolivia 228
Bolton 531
Bonnie Doone 3,893
Boone 12,915
Boonville 1,009
Bostic 371
Brevard 5,388
Bridgeton 453
Broadway 973
Brogden 3,246
Brookford 451
Brunswick 302
Bryson City 1,145
Buies Creek 2,085
Bunn 364
Burgaw 1,807
Burlington 39,498
Burnsville 1,482
Butner 4,679
Cajah's Mountain ... 2,429
Calabash 1,210
Calypso 481
Cameron 215
Camp Lejeune 36,716
Candor 748
Canton 3,790
Cape Carteret 1,008
Carolina Beach 3,630
Carrboro 11,553
Carthage 976
Cary 43,858
Casar 328
Castalia 261
Castle Hayne 1,182
Catawba 467
Cerro Gordo 227
Chadbourn 2,005
Chapel Hill 38,719
Charlotte 395,934
Cherryville 4,756
China Grove 2,732
Chocowinity 624
Claremont 980
Clarkton 739
Clayton 4,756
Clemmons 6,020
Cleveland 696
Clinton 8,204
Clyde 1,041
Coats 1,493
Cofield 407
Columbia 836
Columbus 812
Concord 27,347
Conetoe 292
Conover 5,465
Conway 759
Cooleemee 971
Cornelius 2,581
Cove City 497
Cramerton 2,371
Creedmoor 1,504
Creswell 361
Cricket 2,015
Crossnore 271
Cullowhee 4,029
Dallas 3,012
Davidson 4,046
Denton 1,292
Dobson 1,195
Dortches 840
Dover 451
Drexel 1,746
Dublin 246
Dunn 8,336
Durham 136,611
Earl 230
East Arcadia 468
East Bend 619
East Flat Rock 3,218
East Laurinburg 302
East Rockingham ... 4,158
East Spencer 2,055
Eastover 1,243
Eden 15,238
Edenton 5,268
Elizabeth City 14,292
Elizabethtown 3,704
Elk Park 486
Elkin 3,790
Ellenboro 514
Ellerbe 1,132
Elm City 1,624
Elon College 4,394
Elroy 4,028
Emerald Isle 2,434
Enfield 3,082
Enochville 2,901
Erwin 4,061
Etowah 1,997
Eureka 282
Fair Bluff 1,068
Fairmont 2,489
Fairplains 2,339
Fairview 1,830
Faison 701
Faith 553
Falcon 216
Fallston 498
Farmville 4,392
Fayetteville 75,695
Flat Rock 1,812
Fletcher 2,787
Forest City 7,475
Forest Oaks 3,054
Fort Bragg 34,744
Fountain 445
Four Oaks 1,308
Foxfire 334
Franklin 2,873
Franklinton 1,615
Franklinville 666
Fremont 1,710
Fuquay-Varina 4,562
Gamewell 3,357
Garland 746
Garner 14,967
Garysburg 1,057
Gaston 1,003
Gastonia 54,732
Gatesville 308
Gibson 532
Gibsonville 3,441
Glen Alpine 563
Glen Raven 2,616
Goldsboro 40,709
Goldston 299
Gorman 1,090
Graham 10,426
Granite Falls 3,253
Granite Quarry 1,646
Greenevers 512
Greensboro 183,521
Greenville 44,972
Grifton 2,393
Grimesland 469
Grover 516
Half Moon 6,306
Halifax 327
Hamilton 544
Hamlet 6,196
Harkers Island 1,759
Harmony 431
Harrisburg 1,625
Havelock 20,268
Haw River 1,855
Hayesville 279
Hays 1,522
Hazelwood 1,678
Hemby Bridge 2,876
Henderson 15,655
Hendersonville 7,284
Hertford 2,105
Hickory 28,301
High Point 69,496
High Shoals 605
Highlands 948
Hildebran 790
Hillsborough 4,263
Hobgood 435
Hoffman 348
Holden Beach 626
Holly Ridge 728
Holly Springs 908
Hookerton 422
Hope Mills 8,184
Hot Springs 478
Hudson 2,819
Huntersville 3,014
Icard 2,553
Indian Trail 1,942
Jackson 592
Jacksonville 30,013
James City 4,279
Jamestown 2,600
Jamesville 612
Jefferson 1,300
Jonesville 1,549
Kannapolis 29,696
Kelford 204
Kenansville 856
Kenly 1,549
Kernersville 10,836
Kill Devil Hills 4,238
King 4,059
Kings Mountain 8,763
Kinston 25,295
Kittrell 228
Kitty Hawk 1,937
Knightdale 1,884
Kure Beach 619
La Grange 2,805
Lake Junaluska 2,482
Lake Lure 691
Lake Waccamaw 954
Landis 2,333
Laurel Park 1,322
Laurinburg 11,643
Lawndale 573
Leland 1,801
Lenoir 14,192
Lewiston 788
Lewisville 3,206
Lexington 16,581
Liberty 2,047
Lilesville 468
Lillington 2,048
Lincolnton 6,847
Littleton 691
Locust 1,940
Long Beach 3,816
Longview 3,229
Louisburg 3,037
Lowell 2,704
Lucama 933
Lumberton 18,601
Macclesfield 493
Madison 2,371
Magnolia 747
Maiden 2,574
Manteo 991
Mar-Mac 3,282
Marietta 206
Marion 4,765
Mars Hill 1,611
Marshall 809
Marshville 2,020
Masonboro 7,010
Matthews 13,651
Maxton 2,373
Mayodan 2,471
Maysville 892
McAdenville 830
McLeansville 1,154
Mebane 4,754
Mesic 310
Micro 417
Middlesex 730
Millers Creek 1,787
Minnesott Beach 266
Mint Hill 11,567
Mocksville 3,399
Monroe 16,127
Montreat 693
Mooresboro 294
Mooresville 9,317
Moravian Falls 1,736
Morehead City 6,046
Morganton 15,085
Morrisville 1,022
Morven 590
Mount Airy 7,156
Mount Gilead 1,336
Mount Holly 7,710
Mount Olive 4,582

North Carolina (continued)

Mount Pleasant 1,027
Mountain Home 1,898
Mulberry 2,339
Murfreesboro 2,580
Murphy 1,575
Myrtle Grove 4,275
Nags Head 1,838
Nashville 3,617
Navassa 445
New Bern 17,363
New Hope 5,694
New Hope 4,491
New London 414
New River Station 9,732
Newland 645
Newport 2,516
Newton 9,304
Newton Grove 511
Norlina 996
North Wilkesboro 3,384
Norwood 1,617
Oak City 389
Oakboro 600
Ocean Isle Beach 523
Ogden 3,228
Old Fort 720
Oriental 786
Oxford 7,913
Parkton 367
Parkwood 4,123
Parmele 321
Patterson Springs 690
Peachland 384
Pembroke 2,241
Pikeville 598
Pilot Mountain 1,181
Pine Knoll Shores 1,360
Pine Level 1,217
Pinebluff 876
Pinehurst 5,103
Pinetops 1,514
Pineville 2,970
Piney Green 8,999
Pink Hill 547
Pittsboro 1,436
Pleasant Garden 2,228
Pleasant Hill 1,114
Plymouth 4,328
Polkton 662
Polkville 1,514
Pollocksville 299
Pope AFB 2,857
Poplar Tent 3,872
Princeton 1,181
Princeville 1,652
Pumpkin Center 2,857
Raeford 3,469
Raleigh 207,951
Ramseur 1,186
Randleman 2,612
Ranlo 1,650
Red Oak 280
Red Springs 3,799
Reidsville 12,183
Rennert 217
Rhodhiss 638
Rich Square 1,058
Richfield 535
Richlands 996
Roanoke Rapids 15,722
Robbins 970
Robbinsville 709
Robersonville 1,940
Rockingham 9,399
Rockwell 1,598
Rocky Mount 48,997
Rolesville 572
Ronda 367
Roper 669
Rose Hill 1,287
Roseboro 1,441
Rosman 385
Rowland 1,139
Roxboro 7,332
Roxobel 244
Rural Hall 1,652
Ruth 366
Rutherford College 1,126
Rutherfordton 3,617
St. Pauls 1,992
St. Stephens 8,734
Salem 2,271
Salemburg 409
Salisbury 23,087
Saluda 488
Sanford 14,475
Saratoga 342
Sawmills 4,088
Saxapahaw 1,178
Scotland Neck 2,575
Seaboard 791
Seagate 5,444
Seagrove 244
Selma 4,600
Severn 260
Shallotte 965
Sharpsburg 1,536
Shelby 14,669
Sherrills Ford 3,185
Siler City 4,808
Silver City 1,343
Silver Lake 4,071
Simpson 410
Smithfield 7,540
Sneads Ferry 2,031
Snow Hill 1,378
South Gastonia 5,487
South Henderson 1,374
South Weldon 1,640
Southern Pines 9,129
Southern Shores 1,447
Southport 2,369
Sparta 1,957
Spencer 3,219
Spindale 4,040
Spring Hope 1,221
Spring Lake 7,524
Spruce Pine 2,010
Staley 204
Stallings 2,132
Stanfield 517
Stanley 2,823
Stanleyville 4,779
Stantonsburg 782
Star 775
Statesville 17,567
Stedman 577
Stem 249
Stokesdale 2,134
Stoneville 1,109
Stonewall 279
Stony Point 1,286
Stovall 409
Summerfield 2,051
Sunset Beach 311
Surf City 970
Swannanoa 3,538
Swansboro 1,165
Swepsonville 1,195
Sylva 1,809
Tabor City 2,330
Tarboro 11,037
Taylorsville 1,566
Teachey 244
Thomasville 15,915
Toast 2,125
Topsail Beach 346
Trent Woods 2,366
Trenton 248
Trinity 5,469
Troutman 1,493
Troy 3,404
Tryon 1,680
Turkey 234
Valdese 3,914
Valley Hill 1,802
Vanceboro 946
Vandemere 299
Vander 1,179
Vass 670
Waco 320
Wade 238
Wadesboro 3,645
Wagram 480
Wake Forest 5,769
Walkertown 1,200
Wallace 2,939
Walnut Cove 1,088
Walnut Creek 623
Wanchese 1,380
Warrenton 949
Warsaw 2,859
Washington 9,075
Washington Park 403
Waxhaw 1,294
Waynesville 6,758
Weaverville 2,107
Webster 410
Weddington 3,803
Welcome 3,377
Weldon 1,392
Wendell 2,822
West Canton 1,119
West Jefferson 1,002
West Marion 1,291
Whispering Pines 1,243
Whitakers 860
White Lake 390
White Plains 1,027
Whiteville 5,078
Wilkesboro 2,573
Williamston 5,503
Wilmington 55,530
Wilson 36,930
Windmere 4,604
Windsor 2,056
Winfall 501
Wingate 2,821
Winston-Salem 143,485
Winterville 2,816
Winton 796
Woodfin 2,736
Woodland 760
Wrightsboro 4,752
Wrightsville Beach 2,937
Yadkinville 2,525
Yanceyville 1,973
Yaupon Beach 734
Youngsville 424
Zebulon 3,173

North Dakota ■ population 641,364

Metropolitan areas

Bismarck 83,831
Fargo-Moorhead (Minn.) 153,296 (102,874 in N. Dak.; 50,422 in Minn.)
Grand Forks 70,683

Counties

Adams 3,174
Barnes 12,545
Benson 7,198
Billings 1,108
Bottineau 8,011
Bowman 3,596
Burke 3,002
Burleigh 60,131
Cass 102,874
Cavalier 6,064
Dickey 6,107
Divide 2,899
Dunn 4,005
Eddy 2,951
Emmons 4,830
Foster 3,983
Golden Valley 2,108
Grand Forks 70,683
Grant 3,549
Griggs 3,303
Hettinger 3,445
Kidder 3,332
La Moure 5,383
Logan 2,847
McHenry 6,528
McIntosh 4,021
McKenzie 6,383
McLean 10,457
Mercer 9,808
Morton 23,700
Mountrail 7,021
Nelson 4,410
Oliver 2,381
Pembina 9,238
Pierce 5,052
Ramsey 12,681
Ransom 5,921
Renville 3,160
Richland 18,148
Rolette 12,772
Sargent 4,549
Sheridan 2,148
Sioux 3,761
Slope 907
Stark 22,832
Steele 2,420
Stutsman 22,241
Towner 3,627
Traill 8,752
Walsh 13,840
Ward 57,921
Wells 5,864
Williams 21,129

Cities

Abercrombie 252
Adams 248
Alexander 216
Anamoose 277
Aneta 314
Arthur 400
Ashley 1,052
Beach 1,205
Belcourt 2,458
Belfield 887
Berthold 409
Beulah 3,363
Binford 233
Bisbee 227
Bismarck 49,256
Bottineau 2,598
Bowbells 498
Bowman 1,741
Buffalo 204
Burlington 995
Buxton 343
Cando 1,564
Cannon Ball 702
Carrington 2,267
Carson 383
Casselton 1,601
Cavalier 1,508
Center 826
Columbus 223
Cooperstown 1,247
Crosby 1,312
Davenport 218
Des Lacs 216
Devils Lake 7,782
Dickinson 16,097
Drake 361
Drayton 961
Dunseith 723
Edgeley 680
Edinburg 284
Edmore 329
Ellendale 1,798
Emerado 483
Enderlin 997
Fairmount 427
Fargo 74,111
Fessenden 655
Finley 543
Flasher 317
Fordville 299
Forman 586
Fort Totten 867
Frontier 218
Gackle 450
Garrison 1,530
Gilby 262
Gladstone 224
Glen Ullin 927
Glenburn 439
Golden Valley 239
Grafton 4,840
Grand Forks 49,425
Grand Forks AFB 9,343
Grandin 213
Granville 236
Grenora 261
Gwinner 585
Halliday 288
Hankinson 1,038
Hannaford 204
Harvey 2,263
Harwood 590
Hatton 800
Hazelton 240
Hazen 2,818
Hebron 888
Hettinger 1,574
Hillsboro 1,488
Hoople 310
Hope 281
Horace 662
Hunter 341
Jamestown 15,571
Kenmare 1,214
Killdeer 722
Kindred 569
Kulm 514
Lakota 898
LaMoure 970
Langdon 2,241
Lansford 249
Larimore 1,464
Leeds 542
Leonard 310
Lidgerwood 799
Lignite 242
Lincoln 1,132
Linton 1,410
Lisbon 2,177
Litchville 205
Maddock 559
Mandan 15,177
Mandaree 367
Manvel 333
Mapleton 682
Max 301
Mayville 2,092
McClusky 492
McVille 559
Medina 387
Michigan 413
Milnor 651
Minnewaukan 401
Minot 34,544
Minot AFB 9,095
Minto 560
Mohall 931
Mott 1,019
Munich 310
Napoleon 930
Neche 434
New England 663
New Leipzig 326
New Rockford 1,604
New Salem 909
New Town 1,388
Noonan 231
Northwood 1,166
Oakes 1,775
Osnabrock 214
Page 266
Park River 1,725
Parshall 943
Pembina 642
Petersburg 219
Pick City 203
Portland 602
Powers Lake 408
Ray 603
Reeder 252
Regent 268
Reile's Acres 210
Reynolds 299
Richardton 625
Riverdale 283
Rock Lake 221
Rolette 623
Rolla 1,286
Rugby 2,909
Rutland 212
St. John 368
St. Thomas 444
Sawyer 319
Scranton 294
Selfridge 242
Sherwood 286
Sheyenne 272
South Heart 322
Stanley 1,371
Stanton 517
Steele 762
Strasburg 553
Surrey 856
Tappen 239
Thompson 930
Tioga 1,278
Tolna 230
Tower City 233
Towner 669
Turtle Lake 681
Underwood 976
Upham 205
Valley City 7,163
Velva 968
Wahpeton 8,751
Walhalla 1,131
Washburn 1,506
Watford City 1,784
West Fargo 12,287
Westhope 578
White Shield 274
Williston 13,131
Willow City 281
Wilton 728
Wimbledon 275
Wing 208
Wishek 1,171
Wyndmere 501
Zap 287

Ohio ■ population 10,887,325

Metropolitan areas

Akron 657,575
Canton 394,106
Cincinnati 1,452,645 (1,130,324 in O.; 283,486 in Ky.; 38,835 in Ind.)
Cleveland 1,831,122
Columbus 1,377,419
Dayton-Springfield 951,270
Hamilton-Middletown 291,479
Huntington (W. Va.)-Ashland (Ky.) 312,529 (138,463 in W. Va.; 112,232 in Ky.; 61,834 in O.)
Lima 154,340
Lorain-Elyria 271,126
Mansfield 126,137
Parkersburg (W. Va.)-Marietta 149,169 (86,915 in W. Va.; 62,254 in O.)
Steubenville-Weirton (W. Va.) 142,523 (80,298 in O.; 62,225 in W. Va.)
Toledo 614,128
Wheeling (W. Va.) 159,301 (82,227 in W. Va.; 71,074 in O.)
Youngstown-Warren 492,619

Counties

Adams 25,371
Allen 109,755
Ashland 47,507
Ashtabula 99,821
Athens 59,549
Auglaize 44,585
Belmont 71,074
Brown 34,966
Butler 291,479
Carroll 26,521
Champaign 36,019
Clark 147,548
Clermont 150,187
Clinton 35,415
Columbiana 108,276
Coshocton 35,427
Crawford 47,870
Cuyahoga 1,412,140
Darke 53,619
Defiance 39,350
Delaware 66,929
Erie 76,779
Fairfield 103,461
Fayette 27,466
Franklin 961,437
Fulton 38,498
Gallia 30,954
Geauga 81,129
Greene 136,731
Guernsey 39,024
Hamilton 866,228
Hancock 65,536
Hardin 31,111
Harrison 16,085
Henry 29,108
Highland 35,728
Hocking 25,533
Holmes 32,849
Huron 56,240
Jackson 30,230
Jefferson 80,298
Knox 47,473
Lake 215,499
Lawrence 61,834
Licking 128,300
Logan 42,310
Lorain 271,126
Lucas 462,361
Madison 37,068
Mahoning 264,806
Marion 64,274
Medina 122,354
Meigs 22,987
Mercer 39,443
Miami 93,182
Monroe 15,497
Montgomery 573,809
Morgan 14,194
Morrow 27,749
Muskingum 82,068
Noble 11,336
Ottawa 40,029
Paulding 20,488
Perry 31,557
Pickaway 48,255
Pike 24,249
Portage 142,585
Preble 40,113
Putnam 33,819
Richland 126,137
Ross 69,330
Sandusky 61,963
Scioto 80,327
Seneca 59,733
Shelby 44,915
Stark 367,585
Summit 514,990
Trumbull 227,813
Tuscarawas 84,090
Union 31,969
Van Wert 30,464
Vinton 11,098
Warren 113,909
Washington 62,254
Wayne 101,461
Williams 36,956
Wood 113,269
Wyandot 22,254

Cities and villages

Aberdeen 1,329
Ada 5,413
Addyston 1,198
Adelphi 398
Adena 842
Akron 223,019
Albany 795
Alexandria 468
Alger 864
Alliance 23,376
Alvordton 298
Amanda 729
Amberly 3,108
Amelia 1,837
Amherst 10,332
Amsterdam 669
Andover 1,216
Anna 1,164
Ansonia 1,279
Antwerp 1,677
Apple Creek 860
Aquilla 360
Arcadia 546
Arcanum 1,953
Archbold 3,440
Arlington 1,267
Arlington Heights 1,084
Ashland 20,079
Ashley 1,059
Ashtabula 21,633
Ashville 2,254
Athalia 346
Athens 21,265
Attica 944
Aurora 9,192
Austintown 32,371
Avon 7,337
Avon Lake 15,066
Bailey Lakes 367
Bainbridge 3,602
Ballville 3,083
Baltic 659

Baltimore 2,971
Barberton 27,623
Barnesville 4,326
Batavia 1,700
Bay View 739
Bay Village 17,000
Beach City 1,051
Beachwood 10,677
Beallsville 464
Beaver 336
Beavercreek 33,626
Beaverdam 467
Bedford 14,822
Bedford Heights 12,131
Bellaire 6,028
Bellbrook 6,511
Belle Center 796
Belle Valley 267
Bellefontaine 12,142
Bellevue 8,146
Bellville 1,568
Belmont 471
Beloit 1,037
Belpre 6,796
Benton Ridge 351
Berea 19,051
Bergholz 713
Berlin Heights 691
Bethel 2,407
Bethesda 1,161
Bettsville 752
Beverly 1,444
Bexley 13,088
Blacklick Estates 10,080
Blanchester 4,206
Bloomdale 632
Bloomingburg 769
Bloomville 949
Blue Ash 11,860
Bluffton 3,367
Boardman 38,596
Bolivar 914
Boston Heights 733
Botkins 1,340
Bowerston 343
Bowersville 225
Bowling Green 28,176
Bradford 2,005
Bradner 1,093
Brady Lake 490
Bratenahl 1,356
Brecksville 11,818
Bremen 1,386
Brentwood 3,568
Brewster 2,307
Briarwood Beach 682
Bridgeport 2,318
Bridgetown 11,748
Brilliant 1,672
Brimfield 3,223
Broadview
Heights 12,219
Brook Park 22,865
Brookfield 1,396
Brooklyn 11,706
Brooklyn Heights 1,450
Brookside 703
Brookville 4,621
Brunswick 28,230
Bryan 8,348
Buchtel 640
Buckeye Lake 2,986
Bucyrus 13,496
Burbank 289
Burlington 3,003
Burton 1,349
Butler 968
Byesville 2,435
Cadiz 3,439
Cairo 473
Calcutta 1,212
Caldwell 1,786
Caledonia 644
Cambridge 11,748
Camden 2,210
Campbell 10,038
Canal Fulton 4,157
Canal Winchester 2,617
Canfield 5,409
Canton 84,161
Cardington 1,770
Carey 3,684
Carlisle 4,872
Carroll 558
Carrollton 3,042
Casstown 246
Castalia 915
Cecil 249
Cedarville 3,210
Celina 9,650
Centerburg 1,323
Centerville 21,082
Chagrin Falls 4,146
Champion Heights 4,665
Chardon 4,446
Chauncey 980
Cherry Grove 4,972
Chesapeake 1,073
Chesterhill 309
Chesterland 2,078
Cheviot 9,616
Chickasaw 378
Chillicothe 21,923
Christiansburg 599
Cincinnati 364,040
Circleville 11,666
Clarington 406
Clarksburg 523
Clarksville 485
Clay Center 289
Clayton 713
Cleveland 505,616
Cleveland
Heights 54,052
Cleves 2,208
Clinton 1,175
Cloverdale 270
Clyde 5,776
Coal Grove 2,251
Coalton 553
Coldwater 4,335
College Corner 379
Columbiana 4,961
Columbus 632,910
Columbus Grove 2,231
Commercial Point 405
Conesville 420
Conneaut 13,241
Continental 1,214
Convoy 1,200
Coolville 663
Corning 703
Cortland 5,666
Coshocton 12,193
Covedale 6,669
Covington 2,603
Craig Beach 1,402
Crestline 4,934
Creston 1,848
Cridersville 1,885
Crooksville 2,601
Crown City 445
Crystal Lakes 1,613
Cumberland 318
Cuyahoga Falls 48,950
Cuyahoga Heights 682
Cygnet 560
Dalton 1,377
Danville 1,001
Darbydale 272
Day Heights 2,812
Dayton 182,044
Deer Park 6,181
Defiance 16,768
De Graff 1,331
Delaware 20,030
Dellroy 314
Delphos 7,093
Delta 2,849
Dennison 3,282
Dent 6,416
Deshler 1,876
Devola 2,736
Dillonvale 857
Dover 11,329
Doylestown 2,668
Dresden 1,581
Drexel 5,143
Dry Run 5,389
Dublin 16,366
Dunkirk 869
Dupont 279
East Canton 1,742
East Cleveland 33,096
East Liverpool 13,654
East Palestine 5,168
East Sparta 771
Eastlake 21,161
Eaton 7,396
Eaton Estates 1,586
Edgerton 1,896
Edgewood 5,189
Edison 488
Edon 880
Eldorado 549
Elida 1,486
Elmore 1,334
Elmwood Place 2,937
Elyria 56,746
Empire 364
Englewood 11,432
Enon 2,605
Euclid 54,875
Evendale 3,175
Fairborn 31,300
Fairfax 2,029
Fairfield 39,729
Fairlawn 5,779
Fairport Harbor 2,978
Fairview Lanes 1,120
Fairview Park 18,028
Farmersville 932
Fayette 1,248
Fayetteville 393
Felicity 856
Findlay 35,703
Finneytown 13,096
Fletcher 545
Flushing 1,042
Forest 1,594
Forest Park 18,609
Forestville 9,185
Fort Jennings 436
Fort Loramie 1,042
Fort McKinley 9,740
Fort Recovery 1,313
Fort Shawnee 4,128
Fostoria 14,983
Frankfort 1,065
Franklin 11,026
Franklin Furnace 1,212
Frazeysburg 1,165
Fredericksburg 502
Fredericktown 2,443
Freeport 475
Fremont 17,648
Fruit Hill 4,101
Fulton 325
Gahanna 27,791
Galena 361
Galion 11,859
Gallipolis 4,831
Gambier 2,073
Garfield Heights 31,739
Garrettsville 2,014
Gates Mills 2,508
Geneva 6,597
Geneva-on-
the-Lake 1,626
Genoa 2,262
Georgetown 3,627
Germantown 4,916
Gettysburg 539
Gibsonburg 2,579
Girard 11,304
Glandorf 829
Glendale 2,445
Glenmoor 2,307
Glenwillow 455
Gloria Glens Park 446
Glouster 2,001
Gnadenhutten 1,226
Golf Manor 4,154
Grafton 3,344
Grand Rapids 955
Grand River 297
Grandview
Heights 7,010
Granville 4,353
Gratis 998
Green Camp 393
Green Meadows 2,526
Green Springs 1,446
Greenfield 5,172
Greenhills 4,393
Greensburg 3,306
Greenville 12,863
Greenwich 1,442
Groesbeck 6,684
Grove City 19,661
Groveport 2,948
Grover Hill 518
Hamden 877
Hamersville 586
Hamilton 61,368
Hamler 623
Hanging Rock 306
Hanover 803
Hanoverton 434
Harrisburg 340
Harrison 7,518
Harrisville 308
Harrod 537
Hartford 418
Hartville 2,031
Harveysburg 437
Haskins 549
Hayesville 457
Heath 7,231
Hebron 2,076
Helena 267
Hicksville 3,664
Higginsport 298
Highland Heights 6,249
Hilliard 11,796
Hillsboro 6,235
Hiram 1,330
Holgate 1,290
Holland 1,210
Hollansburg 300
Holloway 354
Holmesville 419
Hopedale 685
Howland 6,732
Hoytville 301
Hubbard 8,248
Huber Heights 38,696
Huber Ridge 5,255
Hudson 5,159
Hunting Valley 799
Huntsville 343
Huron 7,030
Independence 6,500
Indian Hill 5,383
Irondale 382
Ironton 12,751
Jackson 6,144
Jackson Center 1,398
Jacksonville 544
Jamestown 1,794
Jefferson 3,331
Jefferson 4,505
Jeffersonville 1,281
Jeromesville 582
Jerry City 517
Jewett 778
Johnstown 3,237
Junction City 770
Kalida 947
Kent 28,835
Kenton 8,356
Kenwood 7,469
Kettering 60,569
Killbuck 809
Kingston 1,153
Kipton 283
Kirkersville 563
Kirtland 5,881
Kirtland Hills 628
La Croft 1,427
Lafayette 449
Lagrange 1,199
Lake Darby 2,798
Lakemore 2,684
Lakeview 1,056
Lakewood 59,718
Lancaster 34,507
Landen 9,263
La Rue 802
Laura 483
Laurelville 605
Lawrenceville 304
Lebanon 10,453
Leesburg 1,063
Leetonia 2,070
Leipsic 2,203
Lewisburg 1,584
Lexington 4,124
Liberty Center 1,084
Lima 45,549
Lincoln Heights 4,805
Lincoln Village 9,958
Lindsey 529
Lisbon 3,037
Lithopolis 563
Lockland 4,357
Lodi 3,042
Logan 6,725
London 7,807
Lorain 71,245
Lordstown 3,404
Lore City 384
Loudonville 2,915
Louisville 8,087
Loveland 9,990
Loveland Park 1,357
Lowell 617
Lowellville 1,349
Lucas 730
Lucasville 1,575
Luckey 848
Lynchburg 1,212
Lyndhurst 15,982
Lyons 579
Macedonia 7,509
Mack North 5,767
Macksburg 218
Madeira 9,141
Madison 2,477
Magnetic Springs 373
Magnolia 937
Malinta 294
Malta 802
Malvern 1,112
Manchester 2,223
Mansfield 50,627
Mantua 1,178
Maple Heights 27,089
Marble Cliff 633
Marblehead 745
Marengo 393
Mariemont 3,118
Marietta 15,026
Marion 34,075
Marshallville 758
Martins Ferry 7,990
Martinsville 476
Marysville 9,656
Mason 11,452
Massillon 31,007
Maumee 15,561
Mayfield 3,462
Mayfield Heights 19,847
McArthur 1,541
McClure 781
McComb 1,544
McConnelsville 1,804
McDonald 3,526
McGuffey 550
Mechanicsburg 1,803
Medina 19,231
Melrose 307
Mendon 717
Mentor 47,358
Mentor-on-
the-Lake 8,271
Metamora 543
Miamisburg 17,834
Middleburg
Heights 14,702
Middlefield 1,898
Middle Point 639
Middleport 2,725
Middletown 46,022
Midland 319
Midvale 575
Midway 289
Milan 1,464
Milford 5,660
Milford Center 651
Millbury 1,081
Millersburg 3,051
Millersport 1,010
Millville 755
Mineral City 725
Mineral Ridge 3,928
Minerva 4,318
Minerva Park 1,463
Mingo Junction 4,297
Minster 2,650
Mogadore 4,008
Monfort Heights
East 3,661
Monfort Heights
South 4,587
Monroe 4,490
Monroeville 1,381
Montgomery 9,753
Montpelier 4,299
Montrose-Ghent 4,906
Moraine 5,989
Moreland Hills 3,354
Morral 373
Morristown 296
Morrow 1,206
Moscow 279
Mount Blanchard 491
Mount Carmel 4,462
Mount Gilead 2,846
Mount Healthy 7,580
Mount Healthy
Heights 3,863
Mount Orab 1,929
Mount Pleasant 498
Mount Sterling 1,647
Mount Vernon 14,550
Mount Victory 551
Mowrystown 460
Munroe Falls 5,359
Murray City 499
Napoleon 8,884
Navarre 1,635
Neffs 1,213
Nelsonville 4,563
Nevada 849
New Albany 1,621
New Alexandria 257
New Athens 370
New Boston 2,717
New Bremen 2,558
New Carlisle 6,049
New Concord 2,086
New Holland 841
New Knoxville 838
New Lebanon 4,323
New Lexington 5,117
New London 2,642
New Madison 928
New Miami 2,555
New Middletown 1,912
New Paris 1,801
New Phila-
delphia 15,698
New Richmond 2,408
New Riegel 298
New Straitsville 865
New Vienna 932
New Washington 1,057
New Waterford 1,278
Newark 44,389
Newburgh
Heights 2,310
Newcomerstown 4,012
Newton Falls 4,866
Newtonsville 427
Newtown 1,589
Ney 331
Niles 21,128
North Baltimore 3,139
North Bend 541
North Canton 14,748
North College
Hill 11,002
North Fairfield 504
North Hampton 417
North Kingsville 2,672
North Lewisburg 1,160
North Madison 8,699
North Olmsted 34,204
North Perry 824
North Randall 977
North Ridgeville 21,564
North Robinson 216
North Royalton 23,197
North Zanesville 2,121
Northbrook 11,471
Northfield 3,624
Northridge 5,939
Northridge 9,448
Northview 10,337
Northwood 5,506
Norton 11,477
Norwalk 14,731
Norwood 23,674
Oak Harbor 2,637
Oak Hill 1,831
Oakwood 3,392
Oakwood 709
Oakwood 8,957
Oberlin 8,191
Obetz 3,167
Ohio City 899
Olmsted Falls 6,741
Ontario 4,026
Orange 2,810
Oregon 18,334
Orrville 7,712
Orwell 1,258
Osgood 255
Ostrander 431
Ottawa 3,999
Ottawa Hills 4,543
Ottoville 842
Overlook
[-Page Manor] 13,242
Owensville 1,019
Oxford 18,937
Painesville 15,699
Pandora 1,009
Park Layne 4,795
Parma 87,876
Parma Heights 21,448
Pataskala 3,046
Paulding 2,605
Payne 1,244
Peebles 1,782
Pemberville 1,279
Peninsula 562
Pepper Pike 6,185
Perry 1,012
Perry Heights 9,055
Perrysburg 12,551
Perrysville 691
Phillipsburg 644
Philo 810
Pickerington 5,668
Piketon 1,717
Pioneer 1,287
Piqua 20,612
Pitsburg 425
Plain City 2,278
Plains, The 2,644
Pleasant City 419
Pleasant Hill 1,066
Pleasant Run 4,964
Pleasantville 926
Plymouth 1,942
Poland 2,992
Polk 355
Pomeroy 2,259
Port Clinton 7,106
Port Jefferson 381
Port Washington 513
Portage 469
Portage Lakes 13,373
Portsmouth 22,676
Potsdam 250
Powell 2,154
Powhatan Point 1,807
Proctorville 765
Prospect 1,148
Quaker City 560
Quincy 697
Racine 729
Ravenna 12,069
Rawson 482
Rayland 490
Reading 12,038
Reminderville 2,163
Republic 611
Reynoldsburg 25,748
Richfield 3,117
Richmond 446
Richmond Heights 9,611
Richwood 2,186
Ridgeway 378
Rio Grande 995
Ripley 1,816
Risingsun 659
Rittman 6,147
Riverlea 503
Riverside 1,471
Roaming Shores 775
Rock Creek 553
Rockford 1,119
Rocky Ridge 425
Rocky River 20,410
Rosemount 1,926
Roseville 1,847
Ross 2,124
Rossford 5,861
Rushsylvania 573
Russells Point 1,504
Russellville 459
Russia 442
Rutland 469
Sabina 2,662
St. Bernard 5,344
St. Clairsville 5,162
St. Henry 1,907
St. Louisville 372
St. Marys 8,441
St. Paris 1,842
Salem 12,233
Salineville 1,474
Sandusky 29,764
Sandusky South 6,336
Sardinia 792
Savannah 363
Scio 856
Sciotodale 1,128
Scott 339
Seaman 1,013
Sebring 4,848
Senecaville 434
Seven Hills 12,339
Seven Mile 804
Seville 1,810
Shadyside 3,934
Shaker Heights 30,831
Sharonville 13,153
Shawnee 742
Shawnee Hills 423
Shawnee Hills 2,199
Sheffield 1,943
Sheffield Lake 9,825
Shelby 9,564
Sherrodsville 284
Sherwood 828
Shiloh 778
Shiloh 11,607
Shreve 1,584
Sidney 18,710
Silver Lake 3,052
Silverton 5,859
Smithfield 722
Smithville 1,354
Solon 18,548
Somerset 1,390
Somerville 279
South Amherst 1,765
South Bloomfield 900
South Charleston 1,626
South Euclid 23,866
South Lebanon 2,696
South Point 3,823
South Russell 3,402
South Solon 379
South Vienna 550
South Webster 806
South Zanesville 1,969
Spencer 726
Spencerville 2,288
Spring Valley 507

Ohio (continued)

Springboro 6,590
Springdale 10,621
Springfield 70,487
Steubenville 22,125
Stockport 462
Stony Prairie 1,536
Stoutsville 518
Stow 27,702
Strasburg 1,995
Stratton 278
Streetsboro 9,932
Strongsville 35,308
Struthers 12,284
Stryker 1,468
Sugar Grove 465
Sugarcreek 2,062
Summerfield 295
Summerside 4,573
Sunbury 2,046
Swanton 3,557
Sycamore 919
Sylvania 17,301
Syracuse 827
Tallmadge 14,870
Tarlton 315
Terrace Park 2,133
Thornville 758
Thurston 539
Tiffin 18,604
Tiltonsville 1,517
Timberlake 833
Tipp City 6,027
Toledo 332,943
Tontogany 364
Toronto 6,127
Tremont City 493
Trenton 6,189
Trimble 441
Trotwood 8,816
Troy 19,478
Turpin Hills 4,927
Tuscarawas 826
Twinsburg 9,606
Uhrichsville 5,604
Union 5,501
Union City 1,984
University Heights 14,790
Upper Arlington 34,128
Upper Sandusky 5,906
Urbana 11,353
Urbancrest 862
Utica 1,997
Valley View 2,137
Valleyview 604
Van Buren 337
Van Wert 10,891
Vandalia 13,882
Vanlue 373
Vermilion 11,127
Verona 472
Versailles 2,351
Vinton 293
Wadsworth 15,718
Waite Hill 454
Wakeman 948
Walbridge 2,736
Waldo 340
Walton Hills 2,371
Wapakoneta 9,214
Warren 50,793
Warrensville Heights 15,745
Warsaw 699
Washington Court House 12,983
Washingtonville 894
Waterville 4,517
Wauseon 6,322
Waverly 4,477
Wayne 803
Waynesburg 1,068
Waynesfield 831
Waynesville 1,949
Wellington 4,140
Wellston 6,049
Wellsville 4,532
West Alexandria 1,460
West Carrollton 14,403
West Farmington 542
West Lafayette 2,129
West Liberty 1,613
West Manchester 464
West Mansfield 830
West Milton 4,348
West Portsmouth 3,551
West Salem 1,534
West Union 3,096
West Unity 1,677
Westerville 30,269
Westfield Center 784
Westlake 27,018
Weston 1,716
Wharton 378
Wheelersburg 5,113
White Oak 12,430
Whitehall 20,572
Whitehouse 2,528
Wickliffe 14,558
Wilberforce 2,639
Willard 6,210
Williamsburg 2,322
Williamsport 851
Willoughby 20,510
Willoughby Hills 8,427
Willowick 15,269
Willshire 541
Wilmington 11,199
Wilmot 261
Winchester 978
Windham 2,943
Wintersville 4,102
Woodbourne [-Hyde Park] 7,837
Woodlawn 2,674
Woodmere 834
Woodsfield 2,832
Woodville 1,953
Wooster 22,191
Worthington 14,869
Wright-Patterson AFB 8,579
Wyoming 8,128
Xenia 24,664
Yellow Springs 3,973
Yorkville 1,246
Youngstown 95,732
Zaleski 294
Zanesville 26,778

Oklahoma ■ population 3,157,604

Metropolitan areas

Enid 56,735
Fort Smith (Ark.) 175,911
(142,083 in Ark.; 33,828 in Okla.)
Lawton 111,486
Oklahoma City 958,839
Tulsa 708,954

Counties

Adair 18,421
Alfalfa 6,416
Atoka 12,778
Beaver 6,023
Beckham 18,812
Blaine 11,470
Bryan 32,089
Caddo 29,550
Canadian 74,409
Carter 42,919
Cherokee 34,049
Choctaw 15,302
Cimarron 3,301
Cleveland 174,253
Coal 5,780
Comanche 111,486
Cotton 6,651
Craig 14,104
Creek 60,915
Custer 26,897
Delaware 28,070
Dewey 5,551
Ellis 4,497
Garfield 56,735
Garvin 26,605
Grady 41,747
Grant 5,689
Greer 6,559
Harmon 3,793
Harper 4,063
Haskell 10,940
Hughes 13,023
Jackson 28,764
Jefferson 7,010
Johnston 10,032
Kay 48,056
Kingfisher 13,212
Kiowa 11,347
Latimer 10,333
Le Flore 43,270
Lincoln 29,216
Logan 29,011
Love 8,157
Major 8,055
Marshall 10,829
Mayes 33,366
McClain 22,795
McCurtain 33,433
McIntosh 16,779
Murray 12,042
Muskogee 68,078
Noble 11,045
Nowata 9,992
Okfuskee 11,551
Oklahoma 599,611
Okmulgee 36,490
Osage 41,645
Ottawa 30,561
Pawnee 15,575
Payne 61,507
Pittsburg 40,581
Pontotoc 34,119
Pottawatomie 58,760
Pushmataha 10,997
Roger Mills 4,147
Rogers 55,170
Seminole 25,412
Sequoyah 33,828
Stephens 42,299
Texas 16,419
Tillman 10,384
Tulsa 503,341
Wagoner 47,883
Washington 48,066
Washita 11,441
Woods 9,103
Woodward 18,976

Cities and towns

Achille 491
Ada 15,820
Adair 685
Afton 915
Agra 334
Alderson 395
Alex 639
Aline 295
Allen 972
Altus 21,910
Alva 5,495
Amber 418
Ames 268
Anadarko 6,586
Antlers 2,524
Apache 1,591
Arapaho 802
Arcadia 320
Ardmore 23,079
Arkoma 2,393
Arnett 547
Asher 449
Atoka 3,298
Avant 369
Barnsdall 1,316
Bartlesville 34,256
Beaver 1,584
Beggs 1,150
Bennington 251
Bernice 330
Bessie 248
Bethany 20,075
Bethel Acres 2,505
Big Cabin 271
Billings 555
Binger 724
Bixby 9,502
Blackwell 7,538
Blair 922
Blanchard 1,922
Boise City 1,509
Bokchito 576
Bokoshe 403
Boley 908
Boswell 643
Bowlegs 398
Boynton 391
Braggs 308
Braman 251
Bray 925
Breckenridge 251
Bristow 4,062
Broken Arrow 58,043
Broken Bow 3,961
Buffalo 1,312
Burns Flat 1,027
Butler 341
Byars 263
Byng 755
Cache 2,251
Caddo 918
Calera 1,536
Calumet 560
Calvin 251
Cameron 327
Canadian 261
Canton 632
Canute 538
Carmen 459
Carnegie 1,593
Carney 558
Carter 286
Cashion 430
Catoosa 2,954
Cement 642
Chandler 2,596
Chattanooga 437
Checotah 3,290
Chelsea 1,620
Cherokee 1,787
Cheyenne 948
Chickasha 14,988
Choctaw 8,545
Chouteau 1,771
Claremore 13,280
Clayton 636
Cleo Springs 359
Cleveland 3,156
Clinton 9,298
Coalgate 1,895
Colbert 1,043
Colcord 628
Cole 355
Collinsville 3,612
Comanche 1,695
Commerce 2,426
Copan 809
Corn 548
Covington 590
Coweta 6,159
Cowlington 756
Coyle 289
Crescent 1,236
Cromwell 268
Crowder 339
Cushing 7,218
Custer City 443
Cyril 1,072
Davenport 979
Davidson 473
Davis 2,543
Del City 23,928
Delaware 434
Depew 502
Dewar 921
Dewey 3,326
Dickson 942
Dill City 622
Disney 257
Dover 376
Drummond 408
Drumright 2,799
Duncan 21,732
Durant 12,823
Dustin 429
Eakly 277
Earlsboro 535
East Ninnekah 1,016
Edmond 52,315
Eldorado 573
Elgin 975
Elk City 10,428
Elmore City 493
El Reno 15,414
Empire City 219
Enid 45,309
Erick 1,083
Eufaula 2,652
Fair Oaks 1,133
Fairfax 1,749
Fairland 916
Fairview 2,936
Fanshawe 331
Fargo 299
Fletcher 1,002
Forest Park 1,249
Forgan 489
Fort Cobb 663
Fort Gibson 3,359
Fort Sill 12,107
Fort Supply 369
Fort Towson 568
Francis 346
Frederick 5,221
Freedom 264
Gage 473
Gans 218
Garber 959
Geary 1,347
Geronimo 990
Glencoe 473
Glenpool 6,688
Goldsby 816
Goltry 297
Goodwell 1,065
Gore 690
Gotebo 370
Gould 237
Gracemont 339
Grandfield 1,224
Granite 1,844
Greenfield 200
Grove 4,020
Guthrie 10,518
Guymon 7,803
Haileyville 918
Hall Park 1,090
Hammon 611
Hardesty 228
Harrah 4,206
Hartshorne 2,120
Haskell 2,143
Haworth 293
Healdton 2,872
Heavener 2,601
Helena 1,043
Hennessey 1,902
Henryetta 5,872
Hinton 1,233
Hobart 4,305
Holdenville 4,792
Hollis 2,584
Hominy 2,342
Hooker 1,551
Howe 510
Hugo 5,978
Hulbert 499
Hunter 218
Hydro 977
Idabel 6,957
Indiahoma 337
Inola 1,444
Jay 2,220
Jenks 7,493
Jennings 381
Jet 272
Jones 2,424
Kansas 556
Kaw City 314
Kellyville 984
Keota 625
Ketchum 263
Keyes 454
Kiefer 962
Kingfisher 4,095
Kingston 1,237
Kinta 233
Kiowa 718
Konawa 1,508
Krebs 1,955
Kremlin 243
Lahoma 645
Lamont 454
Langley 526
Langston 1,471
Laverne 1,269
Lawton 80,561
Leedey 468
Lehigh 303
Lenapah 253
Lexington 1,776
Lindsay 2,947
Locust Grove 1,326
Lone Grove 4,114
Lone Wolf 576
Longdale 281
Luther 1,560
Madill 3,069
Mangum 3,344
Manitou 244
Mannford 1,826
Mannsville 396
Marble City 232
Marietta 2,306
Marland 280
Marlow 4,416
Marshall 288
Martha 217
Maud 1,204
Maysville 1,203
McAlester 16,370
McCurtain 465
McLoud 2,493
Medford 1,172
Medicine Park 285
Meeker 1,003
Miami 13,142
Midwest City 52,267
Milburn 264
Mill Creek 336
Millerton 234
Minco 1,411
Moffett 219
Moore 40,318
Mooreland 1,157
Morris 1,216
Morrison 640
Mounds 980
Mountain Park 473
Mountain View 1,086
Muldrow 2,889
Muskogee 37,708
Mustang 10,434
Nash 281
New Tulsa 272
Newcastle 4,214
Newkirk 2,168
Nichols Hills 4,020
Nicoma Park 2,353
Noble 4,710
Norman 80,071
North Enid 874
North Miami 450
Nowata 3,896
Oakhurst 3,030
Oakland 602
Oaks 431
Ochelata 441
Oilton 1,060
Okarche 1,160
Okay 528
Okeene 1,343
Okemah 3,085
Oklahoma City 444,719
Okmulgee 13,441
Oktaha 266
Olustee 701
Oolagah 828
Owasso 11,151
Paden 400
Panama 1,528
Paoli 574
Pauls Valley 6,150
Pawhuska 3,825
Pawnee 2,197
Perkins 1,925
Perry 4,978
Picher 1,714
Piedmont 2,522
Pink 1,020
Pittsburg 249
Pocola 3,664
Ponca City 26,359
Pond Creek 982
Porter 588
Porum 851
Poteau 7,210
Prague 2,308
Prue 346
Pryor 8,327
Purcell 4,784
Quapaw 928
Quinton 1,133
Ralston 405
Ramona 508
Randlett 458
Rattan 257
Ravia 404
Red Oak 602
Red Rock 321
Reydon 200
Ringling 1,250
Ringwood 394
Ripley 376
Rock Island 478
Roff 717
Roland 2,481
Roosevelt 323
Rush Springs 1,229
Ryan 945
Salina 1,153
Sallisaw 7,122
Sand Springs 15,346
Sapulpa 18,074
Savanna 869
Sayre 2,881
Seiling 1,031
Seminole 7,071
Sentinel 960
Shady Point 597
Shattuck 1,454
Shawnee 26,017
Shidler 487
Silo 249
Skiatook 4,910
Slaughterville 1,843
Snyder 1,619
Soper 305
South Coffeyville 791
Sparks 202
Spavinaw 432
Spencer 3,972
Sperry 937
Spiro 2,146
Springer 485
Sterling 684
Stigler 2,574
Stillwater 36,676
Stilwell 2,663
Stonewall 519
Stratford 1,404
Stringtown 366
Stroud 2,666
Stuart 228
Sulphur 4,824
Taft 400
Tahlequah 10,398
Talala 206
Talihina 1,297
Taloga 415
Tecumseh 5,750
Temple 1,223
Terral 469
Texhoma 746
Thackerville 290
Thomas 1,246
Tipton 1,043
Tishomingo 3,116
Tonkawa 3,127
Tribbey 288
Tryon 514
Tulsa 367,302
Tupelo 323
Turley 2,930
Tushka 256
Tuttle 2,807
Tyrone 880
Union City 1,000
Valley Brook 744
Valliant 873
Velma 661
Verden 546
Vian 1,414
Vici 751
Village, The 10,353
Vinita 5,804
Wagoner 6,894
Wainwright 223
Wakita 453
Walters 2,519
Wanette 346
Wapanucka 402
Warner 1,479
Warr Acres 9,288
Washington 279
Watonga 3,408
Watts 303
Waukomis 1,322
Waurika 2,088
Wayne 519
Waynoka 947
Weatherford 10,124
Webbers Falls 722
Welch 499
Weleetka 1,112
Wellston 912
West Siloam Springs 539
Westport 326
Westville 1,374
Wetumka 1,427
Wewoka 4,050
Whitefield 253
Wilburton 3,092
Wilson 1,639
Winchester 301
Wister 956
Woodward 12,340
Wright City 836
Wyandotte 366
Wynnewood 2,451
Wynona 531
Yale 1,392
Yukon 20,935

Oregon ■ population 2,853,733

Metropolitan areas

Eugene-Springfield 282,912
Medford 146,389
Portland 1,239,842
Salem 278,024

Counties

Baker 15,317
Benton 70,811
Clackamas 278,850
Clatsop 33,301
Columbia 37,557
Coos 60,273
Crook 14,111
Curry 19,327
Deschutes 74,958
Douglas 94,649
Gilliam 1,717
Grant 7,853
Harney 7,060
Hood River 16,903
Jackson 146,389
Jefferson 13,676
Josephine 62,649
Klamath 57,702
Lake 7,186
Lane 282,912
Lincoln 38,889
Linn 91,227
Malheur 26,038
Marion 228,483
Morrow 7,625
Multnomah 583,887
Polk 49,541
Sherman 1,918
Tillamook 21,570
Umatilla 59,249
Union 23,598
Wallowa 6,911
Wasco 21,683
Washington 311,554
Wheeler 1,396
Yamhill 65,551

Cities and towns

Adair Village 554
Adams 223
Albany 29,462
Aloha 34,284
Altamont 18,591
Amity 1,175
Arlington 425
Ashland 16,234
Astoria 10,069
Athena 997
Aumsville 1,650
Aurora 567
Baker 9,140
Bandon 2,215
Banks 563
Barview 1,402
Bay City 1,027
Beaverton 53,310
Bend 20,469
Boardman 1,387
Bonanza 323
Brookings 4,400
Brownsville 1,281
Bunker Hill 1,242
Burns 2,913
Butte Falls 252
Canby 8,983
Cannon Beach 1,221
Canyon City 648
Canyonville 1,219
Carlton 1,289
Cascade Locks 930
Cave Junction 1,126
Cedar Hills 9,294
Cedar Mill 9,697
Central Point 7,509
Chenoweth 3,246
Chiloquin 673
Clackamas 2,578
Clatskanie 1,629
Coburg 763
Columbia City 1,003
Condon 635
Coos Bay 15,076
Coquille 4,121
Cornelius 6,148
Corvallis 44,757
Cottage Grove 7,402
Cove 507
Creswell 2,431
Culver 570
Dallas 9,422
Dalles, The 11,060
Dayton 1,526
Depoe Bay 870
Deschutes River Woods 2,373
Detroit 331
Donald 316
Drain 1,011
Dufur 527
Dundee 1,663
Dunes City 1,081
Durham 748
Eagle Point 3,008
Echo 499
Elgin 1,586
Enterprise 1,905
Estacada 2,016
Eugene 112,669
Fairview 2,391
Falls City 818
Florence 5,162
Forest Grove 13,559
Fossil 399
Four Corners 12,156
Garden Home [-Whitford] 6,652
Garibaldi 877
Gaston 563
Gates 499
Gearhart 1,027
Gervais 992
Gladstone 10,152
Glendale 707
Gold Beach 1,546
Gold Hill 964
Grants Pass 17,488
Green 5,076
Gresham 68,235
Haines 405
Halfway 311
Halsey 667
Hammond 589
Happy Valley 1,519
Harbeck [-Fruitdale] 3,982
Harbor 2,143
Harrisburg 1,939
Hayesville 14,318
Hazelwood 11,480
Heppner 1,412
Hermiston 10,040
Hillsboro 37,520
Hines 1,452
Hood River 4,632
Hubbard 1,881
Huntington 522
Idanha 289
Imbler 299
Independence 4,425
Ione 255
Irrigon 737
Island City 696
Jacksonville 1,896
Jefferson 1,805
Jennings Lodge 6,530
John Day 1,836
Johnson City 586
Jordan Valley 364
Joseph 1,073
Junction City 3,670
Keizer 21,884
King City 2,060
Klamath Falls 17,737
Lafayette 1,292
La Grande 11,766
Lake Oswego 30,576
Lakeside 1,437
Lakeview 2,526
Lebanon 10,950
Lexington 286
Lincoln Beach 1,507
Lincoln City 5,892
Long Creek 249
Lostine 231
Lowell 785
Lyons 938
Madras 3,443
Malin 725
Manzanita 513
Maupin 456
Maywood Park 781
McMinnville 17,894
Medford 46,951
Merrill 837
Metolius 450
Metzger 3,149
Mill City 1,555
Millersburg 715
Milton-Freewater 5,533
Milwaukie 18,692
Mission 664
Molalla 3,651
Monmouth 6,288
Monroe 448
Moro 292
Mosier 244
Mount Angel 2,778
Mount Hood Village 2,234
Mount Vernon 538
Myrtle Creek 3,063
Myrtle Point 2,712
Nehalem 232
Newberg 13,086
Newport 8,437
North Albany 4,325
North Bend 9,614
North Plains 972
North Powder 448
North Springfield 5,451
Nyssa 2,629
Oak Grove 12,576
Oak Hills 6,450
Oakland 844
Oakridge 3,063
Oatfield 15,348
Ontario 9,392
Oregon City 14,698
Paisley 350
Pendleton 15,126
Philomath 2,983
Phoenix 3,239
Pilot Rock 1,478
Port Orford 1,025
Portland 437,319
Powellhurst [-Centennial] 28,756
Powers 682
Prairie City 1,117
Prineville 5,355
Rainier 1,674
Raleigh Hills 6,066
Redmond 7,163
Redwood 3,702
Reedsport 4,796
Riddle 1,143
River Road 9,443
Rivergrove 294
Rockaway 970
Rockcreek 8,282
Rogue River 1,759
Rose Lodge 1,257
Roseburg 17,032
Roseburg North 6,831
Rufus 295
St. Helens 7,535
St. Paul 322
Salem 107,786
Sandy 4,152
Santa Clara 12,834
Scappoose 3,529
Scio 623
Scotts Mills 283
Seaside 5,359
Shady Cove 1,351
Sheridan 3,979
Sherwood 3,093
Siletz 926
Silverton 5,635
Sisters 679
South Lebanon 1,203
Springfield 44,683
Stanfield 1,568
Stayton 5,011
Sublimity 1,491
Sunnyside 4,423
Sutherlin 5,020
Sweet Home 6,850
Talent 3,274
Tangent 556
Terrebonne 1,143
Three Rivers 1,268
Tigard 29,344
Tillamook 4,001
Toledo 3,174
Tri City 3,585
Troutdale 7,852
Tualatin 15,013
Turner 1,281
Ukiah 250
Umatilla 3,046
Umatilla Reservation 2,502
Union 1,847
Vale 1,491
Veneta 2,519
Vernonia 1,808
Waldport 1,595
Wallowa 748
Warm Springs 2,287
Warm Springs Reservation 3,076
Warrenton 2,681
Wasco 374
West Haven [-Sylvan] 6,009
West Linn 16,367
West Slope 7,959
Westfir 278
Weston 606
Wheeler 335
White City 5,891
Willamina 1,717
Wilsonville 7,106
Winston 3,773
Wood Village 2,814
Woodburn 13,404
Yachats 533
Yamhill 867
Yoncalla 919

Pennsylvania ■ population 11,924,710

Metropolitan areas

Allentown-Bethlehem-Easton 686,688 (595,081 in Pa.; 91,607 in N.J.)
Altoona 130,542
Beaver County 186,093
Erie 275,572
Harrisburg-Lebanon-Carlisle 587,986
Johnstown 241,247
Lancaster 422,822
Philadelphia 4,856,881 (3,728,909 in Pa.; 1,127,972 in N.J.)
Pittsburgh 2,056,705
Reading 336,523
Scranton-Wilkes Barre 734,175
Sharon 121,003
State College 123,786
Williamsport 118,710
York 417,848

Counties

Adams 78,274
Allegheny 1,336,449
Armstrong 73,478
Beaver 186,093
Bedford 47,919
Berks 336,523
Blair 130,542
Bradford 60,967
Bucks 541,174
Butler 152,013
Cambria 163,029
Cameron 5,913
Carbon 56,846
Centre 123,786
Chester 376,396
Clarion 41,699
Clearfield 78,097
Clinton 37,182
Columbia 63,202
Crawford 86,169
Cumberland 195,257
Dauphin 237,813
Delaware 547,651
Elk 34,878
Erie 275,572
Fayette 145,351
Forest 4,808
Franklin 121,082
Fulton 13,837
Greene 39,550
Huntingdon 44,164
Indiana 89,994
Jefferson 46,083
Juniata 20,625
Lackawanna 219,039
Lancaster 422,822
Lawrence 96,246
Lebanon 113,744
Lehigh 291,130
Luzerne 328,149
Lycoming 118,710
McKean 47,131
Mercer 121,003
Mifflin 46,197
Monroe 95,709
Montgomery 678,111
Montour 17,735
Northampton 247,105
Northumberland 96,771
Perry 41,172
Philadelphia 1,585,577
Pike 27,966
Potter 16,717
Schuylkill 152,585
Snyder 36,680
Somerset 78,218
Sullivan 6,104
Susquehanna 40,380
Tioga 41,126
Union 36,176
Venango 59,381
Warren 45,050
Washington 204,584
Wayne 39,944
Westmoreland 370,321
Wyoming 28,076
York 339,574

Cities and boroughs

Adamstown 1,108
Akron 3,869
Albion 1,575
Alburtis 1,415
Aldan 4,549
Aliquippa 13,374
Allentown 105,090
Almedia 1,116
Altoona 51,881
Ambler 6,609
Ambridge 8,133
Annville 4,294
Apollo 1,895
Archbald 6,291
Arlington Heights 4,768
Arnold 6,113
Ashland 3,859
Ashley 3,291
Aspinwall 2,880
Athens 3,468
Auburn 913
Avalon 5,784
Avis 1,506
Avoca 2,897
Avonia 1,336
Avonmore 1,089
Baden 5,074
Baldwin 21,923
Bally 973
Bangor 5,383
Barnesboro 2,530
Bath 2,358
Beaver 5,028
Beaver Falls 10,687
Beaver Meadows 985
Beaverdale [-Lloydell] 1,278
Bedford 3,137
Bell Acres 1,436
Belle Vernon 1,213
Bellefonte 6,358
Belleville 1,589
Bellevue 9,126
Bellwood 1,976
Belmont 3,184
Ben Avon 2,096
Bentleyville 2,673
Benton 958
Berlin 2,064
Berwick 10,976
Bessemer 1,196
Bethel Park 33,823
Bethlehem 71,428
Big Beaver 2,298
Biglerville 993
Birdsboro 4,222
Black Lick 1,100
Blairsville 3,595
Blakely 7,222
Blawnox 1,626
Bloomsburg 12,439
Blossburg 1,571
Boalsburg 2,206
Boiling Springs 1,978
Boswell 1,485
Bowmanstown 888
Boyertown 3,759
Brackenridge 3,784
Braddock 4,682
Braddock Hills 2,026
Bradford 9,625
Bradford Woods 1,329
Brentwood 10,823
Bridgeport 4,292
Bridgeville 5,445
Bristol 10,405
Brockway 2,207
Brookhaven 8,567
Brookville 4,184
Brownsville 3,164
Burgettstown 1,634
Burnham 2,197
Butler 15,714
California 5,748
Calumet [-Norvelt] 1,790
Cambridge Springs 1,837
Camp Hill 7,831
Campbelltown 1,609
Canonsburg 9,200
Canton 1,966
Carbondale 10,664
Carlisle 18,419
Carnegie 9,278
Carnot [-Moon] 10,187
Carrolltown 1,286
Castenea 1,123
Castle Shannon 9,135
Catasauqua 6,662
Catawissa 1,683
Centerville 3,842
Central City 1,246
Centre Hall 1,203
Chalfant 959
Chalfont 3,069
Chambersburg 16,647
Charleroi 5,014
Chester 41,856
Chester Heights 2,273
Chester Hill 945
Cheswick 1,971
Chevy Chase Heights 1,535
Chicora 1,058
Christiana 1,045
Churchill 3,883
Clairton 9,656
Clarion 6,457
Clarks Green 1,603
Clarks Summit 5,433
Claysburg 1,399
Claysville 962
Clearfield 6,633
Cleona 2,322
Clifton Heights 7,111
Clymer 1,499
Coaldale 2,531
Coatesville 11,038
Cochranton 1,174
Collegeville 4,227
Collingdale 9,175
Columbia 10,701
Colver 1,024
Colwyn 2,613
Connellsville 9,229
Conshohocken 8,064
Conway 2,424
Conyngham 2,060
Coopersburg 2,599
Coplay 3,267
Coraopolis 6,747
Cornwall 3,231
Corry 7,216
Coudersport 2,854
Crafton 7,188
Cresson 1,784
Cressona 1,694
Curtisville 1,285
Curwensville 2,924
Dale 1,642
Dallas 2,567
Dallastown 3,974
Dalton 1,369
Danville 5,165
Darby 11,140
Davidsville 1,167
Delmont 2,041
Denver 2,861
Derry 2,950
Devon [-Berwyn] 5,019
Dickson City 6,276
Dillsburg 1,925
Donora 5,928
Dormont 9,772
Dover 1,884
Downingtown 7,749
Doylestown 8,575
Dravosburg 2,377
Dublin 1,985
Du Bois 8,286
Duboistown 1,201
Dunbar 1,213
Duncannon 1,450
Duncansville 1,309
Dunmore 15,403
Dunnstown 1,486
Dupont 2,984
Duquesne 8,525
Duryea 4,869
East Bangor 1,006
East Berlin 1,175
East Brady 1,047
East Conemaugh 1,470
East Greenville 3,117
East Lansdowne 2,691
East McKeesport 2,678
East Petersburg 4,197
East Pittsburgh 2,160
East Stroudsburg 8,781
East Uniontown 2,822
East Washington 2,126
Eastlawn Gardens 1,794
Easton 26,276
Ebensburg 3,872
Economy 9,519
Eddystone 2,446
Edgewood 3,581
Edgewood 2,719
Edgeworth 1,670
Edinboro 7,736
Edwardsville 5,399
Eldred 869
Elim 3,861
Elizabeth 1,610
Elizabethtown 9,952
Elizabethville 1,467
Elkland 1,849
Ellport 1,243
Ellsworth 1,048
Ellwood City 8,894
Elysburg 1,890
Emigsville 2,580
Emmaus 11,157
Emporium 2,513
Emsworth 2,892
Ephrata 12,133
Erie 108,718
Espy 1,430
Etna 4,200
Evans City 2,054
Evansburg 1,047
Everett 1,777
Everson 939
Exeter 5,691
Export 981
Exton 2,550
Fairchance 1,918
Fairdale 2,049
Fairview 1,988
Fairview [-Ferndale] 2,895
Falls Creek 1,087
Farrell 6,841
Fayetteville 3,033
Ferndale 2,020
Fernway 9,072
Fleetwood 3,478
Flemington 1,321
Folcroft 7,506
Ford City 3,413
Forest City 1,846
Forest Hills 7,335
Forty Fort 5,049
Fountain Hill 4,637
Fox Chapel 5,319
Frackville 4,700
Franklin 7,329
Franklin Park 10,109
Fredericksburg 1,202
Fredericktown 1,237
Freedom 1,897
Freeland 3,909
Freemansburg 1,946
Freeport 1,983
Friedens 1,576
Fullerton 13,127

Pennsylvania (continued)

Galeton 1,370
Gallitzin 2,003
Garden View 2,687
Geistown 2,749
Gettysburg 7,025
Gilberton 953
Gilbertsville 3,994
Girard 2,879
Girardville 1,889
Glassport 5,582
Glen Lyon 2,082
Glen Rock 1,688
Glenolden 7,260
Grandview Park 2,170
Green Tree 4,905
Greencastle 3,600
Greensburg 16,318
Greenville 6,734
Greenville East 1,419
Grove City 8,240
Guilford 1,618
Halfway House 1,415
Hallam 1,375
Hallstead 1,274
Hamburg 3,987
Hanover 14,399
Harleysville 7,405
Harmony 1,054
Harrisburg 52,376
Harrisville 862
Harveys Lake 2,746
Hasson Heights 1,610
Hastings 1,431
Hatboro 7,382
Hatfield 2,650
Hawley 1,224
Hazleton 24,730
Heidelberg 1,238
Hellertown 5,662
Hershey 11,860
Highland Park 1,583
Highspire 2,668
Hiller 1,401
Hollidaysburg 5,624
Homeacre [-Lyndora] 7,511
Homer City 1,809
Homestead 4,179
Hometown 1,545
Honesdale 4,972
Honey Brook 1,184
Hopwood 2,021
Horsham 15,051
Houston 1,445
Houtzdale 1,204
Hughestown 1,734
Hughesville 2,049
Hulmville 916
Hummels Wharf 1,069
Hummelstown 3,981
Huntingdon 6,843
Hyde 1,643
Hyndman 1,019
Imperial [-Enlow] 3,449
Indiana 15,174
Industry 2,124
Ingram 3,901
Irwin 4,604
Jacobus 1,370
Jeannette 11,221
Jefferson 9,533
Jenkintown 4,574
Jermyn 2,263
Jerome 1,074
Jersey Shore 4,353
Jessup 4,605
Jim Thorpe 5,048
Johnsonburg 3,350
Johnstown 28,134
Juniata Terrace 556
Kane 4,590
Kenhorst 2,918
Kenilworth 1,890
Kennett Square 5,218
Kingston 14,507
Kittanning 5,120
Knox 1,182
Koppel 1,024
Kulpmont 3,233
Kutztown 4,704
Laflin 1,498
Lake City 2,519
Lancaster 55,551
Langhorne 1,361
Langhorne Manor 807
Langloth 1,112
Lansdale 16,362
Lansdowne 11,712
Lansford 4,583
Laporte 328
Larksville 4,700
Latrobe 9,265
Laureldale 3,726
Lawrence Park 4,310
Lawson Heights 2,464
Lebanon 24,800
Lebanon South 1,764
Leechburg 2,504
Leesport 1,270
Leetsdale 1,387
Lehighton 5,914
Leith [-Hatfield] 2,437
Lemoyne 3,959
Lenape Heights 1,355
Lewisburg 5,785
Lewistown 9,341
Liberty 2,744
Ligonier 1,638
Lilly 1,162
Lincoln 1,187
Linesville 1,166
Linntown 1,640
Lititz 8,280
Littlestown 2,974
Lock Haven 9,230
Loganville 954
Lorain 824
Loretto 1,072
Lower Burrell 12,251
Lucerne Mines 1,074
Luzerne 3,206
Lykens 1,986
Lynnwood [-Pricedale] 2,664
Macungie 2,597
Mahanoy City 5,209
Malvern 2,944
Manchester 1,830
Manheim 5,011
Manor 2,627
Mansfield 3,538
Marcus Hook 2,546
Marietta 2,778
Mars 1,713
Marshallton 1,482
Martinsburg 2,119
Marysville 2,425
Masontown 3,759
Matamoras 1,934
Mayfield 1,890
Maytown 1,720
McAdoo 2,459
McChesneytown [-Loyalhanna] 3,708
McClure 1,070
McConnellsburg 1,106
McDonald 2,252
McKees Rocks 7,691
McKeesport 26,016
McSherrystown 2,769
Meadowood 3,011
Meadville 14,318
Mechanicsburg 9,452
Mechanicsville 2,803
Media 5,957
Mercer 2,444
Mercersburg 1,640
Meridian 3,473
Meyersdale 2,518
Middleburg 1,422
Middletown 9,254
Midland 3,321
Midway 1,043
Mifflinburg 3,480
Mifflintown 866
Mifflinville 1,329
Milesburg 1,144
Milford 1,064
Mill Hall 1,702
Millersburg 2,729
Millersville 8,099
Millvale 4,341
Millville 969
Milroy 1,456
Milton 6,746
Minersville 4,877
Mohnton 2,484
Monaca 6,739
Monessen 9,901
Monongahela 4,928
Monroeville 29,169
Mont Alto 1,395
Montgomery 1,631
Montoursville 4,983
Montrose 1,982
Moosic 5,339
Morrisville 9,765
Morrisville 1,365
Morton 2,851
Moscow 1,527
Mount Carmel 7,196
Mount Holly Springs 1,925
Mount Jewett 1,029
Mount Joy 6,398
Mount Lebanon 33,362
Mount Oliver 4,160
Mount Penn 2,883
Mount Pleasant 4,787
Mount Pocono 1,795
Mount Union 2,878
Mount Wolf 1,365
Mountville 1,977
Muncy 2,702
Munhall 13,158
Murrysville 17,240
Myerstown 3,236
Nanticoke 12,267
Nanty-Glo 3,190
Narberth 4,278
Nazareth 5,713
Nemacolin 1,097
Nescopeck 1,651
Nesquehoning 3,364
New Beaver 1,736
New Berlin 892
New Bethlehem 1,151
New Brighton 6,854
New Britain 2,174
New Castle 28,334
New Castle Northwest 1,515
New Cumberland 7,665
New Eagle 2,172
New Freedom 2,920
New Holland 4,484
New Hope 1,400
New Kensington 15,894
New Milford 953
New Oxford 1,617
New Philadelphia 1,283
New Salem [-Buffington] 1,169
New Stanton 2,081
New Wilmington 2,706
Newmanstown 1,410
Newport 1,568
Newtown 2,565
Newville 1,349
Nixon 1,342
Norristown 30,749
North Apollo 1,391
North Belle Vernon 2,112
North Braddock 7,036
North Catasauqua 2,867
North Charleroi 1,562
North East 4,617
North Irwin 956
North Vandergrift [-Pleasant View] 1,431
North Wales 3,802
North York 1,689
Northampton 8,717
Northumberland 3,860
Northwest Harborcreek 6,662
Norwood 6,162
Oakdale 1,752
Oakland 1,766
Oakmont 6,961
Oakwood 2,541
Ohioville 3,865
Oil City 11,949
Oklahoma 977
Old Forge 8,834
Oliver 3,271
Olyphant 5,222
Orchard Hills 2,019
Orwigsburg 2,780
Osceola 1,310
Oxford 3,769
Paint 1,091
Palmerton 5,394
Palmyra 6,910
Palo Alto 1,192
Paoli 5,603
Paradise 1,043
Parkesburg 2,981
Parkside 2,369
Parkville 6,014
Patton 2,206
Paxtang 1,599
Pen Argyl 3,492
Penbrook 2,791
Penndel 2,703
Pennsburg 2,460
Pennville 1,336
Perkasie 7,878
Perryopolis 1,833
Philadelphia 1,585,577
Philipsburg 3,048
Phoenixville 15,066
Pine Grove 2,118
Pine Grove Mills 1,129
Pitcairn 4,087
Pittsburgh 369,879
Pittston 9,389
Plains 4,694
Pleasant Gap 1,699
Pleasant Hill 1,659
Pleasant Hills 8,884
Pleasantville 991
Plum 25,609
Plymouth 7,134
Plymptonville 1,074
Point Marion 1,344
Polk 1,267
Port Allegany 2,391
Port Carbon 2,134
Port Vue 4,641
Portage 3,105
Pottsgrove 3,122
Pottstown 21,831
Pottsville 16,603
Pringle 1,161
Prospect 1,122
Prospect Park 6,764
Punxsutawney 6,782
Quakertown 8,982
Quarryville 1,642
Rankin 2,503
Reading 78,380
Reamstown 2,649
Red Hill 1,794
Red Lion 6,130
Reedsville 1,030
Renovo 1,526
Republic [-Merritstown] 1,603
Reynoldsville 2,818
Rheems 1,044
Richboro 5,332
Richland 1,457
Richlandtown 1,195
Ridgway 4,793
Ridley Park 7,592
Riegelsville 912
Rimersburg 1,053
Riverside 1,991
Roaring Spring 2,615
Robesonia 1,944
Rochester 4,156
Rockledge 2,679
Rockwood 1,014
Roscoe 872
Rose Valley 982
Roseto 1,555
Rouzerville 1,188
Royalton 1,120
Royersford 4,458
Rural Valley 957
Russellton 1,691
Rutledge 843
Saegertown 1,066
St. Clair 3,524
St. Lawrence 1,542
St. Marys 5,511
St. Michael [-Sidman] 1,189
Saltsburg 990
Sanatoga 5,534
Sand Hill 2,307
Sandy 1,795
Saxonburg 1,345
Sayre 5,791
Scalp Level 1,158
Schuylkill Haven 5,610
Schwenksville 1,326
Scottdale 5,184
Scranton 81,805
Selinsgrove 5,384
Sellersville 4,479
Sewickley 4,134
Shamokin 9,184
Shamokin Dam 1,690
Sharon 17,493
Sharon Hill 5,771
Sharpsburg 3,781
Sharpsville 4,729
Sheffield 1,294
Shenandoah 6,221
Shenandoah Heights 1,386
Shickshinny 1,108
Shillington 5,062
Shiloh 8,245
Shinglehouse 1,243
Shippensburg 5,331
Shiremanstown 1,567
Shoemakersville 1,443
Shrewsbury 2,672
Sinking Spring 2,467
Skyline View 2,370
Slatington 4,678
Slippery Rock 3,008
Smethport 1,734
Smithfield 1,000
Somerset 6,454
Souderton 5,957
South Coatesville 1,026
South Connellsville 2,204
South Fork 1,197
South Greensburg 2,293
South Pottstown 1,966
South Waverly 1,049
South Williamsport 6,496
Southmont 2,415
Southwest Greensburg 2,456
Spangler 2,068
Speers 1,284
Spring City 3,433
Spring Grove 1,863
Spring Hill 1,014
Springdale 3,992
Springfield 24,160
State College 38,923
Steelton 5,152
Stewartstown 1,308
Stoneboro 1,091
Stowe 3,598
Strasburg 2,568
Stroudsburg 5,312
Sturgeon [-Noblestown] 1,350
Sugar Notch 1,044
Sugarcreek 5,532
Summit Hill 3,332
Sunbury 11,591
Susquehanna Depot 1,760
Swarthmore 6,157
Swissvale 10,637
Swoyersville 5,630
Sykesville 1,387
Tamaqua 7,943
Tarentum 5,674
Tatamy 873
Taylor 6,941
Telford 4,238
Temple 1,491
Terre Hill 1,282
Throop 4,070
Tionesta 634
Tipton 1,194
Titusville 6,434
Topton 1,987
Toughkenamon 1,273
Towanda 3,242
Trafford 3,345
Trainer 2,271
Trappe 2,115
Tremont 1,814
Tresckow 1,033
Trevorton 2,058
Trooper 5,137
Troy 1,262
Tullytown 2,339
Tunkhannock 2,251
Turtle Creek 6,556
Tyrone 5,743
Union City 3,537
Uniontown 12,034
Upland 3,334
Upper Darby 81,177
Upper Merion 25,722
Upper St. Clair 19,692
Valley View 1,749
Vandergrift 5,904
Vanport 1,700
Verona 3,260
Versailles 1,821
Wall 853
Walnutport 2,055
Warren 11,122
Warren South 1,780
Washington 15,864
Waterford 1,492
Watsontown 2,310
Waymart 1,337
Wayne Heights 1,683
Waynesboro 9,578
Waynesburg 4,270
Weatherly 2,640
Weigelstown 8,665
Weissport East 1,843
Wellsboro 3,430
Wernersville 1,934
Wesleyville 3,655
West Brownsville 1,170
West Chester 18,041
West Conshohocken 1,294
West Easton 1,163
West Fairview 1,403
West Goshen 8,948
West Grove 2,128
West Hazleton 4,136
West Homestead 2,495
West Kittanning 1,253
West Lawn 1,606
West Leechburg 1,359
West Mayfield 1,312
West Middlesex 982
West Mifflin 23,644
West Newton 3,152
West Norriton 15,209
West Pittston 5,590
West Reading 4,142
West View 7,734
West Wyoming 3,117
West York 4,283
Westfield 1,119
Westmont 5,789
Wheatland 760
Whitaker 1,416
White Haven 1,132
White Oak 8,761
Whitehall 14,451
Wiconisco 1,372
Wilkes-Barre 47,523
Wilkinsburg 21,080
Williamsburg 1,456
Williamsport 31,933
Williamstown 1,509
Wilmerding 2,222
Wilson 7,830
Wind Gap 2,741
Windber 4,756
Windsor 1,355
Womelsdorf 2,270
Woodland Heights 1,471
Woodside [-Drifton] 1,360
Wormleysburg 2,847
Wrightsville 2,396
Wyoming 3,255
Wyomissing 7,332
Wyomissing Hills 2,469
Yardley 2,288
Yeadon 11,980
Yeagertown 1,150
Yoe 947
York 42,192
Youngsville 1,775
Youngwood 3,372
Zelienople 4,158

Puerto Rico ■ population 3,522,037

Population

3,522,037 ..Census .. 1990
3,196,520 ....."...... 1980
2,712,033 ....."...... 1970
2,349,544 ....."...... 1960
2,210,703 ....."...... 1950
1,869,255 ....."...... 1940
1,543,913 ....."...... 1930
1,299,809 ....."...... 1920
1,118,012 ....."...... 1910

Metropolitan areas

Aguadilla 167,319
Arecibo 176,430
Caguas 304,925
Mayagüez 214,300
Ponce 232,947
San Juan 1,689,077

Municipalities

Adjuntas 19,451
Aguada 35,911
Aguadilla 59,335
Aguas Buenas 25,424
Aibonito 24,971
Añasco 25,234
Arecibo 93,385
Arroyo 18,910
Barceloneta 20,947
Barranquitas 25,605
Bayamón 220,262
Cabo Rojo 38,521
Caguas 133,447
Camuy 28,917
Canóvanas 36,816
Carolina 177,806
Cataño 34,587
Cayey 46,553
Ceiba 17,145
Ciales 18,084
Cidra 35,601
Coamo 33,837
Comerío 20,265
Corozal 33,095
Culebra 1,542
Dorado 30,759
Fajardo 36,882
Florida 8,689
Guánica 19,984
Guayama 41,588
Guayanilla 21,581
Guaynabo 92,886
Gurabo 28,737
Hatillo 32,703
Hormigueros 15,212
Humacao 55,203
Isabela 39,147
Jayuya 15,527
Juana Díaz 45,198
Juncos 30,612
Lajas 23,271
Lares 29,015
Las Marías 9,306
Las Piedras 27,896
Loíza 29,307
Luquillo 18,100
Manatí 38,692
Maricao 6,206
Maunabo 12,347
Mayagüez 100,371
Moca 32,926
Morovis 25,288
Naguabo 22,620
Naranjito 27,914
Orocovis 21,158
Patillas 19,633
Peñuelas 22,515
Ponce 187,749
Quebradillas 21,425
Rincón 12,213
Río Grande 45,648
Sabana Grande 22,843
Salinas 28,335
San Germán 34,962
San Juan 437,745
San Lorenzo 35,163
San Sebastián 38,799
Santa Isabel 19,318
Toa Alta 44,101
Toa Baja 89,454
Trujillo Alto 61,120
Utuado 34,980
Vega Alta 34,559
Vega Baja 55,997
Vieques 8,602
Villalba 23,559
Yabucoa 36,483
Yauco 42,058

Cities, towns, and villages

Adjuntas 5,239
Aguadilla 22,039
Aibonito 9,331
Arecibo 48,779
Arroyo 8,435
Bayamón 185,087
Cabo Rojo 10,292
Caguas 87,214
Canóvanas 7,260
Carolina 147,835
Cataño 26,243
Cayey 23,305
Cidra 6,069
Coamo 12,851
Comerío 5,736
Corozal 5,889
Dorado 10,203
Fajardo 26,928
Guánica 9,628

Guayama 21,097
Guayanilla 6,163
Guaynabo 65,075
Gurabo 7,645
Hormigueros 12,031
Humacao 19,147
Isabela 12,087
Juana Díaz 10,469
Juncos 7,851
Manatí 17,347
Mayagüez 82,968
Ponce 161,739
Río Grande 12,047
Sabana
Grande 7,435
Salinas 6,220
San Germán 13,054
San Juan 424,600
San Lorenzo 8,880
San Sebastián 10,619
Santa Isabel 6,948
Trujillo Alto 41,141
Utuado 11,113
Vega
Alta 10,582
Vega
Baja 18,233
Yabucoa 6,797
Yauco 14,594

Rhode Island ■ population 1,005,984

Metropolitan areas

Fall River 157,272
(139,621 in Mass.;
17,651 in R.I.)
New London-Norwich 266,819
(238,341 in Conn.;
28,478 in R.I.)
Pawtucket-Woonsocket-
Attleboro 329,384
(227,131 in R.I.;
102,253 in Mass.)
Providence 654,854

Counties

Bristol 48,859
Kent 161,135
Newport 87,194
Providence 596,270
Washington 110,006

Cities and towns

Ashaway 1,584
Barrington 15,849
Bradford 1,604
Bristol 21,625
Burrillville 16,230
Central Falls 17,637
Charlestown 6,478
Coventry 31,083
Cranston 76,060
Cumberland 29,038
Cumberland Hill 6,379
East Greenwich 11,865
East Providence 50,380
Exeter 5,461
Foster 4,316
Glocester 9,227
Greenville 8,303
Harrisville 1,654
Hope Valley 1,446
Hopkinton 6,873
Jamestown 4,999
Johnston 26,542
Kingston 6,504
Lincoln 18,045
Little Compton 3,339
Melville 4,426
Middletown 19,460
Narragansett 14,985
Narragansett Pier 3,721
Narragansett
Reservation 31
New Shoreham 836
Newport 28,227
Newport East 11,080
North Kingstown 23,786
North Providence 32,090
North Smithfield 10,497
Pascoag 5,011
Pawtucket 72,644
Portsmouth 16,857
Providence 160,728
Richmond 5,351
Scituate 9,796
Smithfield 19,163
South Kingstown 24,631
Tiverton 7,259
▲14,312
Valley Falls 11,175
Wakefield
(-Peacedale) 7,134
Warren 11,385
Warwick 85,427
West Greenwich 3,492
West Warwick 29,268
Westerly 16,477
▲21,605
Woonsocket 43,877

▲ Entire township, including rural area.

South Carolina ■ population 3,505,707

Metropolitan areas

Anderson 145,196
Augusta (Ga.) 396,809
(275,869 in Ga.;
120,940 in S.C.)
Charleston 506,875
Charlotte-Gastonia (N.C.)-
Rock Hill 1,162,093
(1,030,596 in N.C.;
131,497 in S.C.)
Columbia 453,331
Florence 114,344
Greenville-Spartanburg 640,861

Counties

Abbeville 23,862
Aiken 120,940
Allendale 11,722
Anderson 145,196
Bamberg 16,902
Barnwell 20,293
Beaufort 86,425
Berkeley 128,776
Calhoun 12,753
Charleston 295,039
Cherokee 44,506
Chester 32,170
Chesterfield 38,577
Clarendon 28,450
Colleton 34,377
Darlington 61,851
Dillon 29,114
Dorchester 83,060
Edgefield 18,375
Fairfield 22,295
Florence 114,344
Georgetown 46,302
Greenville 320,167
Greenwood 59,567
Hampton 18,191
Horry 144,053
Jasper 15,487
Kershaw 43,599
Lancaster 54,516
Laurens 58,092
Lee 18,437
Lexington 167,611
Marion 33,899
Marlboro 29,361
McCormick 8,868
Newberry 33,172
Oconee 57,494
Orangeburg 84,803
Pickens 93,894
Richland 285,720
Saluda 16,357
Spartanburg 226,800
Sumter 102,637
Union 30,337
Williamsburg 36,815
York 131,497

Cities and towns

Abbeville 5,778
Aiken 19,872
Allendale 4,410
Anderson 26,184
Andrews 3,050
Arcadia Lakes 899
Arial 2,604
Atlantic Beach 446
Aynor 470
Bamberg 3,843
Barnwell 5,255
Batesburg 4,082
Bath 2,242
Beaufort 9,576
Belton 4,646
Belvedere 6,133
Bennettsville 9,345
Berea 13,535
Bethune 405
Bishopville 3,560
Blacksburg 1,907
Blackville 2,688
Bluffton 738
Boiling Springs 3,522
Bonneau 374
Bowman 1,063
Branchville 1,107
Briarcliffe Acres 552
Brookdale 5,339
Brunson 587
Bucksport 1,022
Buffalo 1,569
Burnettown 493
Burton 6,917
Calhoun Falls 2,328
Camden 6,696
Cameron 504
Campobello 465
Carlisle 470
Cayce 11,163
Central 2,438
Central Pacolet 257
Chapin 282
Charleston 80,414
Chreaw 5,505
Chesnee 1,280
Chester 7,158
Chesterfield 1,373
City View 1,490
Clearwater 4,731
Clemson 11,096
Clinton 7,987
Clio 882
Clover 3,422
Columbia 98,052
Conway 9,819
Cottageville 572
Coward 532
Cowpens 2,176
Cross Hill 469
Darlington 7,311
Denmark 3,762
Dentville 11,839
Dillon 6,829
Donalds 326
Due West 1,220
Duncan 2,152
Dunean 4,637
Easley 15,195
East Gaffney 3,278
East Sumter 1,590
Eastover 1,044
Edgefield 2,563
Edisto Beach 340
Ehrhardt 442
Elgin 622
Elko 214
Elloree 939
Estill 2,387
Eutawville 350
Fairfax 2,317
Florence 29,813
Folly Beach 1,398
Forest Acres 7,197
Forestbrook 2,502
Fort Lawn 718
Fort Mill 4,930
Fountain Inn 4,388
Gaffney 13,145
Gantt 13,891
Gaston 984
Georgetown 9,517
Gifford 313
Gilbert 324
Gloverville 2,753
Golden Grove 2,055
Goose Creek 24,692
Gray Court 914
Great Falls 2,307
Greeleyville 464
Greenville 58,282
Greenwood 20,807
Greer 10,322
Hampton 2,997
Hanahan 13,176
Hardeeville 1,583
Harleyville 633
Hartsville 8,372
Health Springs 907
Hemingway 829
Hickory Grove 287
Hilda 342
Hilton Head
Island 23,694
Holy Hill 1,478
Hollywood 2,094
Homeland Park 6,569
Honea Path 3,841
Inman 1,742
Inman Mills 1,571
Irmo 11,280
Irwin 1,296
Isle of Palms 3,680
Iva 1,174
Jackson 1,681
Jefferson 745
Joanna 1,735
Johnsonville 1,415
Johnston 2,688
Jonesville 1,205
Kershaw 1,814
Kingstree 3,858
Kline 285
Ladson 13,540
Lake City 7,153
Lake View 872
Lamar 1,125
Lancaster 8,914
Landrum 2,347
Lane 523
Latta 1,565
Laurel Bay 4,972
Laurens 9,694
Leesville 2,025
Lexington 3,289
Liberty 3,228
Lincolnville 716
Little Mountain 235
Little River 3,470
Loris 2,067
Lowrys 200
Lugoff 3,211
Lyman 2,271
Lynchburg 475
Manning 4,428
Marion 7,658
Mauldin 11,587
Mayesville 694
Mayo 1,569
McBee 715
McClellanville 333
McColl 2,685
McCormick 1,659
Meggett 787
Millwood 1,070
Monarch Mills 2,214
Moncks Corner 5,607
Monetta 285
Mount Pleasant 30,108
Mulberry 1,097
Mullins 5,910
Murrells Inlet 3,334
Myrtle Beach 24,848
Neeses 410
New Ellenton 2,515
Newberry 10,542
Nichols 528
Ninety Six 2,099
Norris 884
North 809
North Augusta 15,351
North Charleston 70,218
North Hartsville 2,906
North Myrtle
Beach 8,636
Norway 401
Oak Grove 7,173
Oakland 1,298
Olanta 687
Olar 391
Orangeburg 13,739
Pacolet 1,736
Pacolet Mills 696
Pageland 2,666
Pamplico 1,314
Parris Island 7,172
Patrick 368
Paxville 218
Pelion 336
Pendleton 3,314
Perry 241
Pickens 3,042
Piedmont 4,143
Pineridge 1,731
Pinewood 600
Pomaria 267
Port Royal 2,985
Prosperity 1,116
Quinby 865
Ravenel 2,165
Red Bank 5,950
Reevesville 244
Richburg 405
Ridge Spring 861
Ridgeland 1,071
Ridgeville 1,625
Ridgeway 407
Rock Hill 41,643
Roebuck 1,966
Rowesville 316
Ruby 300
St. Andrews 25,692
St. George 2,077
St. Matthews 2,345
St. Stephen 1,697
Salley 451
Saluda 2,798
Sans Souci 7,612
Santee 638
Saxon 4,002
Scranton 802
Sellers 358
Seneca 7,726
Seven Oaks 15,722
Sharon 270
Shell Point 2,885
Simpsonville 11,708
Six Mile 562
Slater (-Marietta) 2,245
Socastee 10,426
Society Hill 686
South Congaree 2,406
South Sumter 4,371
Southern Shops 3,378
Spartanburg 43,467
Springdale 2,643
Springdale 3,226
Springfield 523
Startex 1,162
Stuckey 311
Sullivans Island 1,623
Summerton 975
Summerville 22,519
Summit 242
Sumter 41,943
Surfside Beach 3,845
Swansea 527
Sycamore 208
Taylors 19,619
Tega Cay 3,016
Timmonsville 2,182
Travelers Rest 3,069
Trenton 303
Turbeville 698
Union 9,836
Utica 1,478
Valencia Heights 4,122
Valley Falls 3,504
Vance 214
Varnville 1,970
Wade Hampton 20,014
Wagener 731
Walhalla 3,755
Walterboro 5,492
Ware Shoals 2,497
Watts Mills 1,535
Welcome 6,560
Wellford 2,511
West Columbia 10,588
West Pelzer 989
West Union 260
Westminster 3,120
Whitmire 1,702
Wilkinson Heights 3,394
Williamston 3,876
Williston 3,099
Winnsboro 3,475
Winnsboro Mills 2,275
Woodfield 8,862
Woodford 200
Woodruff 4,365
Yemassee 728
York 6,709

South Dakota ■ population 699,999

Metropolitan areas

Rapid City 81,343
Sioux Falls 123,809

Counties

Aurora 3,135
Beadle 18,253
Bennett 3,206
Bon Homme 7,089
Brookings 25,207
Brown 35,580
Brule 5,485
Buffalo 1,759
Butte 7,914
Campbell 1,965
Charles Mix 9,131
Clark 4,403
Clay 13,186
Codington 22,698
Corson 4,195
Custer 6,179
Davison 17,503
Day 6,978
Deuel 4,522
Dewey 5,523
Douglas 3,746
Edmunds 4,356
Fall River 7,353
Faulk 2,744
Grant 8,372
Gregory 5,359
Haakon 2,624
Hamlin 4,974
Hand 4,272
Hanson 2,994
Harding 1,669
Hughes 14,817
Hutchinson 8,262
Hyde 1,696
Jackson 2,811
Jerauld 2,425
Jones 1,324
Kingsbury 5,925
Lake 10,550
Lawrence 20,655
Lincoln 15,427
Lyman 3,638
Marshall 4,844
McCook 5,688
McPherson 3,228
Meade 21,878
Mellette 2,137
Miner 3,272
Minnehaha 123,809
Moody 6,507
Pennington 81,343
Perkins 3,932
Potter 3,190
Roberts 9,914
Sanborn 2,833
Shannon 9,902
Spink 7,981
Stanley 2,453
Sully 1,589
Todd 8,352
Tripp 6,924
Turner 8,576
Union 10,189
Walworth 6,087
Yankton 19,252
Ziebach 2,220

Cities and towns

Aberdeen 24,927
Alcester 843
Alexandria 518
Alpena 251
Antelope 744
Arlington 908
Armour 854
Artesian 217
Aurora 619
Avon 576
Baltic 666
Belle Fourche 4,335
Beresford 1,849
Big Stone City 669
Bison 451
Black Hawk 1,995
Blunt 342
Bonesteel 297
Bowdle 589
Box Elder 2,680
Brandon 3,543
Bridgewater 533
Bristol 419
Britton 1,394
Brookings 16,270
Bruce 235
Bryant 374
Buffalo 488
Burke 756
Canistota 608
Canton 2,787
Carthage 221
Castlewood 549
Centerville 887
Chamberlain 2,347
Chancellor 276
Cheyenne River
Reservation 7,743
Clark 1,292
Clear Lake 1,247
Colman 482
Colome 309
Colonial Pine Hills 1,553
Colton 657
Conde 203
Corsica 619
Crooks 671
Crow Creek
Reservation 1,756

South Dakota (continued)

Custer 1,741
Deadwood 1,830
Dell Rapids 2,484
Delmont 235
De Smet 1,172
Doland 306
Dupree 484
Eagle Butte 489
Edgemont 906
Egan 208
Elk Point 1,423
Elkton 602
Ellsworth 7,017
Emery 417
Estelline 658
Ethan 312
Eureka 1,197
Faith 548
Faulkton 809
Flandreau 2,311
Flandreau Reservation 279
Fort Pierre 1,854
Fort Thompson 1,088
Frederick 241
Freeman 1,293
Garretson 924
Gary 274
Gayville 401
Geddes 280
Gettysburg 1,510
Gregory 1,384
Groton 1,196
Harrisburg 727
Hartford 1,262
Hayti 372
Hecla 398
Henry 215
Hermosa 242
Herreid 488
Highmore 835
Hill City 650
Hosmer 310
Hot Springs 4,325
Hoven 522
Howard 1,156
Hudson 332
Humboldt 468
Hurley 372
Huron 12,448
Ipswich 965
Irene 464
Iroquois 328
Isabel 319
Jefferson 527
Kadoka 736
Kennebec 284
Keystone 232
Kimball 743
Kyle 914
Lake Andes 846
Lake Norden 427
Lake Preston 663
Lake Traverse Reservation 10,496
Langford 298
Lead 3,632
Lemmon 1,614
Lennox 1,767
Leola 521
Little Eagle 294
Lower Brule 655
Lower Brule Reservation 1,123
Madison 6,257
Marion 831
Martin 1,151
Marty 436
McIntosh 302
McLaughlin 780
Menno 768
Midland 233
Milbank 3,879
Miller 1,678
Mission 730
Mitchell 13,798
Mobridge 3,768
Montrose 420
Mount Vernon 368
Murdo 679
New Effington 219
New Underwood 553
Newell 675
North Eagle Butte 1,423
North Sioux City 2,019
North Spearfish 2,274
Oacoma 367
Oglala 422
Onida 761
Parker 984
Parkston 1,572
Parmelee 618
Philip 1,077
Pierre 12,906
Pine Ridge 2,596
Pine Ridge Reservation 11,385
Pine Ridge Trust Lands 804
Plankinton 604
Platte 1,311
Pollock 379
Porcupine 783
Presho 654
Pukwana 263
Rapid City 54,523
Rapid Valley 5,968
Redfield 2,770
Roscoe 362
Rosebud 1,538
Rosebud Reservation 8,352
Rosebud Trust Lands 1,344
Rosholt 408
Roslyn 251
St. Francis 815
St. Lawrence 223
Salem 1,289
Scotland 968
Selby 707
Sioux Falls 100,814
Sisseton 2,181
South Shore 260
Spearfish 6,966
Spencer 317
Spring Creek 231
Springfield 834
Standing Rock Reservation 4,195
Stickney 323
Sturgis 5,330
Summit 267
Tabor 403
Tea 786
Timber Lake 517
Toronto 201
Trent 211
Tripp 664
Tulare 244
Tyndall 1,201
Valley Springs 739
Veblen 321
Vermillion 10,034
Viborg 763
Volga 1,263
Wagner 1,462
Wakonda 329
Wall 834
Wanblee 654
Warner 336
Watertown 17,592
Waubay 647
Webster 2,017
Wessington 265
Wessington Springs 1,083
White 536
White Lake 419
White River 595
Whitewood 891
Willow Lake 317
Wilmot 566
Winner 3,354
Wolsey 442
Woonsocket 766
Worthing 371
Yankton 12,703
Yankton Reservation 6,269

Tennessee ■ population 4,896,641

Metropolitan areas

Chattanooga 433,210 (319,259 in Tenn.; 113,951 in Ga.)
Clarksville-Hopkinsville 169,439 (100,498 in Tenn.; 68,941 in Ky.)
Jackson 77,982
Johnson City-Kingsport-Bristol (Va.) 436,047 (348,530 in Tenn.; 87,517 in Va.)
Knoxville 604,816
Memphis 981,747 (863,898 in Tenn.; 49,939 in Ark.; 67,910 in Miss.)
Nashville 985,026

Counties

Anderson 68,250
Bedford 30,411
Benton 14,524
Bledsoe 9,669
Blount 85,969
Bradley 73,712
Campbell 35,079
Cannon 10,467
Carroll 27,514
Carter 51,505
Cheatham 27,140
Chester 12,819
Claiborne 26,137
Clay 7,238
Cocke 29,141
Coffee 40,339
Crockett 13,378
Cumberland 34,736
Davidson 510,784
Decatur 10,472
De Kalb 14,360
Dickson 35,061
Dyer 34,854
Fayette 25,559
Fentress 14,669
Franklin 34,725
Gibson 46,315
Giles 25,741
Grainger 17,095
Greene 55,853
Grundy 13,362
Hamblen 50,480
Hamilton 285,536
Hancock 6,739
Hardeman 23,377
Hardin 22,633
Hawkins 44,565
Haywood 19,437
Henderson 21,844
Henry 27,888
Hickman 16,754
Houston 7,018
Humphreys 15,795
Jackson 9,297
Jefferson 33,016
Johnson 13,766
Knox 335,749
Lake 7,129
Lauderdale 23,491
Lawrence 35,303
Lewis 9,247
Lincoln 28,157
Loudon 31,255
Macon 15,906
Madison 77,982
Marion 24,860
Marshall 21,539
Maury 54,812
McMinn 42,383
McNairy 22,422
Meigs 8,033
Monroe 30,541
Montgomery 100,498
Moore 4,721
Morgan 17,300
Obion 31,717
Overton 17,636
Perry 6,612
Pickett 4,548
Polk 13,643
Putnam 51,373
Rhea 24,344
Roane 47,227
Robertson 41,494
Rutherford 118,570
Scott 18,358
Sequatchie 8,863
Sevier 51,043
Shelby 826,330
Smith 14,143
Stewart 9,479
Sullivan 143,596
Sumner 103,281
Tipton 37,568
Trousdale 5,920
Unicoi 16,549
Union 13,694
Van Buren 4,846
Warren 32,992
Washington 92,315
Wayne 13,935
Weakley 31,972
White 20,090
Williamson 81,021
Wilson 67,675

Cities and towns

Adams 587
Adamsville 1,745
Alamo 2,426
Alcoa 6,400
Alexandria 730
Algood 2,399
Allardt 609
Altamont 679
Ardmore 866
Arlington 1,541
Ashland City 2,552
Athens 12,054
Atoka 659
Atwood 1,066
Auburntown 240
Baileyton 309
Banner Hill 1,717
Bartlett 26,989
Baxter 1,289
Beersheba Springs 596
Bell Buckle 326
Belle Meade 2,839
Bells 1,643
Benton 992
Berry Hill 802
Bethel Springs 755
Big Sandy 505
Blaine 1,326
Bloomingdale 10,953
Blountville 2,605
Bluff City 1,390
Bolivar 5,969
Braden 354
Bradford 1,154
Brentwood 16,392
Brighton 717
Bristol 23,421
Brownsville 10,019
Bruceton 1,586
Bulls Gap 659
Burlison 394
Burns 1,127
Byrdstown 998
Calhoun 552
Camden 3,643
Carthage 2,386
Caryville 1,751
Cedar Hill 347
Celina 1,493
Centertown 332
Centerville 3,616
Central 2,635
Chapel Hill 833
Charleston 653
Charlotte 854
Chattanooga 152,466
Church Hill 4,834
Clarksburg 321
Clarksville 75,494
Cleveland 30,354
Clifton 620
Clinton 8,972
Coalmont 813
Collegedale 5,048
Collierville 14,427
Collinwood 1,014
Colonial Heights 6,716
Columbia 28,583
Cookeville 21,744
Copperhill 362
Cornersville 683
Covington 7,487
Cowan 1,738
Crab Orchard 876
Cross Plains 1,025
Crossville 6,930
Crump 2,028
Cumberland City 319
Cumberland Gap 210
Dandridge 1,540
Dayton 5,671
Decatur 1,361
Decaturville 879
Decherd 2,196
Dickson 8,791
Dover 1,341
Dowelltown 308
Doyle 345
Dresden 2,488
Ducktown 421
Dunlap 3,731
Dyer 2,204
Dyersburg 16,317
Eagleton Village 5,169
Eagleville 462
East Brainerd 11,594
East Cleveland 1,249
East Ridge 21,101
Eastview 563
Elizabethton 11,931
Elkton 448
Englewood 1,611
Enville 211
Erin 1,586
Erwin 5,015
Estill Springs 1,408
Ethridge 565
Etowah 3,815
Fairfield Glade 2,209
Fairmount 1,578
Fairview 4,210
Fall Branch 1,203
Farragut 12,793
Fayetteville 6,921
Finger 279
Forest Hills 4,231
Franklin 20,098
Friendship 467
Friendsville 792
Gadsden 561
Gainesboro 1,002
Gallatin 18,794
Gallaway 762
Gates 608
Gatlinburg 3,417
Germantown 32,893
Gibson 281
Gilt Edge 447
Gleason 1,402
Goodlettsville 11,219
Gordonsville 891
Grand Junction 365
Gray 1,071
Graysville 1,301
Greenback 611
Greenbrier 2,873
Greeneville 13,532
Greenfield 2,105
Guys 497
Halls 2,431
Halls Crossroads 6,450
Harriman 7,119
Harrison 7,191
Harrogate [-Shawnee] 2,657
Hartsville 2,188
Henderson 4,760
Hendersonville 32,188
Henning 802
Henry 317
Hohenwald 3,760
Hollow Rock 902
Hornbeak 445
Hornsby 313
Humboldt 9,651
Hunter 1,602
Huntingdon 4,180
Huntland 885
Huntsville 660
Iron City 402
Jacksboro 1,568
Jackson 48,949
Jamestown 1,862
Jasper 2,780
Jefferson City 5,494
Jellico 2,447
Johnson City 49,381
Jonesborough 3,091
Karns 1,458
Kenton 1,366
Kimball 1,243
Kingsport 36,365
Kingston 4,552
Kingston Springs 1,529
Knoxville 165,121
Lafayette 3,641
La Follette 7,192
Lake City 2,166
Lakeland 1,204
Lakesite 732
Lakewood 2,009
La Vergne 7,499
Lawrenceburg 10,412
Lebanon 15,208
Lenoir City 6,147
Lewisburg 9,879
Lexington 5,810
Liberty 391
Linden 1,099
Livingston 3,809
Lobelville 830
Lookout Mountain 1,901
Loretto 1,515
Loudon 4,026
Luttrell 812
Lynchburg 4,721
Lynnville 344
Madisonville 3,033
Manchester 7,709
Martin 8,600
Maryville 19,208
Mascot 2,138
Mason 337
Maury City 782
Maynardville 1,298
McEwen 1,442
McKenzie 5,168
McLemoresville 280
McMinnville 11,194
Medina 658
Memphis 610,337
Michie 677
Middle Valley 12,255
Middleton 536
Midway 2,953
Milan 7,512
Milledgeville 279
Millersville 2,575
Millington 17,866
Minor Hill 372
Monteagle 1,138
Monterey 2,559
Morrison 570
Morristown 21,385
Moscow 384
Mosheim 1,451
Mount Carmel 4,082
Mount Juliet 5,389
Mount Pleasant 4,278
Mountain City 2,169
Munford 2,326
Murfreesboro 44,922
Nashville 510,784
New Hope 854
New Johnsonville 1,643
New Market 1,086
New Tazewell 1,864
Newbern 2,515
Newport 7,123
Niota 745
Nolensville 1,570
Norris 1,303
Oak Grove 3,498
Oak Hill 4,301
Oak Ridge 27,310
Oakdale 268
Oakland 392
Obion 1,241
Oliver Springs 3,433
Oneida 3,502
Ooltewah 4,903
Orlinda 469
Palmer 769
Paris 9,332
Parsons 2,033
Pegram 1,371
Petersburg 514
Philadelphia 463
Pigeon Forge 3,027
Pikeville 1,771
Pine Crest 3,821
Piperton 612
Pittman Center 478
Pleasant Hill 494
Portland 5,165
Powell 7,534
Powells Crossroads 1,098
Pulaski 7,895
Puryear 592
Ramer 337
Red Bank 12,322
Red Boiling Springs 905
Ridgely 1,775
Ridgeside 400
Ridgetop 1,132
Ripley 6,188
Rives 344
Roan Mountain 1,220
Rockford 646
Rockwood 5,348
Rogersville 4,149
Rossville 291
Rutherford 1,303
Rutledge 903
St. Joseph 789
Saltillo 383
Samburg 374
Sardis 305
Savannah 6,547
Scotts Hill 594
Selmer 3,838
Sevierville 7,178
Sewanee 2,128
Seymour 7,026
Sharon 1,047
Shelbyville 14,049
Signal Mountain 7,034
Smithville 3,791
Smyrna 13,647
Sneedville 1,446
Soddy-Daisy 8,240
Somerville 2,047
South Carthage 851
South Cleveland 5,372
South Fulton 2,688
South Pittsburg 3,295
Sparta 4,681
Spencer 1,125
Spring City 2,199
Spring Hill 1,464
Springfield 11,227
Spurgeon 3,149
Stanton 487
Stantonville 264
Surgoinsville 1,499
Sweetwater 5,066
Tazewell 2,150
Tellico Plains 657
Tennessee Ridge 1,271
Tiptonville 2,149
Toone 279
Townsend 329
Tracy City 1,556
Trenton 4,836
Trezevant 874
Trimble 694
Troy 1,047
Tullahoma 16,761
Tusculum 1,918
Union City 10,513
Vanleer 369
Vonore 605
Walden 1,523
Walnut Hill 3,332
Wartburg 932
Wartrace 494
Watauga 389
Watertown 1,250
Waverly 3,925
Waynesboro 1,824
Westmoreland 1,726
White Bluff 1,988
White House 2,987
White Pine 1,771
Whiteville 1,050
Whitwell 1,622
Wildwood Lake 2,680
Williston 427
Winchester 6,305
Winfield 564
Woodbury 2,287
Woodland Mills 398
Yorkville 347

Texas ■ population 17,059,805

Metropolitan areas

Abilene 119,655
Amarillo 187,547
Austin 781,572
Beaumont-Port Arthur 361,226
Brazoria 191,707
Brownsville-Harlingen 260,120
Bryan-College Station 121,862
Corpus Christi 349,894
Dallas 2,553,362
El Paso 591,610
Fort Worth-Arlington 1,332,053
Galveston-Texas City 217,399
Houston 3,301,937
Killeen-Temple 255,301
Laredo 133,239
Longview-Marshall 162,431
Lubbock 222,636
McAllen-Edinburg-Mission 383,545
Midland 106,611
Odessa 118,934
San Angelo 98,458
San Antonio 1,302,099
Sherman-Denison 95,021
Texarkana-Texarkana (Ark.) 120,132 (81,665 in Tex.; 38,467 in Ark.)
Tyler 151,309
Victoria 74,361
Waco 189,123
Wichita Falls 122,378

Counties

Anderson 48,024
Andrews 14,338
Angelina 69,884
Aransas 17,892
Archer 7,973
Armstrong 2,021
Atascosa 30,533
Austin 19,832
Bailey 7,064
Bandera 10,562
Bastrop 38,263
Baylor 4,385
Bee 25,135
Bell 191,088
Bexar 1,185,394
Blanco 5,972
Borden 799
Bosque 15,125
Bowie 81,665
Brazoria 191,707
Brazos 121,862
Brewster 8,681
Briscoe 1,971
Brooks 8,204
Brown 34,371
Burleson 13,625
Burnet 22,677
Caldwell 26,392
Calhoun 19,053
Callahan 11,859
Cameron 260,120
Camp 9,904
Carson 6,576
Cass 29,982
Castro 9,070
Chambers 20,088
Cherokee 41,049
Childress 5,953
Clay 10,024
Cochran 4,377
Coke 3,424
Coleman 9,710
Collin 264,036
Collingsworth 3,573
Colorado 18,383
Comal 51,832
Comanche 13,381
Concho 3,044
Cooke 30,777
Coryell 64,213
Cottle 2,247
Crane 4,652
Crockett 4,078
Crosby 7,304
Culberson 3,407
Dallam 5,461
Dallas 1,852,810
Dawson 14,349
Deaf Smith 19,153
Delta 4,857
Denton 273,525
De Witt 18,840
Dickens 2,571
Dimmit 10,433
Donley 3,696
Duval 12,918
Eastland 18,488
Ector 118,934
Edwards 2,266
Ellis 85,167
El Paso 591,610
Erath 27,991
Falls 17,712
Fannin 24,804
Fayette 20,095
Fisher 4,842
Floyd 8,497
Foard 1,794
Fort Bend 225,421
Franklin 7,802
Freestone 15,818
Frio 13,472
Gaines 14,123
Galveston 217,399
Garza 5,143
Gillespie 17,204
Glasscock 1,447
Goliad 5,980
Gonzales 17,205
Gray 23,967
Grayson 95,021
Gregg 104,948
Grimes 18,828
Guadalupe 64,873
Hale 34,671
Hall 3,905
Hamilton 7,733
Hansford 5,848
Hardeman 5,283
Hardin 41,320
Harris 2,818,199
Harrison 57,483
Hartley 3,634
Haskell 6,820
Hays 65,614
Hemphill 3,720
Henderson 58,543
Hidalgo 383,545
Hill 27,146
Hockley 24,199
Hood 28,981
Hopkins 28,833
Houston 21,375
Howard 32,343
Hudspeth 2,915
Hunt 64,343
Hutchinson 25,689
Irion 1,629
Jack 6,981
Jackson 13,039
Jasper 31,102
Jeff Davis 1,946
Jefferson 239,397
Jim Hogg 5,109
Jim Wells 37,679
Johnson 97,165
Jones 16,490
Karnes 12,455
Kaufman 52,220
Kendall 14,589
Kenedy 460
Kent 1,010
Kerr 36,304
Kimble 4,122
King 354
Kinney 3,119
Kleberg 30,274
Knox 4,837
Lamar 43,949
Lamb 15,072
Lampasas 13,521
La Salle 5,254
Lavaca 18,690
Lee 12,854
Leon 12,665
Liberty 52,726
Limestone 20,946
Lipscomb 3,143
Live Oak 9,556
Llano 11,631
Lubbock 222,636
Lynn 6,758
Madison 10,931
Marion 9,984
Martin 4,956
Mason 3,423
Matagorda 36,928
Maverick 36,378
McCulloch 8,778
McLennan 189,123
McMullen 817
Medina 27,312
Menard 2,252
Midland 106,611
Milam 22,946
Mills 4,531
Mitchell 8,016
Montague 17,274
Montgomery 182,201
Moore 17,865
Morris 13,200
Motley 1,532
Nacogdoches 54,753
Navarro 39,926
Newton 13,569
Nolan 16,594
Nueces 291,145
Ochiltree 9,128
Oldham 2,278
Orange 80,509
Palo Pinto 25,055
Panola 22,035
Parker 64,785
Parmer 9,863
Pecos 14,675
Polk 30,687
Potter 97,874
Presidio 6,637
Rains 6,715
Randall 89,673
Reagan 4,514
Real 2,412
Red River 14,317
Reeves 15,852
Refugio 7,976
Roberts 1,025
Robertson 15,511
Rockwall 25,604
Runnels 11,294
Rusk 43,735
Sabine 9,586
San Augustine 7,999
San Jacinto 16,372
San Patricio 58,749
San Saba 5,401
Schleicher 2,990
Scurry 18,634
Shackelford 3,316
Shelby 22,034
Sherman 2,858
Smith 151,309
Somervell 5,360
Starr 40,518
Stephens 9,010
Sterling 1,438
Stonewall 2,013
Sutton 4,135
Swisher 8,133
Tarrant 1,170,103
Taylor 119,655
Terrell 1,410
Terry 13,218
Throckmorton 1,880
Titus 24,009
Tom Green 98,458
Travis 576,407
Trinity 11,445
Tyler 16,646
Upshur 31,370
Upton 4,447
Uvalde 23,340
Val Verde 38,721
Van Zandt 37,944
Victoria 74,361
Walker 50,917
Waller 23,390
Ward 13,115
Washington 26,154
Webb 133,239
Wharton 39,955
Wheeler 5,879
Wichita 122,378
Wilbarger 15,121
Willacy 17,705
Williamson 139,551
Wilson 22,650
Winkler 8,626
Wise 34,679
Wood 29,380
Yoakum 8,786
Young 18,126
Zapata 9,279
Zavala 12,162

Cities, towns, and villages

Abernathy 2,720
Abilene 106,654
Addison 8,783
Agua Dulce 794
Alamo 8,210
Alamo Heights 6,502
Albany 1,962
Aldine 11,133
Aledo 1,169
Alice 19,788
Allen 18,309
Alpine 5,637
Alto 1,027
Alton 3,069
Alvarado 2,918
Alvin 19,220
Alvord 865
Amarillo 157,615
Ames 989
Amherst 742
Anahuac 1,993
Andrews 10,678
Angleton 17,140
Anna 904
Anson 2,644
Anthony 3,328
Anton 1,212
Aransas Pass 7,180
Archer City 1,748
Argyle 1,575
Arlington 261,721
Arp 812
Asherton 1,608
Aspermont 1,214
Athens 10,967
Atlanta 6,118
Aubrey 1,138
Austin 465,622
Azle 8,868
Bacliff 5,549
Baird 1,658
Balch Springs 17,406
Balcones Heights 3,022
Ballinger 3,975
Bandera 877
Bangs 1,555
Barrett 3,052
Bartlett 1,439
Bastrop 4,044
Bay City 18,170
Baytown 63,850
Beach City 852
Beaumont 114,323
Beckville 783
Bedford 43,762
Beeville 13,547
Bellaire 13,842
Bellmead 8,336
Bellville 3,378
Belton 12,476
Benavides 1,788
Benbrook 19,564
Benjamin 225
Bertram 849
Beverly Hills 2,048
Bevil Oaks 1,350
Big Lake 3,672
Big Sandy 1,185
Big Spring 23,093
Big Wells 756
Bishop 3,337
Blanco 1,238
Blossom 1,440
Blue Mound 2,133
Boerne 4,274
Bogata 1,421
Bonham 6,686
Booker 1,236
Borger 15,675
Bovina 1,549
Bowie 4,990
Boyd 1,041
Brackettville 1,740
Brady 5,946
Brazoria 2,717
Breckenridge 5,665
Bremond 1,110
Brenham 11,952
Briar 3,899
Bridge City 8,034
Bridgeport 3,581
Bronte 962
Brookshire 2,922
Brookside Village 1,470
Brownfield 9,560
Brownsville 98,962
Brownwood 18,387
Bruceville-Eddy 1,075
Bryan 55,002
Buffalo 1,555
Bunker Hill 3,391
Burkburnett 10,145
Burleson 16,113
Burnet 3,423
Cactus 1,529
Caddo Mills 1,068
Caldwell 3,181
Calvert 1,536
Cameron 5,580
Canadian 2,417
Canton 2,949
Canyon 11,365
Carrizo Springs 5,745
Carrollton 82,169
Carthage 6,496
Castle Hills 4,198
Castroville 2,159
Cedar Hill 19,976
Cedar Park 5,161
Celina 1,737
Center 4,950
Centerville 812
Chandler 1,630
Channelview 25,564
Channing 277
Charlotte 1,475
Chico 800
Childress 5,055
Chillicothe 816
China 1,144
Cisco 3,813
Clarendon 2,067
Clarksville 4,311
Claude 1,199
Clear Lake Shores 1,096
Cleburne 22,205
Cleveland 7,124
Clifton 3,195
Clint 1,035
Cloverleaf 18,230
Clute 8,910
Clyde 3,002
Coahoma 1,133
Cockrell Hill 3,746
Coldspring 538
Coleman 5,410
College Station 52,456
Colleyville 12,724
Colorado City 4,749
Columbus 3,367
Comanche 4,087
Combes 2,042
Comfort 1,477
Commerce 6,825
Conroe 27,610
Converse 8,887
Cooper 2,153
Coppell 16,881
Copperas Cove 24,079
Corinth 3,944
Corpus Christi 257,453
Corrigan 1,764
Corsicana 22,911
Cotulla 3,694
Cove 402
Crandall 1,652
Crane 3,533
Crockett 7,024
Crosbyton 2,026
Cross Plains 1,063
Crowell 1,230
Crowley 6,974
Crystal City 8,263
Cuero 6,700
Cut and Shoot 903
Daingerfield 2,572
Daisetta 969
Dalhart 6,246
Dallas 1,006,877
Dalworthington Gardens 1,758
Danbury 1,447
Dawson 766
Dayton 5,151
Decatur 4,252
Deer Park 27,652
De Kalb 1,976
De Leon 2,190
Del Rio 30,705
Denison 21,505
Denton 66,270
Denver City 5,145
De Soto 30,544
Detroit 706
Devine 3,928
Diboll 4,341
Dickens 322
Dickinson 9,497
Dilley 2,632
Dimmitt 4,408
Donna 12,652
Dublin 3,190
Dumas 12,871
Duncanville 35,748
Eagle Lake 3,551
Eagle Pass 20,651
Early 2,380
Earth 1,228
Eastland 3,690
Edcouch 2,878
Eden 1,567
Edgecliff 2,715
Edgewood 1,284
Edinburg 29,885
Edna 5,343
El Campo 10,511
Eldorado 2,019
Electra 3,113
Elgin 4,846
Elkhart 1,076
El Lago 3,269
El Paso 515,342
Elsa 5,242
Emory 963
Ennis 13,883
Euless 38,149
Everman 5,672
Fabens 5,599
Fairfield 3,234
Fairview 1,554
Falfurrias 5,788
Farmers Branch 24,250
Farmersville 2,640
Farwell 1,373
Ferris 2,212
Flatonia 1,295
Florence 829
Floresville 5,247
Flower Mound 15,527
Floydada 3,896
Forest Hill 11,482
Forney 4,070
Fort Bliss 13,915
Fort Hood 35,580
Fort Stockton 8,524
Fort Worth 447,619
Franklin 1,336
Frankston 1,127
Fredericksburg 6,934
Freeport 11,389
Freer 3,271
Friendswood 22,814
Friona 3,688
Frisco 6,141
Fritch 2,335
Gainesville 14,256
Galena Park 10,033
Galveston 59,070
Ganado 1,701
Garland 180,650
Garrison 883
Gatesville 11,492
George West 2,586
Georgetown 14,842
Giddings 4,093
Gilmer 4,822
Gladewater 6,027
Glenn Heights 4,564
Glen Rose 1,949
Goldthwaite 1,658
Goliad 1,946
Gonzales 6,527
Gorman 1,290
Graham 8,986
Granbury 4,045
Grand Prairie 99,616
Grand Saline 2,630
Grandview 1,245
Granger 1,190
Grapeland 1,450
Grapevine 29,202
Greenville 23,071
Gregory 2,458
Grey Forest 425
Groesbeck 3,185
Groom 613
Groves 16,513
Groveton 1,071
Gruver 1,172
Gun Barrel City 3,526
Gunter 898
Hale Center 2,067
Hallettsville 2,718
Hallsville 2,288
Haltom City 32,856
Hamilton 2,937
Hamlin 2,791
Hardin 563
Harker Heights 12,841
Harlingen 48,735
Hart 1,221
Haskell 3,362
Hawkins 1,309
Hearne 5,132
Heath 2,108
Hebbronville 4,465
Hedwig Village 2,616
Hemphill 1,182
Hempstead 3,551
Henderson 11,139
Henrietta 2,896
Hereford 14,745
Hewitt 8,983
Hickory Creek 1,893
Hico 1,342
Hidalgo 3,292
Highland Park 8,739
Highland Village 7,027
Highlands 6,632
Hill County Village 1,038
Hillcrest 695
Hillsboro 7,072
Hitchcock 5,868
Holland 1,118
Holliday 1,475
Hollywood Park 2,841
Hondo 6,018
Honey Grove 1,681
Hooks 2,684
Houston 1,630,553
Howe 2,173
Hubbard 1,589
Hudson 2,374
Hughes Springs 1,938
Humble 12,060
Hunters Creek Village 3,954
Huntington 1,794
Huntsville 27,925
Hurst 33,574
Hutchins 2,719
Idalou 2,074
Ingleside 5,696
Iowa Park 6,072
Iraan 1,322
Irving 155,037
Italy 1,699
Itasca 1,523
Jacinto City 9,343
Jacksboro 3,350
Jacksonville 12,765
Jasper 6,959
Jayton 608
Jefferson 2,199
Jersey Village 4,826
Joaquin 805
Johnson City 932
Jones Creek 2,160
Joshua 3,828
Jourdanton 3,220
Junction 2,654
Justin 1,234
Karnes City 2,916
Katy 8,005
Kaufman 5,238
Keene 3,944
Keller 13,683
Kemah 1,094
Kemp 1,184
Kenedy 3,763
Kenefick 435
Kennedale 4,096
Kerens 1,702
Kermit 6,875
Kerrville 17,384
Kilgore 11,066
Killeen 63,535
Kingsland 2,725
Kingsville 25,276
Kingwood 37,397
Kirby 8,326
Kirbyville 1,871
Knox City 1,440
Kountze 2,056
Kress 739
Krum 1,542
Kyle 2,225
Lackland Air Force Base 9,352
La Coste 1,021
Lacy-Lakeview 3,617
La Feria 4,360
La Grange 3,951
La Joya 2,604
Lake Dallas 3,656
Lake Jackson 22,776
Lake Worth Village 4,591
Lakeport 710
Lakeside 816
Lakeway 4,044
La Marque 14,120
Lamesa 10,809
Lampasas 6,382
Lancaster 22,117
La Porte 27,910
La Pryor 1,343
Laredo 122,899
Laughlin Air Force Base 2,556
La Villa 1,388
League City 30,159

Texas (continued)

Leakey 399
Leander 3,398
Lefors 656
Leon Valley 9,581
Leonard 1,744
Levelland 13,986
Lewisville 46,521
Lexington 953
Liberty 7,733
Liberty City 1,607
Lindale 2,428
Linden 2,375
Little Elm 1,255
Little River-Academy 1,390
Littlefield 6,489
Live Oak 10,023
Livingston 5,019
Llano 2,962
Lockhart 9,205
Lockney 2,207
Lone Star 1,615
Longview 70,311
Loraine 731
Lorenzo 1,208
Los Fresnos 2,473
Lott 775
Lowry Crossing 865
Lubbock 186,206
Lucas 2,205
Lufkin 30,206
Luling 4,661
Lumberton 6,640
Lyford 1,674
Lytle 2,255
Mabank 1,739
Madisonville 3,569
Magnolia 940
Malakoff 2,038
Manor 1,041
Mansfield 15,607
Manvel 3,733
Marble Falls 4,007
Marfa 2,424
Marlin 6,386
Marshall 23,682
Mart 2,004
Mason 2,041
Matador 790
Mathis 5,423
Maud 1,049
McAllen 84,021
McCamey 2,493
McGregor 4,683
McKinney 21,283
McLean 849
McLendon-Chisholm 646
McQueeney 2,063
Memphis 2,465
Menard 1,606
Mercedes 12,694
Meridian 1,390
Merkel 2,469
Mertzon 778
Mesquite 101,484
Mexia 6,933
Miami 675
Midland 89,443
Midlothian 5,141
Mineola 4,321
Mineral Wells 14,870
Mission 28,653
Missouri City 36,176
Monahans 8,101
Mont Belvieu 1,323
Moody 1,329
Morgan's Point Resort 1,766
Morton 2,597
Moulton 923
Mount Pleasant 12,291
Mount Vernon 2,219
Muenster 1,387
Muleshoe 4,571
Munday 1,600
Murphy 1,547
Nacogdoches 30,872
Naples 1,508
Nash 2,162
Nassau Bay 4,320
Natalia 1,216
Navasota 6,296
Nederland 16,192
Needville 2,199
New Boston 5,057
New Braunfels 27,334
New London 926
New Waverly 936
Newton 1,885
Nixon 1,995
Nocona 2,870
Nolanville 1,834
North Richland Hills 45,895
North San Pedro 953
Northcrest 1,725
O'Donnell 1,102
Oak Ridge North 2,454
Odem 2,366
Odessa 89,699
Old River-Winfree 1,233
Olmos Park 2,161
Olney 3,519
Olton 2,116
Orange 19,381
Orange Grove 1,175
Ore City 898
Overton 2,105
Ovilla 2,027
Oyster Creek 912
Ozona 3,181
Paducah 1,788
Paint Rock 227
Palacios 4,418
Palestine 18,042
Palmer 1,659
Pampa 19,959
Panhandle 2,353
Panorama Village 1,556
Pantego 2,371
Paris 24,699
Parker 1,235
Pasadena 119,363
Patton 1,155
Pearland 18,697
Pearsall 6,924
Pecos 12,069
Perryton 7,607
Petersburg 1,292
Petrolia 762
Pharr 32,921
Pilot Point 2,538
Pinehurst 2,682
Pineland 882
Piney Point Village 3,197
Pittsburg 4,007
Plains 1,422
Plainview 21,700
Plano 128,713
Pleasanton 7,678
Point Comfort 956
Port Aransas 2,233
Port Arthur 58,724
Port Isabel 4,467
Port Lavaca 10,886
Port Neches 12,974
Portland 12,224
Post 3,768
Post Oak Bend City 264
Poteet 3,206
Poth 1,642
Pottsboro 1,177
Prairie View 4,004
Premont 2,914
Presidio 3,072
Primera 2,030
Princeton 2,321
Quanah 3,413
Queen City 1,748
Quinlan 1,360
Quitman 1,684
Ralls 2,172
Ranger 2,803
Rankin 1,011
Raymondville 8,880
Red Oak 3,124
Refugio 3,158
Reno 1,784
Reno 2,322
Richardson 74,840
Richland Hills 7,978
Richmond 9,801
Richwood 2,732
Rio Grande City 9,891
Rio Hondo 1,793
Rising Star 859
River Oaks 6,580
Roanoke 1,616
Robert Lee 1,276
Robinson 7,111
Robstown 12,849
Roby 616
Rockdale 5,235
Rockport 4,753
Rocksprings 1,339
Rockwall 10,486
Rogers 1,131
Rollingwood 1,388
Roman Forest 1,033
Roscoe 1,446
Rosebud 1,638
Rosenberg 20,183
Rotan 1,913
Round Rock 30,923
Rowlett 23,260
Royse City 2,206
Rule 783
Runge 1,139
Rusk 4,366
Sabinal 1,584
Sachse 5,346
Saginaw 8,551
St. Jo 1,048
San Angelo 84,474
San Antonio 935,933
San Augustine 2,337
San Benito 20,125
San Diego 4,983
San Elizario 4,385
San Juan 10,815
San Leon 3,328
San Marcos 28,743
San Saba 2,626
Sanderson 1,128
Sanger 3,508
Sansom Park Village 3,928
Santa Anna 1,249
Santa Fe 8,429
Santa Rosa 2,223
Savoy 877
Schertz 10,555
Schulenburg 2,455
Seabrook 6,685
Seadrift 1,277
Seagoville 8,969
Seagraves 2,398
Sealy 4,541
Seguin 18,853
Seminole 6,342
Seth Ward 1,402
Seven Points 723
Seymour 3,185
Shady Shores 1,045
Shallowater 1,708
Shamrock 2,286
Shavano Park 1,708
Shenandoah 1,718
Shepherd 1,812
Sherman 31,601
Shiner 2,074
Shoreacres 1,316
Silsbee 6,368
Silverton 779
Sinton 5,549
Skellytown 664
Slaton 6,078
Smithville 3,196
Snyder 12,195
Somerset 1,144
Somerville 1,542
Sonora 2,751
Sour Lake 1,547
South Houston 14,207
South Padre Island 1,677
Southlake 7,065
Southside Place 1,392
Spearman 3,197
Spring Valley 3,392
Springtown 1,740
Spur 1,300
Stafford 8,397
Stamford 3,817
Stanton 2,576
Stephenville 13,502
Sterling City 1,096
Stinnett 2,166
Stockdale 1,268
Stratford 1,781
Sudan 983
Sugar Land 24,529
Sulphur Springs 14,062
Sundown 1,759
Sunnyvale 2,228
Sunray 1,729
Sunset Valley 327
Surfside Beach 611
Sweeny 3,297
Sweetwater 11,967
Taft 3,222
Tahoka 2,868
Talco 592
Tatum 1,289
Taylor 11,472
Taylor Lake Village 3,394
Teague 3,268
Temple 46,109
Tenaha 1,072
Terrell 12,490
Terrell Hills 4,592
Texarkana 31,656
Texas City 40,822
The Colony 22,113
The Woodlands 29,205
Thorndale 1,092
Three Rivers 1,889
Throckmorton 1,036
Timpson 1,029
Tomball 6,370
Tool 1,712
Trinidad 1,056
Trinity 2,648
Troup 1,659
Troy 1,395
Tulia 4,699
Tye 1,088
Tyler 75,450
Universal City 13,057
University Park 22,259
Uvalde 14,729
Valley Mills 1,085
Van 1,854
Van Alstyne 2,090
Van Horn 2,930
Vega 840
Vernon 12,001
Victoria 55,076
Vidor 10,935
Waco 103,590
Waelder 745
Wake Village 4,757
Waller 1,493
Wallis 1,001
Waskom 1,812
Watauga 20,009
Waxahachie 18,168
Weatherford 14,804
Webster 4,678
Weimar 2,052
Wellington 2,456
Wells 761
Weslaco 21,877
West 2,515
West Columbia 4,372
West Lake Hills 2,542
West Orange 4,187
West University Place 12,920
Westworth 2,350
Wharton 9,011
Wheeler 1,393
White Deer 1,125
White Oak 5,136
White Settlement 15,472
Whitehouse 4,032
Whitesboro 3,209
Whitewright 1,713
Whitney 1,626
Wichita Falls 96,259
Willis 2,764
Willow Park 2,328
Wills Point 2,986
Wilmer 2,479
Windcrest 5,331
Wink 1,189
Winnsboro 2,904
Winters 2,905
Wolfe City 1,505
Wolfforth 1,941
Woodsboro 1,731
Woodville 2,636
Woodway 8,695
Wortham 1,020
Wylie 8,716
Yoakum 5,611
Yorktown 2,207
Zapata 7,119

Utah ■ population 1,727,784

Metropolitan areas

Provo-Orem 263,590
Salt Lake City-Ogden 1,072,227

Counties

Beaver 4,765
Box Elder 36,485
Cache 70,183
Carbon 20,228
Daggett 690
Davis 187,941
Duchesne 12,645
Emery 10,332
Garfield 3,980
Grand 6,620
Iron 20,789
Juab 5,817
Kane 5,169
Millard 11,333
Morgan 5,528
Piute 1,277
Rich 1,725
Salt Lake 725,956
San Juan 12,621
Sanpete 16,259
Sevier 15,431
Summit 15,518
Tooele 26,601
Uintah 22,201
Utah 263,590
Wasatch 10,089
Washington 48,560
Wayne 2,177
Weber 158,330

Cities and towns

Alpine 3,492
Alta 397
Amalga 366
American Fork 15,696
Annabella 487
Aurora 911
Ballard 644
Bear River City 700
Beaver 1,998
Bicknell 327
Blanding 3,162
Bluffdale 2,152
Bountiful 36,659
Brigham City 15,644
Castle Dale 1,704
Cedar City 13,443
Cedar Fort 284
Cedar Hills 769
Centerfield 766
Centerville 11,500
Charleston 336
Circleville 417
Clarkston 645
Clearfield 21,435
Cleveland 498
Clinton 7,945
Coalville 1,065
Corinne 639
Cornish 205
Cottonwood Heights 28,766
Delta 2,998
Deweyville 318
Draper 7,257
Duchesne 1,308
Dugway 1,761
East Carbon 1,270
East Millcreek 21,184
Elk Ridge 771
Elmo 267
Elsinore 608
Elwood 575
Emery 300
Enoch 1,947
Enterprise 936
Ephraim 3,363
Escalante 818
Eureka 562
Fairview 960
Farmington 9,028
Ferron 1,606
Fielding 422
Fillmore 1,956
Fort Duchesne 655
Fountain Green 578
Francis 381
Fruit Heights 3,900
Garland 1,637
Genola 803
Glendale 282
Glenwood 437
Goshen 578
Grantsville 4,500
Green River 866
Gunnison 1,298
Harrisville 3,004
Heber City 4,782
Helper 2,148
Henefer 554
Highland 5,002
Hildale 1,325
Hinckley 658
Holden 402
Holladay (Cottonwood) 14,095
Honeyville 1,112
Hooper 3,468
Howell 237
Huntington 1,875
Huntsville 561
Hurricane 3,915
Hyde Park 2,190
Hyrum 4,829
Ivins 1,630
Kamas 1,061
Kanab 3,289
Kanarraville 228
Kanosh 386
Kaysville 13,961
Kearns 28,374
Koosharem 266
Laketown 261
La Verkin 1,771
Layton 41,784
Leamington 253
Leeds 254
Lehi 8,475
Levan 416
Lewiston 1,532
Lindon 3,818
Loa 444
Logan 32,762
Maeser 2,598
Magna 17,829
Manila 207
Manti 2,268
Mantua 665
Mapleton 3,572
Marysvale 364
Mayfield 438
Meadow 250
Mendon 684
Mexican Hat 259
Midvale 11,886
Midway 1,554
Milford 1,107
Millcreek 32,230
Millville 1,202
Minersville 608
Moab 3,971
Mona 584
Monroe 1,472
Monticello 1,806
Morgan 2,023
Moroni 1,115
Mount Olympus 7,413
Mount Pleasant 2,092
Murray 31,282
Myton 468
Neola 511
Nephi 3,515
Newton 659
Nibley 1,167
North Logan 3,768
North Ogden 11,668
North Salt Lake 6,474
Oak City 587
Oakley 522
Ogden 63,909
Orangeville 1,459
Orderville 422
Orem 67,561
Panguitch 1,444
Paradise 561
Paragonah 307
Park City 4,468
Parowan 1,873
Payson 9,510
Perry 1,211
Plain City 2,722
Pleasant Grove 13,476
Pleasant View 3,603
Plymouth 267
Portage 218
Price 8,712
Providence 3,344
Provo 86,835
Randlett 283
Randolph 488
Redmond 648
Richfield 5,593
Richmond 1,955
River Heights 1,274
Riverdale 6,419
Riverton 11,261
Roosevelt 3,915
Roy 24,603
Rush Valley 339
St. George 28,502
Salem 2,284
Salina 1,943
Salt Lake City 159,936
Sandy 75,058
Santa Clara 2,322
Santaquin 2,336
Scipio 291
Sigurd 385
Smithfield 5,566
Snowville 251
South Jordan 12,220
South Ogden 12,105
South Salt Lake 10,129
South Weber 2,863
Spanish Fork 11,272
Spring City 715
Springdale 275
Springville 13,950
Stockton 426
Sunnyside 339
Sunset 5,128
Syracuse 4,658
Taylorsville (-Bennion) 52,351
Tooele 13,887
Toquerville 488
Tremonton 4,264
Trenton 464
Tropic 374
Uintah 760
Union 13,684
Val Verda 3,712
Vernal 6,644
Virgin 229
Wallsburg 252
Washington 4,198
Washington Terrace 8,189
Wellington 1,632
Wellsville 2,206
Wendover 1,127
West Bountiful 4,477
West Jordan 42,892
West Point 4,258
West Valley City 86,976
White City 6,506
Whiterocks 312
Willard 1,298
Woodland Hills 301
Woods Cross 5,384

Vermont ■ population 564,964

Metropolitan area

Burlington 131,439

Counties

Addison 32,953
Albany 180 ▲782
Bennington 35,845
Caledonia 27,846
Chittenden 131,761
Essex 6,405
Franklin 39,980
Grand Isle 5,318
Lamoille 19,735
Orange 26,149
Orleans 24,053
Rutland 62,142
Washington 54,928
Windham 41,588
Windsor 54,055

Cities, towns, and villages

Addison 1,023
Alburg 436 ▲1,362
Andover 373
Arlington 1,311 ▲2,299
Athens 313
Bakersfield 977
Barnard 872
Barnet 1,415
Barre 7,411
Barre 9,482
Barton 908 ▲2,967
Bellows Falls 3,313
Belvidere 228
Bennington 9,532 ▲16,451
Benson 847
Berkshire 1,190
Berlin 2,561
Bethel 1,866
Bloomfield 253
Bolton 971
Bradford 672 ▲2,522
Braintree 1,174
Brandon 1,902 ▲4,223
Brattleboro 8,612 ▲12,241
Bridgewater 895
Bridport 1,137
Brighton 1,562
Bristol 1,801 ▲3,762
Brookfield 1,089
Brookline 403
Brownington 705
Burke 1,406
Burlington 39,127
Cabot 220 ▲1,043
Calais 1,521
Cambridge 292 ▲2,667
Canaan 1,121
Castleton 4,278
Cavendish 1,323
Charleston 844
Charlotte 3,148
Chelsea 1,166
Chester 2,832
Chester (-Chester Depot) 1,057
Chittenden 1,102
Clarendon 2,835
Colchester 14,731
Concord 1,093
Corinth 1,244
Cornwall 1,101
Coventry 806
Craftsbury 994
Danby 1,193
Danville 1,917
Derby 4,479
Derby Center 684
Derby Line 855
Dorset 1,918
Dover 994
Dummerston 1,863
Duxbury 976
East Haven 269
East Montpelier 2,239
Eden 840
Elmore 573
Enosburg 2,535
Enosburg Falls 1,350
Essex 16,498
Essex Junction 8,396
Fair Haven 2,432 ▲2,887
Fairfax 2,486
Fairfield 1,680
Fairlee 883
Fayston 846
Ferrisburg 2,317
Fletcher 941
Franklin 1,068
Georgia 3,753
Glover 820
Goshen 226
Grafton 602
Grand Isle 1,642
Graniteville (-East Barre) 2,189
Granville 309
Greensboro 717
Groton 862
Guildhall 270
Guilford 1,941
Halifax 588
Hancock 340
Hardwick 2,964
Hartford 9,404
Hartland 2,988
Highgate 3,020
Hinesburg 3,780
Holland 423
Hubbardton 576
Huntington 1,609
Hyde Park 457 ▲2,344
Ira 426
Irasburg 907
Island Pond 1,222
Isle La Motte 408
Jacksonville 244
Jamaica 754
Jay 381
Jeffersonville 462
Jericho 1,405 ▲4,302
Johnson 1,470 ▲3,156
Kirby 347
Leicester 871
Lincoln 974
Londonderry 1,506
Lowell 594
Ludlow 1,123 ▲2,302
Lunenburg 1,176
Lyndon 5,371
Lyndonville 1,255
Manchester 561 ▲3,622
Manchester Center 1,574
Marlboro 924
Marshfield 257 ▲1,331
Mendon 1,049
Middlebury 6,007 ▲8,034
Middlesex 1,514
Middletown Springs 686
Milton 1,578 ▲8,404
Monkton 1,482
Montgomery 823
Montpelier 8,247
Moretown 1,415
Morgan 497
Morristown 4,733
Morrisville 1,984
Mount Holly 1,093
Mount Tabor 214
New Haven 1,375
Newark 354
Newbury 412 ▲1,985
Newfane 164 ▲1,555
Newport 1,367 ▲4,434
North Bennington 1,520
North Hero 502
North Troy 723
North Westminster 268
Northfield 1,889 ▲5,610
Norwich 3,093
Old Bennington 279
Orange 915
Orleans 806
Orwell 1,114
Panton 606
Pawlet 1,314
Peacham 627
Peru 324
Pittsfield 389
Pittsford 2,919
Plainfield 1,302
Plymouth 440
Pomfret 874
Poultney 1,731 ▲3,498
Pownal 3,485
Proctor 1,979
Putney 2,352
Randolph 4,764
Reading 614
Readsboro 762
Richford 1,425 ▲2,178
Richmond 3,729
Ripton 444
Rochester 1,181
Rockingham 5,484
Roxbury 575
Royalton 2,389
Rupert 654
Rutland 3,781
Rutland 18,230
Ryegate 1,058
St. Albans 4,606
St. Albans 7,339
St. George 705
St. Johnsbury 6,424 ▲7,608
Salisbury 1,024
Sandgate 278
Saxtons River 541
Shaftsbury 3,368
Sharon 1,211
Sheffield 541
Shelburne 5,871
Sheldon 1,748
Sherburne 738
Shoreham 1,115
Shrewsbury 1,107
South Barre 1,314
South Burlington 12,809
South Hero 1,404
Springfield 4,207 ▲9,579
Stamford 773
Starksboro 1,511
Stockbridge 618
Stowe 450 ▲3,433
Strafford 902
Sudbury 516
Sunderland 872
Sutton 854
Swanton 2,360 ▲5,636
Thetford 2,438
Tinmouth 455
Topsham 944
Townshend 1,019
Troy 1,609
Tunbridge 1,154
Underhill 2,799
Vergennes 2,578
Vernon 1,850
Vershire 560
Waitsfield 1,422
Walden 703
Wallingford 1,148 ▲2,184
Waltham 454
Wardsboro 654
Warren 1,172
Washington 937
Waterbury 1,702 ▲4,589
Waterford 1,190
Waterville 532
Weathersfield 2,674
Wells 902
Wells River 424
West Brattleboro 3,135
West Burke 353
West Fairlee 633
West Haven 273
West Rutland 2,246 ▲2,448
West Windsor 923
Westfield 422
Westford 1,740
Westminster 399 ▲3,026
Westmore 305
Weston 488
Weybridge 749
Wheelock 481
White River Junction 2,521
Whiting 407
Whitingham 1,177
Wilder 1,576
Williamstown 2,839
Williston 4,887
Wilmington 1,968
Windham 251
Windsor 3,714
Winhall 482
Winooski 6,649
Wolcott 1,229
Woodbury 766
Woodford 331
Woodstock 1,037 ▲3,212
Worcester 906

▲ Entire township, including rural area.

Virginia ■ population 6,216,568

Metropolitan areas

Charlottesville 131,107
Danville 108,711
Johnson City-Kingsport (Tenn.)-Bristol 436,047 (348,530 in Tenn.; 87,517 in Va.)
Lynchburg 142,199
Norfolk-Virginia Beach-Newport News 1,396,107
Richmond-Petersburg 865,640
Roanoke 224,477
Washington, D.C. 3,923,574 (1,789,029 in Md.; 1,527,645 in Va.; 606,900 in D.C.)

Counties

Accomack 31,703
Albemarle 68,040
Alleghany 13,176
Amelia 8,787
Amherst 28,578
Appomattox 12,298
Arlington 170,936
Augusta 54,677
Bath 4,799
Bedford 45,656
Bland 6,514
Botetourt 24,992
Brunswick 15,987
Buchanan 31,333
Buckingham 12,873
Campbell 47,572
Caroline 19,217
Carroll 26,594
Charles City 6,282
Charlotte 11,688
Chesterfield 209,274
Clarke 12,101
Craig 4,372
Culpeper 27,791
Cumberland 7,825
Dickenson 17,620
Dinwiddie 20,960
Essex 8,689
Fairfax 818,584
Fauquier 48,741
Floyd 12,005
Fluvanna 12,429
Franklin 39,549
Frederick 45,723
Giles 16,366
Gloucester 30,131
Goochland 14,163
Grayson 16,278
Greene 10,297
Greensville 8,853
Halifax 29,033
Hanover 63,306
Henrico 217,881
Henry 56,942
Highland 2,635
Isle of Wight 25,053
James City 34,859
King and Queen 6,289
King George 13,527
King William 10,913
Lancaster 10,896
Lee 24,496
Loudoun 86,129
Louisa 20,325
Lunenburg 11,419
Madison 11,949
Mathews 8,348
Mecklenburg 29,241
Middlesex 8,653
Montgomery 73,913
Nelson 12,778
New Kent 10,445
Northampton 13,061
Northumberland 10,524
Nottoway 14,993
Orange 21,421
Page 21,690
Patrick 17,473
Pittsylvania 55,655
Powhatan 15,328
Prince Edward 17,320
Prince George 27,394
Prince William 215,686
Pulaski 34,496
Rappahannock 6,622
Richmond 7,273
Roanoke 79,332
Rockbridge 18,350
Rockingham 57,482
Russell 28,667
Scott 23,204
Shenandoah 31,636
Smyth 32,370
Southampton 17,550
Spotsylvania 57,403
Stafford 61,236
Surry 6,145
Sussex 10,248
Tazewell 45,960
Warren 26,142
Washington 45,887
Westmoreland 15,480
Wise 39,573
Wythe 25,466
York 42,422

Cities and towns

Abingdon 7,003
Accomac 466
Alberta 337
Alexandria 111,183
Altavista 3,686
Amherst 1,060
Annandale 50,975
Appalachia 1,994
Appomattox 1,707
Aquia Harbor 6,308
Arlington 170,936
Ashburn 3,393
Ashland 5,864
Atkins 1,130
Bailey's Crossroads 19,507
Bassett 1,579
Bedford 6,073
Belle Haven 526
Belle Haven 6,427
Bellwood 6,178
Bensley 5,093
Berryville 3,097
Big Stone Gap 4,748
Blacksburg 34,590
Blackstone 3,497
Bloxom 357
Blue Ridge 2,840
Bluefield 5,363
Bon Air 16,413
Boones Mill 239
Bowling Green 727
Boyce 520
Boydton 453
Boykins 658
Bridgewater 3,918
Bristol 18,426
Broadway 1,209
Brodnax 388
Brookneal 1,344
Buchanan 1,222
Buena Vista 6,406
Burke 57,734
Burkeville 535
Cape Charles 1,398
Castlewood 2,110
Cave Spring 24,053
Cedar Bluff 1,290
Centreville 26,585
Chamberlayne 4,577
Chantilly 29,337
Charlotte Court House 531
Charlottesville 40,341
Chase City 2,442
Chatham 1,354
Cheriton 515
Chesapeake 151,976
Chester 14,986
Chilhowie 1,971
Chincoteague 3,572
Christiansburg 15,004
Claremont 358
Clarksville 1,243
Claypool Hill 1,468
Cleveland 214
Clifton Forge 4,679
Clintwood 1,542
Cloverdale 1,689
Coeburn 2,165
Collinsville 7,280
Colonial Beach 3,132
Colonial Heights 16,064
Commonwealth 5,538
Courtland 819
Covington 6,991
Craigsville 812
Crewe 2,276
Crimora 1,752
Crozet 2,256
Culpeper 8,581
Dale City 47,170
Daleville 1,163
Damascus 918
Danville 53,056
Dayton 921
Dendron 305
Dillwyn 458
Dooms 1,307
Drakes Branch 565
Dublin 2,012
Dumbarton 8,526
Dumfries 4,282
Dungannon 250
Dunn Loring 6,509
East Highland Park 11,850
Edinburg 860
Elkton 1,935
Elliston (-Lafayette) 1,243
Emory (-Meadow View) 2,248
Emporia 5,306
Ettrick 5,290
Exmore 1,115
Fairfax 19,622
Fairlawn 2,399
Falls Church 9,578
Falmouth 3,541
Farmville 6,046
Ferrum 1,514
Fieldale 1,018
Fincastle 236
Fishersville 3,230
Floyd 396
Forest 5,624
Fort Belvoir 8,590
Fort Hunt 12,989
Fort Lee 6,895
Franconia 19,882
Franklin 7,864
Fredericksburg 19,027
Fries 690
Front Royal 11,880
Galax 6,670
Gate City 2,214
Glade Spring 1,435
Glasgow 1,140
Glen Allen 9,010
Gloucester Point 8,509
Gordonsville 1,351
Goshen 366
Great Falls 6,945
Gretna 1,339
Grottoes 1,455
Groveton 19,997
Grundy 1,305
Halifax 688
Hallwood 228
Hamilton 700
Hampden Sydney 1,240
Hampton 133,793
Harrisonburg 30,707
Haymarket 483
Haysi 222
Herndon 16,139
Highland Springs 13,823
Hillsville 2,008
Hollins 13,305
Hollymead 2,628
Honaker 950
Hopewell 23,101
Horse Pasture 2,224
Huntington 7,489
Hurt 1,294
Hybla Valley 15,491
Idylwood 14,710
Independence 988
Iron Gate 417
Irvington 496
Isle of Wight
Ivor 324
Jarratt 556
Jefferson 25,782
Jonesville 927
Keller 235
Kenbridge 1,264
Keysville 606
Kilmarnock 1,109
La Crosse 549
Lake Barcroft 8,686
Lake Ridge 23,862
Lakeside 12,081
Laurel 13,011
Lawrenceville 1,486
Lebanon 3,386
Leesburg 16,202
Lexington 6,959
Lincolnia 13,041
Loch Lomond 3,292
Lorton 15,385
Louisa 1,088
Lovettsville 749
Luray 4,587
Lynchburg 66,049
Madison 307
Madison Heights 11,700
Manassas 27,957
Manassas Park 6,734
Mantua 6,804
Marion 6,630
Martinsville 16,162
McKenney 386
McLean 38,168
Mechanicsville 22,027
Melfa 428
Merrifield 8,399
Middleburg 549
Middletown 1,061
Mineral 471
Monterey 222
Montrose 6,405
Montross 359
Mount Crawford 228
Mount Jackson 1,583
Mount Vernon 27,485
Narrows 2,082
Nassawadox 564
New Market 1,435
Newington 17,965
Newport News 170,045
Newsoms 337
Nickelsville 411
Norfolk 261,229
North Springfield 8,996
Norton 4,247
Oakton 24,610
Occoquan 361
Onancock 1,434
Onley 532
Orange 2,582
Painter 259
Pamplin 208
Parksley 779
Pearisburg 2,064

Virginia (continued)

Pembroke 1,064
Pennington Gap 1,922
Petersburg 38,386
Phenix 260
Pimmit Hills 6,019
Plains, The 219
Pocahontas 513
Poquoson 11,005
Port Royal 204
Portsmouth 103,907
Pound 995
Pulaski 9,985
Purcellville 1,744
Quantico 670
Quantico Station 7,425
Radford 15,940
Raven 2,640
Remington 460
Reston 48,556
Rich Creek 670
Richlands 4,456
Richmond 203,056
Ridgeway 752
Rio 5,133
Roanoke 96,397
Rocky Mount 4,098
Rose Hill 12,675
Round Hill 514
Rural Retreat 972
Rushmere 1,064
St. Charles 206
St. Paul 1,007
Salem 23,756
Saltville 2,300
Saxis 367
Scottsville 239
Seven Corners 7,280
Shawsville 1,260
Shenandoah 2,213
Smithfield 4,686
South Boston 6,997
South Hill 4,217
Springfield 23,706
Stanardsville 257
Stanley 1,186
Stanleytown 1,563
Staunton 24,461
Stephens City 1,186
Sterling 20,512
Stony Creek 271
Strasburg 3,762
Stuart 965
Stuarts Draft 5,087
Suffolk 52,141
Sugarland Run 9,357
Tangier 659
Tappahannock 1,550
Tazewell 4,176
Timberlake 10,314
Timberville 1,596
Toms Brook 227
Triangle 4,740
Troutville 455
Tuckahoe 42,629
Tysons Corner 13,124
University Heights 6,900
Urbanna 529
Vansant 1,187
Verona 3,479
Victoria 1,830
Vienna 14,852
Vila Heights 1,021
Vint Hill Farms Station 1,332
Vinton 7,665
Virginia Beach 393,069
Wachapreague 291
Wakefield 1,070
Warrenton 4,830
Warsaw 961
Waverly 2,223
Waynesboro 18,549
Weber City 1,377
West Gate 6,565
West Point 2,938
West Springfield 28,126
White Stone 372
Williamsburg 11,530
Winchester 21,947
Windsor 1,025
Wise 3,193
Wolf Trap 13,133
Woodbridge 26,401
Woodstock 3,182
Wytheville 8,038
Yorkshire 5,699

Washington ■ population 4,887,941

Metropolitan areas

Bellingham 127,780
Bremerton 189,731
Olympia 161,238
Richland-Kennewick-Pasco 150,033
Seattle 1,972,961
Spokane 361,364
Tacoma 586,203
Vancouver 238,053
Yakima 188,823

Counties

Adams 13,603
Asotin 17,605
Benton 112,560
Chelan 52,250
Clallam 56,464
Clark 238,053
Columbia 4,024
Cowlitz 82,119
Douglas 26,205
Ferry 6,295
Franklin 37,473
Garfield 2,248
Grant 54,758
Grays Harbor 64,175
Island 60,195
Jefferson 20,146
King 1,507,319
Kitsap 189,731
Kittitas 26,725
Klickitat 16,616
Lewis 59,358
Lincoln 8,864
Mason 38,341
Okanogan 33,350
Pacific 18,882
Pend Oreille 8,915
Pierce 586,203
San Juan 10,035
Skagit 79,555
Skamania 8,289
Snohomish 465,642
Spokane 361,364
Stevens 30,948
Thurston 161,238
Wahkiakum 3,327
Walla Walla 48,439
Whatcom 127,780
Whitman 38,775
Yakima 188,823

Cities and towns

Aberdeen 16,565
Airway Heights 1,971
Albion 632
Algona 1,694
Almira 310
Anacortes 11,451
Arlington 4,037
Asotin 981
Auburn 33,102
Ault Field 3,795
Battle Ground 3,758
Beaux Arts 303
Bellevue 86,874
Bellingham 52,179
Benton City 1,806
Bingen 645
Birch Bay 2,656
Black Diamond 1,422
Blaine 2,489
Bonney Lake 7,494
Bothell 12,345
Bremerton 38,142
Brewster 1,633
Bridgeport 1,498
Brier 5,633
Brush Prairie 2,650
Buckley 3,516
Bucoda 536
Burbank 1,745
Burien 25,089
Burlington 4,349
Camas 6,442
Carbonado 495
Carnation 1,243
Cashmere 2,544
Castle Rock 2,067
Cathlamet 508
Central Park 2,669
Centralia 12,101
Chehalis 6,527
Chelan 2,969
Cheney 7,723
Chewelah 1,945
Clarkston 6,753
Cle Elum 1,778
Clinton 1,564
Clyde Hill 2,972
Colfax 2,713
College Place 6,308
Colton 325
Colville 4,360
Concrete 735
Connell 2,005
Cosmopolis 1,372
Coulee City 568
Coulee Dam 1,087
Country Homes 5,126
Coupeville 1,377
Creston 230
Darrington 1,042
Davenport 1,502
Dayton 2,468
Deer Park 2,278
Des Moines 17,283
Dishman 9,671
Dupont 592
Duvall 2,770
East Port Orchard 5,409
East Renton Highlands 13,218
East Wenatchee 2,701
East Wenatchee Bench 12,539
Eatonville 1,374
Edmonds 30,744
Electric City 910
Ellensburg 12,361
Elma 3,011
Elmer City 290
Endicott 320
Entiat 449
Enumclaw 7,227
Ephrata 5,349
Esperance 11,236
Everett 69,961
Everson 1,490
Fairfield 446
Fairwood 5,807
Fall City 1,582
Federal Way 67,554
Ferndale 5,398
Fife 3,864
Fircrest 5,258
Fords Prairie 2,480
Forks 2,862
Fort Lewis 22,224
Fox Island 2,017
Freeland 1,278
Friday Harbor 1,492
Fruitvale 4,125
Garfield 544
Garrett 1,004
George 253
Gig Harbor 3,236
Gold Bar 1,078
Goldendale 3,319
Grand Coulee 984
Grandview 7,169
Granger 2,053
Granite Falls 1,060
Green Acres 4,626
Hadlock [-Irondale] 2,742
Hamilton 228
Harrah 341
Harrington 449
Hoquiam 8,972
Hunts Point 513
Ilwaco 815
Inchelium 393
Indianola 1,729
Ione 507
Issaquah 7,786
Kalama 1,210
Kelso 11,820
Kenmore 8,917
Kennewick 42,155
Kent 37,960
Kettle Falls 1,272
Kingsgate 14,259
Kingston 1,270
Kirkland 40,052
Kittitas 843
La Center 451
Lacey 19,279
La Conner 656
La Crosse 336
Lake Forest North 8,002
Lake Forest Park 4,031
Lake Stevens 3,380
Lakeland North 14,402
Lakeland South 9,027
Lakewood 58,412
Langley 845
Leavenworth 1,692
Liberty Lake 2,015
Lind 472
Long Beach 1,236
Longview 31,499
Lyman 275
Lynden 5,709
Lynnwood 28,695
Mabton 1,482
Manchester 4,031
Mansfield 311
Maple Valley 1,211
Marietta [-Alderwood] 2,766
Martha Lake 10,155
Marysville 10,328
Mattawa 941
McCleary 1,235
Medical Lake 3,664
Medina 2,981
Mercer Island 20,816
Mesa 252
Metaline Falls 210
Millwood 1,559
Milton 4,995
Minnehaha 9,661
Monroe 4,278
Montesano 3,064
Morton 1,130
Moses Lake 11,235
Moses Lake North 3,677
Mossyrock 452
Mount Vernon 17,647
Mountlake Terrace 19,320
Moxee City 814
Mukilteo 7,007
Naches 596
Napavine 745
Navy Yard City 2,905
Neah Bay 916
Newport 1,691
Newport Hills 14,736
Nooksack 584
Normandy Park 6,709
North Bend 2,578
North Bonneville 411
North Hill 5,706
North Marysville 18,711
Northport 308
Oak Harbor 17,176
Oakesdale 346
Oakville 493
Ocean Park 1,409
Ocean Shores 2,301
Odessa 935
Okanogan 2,370
Olympia 33,840
Omak 4,117
Opportunity 22,326
Oroville 1,505
Orting 2,106
Othello 4,638
Otis Orchards [-East Farms] 5,811
Pacific 4,622
Palouse 915
Parkland 20,882
Parkwood 6,853
Pasco 20,337
Pateros 570
Pe Ell 547
Pomeroy 1,393
Port Angeles 17,710
Port Angeles East 2,672
Port Orchard 4,984
Port Townsend 7,001
Poulsbo 4,848
Prescott 267
Prosser 4,476
Pullman 23,478
Puyallup 23,875
Quincy 3,738
Rainier 991
Raymond 2,901
Reardan 482
Redmond 35,800
Renton 41,688
Republic 940
Richland 32,315
Richmond Highlands 26,037
Ridgefield 1,297
Ritzville 1,725
Riverside 223
Rochester 1,250
Rock Island 524
Rockford 481
Rosalia 552
Roslyn 869
Roy 258
Royal City 1,104
Ruston 693
St. John 499
Seattle 516,259
Sedro-Woolley 6,031
Selah 5,113
Sequim 3,616
Shelton 7,241
Sheridan Beach 6,518
Silverdale 7,660
Skykomish 273
Snohomish 6,499
Snoqualmie 1,546
Soap Lake 1,149
South Bend 1,551
South Broadway 2,735
South Cle Elum 457
South Wenatchee 1,207
Spanaway 15,001
Spangle 229
Spokane 177,196
Sprague 410
Springdale 260
Stanwood 1,961
Steilacoom 5,728
Stevenson 1,147
Sultan 2,236
Sumas 744
Sumner 6,281
Sunnyside 11,238
Sunnyslope 1,907
Suquamish 3,105
Tacoma 176,664
Taholah 788
Tanglewilde [-Thompson Place] 6,061
Tekoa 750
Tenino 1,292
Terrace Heights 4,223
Tieton 693
Toledo 586
Tonasket 847
Toppenish 7,419
Town and Country 4,921
Tracyton 2,621
Trentwood 4,060
Tukwila 11,874
Tumwater 9,976
Twisp 872
Union Gap 3,120
Uniontown 277
University Place 27,701
Vader 414
Vancouver 46,380
Veradale 7,836
Waitsburg 990
Walla Walla 26,478
Walla Walla East 2,959
Wapato 3,795
Warden 1,639
Washougal 4,764
Washtucna 231
Waterville 995
Wenatchee 21,756
West Clarkston [-Highland] 3,913
West Pasco 7,312
West Richland 3,962
West Wenatchee 2,220
Westport 1,892
White Center [-Shorewood] 20,531
White Salmon 1,861
White Swan 2,669
Wilbur 863
Wilkeson 366
Winlock 1,027
Winslow 3,081
Winthrop 302
Woodinville 23,654
Woodland 2,500
Woodway 914
Yacolt 600
Yakima 54,827
Yarrow Point 962
Yelm 1,337
Zillah 1,911

West Virginia ■ population 1,801,625

Metropolitan areas

Charleston 250,454
Cumberland (Md.) 101,643 (74,946 in Md.; 26,697 in W. Va.)
Huntington-Ashland (Ky.) 312,529 (138,463 in W. Va.; 61,834 in O.; 112,232 in Ky.)
Parkersburg-Marietta (O.) 149,619 (86,915 in W. Va.; 62,254 in O.)
Weirton-Steubenville (O.) 142,523 (80,298 in O.; 62,225 in W. Va.)
Wheeling 159,301 (88,227 in W. Va.; 71,074 in O.)

Counties

Barbour 15,699
Berkeley 59,253
Boone 25,870
Braxton 12,998
Brooke 26,992
Cabell 96,827
Calhoun 7,885
Clay 9,983
Doddridge 6,994
Fayette 47,952
Gilmer 7,669
Grant 10,428
Greenbrier 34,693
Hampshire 16,498
Hancock 35,233
Hardy 10,977
Harrison 69,371
Jackson 25,938
Jefferson 35,926
Kanawha 207,619
Lewis 17,223
Lincoln 21,382
Logan 43,032
Marion 57,249
Marshall 37,356
Mason 25,178
McDowell 35,233
Mercer 64,980
Mineral 26,697
Mingo 33,739
Monongalia 75,509
Monroe 12,406
Morgan 12,128
Nicholas 26,775
Ohio 50,871
Pendleton 8,054
Pleasants 7,546
Pocahontas 9,008
Preston 29,037
Putnam 42,835
Raleigh 76,819
Randolph 27,803
Ritchie 10,233
Roane 15,120
Summers 14,204
Taylor 15,144
Tucker 7,728
Tyler 9,796
Upshur 22,867
Wayne 41,636
Webster 10,729
Wetzel 19,258
Wirt 5,192
Wood 86,915
Wyoming 28,990

Cities, towns, and villages

Alderson 1,152
Alum Creek 1,602
Amherstdale [-Robinette] 2,435
Anawait 329
Anmoore 686
Ansted 1,643
Athens 741
Bancroft 381
Barboursville 2,774
Barrackville 1,443
Bayard 414
Beaver 1,244
Beckley 18,296
Beech Bottom 415
Belington 1,850
Belle 1,421
Belmont 912
Benwood 1,669
Berkeley Springs 735
Bethany 1,139
Bethlehem 2,694
Beverly 696
Blennerhassett 2,924
Bluefield 12,756
Bolivar 1,013
Bradley 2,144
Bradshaw 394
Bramwell 620
Bridgeport 6,739
Brookhaven 3,836
Buckhannon 5,909
Buffalo 969
Burnsville 495
Cairo 290
Cameron 1,177
Cassville 1,458
Cedar Grove 1,213
Ceredo 1,916
Chapmanville 1,110
Charles Town 3,122
Charleston 57,287
Chattaroy 1,182
Chesapeake 1,896
Chester 2,905
Clarksburg 18,059
Clay 592
Clearview 622
Clendenin 1,203
Coal City 1,876
Coal Fork 2,100
Cowen 549
Crab Orchard 2,919

Craigsville 1,955
Culloden 2,907
Daniels 1,714
Danville 595
Davis 799
Davy 403
Delbarton 705
Despard 1,018
Dunbar 8,697
Durbin 278
East Bank 892
Eleanor 1,256
Elizabeth 900
Elk Garden 261
Elkins 7,420
Elkview 1,047
Ellenboro 453
Enterprise 1,058
Fairlea 1,743
Fairmont 20,210
Fairview 513
Farmington 414
Fayetteville 2,182
Flatwoods 324
Flemington 352
Follansbee 3,339
Fort Ashby 1,288
Fort Gay 852
Franklin 914
Gary 1,355
Gassaway 946
Gauley Bridge 691
Gilbert 456
Glasgow 906
Glen Dale 1,612
Glenville 1,923
Grafton 5,524
Grant Town 694
Grantsville 671
Granville 798
Hambleton 265
Hamlin 1,030
Handley 334
Harpers Ferry 308
Harrisville 1,839
Hartford 487
Harts 2,332
Hedgesville 227
Henderson 549
Hendricks 303
Hinton 3,433
Holden 1,246
Hooverson Heights 3,056
Hundred 386
Huntington 54,844
Hurricane 4,461
Huttonsville 211
Iaeger 551
Inwood 1,360
Jane Lew 439
Junior 542
Kenova 3,748
Kermit 342
Keyser 5,870
Keystone 627
Kimball 550
Kingwood 3,243
Lester 420
Lewisburg 3,598
Logan 2,206
Lost Creek 413
Lubeck 1,579
Lumberport 1,014
Mabscott 1,543
MacArthur 1,595
Madison 3,051
Mallory 1,126
Man 914
Mannington 2,184
Marlinton 1,148
Marmet 1,879
Martinsburg 14,073
Mason 1,053
Masontown 737
Matewan 619
Matoaka 366
McMechen 2,130
Meadow Bridge 325
Middlebourne 922
Mill Creek 685
Milton 2,242
Mineralwells 1,698
Mitchell Heights 265
Monongah 1,018
Montcalm 1,023
Montgomery 2,449
Moorefield 2,148
Morgantown 25,879
Moundsville 10,753
Mount Gay (-Shamrock) 3,377
Mount Hope 1,573
Mullens 2,006
New Cumberland 1,363
New Haven 1,632
New Martinsville 6,705
Newburg 378
Newell 1,724
Nitro 6,851
North Hills 849
Northfork 656
Nutter Fort 1,819
Oak Hill 6,812
Oceana 1,791
Paden City 2,862
Parkersburg 33,862
Parsons 1,453
Paw Paw 538
Pennsboro 1,282
Petersburg 2,360
Peterstown 550
Philippi 3,132
Piedmont 1,094
Pinch 2,695
Pine Grove 701
Pineville 865
Piney View 1,085
Poca 1,124
Point Pleasant 4,996
Powellton 1,905
Pratt 640
Princeton 7,043
Prosperity 1,322
Quinwood 559
Rainelle 1,681
Ranson 2,890
Ravenswood 4,189
Reedsville 482
Reedy 271
Rhodell 221
Richwood 2,808
Ridgeley 779
Ripley 3,023
Rivesville 1,064
Romney 1,966
Ronceverte 1,754
Rowlesburg 648
Rupert 1,104
St. Albans 11,194
St. Marys 2,148
Salem 2,063
Shady Spring 1,929
Shepherdstown 1,287
Shinnston 2,543
Sissonville 4,290
Sistersville 1,797
Smithers 1,162
Smithfield 205
Sophia 1,182
South Charleston 13,645
Spencer 2,279
Stanaford 1,706
Star City 1,251
Stonewood 1,996
Summersville 2,906
Sutton 939
Switzer 1,004
Terra Alta 1,713
Thomas 573
Tornado 1,006
Triadelphia 835
Tunnelton 331
Union 566
Valley Grove 569
Vienna 10,862
War 1,081
Washington 1,030
Wayne 1,128
Webster Springs 674
Weirton 22,124
Welch 3,028
Wellsburg 3,385
West Hamlin 423
West Liberty 1,434
West Logan 524
West Milford 519
West Union 830
Weston 4,994
Westover 4,201
Wheeling 34,882
White Sulphur Springs 2,779
Whitesville 486
Williamson 4,154
Williamstown 2,774
Winfield 1,164
Womelsdorf 277
Worthington 233

Wisconsin ■ population 4,906,745

Metropolitan areas

Appleton-Oshkosh 315,121
Duluth (Minn.) 239,971 (198,213 in Minn.; 41,758 in Wis.)
Eau Claire 137,543
Green Bay 194,594
Janesville-Beloit 139,510
Kenosha 128,181
La Crosse 97,904
Madison 367,085
Milwaukee 1,432,149
Minneapolis-St. Paul (Minn.) 2,464,124 (2,413,873 in Minn.; 50,251 in Wis.)
Racine 175,034
Sheboygan 103,877
Wausau 115,400

Counties

Adams 15,682
Ashland 16,307
Barron 40,750
Bayfield 14,008
Brown 194,594
Buffalo 13,584
Burnett 13,084
Calumet 34,291
Chippewa 52,360
Clark 31,647
Columbia 45,088
Crawford 15,940
Dane 367,085
Dodge 76,559
Door 25,690
Douglas 41,758
Dunn 35,909
Eau Claire 85,183
Florence 4,590
Fond du Lac 90,083
Forest 8,776
Grant 49,264
Green 30,339
Green Lake 18,651
Iowa 20,150
Iron 6,153
Jackson 16,588
Jefferson 67,783
Juneau 21,650
Kenosha 128,181
Kewaunee 18,878
La Crosse 97,904
Lafayette 16,076
Langlade 19,505
Lincoln 26,993
Manitowoc 80,421
Marathon 115,400
Marinette 40,548
Marquette 12,321
Menominee 3,890
Milwaukee 959,275
Monroe 36,633
Oconto 30,226
Oneida 31,679
Outagamie 140,510
Ozaukee 72,831
Pepin 7,107
Pierce 32,765
Polk 34,773
Portage 61,405
Price 15,600
Racine 175,034
Richland 17,521
Rock 139,510
Rusk 15,079
St. Croix 50,251
Sauk 46,975
Sawyer 14,181
Shawano 37,157
Sheboygan 103,877
Taylor 18,901
Trempealeau 25,263
Vernon 25,617
Vilas 17,707
Walworth 75,000
Washburn 13,772
Washington 95,328
Waukesha 304,715
Waupaca 46,104
Waushara 19,385
Winnebago 140,320
Wood 73,605

Cities and villages

Abbotsford 1,916
Adams 1,715
Adell 510
Albany 1,140
Algoma 3,353
Allouez 14,431
Alma 790
Alma Center 416
Almena 625
Almond 455
Altoona 5,889
Amery 2,657
Amherst 792
Amherst Junction 269
Aniwa 249
Antigo 8,276
Appleton 65,695
Arcadia 2,166
Arena 525
Argyle 798
Arlington 440
Arpin 312
Ashland 8,695
Ashwaubenon 16,376
Athens 951
Auburndale 665
Augusta 1,510
Avoca 474
Bad River Reservation 1,070
Bagley 306
Baldwin 2,022
Balsam Lake 792
Bangor 1,076
Baraboo 9,203
Barneveld 660
Barron 2,986
Bay City 578
Bayfield 686
Bayside 4,789
Bear Creek 418
Beaver Dam 14,196
Belgium 928
Belleville 1,456
Belmont 823
Beloit 35,573
Benton 898
Berlin 5,371
Big Bend 1,299
Birchwood 443
Birnamwood 693
Biron 794
Black Creek 1,152
Black Earth 1,248
Black River Falls 3,490
Blair 1,126
Blanchardville 802
Bloomer 3,085
Bloomington 776
Blue Mounds 446
Blue River 438
Bohners Lake 1,553
Bonduel 1,210
Boscobel 2,706
Bowler 279
Boyceville 913
Boyd 683
Brandon 872
Brillion 2,840
Brodhead 3,165
Brokaw 224
Brookfield 35,184
Brooklyn 789
Brown Deer 12,236
Browns Lake 1,725
Browntown 256
Bruce 844
Buffalo 915
Burlington 8,855
Butler 2,079
Butternut 416
Cadott 1,328
Cambria 768
Cambridge 963
Cameron 1,273
Camp Douglas 512
Camp Lake 2,291
Campbellsport 1,732
Cascade 620
Casco 544
Cashton 780
Cassville 1,144
Cazenovia 288
Cecil 373
Cedar Grove 1,521
Cedarburg 9,895
Centuria 790
Chaseburg 365
Chenequa 601
Chetek 1,953
Chilton 3,240
Chippewa Falls 12,727
Clayton 450
Clear Lake 932
Cleveland 1,398
Clinton 1,849
Clintonville 4,351
Clyman 370
Cobb 440
Cochrane 475
Colby 1,532
Coleman 839
Colfax 1,110
Coloma 383
Columbus 4,093
Combined Locks 2,190
Como 1,353
Coon Valley 817
Cornell 1,541
Cottage Grove 1,131
Crandon 1,958
Crivitz 996
Cross Plains 2,098
Cuba City 2,024
Cudahy 18,659
Cumberland 2,163
Dallas 452
Dane 621
Darien 1,158
Darlington 2,235
Deer Park 237
Deerfield 1,617
De Forest 4,882
Delafield 5,347
Delavan 6,073
Delavan Lake 2,177
Denmark 1,612
De Pere 16,569
De Soto 326
Dickeyville 862
Dodgeville 3,882
Dorchester 697
Dousman 1,277
Downing 250
Doylestown 316
Dresser 614
Durand 2,003
Eagle 1,182
Eagle River 1,374
East Troy 2,664
Eastman 369
Eau Claire 56,856
Eden 610
Edgar 1,318
Edgerton 4,254
Eland 247
Eleva 491
Elk Mound 765
Elkhart Lake 1,019
Elkhorn 5,337
Ellsworth 2,706
Elm Grove 6,261
Elmwood 775
Elmwood Park 534
Elroy 1,533
Embarrass 461
Endeavor 316
Ephraim 261
Ettrick 461
Evansville 3,174
Evergreen 3,423
Fairchild 504
Fairwater 302
Fall Creek 1,034
Fall River 842
Fennimore 2,378
Fenwood 214
Fond du Lac 37,757
Fontana 1,635
Footville 764
Forestville 470
Fort Atkinson 10,227
Fountain City 938
Fox Lake 1,269
Fox Point 7,238
Francis Creek 562
Franklin 21,855
Frederic 1,124
Fredonia 1,558
Fremont 632
French Island 4,478
Friendship 728
Friesland 271
Galesville 1,278
Gays Mills 578
Genoa 266
Genoa City 1,277
Germantown 13,658
Gillett 1,303
Gilman 412
Glenbeulah 386
Glendale 14,088
Glenwood City 1,026
Grafton 9,340
Granton 379
Grantsburg 1,144
Gratiot 207
Green Bay 96,466
Green Lake 1,064
Greendale 15,128
Greenfield 33,403
Greenwood 969
Gresham 515
Hales Corners 7,623
Hammond 1,097
Hancock 382
Hartford 8,188
Hartland 6,906
Hatley 295
Haugen 305
Hawkins 375
Hayward 1,897
Hazel Green 1,171
Hewitt 595
Highland 799
Hilbert 1,211
Hillsboro 1,288
Hixton 345
Hollandale 256
Holmen 3,220
Horicon 3,873
Hortonville 2,029
Howard 9,874
Howards Grove 2,329
Hudson 6,378
Hurley 1,782
Hustisford 979
Independence 1,041
Iola 1,125
Iron Ridge 887
Ironton 200
Jackson 2,486
Janesville 52,133
Jefferson 6,078
Johnson Creek 1,259
Junction City 502
Juneau 2,157
Kaukauna 11,982
Kellnersville 350
Kendall 453
Kenosha 80,352
Keshena 685
Kewaskum 2,515
Kewaunee 2,750
Kiel 2,910
Kimberly 5,406
Kingston 346
Knapp 419
Kohler 1,817
Lac Courte Oreilles Reservation 2,409
Lac du Flambeau Reservation 2,434
Lac La Belle 258
La Crosse 51,003
Ladysmith 3,938
La Farge 766
Lake Delton 1,470
Lake Geneva 5,979
Lake Mills 4,143
Lake Nebagamon 900
Lake Wazeecha 2,278
Lake Wissota 2,175
Lancaster 4,192
Lannon 924
La Valle 446
Lena 590
Linden 429
Little Chute 9,207
Livingston 576
Lodi 2,093
Loganville 228
Lohrville 368
Lomira 1,542
Lone Rock 641
Lowell 300
Loyal 1,244
Luck 1,022
Luxemburg 1,151
Lyndon Station 474
Madison 191,262
Manawa 1,169
Manitowoc 32,520
Maple Bluff 1,352
Marathon City 1,606
Maribel 372
Marinette 11,843
Marion 1,242
Markesan 1,496
Marshall 2,329
Marshfield 19,291
Mattoon 431
Mauston 3,439
Mayville 4,374
Mazomanie 1,377
McFarland 5,232
Medford 4,283
Mellen 935
Melrose 551
Menasha 14,711
Menomonee Falls 26,840
Menominee Reservation 3,397
Menomonie 13,547
Mequon 18,885
Merrill 9,860
Merrillan 553
Merrimac 392
Merton 1,199
Middleton 13,289
Milladore 314
Milltown 786
Milton 4,434
Milwaukee 628,088
Mineral Point 2,428
Minong 521
Mishicot 1,296
Mondovi 2,491
Monona 8,637
Monroe 10,241
Montello 1,329
Montfort 676
Monticello 1,140
Montreal 838
Mosinee 3,820
Mount Calvary 558
Mount Horeb 4,182
Mount Sterling 217
Mukwonago 4,457
Muscoda 1,287
Muskego 16,813
Nashotah 567
Necedah 743
Neenah 23,219
Neillsville 2,680
Nekoosa 2,557
Nelson 388
Neopit 615
Neosho 658
Neshkoro 384
New Auburn 485
New Berlin 33,592
New Glarus 1,899
New Holstein 3,342
New Lisbon 1,491
New London 6,658
New Richmond 5,106
Newburg 875
Niagara 1,999
Nichols 254
North Bay 246
North Fond du Lac 4,292
North Freedom 591
North Hudson 3,101
North Prairie 1,322
Norwalk 564
Oak Creek 19,513
Oakfield 1,003
Oconomowoc 10,993
Oconomowoc Lake 493
Oconto 4,474
Oconto Falls 2,584
Ogdensburg 220

Wisconsin (continued)

Okauchee 3,819
Oliver 265
Omro 2,836
Onalaska 11,284
Oneida 808
Oneida Reservation 18,033
Ontario 407
Oostburg 1,931
Oregon 4,519
Orfordville 1,219
Osceola 2,075
Oshkosh 55,006
Osseo 1,551
Owen 895
Oxford 499
Paddock Lake 2,662
Palmyra 1,539
Pardeeville 1,630
Park Falls 3,104
Park Ridge 546
Patch Grove 202
Pell Lake 2,018
Pepin 873
Peshtigo 3,154
Pewaukee 4,941
Phillips 1,592
Pigeon Falls 289
Pittsville 838
Plain 691
Plainfield 839
Platteville 9,708
Pleasant Prairie 11,961
Plover 8,176
Plum City 534
Plymouth 6,769
Poplar 516
Port Edwards 1,848
Port Washington 9,338
Portage 8,640
Potawatomie Reservation 279
Potosi 654
Potter 252
Potter Lake 1,096
Pound 434
Powers Lake 1,044
Poynette 1,662
Prairie du Chien 5,659
Prairie du Sac 2,380
Prairie Farm 494
Prentice 571
Prescott 3,243
Princeton 1,458
Pulaski 2,200
Racine 84,298
Radisson 237
Randolph 1,729
Random Lake 1,439
Readstown 420
Red Cliff Reservation 857
Redgranite 1,009
Reedsburg 5,834
Reedsville 1,182
Reeseville 673
Reserve 371
Rewey 220
Rhinelander 7,427
Rib Lake 887
Rice Lake 7,998
Richland Center 5,018
Ridgeland 246
Ridgeway 577
Rio 768
Ripon 7,241
River Falls 10,610
River Hills 1,612
Roberts 1,043
Rochester 978
Rock Springs 432
Rockdale 235
Rockland 509
Rosendale 777
Rosholt 512
Rothschild 3,310
Rudolph 451
St. Cloud 494
St. Croix Falls 1,640
St. Croix Reservation 505
St. Francis 9,245
St. Nazianz 693
Sauk City 3,019
Saukville 3,695
Scandinavia 298
Schofield 2,415
Seymour 2,782
Sharon 1,250
Shawano 7,598
Sheboygan 49,676
Sheboygan Falls 5,823
Sheldon 268
Shell Lake 1,161
Sherwood 837
Shiocton 913
Shorewood 14,116
Shorewood Hills 1,680
Shullsburg 1,236
Silver Lake 1,801
Siren 863
Sister Bay 675
Slinger 2,340
Sokaogon Chippewa Reservation 216
Soldiers Grove 564
Solon Springs 575
Somerset 1,065
South Milwaukee 20,958
South Wayne 478
Sparta 7,788
Spencer 1,757
Spooner 2,464
Spring Green 1,283
Spring Valley 1,051
Stanley 2,011
Star Prairie 507
Stetsonville 511
Stevens Point 23,006
Stockbridge 579
Stockbridge Reservation 581
Stoddard 775
Stoughton 8,786
Stratford 1,515
Strum 949
Sturgeon Bay 9,176
Sturtevant 3,803
Sullivan 432
Sun Prairie 15,333
Superior 27,134
Superior 481
Suring 626
Sussex 5,039
Taylor 419
Tennyson 378
Theresa 771
Thiensville 3,301
Thorp 1,657
Tigerton 815
Tomah 7,570
Tomahawk 3,328
Trempealeau 1,039
Turtle Lake 817
Twin Lakes 3,989
Two Rivers 13,030
Union Grove 3,669
Unity 452
Valders 905
Verona 5,374
Vesper 598
Viola 644
Viroqua 3,922
Waldo 442
Wales 2,471
Walworth 1,614
Warrens 343
Washburn 2,285
Waterford 2,431
Waterloo 2,712
Watertown 19,142
Waukesha 56,958
Waunakee 5,897
Waupaca 4,957
Waupun 8,207
Wausau 37,060
Wausau West (Rib Mountain) 4,634
Wausaukee 656
Wautoma 1,784
Wauwatosa 49,366
Wauzeka 595
Webster 623
West Allis 63,221
West Baraboo 1,021
West Bend 23,916
West Milwaukee 3,973
West Salem 3,611
Westby 1,866
Westfield 1,125
Weston 9,714
Weyauwega 1,665
Weyerhaeuser 283
Wheeler 348
White Lake 304
Whitefish Bay 14,272
Whitehall 1,494
Whitelaw 700
Whitewater 12,636
Whiting 1,838
Wild Rose 676
Williams Bay 2,108
Wilton 478
Wind Lake 3,748
Wind Point 1,941
Windsor 2,182
Winneconne 2,059
Winter 383
Wisconsin Dells 2,393
Wisconsin Rapids 18,245
Wisconsin Winnebago Reservation 506
Withee 503
Wittenberg 1,145
Wonewoc 793
Woodville 942
Wrightstown 1,262
Wyocena 620

Wyoming ■ population 455,975

Metropolitan area

Casper 61,226
Cheyenne 73,142

Counties

Albany 30,797
Big Horn 10,525
Campbell 29,370
Carbon 16,659
Converse 11,128
Crook 5,294
Fremont 33,662
Goshen 12,373
Hot Springs 4,809
Johnson 6,145
Laramie 73,142
Lincoln 12,625
Natrona 61,226
Niobrara 2,499
Park 23,178
Platte 8,145
Sheridan 23,562
Sublette 4,843
Sweetwater 38,823
Teton 11,172
Uinta 18,705
Washakie 8,388
Weston 6,518

Cities and towns

Afton 1,394
Albin 120
Arapahoe 393
Baggs 272
Bairoil 228
Basin 1,180
Big Piney 454
Buffalo 3,302
Burlington 184
Burns 254
Byron 470
Casper 46,742
Cheyenne 50,008
Chugwater 192
Clearmont 119
Cody 7,897
Cokeville 493
Cowley 477
Dayton 565
Deaver 199
Diamondville 864
Dixon 70
Douglas 5,076
Dubois 895
East Thermopolis 221
Edgerton 247
Elk Mountain 174
Ethete 1,059
Evanston 10,903
Evansville 1,403
Fort Laramie 243
Fort Washakie 1,334
Fox Farm (-College) 2,965
Frannie 148
Gillette 17,635
Glendo 195
Glenrock 2,153
Granger 126
Green River 12,711
Greybull 1,789
Guernsey 1,155
Hanna 1,076
Hartville 78
Hudson 392
Hulett 429
Jackson 4,472
Kaycee 256
Kemmerer 3,020
Kirby 59
La Barge 493
La Grange 224
Lander 7,023
Laramie 26,687
Lingle 473
Lost Springs 4
Lovell 2,131
Lusk 1,504
Lyman 1,896
Manderson 83
Manville 97
Marbleton 634
Medicine Bow 389
Meeteetse 368
Midwest 495
Mills 1,574
Moorcroft 768
Mountain View 1,189
Mountain View 1,345
Newcastle 3,003
Opal 95
Pavillion 126
Pine Bluffs 1,054
Pinedale 1,181
Powell 5,292
Ranchester 676
Rawlins 9,380
Riverside 85
Riverton 9,202
Rock River 190
Rock Springs 19,050
Saratoga 1,969
Sheridan 13,900
Shoshoni 497
Sinclair 500
Sundance 1,139
Superior 273
Ten Sleep 311
Thayne 267
Thermopolis 3,247
Torrington 5,651
Upton 980
Van Tassell 8
Wamsutter 240
Warren AFB 3,832
Wheatland 3,271
Wind River Reservation 21,851
Worland 5,742
Wright 1,236
Yoder 136

Index

How to use the index

This index covers the contents of the 1990, 1991, and 1992 editions of *The World Book Year Book.*

Koskotas, George, 92: 234, **90:** 318
Kosovo, 92: 474, **91:** 480, **90:** 485
Kozol, Jonathan, 92: 191
Kraft USA, 90: 394
Kravchuk, Leonid M., 92: 438
Kreimer, Richard, 92: 280
Kreisky, Bruno, 91: 183
Krenz, Egon, 90: 313-314
Krishna Prasad Bhattarai, 91: 379
Kronberger, Petra, 92: 390, **91:** 427
Kryuchkov, Vladimir A., 92: 432-435
Krzysztof, Jan, 92: 204 (il.)
Kuomintang, 92: 413, **91:** 447, **90:** 452, 453
Kurds: Iran, **92:** 250; Iraq, **92:** 252-253, 314, 355, 447-448, **90:** 336; Turkey, **92:** 430-431, **91:** 459, **90:** 468
Kuril Islands, 92: 71, **91:** 177
KUWAIT, 92: 266-268, **91:** 340; immigration to U.S., **92:** 243; oil supply, **92:** 357; Persian Gulf crisis and War, **92:** 251, 266-268, 342-355, 447, **91:** 329-330, 340, 366-368; reconstruction, **92:** 99; Saudi Arabia, **91:** 427, **90:** 432-433; tables, **92:** 316, **91:** 370, **90:** 378. See also **Hussein, Saddam; Persian Gulf crisis and War.**
Kyrgyzstan, 92: 438

L

LABOR, 92: 268-271, **91:** 340-342, **90:** 346-349; airline strikes, **90:** 192, 346-347; baseball contract, **91:** 198, 341; Chile mining strikes, **92:** 140; Los Angeles health care workers' strike, **92:** 291; Manitoba nurses' strike, **92:** 293; Montreal city workers' strike, **92:** 318; Postal Service contract, **92:** 372; productivity, **90:** 282-283; railroad strikes, **92:** 379-380; San Francisco Opera contract, **91:** 243; Soviet mining strike, **90:** 380-381
Labor Party: Australia, **92:** 76; Norway, **91:** 390
Labour Party (Great Britain), 91: 310-311, **90:** 316, 317
Lacalle, Luis Alberto, 91: 472, **90:** 477
Lacroix, Christian, 90: 304
Lacrosse, 92: 401, **91:** 435, **90:** 441
Ladies Professional Bowlers Tour. See **Bowling.**
Ladies Professional Golfers Association. See **Golf.**
Laetare Medal, 92: 386
Lagerfeld, Karl, 91: 299
La Jolla Playhouse, 90: 460-461
LAMER, ANTONIO, 91: 343
***Land Before Time, The* (film), 91:** 136, 150, 151
Landfills, 92: 461 (il.), 462
Landslides, 91: 307
Lanier, Bob, 92: 240, 241
Lao People's Revolutionary Party, 92: 271
LAOS, 92: 271, **91:** 343, **90:** 349; ivory trade, **91:** 50-51; tables, **92:** 73, **91:** 179, **90:** 182; Thailand, **92:** 417
Laptop computers, 92: 152, **90:** 245
LaRouche, Lyndon H., Jr., 90: 257
Lasers, 92: 350, 428
Latifah, Queen, 92: 369
LATIN AMERICA, 92: 272-275, **91:** 343-347, **90:** 350-354; foreign debt, **91:** 281, 343-344; life expectancy, **90:** 415; Protestantism, **92:** 384, **90:** 419; trade agreements, **92:** 249; U.S. policy, **91:** 215, 326-327, 346, **90:** 350, 476
LATVIA, 92: 276-277; ethnic unrest, **91:** 462, 464, **90:** 67, 469; independence, **92:** 202 (il.), 435; tables, **92:** 205; United Nations membership, **92:** 448; *WBE,* **92:** 500
Lauda-Air, 92: 83
Law enforcement. See **Police.**
Law of Return (Israel), 90: 343
Laws. See **Congress of the U.S.; Courts; Crime; State government; Supreme Court of the U.S.; United States, Government of the;** and specific countries.

Each index entry gives the edition year and the page number or numbers—for example, **Kravchuk, Leonid M., 92:** 438. This means that information on Kravchuk may be found on page 438 of the 1992 *Year Book.*

When there are many references to a topic, they are grouped alphabetically by clue words under the main topic. For example, the clue words under **Kurds** group the references to that topic under three subtopics.

When a topic such as **LABOR** appears in all capital letters, this means that there is a *Year Book* Update article entitled Labor in at least one of the three volumes covered by this index. References to the topic in other articles may also appear after the topic name.

When only the first letter of a topic such as **Labor Party** is capitalized, this means that there is no article entitled Labor Party, but that information on this topic may be found in the edition and on the pages listed.

The "see" and "see also" cross references are to other entries in the index—for example, **Ladies Professional Bowlers Tour,** see **Bowling.**

The indication (il.) means that the reference is to an illustration only, as in the **Landfill** picture on page 461 of the 1992 edition.

An index entry followed by *WBE* refers to a new or revised *World Book Encyclopedia* article in the supplement section, as: **LATVIA, 92:** 500. This means that a *World Book Encyclopedia* article on Latvia begins on page 500 of the 1992 *Year Book.*

Index

A

A-12 attack jet, 92: 450, 91: 172
Abassid Caliphate, 92: 57
Abbado, Claudio, 92: 149, 90: 239
ABC. See **American Broadcasting Companies**
Abdallah Abderemane, Ahmed, 90: 162
Abdul-Jabbar, Kareem, 90: 205
Abedi, Agha Hasan, 92: 86
Aborigines, 92: 77, 90: 187
Abortion: Belgium, 91: 203; Canada, 91: 222; Eastern Orthodox Churches, 90: 281; Germany, 91: 418; Judaism, 90: 343; laws and court cases, 92: 157-158, 161-162, 407, 91: 438, 443, 90: 256, 425, 445, 449; Protestant churches, 92: 376, 91: 411, 90: 419; Roman Catholic Church, 92: 384, 385, 90: 429
Abraham, E. Spencer, 92: 382-383
Abrams, Elliot, 92: 251, 451
Abu Bakr, Iman Yasin, 91: 478-479
Academy Awards, 92: 320, 91: 189, 90: 193
Accidents. See **Disasters; Safety**
Aceh Province, Indonesia, 92: 247
Acetaminophen, 90: 321
Acid rain, 92: 112, 91: 290, 90: 111, 292
Acquired immune deficiency syndrome. See **AIDS**
ADA. See **Adenosine deaminase deficiency**
Adamec, Ladislav, 90: 260-261
Adams, Randall Dale, 90: 393
Addiction. See **Alcoholism; Drug abuse; Smoking**
Aden. See **Yemen**
Adenosine deaminase deficiency, 92: 305-306, 91: 362
Adolescents, 92: 376-377, 91: 478
ADVERTISING, 92: 40, 91: 154-155, 90: 156-157; laws, 91: 257; magazine, 90: 368; television, 90: 74-75, 84-85
Aerospace industry. See **Aviation; Space exploration**
Affirmative action: elections, 91: 285; Supreme Court rulings, 91: 240, 442, 90: 237-238, 449-450. See also **Civil rights**
AFGHANISTAN, 92: 41, 91: 155, 90: 157; facts in brief, 92: 73, 91: 179, 90: 182; land mines, 92: 72; refugees, 90: 180, 472; Saudi Arabia, 90: 432; Soviet withdrawal, 90: 155, 179, 470; UN peace plan, 92: 41, 71
Aflatoxin, 90: 306
AFRICA, 92: 42-48, 91: 156-161, 90: 158-164; AIDS, 91: 161; elephant poaching, 91: 36-51, 90: 253; life expectancy, 90: 415; prehuman fossils, 92: 51-52
African National Congress, 92: 393, 91: 156, 360, 430-431, 90: 158, 436
Agent Orange, 91: 415, 90: 478
Aging: drugs, 90: 280; human growth hormone, 91: 363-364; hypertension, 92: 297; memory loss, 91: 128; population changes, 92: 129, 130, 133
Agriculture. See **Farm and farming**
Ahmed, Shahabuddin, 92: 83, 84
Aho, Esko, 92: 219
Aideed, Mohamed Farah, 92: 392
AIDS, 92: 48, 91: 161-162, 90: 164-165; Africa, 92: 331, 91: 161; drug abuse, 91: 277; immigration ban, 92: 243; Latin America, 92: 274; mandatory testing, 92: 240; New York City, 92: 324; pediatric treatment, 91: 162, 90: 228; plays, 92: 420; prisons, 92: 372; research funding, 91: 253; school condom distribution, 92: 191; Thailand, 91: 452; virus in disguise, 92: 138
Ailey, Alvin, 91: 264
Air Force, U.S. See **Armed forces**
Air pollution. See **Environmental pollution**
Airbags, 91: 424
Aircraft crashes. See **Aviation disasters**
Airlines. See **Aviation**
AKIHITO, 91: 335, 418, 90: 165, 339-340
Akkad, 92: 56, 57
Alabama, 92: 404, 91: 439, 90: 444; energy supply, 92: 195, 196 (il.)
Alar, 90: 293, 301, 305-306, 421
Alaska, 92: 404, 91: 439, 90: 444; census, 91: 227; consumer fraud, 90: 255; oil spill, 90: 294-295, 406; weather, 91: 477, 90: 481
ALBANIA, 92: 48-49, 91: 162-163, 90: 165; facts in brief, 92: 205, 91: 295, 90: 298; refugees, 92: 234, 259; Roman Catholic Church, 92: 384
Albanians, Kosovo, 91: 480, 90: 485
Al-Bashir, Umar Hasan Ahmad, 92: 406, 91: 157, 442, 90: 448
ALBERTA, 92: 50, 91: 163, 90: 166
Alberta Heritage Savings Trust Fund, 92: 50
Alcohol consumption, 92: 185, 91: 129, 277, 90: 450
Alcoholism, 92: 185, 91: 315, 90: 101
Alcott, Amy, 92: 230
Aleksei II, 92: 188, 91: 279
ALEXANDER, LAMAR, 92: 50, 148, 190, 91: 281
Alexander I of Yugoslavia, 92: 473
Al-Fatah, 92: 278
Alfonsín, Raúl Ricardo, 90: 173
ALGERIA, 92: 50-51, 91: 164, 90: 166; facts in brief, 92: 46, 91: 158, 90: 160; Islamic movements, 92: 254; Morocco, 90: 382; Persian Gulf crisis, 91: 366, 368; political reforms, 90: 380
Al-Huss, Salim, 90: 355
Ali, Abduraham Ahmed, 92: 392
Alia, Ramiz, 91: 162-163
Aliens. See **Immigration**
Allaire report, 92: 120-121
Allen, William Barclay, 90: 238
Allison, Gray D., 90: 357
***Allure* (magazine),** 92: 292
Al-Mahdi, Al-Sadiq, 90: 448
Al-Megrahi, Abdel Basset Ali, 92: 280-281
Alpha interferon, 92: 186
Al-Sabah, Jabir al-Ahmad al-Jabir, 92: 266, 91: 340
Al-Sayed, Refaat, 90: 451
Alzheimer's disease, 92: 93, 236, 91: 129, 278
Amal (militia), 92: 278
Amazon region, 92: 98, 91: 371. See also **Rain forest**
America 2000 (plan), 92: 190
American Airlines, 92: 83, 270
American Ballet Theatre, 92: 168, 91: 263-264, 90: 262
American Bible Society, 92: 382
American Broadcasting Companies, 92: 40, 222-224, 414-416, 91: 434, 449-450, 90: 73-86, 454-457
American Family Association, 91: 174
American Hospital Association. See **Hospital**
American Immigrant Wall of Honor, 91: 101
American Indian. See **Indian, American**
American Kennel Club. See **Dog**
American Library Association. See **Library**
American Psychiatric Association, 91: 364
American Psychological Association, 91: 364
American Red Cross, 92: 377
***American Tail, An* (film),** 91: 136, 150, 151
American Telephone and Telegraph Co., 90: 243-244, 338, 348
Americans with Disabilities Act (1990), 92: 235-236, 271, 91: 249, 314, 457
America's Cup. See **Boating**
"America's Funniest Home Videos," 91: 449
Amnesia, 91: 129
Amnesty International, 92: 148
Amphibians, 91: 254
Ampligen, 92: 186
AMU. See **Arab Maghreb Union**
Amyotrophic lateral sclerosis, 92: 93
Anabolic steroids, 92: 185, 90: 464
Anafranil, 91: 364
Anan Panyarachun, 92: 417
ANAP, 92: 431, 91: 459
ANC. See **African National Congress**
Anderson, Marian, 90: 241
Anderson, Terry A., 92: 315 (il.), 316-317
Anderson, Vinton, 92: 382
Ando, Tadao, 92: 61
Andorra, 92: 205, 91: 295, 90: 298
Andreotti, Giulio, 92: 257-258, 91: 332, 333, 90: 339
Andretti, Michael, 92: 80
Andrew, Prince, 90: 318
Anemia, 90: 207, 280
Anglicans. See **England, Church of**
ANGOLA, 91: 165, 90: 166-167; civil war, 92: 44, 91: 157, 165, 90: 158, 166-167; Cuba, 92: 165, 90: 260; facts in brief, 92: 46, 91: 158, 90: 160; Namibia, 90: 387
Animal. See **Cat; Conservation; Dog; Endangered species; Farm and farming; Zoology; Zoos**
Animated film, 92: 320-321, 91: 135-151, 375; "Simpsons, The," 91: 136, 137, 313, 448, 455; voice artists, 90: 385
Anne, Princess, 90: 317
Antall, Jozsef, 91: 321
Antarctica: conservation, 90: 125-139, 293, 294; explorers, 91: 383-384; ozone hole, 92: 199, 91: 289, 90: 130-132, 292
Anthony, Beryl F., Jr., 90: 272
Anthony, Earl, 92: 95
ANTHROPOLOGY, 92: 51-52, 91: 165-166, 90: 167-169. See also **Fossils**
Antibodies, Plant, 90: 207
Antigua and Barbuda: election, 90: 484; facts in brief, 92: 275, 91: 345, 90: 353
Aouita, Said, 90: 464
Aoun, Michel. See **Awn, Michel**
Aozou Strip, 91: 156, 229, 90: 358
Apartheid. See **South Africa**
Apple Computer, Inc., 92: 152, 91: 248, 90: 245
Appling, Luke, 92: 171
Aquariums. See **Zoos**
Aquifers, 92: 457-467
Aquino, Benigno S., Jr., 91: 402
Aquino, Corazon C., 92: 360, 361, 91: 401-402, 90: 409-410
Arab Cooperation Council, 90: 380
Arab League, 92: 193, 91: 284, 90: 355-356, 379
Arab Maghreb Union, 90: 166, 358, 380
Arabs. See **Islam; Middle East; Palestinians**
Arachnids, 90: 404
Arafat, Yasir, 92: 314, 90: 377
Arazi (horse), 92: 239
ARCHAEOLOGY, 92: 52-53, 91: 166-168, 90: 169-171; Persian Gulf War damage, 92: 56-59
Archery, 92: 401, 91: 434, 90: 440
ARCHITECTURE, 92: 60-62, 91: 168-169, 90: 171-173; awards, 91: 189, 90: 193. See also **Building and construction**
Arco Chemical Co., 92: 387, 91: 423
ARENA (party), 90: 289
ARGENTINA, 92: 62, 91: 170, 90: 173; facts in brief, 92: 275, 91: 345, 90: 353; free-trade zone, 92: 273, 91: 346; military spending, 92: 274; transportation, 90: 354. See also **Menem, Carlos Saúl**
***Ariane* (rocket),** 91: 433, 90: 439
Arias Sánchez, Oscar, 91: 216
ARISTIDE, JEAN-BERTRAND, 92: 63, 234, 235, 470, 91: 313
Arizona, 92: 404, 91: 439, 90: 444; elections, 92: 194; King holiday, 91: 302, 440; political scandal, 92: 405
Arkansas, 92: 404, 91: 439, 90: 444
***Arkansas Gazette*,** 92: 329
ARMED FORCES, 92: 63-67, 91: 170-173, 90: 173-177; construction projects, 91: 209-210; manufacturing, 92: 295. See also **Defense, U.S. Department of** and specific countries
Armenia: ethnic unrest, 91: 464, 90: 65-67, 469; independence, 92: 438
Arms control: European security, 91: 294; NATO summit, 90: 215-216, 310; U.S.-Soviet talks, 92: 63-65, 91: 171-172, 90: 67-69, 470, 465-466. See also **Nuclear weapons; Strategic Arms Reduction Treaty**
Army, U.S. See **Armed forces**
Arnett, Peter, 92: 414
Arpino, Gerald, 91: 263
ART, 92: 67-69, 91: 173-175, 90: 177-179; cave, 92: 53; Iraq ancient treasures, 92: 56-59; Latin America, 91: 347
Art Institute of Chicago, 92: 69, 90: 177
Arthritis, 91: 315-316, 90: 321
Arts. See **Awards and prizes** and specific arts
Artsebarsky, Anatoly, 92: 396
Arumainayagam, Raja, 92: 244
***As Nasty as They Wanna Be* (recording),** 92: 370, 91: 406
Asbestos, 90: 421
Ash, John, 92: 363
Ashbery, John, 92: 362
Ashcroft, Dame Peggy, 92: 171
ASIA, 92: 70-74, 91: 176-179, 90: 179-183; automobiles, 90: 188; elephants, 91: 40; life expectancy, 90: 415; Pacific rim nations, 91: 103-119
Asian Americans: immigration, 92: 242-243; *Miss Saigon*, 91: 452-453; *WBE*, 91: 537
Asian Games, 91: 236
Assad, Hafez al-, 92: 412-413, 91: 446, 90: 452
Assam, India, 90: 329
Assault weapons. See **Firearms**
Assembly of First Nations, 92: 110, 111
Association of Southeast Asian Nations, 92: 71
Assyria, 92: 56, 58
Asteroid, 92: 394
Astronauts. See **Space exploration**
ASTRONOMY, 92: 74-76, 91: 180-181, 90: 183-185. See also **Space exploration**
Asunción, Treaty of, 92: 273
AT&T. See **American Telephone and Telegraph Co.**
Atatürk Dam, 91: 459
Athanassopoulos, Nikos, 91: 312
Atherosclerosis, 92: 237
Athletics. See **Olympic Games; Sports**
Atlanta Braves, 92: 86-88
Atlantic Ocean. See **Ocean**
***Atlantis* (space shuttle),** 92: 394, 90: 437-438
ATM's. See **Automatic teller machines**
Atomic energy. See **Nuclear energy**
Atwater, Lee, 92: 382, 383, 91: 419, 420, 90: 426-427
Auctions and sales. See **Art; Coin collecting; Stamp collecting**

Auguin, Christophe, 92: 95
Aulby, Mike, 90: 209
Auschwitz, 91: 421-422, **90:** 342-343, 428
AUSTRALIA, 92: 76-77, **91:** 181-183, **90:** 185-187; facts in brief, **92:** 338, **91:** 179, **90:** 182; gold mining, **90:** 381; Nauru, **91:** 394-395, **90:** 403
***Australopithecus*, 92:** 51-52, **91:** 165
AUSTRIA, 92: 78, **91:** 183, **90:** 187-188; European trade, **92:** 206, **91:** 296; facts in brief, **92:** 205, **91:** 295, **90:** 298; Hungary, **90:** 187-188, 326-327
Automatic teller machines, 91: 436
Automation. See **Computer; Office automation**
AUTOMOBILE, 92: 78-80, **91:** 183-185, **90:** 188-189; alternative energy sources, **92:** 196, **91:** 287, **90:** 290; Detroit, **91:** 274, **90:** 274; fuel efficiency bills, **92:** 161, **91:** 257; manufacturing, **92:** 293, **90:** 369-370; safety, **92:** 162, **91:** 423-424, **90:** 431-432
AUTOMOBILE RACING, 92: 80-81, **91:** 185-186, **90:** 189-190
Avalanches, 92: 184
Avery, Cheryl and Dennis, 91: 259
AVIATION, 92: 81-83, **91:** 186-188, **90:** 190-192; Argentina, **90:** 354; Australia, **90:** 185; Chicago airport plan, **91:** 232; disabled, seating for, **91:** 314; labor issues, **92:** 270-271, **90:** 192, 346-347; liquefied natural gas plane, **90:** 290; manufacturing, **90:** 369; Trump Shuttle, **90:** 467. See also **Armed forces**
Aviation disasters, 92: 83, 182-184, **91:** 187-188, 274, **90:** 190-191, 275-276; China, **91:** 235; defects and failures, **90:** 431; Italy, **90:** 339; Lockerbie, Scotland, **92:** 81-82, 280-281, **90:** 195, 209, 282-283; Saudi Arabia, **92:** 389; Sweden, **90:** 451
Avril, Prosper, 90: 352
***Awakenings* (film), 92:** 329
Awami League, 92: 83, **91:** 194
AWARDS AND PRIZES, 91: 189-193, **90:** 193-197. See also **Nobel Prizes; Pulitzer Prizes**
Awn, Michel, 92: 278, **91:** 347-348, 446, **90:** 355-356, 378-379
Aya, Prince, 91: 384
AYLWIN AZÓCAR, PATRICIO, 91: 194, 233, **90:** 229
Azerbaijan: ethnic conflict, **91:** 418, 464, **90:** 65, 469; independence, **92:** 435, 438
Aziz, Tariq, 91: 329-330, 366
Azlan Muhibbuddin Shah ibni Sultan Yusof Izzudin, 90: 368
AZT (drug), 92: 48, **91:** 161-162, **90:** 164
Aztecs, 90: 354

B

B-1B bomber, 92: 66, **91:** 172, **90:** 175
B-2 bomber, 92: 65, 66, 450, **91:** 172, **90:** 175
Babangida, Ibrahim, 92: 331, **91:** 387-388, **90:** 396
Baby boomers, 92: 129, 130, 133, **91:** 136, 151
Babylonia, 92: 56, 57
Bach, Tran Xuan, 91: 473
Backley, Steve, 91: 457
Backus, Jim, 90: 385
BACON, ROGER STUART, 92: 335, **91:** 194, 390
Bacteria: food irradiation, **92:** 221; ground water, **92:** 466; stomach cancer, **92:** 93
Badminton, 92: 401, **91:** 434, **90:** 440
Badr, Zaki, 91: 284
Badran, Mudar, 90: 343
Baghdad. See **Iraq; Persian Gulf crisis and War**
Bahamas, 92: 275, **91:** 345, **90:** 353
***Bahía Paraíso* (ship), 90:** 126, 294
Bahrain, 92: 316, **91:** 370, **90:** 378
Bailey, Pearl, 91: 265
BAKER, JAMES ADDISON, III, 90: 198; China, **92:** 141; Mexico, **92:** 311; Middle East, **92:** 262 (il.), 314, 315, 412 (il.), **90:** 377; U.S.S.R., **92:** 438-439, 440, **90:** 470; Vietnam, **91:** 177, 473
Baker, Kristin M., 90: 394
Baker-Finch, Ian, 92: 230
Bakhtiar, Shahpour, 92: 250
Bakker, Jim, 92: 162, **90:** 419
Balaguer Ricardo, Joaquín, 91: 479
Bald eagle, 90: 40-42, 47 (il.), 51-53
Baldness, 90: 280
Balkanization, 92: 473
Ball, Lucille, 90: 455
Ball, William, 92: 418
Ballet. See **Dancing**
Baltimore, 92: 62, 194, 424, **90:** 466
Bangkok, 92: 417, **91:** 110, **90:** 459
BANGLADESH, 92: 83-84, **91:** 194, **90:** 198; cyclone, **92:** 70, 84, 469; facts in brief, **92:** 73, **91:** 179, **90:** 182; India, **90:** 181
Bangladesh Nationalist Party, 92: 83-84
BANK, 92: 85-86, **91:** 195-198, **90:** 199-200; Australia, **92:** 77; check clearing, **91:** 257; congressional reform plan, **92:** 158; credit requirements, **92:** 160-161; crises and bailouts, **92:** 85, 451; European unification, **92:** 206; Japan scandals, **92:** 261; Panama, **91:** 398; Switzerland, **90:** 452. See also **Interest rates; Savings and loan associations**
Bank of Canada, 92: 109
Bank of Credit and Commerce International, 92: 85-86, 234, 276, 317
Baptists, 92: 376, **91:** 412
Barbados, 92: 275, **91:** 345, **90:** 353
Barbie (doll), 90: 392, 463
Barbie, Klaus, 92: 171
Barcelona, 92: 397-399
Barco Vargas, Virgilio, 90: 242, 350
Bardeen, John, 92: 171
Barenboim, Daniel, 92: 149, **90:** 239
Barnes, Randy, 91: 456
Barnett, Marguerite Ross, 91: 319
Barqueta Bridge, 92: 100 (il.)
BARR, ROSEANNE, 91: 385, **90:** 200
BARR, WILLIAM P., 92: 86
Barre, Mohamed Siad, 92: 44, 392, **91:** 157
Barrette, Leanne, 92: 95
Barrowman, Mike, 92: 411, **91:** 445, **90:** 451
Barry, Dave, 92: 329
Barry, Marion S., Jr., 92: 453, 454, **91:** 473-474, **90:** 479
Bartholomew I, 92: 187
Baryshnikov, Mikhail, 91: 263-264, **90:** 262, 459
Barzani, Massoud, 92: 253
BASEBALL, 92: 86-88, **91:** 198-200, **90:** 200-203; contract, **91:** 198, 341; Little League, **92:** 401; new teams, **92:** 146; parks, **92:** 62. See also names of players
Baseball cards, 92: 327
Basilica of Our Lady of Peace, 91: 333, 420-421, **90:** 212-213
***Basilosaurus*, 91:** 396
Basinger, Kim, 91: 383
BASKETBALL, 92: 89-91, **91:** 200-203, **90:** 203-205; college academic standards, **90:** 440; college finances, **91:** 434. See also names of players
Basques, 91: 433
Batchelder Award. See **Literature for children**
BATES, KATHY, 92: 92
Batista, Eike, 92: 95
***Batman* (film), 90:** 383, 462
Batmonh, Jambyn, 91: 371
Baudouin I, 91: 203
Bauxite, 91: 371
Bavadra, Timoci, 90: 403
Bazoft, Farzad, 91: 330
BCCI. See **Bank of Credit and Commerce International**
Bear poaching, 90: 253
Beastie Boys, 92: 368
Beauty, Facial, 91: 413 (il.), 414
***Beauty and the Beast* (film), 92:** 319 (il.), 320
Becker, Boris, 92: 416, 417, **91:** 450, 451, **90:** 457, 458
***Becoming Light* (Jong), 92:** 363
Beene, Geoffrey, 92: 218
Bees, Africanized, 92: 477, **91:** 385
Beg, Mirza Aslam, 92: 339
Beijing, 92: 140-141, **91:** 233-236, **90:** 230-232
Beirut, 92: 278, **91:** 347, **90:** 355, 356
Belfour, Ed, 92: 238
BELGIUM, 92: 92, **91:** 203, **90:** 206; facts in brief, **92:** 205, **91:** 295, **90:** 298
Belize: conservation, **91:** 256; election, **90:** 484; facts in brief, **92:** 275, **91:** 345, **90:** 353; Guatemala, **92:** 274
Bellamy, Ralph Rexford, 92: 171
Ben Ali, Zine El-Abidine, 92: 254, 430, **91:** 458-459, **90:** 467
Benavides Moreno, Guillermo Alfredo, 92: 195
Bendjedid, Chadli, 92: 50, **91:** 164, 426, **90:** 166, 380
Benin: civil unrest, **91:** 157; election, **92:** 45; facts in brief, **92:** 46, **91:** 158, **90:** 160
Bennett, William J., 90: 218
Bensonhurst (New York City), 92: 148, **91:** 242, 257-258
Bentsen, Lloyd Millard, Jr., 91: 272
Benzine pollution, 90: 292-293
Bergalis, Kimberly, 92: 48
Berlin: unification, **91:** 308; Wall, **91:** 382 (il.), **90:** 299, 312, 314, 454
Berlin Philharmonic, 90: 239
Bermuda Triangle, 92: 327
Bernardin, Joseph Cardinal, 91: 421
Bernstein, Leonard, 91: 243
Berton, Pierre, 91: 225
Best sellers. See **Literature**
Beta-amyloid, 92: 93
Beta decay, 92: 362
Beta Pictoris (star), 91: 85
BEVILACQUA, ANTHONY J. CARDINAL, 92: 92
Bharatiya Janata Party, 92: 244, **91:** 322, 323
Bhopal, India, 90: 330
Bhutan: ethnic conflict, **92:** 71-73, **91:** 178; facts in brief, **92:** 73, **91:** 179, **90:** 182
Bhutto, Benazir, 92: 339, **91:** 395-396, **90:** 403
Biathlon, 92: 401, **91:** 435, **90:** 440
Bible, 91: 413
Bidart, Frank, 91: 404
"Big Green" (bill), 91: 298, 438
Bildt, Carl, 92: 411
Bilingualism, Canadian, 92: 107, 114, **91:** 221, **90:** 382
***Billboard*, 92:** 364
Billiards, 92: 401, **91:** 435, **90:** 440
Bilzerian, Paul A., 90: 257
Bin Shakir, Zayd, 90: 343
Biography. See **Canadian literature; Deaths; Literature; Newsmakers**
BIOLOGY, 92: 93, **91:** 203-204, **90:** 206-207
Biomineralization, 92: 137
Biondi, Matt, 90: 451
Biosphere II, 92: 61, 326
Bird, Vere C., 90: 484
Birds: ancient, **91:** 396; endangered species, **91:** 254, **90:** 38-53, 254-256
Birendra Bir Bikram Shah Dev, 91: 178, 379, **90:** 181
Birmingham, Ala., 92: 194
Birmingham Six, 92: 333, **91:** 389
Birth control, 91: 365, **90:** 415
Birth rate. See **Population**
Bishop, André, 92: 418
Bishop, Maurice, 92: 470
Biswas, Abdur Rahman, 92: 84
***Black and White* (Macaulay), 92:** 286, 288
Black lung disease, 92: 151
Black Tie Affair (horse), 92: 239
Blacks: athlete academic standards, **90:** 440; census and population, **92:** 126, 128, 130, 132, 145; Dahmer murders, **92:** 163-164; education, **92:** 192-193; imprisonment, **91:** 409-410; job bias, **92:** 148; Montreal, **92:** 318; motion pictures, **92:** 321-322; Namibia, **91:** 378; New York City, **92:** 323; popular music, **92:** 367, **91:** 407-408, **90:** 414; Republican Party, **90:** 426; Roman Catholic Church, **90:** 428; theater, **92:** 420. See also **Aborigines; Civil rights; Integration; Race relations; South Africa**
Blanc, Mel, 90: 385
Bleaching of reefs, 92: 335
Bloc Québécois, 91: 221
Block, Sherman, 92: 290
Blood: safety, **92:** 377; *WBE*, **91:** 544
Blood poisoning, 92: 186
Bluth, Don, 91: 149-150
Boat people, 92: 72-74, **91:** 177, **90:** 180-181
BOATING, 92: 95, **91:** 204-205, **90:** 207-208; San Diego, **92:** 387
Bobsledding, 92: 401, **91:** 435, **90:** 440
Bodo, 90: 329
Body odor, 91: 230
Boeing Co., 91: 187-188, **90:** 474
Boesak, Allan, 91: 410-411
Bofill, Ricardo, 92: 60
Boggs, Corinne C., 92: 386
BOLGER, JAMES BRENDAN, 92: 325, **91:** 205, 381
BOLIVIA, 91: 206, **90:** 208; facts in brief, **92:** 275, **91:** 345, **90:** 353; free-trade zone, **92:** 249, 273
Bolsheviks, 92: 442
Bond, Alan, 91: 174-175, **90:** 186-187
Bonds. See **Bank; Stocks and bonds**
Bonilla, Bobby, 92: 86
Bonior, David E., 92: 158
Books. See **Canadian literature; Literature; Literature for children; Poetry**
Bosnia and Hercegovina, 92: 473-475
Boston, 92: 194, **90:** 234
BOTANY, 91: 206, **90:** 208
Botha, Pieter Willem, 90: 162, 264, 436
Botswana: elephants, **91:** 49, 50, **90:** 253; facts in brief, **92:** 46, **91:** 158, **90:** 160; student unrest, **90:** 163
Bougainville, 92: 337-338, **91:** 394, **90:** 402
Bouknight, Jacqueline, 91: 444
Bourassa, Robert, 92: 107, 120, 379, **91:** 218, 220-221, 416, **90:** 422
BOWLING, 92: 95, **91:** 206-207, **90:** 209
Bowman, Christopher, 91: 321, 322
Bowman, Patricia, 92: 161
BOXING, 92: 96-97, **91:** 207-208, **90:** 210. See also names of boxers
Boyd Theater, 92: 62
Brabham, Geoff, 92: 81, **91:** 186
Bradley, Pat, 92: 230
Bradley, Thomas, 91: 357, **90:** 366

Brady, James, 92: 142-143
Brady, Nicholas Frederick, 91: 281, 344, **90:** 332, 476
Brain: early man, **91:** 165; memory, **91:** 122, 128-129; rheumatoid arthritis, **90:** 321; sex differences, **90:** 420; sexual orientation, **92:** 93. See also **Alzheimer's disease**
Braithwaite, Nicholas, 92: 470
Branagh, Kenneth, 90: 386
Brandt, Willy, 92: 204 (il.)
Braselton, Ga., 91: 383
BRAZIL, 92: 97-98, **91:** 208-209, **90:** 211-212; facts in brief, **92:** 275, **91:** 345, **90:** 353; foreign debt, **90:** 352; military spending, **92:** 274; pope's visit, **92:** 384; rare monkey, **91:** 481-482; trade, **92:** 273, **90:** 333. See also **Collor de Mello, Fernando; Rain forest**
Breast cancer, 92: 199, **90:** 372
Breast implants, 92: 297
Breeders' Cup Series. See **Horse racing**
Breeding. See **Farm and farming; Zoos**
Brennan, William J., Jr., 91: 444
Brezhnev, Leonid, 92: 443
Bridgeport, Conn., 92: 142, 143
Bridges. See **Building and construction**
Bridgestone-Firestone Inc., 92: 271
BRITISH COLUMBIA, 92: 98, **91:** 209, **90:** 212; Johnston, Rita, **92:** 98, 262
British North America Act, 92: 117, 119
Broadway. See **Theater**
Brodsky, Joseph, 92: 363
Bronk, William, 92: 362
Bronze Age, 90: 170-171
Brooks, Garth, 92: 366
Brouwer, Arie R., 90: 419
BROWN, EDMUND GERALD, JR., 92: 98
Brown, Ronald H., 91: 272, 380 (il.), **90:** 272
Brown dwarf, 90: 185
Browning, Kurt, 92: 242, **91:** 321, 322, **90:** 327
Brundtland, Gro Harlem, 92: 334, **91:** 390
Brunei: facts in brief, **92:** 73, **91:** 179, **90:** 182; free-trade area, **92:** 71
Brussels summit, 90: 215-216, 310
Bubiyan (Kuwait), 92: 344-345
Bubka, Sergei, 92: 423
Buchanan, John, 90: 399
BUCHANAN, PATRICK J., 92: 99, 383, **91:** 390
Buchwald, Art, 91: 384
Buckey, Peggy McMartin and Raymond, 91: 258
Buckyballs, 92: 362
Buddhists, 92: 71, 164-165, **91:** 213, **90:** 198
Budget, Defense. See **Armed forces**
Budget deficit. See **Federal budget deficit**
Buffalo Bills, 91: 302
Bufi, Ylli, 92: 49
BUILDING AND CONSTRUCTION, 92: 99-100, **91:** 209-211, **90:** 212-213. See also **Architecture; Housing**
BULGARIA, 92: 101, **91:** 212, **90:** 214; facts in brief, **92:** 205, **91:** 295, **90:** 298; Turks, **90:** 214, 467-468; U.S. trade, **92:** 249, **91:** 327
Bull, Gerald, 91: 203
Bunya-bunya tree, 90: 208
Buprenorphine, 90: 226
Bureau of Indian Affairs. See **Indian, American**
Burkina Faso: coup attempts, **90:** 162; facts in brief, **92:** 46, **91:** 158, **90:** 160
BURMA, 92: 101, **91:** 212-213, **90:** 214; election, **92:** 72; facts in brief, **92:** 73, **91:** 179, **90:** 182
Burnt Pages, The **(Ash), 92:** 363
Burrell, Leroy, 92: 422, **91:** 456-457
Burundi: facts in brief, **92:** 46, **91:** 158, **90:** 160; ivory trade, **91:** 48
Busey, James B., IV, 90: 192
Bush, Barbara, 92: 102 (il.), 104, **91:** 214, 215, 276, **90:** 217, 278 (il.)
BUSH, GEORGE HERBERT WALKER, 92: 102-104, **91:** 213-215, **90:** 215-217; armed forces, **92:** 63-65, 67, **91:** 170-172, **90:** 173-177; arts funding, **91:** 174; banking, **92:** 85, 86, 160-161, **91:** 196-197; budget deficit, **91:** 468-470, **90:** 473, 474; Canada, **92:** 112, **91:** 224, **90:** 223; China, **92:** 141; civil rights, **92:** 146, **91:** 240, 249; Congress, U.S., **92:** 153-158, **91:** 248-249, **90:** 250-253; Democratic Party, **92:** 179-180, **91:** 213, 272, **90:** 272; Denmark, **92:** 181 (il.); drug war, **90:** 279; economy, **92:** 103, 188, 189; education, **92:** 190, **91:** 281, **90:** 229, 283, 285; energy policy, **92:** 161, 195; environmental issues, **92:** 158-159, 217, **91:** 254; Greece, **92:** 233 (il.); health, personal, **92:** 104, 379; Japan, **92:** 261; Jordan, **92:** 263; labor issues, **92:** 269-271, **91:** 342, **90:** 252; Latin America policy, **92:** 97, 273, 310, **91:** 326, 346, **90:** 350; Middle East peace conference, **92:** 103, 255-256, 314, 315; NATO summit, **90:** 297; Nicaragua, **92:** 330; nominations and appointments, **92:** 451-453, **91:** 241, 470, **90:** 238, 473-474; Panama invasion, **90:** 216, 404-405; Persian Gulf crisis and War, **92:** 102-103, 179, 180, 345, 347, 351, 355, 414, **91:** 213-214, 329, 426; presidential campaign, **92:** 449; Republican Party, **92:** 382, 383, **91:** 419; summer home destruction, **92:** 146; Sununu, John, **92:** 103, 406; tax policy, **92:** 413, 414, **91:** 285, 419, 420, 469-470; trade policy, **92:** 249, **91:** 326-327, 472, **90:** 333; transit, **92:** 424; U.S.S.R., **92:** 103, 216, 249, **91:** 214-215, **90:** 297; Zionism resolution, **92:** 449
Bush, Neil, 91: 197
Business. See **Economics; International trade; Labor; Manufacturing;** and specific industries
Busing. See **Integration**
Butcher, Susan, 91: 384 (il.)
Buthelezi, Mangosuthu Gatsha, 92: 394, **91:** 410
Buzz **(magazine), 92:** 292
Byelarus, 92: 438, 447
Byelorussia. See **Byelarus**

C

Caan, James, 92: 321 (il.)
CABINET, U.S., 92: 104, **90:** 217-218; changes, **92:** 451, **91:** 470, **90:** 473
Cable News Network, 92: 40, 390, 414, **90:** 454
Cable television, 91: 450, **90:** 457; network competition, **90:** 76-86; regulation, **92:** 161, 416, **91:** 257
CAD-CAM, 90: 273-274, 371
Cadilhe, Miguel Ribeiro, 91: 408
Calcavecchia, Mark, 90: 315
Caldecott Medal. See **Literature for children**
CALDERÓN FOURNIER, RAFAEL ANGEL, 91: 216, 257
Calfa, Marián, 91: 262, **90:** 261
Calgary Flames, 90: 321
California, 92: 402, 404, **91:** 439, **90:** 444; earthquake, **91:** 238-239, **90:** 202, 213, 235-237, 312, 454; education, **92:** 403, **90:** 284; energy supply, **91:** 287, 288; environment, **91:** 298, 438; gun control, **90:** 445; libraries, **92:** 280; population growth, **92:** 128, 276, **91:** 227; transit, **91:** 457-458; water supply, **92:** 455, 456-457, 464, 468, **91:** 474-475
California **(magazine), 92:** 292
Callaghan, Morley, 91: 265
Callejas, Rafael Leonardo, 91: 317, **90:** 323
Calvert, Crispina and Mark, 91: 259
CAMBODIA, 92: 105, **91:** 216-217, **90:** 218; facts in brief, **92:** 73, **91:** 179, **90:** 182; land mines, **92:** 72; peace agreement, **92:** 70-71, 448, 453; Thailand, **92:** 417, **90:** 459; Vietnam occupation, **90:** 179, 478
Cambrian Period, 92: 340
Camcorders, 92: 195, **91:** 286
CAMERON, DONALD, 92: 105, 335
Cameroon, 92: 46, **91:** 158, **90:** 160
Campbell, Kim, 91: 222
CANADA, 92: 107-112, **91:** 217-224, **90:** 219-223; coin, **91:** 245; dancing, **91:** 264; farming, **92:** 216, **90:** 303; football, **92:** 222, **91:** 303, **90:** 308; free-trade area, **92:** 249, 273; Indian affairs, **92:** 111-112, **91:** 217-219, **90:** 331; insanity committal law, **92:** 310; petroleum and gas, **91:** 400, **90:** 408; Quebec controversy, **92:** 107-110, 113-124, **91:** 219-222, **90:** 221; rail system, **91:** 210; strikes, **92:** 106-107 (il.), **90:** 325; television, **90:** 87, 91; tobacco advertising, **92:** 40. See also **Meech Lake Accord; Mulroney, Brian;** and names of provinces and territories
CANADIAN LITERATURE, 92: 125-126, **91:** 224-226, **90:** 224-225. See also **Awards and prizes**
Cancer: death rates, **91:** 415; dental treatment, **90:** 274; depression, **90:** 421; drugs, **92:** 186, **91:** 278; fluoride in water, **91:** 475; genetics, **92:** 236, 304, 306, 308, **91:** 362, **90:** 206, 320; Nobel Prize, **90:** 397; radiation deaths, **92:** 199. See also specific types of cancer
Cannes International Film Festival, 91: 189, **90:** 193
Canoeing, 92: 401, **91:** 435, **90:** 441
Canon Corp., 92: 195
CANSECO, JOSÉ, JR., 91: 226
Cape Verde: election, **92:** 45; facts in brief, **92:** 46, **91:** 158, **90:** 160
Capital gains tax, 90: 453-454
Capital investment. See **Manufacturing**
Capital punishment, 92: 373, 407, **91:** 410, **90:** 450
Capra, Frank, 92: 171
CAPRIATI, JENNIFER, 91: 226, 451
Carbamazepine, 91: 278
Carbon, 92: 137 (il.), 362, **91:** 230-231
Carbon dioxide: global warming, **92:** 197, 228, **90:** 111; planet atmospheres, **91:** 73-77
Cardoso de Mello, Zelia, 92: 97
CAREY, GEORGE LEONARD, 92: 374 (il.), 376, **91:** 226
Carey, Ron, 92: 270
Caribbean Community and Common Market, 91: 346
Caribou, 92: 476
Carlsson, Ingvar, 92: 411, **91:** 444
Carnegie Hall, 92: 148-150, **91:** 242
Carpio Nicolle, Jorge, 91: 313
Carter, Asa, 92: 285
Carter, Jimmy, 92: 104 (il.), **91:** 382
Cartoons. See **Animated film**
Casiraghi, Stefano, 91: 205
Castle Garden, 91: 89-90
Castro, Fidel, 92: 165, **91:** 261, **90:** 260
CAT, 92: 126, **91:** 227, **90:** 225
Catastrophic health insurance law, 90: 436
Caterpillar Inc., 92: 296
Catholic University of America, 90: 429
Catholics. See **Roman Catholic Church**
Cavaço Silva, Aníbal, 92: 371, **91:** 408, **90:** 415
Cavallo, Domingo Felipe, 92: 62
CBS Inc., 92: 415-416, **91:** 449-450, **90:** 73-86, 157, 454-457
CD-I (television), 92: 195
CD's. See **Compact discs**
CDTV (television), 92: 195
Ceausescu, Nicolae, 92: 386, **91:** 422, **90:** 430
Cedras, Raoul, 92: 234
Cel animation, 91: 137, 142
Celibacy, 91: 421
Cemetery desecration, 91: 336
Censorship: arts funding, **91:** 173-174; books, **90:** 357-358. See also **Obscenity**
CENSUS, 92: 126, 127-136, **91:** 227-229; American Indians, **92:** 246-247; American self-portrait, **92:** 127-136; city disputes, **92:** 139, 145, **91:** 232, 236, 273. See also **Population**
Center Party (Finland), 92: 219
Centoxin, 92: 186
Central African Republic: facts in brief, **92:** 46, **91:** 158, **90:** 160; political changes, **92:** 45
Central America. See **Latin America**
Central America **(ship), 91:** 392, **90:** 400
Central Intelligence Agency, 92: 226
Central planning, in U.S.S.R., 90: 57-60
Cerezo Arévalo, Vinicio, 92: 234, **90:** 319
Ceylon. See **Sri Lanka**
CFA. See **College Football Association**
CFC's. See **Chlorofluorocarbons**
CHAD, 91: 229; civil war, **91:** 156-157, 229, 305, **90:** 162; facts in brief, **92:** 46, **91:** 158, **90:** 160; Libya, **90:** 358
CHAMORRO, VIOLETA BARRIOS DE, 92: 330, **91:** 229, 386-387, **90:** 395-396
Championship Auto Racing Teams. See **Automobile racing**
Chaovalit Yongchaiyut, 92: 417, **91:** 451, **90:** 459
Chapman, Morris H., 92: 376, **91:** 412
Charity, 91: 418, **90:** 425
Charles, Prince, 90: 171, 317
Charleston, S.C., 90: 237
Charon (moon), 91: 85
Chatchai Chunhawan, 92: 417, **91:** 451-452, **90:** 459
Chávez Araujo, Oliverio, 92: 311
Chelsea, Mass., 90: 284
Chemical flooding, 91: 400
CHEMISTRY, 92: 137-138, **91:** 230-231, **90:** 225-226; Nobel Prize, **92:** 332, **91:** 389, **90:** 397
Chemotherapy, 92: 186
Chen Jinhua, 91: 235
Chen Yun, 91: 233-235
CHENEY, RICHARD BRUCE, 91: 170, **90:** 175, 226
CHESS, 92: 138, **91:** 231, **90:** 227
Chevron Corp., 91: 287
Cheyenne Mountain Zoo, 92: 477-478
CHICAGO, 92: 139-140, **91:** 232-233, **90:** 227-228; aquarium, **92:** 478; art, **92:** 69, **90:** 177, 228; buildings, **92:** 62, 279, **90:** 213; census and population, **92:** 145, **91:** 227, 232; classical music, **92:** 148, 149, **91:** 242, 243, **90:** 239, 241; commodities scandal, **90:** 259; schools, **91:** 232-233, 282, 421, **90:** 285. See also **Daley, Richard Michael**
Chicago Board of Trade, 90: 301
Chicago Bulls, 92: 91
Chicago Symphony Orchestra, 92: 149
Chicago White Sox, 91: 233
Child abuse: Iraq, **90:** 336; McMartin Pre-School, **91:** 258; Steinberg case, **90:** 256-257; Supreme Court cases, **91:** 444
CHILD WELFARE, 90: 228-229; child care laws, **91:** 249, 342; homelessness, **90:** 100-101, 104 (il.); Israel, **91:** 332; mental disorders, **90:** 374;

program consolidation, **92:** 469; UN actions, **91:** 421, 468, **90:** 472. See also **Education; Welfare**
Childbirth, 91: 277, 316, 364
Children: AIDS, **91:** 162, **90:** 228; alcoholism exposure, **92:** 185; animated films, **91:** 147-149, 151; car-seat homicide case, **92:** 162; disabilities, **92:** 236; lead exposure, **92:** 199; libraries, **90:** 357; literature topic, **91:** 353; memory studies, **91:** 413-414. See also **Adolescents; Child abuse; Child welfare; Literature for children**
CHILE, 92: 140, **91:** 233, **90:** 229; facts in brief, **92:** 275, **91:** 345, **90:** 353; fruit scare, **90:** 229, 305, 421; Hudson volcano, **92:** 226-228; military spending, **92:** 274. See also **Aylwin Azócar, Patricio**
Chiluba, Frederick, 92: 45
Chimpanzee, 90: 486-487
CHINA, 92: 140-142, **91:** 233-236, **90:** 230-233; archaeology, **92:** 53 (il.), **91:** 166; Cambodia, **91:** 216-217; facts in brief, **92:** 73, **91:** 179, **90:** 182; Hong Kong, **92:** 72, **91:** 178, 234 (il.), **90:** 181; Indonesia, **91:** 176, 325; ivory trade, **91:** 50; Japan, **92:** 140, **91:** 177; Korea, North, **92:** 141, **91:** 338; Korea, South, **92:** 264, **91:** 339; Mongolia, **91:** 372; prodemocracy demonstrations, **92:** 141, **91:** 177, 234, **90:** 216-217, 230-233; Protestant churches, **91:** 411, **90:** 418-419; satellite launch, **91:** 433; stamp, **90:** 442-443; Taiwan, **92:** 413, **90:** 452-453; U.S. relations, **92:** 140-141, 249-250, **90:** 216-217; U.S.S.R., **92:** 71, 140, **91:** 236, **90:** 233, 470-471; Vietnam, **92:** 141, **91:** 176; wildlife sanctuary, **91:** 256. See also **Deng Xiaoping; Jiang Zemin; Li Peng**
Chippewa Indians, 92: 247, **91:** 324
Chirac, Jacques, 92: 225
Chiron (comet), 90: 184-185
Chissano, Joaquím Alberto, 91: 157, 377, **90:** 387
Chlorofluorocarbons, 91: 289-290, **90:** 292, 390
Choctaw Indians, 92: 246 (il.)
Choice (education), 92: 50, 190
Cholera, 92: 274, 331, 356, 377
Cholesterol, 92: 220, 306, **91:** 414-415, **90:** 372
CHRÉTIEN, JEAN JOSEPH-JACQUES, 91: 219-222, 236
Christian Democratic Union, 92: 228, **91:** 307
Christian fundamentalists, 92: 376, **91:** 412
Christian Science, 91: 412-413, **90:** 425
Christie's, 92: 67-68, **90:** 179
Christo, 92: 67, 69 (il.)
Chromosomes, 92: 236, 301
Chronic fatigue syndrome, 92: 186, 297 (il.), **91:** 364
Chrysler Corp., 92: 78, 79, **91:** 183-185, 274, 424, **90:** 188-189, 274
Chunnel. See **English Channel Tunnel**
Churches. See **Religion** and specific churches and religions
***Church's Missionary Mandate, The* (encyclical), 92:** 384
CIA. See **Central Intelligence Agency**
Cicippio, Joseph J., 92: 317, **90:** 216
Cigarettes. See **Smoking**
Cincinnati, 91: 174, **90:** 487
Cincinnati Reds, 91: 198-200
CITES. See **Convention on International Trade in Endangered Species**
Citicorp, 92: 190
Citizen's Charter, 92: 232
Citizens' Forum on Canada's Future, 92: 107
CITY, 92: 142-146, **91:** 236-239, **90:** 234-237; census data, **92:** 128, **91:** 228, 236; homelessness, **90:** 97-107; mayoral elections, **92:** 194, **91:** 285, **90:** 287-288. See also **Transit** and specific cities
***City of Angels* (musical), 91:** 453
Civic Forum, 92: 166, **91:** 262
CIVIL RIGHTS, 92: 146-148, **91:** 240-242, **90:** 237-239; congressional bills, **92:** 157, **91:** 249, 253; criminal defendants, **92:** 407-408; golf club membership case, **91:** 309; labor issues, **91:** 342; Los Angeles voting, **92:** 290; Supreme Court changes, **92:** 407, 409-410. See also **Affirmative action; Job discrimination; Human rights; Integration; Supreme Court of the U.S.**
Civil Rights Act (1964), 92: 147
Civil Rights Act (1991), 92: 146, 157, 271
Civil Rights Bill (1990), 91: 240, 342
***Civil War, The* (TV series), 91:** 450
Clark, Charles Joseph, 92: 110
Clark, Dick, 90: 391
Clarke, Robert L., 92: 85, 451
Clarridge, Duane R., 92: 251, 451
CLASSICAL MUSIC, 92: 148-150, **91:** 242-244, **90:** 239-241. See also **Awards and prizes**
Clay, Andrew Dice, 91: 450
Claymation, 91: 139 (il.), 140
Clean Air Act (1990), 91: 249, 288-289, 298, 417
Clifford, Clark M., 92: 85 (il.)
Climate: Antarctica, **90:** 127; global, **91:** 391-392. See also **Global warming; Greenhouse effect; Weather**
CLINTON, WILLIAM JOSEPH, 92: 150
Clio Awards, 92: 40
Clomipramine, 91: 364
Closed-captioned television, 91: 314
Clothing. See **Fashion**
Co2. See **Carbon dioxide**
COAL, 92: 151, **91:** 244-245, **90:** 242; energy crisis, **90:** 111, 114-115 (ils.); ground water pollution, **92:** 462. See also **Mining**
Coalition for Democratic Values, 92: 180, **91:** 272
Coase, Ronald H., 92: 332
Coca-Cola Co., 92: 40, 396, **91:** 383
Cocaine: drug to reduce dependency, **90:** 226; Latin America drug trade, **92:** 341, **90:** 260, 350, 406; record seizure, **90:** 259; usage, **92:** 185, **91:** 277, **90:** 279. See also **Crack**
Coelho, Tony, 90: 246, 272-273
Coffee, 90: 354
COIN COLLECTING, 91: 245-246, **90:** 242
Cold fusion, 90: 121-122
Cold War. See **Communism**
Colds, 92: 310, 376
Cole, Natalie, 92: 366
Collecting. See **Coin collecting; Stamp collecting**
College Football Association, 91: 434
Colleges. See **Universities and colleges**
Collins, Robert F., 92: 453
COLLOR DE MELLO, FERNANDO, 92: 97, 159-160, **91:** 208, 209, 246, **90:** 211, 354
COLOMBIA, 92: 151, **91:** 246, **90:** 242-243; cholera, **92:** 274; coffee, **90:** 354; constitution, **92:** 274; drug trafficking, **92:** 151, 276, **91:** 246, 446, **90:** 175, 242-243, 350; facts in brief, **92:** 275, **91:** 345, **90:** 353; free-trade zone, **92:** 249, 273-274; kidnapping, **91:** 385
Colon cancer, 92: 236, **91:** 278, **90:** 373-374
Colonias, 90: 480
Colorado, 92: 404, **91:** 439, **90:** 444
Colorado, University of, 91: 302-305, **90:** 308, 310
***Columbia* (space shuttle), 92:** 394, 451, **91:** 431, 432, **90:** 438
Columbia University, 91: 349
Columbus, Christopher, 92: 100, 276, 398
Comaneci, Nadia, 90: 392-393
Comecon, 92: 101
Comet, 90: 184-185
***Coming to America* (film), 91:** 384
Comiskey Park (Chicago), 92: 62, 140, **91:** 233, 239 (il.)
Commerce. See **Economics; International trade**
Commodities scandal, 90: 259
Common Agricultural Policy, 92: 212
Common Market. See **European Community**
Commonwealth, British. See **Great Britain** and other Commonwealth countries
Commonwealth Edison Co., 92: 139
Commonwealth of Independent States, 92: 65, 103, 202, 432, 438-440, 447. See also **Union of Soviet Socialist Republics**
Commonwealth status for Puerto Rico, 91: 52-67
COMMUNICATIONS, 90: 243-244; labor contracts, **90:** 348-349. See also **Literature; Motion pictures; Postal Service, U.S.; Television**
Communications satellites. See **Satellites, Artificial**
Communism: collapse in Europe, **92:** 202-204, **91:** 292, **90:** 296; collapse in U.S.S.R., **92:** 71, 202-204, 432-440, 441-446; undesirable aliens list, **92:** 242. See also specific countries
Comoros: coup, **90:** 162; facts in brief, **92:** 46, **91:** 158, **90:** 160
Compact discs, 92: 195, **91:** 286
***Company B* (dance), 92:** 168
Compressed air energy storage plant, 92: 195
COMPUTER, 92: 152, **91:** 247-248, **90:** 244-245; animated film, **91:** 136, 140-143
Computer-assisted design and manufacturing. See **CAD-CAM**
Computer chips, 92: 138, **90:** 226
Conable, Barber B., Jr., 91: 194
CONCACAF Gold Cup. See **Soccer**
Condoms, 92: 191
Condor, California, 92: 160, **90:** 40-46, 254
Confederation of Regions Party, 92: 323
Conference on Security and Cooperation in Europe, 91: 162, 273, 294, 305
Congo, 92: 46, **91:** 158, **90:** 160
Congo (Kinshasa). See **Zaire**
Congregation Hineni, 92: 263
Congress of People's Deputies (U.S.S.R), 92: 435, **90:** 54-56, 67
CONGRESS OF THE UNITED STATES, 92: 153-158, **91:** 248-253, **90:** 246-253; Bush, George, **92:** 153-158, **91:** 213, 248-249, **90:** 250-253; census data, **92:** 136; ethics investigations, **92:** 158, **91:** 253, **90:** 246-247; Persian Gulf crisis and War, **92:** 153, **91:** 214; savings and loan scandal, **91:** 197. See also **Democratic Party; Elections; Republican Party; United States, Government of the**
Congress Party (India), 92: 243-244
Connecticut, 92: 404, **91:** 439, **90:** 444; abortion law, **91:** 438; taxes, **92:** 402
Conner, Dennis, 92: 95
Connors, Jimmy, 92: 417
CONSERVATION, 92: 158-160, **91:** 254-256, **90:** 253-255; Africa, **92:** 48; architecture, **92:** 61; Canadian literature, **91:** 225; farming, **92:** 216-217; Latin-American alliance, **92:** 276; ocean drift nets, **91:** 254-255, 392, **90:** 253-254. See also **Endangered species; Energy supply; Environmental pollution; Rain forest**
Conservation Reserve Program, 91: 297
Conservative Party: Great Britain, **92:** 231-232, **91:** 310, 311, **90:** 316, 317; Norway, **92:** 335
Constitution: Brazil, **92:** 97; Canada, **92:** 107-110, 119-124, **91:** 220-221; Colombia, **92:** 151, 274; Fiji, **92:** 338; Japan, **92:** 260; Laos, **92:** 271; Namibia, **91:** 378; Portugal, **90:** 415; Puerto Rico, **91:** 60-61; South Africa, **92:** 392; Thailand, **92:** 417; U.S.S.R., **91:** 464-465
Constitution Act (Canada), 92: 119
Construction. See **Building and construction**
Constructive process (memory), 91: 127
Consumer Confidence Index, 92: 160
Consumer Price Index, 92: 111, 160, **91:** 256, **90:** 255
CONSUMERISM, 92: 160-161, **91:** 256-257, **90:** 255
Contact lenses, 90: 372-373
Conte, Silvio O., 92: 158
Continental Airlines, 91: 187
Continental Can Co., 92: 269
***Continuous Life, The* (Strand), 91:** 403
Contraception. See **Birth control**
Contras: demobilization, **91:** 386, 387, 467, **90:** 350-352, 395; Honduras bases, **91:** 317, **90:** 323; rearming, **92:** 330-331; U.S. aid, **90:** 216, 396. See also **Iran-contra affair**
Contreras Sepúlveda, Juan Manuel, 92: 140
Convention on International Trade in Endangered Species, 91: 46, **90:** 253
Convention on the Rights of the Child, 91: 468
Conventional Forces in Europe treaty, 92: 66
Cooper, Bert, 92: 96
Coors Brewing Co., 92: 40
Copland, Aaron, 91: 242
Copper mining, 92: 317
Coral reefs, 92: 335
Corcoran Gallery of Art, 90: 177
Corn, Genetically engineered, 91: 206
Coronary artery disease. See **Heart disease**
Cosmonauts. See **Space exploration**
Cossiga, Francesco, 92: 257, **91:** 332
COSTA RICA, 91: 257; common market, **92:** 274; facts in brief, **92:** 275, **91:** 345, **90:** 353. See also **Calderón Fournier, Rafael Angel**
COSTNER, KEVIN, 92: 161
Counterfeit stamps, 91: 436
Country music. See **Awards and prizes; Popular music**
Courier, Jim, 92: 416, 417
Court of Justice, 92: 214
Court tennis, 92: 401, **91:** 435, **90:** 441
COURTS, 92: 161-162, **91:** 257-259, **90:** 256-257. See also **Congress of the U.S.; State government; Supreme Court of the U.S.; United States, Government of the**
Couture. See **Fashion**
Covenant House, 91: 421
CPI. See **Consumer Price Index**
Crack (cocaine), 92: 185, **91:** 277, **90:** 279, 409
Crane (bird). See **Whooping crane**
Cranston, Alan, 92: 158, **91:** 197, 253
Crawford-Butler Act, 91: 60
Crayola crayons, 92: 329, **91:** 455-456
Cree Indians, 92: 379
CRESSON, EDITH, 92: 163, 224-225
CRIME, 92: 163-165, **91:** 259-261, **90:** 257-259; congressional actions, **92:** 142-143, 158; defendants' rights, **92:** 407-408; drug abuse connection, **91:** 277; state laws, **91:** 438; Washington, D.C., **92:** 455. See also **City; Courts; Drug abuse;** and various countries and cities
CRISTIANI BURKARD, ALFREDO, 92: 195, **91:** 286, **90:** 259, 289
Croatia, 92: 472-475, **91:** 479-480
Cross-country, 92: 401, **91:** 435, **90:** 441

Crown, Dental, 90: 273-274
Crufts dog show, 91: 276
Cruzan, Nancy, 91: 442
Crystal meth, 90: 279
CSCE. See **Conference on Security and Cooperation in Europe**
CSX Corp., 90: 346
CUBA, 92: 165-166, **91:** 261, **90:** 260; ancient meteor impact, **91:** 307; Angola, **92:** 165; facts in brief, **92:** 275, **91:** 345, **90:** 353; immigration to U.S., **92:** 243; Pan American Games, **92:** 165, 400; Sweden, **92:** 411; troops in Angola, **90:** 166-167, 260; U.S. prisoners, **92:** 373
Cuneiform, 92: 56, 57
Cunningham, Merce, 92: 168, **90:** 264
Cunningham, Randall, 92: 221
Cuomo, Andrew, 91: 383
Cuomo, Mario M., 92: 180, 323, **91:** 380 (il.)
Curling, 92: 401, **91:** 435, **90:** 441
Curran, Charles E., 90: 429
Curreri, Steven, 92: 162
Customs union, 92: 209
Cyanide poisonings, 92: 165
Cycling, 92: 401, **91:** 434, **90:** 440
Cyprus, 92: 316, **91:** 370, **90:** 378
***Cyrano de Bergerac* (film), 91:** 375-376
Cystic fibrosis, 91: 203-204, **90:** 206, 320
CZECHOSLOVAKIA, 92: 166-167, **91:** 262, **90:** 260-261; Eastern Orthodox Churches, **92:** 187-188; European trade, **92:** 206; facts in brief, **92:** 205, **91:** 295, **90:** 298; pope's visit, **91:** 420; U.S. trade, **91:** 262, 327. See also **Havel, Václav**

D

D'Aboville, Gerard, 92: 327-328
Dahmer, Jeffrey L., 92: 163-164
Daim Zainuddin, 92: 293
Dalai Lama, 90: 233, 397
DALEY, RICHARD MICHAEL, 92: 139, **91:** 232, 238 (il.), **90:** 227, 261
Dali, Salvador, 90: 439
Dallas, 92: 194, 424, **90:** 212
Dallas Cowboys, 90: 307
Dallas Zoo, 91: 482-483
Daly, John, 92: 230
D'Amato, Alfonse M., 92: 158, 449
Daminozide. See **Alar**
Dance Smartly (horse), 92: 239
Dance Theatre of Harlem, 92: 168, **91:** 263
DANCING, 92: 167-168, **91:** 263-264, **90:** 262-264; awards, **91:** 189, **90:** 193; two dance legends, **92:** 169-170. See also **Popular music**
***Dancing at Lughnasa* (Friel), 92:** 419
Danforth, John C., 92: 157
Daniel, Beth, 91: 309
D'Arco, John A., Jr., 91: 232
***Dark Verses and Light* (Disch), 92:** 363
Darnyi, Tamas, 92: 411
DAT. See **Digital audio tape**
Data Discman, 92: 195
Data processing. See **Computer**
D'Aubuisson, Roberto, 90: 289
Davis, Alan Robert, 92: 164
Davis, Junior L., 91: 259
Davis, Mary Sue. See **Stowe, Mary Sue Davis**
Davis, Miles, 92: 172
Davis Cup. See **Tennis**
DAY-LEWIS, DANIEL, 91: 264
DDB Needham Worldwide, 91: 155
DDI (drug). See **Dideoxyinosine**
DDT, 90: 52-53
Dead Sea Scrolls, 92: 52, 381, 382 (il.)
Death. See **Right to die; Suicide**
***Death of Klinghoffer, The* (opera), 92:** 149-150
Death penalty. See **Capital punishment**
Death rates. See **Mortality rates; Population**
DEATHS, 92: 171-176, **91:** 265-271, **90:** 265-271
Deby, Idriss, 91: 156-157, 229
DeConcini, Dennis, 92: 158, **91:** 197
Defendants' rights, 91: 444
Defense. See **Armed forces**
Defense, U.S. Department of: budget, **92:** 66-67, 450, **91:** 172, **90:** 176, 474; contracting scandal, **92:** 451, **91:** 470, **90:** 474; factory orders, **90:** 369. See also **Armed forces; Cheney, Richard Bruce**
Deficit. See **Economics; Federal budget deficit; Trade, U.S. balance of**
DeFusco, Annette and David, 91: 257, **90:** 255
"Degenerate Art" (exhibit), 92: 69
De Gennes, Pierre-Gilles, 92: 332
Deinstitutionalization, 90: 101-102
DE KLERK, FREDERIK WILLEM, 92: 45-48, 392-393, **91:** 156, 430-431, **90:** 162, 264, 436-437
De la Renta, Oscar, 92: 219
Delaware, 92: 404, **91:** 439, **90:** 444
De Leo, Pasquale F., 92: 140, **91:** 232
Delta Air Lines, 92: 83, 270
DE MAIZIÈRE, LOTHAR, 91: 272
De Michelis, Gianni, 91: 332, 333
Demirel, Suleyman, 92: 431
Democracy: Africa, **92:** 44-45, **91:** 157-160; China demonstrations, **92:** 141, 177, **91:** 234, **90:** 216-217, 230-233. See also **Communism; Glasnost; Perestroika**
Democracy Forum, 92: 247
Democratic Constitutional Rally, 92: 430
Democratic Liberal Party (S. Korea), 91: 338, 339
DEMOCRATIC PARTY, 92: 179-180, **91:** 272-273, **90:** 272-273; Brown, Edmund Gerald, Jr., **92:** 98; budget deficit, **91:** 468-470; Bush, George, **92:** 179-180, **91:** 213, 272, **90:** 272; Clinton, William Joseph, **92:** 150; energy policy, **92:** 195; Harkin, Tom, **92:** 236; Kerrey, Bob, **92:** 264; tax policy, **92:** 413-414; Tsongas, Paul, **92:** 430; Wilder, L. Douglas, **92:** 470. See also **Congress of the U.S.; Elections; Republican Party**
Democratic Party (S. Korea), 92: 264
Democratic Party of the Left, 92: 259
Democratic Progressive Party (Taiwan), 92: 413
Democratic Union, 92: 363
Demography. See **Population**
Dene Indians, 91: 390
Deng Xiaoping, 92: 141, **91:** 233-235, **90:** 230, 232-233
DENMARK, 92: 180-181, **91:** 273, **90:** 273; facts in brief, **92:** 205, **91:** 295, **90:** 298; Great Belt, **92:** 100
DENTISTRY, 90: 273-274; AIDS infection, **92:** 48
Denver, 92: 146, 424, **90:** 255
Denver Broncos, 91: 302
Depression (disorder), 90: 421
Dernier Recours, 92: 318
DeRoburt, Hammer, 90: 403
DERWINSKI, EDWARD JOSEPH, 90: 274
Desalinization, 92: 455
Desegregation. See **Integration**
Détente, 92: 443
Detmer, Ty, 92: 224, **91:** 305
DETROIT, 92: 181-182, **91:** 273-274, **90:** 274-275; building, **91:** 239; classical music, **90:** 239-241; newspapers, **90:** 395; population, **91:** 227, 236, 273; zoos, **90:** 486
Detroit Pistons, 91: 200, 202, **90:** 203-205
Detroit Tigers, 92: 182
Deuterium, in reactors, 90: 118-121
Dev-Sol, 92: 431
Developing countries: foreign debt, **91:** 281, **90:** 332-333, 476; population, **92:** 371; UN action, **91:** 468. See also **Africa; Latin America**
Devil's Night, 91: 274
Devine, Grant, 92: 388, **91:** 425, **90:** 432
Dewhurst, Colleen, 92: 172
Dharsono, Hartono R., 91: 325
***Dick Tracy* (film), 91:** 375
Dictionary: *Oxford English Dictionary,* **90:** 363; *WB Dictionary* supplement, **92:** 479, **91:** 501, **90:** 505
Dideoxyinosine, 92: 48
Diet, 92: 237, **91:** 166, **90:** 421
Digital audio tape, 91: 286, **90:** 288
Digital compact cassette, 92: 195, **91:** 286
Digital Equipment Corp., 90: 245
Digital Video Interactive technology, 91: 248
Dimitrios I, 92: 187, **91:** 279
Dimitrov, Filip, 92: 101
Ding, K. H., 91: 411
DINKINS, DAVID NORMAN, 92: 323, **91:** 228, 380, **90:** 275, 287, 389
Dinosaurs, 92: 340, **90:** 404
Dior, Christian, 90: 304
Diouf, Abdou, 92: 390
Dioxins, 90: 293
Direct-broadcast satellite, 90: 85
Diro, Edward Ramu, 92: 338
Disabilities. See **Handicapped**
Disarmament. See **Arms control**
DISASTERS, 92: 182-184, **91:** 274-275, **90:** 275-277; Asia, **92:** 70; Bangladesh cyclone, **92:** 70, 84, 469; British soccer match, **90:** 316 (il.), 318, 435; Danish ship, **91:** 273; Egyptian ferry, **92:** 193; *Iowa,* U.S.S., **91:** 172, **90:** 175-176, 474; Japan typhoon, **92:** 261; Kentucky mine, **91:** 423, **90:** 380; Kentucky school bus, **90:** 257; Maryland construction, **90:** 213; New York City subway crash, **92:** 323, 324 (il.), 424; Oakland, Calif., fires, **92:** 145-146; Philadelphia skyscraper fire, **92:** 359-360; Philadelphia subway crash, **91:** 401; rock concert deaths and injuries, **92:** 364; Saudi Arabia tunnel, **91:** 426-427; Soviet nuclear submarine, **90:** 401. See also **Aviation disasters; Earthquakes; Oil spills; Oil well fires; Volcanoes; Weather**
Disch, Tom, 92: 363, **90:** 411
Discount rate, 92: 188, 449-450
***Discovery* (space shuttle), 92:** 394, **90:** 437, 438
Discrimination. See **Civil rights; Job discrimination; Sex discrimination**
Disease. See **Health and disease**
Disero, Betty, 92: 420
Disney, Walt, 91: 144-146, 149, **90:** 385. See also **EuroDisneyland; Walt Disney Co.**
Diving, 92: 401, **91:** 434, **90:** 440
Divorce, 92: 135
Dixon, Don R., 91: 197
DIXON, SHARON PRATT, 92: 453-455, **91:** 276, 474
Djibouti, 92: 46, **91:** 158, **90:** 160
Dmitriev, Artur, 92: 242
DNA, 92: 301-302; early man, **92:** 52; gene therapy, **92:** 306, **91:** 203; genetic engineering, **92:** 303, **91:** 204
Do Muoi, 92: 453
***Do the Right Thing* (film), 90:** 356
Doe, Samuel K., 92: 278, 279, **91:** 157, 348-349, **90:** 357
DOG, 92: 185, **91:** 276, 385, **90:** 278
Doi, Takako, 92: 261
DOLE, ELIZABETH HANFORD, 91: 342, **90:** 278
Dollar, U.S., 90: 332, 369
Dolphins, 91: 254-255
Dominica, 92: 275, **91:** 345, **90:** 353
Dominican Republic: Columbus memorials, **92:** 276; election, **91:** 479; facts in brief, **92:** 275, **91:** 345, **90:** 353
Donetsk Ballet, 90: 263-264
Doré, Jean, 92: 318, **91:** 373
Dos Santos, José Eduardo, 91: 165, **90:** 166-167
DOT. See **Transportation, U.S. Department of**
Dotan, Rami, 92: 257
Dotson, Gary E., 90: 393-394
DOUGLAS, JAMES (BUSTER), 92: 96, **91:** 207-208, 276
Dow Jones Averages, 92: 190, 405-406, **91:** 441, **90:** 447
Drama. See **Awards and prizes; Theater**
Drexel Burnham Lambert Inc., 91: 441, **90:** 259
Drinking. See **Alcohol consumption; Alcoholism**
Drought: Australia, **92:** 76; U.S., **92:** 388, 456, 468, **91:** 474-475, **90:** 301-302, 481. See also **Water; Weather**
DRUG ABUSE, 92: 185, **91:** 277, **90:** 279; China, **92:** 142; cities, **91:** 236-237; cocaine stopper, **90:** 226; homelessness, **90:** 101; imprisonment, **92:** 372; memory impairment, **91:** 129; state laws, **91:** 438, **90:** 443-445; testing, **91:** 457, **90:** 239, 424, 450; UN program, **91:** 468. See also **Drug trafficking**
Drug trafficking: Bolivia, **91:** 206; Colombia, **92:** 151, 276, **91:** 246, 446, **90:** 242-243, 350; imprisonment, **92:** 372; Italy, **91:** 332; Los Angeles, **91:** 357; Mexico, **92:** 276, 311, **90:** 375; Pakistan, **90:** 403; Panama, **92:** 276, 341, **91:** 397, **90:** 404; Peru, **92:** 276, 356, **90:** 406; U.S. military programs, **91:** 171, **90:** 175; Washington, D.C., **90:** 479-480
DRUGS, 92: 186, **91:** 278, **90:** 280; genetic engineering, **92:** 302-303; Nobel Prize, **91:** 389; obsessive-compulsive disorder, **91:** 364. See also specific drugs and diseases
Drunken driving, 91: 444, **90:** 421
D'Souza, Dinesh, 92: 192
Duarte, José Napoleon, 91: 266
Dubček, Alexander, 91: 262, **90:** 261
Dubrovnik, Yugoslavia, 92: 471
Duchesnay, Isabelle and Paul, 92: 242
Dugan, Michael J., 91: 170
Duggan, Anne Marie, 92: 95
Dukakis, Michael Stanley, 90: 445
DUKE, DAVID E., 92: 157, 186, 383, **91:** 419-420
Duke University, 92: 89, 91
Dumping (economics), 92: 77
Dunne, John R., 91: 241
Duplessis, Maurice, 92: 118
Durable goods. See **Manufacturing**
Durán, Roberto, 90: 210
Durenberger, David F., 91: 253
Durocher, Leo Ernest, 92: 172
Dwarf lemur, 91: 481
Dystrophin, 92: 305

E

Eagle, Bald. See **Bald eagle**
Eagleburger, Lawrence, 90: 217
Earhart, Amelia, 90: 392
Earnhardt, Dale, 92: 81, **91:** 185-186
Earth, as a planet, 91: 70-73, 76
Earth Day, 92: 159 (il.), **91:** 288
Earthquakes, 92: 184, **91:** 274, **90:** 276; Asia, **92:** 70; California, **91:** 238-239, **90:** 202, 213, 235-

237, 312, 454; Iran, **91:** 274, 327; Philippines, **91:** 401
Eastern Airlines, 92: 82, **91:** 187, **90:** 346-347
Eastern Europe. See **Europe** and individual countries
EASTERN ORTHODOX CHURCHES, 92: 187-188, **91:** 279, 466, **90:** 281
Easy Goer (horse), 91: 317, **90:** 323, 324
Eating Right Pyramid, 92: 221
EC. See **European Community**
Ecology. See **Conservation; Endangered species; Environmental pollution**
Economic and Monetary Union, 92: 206, **91:** 292
Economic Commission of West African States, 91: 160
ECONOMICS, 92: 188-190, **91:** 279-281, **90:** 282-283; Latin America common markets, **92:** 249, 273-274, 470; Nobel Prize, **92:** 332, **91:** 388, **90:** 397; Pacific rim nations, **91:** 103-119. See also **Bank; European Community; Federal budget deficit; Inflation; International trade; Labor; Manufacturing; Prices; Recession;** and specific countries, provinces, and cities
ECU. See **European Currency Unit**
Ecuador: cholera, **92:** 274; facts in brief, **92:** 275, **91:** 345, **90:** 353; Peru, **92:** 274; trade agreements, **92:** 249, 273
Edberg, Stefan, 92: 416, 417, **91:** 450, 451
Edmonton Oilers, 91: 316
EDUCATION, 92: 190-193, **91:** 281-283, **90:** 283-286; Catholic school closings, **91:** 421; handicapped, **90:** 320; minority scholarships, **92:** 148; national policy, **92:** 190-191, **90:** 229; state laws and programs, **92:** 402-403, **91:** 437-438, **90:** 445; UN conference, **91:** 468. See also **Alexander, Lamar; Integration; Universities and colleges;** and specific cities and countries
***Education of Little Tree, The* (Carter), 92:** 285
Edwards, Edwin W., 92: 383, 405
Eelam People's Revolutionary Liberation Front, 91: 436
EFTA. See **European Free Trade Association**
Egerszegi, Krisztina, 92: 411
Eggleton, Arthur, 92: 420
EGYPT, 92: 193, **91:** 284, **90:** 286; facts in brief, **92:** 46, 316, **91:** 158, **90:** 160; Ghali appointment to UN, **92:** 449; Middle East peace, **92:** 314-315, **90:** 377; regional bloc, **90:** 380; Syria, **91:** 446
Egypt, Ancient, 90: 170
Eisenhower, Dwight D., 91: 245
Elderly. See **Aging**
ELECTIONS, 92: 194, **91:** 284-285, **90:** 287-288. See also **City; Democratic Party; Republican Party; State government; Voting rights;** and specific countries, provinces, and cities
Electric power. See **Energy supply**
Electric shocks, 92: 387
Electro-rheological fluid, 91: 230
ELECTRONICS, 92: 195, **91:** 286, **90:** 226, 288
Elephant man's disease. See **Neurofibromatosis**
Elephants: conservation, **91:** 36-51, **90:** 253; zoos, **90:** 486
Elizabeth II, 92: 326, **91:** 163 (il.), **90:** 318, 424
Ellis Island, 91: 87-101, 322
El-Mahdi, Sadiq. See **Al-Mahdi, Al-Sadiq**
EL SALVADOR, 92: 195, **91:** 286, **90:** 289; common market, **92:** 274; facts in brief, **92:** 275, **91:** 345, **90:** 352; Jesuit murders, **92:** 195, 381, **91:** 418; UN actions, **92:** 195, 448, **91:** 467. See also **Cristiani Burkard, Alfredo**
Embryo, Frozen, 91: 259, **90:** 256
Emergency Quota Act, 91: 91
Emigration. See **Immigration**
Emmy Awards, 92: 414, **91:** 190, **90:** 194
Emotional disorders. See **Mental health**
Employment. See **Economics; Job discrimination; Labor; Manufacturing; Social security; Unemployment; Welfare**
EMS. See **European Monetary System**
Emtman, Steve, 92: 224
Enalapril, 92: 186
Endangered species: birds, **91:** 254, **90:** 38-53, 254-259; elephants, **91:** 36-51, **90:** 253. See also **Conservation**
ENDARA, GUILLERMO, 91: 287, 397, **90:** 405
***Endeavor* (space shuttle), 92:** 394
Energy, U.S. Department of. See **Coal; Energy supply**
Energy Foundation, 92: 197
ENERGY SUPPLY, 92: 195-197, **91:** 287-288, **90:** 290-291; car mileage requirements, **92:** 161; Chicago power outages, **91:** 233; energy crisis, **90:** 108-123. See also **Coal; Nuclear energy; Petroleum and gas**
Engineering. See **Building and construction**
England. See **Great Britain**
England, Church of, 92: 376, **91:** 226
English Channel Tunnel, 92: 425-429, **91:** 210, 296, **90:** 212
Ennahda, 90: 380, 467
Enterprise for the Americas, 91: 326
Entertainment. See **Awards and prizes; Classical music; Dancing; Motion pictures; Popular music; Sports; Television; Theater**
ENVIRONMENTAL POLLUTION, 92: 197-199, **91:** 288-290, **90:** 292-293; Adriatic slime, **90:** 339; Antarctica, **90:** 126, 130-139; Australia, **91:** 182, **90:** 185; endangered species, **90:** 51-53; energy sources, **90:** 108-123, 290, 407; farming, **92:** 217, **91:** 297; federal policy, **91:** 249, 470; ground water, **92:** 459-467; Mexico, **92:** 311; Netherlands, **91:** 379; ocean, **92:** 336; Persian Gulf War, **92:** 335, 355, 389, 455; pope's world peace message, **91:** 420; Quebec protests, **90:** 422; state laws, **91:** 438; transit, **92:** 424. See also **Conservation; Energy supply; Oil spills; Oil well fires**
Environmental Protection Agency. See **Conservation; Environmental pollution**
Enzyme replacement therapy, 91: 278
Epilepsy, 91: 204, 278
Episcopal Church, 92: 375, 381-382, **90:** 320, 418
EPO. See **Epoetin**
Epoetin, 90: 206-207, 280
EPRLF. See **Eelam People's Revolutionary Liberation Front**
Equal Employment Opportunity Commission, U.S., 92: 235-236, 271
Equality Party, 90: 422
Equatorial Guinea, 92: 46, **91:** 158, **90:** 160
Equestrian events, 92: 401, **91:** 435, **90:** 441
Erick Hawkins Dance Co., 91: 263 (il.)
***Eric's Reality* (boat), 90:** 208
Eritrea, 92: 201, **91:** 157, 291, **90:** 162, 296
Ernst, Richard R., 92: 332
Ershad, Hussain Mohammad, 92: 83, **91:** 194, **90:** 198
ESA. See **European Space Agency**
Escobar Gaviria, Pablo, 92: 151, 276
Eskimos. See **Inuit**
ESTONIA, 92: 200; facts in brief, **92:** 205; independence, **92:** 103, 435; UN membership, **92:** 447 (il.), 448; U.S.S.R. conflict, **91:** 462, 464, **90:** 67, 304, 469; *WBE*, **92:** 483
Estrogen, 92: 236-237
***Ether Dome, The* (Grossman), 92:** 362-363
ETHIOPIA, 92: 201, **91:** 291, **90:** 296; civil war, **92:** 42-44, 201, **91:** 157, 291, **90:** 162, 296; democratic reform meeting, **91:** 157; facts in brief, **92:** 46, **91:** 158, **90:** 160; prehuman fossils, **92:** 51; refugees to Israel, **92:** 255, 256 (il.); Somalia, **91:** 157
Ethnic conflict: Bangladesh, **91:** 194; Bhutan, **92:** 71-72; China, **91:** 235-236; Malaysia, **91:** 110-111; Nigeria, **92:** 331; Pakistan, **90:** 403; Romania, **91:** 321; U.S.S.R., **91:** 462-463, **90:** 65-67, 469; Yugoslavia, **92:** 472-475
Etidronate, 91: 278
Eugenie, Princess, 91: 311 (il.)
Euratom, 92: 209, 212
EuroDisneyland, 92: 60, **91:** 168
Europa (moon), 91: 79, 83 (il.)
EUROPE, 92: 202-207, **91:** 292-296, **90:** 296-300; economic unification, **92:** 208-215; sports, **92:** 400; television, **90:** 87-91
European Atomic Energy Community. See **Euratom**
European Bank for Reconstruction and Development, 92: 206, **91:** 327
European Coal and Steel Community, 92: 209, 212
European Commission. See **European Community**
European Community: Albania, **91:** 163, **90:** 165; Austria, **92:** 78, **91:** 183, **90:** 187; Belgium, **92:** 92, **91:** 203; Denmark, **92:** 180-181, **91:** 273, **90:** 273; Estonia, **92:** 200; European unification, **92:** 202-206, 208-215, 248-249, **91:** 292-296, **90:** 297-300; Finland, **92:** 219, **91:** 300; France, **92:** 224, 225, **91:** 305; Germany, **91:** 292, 307-308; Great Britain, **92:** 231-232, **91:** 310, 311, **90:** 317; Greece, **92:** 233, **91:** 312; Hungary, **92:** 241; Italy, **92:** 258-259, **91:** 332, **90:** 339; ivory trade ban, **91:** 48; Netherlands, **92:** 322-323; Norway, **92:** 334-335, **91:** 390; Portugal, **92:** 371, **91:** 408, **90:** 415, 416; Spain, **92:** 396; Sweden, **92:** 411; Switzerland, **92:** 412; television regulation, **90:** 90; Turkey, **92:** 430, **91:** 459; United States, **91:** 326. See also member nations
European Cup. See **Soccer**
European Currency Unit, 92: 212-213, 219, 334
European Free Trade Association, 92: 206, 248-249, 412, **91:** 296, 300, **90:** 299-300
European Monetary System, 92: 212-213
European Parliament, 92: 204, 214, **90:** 300
European Space Agency, 92: 396, **91:** 432, 433
Eurotunnel, 92: 426-427
Evangelical Lutheran Church in America, 92: 376, 381-382, **91:** 412
Evangelists, 92: 373-374, **90:** 419
Evans, Donald Leroy, 92: 164
Evans, Janet, 92: 411, **91:** 434, 445, **90:** 451
Eveready Battery Co., 92: 40
Everglades, 92: 159
Evert, Chris, 90: 457, 458 (il.)
Evolution of man, 92: 52
Exchange rates, 92: 212-213, **91:** 311, **90:** 332
Excise tax, 91: 448
Exhibitions. See **Art**
Exosurf Neonatal, 91: 278
Expendable launch vehicle, 91: 433
Explosions. See **Disasters**
Expo '92, 92: 99-100, 397-399
Export-Import Bank, U.S., 92: 249
Exports. See **Economics; Farm and farming; International trade**
Extinctions, 92: 340, **91:** 306-307. See also **Conservation; Endangered species**
Exurbia, 91: 227
***Exxon Valdez* (ship), 91:** 259, 290, **90:** 108, 294-295, 406
***Eyes of the Goddess, The* (dance), 92:** 168

F

F-22 Advanced Tactical Fighter, 92: 66
F-117A Stealth fighter, 92: 65-66, 348 (il.), 350
Fading kitten syndrome, 91: 227
Fahd bin Abd al-Aziz Al-Saud, 92: 388, **91:** 370, 427, **90:** 432
Fair Tower, 91: 211
Falcon, Joe, 91: 456, 457
Faldo, Nick, 91: 309, **90:** 315
Falkland Islands, 91: 437, **90:** 173
Falwell, Jerry, 90: 419
Fama, Joseph, 91: 257-258
Familial hypercholesterolemia, 92: 306
Family: size, **92:** 130, 134, **90:** 420-421; violence, **90:** 450; warm parenting, **92:** 310
Family and Medical Leave Act, 91: 342
Family Media Inc., 92: 291
Famine: Afghanistan, **92:** 41; Africa, **91:** 160-161, 165, 442, **90:** 163
Fang Lizhi, 91: 235
FAO. See **Food and Agriculture Organization**
FARM AND FARMING, 92: 216-217, **91:** 297-298, **90:** 301-303; European economic unity, **92:** 212; federal subsidies, **91:** 253; U.S.S.R., **90:** 56, 62; Yeutter, Clayton K., **90:** 485. See also **Food** and individual countries
Farmer, Robert, 90: 272
Farooq, Mohammad, 91: 323
FASHION, 92: 218-219, **91:** 299-300, **90:** 303-304
Fat, Dietary, 92: 220, **91:** 414
Fatherland Party (Afghanistan), 91: 155
Faulk, Marshall, 92: 224
Fay, Michael, 91: 204
FBI. See **Federal Bureau of Investigation**
FCC. See **Federal Communications Commission**
FDA. See **Drugs; Food**
Federal Aviation Administration. See **Aviation**
Federal budget deficit, 92: 189, 450, **91:** 280-281; congressional debates, **91:** 248, 468-469, **90:** 473; tax policy, **91:** 447-448, **90:** 453-454
Federal Bureau of Investigation, 92: 68, 147, 162, 181, **90:** 358
Federal Communications Commission: affirmative action, **91:** 442; new chairman, **90:** 244; television regulations, **92:** 416, **90:** 75-76, 86, 94
Federal Deposit Insurance Corporation. See **Bank**
Federal Emergency Management Agency, 90: 477
Federal funds rate, 92: 188, **91:** 281, **90:** 199
Federal Republic of Germany. See **Germany, West**
Federal Reserve System. See **Bank; Economics**
Federal Savings and Loan Insurance Corporation. See **Savings and loan associations**
Federal Trade Commission, 92: 222-224, **91:** 245-246, 257, **90:** 255
Feld Ballets/NY, 92: 167 (il.)
Felix the Cat, 91: 144
Fencing, 92: 401, **91:** 434, **90:** 440
Ferguson, Sarah. See **York, Duchess of**
Ferraro, Dave, 91: 206
Ferré, Gianfranco, 90: 304
Ferret, Black-footed, 92: 160
Fertilization, Laboratory, 92: 309

Fertilizers, 92: 462
Festival seating, 92: 364
Fetal surgery, 91: 362-363
Fhimah, Lamen Khalifa, 92: 280-281
Fianna Fáil, 92: 253, 90: 336-337
Fiat (car), 90: 338
Fiber optics, 90: 85
Fiction. See **Canadian literature; Literature; Literature for children**
Field hockey, 92: 401, 91: 435, 90: 441
Fielder, Cecil, 91: 200
Fiers, Alan D., Jr., 92: 251, 451
Figure skating. See **Ice skating**
Fiji: facts in brief, 92: 338, 91: 394, 90: 402; interim government, 92: 338, 91: 393-394, 90: 403
Filmon, Gary Albert, 91: 360
Films. See **Motion pictures**
Financial Institutions Reform, Recovery and Enforcement Act, 91: 196
FINLAND, 92: 219, 91: 300, 90: 304; European trade, 92: 206; facts in brief, 92: 205, 91: 295, 90: 298
Finley, Karen, 91: 174
Firearms: assault rifles, 91: 438, 90: 258-259, 445, 476-477; city gun control, 92: 142-143; scandals, 90: 329, 451; schools, 92: 191; Washington, D.C., 92: 455
Fires. See **Disasters; Forests; Oil well fires**
FIS. See **Islamic Salvation Front**
Fish, Susan, 92: 420
Fish and Wildlife Service, U.S. See **Conservation**
Fishing industry: Antarctica, 90: 136; British Columbia, 90: 212; drift nets, 91: 254-255, 392, 90: 253-254; Newfoundland, 91: 381, 90: 390
Fittipaldi, Emerson, 91: 185, 90: 189
Five, Kaci Kullmann, 92: 335
FK506 (drug), 91: 278
Flag, U.S.: Chicago art exhibit, 90: 177, 228; Supreme Court flag burning rulings, 91: 241, 253, 443, 90: 238, 252-253, 449
Flake, Floyd H., 91: 253
Fleck, John, 91: 174
Fleischmann, Martin, 90: 121-122
Flemings. See **Belgium**
Fletcher, Arthur A., 91: 241
FLN, 91: 164, 90: 166
Floods, 92: 184, 91: 275, 90: 276; Asia, 92: 70, 141; Tunisia, 91: 458-459; U.S., 92: 468, 91: 477
Florida, 92: 404, 91: 439, 90: 444; abortion law, 90: 445; murders, 92: 164, 91: 259; zoos, 92: 478
Florida, University of, 91: 259
Florida Suncoast Dome, 90: 212
Florio, James J., 92: 405
***Flow Chart* (Ashbery),** 92: 362
Flutie, Doug, 92: 222
FOLEY, THOMAS STEPHEN, 92: 405, 90: 305, 426-427
Follini, Stefania, 90: 391-392
Fonteyn, Margot, 92: 169-170
FOOD, 92: 220-221, 91: 300-301, 90: 305-306; contaminated grapes, 90: 229, 305; hungry children, 92: 469; Iraq shortages, 92: 253; labeling, 92: 40, 160, 216, 220, 91: 257; Latin-American coffee, 90: 354; pesticide scare, 90: 293, 421, 432; Prince Edward Island potatoes, 92: 372; U.S.S.R. shortages, 92: 206, 216, 439, 440. See also **Diet; Famine; Farm and farming**
Food, Agriculture, Conservation and Trade Act (1990), 91: 297-298
Food and Agriculture Organization, 92: 281, 90: 473
Food and Drug Administration, U.S. See **Drugs; Food**
Food stamps, 91: 478
FOOTBALL, 92: 221-224, 91: 302-305, 90: 306-310; college football issues, 91: 434, 90: 440. See also names of players
***For the Boys* (film),** 92: 321 (il.)
Foraker Act, 91: 55-56, 61
Forbes, Malcolm S., 91: 267
Ford, Gerald, 92: 104 (il.)
Ford, Tennessee Ernie, 92: 173
Ford Motor Co., 92: 78, 79, 91: 183-185, 424, 90: 188, 189
Fordice, Kirk, 92: 383
Foreman, George, 92: 96, 91: 208
Forests, 91: 254, 90: 254, 292; fires, 92: 145-146, 468, 90: 354, 369, 399. See also **Rain forest**
Foretich, Hilary, 91: 383
Forget, Guy, 92: 417
Formula One series. See **Automobile racing**
Fort Worth, Tex., 92: 194, 90: 173
Fortensky, Larry, 92: 328
Fossil fuels. See **Coal; Petroleum and gas**
Fossils: early man, 92: 51-52, 91: 165, 90: 167-168; marine, 92: 340; plant, 91: 206; prehistoric animal, 91: 396, 90: 404
FOSTER, JODIE, 90: 310
Fox Broadcasting Co., 92: 415, 91: 448, 90: 82-84
Foxx, Redd, 92: 173
Fragile X syndrome, 92: 93, 236
FRANCE, 92: 224-225, 91: 305, 90: 310-311; Canada, 92: 114-117, 90: 222-223; cave art, 92: 53; English Channel Tunnel, 92: 425-429, 91: 296, 90: 212; European unity, 92: 202, 204, 213 (il.), 91: 292, 305, 90: 299; facts in brief, 92: 205, 91: 295, 90: 298; French Revolution Bicentennial, 90: 241, 310, 442; German unification, 91: 305, 307; Jewish cemetery vandalism, 91: 336; Libya terrorism, 92: 281; Persian Gulf crisis and War, 92: 224, 91: 224, 294, 305; television, 90: 90, 91. See also **Cresson, Edith; Mitterrand, François**
Francois, Marcellus, 92: 318
Frank, Anthony M., 92: 371, 372, 90: 409, 416
Frank, Barney, 91: 253, 90: 250
Franklin, Barbara, 92: 104
Franklin, Benjamin, 91: 401
Fraternities, 90: 285
Fraud: banking, 92: 85-86, 356, 91: 196-197; consumer, 90: 255
Free agency, 92: 222, 90: 308
***Freedom* (space station),** 92: 396
Freedom of Conscience law, 91: 420
Freedom of speech, 92: 192. See also **Censorship; Flag, U.S.**
Freedom of the press. See **Censorship; Libel**
Freedom Party (Austria), 91: 183, 90: 188
Frelimo, 91: 377
Fricker, Werner, 91: 428-429
Friedman, Jerome I., 91: 388-389
Friedman, Thomas L., 90: 361
Friel, Brian, 92: 419
Front de Libération du Québec, 92: 119
FSX (plane), 90: 341
FTC. See **Federal Trade Commission**
Fuel. See **Coal; Conservation; Energy supply; Petroleum and gas**
Fuel cells, 92: 196
FUJIMORI, ALBERTO, 92: 160, 357, 91: 306, 343, 398
Fujitsu Limited, 91: 247
Fullerite, 91: 230-231
Fundamentalists. See **Christian fundamentalists; Islamic fundamentalists**
Furans, 90: 293
Futures market, 90: 228, 259, 301

G

Gabon: facts in brief, 92: 46, 91: 158, 90: 160; political changes, 92: 45, 91: 157, 90: 163
Gabor, Zsa Zsa, 91: 384, 90: 394
Gadhafi, Muammar Muhammad al-. See **Qadhafi, Muammar Muhammad al-**
***Gaia* (ship),** 92: 325
Gainesville, Fla., 92: 164, 91: 259
Galán, Luís Carlos, 90: 242
Galanos, James, 92: 218
Galaxies, 91: 181
***Galileo* (spacecraft),** 92: 74, 76, 394, 90: 438
Gallina, Juliane, 92: 67
Gallium, 91: 403
Gambia: facts in brief, 92: 46, 91: 158, 90: 160; ivory, 91: 48; Senegal, 90: 162
Gambling, 92: 402, 91: 325, 90: 331
Games. See **Chess; Sports; Toys and games**
Gamma Ray Observatory, 92: 76, 394
Gamsakhurdia, Zviad K., 92: 439
Gandhi, Rajiv, 92: 243-244, 91: 322, 90: 329
Gandhi, Sonia, 92: 244
Ganilau, Ratu Sir Penaia, 91: 394
Garba, Joseph Nanven, 90: 396, 471
Garbrecht, Monique, 92: 242
Garcia, Robert, 91: 253, 90: 250, 389
García Márquez, Gabriel, 91: 352
García Pérez, Alan, 92: 276, 356, 90: 406
Gas and gasoline. See **Petroleum and gas**
Gates, Daryl F., 92: 290
GATES, ROBERT, 92: 226
Gathers, Hank, 91: 201, 90: 204
GATT. See **General Agreement on Tariffs and Trade**
Gaviria Trujillo, César, 92: 151, 91: 246
Gay rights. See **Homosexuality**
Gaza Strip and West Bank, 92: 255-257, 91: 331-332, 368-369, 90: 286, 337, 338, 376-378
Gemayel, Amin, 90: 355
Gene therapy, 92: 298, 300; adenosine deaminase deficiency, 92: 305-306, 91: 203, 362; cancer, 92: 306, 91: 362
General Agreement on Tariffs and Trade, 92: 206, 212, 216, 248, 91: 326, 90: 302-303, 333
General Electric Co., 92: 271
General Motors Corp., 92: 78-79, 91: 183-185, 90: 188-189; labor, 92: 296, 91: 184, 341; safety, 91: 424; TV advertising, 91: 155
Genes, 92: 300-301; twins, 90: 140-153. See also **Gene therapy; Genetic engineering; Genetic medicine**
Genetic engineering, 92: 302; cow hormone, 90: 303; cystic fibrosis, 91: 203-204; drugs, 92: 302-303, 90: 206-207; farming, 91: 298
Genetic medicine, 92: 298-309; gene mapping, 92: 306-309; gene testing, 92: 303, 307-309. See also **Biology; Cancer; Gene therapy; Health and disease**
Genscher, Hans-Dietrich, 92: 228, 91: 296, 307
GEOLOGY, 92: 226-228, 91: 306-307, 90: 312. See also **Ocean**
George, Clair E., 92: 251, 451
Georgia (republic): ethnic unrest, 90: 67; independence, 92: 202, 435; violence, 92: 439
Georgia (state), 92: 404, 91: 439, 90: 444; drug testing law, 91: 438
Georgia Institute of Technology, 91: 302-305
Geothermal heat, 90: 117-118
Gephardt, Richard A., 92: 179
German Democratic Republic. See **Germany, East**
German measles. See **Rubella**
GERMANY, 92: 228-229, 91: 307-309; automobiles, 92: 78; economy, 92: 190; European unity, 92: 204, 206; facts in brief, 92: 205, 91: 295; reunification, 92: 228, 91: 292-296, 305, 307-309, 405, 418, 465; Soviet aid, 92: 206; sports, 92: 400; trains, 92: 380 (il.); *WBE,* 91: 508. See also **Kohl, Helmut Michael**
GERMANY, EAST, 90: 312-314; Austria, 90: 188; European economic unity, 90: 299; facts in brief, 90: 298; Hungary, 90: 327; Protestantism, 90: 419. See also **De Maizière, Lothar; Germany**
GERMANY, WEST, 90: 314-315; European economic unity, 90: 299; facts in brief, 90: 298; France, 90: 310; IRA terrorism, 90: 398; soccer, 91: 428; U.S. troops, 90: 216. See also **Germany; Kohl, Helmut Michael**
Getty, Donald R., 91: 163, 90: 166
Getty Center, 92: 61
Ghali, Boutros, 92: 449
GHANA, 92: 230; facts in brief, 92: 46, 91: 158, 90: 160; Nigeria, 90: 396; political reforms, 90: 162
Ghiz, Joseph A., 92: 372, 91: 409, 90: 417
***Ghost* (film),** 91: 374
Ghozali, Sid Ahmed, 92: 50
Giamatti, A. Bartlett, 90: 200-201
Gianulias, Nikki, 91: 206, 207
Gigantopithecus, 91: 166
Gingrich, Newt, 92: 413, 91: 420, 90: 246, 250
Gioia, Dana, 92: 363
Girardelli, Marc, 92: 390-391, 90: 434
Girija Prasad Koirala, 92: 72
Giroldi Vega, Moisés, 90: 404-405
Giscard d'Estaing, Valéry, 92: 225
Giuliani, Rudolph W., 90: 275
"Give Peace a Chance" (song), 92: 364
Givenchy, Hubert de, 92: 218
Gladio, 91: 333
Glasnost: arts, 90: 386, 461; Jewish emigration, 92: 263, 91: 336, 90: 342; political reforms, 92: 444, 91: 462, 90: 54-69, 468
Glass-Steagall Banking Act, 91: 198
Glemp, Jozef Cardinal, 90: 428
Glenn, John H., Jr., 92: 158, 91: 197
Global warming: experiment, 92: 335; ocean studies, 91: 391-392; rate, 90: 312; record temperatures, 92: 469; reef bleaching, 92: 335; superplumes, 92: 228. See also **Greenhouse effect**
Globe Theatre, 90: 169, 170
GM. See **General Motors Corp.**
GM-1 ganglioside (drug), 92: 186
Goddess of Democracy (statue), 90: 230
Goh Chok Tong, 92: 72, 91: 178
Gold, 90: 400. See also **Coin collecting**
GOLF, 92: 230, 91: 309, 90: 315; racial exclusion, 91: 154-155, 309
Goncz, Arpad, 91: 321
Gondwanaland, 90: 135-136
Gong Pin Mei, 92: 385-386
González, Antonio Ermán, 92: 62
Gonzalez, Julio, 92: 162, 91: 260
González Márquez, Felipe, 92: 396, 91: 433, 90: 439
Goode, W. Wilson, 91: 400, 401
Goods and services tax (Canada), 92: 111, 388, 91: 219, 416, 90: 219-220
Goodwill Games, 91: 203, 242, 392, 445

Gooley, Kathleen, 91: 382
Gorbachev, Mikhail Sergeyevich: China, **92:** 71, **90:** 233; coup attempt, **92:** 140, 263, 384, 432-435, 440 (il.), 446; efforts to preserve U.S.S.R., **92:** 435-440; Germany, **91:** 308, **90:** 314; Japan, **92:** 71, 261; John Paul II meeting, **91:** 417, **90:** 428, 471; Korea, South, **91:** 177; Lithuania, **92:** 288-289; Middle East peace conference, **92:** 103, 314; Nobel Peace Prize, **91:** 388, 460; political and economic reforms, **92:** 444-446, **91:** 460-465, **90:** 54-69, 468-470; resignation, **92:** 432; U.S.-Soviet relations, **92:** 63-65, **91:** 214-215, **90:** 215-216, 297
Gorbachev, Raisa, 92: 440 (il.)
Gordimer, Nadine, 92: 283 (il.), 331-332
Goren, Charles H., 92: 173
Gotti, John, 91: 259
Government. See **City; State government; United States, Government of the;** and specific countries
Governor General's Literary Awards. See **Canadian literature**
gp120 (genetic feature), 92: 138
Graf, Steffi, 92: 417, **91:** 450, 451, **90:** 457, 458
Graham, Martha, 92: 168-170, **91:** 264, **90:** 264
Graham, William, 92: 365
Grain. See **Farm and farming**
Gramm-Rudman law, 90: 473
Grammy Awards, 92: 366, **91:** 189-190, 407, **90:** 193
Grand Canyon, 92: 159
Grand Prix. See **Automobile racing**
Grand Slam. See **Golf; Tennis**
Grange, Red, 92: 173
Granulocyte colony stimulating factor, 92: 186
Graves' disease, 92: 104
Gray, C. Boyden, 92: 157
Gray, William H., III, 92: 158, 358-359, **90:** 246
Great American Bank, 91: 425
Great Belt project, 92: 100
GREAT BRITAIN, 92: 231-233, **91:** 310-312, **90:** 316-318; economy, **90:** 283; English Channel Tunnel, **92:** 425-429, **91:** 210, 296, **90:** 212; European unity, **92:** 202, 204, **91:** 292, 296, **90:** 299; facts in brief, **92:** 205, **91:** 295, **90:** 298; German reunification, **91:** 292, 307; health care plan, **92:** 232, **90:** 317, 325; Hong Kong, **92:** 72, **91:** 178, **90:** 181; Ireland, **91:** 330; ivory trade, **91:** 50; motion pictures, **90:** 384-386; Northern Ireland, **92:** 333, **91:** 389, **90:** 398; Persian Gulf crisis and War, **92:** 231, 232, **91:** 294; petroleum and gas, **90:** 408; Quebec history, **92:** 114-117; Shakespeare's theaters, **90:** 169-170; soccer, **92:** 391, **91:** 428, 429, **90:** 318, 435; stamps, **90:** 442; U.S.S.R. collapse, **92:** 440; Vietnamese refugees, **92:** 74. See also **Major, John; Thatcher, Margaret H.**
Great Dark Spot (Neptune), 91: 84
Great Man-Made River (Libya), 92: 455, **90:** 359
Great Purge (U.S.S.R.), 92: 442
Great Red Spot (Jupiter), 91: 78
Great Whale project, 92: 379
GREECE, 92: 233-234, **91:** 312, **90:** 318; democracy birthday, **92:** 327; facts in brief, **92:** 205, **91:** 295, **90:** 298. See also **Mitsotakis, Constantine**
Greek Orthodox Church. See **Eastern Orthodox Churches**
Green, Richard R., 90: 389
Greene, Graham, 92: 173
Greenhouse effect: Earth, **92:** 197, 469, **90:** 108, 111, 129, 132; Venus, **91:** 73-76
Greenspan, Alan, 92: 451
Grenada: coup attempt, **92:** 470; facts in brief, **92:** 275, **91:** 345, **90:** 353
Gretzky, Wayne, 92: 238, **91:** 316, **90:** 321-322
Grey Cup. See **Football**
Greyhound Bus Lines, 91: 341
Griff, Professor, 92: 370
Griffin, Eric, 90: 210
Griffith Joyner, Florence, 90: 440
GROENING, MATT, 91: 313
Gross national product. See **Bank; Economics**
Grossman, Allen, 92: 362-363
Ground water, 92: 456-467
Group of 50, 92: 247
Group of Seven, 92: 231, 440
***Groupe Sceta* (boat), 92:** 95
Guare, John, 91: 453
GUATEMALA, 92: 234, **91:** 313, **90:** 319; Belize, **92:** 274; common market, **92:** 274; evangelical right, **91:** 411; facts in brief, **92:** 275, **91:** 345, **90:** 353; Maya artifacts, **92:** 53
Guerra González, Juan, 91: 433
Guggenheim Museum, 92: 68, **91:** 175
Guinea, 92: 46, **91:** 158, **90:** 160
Guinea-Bissau: facts in brief, **92:** 46, **91:** 158, **90:** 160; Senegal, **90:** 433
Gulf of the Farallones, 92: 336
Gum disease, 90: 274
Gumbel, Bryant, 90: 393
Gun control. See **Firearms**
Guns N' Roses, 92: 364, 365, **90:** 413
Gupta, Viswa Jit, 90: 404
Gurganus, Allan, 90: 359
Guthrie Theater, 90: 461
GUYANA, 92: 234; facts in brief, **92:** 275, **91:** 345, **90:** 353
Gwich'in Indians, 92: 334
Gymnastics, 92: 400, 401, **91:** 434, **90:** 440
Gysi, Gregor, 90: 314

H

HA-1A (drug), 92: 186
Haavelmo, Trygve, 90: 397
Habré, Hissein, 91: 156-157, 229
Habyarimana, Juvénal, 91: 157
Hagen, Carl I., 90: 399
Haislett, Nicole, 92: 411
HAITI, 92: 234-235, **91:** 313; ancient meteor impact, **91:** 307; corruption, **90:** 352-354; coup, **92:** 234-235, 272-273 (il.), 470; facts in brief, **92:** 275, **91:** 345, **90:** 353; U.S. trade embargo, **92:** 250. See also **Aristide, Jean-Bertrand**
Hakim, Albert A., 91: 329, **90:** 335
Halkieriid, 91: 396
Hall, Arsenio, 90: 457
Hammadi, Sa'doun, 92: 253
Hammer, M. C., 92: 369 (il.), 370
Handball, 92: 401, **91:** 435, **90:** 441
Handegard, John, 92: 95
Handgun. See **Firearms**
HANDICAPPED, 92: 235-236, **91:** 314, **90:** 319-320; Civil Rights Act, **92:** 146; mass transit, **90:** 466; Ontario, **90:** 401. See also **Americans with Disabilities Act**
Hanson, P. L. C. (firm), 91: 245
Hao Po-ts'un, 91: 447
Happy Land Social Club, 92: 162, **91:** 260
Harald V, 92: 335
Harawi, Ilyas, 91: 347, 348
Harcourt, Michael, 92: 98
HARKIN, TOM, 92: 236
Harness racing. See **Horse racing**
Harold Washington Library Center, 92: 279
Harper, Elijah, 91: 221
HARRIS, BARBARA CLEMENTINE, 90: 320
Harris, Joseph M., 92: 164
Hart, William L., 92: 181
Hartwig, Clayton M., 92: 66, **91:** 172, **90:** 175
Harvard Medical School, 92: 192
Hashimoto, Ryutaro, 92: 261
Hassan II, 92: 318-319, **91:** 373-374, **90:** 382, 391
Hate crimes, 92: 147, **91:** 241-242, **90:** 238-239
Hate speech, 92: 162
Haughey, Charles James, 92: 253-254, **91:** 330, **90:** 336-337
HAVEL, VÁCLAV, 92: 166-167, **91:** 262, 315, **90:** 261
Hawaii, 92: 404, **91:** 439, **90:** 444
Hawke, Robert James Lee, 92: 76, **91:** 181, **90:** 185-187
Hawkins, Yusuf K., 92: 148, 162, **91:** 242, 257-258, **90:** 390
Hazardous wastes. See **Environmental pollution**
Hazeltine Corp., 90: 474
Hazelwood, Joseph J., 91: 259
HBO. See **Home Box Office**
HCFA. See **Health Care Financing Administration**
HDTV. See **High-definition television**
HEALTH AND DISEASE, 92: 236-237, **91:** 315-316, **90:** 320-321; African programs, **92:** 48; air pollution, **92:** 198-199; food health claims, **90:** 156, 306; memory loss, **91:** 128-129; state laws and programs, **92:** 403, **91:** 438; veterans, **90:** 478. See also **Dentistry; Drugs; Gene therapy; Genetic medicine; Handicapped; Hospital; Medicine; Mental health; Public health;** and specific diseases
Health Care Financing Administration, 92: 392
Hearns, Thomas, 92: 96
Heart, Artificial, 91: 363
Heart-assist device, 92: 297
Heart disease: arrhythmia drugs, **90:** 280; diet effects, **91:** 414-415; hypertension, **92:** 297; prevention, **92:** 237; smoking, **90:** 321; women, **92:** 236-237, 297, **91:** 363
Heart failure, 92: 186
Heath, Edward, 92: 232
Hebrew Union College, 92: 52
Hecht, Anthony E., 91: 403
Hedgecock, Roger, 91: 425
Hefner, Hugh M., 90: 393
***Heidi Chronicles, The* (Wasserstein), 90:** 460
Heimdal, Scott, 91: 385
Heinz, John H., III, 92: 83, 358-359
Heisman Trophy. See **Football**
***Helicobacter pylori* (bacteria), 92:** 93
Helmick, Robert H., 92: 336
Helmsley, Leona, 90: 257
Helprin, Mark, 92: 282
HENDERSON, RICKEY, 92: 88, 237
Hennard, George J., 92: 164
***Henry V* (film), 90:** 386
Henson, Jim, 92: 329, **91:** 268-269
Hepatitis, 92: 186, 377, **91:** 363
Hereditary diseases, 92: 303-304. See also **Genetic medicine; Health and disease**
Hermann, Jane, 91: 263-264
Hernández Colón, Rafael, 92: 378, **91:** 52, 64
Hernia of the diaphragm, 91: 362-363
Herpes, 91: 316
Herrhausen, Alfred, 90: 315
Hezbollah, 92: 277-278, **90:** 356, 379
Hibernation, 90: 486
Higgins, William R., 90: 216, 356
High-definition television, 92: 195, **90:** 92-95, 288
Highway of death, 92: 343 (il.), 353
Highways. See **Transit**
Hijuelos, Oscar, 90: 359
Hill, Anita F., 92: 147, 157, 407, 408 (il.)
Hill, Mike, 92: 230
Hindus, 92: 71, **91:** 178, 322-323, **90:** 198
Hirohito, 90: 339
Hispanic Americans: census and population, **92:** 126, 128, 130, 132, 145, 276; job bias, **92:** 148; Los Angeles, **92:** 290, **91:** 241, 356; New York City, **92:** 323; Protestantism, **90:** 419; Washington, D.C., **92:** 454-455; *WBE*, **90:** 540
HIV. See **AIDS**
HNATYSHYN, RAMON JOHN, 91: 218 (il.), 316, **90:** 222
Hoar, Joseph P., 92: 67
Hobbies. See **Coin collecting; Stamp collecting; Toys and games**
HOCKEY, 92: 237-238, **91:** 316, **90:** 321-322
HOFFMAN, DUSTIN, 90: 323, 459
Hoffmann, Joerg, 92: 411
Holland. See **Netherlands**
Holliman, John, 92: 414
Hologram, 90: 95
Holyfield, Evander, 92: 96, **91:** 207-208, **90:** 210
Home Box Office, 90: 76
Homelessness, 90: 97-107; census data, **92:** 129, **91:** 228; city programs, **90:** 235, 409; libraries, **92:** 280; mental illness, **90:** 101-102, 374; New York City, **92:** 146 (il.); woman feeds homeless, **91:** 382
***Homo erectus*, 90:** 168
***Homo habilis*, 90:** 168
Homosexuality: armed forces, **91:** 173; arts funding, **91:** 453; brain structure, **92:** 93; marriage in Denmark, **90:** 273; Massachusetts law, **90:** 239; ordination, **92:** 375, **91:** 412, **90:** 418; Protestant attitudes, **92:** 375
Honasan, Gregorio, 90: 409
Honda Motor Co., 91: 184-185, **90:** 188, 189
HONDURAS, 91: 317, **90:** 323; AIDS, **92:** 274; common market, **92:** 274; contra bases, **90:** 352; facts in brief, **92:** 275, **91:** 345, **90:** 353
Honecker, Erich, 92: 229, **90:** 312-314
Hong Kong: boat people, **90:** 180-181; Chinese control, **92:** 72, **91:** 178, 234 (il.), **90:** 181; construction, **91:** 211; ivory trade, **91:** 46-48; Pacific rim economies, **91:** 103; Vietnamese refugees, **92:** 74
Honiara Declaration, 92: 337
Honorat, Jean-Jacques, 92: 235
Hooker, John Lee, 91: 193 (il.)
Hopkins, Ann B., 91: 241
HORSE RACING, 92: 239-240, **91:** 317-318, **90:** 323-324
Horseback riding, 91: 167-168
Horseshoe pitching, 92: 401, **91:** 435, **90:** 441
Horticulture. See **Botany**
HOSPITAL, 92: 240, **91:** 318, **90:** 324-325; veteran death rates, **90:** 478. See also **Drugs; Health and disease; Medicine; Public health**
Hostages: Iraq, **92:** 345-346, **91:** 329, 366; Lebanon, **92:** 233, 250, 257, 277, 316-317, 448-449, **91:** 328, **90:** 216, 356, 379
Hot poles (Mercury), 91: 181
Houphouët-Boigny, Félix, 92: 44, **91:** 160, 333, 420-421
House of Representatives. See **Congress of the U.S.; Democratic Party; Elections; Republican Party**
Housing: immigrants to Israel, **91:** 332; National Affordable Housing Act, **91:** 253; Toronto, **90:** 462. See also **Building and construction; City; Homelessness**

Index

Housing and Urban Development, U.S. Department of, 91: 470, **90:** 474
HOUSTON, 92: 240-241, **91:** 319, **90:** 325-326; economic summit, **91:** 238, 319; Republican National Convention, **92:** 241, 383
Houston Ballet, 92: 168
Houston Grand Opera, 90: 241
Howard, Desmond, 92: 222 (il.), 224
Howard University, 90: 426
Howe, Sir Geoffrey, 90: 317
Hrawi, Ilyas, 92: 278, **90:** 379
Hu Yaobang, 90: 230
Hubbard Street Dance Co., 91: 264
***Hubble Space Telescope*, 92:** 74, **91:** 180, 431-432, 472
HUD. See **Housing and Urban Development, U.S. Department of**
Hudson volcano, 92: 62, 226-228
Hughes, Holly, 91: 174
Hull, Brett, 92: 238
Human Genome Initiative, 92: 307, 309
Human growth hormone, 91: 363-364
Human immunodeficiency virus. See **AIDS**
Human rights: Amnesty International report, **92:** 148; Argentina, **90:** 173; Burma, **92:** 101, **91:** 213; China, **92:** 140-141, **91:** 235, **90:** 230-232; Cuba, **90:** 260; Denmark meeting, **91:** 273; Indonesia, **92:** 247; Iran, **91:** 327; Iraq, **92:** 266; Israel, **91:** 332, 369, **90:** 378; Kenya, **92:** 263; Korea, North, **90:** 344; Kuwait, **92:** 268; Middle East, **91:** 369; Morocco, **92:** 318-319; Peru, **92:** 357; Romania, **92:** 386; Somalia, **92:** 392. See also **Civil rights**
Humbert gold piece, 90: 242
Hun Sen, 92: 105, **90:** 218, 459
***Hundredth Year, The* (encyclical), 92:** 384-385
Hungarian Democratic Forum, 92: 241
HUNGARY, 92: 241, **91:** 320-321, **90:** 326-327; Austria, **90:** 187-188, 326-327; European trade, **92:** 206; facts in brief, **92:** 205, **91:** 295, **90:** 298; pope's visit, **92:** 384; swimming, **92:** 411; U.S. trade, **90:** 333
Hunger. See **Famine; Food**
Huntington Beach, Calif., 91: 289 (il.)
Huntington Library, 92: 52
Huntsville, Ala., 90: 481
Hurricanes, 92: 468-469, **91:** 478, **90:** 481; Bob, **92:** 146, 468; Grace, **92:** 468-469; Hugo, **90:** 213, 237, 477, 481, 483; Jerry, **90:** 481
Husák, Gustáv, 92: 173, **90:** 261
Hussein I, 92: 262-263, **91:** 337, **90:** 343
HUSSEIN, SADDAM, 91: 321; book, **91:** 353; Iraq reforms, **92:** 253, **90:** 336; Islamic support, **92:** 254; Persian Gulf crisis and War, **92:** 102-103, 251, 255, 313-314, 344-355, **91:** 329, 366-368, 399, 466-467; Syria, **91:** 446
Hybl, William J., 92: 336
Hydergine, 91: 278
Hydrochlorofluorocarbons, 91: 290
Hydrogen fuel, 90: 290
Hydrologic cycle, 92: 459 (il.)
Hydroplane. See **Boating**
Hyenas, 92: 477
Hypercar, 90: 463
Hypertension, 92: 297

I

"I Love Lucy," 90: 455
IACOBUCCI, FRANK, 92: 109 (il.), 242
Ibarruri Gómez, Dolores, 90: 439
Ibero-American Summit, 92: 274-276
IBM. See **International Business Machines Corp.**
Ice (drug). See **Crystal meth**
Ice hockey. See **Hockey**
ICE SKATING, 92: 242, **91:** 321-322, **90:** 327-328
Iceland: facts in brief, **92:** 205, **91:** 295, **90:** 298; free-trade zone, **92:** 206
Idaho, 92: 404, **91:** 438, **90:** 444
Iliescu, Ion, 92: 386, **91:** 422, **90:** 430
Illegal aliens. See **Immigration**
***Illiberal Education* (D'Souza), 92:** 192
Illinois, 92: 404, **91:** 439, **90:** 444; education, **92:** 403; patronage, **91:** 442-443
Imani Temple, 91: 422, **90:** 428
IMF. See **International Monetary Fund**
IMMIGRATION, 92: 242-243, **91:** 322, **90:** 328; Africans in Spain, **92:** 396; Arabs in France, **92:** 225, **91:** 305; Australia, **92:** 77; Belgium, **92:** 92; census, **91:** 227; Ellis Island, **91:** 87-101; Europe, **92:** 207, **90:** 300; Hispanics in U.S., **90:** 354; Soviet bloc Jews, **92:** 255, **91:** 331-332, 368, **90:** 342. See also **Refugees**
Immigration Act (1990), 92: 242, **91:** 249, 322
Implicit Price Index. See **Economics**
Imports. See **Economics; International trade**
Incas, 90: 354
Income, Personal. See **Labor; Welfare**
Income tax. See **Taxation**
INDIA, 92: 243-245, **91:** 322-323, **90:** 329-330; facts in brief, **92:** 73, **91:** 179, **90:** 182; relations with neighbors, **90:** 181; Soviet collapse, **92:** 71; Sri Lanka, **92:** 402; U.S. trade, **90:** 333. See also **Gandhi, Rajiv; Rao, P. V. Narasimha**
INDIAN, AMERICAN, 92: 246-247, **91:** 324-325, **90:** 330-331; Alberta, **90:** 331; art, **92:** 68; British Columbia, **91:** 209; Canadian laws, **92:** 108, 110-112; census and population, **92:** 128, 130, 132, 246-247; Latin America, **91:** 209, **90:** 354; Manitoba, **90:** 331; museum reburials, **91:** 166, **90:** 168-169, 330; Northwest Territories, **92:** 334; Ontario, **92:** 246, 337; Quebec, **92:** 124, 324, **91:** 217-218; Yukon Territory, **92:** 476
Indiana, 92: 404, **91:** 439, **90:** 444
Indianapolis, 92: 194, **91:** 483, **90:** 234
Indianapolis 500. See **Automobile racing**
INDONESIA, 92: 247, **91:** 325, **90:** 331-332; China, **91:** 176; facts in brief, **92:** 73, **91:** 179, **90:** 182; free-trade area, **92:** 71; industrialization, **91:** 103-104, 110-111, 115-119; U.S. bases in Philippines, **90:** 183
Industry. See **Economics; International trade; Labor; Manufacturing;** and specific industries, countries, and provinces
Inertial confinement, 90: 119-121
Inflation: Peru, **92:** 357; U.S., **92:** 160, 189, **91:** 279, **90:** 199; world, **91:** 281, **90:** 283
Infomercials, 91: 257
Inkatha Freedom Party, 92: 393-394
Inland Steel Industries, 91: 440
Insanity committal law, 92: 310
Insecticides. See **Pesticides**
Institute of Contemporary Art, 91: 174
***Instruction on the Ecclesiastical Vocation of the Theologian, An*, 91:** 421
Insurance: automobile, **90:** 401, 446; national health plan, **92:** 383, **91:** 318; property and casualty, **90:** 446. See also **Social security**
Integration: housing, **91:** 241; school, **92:** 408, **91:** 237-238, 240, 282, 443
Intelligence, 91: 364, **90:** 147
Interactive television, 90: 95
Intercontinental ballistic missiles, 92: 63-65
Interest rates: banking, **92:** 86, 188-189, 449, **91:** 196, 198, **90:** 199; bond, **92:** 406, **91:** 281, 441, **90:** 448; trends, **91:** 281
Interference, Memory, 91: 124-126
Interferon, 91: 363
Internal Revenue Service. See **Taxation**
International Business Machines Corp., 92: 152, 296, **91:** 247-248, **90:** 244-245
International Energy Agency, 92: 358
International Monetary Fund: Africa, **90:** 164; Argentina, **92:** 62; Egypt, **92:** 193; funding increase, **91:** 327, **90:** 332; Hungary, **92:** 241; Peru, **91:** 398; Poland, **92:** 364, **91:** 405; U.S.S.R., **92:** 190
INTERNATIONAL TRADE, 92: 248-250, **91:** 325-327, **90:** 332-333; agriculture, **90:** 302-303; automobiles, **91:** 183-185, **90:** 188; manufacturing, **91:** 361-362, **90:** 369; Pacific rim nations, **91:** 103-119. See also **European Community; Trade, U.S. balance of;** and specific continents and countries
Intifada, 91: 331, 369, **90:** 377-378
Inuit, 92: 334, **91:** 390, **90:** 399
Investments. See **Bank; Economics; International trade; Loans; Stocks and bonds**
Io (moon), 91: 78-79, 81 (il.)
Ions, 92: 333
Iowa, 92: 404, **91:** 439, **90:** 444
Iowa, University of, 92: 164
***Iowa*, U.S.S., 92:** 66, **91:** 172, **90:** 175-176, 474
IRA (organization). See **Irish Republican Army**
IRAN, 92: 250, **91:** 327-328, **90:** 333-335; Afghanistan, **92:** 41; earthquake, **91:** 274, 327; facts in brief, **92:** 316, **91:** 370, **90:** 378; Iraq, **91:** 328, **90:** 336, 380, 471; Persian Gulf crisis and War, **92:** 344, 345, **91:** 328; regional bloc, **90:** 380; religious repression, **90:** 426; Rushdie affair, **91:** 311-312, **90:** 317, 332, 334, 362; Saudi Arabia, **90:** 432-433; U.S. hostages, **92:** 316-317. See also **Rafsanjani, Ali Akbar Hashemi**
IRAN-CONTRA AFFAIR, 92: 251, 276, 451, **91:** 328-329, **90:** 335
IRAQ, 92: 251-253, **91:** 329-330, **90:** 336; ancient treasures, **92:** 56-59; facts in brief, **92:** 316, **91:** 370, **90:** 378; immigration to U.S., **92:** 243; Iran, **91:** 328, **90:** 336, 380, 471; Kuwait abuses, **92:** 266; oil supply, **92:** 357; Persian Gulf crisis and War, **92:** 313-314, 342-355, 447, **91:** 329-330, 340, 366-368; political liberalization, **90:** 380; regional bloc, **90:** 380; Saudi Arabia, **91:** 426; Syria, **90:** 452; television coverage, **92:** 414; UN actions, **92:** 447, 448; *WBE*, **92:** 486. See also **Hussein, Saddam; Persian Gulf crisis and War**
IRELAND, 92: 253-254, **91:** 330, **90:** 336-337; facts in brief, **92:** 205, **91:** 295, **90:** 298; Northern Ireland, **92:** 333
Ireland, Northern. See **Northern Ireland**
Ireland, Patricia, 92: 327
Irish Republican Army, 92: 233, 333, **91:** 389, **90:** 398
Iron and steel. See **Steel industry**
IRONS, JEREMY, 92: 254
Irwin, James B., 92: 173
Isa, Maria and Zein, 92: 162
Ishaq Khan, Ghulam, 91: 395
ISLAM, 92: 254; Bulgaria, **91:** 212; Burma, **92:** 101; denominational survey, **92:** 376; France, **92:** 225, **91:** 305, **90:** 311; India, **92:** 244-245, **91:** 322-323; Indonesia, **91:** 325, **90:** 331-332; Lebanon, **91:** 347-348, **90:** 355-356, 378-379; Nigeria, **92:** 331; Persian Gulf crisis, **91:** 368; Rushdie affair, **91:** 311-312, **90:** 317, 334, 362; Sri Lanka, **91:** 436; U.S.S.R., **91:** 417-418, 466; West Indies, **91:** 478-479; Yugoslavia, **92:** 473. See also **Islamic fundamentalists; Shiite Muslims**
Islamic Democratic Alliance, 92: 339, **91:** 395-396
Islamic fundamentalists: Algeria, **92:** 50, **91:** 164; Egypt, **91:** 284, **90:** 286; Iran, **92:** 250; Jordan, **92:** 263; Middle East gains, **91:** 369-370; Sudan, **91:** 442; Tunisia, **92:** 254, 430, **91:** 458, **90:** 380
Islamic Salvation Front, 92: 50-51, 254, **91:** 164
Ismail, Raghib (Rocket), 92: 222, **91:** 305
Isozaki, Arata, 92: 60, 61
ISRAEL, 92: 255-257, **91:** 331-332, **90:** 337-338; archaeology, **92:** 52, **91:** 167; Egypt, **91:** 284, **90:** 286; Ethiopia, **92:** 201, **91:** 291; facts in brief, **92:** 316, **91:** 370, **90:** 378; hospice occupation, **91:** 279; hostages, **92:** 316-317, 449; Iraqi spy case, **91:** 330; Lebanon, **92:** 278; Middle East peace conference, **92:** 103, 314-316; Palestinian conflict, **92:** 256-257, **91:** 331-332, 368-369, 467-468, **90:** 337-338, 376-378; Persian Gulf War, **92:** 255, 257, 346, 350; U.S. relations, **92:** 255-256, **91:** 215, 332, 368-369, **90:** 377-378, 473. See also **Gaza Strip and West Bank; Judaism; Shamir, Yitzhak**
***It Takes a Nation of Millions to Hold Us Back* (recording), 92:** 369-370
ITALY, 92: 257-259, **91:** 332-333, **90:** 338-339; Albania, **92:** 48, **90:** 165; facts in brief, **92:** 205, **91:** 295, **90:** 298; railroad station, **91:** 210-211. See also **Andreotti, Giulio; Cossiga, Francesco**
Ito, Midori, 92: 242, **91:** 321, **90:** 327, 328 (il.)
Ivan, Paula, 90: 464
IVORY COAST, 91: 333; church, **91:** 333, 420-421, **90:** 212-213; facts in brief, **92:** 46, **91:** 158, **90:** 160; political changes, **92:** 44, **91:** 157-160, **90:** 163
Ivory trade, 92: 328-329, **91:** 36-51, **90:** 253

J

J. P. Morgan & Company, Inc., 91: 198
JACKSON, BO, 92: 88, **90:** 339
Jackson, Jesse Louis, 92: 142, 180, **91:** 273, 474, **90:** 479
Jackson, Michael, 92: 365
Jagan, Cheddi B., 92: 234
Jager, Tom, 92: 411, **91:** 445, **90:** 451
Jamaica: election, **90:** 483-484; facts in brief, **92:** 275, **91:** 345, **90:** 353
Janata Dal Party, 92: 243-244
JAPAN, 92: 259-261, **91:** 333-335, **90:** 339-341; art scandal, **92:** 68; automobiles, **92:** 79-80, **91:** 183-185, **90:** 188-189; buildings, **91:** 168, 211; China, **92:** 140, **91:** 177; economy, **92:** 190, **91:** 281, 335, **90:** 283; European trade, **92:** 206, 214-215, **90:** 300; facts in brief, **92:** 73, **91:** 179, **90:** 182; fishing nets, **91:** 254, **90:** 253; ivory trade, **91:** 50; Latin America, **91:** 344-346; manufacturing system, **90:** 371; motion pictures, **92:** 321; Mt. Unzen, **92:** 226; nuclear power accident, **92:** 197; Olympic Games, **92:** 336; Osaka Aquarium, **91:** 168, 482; Pacific rim nations, **91:** 103, 106-107, 111-119; Reagan visit, **90:** 424; Rockefeller Center purchase, **90:** 390; space missions, **92:** 396, **91:** 433; sports, **92:** 400; steel industry, **90:** 446; U.S. trade, **92:** 248, 261, **91:** 326, 472, **90:** 333, 340-341; U.S.S.R., **92:** 71, 261, **91:** 177, 335; World War II soldiers, **91:** 382. See also **Akihito; Kaifu, Toshiki; Miyazawa, Kiichi**
Japanese-American reparations, 91: 241
Jatoi, Ghulam Mustafa, 91: 395, 396

Java, 92: 247
Jazz, *WBE,* **92:** 493. See also **Awards and prizes; Popular music**
Jennings, Lynn, 92: 401, **91:** 457
Jersey City, N.J., 90: 284
Jerusalem, 91: 331, 368
Jeu de Paume, 92: 68
Jews. See **Israel; Judaism**
***JFK* (film), 92:** 319
Jiang Qing, 92: 142
JIANG ZEMIN, 92: 140, 141, **91:** 235, **90:** 232-233, 343
Jigme Singye Wangchuk, 92: 71-73, **91:** 178
Job discrimination: blacks, **92:** 148; genetic testing, **92:** 308-309; handicapped, **92:** 236; large companies, **92:** 269; Supreme Court cases, **90:** 237-238, 449-450. See also **Affirmative action**
Joffrey Ballet, 92: 168, **91:** 263, **90:** 264
John Fairfax Group, 92: 77
John G. Shedd Aquarium, 92: 478
John Paul II, 92: 384-386, **91:** 420-421, **90:** 428-429; Gorbachev meeting, **91:** 417, **90:** 428, 471; Mexico visit, **91:** 365; Poland visit, **92:** 364 (il.); Runcie meeting, **90:** 418
Johnson, Anna L., 91: 259
Johnson, Ben, 91: 457, **90:** 464
Johnson, Earvin (Magic), Jr., 92: 48, 89 (il.), 91, **90:** 205
Johnson, Larry, 92: 90
Johnson, Prince Yormie, 92: 278, **91:** 349
JOHNSTON, RITA, 92: 98, 262
***JOIDES Resolution* (ship), 91:** 306, 392, **90:** 400
Joint Chiefs of Staff, 90: 416
Joint Global Ocean Flux Study, 91: 391-392
Joint operating agreement, 91: 386, **90:** 395
Joint venture, 90: 60, 188, 446
Jones, Brereton C., 92: 405
Jones Act (Puerto Rico), 91: 59
Jong, Erica, 92: 363
JORDAN, 92: 262-263, **91:** 337, **90:** 343; facts in brief, **92:** 316, **91:** 370, **90:** 378; Middle East peace conference, **92:** 314-315; Persian Gulf crisis and War, **92:** 262, **91:** 337, 367; *WBE,* **90:** 512
Jordan, Michael, 92: 89 (il.), 91, **90:** 205
Journalism. See **Awards and prizes; Magazine; Newspaper**
Jovan The Legend (cat), 92: 126
***Joy Luck Club, The* (Tan), 90:** 359
Joyner-Kersee, Jackie, 92: 423, 424
JUDAISM, 92: 263, **91:** 336, **90:** 342-343; Auschwitz convent, **91:** 421-422, **90:** 342-343, 428; denominational survey, **92:** 376; evangelical relations, **90:** 419; New York City race relations, **92:** 324; Spain, **91:** 433. See also **Israel**
Judas Priest, 91: 406-407
Judo, 91: 435, **90:** 441
Junior Black Mafia, 90: 409
Junk bonds, 92: 406, **91:** 441, **90:** 448, 476
Jupiter, 91: 69-79
Jury selection, 92: 408
Justice, U.S. Department of, 92: 86, 147

K

Kahane, Meir, 91: 336
Kahn, Louis I., 92: 61
KAIFU, TOSHIKI, 92: 140, 259-261, **91:** 333-334, **90:** 340, 344
Kalpokas, Donald, 92: 339
Kampuchea. See **Cambodia**
Kamsky, Gata, 92: 138
Kanaks, 91: 395, **90:** 402-403
Kanemaru, Shin, 92: 261
Kang Kyung Dae, 92: 265
Kansas, 92: 404, **91:** 439, **90:** 444
Kansas City, Mo.: election, **92:** 194; murders, **90:** 237; newspapers, **91:** 386, **90:** 395; school integration, **91:** 237
Kapolei, Hawaii, 91: 239
Karajan, Herbert von, 90: 239
Karamanlis, Constantine, 91: 312
Karami, Omar, 91: 348
Karmal, Babrak, 92: 41
Karpov, Anatoly, 92: 138, **91:** 231, **90:** 227
Kashmir, India, 92: 244-245, **91:** 323, **90:** 329-330
Kasparov, Garry, 92: 138, **91:** 231, **90:** 227
Kaunda, Kenneth David, 92: 45, **91:** 160, 481
Kawashima, Kiko, 91: 384
Kaysone Phomvihan, 92: 271, **91:** 343, **90:** 349
Kazakhstan, 92: 438, 439
Keating, Charles H., Jr., 92: 158, 162, **91:** 197, 261
Keating, Paul, 92: 76
Keenan, Brian, 91: 330
Kelly, Jim, 92: 221
Kelly, Patrick F., 92: 162
Kelly, Sharon Pratt. See **Dixon, Sharon Pratt**
KEMP, JACK FRENCH, 90: 344, 474
Kendall, Henry W., 91: 388-389
Kennedy, Donald, 92: 192, **91:** 282
Kennedy, John F., 92: 319
Kennedy, Kerry, 91: 383
Kennedy Stadium, 90: 409
Kent, Doug, 92: 95
Kentucky, 92: 404, **91:** 439, **90:** 444; disasters, **90:** 257, 380; elections, **92:** 194, 405; lottery, **90:** 446; schools, **91:** 283, 437, **90:** 285
Kentucky Derby. See **Horse racing**
KENYA, 92: 263, **91:** 338, **90:** 344; elephants, **91:** 40, 46-51, **90:** 253; facts in brief, **92:** 46, **91:** 158, **90:** 160; political repression, **92:** 44, **91:** 160
Kérékou, Mathieu, 92: 45
KERREY, BOB, 92: 264
Keshtmand, Soltan Ali, 90: 157
Kessler, David A., 92: 40
Kevorkian, Jack, 92: 296, **91:** 260-261
KGB, 92: 277 (il.), 432, 435
Khaliqyar, Fazil Haq, 92: 41
Khamenei, Ali Hoseini, 92: 51, 254, **91:** 327, **90:** 333
Khieu Samphan, 92: 105
Khmer Rouge, 92: 70-71, 105, **91:** 216-217, **90:** 179, 218
Khomeini, Ayatollah Ruhollah, 92: 250, **91:** 327, 328 (il.), **90:** 333, 335, 362, 423
Khrushchev, Nikita S., 92: 443
Kidney disease, 90: 321
Kiet Muoi, Vo Van, 92: 453
Killeen, Tex., 92: 163 (il.), 164
Kim Dae Jung, 92: 264, **91:** 338-339, **90:** 345
Kim Il-sŏng, 92: 141, **91:** 338, 339
Kim Young Sam, 91: 338
Kimbrough, Ted D., 90: 227
King, Betsy, 91: 309, **90:** 315
King, Gwendolyn S., 90: 436
King, Martin Luther, Jr., 91: 302, 440
King, Rodney G., 92: 290
King, Tom, 91: 389
Kingdom, Roger, 90: 464, 465
Kinnock, Neil Gordon, 91: 311
Kirghiz. See **Kyrgyzstan**
Kiribati, 92: 338, **91:** 394, **90:** 402
Kirov Ballet, 90: 263
Kitingan, Jeffrey, 92: 293
Kleeman, Gunda, 92: 242
Klinghoffer, Leon, 92: 150
KLM Royal Dutch Airlines, 90: 192
KMT. See **Kuomintang**
Koch, Bill, 92: 95
Koch, Edward I., 90: 389
Kohl, Helmut Michael, 92: 228, 229, **91:** 292-296, 307-308, 465, **90:** 300 (il.), 314
Kondrusiewicz, Tadeusz, 92: 384
Koop, C. Everett, 90: 421
Kopp, Elisabeth and Hans, 91: 446, **90:** 452
KOREA, NORTH, 92: 264, **91:** 338, **90:** 344; China, **92:** 141, **91:** 338; facts in brief, **92:** 73, **91:** 179, **90:** 182; South Korea, **92:** 264, **91:** 338, 339, **90:** 345; Soviet collapse, **92:** 71
KOREA, SOUTH, 92: 264-265, **91:** 338, **90:** 345; China and U.S.S.R. trade, **91:** 177; facts in brief, **92:** 73, **91:** 179, **90:** 182; ivory trade, **91:** 50; Japan, **91:** 335; North Korea, **92:** 264, **91:** 338, 339, **90:** 345; Pacific rim nations, **91:** 103, 106-109, 119
Koskotas, George, 92: 234, **90:** 318
Kosovo, 92: 474, **91:** 480, **90:** 485
Koss, Johann Olav, 92: 242
Kozol, Jonathan, 92: 191
Kraft USA, 90: 394
Kravchuk, Leonid M., 92: 438
Kreimer, Richard, 92: 280
Kreisky, Bruno, 91: 183
Krenz, Egon, 90: 313-314
Krishna Prasad Bhattarai, 91: 379
Kronberger, Petra, 92: 390, **91:** 427
Kryuchkov, Vladimir A., 92: 432-435
Krzysztof, Jan, 92: 204 (il.)
Kuomintang, 92: 413, **91:** 447, **90:** 452, 453
Kurds: Iran, **92:** 250; Iraq, **92:** 103, 252-253, 314, 355, 447-448, **90:** 336; Turkey, **92:** 430-431, **91:** 459, **90:** 468
Kuril Islands, 92: 71, **91:** 177
KUWAIT, 92: 266-268, **91:** 340; environmental damage, **92:** 197-198; facts in brief, **92:** 316, **91:** 370, **90:** 378; immigration to U.S., **92:** 243; oil supply, **92:** 357; Persian Gulf crisis and War, **92:** 251, 266-268, 342-355, 447, **91:** 329-330, 340, 366-368; reconstruction, **92:** 99; Saudi Arabia, **91:** 427, **90:** 432-433. See also **Hussein, Saddam; Persian Gulf crisis and War**
Kyrgyzstan, 92: 438

L

LABOR, 92: 268-271, **91:** 340-342, **90:** 346-349; airline strikes, **90:** 192, 346-347; baseball contract, **91:** 198, 341; Chile mining strikes, **92:** 140; Los Angeles health-care workers' strike, **92:** 291; Manitoba nurses' strike, **92:** 293; Montreal city workers' strike, **92:** 318; Postal Service contract, **92:** 372; productivity, **90:** 282-283; railroad strikes, **92:** 379-380; San Francisco Opera contract, **91:** 243; Soviet mining strike, **90:** 380-381
Labor Party: Australia, **92:** 76; Norway, **91:** 390
Labour Party (Great Britain), 91: 310-311, **90:** 316, 317
Lacalle, Luis Alberto, 91: 472, **90:** 477
Lacroix, Christian, 90: 304
Lacrosse, 92: 401, **91:** 435, **90:** 441
Ladies Professional Bowlers Tour. See **Bowling**
Ladies Professional Golfers Association. See **Golf**
Laetare Medal, 92: 386
Lagerfeld, Karl, 91: 299
La Jolla Playhouse, 90: 460-461
LAMER, ANTONIO, 91: 343
***Land Before Time, The* (film), 91:** 136, 150, 151
Landfills, 92: 461 (il.), 462
Landmark Tower, 91: 211
Landon, Michael, 92: 174
Landslides, 92: 184, **91:** 307
Lane Publishing Co., 91: 358
Lange, David R., 90: 390
Lanier, Bob, 92: 240, 241
Lao People's Revolutionary Party, 92: 271
LAOS, 92: 271, **91:** 343, **90:** 349; facts in brief, **92:** 73, **91:** 179, **90:** 182; ivory trade, **91:** 50-51; Thailand, **92:** 417
Laptop computers, 92: 152, **90:** 245
LaRouche, Lyndon H., Jr., 90: 257
Lasers, 92: 350, 428
Latifah, Queen, 92: 369
LATIN AMERICA, 92: 273-276, **91:** 343-347, **90:** 350-354; foreign debt, **91:** 281, 343-344; life expectancy, **90:** 415; Protestantism, **92:** 384, **90:** 419; trade agreements, **92:** 249, 273-274, 470; U.S. policy, **92:** 273, **91:** 215, 326-327, 346, **90:** 350, 476
Latin American Integration Association, 91: 346
LATVIA, 92: 276-277; ethnic unrest, **91:** 462, 464, **90:** 67, 469; facts in brief, **92:** 205; independence, **92:** 103, 202 (il.), 435; UN membership, **92:** 448; *WBE,* **92:** 500
Lauda-Air, 92: 83
Law enforcement. See **Police**
Law of Return (Israel), 90: 343
Laws. See **Congress of the U.S.; Courts; Crime; State government; Supreme Court of the U.S.; United States, Government of the;** and specific countries
Layoffs. See **Unemployment**
Layton, Jack, 92: 420
Lead: exposure, **92:** 199, 221; poisoning, **92:** 386
Leakey, Richard E. F., 91: 51
Lean, Sir David, 92: 174
Leaning Tower of Pisa, 91: 384
LEBANON, 92: 277-278, **91:** 347-348, **90:** 355-356; cease-fire efforts, **90:** 378-379; facts in brief, **92:** 316, **91:** 370, **90:** 378; Middle East peace conference, **92:** 314-315; Swiss drug case, **90:** 452. See also **Hostages**
Le Carré, John, 90: 359 (il.), 363
Leconte, Henri, 92: 417
LEE, SPIKE, 90: 356
Lee Hsien Loong, 91: 178
Lee Kuan Yew, 91: 178
Lee Teng-hui. See **Li Teng-hui**
Lefebvre, Marcel, 92: 386
Leland, Mickey, 90: 191, 325
Lemieux, Mario, 92: 238, **90:** 321, 322
Lemur, 91: 481
Lendl, Ivan, 91: 450, 451, **90:** 457, 458
Lenihan, Brian, 91: 330
Lenin, Vladimir I., 92: 442
LENO, JAY, 92: 278
Leonard, Sugar Ray, 92: 96, **90:** 210
Lepine, Marc, 90: 381
Lesage, Jean, 92: 118
Lesbianism. See **Homosexuality**
Lesotho: coup, **92:** 44; facts in brief, **92:** 46, **91:** 158, **90:** 160
Letelier, Orlando, 92: 140, **90:** 229
Levamisole, 91: 278
Lévesque, René, 92: 119
Levi, Wayne, 91: 309
Levine, Philip, 92: 362
Lewis, Carl, 92: 422, 424
Lewis, Charles, 90: 479

Lewis, Hayley, 91: 445
Li Huan, 90: 453
Li Peng, 92: 140, 141, **91:** 176, 234-235, 325, **90:** 183 (il.), 230
Li Teng-hui, 92: 413, **91:** 447, **90:** 453
Libel, 90: 395
Liberal Democratic Party (Japan), 92: 259, 261, 317, **91:** 333, 334, **90:** 340
Liberal Party (Canada), 91: 219-222; New Brunswick, **92:** 323; Ontario, **91:** 392; Prince Edward Island, **92:** 372; Quebec, **92:** 118, 120, 379; Toronto, **92:** 420. See also **Chrétien, Jean Joseph-Jacques**
Liberation theology, 91: 313
Liberation Tigers of Tamil Eelam, 92: 244, 402, **91:** 436, **90:** 442
LIBERIA, 92: 278-279, **91:** 348-349, **90:** 357; civil war, **92:** 44, **91:** 157, 171, 348-349; facts in brief, **92:** 46, **91:** 158, **90:** 160
LIBRARY, 92: 279-280, **91:** 349-350, **90:** 357-359; Bush presidential library, **92:** 104
LIBYA, 92: 280-281, **91:** 350, **90:** 358-359; Chad, **91:** 229; facts in brief, **92:** 46, **91:** 158, **90:** 160; irrigation project, **92:** 455, **90:** 359; Persian Gulf crisis, **91:** 350, 368
Liechtenstein: European trade, **92:** 206; facts in brief, **92:** 205, **91:** 295, **90:** 298
Life: chemistry, **91:** 231; development, **92:** 340
Life expectancy: Thailand, **91:** 107; world, **91:** 408, **90:** 415
Lifsh, Yosef, 92: 324
Ligachev, Yegor, 92: 445
Light rapid transit, 92: 424, **91:** 457-458
"Like a Prayer" (recording), 90: 413
Likud bloc, 91: 331, **90:** 337-338
Lin, Maya Ying, 90: 171
Lincoln Center, 92: 148, 149
Lincoln Center Theater, 92: 418, 419
Lincoln Savings & Loan Association, 92: 158, 162, **91:** 261
Linh, Nguyen Van, 92: 453, **90:** 478
Lini, Walter, 92: 338-339
Lipstein, Owen J., 91: 358
List, John E., 91: 258
Literacy, 91: 115, 349
LITERATURE, 92: 282-285, **91:** 350-353, **90:** 359-363; Nobel Prizes, **92:** 331-332, **91:** 388, **90:** 397. See also **Awards and prizes; Canadian literature; Literature for children**
LITERATURE FOR CHILDREN, 92: 285-288, **91:** 354-356, **90:** 363-366; Dr. Seuss, **92:** 177-178
LITHUANIA, 92: 288-289; ethnic conflict, **91:** 462, 464, **90:** 67, 469; facts in brief, **92:** 205; independence, **92:** 103, 435; UN membership, **92:** 448; *WBE*, **92:** 503
Little Bighorn Battlefield National Monument, 92: 247
***Little Mermaid, The* (film), 91:** 136, 150, **90:** 384
***Little Vera* (film), 90:** 386
Liver cancer, 92: 236
Liver transplant, 90: 373
***Liverpool Oratorio* (McCartney), 92:** 150
Living wills, 92: 240
Lizards, 92: 477
Lloyd Webber, Andrew, 91: 453
Loans: bank, **91:** 195; building, **91:** 209; education, **91:** 282-283
Lockerbie, Scotland, air disaster, 92: 81-82, 280-281, **91:** 350, **90:** 191, 431
London, 92: 233, **91:** 310, **90:** 304
***Lonesome Dove* (TV series), 90:** 457
Long, Vicki, 91: 421
***Looking to the Future* (report), 91:** 311
Lopez, Stephen, 92: 162
Lorenzo, Frank, 91: 187, **90:** 346-347
LOS ANGELES, 92: 290-291, **91:** 356-357, **90:** 366-367; air pollution, **92:** 199; architecture, **92:** 61; art, **92:** 69; census and population, **92:** 126, 145; police contract, **90:** 348; water supply, **91:** 357, **90:** 480; zoo, **90:** 486
Los Angeles Lakers, 92: 90-91, **90:** 203, 205
Los Angeles Philharmonic, 90: 239
***Lost in Yonkers* (Simon), 92:** 418-419
Lost Squadron, 92: 326-327
Lottery: immigration, **92:** 242; states, **90:** 391
Lotus Development Corp., 91: 248
Lou Gehrig's disease. See **Amyotrophic lateral sclerosis**
Louisiana, 92: 404, **91:** 439, **90:** 444; abortion bill, **91:** 438; elections, **92:** 383, 403-404; nuclear power plant, **90:** 291; tax plan, **90:** 445; voting rights, **92:** 408
Louvre, 90: 171, 179
Loyalty oath, 91: 173
Lozano, William, 91: 259, **90:** 257
Lu, Gang, 92: 164
Lubbers, Ruud, 92: 322-323, **91:** 379, **90:** 388
Lubicon Lake Indians, 90: 331
Lucas, William C., 90: 473
Luge, 92: 401, **91:** 435, **90:** 441
LUJAN, MANUEL, JR., 91: 470, **90:** 367
Lukanov, Andrey K., 91: 212
Lukens, Donald E. (Buz), 91: 253
Lundgren, Jeffrey, 91: 259
Lung cancer, 91: 315, 415
Luxembourg, 92: 205, **91:** 295, **90:** 298
Luxor statues, 90: 170
Luyendyk, Arie, 91: 185
Lymphoma, 91: 161-162
LYNCH, DAVID, 91: 358
Lyric Opera of Chicago, 91: 242, **90:** 239

M

M1 and M2. See **Bank; Economics**
Mabus, Ray, 92: 405
Macaulay, David, 92: 286, 288
MacDonald, Peter, 92: 247, **91:** 324, **90:** 331
Macedonia, 92: 473, 475
MacGuire Seven, 91: 389
Machine tools. See **Manufacturing**
Mackenzie River Valley, 91: 390
Mackintosh, Cameron, 91: 452-453
MacMurray, Fred, 92: 174
Mad cow disease, 91: 312
Madagascar: demonstrations, **92:** 44-45; elections, **90:** 162; facts in brief, **92:** 47, **91:** 159, **90:** 161
Madani, Abassi, 92: 50-51
MADIGAN, EDWARD R., 92: 291
Madison, Wis., 92: 329
Madonna (singer), 91: 408, **90:** 156, 413
Madrid peace conference, 92: 314-315
Mafia, 92: 257, **91:** 259, 261, 332, **90:** 339
MAGAZINE, 92: 291-292, **91:** 358-359, **90:** 367-368. See also **Awards and prizes**
***Magellan* (spacecraft), 92:** 75-76, **91:** 76, 180-181, 432, **90:** 437-438
Magharian, Barkev and Jean, 91: 446, **90:** 452
Maglev train, 91: 238, 417
Magnetic confinement, 90: 119-121
Magnetic field of Earth, 92: 228
Mahathir bin Mohamad, 92: 292-293, **91:** 359, **90:** 183, 368
Mahgoub, Rifaat, 91: 284
Mahoney, Larry W., 90: 257
MAHONY, ROGER M. CARDINAL, 92: 292
Maida, Adam, 91: 274
Mail bombs, 90: 259
Maine, 92: 404, **91:** 439, **90:** 444
MAJOR, JOHN, 92: 140, 231-232, **91:** 310, 311, 359
Major Indoor Soccer League, 91: 429
Malawi: facts in brief, **92:** 47, **91:** 159, **90:** 161; life expectancy, **90:** 415; Mozambique, **91:** 377
MALAYSIA, 92: 292-293, **91:** 359, **90:** 368; boat people, **91:** 177; facts in brief, **92:** 73, **91:** 179, **90:** 182; free-trade area, **92:** 71; industrialization, **91:** 103-104, 110-111, 115-119; refugees, **92:** 72; U.S. bases in Philippines, **90:** 183
Maldives: facts in brief, **92:** 73, **91:** 179, **90:** 182; India troops, **90:** 181
Mali: facts in brief, **92:** 47, **91:** 159, **90:** 161; rebellion, **92:** 42, 44
Mallon, Meg, 92: 230
Malta: Bush-Gorbachev summit, **90:** 216; facts in brief, **92:** 205, **91:** 295, **90:** 298
***Mambo Kings Play Songs of Love, The* (Hijuelos), 90:** 359
Mammograms, 90: 372
Mammoth ivory, 92: 328-329
Manatees, 92: 478
MANDELA, NELSON, 92: 393-394, **91:** 156, 249 (il.), 274, 360, 383, 430, **90:** 436
Mandela, Winnie, 92: 394
***Maniac Magee* (Spinelli), 92:** 288
MANITOBA, 92: 293, **91:** 360, **90:** 369; American Indians, **90:** 331; Meech Lake Accord, **91:** 220-221, **90:** 221
Manley, Michael N., 90: 483-484
Mann, Jack, 92: 233, 317
Manning, Patrick, 92: 470
Manuel Rodríguez Patriot Front, 92: 140
MANUFACTURING, 92: 293-296, **91:** 360-362, **90:** 369-371; U.S.S.R., **90:** 56-63. See also **Labor; Technology**
Mao Zedong, 92: 142
Maoris, 91: 381
Mapplethorpe, Robert, 91: 174, **90:** 177
Mara, Ratu Sir Kamisese, 92: 338, **91:** 393, **90:** 403
Maradona, Diego, 92: 391
Marcos, Ferdinand E., 92: 361, **91:** 259, 402, **90:** 409, 410
Marcos, Imelda, 92: 68, 361, **91:** 258-259, 402, **90:** 410 (il.)
Marcy, Pat, 91: 232
Marfan's syndrome, 92: 93, 236
Margrethe II, 92: 181 (il.)
Marijuana, 92: 185, **91:** 277, **90:** 279
Marine Corps, U.S. See **Armed forces**
***Mariner* space probes, 91:** 73, 76-77
Marino, Eugene A., 91: 421
Marković, Ante, 92: 471, **91:** 479-480, **90:** 485
Markowitz, Harry M., 91: 388
Maronite Christians, 90: 355-356
Marriage age, 92: 134
"Married...With Children," 90: 456
Mars, 91: 69-78, **90:** 184, 438
Marshall, Donald, Jr., 91: 390
Marshall, Thurgood, 92: 409-410
Marshall Islands, 92: 339, 448
Martens, Wilfried, 92: 92
***Martha Stewart Living* (magazine), 92:** 292
MARTIN, LYNN M., 92: 269, 296, **91:** 470
Martin, Mary, 91: 269
Martinez, Bob, 90: 445
Martins, Peter, 92: 167-168
Marxist People's Liberation Front, 91: 436
Maryland, 92: 404, **91:** 439, **90:** 444
Masloff, Sophie, 90: 237
Mass transit. See **Transit**
Massachusetts, 92: 404, **91:** 439, **90:** 444; art, **92:** 67; economy and taxes, **91:** 438, **90:** 445; election, **92:** 194; gay rights, **90:** 239; health, **92:** 403; libraries, **92:** 280; schools, **90:** 284
Massachusetts Institute of Technology, 92: 192
Massawa, 91: 291
Masters tournament. See **Golf**
Masur, Kurt, 92: 149
Mathematics ability, 90: 420
Matignon Accord, 90: 402
Matsushita Electrical Industrial Co., 91: 286
Mauritania: facts in brief, **92:** 47, **91:** 159, **90:** 161; Senegal, **92:** 390, **90:** 162, 433
Mauritius: assassination attempt, **90:** 162; facts in brief, **92:** 47, **91:** 159, **90:** 161
Maxwell, Robert, 92: 174, 269, 329
Maya, 92: 53
Mazankowski, Donald F., 92: 110
Mazda Motor Corp., 91: 185, **90:** 188, 189
MAZOWIECKI, TADEUSZ, 91: 404-405, **90:** 371, 412
MCA Inc., 91: 286
McBride, Patricia, 90: 262
McCain, John, III, 92: 158, **91:** 197
McCarthy, John, 92: 233, 314 (il.), 316, 449
McCartney, Paul, 92: 150
McCray, Anton, 91: 257
McDougall, Barbara J., 92: 110
McEntire, Reba, 92: 366
McFarlane, Robert C., 90: 335
McGriff, Deborah, 92: 182
McIlvane, Thomas, 92: 164
McKee, Rae Ellen, 92: 191 (il.)
McKenna, Frank J., 92: 323, **91:** 379
McKinney, Tamara, 91: 427, **90:** 434
McKinney Homeless Assistance Act, 90: 106
McKissick, Floyd B., 92: 174
McLACHLIN, BEVERLEY MARY, 90: 371
McMartin Pre-School, 91: 258
Mears, Rick, 92: 80, **90:** 189
Measles, 91: 415, **90:** 421
Mecca, 91: 426, **90:** 432
Medellín drug cartel, 92: 151, 276, **91:** 332
Medfly, 91: 357, **90:** 367
Media. See **Communications; Magazine; Newspaper; Television**
Medicaid, 92: 240, 403
Medical waste, 90: 324-325
Medicare, 92: 240, 392, **91:** 318, 429, 447-448
MEDICINE, 92: 296-297, **91:** 362-364, **90:** 372-374; labor disputes, **92:** 291, 293; Nobel Prizes, **92:** 332-333, **91:** 389, **90:** 397. See also **Drugs; Genetic medicine; Health and disease; Hospital; Mental health; Nobel Prizes; Social security**
Medina, Saudi Arabia, 91: 426
Meech Lake Accord, 92: 107-110, 120, **91:** 220-221, 360, 416, **90:** 221
Meese, Edwin, III, 90: 476
Mehta, Zubin, 92: 149
Meier, Richard, 92: 61
Melanoma, 92: 306, **90:** 320
Meles Zenawi, 92: 201
Memory, 91: 121-133, 413-414
Memphis, 92: 194, 424, **90:** 234
Mendes, Francisco (Chico), 91: 346-347
Mendoza Vallecillos, Yusshy René, 92: 195
MENEM, CARLOS SAÚL, 92: 62, **91:** 170, **90:** 173, 374
Mengistu Haile-Mariam, 92: 42-44, 201, **91:** 157, 291, **90:** 162, 296
MENTAL HEALTH, 92: 310, **91:** 364, **90:** 374-375; homelessness, **90:** 101-102, 374
Mental illness. See **Mental health; Psychology**

Mental retardation, 92: 236, **90:** 374
Mercosur, 92: 273
Mercredi, Ovide, 92: 111-112
Mercury (planet), 91: 70-73, 181
Mergers and acquisitions: airlines, **90:** 191-192; bank, **92:** 86; communications media, **91:** 358, **90:** 244; electronics industry, **91:** 286; Japanese investment in U.S., **90:** 341, 390; San Diego utility proposal, **92:** 387
Mesić, Stjepan, 92: 470-471
Mesopotamia, 92: 56-57
Messeturm, 91: 211
Meteorites: Antarctica, **90:** 129; extinctions, **92:** 340, **91:** 306-307
Meteorology. See **Weather**
Methanol, 90: 242, 290-291
Methodist Church, 92: 375
Métis, 91: 390
Metro Blue Line, 91: 458
Metropolitan Museum of Art, 92: 68
Metropolitan Opera, 92: 149
MEXICO, 92: 310-311, **91:** 365, **90:** 375; drug trafficking, **92:** 276, 311, **90:** 375; facts in brief, **92:** 275, **91:** 345, **90:** 353; foreign debt, **90:** 332, 375; free-trade areas, **92:** 249, 273-274, 310; illegal immigration, **91:** 322, **90:** 328; Japanese investments, **91:** 344-346; mining strike, **90:** 381; Spain, **91:** 433; U.S. trade, **92:** 310, **91:** 326-327, 365, **90:** 375. See also **Salinas de Gortari, Carlos**
Meyerbeer, Giacomo, 92: 148
Meyerson Symphony Center, 90: 212
Miami, 92: 146, 424, **90:** 235
Miami, University of, 90: 306, 308, 310
Miami Metrozoo, 91: 483
MIA's. See **Missing in action**
Michelangelo, 91: 173 (il.)
Michigan, 92: 404, **91:** 439, **90:** 444; welfare, **92:** 469
Mickey Mouse, 91: 144
Micronesia, 92: 339, 448
Microsoft Corp., 92: 152
MIDDLE EAST, 92: 313-317, **91:** 366-370, **90:** 376-380; ivory trade, **91:** 46; peace conference, **92:** 103, 193, 255-256, 313-316, 389, 412-413. See also **Islam; Persian Gulf crisis and War; Petroleum and gas;** and specific countries
Midgetman missile, 90: 175
Midland Cogeneration Venture, 91: 287-288
Midler, Bette, 92: 321 (il.)
Midway Airlines, 92: 82
Milk production, 90: 303
Milken, Michael R., 91: 258, 441, **90:** 259
Milky Way galaxy, 91: 181
Miller, Merton H., 91: 388
Miller, Mike, 92: 95
Miller, Tim, 91: 174
Miller-Mackie, Dana, 91: 207
Milli Vanilli, 91: 407
Millie (dog), 91: 276, **90:** 278 (il.)
Milośević, Slobodan, 92: 471, 475
Milutinovic, Bora, 92: 391
Milwaukee, 92: 163-164, **91:** 238
Mimas (moon), 91: 83 (il.)
Mini Disc, 92: 195
Minimum wage, 90: 252, 349
MINING, 92: 317, **91:** 371, **90:** 380-381; ancient mines, **90:** 170-171; Antarctica, **90:** 135-136; Australia, **92:** 77; Bougainville, **90:** 402; disaster in Kentucky, **91:** 423, **90:** 380. See also **Coal; Labor; Petroleum and gas**
Minneapolis, Minn., 90: 234-235
Minnesota, 92: 404, **91:** 439, **90:** 444; abortion law, **91:** 438, 443; zoos, **92:** 478
Minnesota North Stars, 92: 237-238
Minnesota Twins, 92: 86-87
Minority groups. See **Blacks; Civil rights; Hispanic Americans; Indian, American**
Mir **(space station), 92:** 327 (il.), 396, **90:** 438
Miranda (moon), 91: 70, 84
Mishkutienok, Natalia, 92: 242
Miss America pageant, 91: 385
Miss Saigon **(musical), 92:** 418, **91:** 452-453
Missiles. See **Armed forces; Nuclear weapons; Patriot missile; Scud missiles; Tomahawk cruise missile**
Missing in action, 92: 453, **91:** 343, **90:** 349
Mississippi, 92: 404, **91:** 439, **90:** 444; elections, **92:** 383, 405; Indian protest, **92:** 246 (il.); voting rights, **90:** 238
Missouri, 92: 404, **91:** 439, **90:** 444; abortion law, **90:** 425; right-to-die case, **91:** 442
MITCHELL, GEORGE JOHN, 90: 381
Mitochondrial DNA, 92: 52, **91:** 204
MITSOTAKIS, CONSTANTINE, 92: 233, **91:** 312, 371
Mitterrand, François, 92: 163, 225, **91:** 292, 296, 305, **90:** 299, 310-311
MIYAZAWA, KIICHI, 92: 259, 261, 317
Mladenov, Petur T., 91: 212, **90:** 214
Mnemonic devices, 91: 132-133
Moawad, René, 90: 356, 379
Mobil Corp., 90: 407
Mobile computers, 92: 152
Mobutu Sese Seko, 92: 45, 476
Moderate Party (Sweden), 92: 411
Modern pentathlon, 92: 401, **91:** 435, **90:** 441
Modrow, Hans, 90: 314
Mohamed, Ali Mahdi, 92: 392
Mohawk Indians, 91: 217-219, 325, 372-373, **90:** 331
Moi, Daniel T. arap, 92: 44, 263, **91:** 46, 160, 338, **90:** 253, 344
Moldavia, 92: 202, 435, **91:** 296 (il.). See also **Moldova**
Moldova, 92: 435, 438
Mole (machine), 92: 427-428
Molecular biology, 92: 302
Molina, Gloria, 92: 290
Momenta International, 92: 152
Monaco, 92: 205, **91:** 295, **90:** 298
Mondello, Keith, 91: 258
Monet, Claude, 91: 175
Money. See **Bank; Economics; International trade**
Mongol People's Revolutionary Party, 91: 371-372
MONGOLIA, 91: 371-372; facts in brief, **92:** 73, **91:** 179, **90:** 182; U.S.S.R., **92:** 71, **90:** 181
Moniba, Harry, 92: 278
Monkey, Rare, 91: 481-482
Monnaie Dance Group, 91: 264
Monrovia, Liberia, 92: 279, **91:** 348-349
Montana, 92: 404, **91:** 439, **90:** 444; schools, **90:** 445
Montana, Claude, 92: 218 (il.), **91:** 299-300
Montana, Joe, 92: 221, **91:** 302
Montand, Yves, 92: 175
Montazeri, Ayatollah Hussein Ali, 90: 333
Montenegro, 92: 473-475
MONTREAL, 92: 318, **91:** 372-373, **90:** 381-382; Indian affairs, **91:** 217-218, 372-373
Montreal, University of, 90: 222, 258, 381
Montreal Expos, 92: 318, **91:** 373
Montreal Protocol, 90: 292
Moody, Orville, 90: 315
Moon, 91: 70, 433
Moon Ik Hwan, 90: 345
Moons, in solar system, 91: 78-85
Moore, Charles W., 92: 61
Moore, Michael K., 91: 381
Moran, Mary C., 92: 142, 143
More Opposites **(Wilbur), 92:** 363
Moreira, Marcilio Marques, 92: 97
Morgan, Elizabeth, 91: 383
Moriyama, Mayumi, 90: 340
MOROCCO, 92: 318-319, **91:** 373-374, **90:** 382; facts in brief, **92:** 47, **91:** 159, **90:** 161; Western Sahara, **92:** 44, 319, 448, **91:** 374, **90:** 382
Morris, Jack, 92: 86-88
Morris, Mark, 91: 264, **90:** 264
Mortality rates: cancer, **91:** 415; veterans hospitals, **90:** 478
MOSBACHER, ROBERT ADAM, 92: 126, **90:** 383
Moscow: coup attempt, **92:** 432-435; Eastern Orthodox patriarch, **91:** 279; Gorbachev policies, **90:** 54, 56; nuclear safety meeting, **90:** 291
Moser, Constanze, 90: 328
Motherland Party. See **ANAP**
MOTION PICTURES, 92: 319-322, **91:** 374-377, **90:** 383-386; awards, **92:** 320, **91:** 189, **90:** 193; Bates, Kathy, **92:** 92; commercials, **91:** 155; Costner, Kevin, **92:** 161; Hoffman, Dustin, **90:** 323; Irons, Jeremy, **92:** 254; Japanese moviemaking, **90:** 288; Lee, Spike, **90:** 356; Roberts, Julia, **92:** 383. See also **Animated film**
Motivated forgetting, 91: 126-127
Motorcycle racing, 92: 401, **91:** 435, **90:** 441
Motorcycle safety helmets, 92: 387
Mount Pinatubo, 92: 199, 226, 360, 361
Mount Unzen, 92: 226
Movement for Rights and Freedom, 92: 101
Moynihan, Daniel Patrick, 92: 391-392, 414, **91:** 272, 468-469
MOZAMBIQUE, 91: 377, **90:** 387; civil war, **92:** 44, **91:** 157, **90:** 158-162; facts in brief, **92:** 47, **91:** 159, **90:** 161; ivory trade, **90:** 253
Mozambique National Resistance. See **Renamo**
Mozart, Wolfgang Amadeus, 92: 148
MPLA, 91: 165, **90:** 166-167
Ms. **magazine, 92:** 292
Mubarak, Hosni, 92: 193, **91:** 284, **90:** 286, 377
Mugabe, Robert Gabriel, 91: 481, **90:** 163
MULRONEY, BRIAN, 92: 322, **91:** 377, **90:** 387; appointments, **92:** 110-111, **91:** 219, 222, **90:** 222; economic issues, **91:** 219, **90:** 219; foreign relations, **92:** 112, **91:** 223, **90:** 219 (il.), 223; popularity, **91:** 217, **90:** 219; Prince Edward Island, **91:** 409; Quebec controversy, **92:** 107, 120, **91:** 220-221
Multimedia technology, 92: 152, **91:** 248
Multistage flash distillation, 92: 455
Mundy, Carl E., Jr., 92: 67
Muñoz Marín, Luis, 91: 60
Munro, Alice, 91: 224
Muon, 90: 122-123
Muppets, 91: 268-269, **90:** 463
Murder. See **Crime**
Murdoch, Rupert, 90: 82-83, 89, 367
Murphy, Eddie, 91: 384
Murray, Joseph E., 91: 389
Musa Hitam, 90: 368
Muscular dystrophy, 92: 304-305
Museum of Contemporary Art (Los Angeles), 92: 61, 69
Museum of Modern Art (New York City), 92: 69
Museums. See **Art**
Music. See **Classical music; Popular music**
Music videos. See **Popular music**
Musicals. See **Theater**
Muslims. See **Islam; Islamic fundamentalists**
My Left Foot **(film), 91:** 264
Myanmar. See **Burma**

N

Nagorno-Karabakh, 91: 464, **90:** 65, 469
Najibullah, 92: 41, **91:** 155, **90:** 157
Namaliu, Rabbie, 91: 394
NAMIBIA, 91: 378, **90:** 387-388; facts in brief, **92:** 47, **91:** 159, **90:** 161; prehuman fossils, **92:** 52; Protestantism, **91:** 411; UN actions, **91:** 467, **90:** 471. See also **Nujoma, Sam**
NASA. See **National Aeronautics and Space Administration**
NASCAR. See **Automobile racing**
Nash, Clarence, 90: 385
Nashville Zoo, 92: 477
National, The **(newspaper), 92:** 329, **91:** 386
National Academy of Recording Arts and Sciences. See **Grammy Awards**
National Academy of Television Arts and Sciences. See **Emmy Awards**
National Aeronautics and Space Administration: satellites, **92:** 394, 396, **91:** 433, **90:** 439; space probes, **92:** 394, **91:** 181, **90:** 183; space station, **92:** 394-396, 451. See also ***Hubble Space Telescope;*** **Space shuttle**
National Affordable Housing Act (1990), 91: 253
National Association of Purchasing Management index. See **Manufacturing**
National Basketball Association. See **Basketball**
National Board for Professional Teaching Standards, 90: 284
National Broadcasting Co., 92: 40, 415-416, **91:** 448-450, **90:** 73-86, 454-457
National Civil Rights Museum, 92: 147
National Coal Association. See **Coal**
National Collegiate Athletic Association, 92: 89-91, 400-401, **91:** 200-201, 434, **90:** 203-204, 440
National Council of Churches, 90: 419
National defense. See **Armed forces** and specific countries
National Educational Goals Panel, 92: 190
National Endowment for the Arts, 92: 67, 68, **91:** 173-174, 411-412, 453, **90:** 177-178
National Film Registry, 92: 322, **90:** 384
National Football League. See **Football**
National Gallery (London), 92: 60
National Health Service (Great Britain), 92: 232, **90:** 317, 325
National Hockey League. See **Hockey**
National Institutes of Health, 92: 300, 303, 305-306
National Islamic Front, 91: 442
National League of Democracy, 92: 101, **91:** 212-213
National Organization for Women, 92: 327
National Origins Act, 91: 91-93
National Party: New Zealand, **91:** 381; South Africa, **91:** 431, **90:** 436-437
National Patriotic Front of Liberia, 92: 278-279, **91:** 348
National Salvation Front, 92: 386, **91:** 422
Native Americans Day, 91: 324
NATO. See **North Atlantic Treaty Organization**
Natural gas. See **Energy supply; Petroleum and gas**
Nauru, 91: 394-395, **90:** 403; facts in brief, **92:** 338, **91:** 394, **90:** 402
Navajo, 92: 247, **91:** 324, **90:** 331
Navarro Wolff, Antonio, 92: 151

Navratilova, Martina, 92: 416, 417, **91:** 450, 451, **90:** 458
Navy, U.S. See **Armed forces**
NBA. See **Basketball**
NBC. See **National Broadcasting Co.**
NCA. See **Coal**
NCAA. See **National Collegiate Athletic Association**
NCC. See **National Council of Churches**
NDP. See **New Democratic Party**
Ne Win, 90: 214
NEA. See **National Endowment for the Arts**
Neanderthals, 90: 168
Nebraska, 92: 404, **91:** 439, **90:** 444
Neghme, Jacar, 90: 229
Neher, Erwin, 92: 333
NEPAL, 91: 379; elections, **92:** 72; facts in brief, **92:** 73, **91:** 179, **90:** 182; India, **90:** 181
Neptune, 91: 69-73, 84-85, **90:** 183-184, 312, 437
Nerette, Joseph, 92: 234
Nesty, Anthony, 92: 411
NETHERLANDS, 92: 322-323, **91:** 379, **90:** 388; facts in brief, **92:** 205, **91:** 295, **90:** 298
Neurofibromatosis, 91: 315
Neutrino, 92: 362, **91:** 402-403, **90:** 410-411
Neutron stars, 92: 76
Nevada, 92: 404, **91:** 439, **90:** 444; population growth, **92:** 131, **91:** 227
NEW BRUNSWICK, 92: 323, **91:** 220, 379, **90:** 389
New Caledonia, 91: 395, **90:** 402-403
New Democratic Party (Canada), 91: 219, 222, **90:** 219; Alberta, **90:** 166; British Columbia, **92:** 98; Ontario, **92:** 336, **91:** 392-393; Saskatchewan, **92:** 388; Toronto, **91:** 454; Yukon Territory, **90:** 485
New Hampshire, 92: 404, **91:** 439, **90:** 444
New Jersey, 92: 404, **91:** 439, **90:** 444; art, **92:** 67; education, **91:** 283, 437-438, **90:** 284, 445; elections, **92:** 194, 383, 405, **90:** 287; gun control, **91:** 438
New Kids on the Block, 91: 407, 455, **90:** 414
New Mexico, 92: 404, **91:** 439, **90:** 444
New Orleans, 92: 424, **91:** 237, 482
New People's Army (Philippines), 91: 401
New Progressive Party (Puerto Rico), 91: 65
New York (state), 92: 404, **91:** 439, **90:** 444; art, **92:** 67; Ellis Island, **91:** 87-101
NEW YORK CITY, 92: 323-324, **91:** 380-381, **90:** 389-390; architecture, **92:** 61-62, **91:** 169, **90:** 173; art, **92:** 68, 69, **91:** 174, 175, **90:** 177; census and population, **92:** 126, 145, **91:** 227, 228; classical music, **92:** 148-150, **90:** 239, 241; crime, **92:** 162, **91:** 242, 257-259, **90:** 238-239, 258-259, 390; Democratic National Convention, **91:** 272-273; libraries, **92:** 279, **91:** 349; newspapers, **92:** 269, **91:** 341-342, 381, 386; schools, **92:** 192; subway crash, **92:** 323, 324 (il.), 424; theater, **92:** 418-420; transit, **90:** 465; zoos, **92:** 477, **91:** 483, **90:** 486. See also **Dinkins, David Norman**
New York City Ballet, 92: 167-168, **91:** 264, **90:** 262-263
***New York Daily News,* 92:** 269, 329
New York Giants, 92: 221, **91:** 302
New York Shakespeare Festival, 92: 418, **91:** 453
NEW ZEALAND, 92: 325, **91:** 381, **90:** 390; boating, **90:** 207; facts in brief, **92:** 338, **91:** 394, **90:** 402. See also **Bolger, James Brendan**
Newark, N.J., 91: 239, **90:** 235
Newbery Medal. See **Literature for children**
NEWFOUNDLAND, 92: 325, **91:** 381, **90:** 390; Meech Lake Accord, **91:** 221. See also **Wells, Clyde Kirby**
News re-creations, 90: 456
NEWSMAKERS, 92: 325-329, **91:** 382-385, **90:** 391-394. See also **Deaths**
NEWSPAPER, 92: 329, **91:** 386, **90:** 395; Los Angeles, **90:** 367; New York City, **92:** 269, **91:** 341-342, 381, 386; U.S.S.R., **90:** 64. See also **Awards and prizes**
NFL. See **Football**
NICARAGUA, 92: 330-331, **91:** 386-387, **90:** 395-396; cease-fire with contras, **91:** 467, **90:** 350-352; common market, **92:** 274; El Salvador, **90:** 289; facts in brief, **92:** 275, **91:** 345, **90:** 353; U.S. aid to contras, **90:** 216, 396. See also **Chamorro, Violeta B. de; Contras**
***Nick and Nora* (musical), 92:** 418
Nicklaus, Jack, 92: 230, **91:** 309
Nielsen, Leslie, 92: 40
Nielsen ratings, 92: 415, **91:** 449
Niger, 92: 47, **91:** 159, **90:** 161
NIGERIA, 92: 331, **91:** 387-388, **90:** 396; democratic reform, **91:** 157; facts in brief, **92:** 47, **91:** 159, **90:** 161
Night Stalker murders, 90: 257
Nightmares, 91: 413
NIH. See **National Institutes of Health**
Nikkei stock index. See **Stocks and bonds**
Ninn-Hansen, Erik, 92: 180
Nintendo of America, Inc., 92: 421, **90:** 462
Nippon Steel Corp., 91: 440
Nissan Motor Co., 92: 196, **91:** 185, **90:** 188, 189, 346
Nitrates, 92: 462
Nitrogen-fixing bacteria, 90: 208
Nixon, Richard, 92: 104 (il.)
Nixon, Walter L., Jr., 90: 476
NOBEL PRIZES, 92: 331-333, **91:** 388-389, **90:** 397
Noble, Alexandre, 91: 401
Nofziger, Lyn, 90: 476
Noise, Aircraft, 92: 83, **91:** 188
Nondurable goods. See **Manufacturing**
Nonsteroidal anti-inflammatory drugs, 90: 280
Noriega, Manuel Antonio, 92: 162, 276, 341, **91:** 397-398, **90:** 216, 404
North, Oliver L., 92: 251, 451, **91:** 329, **90:** 335
North American Free Trade Agreement, 92: 249, 273, 310
North Atlantic Treaty Organization: France, **91:** 305, **90:** 310; future role, **92:** 202-204, **91:** 292-294, **90:** 297-299; German reunification, **91:** 292, 307-309; U.S. troop cut plan, **90:** 175, 215-216
North Carolina, 92: 404, **91:** 439, **90:** 444
North Dakota, 92: 404, **91:** 439, **90:** 444
North Korea. See **Korea, North**
"Northern Exposure," 92: 415 (il.)
NORTHERN IRELAND, 92: 333, **91:** 389, **90:** 398
Northern Rhodesia. See **Zambia**
Northwest Airlines, 92: 82-83
NORTHWEST TERRITORIES, 92: 334, **91:** 390, **90:** 399
Norton, Eleanor Holmes, 91: 474
Norville, Deborah, 90: 454
NORWAY, 92: 334-335, **91:** 390, **90:** 399; European trade, **92:** 206; facts in brief, **92:** 205, **91:** 295, **90:** 298
Notre Dame, University of, 91: 434, **90:** 308, 310
Nouhak Phounsavanh, 90: 349
NOVA SCOTIA, 92: 335, **91:** 390, **90:** 399. See also **Bacon, Roger Stuart; Cameron, Donald**
Novello, Antonia C., 91: 414 (il.), **90:** 421, 473
Novotna, Jana, 92: 417
NOW. See **National Organization for Women**
NSAID's. See **Nonsteroidal anti-inflammatory drugs**
Nuclear energy, 92: 196-197, **91:** 287-288, **90:** 291; Cuba, **92:** 166; energy crisis, **90:** 110, 112. See also **Nuclear fusion**
Nuclear fission. See **Nuclear energy**
Nuclear fusion, 90: 118-123, 225-226
Nuclear magnetic resonance spectroscopy, 92: 332
Nuclear weapons: Brazil, **91:** 209; Germany, West, **90:** 314; Iraq, **92:** 313, **91:** 330; Korea, North, **92:** 264; plant safety, **90:** 432; U.S.S.R. collapse, **92:** 103, 439-440. See also **Arms control; Strategic Defense Initiative**
NUJOMA, SAM, 91: 378, 391, **90:** 388, 471
***Numbat* (rescue vehicle), 92:** 317
Nureyev, Rudolf, 90: 263, 264
Nursing homes, 90: 375
Nussbaum, Hedda, 90: 256-257
Nutrition and Labeling Act (1990), 92: 216, 220
N.W.A. (pop group), 92: 370
NWA Inc., 90: 192, 347
Nyers, Rezso, 90: 326

O

Oakland, Calif., 92: 143 (il.), 145-146, **91:** 238-239, **90:** 235-237
Oakland Athletics, 92: 237, **91:** 198-200, **90:** 201-202
OAS. See **Organization of American States**
OAU. See **Organization of African Unity**
Obeid, Abdul-Karim, 90: 356, 379
Obesity, 92: 377
Obituaries. See **Deaths**
O'Brien, Dan, 92: 423, 424
Obscenity: art, **92:** 68, **91:** 173-174, 411-412, 453; popular music, **92:** 370, **91:** 406; telephone pornography, **90:** 244
Obsessive-compulsive disorder, 91: 364
Occupational Safety and Health Administration. See **Safety**
OCEAN, 92: 335-336, **91:** 391-392, **90:** 400-401; Antarctica, **90:** 127, 136; geological studies, **91:** 306, 392, **90:** 400; *WBE,* **90:** 518. See also **Fishing industry**
O'Connor, Sinéad, 91: 407
Odinga, Oginga, 92: 263
Office automation, 90: 245
Office of Management and Budget, 92: 391
Ohio, 92: 404, **91:** 439, **90:** 444; abortion law, **91:** 443
Oil. See **Petroleum and gas**
Oil spills: *Bahia Paraiso,* **90:** 126, 294; cleanup plan, **91:** 400; *Exxon Valdez,* **91:** 259, 290, **90:** 108, 294-295, 406; Persian Gulf War, **92:** 197-198, 335, 355, 389, 455
Oil well fires, 92: 197-198, 266, 355, 357
Oklahoma, 92: 404, **91:** 439, **90:** 444
Olav V, 92: 335
Old age. See **Aging; Social security**
Old-Age and Survivors Insurance Trust Fund. See **Social security**
Older Workers Benefit Protection Act (1990), 91: 240
***Oldest Living Confederate Widow Tells All* (Gurganus), 90:** 359
Olivier, Laurence, 90: 268
Olson, Lisa, 91: 302
OLYMPIC GAMES, 92: 336, **91:** 392, **90:** 401; Atlanta, **91:** 239; Spain, **92:** 397, 399; Toronto bid, **91:** 454, **90:** 462
Olympic Stadium (Montreal), 92: 318
Olympus Mons (Mars), 91: 77, 80 (il.)
Omaha, Nebr., 91: 483
O'Malley, Desmond, 90: 337
Oman: facts in brief, **92:** 316, **91:** 370, **90:** 378; methanol, **90:** 290-291
"One Nation, Many Peoples" (report), 92: 192
Ong Teng Cheong, 91: 178
ONTARIO, 92: 336-337, **91:** 392-393, **90:** 401; Indian affairs, **92:** 246, 337. See also **Rae, Robert Keith**
OPEC. See **Petroleum and gas**
Opera. See **Classical music**
Operation Desert Shield, 92: 345, **91:** 170, 214. See also **Persian Gulf crisis and War**
Operation Desert Storm, 92: 342-355. See also **Persian Gulf crisis and War**
Operation Greylord, 92: 140
Operation Just Cause, 90: 173, 404
Optometry, 91: 257
Orchirbat, Punsalmaagiyn, 91: 371, 372
Oregon, 92: 404, **91:** 439, **90:** 444; education, **92:** 402; health, **92:** 403
Organ transplantation, 91: 204, 278, 389, **90:** 373
Organic Act. See **Foraker Act**
Organization of African Unity, 92: 48, 449, **91:** 157
Organization of American States, 92: 234, 235, 470, **90:** 352
Organization of Petroleum Exporting Countries. See **Petroleum and gas**
Organization of the Islamic Conference, 92: 331
Oriental Orthodox churches, 90: 281
Oriole Park at Camden Yards, 92: 62
Orlando, Fla., 91: 383
Ortega, Daniel, 92: 331, **91:** 229, **90:** 352, 395
Ortega Saavedra, Humberto, 91: 386
"Oscars." See **Academy Awards**
OSHA. See **Safety**
Osteoporosis, 91: 278, **90:** 373
Oświęcim. See **Auschwitz**
Otto, Kristin, 90: 451
Oueddei, Goukouni, 91: 229
***Ouranopithecus,* 91:** 165
Overdraft of aquifer, 92: 464
***Oxford English Dictionary,* 90:** 363
Özal, Turgut, 92: 430, 431, **91:** 459, **90:** 467
Ozawa, Ichiro, 92: 261
Ozio, David, 92: 95
Ozone hole, 92: 199, **91:** 289-290, **90:** 130-132, 292

P

PACIFIC ISLANDS, 92: 337-339, **91:** 393-395, **90:** 402-403
Pacific Ocean. See **Ocean**
Pacific rim nations, 91: 103-119
Packer, Kerry F. B., 91: 182
Paddle tennis, 90: 441
Page, Ruth, 92: 175
Paisley, Melvin R., 92: 451
PAKISTAN, 92: 339, **91:** 395-396, **90:** 403; Afghanistan, **92:** 41, **91:** 155, 177-178; facts in brief, **92:** 73, **91:** 179, **90:** 182; Rushdie affair, **90:** 362. See also **Sharif, Nawaz**
Palau, 91: 395
PALEONTOLOGY, 92: 340, **91:** 396, **90:** 404. See also **Anthropology; Archaeology; Fossils; Geology**
Palestine. See **Israel; Jordan; Middle East**

Palestine Liberation Organization: Arab-Israeli conflict, **92:** 256, **90:** 337, 376-377, 432; Lebanon, **92:** 278; Middle East peace conference, **92:** 314, 315; Persian Gulf crisis and War, **92:** 345, **91:** 368; Syria, **90:** 452; United Nations, **90:** 472-473
Palestinians: Egypt, **91:** 284; Jewish attitudes toward Israel, **91:** 336; Jordan, **90:** 343; Middle East peace conference, **92:** 314-316; occupied territories, **92:** 256-257, **91:** 331-332, 368-369, **90:** 337-338, 376-378; Saudi Arabia, **90:** 432; UN action, **91:** 467-468. See also **Gaza Strip and West Bank**
Palme, Olof, 90: 451
Pamyat, 91: 336
Pan American Games, 92: 165, 400
Pan American World Airways, 92: 82, 83, 271, **91:** 186
PANAMA, 92: 341, **91:** 397-398, **90:** 404-405; common market, **92:** 274; facts in brief, **92:** 275, **91:** 345, **90:** 353; U.S. invasion, **90:** 173, 216, 352, 404-405; U.S. withdrawal, **91:** 171. See also **Endara, Guillermo; Noriega, Manuel Antonio**
Panda, 90: 487
Panhellenic Socialist Movement, 92: 234, **91:** 312, **90:** 318
Panza di Biumo, Giuseppe, 91: 175
Papandreou, Andreas, 92: 233-234, **90:** 318
Paperback Software International, 91: 248
Papp, Joseph, 92: 418, **91:** 453
Papua New Guinea: Bougainville rebellion, **92:** 337-338, **91:** 394, **90:** 402; facts in brief, **92:** 73, 338, **91:** 394, **90:** 402
Parachute jumping, 92: 401, **91:** 435, **90:** 441
PARAGUAY, 90: 405; facts in brief, **92:** 275, **91:** 345, **90:** 353; free-trade zone, **92:** 273
Paramount Communications Inc., 90: 244
Paris: architecture, **91:** 168; art, **92:** 68, 69; farm protest, **92:** 213 (il.); fashion, **91:** 299, **90:** 303, 304
Parizeau, Jacques, 91: 416, **90:** 422
Parkinson's disease, 90: 372
Parks, Bert, 91: 385
Parti Québécois, 92: 119, 379, **91:** 416, **90:** 422
Particle accelerator, 90: 410-411
Partisans (Yugoslavia), 92: 474, 475
Party of God. See **Hezbollah**
PASOK. See **Panhellenic Socialist Movement**
Patent genes, 92: 303
Patriarca, Raymond J., Jr., 91: 261
Patrick, Dennis R., 90: 244
Patriot missile, 92: 66, 349 (il.)
Patronage, 91: 442-443
Paul, Wolfgang, 90: 397
Pauley, Jane, 90: 454
Pavin, Corey, 92: 230
Pay-per-view television, 90: 84
Payments, U.S. balance of, 92: 248, **90:** 332
Paz, Octavio, 91: 388
Paz Zamora, Jaime, 91: 206, **90:** 208
PBA. See **Bowling**
PBS. See **Public Broadcasting Service**
PCB's. See **Polychlorinated biphenyls**
Peabody Coal Co., 91: 245
Peace, Nobel Prize for, 92: 331, **91:** 388, **90:** 397
Peace Corps (horse), 90: 324
Pearl Harbor, 92: 261
Peary, Robert E., 90: 391
Pei, I. M., 90: 171
Pen-top computers, 92: 152
Pencak, Jim, 91: 206
Penikett, Antony, 90: 485
Pennsylvania, 92: 404, **91:** 439, **90:** 444; abortion law, **92:** 161, **90:** 445; elections, **92:** 194
Pennsylvania Ballet, 92: 168, 360
Pentagon. See **Armed forces; Defense, U.S. Department of**
Pentagonal (organization), 91: 183
People's Action Party (Singapore), 92: 72
People's Liberation Front (Sri Lanka), 90: 442
People's National Congress Party (Guyana), 92: 234
People's Republic of China. See **China**
Peoria, Ill., 91: 385
PepsiCo Inc., 92: 40
Perestroika: Gorbachev policies, **92:** 444, **91:** 460, 462, 465, **90:** 54-69, 468; Judaism in U.S.S.R., **92:** 263
Pérez, Carlos Andrés, 92: 274, 470, **91:** 472, **90:** 352, 477
Pérez de Cuéllar, Javier, 92: 41, 447-449, **91:** 467, **90:** 471
Perkins, Kieren, 92: 411
Permeable rock, 92: 458
Peronist Party, 92: 62
Perrier mineral water, 91: 475
Persian Gulf crisis and War (1990-1991), 92: 342-355, **91:** 366-370; advertising, **92:** 40; African economies, **91:** 160; aftermath, **92:** 313-314; airlines, **92:** 81; ancient treasure damage, **92:** 56-59; armed forces, **92:** 65-67, **91:** 170-171; Asian economies, **91:** 178; Brazil, **91:** 209; Canada, **92:** 112, **91:** 223-224; congressional debate, **92:** 153; Denmark, **91:** 273; Egypt, **92:** 193, **91:** 284; environmental damage, **92:** 197-198, 266, 335, 355, 389, 455; European security concerns, **91:** 294; France, **92:** 224, **91:** 294, 305; Germany, **92:** 228-229; Great Britain, **92:** 231, 232, **91:** 294; Greece, **92:** 234, **91:** 312; Iran, **92:** 344, 345, **91:** 328; Islam, **92:** 254; Israel, **92:** 255, 257, 346, 350; Italy, **91:** 332; Japan, **92:** 259-260, **91:** 334; Jordan, **92:** 262, **91:** 337, 367; Latin-American economies, **91:** 346; Libya, **91:** 350, 368; manufacturing, **92:** 295; Morocco, **92:** 318; New Zealand, **92:** 325; oil supply, **92:** 357, 358, **91:** 186, 399; popular music, **92:** 364; Protestant reactions, **92:** 374; Roman Catholic reactions, **92:** 384; Romania, **91:** 423; Saudi Arabia, **92:** 344, 353, 388, **91:** 366, 426; Shaw, Bernard, **92:** 390; Spain, **92:** 396, **91:** 433; stocks and bonds, **92:** 405, **91:** 441; Sudan, **92:** 406; Syria, **92:** 412, **91:** 446; tax break, **92:** 414; television coverage, **92:** 414; toys, **92:** 421; Tunisia, **92:** 430, **91:** 458; Turkey, **92:** 430-431, **91:** 367, 459; United Nations, **92:** 251, 253, 345, 347, 355, 447, **91:** 330, 366, 466-467; U.S. economy, **91:** 279-280; U.S.S.R., **91:** 465; Venezuela, **91:** 472; Yemen, **91:** 479. See also **Bush, George H. W.; Hussein, Saddam; Iraq; Kuwait; Schwarzkopf, H. Norman, Jr.**
Persistence of vision, 91: 137
Personal computer. See **Computer**
PERU, 92: 356-357, **91:** 398, **90:** 406; ancient buildings, **90:** 354; cholera, **92:** 274, 377; drug trafficking, **92:** 276, 356, **90:** 406; Ecuador, **92:** 274; facts in brief, **92:** 275, **91:** 345, **90:** 353; free-trade zone, **92:** 249, 273; rain forest drilling, **92:** 160. See also **Fujimori, Alberto**
Pesticides, 92: 221, 459-462, **91:** 298, **90:** 293, 301
Petén region, 92: 53
Peterson, David, 91: 392-393, **90:** 401
Petipa, Marius, 92: 167-168
PETROLEUM AND GAS, 92: 357-358, **91:** 399-400, **90:** 406-408; Africa, **91:** 160; Antarctica, **90:** 136; energy crisis, **90:** 108-111; ground water pollution, **92:** 464; jet fuel prices, **91:** 186; labor agreement, **91:** 340; Mexico, **92:** 311; offshore drilling, **92:** 159, **91:** 381, 400; U.S. and foreign oil, **92:** 161, 195, 197; Yukon Territory, **92:** 476. See also **Energy supply; Middle East; Oil spills; Oil well fires; Persian Gulf crisis and War;** and specific countries, provinces, and cities
Pettersson, Carl Gustav Christer, 90: 451
PHILADELPHIA, 92: 358-360, **91:** 400-401, **90:** 408-409; architecture, **92:** 62
Philip Morris Companies, Inc., 90: 157
PHILIPPINES, 92: 360-361, **91:** 401-402, **90:** 409-410; facts in brief, **92:** 73, **91:** 179, **90:** 182; free-trade area, **92:** 71; Mt. Pinatubo, **92:** 199, 226; U.S. bases, **92:** 67, 360-361, **91:** 173, **90:** 181-183
Philips Electronics N. V., 92: 195, **91:** 379
Phillips, Mark, 90: 317
Phillips Petroleum Co., 91: 423
Phobia, 91: 364
***Phobos 2* (spacecraft), 90:** 184, 438
Phoenix, 92: 164-165, **91:** 302
Photography, Newspaper, 90: 395
Photolithography, 92: 138
Photopheresis, 91: 162
Photovoltaic cell, 90: 290
PHYSICS, 92: 362, **91:** 402-403, **90:** 410-411; Nobel Prize, **92:** 332, **91:** 388-389, **90:** 397
Physiology, Nobel Prize for, 92: 332-333, **91:** 389, **90:** 397. See also **Medicine**
Picasso, Pablo, 90: 178
Pierce, Samuel R., Jr., 91: 470, **90:** 474
Pincham, R. Eugene, 92: 139
Pinochet Ugarte, Augusto, 91: 194, 233, **90:** 229
***Pioneer Venus* (spacecraft), 91:** 73, 76
Pit bulls, 91: 276, **90:** 278
Pittsburgh, Pa., 91: 238, **90:** 234
Pittsburgh Penguins, 92: 237-238
***Pittsburgh Post-Gazette*, 90:** 395
Pittsburgh Zoo, 92: 477
Piva, Hugo de Oliveira, 91: 209
Planetesimal, 91: 72
Planets, 92: 76, **91:** 69-85. See also individual planets
Plant. See **Botany; Farm and farming; Forests**
Plate tectonics, 90: 400
Platform tennis, 92: 401, **91:** 435, **90:** 441
PLO. See **Palestine Liberation Organization**
Pluto, 91: 72, 85
Poaching: bear, **90:** 253; elephant, **91:** 36-51, **90:** 253
Poet laureate. See **Poetry**
POETRY, 92: 362-363, **91:** 403-404, **90:** 411. See also **Canadian literature; Literature for children**
Poindexter, John M., 92: 251, 451, **91:** 328, **90:** 335
POLAND, 92: 363-364, **91:** 404-405, **90:** 412; Auschwitz convent, **91:** 421-422, **90:** 342-343, 428; Dutch air pollution plan, **91:** 379; European trade, **92:** 206; facts in brief, **92:** 205, **91:** 295, **90:** 298; mining strike, **90:** 381; pope's visits, **92:** 384; U.S. aid, **90:** 216, 333. See also **Mazowiecki, Tadeusz; Walesa, Lech**
Polhill, Robert, 91: 328
Police: Detroit, **91:** 274; Houston, **90:** 326; Los Angeles, **92:** 290; Miami, **90:** 235; Montreal, **92:** 318; San Diego, **92:** 387, **91:** 425
Polisario Front, 92: 44, **91:** 157, **90:** 166, 380, 382
Politburo (U.S.S.R.), 92: 442, 445, **91:** 465
Political correctness, 92: 192
Political parties. See **Democratic Party; Republican Party;** and other parties
Poll tax (Great Britain), 92: 232, **91:** 310
Pollution. See **Environmental pollution**
Polychlorinated biphenyls, 90: 422
Pons, B. Stanley, 90: 121-122
Pope. See **John Paul II**
Popular Democratic Party (Puerto Rico), 91: 64
POPULAR MUSIC, 92: 364-366, **91:** 406-408, **90:** 413-415; *WBE*, **91:** 538. See also **Jazz; Rap music**
POPULATION, 92: 371, **91:** 408, **90:** 415; cities, **92:** 145; U.S. center, **92:** 325-326. See also **Census; City;** and specific continents, countries, and regions
Pornography. See **Obscenity**
Porous rock, 92: 458
Porter, Cole, 92: 148
Porter, John W., 90: 275
Porter, Sylvia, 92: 175
PORTUGAL, 92: 371, **91:** 408, **90:** 415-416; facts in brief, **92:** 205, **91:** 295, **90:** 298; Ibero-American Summit, **92:** 274-276; pope's visit, **92:** 385 (il.)
Post-Modern architecture, 92: 61
Post-traumatic stress disorder, 92: 310
POSTAL SERVICE, UNITED STATES, 92: 371-372, **91:** 409, **90:** 416; labor pact, **92:** 271; murders, **92:** 164. See also **Stamp collecting**
Potash Corp., 90: 432
Pough, James E., 91: 259
Poverty. See **Homelessness; Welfare**
POWELL, COLIN LUTHER, 92: 66 (il.), 67, 450, **90:** 416
Powell, Mel, 91: 243
Powell, Mike, 92: 422, 424
Power (energy). See **Energy supply**
Powerboating. See **Boating**
Powers, Larry J., 92: 408
Poynter, Jane, 92: 326
PPV. See **Pay-per-view television**
Precious Bunny (horse), 92: 240
Pregnancy, 91: 278, 364, **90:** 142, 279. See also **Childbirth**
Prehistoric people. See **Anthropology; Archaeology**
Premadasa, Ranasinghe, 92: 402, **90:** 442
Presbyterian Church (U.S.A.), 92: 375
President of the U.S. See **Bush, George H. W.**
Press. See **Censorship; Newspaper**
***Pretty Woman* (film), 91:** 374
Previn, André, 90: 239
Price, George C., 90: 484
Prices: oil, **92:** 358, **91:** 399, **90:** 407; stocks, **92:** 405-406, **91:** 441, **90:** 447-448; U.S.S.R., **90:** 60, 63. See also **Consumerism; Economics; Inflation**
Prime interest rate. See **Bank; Interest rates**
PRINCE EDWARD ISLAND, 92: 372, **91:** 409, **90:** 417
Prince William Sound. See ***Exxon Valdez***
PRISON, 92: 372-373, **91:** 409-410, **90:** 417; Great Britain siege, **91:** 312; Mexico drug corruption, **92:** 311
Privatization: Great Britain, **91:** 311; Portugal, **90:** 416; Saskatchewan, **90:** 432
Prizes. See **Awards and prizes**
Procter & Gamble Co., 92: 40
Production sharing (theater), 90: 460-461
Productivity. See **Economics; Manufacturing**
Professional Bowlers Association. See **Bowling**
Professional Coin Grading Service, 91: 245-246
Professional Golfers' Association. See **Golf**
Progressive Conservative Party (Canada), 92: 107, **91:** 217-222, **90:** 219; Alberta, **92:** 50, **91:**

163, **90:** 166; Manitoba, **91:** 360; Nova Scotia, **92:** 335; Saskatchewan, **92:** 388. See also **Bacon, Roger Stuart; Cameron, Donald; Mulroney, Brian**
Prokofiev, Sergei, 92: 148
Property taxes, 92: 191, **90:** 443
Proposition 42, 90: 440
Proposition 103 (California), 90: 446
Prost, Alain, 91: 185, **90:** 189-190
Protein synthesis. See **DNA**
PROTESTANTISM, 92: 373-376, **91:** 410-413, **90:** 418-419; Latin America, **92:** 384, **90:** 419; Spain, **91:** 433. See also **Harris, Barbara C.**
PS/1 Computer, 91: 247-248
Psychiatry. See **Medicine; Mental health**
PSYCHOLOGY, 92: 376-377, **91:** 413-414, **90:** 420-421; twins, **90:** 140-153
Public Against Violence, 92: 166, **91:** 262
Public Broadcasting Service, 92: 149, **91:** 450, **90:** 457
Public Enemy, 92: 368 (il.), 369-370, **90:** 413
PUBLIC HEALTH, 92: 377, **91:** 414-415, **90:** 421
Public transportation. See **City; Transit**
Publishing. See **Canadian literature; Literature; Magazine; Newspaper**
Puerto Rican Federal Relations Act, 91: 61
PUERTO RICO, 92: 378, **91:** 415, **90:** 422; facts in brief, **92:** 275, **91:** 345, **90:** 353; statehood issue, **91:** 52-61
Pugo, Boris K., 92: 432-435
PULITZER PRIZES, 92: 378, **91:** 192-193, **90:** 197
Punjab, India, 92: 245, **91:** 323, **90:** 329
Puppet animation, 91: 137-140
Purdy, Patrick E., 90: 257-258
Puyallup Indians, 91: 324
Pyro Mining Co., 91: 423

Q

Qaboos bin Said, 91: 370
Qadhafi, Muammar Muhammad al-, 92: 455, **91:** 156, 229, 350, **90:** 358-359
Qatar, 92: 316, **91:** 370, **90:** 378
Quaker Oats Co., 90: 156
Quark, 91: 389, **90:** 410
QUAYLE, DAN, 92: 379, **91:** 415, **90:** 422; Republican Party, **92:** 383
QUEBEC, 92: 379, **91:** 416, **90:** 422; energy supply, **90:** 291; secession issue, **92:** 107-110, 113-124, **91:** 219-222, **90:** 221
Quiet Revolution, 92: 118
Quirot, Ana, 90: 465

R

***Rabbit at Rest* (Updike), 91:** 350
Rabies, 91: 204
Rabuka, Sitiveni, 92: 338, **90:** 403
Race relations: Australia, **90:** 187; Belgium, **92:** 92; Hispanic immigration, **92:** 276; Miami, **90:** 235; New York City, **92:** 324, **91:** 380, **90:** 390; pope on racism, **90:** 429; Republican Party, **91:** 419-421; school curricula, **92:** 192; South Africa, **92:** 392-394, **91:** 430-431, **90:** 436; universities, **90:** 285; Washington, D.C., **92:** 454-455. See also **Affirmative action; Blacks; Civil rights; Hate crimes**
Races, Human, *WBE,* **92:** 506
Racquetball, 92: 401, **91:** 435, **90:** 441
Racquets, 92: 401, **91:** 435, **90:** 441
Radiation dangers, 92: 199
Radio. See **Awards and prizes**
Radioactive wastes, 90: 110, 112
RAE, ROBERT KEITH, 92: 336, 337, 421, **91:** 392-393, 417
RAFSANJANI, ALI AKBAR HASHEMI, 92: 250, **91:** 327, 328, **90:** 333-334, 379, 423
RAILROAD, 92: 379-380, **91:** 417, **90:** 423-424; Canada, **91:** 373, **90:** 221, 424; labor pacts, **92:** 269-270, **90:** 346; Los Angeles, **91:** 356-357, 457-458; maglev, **91:** 238, 417. See also **Disasters; English Channel Tunnel; Transit**
Rain forest: Brazil protection program, **92:** 97, 159-160; destruction, **91:** 255-256, 346, **90:** 111, 253, 354; Yanomami Indians, **91:** 209
***Raising Hell* (recording), 92:** 368
Raitt, Bonnie, 91: 193 (il.), 407
Rakolta, Terry, 90: 456
Rakowski, Mieczysław, 90: 412
Ramirez, Richard, 90: 257
Ramsey, Norman F., Jr., 90: 397
Ranford, Bill, 91: 316
RAO, P. V. NARASIMHA, 92: 243-244, 380
Rap music, 92: 366, 367-370, **91:** 406, 407, **90:** 413, 414
Rape. See **Crime; Courts**
Ratings, Motion-picture, 91: 376
Ratsiraka, Didier, 92: 44-45
Ratzinger, Joseph Cardinal, 91: 421
Raucci, Pasquale, 92: 148, 162
Rawlings, Jerry John, 92: 230, **90:** 162
Rawlins, Dennis, 90: 391
Ray, Robert, 92: 323
Raycroft Socialite (dog), 92: 185
Razaleigh Hamzah, 91: 359
Reagan, Nancy, 90: 424
REAGAN, RONALD WILSON, 92: 104 (il.), 251, **91:** 328, **90:** 424
Reasoner, Harry, 92: 175
Recession: Argentina, **92:** 62; Brazil, **91:** 208; Canada, **92:** 111, 318, 336, **91:** 222, 373; Great Britain, **92:** 232-233, **91:** 311; Italy, **92:** 258; Poland, **92:** 364
Recession, U.S., 92: 188-190, **91:** 280; automobiles, **92:** 78-79, **91:** 183-184; aviation, **92:** 81; banks, **91:** 195; building, **92:** 99; cities, **92:** 142; consumerism, **92:** 160; labor, **92:** 268; libraries, **92:** 279; magazines, **92:** 291; manufacturing, **92:** 293-296, **91:** 360; oil demand, **92:** 357-358; popular music, **92:** 364-365; San Diego, **92:** 388; state governments, **92:** 402; stocks and bonds, **92:** 405; U.S. government programs, **92:** 103, 449-450
Recordings. See **Classical music; Popular music**
Recruit Co., 92: 259, **90:** 340
Recycling, 91: 440
Red Dog Mine, 92: 317
Reduced Instruction Set Chip, 92: 152
Reebok International Limited, 91: 154
Reed, Frank H., 91: 328
Refugees: African, **91:** 160-161; Albanian, **92:** 48, 234, 259, **91:** 163; Asian, **92:** 72-74, **91:** 155, 177-178, **90:** 180-181; Burmese, **92:** 101; Cambodian, **92:** 105; German nonnationals, **92:** 229; Haitian, **92:** 234-235; Kurds, **92:** 103, 355, 430-431, 447-448; UN actions, **90:** 472; Vietnamese, **92:** 453. See also **Boat people; Immigration**
Refuseniks, 90: 342
Regional holding companies, 90: 243
Rehabilitation. See **Handicapped**
Rehnquist, William H., 90: 449
Reid, James Earl, 90: 178
Reinhardt, Ad, 92: 69
RELIGION, 92: 381-382, **91:** 417-418, **90:** 425-426; Africa conflicts, **90:** 163; Albania, **91:** 163; church-state in U.S., **91:** 443-444, **90:** 450; U.S.S.R., **91:** 466, **90:** 471. See also specific religions and churches
Remick, Lee, 92: 175
Renamo, 92: 44, **91:** 157, 377, **90:** 158-162, 387
Rendell, Edward G., 92: 358
Republican Guards (Iraq), 92: 347, 353
REPUBLICAN PARTY, 92: 382-383, **91:** 419-420, **90:** 426-427; Buchanan, Patrick, **92:** 99, 383, 390; Bush, George, **92:** 382, 383, **91:** 213; Duke, David E., **92:** 157, 186, 383, **91:** 419-420; National Convention, **92:** 241, 383; tax policy, **92:** 413. See also **Congress of the U.S.; Democratic Party; Elections**
Resolution Trust Corp., 92: 86, 451, **91:** 196
Respiratory distress syndrome, 91: 278
Restriction enzymes, 92: 302
Retinitis pigmentosa, 90: 206, 321
Retrieval failure (memory), 91: 126
Retrosynthetic analysis, 91: 389
Revelle, Roger, 92: 175
Reverse osmosis, 92: 455
Reyes, Virgilio Godoy, 91: 386
Reynolds Tobacco Co., 91: 154
Rheumatoid arthritis, 90: 321
Rhode Island, 92: 404, **91:** 439, **90:** 444
Rhythmic gymnastics, 92: 401, **91:** 435, **90:** 441
Richards, Ann W., 92: 403 (il.), **91:** 285 (il.)
Richards, Pamela, 91: 384
***Richmond v. Croson,* 90:** 237
Ridley, Nicholas, 91: 311
Riegle, Donald W., Jr., 92: 158, **91:** 197
Riga, 92: 276-277
Riggs, Anthony and Toni Cato, 92: 182
Right to die, 92: 296, **91:** 260-261, 406-407, 442. See also **Suicide**
Rio de Janeiro, 90: 212
Ríos Montt, Efraín, 91: 411, **90:** 319
Ripken, Cal, Jr., 92: 88
Ritter, Bruce, 91: 421
Rizzo, Frank L., 92: 358
RNA, 91: 204
Ro Jai Bong, 92: 265
Robbins, Jerome, 91: 264, **90:** 262
ROBERTS, JULIA, 92: 383
Roberts, Oral, 90: 324, 419
Robinson, Arthur Napoleon Raymond, 92: 470, **91:** 478
Robinson, Mary, 92: 254, **91:** 330
Rocard, Michel, 91: 305, **90:** 311
Rochon, Donald, 92: 147
Rock music. See **Popular music**
Rockefeller Center, 90: 390
Rodeo, 92: 401, **91:** 435, **90:** 441
Rodriguez, Juan, 92: 230
Rodriguez, Ramiro de Jesus, 92: 162
Rodríguez Pedotti, Andrés, 90: 405
***Roe v. Wade,* 90:** 449
Roemer, Charles E., III, 92: 403-404
Roh Tae Woo, 92: 264, 265, **91:** 338, 339, **90:** 345, 346
Rohwedder, Detlev, 92: 229
Rolling, Danny H., 92: 164
Rollins, Edward J., Jr., 92: 382, **91:** 420
Roman, Petre, 92: 386, **91:** 422-423
ROMAN CATHOLIC CHURCH, 92: 384-386, **91:** 420-422, **90:** 428-429; Auschwitz convent dispute, **91:** 421-422, **90:** 342-343, 428; elevations to cardinal, **92:** 92, 292; Poland, **90:** 412, 428; Protestant relations, **92:** 381, **90:** 418; Quebec, **92:** 114-118
ROMANIA, 92: 386, **91:** 422-423, **90:** 430; Eastern Orthodox Churches, **92:** 187-188; facts in brief, **92:** 205, **91:** 295, **90:** 298; libraries, **91:** 349; trade, **92:** 249 (il.)
Romanow, Roy, 92: 388
Rome Treaties, 92: 209, 215
Romeo, Robin, 91: 206, 207, **90:** 209
Rooney, Andy, 91: 385
***Rosat* (observatory), 91:** 180, 433
Rose, Pete, 91: 198, **90:** 200-201
Rose Theatre, 90: 169-170
Rosenbaum, Yankel, 92: 324
Ross, David, 92: 68
Rostenkowski, Dan, 92: 413-414, **91:** 469
Rostropovich, Mstislav, 91: 244
Roti, Fred B., 91: 232
Roundabout Theater Co., 92: 419
Rouse, Jeff, 92: 411
Rowing, 92: 401, **91:** 434, **90:** 440
Rowlands, June, 92: 420
Royal Ballet, 92: 168
Rozelle, Pete, 90: 307
Rozsa, Norbert, 92: 411
Rubella, 92: 377
Ruddock, Donovan (Razor), 92: 96
Rugby, 92: 401
Run-D.M.C. (pop group), 92: 368
Runcie, Robert A. K., 90: 418
Rushdie, Salman, 92: 250, **91:** 311-312, 351, **90:** 317, 334, 362
Russia: ethnic unrest, **91:** 462-464; Judaism, **92:** 263; UN membership, **92:** 447; U.S.S.R. collapse, **92:** 438, 439. See also **Union of Soviet Socialist Republics; Yeltsin, Boris Nikolayevich**
Russian Orthodox Church. See **Eastern Orthodox Churches**
Russian Revolution, 92: 442
Rwanda: civil war, **91:** 157; facts in brief, **92:** 47, **91:** 159, **90:** 161
RYAN, NOLAN, 92: 88, **91:** 198, 200, 423, **90:** 203
Ryan, Sheelah, 90: 391
Ryskamp, Kenneth L., 92: 453
Ryzhkov, Nikolay I., 90: 468

S

Saatchi & Saatchi PLC, 90: 157
Sabah family, 92: 266
Sabatini, Gabriela, 91: 450, 451
Sacks, Oliver, 92: 329
Sacramento, Calif., 90: 291, 466
SAFETY, 92: 386-387, **91:** 423-424, **90:** 431-432; aviation, **90:** 191; food, **92:** 220-221, **91:** 301; health-care workers, **90:** 349; mining, **92:** 151; nuclear plant, **90:** 291; railroad, **91:** 417, **90:** 423-424; U.S. Navy, **90:** 176, 474. See also **Disasters**
Safety of Pesticides in Food Act (1991), 92: 221
Sailing. See **Boating**
St. Bartholomew's Church, 92: 61-62, **91:** 169
St. Basil's Cathedral, 92: 187 (il.)
St. Christopher and Nevis: election, **90:** 484; facts in brief, **92:** 275, **91:** 345, **90:** 353
Saint Laurent, Yves, 90: 304
***St. Louis Sun,* 91:** 386, **90:** 395
St. Louis Zoo, 90: 486
St. Lucia, 92: 275, **91:** 345, **90:** 353
St. Vincent and the Grenadines, 92: 275, **91:** 345, **90:** 353
Sajak, Pat, 90: 457
Sakmann, Bert, 92: 333
Salaam, Yusef, 91: 257
Salaries. See **Wages**
Salih, Ali Abdallah, 91: 479
Salinas de Gortari, Carlos, 92: 273, 310-311, **91:**

344, 365, **90:** 375
Salmon, Sockeye, 92: 217
Salomon Brothers, 92: 406
Saltwater intrusion, 92: 465
***Salyut 7* (space station), 92:** 396
Samarra, 92: 57-58
Sampling (electronics), 92: 368-369
SAMPRAS, PETE, 92: 417, **91:** 424, 450, 451
San Andreas Fault, 90: 312
SAN DIEGO, 92: 387-388, **91:** 425; population, **90:** 237; transit, **90:** 466
San Diego Sockers, 92: 391
San Diego Zoo, 92: 477, **90:** 486
San Francisco: architecture, **91:** 168; earthquake, **91:** 238-239, **90:** 213, 235-237, 275; theater, **92:** 418; transit, **92:** 424
San Francisco 49ers, 91: 302, **90:** 306-307
San Francisco Giants, 90: 202
San Jose, 91: 237, **90:** 237
San Marino, 92: 205, **91:** 295, **90:** 298
Sánchez Vicario, Arantxa, 90: 457, 458
Sanders, Summer, 92: 411, **91:** 445
Sandinista National Liberation Front, 92: 331, **91:** 229, 386-387, **90:** 395-396
Sanguinetti, Julio María, 90: 477
Santa Barbara, Calif., 92: 455, **91:** 474-475
Santa Cruz, Calif., 91: 238-239
Santana, Raymond, 91: 257
São Tomé and Príncipe: election, **92:** 45; facts in brief, **92:** 47, **91:** 159, **90:** 161
Sarney Costa, José, 90: 352
SASKATCHEWAN, 92: 388, **91:** 425, **90:** 432
***Sassy* (magazine), 92:** 291-292
***Satanic Verses, The* (Rushdie), 92:** 250, **91:** 311-312, **90:** 317, 362
Satellites, Artificial, 91: 180; launches, **92:** 394, 396, **91:** 431, 432, **90:** 437; television, **90:** 76-79, 85, 87-89. See also ***Hubble Space Telescope;* Space exploration**
Saturn (car), 91: 183, 361 (il.)
Saturn (planet), 91: 69-73, 79-82
SAUDI ARABIA, 92: 388-389, **91:** 426-427, **90:** 432-433; facts in brief, **92:** 316, **91:** 370, **90:** 378; Iran, **92:** 250; oil supply, **92:** 357, **91:** 399-400, **90:** 408; Persian Gulf crisis and War, **92:** 344, 353, 388, **91:** 366, 426; water supply, **92:** 455; Yemen, **91:** 479
SAUVÉ, JEANNE MATHILDE, 90: 433
Savage, Gus, 91: 253
***Savage Inequalities* (Kozol), 92:** 191
"Save Our Cities" march, 92: 142
Savimbi, Jonas, 91: 165, **90:** 166-167
Savings and loan associations: crises and bailouts, **92:** 86, 451, **91:** 196-197, 470, **90:** 199-200; Keating investigation, **92:** 158, **91:** 197, 261, **90:** 250
Savisaar, Edgar, 92: 200
Sawallisch, Wolfgang, 91: 401
Sawyer, Amos, 92: 278-279, **91:** 349
Sayin, Hulusi, 92: 431
Scaasi, Arnold, 91: 300
Scandinavia. See **Denmark; Norway; Sweden**
***Scandinavian Star* (ship), 91:** 273
Scarfo, Nicodemo, Jr., 90: 409
Schengen treaty, 91: 203, 379
Schizophrenia, 91: 364, **90:** 374
Schlüter, Poul, 92: 180, 181, **91:** 273, **90:** 273
Schmoke, Kurt L., 92: 142, 194
Schneider, Vreni, 90: 434
Scholastic Aptitude Test, 91: 281
Schools. See **Education**
Schuller, Robert, 90: 419
Schulz, Charles, 91: 191 (il.)
Schuylkill Expressway, 90: 408-409
SCHWARZKOPF, H. NORMAN, JR., 92: 63 (il.), 326, 351, 353, 389
Schweitzer, Arlette, 92: 327
Science and research: awards, **91:** 193, **90:** 197; literature, **91:** 353. See also **Nobel Prizes** and specific sciences
Scowcroft, Brent, 90: 217
Scranton, Nancy, 92: 230
Screwworm fly, 92: 281
Scud missiles, 92: 66, 350-351, 414, 421
SDI. See **Strategic Defense Initiative**
Sea World (Orlando, Fla.), 92: 478
Seabrook Nuclear Power Station, 91: 288
Seafood inspection, 91: 301
Sears, Roebuck and Co., 90: 416
Seat belts, 90: 432
Seattle: building, **90:** 212; business city poll, **91:** 239; crime, **91:** 237; transit, **91:** 458, **90:** 465-466
Second Organic Act, 91: 59
Secord, Richard V., 91: 329, **90:** 335
***Secret Garden, The* (musical), 92:** 418
Secretariat (horse), 90: 394
Segregation. See **Civil rights; Integration**
Séguin, Yves, 91: 416
Seidman, L. William, 92: 451
SELES, MONICA, 92: 389, 416-417
Self-esteem, 92: 376-377
Selma, Ala., 91: 242
Semiautomatic weapons. See **Firearms**
Semiconductor chip, 90: 371
Senate. See **Congress of the U.S.; Democratic Party; Elections; Republican Party**
SENEGAL, 92: 390, **90:** 433; facts in brief, **92:** 47, **91:** 159, **90:** 161; relations with neighbors, **90:** 162, 433
Senkaku Islands, 92: 71, **91:** 178
Senna, Ayrton, 92: 80, 81, **91:** 185, **90:** 189-190
Serbia. See **Yugoslavia**
Serkin, Rudolf, 92: 175
Serra, Richard, 90: 177
Serrano, Andres, 90: 177
Serrano Elías, Jorge, 92: 234, 274, **91:** 313
"Sesame Street," 91: 268-269
Set-aside plans. See **Affirmative action**
Seurat, Georges, 92: 69
Seuss, Dr., 92: 177-178
Severe combined immunodeficiency disease, 91: 278
Seville, Spain, 92: 99-100, 397-399
Sex cells, 92: 301, 307 (il.), 309
Sex discrimination, 92: 193, **91:** 241, **90:** 237-238
Sexual harassment, 92: 157, 407, **91:** 302-303
Sexuality, 92: 375. See also **Homosexuality**
Seychelles, 92: 47, **91:** 159, **90:** 161
Shadow senator, 91: 474
Shakespeare, William, 92: 418, **90:** 169-170. See also **New York Shakespeare Festival**
Shamir, Yitzhak, 92: 255, 315, **91:** 331, 332, **90:** 337-338, 377
SHARIF, NAWAZ, 92: 339, **91:** 427
Sharman, Helen, 92: 396
Sharpe, William, 91: 388
Sharq, Mohammad Hassan, 90: 157
Shatalin, Stanislav S., 91: 460
SHAW, BERNARD, 92: 390, 414
Sheep, Peelable, 92: 217 (il.)
Shekhar, Chandra, 92: 243-244, **91:** 322
Shell, Art, 90: 308
Shevardnadze, Eduard A., 92: 445, **91:** 335, 460, **90:** 174, 470, 472
Shields, David J., 92: 140, **91:** 232
Shields, Jill, 92: 328
Shihabi, Samir, 92: 448
Shiite Muslims: Egypt, **90:** 286; Iraq, **92:** 252; Lebanon, **90:** 356, 379; Persian Gulf War, **92:** 102-103, 355; Western hostages, **92:** 257, 277, 316
Shining Path, 92: 356, **90:** 406
Shinto, 91: 418
Ship and shipping. See **Disasters; Oil spills**
Shock incarceration, 90: 417
Shoemaker, Bill, 92: 240
Shooting (sport), 92: 401, **91:** 435, **90:** 441
Short, Nigel, 92: 138
Shostakovich, Maxim, 92: 149
Shuttle, Space. See **Space shuttle**
Siam. See **Thailand**
Siberia, 92: 439
Sierra Leone, 92: 47, **91:** 159, **90:** 161
Sihanouk, Norodom, 92: 105, **91:** 216, **90:** 218
Sikes, Alfred C., 90: 244
Sikhs, 92: 245, **90:** 329
Silberman, Richard T., 91: 425
Silver mines, 90: 485. See also **Coin collecting**
Simic, Charles, 91: 403-404
Simmonds, Kennedy Alphonse, 90: 484
Simon, Neil, 92: 418-419
Simon, Paul, 92: 365
"Simple Truth, The" (concert), 92: 365
Simplesse, 91: 300
"Simpsons, The," 91: 136, 137, 313, 448, 455
Singapore: China, **91:** 176-177; elections, **92:** 72; facts in brief, **92:** 73, **91:** 179, **90:** 182; free-trade area, **92:** 71; Pacific rim nations, **91:** 103, 107; U.S. bases, **90:** 181
Singer, Isaac Bashevis, 92: 176
Singh, Vishwanath Pratap, 92: 243-244, **91:** 322-323, **90:** 329
Single European Act, 92: 209, 214-215
Sinhalese. See **Sri Lanka**
Sinkholes, 92: 463 (il.), 464
Sinn Féin. See **Irish Republican Army**
Sioux Indians, 91: 324-325
Siphandon, Khamtai, 92: 271
Sir Serei Eri, 92: 337-338
Sitthi Sawetsila, 90: 459
"60 Minutes," 91: 385
Skating. See **Hockey; Ice skating**
SKIING, 92: 390-391, **91:** 427, **90:** 434
Skin cancer, 92: 199. See also **Melanoma**
Skinner, B. F., 91: 271
SKINNER, SAMUEL KNOX, 92: 83, **90:** 435
SkyDome (Toronto), 92: 421, **91:** 454, **90:** 213 (il.), 462
***Sleeping Beauty, The* (ballet), 92:** 167-168
Slovaks. See **Czechoslovakia**
Slovenia. See **Yugoslavia**
Smart, Pamela, 92: 162
Smart bombs, 92: 65, 350
Smith, John, 92: 401
Smith, Larkin I., 90: 191
Smith, William Kennedy, 92: 161
Smithsonian Institution, 92: 68-69, **90:** 330-331
Smog, 92: 199, 311, **90:** 292
Smoking: advertising, **91:** 154; airline ban, **90:** 192; disease and deaths, **91:** 415, **90:** 321; high-school students, **92:** 185, **91:** 277
Smurfitt, Michael, 92: 254
So Kyong Won, 90: 345
Soares, Mário Alberto, 92: 371, **91:** 408
SOCCER, 92: 391, **91:** 428-429, **90:** 435; English riot, **90:** 316 (il.), 318, 435
Social Credit Party (Canada), 92: 98
Social Democratic Party: Germany, **92:** 228; Japan, **92:** 261; Portugal, **92:** 371, **91:** 408; Sweden, **92:** 411, **91:** 444
SOCIAL SECURITY, 92: 391-392, **91:** 429, **90:** 435-436; benefits to disabled, **92:** 236, **90:** 319; Moynihan plan, **91:** 272, 468-469; taxes, **92:** 391-392, 414, **91:** 272, 429, 468-469
Socialist Party: Austria, **91:** 183; France, **92:** 225, **90:** 311; Hungary, **90:** 326; Japan, **92:** 261, **91:** 333; Portugal, **92:** 371
Socialist Unity Party (Germany), 90: 312, 314
Socialist Workers' Party (Spain), 92: 396
Sodium fluoride, 91: 475, **90:** 373
Softball, 92: 401, **91:** 435, **90:** 441
Soglo, Nicephore, 92: 45
Sokomanu, Ati George, 90: 403
Solar energy, 92: 196, **90:** 112-117, 290
***Solar Maximum Mission* satellite, 90:** 438-439
Solar nebula, 91: 72-73
Solar system, 91: 69-85
***Soldier of the Great War, A* (Helprin), 92:** 282
Soldiers of Destiny party. See **Fianna Fáil**
Solidarity (Poland), 92: 363, **91:** 404-405, 473, **90:** 371, 412
Solomon Islands, 92: 338, **91:** 394, **90:** 402
Solti, Sir Georg, 92: 149
Somali National Movement, 92: 392
SOMALIA, 92: 392; civil war, **92:** 44, 392, **91:** 157; facts in brief, **92:** 47, **91:** 159, **90:** 161; ivory trade, **91:** 48; religious conflict, **90:** 163
Sony Corp., 92: 195, **91:** 286, **90:** 288
Sorrell, Martin, 90: 157
Sotheby's, 92: 67-68, **91:** 174-175, 246, **90:** 179
Sotomayor, Javier, 90: 464, 465
SOUTER, DAVID HACKETT, 91: 429, 444
SOUTH AFRICA, 92: 392-394, **91:** 430-431, **90:** 436-437; Angola, **90:** 166; apartheid law changes, **92:** 42 (il.), 45-48, 392; facts in brief, **92:** 47, **91:** 159, **90:** 161; ivory trade, **91:** 49, **90:** 253; library boycott, **91:** 350; Mobil Corp. withdrawal, **90:** 407; Namibia, **91:** 378, 411, 467, **90:** 158, 387, 471; Protestantism, **91:** 410-411; sports, **92:** 400, **90:** 401; steel imports, **91:** 440; trade ban, **92:** 250. See also **De Klerk, Frederik W.; Mandela, Nelson**
South America. See **Latin America**
South Carolina, 92: 404, **91:** 439, **90:** 444; abortion law, **91:** 438; bridge disaster, **90:** 213; political scandal, **92:** 405
South Dakota, 92: 404, **91:** 439, **90:** 444; Native Americans Day, **91:** 324
South Korea. See **Korea, South**
South West African People's Organization, 91: 378, **90:** 158, 387-388, 471
Southern California Edison Co., 92: 196
Southern Ocean Racing Conference. See **Boating**
Soviet Union. See **Union of Soviet Socialist Republics**
Soybean futures, 90: 301
SPACE EXPLORATION, 92: 394-396, **91:** 431-433, **90:** 437-439; Mars probe, **90:** 184; Neptune probe, **90:** 183; solar system, **91:** 69-85; Venus probe, **91:** 180-181. See also **Astronomy**
Space shuttle, 92: 394, 451, **91:** 432, 472, **90:** 437-438
SPAIN, 92: 396, **91:** 433, **90:** 439; Expo '92, **92:** 99-100, 397-399; facts in brief, **92:** 205, **91:** 295, **90:** 298; Ibero-American Summit, **92:** 274-276; Madrid peace conference, **92:** 314-315; Olympics, **92:** 397, 399; Puerto Rico, **91:** 54-55
Spanish Sahara. See **Western Sahara**
Specialty Metals Processing Consortium, Inc., 91: 440
Speck, Richard, 92: 176
Speed skating. See **Ice skating**
Spielberg, Steven, 92: 321, **90:** 384

Spinal cord injuries, 92: 186
Spinal osteoporosis, 90: 373
Spinelli, Jerry, 92: 288
***Spirit of the Amazon* (boat), 92:** 95
SPORTS, 92: 400-401, **91:** 434-435, **90:** 440-441; intercollegiate sports, **90:** 285-286, 440; Pan American Games, **92:** 165, 400; Philadelphia sports arena, **90:** 409. See also **Goodwill Games; Olympic Games;** and specific sports
Spotted owl, 91: 254, **90:** 254
SRI LANKA, 92: 402, **91:** 436, **90:** 442; facts in brief, **92:** 73, **91:** 179, **90:** 182; Gandhi death, **92:** 244
Sri Lanka Freedom Party, 92: 402
SSC. See **Superconducting Super Collider**
Staley, Dawn, 92: 90
Stalin, Joseph, 92: 442-444
Stallings, George A., 91: 422, **90:** 428
STAMP COLLECTING, 91: 436-437, **90:** 442-443
Standard & Poor's indexes. See **Stocks and bonds**
Stanford University, 92: 192
Stanley Cup. See **Hockey**
"Star-Spangled Banner, The," 91: 385
"Star Wars" (defense). See **Strategic Defense Initiative**
***Stark*, U.S.S., 90:** 336
Starr, Patricia, 90: 401
START. See **Strategic Arms Reduction Treaty**
State Committee for the State of Emergency, 92: 432-435
STATE GOVERNMENT, 92: 402-405, **91:** 437-440, **90:** 443-446; education reform proposals, **91:** 281; Puerto Rico statehood issue, **91:** 52-67, 415. See also **Elections** and specific states
State Law and Order Restoration Council, 92: 101
Statement of Political Relationship, 92: 246
Staten Island, 90: 389
Stealth. See **A-2 attack jet; B-2 bomber; F-117A Stealth fighter**
STEEL INDUSTRY, 91: 440, **90:** 446; labor contracts, **90:** 348
Steelville, Mo., 92: 326
Steen, Alann, 92: 317
Steeplechasing. See **Horse racing**
Steinberg, Joel B., 90: 256-257
Steinbrenner, George, 91: 198
***Steinlager 2* (boat), 91:** 205
Stem cells, 92: 306
Steroids, Anabolic. See **Anabolic steroids**
Stewart, Melvin, 92: 411
Stewart, Payne, 92: 230, **90:** 315
Still video, 90: 395
Sting, 90: 459
Stirling, James, 90: 171
Stock cars. See **Automobile racing**
STOCKS AND BONDS, 92: 405-406, **91:** 441, **90:** 447-448; fraud, **90:** 257, 259, 448; Japan scandals, **92:** 261; Treasury bond sale, **91:** 281. See also **Economics; Interest rates; Junk bonds; Prices**
Stolojan, Theodor, 92: 386
Stomach cancer, 92: 93
Stone, Oliver, 92: 319, 321
Storms. See **Disasters; Weather**
Stowe, Mary Sue Davis, 91: 259, **90:** 256
***Straight Outta Compton* (recording), 92:** 370
Strand, Mark, 91: 403
Strange, Curtis, 90: 315
Stratcom, 92: 65
Strategic Air Command, 92: 65
Strategic Arms Reduction Treaty, 92: 64, 65, 103, 440, **91:** 171, 466, **90:** 173-174
Strategic Defense Initiative, 92: 65, 394, 450, **91:** 171, **90:** 474
Strauss, Robert S., 92: 103
Stress, 92: 310, 376, **91:** 131
Stressler, Charles, 92: 162
Strike the Gold (horse), 92: 239 (il.), 240
Strikes. See **Labor**
Stroessner, Alfredo, 90: 405
Stroke, 92: 297
Structural funds, 92: 213
Structural Impediments Initiative, 91: 326
Stuart, Carol and Charles, 91: 261
Sturges, Jock, 92: 68
Stus, Gene, 92: 95
Stuttgart Opera, 91: 242
Subatomic particles. See **Physics**
Subliminal messages, in music, 91: 406-407
Submarine disaster, 90: 401
Substance abuse. See **Alcoholism; Drug abuse**
Suburban population growth, 92: 128
Suchinda Kraprayoon, 92: 417
Sudafed, 92: 165
SUDAN, 92: 406, **91:** 442, **90:** 448; civil war, **92:** 44, 406, **91:** 157, 447, **90:** 442; facts in brief, **92:** 47, 316, **91:** 159, **90:** 161; human rights, **91:** 369
Suharto, 92: 247, **91:** 114-115, 325, **90:** 331, 332
Suicide, 92: 296, **91:** 260-261, 406-407
Sullivan, Gordon R., 92: 67
SULLIVAN, LOUIS WADE, 90: 448
Sullivan Award, 92: 401
Sumer, 92: 56
Sun: neutrino emissions, **91:** 402-403; solar eclipse, **92:** 74-75; solar system features and origin, **91:** 70-73; *Ulysses* probe, **91:** 432. See also **Solar energy**
Sun Microsystems, 90: 245
Sunday Silence (horse), 91: 317, **90:** 323-324
Sunglasses, 90: 373
Sunken treasure, 91: 392, **90:** 400
Sunspots, 91: 403
SUNUNU, JOHN, 92: 103, 104, 406
Super Bowl. See **Football**
Superconducting Super Collider, 90: 411
Superconductors, 92: 362
Superfund sites, 92: 464
Superplumes, 92: 228
Supreme Court of Canada, 92: 109, 242
SUPREME COURT OF THE UNITED STATES, 92: 407-408, **91:** 442-444, **90:** 449-450; abortion, **92:** 157-158, 407, **91:** 443, **90:** 419, 425, 429, 445, 449; civil rights, **92:** 147, 407-408, **91:** 240-241, 342, 442, **90:** 237-238; copyright on artwork, **90:** 178; death penalty, **92:** 407, **90:** 417; drugs for mentally ill, **91:** 364; flag burning, **91:** 241, 253, 443, **90:** 238, 252-253, 449; historic church, **92:** 61-62; Marshall retirement, **92:** 409-410; New York City charter revision, **90:** 389; newspaper libel award, **90:** 395; obscenity, **90:** 244; prison conditions, **92:** 373; religious freedom, **91:** 325, 443-444, **90:** 425, 450; Souter confirmation, **92:** 147, **91:** 429, 470; Thomas confirmation, **92:** 153-157, 407, 420
Supreme National Council (Cambodia), 92: 105
Surface Transportation Efficiency Act (1991), 92: 424
Surfing, 92: 401, **91:** 435, **90:** 441
Surgery. See **Medicine; Organ transplantation**
Suriname: election, **92:** 274; facts in brief, **92:** 275, **91:** 345, **90:** 353
Surrogate motherhood, 91: 259
Sutherland, Joan, 91: 182 (il.), **90:** 241
Sutherland, Thomas, 92: 317
Suu Kyi, Aung San, 92: 72, 101, 331, 332 (il.), **91:** 212-213, **90:** 214
Suzuki, Shunichi, 92: 261
***Swan Lake* (ballet), 90:** 262
SWAPO. See **South West African People's Organization**
Swaziland, 92: 47, **91:** 159, **90:** 161
SWEDEN, 92: 411, **91:** 444, **90:** 451; European unity, **92:** 206, **91:** 296; facts in brief, **92:** 205, **91:** 295, **90:** 298; hockey, **92:** 238
SWIMMING, 92: 411, **91:** 445, **90:** 451. See also **Synchronized swimming**
SWITZERLAND, 92: 412, **91:** 446, **90:** 452; European unity, **92:** 206, **91:** 296; facts in brief, **92:** 205, **91:** 295, **90:** 298
Synchronized swimming, 92: 401, **91:** 435, **90:** 441
Synfuels. See **Energy supply**
Syphilis, 91: 415
SYRIA, 92: 412-413, **91:** 446, **90:** 452; facts in brief, **92:** 316, **91:** 370, **90:** 378; Lebanon, **92:** 277, **91:** 347-348, **90:** 355-356, 378-379; Middle East peace conference, **92:** 314-315; U.S. hostages, **92:** 316
Syse, Jan P., 92: 335, **91:** 390, **90:** 399
Szoka, Edmund Cardinal, 90: 275

T

Taba (resort), 90: 286
Table tennis, 92: 401, **91:** 435, **90:** 441
Tadzhik republic, 91: 418. See also **Tadzhikistan**
Tadzhikistan, 92: 438
Tae kwan do, 92: 401, **91:** 435, **90:** 441
Tafero, Jessie J., 91: 410
Tagliabue, Paul J., 91: 302-303, **90:** 307
TAIWAN, 92: 413, **91:** 447, **90:** 452-453; facts in brief, **92:** 73, **91:** 179, **90:** 182; fishing drift nets, **91:** 254; Pacific rim nations, **91:** 103-104, 111-119
Takeshita, Noboru, 90: 340
Talent, John A., 90: 404
Talmud, 92: 263
Tamarin, 91: 481-482
Tamils, 92: 180, 244, 402, **91:** 436, **90:** 442
Tan, Amy, 90: 359
Tanai, Shahnawaz, 91: 155
TANDY, JESSICA, 91: 189 (il.), 447
Tandy Corp., 92: 152, **91:** 248
Tanzania: elephants, **91:** 40; facts in brief, **92:** 47, **91:** 159, **90:** 161; political repression, **91:** 160; *WBE*, **90:** 534
Tariffs, 92: 209. See also **International trade**
Tarkanian, Jerry, 92: 89, 91, **91:** 201
Tartikoff, Brandon, 92: 416
Tax Reform Act (1986), 92: 68
TAXATION, 92: 413-414, **91:** 447-448, **90:** 453-454; Bush campaign pledge, **91:** 272, 419, 420, 468; consumer items, **91:** 256; education, **92:** 191, **91:** 240, 443; governorship election issue, **91:** 285; social security, **92:** 391-392, 414, **91:** 272, 429, 468-469. See also **Congress of the U.S.; Goods and services tax; State government;** and individual countries
Taylor, Charles, 92: 278-279, **91:** 348-349
Taylor, Elizabeth, 92: 328
Taylor, Paul, 92: 168, **91:** 264
Taylor, Richard E., 91: 388-389
Taylor, Zachary, 92: 325
Teach for America, 91: 282
Teachers. See **Education**
Teamsters Union, 92: 270, **91:** 341, **90:** 349
Technology: awards, **91:** 193, **90:** 197; television, **90:** 85-86, 92-95. See also **Computer; Manufacturing**
Teenage Mutant Ninja Turtles, 91: 375, 455
Tekere, Edgar Z., 90: 163
Teledyne Industries, 90: 474
Telemarketing, 90: 255
Telephone: pornography, **90:** 244; television market, **92:** 161, 416; television technology, **90:** 85. See also **American Telephone and Telegraph Co.**
Telescope, Space. See ***Hubble Space Telescope***
TELEVISION, 92: 414-416, **91:** 448-450, **90:** 454-457; animation, **91:** 136; closed-caption law, **91:** 314; Cuba broadcasts, **90:** 260; Europe, **90:** 87-91; labor agreement, **90:** 348; Latin-American politics, **90:** 211, 352-354; Leno, Jay, **92:** 278; network problems, **90:** 73-86; new technology, **92:** 195, **90:** 92-95, 288; regulations, **92:** 161, **91:** 257; sports, **92:** 222-224, **91:** 302, 434; televangelists, **90:** 419. See also **Advertising; Awards and prizes**
Temple Mount, 91: 331, 368, 369
Teng Hsiao-p'ing. See **Deng Xiaoping**
Tennessee, 92: 404, **91:** 439, **90:** 444
TENNIS, 92: 416-417, **91:** 450-451, **90:** 457-458. See also names of players
Teresa, Mother, 90: 165
Terrorism: airlines, **92:** 81-82, **90:** 431; Colombia, **90:** 243; energy supply system, **90:** 291; Germany, **92:** 229, **90:** 315; India, **91:** 323; Iran, **91:** 327; Libya, **92:** 280-281, **91:** 350, **90:** 359; Mozambique, **90:** 387; Northern Ireland, **92:** 231 (il.), 333, **91:** 389, **90:** 398; Philippines, **90:** 409; Rushdie affair, **90:** 362; Spain, **91:** 433; Sri Lanka, **91:** 436, **90:** 442; Syria, **92:** 413, **91:** 446; Turkey, **92:** 431
Terry, Randall, 90: 419
Terry, Sir Peter, 91: 389
Testing, Drug. See **Drug abuse**
Texas, 92: 404, **91:** 439, **90:** 444; education, **92:** 402, **91:** 283, **90:** 285; election, **92:** 194; voting rights, **92:** 408; water supply, **90:** 480; zoos and aquariums, **91:** 482-483
Texas Air Corp., 90: 346-347
Texas Rangers (team), 91: 423
***Texas v. Johnson*, 90:** 449
TGV (train), 90: 424
THAILAND, 92: 417, **91:** 451-452, **90:** 459; Burma, **92:** 101; facts in brief, **92:** 73, **91:** 179, **90:** 182; free-trade area, **92:** 71; industrialization, **91:** 103-110, 115-119; jetliner explosion, **92:** 182-183 (il.); Laos, **90:** 349; Vietnam refugees, **91:** 177
Tharp, Twyla, 92: 168, **91:** 263-264, **90:** 262
Thatcher, Margaret Hilda, 92: 231, 232, **91:** 292, 296, 310-311, **90:** 299, 300 (il.), 316-317
THEATER, 92: 418-420, **91:** 452-454, **90:** 459-461; Shakespeare's theaters, **90:** 169-170. See also **Awards and prizes**
***Thelma and Louise* (film), 92:** 319
Theodore, Rene, 92: 470
Thermal Neutron Analysis device, 90: 431
Thiam, Habib, 92: 390
Third World. See **Developing countries**
Tho, Le Duc, 91: 473, **90:** 478
THOMAS, CLARENCE, 92: 147, 153-157, 414, 420
Thomas, Danny, 92: 176
Thomas, E. Donnall, 91: 389
Thomas, Thurman, 92: 221
Thompson, Jack, 91: 406
Thompson, James R., 91: 442-443
Thornburgh, Richard L., 92: 179, 383, 449, 451
Thorncrown Chapel, 92: 60-61 (il.)
Thornhill, Roland, 92: 335

Thoroughbreds. See **Horse racing**
Threatened species. See **Endangered species**
3-D television, 90: 95
Tiananmen Square demonstrations, 91: 177, 234, **90:** 216-217, 230-233
Tibet, 92: 142, **91:** 235, **90:** 233
Tidal energy, 90: 117-118
Tigre, 92: 201, **91:** 157, 291, **90:** 162, 296
***Tilted Arc* (Serra), 90:** 177
Timakata, Fred, 90: 403
Time-share real estate, 90: 255
Time Warner Inc., 91: 358, **90:** 244
Timman, Jan, 92: 138
Timor, 92: 247
***Tin Toy* (film), 91:** 136, 142
Tippett, Sir Michael, 90: 241
Titan (moon), 91: 82
Tito, Josip Broz, 92: 470, 474
Tjibaou, Jean-Marie, 90: 402
Tobacco. See **Smoking**
Tobago. See **Trinidad and Tobago**
"Today" show, 90: 454
Toekes, Laszlo, 90: 430
Tofilau Eti Alesana, 92: 339
Togo, 92: 47, **91:** 159, **90:** 161
Tomahawk cruise missile, 92: 65, 348 (il.), 350
Tomba, Alberto, 92: 391
Tomlin, Garland L., Jr., 90: 474
Tonga, 92: 338, **91:** 394, **90:** 402
***Tongues of Angels, The* (Price), 91:** 350
"Tonight Show," 92: 278
Tools, Prehistoric. See **Anthropology**
Tornadoes, 92: 184, 468, **91:** 275, 476, **90:** 276, 481
TORONTO, 92: 420-421, **91:** 454, **90:** 462; SkyDome, **92:** 421, **91:** 454, **90:** 213 (il.), 462
Toronto Argonauts, 92: 222
Toronto Blue Jays, 90: 202
Toshika's Secret Desire (cat), 92: 126
***Total Ozone Mapping Spectrometer,* 92:** 396
Tower, John G., 92: 83, **90:** 176-177, 217-218, 473
Toxic wastes. See **Environmental pollution**
Toyota Motor Corp., 92: 80, **91:** 185, **90:** 188, 189
TOYS AND GAMES, 92: 421-422, **91:** 455-456, **90:** 462-463
TRACK AND FIELD, 92: 422-424, **91:** 456-457, **90:** 464-465
***Trackers* (dance), 92:** 168
***Tracking and Data Relay Satellite,* 92:** 394
Tracy, Edward Austin, 92: 317
Trade. See **Economics; International trade**
Trade, U.S. balance of, 92: 248, 250, **91:** 325, 472, **90:** 332
Trade unions. See **Labor**
Trains. See **Disasters; Railroad; Transit**
Trans World Airlines, 92: 82-83
TRANSIT, 92: 424, **91:** 457-458, **90:** 465-466; federal program, **92:** 158; Houston, **92:** 241. See also **Automobile; Aviation; English Channel Tunnel; Railroad**
***Transparent Man, The* (Hecht), 91:** 403
Transportation. See **Transit**
Transportation, U.S. Department of, 90: 424
Treasury bills. See **Bank**
Trees. See **Botany; Forests**
Trenary, Jill, 91: 321-322
Trevino, Lee, 92: 230, **91:** 309
Triathlon, 92: 401, **91:** 435, **90:** 441
Trinidad and Tobago: coup attempt, **91:** 478-479; elections, **92:** 470; facts in brief, **92:** 275, **91:** 345, **90:** 353
Triple Crown. See **Horse racing**
Triton, 91: 70, 80 (il.), 84-85, **90:** 184, 312
Trolley buses, 91: 458, **90:** 465-466
Tropical rain forest. See **Rain forest**
Tropical Storm Allison, 90: 481
Trucks and trucking, 92: 270, 380, **91:** 417
Trudeau, Pierre Elliott, 92: 119, **91:** 220, 225
TRUMP, DONALD JOHN, 92: 327, **91:** 211, 382, **90:** 192, 347, 467
Trump, Ivana, 92: 327
Tshisekedi, Etienne, 92: 476
TSONGAS, PAUL, 92: 179, 430
Tudjman, Franjo, 92: 475
Tumor-suppressor genes, 92: 304
TUNISIA, 92: 430, **91:** 458-459, **90:** 467; facts in brief, **92:** 47, **91:** 159, **90:** 161; Islamic movements, **92:** 254; regional bloc, **90:** 380
Tunnel. See **English Channel Tunnel**
TURKEY, 92: 430-431, **91:** 459, **90:** 467-468; Bronze-Age tin mines, **90:** 170-171; facts in brief, **92:** 205, **91:** 295, **90:** 298; Persian Gulf crisis and War, **92:** 430-431, **91:** 367, 459
Turkmenistan, 92: 438
Turks, in Bulgaria, 92: 101, **90:** 214
Turner, Jesse, 92: 317
Turner, John N., 91: 236, **90:** 219
Turner, Maurice T., Jr., 90: 479
Turtle excluder device, 90: 254
Tuvalu, 92: 338, **91:** 394, **90:** 402
"Twin Peaks," 91: 358, 449
Twins, 90: 140-153
Twitchell, David and Ginger, 91: 412-413
Two Forks Dam, 90: 255
2 Live Crew, 92: 370, **91:** 406
Tyler, Scott, 90: 177
Tyminski, Stanislaw, 91: 404-405
Typhoons. See **Disasters; Weather**
***Tyrannosaurus rex,* 90:** 404
Tyson, Mike, 92: 96, **91:** 207-208, 276, **90:** 210
Tzannetakis, Tzannis, 90: 318

U

UAL Corp.. See **United Airlines**
UAW. See **United Automobile Workers**
Ueberroth, Peter V., 90: 200, 201, 347
Uganda: elephants, **91:** 40; facts in brief, **92:** 47, **91:** 159, **90:** 161; rebellion, **92:** 44
Ukraine, 92: 435-438, 447
Ukrainian Catholic Church, 91: 420, **90:** 428
Ulcerative keratitis, 90: 372-373
Ulster. See **Northern Ireland**
***Ulysses* (space probe), 91:** 432
UMNO, 91: 359, **90:** 368
UMTA. See **Urban Mass Transportation Administration**
UMW. See **United Mine Workers of America**
UN. See **United Nations**
Unbridled (horse), 91: 317-318
Unemployment: benefits, **92:** 271; congressional actions, **92:** 157; handicapped, **90:** 319-320; Houston, **91:** 238; manufacturing, **90:** 370; U.S. rates, **92:** 189, 268, 296, **91:** 279, **90:** 282. See also individual cities, provinces, and countries
UNESCO, 91: 468, **90:** 473
Ungaro, Emanuel, 91: 299 (il.)
UNICEF, 91: 421, 468, **90:** 473
Union of Democratic Forces, 92: 101, **91:** 212
UNION OF SOVIET SOCIALIST REPUBLICS, 92: 432-440, **91:** 460-466, **90:** 468-471; Afghanistan, **92:** 41, **91:** 155, **90:** 157, 179, 470; chess, **92:** 138, **91:** 231, **90:** 227; China, **92:** 71, 140, **91:** 236, **90:** 233, 470-471; collapse, **92:** 103, 202-204, 435-446; coup attempt, **92:** 432-435, 446; Cuba, **92:** 165-166, 440, **91:** 261; Czechoslovakia, **91:** 262; dancing, **91:** 264; Eastern Orthodox Churches, **92:** 187-188, **91:** 279, **90:** 281; economic aid, **92:** 190; Estonia, **92:** 200; Ethiopia, **92:** 201; ethnic conflict, **91:** 462-463, **90:** 65-67, 469; facts in brief, **92:** 205, **91:** 295, **90:** 298; farming and food production, **92:** 206, 216, 439, 440, **91:** 298; Finland, **92:** 219, **91:** 300, **90:** 304; Germany, **91:** 292, 296, 307-308; human rights pacts, **90:** 239; Hungary, **90:** 327; Israel, **92:** 255, 256, **91:** 331, 336, **90:** 342; ivory, **92:** 328-329; Japan, **92:** 71, 261, **91:** 177, 335; Jews, **92:** 263, **91:** 336, **90:** 342; Korea, North and South, **92:** 264, **91:** 177, 338, 339; Latvia, **92:** 276-277; Lithuania, **92:** 288-289; Middle East peace conference, **92:** 103, 314; mining strikes, **90:** 380; Mongolia, **91:** 371, **90:** 181; motion pictures, **90:** 386; oil, **92:** 358, **91:** 400; Poland, **91:** 405; political reforms, effects of, **90:** 54-69; popular music, **90:** 414; Protestantism, **92:** 373-374, **91:** 410, **90:** 419; religious freedom, **91:** 417-418, 466; Roman Catholic Church, **92:** 384, **91:** 420, **90:** 428; space missions, **92:** 396, **91:** 432-433, **90:** 184, 438, 439; technology, **90:** 290, 401; theater, **90:** 461; United Nations, **92:** 447; U.S. relations, **92:** 63-65, 216, 249, 439-440, **91:** 171-172, 214-215, 465-466, **90:** 67-69, 173-174, 215-216, 470; Vietnam, **92:** 453, **91:** 473. See also **Gorbachev, Mikhail S.; Yeltsin, Boris N.**
Unions. See **Labor**
UNITA, 91: 165, **90:** 158, 166-167
United Airlines, 92: 83, 270, **91:** 186, 342, **90:** 192, 347
United Arab Emirates: facts in brief, **92:** 316, **91:** 370, **90:** 378; Iraq conflict, **92:** 344, 345, **91:** 329, 399; oil supply, **92:** 357
United Automobile Workers, 91: 184, 341, **90:** 346
United Church of Canada, 90: 418
United Kingdom. See **Great Britain; Northern Ireland**
United Mine Workers of America, 91: 244-245, 340, **90:** 347
United National Independence Party (Zambia), 91: 481
United National Party (Sri Lanka), 92: 402, **90:** 442
UNITED NATIONS, 92: 447-449, **91:** 466-468, **90:** 471-473; Afghanistan, **92:** 71; Cambodia, **92:** 71, 105, 448, **91:** 216, 467; El Salvador, **92:** 195; Korea, North and South, **92:** 264; Latin America, **92:** 274; Middle East peace conference, **92:** 314-315; Pacific Islands, **92:** 339; Persian Gulf crisis and War, **92:** 251, 253, 345, 347, 355, 447, **91:** 330, 366; Taiwan, **92:** 413
United Rubber Workers, 92: 271
United Somali Congress, 92: 392
UNITED STATES, GOVERNMENT OF THE, 92: 449-453, **91:** 468-472, **90:** 473-477; conservation, **91:** 48, **90:** 253-254; Eastern Europe trade, **92:** 249; Ellis Island immigration, **91:** 87-101; Latin-American debt plan, **91:** 281, 344; Middle East peace conference, **92:** 314-315; North American free-trade area, **92:** 249, 273, 310; Pacific rim nations, **91:** 104-107, 119; Persian Gulf crisis and War, **92:** 251, **91:** 329-330, 366-368; Puerto Rico statehood issue, **91:** 52-67. See also **Armed forces; Bush, George H. W.; Congress of the U.S.; State government; Supreme Court of the U.S.;** and specific foreign countries
United Steelworkers of America, 92: 269, **90:** 348
Universal Ballet Academy, 91: 264
Universal Pictures, 92: 321
Universe, Age of, 92: 76
Universities and colleges: basketball, **92:** 89-90, **91:** 200-202, 434, **90:** 203-204, 440; costs, **91:** 282-283, **90:** 285; enrollments, **92:** 193, **91:** 283, **90:** 286; football, **92:** 222-224, **91:** 303-305, 434, **90:** 308-310, 440; funding scandals, **92:** 191-192; magazine for students, **90:** 367-368; NCAA reforms, **92:** 400-401, **90:** 440; quality of campus life, **90:** 285-286; research versus teaching, **91:** 282; South Korea protests, **92:** 264-265
University of Miami, 92: 224
University of Nevada, Las Vegas, 92: 89-90
University of Washington, 92: 224
University of Wisconsin, 92: 162, 192
Uno, Sosuke, 90: 340
Unser, Al, Jr., 91: 185, **90:** 189
UNTAG (organization), 90: 471
Updike, John, 91: 350
***Upper Atmosphere Research Satellite (UARS),* 92:** 394
Upper Volta. See **Burkina Faso**
Uranus, 91: 69-73, 82-84
Urban Mass Transportation Administration, 91: 457, **90:** 466
URUGUAY, 91: 472, **90:** 477; facts in brief, **92:** 275, **91:** 345, **90:** 353; free-trade zone, **92:** 273, **91:** 346
Uruguay Round, 92: 216, 248
U.S. Patient Self-Determination Act (1991), 92: 240
USAir, 92: 83
***Use Your Illusion* (recordings), 92:** 365
U.S.S.R. See **Union of Soviet Socialist Republics**
USX Corp., 92: 269, **90:** 446
Utah, 92: 404, **91:** 439, **90:** 444
Uzbekistan, 92: 438

V

VA. See **Veterans**
Vaccine: AIDS, **91:** 162, **90:** 164-165; wildlife rabies, **91:** 204
Valentino, 92: 218, **90:** 303
Value added tax, 92: 213, 215
Van Gogh, Vincent, 92: 323, **91:** 174
Vanden Boeynants, Paul, 90: 206
Vander Zalm, William N., 92: 98, 262, **91:** 209, **90:** 212
Vanuatu: election, **92:** 338-339; facts in brief, **92:** 338, **91:** 394, **90:** 402; mutiny trial, **90:** 403
Vargas Llosa, Mario, 91: 398, **90:** 406
Varmus, Harold E., 90: 397
Vásquez, Tabaré, 91: 472, **90:** 477
Vatican. See **Roman Catholic Church**
VCR's. See **Videocassette recorders**
Venetiaan, Ronald, 92: 274
VENEZUELA, 91: 472, **90:** 477; Brady plan, **91:** 344; facts in brief, **92:** 275, **91:** 345, **90:** 353; free-trade zone, **92:** 249, 273-274, 470; oil, **92:** 274, 357
Vento, John S., 91: 258
Venturi, Robert, 92: 60, 61
Venus, 92: 75-76, **91:** 69-76, 180-181, 432
Verbal ability, 90: 420-421
Vergara, Ramón González, 91: 261
Vermont, 92: 404, **91:** 439, **90:** 444
Versace, Gianni, 90: 303
VETERANS, 90: 478
Veterans Administration. See **Veterans**
Veterans Affairs, Department of, 90: 274, 478

Vice President of the U.S. See **Quayle, Dan**
Video games, 91: 455, **90:** 462
Videocassette recorders, 91: 286, **90:** 73, 81, 85
Viehboeck, Franz, 92: 396
VIETNAM, 92: 453, **91:** 473, **90:** 478; Cambodia, **92:** 105, **91:** 216-217, **90:** 179-180, 218; China, **92:** 141, **91:** 176; facts in brief, **92:** 73, **91:** 179, **90:** 182; ivory trade, **91:** 51; refugees, **92:** 72-74, **91:** 177; Soviet collapse, **92:** 71
Vietnam War, 90: 386. See also **Missing in action**
***Viking* space probes, 91:** 76-77
***Vineland* (Pynchon), 91:** 350
Virginia, 92: 404, **91:** 439, **90:** 444; elections, **92:** 383. See also **Wilder, L. Douglas**
Viruses, 92: 137-138, 372. See also **AIDS; Health and disease; Public health**
Vision, 92: 377, **90:** 206, 321, 372-273, 486
***Vision of Britain, A* (Charles), 90:** 171
Visser, Leo, 90: 328
Visual Artist's Rights Act (1991), 92: 68
"Voices That Care" (recording), 92: 364
Vojvodina, 92: 474
Volcanoes: Asia, **92:** 70; Hudson, **92:** 62, 226-228; Mt. Pinatubo, **92:** 199, 226, 360, 361; Mt. Unzen, **92:** 226; ocean landslides, **91:** 307; solar system, **91:** 77-79, 85, **90:** 184
Volleyball, 92: 401, **91:** 435, **90:** 441
Volvo (car), 91: 154
Voting rights, 92: 147, 290, 408, **91:** 241, 356, **90:** 238
Voting Rights Act (1965), 92: 147
***Voyager 1* (space probe), 91:** 78-82
***Voyager 2* (space probe), 91:** 77 (il.), 78-84, **90:** 183-184, 437
Vranitzky, Franz, 92: 78, **90:** 187
Vukovich, Bill, III, 91: 185

W

WA Inc., 91: 182
Wages, 92: 268-269, **91:** 340, **90:** 346. See also **Minimum wage**
Wagner, Lisa, 91: 207
Wahid, Abdurrahman, 92: 247
Waitangi, Treaty of, 91: 381
Waite, Terry, 92: 233, 317
Wajed, Hasina, 90: 198
Waldheim, Kurt, 92: 78, **91:** 183
WALESA, LECH, 92: 363-364, **91:** 404-405, 473, **90:** 412
Walker, Mort, 91: 385 (il.)
Wallace, Irving, 91: 271
Wallace, Rusty, 90: 190
Walloons. See **Belgium**
Walt Disney Co., 92: 320, 329, **91:** 168, **90:** 393
Walters, Rita, 92: 291
War. See **Ethnic conflict; Persian Gulf crisis and War;** and specific countries and regions
Warba (Kuwait), 92: 344-345
Ware, Andre, 90: 310
Warhol, Andy, 90: 178
Warner Brothers, 91: 146, 150
Warner Communications Inc., 90: 244
Warren, Chris, 91: 206
Warsaw Pact, 92: 204, **91:** 294, **90:** 296, 297
Washington (state), 92: 404, **91:** 439, **90:** 444; elections, **92:** 405
WASHINGTON, D.C., 92: 453-455, **91:** 473-474, **90:** 479-480; architecture, **90:** 171; art, **90:** 177; riots, **92:** 276; theater, **92:** 418; transit, **92:** 424, **91:** 458, **90:** 465; zoo, **90:** 487. See also **Dixon, Sharon Pratt**
Washington Cathedral, 91: 411 (il.)
Washington Redskins, 92: 221
WATER, 92: 455, **91:** 474-475, **90:** 480; ground water, **92:** 456-467; Los Angeles, **91:** 357, **90:** 480; Middle East, **91:** 370; San Diego, **91:** 425; wettability, **92:** 137. See also **Drought; Environmental pollution; Oil spills**
Water polo, 92: 401, **91:** 435, **90:** 441
Water skiing, 92: 401, **91:** 435, **90:** 441
Waters, Stanley, 91: 163
Watkins, Brian, 91: 380
WATKINS, JAMES DAVID, 91: 287, **90:** 480
Watson, Elizabeth M., 91: 319
Weapons. See **Armed forces; Arms control; Firearms; Nuclear weapons**
WEATHER, 92: 468-469, **91:** 476-478, **90:** 481-482; Asia storms, **92:** 70; farm production, **92:** 217; U.S. storms, **92:** 146. See also **Climate**
Weber, Pete, 92: 95, **90:** 209
***Webster v. Reproductive Health Services*, 90:** 449
Wedtech Corp., 90: 250, 389
Weightlifting, 92: 401, **91:** 435, **90:** 441
Weiner, Kenneth, 92: 181, **91:** 274
WELFARE, 92: 469, **91:** 478, **90:** 483; census data, **92:** 130; city ills, **92:** 142; New York City, **92:** 323. See also **Child welfare; Homelessness**
Wellman, Mark, 90: 393
Wells (water), 92: 459, 462, 463
WELLS, CLYDE KIRBY, 91: 221, **90:** 483
Wells, Denise, 91: 384-385
Wellstone, Paul, 92: 40
Wesbecker, Joseph T., 90: 258
"West as America" (exhibit), 92: 68-69
West Bank. See **Gaza Strip and West Bank**
WEST INDIES, 92: 470, **91:** 478-479, **90:** 483-484
West Virginia, 92: 404, **91:** 439, **90:** 444; taxes, **90:** 445
Western European Union, 91: 294
Western Sahara, 92: 44, 319, 448, **91:** 157, 374, **90:** 166, 382
Western Samoa: election, **92:** 339; facts in brief, **92:** 338, **91:** 394, **90:** 402
Westinghouse Electric Corp., 91: 288
Westminster Kennel Club. See **Dog**
Wetlands, 92: 158, 216-217
Wexner Center for the Visual Arts, 90: 171
Whales, 92: 477, 478, **91:** 396, 482
Wharton, David, 90: 451
***What Is the Proper Way to Display a U.S. Flag?* (Tyler), 90:** 177
***What Work Is* (Levine), 92:** 362
Whisperwind on a Carousel (dog), 92: 185
Whitaker, Pernell, 92: 96, **91:** 208
Whitbread Round the World Race, 91: 205
WHITE, BILL, 90: 484
White, Patrick, 91: 183
White, Ryan, 91: 271
White-collar crime. See **Crime**
White House Conference on Libraries and Information Services, 92: 280
Whitmire, Kathryn J., 92: 240, 241, **90:** 325
Whitney Museum of American Art, 92: 68, **91:** 175
WHO. See **World Health Organization**
***Who Framed Roger Rabbit* (film), 91:** 136, 150-151
Whooping crane, 90: 40-42, 46 (il.), 48-51
Wichita, Kans., 92: 161-162
Wijeratne, Ranjan, 92: 402
Wijeweera, Rohana, 90: 442
Wilbur, Richard, 92: 363
***Wild at Heart* (film), 91:** 358
WILDER, L. DOUGLAS, 92: 180, 470, **91:** 437 (il.), **90:** 287, 484
Wilderness areas. See **Conservation**
"Wilding," 91: 257, **90:** 259
Wildlife. See **Conservation; Endangered species; Zoology**
Wildmon, Donald E., 91: 174
***Will Rogers Follies, The* (musical), 92:** 418
William Station Mine, 90: 380
Williams, Robert, 91: 412
Williams, Walter Ray, 92: 95
Wilson, Edward O., 92: 378
Wilson, Michael Holcombe, 92: 110, 111, **91:** 223, **90:** 219-221
Wilson, Sir David, 92: 72
Winchester Three, 91: 389
Wind energy, 91: 288, **90:** 117, 118
Windows (software), 92: 152
Winnipeg Blue Bombers, 91: 303
Winter Olympics. See **Olympic Games**
Wisconsin, 92: 404, **91:** 439, **90:** 444; Chippewa dispute, **92:** 247; education, **91:** 282
"Witnesses: Against Our Vanishing" (artwork), 90: 177-178
Wofford, Harris L., 92: 179, 383, 449
Wojewodski, Stan, Jr., 92: 418
Wojnarowicz, David, 91: 174
Wolfe, George C., 91: 453
Wolff, Antonio Navarro, 91: 246
Women: armed forces, **92:** 67, **91:** 173; civil rights, **92:** 146, 408, **91:** 249, 342, 369; election gains, **92:** 145; health studies, **92:** 297; heart disease, **92:** 236-237, 297, **91:** 363; literature topic, **91:** 353; Protestant clergy role, **90:** 418; rap music, **92:** 369; sex and brain structure differences, **90:** 420; sex and self-esteem, **92:** 376-377. See also **Abortion; Sex discrimination; Sexual harassment; Surrogate motherhood**
Wool, 92: 77
Woosnam, Ian, 92: 230
World Association of Nuclear Operators, 90: 291
World Bank, 92: 62, 190, 250, **90:** 332
***World Book* supplements:** *Dictionary*, **92:** 479, **91:** 501, **90:** 505; *Encyclopedia*, **92:** 482, **91:** 506, **90:** 510
World Council of Churches, 92: 187, 382
World Cup. See **Skiing; Soccer; Track and field**
World Day of Youth, 92: 384
***World Doesn't End, The* (Simic), 91:** 403-404
World Festival of Youth and Students, 90: 344
World Gymnastics Championships, 92: 400
World Health Organization, 90: 472-473
World League of American Football, 92: 222
World Ocean Circulation Experiment, 91: 391
World Series. See **Baseball**
World University Games, 92: 400
World's Fair (1992). See **Expo '92**
Wrestling, 92: 401, **91:** 434, **90:** 440
Wright, Frank Lloyd, 91: 169
Wright, James C., Jr., 90: 246, 272 (il.)
Wrzesinski, Bryan, 92: 327
Wuornos, Aileen Carol, 92: 164
Wyoming, 92: 404, **91:** 439, **90:** 444; conservation, **92:** 160

X

X-ray telescope, 91: 180, 433
Xie Jun, 92: 138
Xinjiang province, 91: 235-236

Y

Yachting. See **Boating**
Yakovlev, Alexander, 92: 445
Yamaguchi, Kristi, 92: 242, **91:** 321-322, **90:** 328
Yanayev, Gennady I., 92: 432-435
Yang Shangkun, 90: 230, 232
Yankee Rowe nuclear power station, 92: 197
Yanomami Indians, 91: 209, 371
Yazov, Dimitry T., 92: 432-435
YELTSIN, BORIS NIKOLAYEVICH, 91: 479; Bush meeting, **92:** 103; coup attempt, **92:** 434, 435, 438 (il.); U.S.S.R. collapse, **92:** 438-440; U.S.S.R. political changes, **92:** 445, **91:** 460-465
YEMEN, 91: 479; facts in brief, **92:** 316, **91:** 370, **90:** 378
YEUTTER, CLAYTON KEITH, 92: 382, 383, 451, **91:** 297, **90:** 485
Yo-yo dieting, 92: 237
Yoma, Amira, 92: 62
Yoma de Menem, Zulema, 91: 170
Yonkers, N.Y., 91: 241
York, Duchess of, 90: 318
Young, Coleman A., 92: 181, **91:** 273, 274, **90:** 274
Young, W. Dale, 90: 256
***YSB* (magazine), 92:** 292
YUGOSLAVIA, 92: 470-471, **91:** 479-480, **90:** 485; Austria, **92:** 78; Eastern Orthodox Churches, **92:** 187-188; ethnic conflicts, **92:** 472-475; facts in brief, **92:** 205, **91:** 295, **90:** 298; Netherlands, **92:** 322; sports, **92:** 400; U.S. trade, **92:** 250
Yukon Indians, 91: 481
YUKON TERRITORY, 92: 476, **91:** 481, **90:** 485
Yusupov, Artur, 92: 138

Z

Zag (automobile), 92: 79 (il.)
Zah, Peterson, 92: 247
ZAIRE, 92: 476; Belgium, **91:** 203; facts in brief, **92:** 47, **91:** 159, **90:** 161; ivory trade, **91:** 48; political changes, **92:** 45, **91:** 157, **90:** 163
ZAMBIA, 91: 481; election, **92:** 45; facts in brief, **92:** 47, **91:** 159, **90:** 161
Zardari, Asif Ali, 91: 395
Zebra mussels, 91: 475
Zhao Ziyang, 90: 230, 232
Zhelesovski, Igor, 92: 242
Zhelev, Zhelyu, 92: 101, **91:** 212
Zhivkov, Todor, 91: 212, **90:** 214
Zhu Rongji, 92: 141
Zia, Khaleda. See **Ziaur Rahman, Khaleda**
ZIAUR RAHMAN, KHALEDA, 92: 83-84, 476, **90:** 198
Zidovudine. See **AZT**
ZIMBABWE, 91: 481; facts in brief, **92:** 47, **91:** 159, **90:** 161; ivory trade, **91:** 49, **90:** 253; Zimbabwe Unity Movement, **90:** 163
Zimbabwe African National Union, 91: 481, **90:** 163
Zinc mining, 92: 317
Zionism, 92: 315, 449
Zmeskal, Kim, 92: 400 (il.)
ZOOLOGY, 92: 477, **91:** 481-482, **90:** 486
ZOOS, 92: 477-478, **91:** 482-483, **90:** 486-487
Zou Jiahua, 92: 141
Zubero, Martin, 92: 411
Zulus, 92: 393-394, **91:** 431
Zurbriggen, Pirmin, 91: 427

Acknowledgments

The publishers acknowledge the following sources for illustrations. Credits read from top to bottom, left to right, on their respective pages. An asterisk (*) denotes illustrations and photographs that are the exclusive property of *The Year Book*. All maps, charts, and diagrams were prepared by *The Year Book* staff unless otherwise noted.

4 Reuters/Bettmann
6 © Robert Trippett, Sipa Press; From *The Cat in the Hat* by Dr. Seuss. Copyright © 1987 by Dr. Seuss. Copyright renewed 1985 Theodor S. Geisel and Audrey S. Geisel. Reprinted by permission of Random House, Inc.; © E. Adams, Sygma
7 © Louise Gubb, JB Pictures; Jet Propulsion Laboratory; Anatoly Sapronyenko, Agence France-Presse
11 © J. Langevin, Sygma
12 © Bruno Barbey, Magnum; AP/Wide World; © Trippett, Sipa Press
13 © Apesteguy/Merillon/Simon, Gamma/Liaison; © Antonio Emerito, Sipa Press;
14 Focus on Sports; © Sygma
15 © East News from Sipa Press
16 © J. Langevin, Sygma
18 © Orion from Shooting Star
19 © John Mandel, Sipa Press
20 © Kees, Sygma
21 Focus on Sports
22 © Stefan Ellis, Agence France-Presse
23 © Les Stone, Sygma
24 © Andrew D. Bernstein, NBA Photos
25 © Robert Trippett, Sipa Press; © Antonio Emerito, Sipa Press
26 © De Keerle, Sygma
27 © Burr, Gamma/Liaison; Reuters/Bettmann
28 © Shepard Sherbell, SABA
30 © Esaias Baitel, Gamma/Liaison; AP/Wide World
32 © Ronald D. Modra, *Sports Illustrated*; © B. Ward, *San Francisco Chronicle*
33 © Trippett, Sipa Press
34 AP/Wide World; © Bill Nation, Sygma
35-37 AP/Wide World
39 © A. Hernandez
41 Agence France-Presse
42 © Louise Gubb, JB Pictures
45 © Daniel Geerarerts, Gamma/Liaison
49 AP/Wide World
50 Abdelak Senna, Agence France-Presse
51 © Hinterleitner, Gamma/Liaison
53 Xinhua News Agency
54 © Bill Lyons
55 © Bill Lyons; © Barry Iverson, *Time* Magazine; © Bill Lyons
57 © Barry Iverson, *Time* Magazine
58 Iraq Museum, Baghdad; David Stronach, University of California at Berkeley; David Stronach, University of California at Berkeley
59 Elizabeth Stone, State University of New York at Stony Brook
60 © Greg Hursley
63-64 AP/Wide World
66 U.S. Department of Defense
69 Agence France-Presse
70 © James Nachtwey, Magnum
72 Reuters/Bettmann
74 Jet Propulsion Laboratory
79 Ford Motor Company
80 Reuters/Bettmann
82 © Emmanuel Joffet, Sipa Press
84 Rahman, Sipa Press
85-88 AP/Wide World
89 © Andrew D. Bernstein, NBA Photos
94 © Mike Powell, Allsport
96 © John Biever, *Sports Illustrated*
98 Bayne Stanley
100 © Peter Reina
102 Susan Biddle, The White House
104 AP/Wide World
106 Michel Tessier, Ponopresse
109 Canapress
111 © Mark O'Neill, Canada Wide
113 Paul Chiasson, Canapress
116 Canapress; © John Gillmore, The Stock Market
117 Confederation Life Collection. Detail from "Champlain in Huronia" painting by Rex Woods
118 National Archives of Canada
120 Canapress
122 Quebec and Ontario Paper Company, Ltd.; Canapress
127 U.S. Census Bureau; K&S Galvin, H. Armstrong Roberts
131 From the *Road Atlas* © 1991 by Rand McNally R.L. 91-S-188; JAK Graphics*
132 K&S Galvin, H. Armstrong Roberts; JAK Graphics*
134 R. Downs, H. Armstrong Roberts; JAK Graphics*
137 International Business Machines; Rice University
139 © Antonio Dickey, City of Chicago
143 AP/Wide World
146 Cynthia Carris
147 The National Civil Rights Museum
149 AP/Wide World
153 © Paul Hosefros, NYT Pictures
159 AP/Wide World
163 © Gaylon Wamplet, *The Houston Post*
165 Tim Davis, Duomo
166 © Tom Brazil
169 *London Daily Express* from Archive Photos; Bettmann
171 UPI/Bettmann; Bettmann; AP/Wide World; UPI/Bettmann
172 Bettmann; UPI/Bettmann; UPI/Bettmann; Archive Photos
173 UPI/Bettmann
174 Reuters/Bettmann; UPI/Bettmann; UPI/Bettmann; UPI/Bettmann
175 *World Book* photo by Dennis Brack; Reuters/Bettmann; The Ruth Page Foundation; UPI/Bettmann
176 UPI/Bettmann
177 From *The Cat in the Hat* by Dr. Seuss. Copyright © 1987 by Dr. Seuss. Copyright renewed 1985 by Theodor S. Geisel and Audrey S. Geisel. Reprinted by permission of Random House, Inc.
178 UPI/Bettmann
179 Agence France-Presse
180 © Ira Wyman, Sygma
181 AP/Wide World
183 Sipa Press
187 © East News from Sipa Press
189 Rodney Curtis
191 UPI/Bettmann
192 © Michael Sieron
196 © Craig Beasley, Tennessee Valley Authority
198 AP/Wide World
200 © Peter Stone, Black Star
201 © Jerome Delay, Agence France-Presse
202 Reuters/Bettmann
204 © DPA from Photoreporters
207 Reuters/Bettmann
208 © Grant V. Faint, The Image Bank
210 JAK Graphics*
213 © Patrick Kovarik, Agence France-Presse
214 © Ken Kerbs, DOT
217 CSIRO Australia
218 AP/Wide World
220 Walt Handelsman © 1991 *The Times-Picayune* from Tribune Media Service
222 © Per H. Kjeldsen, University of Michigan
225 © Witt/Chamussy/Stevens, Sipa Press
226 Sygma
229 Photoreporters
231 © Jason Fraser, Sipa Press
233 © Dirck Halstead, Gamma/Liaison
235 Winter, Gamma/Liaison
238-239 AP/Wide World
243 Baldev, Sygma
244 AP/Wide World
246 Barbara Rascher
249 AP/Wide World
251 © Craig Porter, Black Star
252 AP/Wide World
255 Reuters/Bettmann
256 © Esaias Baitel, Gamma/Liaison
258 © Susanna Rebuffi, Grazia Neri
259 © M. Hasimoto, Sygma
260 © Torin Boyd, Gamma/Liaison
262 AP/Wide World
265 Agence France-Presse
266 © Bruno Barbey, Magnum
270 © Mario Villafuerte, Picture Group

272 © Christopher Brown, Sipa Press
277 © Peter Stone, Black Star
279 Phil Moloitis and Gary Degnan, Chicago Public Library
280-283 Agence France-Presse
286 Illustration by David Macaulay from *Black and White*, © 1990 by David Macaulay. Reprinted by permission from Houghton Mifflin Company.
288 Juraatis, Sipa Press
290 © Ted Soqui, Impact Visuals
291 AP/Wide World
294 © Gary Gladstone
297 © John Barr, Gamma/Liaison
298-307 Art: Cary Henrie*—photo: © Kay Chernush
311 © Larry Reiter, Sipa Press
313 © Apesteguy/Merillon/Simon, Gamma/Liaison
314-315 AP/Wide World
321 © 20th Century Fox from Shooting Star
324 Agence France-Presse
326 AP/Wide World
327 Sovfoto
328 AP/Wide World
330 © Ernie Cox, Jr., Chicago Tribune Company, all rights reserved, used with permission
332 © Steven Erlanger, NYT Pictures
333 © Francis Apesteguy, Gamma/Liaison
334 © Holmuarig, Sipa Press
336 © Peter Sibbald
339 AP/Wide World
340 © Uno Samuelsson, National Geographic Society
341 Chris Brown, Sipa Press
342 © E. Adams, Sygma
348 © Sipa Press; © J. Witt, Sipa Press; © Photri from Sygma; © J. Witt, Sipa Press
349 © Natsuko Utsumi, Gamma/Liaison; Reuters/Bettmann
351 © Kenneth Jarecke, Contact
352 © J. Langevin, Sygma
354 © J. Mantel, Sipa Press; © Patrick Robert, Sygma; © Peter Jordan, Gamma/Liaison
356 © Alejandro Balaguer, Sygma
359 AP/Wide World
360 Reuters/Bettmann
361 © Alberto Garcia, SABA
363 Reid Baker, Library of Congress
364 Sygma
365 AP/Wide World
367 Robin Holland, Onyx
369 Cleriot, UK Press from Gamma/Liaison; Todd Kaplan, Star File
373 AP/Wide World
374 © Harvey/Cherruault, Sipa Press
378 *World Book* photo by Christopher Morrow
380 © Patrick Piel, Gamma/Liaison
382 Huntington Library
385-389 AP/Wide World
390 © Rick Rickman, Duomo
393 Reuters/Bettmann
395 NASA
397 EXPO '92
398 Sygma
400 Agence France-Presse
403 © Donna Bagby, SABA
407 Reuters/Bettmann
408 AP/Wide World
409 UPI/Bettmann
412 AP/Wide World
415 Tony Esparza, CBS
416 © Dan Smith, Allsport
419 Michael LePoer Trench
422 © Billy Stickland, Allsport
423 AP/Wide World
425-428 © Raphael Gaillarde, Gamma/Liaison
431 Nabil Ismail, Agence France-Presse
432 © A. Hernandez, Sipa Press
434 © Deborah Copaken, Contact Press
438 © W. Laski, Sipa Press
440 © Gamma Moscow from Gamma/Liaison
441 © Anatoly Sapronyenko, Agence France-Presse
443 Bettmann
444 Bettmann; UPI/Bettmann; Sipa Press; Sipa Press
445 © F. Apesteguy, Gamma/Liaison; © Peter Turnley, Black Star
447 © R. Maiman, Sygma
448 UPI/Bettmann
454 © David Aaron, Sipa Press
456 Stanley N. Davis
459 Nancy Lee Walter*
460 JAK Graphics*; © Bill Campbell, Picture Group; JAK Graphics*
461 U.S. Department of Agriculture; Nancy Lee Walter*; © Louie Psihoyos, Matrix
463 AP/Wide World; U.S. Air Force; Harris-Galveston Coastal Subsidence District
465 U.S. Department of Agriculture
468 AP/Wide World
471 © Jasmin You, Gamma/Liaison
472 © Luc Delahaye, Sipa Press
474 JAK Graphics*
478 © Chicago Tribune Company, all rights reserved, used with permission

Family Milestones of 1991

In the preceding pages, *The World Book Year Book* reported the major events and trends of 1991. Use these two pages to record the developments that made the year memorable for *your* family.

Family members (names)	Ages	Family pets

Births (name)	Date	Where born	Weight	Height

Weddings (names)	Date	Where held

Religious events

Graduations

Anniversaries

In memoriam

Awards, honors, and prizes

Sports and club achievements

Vacations and trips

Most enjoyable books

Most-played recordings and tapes

Most unforgettable motion pictures

Most-watched television programs

Paste a favorite family photograph or snapshot here.

Date

Location

Occasion